Readings in Database Systems

Readings in Database Systems
4th edition

edited by Joseph M. Hellerstein and Michael Stonebraker

The MIT Press
Cambridge, Massachusetts
London, England

MIT Press books may be purchased at special quantity discounts for business or sales promotional use. For information, please email special_sales@mitpress.mit.edu or write to Special Sales Department, The MIT Press, 5 Cambridge Center, Cambridge, MA 02142.

Printed and bound in the United States of America.

ISBN: 978-0-262-69314-1 (pbk. : alk. paper)
Library of Congress Control Number: 2004113624

10 9 8 7 6 5 4 3

Contents

Chapter 4: Transaction Management

Chapter 5: Extensibility

Chapter 6: Database Evolution

Chapter 7: Data Warehousing

Preface

This fourth edition of *Readings in Database Systems* is being issued at an interesting time in the history of the field. The database industry has undergone significant consolidation in recent years. It is now dominated by three companies, two of which are not database vendors per se. IBM and Microsoft manage large portfolios of products and services; database systems are one—but only one—of their crown jewels. The third major player, Oracle, is nominally a database company, but is as active in enterprise applications as it is in core database systems. The era of the "database wars" is over, and it has been a long time since a database startup company has made major noise. The argument is sometimes made that database management systems—like many other components in the computing industry—are a victim of their own success: they have reached a level of maturity at which significant industrial innovation has become impossible.

Even if this were an accurate assessment of the entrenched database industry, it is a very narrow view of database research. The research field itself is healthier than it has ever been. There has been a surge of database faculty hiring in recent years, including at some of the leading research institutions that traditionally ignored the field. New conferences have emerged both in database systems design, and in more algorithmic fields like data mining. Lessons from the database literature are being applied in a host of forward-looking research areas at universities, from bioinformatics to sensor networks to next-generation Internet architectures.

This external interest in database technologies is not confined to academia. Industrial software systems are increasingly turning to database system innovations to solve other problems. Rumor has it, for example, that Microsoft's next operating system will have a single unified store for all files and data, based on their database engine. Web-based e-commerce services depend to a large extent on transactional messaging technologies developed in the database community. Text-based web services like search engines also owe a debt to database innovations in parallel query processing. The list goes on.

It would seem, then, that while the core industrial database products have gelled, the ideas that they encapsulate have become increasingly influential. A much more optimistic and realistic view of database research is that the field is in a position to make a bigger impact on computing in the large than it ever has before, in part because the community has solved many of its own challenges and is courting other areas for collaborations. This cross-fertilization could result in major changes in the traditional database industry, and in other aspects of computing.

This book is intended to provide software technologists—both professionals and students—with a grounding in database research past and present, and a technical context for understanding new innovations. It is also designed to be a reference for anyone already active in database systems. This set of readings represents what we perceive to be the most important issues in the database area: the core material for any DBMS professional to study.

The book opens with two introductory articles we wrote to set the stage for the research papers collected here. The first article presents a historical perspective on the design of data models and query languages; the second provides an architectural overview of the anatomy of a database system. These articles are intended to provide an organized, modern introduction to basic knowledge of the field, which in previous editions was represented by a sampling of seminal research papers from the late Ted Codd and the pioneering INGRES and System R projects. A true database aficionado should still read those original papers [Cod70,ABC+76, SWK76, Sto80, CPS+81], since they give a snapshot of the excitement and challenges of the time. However we felt that after three decades it was hard for readers to get a substantive basis for the field in its current richness by reading the early papers. Hence with some notable regret we chose not to include them in this edition.

For the remaining papers we have selected, we provide chapter introductions to discuss the context, motivation, and, when relevant, the controversy in the area. These introductions summarize the comments we make during lectures in our graduate courses, and place the papers in the broader perspective of database research. The comments are often explicitly intended to be *opinions*, not necessarily statements of fact—they are intended as conversation-starters. We hope this style encourages students and independent readers to critically evaluate both the papers and our editorial remarks.

This edition of the book contains a host of new papers, including a number of chapters in new areas. Four of the papers were written expressly for the book: the two introductory articles, Brewer's paper on search engine architecture, and Jacobs' paper on application servers. The remaining papers we chose from both the classical literature and from recent hot topics. We selected papers based on our assessment both of the quality of research and its potential for lasting importance. We have tried to assemble a collection of papers that are both seminal in nature and accessible to a reader who has a basic familiarity with database systems. We often had two or more papers to choose from. In such cases we selected what we felt was the best one or the one discussing the broadest variety of issues. In some areas such as transaction management, all of the research is very detail-oriented. In these cases we tried to favor papers that are accessible. In areas like data mining with a strong mathematical component, we tried to select papers that are both accessible to software systems experts, and that deal non-trivially with systems challenges.

This book has been greatly improved by the input of many colleagues, including: Paul Aoki, Eric Brewer, David DeWitt, Mike Franklin, Johannes Gehrke, Jim Gray, James Hamilton, Wei Hong, Guy Lohman, Sam Madden, Chris Olston, Tamer Ozsu, Raghu Ramakrishnan, Andreas Reuter, and Stuart Russell. We particularly thank Eric Brewer and Dean Jacobs for their contributions of new material. Thanks are also due to the students of CS286 and CS262 at Berkeley, and 689.3 at MIT; their comments have been a major influence on our choice of papers and our presentation of the material.

References

[ABC+76] Morton M. Astrahan, Mike W. Blasgen, Donald D. Chamberlin, Kapali P. Eswaran, Jim Gray, Patricia P. Griffiths, W. Frank King III, Raymond A. Lorie, Paul R. McJones, James W. Mehl, Gianfranco R. Putzolu, Irving L. Traiger, Bradford W. Wade, and Vera Watson. System R: Relational Approach to Database Management. *ACM Transactions on Database Systems (TODS),* 1(2):97-137, 1976.

[CPS+81] Donald D. Chamberlin, Franco Putzolu, Patricia Griffiths Selinger, Mario Schkolnick, Donald R. Slutz, Irving L. Traiger, Bradford W. Wade, Robert A. Yost, Morton M. Astrahan, Michael W. Blasgen, James N. Gray, W. Frank King, Bruce G. Lindsay, Raymond Lorie, James W. Mehl and Thomas G. Price. A History and Evaluation of System R, *Communications of the ACM* 24:10 (1981), 632-646.

[Cod70] E. F. Codd. A Relational Model of Data for Large Shared Data Banks, *Comm. ACM* 13(6), June 1970, p377-387.

[SWK76] M.R. Stonebraker, E. Wong, and P. Kreps. The Design and Implementation of INGRES. *ACM Transactions on Database Systems (TODS)*, 1(3):189-222, September 1976.

[Sto80] M. Stonebraker. Retrospection on a Database System. *ACM Transactions on Database Systems (TODS)*, 5(2):225-240, 1980.

Chapter 1
Data Models and DBMS Architecture

What Goes Around Comes Around

Michael Stonebraker
Joseph M. Hellerstein

Abstract

This paper provides a summary of 35 years of data model proposals, grouped into 9 different eras. We discuss the proposals of each era, and show that there are only a few basic data modeling ideas, and most have been around a long time. Later proposals inevitably bear a strong resemblance to certain earlier proposals. Hence, it is a worthwhile exercise to study previous proposals.

In addition, we present the lessons learned from the exploration of the proposals in each era. Most current researchers were not around for many of the previous eras, and have limited (if any) understanding of what was previously learned. There is an old adage that he who does not understand history is condemned to repeat it. By presenting "ancient history", we hope to allow future researchers to avoid replaying history.

Unfortunately, the main proposal in the current XML era bears a striking resemblance to the CODASYL proposal from the early 1970's, which failed because of its complexity. Hence, the current era is replaying history, and "what goes around comes around". Hopefully the next era will be smarter.

I Introduction

Data model proposals have been around since the late 1960's, when the first author "came on the scene". Proposals have continued with surprising regularity for the intervening 35 years. Moreover, many of the current day proposals have come from researchers too young to have learned from the discussion of earlier ones. Hence, the purpose of this paper is to summarize 35 years worth of "progress" and point out what should be learned from this lengthy exercise.

We present data model proposals in nine historical epochs:

Hierarchical (IMS): late 1960's and 1970's
Network (CODASYL): 1970's
Relational: 1970's and early 1980's
Entity-Relationship: 1970's
Extended Relational: 1980's
Semantic: late 1970's and 1980's
Object-oriented: late 1980's and early 1990's
Object-relational: late 1980's and early 1990's

Semi-structured (XML): late 1990's to the present

In each case, we discuss the data model and associated query language, using a neutral notation. Hence, we will spare the reader the idiosyncratic details of the various proposals. We will also attempt to use a uniform collection of terms, again in an attempt to limit the confusion that might otherwise occur.

Throughout much of the paper, we will use the standard example of suppliers and parts, from [CODD70], which we write for now in relational form in Figure 1.

Supplier (sno, sname, scity, sstate)
Part (pno, pname, psize, pcolor)
Supply (sno, pno, qty, price)

A Relational Schema
Figure 1

Here we have Supplier information, Part information and the Supply relationship to indicate the terms under which a supplier can supply a part.

II IMS Era

IMS was released around 1968, and initially had a hierarchical data model. It understood the notion of a **record type,** which is a collection of named fields with their associated data types. Each **instance** of a record type is forced to obey the data description indicated in the definition of the record type. Furthermore, some subset of the named fields must uniquely specify a record instance, i.e. they are required to be a **key**. Lastly, the record types must be arranged in a **tree**, such that each record type (other than the root) has a unique **parent** record type. An IMS data base is a collection of instances of record types, such that each instance, other than root instances, has a single parent of the correct record type.

This requirement of tree-structured data presents a challenge for our sample data, because we are forced to structure it in one of the two ways indicated in Figure 2. These representations share two common undesirable properties:

1) **Information is repeated**. In the first schema, Part information is repeated for each Supplier who supplies the part. In the second schema, Supplier information is repeated for each part he supplies. Repeated information is undesirable, because it offers the possibility for inconsistent data. For example, a repeated data element could be changed in some, but not all, of the places it appears, leading to an inconsistent data base.
2) **Existence depends on parents**. In the first schema it is impossible for there to be a part that is not currently supplied by anybody. In the second schema, it is impossible to have a supplier which does not currently supply anything. There is no support for these "corner cases" in a strict hierarchy.

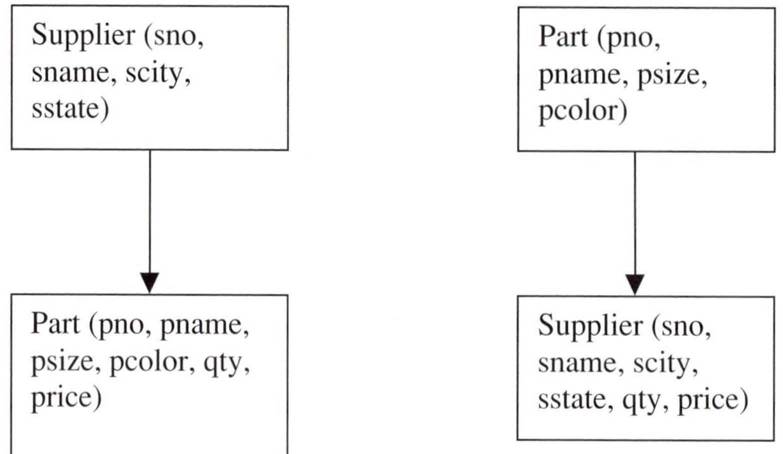

Two Hierarchical Organizations
Figure 2

IMS chose a hierarchical data base because it facilitates a simple data manipulation language, DL/1. Every record in an IMS data base has a **hierarchical sequence key** (HSK). Basically, an HSK is derived by concatenating the keys of ancestor records, and then adding the key of the current record. HSK defines a natural order of all records in an IMS data base, basically depth-first, left-to-right. DL/1 intimately used HSK order for the semantics of commands. For example, the "get next" command returns the next record in HSK order. Another use of HSK order is the "get next within parent" command, which explores the subtree underneath a given record in HSK order.

Using the first schema, one can find all the red parts supplied by Supplier 16 as:

```
Get unique Supplier (sno = 16)
Until failure do
        Get next within parent (color = red)
        Enddo
```

The first command finds Supplier 16. Then we iterate through the subtree underneath this record in HSK order, looking for red parts. When the subtree is exhausted, an error is returned.

Notice that DL/1 is a "record-at-a-time" language, whereby the programmer constructs an algorithm for solving his query, and then IMS executes this algorithm. Often there are multiple ways to solve a query. Here is another way to solve the above specification:

```
Until failure do
        Get next Part (color = red)
        Enddo
```

Although one might think that the second solution is clearly inferior to the first one; in fact if there is only one supplier in the data base (number 16), the second solution will outperform the first. The DL/1 programmer must make such optimization tradeoffs.

IMS supported four different storage formats for hierarchical data. Basically root records can either be:

Stored sequentially
Indexed in a B-tree using the key of the record
Hashed using the key of the record

Dependent records are found from the root using either

Physical sequentially
Various forms of pointers.

Some of the storage organizations impose restrictions on DL/1 commands. For example the purely sequential organization will not support record inserts. Hence, it is appropriate only for batch processing environments in which a change list is sorted in HSK order and then a single pass of the data base is made, the changes inserted in the correct place, and a new data base written. This is usually referred to as "old-master-new-master" processing. In addition, the storage organization that hashes root records on a key cannot support "get next", because it has no easy way to return hashed records in HSK order.

These various "quirks" in IMS are designed to avoid operations that would have impossibly bad performance. However, this decision comes at a price: One cannot freely change IMS storage organizations to tune a data base application because there is no guarantee that the DL/1 programs will continue to run.

The ability of a data base application to continue to run, regardless of what tuning is performed at the physical level will be called **physical data independence**. Physical data independence is important because a DBMS application is not typically written all at once. As new programs are added to an application, the tuning demands may change, and better DBMS performance could be achieved by changing the storage organization. IMS has chosen to limit the amount of physical data independence that is possible.

In addition, the logical requirements of an application may change over time. New record types may be added, because of new business requirements or because of new government requirements. It may also be desirable to move certain data elements from one record type to another. IMS supports a certain level of **logical data independence**, because DL/1 is actually defined on a **logical data base**, not on the actual physical data base that is stored. Hence, a DL/1 program can be written initially by defining the logical data base to be exactly same as the physical data base. Later, record types can be added to the physical data base, and the logical data base redefined to exclude them. Hence, an IMS data base can grow with new record types, and the initial DL/1 program will continue to operate correctly. In general, an IMS logical data base can be a subtree of a physical data base.

It is an excellent idea to have the programmer interact with a logical abstraction of the data, because this allows the physical organization to change, without compromising the runability of DL/1 programs. Logical and physical data independence are important because DBMS application have a much longer lifetime (often a quarter century or more) than the data on which they operate. Data independence will allow the data to change without requiring costly program maintenance.

One last point should be made about IMS. Clearly, our sample data is not amenable to a tree structured representation as noted earlier. Hence, there was quickly pressure on IMS to represent our sample data without the redundancy or dependencies mentioned above. IMS responded by extending the notion of logical data bases beyond what was just described.

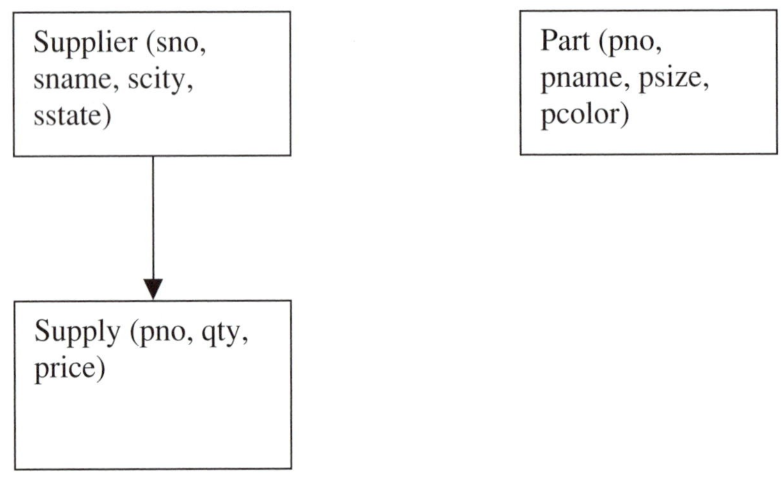

Two IMS Physical Data Bases
Figure 3

Suppose one constructs two physical data bases, one containing only Part information and the second containing Supplier and Supply information as shown in the diagram of Figure 3. Of course, DL/1 programs are defined on trees; hence they cannot be used directly on the structures of Figure 3. Instead, IMS allowed the definition of the logical data base shown in Figure 4. Here, the Supply and Part record types from two different data bases are "fused" (joined) on the common value of part number into the hierarchical structure shown.

Basically, the structure of Figure 3 is actually stored, and one can note that there is no redundancy and no bad existence dependencies in this structure. The programmer is presented with the hierarchical view shown in Figure 4, which supports standard DL/1 programs.

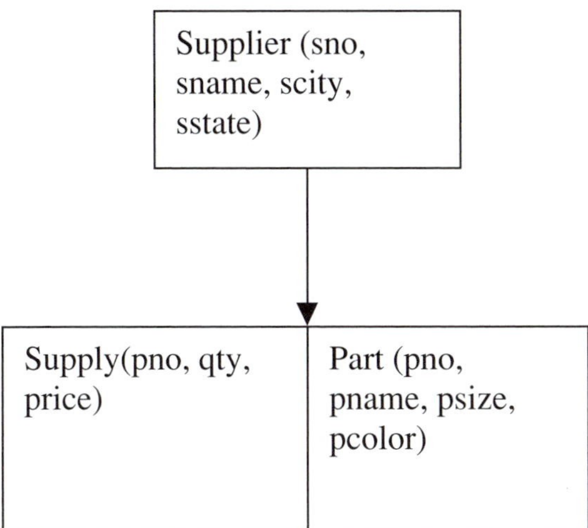

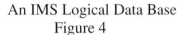

An IMS Logical Data Base
Figure 4

Speaking generally, IMS allow two different tree-structured physical data bases to be "grafted" together into a logical data base. There are many restrictions (for example in the use of the delete command) and considerable complexity to this use of logical data bases, but it is a way to represent non-tree structured data in IMS.

The complexity of these logical data bases will be presently seen to be pivotial in determining how IBM decided to support relational data bases a decade later.

We will summarize the lessons learned so far, and then turn to the CODASYL proposal.

Lesson 1: Physical and logical data independence are highly desirable

Lesson 2: Tree structured data models are very restrictive

Lesson 3: It is a challenge to provide sophisticated logical reorganizations of tree structured data

Lesson 4: A record-at-a-time user interface forces the programmer to do manual query optimization, and this is often hard.

III CODASYL Era

In 1969 the CODASYL (Committee on Data Systems Languages) committee released their first report [CODA69], and then followed in 1971 [CODA71] and 1973 [CODA73] with language specifications. CODASYL was an ad-hoc committee that championed a network data model along with a record-at-a-time data manipulation language.

This model organized a collection of record types, each with keys, into a network, rather than a tree. Hence, a given record instance could have multiple parents, rather than a single one, as in IMS. As a result, our Supplier-Parts-Supply example could be represented by the CODASYL network of Figure 5.

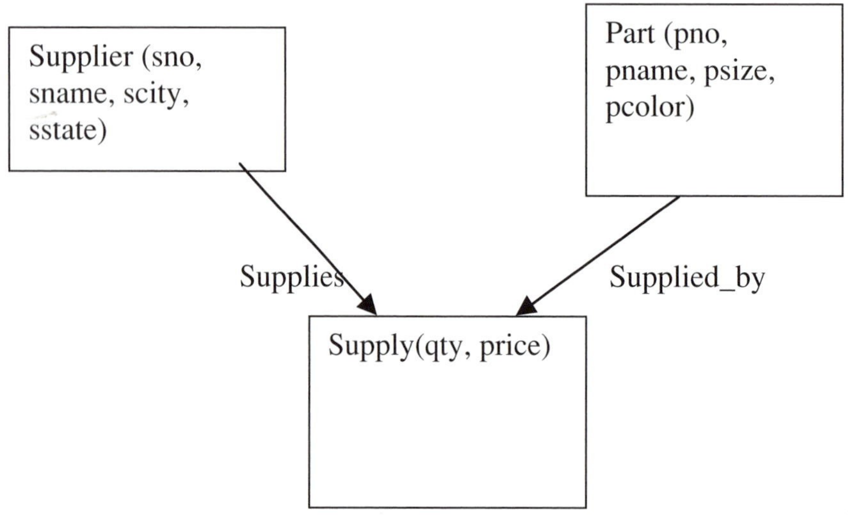

A CODASYL Network
Figure 5

Here, we notice three record types arranged in a network, connected by two named arcs, called Supplies and Supplied_by. A named arc is called a **set** in CODASYL, though it is not technically a set at all. Rather it indicates that for each record instance of the **owner** record type (the tail of the arrow) there is a relationship with zero or more record instances of the **child** record type (the head of the arrow). As such, it is a 1-to-n relationship between owner record instances and child record instances.

A CODASYL network is a collection of named record types and named set types that form a connected graph. Moreover, there must be at least one **entry point** (a record type that is not a child in any set). A CODASYL data base is a collection of record instances and set instances that obey this network description.

Notice that Figure 5 does not have the existence dependencies present in a hierarchical data model. For example, it is ok to have a part that is not supplied by anybody. This will merely be an empty instance of the Supplied_by set. Hence, the move to a network data model solves many of the restrictions of a hierarchy. However, there are still situations that are hard to model in CODASYL. Consider, for example, data about a marriage ceremony, which is a 3-way relationship between a bride, a groom, and a minister. Because CODASYL sets are only two-way relationships, one is forced into the data model indicated in Figure 6.

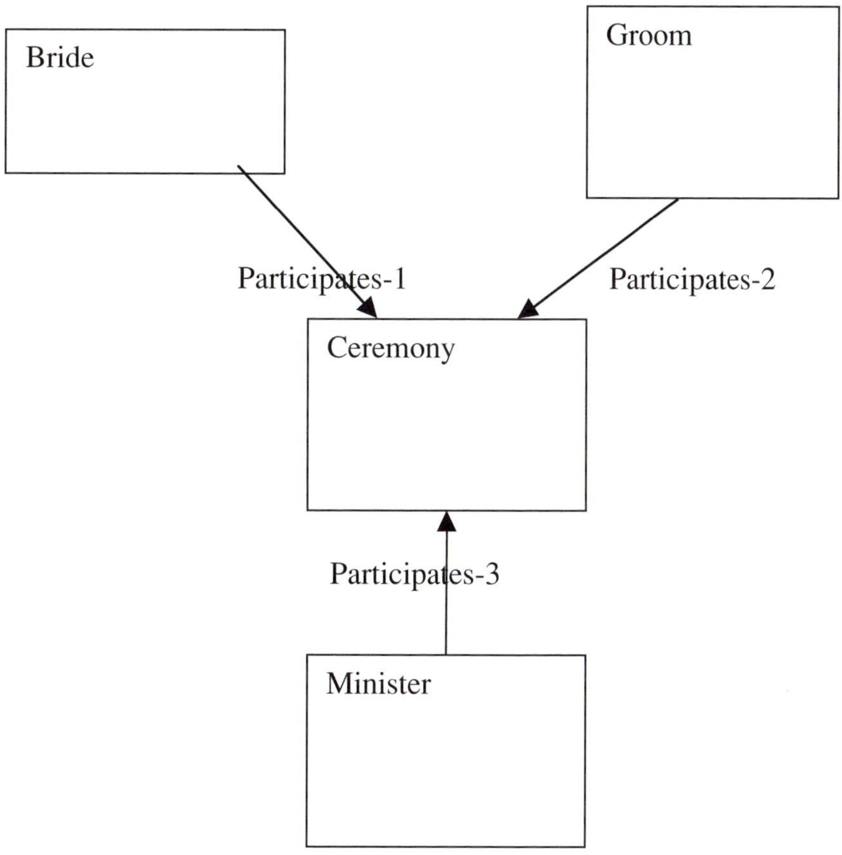

A CODASYL Solution
Figure 6

This solution requires three binary sets to express a three-way relationship, and is somewhat unnatural. Although much more flexible than IMS, the CODASYL data model still had limitations.

The CODASYL data manipulation language is a record-at-a-time language whereby one enters the data base at an entry point and then navigates to desired data by following sets. To find the red parts supplied by Supplier 16 in CODASYL, one can use the following code:

```
Find Supplier (SNO = 16)
Until no-more {
        Find next Supply record in Supplies
        Find owner Part record in Supplied_by
        Get current record
        -check for red—
}
```

One enters the data base at supplier 16, and then iterates over the members of the Supplies set. This will yield a collection of Supply records. For each one, the owner in the Supplied_by set is identified, and a check for redness performed.

The CODASYL proposal suggested that the records in each entry point be hashed on the key in the record. Several implementations of sets were proposed that entailed various combinations of pointers between the parent records and child records.

The CODASYL proposal provided essentially no physical data independence. For example, the above program fails if the key (and hence the hash storage) of the Supplier record is changed from sno to something else. In addition, no logical data independence is provided, since the schema cannot change without affecting application programs.

The move to a network model has the advantage that no kludges are required to implement graph-structured data, such as our example. However, the CODASYL model is considerably more complex than the IMS data model. In IMS a programmer navigates in a hierarchical space, while a CODASYL programmer navigates in a multi-dimensional hyperspace. In IMS the programmer must only worry about his current position in the data base, and the position of a single ancestor (if he is doing a "get next within parent").

In contrast, a CODASYL programmer must keep track of the:

The last record touched by the application
The last record of each record type touched
The last record of each set type touched

The various CODASYL DML commands update these currency indicators. Hence, one can think of CODASYL programming as moving these currency indicators around a CODASYL data base until a record of interest is located. Then, it can be fetched. In addition, the CODASYL programmer can suppress currency movement if he desires. Hence, one way to think of a CODASYL programmer is that he should program looking at a wall map of the CODASYL network that is decorated with various colored pins indicating currency. In his 1973 Turing Award lecture, Charlie Bachmann called this "navigating in hyperspace" [BACH73].

Hence, the CODASYL proposal trades increased complexity for the possibility of easily representing non-hierarchical data. CODASYL offers poorer logical and physical data independence than IMS.

There are also some more subtle issues with CODASYL. For example, in IMS each data base could be independently bulk-loaded from an external data source. However, in CODASYL, all the data was typically in one large network. This much larger object had to be bulk-loaded all at once, leading to very long load times. Also, if a CODASYL data base became corrupted, it was necessary to reload all of it from a dump. Hence, crash recovery tended to be more involved than if the data was divided into a collection of independent data bases.

In addition, a CODASYL load program tended to be complex because large numbers of records had to be assembled into sets, and this usually entailed many disk seeks. As such, it was usually important to think carefully about the load algorithm to optimize performance. Hence, there was no general purpose CODASYL load utility, and each installation had to write its own. This complexity was much less important in IMS.

Hence, the lessons learned in CODASYL were:

Lesson 5: Networks are more flexible than hierarchies but more complex

Lesson 6: Loading and recovering networks is more complex than hierarchies

IV Relational Era

Against this backdrop, Ted Codd proposed his relational model in 1970 [CODD70]. In a conversation with him years later, he indicated that the driver for his research was the fact that IMS programmers were spending large amounts of time doing maintenance on IMS applications, when logical or physical changes occurred. Hence, he was focused on providing better data independence.

His proposal was threefold:

Store the data in a simple data structure (tables)
Access it through a high level set-at-a-time DML
No need for a physical storage proposal

With a simple data structure, one has a better change of providing logical data independence. With a high level language, one can provide a high degree of physical data independence. Hence, there is no need to specify a storage proposal, as was required in both IMS and CODASYL.

Moreover, the relational model has the added advantage that it is flexible enough to represent almost anything. Hence, the existence dependencies that plagued IMS can be easily handled by the relational schema shown earlier in Figure 1. In addition, the three-way marriage ceremony that was difficult in CODASYL is easily represented in the relational model as:

Ceremony (bride-id, groom-id, minister-id, other-data)

Codd made several (increasingly sophisticated) relational model proposals over the years [CODD79, CODDXX]. Moreover, his early DML proposals were the relational calculus (data language/alpha) [CODD71a] and the relational algebra [CODD72a]. Since Codd was originally a mathematician (and previously worked on cellular automata), his DML proposals were rigorous and formal, but not necessarily easy for mere mortals to understand.

Codd's proposal immediately touched off "the great debate", which lasted for a good part of the 1970's. This debate raged at SIGMOD conferences (and it predecessor SIGFIDET). On the one side, there was Ted Codd and his "followers" (mostly researchers and academics) who argued the following points:

a) Nothing as complex as CODASYL can possibly be a good idea
b) CODASYL does not provide acceptable data independence
c) Record-at-a-time programming is too hard to optimize
d) CODASYL and IMS are not flexible enough to easily represent common situations (such as marriage ceremonies)

On the other side, there was Charlie Bachman and his "followers" (mostly DBMS practitioners) who argued the following:

a) COBOL programmers cannot possibly understand the new-fangled relational languages
b) It is impossible to implement the relational model efficiently
c) CODASYL can represent tables, so what's the big deal?

The highlight (or lowlight) of this discussion was an actual debate at SIGMOD '74 between Codd and Bachman and their respective "seconds" [RUST74]. One of us was in the audience, and it was obvious that neither side articulated their position clearly. As a result, neither side was able to hear what the other side had to say.

In the next couple of years, the two camps modified their positions (more or less) as follows:

Relational advocates

a) Codd is a mathematician, and his languages are not the right ones. SQL [CHAM74] and QUEL [STON76] are much more user friendly.

b) System R [ASTR76] and INGRES [STON76] prove that efficient implementations of Codd's ideas are possible. Moreover, query optimizers can be built that are competitive with all but the best programmers at constructing query plans.

c) These systems prove that physical data independence is achievable. Moreover, relational views [STON75] offer vastly enhanced logical data independence, relative to CODASYL.

d) Set-at-a-time languages offer substantial programmer productivity improvements, relative to record-at-a-time languages.

CODASYL advocates

a) It is possible to specify set-at-a-time network languages, such as LSL [TSIC76], that provide complete physical data independence and the possibility of better logical data independence.

b) It is possible to clean up the network model [CODA78], so it is not so arcane.

Hence, both camps responded to the criticisms of the other camp. The debate then died down, and attention focused on the commercial marketplace to see what would happen.

Fortuitously for the relational camp, the minicomputer revolution was occurring, and VAXes were proliferating. They were an obvious target for the early commercial relational systems, such as Oracle and INGRES. Happily for the relational camp, the major CODASYL systems, such as IDMS from Culinaine Corp. were written in IBM assembler, and were not portable. Hence, the early relational systems had the VAX market to themselves. This gave them time to improve the performance of their products, and the success of the VAX market went hand-in-hand with the success of relational systems.

On mainframes, a very different story was unfolding. IBM sold a derivative of System R on VM/370 and a second derivative on VSE, their low end operating system. However, neither platform was used by serious business data processing users. All the action was on MVS, the high-end operating system. Here, IBM continued to sell IMS, Cullinaine successfully sold IDMS, and relational systems were nowhere to be seen.

Hence, VAXes were a relational market and mainframes were a non-relational market. At the time all serious data management was done on mainframes.

This state of affairs changed abruptly in 1984, when IBM announced the upcoming release of DB/2 on MVS. In effect, IBM moved from saying that IMS was their serious DBMS to a dual data base strategy, in which both IMS and DB/2 were declared strategic. Since DB/2 was the new technology and was much easier to use, it was crystal clear to everybody who the long-term winner was going to be.

IBM's signal that it was deadly serious about relational systems was a watershed moment. First, it ended once-and-for-all "the great debate". Since IBM held vast marketplace power at the time, they effectively announced that relational systems had won and CODASYL and hierarchical systems had lost. Soon after, Cullinaine and IDMS went into a marketplace swoon. Second, they effectively declared that SQL was the de facto standard relational language. Other (substantially better) query languages, such as QUEL, were immediately dead. For a scathing critique of the semantics of SQL, consult [DATE84].

A little known fact must be discussed at this point. It would have been natural for IBM to put a relational front end on top of IMS, as shown in Figure 7. This architecture would have allowed IMS customers to continue to run IMS. New application could be written to the relational interface, providing an elegant migration path to the new technology. Hence, over time a gradual shift from DL/1 to SQL would have occurred, all the while preserving the high-performance IMS underpinnings

In fact, IBM attempted to execute exactly this strategy, with a project code-named Eagle. Unfortunately, it proved too hard to implement SQL on top of the IMS notion of logical data bases, because of semantic issues. Hence, the complexity of logical data bases in IMS came back to haunt IBM many years later. As a result, IBM was forced to move to the dual data base strategy, and to declare a winner of the great debate.

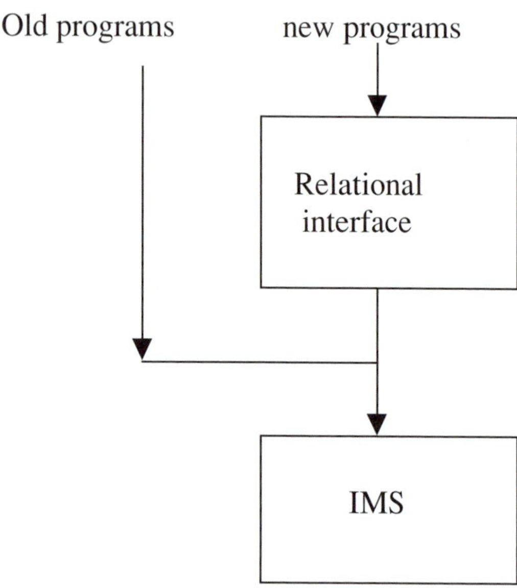

The Architecture of Project Eagle
Figure 7

In summary, the CODASL versus relational argument was ultimately settled by three events:

a) the success of the VAX
b) the non-portability of CODASYL engines
c) the complexity of IMS logical data bases

The lessons that were learned from this epoch are:

Lesson 7: Set-a-time languages are good, regardless of the data model, since they offer much improved physical data independence.

Lesson 8: Logical data independence is easier with a simple data model than with a complex one.

Lesson 9: Technical debates are usually settled by the elephants of the marketplace, and often for reasons that have little to do with the technology.

Lesson 10: Query optimizers can beat all but the best record-at-a-time DBMS application programmers.

V The Entity-Relationship Era

In the mid 1970's Peter Chen proposed the entity-relationship (E-R) data model as an alternative to the relational, CODASYL and hierarchical data models [CHEN76]. Basically, he proposed that a data base be thought of a collection of instances of **entities**. Loosely speaking these are objects that have an existence, independent of any other entities in the data base. In our example, Supplier and Parts would be such entities.

In addition, entities have **attributes**, which are the data elements that characterize the entity. In our example, the attributes of Part would be pno, pname, psize, and pcolor. One or more of these attributes would be designated to be unique, i.e. to be a key. Lastly, there could be **relationships** between entities. In our example, Supply is a relationship between the entities Part and Supplier. Relationships could be 1-to-1, 1-to-n, n-to-1 or m-to-n, depending on how the entities participate in the relationship. In our example, Suppliers can supply multiple parts, and parts can be supplied by multiple suppliers. Hence, the Supply relationship is m-to-n. Relationships can also have attributes that describe the relationship. In our example, qty and price are attributes of the relationship Supply.

A popular representation for E-R models was a "boxes and arrows" notation as shown in Figure 8. The E-R model never gained acceptance as the underlying data model that is implemented by a DBMS. Perhaps the reason was that in the early days there was no query language proposed for it. Perhaps it was simply overwhelmed by the interest in the relational model in the 1970's. Perhaps it looked too much like a "cleaned up" version of the CODASYL model. Whatever the reason, the E-R model languished in the 1970's.

An E-R Diagram
Figure 8

There is one area where the E-R model has been wildly successful, namely in data base (schema) design. The standard wisdom from the relational advocates was to perform data base design by constructing an initial collection of tables. Then, one applied normalization theory to this initial design. Throughout the decade of the 1970's there were a collection of normal forms proposed, including second normal form (2NF) [CODD71b], third normal form [CODD71b], Boyce-Codd normal form (BCNF) [CODD72b], fourth normal form (4NF) [FAGI77a], and project-join normal form [FAGI77b].

There were two problems with normalization theory when applied to real world data base design problems. First, real DBAs immediately asked "How do I get an initial set of tables?" Normalization theory had no answer to this important question. Second, and perhaps more serious, normalization theory was based on the concept of functional dependencies, and real world DBAs could not understand this construct. Hence, data base design using normalization was "dead in the water".

In contrast, the E-R model became very popular as a data base design tool. Chen's papers contained a methodology for constructing an initial E-R diagram. In addition, it was straightforward to convert an E-R diagram into a collection of tables in third normal form [WONG79]. Hence, a DBA tool could perform this conversion automatically. As such, a DBA could construct an E-R model of his data, typically using a boxes and arrows drawing tool, and then be assured that he would automatically get a good relational schema. Essentially all data base design tools, such as Silverrun from Magna Solutions, ERwin from Computer Associates, and ER/Studio from Embarcadero work in this fashion.

Lesson 11: Functional dependencies are too difficult for mere mortals to understand. Another reason for KISS (Keep it simple stupid).

VI R++ Era

Beginning in the early 1980's a (sizeable) collection of papers appeared which can be described by the following template:

Consider an application, call it X
Try to implement X on a relational DBMS
Show why the queries are difficult or why poor performance is observed
Add a new "feature" to the relational model to correct the problem

Many X's were investigated including mechanical CAD [KATZ86], VLSI CAD [BATO85], text management [STON83], time [SNOD85] and computer graphics [SPON84]. This collection of papers formed "the R++ era", as they all proposed additions to the relational model. In our opinion, probably the best of the lot was Gem [ZANI83]. Zaniolo proposed adding the following constructs to the relational model, together with corresponding query language extensions:

1) **set-valued attributes**. In a Parts table, it is often the case that there is an attribute, such as available_colors, which can take on a set of values. It would be nice to add a data type to the relational model to deal with sets of values.

2) aggregation (tuple-reference as a data type). In the Supply relation noted above, there are two **foreign keys**, sno and pno, that effectively point to tuples in other tables. It is arguably cleaner to have the Supply table have the following structure:

Supply (PT, SR, qty, price)

Here the data type of PT is "tuple in the Part table" and the data type of SR is "tuple in the Supplier table". Of course, the expected implementation of these data types is via some sort of pointer. With these constructs however, we can find the suppliers who supply red parts as:

```
Select Supply.SR.sno
From Supply
Where Supply.PT.pcolor = "red"
```

This "cascaded dot" notation allowed one to query the Supply table and then effectively reference tuples in other tables. This cascaded dot notation is similar to the path expressions seen in high level network languages such as LSL. It allowed one to traverse between tables without having to specify an explicit join.

3) generalization. Suppose there are two kinds of parts in our example, say electrical parts and plumbing parts. For electrical parts, we record the power consumption and the voltage. For plumbing parts we record the diameter and the material used to make the part. This is shown pictorially in Figure 9, where we see a root part with two specializations. Each specialization **inherits** all of the data attributes in its ancestors.

Inheritance hierarchies were put in early programming languages such as Planner [HEWI69] and Conniver [MCDO73]. The same concept has been included in more recent programming languages, such as C++. Gem merely applied this well known concept to data bases.

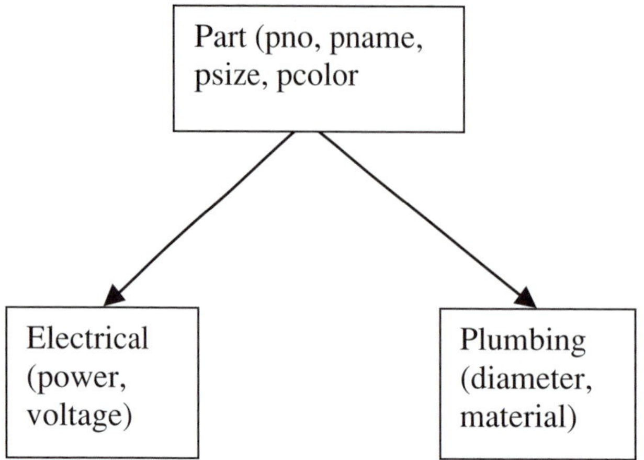

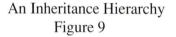

An Inheritance Hierarchy
Figure 9

In Gem, one could reference an inheritance hierarchy in the query language. For example to find the names of Red electrical parts, one would use:

```
Select E.pname
From Electrical E
Where E.pcolor = “red”
```

In addition, Gem had a very elegant treatment of null values.

The problem with extensions of this sort is that while they allowed easier query formulation than was available in the conventional relational model, they offered very little performance improvement. For example, primary-key-foreign-key relationships in the relational model easily simulate tuple as a data type. Moreover, since foreign keys are essentially logical pointers, the performance of this construct is similar to that available from some other kind of pointer scheme. Hence, an implementation of Gem would not be noticeably faster than an implementation of the relational model

In the early 1980’s, the relational vendors were singularly focused on improving transaction performance and scalability of their systems, so that they could be used for large scale business data processing applications. This was a very big market that had major revenue potential. In contrast, R++ ideas would have minor impact. Hence, there was little technology transfer of R++ ideas into the commercial world, and this research focus had very little long-term impact.

Lesson 12: Unless there is a big performance or functionality advantage, new constructs will go nowhere.

VII The Semantic Data Model Era

At around the same time, there was another school of thought with similar ideas, but a different marketing strategy. They suggested that the relational data model is "semantically impoverished", i.e. it is incapable of easily expressing a class of data of interest. Hence, there is a need for a "post relational" data model.

Post relational data models were typically called semantic data models. Examples included the work by Smith and Smith [SMIT77] and Hammer and McLeod [HAMM81]. SDM from Hammer and McLeod is arguably the more elaborate semantic data model, and we focus on its concepts in this section.

SDM focuses on the notion of **classes**, which are a collection of records obeying the same schema. Like Gem, SDM exploited the concepts of aggregation and generalization and included a notion of sets. Aggregation is supported by allowing classes to have attributes that are records in other classes. However, SDM generalizes the aggregation construct in Gem by allowing an attribute in one class to be a **set** of instances of records in some class. For example, there might be two classes, Ships and Countries. The Countries class could have an attribute called Ships_registered_here, having as its value a collection of ships. The **inverse** attribute, country_of_registration can also be defined in SDM.

In addition, classes can generalize other classes. Unlike Gem, generalization is extended to be a graph rather than just a tree. For example, Figure 10 shows a generalization graph where American_oil_tankers inherits attributes from both Oil_tankers and American_ships. This construct is often called **multiple inheritance**. Classes can also be the union, intersection or difference between other classes. They can also be a subclass of another class, specified by a predicate to determine membership. For example, Heavy_ships might be a subclass of Ships with weight greater than 500 tons. Lastly, a class can also be a collection of records that are grouped together for some other reason. For example Atlantic_convoy might be a collection of ships that are sailing together across the Atlantic Ocean.

Lastly, classes can have class variables, for example the Ships class can have a class variable which is the number of members of the class.

Most semantic data models were very complex, and were generally paper proposals. Several years after SDM was defined, Univac explored an implementation of Hammer and McLeod's ideas. However, they quickly discovered that SQL was an intergalactic standard, and their incompatible system was not very successful in the marketplace.

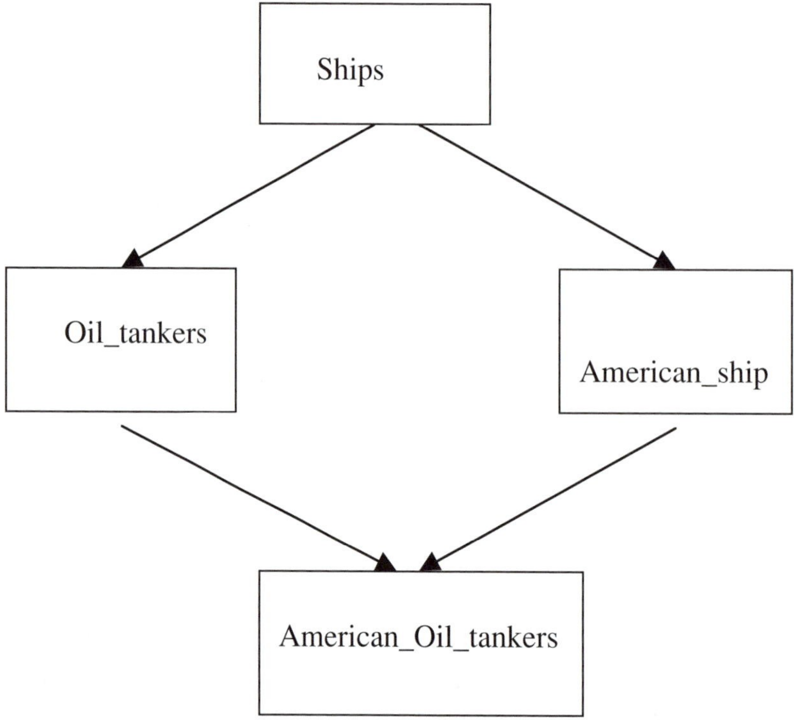

A Example of Multiple Inheritance
Figure 10

In our opinion, SDMs had the same two problems that faced the R++ advocates. Like the R++ proposals, they were a lot of machinery that was easy to simulate on relational systems. Hence, there was very little leverage in the constructs being proposed. The SDM camp also faced the second issue of R++ proposals, namely that the established vendors were distracted with transaction processing performance. Hence, semantic data models had little long term influence.

VIII OO Era

Beginning in the mid 1980's there was a "tidal wave" of interest in Object-oriented DBMSs (OODB). Basically, this community pointed to an "impedance mismatch" between relational data bases and languages like C++.

In practice, relational data bases had their own naming systems, their own data type systems, and their own conventions for returning data as a result of a query. Whatever programming language was used alongside a relational data base also had its own version of all of these facilities. Hence, to bind an application to the data base required a conversion from "programming language speak" to "data base speak" and back. This was like "gluing an apple onto a pancake", and was the reason for the so-called impedance mismatch.

For example, consider the following C++ snippet which defines a Part Structure and then allocates an Example_part.

```
Struct Part {
        Int number;
        Char* name;
        Char* bigness;
        Char* color;
} Example_part;
```

All SQL run-time systems included mechanisms to load variables in the above Struct from values in the data base. For example to retrieve part 16 into the above Struct required the following stylized program:

```
Define cursor P as
        Select *
        From Part
        Where pno = 16;

Open P into Example_part
Until no-more{
        Fetch P (Example_part.number = pno,
                Example_name = pname
                Example_part.bigness = psize
                Example_part.color = pcolor)
}
```

First one defined a cursor to range over the answer to the SQL query. Then, one opened the cursor, and finally fetched a record from the cursor and bound it to programming language variables, which did not need to be the same name or type as the corresponding data base objects. If necessary, data type conversion was performed by the run-time interface.

The programmer could now manipulate the Struct in the native programming language. When more than one record could result from the query, the programmer had to iterate the cursor as in the above example.

It would seem to be much cleaner to integrate DBMS functionality more closely into a programming language. Specifically, one would like a **persistent programming language**, i.e. one where the variables in the language could represent disk-based data as well as main memory data and where data base search criteria were also language constructs. Several prototype persistent languages were developed in the late 1970's, including Pascal-R [SCHM77], Rigel [ROWE79], and a language embedding for PL/1 [DATE76]. For example, Rigel allowed the above query to be expressed as:

```
For P in Part where P.pno = 16{
        Code_to_manipulate_part
}
```

In Rigel, as in other persistent languages, variables (in this case pno) could be declared. However, they only needed to be declared once to Rigel, and not once to the language and a second time to the DBMS. In addition, the predicate p.no = 16 is part of the Rigel programming language. Lastly, one used the standard programming language iterators (in this case a For loop) to iterate over qualifying records.

A persistent programming language is obviously much cleaner than a SQL embedding. However, it requires the compiler for the programming language to be extended with DBMS-oriented functionality. Since there is no programming language Esperanto, this extension must be done once per complier. Moreover, each extension will likely be unique, since C++ is quite different from, for example, APL.

Unfortunately, programming language experts have consistently refused to focus on I/O in general and DBMS functionality in particular. Hence, all programming languages that we are aware of have no built-in functionality in this area. Not only does this make embedding data sublanguages tedious, but also the result is usually difficult to program and error prone. Lastly, language expertise does not get applied to important special purpose data-oriented languages, such as report writers and so-called fourth generation languages.

Hence, there was no technology transfer from the persistent programming language research efforts of the 1970's into the commercial marketplace, and ugly data-sublanguage embeddings prevailed.

In the mid 1980's there was a resurgence of interest in persistent programming languages, motivated by the popularity of C++. This research thrust was called Object-Oriented Data Bases (OODB), and focused mainly on persistent C++. Although the early work came from the research community with systems like Garden [SKAR86] and Exodus [RICH87], the primary push on OODBs came from a collection of start-ups, including Ontologic, Object Design and Versant. All built commercial systems that supported persistent C++.

The general form of these systems was to support C++ as a data model. Hence, any C++ structure could be persisted. For some reason, it was popular to extend C++ with the notion of relationships, a concept borrowed directly from the Entity-Relationship data model a decade earlier. Hence, several systems extended the C++ run-time with support for this concept.

Most of the OODB community decided to address engineering data bases as their target market. One typical example of this area is engineering CAD. In a CAD application, an engineer opens an engineering drawing, say for an electronic circuit, and then modifies the engineering object, tests it, or runs a power simulator on the circuit. When he is done he closes the object. The general form of these applications is to open a large engineering object and then process it extensively before closing it.

Historically, such objects were read into virtual memory by a load program. This program would "swizzle" a disk-based representation of the object into a virtual memory C++ object. The word "swizzle" came from the necessity of modifying any pointers in the object when loading. On disk, pointers are typically some sort of logical reference such as a foreign key, though they can also be disk pointers, for example (block-number, offset). In virtual memory, they should be virtual memory pointers. Hence, the loader had to swizzle the disk representation to a virtual memory representation. Then, the code would operate on the object, usually for a long time. When finished, an unloader would linearize the C++ data structure back into one that could persist on the disk.

To address the engineering market, an implementation of persistent C++ had the following requirements:

1) no need for a declarative query language. All one needed was a way to reference large disk-based engineering objects in C++.
2) no need for fancy transaction management. This market is largely one-user-at-a-time processing large engineering objects. Rather, some sort of versioning system would be nice.
3) The run-time system had to be competitive with conventional C++ when operating on the object. In this market, the performance of an algorithm using persistent C++ had to be competitive with that available from a custom load program and conventional C++

Naturally, the OODB vendors focused on meeting these requirements. Hence, there was weak support for transactions and queries. Instead, the vendors focused on good performance for manipulating persistent C++ structures. For example, consider the following declaration:

```
Persistent int I;
```

And then the code snippet:

```
I =: I+1;
```

In conventional C++, this is a single instruction. To be competitive, incrementing a persistent variable cannot require a process switch to process a persistent object. Hence, the DBMS must run in the same address space as the application. Likewise, engineering objects must be aggressively cached in main memory, and then "lazily" written back to disk.

Hence, the commercial OODBs, for example Object Design [LAMB91], had innovative architectures that achieved these objectives.

Unfortunately, the market for such engineering applications never got very large, and there were too many vendors competing for a "niche" market. At the present time, all of the OODB vendors have failed, or have repositioned their companies to offer something other than and OODB. For example, Object Design has renamed themselves Excelon, and is selling XML services

In our opinion, there are a number of reasons for this market failure.

1) absence of leverage. The OODB vendors presented the customer with the opportunity to avoid writing a load program and an unload program. This is not a major service, and customers were not willing to pay big money for this feature.
2) No standards. All of the OODB vendor offerings were incompatible.
3) Relink the world. In anything changed, for example a C++ method that operated on persistent data, then all programs which used this method had to be relinked. This was a noticeable management problem.
4) No programming language Esperanto. If your enterprise had a single application not written in C++ that needed to access persistent data, then you could not use one of the OODB products.

Of course, the OODB products were not designed to work on business data processing applications. Not only did they lack strong transaction and query systems but also they ran in the same address space as the application. This meant that the application could freely manipulate all disk-based data, and no data protection was possible. Protection and authorization is important in the business data processing market. In addition, OODBs were clearly a throw back to the CODASYL days, i.e. a low-level record at a time language with the programmer coding the query optimization algorithm. As a result, these products had essentially no penetration in this very large market.

There was one company, O2, that had a different business plan. O2 supported an object-oriented data model, but it was not C++. Also, they embedded a high level declarative language called OQL into a programming language. Hence, they proposed what amounted to a semantic data model with a declarative query language, but marketed it as an OODB. Also, they focused on business data processing, not on the engineering application space.

Unfortunately for O2, there is a saying that "as goes the United States goes the rest of the world". This means that new products must make it in North America, and that the rest of the world watches the US for market acceptance. O2 was a French company, spun out of Inria by Francois Bancilhon. It was difficult for O2 to get market traction in Europe with an advanced product, because of the above adage. Hence, O2 realized they had to attack the US market, and moved to the United States rather late in the game. By then, it was simply too late, and the OODB era was on a downward spiral. It is interesting to conjecture about the marketplace chances of O2 if they had started initially in the USA with sophisticated US venture capital backing.

Lesson 13: Packages will not sell to users unless they are in "major pain"

Lesson 14: Persistent languages will go nowhere without the support of the programming language community.

IX The Object-Relational Era

The Object-Relational (OR) era was motivated by a very simple problem. In the early days of INGRES, the team had been interested in geographic information systems (GIS) and had suggested mechanisms for their support [GO75]. Around 1982, the following simple GIS issue was haunting the INGRES research team. Suppose one wants to store geographic positions in a data base. For example, one might want to store the location of a collection of intersections as:

Intersections (I-id, long, lat, other-data)

Here, we require storing geographic points (long, lat) in a data base. Then, if we want to find all the intersections within a bounding rectangle, (X0, Y0, X1, Y1), then the SQL query is:

Select I-id
From Intersections
Where X0 < long < X1 and Y0 < lat < Y1

Unfortunately, this is a two dimensional search, and the B-trees in INGRES are a one-dimensional access method. One-dimensional access methods do not do two-dimensional searches efficiently, so there is no way in a relational system for this query to run fast.

More troubling was the "notify parcel owners" problem. Whenever there is request for a variance to the zoning laws for a parcel of land in California, there must be a public hearing, and all property owners within a certain distance must be notified.

Suppose one assumes that all parcels are rectangles, and they are stored in the following table.

Parcel (P-id, Xmin, Xmax, Ymin, Ymax)

Then, one must enlarge the parcel in question by the correct number of feet, creating a "super rectangle" with co-ordinates X0, X1, Y0, Y1. All property owners whose parcels intersect this super rectangle must be notified, and the most efficient query to do this task is:

Select P-id
From Parcel
Where Xmax > X0 and Ymax > Y0 and Xmin < X1 and Ymax < Y1

Again, there is no way to execute this query efficiency with a B-tree access method. Moreover, it takes a moment to convince oneself that this query is correct, and there are several other less efficient representations. In summary, simple GIS queries are difficult to express in SQL, and they execute on standard B-trees with unreasonably bad performance.

The following observation motivates the OR proposal. Early relational systems supported integers, floats, and character strings, along with the obvious operators, primarily because these were the data types of IMS, which was the early competition. IMS chose these data types because that was what the business data processing market wanted, and that was their market focus. Relational systems also chose B-trees because these facilitate the searches that are common in business data processing. Later relational systems expanded the collection of business data processing data types to include date, time and money. More recently, packed decimal and blobs have been added.

In other markets, such as GIS, these are not the correct types, and B-trees are not the correct access method. Hence, to address any given market, one needs data types and access methods appropriate to the market. Since there may be many other markets one would want to address, it is inappropriate to "hard wire" a specific collection of data types and indexing strategies. Rather a sophisticated user should be able to add his own; i.e. to customize a DBMS to his particular needs. Such customization is also helpful in business data processing, since one or more new data types appears to be needed every decade.

As a result, the OR proposal added

user-defined data types,
user-defined operators,
user-defined functions, and
user-defined access methods

to a SQL engine. The major OR research prototype was Postgres [STON86].

Applying the OR methodology to GIS, one merely adds geographic points and geographic boxes as data types. With these data types, the above tables above can be expressed as:

Intersections (I-id, point, other-data)
Parcel (P-id, P-box)

Of course, one must also have SQL operators appropriate to each data type. For our simple application, these are !! (point in rectangle) and ## (box intersects box). The two queries now become

```
Select I-id
From Intersections
Where point !! "X0, X1, Y0, Y1"
```

and

```
Select P-id
From Parcel
Where  P-box ## "X0, X1, Y0, Y1"
```

To support the definition of user-defined operators, one must be able to specify a user-defined function (UDF), which can process the operator. Hence, for the above examples, we require functions

Point-in-rect (point, box)

and

Box-int-box (box, box)

which return Booleans. These functions must be called whenever the corresponding operator must be evaluated, passing the two arguments in the call, and then acting appropriately on the result.

To address the GIS market one needs a multi-dimensional indexing system, such as Quad trees [SAME84] or R-trees [GUTM84]. In summary, a high performance GIS DBMS can be constructed with appropriate user-defined data types, user-defined operators, user-defined functions, and user-defined access methods.

The main contribution of Postgres was to figure out the engine mechanisms required to support this kind of extensibility. In effect, previous relational engines had hard coded support for a specific set of data types, operators and access methods. All this hard-coded logic must be ripped out and replaced with a much more flexible architecture. Many of the details of the Postgres scheme are covered in [STON90].

There is another interpretation to UDFs which we now present. In the mid 1980's Sybase pioneered the inclusion of **stored procedures** in a DBMS. The basic idea was to offer high performance on TPC-B, which consisted of the following commands that simulate cashing a check:

```
Begin transaction

Update account set balance = balance – X
Where account_number = Y
```

```
Update Teller set cash_drawer = cash_drawer – X
Where Teller_number = Z

Update bank set cash – cash – Y

Insert into log (account_number = Y, check = X, Teller= Z)

Commit
```

This transaction requires 5 or 6 round trip messages between the DBMS and the application. Since these context switches are expensive relative to the very simple processing which is being done, application performance is limited by the context switching time.

A clever way to reduce this time is to define a stored procedure:

```
Define cash_check (X, Y, Z)
        Begin transaction

        Update account set balance = balance – X
        Where account_number = Y

        Update Teller set cash_drawer = cash_drawer – X
        Where Teller_number = Z

        Update bank set cash – cash – Y

        Insert into log (account_number = Y, check = X, Teller= Z)

        Commit

        End cash_check
```

Then, the application merely executes the stored procedure, with its parameters, e.g:

```
Execute cash_check ($100, 79246, 15)
```

This requires only one round trip between the DBMS and the application rather than 5 or 6, and speeds up TPC-B immensely. To go fast on standard benchmarks such as TPC-B, all vendors implemented stored procedures. Of course, this required them to define proprietary (small) programming languages to handle error messages and perform required control flow. This is necessary for the stored procedure to deal correctly with conditions such as "insufficient funds" in an account.

Effectively a stored procedure is a UDF that is written in a proprietary language and is "brain dead", in the sense that it can only be executed with constants for its parameters.

The Postgres UDTs and UDFs generalized this notion to allow code to be written in a conventional programming language and to be called in the middle of processing conventional SQL queries.

Postgres implemented a sophisticated mechanism for UDTs, UDFs and user-defined access methods. In addition, Postgres also implemented less sophisticated notions of inheritance, and type constructors for pointers (references), sets, and arrays. This latter set of features allowed Postgres to become "object-oriented" at the height of the OO craze.

Later benchmarking efforts such as Bucky [CARE97] proved that the major win in Postgres was UDTs and UDFs; the OO constructs were fairly easy and fairly efficient to simulate on conventional relational systems. This work demonstrated once more what the R++ and SDM crowd had already seen several years earlier; namely built-in support for aggregation and generalization offer little performance benefit. Put differently, the major contribution of the OR efforts turned out to be a better mechanism for stored procedures and user-defined access methods.

The OR model has enjoyed some commercial success. Postgres was commercialized by Illustra. After struggling to find a market for the first couple of years, Illustra caught "the internet wave" and became "the data base for cyberspace". If one wanted to store text and images in a data base and mix them with conventional data types, then Illustra was the engine which could do that. Near the height of the internet craze, Illustra was acquired by Informix. From the point of view of Illustra, there were two reasons to join forces with Informix:

a) inside every OR application, there is a transaction processing sub-application. In order to be successful in OR, one must have a high performance OLTP engine. Postgres had never focused on OLTP performance, and the cost of adding it to Illustra would be very high. It made more sense to combine Illustra features into an existing high performance engine.

b) To be successful, Illustra had to convince third party vendors to convert pieces of their application suites into UDTs and UDFs. This was a non-trivial undertaking, and most external vendors balked at doing so, at least until Illustra could demonstrate that OR presented a large market opportunity. Hence, Illustra had a "chicken and egg" problem. To get market share they needed UDTs and UDFs; to get UDTs and UDFs they needed market share.

Informix provided a solution to both problems, and the combined company proceeded over time to sell OR technology fairly successfully into the GIS market and into the market for large content repositories (such as those envisoned by CNN and the British Broadcasting Corporation). However, widescale adoption of OR in the business data processing market remained elusive. Of course, the (unrelated) financial difficulties at Informix made selling new technology such as OR extremely difficult. This certainly hindered wider adoption.

OR technology is gradually finding market acceptance. For example, it is more effective to implement data mining algorithms as UDFs, a concept pioneered by Red Brick and recently adopted by Oracle. Instead of moving a terabyte sized warehouse up to mining code in middleware, it is more efficient to move the code into the DBMS and avoid all the message overhead. OR technology is also being used to support XML processing, as we will see presently.

One of the barriers to acceptance of OR technology in the broader business market is the absence of standards. Every vendor has his own way of defining and calling UDFs, In addition, most vendors support Java UDFs, but Microsoft does not. It is plausible that OR technology will not take off unless (and until) the major vendors can agree on standard definitions and calling conventions.

Lesson 14: The major benefits of OR is two-fold: putting code in the data base (and thereby bluring the distinction between code and data) and user-defined access methods.

Lesson 15: Widespread adoption of new technology requires either standards and/or an elephant pushing hard.

X Semi Structured Data

There has been an avalanche of work on "semi-structured" data in the last five years. An early example of this class of proposals was Lore [MCHU97]. More recently, the various XML-based proposals have the same flavor. At the present time, XMLSchema and XQuery are the standards for XML-based data.

There are two basic points that this class of work exemplifies.

1) schema last
2) complex network-oriented data model

We talk about each point separately in this section.

10.1 Schema Last

The first point is that a schema is not required in advance. In a "**schema first**" system the schema is specified, and instances of data records that conform to this schema can be subsequently loaded. Hence, the data base is always consistent with the pre-existing schema, because the DBMS rejects any records that are not consistent with the schema. All previous data models required a DBA to specify the schema in advance.

In this class of proposals the schema does not need to be specified in advance. It can be specified last, or even not at all. In a "**schema last**" system, data instances must be self-describing, because there is not necessarily a schema to give meaning to incoming records. Without a self-describing format, a record is merely "a bucket of bits".

To make a record self-describing, one must tag each attribute with metadata that defines the meaning of the attribute. Here are a couple of examples of such records, using an artificial tagging system:

Person:
    Name: Joe Jones
    Wages: 14.75
    Employer: My_accounting
    Hobbies: skiing, bicycling
    Works for: ref (Fred Smith)
    Favorite joke: Why did the chicken cross the road? To get to the other side
    Office number: 247
    Major skill: accountant
End Person

Person:
    Name: Smith, Vanessa
    Wages: 2000
    Favorite coffee: Arabian
    Passtimes: sewing, swimming
    Works_for: Between jobs
    Favorite restaurant: Panera
    Number of children: 3
End Person:

As can be seen, these two records each describe a person. Moreover, each attribute has one of three characteristics:

1) it appears in only one of the two records, and there is no attribute in the other record with the same meaning.
2) it appears in only one of the two records, but there is an attribute in the other record with the same meaning (e.g. passtimes and hobbies).
3) it appears in both records, but the format or meaning is different (e.g. Works_for, Wages)

Clearly, comparing these two persons is a challenge. This is an example of **semantic heterogeneity**, where information on a common object (in this case a person) does not conform to a common representation. Semantic heterogeneity makes query processing a big challenge, because there is no structure on which to base indexing decisions and query execution strategies.

The advocates of "schema last" typically have in mind applications where it is natural for users to enter their data as free text, perhaps through a word processor (which may annotate the text with some simple metadata about document structure). In this case, it is an imposition to require a schema to exist before a user can add data. The "schema last" advocates then have in mind automatically or semi-automatically tagging incoming data to construct the above semi-structured records.

In contrast, if a business form is used for data entry, (which would probably be natural for the above Person data), then a "schema first" methodology is being employed, because the person who designed the form is, in effect, also defining the schema by what he allows in the form. As a result, schema last is appropriate mainly for applications where free text is the mechanism for data entry.

To explore the utility of schema-last, we present the following scheme that classifies applications into four buckets.

Ones with rigidly structured data
Ones with rigidly structured data with some text fields
Ones with semi-structured data
Ones with text

Rigidly structured data encompasses data that must conform to a schema. In general, this includes essentially all data on which business processes must operate. For example, consider the payroll data base for a typical company. This data must be rigidly structured, or the check-printing program might produce erroneous results. One simply cannot tolerate missing or badly formatted data that business processes depends on. For rigidly structured data, one should insist on schema-first.

The personnel records of a large company are typical of the second class of data base applications that we consider. There is a considerable amount of rigidly structured data, such as the health plan each employee is enrolled in, and the fringe benefits they are entitled to. In addition, there are free text fields, such as the comments of the manager at the last employee review. The employee review form is typically rigidly structured; hence the only free text input is into specific comment fields. Again schema first appears the right way to go, and this kind of application is easily addressed by an Object-Relational DBMS with an added text data type.

The third class of data is termed semi-structured. The best examples we can think of are want ads and resumes. In each of these cases, there is some structure to the data, but data instances can vary in the fields that are present and how they are represented. Moreover, there is no schema to which instances necessarily conform. Semi-structured instances are often entered as a text document, and then parsed to find information of interest, which is in turn "shredded" into appropriate fields inside the storage engine. In this case, schema last is a good idea.

The fourth class of data is pure text, i.e. documents with no particular structure. In this bucket, there is no obvious structure to exploit. Information Retrieval (IR) systems have focused on this class of data for several decades. Few IR researchers have any interest in semi-structured data; rather they are interested in document retrieval based on the textual content of the document. Hence, there is no schema to deduce in this bucket, and this corresponds to "schema not at all".

As a result, schema-last proposals deal only with the third class of data in our classification system. It is difficult to think up very many examples of this class, other than resumes and advertisements. The proponents (many of whom are academics) often suggest that college course descriptions fit this category. However, every university we know has a rigid format for course descriptions, which includes one or more text fields. Most have a standard form for entering the data, and a system (manual or automatic) to reject course descriptions that do not fit this format. Hence, course descriptions are an example of the second class of data, not the third. In our opinion, a careful examination of the claimed instances of class 3 applications will yield many fewer actual instances of the class. Moreover, the largest web site specializing in resumes (Monster.com) has recently adopted a business form through which data entry occurs. Hence, they have switched from class 3 to class 2, presumably to enforce more uniformity on their data base (and thereby easier comparability).

Semantic heterogeneity has been with enterprises for a very long time. They spend vast sums on warehouse projects to design standard schemas and then convert operational data to this standard. Moreover, in most organizations semantic heterogeneity is dealt with on a data set basis; i.e. data sets with different schemas must be homogenized. Typical warehouse projects are over budget, because schema homogenization is so hard. Any schema-last application will have to confront semantic heterogeneity on a record-by-record basis, where it will be even more costly to solve. This is a good reason to avoid "schema last" if at all possible.

In summary, schema last is appropriate only for the third class of applications in our classification scheme. Moreover, it is difficult to come up with very many convincing examples in this class. If anything, the trend is to move class three applications into class 2, presumably to make semantic heterogeneity issues easier to deal with. Lastly, class three applications appear to have modest amounts of data. For these reasons, we view schema last data bases as a niche market.

10.2 XML Data Model

We now turn to the XML data model. In the past, the mechanism for describing a schema was Document Type Definitions (DTDs), and in the future the data model will be specified in XMLSchema. DTDs and XMLSchema were intended to deal with the structure of formatted documents (and hence the word "document" in DTDs). As a result, they look like a document markup language, in particular a subset of SGML]. Because the structure of a document can be very complex, these document specification standards are necessarily very complex. As a document specification system, we have no quarrel with these standards.

After DTDs and XMLSchema were "cast into cement", members of the DBMS research community decided to try and use them to describe structured data. As a data model for structured data, we believe both standards are seriously flawed. To a first approximation, these standards have everything that was ever specified in any previous data model proposal. In addition, they contain additional features that are complex enough, that nobody in the DBMS community has ever seriously proposed them in a data model.

For example, the data model presented in XMLSchema has the following characteristics:

1) XML records can be hierarchical, as in IMS
2) XML records can have "links" (references to) other records, as in CODASYL, Gem and SDM
3) XML records can have set-based attributes, as in SDM
4) XML records can inherit from other records in several ways, as in SDM

In addition, XMLSchema also has several features, which are well known in the DBMS community but never attempted in previous data models because of complexity. One example is **union types**, that is, an attribute in a record can be of one of a set of possible types. For example, in a personnel data base, the field "works-for" could either be a department number in the enterprise, or the name of an outside firm to whom the employee is on loan. In this case works-for can either be a string or an integer, with different meanings.

Note that B-tree indexes on union types are complex. In effect, there must be an index for each base type in the union. Moreover, there must be a different query plan for each query that touches a union type. If two union types containing N and M base types respectively, are to be joined, then there will be at least Max (M, N) plans to co-ordinate. For these reasons, union types have never been seriously considered for inclusion in a DBMS.

Obviously, XMLSchema is far and away the most complex data model ever proposed. It is clearly at the other extreme from the relational model on the "keep it simple stupid" (KISS) scale. It is hard to imaging something this complex being used as a model for structured data. We can see three scenarios off into the future.

Scenario 1: XMLSchema will fail because of excessive complexity

Scenario 2: A "data-oriented" subset of XMLSchema will be proposed that is vastly simpler.

Scenario 3: XMLSchema will become popular. Within a decade all of the problems with IMS and CODASYL that motivated Codd to invent the relational model will resurface. At that time some enterprising researcher, call him Y, will "dust off" Codd's original paper, and there will be a replay of the "Great Debate". Presumably it will end the same way as the last one. Moreover, Codd won the Turing award in 1981 [CODD82] for his contribution. In this scenario, Y will win the Turing award circa 2015.

In fairness to the proponents of " X stuff", they have learned something from history. They are proposing a set-at-a-time query language, Xquery, which will provide a certain level of data independence. As was discovered in the CODASYL era, providing views for a network data model will be a challenge (and will be much harder than for the relational model).

10.3 Summary

Summarizing XML/XML-Schema/Xquery is a challenge, because it has many facets. Clearly, XML will be a popular "on-the-wire" format for data movement across a network. The reason is simple: XML goes through firewalls, and other formats do not. Since there is always a firewall between the machines of any two enterprises, it follows that cross-enterprise data movement will use XML. Because a typical enterprise wishes to move data within the enterprise the same way as outside the enterprise, there is every reason to believe that XML will become an intergalactic data movement standard.

As a result, all flavors of system and application software must be prepared to send and receive XML. It is straightforward to convert the tuple sets that are produced by relational data bases into XML. If one has an OR engine, this is merely a user-defined function. Similarly, one can accept input in XML and convert it to tuples to store in a data base with a second user-defined function. Hence OR technology facilitates the necessary format conversions. Other system software will likewise require a conversion facility.

Moreover, higher level data movement facilities built on top of XML, such as SOAP, will be equally popular. Clearly, remote procedure calls that go through firewalls are much more useful than ones that don't. Hence, SOAP will dominate other RPC proposals.

It is possible that native XML DBMSs will become popular, but we doubt it. It will take a decade for XML DBMSs to become high performance engines that can compete with the current elephants. Moreover, schema-last should only be attractive in limited markets, and the overly complex network model are the antithesis of KISS. XMLSchema cries out for subsetting.. A clean subset of XML-schema would have the characteristic that it maps easily to current relational DBMSs. In which case, what is the point of implementing a new engine? Hence, we expect native XML DBMSs to be a niche market.

Consider now Xquery. A (sane) subset is readily mappable to the OR SQL systems of several of the vendors. For example, Informix implemented the Xquery operator "//" as a user-defined function. Hence, it is fairly straightforward to implement a subset of Xquery on top of most existing engines. As a result, it is not unlikely that the elephants will support both SQL and a subset of XMLSchema and XQuery. The latter interface will be translated into SQL.

XML is sometimes marketed as the solution to the semantic heterogeneity problem, mentioned earlier. Nothing could be further from the truth. Just because two people tag a data element as a salary does not mean that the two data elements are comparable. One can be salary after taxes in French Francs including a lunch allowance, while the other could be salary before taxes in US dollar. Furthermore, if you call them "rubber gloves" and I call them "latex hand protectors", then XML will be useless in deciding that they are the same concept. Hence, the role of XML will be limited to providing the vocabulary in which common schemas can be constructed.

In addition, we believe that cross-enterprise data sharing using common schemas will be slow in coming, because semantic heterogeneity issues are so difficult to resolve. Although W3C has a project in this area, the so-called semantic web, we are not optimistic about its future impact. After all, the AI community has been working on knowledge representation systems for a couple of decades with limited results. The semantic web bears a striking resemblance to these past efforts. Since web services depend on passing information between disparate systems, don't bet on the early success this concept.

More precisely, we believe that cross-enterprise information sharing will be limited to:

Enterprises that have high economic value in co-operating. After all, the airlines have been sharing data across disparate reservation systems for years.

Applications that are semantically simple (such as e-mail) where the main data type is text and there are no complex semantic mappings involved.

Applications where there is an "elephant" that controls the market. Enterprises like WalMart and Dell have little difficulty in sharing data with their suppliers. They simply say "if you want to sell to me; here is how you will interact with my information systems". When there is an elephant powerful enough to dictate standards, then cross enterprise information sharing can be readily accomplished.

We close with one final cynical note. A couple of years ago OLE-DB was being pushed hard by Microsoft; now it is "X stuff". OLE-DB was pushed by Microsoft, in large part, because it did not control ODBC and perceived a competitive advantage in OLE-DB. Now Microsoft perceives a big threat from Java and its various cross platform extensions, such as J2EE. Hence, it is pushing hard on the XML and Soap front to try to blunt the success of Java.

There is every reason to believe that in a couple of years Microsoft will see competitive advantage in some other DBMS-oriented standard. In the same way that OLE-DB was sent to an early death, we expect Microsoft to send "X stuff" to a similar fate, the minute marketing considerations dictate a change.

Less cynically, we claim that technological advances keep changing the rules. For example, it is clear that the micro-sensor technology coming to the market in the next few years will have a huge impact on system software, and we expect DBMSs and their interfaces to be affected in some (yet to be figured out) way.

Hence, we expect a succession of new DBMS standards off into the future. In such an ever changing world, it is crucial that a DBMS be very adaptable, so it can deal with whatever the next "big thing" is. OR DBMSs have that characteristic; native XML DBMSs do not.

Lesson 16: Schema-last is a probably a niche market

Lesson 17: XQuery is pretty much OR SQL with a different syntax

Lesson 18: XML will not solve the semantic heterogeneity either inside or outside the enterprise.

XI Full Circle

This paper has surveyed three decades of data model thinking. It is clear that we have come "full circle". We started off with a complex data model, which was followed by a great debate between a complex model and a much simpler one. The simpler one was shown to be advantageous in terms of understandability and its ability to support data independence.

Then, a substantial collection of additions were proposed, none of which gained substantial market traction, largely because they failed to offer substantial leverage in exchange for the increased complexity. The only ideas that got market traction were user-defined functions and user-defined access methods, and these were performance constructs not data model constructs. The current proposal is now a superset of the union of all previous proposals. I.e. we have navigated a full circle.

The debate between the XML advocates and the relational crowd bears a suspicious resemblance to the first "Great Debate" from a quarter of a century ago. A simple data model is being compared to a complex one. Relational is being compared to "CODASYL II". The only difference is that "CODASYL II" has a high level query language. Logical data independence will be harder in CODASYL II than in its predecessor, because CODASYL II is even more complex than its predecessor.

We can see history repeating itself. If native XML DBMSs gain traction, then customers will have problems with logical data independence and complexity.

To avoid repeating history, it is always wise to stand on the shoulders of those who went before, rather than on their feet. As a field, if we don't start learning something from history, we will be condemned to repeat it yet again.

More abstractly, we see few new data model ideas. Most everything put forward in the last 20 years is a reinvention of something from a quarter century ago. The only concepts noticeably new appear to be:

Code in the data base (from the OR camp)
Schema last (from the semi-structured data camp)

Schema last appears to be a niche market, and we don't see it as any sort of watershed idea. Code in the data base appears to be a really good idea. Moreover, it seems to us that designing a DBMS which made code and data equal class citizens would be a very helpful. If so, then add-ons to DBMSs such as stored procedures, triggers, and alerters would become first class citizens. The OR model got part way there; maybe it is now time to finish that effort.

References

[ASTR76] Morton M. Astrahan, Mike W. Blasgen, Donald D. Chamberlin, Kapali P. Eswaran, Jim Gray, Patricia P. Griffiths, W. Frank King, Raymond A. Lorie, Paul R. McJones, James W. Mehl, Gianfranco R. Putzolu, Irving L. Traiger, Bradford W. Wade, Vera Watson: System R: Relational Approach to Database Management. TODS 1(2): 97-137 (1976)

[BACH73] Charles W. Bachman: The Programmer as Navigator. CACM 16(11): 635-658 (1973)

[BATO85] Don S. Batory, Won Kim: Modeling Concepts for VLSI CAD Objects. TODS 10(3): 322-346 (1985)

[CARE97] Michael J. Carey, David J. DeWitt, Jeffrey F. Naughton, Mohammad Asgarian, Paul Brown, Johannes Gehrke, Dhaval Shah: The BUCKY Object-Relational Benchmark (Experience Paper). SIGMOD Conference 1997: 135-146

[CHAM74] Donald D. Chamberlin, Raymond F. Boyce: SEQUEL: A Structured English Query Language. SIGMOD Workshop, Vol. 1 1974: 249-264

[CHEN76] Peter P. Chen: The Entity-Relationship Model - Toward a Unified View of Data. TODS 1(1): 9-36 (1976)

[CODA69] CODASYL: Data Base Task Group Report. ACM, New York, N.Y., October 1969

[CODA71] CODASYL: Feature Analysis of Generalized Data Base Management Systems. ACM, New York, N.Y., May 1971

[CODA73] CODASYL: Data Description Language, Journal of Development. National Bureau of Standards, NBS Handbook 113, June 1973

[CODA78] CODASYL: Data Description Language, Journal of Development. Information Systems, January 1978

[CODD70] E. F. Codd: A Relational Model of Data for Large Shared Data Banks. CACM 13(6): 377-387 (1970)

[CODD71a] E. F. Codd: A Database Sublanguage Founded on the Relational Calculus. SIGFIDET Workshop 1971: 35-68

[CODD71b] E. F. Codd: Normalized Data Structure: A Brief Tutorial. SIGFIDET Workshop 1971: 1-17

[CODD72a] E. F. Codd: Relational Completeness of Data Base Sublanguages. IBM Research Report RJ 987, San Jose, California: (1972)

[CODD72b] E.F. Codd: Further Normalization of the Data Base Relational Model. In Data Base Systems ed. Randall Rustin, Prentice-Hall 1972

[CODD79] E. F. Codd: Extending the Database Relational Model to Capture More Meaning. TODS 4(4): 397-434 (1979)

[CODD82] E. F. Codd: Relational Database: A Practical Foundation for Productivity. CACM 25(2): 109-117 (1982)

[DATE76] C. J. Date: An Architecture for High-Level Language Database Extensions. SIGMOD Conference 1976: 101-122

[DATE84] C. J. Date: A Critique of the SQL Database Language. SIGMOD Record 14(3): 8-54, 1984.

[FAGI77a] Ronald Fagin: Multivalued Dependencies and a New Normal Form for Relational Databases. TODS 2(3): 262-278 (1977)

[FAGI77b] Ronald Fagin: Normal Forms and Relational Database Operators. SIGMOD Conference 1977: 153-160

[GO75] Angela Go, Michael Stonebraker, Carol Williams: An Approach to Implementing a Geo-Data System. Data Bases for Interactive Design 1975: 67-77

[GUTM84] Antonin Guttman: R-Trees: A Dynamic Index Structure for Spatial Searching. SIGMOD Conference 1984: 47-57

[HAMM81] Michael Hammer, Dennis McLeod: Database Description with SDM: A Semantic Database Model. TODS 6(3): 351-386 (1981)

[HEWI69] Carl Hewit: PLANNER: A Language for Proving Theorems in Robots. Proceedings of' IJCAI-69, IJCAI, Washington D.C.: May, 1969.

[KATZ86] Randy H. Katz, Ellis E. Chang, Rajiv Bhateja: Version Modeling Concepts for Computer-Aided Design Databases. SIGMOD Conference 1986: 379-386

[LAMB91] Charles Lamb, Gordon Landis, Jack A. Orenstein, Danel Weinreb: The ObjectStore System. CACM 34(10): 50-63 (1991)

[MCDO73] D. McDermott & GJ Sussman: The CONNIVER Reference Manual. AI Memo 259, MIT AI Lab, 1973.

[MCHU97] Jason McHugh, Serge Abiteboul, Roy Goldman, Dallan Quass, Jennifer Widom: Lore: A Database Management System for Semistructured Data. SIGMOD Record 26(3): 54-66 (1997)

[RICH87] Joel E. Richardson, Michael J. Carey: Programming Constructs for Database System Implementation in EXODUS. SIGMOD Conference 1987: 208-219

[ROWE79] Lawrence A. Rowe, Kurt A. Shoens: Data Abstractions, Views and Updates in RIGEL. SIGMOD Conference 1979: 71-81

[RUST74] Randall Rustin (ed): Data Models: Data-Structure-Set versus Relational. ACM SIGFIDET 1974

[SAME84] Hanan Samet: The Quadtree and related Hierarchical Data Structures. Computing Surveys 16(2): 187-260 (1984)

[SCHM77] Joachim W. Schmidt: Some High Level Language Constructs for Data of Type Relation. TODS 2(3): 247-261 (1977)

[SKAR86] Andrea H. Skarra, Stanley B. Zdonik, Stephen P. Reiss: An Object Server for an Object-Oriented Database System. OODBS 1986: 196-204

[SMIT77] John Miles Smith, Diane C. P. Smith: Database Abstractions: Aggregation and Generalization. TODS 2(2): 105-133 (1977)

[SNOD85] Richard T. Snodgrass, Ilsoo Ahn: A Taxonomy of Time in Databases. SIGMOD Conference 1985: 236-246

[SPON84] David L. Spooner: Database Support for Interactive Computer Graphics. SIGMOD Conference 1984: 90-99

[STON75] Michael Stonebraker: Implementation of Integrity Constraints and Views by Query Modification. SIGMOD Conference 1975: 65-78

[STON76] Michael Stonebraker, Eugene Wong, Peter Kreps, Gerald Held: The Design and Implementation of INGRES. TODS 1(3): 189-222 (1976)

[STON83] Michael Stonebraker, Heidi Stettner, Nadene Lynn, Joseph Kalash, Antonin Guttman: Document Processing in a Relational Database System. TOIS 1(2): 143-158 (1983)

[STON86] Michael Stonebraker, Lawrence A. Rowe: The Design of Postgres. SIGMOD Conference 1986: 340-355

[STON90] Michael Stonebraker, Lawrence A. Rowe, Michael Hirohama: The Implementation of Postgres. TKDE 2(1): 125-142 (1990)

[TSIC76] Dennis Tsichritzis: LSL: A Link and Selector Language. SIGMOD Conference 1976: 123-133

[WONG79] Eugene Wong, R. H. Katz: Logical Design and Schema Conversion for Relational and DBTG Databases. ER 1979: 311-322

[ZANI83] Carlo Zaniolo: The Database Language GEM. SIGMOD Conference 1983: 207-218

Anatomy of a Database System

Joseph M. Hellerstein and Michael Stonebraker

1 Introduction

Database Management Systems (DBMSs) are complex, mission-critical pieces of software. Today's DBMSs are based on decades of academic and industrial research, and intense corporate software development. Database systems were among the earliest widely-deployed online server systems, and as such have pioneered design issues spanning not only data management, but also applications, operating systems, and networked services. The early DBMSs are among the most influential software systems in computer science. Unfortunately, many of the architectural innovations implemented in high-end database systems are regularly reinvented both in academia and in other areas of the software industry.

There are a number of reasons why the lessons of database systems architecture are not widely known. First, the applied database systems community is fairly small. There are only a handful of commercial-grade DBMS implementations, since market forces only support a few competitors at the high end. The community of people involved in designing and implementing database systems is tight: many attended the same schools, worked on the same influential research projects, and collaborated on the same commercial products.

Second, academic treatment of database systems has often ignored architectural issues. The textbook presentation of database systems has traditionally focused on algorithmic and theoretical issues – which are natural to teach, study and test – without a holistic discussion of system architecture in full-fledged implementations. In sum, there is a lot of conventional wisdom about how to build database systems, but much of it has not been written down or communicated broadly.

In this paper, we attempt to capture the main architectural aspects of modern database systems, with a discussion of advanced topics. Some of these appear in the literature, and we provide references where appropriate. Other issues are buried in product manuals, and some are simply part of the oral tradition of the community. Our goal here is not to glory in the implementation details of specific components. Instead, we focus on overall system design, and stress issues not typically discussed in textbooks. For cognoscenti, this paper should be entirely familiar, perhaps even simplistic. However, our hope is that for many readers this paper will provide useful context for the algorithms and techniques in the standard literature. We assume that the reader is familiar with textbook database systems material (e.g. [53] or [61]), and with the basic facilities of modern operating systems like Solaris, Linux, or Windows.

1.1 Context

The most mature database systems in production are relational database management systems (RDBMSs), which serve as the backbone of infrastructure applications including banking, airline reservations, medical records, human resources, payroll, telephony, customer relationship management and supply chain management, to name a few. The advent of web-based interfaces has only increased the volume and breadth of use of relational systems, which serve as the repositories of record behind essentially all online commerce. In addition to being very important software infrastructure today, relational database systems serve as a well-understood point of reference for new extensions and revolutions in database systems that may arise in the future.

In this paper we will focus on the architectural fundamentals for supporting core relational features, and bypass discussion of the many extensions present in modern RDBMSs. Many people are unaware that commercial relational systems now encompass enormous feature sets, with support for complex data types, multiple programming languages executing both outside and inside the system, gateways to various external data sources, and so on. (The current SQL standard specification stacks up to many inches of printed paper in small type!) In the interest of keeping our discussion here manageable, we will gloss over most of these features; in particular we will not discuss system extensions for supporting complex code (stored procedures, user-defined functions, Java Virtual Machines, triggers, recursive queries, etc.) and data types (Abstract Data Types, complex objects, XML, etc.)

At heart, a typical database system has four main pieces as shown in Figure 1: a process manager that encapsulates and schedules the various tasks in the system; a statement-at-a-time query processing engine; a shared transactional storage subsystem that knits together storage, buffer management, concurrency control and recovery; and a set of shared utilities including memory management, disk space management, replication, and various batch utilities used for administration.

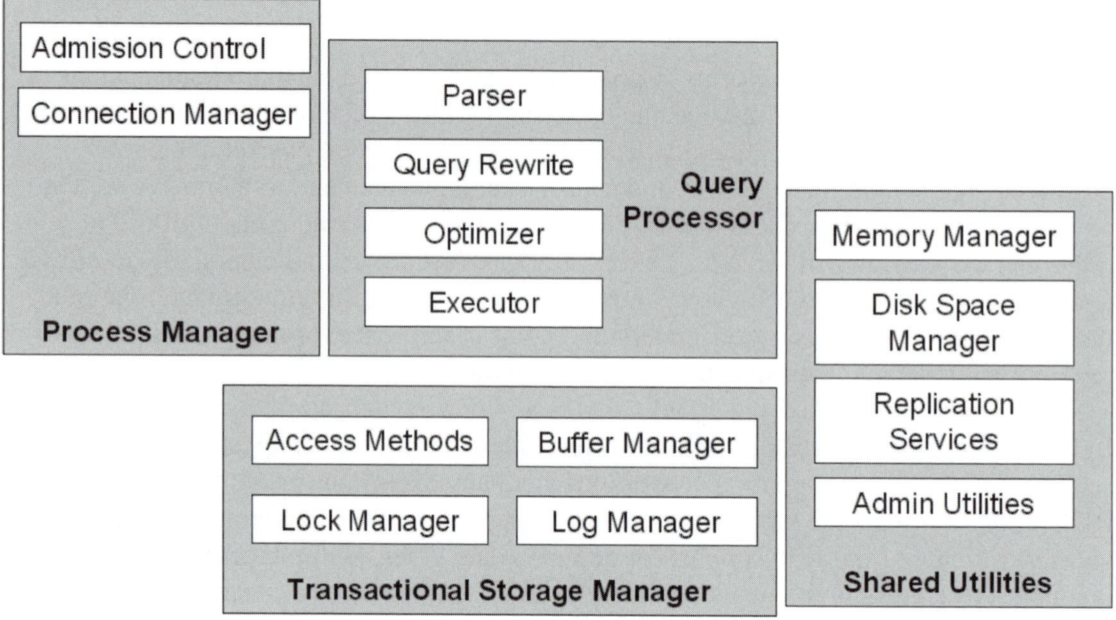

Figure 1: Main Components of a DBMS

1.2 Structure of the Paper

We begin our discussion with overall architecture of DBMS processes, including coarse structure of the software and hardware configurations of various systems, and details about the allocation of various database tasks to threads or processes provided by an operating system. We continue with the storage issues in a DBMS. In the next section we take a single query's view of the system, focusing on the query processing engine. The subsequent section covers the architecture of a transactional storage manager. Finally, we present some of the shared utilities that exist in most DBMSs, but are rarely discussed in textbooks.

2 Process Models and Hardware Architectures

When building any multi-user server, decisions have to be made early on regarding the organization of processes in the system. These decisions have a profound influence on the software architecture of the system, and on its performance, scalability, and portability across operating systems[1]. In this section we survey a number of options for DBMS process models. We begin with a simplified framework, assuming the availability of good operating system support for lightweight threads in a uniprocessor architecture. We then expand on this simplified discussion to deal with the realities of how DBMSs implement their own threads and map them to the OS facilities, and how they manage multiprocessor configurations.

[1] Most systems are designed to be portable, but not all. Notable examples of OS-specific DBMSs are DB2 for MVS, and Microsoft SQL Server. These systems can exploit (and sometimes add!) special OS features, rather than using DBMS-level workarounds.

2.1 Uniprocessors and OS Threads

In this subsection we outline a somewhat simplistic approach to process models for DBMSs. Some of the leading commercial DBMSs are *not* architected this way today, but this introductory discussion will set the stage for the more complex details to follow in the remainder of Section 2.

We make two basic assumptions in this subsection, which we will relax in the subsections to come:

1. **High-performance OS threads:** We assume that the operating system provides us with a very efficient *thread* package that allows a process to have a very large number of threads. We assume that the memory overhead of each thread is small, and that context switches among threads are cheap. This is arguably true on a number of the modern operating systems, but was certainly not true when most DBMSs were first built. In subsequent sections we will describe how DBMS implementations actually work with OS threads and processes, but for now we will assume that the DBMS designers had high-performance threads available from day one.
2. **Uniprocessor Hardware:** We will assume that we are designing for a single machine with a single CPU. Given the low cost of dual-processor and four-way server PCs today, this is an unrealistic assumption even at the low end. However, it will significantly simplify our initial discussion.

In this simplified context, there are three natural process model options for a DBMS. From simplest to most sophisticated, these are:

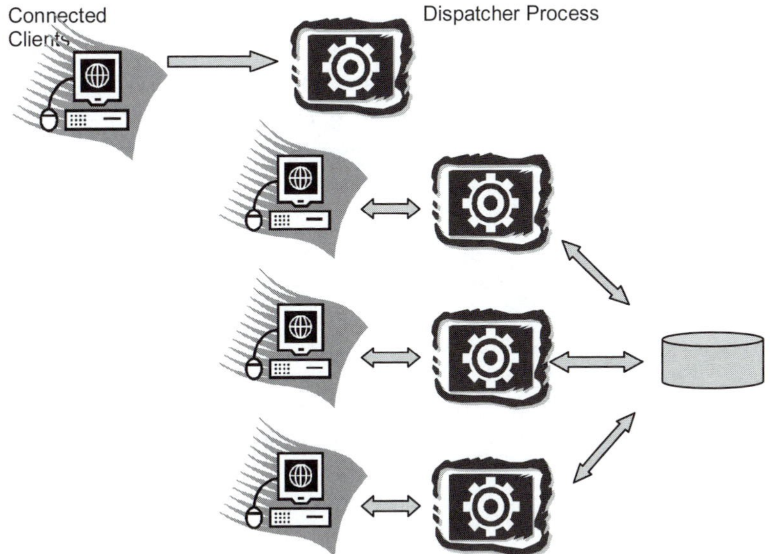

Figure 2: Process per connection model. Each gear icon represents a process.

1. **Process per Connection:** This was the model used in early DBMS implementations on UNIX. In this model, users run a client tool, typically on a machine across a network from the DBMS server. They use a database

connectivity protocol (e.g., ODBC or JDBC) that connects to a main dispatcher process at the database server machine, which forks a separate *process* (not a thread!) to serve that connection. This is relatively easy to implement in UNIX-like systems, because it maps DBMS units of work directly onto OS processes. The OS scheduler manages timesharing of user queries, and the DBMS programmer can rely on OS protection facilities to isolate standard bugs like memory overruns. Moreover, various programming tools like debuggers and memory checkers are well-suited to this process model. A complication of programming in this model regards the data structures that are shared across connections in a DBMS, including the lock table and buffer pool. These must be explicitly allocated in OS-supported "shared memory" accessible across processes, which requires a bit of special-case coding in the DBMS.

In terms of performance, this architecture is not attractive. It does not scale very well in terms of the number of concurrent connections, since processes are heavyweight entities with sizable memory overheads and high context-switch times. Hence this architecture is inappropriate for one of the bread-and-butter applications of commercial DBMSs: high-concurrency transaction processing. This architecture was replaced in the commercial DBMS vendors long ago, though it is still a compatibility option in many systems (and in fact the default option on installation of Oracle for UNIX).

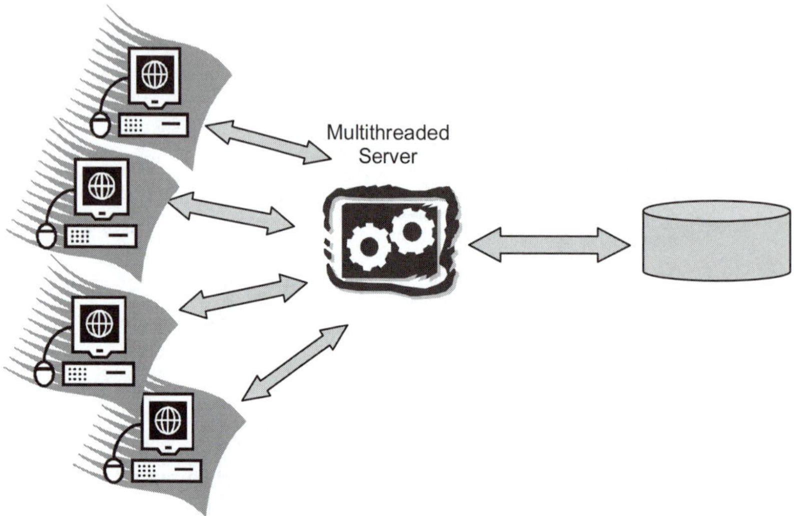

Figure 3: Server Process model. The multiple-gear icon represents a multithreaded process.

2. **Server Process:** This is the most natural architecture for efficiency today. In this architecture, a single multithreaded process hosts all the main activity of the DBMS. A *dispatcher* thread (or perhaps a small handful of such threads) listens for SQL commands. Typically the process keeps a pool of idle *worker threads* available, and the dispatcher assigns incoming SQL commands to idle worker threads, so that each command runs in its own thread. When a command is completed, it clears its state and returns its worker thread to the thread pool.

Shared data structures like the lock table and buffer pool simply reside in the process' heap space, where they are accessible to all threads.

The usual multithreaded programming challenges arise in this architecture: the OS does not protect threads from each other's memory overruns and stray pointers, debugging is tricky especially with race conditions, and the software can be difficult to port across operating systems due to differences in threading interfaces and multi-threaded performance. Although thread API differences across operating systems have been minimized in recent years, subtle distinctions across platforms still cause hassles in debugging and tuning.

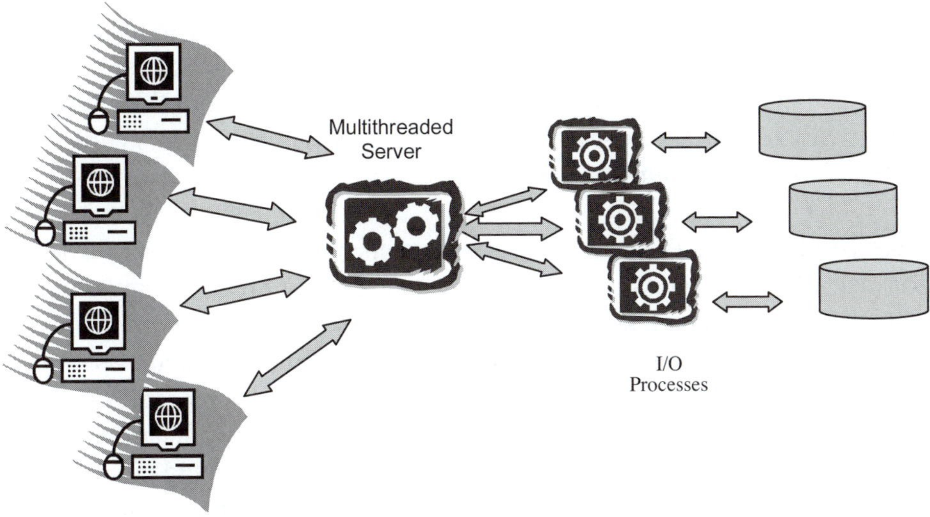

Figure 4: Server process + I/O processes. Note that each disk has a dedicated, single-threaded I/O process.

3. **Server Process + I/O Processes:** The Server Process model makes the important assumption that *asynchronous I/O* is provided by the operating system. This feature allows the DBMS to issue a read or write request, and work on other things while the disk device works to satisfy the request. Asynchronous I/O can also allow the DBMS to schedule an I/O reques to each of multiple disk devices; and have the devices all working in parallel; this is possible even on a uniprocessor system, since the disk devices themselves work autonomously, and in fact have their own microprocessors on board. Some time after a disk request is issued, the OS interrupts the DBMS with a notification the request has completed. Because of the separation of requests from responses, this is sometimes called a *split-phase* programming model.

   Unfortunately, asynchronous I/O support in the operating system is a fairly recent development: Linux only included asynchronous disk I/O support in the standard kernel in 2002. Without asynchronous I/O, all threads of a process must block while waiting for any I/O request to complete, which can unacceptably limit both system throughput and per-transaction latency. To work around this issue on older OS versions, a minor modification to the Server Process model is used. Additional *I/O Processes* are introduced to provide asynchronous I/O features outside the OS. The main Server threads queue I/O requests to an I/O Process via shared memory or network sockets, and the I/O Process queues responses back to the main Server Process in a similar fashion. There is typically about one I/O Process per disk in this environment, to ensure that the system can handle multiple requests to separate devices in parallel.

2.1.1 Passing Data Across Threads

A good Server Process architecture provides non-blocking, asynchronous I/O. It also has dispatcher threads connecting client requests to worker threads. This design begs the question of how data is passed across these thread or process boundaries. The short answer is that various buffers are used. We describe the typical buffers here, and briefly discuss policies for managing them.

- **Disk I/O buffers:** The most common asynchronous interaction in a database is for disk I/O: a thread issues an asynchronous disk I/O request, and engages in other tasks pending a response. There are two separate I/O scenarios to consider:
    - **DB I/O requests: The Buffer Pool.** All database data is staged through the DBMS *buffer pool*, about which we will have more to say in Section 3.3. In Server Process architectures, this is simply a heap-resident data structure. To flush a buffer pool page to disk, a thread generates an I/O request that includes the page's current location in the buffer pool (the *frame*), and its destination address on disk. When a thread needs a page to be read in from the database, it generates an I/O request specifying the disk address, and a handle to a free frame in the buffer pool where the result can be placed. The actual reading and writing and pages into and out of frames is done asynchronously.
    - **Log I/O Requests: The Log Tail.** The database log is an array of entries stored on a set of disks. As log entries are generated during transaction processing, they are staged in a memory queue that is usually called the *log tail,* which is periodically flushed to the log disk(s) in FIFO order. In many systems, a separate thread is responsible for periodically flushing the log tail to the disk.

      The most important log flushes are those that commit transactions. A transaction cannot be reported as successfully committed until a commit log record is flushed to the log device. This means both that client code waits until the commit log record is flushed, and that DBMS server code must hold resources (e.g. locks) until that time as well. In order to amortize the costs of log writes, most systems defer them until enough are queued up, and then do a "group commit" [27] by flushing the log tail. Policies for group commit are a balance between keeping commit latency low (which favors flushing the log tail more often), and maximizing log throughput (which favors postponing log flushes until the I/O can be amortized over many bytes of log tail).

- **Client communication buffers:** SQL typically is used in a "pull" model: clients consume result tuples from a query cursor by repeatedly issuing the SQL `FETCH` request, which may retrieve one or more tuples per request. Most DBMSs try to work ahead of the stream of `FETCH` requests, enqueuing results in advance of client requests.

  In order to support this workahead behavior, the DBMS worker thread for a query contains a pointer to a location for enqueuing results. A simple option is to assign each client to a network socket. In this case, the worker thread can use the socket as a queue for the tuples it produces. An alternative is to multiplex a network socket across multiple clients. In this case, the server process must (a) maintain its own state per client, including a communication queue for each client's SQL results, and (b) have a "coordinator agent" thread (or set of threads) available to respond to client `FETCH` requests by pulling data off of the communication queue.

2.2 DBMS Threads, OS Processes, and Mappings Between Them

The previous section provided a simplified description of DBMS threading models. In this section we relax the first of our assumptions above: the need for high-performance OS thread packages. We provide some historical perspective on how the problem was solved in practice, and also describe the threading in modern systems.

Most of today's DBMSs have their roots in research systems from the 1970's, and commercialization efforts from the '80's. Many of the OS features we take for granted today were unavailable to DBMS developers at the time the original database systems were built. We touched on some of these above: buffering control in the filesystem, and asynchronous I/O service. A more fundamental issue that we ignored above was the lack of high-performance threading packages. When such packages started to become available in the 1990's, they were typically OS-specific. Even the current POSIX thread standard is not entirely predictable across platforms, and recent OS research suggests that OS threads still do not scale as well as one might like ([23][37][67][68], etc.)

Hence for legacy, portability, and performance reasons, many commercial DBMSs provide their own lightweight, logical thread facility at application level (i.e. outside of the OS) for the various concurrent tasks in the DBMS. We will use the term *DBMS thread* to refer to one of these DBMS-level tasks. These DBMS threads replace the role of the OS threads described in the previous section. Each DBMS thread is programmed to manage its own state, to do all slow activities (e.g. I/Os) via non-blocking, asynchronous interfaces, and to frequently yield control to a scheduling routine (another DBMS thread) that dispatches among these tasks. This is an old idea, discussed in a retrospective sense in [38], and widely used in event-loop programming for user interfaces. It has been revisited quite a bit in the recent OS literature [23][37][67][68].

This architecture provides fast task-switching and ease of porting, at the expense of replicating a good deal of OS logic in the DBMS (task-switching, thread state management, scheduling, etc.) [64].

Using a DBMS-level thread package raises another set of design questions. Given DBMS threads and OS process facilities (but *no* OS threads), it is not obvious how to map DBMS threads into OS processes: How many OS processes should there be? What DBMS tasks should get their own DBMS threads? How should threads be assigned to the processes? To explore this design space, we simplify things by focusing on the case where there are only two units of scheduling: DBMS threads and OS processes. We will reintroduce OS threads into the mix in Section 2.2.1.

In the absence of OS thread support, a good rule of thumb is to have one process per physical device (CPU, disk) to maximize the physical parallelism inherent in the hardware, and to ensure that the system can function efficiently in the absence of OS support for asynchronous I/O. To that end, a typical DBMS has the following set of processes:

- **One or more processes to host DBMS threads for SQL processing**. These processes host the worker DBMS threads for query processing. In some cases it is beneficial to allocate more than one such process per CPU; this is often a "tuning knob" that can be set by the database administrator.
- **One or more "dispatcher" processes.** These processes listen on a network port for new connections, and dispatch the connection requests to a DBMS thread in another process for further processing. The dispatcher also sets up session state (e.g. communication queues) for future communication on the connection. The number of dispatchers is typically another knob that can be set by the database administrator; a rule of thumb is to set the number of dispatchers to be the expected peak number of concurrent connections divided by a constant (Oracle recommends dividing by 1000.)
- **One process per database disk (I/O Process Architectures).** For platforms where the OS does not supply efficient asynchronous I/O calls, the lack of OS threads requires multiple I/O Processes, one per database disk, to service I/O requests.
- **One process per log disk (I/O Process Architectures).** For platforms with I/O Processes, there will be a process per log disk, to flush the log tail, and to read the log in support of transaction rollback.
- **One coordinator agent process per client session.** In some systems, a process is allocated for each client session, to maintain session state and handle client communication. In other systems this state is encapsulated in a data structure that is available to the DBMS threads in the SQL processes.
- **Background Utilities:** As we discuss in Section 6, DBMSs include a number of background utilities for system maintenance, including database statistics-gathering, system monitoring, log device archiving, and physical reorganization. Each of these typically runs in its own process, which is typically spawned dynamically on a schedule.

2.2.1 DBMS Threads, OS Threads and Current Commercial Systems

The preceding discussion assumes no support for OS threads. In fact, most modern operating systems now support reasonable threads packages. They may not provide the degree of concurrency needed by the DBMS (Linux threads were very heavyweight until recently), but they are almost certainly more efficient than using multiple processes as described above.

Since most database systems evolved along with their host operating systems, they were originally architected for single-threaded processes as we just described. As OS threads matured, a natural form of evolution was to modify the DBMS to be a single process, using an OS *thread* for each unit that was formerly an OS process. This approach continues to use the DBMS threads, but maps them into OS threads rather than OS processes. This evolution is relatively easy to code, and leverages the code investment in efficient DBMS threads, minimizing the dependency on high-end multithreading in the OS.

In fact, most of today's DBMSs are written in this manner, and can be run over either processes or threads. They abstract the choice between processes and threads in the code, mapping DBMS threads to OS-provided "dispatchable units" (to use DB2 terminology), be they processes or threads.

Current hardware provides one reason to stick with processes as the "dispatchable unit". On many architectures today, the addressable memory per process is not as large as available physical memory – for example, on Linux for x86 only 3GB of RAM is available per process. It is certainly possible to equip a modern PC with more physical memory than that, but no individual process can address all of the memory. Using multiple processes alleviates this problem in a simple fashion.

There are variations in the threading models in today's leading systems. Oracle on UNIX is configured by default to run in Process-Per-User mode, but for better performance can run in the Server Process fashion described at the beginning of Section 2.2: DBMS threads multiplexed across a set of OS processes. On Windows, Oracle uses a single OS process with multiple threads as dispatchable units: DBMS threads are multiplexed across a set of OS threads. DB2 does not provide its own DBMS threads. On UNIX platforms DB2 works in a Process-per-User mode: each user's session has its own agent process that executes the session logic. DB2 on Windows uses OS threads as the dispatchable unit, rather than multiple processes. Microsoft SQL Server only runs on Windows; it runs an OS thread per session by default, but can be configured to multiplex various "DBMS threads" across a single OS thread; in the case of SQL Server the "DBMS threads" package is actually a Windows-provided feature known as *fibers*.

2.3 Parallelism, Process Models, and Memory Coordination

In this section, we relax the second assumption of Section 3.1, by focusing on platforms with multiple CPUs. Parallel hardware is a fact of life in modern server situations, and comes in a variety of configurations. We summarize the standard DBMS terminology (introduced in [65]), and discuss the process models and memory coordination issues in each.

2.3.1 Shared Memory

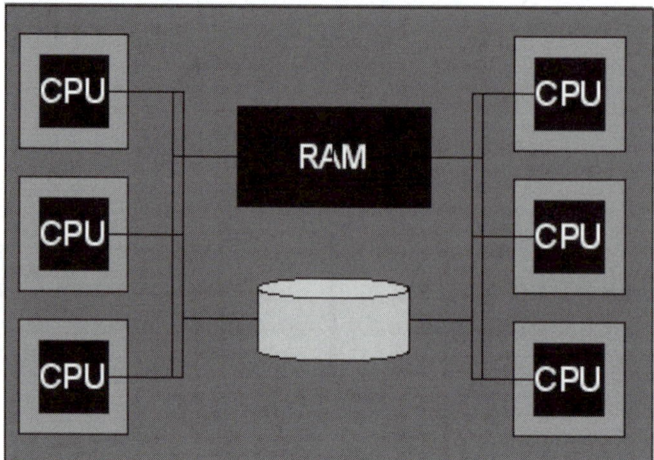

Figure 5: Shared Memory Architecture

A *shared-memory* parallel machine is one in which all processors can access the same RAM and disk with about the same performance. This architecture is fairly standard today – most server hardware ships with between two and eight processors. High-end machines can ship with dozens to hundreds of processors, but tend to be sold at an enormous premium relative to the number of compute resources provided. Massively parallel shared-memory machines are one of the last remaining "cash cows" in the hardware industry, and are used heavily in high-end online transaction processing applications. The cost of hardware is rarely the dominant factor in most companies' IT ledgers, so this cost is often deemed acceptable[2].

The process model for shared memory machines follows quite naturally from the uniprocessor Server Process approach – and in fact most database systems evolved from their initial uniprocessor implementations to shared-memory implementations. On shared-memory machines, the OS typically supports the transparent assignment of dispatchable units (processes or threads) across the processors, and the shared data structures continue to be accessible to all. Hence the Server Process architecture parallelizes to shared-memory machines with minimal effort. The main challenge is to modify the query execution layers described in Section 3 to take advantage of the ability to parallelize a single query across multiple CPUs.

[2] The dominant cost for DBMS customers is typically paying qualified people to administer high-end systems. This includes Database Administrators (DBAs) who configure and maintain the DBMS, and System Administrators who configure and maintain the hardware and operating systems. Interestingly, these are typically very different career tracks, with very different training, skill sets, and responsibilities.

2.3.2 Shared Nothing

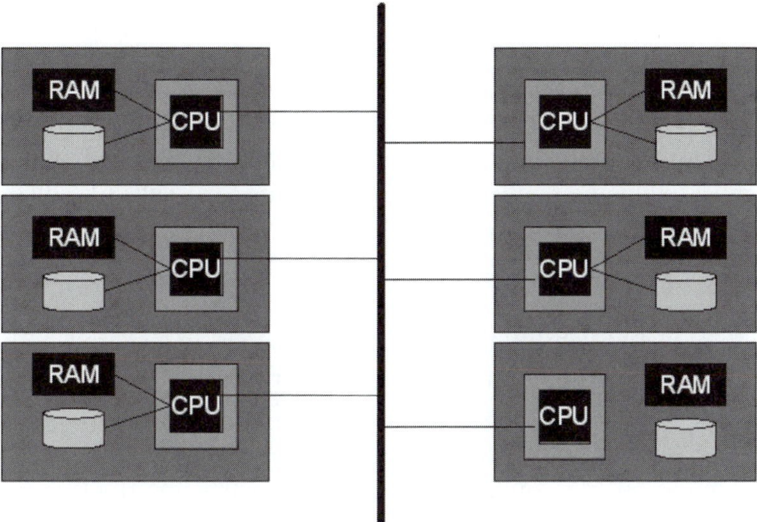

Figure 6: Shared Nothing Architecture

A *shared-nothing* parallel machine is made up of a cluster of single-processor machines that communicate over a high-speed network interconnect. There is no way for a given processor to directly access the memory or disk of another processor. This architecture is also fairly standard today, and has unbeatable scalability and cost characteristics. It is mostly used at the extreme high end, typically for decision-support applications on data warehouses. Shared nothing machines can be cobbled together from individual PCs, but for database server purposes they are typically sold (at a premium!) as packages including specialized network interconnects (e.g. the IBM SP2 or the NCR WorldMark machines.) In the OS community, these platforms have been dubbed "clusters", and the component PCs are sometimes called "blade servers".

Shared nothing systems provide no hardware sharing abstractions, leaving coordination of the various machines entirely in the hands of the DBMS. In these systems, each machine runs its own Server Process as above, but allows an individual query's execution to be parallelized across multiple machines. The basic architecture of these systems is to use *horizontal data partitioning* to allow each processor to execute independently of the others. For storage purposes, each tuple in the database is assigned to an individual machine, and hence each table is sliced "horizontally" and spread across the machines (typical data partitioning schemes include hash-based partitioning by tuple attribute, range-based partitioning by tuple attribute, or round-robin). Each individual machine is responsible for the access, locking and logging of the data on its local disks. During query execution, the query planner chooses how to horizontally re-partition tables across the machines to satisfy the query, assigning each machine a logical partition of the work. The query executors on the various machines ship data requests and tuples to each other, but do not need to transfer any thread state or other low-level information. As a result of this value-based partitioning of the database tuples, minimal coordination is required in these systems. However, good partitioning of the data is required for good performance, which places a significant burden on the DBA to lay out tables intelligently, and on the query optimizer to do a good job partitioning the workload.

This simple partitioning solution does not handle all issues in the DBMS. For example, there has to be explicit cross-processor coordination to handle transaction completion, to provide load balancing, and to support certain mundane maintenance tasks. For example, the processors must exchange explicit control messages for issues like distributed deadlock detection and two-phase commit [22]. This requires additional logic, and can be a performance bottleneck if not done carefully.

Also, *partial failure* is a possibility that has to be managed in a shared-nothing system. In a shared-memory system, the failure of a processor typically results in a hardware shutdown of the entire parallel computing machine. In a shared-nothing system, the failure of a single node will not necessarily affect other nodes, but will certainly affect the overall behavior of the DBMS, since the failed node hosts some fraction of the data in the database. There are three possible approaches in this scenario. The first is to bring down all nodes if any node fails; this in essence emulates what would happen in a shared-memory system. The second approach, which Informix dubbed "Data Skip", allows queries to be executed on any nodes that are up, "skipping" the data on the failed node. This is of use in scenarios where *availability* trumps *consistency*, but the best effort results generated do not have any well-defined semantics. The third approach is to employ redundancy schemes like *chained declustering* [32], which spread copies of tuples across multiple nodes in the cluster. These techniques are designed to tolerate a number of failures without losing data. In practice, however, these techniques are not provided; commercial vendors offer coarser-grained redundancy solutions like database replication (Section 6.3), which maintain a copy of the entire database in a separate "standby" system.

2.3.3 Shared Disk

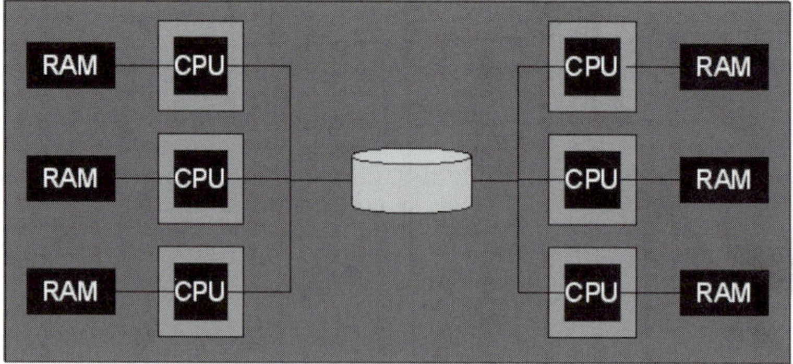

Figure 7: Shared Disk Architecture

A *shared-disk* parallel machine is one in which all processors can access the same disks with about the same performance, but are unable to access each other's RAM. This architecture is quite common in the very largest "single-box" (non-cluster) multiprocessors, and hence is important for very large installations – especially for

Oracle, which does not sell a shared-nothing software platform. Shared disk has become an increasingly attractive approach in recent years, with the advent of Network Attached Storage devices (NAS), which allow a storage device on a network to be mounted by a set of nodes.

One key advantage of shared-disk systems over shared-nothing is in usability, since DBAs of shared-disk systems do not have to consider partitioning tables across machines. Another feature of a shared-disk architecture is that the failure of a single DBMS processing node does not affect the other nodes' ability to access the full database. This is in contrast to both shared-memory systems that fail as a unit, and shared-nothing systems that lose at least some data upon a node failure. Of course this discussion puts more emphasis on the reliability of the storage nodes.

Because there is no partitioning of the data in a shared disk system, data can be copied into RAM and modified on multiple machines. Unlike shared-memory systems there is no natural place to coordinate this sharing of the data – each machine has its own local memory for locks and buffer pool pages. Hence there is a need to explicitly coordinate data sharing across the machines. Shared-disk systems come with a distributed lock manager facility, and a *cache-coherency* protocol for managing the distributed buffer pools [7]. These are complex pieces of code, and can be bottlenecks for workloads with significant contention.

2.3.4 NUMA

Non-Uniform Memory Access (NUMA) architectures are somewhat unusual, but available from vendors like IBM. They provide a shared memory system where the time required to access some remote memory can be much higher than the time to access local memory. Although NUMA architectures are not especially popular today, they do bear a resemblance to shared-nothing clusters in which the basic building block is a small (e.g. 4-way) multiprocessor. Because of the non-uniformity in memory access, DBMS software tends to ignore the shared memory features of such systems, and treats them as if they were (expensive) shared-nothing systems.

2.4 Admission Control

We close this section with one remaining issue related to supporting multiple concurrent requests. As the workload is increased in any multi-user system, performance will increase up to some maximum, and then begin to decrease radically as the system starts to "thrash". As in operating system settings, thrashing is often the result of memory pressure: the DBMS cannot keep the "working set" of database pages in the buffer pool, and spends all its time replacing pages. In DBMSs, this is particularly a problem with query processing techniques like sorting and hash joins, which like to use large amounts of main memory. In some cases, DBMS thrashing can also occur due to contention for locks; transactions continually deadlock with each other and need to be restarted [2]. Hence any good multi-user system has an *admission* control policy, which does not admit new clients unless the workload will stay safely below the maximum that can be handled without thrashing. With a good admission controller, a system will display *graceful degradation* under overload: transactions latencies will increase proportionally to their arrival rate, but throughput will remain at peak.

Admission control for a DBMS can be done in two tiers. First, there may be a simple admission control policy in the dispatcher process to ensure that the number of client connections is kept below a threshold. This serves to prevent overconsumption of basic resources like network connections, and minimizes unnecessary invocations of the query parser and optimizer. In some DBMSs this control is not provided, under the assumption that it is handled by some other piece of software interposed between clients and the DBMS: e.g. an application server, transaction processing monitor, or web server.

The second layer of admission control must be implemented directly within the core DBMS query processor. This *execution* admission controller runs after the query is parsed and optimized, and determines whether a query is postponed or begins execution. The execution admission controller is aided by information provided by the query optimizer, which can estimate the resources that a query will require. In particular, the optimizer's query plan can specify (a) the disk devices that the query will access, and an estimate of the number of random and sequential I/Os per device (b) estimates of the CPU load of the query, based on the operators in the query plan and the number of tuples to be processed, and most importantly (c) estimates about the memory footprint of the query data structures, including space for sorting and hashing tables. As noted above, this last metric is often the key for an admission controller, since memory pressure is often the main cause of thrashing. Hence many DBMSs use memory footprint as the main criterion for admission control.

2.5 Standard Practice

As should be clear, there are many design choices for process models in a DBMS, or any large-scale server system. However due both to historical legacy and the need for extreme high performance, a few standard designs have emerged

To summarize the state of the art for uniprocessor process models:

- Modern DBMSs are built using both "Process-per-User" and "Server Process" models; the latter is more complex to implement but allows for higher performance in some cases.
- Some Server Process systems (e.g. Oracle and Informix) implement a DBMS thread package, which serves the role taken by OS threads in the model of Section 3.1. When this is done, DBMS threads are mapped to a smaller set of "dispatchable units" as described in Section 3.2.
- Dispatchable units can be different across OS platforms as described in Section 3.2.1: either processes, or threads within a single process.

In terms of parallel architectures, today's marketplace supports a mix of Shared-Nothing, Shared-Memory and Shared-Disk architectures. As a rule, Shared-Nothing architectures excel on price-performance for running complex queries on very large databases, and hence they occupy a high-end niche in corporate decision support systems. The other two typically perform better at the high end for processing multiple small transactions. The evolution from a uniprocessor DBMS implementation to a Shared-Nothing implementation is quite difficult, and at most companies was done by spawning a new product line that was only later merged back into the core product. Oracle still does not ship a Shared-Nothing implementation.

3 Storage Models

In addition to the process model, another basic consideration when designing a DBMS is the choice of the persistent storage interface to use. There are basically two options: the DBMS can interact directly with the device drivers for the disks, or the DBMS can use the typical OS file system facilities. This decision has impacts on the DBMS's ability to control storage in both space and time. We consider these two dimensions in turn, and proceed to discuss the use of the storage hierarchy in more detail.

3.1 Spatial Control

Sequential access to disk blocks is between 10 and 100 times faster than random access. This gap is increasing quickly. Disk density – and hence sequential bandwidth – improves following Moore's Law, doubling every 18 months. Disk arm movement is improving at a much slower rate. As a result, it is critical for the DBMS storage manager to place blocks on the disk so that important queries can access data sequentially. Since the DBMS can understand its workload more deeply than the underlying OS, it makes sense for DBMS architects to exercise full control over the spatial positioning of database blocks on disk.

The best way for the DBMS to control spatial locality of its data is to issue low-level storage requests directly to the "raw" disk device interface, since disk device addresses typically correspond closely to physical proximity of storage locations. Most commercial database systems offer this functionality for peak performance. Although quite effective, this technique has some drawbacks. First, it requires the DBA to devote entire disks to the DBMS; this used to be frustrating when disks were very expensive, but it has become far less of a concern today. Second, "raw disk" access interfaces are often OS-specific, which can make the DBMS more difficult to port. However, this is a hurdle that most commercial DBMS vendors chose to overcome years ago. Finally, developments in the storage industry like RAID, Storage Area Networks (SAN), and Network-Attached Storage (NAS) have become popular, to the point where "virtual" disk devices are the norm in many scenarios today – the "raw" device interface is actually being intercepted by appliances or software that reposition data aggressively on one or more physical disks. As a result, the benefits of explicit physical control by the DBMS have been diluted over time. We discuss this issue further in Section 6.2.

An alternative to raw disk access is for the DBMS to create a very large file in the OS file system, and then manage positioning of data in the offsets of that file. This offers reasonably good performance. In most popular filesystems, if you allocate a very large file on an empty disk, the offsets in that file will correspond fairly well to physical proximity of storage regions. Hence this is a good approximation to raw disk access, without the need to go directly to the device interface. Most virtualized storage systems are also designed to place close offsets in a file in nearby physical locations. Hence the relative control lost when using large files rather than raw disks is becoming less significant over time. However, using the filesystem interface has other ramifications, which we discuss in the next subsection.

It is worth noting that in either of these schemes, the size of a database page is a tunable parameter that can be set at the time of database generation; it should be a multiple of the sized offered by typical disk devices. If the filesystem is being used, special interfaces may be required to write pages of a different size than the filesystem default; the POSIX *mmap/msync* calls provide this facility. A discussion of the appropriate choice of page sizes is given in the paper on the "5-minute rule" [20].

3.2 Temporal Control: Buffering

In addition to controlling *where* on the disk data should lie, a DBMS must control *when* data gets physically written to the disk. As we will discuss in Section 5, a DBMS contains critical logic that reasons about when to write blocks to disk. Most OS file systems also provide built-in I/O buffering mechanisms to decide when to do reads and writes of file blocks. If the DBMS uses standard file system interfaces for writing, the OS buffering can confound the intention of the DBMS logic by silently postponing or reordering writes. This can cause major problems for the DBMS.

The first set of problems regard the *correctness* of the database: the DBMS cannot ensure correct transactional semantics without explicitly controlling the timing of disk writes. As we will discuss in Section 5, writes to the log device must precede corresponding writes to the database device, and commit requests cannot return to users until commit log records have been reliably written to the log device.

The second set of problems with OS buffering concern *performance*, but have no implications on correctness. Modern OS file systems typically have some built-in support for *read-ahead* (speculative reads) and *write-behind* (postponed, batched writes), and these are often poorly-suited to DBMS access patterns. File system logic depends on the contiguity of *physical* byte offsets in files to make decisions about reads and writes. DBMS-level I/O facilities can support *logical* decisions based on the DBMS' behavior. For example, the stream of reads in a query is often predictable to the DBMS, but not physically contiguous on the disk, and hence not visible via the OS read/write API. Logical DBMS-level read-ahead can occur when scanning the leaves of a B+-tree, for example. Logical read-aheads are easily achieved in DBMS logic by a query thread issuing I/Os in advance of its needs – the query plan contains the relevant information about data access algorithms, and has full information about future access patterns for the query. Similarly, the DBMS may want to make its own decisions about when to flush the log buffer (often called the log "tail"), based on considerations that mix issues like lock contention with I/O throughput. This mix of information is available to the DBMS, but not to the OS file system.

The final performance issues are "double buffering" and the extreme CPU overhead of memory copies. Given that the DBMS has to do its own buffering carefully for correctness, any additional buffering by the OS is redundant. This redundancy results in two costs. First, it wastes system memory, effectively limiting the memory available for doing useful work. Second, it wastes time, by causing an additional copying step: on reads, data is first copied from the disk to the OS buffer, and then copied again to the DBMS buffer pool, about which we will say more shortly. On writes, both of these copies are required in reverse. Copying data in memory can be a serious bottleneck in DBMS software today. This fact is often a surprise to database students, who assume that main-memory operations are "free" compared to disk I/O. But in practice, *a well-tuned database installation is typically not I/O-bound.* This is achieved in high-end installations by purchasing the right mix of disks and RAM so that repeated page requests are absorbed by the buffer pool, and disk I/Os are shared across the disk arms at a rate that can feed the appetite of all the processors in the system. Once this kind of "system balance" is achieved, I/O latencies cease to be a bottleneck, and the remaining main-memory bottlenecks become the limiting factors in the system. Memory copies are becoming a dominant bottleneck in computer architectures: this is due to the gap in performance evolution between raw CPU cycles per second (which follows Moore's law) and RAM access speed (which trails Moore's law significantly).

The problems of OS buffering have been well-known in the database research literature [64] and the industry for some time. Most modern operating systems now provide hooks (e.g. the POSIX *mmap/msync/madvise* calls) for programs like database servers to circumvent double-buffering the file cache, ensuring that writes go through to disk when requested, that double buffering is avoided, and that some alternate replacement strategies can be hinted at by the DBMS.

3.3 Buffer Management

In order to provide efficient access to database pages, every DBMS implements a large shared buffer pool in its own memory space. The buffer pool is organized as an array of *frames*, each frame being a region of memory the size of a database disk block. Blocks are copied in native format from disk directly into frames, manipulated in memory in native format, and written back. This translation-free approach avoids CPU bottlenecks in "marshalling" and "unmarshalling" data to/from disk; perhaps more importantly, the fixed-sized frames sidestep complexities of external memory fragmentation and compaction that are associated with generic memory management.

Associated with the array of frames is an array of metadata called a *page table*, with one entry for each frame. The page table contains the disk location for the page currently in each frame, a *dirty bit* to indicate whether the page has changed since it was read from disk, and any information needed by the *page replacement policy* used for choosing pages to evict on overflow. It also contains a *pin count* for the page in the frame; the page is not candidate for page replacement unless the pin count is 0. This allows tasks to (hopefully briefly) "pin" pages into the buffer pool by incrementing the pin count before manipulating the page, and decrementing it thereafter.

Much research in the early days of relational systems focused on the design of page replacement policies. The basic tension surrounded the looping access patterns resulting from nested-loops joins, which scanned and rescanned a heap file larger than the buffer pool. For such looping patterns, recency of reference is a pessimal predictor of future reuse, so OS page replacement schemes like LRU and CLOCK were well known to perform poorly for database queries [64]. A variety of alternative schemes were proposed, including some that attempted to tune the replacement strategy via query plan information [10]. Today, most systems use simple enhancements to LRU schemes to account for the case of nested loops; one that appears in the research literature and has been implemented in commercial systems is LRU-2 [48]. Another scheme used in commercial systems is to have a the replacement policy depend on the page type: e.g. the root of a B+-tree might be replaced with a different strategy than a page in a heap file. This is reminiscent of Reiter's Domain Separation scheme [55][10].

3.4 Standard Practice

In the last few years, commercial filesystems have evolved to the point where they can now support database storage quite well. The standard usage model is to allocate a single large file in the filesystem on each disk, and let the DBMS manage placement of data within that file via interfaces like the *mmap* suite. In this configuration, modern filesystems now offer reasonable spatial and temporal control to the DBMS. This storage model is available in essentially all database system implementations. However, the raw disk code in many of the DBMS products long predates the maturation of filesystems, and provides explicit performance control to the DBMS without any worry about subtle filesystem interactions. Hence raw disk support remains a common high-performance option in most database systems.

4 Query Processor

The previous sections stressed the macro-architectural design issues in a DBMS. We now begin a sequence of sections discussing design at a somewhat finer grain, addressing each of the main DBMS components in turn. We start with the query processor.

A relational query engine takes a declarative SQL statement, validates it, optimizes it into a procedural dataflow implementation plan, and (subject to admission control) executes that dataflow on behalf of a client program, which fetches ("pulls") the result tuples, typically one at a time or in small batches. The components of a relational query engine are shown in Figure 1; in this section we concern ourselves with both the query processor and some non-transactional aspects of the storage manager's access methods. In general, relational query processing can be viewed as a single-user, single-threaded task – concurrency control is managed transparently by lower layers of the system described in Section 5. The only exception to this rule is that the query processor must explicitly pin and unpin buffer pool pages when manipulating them, as we note below. In this section we focus on the common case SQL commands: "DML" statements including SELECT, INSERT, UPDATE and DELETE.

4.1 Parsing and Authorization

Given an SQL statement, the main tasks for the parser are to check that the query is correctly specified, to convert it into an internal format, and to check that the user is authorized to execute the query. Syntax checking is done naturally as part of the parsing process, during which time the parser generates an internal representation for the query.

The parser handles queries one "SELECT" block at a time. First, it considers each of the table references in the FROM clause. It canonicalizes each table name into a *schema.tablename* format; users have default schemas which are often omitted from the query specification. It then invokes the *catalog manager* to check that the table is registered in the system catalog; while so checking it may also cache metadata about the table in internal query data structures. Based on information about the table, it then uses the catalog to check that attribute references are correct. The data types of attributes are used to drive the (rather intricate) disambiguation logic for overloaded functional expressions, comparison operators, and constant expressions. For example, in the expression "(EMP.salary * 1.15) < 75000", the code for the multiplication function and comparison operator – and the assumed data type and internal format of the strings "1.15" and "75000" – will depend upon the data type of the EMP.salary attribute, which may be an integer, a floating-point number, or a "money" value. Additional standard SQL syntax checks are also applied, including the usage of tuple variables, the compatibility of tables combined via set operators (UNION/INTERSECT/EXCEPT), the usage of attributes in the SELECT list of aggregation queries, the nesting of subqueries, and so on.

If the query parses correctly, the next phase is to check authorization. Again, the catalog manager is invoked to ensure that the user has the appropriate permissions (SELECT/DELETE/INSERT/UPDATE) on the tables in the query. Additionally, integrity constraints are consulted to ensure that any constant expressions in the query do not result in constraint violations. For example, an UPDATE command may have a clause of the form "SET EMP.salary = -1". If there is an integrity constraint specifying positive values for salaries, the query will not be authorized for execution.

If a query parses and passes authorization checks, then the internal format of the query is passed on to the query rewrite module for further processing.

4.1.1 A Note on Catalog Management

The database catalog is a form of *metadata:* information about the data in the system. The catalog is itself stored as a set of tables in the database, recording the names of basic entities in the system (users, schemas, tables, columns, indexes, etc.) and their relationships. By keeping the metadata in the same format as the data, the system is made both more compact and simpler to use: users can employ the same language and tools to investigate the metadata that they use for other data, and the internal system code for managing the metadata is largely the same as the code for managing other tables. This code and language reuse is an important lesson that is often overlooked in early-stage implementations, typically to the significant regret of developers later on. (One of the authors witnessed this mistake yet again in an industrial setting within the last few years!)

For efficiency, basic catalog data is treated somewhat differently from normal tables. High-traffic portions of the catalog are often materialized in main memory at bootstrap time, typically in data structures that "denormalize" the flat relational structure of the catalogs into a main-memory network of objects. This lack of data independence in memory is acceptable because the in-memory data structures are used in a stylized fashion only by the query parser and optimizer. Additional catalog data is cached in query plans at parsing time, again often in a denormalized form suited to the query. Moreover, catalog tables are often subject to special-case transactional tricks to minimize "hot spots" in transaction processing.

It is worth noting that catalogs can become formidably large in commercial applications. One major Enterprise Resource Planning application generates over 30,000 tables, with between 4 and 8 columns per table, and typically two or three indexes per table.

4.2 Query Rewrite

The query rewrite module is responsible for a number of tasks related to simplifying and optimizing the query, typically without changing its semantics. The key in all these tasks is that they can be carried out without accessing the data in the tables – all of these techniques rely only on the query and on metadata in the catalog. Although we speak of "rewriting" the query, in fact most rewrite systems operate on internal representations of the query, rather than on the actual text of a SQL statement.

- **View rewriting:** The most significant role in rewriting is to handle views. The rewriter takes each view reference that appeared in the FROM clause, and gets the view definition from the catalog manager. It then rewrites the query to remove the view, replacing it with the tables and predicates referenced by the view, and rewriting any predicates that reference the view to instead reference columns from the tables in the view. This process is applied recursively until the query is expressed exclusively over base tables. This view expansion technique, first proposed for the set-based QUEL language in INGRES [63], requires some care in SQL to correctly handle duplicate elimination, nested queries, NULLs, and other tricky details [51].
- **Constant arithmetic evaluation:** Query rewrite can simplify any arithmetic expressions that do not contain tuple variables: e.g. "R.x < 10+2" is rewritten as "R.x < 12".
- **Logical rewriting of predicates:** Logical rewrites are applied based on the predicates and constants in the WHERE clause. Simple Boolean logic is often applied to improve the match between expressions and the capabilities of index-based access methods: for example, a predicate like "NOT Emp.Salary >

1000000" may be rewritten as "Emp.Salary <= 1000000". These logical rewrites can even short-circuit query execution, via simple satisfiability tests: for example, the expression "Emp.salary < 75000 AND Emp.salary > 1000000" can be replaced with FALSE, possibly allowing the system to return an empty query result without any accesses to the database. Unsatisfiable queries may seem implausible, but recall that predicates may be "hidden" inside view definitions, and unknown to the writer of the outer query – e.g. the query above may have resulted from a query for low-paid employees over a view called "Executives".

An additional, important logical rewrite uses the transitivity of predicates to induce new predicates: e.g. "R.x < 10 AND R.x = S.y" suggests adding the additional predicate "AND S.y < 10". Adding these transitive predicates increases the ability of the optimizer to choose plans that filter data early in execution, especially through the use of index-based access methods.

- **Semantic optimization:** In many cases, integrity constraints on the schema are stored in the catalog, and can be used to help rewrite some queries. An important example of such optimization is *redundant join elimination*. This arises when there are foreign key constraints from a column of one table (e.g. Emp.deptno) to another table (Dept). Given such a foreign key constraint, it is known that there is exactly one Dept for each Emp. Consider a query that joins the two tables but does not make use of the Dept columns:
```
SELECT Emp.name, Emp.salary
  FROM Emp, Dept
 WHERE Emp.deptno = Dept.dno
```
Such queries can be rewritten to remove the Dept table, and hence the join. Again, such seemingly implausible scenarios often arise naturally via views – for example, a user may submit a query about employee attributes over a view EMPDEPT that joins those two tables. Semantic optimizations can also lead to short-circuited query execution, when constraints on the tables are incompatible with query predicates.
- **Subquery flattening and other heuristic rewrites:** In many systems, queries are rewritten to get them into a form that the optimizer is better equipped to handle. In particular, most optimizers operate on individual SELECT-FROM-WHERE query blocks in isolation, forgoing possible opportunities to optimize across blocks. Rather than further complicate query optimizers (which are already quite complex in commercial DBMSs), a natural heuristic is to flatten nested queries when possible to expose further opportunities for single-block optimization. This turns out to be very tricky in some cases in SQL, due to issues like duplicate semantics, subqueries, NULLs and correlation [51][58]. Other heuristic rewrites are possible across query blocks as well – for example, predicate transitivity can allow predicates to be copied across subqueries [40]. It is worth noting that the flattening of correlated subqueries is especially important for achieving good performance in parallel architectures, since the "nested-loop" execution of correlated subqueries is inherently serialized by the iteration through the loop.

When complete, the query rewrite module produces an internal representation of the query in the same internal format that it accepted at its input.

4.3 Optimizer

Given an internal representation of a query, the job of the query optimizer is to produce an efficient *query plan* for executing the query (Figure 8). A query plan can be thought of as a dataflow diagram starting from base relations, piping data through a graph of query *operators*. In most systems, queries are broken into SELECT-FROM-WHERE query blocks. The optimization of each individual query block is done using techniques similar to those described in the famous paper by Selinger, et al. on the System R optimizer [57]. Typically, at the top of each query block a few operators may be added as post-processing to compute GROUP BY, ORDER BY, HAVING and DISTINCT clauses if they exist. Then the various blocks are stitched together in a straightforward fashion.

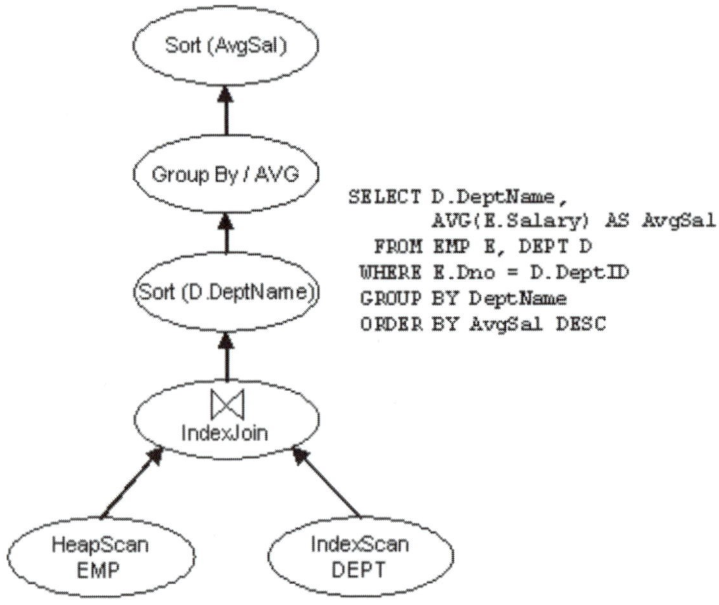
Sort (AvgSal)
Group By / AVG
Sort (D.DeptName)
IndexJoin
HeapScan
EMP
IndexScan
DEPT
SELECT D.DeptName,
AVG(E.Salary) AS AvgSal
FROM EMP E, DEPT D
WHERE E.Dno = D.DeptID
GROUP BY DeptName
ORDER BY AvgSal DESC

Figure 8: A Query Plan. Note that only the main physical operators are shown.

The original System R prototype compiled query plans into machine code, whereas the early INGRES prototype generated an interpretable query plan. Query interpretation was listed as a "mistake" by the INGRES authors in their retrospective paper in the early 1980's [63], but Moore's law and software engineering have vindicated the INGRES decision to some degree. In order to enable cross-platform portability, every system now compiles queries into some kind of interpretable data structure; the only difference across systems these days is the level of abstraction. In some systems the query plan is a very lightweight object, not unlike a relational algebra expression annotated with the names of access methods, join algorithms, and so on. Other systems use a lower-level language of "op-codes", closer in spirit to Java byte codes than to relational algebra expressions. For simplicity in our discussion, we will focus on algebra-like query representations in the remainder of this paper.

Although Selinger's paper is widely considered the "bible" of query optimization, it was preliminary research, and all systems extend it in a number of dimensions. We consider some of the main extensions here.

- **Plan space:** The System R optimizer constrained its plan space somewhat by focusing only on "left-deep" query plans (where the right-hand input to a join must be a base table), and by "postponing Cartesian products" (ensuring that Cartesian products appear only after all joins in a dataflow.) In commercial systems today, it is well known that "bushy" trees (with nested right-hand inputs) and early use of Cartesian products can be useful in some cases, and hence both options are considered in most systems.
- **Selectivity estimation:** The selectivity estimation techniques in the Selinger paper are naïve, based on simple table and index cardinalities. Most systems today have a background process that periodically analyzes and summarizes the distributions of values in attributes via histograms and other summary statistics. Selectivity estimates for joins of base tables can be made by "joining" the histograms on the join columns. To move beyond single-column histograms, more sophisticated schemes have been proposed in the literature in recent years to incorporate issues like dependencies among columns [52] [11]; these innovations have yet to show up in products. One reason for the slow adoption of these schemes is a flaw in the industry benchmarks: the data generators in benchmarks like TPC-H generate independent values in columns, and hence do not encourage the adoption of technology to handle "real" data distributions. Nonetheless, the benefits of improved selectivity estimation are widely recognized: as noted by Ioannidis and Christodoulakis, errors in selectivity early in optimization propagate multiplicatively up the plan tree, resulting in terrible subsequent estimations [32]. Hence improvements in selectivity estimation often merit the modest implementation cost of smarter summary statistics, and a number of companies appear to be moving toward modeling dependencies across columns.
- **Search Algorithms:** Some commercial systems – notably those of Microsoft and Tandem – discard Selinger's dynamic programming algorithm in favor of a goal-directed "top-down" search scheme based on the Cascades framework [17]. Top-down search can in some instances lower the number of plans considered by an optimizer [60], but can also have the negative effect of increasing optimizer memory consumption. If practical success is an indication of quality, then the choice between top-down search and dynamic programming is irrelevant – each has been shown to work well in state-of-the-art optimizers, and both still have runtimes and memory requirements that are exponential in the number of tables in a query.

It is also important to note that some systems fall back on heuristic search schemes for queries with "too many" tables. Although there is an interesting research literature of randomized query optimization heuristics [34][5][62], the heuristics used in commercial systems tend to be proprietary, and (if rumors are to be believed) do not resemble the randomized query optimization literature. An educational exercise is to examine the query "optimizer" of the open-source MySQL engine, which (at last check) is entirely heuristic and relies mostly on exploiting indexes and key/foreign-key constraints. This is reminiscent of early (and infamous) versions of Oracle. In some systems, a query with too many tables in the FROM clause can only be executed if the user explicitly directs the optimizer how to choose a plan (via so-called optimizer "hints" embedded in the SQL).

- **Parallelism:** Every commercial DBMS today has some support for parallel processing, and most support "intra-query" parallelism: the ability to speed up a single query via multiple processors. The query optimizer needs to get involved in determining how to schedule operators – and parallelized operators – across multiple CPUs, and (in the shared-nothing or shared-disk cases) multiple separate computers on a high-speed network. The standard approach was proposed by Hong and Stonebraker [31]and uses two phases: first a traditional single-site optimizer is invoked to pick the best single-site plan, and then this plan is scheduled across the multiple processors. Research has been published on this latter phase [14][15] though it is not clear to what extent these results inform standard practice – currently this seems to be more like art than science.
- **Extensibility:** Modern SQL standards include user-defined types and functions, complex objects (nested tuples, sets, arrays and XML trees), and other features. Commercial optimizers try to handle these extensions with varying degrees of intelligence. One well-scoped issue in this area is to incorporate the costs of expensive functions into the optimization problem as suggested in [29]. In most commercial implementations, simple heuristics are still used, though more thorough techniques are presented in the research literature [28][9]. Support for complex objects is gaining importance as nested XML data is increasingly stored in relational engines. This has generated large volumes of work in the object-oriented [50] and XML [25] query processing literature.

  Having an extensible version of a Selinger optimizer as described by Lohman [42] can be useful for elegantly introducing new operators into the query engine; this is presumably the approach taken in IBM's products. A related approach for top-down optimizers was developed by Graefe [18][17], and is likely used in Microsoft SQL Server.
- **Auto-Tuning:** A variety of ongoing industrial research efforts attempt to improve the ability of a DBMS to make tuning decisions automatically. Some of these techniques are based on collecting a query workload, and then using the optimizer to find the plan costs via various "what-if" analyses: what if other indexes had existed, or the data had been laid out differently. An optimizer needs to be adjusted somewhat to support this activity efficiently, as described by Chaudhuri [8].

4.3.1 A Note on Query Compilation and Recompilation

SQL supports the ability to "prepare" a query: to pass it through the parser, rewriter and optimizer, and store the resulting plan in a catalog table. This is even possible for embedded queries (e.g. from web forms) that have program variables in the place of query constants; the only wrinkle is that during selectivity estimation, the variables that are provided by the forms are assumed by the optimizer to have some "typical" values. Query preparation is especially useful for form-driven, canned queries: the query is prepared when the application is written, and when the application goes live, users do not experience the overhead of parsing, rewriting and optimizing. In practice, this feature is used far more heavily than ad-hoc queries that are optimized at runtime.

As a database evolves, it often becomes necessary to re-optimize prepared plans. At a minimum, when an index is dropped, any plan that used that index must be removed from the catalog of stored plans, so that a new plan will be chosen upon the next invocation.

Other decisions about re-optimizing plans are more subtle, and expose philosophical distinctions among the vendors. Some vendors (e.g. IBM) work very hard to provide *predictable performance*. As a result, they will not reoptimize a plan unless it will no longer execute, as in the case of dropped indexes. Other vendors (e.g. Microsoft) work very hard to make their systems *self-tuning*, and will reoptimize plans quite aggressively: they may even reoptimize, for example, if the value distribution of a column changes significantly, since this may affect the selectivity estimates, and hence the choice of the best plan. A self-tuning system is arguably less predictable, but more efficient in a dynamic environment.

This philosophical distinction arises from differences in the historical customer base for these products, and is in some sense self-reinforcing. IBM traditionally focused on high-end customers with skilled DBAs and application programmers. In these kinds of high-budget IT shops, predictable performance from the database is of paramount importance – after spending months tuning the database design and settings, the DBA does not want the optimizer to change its mind unpredictably. By contrast, Microsoft strategically entered the database market at the low end; as a result, their customers tend to have lower IT budgets and expertise, and want the DBMS to "tune itself" as much as possible.

Over time these companies' business strategies and customer bases have converged so that they compete directly. But the original philosophies tend to peek out in the system architecture, and in the way that the architecture affects the use of the systems by DBAs and database programmers.

4.4 Executor

A query executor is given a fully-specified query plan, which is a fixed, directed dataflow graph connecting operators that encapsulate base-table access and various query execution algorithms. In some systems this dataflow graph is already compiled into op-codes by the optimizer, in which case the query executor is basically a runtime interpreter. In other systems a representation of the dataflow graph is passed to the query executor, which recursively invokes procedures for the operators based on the graph layout. We will focus on this latter case; the op-code approach essentially compiles the logic we described here into a program.

```
class iterator {
  iterator &inputs[];
  void init();
  tuple get_next();
  void close();
}
```

Figure 9: Iterator superclass pseudocode.

Essentially all modern query executors employ the *iterator* model, which was used in the earliest relational systems. Iterators are most simply described in an object-oriented fashion. All operators in a query plan – the nodes in the dataflow graph – are implemented as objects from the superclass `iterator`. A simplified definition for an iterator is given in Figure 9. Each iterator specifies its inputs, which define the edges in the dataflow graph. Each query execution operator is implemented as a subclass of the iterator class: the set of subclasses in a typical system might include filescan, indexscan, nested-loops join, sort, merge-join, hash-join, duplicate-elimination, and grouped-aggregation. An important feature of the iterator model is that any subclass of iterator can be used as input to any other – hence each iterator's logic is independent of its children and parents in the graph, and there is no need to write special-case code for particular combinations of iterators.

Graefe provides more details on iterators in his query processing survey [18]. The interested reader is encouraged to examine the open-source PostgreSQL code base, which includes moderately sophisticated implementations of the iterators for most standard query execution algorithms.

4.4.1 Iterator Discussion

An important property of iterators is that they *couple dataflow with control flow*. The `get_next()` call is a standard procedure call, returning a tuple reference to the callee via the call stack. Hence a tuple is returned to a parent in the graph exactly when control is returned. This implies that only a single DBMS thread is needed to execute an entire query graph, and there is no need for queues or rate-matching between iterators. This makes relational query executors clean to implement and easy to debug, and is a contrast with dataflow architectures in other environments, e.g. networks, which rely on various protocols for queueing and feedback between concurrent producers and consumers.

The single-threaded iterator architecture is also quite efficient for single-site query execution. In most database applications, the performance metric of merit is time to query completion. In a single-processor environment, time to completion for a given query plan is achieved when resources are fully utilized. In an iterator model, since one of the iterators is always active, resource utilization is maximized.[3]

[3] This assumes that iterators never block waiting for I/O requests. As noted above, I/O prefetching is typically handled by a separate thread. In the cases where prefetching is ineffective, there can indeed be inefficiencies in the iterator model. This is typically not a

As we mentioned previously, support for parallel query execution is standard in most modern DBMSs. Fortunately, this support can be provided with essentially no changes to the iterator model or a query execution architecture, by encapsulating parallelism and network communication within special *exchange* iterators, as described by Graefe [16].

4.4.2 Where's the Data?

Our discussion of iterators has conveniently sidestepped any questions of memory allocation for in-flight data; we never specified how tuples were stored in memory, or how they were passed from iterator to iterator. In practice, each iterator has a fixed number of *tuple descriptors* pre-allocated: one for each of its inputs, and one for its output. A tuple descriptor is typically an array of column references, where each column reference is composed of a reference to a tuple somewhere else in memory, and a column offset in that tuple. The basic iterator "superclass" logic never dynamically allocates memory, which raises the question of where the actual tuples being referenced are stored in memory.

There are two alternative answers to this question. The first possibility is that base-table tuples can reside in pages in the buffer pool; we will call these BP-tuples. If an iterator constructs a tuple descriptor referencing a BP-tuple, it must increment the pin count of the tuple's page; it decrements the pin count when the tuple descriptor is cleared. The second possibility is that an iterator implementation may allocate space for a tuple on the memory heap; we will call this an M-tuple, It may construct an M-tuple by copying columns from the buffer pool (the copy bracketed by a pin/unpin pair), and/or by evaluating expressions (e.g. arithmetic expressions like "EMP.sal * 0.1") in the query specification.

An attractive design pitfall is to always copy data out of the buffer pool immediately into M-tuples. This design uses M-tuples as the only in-flight tuple structure, which simplifies the executor code. It also circumvents bugs that can result from having buffer-pool pin and unpin calls separated by long periods of execution (and many lines of code) – one common bug of this sort is to forget to unpin the page altogether (a "buffer leak"). Unfortunately, exclusive use of M-tuples can be a major performance problem, since memory copies are often a serious bottleneck in high-performance systems, as noted in Section 3.2.

On the other hand, there are cases where constructing an M-tuple makes sense. It is sometimes beneficial to copy a tuple out of the buffer pool if it will be referenced for a long period of time. As long as a BP-tuple is directly referenced by an iterator, the page on which the BP-tuple resides must remain pinned in the buffer pool. This consumes a page worth of buffer pool memory, and ties the hands of the buffer replacement policy.

---

big problem in single-site databases, though it arises frequently when executing queries over remote tables [16][43].

The upshot of this discussion is that it is most efficient to support tuple descriptors that can reference both BP-tuples and M-tuples.

4.4.3 Data Modification Statements

Up to this point we have only discussed queries – i.e., read-only SQL statements. Another class of DML statements modify data: INSERT, DELETE and UPDATE statements. Typically, execution plans for these statements look like simple straight-line query plans, with a single access method as the source, and a data modification operator at the end of the pipeline.

In some cases, however, these plans are complicated by the fact that they both query and modify the same data. This mix of reading and writing the same table (possibly multiple times) raises some complications. A simple example is the notorious "Halloween problem", so called because it was discovered on October 31st by the System R group. The Halloween problem arises from a particular execution strategy for statements like "give everyone whose salary is under $20K a 10% raise". A naïve plan for this query pipelines an indexscan iterator over the Emp.salary field into an update iterator (the left-hand side of Figure 10); the pipelining provides good I/O locality, because it modifies tuples just after they are fetched from the B+-tree. However, this pipelining can also result in the indexscan "rediscovering" a previously-modified tuple that moved rightward in the tree after modification – resulting in multiple raises for each employee. In our example, all low-paid employees will receive repeated raises until they earn more than $20K; this is not the intention of the statement.

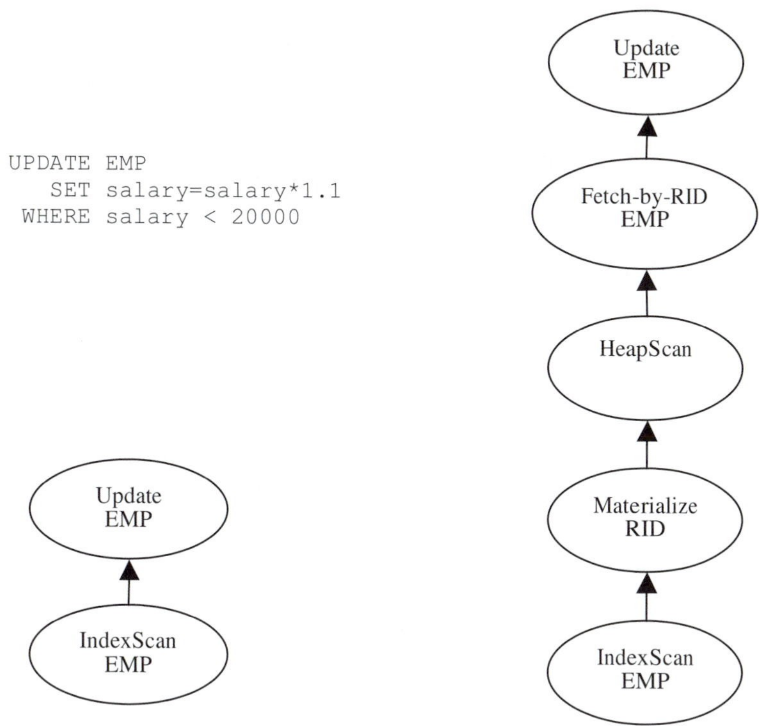

Figure 10: Two query plans for updating a table via an IndexScan. The plan on the left is susceptible to the Halloween problem. The plan on the right is safe, since it identifies all tuples to be updated before doing any updates.

SQL semantics forbid this behavior: an SQL statement is not allowed to "see" its own updates. Some care is needed to ensure that this visibility rule is observed. A simple, safe implementation has the query optimizer choose plans that avoid indexes on the updated column, but this can be quite inefficient in some cases. Another technique is to use a batch read-then-write scheme, which interposes Record-ID materialization and fetching operators between the index scan and the data modification operators in the dataflow (right-hand side of Figure 10.) This materialization operator receives the IDs of all tuples to be modified and stores them in temporary file; it then scans the temporary file and fetches each physical tuple ID by RID, feeding the resulting tuple to the data modification operator. In most cases if an index was chosen by the optimizer, it implies that only a few tuples are being changed, and hence the apparent inefficiency of this technique may be acceptable, since the temporary table is likely to remain entirely in the buffer pool. Pipelined update schemes are also possible, but require (somewhat exotic) multiversion support from the storage engine.[54]

4.5 Access Methods

The access methods are the routines for managing access to the various disk-based data structures supported by the system, which typically included unordered files ("heaps") of tuples, and various kinds of indexes. All commercial database systems include B+-tree indexes and heap files. Most systems are beginning to introduce some rudimentary support for multidimensional indexes like R-trees [24]. Systems targeted at read-mostly data warehousing workloads usually include specialized bitmap variants of indexes as well [49].

The basic API provided by an access method is an iterator API, with the `init()` routine expanded to take a "search predicate" (or in the terminology of System R, a "search argument", or SARG) of the form `column operator constant`. A NULL SARG is treated as a request to scan all tuples in the table. The `get_next()` call at the access method layer returns NULL when there are no more tuples satisfying the search argument.

There are two reasons to pass SARGs into the access method layer. The first reason should be clear: index access methods like B+-trees require SARGs in order to function efficiently. The second reason is a more subtle performance issue, but one that applies to heap scans as well as index scans. Assume that the SARG is checked by the routine that calls the access method layer. Then each time the access method returns from `get_next()`, it must either (a) return a handle to a tuple residing in a frame in the buffer pool, and pin the page in that frame to avoid replacement or (b) make a copy of the tuple. If the caller finds that the SARG is not satisfied, it is responsible for either (a) decrementing the pin count on the page, or (b) deleting the copied tuple. It must then try the next tuple on the page by reinvoking `get_next()`. This logic involves a number of CPU cycles simply doing function call/return pairs, and will either pin pages in the buffer pool unnecessarily (generating unnecessary contention for buffer frames) or create and destroy copies of tuples unnecessarily. Note that a typical heap scan will access all of the tuples on a given page, resulting in multiple iterations of this interaction per page. By contrast, if all this logic is done in the access method layer, the repeated pairs of call/return and either pin/unpin or copy/delete can be avoided by testing the SARGs a page at a time, and only returning from a `get_next()` call for a tuple that satisfies the SARG.

A special SARG is available in all access methods to FETCH a tuple directly by its physical *Record ID (RID)*. FETCH-by-RID is required to support secondary indexes and other schemes that "point" to tuples, and subsequently need to dereference those pointers.

In contrast to all other iterators, access methods have deep interactions with the concurrency and recovery logic surrounding transactions. We discuss these issues next.

5 Transactions: Concurrency Control and Recovery

Database systems are often accused of being enormous, monolithic pieces of software that cannot be split into reusable components. In practice, database systems – and the development teams that implement and maintain them – do break down into independent components with narrow interfaces in between. This is particularly true of the various components of query processing described in the previous section. The parser, rewrite engine, optimizer, executor and access methods all represent fairly independent pieces of code with well-defined, narrow interfaces that are "published" internally between development groups.

The truly monolithic piece of a DBMS is the transactional storage manager, which typically encompasses four deeply intertwined components:

1. A lock manager for concurrency control
2. A log manager for recovery
3. A buffer pool for staging database I/Os
4. Access methods for organizing data on disk.

A great deal of ink has been spilled describing the fussy details of transactional storage algorithms and protocols in database systems. The reader wishing to become knowledgable about these systems should read – at a minimum – a basic undergraduate database textbook [53], the journal article on the ARIES log protocol [45], and one serious article on transactional index concurrency *and* logging [46] [35]. More advanced readers will want to leaf through the Gray and Reuter textbook on transactions [22]. To really become an expert, this reading has to be followed by an implementation effort! We will not focus on algorithms here, but rather overview the roles of these various components, focusing on the system infrastructure that is often ignored in the textbooks, and highlighting the *inter-dependencies* between the components.

5.1 A Note on ACID

Many people are familiar with the term "ACID transactions", a mnemonic due to Härder and Reuter [26]. ACID stands for *Atomicity, Consistency, Isolation,* and *Durability.* These terms were not formally defined, and theory-oriented students sometimes spend a great deal of time trying to tease out exactly what each letter means. The truth is that these are not mathematical axioms that combine to guarantee transactional consistency, so carefully distinguishing the terms may not be a worthwhile exercise. Despite the informal nature, the ACID acronym is useful to organize a discussion of transaction systems.

- Atomicity is the "all or nothing" guarantee for transactions – either all of a transaction's actions are visible to another transaction, or none are.
- Consistency is an application-specific guarantee, which is typically captured in a DBMS by SQL integrity constraints. Given a definition of consistency provided by a set of constraints, a transaction can only commit if it leaves the database in a consistent state.
- Isolation is a guarantee to application writers that two concurrent transactions will not see each other's in-flight updates. As a result, applications need not be coded "defensively" to worry about the "dirty data" of other concurrent transactions.
- Durability is a guarantee that the updates of a committed transaction will be visible in the database to subsequent transactions, until such time as they are overwritten by another committed transaction.

Roughly speaking, modern DBMSs implement Isolation via *locking* and Durability via *logging*; Atomicity is guaranteed by a combination of locking (to prevent visibility of transient database states) and logging (to ensure correctness of data that is visible).

Consistency is managed by runtime checks in the query executor: if a transaction's actions will violate a SQL integrity constraint, the transaction is aborted and an error code returned.

5.2 Lock Manager and Latches

Serializability is the well-defined textbook notion of correctness for concurrent transactions: a sequence of interleaved actions for multiple committing transactions must correspond to some serial execution of the transactions. Every commercial relational DBMS implements serializability via strict two-phase locking (2PL): transactions acquire locks on objects before reading or writing them, and release all locks at the time of transactional commit or abort. The lock manager is the code module responsible for providing the facilities for 2PL. As an auxiliary to database locks, lighter-weight *latches* are also provided for mutual exclusion.

We begin our discussion with locks. Database locks are simply names used by convention within the system to represent either physical items (e.g. disk pages) or logical items (e.g., tuples, files, volumes) that are managed by the DBMS. Note that any name can have a lock associated with it – even if that name represents an abstract concept. The locking mechanism simply provides a place to register and check for these names. Locks come in different lock "modes", and these modes are associated with a lock-mode compatibility table. In most systems this logic is based on the well-known lock modes that are introduced in Gray's paper on granularity of locks [21].

The lock manager supports two basic calls; `lock(lockname, transactionID, mode)`, and `remove_transaction(transactionID)`. Note that because of the strict 2PL protocol, there need not be an individual call to unlock resources individually – the `remove_transaction` call will unlock all resources associated with a transaction. However, as we discuss in Section 5.2.1, the SQL standard allows for lower degrees of consistency than serializability, and hence there is a need for an `unlock(lockname, transactionID)` call as well. There is also a `lock_upgrade(lockname, transactionID, newmode)` call to allow transactions to "upgrade" to higher lock modes (e.g. from shared to exclusive mode) in a two-phase manner, without dropping and re-acquiring locks. Additionally, some systems also support a `conditional_lock(lockname, transactionID, mode)` call. The `conditional_lock` call always returns immediately, and indicates whether it succeeded in acquiring the lock. If it did not succeed, the calling DBMS thread is *not* enqueued waiting for the lock. The use of conditional locks for index concurrency is discussed in [46].

To support these calls, the lock manager maintains two data structures. A global *lock table* is maintained to hold locknames and their associated information. The lock table is a dynamic hash table keyed by (a hash function of) lock names. Associated with each lock is a `current_mode` flag to indicate the lock mode, and a `waitqueue` of lock request pairs `(transactionID, mode)`. In addition, it maintains a *transaction table* keyed by transactionID, which contains two items for each transaction *T*: (a) a pointer to *T*'s DBMS thread state, to allow *T*'s DBMS thread to be rescheduled when it acquires any locks it is waiting on, and (b) a list of pointers to all of *T*'s lock requests in the lock table, to facilitate the removal of all locks associated with a particular transaction (e.g., upon transaction commit or abort).

Internally, the lock manager makes use of a *deadlock detector* DBMS thread that periodically examines the lock table to look for waits-for cycles. Upon detection of a deadlock, the deadlock detector aborts one of the deadlocked transaction (the decision of which deadlocked transaction to abort is based on heuristics that have been studied in the research literature [55].) In shared-nothing and shared-disk systems, distributed deadlock detection facilities are required as well [47]. A more description of a lock manager implementation is given in Gray and Reuter's text [22].

In addition to two-phase locks, every DBMS also supports a lighter-weight mutual exclusion mechanism, typically called a *latch.* Latches are more akin to monitors [30] than locks; they are used to provide exclusive access to internal DBMS data structures. As an example, the buffer pool page table has a latch associated with each frame, to guarantee that only one DBMS thread is replacing a given frame at any time. Latches differ from locks in a number of ways:

- Locks are kept in the lock table and located via hash tables; latches reside in memory near the resources they protect, and are accessed via direct addressing.
- Locks are subject to the strict 2PL protocol. Latches may be acquired or dropped during a transaction based on special-case internal logic.
- Lock acquisition is entirely driven by data access, and hence the order and lifetime of lock acquisitions is largely in the hands of applications and the query optimizer. Latches are acquired by specialized code inside the DBMS, and the DBMS internal code issues latch requests and releases strategically.
- Locks are allowed to produce deadlock, and lock deadlocks are *detected* and resolved via transactional restart. Latch deadlock must be *avoided*; the occurrence of a latch deadlock represents a bug in the DBMS code.
- Latch calls take a few dozen CPU cycles, lock requests take hundreds of CPU cycles.

The latch API supports the routines `latch(object, mode)`, `unlatch(object)`, and `conditional_latch(object, mode)`. In most DBMSs, the choices of latch modes include only Shared or eXclusive. Latches maintain a `current_mode`, and a `waitqueue` of DBMS threads waiting on the latch. The `latch` and `unlatch` calls work as one might expect. The `conditional_latch` call is analogous to the `conditional_lock` call described above, and is also used for index concurrency [46].

5.2.1 Isolation Levels

Very early in the development of the transaction concept, there were attempts to provide more concurrency by providing "weaker" semantics than serializability. The challenge was to provide robust definitions of the semantics in these cases. The most influential effort in this regard was Gray's early work on "Degrees of Consistency" [21]. That work attempted to provide both a declarative definition of consistency degrees, and implementations in terms of locking. Influenced by this work, the ANSI SQL standard defines four "Isolation Levels":

1. READ UNCOMMITTED: A transaction may read any version of data, committed or not. This is achieved in a locking implementation by read requests proceeding without acquiring any locks[4].
2. READ COMMITTED: A transaction may read *any committed* version of data. Repeated reads of an object may result in different (committed) versions. This is achieved by read requests acquiring a read lock before accessing an object, and unlocking it immediately after access.
3. REPEATABLE READ: A transaction will read only one version of committed data; once the transaction reads an object, it will always read the same version of that object. This is achieved by read requests acquiring a read lock before accessing an object, and holding the lock until end-of-transaction.
4. SERIALIZABLE: Fully serializable access is guaranteed.

At first blush, REPEATABLE READ seems to provide full serializability, but this is not the case. Early in the System R project, a problem arose that was dubbed the "phantom problem". In the phantom problem, a transaction accesses a relation more than once with the same predicate, but sees new "phantom" tuples on re-access that were not seen on the first access.[5] This is because two-phase locking at tuple-level granularity does not prevent the insertion of new tuples into a table. Two-phase locking of tables prevents phantoms, but table-level locking can be restrictive in cases where transactions access only a few tuples via an index. We investigate this issue further in Section 5.4.3 when we discuss locking in indexes.

Commercial systems provide the four isolation levels above via locking-based implementations of concurrency control. Unfortunately, as noted in by Berenson, et al. [6], neither the early work by Gray nor the ANSI standard achieve the goal of providing truly declarative definitions. Both rely in subtle ways on an assumption that a locking scheme is used for concurrency control, as opposed to an optimistic [36] or multi-version [54] concurrency scheme. This implies that the proposed semantics are ill-defined. The interested reader is encouraged to look at the Berenson paper which discusses some of the problems in the SQL standard specifications, as well as the research by Adya et al. [1] which provides a new, cleaner approach to the problem.

In addition to the standard ANSI SQL isolation levels, various vendors provide additional levels that have proven popular in various cases.

- CURSOR STABILITY: This level is intended to solve the "lost update" problem of READ COMMITTED. Consider two transactions T1 and T2. T1 runs in READ COMMITTED mode, reads an object X (say the value of a bank account),

---

[4] In all isolation levels, write requests are preceded by write locks that are held until end of transaction.

[5] Despite the spooky similarity in names, the phantom problem has nothing to do with the Halloween problem of Section 4.4.

remembers its value, and subsequently writes object X based on the remembered value (say adding $100 to the original account value). T2 reads and writes X as well (say subtracting $300 from the account). If T2's actions happen between T1's read and T1's write, then the effect of T2's update will be lost – the final value of the account in our example will be up by $100, instead of being down by $200 as desired. A transaction in CURSOR STABILITY mode holds a lock on the most recently-read item on a query cursor; the lock is automatically dropped when the cursor is moved (e.g. via another `FETCH`) or the transaction terminates. CURSOR STABILITY allows the transaction to do read-think-write sequences on individual items without intervening updates from other transactions.

- SNAPSHOT ISOLATION: A transaction running in SNAPSHOT ISOLATION mode operates on a version of the database as it existed at the time the transaction began; subsequent updates by other transactions are invisible to the transaction. When the transaction starts, it gets a unique *start-timestamp* from a monotonically increasing counter; when it commits it gets a unique *end-timestamp* from the counter. The transaction commits only if there is no other transaction with an overlapping *start/end-transaction* pair wrote data that this transaction also wrote. This isolation mode depends upon a multi-version concurrency implementation, rather than locking (though these schemes typically coexist in systems that support SNAPSHOT ISOLATION.)
- READ CONSISTENCY: This is a scheme defined by Oracle; it is subtly different from SNAPSHOT ISOLATION. In the Oracle scheme, each SQL *statement* (of which there may be many in a single transaction) sees the most recently committed values as of the start of the statement. For statements that `FETCH` from cursors, the cursor set is based on the values as of the time it is `open`-ed. This is implemented by maintaining multiple versions of individual tuples, with a single transaction possibly referencing multiple versions of a single tuple. Modifications are maintained via long-term write locks, so when two transactions want to write the same object the first writer "wins", whereas in SNAPSHOT ISOLATION the first committer "wins".

Weak isolation schemes provide higher concurrency than serializability. As a result, some systems even use weak consistency as the default; Oracle defaults to READ COMMITTED, for example. The downside is that Isolation (in the ACID sense) is not guaranteed. Hence application writers need to reason about the subtleties of the schemes to ensure that their transactions run correctly. This is tricky given the operationally-defined semantics of the schemes.

5.3 Log Manager

The log manager is responsible for maintaining the durability of committed transactions, and for facilitating the rollback of aborted transactions to ensure atomicity. It provides these features by maintaining a sequence of log records on disk, and a set of data structures in memory. In order to support correct behavior after crash, the memory-resident data structures obviously need to be re-createable from persistent data in the log and the database.

Database logging is an incredibly complex and detail-oriented topic. The canonical reference on database logging is the journal paper on ARIES [45], and a database expert should be familiar with the details of that paper. The ARIES paper not only explains its protocol, but also provides discussion of alternative design possibilities, and the problems that they can cause. This makes for dense but eventually rewarding reading. As a more digestible introduction, the Ramakrishnan/Gehrke textbook [53] provides a description of the basic ARIES protocol without side discussions or refinements, and we provide a set of powerpoint slides that accompany that discussion on our website (http://redbook.cs.berkeley.edu). Here we discuss some of the basic ideas in recovery, and try to explain the complexity gap between textbook and journal descriptions.

As is well known, the standard theme of database recovery is to use a Write-Ahead Logging (WAL) protocol. The WAL protocol consists of three very simple rules:

1. Each modification to a database page should generate a log record, and the log record must be flushed to the log device *before* the database page is flushed.
2. Database log records must be flushed in order; log record *r* cannot be flushed until all log records preceding *r* are flushed.
3. Upon a transaction commit request, a COMMIT log record must be flushed to the log device *before* the commit request returns successfully.

Many people only remember the first of these rules, but all three are required for correct behavior.

The first rule ensures that the actions of incomplete transactions can be *undone* in the event of a transaction abort, to ensure atomicity. The combination of rules (2) and (3) ensure durability: the actions of a committed transaction can be *redone* after a system crash if they are not yet reflected in the database.

Given these simple principles, it is surprising that efficient database logging is as subtle and detailed as it is. In practice, however, the simple story above is complicated by the need for extreme performance. The challenge is to guarantee efficiency in the "fast path" for transactions that commit, while also providing high-performance rollback for aborted transactions, and quick recovery after crashes. Logging gets even more baroque when application-specific optimizations are added, e.g. to support improved performance for fields that can only be incremented or decremented ("escrow transactions".)

In order to maximize the speed of the fast path, every commercial database system operates in a mode that Härder and Reuter call "DIRECT, STEAL/NOT-FORCE" [26]: (a) data objects are updated in place, (b) unpinned buffer pool frames can be "stolen" (and the modified data pages written back to disk) even if they contain uncommitted data, and (c) buffer pool pages need *not* be "forced" (flushed) to the database before a commit request returns to the user. These policies keep the data in the location chosen by the DBA, and they give the buffer manager and disk schedulers full latitude to decide on memory management and I/O policies without consideration for transactional correctness. These features can have major performance benefits, but require that the log manager efficiently handle all the subtleties of *undoing* the flushes of stolen pages from aborted transactions, and *redoing* the changes to not-forced pages of committed transactions that are lost on crash.

Another fast-path challenge in logging is to keep log records as small as possible, in order to increase the throughput of log I/O activity. A natural optimization is to log *logical* operations (e.g., "insert (Bob, $25000) into EMP") rather than physical operations (e.g., the after-images for all byte ranges modified via the tuple insertion, including bytes on both heap file and index blocks.) The tradeoff is that the logic to redo and undo logical operations becomes quite involved, which can severely degrade performance during transaction abort and database recovery.[6] In practice, a mixture of physical and logical logging (so-called "physiological" logging) is used. In ARIES, physical logging is generally used to support REDO, and logical logging is used to support UNDO – this is part of the ARIES rule of "repeating history" during recovery to reach the crash state, and then rolling back transactions from that point.

Crash recovery performance is greatly enhanced by the presence of database *checkpoints* – consistent versions of the database from the recent past. A checkpoint limits the amount of log that the recovery process needs to consult and process. However, the naïve generation of checkpoints is too expensive to do during regular processing, so some more efficient "fuzzy" scheme for checkpointing is required, along with logic to correctly bring the checkpoint up to the most recent consistent state by processing as little of the log as possible. ARIES uses a very clever scheme in which the actual checkpoint records are quite tiny, containing just enough information to initiate the log analysis process and to enable the recreation of main-memory data structures lost at crash time.

Finally, the task of logging and recovery is further complicated by the fact that a database is not merely a set of user data tuples on disk pages; it also includes a variety of "physical" information that allows it to manage its internal disk-based data structures. We discuss this in the context of index logging in the next section.

5.4 Locking and Logging in Indexes

Indexes are physical storage structures for accessing data in the database. The indexes themselves are invisible to database users, except inasmuch as they improve performance. Users cannot directly read or modify indexes, and hence user code need not be isolated (in the ACID sense) from changes to the index. This allows indexes to be managed via more efficient (and complex) transactional schemes than database data. The only invariant that index concurrency and recovery needs to preserve is that the index always returns transactionally-consistent tuples from the database.

[6] Note also that logical log records must always have well-known inverse functions if they need to participate in undo processing.

5.4.1 Latching in B+-Trees

A well-studied example of this issue arises in B+-tree latching. B+-trees consist of database disk pages that are accessed via the buffer pool, just like data pages. Hence one scheme for index concurrency control is to use two-phase locks on index pages. This means that every transaction that touches the index needs to lock the root of the B+-tree until commit time – a recipe for limited concurrency. A variety of latch-based schemes have been developed to work around this problem without setting any transactional locks on index pages. The key insight in these schemes is that modifications to the tree's *physical structure* (e.g. splitting pages) can be made in a non-transactional manner as long as all concurrent transactions continue to find the correct data at the leaves. There are roughly three approaches to this:

- *Conservative* schemes, which allow multiple transactions to access the same pages only if they can be guaranteed not to conflict in their use of a page's content. One such conflict is that a reading transaction wants to traverse a fully-packed internal page of the tree, and a concurrent inserting transaction is operating below that page, and hence might need to split it [4]. These conservative schemes sacrifice too much concurrency compared with the more recent ideas below.
- *Latch-coupling* schemes, in which the tree traversal logic latches each node before it is visited, only unlatching a node when the next node to be visited has been successfully latched. This scheme is sometimes called latch "crabbing", because of the crablike movement of "holding" a node in the tree, "grabbing" its child, releasing the parent, and repeating. Latch coupling is used in some commercial systems; IBM's ARIES-IM version is well described [46]. ARIES-IM includes some fairly intricate details and corner cases – on occasion it has to restart traversals after splits, and even set (very short-term) tree-wide latches.
- *Right-link* schemes, which add some simple additional structure to the B+-tree to minimize the requirement for latches and retraversals. In particular, a link is added from each node to its right-hand neighbor. During traversal, right-link schemes do no latch coupling – each node is latched, read, and unlatched. The main intuition in right-link schemes is that if a traversing transaction follows a pointer to a node *n* and finds that *n* was split in the interim, the traversing transaction can detect this fact, and "move right" via the rightlinks to find the new correct location in the tree. [39][35]

Kornacker, et al. [35] provide a detailed discussion of the distinctions between latch-coupling and right-link schemes, and points out that latch-coupling is only applicable to B+-trees, and will not work for index trees over more complex data, e.g. multidimensional indexes like R-trees.

5.4.2 Logging for Physical Structures

In addition to special-case concurrency logic, indexes employ special-case logging logic. This logic makes logging and recovery much more efficient, at the expense of more complexity in the code. The main idea is that structural index changes need not be undone when the associated transaction is aborted; such changes may have no effect on the database tuples seen by other transactions. For example, if a B+-tree page is split during an inserting transaction that subsequently aborts, there is no pressing need to undo the split during the abort processing.

This raises the challenge of labeling some log records "redo-only" – during any undo processing of the log, these changes should be left in place. ARIES provides an elegant mechanism for these scenarios called *nested top actions*, which allows the recovery process to "jump over" log records for physical structure modifications without any special case code during recovery.

This same idea is used in other contexts, including in heap files. An insertion into a heap file may require the file to be extended on disk. To capture this, changes must be made to the file's "extent map", a data structure on disk that points to the runs of contiguous blocks that constitute the file. These changes to the extent map need not be undone if the inserting transaction aborts – the fact that the file has become larger is a transactionally invisible side-effect, and may be in fact be useful for absorbing future insert traffic.

5.4.3 Next-Key Locking: Physical Surrogates for Logical Properties

We close this section with a final index concurrency problem that illustrates a subtle but significant idea. The challenge is to provide full seriazability (including phantom protection) while allowing for tuple-level locks and the use of indexes.

The phantom problem arises when a transaction accesses tuples via an index: in such cases, the transaction typically does not lock the entire table, just the tuples in the table that are accessed via the index (e.g. "Name BETWEEN 'Bob' AND 'Bobby'"). In the absence of a table-level lock, other transactions are free to insert new tuples into the table (e.g. Name='Bobbie'). When these new inserts fall within the value-range of a query predicate, they will appear in subsequent accesses via that predicate. Note that the phantom problem relates to visibility of database tuples, and hence is a problem with locks, not just latches. In principle, what is needed is the ability to somehow lock the logical space represented by the original query's search predicate. Unfortunately, it is well known that predicate locking is expensive, since it requires a way to compare arbitrary predicates for overlap – something that cannot be done with a hash-based lock table [2].

The standard solution to the phantom problem in B+-trees is called "next-key locking". In next-key locking, the index insertion code is modified so that an insertion of a tuple with index key *k* is required to allocate an exclusive lock on the "next-key" tuple that exists in the index: the tuple with the lowest key greater than *k*. This protocol ensures that subsequent insertions cannot appear "in between" two tuples that were returned previously to an active transaction; it also ensures that tuples cannot be inserted just below the lowest-keyed tuple previously returned (e.g. if there were no 'Bob' on the 1st access, there should be no 'Bob' on subsequent accesses). One corner case remains: the insertion of tuples just *above* the highest-keyed tuple previously returned. To protect against this case, the next-key locking protocol requires read transactions to be modified as well, so that they must get a shared lock on the "next-key" tuple in the index as well:

the minimum-keyed tuple that does *not* satisfy the query predicate. An implementation of next-key locking is described for ARIES [42].

Next-key locking is not simply a clever hack. It is an instance of using a physical object (a currently-stored tuple) as a *surrogate* for a logical concept (a predicate). The benefit is that simple system infrastructure (e.g. hash-based lock tables) can be used for more complex purposes, simply by modifying the lock protocol. This idea of using physical surrogates for logical concepts is unique to database research: it is largely unappreciated in other systems work on concurrency, which typically does not consider semantic information about logical concepts as part of the systems challenge. Designers of complex software systems should keep this general approach in their "bag of tricks" when such semantic information is available.

5.5 Interdependencies of Transactional Storage

We claimed early in this section that transactional storage systems are monolithic, deeply entwined systems. In this section, we discuss a few of the interdependencies between the three main aspects of a transactional storage system: concurrency control, recovery management, and access methods. In a happier world, it would be possible to identify narrow APIs between these modules, and allow the implementation behind those APIs to be swappable. Our examples in this section show that this is not easily done. We do not intend to provide an exhaustive list of interdependencies here; generating and proving the completeness of such a list would be a very challenging exercise. We do hope, however, to illustrate some of the twisty logic of transactional storage, and thereby justify the resulting monolithic implementations in commercial DBMSs.

We begin by considering concurrency control and recovery alone, without complicating things further with access method details. Even with the simplification, things are deeply intertwined. One manifestation of the relationship between concurrency and recovery is that write-ahead logging makes implicit assumptions about the locking protocol – it requires *strict* two-phase locking, and will not operate correctly with non-strict two-phase locking. To see this, consider what happens during the rollback of an aborted transaction. The recovery code begins processing the log records of the aborted transaction, undoing its modifications. Typically this requires changing pages or tuples that were previously modified by the transaction. In order to make these changes, the transaction needs to have locks on those pages or tuples. In a non-strict 2PL scheme, if the transaction drops any locks before aborting, it is unable to acquire the new locks it needs to complete the rollback process!

Access methods complicate things yet further. It is an enormous intellectual challenge to take a textbook access method (e.g. linear hashing [41] or R-trees [24]) and implement it correctly and efficiently in a transactional system; for this reason, most DBMSs still only implement heap files and B+-trees as native, transactionally protected access methods. As we illustrated above for B+-trees, high-performance implementations of transactional indexes include intricate protocols for latching, locking, and logging. The B+-trees in serious DBMSs are riddled with calls to the concurrency and recovery code. Even simple access methods like heap files have some tricky concurrency and recovery issues surrounding the data structures that describe their contents (e.g. extent maps). This logic is not generic to all access methods – it is very much customized to the specific logic of the access method, and its particular implementation.

Concurrency control in access methods has been well-developed only for locking-oriented schemes. Other concurrency schemes (e.g. Optimistic or Multiversion concurrency control) do not usually consider access methods at all, or if they do mention them it is only in an offhanded and impractical fashion [36]. Hence it is unlikely that one can mix and match different concurrency mechanisms for a given access method implementation.

Recovery logic in access methods is particularly system-specific: the timing and contents of access method log records depend upon fine details of the recovery protocol, including the handling of structure modifications (e.g. whether they get undone upon transaction rollback, and if not how that is avoided), and the use of physical and logical logging.

Even for a specific access method, the recovery and concurrency logic are intertwined. In one direction, the recovery logic depends upon the concurrency protocol: if the recovery manager has to restore a physically consistent state of the tree, then it needs to know what inconsistent states could possibly arise, to bracket those states appropriately with log records (e.g. via nested top actions). In the opposite direction, the concurrency protocol for an access method may be dependent on the recovery logic: for example, the rightlink scheme for B+-trees assumes that pages in the tree never "re-merge" after they split, an assumption that requires the recovery scheme to use a scheme like nested top actions to avoid undoing splits generated by aborted transactions.

The one bright spot in this picture is that buffer management is relatively well-isolated from the rest of the components of the storage manager. As long as pages are pinned correctly, the buffer manager is free to encapsulate the rest of its logic and reimplement it as needed, e.g. the choice of pages to replace (because of the STEAL property), and the scheduling of page flushes (thanks to the NOT FORCE property). Of course achieving this isolation is the direct cause of much of the complexity in concurrency and recovery, so this spot is not perhaps as bright as it seems either.

6 Shared Components

In this section we cover a number of utility subsystems that are present in nearly all commercial DBMS, but rarely discussed in the literature.

6.1 Memory Allocator

The textbook presentation of DBMS memory management tends to focus entirely on the buffer pool. In practice, database systems allocate significant amounts of memory for other tasks as well, and the correct management of this memory is both a programming burden and a performance issue. Selinger-style query optimization can use a great deal of memory, for example, to build up state during dynamic programming. Query operators like hashjoins and sorts allocate significant memory for private space at runtime. In commercial systems, memory allocation is made more efficient and easier to debug via the use of a *context-based* memory allocator.

A memory context is an in-memory data structure that maintains a list of *regions* of contiguous virtual memory, with each region possibly having a small header containing a context label or a pointer to the context header structure.

The basic API for memory contexts includes calls to:

- **Create a context** with a given name or type. The type of the context might advise the allocator how to efficiently handle memory allocation: for example, the contexts for the query optimizer grow via small increments, while contexts for hashjoins allocate their memory in a few large batches. Based on such knowledge, the allocator can choose to allocate bigger or smaller regions at a time.
- **Allocate a chunk of memory within a context**. This allocation will return a pointer to memory (much like the traditional malloc call). That memory may come from an existing region in the context; if no such space exists in any region, the allocator will ask the operating system for a new region of memory, label it, and link it into the context.
- **Delete a chunk of memory within a context.** This may or may not cause the context to delete the corresponding region. Deletion from memory contexts is somewhat unusual – a more typical behavior is to delete an entire context.
- **Delete a context**. This first frees all of the regions associated with the context, and then deletes the context header.
- **Reset a context.** This retains the context, but returns it to the state of original creation – typically by deallocating all previously-allocated regions of memory.

Memory contexts provide important software engineering advantages. The most important is that they serve as a lower-level, programmer-controllable alternative to garbage collection. For example, the developers writing the optimizer can allocate memory in an `optimizer` context for a particular query, without worrying about how to free the memory later on. When the optimizer has picked the best plan, it can make a copy of the plan in memory from a separate `executor` context for the query, and then simply delete the query's `optimizer` context – this saves the trouble of writing code to carefully walk all the optimizer data structures and delete their components. It also avoids tricky memory leaks that can arise from bugs in such code. This feature is very useful for the naturally "phased" behavior of query execution, which proceeds from parser to optimizer to executor, typically doing a number of allocations in each context, followed by a context deletion.

Note that memory contexts actually provide more control than most garbage collectors: developers can control both *spatial* and *temporal* locality of deallocation. Spatial control is provided by the context mechanism itself, which allows the programmer to separate memory into logical units. Temporal control is given by allowing programmers to issue context deletions when appropriate. By contrast, garbage collectors typically work on all of a program's memory, and make their own decisions about when to run. This is one of the frustrations of attempting to write server-quality code in Java [59].

Memory contexts also provide performance advantages in some cases, due to the relatively high overhead for malloc() and free() on many platforms. In particular, memory contexts can use semantic knowledge (via the context type) of how memory will be allocated and deallocated, and may call malloc() and free() accordingly to minimize OS overheads. In particular, some pieces of a database system (e.g. the parser and optimizer) allocate a large number of small objects, and then free them all at once via a context deletion. On most platforms it is rather expensive to call free() on many small objects, so a memory allocator can instead malloc() large regions, and apportion the resulting memory to its callers. The relative lack of memory deallocations means that there is no need for the kind of compaction logic used by malloc() and free(). And when the context is deleted, only a few free() calls are required to remove the large regions.

The interested reader may want to browse the open-source PostgreSQL code, which has a fairly sophisticated memory allocator.

6.1.1 A Note on Memory Allocation for Query Operators

A philosophical design difference among vendors can be seen in the allocation of memory for space-intensive operators like hash joins and sorts. Some systems (e.g. DB2) allow the DBA to control the amount of RAM that will be used by such operations, and guarantee that each query gets that amount of RAM when executed; this guarantee is ensured by the admission control policy. In such systems, the operators allocate their memory off of the heap via the memory allocator. These systems provide good performance stability, but force the DBA to (statically!) decide how to balance physical memory across various subsystems like the buffer pool and the query operators.

Other systems (e.g. MS SQL Server) try to manage these issues automatically, taking the memory allocation task out of the DBA's hands. These systems attempt to do intelligent memory allocation across the various pieces of query execution, including caching of pages in the buffer pool and the use of memory by query operators. The pool of memory used for all of these tasks is the buffer pool itself, and hence in these systems the query operators take memory from the buffer pool, bypassing the memory allocator.

This distinction echoes our discussion of query preparation in Section 4.3.1. The former class of systems assumes that the DBA is engaged in sophisticated tuning, and that the workload for the system will be amenable to one carefully-chosen setting of the DBA's memory "knobs". Under these conditions, these systems should always perform predictably well. The latter class assumes that DBAs either do not or cannot correctly set these knobs, and attempts to replace the DBA wisdom with software logic. They also retain the right to change their relative allocations adaptively, providing the possibility for better performance on changing workloads. As in Section 4.3.1, this distinction says something about how these vendors expect their products to be used, and about the administrative expertise (and financial resources) of their customers.

6.2 Disk Management Subsystems

Textbooks on DBMSs tend to talk about disks as if they were homogeneous objects. In practice, disk drives are complex and heterogeneous pieces of hardware, varying widely in capacity and bandwidth. Hence every DBMS has a disk management subsystem that deals with these issues, managing the allocation of tables and other units of storage across multiple devices.

One aspect of this module is to manage the mapping of tables to devices and or files. One-to-one mappings of tables to files sound natural, but raised problems in early filesystems. First, OS files traditionally could not be larger than a disk, while database tables may need to span multiple disks. Second, it was traditionally bad form to allocate too many OS files, since the OS typically only allowed a few open file descriptors, and many OS utilities for directory management and backup did not scale to very large numbers of files. Hence in many cases a single file is used to hold multiple tables. Over time, most filesystems have overcome these limitations, but it is typical today for OS files to simply be treated by the DBMS as abstract storage units, with arbitrary mappings to database tables.

More complex is the code to handle device-specific details for maintaining temporal and spatial control as described in Section 3. There is a large and vibrant industry today based on complex storage devices that "pretend" to be disk drives, but are in fact large hardware/software systems whose API is a legacy disk drive interface like SCSI. These systems, which include RAID boxes and Network Attached Storage (NAS) devices, tend to have very large capacities, and complex performance characteristics. Users like these systems because they are easy to install, and often provide easily-managed, bit-level reliability with quick or instantaneous failover. These features provide a significant sense of comfort to customers, above and beyond the promises of DBMS recovery subsystems. It is very common to find DBMS installations on RAID boxes, for example.

Unfortunately, these systems complicate DBMS implementations. As an example, RAID systems perform very differently after a fault than they do when all the disks are good, potentially complicating the I/O cost models for the DBMS. Also, these systems – like filesystems before them – tend to want to exercise temporal control over writes by managing their own caching policies, possibly subverting the write-ahead logging protocol. In the case of power failures, this can lead to consistency at the per-bit granularity (storage-oriented consistency), without transactional consistency. It is uncomfortable for the DBMS vendors to point their fingers at the disk vendors in such cases; at the end of the day, DBMS vendors are expected to provide transactional consistency on any popular storage device. Hence DBMSs must understand the ins and outs of the leading storage devices, and manage them accordingly.

RAID systems also frustrate database cognoscenti by underperforming for database tasks.

RAID was conceived for bytestream-oriented storage (a la UNIX files), rather than the tuple-oriented storage used by database systems. Hence RAID devices do not tend to perform as well as database-specific solutions for partitioning and replicating data across multiple physical devices (e.g. the *chained declustering* scheme of Gamma [12] that was roughly coeval with the invention of RAID). Most databases provide DBA commands to control the partitioning of data across multiple devices, but RAID boxes subvert these commands by hiding the multiple devices behind a single interface.

Moreover, many users configure their RAID boxes to minimize space overheads ("RAID level 5"), when the database would perform far, far better via simpler schemes like disk mirroring (a.k.a. "RAID level 1"). A particularly unpleasant feature of RAID level 5 is that writes are much more expensive than reads; this can cause surprising bottlenecks for users, and the DBMS vendors are often on the hook to explain or provide workarounds for these bottlenecks. For better or worse, the use (and misuse) of RAID devices is a fact that commercial systems must take into account, and most vendors spend significant energy tuning their DBMSs to work well on the leading RAID boxes.

6.3 Replication Services

It is often desirable to replicate databases across a network via periodic updates. This is frequently used for an extra degree of reliability – the replicated database serves as a slightly-out-of-date "warm standby" in case the main system goes down. It is advantageous to keep the warm standby in a physically different location, to be able to continue functioning after a fire or other catastrophe. Replication is also often used to provide a pragmatic form of distributed database functionality for large, geographically distributed enterprises. Most such enterprises partition their databases into large geographic regions (e.g. nations or continents), and run all updates locally on the primary copies of the data. Queries are executed locally as well, but can run on a mix of fresh data from their local operations, and slightly-out-of-date data replicated from remote sites regions.

There are three typical schemes for replication, but only the third provides the performance and scalability needed for high-end settings. It is, of course, the most difficult to implement.

1. **Physical Replication:** The simplest scheme is to physically duplicate the entire database every replication period. This scheme does not scale up to large databases, because of the bandwidth for shipping the data, and the cost for reinstalling it at the remote site. Moreover, it is tricky to guarantee a transactionally consistent snapshot of the database; doing so typically requires the unacceptable step of quiescing the source system during the replication process. Physical replication is therefore only used as a client-side hack at the low end; most vendors do not explicitly encourage this scheme via any software support.
2. **Trigger-Based Replication:** In this scheme, triggers are placed on the database tables so that upon any insert, delete, or update to the table, a "difference" record is installed in special replication table. This replication table is shipped to the

remote site, and the modifications are "replayed" there. This scheme solves the problems mentioned above for physical replication, but has a number of performance problems. First, most database vendors provide very limited trigger facilities – often only a single trigger is allowed per table. In such scenarios, it is often not possible to install triggers for replication. Second, database trigger systems cannot usually keep up with the performance of transaction systems. At a minimum, the execution of triggering logic adds approximately 100% more I/Os to each transaction that modifies a database, and in practice even the testing of trigger conditions is quite slow in many systems. Hence this scheme is not desirable in practice, though it is used with some regularity in the field.

3. **Log-Based Replication:** Log-based replication is the replication solution of choice when feasible. In log-based replication, a log "sniffer" process intercepts log writes and ships them to the remote site, where they are "played forward" in REDO mode. This scheme overcomes all of the problems of the previous alternatives. It is low-overhead, providing minimal or invisible peformance burdens on the running system. It provides incremental updates, and hence scales gracefully with the database size and the update rate. It reuses the built-in mechanisms of the DBMS without significant additional logic. Finally, it naturally provides transactionally consistent replicas via the log's built-in logic.

   Most of the major vendors provide log-based replication for their own systems. Providing log-based replication that works across vendors is much more difficult – it requires understanding another vendor's log formats, and driving the vendors replay logic at the remote end.

6.4 Batch Utilities

Every system provides a set of utilities for managing their system. These utilities are rarely benchmarked, but often dictate the manageability of the system. A technically challenging and especially important feature is to make these utilities run *online*, i.e. while user queries and transactions are in flight. This is important in 24x7 operations, which have become much more common in recent years due to the global reach of e-commerce: the traditional "reorg window" in the wee hours is often no-longer available. Hence most vendors have invested significant energy in recent years in providing online utilities. We give a flavor of these utilities here:

- **Optimizer Statistics Gathering:** Every DBMS has a process that sweeps the tables and builds optimizer statistics of one sort or another. Some statistics like histograms are non-trivial to build in one pass without flooding memory; see, for example, the work by Flajolet and Martin on computing the number of distinct values in a column [13].
- **Physical Reorganization and Index Construction:** Over time, access methods can become inefficient due to patterns of insertions and deletions leaving unused space. Also, users may occasionally request that tables be reorganized in the background – e.g. to recluster (sort) them on different columns, or to repartition them across multiple disks. Online reorganization of files and indexes can be tricky, since it must avoid holding locks for any length of time, but still needs to

maintain physical consistency. In this sense it bears some analogies to the logging and locking protocols used for indexes, as described in Section 5.4. This has been the subject of a few research papers [68]. Similar issues arise in the background construction of indexes from scratch.

- **Backup/Export:** All DBMSs support the ability to physically dump the database to backup storage. Again, since this is a long-running process, it cannot naively set locks. Instead, most systems perform some kind of "fuzzy" dump, and augment it with logging logic to ensure transactional consistency. Similar schemes can be used to export the database to an interchange format.

7 Conclusion

As should be clear from this paper, modern commercial database systems are grounded both in academic research and in the experience of developing industrial-strength products for high-end customers. The task of writing and maintaining a high-performance, fully functional relational DBMS from scratch is an enormous investment in time and energy. As the database industry has consolidated to a few main competitors, it has become less and less attractive for new players to enter the main arena. However, many of the lessons of relational DBMSs translate over to new domains: web services, network-attached storage, text and e-mail repositories, notification services, network monitors, and so on. Data-intensive services are at the core of computing today, and knowledge of database system design is a skill that is broadly applicable, both inside and outside the halls of the main database shops. These new directions raise a number of research problems in database management as well, and point the way to new interactions between the database community and other areas of computing.

8 Acknowledgments

The authors would like to thank Rob von Behren, Eric Brewer, Paul Brown, Amol Deshpande, Jim Gray, James Hamilton, Wei Hong, Guy Lohman, Mehul Shah and Matt Welsh for background information and comments on early drafts of this paper.

9 References

[1] Atul Adya, Barbara Liskov, and Patrick O'Neil. Generalized Isolation Level Definitions. In 16th *International Conference on Data Engineering (ICDE),* San Diego, CA, February 2000.

[2] Rakesh Agrawal, Michael J. Carey and Miron Livny. *Concurrency control performance modelling: alternatives and implications, ACM Transactons on Database Systems (TODS)* 12(4):609-654, 1987.

[3] Morton M. Astrahan, Mike W. Blasgen, Donald D. Chamberlin, Kapali P. Eswaran, Jim Gray, Patricia P. Griffiths, W. Frank King III, Raymond A. Lorie, Paul R. McJones, James W. Mehl, Gianfranco R. Putzolu, Irving L. Traiger, Bradford W. Wade, and Vera Watson. System R: Relational Approach to

Database Management. *ACM Transactions on Database Systems (TODS),* 1(2):97-137, 1976.

[4] Rudolf Bayer and Mario Schkolnick. Concurrency of Operations on B-Trees. *Acta Informatica*, 9:1-21, 1977.

[5] Kristin P. Bennett, Michael C. Ferris, and Yannis E. Ioannidis. A Genetic Algorithm for Database Query Optimization. In *Proceedings of the 4th International Conference on Genetic Algorithms*, pages 400-407, San Diego, CA, July 1991.

[6] Hal Berenson, Philip A. Bernstein, Jim Gray, Jim Melton, Elizabeth J. O'Neil, and Patrick E. O'Neil. A Critique of ANSI SQL Isolation Levels. In *Proc. ACM SIGMOD International Conference on Management of Data,* pages 1-10, San Jose, CA, May 1995.

[7] William Bridge, Ashok Joshi, M. Keihl, Tirthankar Lahiri, and Juan Loaiza andgd N. MacNaughton. The Oracle Universal Server Buffer. In *Proc. 23rd International Conference on Very Large Data Bases (VLDB),* pages 590-594, Athens, Greece, August 1997. Morgan Kaufmann.

[8] Surajit Chaudhuri and Vivek R. Narasayya. AutoAdmin 'What-if' Index Analysis Utility. In *Proc. ACM SIGMOD International Conference on Management of Data,* pages 367-378, Seattle, WA, June 1998.

[9] Surajit Chaudhuri and Kyuseok Shim. Optimization of Queries with User-Defined Predicates. *ACM Transactions on Database Systems (TODS),* 24(2):177-228, 1999.

[10] Hong-Tai Chou and David J. DeWitt. An Evaluation of Buffer Management Strategies for Relational Database Systems. In *Proceedings of 11th International Conference on Very Large Data Bases (VLDB),* pages 127-141, Stockholm, Sweden, August 1985.

[11] Amol Desphande, Minos Garofalakis, and Rajeev Rastogi. Independence is Good: Dependency-Based Histogram Synopses for High-Dimensional Data. In *Proceedings of the 18th International Conference on Data Engineering*, San Jose, CA, February 2001.

[12] David J. DeWitt, Robert H. Gerber, Goetz Graefe, Michael L. Heytens, Krishna B. Kumar, and M. Muralikrishna. GAMMA - A High Performance Dataflow Database Machine. *In Twelfth International Conference on Very Large Data Bases (VLDB)*, pages 228-237, Kyoto, Japan, August 1986.

[13] Philippe Flajolet and G. Nigel Martin. Probabilistic Counting Algorithms for Data Base Applications. *Journal of Computing System Science*, 31(2):182-209, 1985.

[14] Sumit Ganguly, Waqar Hasan, and Ravi Krishnamurthy. Query Optimization for Parallel Execution. In *Proceedings of the ACM SIGMOD International Conference on Management of Data*, pages 9-18, San Diego, CA, June 1992.

[15] Minos N. Garofalakis and Yannis E. Ioannidis. Parallel Query Scheduling and Optimization with Time- and Space-Shared Resources. In *Proc. 23rd International Conference on Very Large Data Bases (VLDB)*, pages 296-305, Athens, Greece, August 1997.

[16] G. Graefe. Encapsulation of Parallelism in the Volcano Query Processing System. *In Proc. ACM-SIGMOD International Conference on Management of Data,* pages 102-111, Atlantic City, May 1990.

[17] Goetz Graefe. The Cascades Framework for Query Optimization. *IEEE Data Engineering Bulletin,* 18(3):19-29, 1995.

[18] G. Graefe. Query Evaluation Techniques for Large Databases. *Computing Surveys* 25 (2): 73-170 (1993).

[19] Goetz Graefe and William J. McKenna. The Volcano Optimizer Generator: Extensibility and Efficient Search. In *Proc. 9th International Conference on Data Engineering (ICDE),* pages 209-218, Vienna, Austria, April 1993.

[20] Jim Gray and Goetz Graefe. The Five-Minute Rule Ten Years Later, and Other Computer Storage Rules of Thumb. *ACM SIGMOD Record*, 26(4):63-68, 1997.

[21] Jim Gray, Raymond A. Lorie, Gianfranco R. Putzolu, and Irving L. Traiger. Granularity of Locks and Degrees of Consistency in a Shared Data Base. In *IFIP Working Conference on Modelling in Data Base Management Systems*, pages 365-394, 1976.

[22] Jim Gray and Andreas Reuter. *Transaction Processing: Concepts and Techniques*. Morgan Kaufmann, 1993.

[23] Steven D. Gribble, Eric A. Brewer, Joseph M. Hellerstein, and David Culler. Scalable, Distributed Data Structures for Internet Service Construction. In *Proceedings of the Fourth Symposium on Operating Systems Design and Implementation (OSDI),* 2000. 2

[24] Antonin Guttman. R-Trees: A Dynamic Index Structure For Spatial Searching. In *Proc. ACM-SIGMOD International Conference on Management of Data*, pages 47-57, Boston, June 1984.

[25] Alon Y. Halevy, editor. *The VLDB Journal*, Volume 11(4). The VLDB Foundation, Dec 2002.

[26] Theo Härder and Andreas Reuter. Principles of Transaction-Oriented Database Recovery. *ACM Computing Surveys*, 15(4):287-317, 1983.

[27] Pat Helland, Harald Sammer, Jim Lyon, Richard Carr, Phil Garrett, and Andreas Reuter. Group Commit Timers and High-Volume Transaction Systems. Technical Report TR-88.1, Tandem Computers, March 1988.

[28] Joseph M. Hellerstein. Optimization Techniques for Queries with Expensive Methods. *ACM Transactions on Database Systems (TODS),* 23(2):113-157, 1998.

[29] Joseph M. Hellerstein and Michael Stonebraker. Predicate Migration: Optimizing Queries With Expensive Predicates. In *Proc. ACM-SIGMOD International Conference on Management of Data*, pages 267-276, Washington, D.C., May 1993.

[30] C. Hoare. Monitors: An operating system structuring concept. *Communications of the ACM (CACM)*, 17(10):549-557, 1974.

[31] Wei Hong and Michael Stonebraker. Optimization of Parallel Query Execution Plans in XPRS. In Proceedings of *the First International Conference on Parallel and Distributed Information Systems (PDIS),* pages 218-225, Miami Beach, FL, December 1991.

[32] Hui-I Hsiao and David J. DeWitt. Chained Declustering: A New Availability Strategy for Multiprocessor Database Machines. In *Proc. Sixth International Conference on Data Engineering (ICDE)*, pages 456-465, Los Angeles, CA, November 1990.

[33] Yannis E. Ioannidis and Stavros Christodoulakis. On the Propagation of Errors in the Size of Join Results. In *Proceedings of the ACM SIGMOD International Conference on Management of Data,* pages 268-277, Denver, CO, May 1991.

[34] Yannis E. Ioannidis and Younkyung Cha Kang. Randomized Algorithms for Optimizing Large Join Queries. In *Proc. ACM-SIGMOD International Conference on Management of Data,* pages 312-321, Atlantic City, May 1990.

[35] Marcel Kornacker, C. Mohan, and Joseph M. Hellerstein. Concurrency and Recovery in Generalized Search Trees. In *Proc. ACM SIGMOD International Conference on Management of Data,* pages 62-72, Tucson, AZ, May 1997.

[36] H. T. Kung and John T. Robinson. On Optimistic Methods for Concurrency Control. *ACM Tranactions on Database Systems (TODS)*, 6(2):213-226, 1981.

[37] James R. Larus and Michael Parkes. Using Cohort Scheduling to Enhance Server Performance. In *USENIX Annual Conference*, 2002.

[38] H. C. Lauer and R. M. Needham. On the Duality of Operating System Structures. *ACM SIGOPS Operating Systems Review*, 13(2):3-19, April 1979. 3

[39] Philip L. Lehman and S. Bing Yao. Efficient Locking for Concurrent Operations on B-Trees. *ACM Transactions on Database Systems (TODS)*, 6(4):650-670, December 1981.

[40] Alon Y. Levy, Inderpal Singh Mumick, and Yehoshua Sagiv. Query Optimization by Predicate Move-Around. In *Proc. 20th International Conference on Very Large Data Bases*, pages 96-107, Santiago, September 1994.

[41] Witold Litwin. Linear Hashing: A New Tool for File and Table Addressing. In *Sixth International Conference on Very Large Data Bases (VLDB)*, pages 212-223, Montreal, Quebec, Canada, October 1980.

[42] Guy M. Lohman. Grammar-like Functional Rules for Representing Query Optimization Alternatives. In *Proc. ACM SIGMOD International Conference on Management of Data*, pages 18-27, Chicago, IL, June 1988.

[43] Samuel R. Madden and Michael J. Franklin. Fjording the Stream: An Architecture for Queries over Streaming Sensor Data. In *Proc. 12th IEEE International Conference on Data Engineering (ICDE)*, San Jose, February 2002.

[44] C. Mohan. ARIES/KVL: A Key-Value Locking Method for Concurrency Control of Multiaction Transactions Operating on B-Tree Indexes. In *16th International Conference on Very Large Data Bases (VLDB)*, pages 392-405, Brisbane, Queensland, Australia, August 1990.

[45] C. Mohan, Donald J. Haderle, Bruce G. Lindsay, Hamid Pirahesh, and Peter M. Schwarz. ARIES: A Transaction Recovery Method Supporting Fine- Granularity Locking and Partial Rollbacks Using Write-Ahead Logging. *ACM Transactions on Database Systems (TODS)*, 17(1):94-162, 1992.

[46] C. Mohan and Frank Levine. ARIES/IM: An Efficient and High Concurrency Index Management Method Using Write-Ahead Logging. In Michael Stonebraker, editor, Proc. *ACM SIGMOD International Conference on Management of Data*, pages 371-380, San Diego, CA, June 1992.

[47] C. Mohan, Bruce G. Lindsay, and Ron Obermarck. Transaction Management in the R* Distributed Database Management System. *ACM Transactions on Database Systems (TODS)*, 11(4):378-396, 1986.

[48] Elizabeth J. O'Neil, Patrick E. O'Neil, and Gerhard Weikum. The LRU-K Page Replacement Algorithm For Database Disk Buffering. In *Proceedings ACM SIGMOD International Conference on Management of Data*, pages 297-306, Washington, D.C., May 1993.

[49] Patrick E. O'Neil and Dallan Quass. Improved Query Performance with Variant Indexes. In *Proc. ACM-SIGMOD International Conference on Management of Data*, pages 38-49, Tucson, May 1997.

[50] M. Tamer Ozsu and Jose A. Blakeley. Query Processing in Object-Oriented Database Systems. In Won Kim, editor, *Modern Database Systems.* Addison Wesley, 1995. 4

[51] Hamid Pirahesh, Joseph M. Hellerstein, and Waqar Hasan. Extensible/Rule-Based Query Rewrite Optimization in Starburst. In *Proc. ACM-SIGMOD International Conference on Management of Data*, pages 39-48, San Diego, June 1992.

[52] Viswanath Poosala and Yannis E. Ioannidis. Selectivity Estimation Without the Attribute Value Independence Assumption. In *Proceedings of 23rd International Conference on Very Large Data Bases (VLDB)*, pages 486-495, Athens, Greece, August 1997.

[53] Raghu Ramakrishnan and Johannes Gehrke. *Database Management Systems*, Third Edition. McGraw-Hill, Boston, MA, 2003.

[54] David P. Reed. *Naming and Synchronization in a Decentralized Computer System.* PhD thesis, MIT, Dept. of Electrical Engineering, 1978.

[55] Allen Reiter. A Study of Buffer Management Policies for Data Management Systems. Technical Summary Report 1619, Mathematics Research Center, University of Wisconsin, Madison, 1976.

[56] Daniel J. Rosenkrantz, Richard E. Stearns, and Philip M. Lewis. System Level Concurrency Control for Distributed Database Systems. *ACM Transactions on Database Systems (TODS)*, 3(2):178-198, June 1978.

[57] Patricia G. Selinger, M. Astrahan, D. Chamberlin, Raymond Lorie, and T. Price. Access Path Selection in a Relational Database Management System. In *Proc. ACM-SIGMOD International Conference on Management of Data,* pages 22-34, Boston, June 1979.

[58] Praveen Seshadri, Hamid Pirahesh, and T.Y. Cliff Leung. Complex Query Decorrelation. In *Proc. 12th IEEE International Conference on Data Engineering (ICDE)*, New Orleans, February 1996.

[59] Mehul A. Shah, Samuel Madden, Michael J. Franklin, and Joseph M. Hellerstein. Java Support for Data-Intensive Systems: Experiences Building the Telegraph Dataflow System. *ACM SIGMOD Record*, 30(4):103-114, 2001.

[60] Leonard D. Shapiro. Exploiting Upper and Lower Bounds in Top-Down Query Optimization. *International Database Engineering and Application Symposium (IDEAS)*, 2001.

[61] Abraham Silberschatz, Henry F. Korth, and S. Sudarshan. *Database System Concepts, Fourth Edition.* McGraw-Hill, Boston, MA, 2001.

[62] Michael Steinbrunn, Guido Moerkotte, and Alfons Kemper. Heuristic and Randomized Optimization for the Join Ordering Problem. *VLDB Journal*, 6(3):191-208, 1997.

[63] Michael Stonebraker. Retrospection on a Database System. *ACM Transactions on Database Systems (TODS)*, 5(2):225-240, 1980.

[64] Michael Stonebraker. Operating System Support for Database Management. *Communications of the ACM (CACM)*, 24(7):412-418, 1981.

[65] Michael Stonebraker. The Case for Shared Nothing. *IEEE Database Engineering Bulletin*, 9(1):4-9, 1986. 5

[66] M.R. Stonebraker, E. Wong, and P. Kreps. The Design and Implementation of INGRES. *ACM Transactions on Database Systems*, 1(3):189-222, September 1976.

[67] Matt Welsh, David Culler, and Eric Brewer. SEDA: An Architecture for Well-Conditioned, Scalable Internet Services. In *Proceedings of the 18th Symposium on Operating Systems Principles (SOSP-18)*, Banff, Canada, October 2001.

[68] Rob von Behren, Jeremy Condit, Feng Zhou, George C. Necula, and Eric Brewer. Capriccio: Scalable Threads for Internet Services. In *Proceedings of the Ninteenth Symposium on Operating System Principles (SOSP-19)*, Lake George, New York. October 2003.

[69] Chendong Zou and Betty Salzberg. On-line Reorganization of Sparsely-populated B+trees. In *Proc. ACM SIGMOD International Conference on Management of Data*, pages 115-124, Montreal, Quebec, Canada, 1996.

Chapter 2
Query Processing

This chapter presents a selection of key papers on query processing, starting with single-site query processing, and continuing through parallel and distributed systems. In previous editions we presented the material on parallel and distributed systems in separate sections, but the reality today is that all systems of note have parallel processing features, and most have at least rudimentary distributed functionality as well. Hence we fold the discussion of single-site, parallel, and distributed systems into a single chapter. We will say more about parallelism and distribution soon, but we begin with two foundational issues from a single-site perspective: query optimization, and join algorithms.

Relational query optimization is well known to be a difficult problem, and the theoretical results in the space can be especially discouraging. First, it is computationally complex: Ibaraki and Kameda showed early on that optimizing a query that joins *n* relations is NP-hard [IK84]. Second, it relies on cost estimation techniques that are difficult to get right; and as Christodoulakis and Ioannidis showed, the effects of even small errors can in some circumstances render most optimization schemes no better than random guesses [IC91]. Fortunately, query optimization is an arena where negative theoretical results at the extremes do not spell disaster in most practical cases. In the field, query optimization technology has proved critical to the performance of database systems, and serves as the cornerstone of architectures to achieve Codd's vision of data independence. The limitation on the number of joins is a fact that users have learned to live with, and estimation error is an active area of research and development that has seen significant, continuing improvements over time. In short, query optimizers today do their jobs quite well, based on the foundations developed a quarter century ago. However, the difficulty of the problem has left room for a steady stream of improvements from the research community.

Early innovations in query optimization separated the technologists from the marketeers in the database industry. This culminated in now-famous tales of Oracle's so-called "syntactic optimizer" (which simply ordered joins based on their lexical appearance in the query) and the embarrassment it brought upon them in the days of the Wisconsin Benchmark [BDT83][1]. In practice, a respectable cost-based query optimizer is typically far better than any simple heuristic scheme.

We begin this chapter with the famous Selinger, et al. paper on System R's query optimization scheme, which remains the fundamental reading in this area. The paper does two things remarkably well. First, it breaks down the complex space of query optimization into manageable, independently-addressable problems; this breakdown is not explicit in the paper, but represents its largest contribution. Second, it provides a plausible line of attack for each of the problems. Of

[1] This embarrassment was due only in part to Oracle's poor optimizer and resulting poor performance. Like any good scandal, it was eclipsed by attempts at a cover-up. As the story goes, in the wake of the initial Wisconsin Benchmark results, Oracle's CEO tried to convince the University of Wisconsin to fire benchmark author David DeWitt. This corporate meddling apparently had little influence on UW administrators. Subsequently, Oracle introduced a licensing clause that forbids customers from using the system for purposes of benchmarking. Imagine Ford trying to forbid Consumer Reports from evaluating cars! Sadly, Oracle's competitors all adopted this "DeWitt Clause" as well, and it persists to this day. Although some legal experts question the ability of the DeWitt Clause to stand up in court, it has not been significantly tested to date.

course many of the techniques for attacking these problems have evolved over time – but this is rightly seen as a tribute to the problem breakdown proposed in the paper.

At the highest level, the Selinger paper first simplifies the query optimization problem to focus on individual SQL query "blocks" (SELECT-FROM-WHERE, or *select-project-join* in algebraic terms.) For each query block, it neatly separates three concerns: the *plan space* of legal execution strategies, *cost estimation techniques* for predicting the resource consumption of each plan, and a *search strategy* based on dynamic programming for efficiently considering different options in the search space. These three concerns have each been the subject of significant follow-on work, as mentioned in the second paper of Section 1. Each new benchmark drives the vendors to plug another hole in their optimizer, and commercial optimizer improvement is a slow but continuous process. Perhaps the least robust aspect of the original System R design was its set of formulae for selectivity estimation. But there are numerous other issues glossed over in the paper. An excellent exercise for the research-minded reader is to compile a list of the assumptions built into this paper. Lurking behind each assumption is a research topic: find a plausible scenario where the assumption does not hold, see how that stresses the System R design, and propose a fix. Some of these scenarios will be amenable to evolutionary fixes, others may require more revolutionary changes.

The paper closes with some execution tricks for nested queries. This topic received relatively little attention for quite some time, until it was revisited in the context of query rewriting – especially in Starburst [PHH92,SPL96], the predecessor to recent versions of DB2.

The second paper in this chapter presents Shapiro's description of hash join and sort-merge join algorithms. This paper reviews the earlier GRACE [KTM83] and Hybrid Hash [DKO+84] conference papers, but we include this later paper by Shapiro since it does a nice job placing these algorithms side-by-side with sort-merge join. Shapiro also provides a discussion of possible interactions between hash joins and virtual memory replacement strategies, but this material is of less interest – in practice, these algorithms explicitly manage whatever memory they are granted, without any participation from virtual memory.

Some notes on this paper are in order. First, it presents Hybrid Hash as the most advanced hash join variant, but in practice the advantage of Hybrid over Grace is negligible (especially in the presence of a good optimizer), and hence most commercial systems simply implement Grace hash join. Second, Shapiro's paper does not cover schemes to handle hash *skew*, where some partitions are much larger than others; this tricky issue is addressed in a sequence of papers [NKT88, KNT89, PCL93]. Third, it does not discuss how hash-based schemes akin to Grace's can be used for *unary* operators like grouping, duplicate-elimination, or caching; these topics are addressed in more detail in other work [Bra84, HN96].

Graefe's query processing survey [Gra93] covers various subtleties inherent in the hash- and sort-based operators used in query execution; the reader is especially directed to the discussion of the "duality" between sorting and hashing. The description of Hash Teams in Microsoft's SQL Server [GBC93] covers additional details of both memory management and query optimization that show a number of more holistic details that apply when many hash-based operators are used in the same query plan.

Following the Shapiro paper, the chapter continues with a survey of parallel database technology by DeWitt and Gray, which focuses largely on query processing issues. Historically, parallel database systems arose from earlier research on *database machines*: hardware/software co-designs for database systems [BD83]. These systems investigated designing special devices to accelerate simple database operations like selection, including disks with a processor on each head, or on each track. This research thrust was eventually abandoned when it became clear that specialized database hardware would never keep pace with the exponentially-improving rate of commodity hardware.[2]

The research thread on database machines evolved into research on exploiting multiple commodity processors for query execution. The DeWitt/Gray survey does an excellent job laying out this design space, including the relevant performance metrics and the core architectural ideas. DeWitt and Gray distill out most of the key points from the revolutionary parallel database systems including Gamma [DGG+86], Bubba [BAC+90], XPRS [HS91] and the commercial TeraData system. A deep study of the area should certainly consult the original papers on these systems, but many of the major lessons are covered in the survey.

To flesh out some of the detail in parallel databases, we include two additional papers: Graefe's deceptively simple architectural paper on Exchange provides a flavor of high-level software engineering elegance, whereas the AlphaSort paper gives an example of the significant benefits available by micro-optimizing individual query operators.

Our fourth paper, on Exchange, shows how parallelism can be elegantly retrofitted into a traditional iterator architecture for query execution. The insight is easy to understand, and hence perhaps easy to undervalue, but it can have an important simplifying effect on software implementation. This style of work is typically the domain of Operating Systems research; the database systems literature is perhaps more biased towards feats of complexity than elegance of mechanism. Exchange is a nice example of elegant mechanism design in the database research literature. It weaves hash-partitioning, queuing, networking, and process boundaries into a single iterator that encapsulates them all invisibly. This simplicity is especially attractive when one considers that most parallel DBMS implementations evolved from single-site implementations.

While Exchange is elegant, the reader is also warned that things are not as simple as they appear in the paper. Of course a parallel DBMS needs quite a bit of surrounding technology beyond Exchange: a parallelism-aware optimizer, appropriate support for transactions as discussed in the paper in Section 1, parallel management utilities, and so on. The query executor is probably not the most challenging DBMS component to parallelize. Moreover, even Exchange itself requires somewhat more subtlety in practice than is described here, as Graefe notes elsewhere [GD93], particularly to handle starting up and shutting down the many processes for the Exchange.

The fifth paper in the chapter is on AlphaSort. Parallel sorting has become a competitive sport, grounded in the database research community. Jim Gray maintains a website off of his home page where he keeps the latest statistics on world records in parallel, disk-to-disk sorting (the input begins on disk, and must be output in sorted runs on disk). Since the time of the AlphaSort work, a number of other teams have come along and improved upon the work, both via new software insights and via improvements in hardware over time. While the competition here is stiff, the enthusiastic reader is not discouraged from entering the fray – a number of student

---

[2] Perhaps the most commercially successful and technically impressive of these systems was from a company called Britton-Lee, which was founded by a number of alumi from the INGRES research group. As it became clear that Britton-Lee's hardware would not be competitive in the marketplace, one of the company's founders, Robert Shapiro, left to start a software-only database company called Sybase that was eventually quite successful. Ironically, Sybase was rather late in joining the parallel processing game.

groups have held sorting trophies at various times, and contributed to our understanding of the topic.

AlphaSort also represents a thread of research into the interactions between database systems and computer architecture; this topic has seen increasing interest in recent years (e.g. [ADH02,RR00,CGM01, etc.]) Sorting is an excellent benchmark of both hardware and software *data throughput* – the raw ability to pump data off disk, through various network and memory busses, through some non-trivial code, and eventually back onto disk. As noted in the AlphaSort paper, one of the major bottlenecks to consider in such scenarios is that of processor cache misses. This problem has become even more important since the time of the AlphaSort work. Readers who find the AlphaSort paper intriguing are encouraged to consult a good computer architecture textbook, like that of Patterson and Hennessy, which spells out many of the issues in the paper in more detail.

We conclude the section with two papers on wide-area, distributed query processing. Distributed database systems arose quite separately from the work on parallelism; the leading early distributed DBMS projects were SDD-1 (at the Computer Corporation of America), INGRES* (at Berkeley), and R* (at IBM San Jose). A main goal of the early work on distributed query processing was to minimize network bandwidth consumption during query processing; this was not a main goal of the parallel systems.

Our sixth paper, by Mackert and Lohman, enumerates the space of standard join algorithms for distributed query processing. It also makes a point that was overlooked in SDD-1: bandwidth consumption may be an important cost in distributed query processing, but it is not the *only* cost that should be considered. Instead, a traditional query optimizer should be extended to weigh all of the relevant costs, including I/Os, CPU operations, and network communication (including per-message latencies as well as bandwidth). The Mackert/Lohman paper is ostensibly a micro-benchmark of the R* system, but it should be read largely as an introduction to the various join strategies – particularly the ideas of semi-joins and Bloom joins. It is worth noting that semi-join style techniques recur in the literature even in single-site scenarios, as part of decorrelating subqueries [MFPR90, SPL96]. The lesson there is somewhat subtle and beyond the scope of our discussion; connoisseurs of query processing may choose to investigate those papers further.

We close this chapter with an overview of Mariposa, the most recent distributed database research to be developed to a significant level of functionality. Mariposa's main contribution in query processing is to change the model for cost estimation during query optimization. Instead of a unified, catalog-driven cost estimation module, Mariposa allows each site to declare its own costs for various tasks. Mariposa's approach introduces a computational *marketplace*, where sites can declare their local costs for a query based not only on their estimates of resource consumption, but also on runtime issues such as current system load, and *economic* issues such as their reciprocal relationship with the query site, their relationship with competing sites that could do the work, and so on. Architecturally, Mariposa's changes to the R* optimizer are fairly minimal – they simply add communication rounds to the cost estimation routines. More suggestive is the way that this decoupling of cost estimation enables multiple independent parties (e.g. different companies) to participate in *federated* query processing, wherein each party gets to make autonomous decisions about their participation in any task. The Mariposa system was commercialized as Cohera (later bought by PeopleSoft) and was demonstrated to work across administrative domains in the field. But the flexibility and efficiency of its computational economy ideas have yet to be significantly tested, and it is unclear whether corporate IT is ready for significant investments federated query processing. It is possible that we will see the ideas from Mariposa re-emerge in the peer-to-peer space, where there is significant grassroots interest, a few database-style query systems being proposed [HHL+03, NOTZ03, PMT03], and a number of researchers interested in economic incentives for peer-to-peer (e.g. [Chu03]).

References

[ADH02] A. Ailamaki, D.J. DeWitt, and M.D. Hill. "Data Page Layouts for Relational Databases on Deep Memory Hierarchies." *The VLDB Journal* 11(3), 2002.

[BAC+90] H.Boral,W. Alexander, L. Clay, et al. "Prototyping Bubba, a Highly Parallel Database System. *Transactions on Knowledge and Data Engineering* 2(1), March 1990.

[BD83] Haran Boral and David J. DeWitt. "Database Machines: An Idea Whose Time Passed? A Critique of the Future of Database Machines". In *Proc. International Workshop on Database Machines (IWDM)*, pp 166-187, 1983

[BDT83] Dina Bitton and David J. DeWitt and Carolyn Turbyfill. "Benchmarking Database Systems, a Systematic Approach". In *Proc. 9th International Conference on Very Large Data Bases (VLDB),* Florence, Italy, October, 1983.

[Bra84] Kjell Bratbergsengen. "Hashing Methods and Relational Algebra Operations". In *Proc. 10th International Conference on Management of Data (VLDB),* Singapore, August 1984, pp. 323-333.

[CGM01] Shimin Chen, Phillip B. Gibbons, and Todd C. Mowry, "Improving Index Performance through Prefetching". In *Proc. ACM SIGMOD International Conference on Management of Data,* 2001.

[Chu03] John Chuang, editor. *First Workshop on Economics of Peer-to-Peer Systems.* Berkeley, California, June 5-6 2003.

[DGG+86] David J. DeWitt, Robert H. Gerber, Goetz Graefe, Michael L. Heytens, Krishna B. Kumar, and M. Muralikrishna. GAMMA - A High Performance Dataflow Database Machine. *In Twelfth International Conference on Very Large Data Bases (VLDB)*, pages 228-237, Kyoto, Japan, August 1986.

[DKO+] David J. DeWitt, Randy H. Katz, Frank Olken, Leonard D. Shapiro, Michael R. Stonebraker and David Wood. "Implementation Techniques for Main Memory Database Systems". In *Proc. ACM-SIGMOD International Conference on Management of Data,* Boston, MA, June, 1984, pages 1-8.

[GBC93] G. Graefe, R. Bunker, and S. Cooper. "Hash joins and hash teams in Microsoft SQL Server. In *Proceedings of 24th International Conference on Very Large Data Bases (VLDB)*, August 24-27, 1993.

[GD93] G. Graefe, D.L. Davison. "Encapsulation of Parallelism and Architecture-Independence in Extensible Database Query Execution" *IEEE Transactions on Software Engineering* 19(8) 749-764, August 1993.

[Gra93] G. Graefe. Query Evaluation Techniques for Large Databases. *Computing Surveys* 25 (2): 73-170 (1993).

[HHL+03] Ryan Huebsch, Joseph M. Hellerstein, Nick Lanham, Boon Thau Loo, Scott Shenker and Ion Stoica. "Querying the Internet with PIER." In *Proceedings of 19th International Conference on Very Large Databases (VLDB)*, Berlin, 2003.

[HN96] Joseph M. Hellerstein and Jeffrey F. Naughton. Query Execution Techniques for Caching Expensive Methods. In *Proc. ACM-SIGMOD International Conference on Management of Data,* June 1996, Montreal, pp. 423-424.

[HS91] Wei Hong and Michael Stonebraker. Optimization of Parallel Query Execution Plans in XPRS. In Proceedings of *the First International Conference on Parallel and Distributed Information Systems (PDIS),* pages 218-225, Miami Beach, FL, December 1991.

[IC91] Yannis E. Ioannidis and Stavros Christodoulakis. On the Propagation of Errors in the Size of Join Results. In *Proceedings of the ACM SIGMOD International Conference on Management of Data,* pages 268-277, Denver, CO, May 1991.

[IK84] Toshihide Ibaraki and Tiko Kameda. "Optimal Nesting for Computing N-relational Joins." *ACM Transactions on Database Systems (TODS),* 9(3) 482-502, October, 1984.

[KNT89] Masaru Kitsuregawa, Masaya Nakayama and Mikio Takagi. "The Effect of Bucket Size Tuning in the Dynamic Hybrid GRACE Hash Join Method." *Proceedings of the Fifteenth International Conference on Very Large Data Bases*, August 22-25, 1989, pp. 257-266.

[KTM83] Masaru Kitsuregawa, Hidehiko Tanaka and Tohru Moto-Oka. "Application of Hash to Data Base Machine and Its Architecture". New Generation Comput. 1(1): 63-74, 1983.

[MFPR90] Inderpal Singh Mumick, Sheldon J. Finkelstein, Hamid Pirahesh and Raghu Ramakrishnan. "Magic is Relevant". In *Proceedings of the ACM SIGMOD International Conference on Management of Data,* pages 247-258, Atlantic City, NJ, May 1990.

[NKT88] Masaya Nakayama, Masaru Kitsuregawa and Mikio Takagi. "Hash-Partitioned Join Method Using Dynamic Destaging Strategy". In *Proc. 14th International Conference on Management of Data (VLDB).* Los Angeles, CA, August-September 1988."

[NOTZ03] Wee Siong Ng, Beng Chin Ooi, Kian Lee Tan and AoYing Zhou. "PeerDB: A P2P-based System for Distributed Data Sharing." In *Proc. 19th International Conference on Data Engineering (ICDE),* 2003.

[PCL93] H. Pang, M. Carey, and M. Livny. "Partially preemptible hash joins". In *Proc. ACM SIGMOD International Conference on Management of Data*, pp. 59-68, 1993.

[PHH92] Hamid Pirahesh, Joseph M. Hellerstein, and Waqar Hasan. Extensible/Rule- Based Query Rewrite Optimization in Starburst. In *Proc. ACM-SIGMOD International Conference on Management of Data*, pages 39-48, San Diego, June 1992.

[PMT03] Vassilis Papadimos, David Maier and Kristin Tufte. "Distributed Query Processing and Catalogs for Peer-to-Peer Systems." In *Proc. First Biennial Conference on Innovative Data Systems Research (CIDR)*, Asilomar, CA, January 5-8, 2003.

[RR00] Jun Rao and Kenneth Ross. "Making B+-trees Cache Conscious in Main Memory." In *Proc. of ACM SIGMOD International Conference on Management of Data*, 2000, pp. 475-486.

[SPL96] Praveen Seshadri, Hamid Pirahesh, and T.Y. Cliff Leung. Complex Query Decorrelation. In *Proc. 12th IEEE International Conference on Data Engineering (ICDE)*, New Orleans, February 1996.

Access Path Selection in a Relational Database Management System

P. Griffiths Selinger
M. M. Astrahan
D. D. Chamberlin
R. A. Lorie
T. G. Price

IBM Research Division, San Jose, California 95193

ABSTRACT: In a high level query and data manipulation language such as SQL, requests are stated non-procedurally, without reference to access paths. This paper describes how System R chooses access paths for both simple (single relation) and complex queries (such as joins), given a user specification of desired data as a boolean expression of predicates. System R is an experimental database management system developed to carry out research on the relational model of data. System R was designed and built by members of the IBM San Jose Research Laboratory.

1. Introduction

System R is an experimental database management system based on the relational model of data which has been under development at the IBM San Jose Research Laboratory since 1975 <1>. The software was developed as a research vehicle in relational database, and is not generally available outside the IBM Research Division.

This paper assumes familiarity with relational data model terminology as described in Codd <7> and Date <8>. The user interface in System R is the unified query, data definition, and manipulation language SQL <5>. Statements in SQL can be issued both from an on-line casual-user-oriented terminal interface and from programming languages such as PL/I and COBOL.

In System R a user need not know how the tuples are physically stored and what access paths are available (e.g. which columns have indexes). SQL statements do not require the user to specify anything about the access path to be used for tuple retrieval. Nor does a user specify in what order joins are to be performed. The System R optimizer chooses both join order and an access path for each table in the SQL statement. Of the many possible choices, the optimizer chooses the one which minimizes "total access cost" for performing the entire statement.

This paper will address the issues of access path selection for queries. Retrieval for data manipulation (UPDATE, DELETE) is treated similarly. Section 2 will describe the place of the optimizer in the processing of a SQL statement, and section 3 will describe the storage component access paths that are available on a single physically stored table. In section 4 the optimizer cost formulas are introduced for single table queries, and section 5 discusses the joining of two or more tables, and their corresponding costs. Nested queries (queries in predicates) are covered in section 6.

2. Processing of an SQL statement

A SQL statement is subjected to four phases of processing. Depending on the origin and contents of the statement, these phases may be separated by arbitrary intervals of time. In System R, these arbitrary time intervals are transparent to the system components which process a SQL statement. These mechanisms and a description of the processing of SQL statements from both programs and terminals are further discussed in <2>. Only an overview of those processing steps that are relevant to access path selection will be discussed here.

The four phases of statement processing are parsing, optimization, code generation, and execution. Each SQL statement is sent to the parser. where it is checked for correct syntax. A <u>query block</u> is represented by a SELECT list, a FROM list, and a WHERE tree, containing, respectively the list of items to be retrieved, the table(s) referenced, and the boolean combination of simple predicates specified by the user. A single SQL statement may have many query blocks because a predicate may have one operand which is itself a query.

If the parser returns without any errors detected, the OPTIMIZER component is called. The OPTIMIZER accumulates the names of tables and columns referenced in the query and looks them up in the System R catalogs to verify their existence and to retrieve information about them.

The catalog lookup portion of the OPTIMIZER also obtains statistics about the referenced relations, and the access paths available on each of them. These will be used later in access path selection. After catalog lookup has obtained the datatype and length of each column, the OPTIMIZER rescans the SELECT-list and WHERE-tree to check for semantic errors and type compatibility in both expressions and predicate comparisons.

Finally the OPTIMIZER performs access path selection. It first determines the evaluation order among the query blocks in the statement. Then for each query block, the relations in the FROM list are processed. If there is more than one relation in a block, permutations of the join order and of the method of joining are evaluated. The access paths that minimize total cost for the block are chosen from a tree of alternate path choices. This minimum cost solution is represented by a structural modification of the parse tree. The result is an execution plan in the Access Specification Language (ASL) <10>.

After a plan is chosen for each query block and represented in the parse tree, the CODE GENERATOR is called. The CODE GENERATOR is a table-driven program which translates ASL trees into machine language code to execute the plan chosen by the OPTIMIZER. In doing this it uses a relatively small number of code templates, one for each type of join method (including no join). Query blocks for nested queries are treated as "subroutines" which return values to the predicates in which they occur. The CODE GENERATOR is further described in <9>.

During code generation, the parse tree is replaced by executable machine code and its associated data structures. Either control is immediately transfered to this code or the code is stored away in the database for later execution, depending on the origin of the statement (program or terminal). In either case, when the code is ultimately executed, it calls upon the System R internal storage system (RSS) via the storage system interface (RSI) to scan each of the physically stored relations in the query. These scans are along the access paths chosen by the OPTIMIZER. The RSI commands that may be used by generated code are described in the next section.

3. The Research Storage System

The Research Storage System (RSS) is the storage subsystem of System R. It is responsible for maintaining physical storage of relations, access paths on these relations, locking (in a multi-user environment), and logging and recovery facilities. The RSS presents a tuple-oriented interface (RSI) to its users. Although the RSS may be used independently of System R, we are concerned here with its use for executing the code generated by the processing of SQL statements in System R, as described in the previous section. For a complete description of the RSS, see <1>.

Relations are stored in the RSS as a collection of tuples whose columns are physically contiguous. These tuples are stored on 4K byte pages; no tuple spans a page. Pages are organized into logical units called segments. Segments may contain one or more relations, but no relation may span a segment. Tuples from two or more relations may occur on the same page. Each tuple is tagged with the identification of the relation to which it belongs.

The primary way of accessing tuples in a relation is via an RSS scan. A scan returns a tuple at a time along a given access path. OPEN, NEXT, and CLOSE are the principal commands on a scan.

Two types of scans are currently available for SQL statements. The first type is a segment scan to find all the tuples of a given relation. A series of NEXTs on a segment scan simply examines all pages of the segment which contain tuples from <u>any</u> relation, and returns those tuples belonging to the given relation.

The second type of scan is an index scan. An index may be created by a System R user on one or more columns of a relation, and a relation may have any number (including zero) of indexes on it. These indexes are stored on separate pages from those containing the relation tuples. Indexes are implemented as B-trees <3>, whose leaves are pages containing sets of (key, identifiers of tuples which contain that key). Therefore a series of NEXTs on an index scan does a sequential read along the leaf pages of the index, obtaining the tuple identifiers matching a key, and using them to find and return the data tuples to the user in key value order. Index leaf pages are chained together so that NEXTs need not reference any upper level pages of the index.

In a segment scan, all the non-empty pages of a segment will be touched, regardless of whether there are any tuples from the desired relation on them. However, each page is touched only once. When an entire relation is examined via an index scan, each page of the index is touched only once, but a data page may be examined more than once if it has two tuples on it which are not "close" in the index ordering. If the tuples are inserted into segment pages in the index ordering, and if this physical proximity corresponding to index key value is maintained, we say that the index is <u>clustered</u>. A clustered index has the property that not only each index page, but also each data page containing a tuple from that relation will be touched only once in a scan on that index.

An index scan need not scan the entire relation. Starting and stopping key values may be specified in order to scan only those tuples which have a key in a range of index values. Both index and segment scans may optionally take a set of predicates, called search arguments (or SARGS), which are applied to a tuple before it is returned to the RSI caller. If the tuple satisfies the predicates, it is returned; otherwise the scan continues until it either finds a tuple which satisfies the SARGS or exhausts the segment or the specified index value range. This reduces cost by eliminating the overhead of making RSI calls for tuples which can be efficiently rejected within the RSS. Not all predicates are of the form that can become SARGS. A <u>sargable predicate</u> is one of the form (or which can be put into the form) "column comparison-operator value". SARGS are expressed as a boolean expression of such predicates in disjunctive normal form.

4. <u>Costs for single relation access paths</u>

In the next several sections we will describe the process of choosing a plan for evaluating a query. We will first describe the simplest case, accessing a single relation, and show how it extends and generalizes to 2-way joins of relations, n-way joins, and finally multiple query blocks (nested queries).

The OPTIMIZER examines both the predicates in the query and the access paths available on the relations referenced by the query, and formulates a cost prediction for each access plan, using the following cost formula:

COST = PAGE FETCHES + W * (RSI CALLS).

This cost is a weighted measure of I/O (pages fetched) and CPU utilization (instructions executed). W is an adjustable weighting factor between I/O and CPU. RSI CALLS is the predicted number of tuples returned from the RSS. Since most of System R's CPU time is spent in the RSS, the number of RSI calls is a good approximation for CPU utilization. Thus the choice of a minimum cost path to process a query attempts to minimize total resources required.

During execution of the type-compatibility and semantic checking portion of the OPTIMIZER, each query block's WHERE tree of predicates is examined. The WHERE tree is considered to be in conjunctive normal form, and every conjunct is called a <u>boolean factor</u>. Boolean factors are notable because every tuple returned to the user must satisfy every boolean factor. An index is said to match a boolean factor if the boolean factor is a sargable predicate whose referenced column is the index key; e.g., an index on SALARY matches the predicate 'SALARY = 20000'. More precisely, we say that a predicate or set of predicates <u>matches</u> an index access path when the predicates are sargable and the columns mentioned in the predicate(s) are an initial substring of the set of columns of the index key. For example, a NAME, LOCATION index matches NAME = 'SMITH' AND LOCATION = 'SAN JOSE'. If an index matches a boolean factor, an access using that index is an efficient way to satisfy the boolean factor. Sargable boolean factors can also be efficiently satisfied if they are expressed as search arguments. Note that a boolean factor may be an entire tree of predicates headed by an OR.

During catalog lookup, the OPTIMIZER retrieves statistics on the relations in the query and on the access paths available on each relation. The statistics kept are the following:

For each relation T,
- NCARD(T), the cardinality of relation T.
- TCARD(T), the number of pages in the segment that hold tuples of relation T.
- P(T), the fraction of data pages in the segment that hold tuples of relation T. P(T) = TCARD(T) / (no. of non-empty pages in the segment).

For each index I on relation T,
- ICARD(I), number of distinct keys in index I.
- NINDX(I), the number of pages in index I.

These statistics are maintained in the System R catalogs, and come from several sources. Initial relation loading and index creation initialize these statistics. They are then updated periodically by an UPDATE STATISTICS command, which can be run by any user. System R does not update these statistics at every INSERT, DELETE, or UPDATE because of the extra database operations and the locking bottleneck this would create at the system catalogs. Dynamic updating of statistics would tend to serialize accesses that modify the relation contents.

Using these statistics, the OPTIMIZER assigns a <u>selectivity factor</u> 'F' for each boolean factor in the predicate list. This selectivity factor very roughly corresponds to the expected fraction of tuples which will satisfy the predicate. TABLE 1 gives the selectivity factors for different kinds of predicates. We assume that a lack of statistics implies that the relation is small, so an arbitrary factor is chosen.

TABLE 1 SELECTIVITY FACTORS

column = value

F = 1 / ICARD(column index) if there is an index on column
This assumes an even distribution of tuples among the index key values.
F = 1/10 otherwise

column1 = column2

F = 1/MAX(ICARD(column1 index), ICARD(column2 index))
if there are indexes on both column1 and column2
This assumes that each key value in the index with the smaller cardinality has a matching value in the other index.
F = 1/ICARD(column-i index) if there is only an index on column-i
F = 1/10 otherwise

column > value (or any other open-ended comparison)

F = (high key value - value) / (high key value - low key value)
Linear interpolation of the value within the range of key values yields F if the column is an arithmetic type and value is known at access path selection time.
F = 1/3 otherwise (i.e. column not arithmetic)
There is no significance to this number, other than the fact that it is less selective than the guesses for equal predicates for which there are no indexes, and that it is less than 1/2. We hypothesize that few queries use predicates that are satisfied by more than half the tuples.

column BETWEEN value1 AND value2

F = (value2 - value1) / (high key value - low key value)

A ratio of the BETWEEN value range to the entire key value range is used as the selectivity factor if column is arithmetic and both value1 and value2 are known at access path selection.
F = 1/4 otherwise
Again there is no significance to this choice except that it is between the default selectivity factors for an equal predicate and a range predicate.

column IN (list of values)

F = (number of items in list) * (selectivity factor for column = value)
This is allowed to be no more than 1/2.

columnA IN subquery

F = (expected cardinality of the subquery result) /
(product of the cardinalities of all the relations in the subquery's FROM-list).
The computation of query cardinality will be discussed below.
This formula is derived by the following argument:
Consider the simplest case, where subquery is of the form "SELECT columnB FROM relationC ...". Assume that the set of all columnB values in relationC contains the set of all columnA values. If all the tuples of relationC are selected by the subquery, then the predicate is always TRUE and F = 1. If the tuples of the subquery are restricted by a selectivity factor F', then assume that the set of unique values in the subquery result that match columnA values is proportionately restricted, i.e. the selectivity factor for the predicate should be F'. F' is the product of all the subquery's selectivity factors, namely (subquery cardinality) / (cardinality of all possible subquery answers). With a little optimism, we can extend this reasoning to include subqueries which are joins and subqueries in which columnB is replaced by an arithmetic expression involving column names. This leads to the formula given above.

(pred expression1) OR (pred expression2)

F = F(pred1) + F(pred2) - F(pred1) * F(pred2)

```
(pred1) AND (pred2)
        F = F(pred1) * F(pred2)
        Note that this assumes that column values are independent.

NOT pred
        F = 1 - F(pred)
```

Query cardinality (QCARD) is the product of the cardinalities of every relation in the query block's FROM list times the product of all the selectivity factors of that query block's boolean factors. The number of expected RSI calls (RSICARD) is the product of the relation cardinalities times the selectivity factors of the sargable boolean factors, since the sargable boolean factors will be put into search arguments which will filter out tuples without returning across the RSS interface.

Choosing an optimal access path for a single relation consists of using these selectivity factors in formulas together with the statistics on available access paths. Before this process is described, a definition is needed. Using an index access path or sorting tuples produces tuples in the index value or sort key order. We say that a tuple order is an interesting order if that order is one specified by the query block's GROUP BY or ORDER BY clauses.

For single relations, the cheapest access path is obtained by evaluating the cost for each available access path (each index on the relation, plus a segment scan). The costs will be described below. For each such access path, a predicted cost is computed along with the ordering of the tuples it will produce. Scanning along the SALARY index in ascending order, for example, will produce some cost C and a tuple order of SALARY (ascending). To find the cheapest access plan for a single relation query, we need only to examine the cheapest access path which produces tuples in each "interesting" order and the cheapest "unordered" access path. Note that an "unordered" access path may in fact produce tuples in some order, but the order is not "interesting". If there are no GROUP BY or ORDER BY clauses on the query, then there will be no interesting orderings, and the cheapest access path is the one chosen. If there are GROUP BY or ORDER BY clauses, then the cost for producing that interesting ordering must be compared to the cost of the cheapest unordered path plus the cost of sorting QCARD tuples into the proper order. The cheapest of these alternatives is chosen as the plan for the query block.

The cost formulas for single relation access paths are given in TABLE 2. These formulas give index pages fetched plus data pages fetched plus the weighting factor times RSI tuple retrieval calls. W is the weighting factor between page fetches and RSI calls. Some situations give several alternative formulas depending on whether the set of tuples retrieved will fit entirely in the RSS buffer pool (or effective buffer pool per user). We assume for clustered indexes that a page remains in the buffer long enough for every tuple to be retrieved from it. For non-clustered indexes, it is assumed that for those relations not fitting in the buffer, the relation is sufficiently large with respect to the buffer size that a page fetch is required for every tuple retrieval.

TABLE 2 COST FORMULAS

SITUATION	COST (in pages)
Unique index matching an equal predicate	1 + 1 + W
Clustered index I matching one or more boolean factors	F(preds) * (NINDX(I) + TCARD) + W * RSICARD
Non-clustered index I matching one or more boolean factors	F(preds) * (NINDX(I) + NCARD) + W * RSICARD or F(preds) * (NINDX(I) + TCARD) + W * RSICARD if this number fits in the System R buffer
Clustered index I not matching any boolean factors	(NINDX(I) + TCARD) + W * RSICARD
Non-clustered index I not matching any boolean factors	(NINDX(I) + NCARD) + W * RSICARD or (NINDX(I) + TCARD) + W * RSICARD if this number fits in the System R buffer
Segment scan	TCARD/P + W * RSICARD

5. Access path selection for joins

In 1976, Blasgen and Eswaran <4> examined a number of methods for performing 2-way joins. The performance of each of these methods was analyzed under a variety of relation cardinalities. Their evidence indicates that for other than very small relations, one of two join methods were always optimal or near optimal. The System R optimizer chooses between these two methods. We first describe these methods, and then discuss how they are extended for n-way joins. Finally we specify how the join order (the order in which the relations are joined) is chosen. For joins involving two relations, the two relations are called the outer relation, from which a tuple will be retrieved first, and the inner relation, from which tuples will be retrieved, possibly depending on the values obtained in the outer relation tuple. A predicate which relates columns of two tables to be joined is called a join predicate. The columns referenced in a join predicate are called join columns.

The first join method, called the nested loops method, uses scans, in any order, on the outer and inner relations. The scan on the outer relation is opened and the first tuple is retrieved. For each outer relation tuple obtained, a scan is opened on the inner relation to retrieve, one at a time, all the tuples of the inner relation which satisfy the join predicate. The composite tuples formed by the outer-relation-tuple / inner-relation-tuple pairs comprise the result of this join.

The second join method, called merging scans, requires the outer and inner relations to be scanned in join column order. This implies that, along with the columns mentioned in ORDER BY and GROUP BY, columns of equi-join predicates (those of the form Table1.column1 = Table2.column2) also define "interesting" orders. If there is more than one join predicate, one of them is used as the join predicate and the others are treated as ordinary predicates. The merging scans method is only applied to equi-joins, although in principle it could be applied to other types of joins. If one or both of the relations to be joined has no indexes on the join column, it must be sorted into a temporary list which is ordered by the join column.

The more complex logic of the merging scan join method takes advantage of the ordering on join columns to avoid rescanning the entire inner relation (looking for a match) for each tuple of the outer relation. It does this by synchronizing the inner and outer scans by reference to matching join column values and by "remembering" where matching join groups are located. Further savings occur if the inner relation is clustered on the join column (as would be true if it is the output of a sort on the join column). "Clustering" on a column means that tuples which have the same value in that column are physically stored close to each other so that one page access will retrieve several tuples.

N-way joins can be visualized as a sequence of 2-way joins. In this visualization, two relations are joined together, the resulting composite relation is joined with the third relation, etc. At each step of the n-way join it is possible to identify the outer relation (which in general is composite) and the inner relation (the relation being added to the join). Thus the methods described above for two way joins are easily generalized to n-way joins. However, it should be emphasized that the first 2-way join does not have to be completed before the second 2-way join is started. As soon as we get a composite tuple for the first 2-way join, it can be joined with tuples of the third relation to form result tuples for the 3-way join, etc. Nested loop joins and merge scan joins may be mixed in the same query, e.g. the first two relations of a three-way join may be joined using merge scans and the composite result may be joined with the third relation using a nested loop join. The intermediate composite relations are physically stored only if a sort is required for the next join step. When a sort of the composite relation is not specified, the composite relation will be materialized one tuple at a time to participate in the next join.

We now consider the order in which the relations are chosen to be joined. It should be noted that although the cardinality of the join of n relations is the same regardless of join order, the cost of joining in different orders can be substantially different. If a query block has n relations in its FROM list, then there are n factorial permutations of relation join orders. The search space can be reduced by observing that ~~that~~ once the first k relations are joined, the method to join the composite to the k+1-st relation is independent of the order of joining the first k; i.e. the applicable predicates are the same, the set of interesting orderings is the same, the possible join methods are the same, etc. Using this property, an efficient way to organize the search is to find the best join order for successively larger subsets of tables.

A heuristic is used to reduce the join order permutations which are considered. When possible, the search is reduced by consideration only of join orders which have join predicates relating the inner relation to the other relations already participating in the join. This means that in joining relations t1,t2,...,tn only those orderings ti1,ti2,...,tin are examined in which for all j (j=2,...,n) either
(1) tij has at least one join predicate

with some relation tik, where k < j, or (2) for all k > j, tik has no join predicate with ti1,ti2,...,or ti(j-1). This means that all joins requiring Cartesian products are performed as late in the join sequence as possible. For example, if T1,T2,T3 are the three relations in a query block's FROM list, and there are join predicates between T1 and T2 and between T2 and T3 on different columns than the T1-T2 join, then the following permutations are not considered:

T1-T3-T2
T3-T1-T2

To find the optimal plan for joining n relations, a tree of possible solutions is constructed. As discussed above, the search is performed by finding the best way to join subsets of the relations. For each set of relations joined, the cardinality of the composite relation is estimated and saved. In addition, for the unordered join, and for each interesting order obtained by the join thus far, the cheapest solution for achieving that order and the cost of that solution are saved. A solution consists of an ordered list of the relations to be joined, the join method used for each join, and a plan indicating how each relation is to be accessed. If either the outer composite relation or the inner relation needs to be sorted before the join, then that is also included in the plan. As in the single relation case, "interesting" orders are those listed in the query block's GROUP BY or ORDER BY clause, if any. Also every join column defines an "interesting" order. To minimize the number of different interesting orders and hence the number of solutions in the tree, equivalence classes for interesting orders are computed and only the best solution for each equivalence class is saved. For example, if there is a join predicate E.DNO = D.DNO and another join predicate D.DNO = F.DNO, then all three of these columns belong to the same order equivalence class.

The search tree is constructed by iteration on the number of relations joined so far. First, the best way is found to access each single relation for each interesting tuple ordering and for the unordered case. Next, the best way of joining any relation to these is found, subject to the heuristics for join order. This produces solutions for joining pairs of relations. Then the best way to join sets of three relations is found by consideration of all sets of two relations and joining in each third relation permitted by the join order heuristic. For each plan to join a set of relations, the order of the composite result is kept in the tree. This allows consideration of a merge scan join which would not require sorting the composite. After the complete solutions (all of the relations joined together) have been found, the optimizer chooses the cheapest solution which gives the required order, if any was specified. Note that if a solution exists with the correct order, no sort is performed for ORDER BY or GROUP BY, unless the ordered solution is more expensive than the cheapest unordered solution plus the cost of sorting into the required order.

The number of solutions which must be stored is at most 2**n (the number of subsets of n tables) times the number of interesting result orders. The computation time to generate the tree is approximately proportional to the same number. This number is frequently reduced substantially by the join order heuristic. Our experience is that typical cases require only a few thousand bytes of storage and a few tenths of a second of 370/158 CPU time. Joins of 8 tables have been optimized in a few seconds.

<u>Computation of costs</u>

The costs for joins are computed from the costs of the scans on each of the relations and the cardinalities. The costs of the scans on each of the relations are computed using the cost formulas for single relation access paths presented in section 4.

Let C-outer(path1) be the cost of scanning the outer relation via path1, and N be the cardinality of the outer relation tuples which satisfy the applicable predicates. N is computed by:

N = (product of the cardinalities of all relations T of the join so far) * (product of the selectivity factors of all applicable predicates).

Let C-inner(path2) be the cost of scanning the inner relation, applying all applicable predicates. Note that in the merge scan join this means scanning the contiguous group of the inner relation which corresponds to one join column value in the outer relation. Then the cost of a nested loop join is

C-nested-loop-join(path1,path2)=
    C-outer(path1) + N * C-inner(path2)

The cost of a merge scan join can be broken up into the cost of actually doing the merge plus the cost of sorting the outer or inner relations, if required. The cost of doing the merge is

C-merge(path1,path2)=
    C-outer(path1) + N * C-inner(path2)

For the case where the inner relation is sorted into a temporary relation none of the single relation access path formulas in section 4 apply. In this case the inner scan is like a segment scan except that the merging scans method makes use of the fact that the inner relation is sorted so that it is not necessary to scan the entire inner relation looking for a match. For this case we use the following formula for the cost of the inner scan.

C-inner(sorted list) =
TEMPPAGES/N + W*RSICARD

where TEMPPAGES is the number of pages

required to hold the inner relation. This formula assumes that during the merge each page of the inner relation is fetched once.

It is interesting to observe that the cost formula for nested loop joins and the cost formula for merging scans are essentially the same. The reason that merging scans is sometimes better than nested loops is that the cost of the inner scan may be much less. After sorting, the inner relation is clustered on the join column which tends to minimize the number of pages fetched, and it is not necessary to scan the entire inner relation (looking for a match) for each tuple of the outer relation.

The cost of sorting a relation, C-sort(path), includes the cost of retrieving the data using the specified access path, sorting the data, which may involve several passes, and putting the results into a temporary list. Note that prior to sorting the inner table, only the local predicates can be applied. Also, if it is necessary to sort a composite result, the entire composite relation must be stored in a temporary relation before it can be sorted. The cost of inserting the composite tuples into a temporary relation before sorting is included in C-sort(path).

<u>Example of tree</u>

We now show how the search is done for the example join shown in Fig. 1. First we find all of the reasonable access paths for single relations with only their local predicates applied. The results for this example are shown in Fig. 2. There are three access paths for the EMP table: an index on DNO, an index on JOB, and a segment scan. The interesting orders are DNO and JOB. The index on DNO provides the tuples in DNO order and the index on JOB provides the tuples in JOB order. The segment scan access path is, for our purposes, unordered. For this example we assume that the index on JOB is the cheapest path, so the segment scan path is pruned. For the DEPT relation there are two access paths, an index on DNO and a segment scan. We assume that the index on DNO is cheaper so the segment scan path is pruned. For the JOB relation there are two access paths, an index on JOB and a segment scan. We assume that the segment scan path is cheaper, so both paths are saved. The results just described are saved in the search tree as shown in Fig. 3. In the figures, the notation C(EMP.DNO) or C(E.DNO) means the cost of scanning EMP via the DNO index, applying all predicates which are applicable given that tuples from the specified set of relations have already been fetched. The notation Ni is used to represent the cardinalities of the different partial results.

Next, solutions for pairs of relations are found by joining a second relation to the results for single relations shown in Fig. 3. For each single relation, we find access paths for joining in each second relation for which there exists a predicate connecting it to the first relation. First we consider access path selection for nested loop joins. In this example we assume that the EMP-JOB join is cheapest by accessing JOB on the JOB index. This is

EMP

NAME	DNO	JOB	SAL
SMITH	50	12	8500
JONES	50	5	15000
DOE	51	5	9500

DEPT

DNO	DNAME	LOC
50	MFG	DENVER
51	BILLING	BOULDER
52	SHIPPING	DENVER

JOB

JOB	TITLE
5	CLERK
6	TYPIST
9	SALES
12	MECHANIC

```
SELECT  NAME, TITLE, SAL, DNAME
FROM    EMP, DEPT, JOB
WHERE   TITLE='CLERK'
AND     LOC='DENVER'
AND     EMP.DNO=DEPT.DNO
AND     EMP.JOB=JOB.JOB
```

"Retrieve the name, salary, job title, and department name of employees who are clerks and work for departments in Denver."

Figure 1. JOIN example

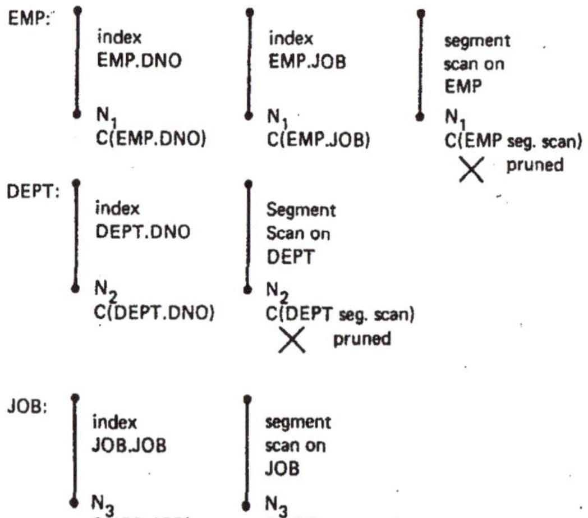

Figure 2.

likely since it can fetch directly the tuples with matching JOB (without having to scan the entire relation). In practice the cost of joining is estimated using the formulas given earlier and the cheapest path is chosen. For joining the EMP relation to the DEPT relation we assume that the DNO index is cheapest. The best access path for each second-level relation is combined with each of the plans in Fig. 3 to form the nested loop solutions shown in Fig. 4.

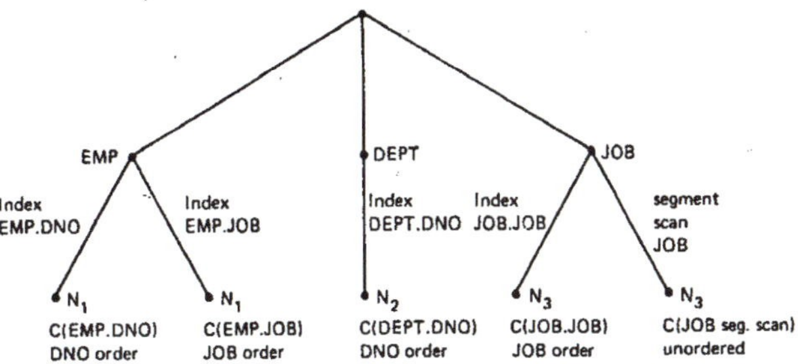

Figure 3. Search tree for single relations

Next we generate solutions using the merging scans method. As we see on the left side of Fig. 3, there is a scan on the EMP relation in DNO order, so it is possible to use this scan and the DNO scan on the DEPT relation to do a merging scans join, without any sorting. Although it is possible to do the merging join without sorting as just described, it might be cheaper to use the JOB index on EMP, sort on DNO, and then merge. Note that we never consider sorting the DEPT table because the cheapest scan on that table is already in DNO order.

For merging JOB with EMP, we only consider the JOB index on EMP since it is the cheapest access path for EMP regardless of order. Using the JOB index on JOB, we can merge without any sorting. However, it might be cheapter to sort JOB using a relation scan as input to the sort and then do the merge.

Referring to Fig. 3, we see that the access path chosen for the DEPT relation is the DNO index. After accessing DEPT via this index, we can merge with EMP using the DNO index on EMP, again without any sorting. However, it might be cheaper to sort EMP first using the JOB index as input to the sort and then do the merge. Both of these cases are shown in Fig. 5.

As each of the costs shown in Figs. 4 and 5 are computed they are compared with the cheapest equivalent solution (same tables and same result order) found so far, and the cheapest solution is saved. After this pruning, solutions for all three relations are found. For each pair of relations, we find access paths for joining in the remaining third relation. As before we will extend the tree using nested loop joins and merging scans to join the third relation. The search tree for three relations is shown in Fig. 6. Note that in one case both the composite relation and the table being added (JOB) are sorted. Note also that for some of the cases no sorts are performed at all. In these cases, the composite result is materialized one tuple at a time and the intermediate composite relation is never stored. As before, as each of the costs are computed they are compared with the cheapest solu-

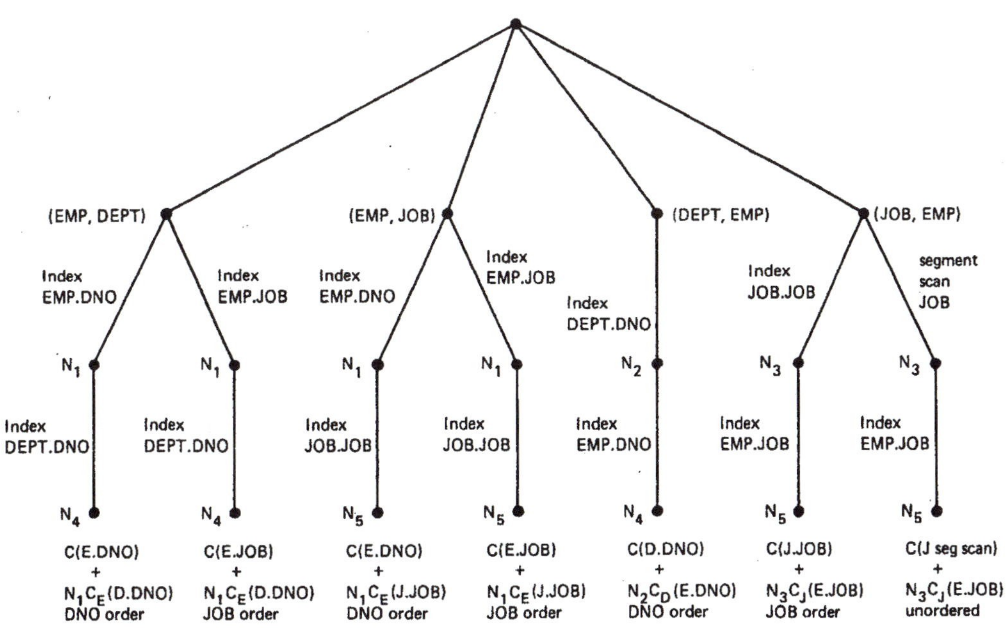

Figure 4. Extended search tree for second relation (nested loop join)

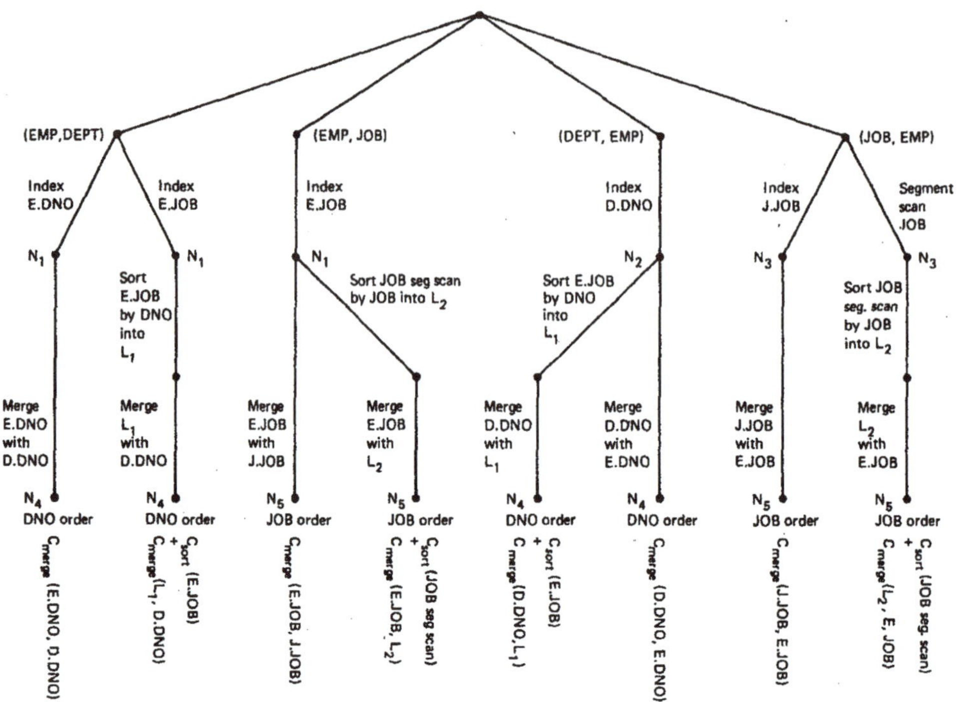

Figure 5. Extended search tree for second relation (merge join)

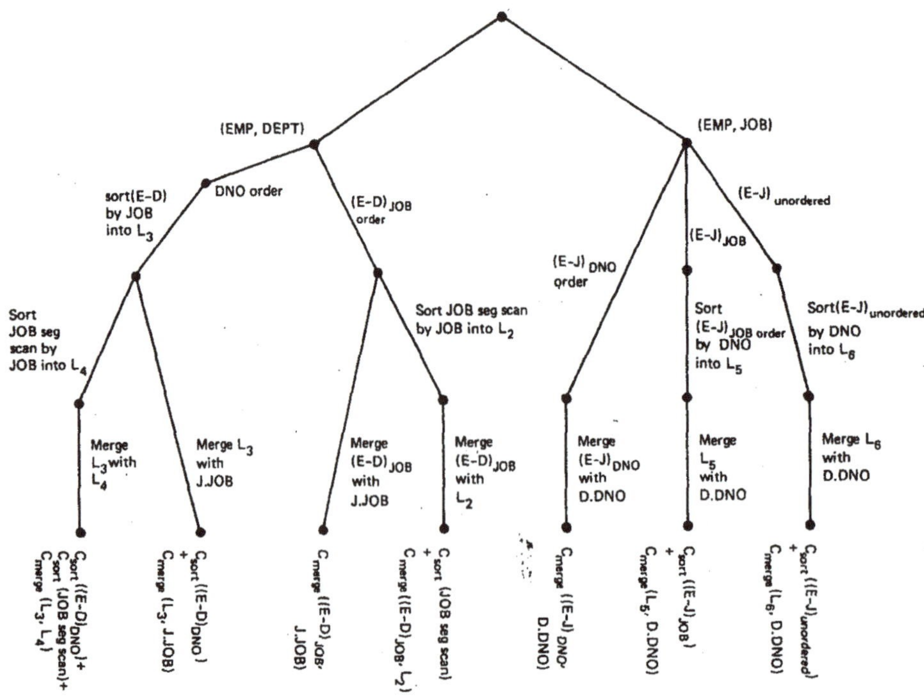

Figure 6. Extended search tree for third relation

6. Nested Queries

A query may appear as an operand of a predicate of the form "expression operator query". Such a query is called a Nested Query or a Subquery. If the operator is one of the six scalar comparisons (=, ¬=, >, >=, <, <=), then the subquery must return a single value. The following example using the "=" operator was given in section 2:

```
SELECT NAME
FROM EMPLOYEE
WHERE SALARY =
    (SELECT AVG(SALARY)
     FROM EMPLOYEE)
```

If the operator is IN or NOT IN then the subquery may return a set of values. For example:

```
SELECT NAME
FROM EMPLOYEE
WHERE DEPARTMENT_NUMBER IN
     (SELECT DEPARTMENT_NUMBER
      FROM DEPARTMENT
      WHERE LOCATION='DENVER')
```

In both examples, the subquery needs to be evaluated only once. The OPTIMIZER will arrange for the subquery to be evaluated before the top level query is evaluated. If a single value is returned, it is incorporated into the top level query as though it had been part of the original query statement; for example, if AVG(SAL) above evaluates to 15000 at execution time, then the predicate becomes "SALARY = 15000". If the subquery can return a set of values, they are returned in a temporary list, an internal form which is more efficient than a relation but which can only be accessed sequentially. In the example above, if the subquery returns the list (17,24) then the predicate is evaluated in a manner similar to the way in which it would have been evaluated if the original predicate had been DEPARTMENT_NUMBER IN (17,24).

A subquery may also contain a predicate with a subquery, down to a (theoretically) arbitrary level of nesting. When such subqueries do not reference columns from tables in higher level query blocks, they are all evaluated before the top level query is evaluated. In this case, the most deeply nested subqueries are evaluated first, since any subquery must be evaluated before its parent query can be evaluated.

A subquery may contain a reference to a value obtained from a candidate tuple of a higher level query block (see example below). Such a query is called a correlation subquery. A correlation subquery must in principle be re-evaluated for each candidate tuple from the referenced query block. This re-evaluation must be done before the correlation subquery's parent predicate in the higher level block can be tested for acceptance or rejection of the candidate tuple. As an example, consider the query:

```
SELECT NAME
FROM EMPLOYEE X
WHERE SALARY > (SELECT SALARY
                FROM EMPLOYEE
                WHERE EMPLOYEE_NUMBER=
                          X.MANAGER)
```

This selects names of EMPLOYEE's that earn more than their MANAGER. Here X identifies the query block and relation which furnishes the candidate tuple for the correlation. For each candidate tuple of the top level query block, the MANAGER value is used for evaluation of the subquery. The subquery result is then returned to the "SALARY >" predicate for testing acceptance of the candidate tuple.

If a correlation subquery is not directly below the query block it references but is separated from that block by one or more intermediate blocks, then the correlation subquery evaluation will be done before evaluation of the highest of the intermediate blocks. For example:

```
level 1    SELECT NAME
           FROM EMPLOYEE X
           WHERE SALARY >
level 2         (SELECT SALARY
                 FROM EMPLOYEE
                 WHERE EMPLOYEE_NUMBER =
level 3              (SELECT MANAGER
                      FROM EMPLOYEE
                      WHERE EMPLOYEE_NUMBER =
                            X.MANAGER))
```

This selects names of EMPLOYEE's that earn more than their MANAGER's MANAGER. As before, for each candidate tuple of the level-1 query block, the EMPLOYEE.MANAGER value is used for evaluation of the level-3 query block. In this case, because the level 3 subquery references a level 1 value but does not reference level 2 values, it is evaluated once for every new level 1 candidate tuple, but not for every level 2 candidate tuple.

If the value referenced by a correlation subquery (X.MANAGER above) is not unique in the set of candidate tuples (e.g., many employees have the same manager), the procedure given above will still cause the subquery to be re-evaluated for each occurrence of a replicated value. However, if the referenced relation is ordered on the referenced column, the re-evaluation can be made conditional, depending on a test of whether or not the current referenced value is the same as the one in the previous candidate tuple. If they are the same, the previous evaluation result can be used again. In some cases, it might even pay to sort the referenced relation on the referenced column in order to avoid re-evaluating subqueries unnecessarily. In order to determine whether or not the referenced column values are unique, the OPTIMIZER can use clues like NCARD > ICARD, where NCARD is the relation cardinality and ICARD is the index cardinality of an index on the referenced column.

7. Conclusion

The System R access path selection has been described for single table queries, joins, and nested queries. Evaluation work on comparing the choices made to the "right" choice is in progress, and will be described in a forthcoming paper. Preliminary results indicate that, although the costs predicted by the optimizer are often not accurate in absolute value, the true optimal path is selected in a large majority of cases. In many cases, the ordering among the estimated costs for all paths considered is precisely the same as that among the actual measured costs.

Furthermore, the cost of path selection is not overwhelming. For a two-way join, the cost of optimization is approximately equivalent to between 5 and 20 database retrievals. This number becomes even more insignificant when such a path selector is placed in an environment such as System R, where application programs are compiled once and run many times. The cost of optimization is amortized over many runs.

The key contributions of this path selector over other work in this area are the expanded use of statistics (index cardinality, for example), the inclusion of CPU utilization into the cost formulas, and the method of determining join order. Many queries are CPU-bound, particularly merge joins for which temporary relations are created and sorts performed. The concept of "selectivity factor" permits the optimizer to take advantage of as many of the query's restriction predicates as possible in the RSS search arguments and access paths. By remembering "interesting ordering" equivalence classes for joins and ORDER or GROUP specifications, the optimizer does more bookkeeping than most path selectors, but this additional work in many cases results in avoiding the storage and sorting of intermediate query results. Tree pruning and tree searching techniques allow this additional bookkeeping to be performed efficiently.

More work on validation of the optimizer cost formulas needs to be done, but we can conclude from this preliminary work that database management systems can support non-procedural query languages with performance comparable to those supporting the current more procedural languages.

Cited and General References

<1> Astrahan, M. M. et al. System R: Relational Approach to Database Management. ACM Transactions on Database Systems, Vol. 1, No. 2, June 1976, pp. 97-137.

<2> Astrahan, M. M. et al. System R: A Relational Database Management System. To appear in Computer.

<3> Bayer, R. and McCreight, E. Organization and Maintenance of Large Ordered Indices. Acta Informatica, Vol. 1, 1972.

<4> Blasgen, M.W. and Eswaran, K.P. On the Evaluation of Queries in a Relational Data Base System. IBM Research Report RJ1745, April, 1976.

<5> Chamberlin, D.D., et al. SEQUEL2: A Unified Approach to Data Definition, Manipulation, and Control. IBM Journal of Research and Development, Vol. 20, No. 6, Nov. 1976, pp. 560-575.

<6> Chamberlin, D.D., Gray, J.N., and Traiger, I.L. Views, Authorization and Locking in a Relational Data Base System. ACM National Computer Conference Proceedings, 1975, pp. 425-430.

<7> Codd, E.F. A Relational Model of Data for Large Shared Data Banks. ACM Communications, Vol. 13, No. 6, June, 1970, pp. 377-387.

<8> Date, C.J. An Introduction to Data Base Systems, Addison-Wesley, 1975.

<9> Lorie, R.A. and Wade, B.W. The Compilation of a Very High Level Data Language. IBM Research Report RJ2008, May, 1977.

<10> Lorie, R.A. and Nilsson, J.F. An Access Specification Language for a Relational Data Base System. IBM Research Report RJ2218, April, 1978.

<11> Stonebraker, M.R., Wong, E., Kreps, P., and Held, G.D. The Design and Implementation of INGRES. ACM Trans. on Database Systems, Vol. 1, No. 3, September, 1976, pp. 189-222.

<12> Todd, S. PRTV: An Efficient Implementation for Large Relational Data Bases. Proc. International Conf. on Very Large Data Bases, Framingham, Mass., September, 1975.

<13> Wong, E., and Youssefi, K. Decomposition - A Strategy for Query Processing. ACM Transactions on Database Systems, Vol. 1, No. 3 (Sept. 1976) pp. 223-241.

<14> Zloof, M.M. Query by Example. Proc. AFIPS 1975 NCC, Vol. 44, AFIPS Press, Montvale, N.J., pp. 431-437.

Join Processing in Database Systems with Large Main Memories

LEONARD D. SHAPIRO
North Dakota State University

We study algorithms for computing the equijoin of two relations in a system with a standard architecture but with large amounts of main memory. Our algorithms are especially efficient when the main memory available is a significant fraction of the size of one of the relations to be joined; but they can be applied whenever there is memory equal to approximately the square root of the size of one relation. We present a new algorithm which is a hybrid of two hash-based algorithms and which dominates the other algorithms we present, including sort-merge. Even in a virtual memory environment, the hybrid algorithm dominates all the others we study.

Finally, we describe how three popular tools to increase the efficiency of joins, namely filters, Babb arrays, and semijoins, can be grafted onto any of our algorithms.

Categories and Subject Descriptors: H.2.0 [**Database Management**]: General; H.2.4 [**Database Management**]: Systems—*query processing*; H.2.6 [**Database Management**]: Database Machines

General Terms: Algorithms, Performance

Additional Key Words and Phrases: Hash join, join processing, large main memory, sort-merge join

1. INTRODUCTION

Database systems are gaining in popularity owing to features such as data independence, high-level interfaces, concurrency control, crash recovery, and so on. However, the greatest drawback to database management systems (other than cost) is the inefficiency of full-function database systems, compared to customized programs; and one of the most costly operations in database processing is the join. Traditionally the most effective algorithm for executing a join (if there are no indices) has been sort-merge [4]. In [6] it was suggested that the existence of increasingly inexpensive main memory makes it possible to use hashing techniques to execute joins more efficiently than sort-merge. Here we extend these results.

Some of the first research on joins using hashing [14, 21] concerned multiprocessor architectures. Our model assumes a "vanilla" computer architecture, that is, a uniprocessor system available in the market today. Although the lack of parallel processing in such systems deprives us of much of the potential speed of

Author's address: Department of Computer Science, North Dakota State University, Fargo, ND 58105.

join processing on multiprocessor systems, our algorithms can be implemented on current systems, and they avoid the complex synchronization problems of some of the more sophisticated multiprocessor algorithms.

Our algorithms require significant amounts of main memory to execute most efficiently. We assume it is not unreasonable to expect that the database system can assign several megabytes of buffer space to executing a join. (Current VAX systems can support 32 megabytes of real memory with 64K chips [8]; and it is argued in [10] that a system can be built with existing technology that will support tens of gigabytes of main memory, and which appears to a programmer to have a standard architecture.)

We will see that our algorithms are most effective when the amount of real memory available to the process is close to the size of one of the relations.

The word "large" in the title refers to a memory size large enough that it is not uncommon for all, or a significant fraction, of one of the relations to be joined to fit in main memory. This is because the minimum amount of memory required to implement our algorithms is approximately the square root of the size of one of the relations (measured in physical blocks). This allows us to process rather large relations in main memories which by today's standards might not be called large. For example, using our system parameters and 4 megabytes of real memory as buffer space, we can join two relations, using our most efficient algorithm, if the smaller of the two relations is at most 325 megabytes.

We show that with sufficient main memory, and for sufficiently large relations, the most efficient algorithms are hash-based. We present two classes of hash-based algorithms, one (simple hash) that is most efficient when most of one relation fits in main memory and another (GRACE) that is most efficient when much less of the smaller relation fits. We then describe a new algorithm, which is a hybrid of simple and GRACE, that is the most efficient of those we study, even in a virtual memory environment. This is in contrast to current commercial database systems, which find sort-merge-join to be most efficient in many situations and do not implement hash joins.

In Section 2 we present four algorithms for computing an equijoin, along with their cost formulas. The first algorithm is sort-merge, modified to take advantage of large main memory. The next is a very simple use of hashing, and another is based on GRACE, the Japanese fifth-generation project's database machine [14]. The last is a hybrid of the simple and GRACE algorithms. We show in Section 3 that for sufficiently large relations the hybrid algorithm is the most efficient, inclusive of sort-merge, and we present some analytic modeling results. All our hashing algorithms are based on the idea of partitioning: we partition each relation into subsets which can (on the average) fit into main memory. In Section 3 we assume that all the partitions can fit into main memory, and in Section 4 discuss how to deal with the problem of partition overflow. In Section 5 we describe the effect of using virtual memory in place of some main memory. In Section 6 we discuss how to include in our algorithms other tools that have become popular in database systems, namely selection filters, semijoin strategies, and Babb arrays.

A description of these algorithms, similar to that in Section 2, and analytic modeling results similar to those in the second half of Section 3, appeared in [6].

In [5] it is shown that hashing is preferable to nested-loop and sort-merge algorithms for a variety of relational algebra operations—results consistent with those we present. In [7] the results of [6] are extended to the multiprocessor environment, and experimental results are reported. These results support the analyses in [6] and in the present paper, and show that, in the cases reported, if a bit-filtering technique is used (see Section 6) the timings of all algorithms are similar above a certain memory size. A related algorithm, the nested-hash algorithm, is also studied there, and is shown to have performance comparable to the hybrid algorithm for large memory sizes, but to be inferior to hybrid for smaller memory sizes. In [22], the GRACE hash algorithm is studied in depth, including an analysis of the case when more than two phases of processing are needed and an analysis of various partitioning schemes. I/O accesses and CPU time are analyzed separately, and it is shown that GRACE hash-join is superior to merge-join.

1.1 Notation and Assumptions

Our goal is to compute the equijoin of two relations labeled **R** and **S**. We use **M** to denote main memory. We do not count initial reads of **R** or **S** or final writes of the join output because these costs are identical for all algorithms. After the initial reads of **R** and **S**, those relations are not referenced again by our algorithms. Therefore, all I/O in the join processing is of temporary relations. We choose to block these temporary relations at one track per physical block, so each I/O which we count will be of an entire track. Therefore, throughout this paper the term "block" refers to a full track of data. Of course, **R** and **S** may be stored with a different blocking factor. In all the cost formulas and analytic modeling in this paper we use the labels given in Figure 1.

In our model we do not distinguish between sequential and random I/O. This is justified because all reads or writes of any temporary file in our algorithms will be sequential from or to that file. If only one file is active, I/O is sequential in the traditional sense, except that because of our full-track blocking an I/O operation is more likely to cause head movement. If more than one file is active there will be more head movement, but the cost of that extra head movement is assumed negligible. This is why we choose a full track as our blocking factor for the temporary relations.

We assume that **S** is the larger relation, that is, $|\mathbf{R}| \leq |\mathbf{S}|$. We use the "fudge factor", **F**, in Figure 1 to calculate values that are small increments of other values. For example, a hash table for **R** is assumed to occupy $|\mathbf{R}| * \mathbf{F}$ blocks.

In our cost formulas we assume that all selections and projections of **R** and **S** have already been done and that neither relation **R** nor **S** is ordered or indexed. We assume no overlap between CPU and I/O processing. We assume each tuple from **S** joins with at most one block of tuples from **R**. If it is expected that there will be few tuples in the resulting join, it may be appropriate to process only tuple IDs instead of projected tuples, and then at the end translate the TIDs that are output into actual tuple values. We view this as a separate process from the actual join; our formulas do not include this final step.

For the first four sections of this paper we assume that the memory manager allocates a fixed amount of real memory to each join process. The process knows

comp	time to compare keys in main memory
hash	time to hash a key that is in main memory
move	time to move a tuple in memory
swap	time to swap two tuples in memory
IO	time to read or write a block between disk and main memory
F	incremental factor (see below)
$\lvert$ **R** $\rvert$	number of blocks in **R** relation (similar for **S** and **M**)
{**R**}	number of tuples in **R** (similar for **S**)
$\{M\}_R$	number of **R** tuples that can fit in **M** (similar for **S**)

Fig. 1. Notation used in cost formulas in this paper.

how much memory is allocated to it, and can use this information in designing a strategy for the join. The amount of real memory allocated is fixed throughout the lifetime of the process. In Section 5 we discuss an alternate to this simple memory management strategy.

2. THE JOIN ALGORITHMS

In this section we present four algorithms for computing the equijoin of relations **R** and **S**. One is a modified sort-merge algorithm and the other three are based on hashing.

Each of the algorithms we describe executes in two phases. In phase 1, the relations **R** and **S** are restructured into runs (for sort-merge) or subsets of a partition (for the three hashing algorithms). In phase 2, the restructured relations are used to compute the join.

2.1 Sort-Merge-Join Algorithm

The standard sort-merge-join algorithm [4] begins by producing sorted runs of tuples of **S**. The runs are on the average (over all inputs) twice as long as the number of tuples that can fit into a priority queue in memory [15, p. 254]. This requires one pass over **S**. In subsequent phases, the runs are sorted using an n-way merge. **R** is sorted similarly. After **R** and **S** are sorted they are merged together and tuples with matching join attributes are output. For a fixed relation size, the CPU time to do a sort with n-way merges is independent of n, but I/O time increases as n decreases and the number of phases increases. One should therefore choose the merging factor n to be as large as possible so that the process will involve as few phases as possible. Ideally, only two phases will be needed, one to construct runs and the other to merge and join them. We show that if $|\mathbf{M}|$ is at least $\sqrt{|S|}$, then only two phases are needed to accomplish the join.

Here are the steps of our version of the sort-merge algorithm in the case where there are at least $\sqrt{|S|}$ blocks of memory for the process. (See Figure 2, sort-merge-join).

In the following analysis we use average (over all inputs) values, for instance, $2 * |\mathbf{M}|$ is the length of a run.

(1) Scan **S** and produce output runs using a heap or some other priority queue structure. Do the same for **R**. A run will be $2 * |\mathbf{M}|$ blocks long. Given

PHASE 1

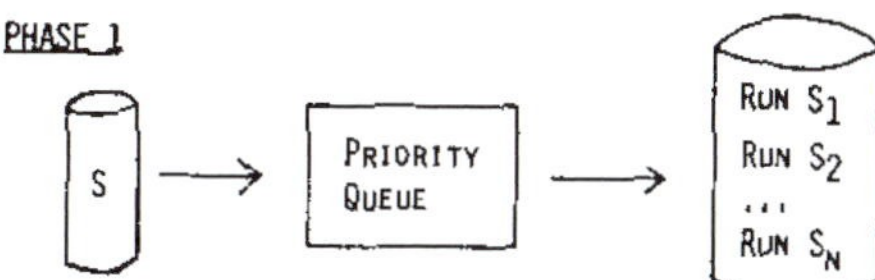

AFTER ALL OF S IS DECOMPOSED INTO RUNS, THE ABOVE IS REPEATED WITH S REPLACED BY R,

Fig. 2. Sort-merge-join.

PHASE 2

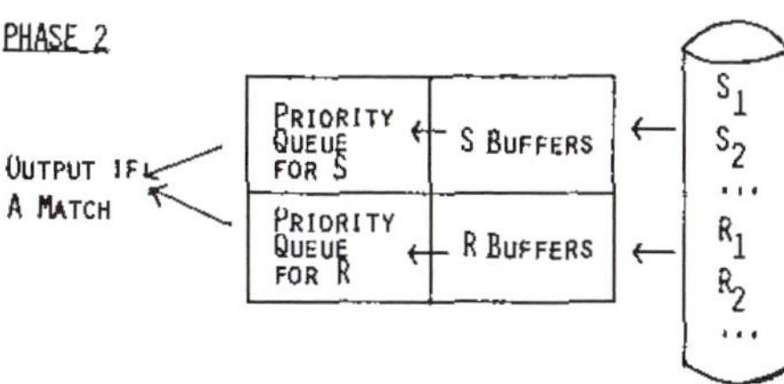

that $|\mathbf{M}| \geq \sqrt{|S|}$, the runs will be at least $2\sqrt{|S|}$ blocks in length. Therefore there will be at most

$$\frac{|S|}{2\sqrt{|S|}} = \frac{1}{2}\sqrt{|S|}$$

distinct runs of **S** on the disk. Since **S** is the larger relation, **R** has at most the same number of runs on disk. Therefore there will be at most $\sqrt{|S|}$ runs of **R** and **S** altogether on the disk at the end of phase 1.

(2) Allocate one block of memory for buffer space for each run of **R** and **S**. Merge all the runs of **R** and concurrently merge all the runs of **S**. As tuples of **R** and **S** are generated in sorted order by these merges, they can be checked for a match. When a tuple from **R** matches one from **S**, output the pair.

In step (2), one input buffer is required per run, and there are at most $\sqrt{|S|}$ runs, so if $|\mathbf{M}| \geq \sqrt{|S|}$, there is sufficient room for the input buffers. Extra space is required for merging, but this is negligible since the priority queue contains only one tuple per run.

If the memory manager allocates fewer than $\sqrt{|S|}$ blocks of memory to the join process, more than two phases are needed. We do not investigate this case further; we assume $|\mathbf{M}| \geq \sqrt{|S|}$. If $|\mathbf{M}|$ is greater than $\sqrt{|S|}$, the extra blocks of real memory can be used to store runs between phases, thus saving I/O costs. This is reflected in the last term of the cost formula.

The cost of this algorithm is

$(\{\mathbf{R}\} \log_2\{\mathbf{R}\} + \{\mathbf{S}\} \log_2\{\mathbf{S}\}) * (\text{comp} + \text{swap})$	Manage priority queues in both phases.
$+ (|\mathbf{R}| + |\mathbf{S}|) * \text{IO}$	Write initial runs.
$+ (|\mathbf{R}| + |\mathbf{S}|) * \text{IO}$	Read initial runs.
$+ (\{\mathbf{R}\} + \{\mathbf{S}\}) * \text{comp}$	Join results of final merge.
$- \min(|\mathbf{R}| + |\mathbf{S}|, |\mathbf{M}| - \sqrt{|S|}) * 2 * \text{IO}$	I/O savings if extra memory is available.

2.2 Hashing Algorithms

The simplest use of hashing as a join strategy is the following algorithm, which we call *classic hashing*: build a hash table, in memory, of tuples from the smaller relation **R**, hashed on the joining attribute(s). Then scan the other relation **S** sequentially. For each tuple in **S**, use the hash value for that tuple to probe the hash table of **R** for tuples with matching key values. If a match is found, output the pair, and if not then drop the tuple from **S** and continue scanning **S**.

This algorithm works best when the hash table for **R** can fit into real memory. When most of a hash table for **R** cannot fit in real memory, this classic algorithm can still be used in virtual memory, but it behaves poorly, since many tuples cause page faults. The three hashing algorithms we describe here each extend the classic hashing approach in some way so as to take into account the possibility that a hash table for **R** will not fit into main memory.

If a hash table for the smaller relation **R** cannot fit into memory, each of the hashing algorithms described in this paper calculates the join by partitioning **R** and **S** into disjoint subsets and then joining corresponding subsets. The size of the subsets varies for different algorithms. For this method to work, one must choose a partitioning of **R** and **S** so that computing the join can be done by just joining corresponding subsets of the two relations. The first mention of this method is in [11], and it also appears in [3]. Our use of it is closely related to the description in [14].

The method of partitioning is first to choose a hash function h, and a partition of the values of h into, say, $H_1, \ldots, H_n$. (For example, the negative and nonnegative values of h constitute a partition of h values into two subsets, H_1 and H_2.) Then, one partitions **R** into corresponding subsets $R_1, \ldots, R_n$, where a tuple r of **R** is in R_i whenever $h(r)$ is in H_i. Here by $h(r)$ we mean the hash function applied to the joining attribute of r. Similarly, one partitions **S** into corresponding subsets $S_1, \ldots, S_n$ with s in S_i when $h(s)$ is in H_i. The subsets R_i and S_i are actually buckets, but we refer to them as subsets of the partition, since they are not used as ordinary hash buckets.

If a tuple r in **R** is in R_i and it joins with a tuple s from **S**, then the joining attributes of r and s must be equal, thus $h(r) = h(s)$ and s is in S_i. This is why, to join **R** and **S**, it suffices to join the subsets R_i and S_i for each i.

In all the hashing algorithms we describe we are required to choose a partitioning into subsets of a specified size (e.g., such that **R** is partitioned into two subsets of equal size). Partitioning into specified size subsets is not easy to accomplish if the distribution of the joining attribute of **R** is not well understood. In this section we describe the hashing algorithms as if bucket overflow never occurs, then in Section 4 we describe how to deal with the problem.

Each of the three algorithms we describe uses partitioning, as described above. Each proceeds in two phases: the first is to partition each relation. The second phase is to build hash table(s) for **R** and probe for matches with each tuple of **S**. The first algorithm we describe, simple hashing, does as little of the first phase—partitioning—as possible on each step, and goes right into building a hash table and probing. It performs well when most of **R** can fit in memory. The next algorithm, GRACE hash, does all of the first phase at once, then turns to the second phase of building hash tables and probing. It performs relatively well when little of **R** can fit in memory. The third algorithm, hybrid hash, combines the two, doing all partitioning on the first pass over each relation and using whatever memory is left to build a hash table. It performs well over a wide range of memory sizes.

2.3 Simple Hash-Join Algorithm

If a hash table containing all of **R** fits into memory (i.e., if $|R| * F \leq |M|$), the simple hash-join algorithm which we define here is identical to what we have called classic hash-join. If there is not enough memory available, our simple hash-join scans **R** repeatedly, each time partitioning off as much of **R** as can fit in a hash table in memory. After each scan of **R**, **S** is scanned and, for tuples corresponding to those in memory, a probe is made for a match (see Figure 3, simple hash-join).

The steps of our simple hash-join algorithm are

(1) Let $\mathbf{P} = \min(|\mathbf{M}|, |\mathbf{R}| * \mathbf{F})$. Choose a hash function h and a set of hash values so that **P/F** blocks of **R** tuples will hash into that set. Scan the (smaller) relation **R** and consider each tuple. If the tuple hashes into the chosen range, insert the tuple into a **P**-block hash table in memory. Otherwise, pass over the tuple and write it into a new file on disk.

(2) Scan the larger relation **S** and consider each tuple. If the tuple hashes into the chosen range, check the hash table of **R** tuples in memory for a match and output the pair if a match occurs. Otherwise, pass over the tuple and write it to disk. Note that if key values of the two relations are distributed similarly, there will be $P/F * |S|/|R|$ blocks of the larger relation **S** processed in this pass.

(3) Repeat steps (1) and (2), replacing each of the relations **R** and **S** by the set of tuples from **R** and **S** that were "passed over" and written to disk in the previous pass. The algorithm ends when no tuples from **R** are passed over.

This algorithm performs particularly well when most of **R** fits into main memory. In that case, most of **R** (and **S**) are touched only once, and only what cannot fit into memory is written out to disk and read in again. On the other hand, when there is little main memory this algorithm behaves poorly, since in that case there are many passes and both **R** and **S** are scanned over and over again. In fact, this algorithm operates as specified for any amount of memory, but to be consistent with the other hash-based algorithms we assume it is undefined for less than $\sqrt{F|R|}$ blocks of memory.

We assume here and elsewhere that the same hash function is used both for partitioning and for construction of the hash tables.

In the following formula and in later formulas we must estimate the number of compares required when the hash table is probed for a match. This amounts to estimating the number of collisions. We have chosen to use the term comp * **F** for the number of compares required. Although this term is too simple to be valid in general, when **F** is 1.4 (which is the value we use in our analytic modeling) it means that for a hash table with a load factor of 71 percent the estimated number of probes is 1.4. This is consistent with the simulations reported in [18].

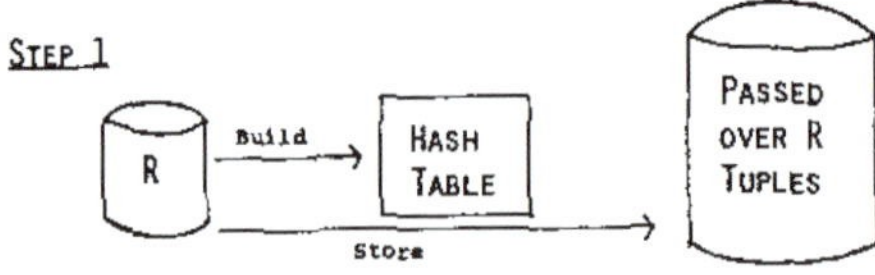

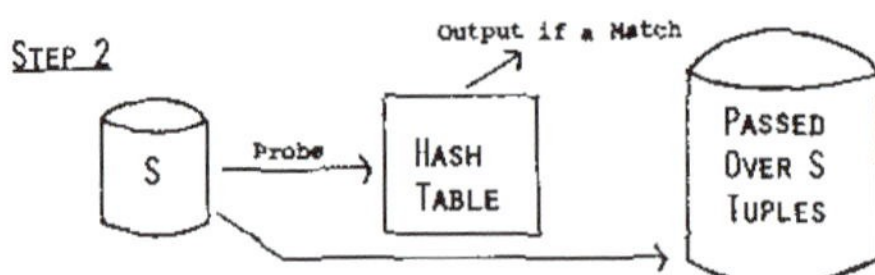

REPEAT STEPS 1 AND 2 WITH R, S REPLACED BY THE PASSED OVER TUPLES.

Fig. 3. Simple hash-join.

The algorithm requires

$$\left\lceil \frac{|R| * F}{|M|} \right\rceil$$

passes to execute, where ⌈ ⌉ denotes the ceiling function. We denote this quantity by **A**. Note that on the ith pass, $i = 1, \ldots, \mathbf{A} - 1$, there are

$$\{R\} - i * \frac{\{M\}_R}{F}$$

tuples of **R** passed over.

The cost of the algorithm is

$$+ \left[A * \{R\} - \frac{A * (A-1)}{2} * \frac{\{M\}_R}{F} \right] * (\text{hash} + \text{move}).$$

Hash and move **R** and passed-over tuples in R.

$$+ \left[A * \{S\} - \frac{A * (A-1)}{2} * \frac{\{M\}_S}{F} \right] * (\text{hash} + \text{move}).$$

Hash and move **S** and passed-over tuples in **S**.

$- \{S\} * \text{move}$ — On each pass, passed-over tuples of **S** are moved into the buffer and others result in probing the hash table for a match. The latter are not moved, yet they are counted as being moved in the previous term. This adjustment corrects that.

$+ \{\mathbf{S}\} * \text{comp} * \mathbf{F}$ — Check each tuple of **S** for a match.

$$+ \left[(A-1) * |R| - \frac{A * (A-1)}{2} * \frac{|M|}{F} \right] * 2 * \text{IO}.$$

Write and read passed-over tuples in **R**.

$$+ \left[(A-1) * |S| - \frac{A * (A-1)}{2} * \frac{|M|}{F} * \frac{|S|}{|R|} \right] * 2 * \text{IO}.$$

Write and read passed-over tuples in **S**.

2.4 GRACE Hash-Join Algorithm

As outlined in [14], the GRACE hash-join algorithm executes as two phases. The first phase begins by partitioning **R** and **S** into corresponding subsets, such that **R** is partitioned into sets of approximately equal size. During the second phase of the GRACE algorithm the join is performed using a hardware sorter to execute a sort-merge algorithm on each pair of sets in the partition.

Our version of the GRACE algorithm differs from that of [14] in two ways. First, we do joining in the second phase by hashing, instead of using hardware sorters. Second, we use only $\sqrt{F|R|}$ blocks of memory for both phases; the rest is used to store as much of the partitions as possible so they need not be written to disk and read back again. The algorithm proceeds as follows, assuming there are $\sqrt{F|R|}$ blocks of memory (see Figure 4):

(1) Choose a hash function h, and a partition of its hash values, so that **R** will be partitioned into $\sqrt{F|R|}$ subsets of approximately equal size.[1] Allocate $\sqrt{F|R|}$ blocks of memory, each to be an output buffer for one subset of the partition of **R**.

(2) Scan **R**. Using h, hash each tuple and place it in the appropriate output buffer. When an output buffer fills, it is written to disk. After **R** has been completely scanned, flush all output buffers to disk.

(3) Scan **S**. Using h, the same function used to partition **R**, hash each tuple and place in the appropriate output buffer. When an output buffer fills, it is written to disk. After **S** has been completely scanned, flush all output buffers to disk.

Steps (4) and (5) below are repeated for each set R_i, $1 \le i \le \sqrt{F|R|}$, in the partition for **R**, and its corresponding set S_i.

(4) Read R_i into memory and build a hash table for it.

We pause to check that a hash table for R_i can fit in memory. Assuming that all the sets R_i are of equal size, since there are $\sqrt{F|R|}$ of them, each of the sets R_i will be

$$\frac{|R|}{\sqrt{F|R|}} = \sqrt{\frac{|R|}{F}}$$

blocks in length. A hash table for each subset R_i will therefore require

$$F\sqrt{\frac{|R|}{F}} = \sqrt{F|R|}$$

blocks of memory, and we have assumed at least this much real memory.

(5) Hash each tuple of S_i with the same hash function used to build the hash table in (4). Probe for a match. If there is one, output the result tuple, otherwise proceed with the next tuple of S_i.

What if there are more or less than $\sqrt{F|R|}$ blocks of memory available? Just as with sort-merge-join, we do not consider the case when less than this minimum

[1] Our assumption, that a tuple of **S** joins with at most one block of tuples of **R**, is used here. If **R** contains many tuples with the same joining attribute value, then this partitioning may not be possible.

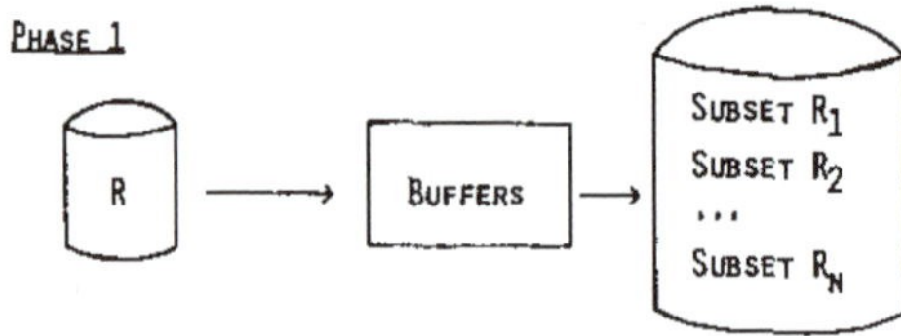

PHASE 1 IS REPEATED WITH S IN PLACE OF R.

Fig. 4. GRACE hash-join.

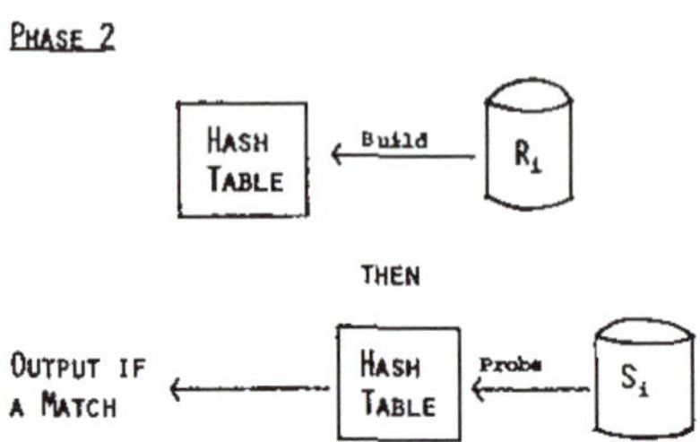

number of blocks is available, and if more blocks are available, we use them to store subsets of **R** and/or **S** so they need not be written to and read from disk.

This algorithm works very well when there is little memory available, because it avoids repeatedly scanning **R** and **S**, as is done in simple hash. Yet when most of **R** fits into memory, GRACE join does poorly since it scans both **R** and **S** twice.

One advantage of using hash in the second phase, instead of sort-merge, as is done by the designers of the GRACE machine, is that subsets of **S** can be of arbitrary size. Only **R** needs to be partitioned into subsets of approximately equal size. Since partition overflow can cause significant problems (see Section 4), this is an important advantage.

The cost of this algorithm is

$(\{\mathbf{R}\} + \{\mathbf{S}\} * (\text{hash} + \text{move})$ — Hash tuple and move to output buffer.

$+ (|\mathbf{R}| + |\mathbf{S}|) * \text{IO}$ — Write partitioned relations to disk.

$+ (|\mathbf{R}| + |\mathbf{S}|) * \text{IO}$ — Read partitioned sets.

$+ \{\mathbf{R}\} * (\text{hash} + \text{move})$ — Build hash tables in memory.

$+ \{\mathbf{S}\} * (\text{hash} + \text{comp} * \mathbf{F})$ — Probe for a match.

$- \min(|\mathbf{R}| + |\mathbf{S}|, |\mathbf{M}| \sqrt{F|R|}) * 2 * \text{IO}$ — IO savings if extra memory is available.

2.5 Hybrid Hash-Join Algorithm

Hybrid hash combines the features of the two preceding algorithms, doing both partitioning and hashing on the first pass over both relations. On the first pass, instead of using memory as a buffer as is done in the GRACE algorithm, only as many blocks (**B**, defined below) as are necessary to partition **R** into sets that can fit in memory are used. The rest of memory is used for a hash table that is processed at the same time that **R** and **S** are being partitioned (see Figure 5).

PHASE 1

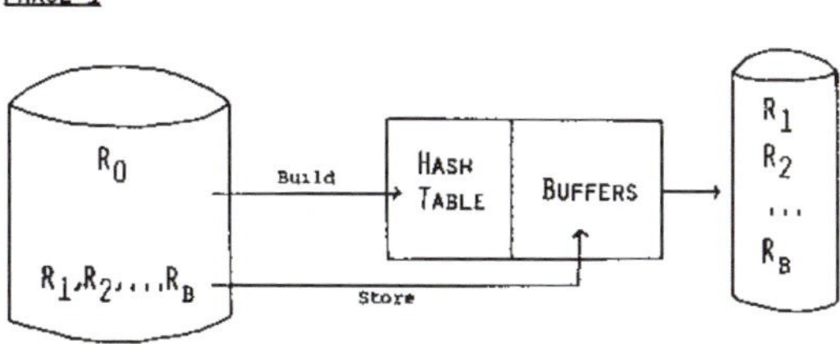

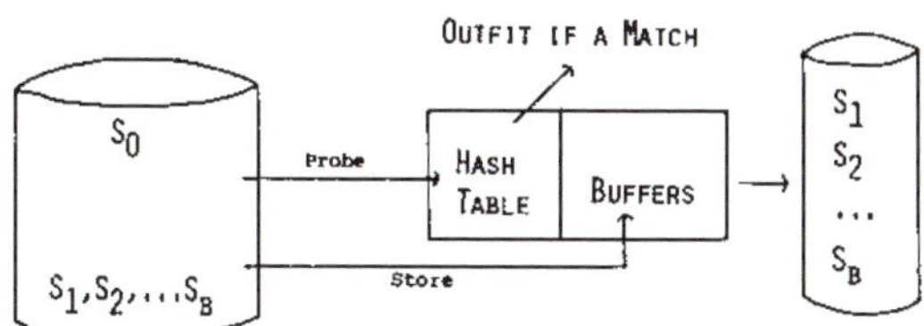

PHASE 2
SAME AS GRACE HASH JOIN.

Fig. 5. Hybrid hash-join.

Here are the steps of the hybrid hash algorithm. If $|R| * F \leq M$, then a hash table for **R** will fit in real memory, and hybrid hash is identical to simple hash in this case.

(1) Let

$$\mathbf{B} = \left\lceil \frac{|R| * F - |M|}{|M| - 1} \right\rceil.$$

There will be **B** + 1 steps in the hybrid hash algorithm. (To motivate the formula for **B**, we note that it is approximately equal to the number of steps in simple hash. The small difference is due to setting aside some real memory in phase 1 for a hash table for R_0.) First, choose a hash function h and a partition of its hash values which will partition **R** into $R_0, \ldots, R_B$, such that a hash table for R_0 has | **M** | − **B** blocks, and $R_1, \ldots, R_B$ are of equal size. Then allocate **B** blocks in memory to **B** output buffers. Assign the other | **M** | − **B** blocks of memory to a hash table for R_0.

(2) Assign the ith output buffer block to R_i for $i = 1, \ldots,$ **B**. Scan **R**. Hash each tuple with h. If it belongs to R_0 it will be placed in memory in a hash table. Otherwise it belongs to R_i for some $i > 0$, so move it to the ith output buffer block. When this step has finished, we have a hash table for R_0 in memory, and $R_1, \ldots, R_B$ are on disk.

(3) The partition of **R** corresponds to a partition of **S** compatible with h, into sets $S_0, \ldots, S_B$. Assign the ith output buffer block to S_i for $i = 1, \ldots,$ **B**. Scan **S**, hashing each tuple with h. If the tuple is in S_0, probe the hash table in memory for a match. If there is a match, output the result tuple, otherwise drop the tuple. If the tuple is not in S_0, it belongs to S_i for some $i > 0$, so move it to the ith output buffer block. Now $R_1, \ldots, R_B$ and $S_1, \ldots, S_B$ are on disk.

Repeat steps (4) and (5) for $i = 1, \ldots, \mathbf{B}$.

(4) Read R_i and build a hash table for it in memory.

(5) Scan S_i, hashing each tuple, and probing the hash table for R_i, which is in memory. If there is a match, output the result tuple, otherwise toss the **S** tuple.

We omit the computation that shows that a hash table for R_i will actually fit in memory. It is similar to the above computation for the GRACE join algorithm.

For the cost computation, denote by q the quotient $|R_0|/|R|$, namely the fraction of **R** represented by R_0. To calculate the cost of this join we need to know the size of S_0, and we estimate it to be $q * |\mathbf{S}|$. Then the fraction of **R** and **S** sets remaining on the disk after step (3) is $1 - q$. The cost of the hybrid hash join is

$(\{\mathbf{R}\} + \{\mathbf{S}\}) * \text{hash}$	Partition **R** and **S**.
$+ (\{\mathbf{R}\} + \{\mathbf{S}\}) * (1 - q) * \text{move}$	Move tuples to output buffers.
$+ (|\mathbf{R}| + |\mathbf{S}|) * (1 - q) * \text{IO}$	Write from output buffers.
$+ (|\mathbf{R}| + |\mathbf{S}|) * (1 - q) * \text{IO}$	Read subsets into memory.
$+ (\{\mathbf{R}\} + \{\mathbf{S}\}) * (1 - q) * \text{hash}$	Build hash tables for **R** and hash to probe for **S** during (4) and (5).
$+ \{\mathbf{R}\} * \text{move}$	Move tuples to hash tables for **R**.
$+ \{\mathbf{S}\} * \text{comp} * F$	Probe for each tuple of **S**.

At the cost of some complexity, each of the above algorithms could be improved by not flushing buffers at the end of phase 1. The effect of this change is analyzed in Section 5.

3. COMPARISON OF THE FOUR JOIN ALGORITHMS

We begin by showing that when **R** and **S** are sufficiently large the hybrid algorithm dominates the other two hash-based join algorithms, then we show that hybrid also dominates sort-merge for sufficiently large relations. In fact, we also show that GRACE dominates sort-merge, except in some cases where **R** and **S** are close in size. Finally, we present results of analytic modeling of the four algorithms. Our assumption that **R** (and therefore **S**) are sufficiently large, along with our previous assumption that $|\mathbf{M}|$ is at least $\sqrt{|S|}$ (sort-merge) of $\sqrt{F\,|R|}$ (hash-based algorithms) means that we can also assume $|\mathbf{M}|$ to be large. The precise definition of "large" depends on system parameters, but it will typically suffice that $\{\mathbf{R}\}$ be at least 1000 and $|\mathbf{M}|$ at least 5.

First we indicate why hybrid dominates simple hash-join. We assume less than half of a hash table for **R** fits in memory because otherwise the hybrid and simple join algorithms are identical. Denoting $|\mathbf{R}| * \mathbf{F}/2 - |\mathbf{M}|$ by **E**, our assumption means that $\mathbf{E} > 0$. If we ignore for a moment the space requirements for the output buffers for both simple and hybrid hash, the I/O and CPU costs for both methods are identical, except that some tuples written to disk in the simple hash-join are processed[2] more than once, whereas each is processed only once in hybrid

[2] By *processing* we mean, for tuples of **R**, one hash and one move of each tuple plus one read and one write for each block. For **S** tuples we mean one hash and one move or compare per tuple plus two I/Os per block.

hash-join. In fact, $|\mathbf{R}| - 2 * |\mathbf{M}|/\mathbf{F} = \mathbf{2} * \mathbf{E}/\mathbf{F}$ blocks of **R** will be processed more than once by simple hash (and similarly for some **S** tuples). So far hybrid is ahead by the cost of processing at least $2 * \mathbf{E}/\mathbf{F}$ blocks of tuples. Now consider the space requirements for output buffers, which we temporarily ignored above. Simple hash uses only one output buffer. Hybrid uses approximately $(|\mathbf{R}| * \mathbf{F}/|\mathbf{M}|) - 1$ output buffers,[3] that is, $(|\mathbf{R}| * \mathbf{F}/\mathbf{M}|) - 2$ more than simple hash-join uses, and $|\mathbf{R}| * \mathbf{F}/|\mathbf{M}| - 2 = 2\mathbf{E}/|\mathbf{M}|$. Therefore hybrid must process the extra $2 * \mathbf{E}/|\mathbf{M}|$ blocks in the second phase, since space for them is taken up by buffers. In total, hybrid is ahead by the cost of processing $(2 * \mathbf{E}/\mathbf{F}) - (2 * \mathbf{E}/|\mathbf{M}|)$ blocks,which is clearly a positive number. We conclude that hybrid dominates simple hash-join.

Next we indicate why hybrid dominates GRACE. If we compare the cost formulas, they are identical in CPU time, except that some terms in the hybrid cost formula are multiplied by $(1 - q)$. Since $q \leq 1$, hybrid dominates GRACE in CPU costs. The two algorithms read and write the following number of blocks:

$$\text{GRACE: } |\mathbf{R}| + |\mathbf{S}| - \min(|\mathbf{R} + |\mathbf{S}|, |\mathbf{M}| - \sqrt{F|R|}).$$
$$\text{Hybrid: } |\mathbf{R}| + |\mathbf{S}| - q * (|\mathbf{R}| + |\mathbf{S}|).$$

To show that I/O costs for GRACE are greater than those for hybrid, it suffices to prove that

$$q * (|\mathbf{R}| + |\mathbf{S}|) > |\mathbf{M}| - \sqrt{F|R|}.$$

Since $|\mathbf{S}| > 0$, we can discard it in the preceding formula. Since $q * |\mathbf{R}| = |R_0| = |\mathbf{M}| - \mathbf{B}$, it suffices to prove that

$$\sqrt{F|R|} \geq \mathbf{B}.$$

But **B** was the least number of buffers necessary to partition $\mathbf{R} - R_0$ into sets which fit in memory. From the description of the GRACE algorithm we know that $\sqrt{F|R|}$ buffers are always enough to partition all of **R** into sets which can fit in memory, so **B** cannot be more than $\sqrt{F|R|}$.

We have proved that hybrid dominates both the simple and the GRACE hash-join algorithms. Now we compare the hash-join algorithms with sort-merge.

When a hash table for **R** can fit in main memory, it is clear that hybrid hash will outperform sort-merge. This is because when a hash table for **R** can fit in real memory there are no I/O costs, and CPU costs are, with slight rearranging:

$$\text{Hybrid: } \begin{cases} \{\mathbf{R}\} * [\text{hash} + \text{move}] + \\ \{\mathbf{S}\} * [\text{hash} + \text{comp} * \mathbf{F}]. \end{cases}$$

$$\text{Sort: } \begin{cases} \{\mathbf{R}\} * [\text{comp} + (\log_2\{\mathbf{R}\}) * (\text{comp} + \text{swap})] + \\ \{\mathbf{S}\} * [\text{comp} + (\log_2\{\mathbf{S}\}) * (\text{comp} + \text{swap})]. \end{cases}$$

Since the times to hash and to compare are similar on any system, and swap is more expensive than move or comp $*$ **F**, the log terms will force sort-merge to be more costly except when **R** is very small.

[3] Here we have used the formula for **B** above, and have assumed $|\mathbf{M}|$ is large enough that $|\mathbf{M}| - 1$ can be approximated by $|\mathbf{M}|$.

comp	compare keys	3 microseconds
hash	hash a key	9 microseconds
move	move a tuple	20 microseconds
swap	swap two tuples	60 microseconds
IO	read/write of a block	30 milliseconds
F	incremental factor	1.4
$\|\mathbf{R}\|$	size of **R**	800 blocks
$\|\mathbf{S}\|$	size of **S**	1600 blocks
$\{\mathbf{R}\}/\|\mathbf{R}\|$	number of **R** tuples/block	250
$\{\mathbf{S}\}/\|\mathbf{S}\|$	number of **S** tuples/block	250
	block size	25,000 bytes

Fig. 6. System parameters used in modeling in this paper.

To show that GRACE typically dominates sort-merge, the previous argument can be extended as follows: first we show that GRACE typically has lower I/O costs than sort-merge. The runs generated by sort-merge and the subsets generated by GRACE are of the same size in total, namely $|\mathbf{R}| + |\mathbf{S}|$, so when memory is at the minimum ($\sqrt{|S|}$ for sort-merge and $\sqrt{F\,|R|}$ for GRACE), I/O costs, which consist of writing and reading the runs or subsets, are identical. More real memory results in equal savings, so GRACE has higher I/O costs only if $\sqrt{F\,|R|} > \sqrt{|S|}$, which is atypical since $|\mathbf{R}|$ is the smaller relation.

Next we compare the CPU costs of GRACE and sort-merge. The CPU cost of GRACE is

$$\text{GRACE: } \begin{cases} \{\mathbf{R}\} * (2 * \text{hash} + 2 * \text{move}) + \\ \{\mathbf{S}\} * (2 * \text{hash} + \text{comp} * \mathbf{F} + \text{move}). \end{cases}$$

As with hybrid's CPU time, the coefficients of $\{\mathbf{R}\}$ and $\{\mathbf{S}\}$ are similar except for the logarithm terms, which force sort-merge to be more costly. We conclude that GRACE dominates sort-merge except when **R** is small or when $\sqrt{F\,|R|} > \sqrt{|S|}$.

We have modeled the performance of the four join algorithms by numerically evaluating our formulas for a sample set of system parameters given in Figure 6. We should note that all the modelings of the hash-based algorithms are somewhat optimistic, since we have assumed no partition overflow. We discuss in Section 4 ways to deal with partition overflow.

In Figure 7 we display the relative performance of the four join algorithms as described above. As we have noted, each algorithm requires a minimum amount of main memory. For the relations modeled in Figure 7, the minimum memory size for sort-merge is 1.1 megabytes, and for hash-based algorithms the minimum memory size is 0.8 megabytes.

Among hash algorithms, simple and our modification of GRACE join each perform as expected, with simple doing well for high memory values and GRACE for low memory. Hybrid dominates both, as we have shown above.

The curves for simple and hybrid hash-join level off at just above 20 megabytes, when a hash table for **R** fits in main memory. It is an easy matter to modify the GRACE hash algorithms so that, if this occurs, then GRACE defaults to the simple algorithm; thus GRACE and simple would be identical above that point.

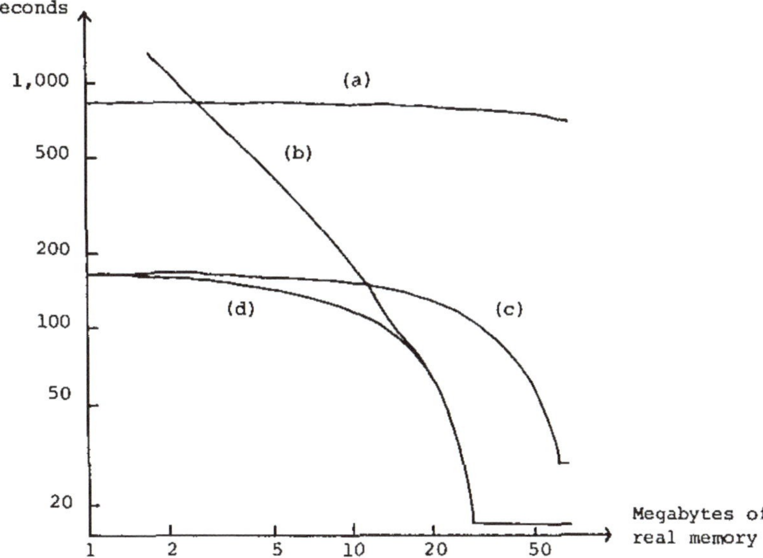

Fig. 7. CPU + I/O times of join algorithms with $|\mathbf{R}| = 20$ megabytes, $|\mathbf{S}| = 40$ megabytes. (a) Sort-merge, (b) simple hash, (c) GRACE hash, (d) hybrid hash. Simple and hybrid hash are identical after 13 megabytes.

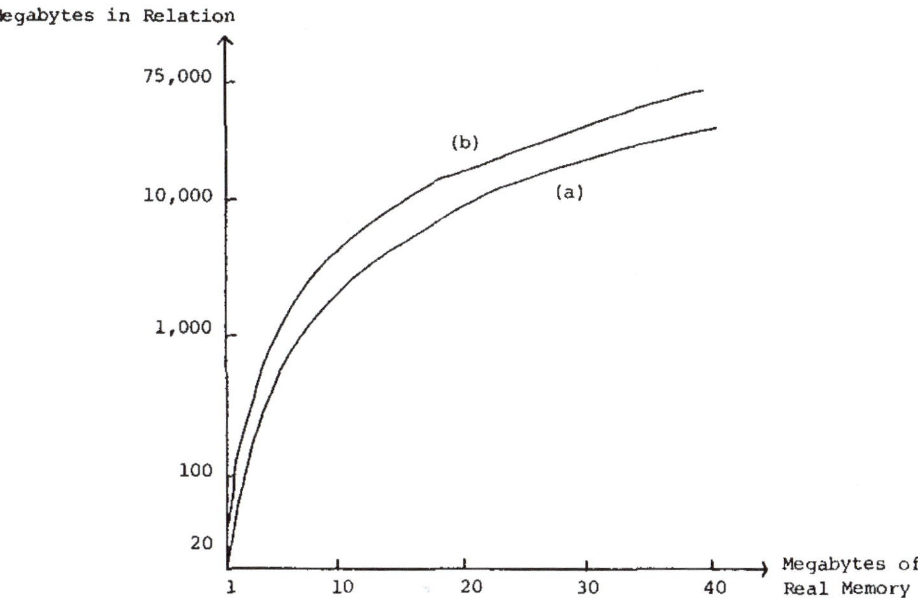

Fig. 8. Maximum relation sizes for varying amounts of main memory. (a) Sort-merge (larger relation), (b) hash-based (smaller relation).

Our algorithms require a minimum number of blocks of real memory, either $\sqrt{|S|}$ (sort-merge) or $\sqrt{F\,|R|}$ (hash-based algorithms). Therefore, for a given number of blocks of main memory there is a maximum relation size that can be processed by these algorithms. Figure 8 shows these maximum sizes when the

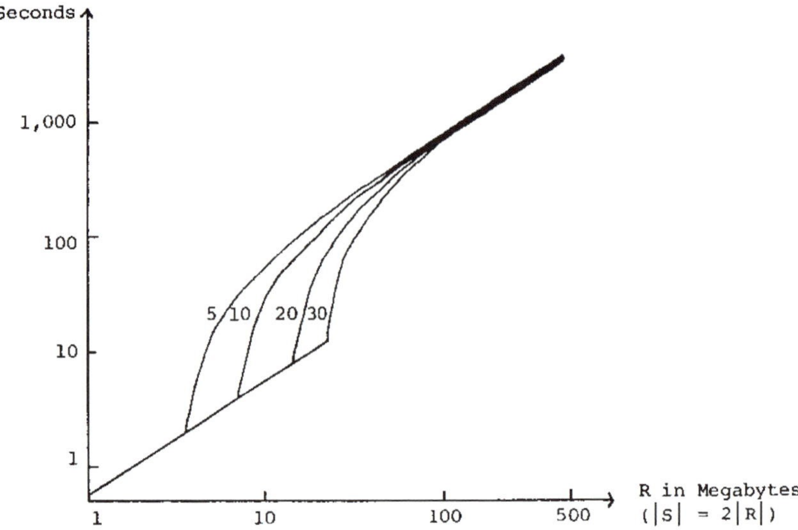

Fig. 9. CPU + I/O time of the hybrid algorithm with 5, 10, 20, and 30 megabytes of real memory.

block size is 25,000 bytes and **F** is 1.4. Note that the sort-merge curve represents the maximum size of the larger relation, while curve (b) shows the maximum size of the smaller relation for the hash-based algorithms.

Figure 9 shows the performance of the hybrid algorithm for a few fixed-memory sizes, as relation sizes vary. Note that when the relation **R** can fit in main memory, the execution time is not very large: less than 12 seconds for relations up to 20 megabytes (excluding, as we always do, the time required to read **R** and **S** and write the result, but assuming no CPU I/O overlap). It is also clear from Figure 9 that when the size of main memory is much less than the size of **R**, performance degrades rapidly.

4. PARTITION OVERFLOW

In all the hashing algorithms that use partitioning, namely simple, GRACE, and hybrid hash, we have made assumptions about the expected size of the subsets of the partitions. For example, in the simple hash-join algorithm, when the relation **R** cannot fit in memory, we assumed that we could choose a hash function *h* and a partition of its hash values that will partition **R** into two subsets, so that a hash table for the first subset would fit exactly into memory. What happens if we guess incorrectly, and memory fills up with the hash table before we are finished processing **R**?

In [14] this problem is called "bucket overflow." We use the term "partition overflow" because we want to distinguish between the subsets of the partitions of **R** and **S**, produced in the first phase of processing, and the buckets of the hash table of **R** tuples, produced in the second phase, even though both are really hash buckets.

The designers of GRACE deal with overflow by the use of "tuning" (i.e., beginning with very small partitions, and then, when the size of the smaller partitions is known, combining them into larger partitions of the appropriate size). This approach is also possible in our environment. We present other approaches below.

In all our hash-based algorithms, each tuple of **S** in phase 1 is either used for probing and then discarded, or copied to disk for later use. In phase 2, the remaining tuples on disk are processed sequentially. Since an entire partition of **S** never needs to reside in main memory (as is the case for partitions of **R**), the size of **S**-partitions is of no consequence. Thus we need only find an accurate partitioning of **R**.

To partition **R**, we can begin by choosing a hash function h with the usual randomizing properties. If we know nothing about the distribution of the joining attribute values in **R**, we can assume a uniform distribution and choose a partition of h's hash values accordingly. It is also possible to store statistics about the distribution of h-values. In [16] a similar distribution statistic is studied, where the identity function is used instead of a hash function, and it is shown that using sampling techniques one can collect such distribution statistics on all attributes of a large commercial database in a reasonable time.

Even with the problem reduced to partitioning **R** only, with a good choice of h and with accurate statistics, overflow will occur. In the remainder of this section we show how to handle the three kinds of partition overflow that occur in our algorithms.

4.1 Partition Overflow on Disk

In two algorithms, GRACE and hybrid hash, partitions of **R** are created in disk files, partitions which will later be required to fit in memory. In both algorithms these partitions were denoted $R_1, \ldots, R_n$, where $n = \sqrt{F\,|R|}$ for GRACE and $n = \mathbf{B}$ for hybrid. After these partitions are created, it is possible that some of them will be so large that a hash table for them cannot fit in memory.

If one **R** partition on disk overflows, that partition can be reprocessed. It can be scanned and partitioned again, into two pieces, so that a hash table for each will fit in memory. Alternatively, an attempt can be made to partition it into one piece that will just fit, and another that can be added to a partition that turned out to be smaller than expected. Note that a similar adjustment must be made to the corresponding partition of **S**, so that the partitions of **R** and **S** will correspond pairwise to the same hash values.

4.2 Partition Overflow in Memory: Simple Hash

In simple hash, as **R** is processed, a hash table of **R** tuples is built in memory. What if the hash table turns out to be too large to fit in memory? The simplest solution is to reassign some buckets, presently in memory, to the set of "passed-over" tuples on disk, then continue processing. This amounts to modifying the partitioning hash function slightly. Then the modified hash function will be used to process **S**.

4.3 Partition Overflow in Memory: Hybrid Hash

In hybrid hash, as **R** is processed on step 1, a hash table is created from tuples of R_0. What if R_0 turns out to be too large to fit into the memory that remains after some blocks are allocated to output buffers? The solution here is similar to the simple hash case: reassign some buckets to a new partition on disk. This new partition can be handled just like the others, or it can be spread over others if some partitions are smaller than expected. All this is done before **S** is processed, so the modified partitioning function can be used to process **S**.

5. MEMORY MANAGEMENT STRATEGIES

In this section we consider an alternate memory management strategy for our algorithms. For simplicity we discuss only sort-merge and hybrid hash-join in this section. The behavior of GRACE and simple hash are similar to the behaviors we describe here. We begin in Section 5.1 by describing the weaknesses of the "all real memory" model of the previous sections, where a process was allocated a fixed amount of real memory for its lifetime and the amount of real memory was known to the process. In Section 5.2 we consider virtual memory as an alternative to this simple strategy, with at least a minimum amount of real memory as a "hot set." In Section 5.3 we describe how parts of the data space are assigned to the hot set and to virtual memory, and in Section 5.4 we analyze the impact of this new model on performance. Section 5.5 presents the results of an analytic modeling of performance.

5.1 Problems with an All Real Memory Strategy

Until this section we have assumed a memory management strategy in which each join operation (which we view as a single process) is assigned a certain amount of real memory and that memory is available to it throughout its life. Based on the amount of memory granted by the memory manager (denoted $|\mathbf{M}|$ in Section 2), a strategy will be chosen for processing the join. The key here is knowledge of the amount of memory available. Each of the algorithms we have described above depends significantly on the amount of memory available to the process. There are several problems inherent in designing such a memory manager.

(1) If only one process requests memory space, how much of available memory should be allocated to it? In order to answer this question the memory manager must predict how many and what kind of other processes will require memory before this process completes.

(2) If several processes request memory, how should it be allocated among them? This is probably a simple optimization problem if each process can present to the memory manager an efficiency graph, telling the time the process will take to complete given various possible memory allocations.

(3) If all of memory is taken by active processes, and a new process requests memory, the new process will have to wait until memory is available. This is an intolerable situation in many scenarios. Swapping out a process is not acceptable in general since such large amounts of memory are involved.

As was shown in Figure 8, our algorithms can join huge relations with only a few megabytes of memory. Thus one might argue that the relatively small amounts of real memory needed are affordable in a system with a large main memory. But as one can see from Figures 7 and 9, excellent performance is achieved only when the amount of real memory is close to the size of the smaller (hybrid) or larger (sort-merge) relation. In general it will not be possible to allocate to each join process an amount of memory near the size of the smaller relation.

5.2 The Hot Set + Virtual Memory Model

One obvious solution to the problems just described is to assign each process all the memory it requests, but in virtual memory, and to let active processes compete for real memory via LRU or some other page-replacement algorithm.

If a process, which is executing a relational operator, is forced to compete for pages with other processes via the usual LRU algorithm, severe thrashing can result. This is pointed out in [17] and in [20], where a variety of relational operators are discussed. Sacco and Scholnick [17] propose to assign each process a certain number of pages (the "hot-set size") which are not subject to demand paging. The hot-set size is estimated by the access planner, and is determined as the point below which a sharp increase in processing time occurs—as the hot-set size varies with each relation and each strategy, it must be estimated by the access planner. Stonebraker [20] proposes allowing the database system to override the usual LRU replacement algorithm when appropriate. We find that a combination of these two approaches best suits our needs.

The algorithms discussed in this paper lend themselves to a hot-set approach since below a certain real memory size ($\sqrt{F \mid R \mid}$ or $\sqrt{\mid S \mid}$) our algorithms behave very poorly.

Therefore, we adopt a similar strategy to that of [17], in that we expect each process to have a certain number of "hot-set" pages guaranteed to it throughout its lifetime. Those hot-set pages will be "wired down" in real memory for the lifetime of the process. A facility for wiring down pages in a buffer is proposed in [9]. The rest of the data space of the process will be assigned to virtual memory. In the next section we describe what is assigned to the hot set and what to virtual memory.

5.3 T and C

Recall that each of the algorithms sort-merge and hybrid hash-join operates in two phases, first processing **R** and **S** and creating either runs or partitions, and secondly reading these runs and partitions and processing them to create the join. Each algorithm's data space also splits into two pieces.

The first piece, which we denote **T** (for Tables), consists of a hash table or a priority queue, plus buffers to input or output the partitions or runs. The second piece of the algorithm's data, which we denote **C** (for Cache), is the partitions or runs generated during phase 1 and read during phase 2.

For sort-merge, as described in Section 2, **T** was fixed in size at $\sqrt{\mid S \mid}$ blocks. If more than $\sqrt{\mid S \mid}$ blocks of real memory were available for sort-merge, the remainder was used to store some or all of **C**, to save I/O costs. The blocks of **C** not assigned to real memory were stored on disk. For hybrid, **T** occupied as much real memory as was available (except that **T** was always between $\sqrt{F \mid R \mid}$ and $\mathbf{F} * \mid \mathbf{R} \mid$ blocks).

Since all of **T** is accessed randomly, and in fact each tuple processed by either algorithm generates a random access to **T**, we assign **T** to the hot set. This means that the join process needs at least $\sqrt{|S|}$ or $\sqrt{F\,|R|}$ blocks of real memory to hold **T**. By Figure 8, we can see that $\sqrt{|S|}$ or $\sqrt{F\,|R|}$ blocks of memory is a reasonable amount. In the case of sort-merge, if additional space is available in the hot set, then some of **C** will be assigned there. For simplicity, henceforth in the case of sort-merge we let **C** refer to the set of runs stored in virtual memory.

For both hybrid and sort-merge join, **C** will be assigned to virtual memory. The hot set + virtual memory model of this section differs from that of the previous sections by substituting virtual memory for disk storage. This allows the algorithms to run with relatively small amounts of wired-down memory, but also to take advantage of other real memory shared with other processes.

To distinguish the algorithms we discuss here from those of Section 2, we append the suffix RM (for Real Memory) to the algorithms of Section 2, which use all real memory, and VM for the variants here, in which **C** is stored in Virtual Memory.

5.4 What Are the Disadvantages of Placing C in Virtual Memory?

Let us suppose that the virtual memory in which **C** resides includes $|\mathbf{C}| * \mathbf{Q}$ blocks of real memory, where $\mathbf{Q} \leq 1$. The quantity **Q** can change during the execution of the algorithm, but for simplicity we assume it to be constant.

What are the potential disadvantages of storing **C** in virtual memory? There are two. The first concerns the blocking factor of one track that we have chosen. In the VM algorithms, where **C** is assigned to virtual memory, during phase 1, in order to take advantage of all $|\mathbf{C}| * \mathbf{Q}$ blocks of real memory, and not knowing what **Q** is, the algorithms should write all $|\mathbf{C}|$ blocks to virtual memory and let the memory manager page out $|\mathbf{C}| * (1 - \mathbf{Q})$ of those blocks. But if the memory manager pages out one page at a time, it may not realize the savings from writing one track at a time. This will result in a higher I/O cost. On the other hand, paging is supported by much more efficient mechanisms than normal I/O. For simplicity, we assume this trade-off results in no net change in I/O costs.

The second possible disadvantage of assigning **C** to virtual memory concerns the usual LRU paging criterion. At the end of phase 1, in the VM algorithms $|\mathbf{C}| * \mathbf{Q}$ blocks of **C** will reside in real memory and $|\mathbf{C}| * (1 - \mathbf{Q})$ blocks on disk. Ideally, all $|\mathbf{C}| * \mathbf{Q}$ blocks will be processed in phase 2 directly from real memory, without having to be written and then read back from disk. As we see below, the usual LRU paging algorithm plays havoc with our plans, paging out many of the $|\mathbf{C}| * \mathbf{Q}$ blocks to disk before they can be processed, and leaving in memory blocks that are no longer of use. This causes a more significant problem. To analyze LRU's behavior more precisely, we must study the access pattern of **C** as it is written to virtual memory and then read back into **T** for processing.

We must estimate how many of the $|\mathbf{C}| * \mathbf{Q}$ blocks in real memory at the end of phase 1 will be paged out before they can be processed. We first consider Hybrid-VM.

In the special case of Hybrid-VM, when $\mathbf{F} * |\mathbf{R}| \leq 2\,|\mathbf{M}|$, that is, when only R_0 and perhaps R_1 are constructed, unnecessary paging can be avoided completely. Then $\mathbf{C} = R_1$, or **C** is empty, so **C** consists of one subset and can be read back in phase 2 in any order. In particular, it can be read back in the opposite order from which it was written, thus reading all the in-memory blocks first. Therefore, for

Hybrid-VM, in case **F** | **R** | ≤ 2 | **M** | and in case the process' resident size does not change, all of the | **C** | * **Q** blocks in real memory at the end of phase 1 will be processed before they are paged out.

In the remaining cases of Hybrid-VM, when **F** | **R** | > 2 | **M** |, there are more than two subsets R_i constructed, that is, **B** > 1 (**B** is defined in Section 2.5). The **B** subsets are produced in parallel in phase 1 and read back serially in phase 2. This parallel/serial behavior will cause poor real-memory usage under LRU, as we shall see. To see this, consider the end of phase 1 in Hybrid-VM, which is the time at which all of **C** has been created. | **C** | * **Q** blocks of **C** are in real memory and | **C** | * (1 − **Q**) blocks are on disk, and the algorithm is about to read **C** for processing. After phase 2 has begun and **C** has been processed for a while, the part of **C** which remains in real memory consists of

C_1: These tuples were on disk at the end of phase 1, and have been read into real memory and processed.

C_2: These tuples were in real memory at the end of phase 1. They have been processed and are no longer needed by the algorithm in phase 2.

C_3: These tuples were in real memory at the end of phase 1. They have not yet been processed in phase 2.

What will happen next, assuming that phase 2 needs to read a block from disk, and therefore to page out a page in memory? If the system uses the usual LRU algorithm, then since the tuples in C_3 were all used less recently than those in C_1 and C_2, the memory manager will choose a page from C_3 to page out, which is exactly the *opposite* of what we would like! This "worst" behavior is pointed out in [20].

Figure 10 gives an intuitive picture of why only | **C** | * Q^2 blocks are read directly from real memory in the case we are discussing, namely Hybrid-VM with **B** > 1. Figure 10 shows the state of the system at the point in phase 2 of Hybrid-VM at which C_3 first becomes empty. After this point all unprocessed tuples of **C** are on disk, and so all requests for tuples from **C** will cause a page fault. Before this point requests for tuples from **C** might not cause a page fault, if those tuples were in real memory at the beginning of phase 2. The set D_1 denotes the location of the tuples of C_1 before they were read onto disk. Since the number of bytes in C_1 and D_1 are equal, a little algebra shows that x must be **Q** * **B**, and then that there are | **C** | * Q^2 blocks in C_2. Thus only | **C** | * Q^2 blocks have been read directly from real memory.

This argument is based on the ideal picture of Figure 10. In practice, the sets C_1, D_1, and C_2 in Figure 10 have jagged edges, and the argument we have given is not precise. However, it can be shown that this argument is valid if **B** is large and if the subsets are created at uniform speed, by the partitioning process in phase 1. This analysis indicates that in Hybrid-VM, at least when **B** is large, only | **C** | * Q^2 blocks are read directly from real memory.

A similar analysis is valid for sort-merge, based on the fact that runs in sort-merge are produced serially and read back in parallel, with a similar | **C** | * Q^2 conclusion.

Is there a way to avoid this poor paging behavior? One relatively simple technique, called "throw immediately" in [20], is to mark a page of **C** as "aged'

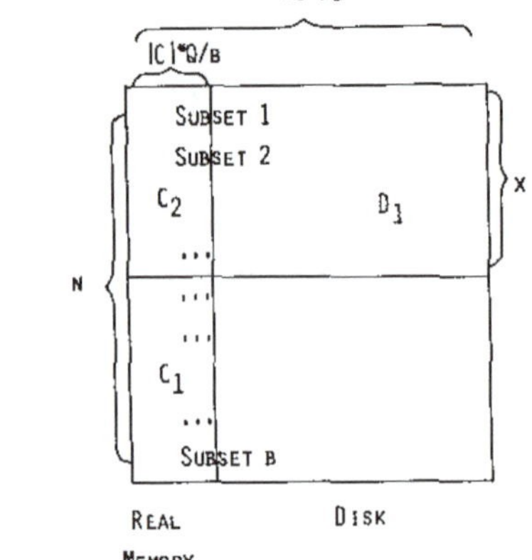

Fig. 10. Hybrid hash-join in virtual memory with LRU.

after it has been read into **T**, so that when part of **C** needs to be paged out the system will take the artificially aged page instead of a yet unprocessed page. With this page-aging facility, a full $|\mathbf{C}| * \mathbf{Q}$ blocks of **C** will be read directly from real memory and will generate I/O savings.

5.5 Performance in the Hot Set + Virtual Memory Model

Figure 11 presents the results of an analytic modeling of Hybrid-VM, assuming that 5 megabytes of real memory are allocated to the hot set where **T** resides, and other real memory is used to support the virtual memory in which **C** resides. In graph (a), we have assumed that only $|\mathbf{C}|\ Q^2$ blocks of $|\mathbf{R}|$ are read directly from real memory, as would be the case if LRU were used. In (b) we assume $|\mathbf{C}| * Q$ blocks of **C** are read from real memory, as would be the case if page-aging were used.

According to Figure 11, the most efficient processing, with all real memory, requires 28 megabytes and takes 16 seconds, compared to 54 megabytes and 25 seconds when virtual memory is used, with the hot-set size of 5 megabytes. More memory is needed when virtual memory is used because in that case subsets from both **R** and **S** are stored.

One way to explain the poorer performance of graph 11(b) compared to graph 11(c) is to view 11(b) as the result of reducing the size of the hot set, and therefore **T**. When the hot set is large (e.g., when it can hold a hash table for **R**) no virtual memory is needed, and performance is given by (c) at its minimum CPU + I/O time. As the hot-set size decreases, performance degrades. At the minimum, when the hot-set size is $\sqrt{F\,|R|}$, hybrid's performance in the hot set + virtual memory model is identical to that of GRACE, since the algorithms for GRACE and hybrid in Section 2 are identical when $|\mathbf{M}| = \sqrt{F\,|R|}$.

The performance of sort-merge in the hot set + virtual memory model with LRU plus page-aging is identical to the all real memory case, because sort-merge uses real memory, beyond the $\sqrt{|S|}$ blocks needed for **T** to store **C** and save I/O. Therefore, only $\sqrt{|S|}$ blocks of real memory should be assigned to the hot set for sort-merge.

We conclude that if page-aging is possible, then the performance of sort-merge is unaffected in the hot set + virtual memory model, but the performance of the

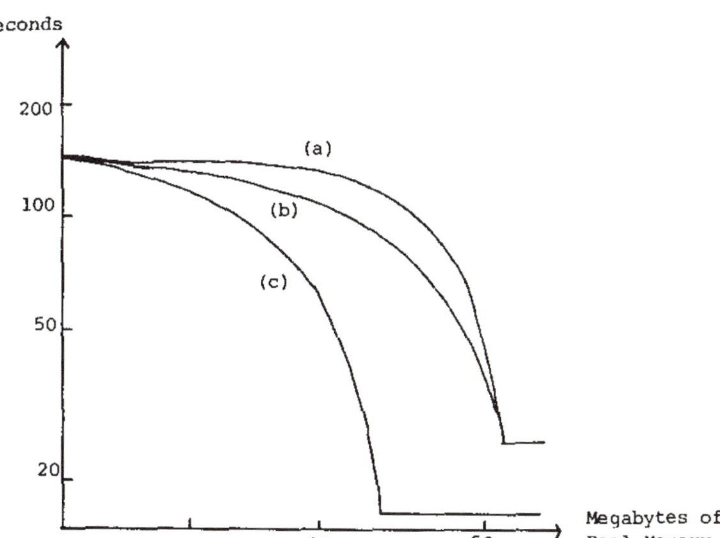

Fig. 11. CPU + I/O time of Hybrid algorithm for varying amounts of memory. | **R** | = 20 megabytes, | **S** | = 40 megabytes. For (a) and (b), hot-set size is 5 megabytes. (a) Hybrid-VM with LRU, (b) Hybrid-VM with page-aging, (c) Hybrid-RM: all real memory.

hybrid join degrades, as the hot-set size decreases, to the performance of GRACE. Since we have shown, in Section 3, that GRACE typically dominates sort-merge, we conclude that hybrid typically dominates sort-merge, even in the hot set + virtual memory model.

6. OTHER TOOLS

In this section we discuss three tools that have been proposed to increase the efficiency of join processing, namely database filters, Babb arrays, and semijoins. Our objective is to show that all of them can be used equally effectively with any of our algorithms.

Database filters [19] are an important tool to make database managers more efficient. Filters are a mechanism to process records as they come off the disk, and send to the database only those which qualify. Filters can be used easily with our algorithms, since we have made no assumption about how the selections and projections of the relations **R** and **S** are made before the join.

Another popular tool is the Babb array [1]. This idea is closely related to the concept of partitioning which we have described in Section 2. As **R** is processed, a boolean array is built. Each bit in the array corresponds to a hash bucket, and the bit is turned on when an **R** tuple hashes into that bucket. Then, as each tuple s from **S** is processed, the boolean array is checked, and if s falls in a bucket for which there are no **R** tuples, the s tuple can be discarded without checking **R** itself. This is a very powerful tool when relatively few tuples qualify for the join.

The Babb array can easily be added to any of our algorithms. The first time **R** is scanned, the array is built, and when **S** is scanned, some tuples can be discarded. Its greatest cost is for space to store the array. Given a limited space in which to store the array, another problem is to find a hash function to use in constructing the array so that the array will carry maximum information. It is possible to use several hash functions and an array for each, to increase the information, but with limited space this alternative allows each hash function a smaller array and therefore less information. Babb arrays are most useful when the join has a high selectivity (i.e., when there are few matching tuples).

Finally, we discuss the semijoin [2]. This is often regarded as an alternative way to do joins, but as we shall see it is a special case of a more general tool. The semijoin is constructed as follows.

(1) Construct the projection of **R** on its joining attributes. We denote this projection by $\pi(R)$.
(2) Join $\pi(R)$ to **S**. The result is called the semijoin of S with R and is denoted $S \ltimes R$. The semijoin of S with R is the set of **S** tuples that participate in the join of **R** and **S**.
(3) Join $S \ltimes R$ to **R**. The result is equal to the join of **R** and **S**.

These steps can be integrated into any of our algorithms. When first scanning **R**, one constructs $\pi(R)$ and, when first scanning **S**, one discards tuples whose joining attribute values do not appear in $\pi(R)$. If the join has a low selectivity, then this will reduce significantly the number of **S** tuples to be processed, and will be a useful tool to add to any of the above algorithms.

The most significant expense of the semijoin tool is space to store $\pi(R)$. For example, in some cases $\pi(R)$ might be almost as large as **R**. Can we minimize the space needed to store $\pi(R)$? One obvious candidate is a Babb array. In fact, the Babb array and semijoins are just two specific examples of a more general tool, which can be described as follows.

(1′) Construct a structure $\sigma(R)$ which contains some information about the relation $\pi(R)$, where $\pi(R)$ is defined in (1) above. In particular, $\sigma(R)$ must contain enough information to tell when a given tuple is *not* in $\pi(R)$.
(2′) Scan **S** and discard those tuples which, given the information in $\sigma(R)$, cannot participate in the join. Denote the set of undiscarded **S** tuples by $\mathbf{R}\ \Sigma\ \mathbf{S}$.
(3′) Join $\mathbf{R}\ \Sigma\ \mathbf{S}$ to **R**. The result is equal to the join of **R** with **S**.

The semijoin tool takes $\sigma(R)$ equal to $\pi(R)$, while the Babb array is another representation of $\sigma(R)$, which may be much more compact than $\pi(R)$. This more general tool is a special case of the Tuneable Dynamic Filter described in [13].

7. CONCLUSIONS

We have defined and analyzed three hash-based equijoin algorithms, plus a version of sort-merge that takes advantage of significant amounts of main memory. These algorithms can also operate efficiently with relatively little main memory. If the relations are sufficiently large, then one hash-based algorithm, a hybrid of the other two, is proved to be the most efficient of all the algorithms we study.

The hash-based join algorithms all partition the relations into subsets which can be processed in main memory. Simple mechanisms exist to minimize overflow of these partitions and to correct it when it occurs, but the quantitative effect of these mechanisms remains to be investigated.

The algorithms we describe can operate in virtual memory with a relatively small "hot set" of nonpageable real memory. If it is possible to age pages, marking them for paging out as soon as possible, then sort-merge has the same performance in the hot set plus virtual memory model as in the all real memory model, while the performance of the hybrid algorithm degrades. If aging is not possible, then the performance of both hybrid and sort-merge degrades. In fact, if a fraction **Q** of the required virtual memory space is supported by real memory, then the absence of an aging facility can result in performance equal to that with only a fraction Q^2 of real pages. In the hot set plus virtual memory model, the hybrid hash-based algorithm still has better performance than sort-merge for sufficiently large relations.

Database filters, Babb arrays, and semijoin strategies can be incorporated into any of our algorithms if they prove to be useful.

We conclude that, with decreasing main memory costs, hash-based algorithms will become the preferred strategy for joining large relations.

REFERENCES

1. BABB, E. Implementing a relational database by means of specialized hardware. *ACM Trans. Database Syst. 4*, 1 (Mar. 1979).
2. BERNSTEIN, P. A. Query processing in a system for distributed databases (SDD-1). *ACM Trans. Database Syst. 6*, 4 (Dec. 1981), 602–625.
3. BITTON, D., BORAL, H., DEWITT, D., AND WILKINSON, W. Parallel algorithms for the execution of relational database operations. *ACM Trans. Database Syst. 8*, 3 (Sept. 1983), 324–353.
4. BLASGEN, M. W., AND ESWARAN, K. P. Storage and access in relational databases. *IBM Syst. J. 16*, 4 (1977).
5. BRATBERGSENGEN, K. Hashing methods and relational algebra operations. In *Proceedings of the Conference on Very Large Data Bases* (Singapore, 1984).
6. DEWITT, D., KATZ, R., OLKEN, F., SHAPIRO, L., STONEBRAKER, M., AND WOOD, D. Implementation techniques for main memory database systems. In *Proceedings of SIGMOD* (Boston, 1984), ACM, New York.
7. DEWITT, D., AND GERBER, R. Multiprocessor hash-based join algorithms. In *Proceedings of the Conference on Very Large Data Bases* (Stockholm, 1985).
8. DIGITAL EQUIPMENT CORP. Product announcement, 1984.
9. EFFELSBERG, W., AND HARDER, T. Principles of database buffer management. *ACM Trans. Databse Syst. 9*, 4 (Dec. 1984), 560–595.
10. GARCIA-MOLINA, H., LIPTON, R., AND VALDES, J. A massive memory machine. *IEEE Trans. Comput. C-33*, 5 (1984), 391–399.
11. GOODMAN, J. R. An investigation of multiprocessor structures and algorithms for data base management. Electronics Research Lab. Memo. ECB/ERL M81/33, Univ. of California, Berkeley, 1981.
12. KERSCHBERG, L., TING, P., AND YAO, S. Query optimization in Star computer networks. *ACM Trans. Database Syst. 7*, 4 (Dec 1982), 678–711.
13. KIESSLING, W. Tuneable dynamic filter algorithms for high performance database systems. In *Proceedings of the International Workshop on High Level Computer Architecture* (May 1984), 6.10–6.20.
14. KITSUREGAWA, M., ET AL. Application of hash to data base machine and its architecture. *New Generation Comput. 1* (1983), 62–74.

15. KNUTH, D. *The Art of Computer Programming: Sorting and Searching, Vol. 3.* Addison-Wesley, Reading, Mass., 1973.
16. PIATETSKY-SHAPIRO, G., AND CONNELL, C. Accurate estimation of the number of tuples satisfying a condition. In *Proceedings of SIGMOD Annual Meeting* (Boston, 1984), ACM, New York.
17. SACCO, G. M., AND SCHOLNICK, M. A mechanism for managing the buffer pool in a relational database system using the hot-set model. Computer Science Res. Rep. RJ-3354, IBM Research Lab., San Jose, Calif., Jan. 1982.
18. SEVERANCE, D., AND DUEHNE, R. A practitioners guide to addressing algorithms. *Commun. ACM 19*, 6 (June 1976), 314–326.
19. SLOTNICK, D. Logic per track devices. In *Advances in Computers*, Vol. 10, J. Tou, Ed., Academic Press, New York, 1970, 291–296.
20. STONEBRAKER, M. Operating system support for database management. *Commun. ACM 24*, 7 (July 1981), 412–418.
21. VALDURIEZ, P., AND GARDARIN, G. Join and semijoin algorithms for a multiprocessor database machine. *ACM Trans. Database Syst. 9*, 1 (Mar. 1984), 133–161.
22. YAMANE, Y. A hash join technique for relational database systems. In *Proceedings of the International Conference on Foundations of Data Organization* (Kyoto, May 1985).

Received August 1984; revised December 1985; accepted December 1985.

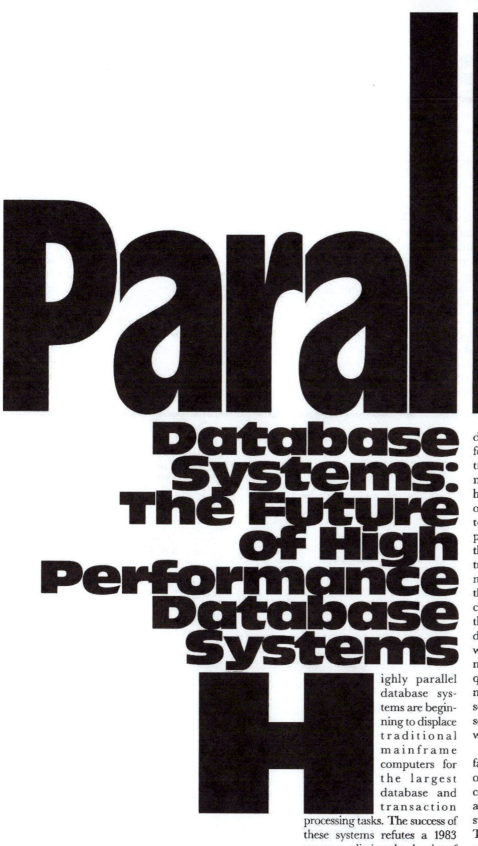

Parallel Database Systems: The Future of High Performance Database Systems

Highly parallel database systems are beginning to displace traditional mainframe computers for the largest database and transaction processing tasks. The success of these systems refutes a 1983 paper predicting the demise of database machines [3]. Ten years ago the future of highly parallel database machines seemed gloomy, even to their staunchest advocates. Most database machine research had focused on specialized, often trendy, hardware such as CCD memories, bubble memories, head-per-track disks, and optical disks. None of these technologies fulfilled their promises; so there was a sense that conventional CPUs, electronic RAM, and moving-head magnetic disks would dominate the scene for many years to come. At that time, disk throughput was predicted to double while processor speeds were predicted to increase by much larger factors. Consequently, critics predicted that multiprocessor systems would soon be I/O limited unless a solution to the I/O bottleneck was found.

While these predictions were fairly accurate about the future of hardware, the critics were certainly wrong about the overall future of parallel database systems. Over the last decade Teradata, Tandem, and a host of startup companies have successfully developed and marketed highly parallel machines.

David DeWitt and Jim Gray

Parallel Database Systems

Why have parallel database systems become more than a research curiosity? One explanation is the widespread adoption of the relational data model. In 1983 relational database systems were just appearing in the marketplace; today they dominate it. Relational queries are ideally suited to parallel execution; they consist of uniform operations applied to uniform streams of data. Each operator produces a new relation, so the operators can be composed into highly parallel dataflow graphs. By streaming the output of one operator into the input of another operator, the two operators can work in series giving *pipelined parallelism.* By partitioning the input data among multiple processors and memories, an operator can often be split into many independent operators each working on a part of the data. This partitioned data and execution gives *partitioned parallelism* (Figure 1).

The dataflow approach to database system design needs a message-based client-server operating system to interconnect the parallel processes executing the relational operators. This in turn requires a high-speed network to interconnect the parallel processors. Such facilities seemed exotic a decade ago, but now they are the mainstream of computer architecture. The client-server paradigm using high-speed LANs is the basis for most PC, workstation, and workgroup software. Those same client-server mechanisms are an excellent basis for distributed database technology.

Mainframe designers have found it difficult to build machines powerful enough to meet the CPU and I/O demands of relational databases serving large numbers of simultaneous users or searching terabyte databases. Meanwhile, multiprocessors based on fast and inexpensive microprocessors have become widely available from vendors including Encore, Intel, NCR, nCUBE, Sequent, Tandem, Teradata, and Thinking Machines. These machines provide more total power than their mainframe coun-

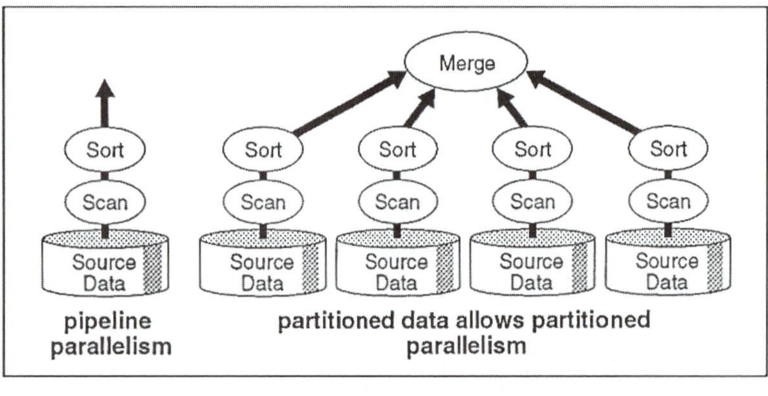

Figure 1.
The dataflow approach to relational operators gives both pipelined and partitioned parallelism. Relational data operators take relations (uniform sets of records) as input and produce relations as outputs. This allows them to be composed in dataflow graphs that allow *pipeline parallelism* (left) in which the computation of one operator proceeds in parallel with another, and *partitioned parallelism* in which operators (sort and scan in the diagram at the right) are replicated for each data source, and the replicas execute in parallel.

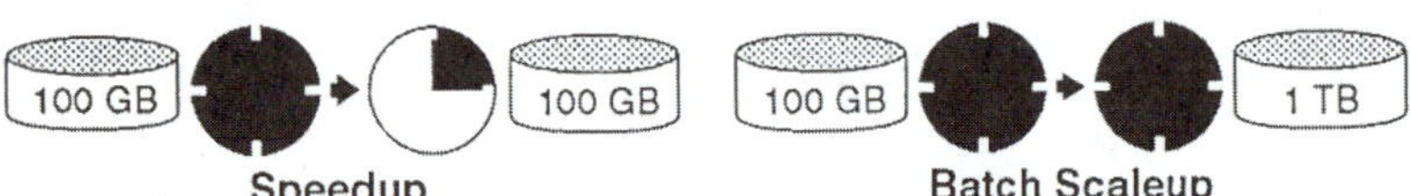

Figure 2.
Speedup and Scaleup. A speedup design performs a one-hour job four times faster when run on a four-times larger system. A scaleup design runs a ten-times bigger job is done in the same time by a ten-times bigger system.

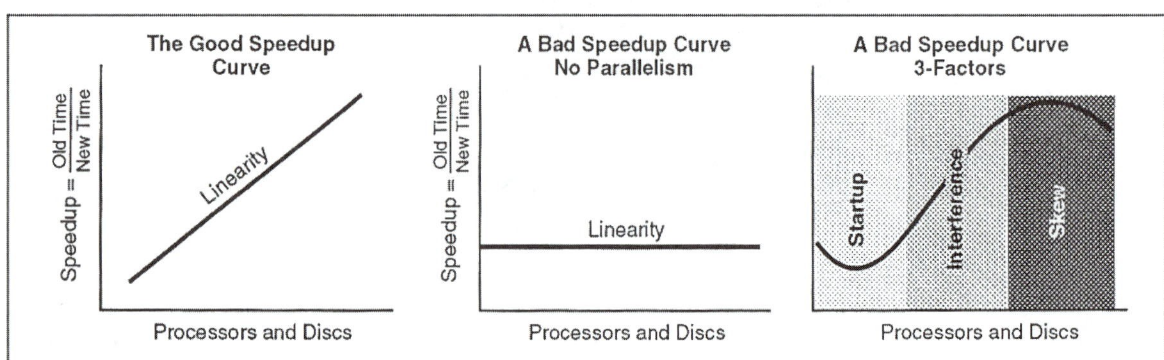

Figure 3.
Good and bad speedup curves. The standard speedup curves. The left curve is the ideal. The middle graph shows no speedup as hardware is added. The right curve shows the three threats to parallelism. Initial startup costs may dominate at first. As the number of processes increase, interference can increase. Ultimately, the job is divided so finely, that the variance in service times (skew) causes a slowdown.

terparts at a lower price. Their modular architectures enable systems to grow incrementally, adding MIPS, memory, and disks either to speedup the processing of a given job, or to scaleup the system to process a larger job in the same time.

In retrospect, special-purpose database machines have indeed failed; but parallel database systems are a big success. The successful parallel database systems are built from conventional processors, memories, and disks. They have emerged as major consumers of highly parallel architectures, and are in an excellent position to exploit massive numbers of fast-cheap commodity disks, processors, and memories promised by current technology forecasts.

A consensus on parallel and distributed database system architecture has emerged. This architecture is based on a *shared-nothing* hardware design [29] in which processors communicate with one another only by sending messages via an interconnection network. In such systems, tuples of each relation in the database are *partitioned (declustered)* across disk storage units[1] attached directly to each processor. Partitioning allows multiple processors to scan large relations in parallel without needing any exotic I/O devices. Such architectures were pioneered by Teradata in the late 1970s and by several research projects. This design is now used by Teradata, Tandem, NCR, Oracle-nCUBE, and several other products currently under development. The research community has also embraced this shared-nothing dataflow architecture in systems like Arbre, Bubba, and Gamma.

The remainder of this article is organized as follows: The next section describes the basic architectural concepts used in these parallel database systems. This is followed by a brief presentation of the unique features of the Teradata, Tandem, Bubba, and Gamma systems in the following section, entitled "The State of the Art." Several areas for future research are described in "Future Directions and Research Problems" prior to the conclusion of this article.

Basic Techniques for Parallel Database Machine Implementation

Parallelism Goals and Metrics: Speedup and Scaleup

The ideal parallel system demonstrates two key properties: (1) *linear speedup:* Twice as much hardware can perform the task in half the elapsed time, and (2) *linear scaleup:* Twice as much hardware can perform twice as large a task in the same elapsed time (see Figures 2 and 3).

More formally, given a fixed job run on a small system, and then run on a larger system, the *speedup* given by the larger system is measured as:

$$Speedup = \frac{small\_system\_elapsed\_time}{big\_system\_elapsed\_time}$$

Speedup is said to be linear, if an N-times large or more expensive system yields a speedup of N.

Speedup holds the problem size constant, and grows the system. Scaleup measures the ability to grow both the system and the problem. *Scaleup* is defined as the ability of an N-times larger system to perform an N-times larger job in the same elapsed time as the original system. The scaleup metric is:

$$Scaleup = \frac{small\_system\_elapsed\_time\_on\_small\_problem}{big\_system\_elapsed\_time\_on\_big\_problem}$$

If this scaleup equation evaluates to 1, then the scaleup is said to be linear[2]. There are two distinct kinds of scaleup, batch and transactional. If the job consists of performing many small independent requests submitted by many clients and operating on a shared database, then scaleup consists of N-times as many clients, submitting N-times as many requests against an N-times larger database. This is the scaleup typically found in transaction processing systems and timesharing systems. This form of scaleup is used by the Transaction Processing Performance Council to scaleup their transaction processing benchmarks [36]. Consequently, it is called *transaction scaleup.* Transaction scaleup is ideally suited to parallel systems since each transaction is typically a small independent job that can be run on a separate processor.

A second form of scaleup, called *batch scaleup,* arises when the scaleup task is presented as a single large job. This is typical of database queries and is also typical of scientific simulations. In these cases, scaleup consists of using an N-times larger computer to solve an N-times larger problem. For database systems batch scaleup translates to the same query on an N-times larger database; for scientific problems, batch scaleup translates to the same calculation on an N-times finer grid or on an N-times longer simulation.

The generic barriers to linear speedup and linear scaleup are the triple threats of:

startup: The time needed to start a parallel operation. If thousands of processes must be started, this can easily dominate the actual computation time.

interference: The slowdown each new process imposes on all others when accessing shared resources.

skew: As the number of parallel steps increases, the average size of each step decreases, but the variance can well exceed the mean. The service time of a job is the service time of the slowest step of the job. When the variance dominates the mean, increased parallelism improves elapsed time only slightly.

The subsection "A Parallel

[1]The term disk is used here as a shorthand for disk or other nonvolatile storage media. As the decade proceeds, nonvolatile electronic storage or some other media may replace or augment disks.

[2]The execution cost of some operators increases super-linearly. For example, the cost of sorting n-tuples increases as *nlog(n)*. When n is in the billions, scaling up by a factor of a thousand, causes *nlog(n)* to increase by 3,000. This 30% deviation from linearity in a three-orders-of-magnitude scaleup justifies the use of the term *near-linear* scaleup.

Dataflow Approach to SQL Software" describes several basic techniques widely used in the design of shared-nothing parallel database machines to overcome these barriers. These techniques often achieve linear speedup and scaleup on relational operators.

Hardware Architecture, the Trend to Shared-Nothing Machines

The ideal database machine would have a single infinitely fast processor with an infinite memory with infinite bandwidth—and it would be infinitely cheap (free). Given such a machine, there would be no need for speedup, scaleup, or parallelism. Unfortunately, technology is not delivering such machines—but it is coming close. Technology is promising to deliver fast one-chip processors, fast high-capacity disks, and high-capacity electronic RAM. It also promises that each of these devices will be very inexpensive by today's standards, costing only hundreds of dollars each.

So, the challenge is to build an infinitely fast processor out of infinitely many processors of finite speed, and to build an infinitely large memory with infinite memory bandwidth from infinitely many storage units of finite speed. This sounds trivial mathematically; but in practice, when a new processor is added to most computer designs, it slows every other computer down just a little bit. If this slowdown (interference) is 1%, then the maximum speedup is 37 and a 1,000-processor system has 4% of the effective power of a single-processor system.

How can we build scaleable multiprocessor systems? Stonebraker suggested the following simple taxonomy for the spectrum of designs (see Figures 4 and 5) [29][3]:

shared-memory: All processors share direct access to a common global memory and to all disks. The IBM/370, Digital VAX, and Sequent Symmetry multiprocessors typify this design.

shared-disks: Each processor has a private memory but has direct access to all disks. The IBM Sysplex and original Digital VAXcluster typify this design.

shared-nothing: Each memory and disk is owned by some processor that acts as a server for that data. Mass storage in such an architecture is distributed among the processors by connecting one or more disks. The Teradata, Tandem, and nCUBE machines typify this design.

Shared-nothing architectures minimize interference by minimizing resource sharing. They also exploit commodity processors and memory without needing an incredibly powerful interconnection network. As Figure 5 suggests, the other architectures move large quantities of data through the interconnection network. The shared-nothing design moves only questions and answers through the network. Raw memory accesses and raw disk accesses are performed locally in a processor, and only the filtered (reduced) data is passed to the client program. This allows a more scaleable design by minimizing traffic on the interconnection network.

Shared-nothing characterizes the database systems being used by Teradata [33], Gamma [8, 9], Tandem [32], Bubba [1], Arbre [21], and nCUBE [13]. Significantly, Digital's VAXcluster has evolved to this design. DOS and UNIX workgroup systems from 3com, Borland, Digital, HP, Novell, Microsoft, and Sun also adopt a shared-nothing client-server architecture.

The actual interconnection networks used by these systems vary enormously. Teradata employs a redundant tree-structured communication network. Tandem uses a three-level duplexed network, two levels within a cluster, and rings connecting the clusters. Arbre, Bubba, and Gamma are independent of the underlying interconnection network, requiring only that the network allow any two nodes to communicate with one another. Gamma operates on an Intel Hypercube. The Arbre prototype was implemented using IBM 4381 processors connected to one another in a point-to-point network. Workgroup systems are currently making a transition from Ethernet to higher speed local networks.

The main advantage of shared-nothing multiprocessors is that they can be scaled up to hundreds and probably thousands of processors that do not interfere with one another. Teradata, Tandem, and Intel have each shipped systems with more than 200 processors. Intel is implementing a 2,000-node hypercube. The largest shared-memory multiprocessors currently available are limited to about 32 processors.

These shared-nothing architectures achieve near-linear speedups and scaleups on complex relational queries and on on-line transaction processing workloads [9, 10, 32]. Given such results, database machine designers see little justification for the hardware and software complexity associated with shared-memory and shared-disk designs.

Shared-memory and shared-disk systems do not scale well on database applications. Interference is a major problem for shared-memory multiprocessors. The interconnection network must have the bandwidth of the sum of the processors and disks. It is difficult to build such networks that can scale to thousands of nodes. To reduce network traffic and to minimize latency, each processor is given a large private cache. Measurements of shared-memory multiprocessors running database workloads show that loading and flushing these caches considerably degrades processor performance [35]. As parallelism increases, interference on shared resources limits performance. Multiprocessor systems

[3]Single Instruction stream, Multiple Data stream (SIMD) machines such as ILLIAC IV and its derivatives like MASSPAR and the "old" Connection Machine are ignored here because to date they have few successes in the database area. SIMD machines seem to have application in simulation, pattern matching, and mathematical search, but they do not seem to be appropriate for the multiuser, I/O intensive, and dataflow paradigm of database systems.

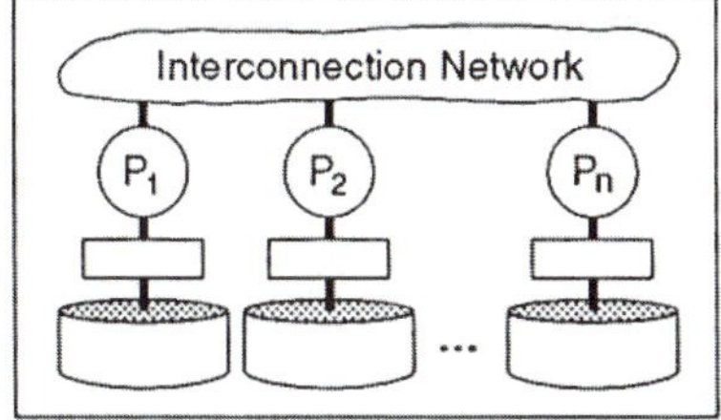

Figure 4.
The basic shared-nothing design. Each processor has a private memory and one or more disks. Processors communicate via a high-speed interconnect network. Teradata, Tandem, nCUBE, and the newer VAXclusters typify this design.

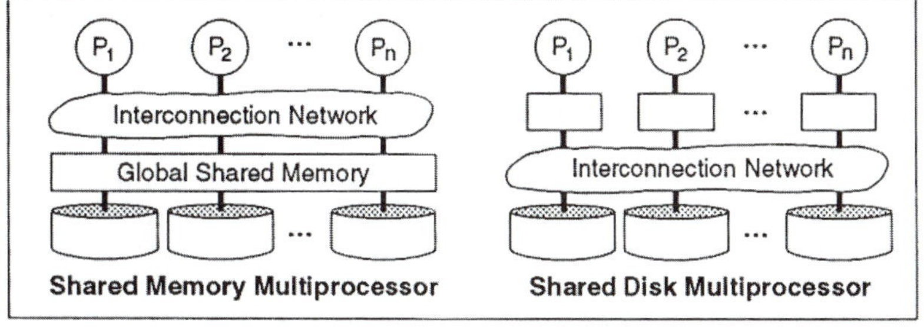

Figure 5.
The shared-memory and shared-disk designs. A shared-memory multiprocessor connects all processors to a globally shared memory. Multiprocessor IBM/370, VAX, and Sequent computers are typical examples of shared-memory designs. Shared-disk systems give each processor a private memory, but all the processors can directly address all the disks. Digital's VAXcluster and IBM's Sysplex typify this design.

Figure 6.
Example of a scan of a telephone relation to find the phone numbers of all people named Smith.

```
SELECT telephone_number        /* the output attribute(s) */
FROM   telephone_book          /* the input relation      */
WHERE  last_name = 'Smith';    /* the predicate           */
```

often use an affinity scheduling mechanism to reduce this interference; giving each process an affinity to a particular processor. This is a form of data partitioning; it represents an evolutionary step toward the shared-nothing design. Partitioning a shared-memory system creates many of the skew and load balancing problems faced by a shared-nothing machine; but reaps none of the simpler hardware interconnect benefits. Based on this experience, we believe high-performance shared-memory machines will not economically scale beyond a few processors when running database applications.

To ameliorate the interference problem, most shared-memory multiprocessors have adopted a shared-disk architecture. This is the logical consequence of affinity scheduling. If the disk interconnection network can scale to thousands of disks and processors, then a shared-disk design is adequate for large read-only databases and for databases where there is no concurrent sharing. The shared-disk architecture is not very effective for database applications that read and write a shared database. A processor wanting to update some data must first obtain the current copy of that data. Since others might be updating the same data concurrently, the processor must declare its intention to update the data. Once this declaration has been honored and acknowledged by all the other processors, the updator can read the shared data from disk and update it. The processor must then write the shared data to disk so that subsequent readers and writers will be aware of the update. There are many optimizations of this protocol, but they all end up exchanging reservation messages and exchanging large physical data pages. This creates processor interference and delays. It creates heavy traffic on the shared interconnection network.

For shared database applications, the shared-disk approach is much more expensive than the shared-nothing approach of exchanging small high-level logical questions and answers among clients and servers. One solution to this interference has been to give data a processor affinity; other processors wanting to access the data send messages to the server managing the data. This has emerged as a major application of transaction processing monitors that partition the load among partitioned servers, and is also a major application for remote procedure calls. Again, this trend toward the partitioned data model and shared-nothing architecture on a shared-disk system reduces interference. Since the shared-disk system interconnection network is difficult to scale to thousands of processors and disks, many conclude that it would be better to adopt the shared-nothing architecture from the start.

Given the shortcomings of shared-disk and shared-memory architectures, why have computer architects been slow to adopt the shared-nothing approach? The first answer is simple, high-performance, low-cost commodity components have only recently become available. Traditionally, commodity components provided relatively low performance and low quality.

Today, old software is the most significant barrier to the use of parallelism. Old software written for uniprocessors gets no speedup or scaleup when put on any kind of multiprocessor. It must be rewritten to benefit from parallel processing and multiple disks. Database applications are a unique exception to this. Today, most database programs are written in the relational language SQL that has been standardized by both ANSI and ISO. It is possible to take standard SQL applications written for uniprocessor systems and execute them in parallel on shared-nothing database machines. Database systems can automatically distribute data among multiple processors. Teradata and Tandem routinely port SQL applications to their system and demonstrate near-linear speedups and scaleups. The following subsection explains the basic techniques used by such parallel database systems.

A Parallel Dataflow Approach to SQL Software

Terabyte on-line databases, consisting of billions of records, are becoming common as the price of online storage decreases. These databases are often represented and manipulated using the SQL relational model. The next few paragraphs give a rudimentary introduction to relational model concepts needed to understand the remainder of this article.

A relational database consists of *relations* (*files* in COBOL terminology) that in turn contain *tuples* (*records* in COBOL terminology). All the tuples in a relation have the same set of *attributes* (*fields* in COBOL terminology).

Relations are created, updated, and queried by writing SQL statements. These statements are syntactic sugar for a simple set of operators chosen from the relational algebra. *Select-project,* here called *scan,* is the simplest and most common operator—it produces a row-and-column subset of a relational table. A scan of relation R using predicate P and attribute list L produces a relational data stream as output. The scan reads each tuple, t, of R and applies the predicate P to it. If $P(t)$ is true, the scan discards any attributes of t not in L and inserts the resulting tuple in the scan output stream. Expressed in SQL, a scan of a telephone book relation to find the phone numbers of all people named Smith would be written as shown in Figure 6. A scan's output stream can be sent to another relational operator, returned to an application, displayed on a terminal, or printed in a report. Therein lies the beauty and utility of the relational model. The uniformity of the data and operators allow them to be arbitrarily composed into dataflow graphs.

The output of a scan may be sent to a *sort* operator that will reorder the tuples based on an attribute sort criteria, optionally eliminating duplicates. SQL defines several *aggregate* operators to summarize attributes into a single value, for example, taking the sum, min, or max of an attribute, or counting the number of distinct values of the attribute. The *insert* operator adds tuples from a stream to an existing relation. The *update* and *delete* operators alter and delete tuples in a relation matching a scan stream.

The relational model defines several operators to combine and compare two or more relations. It provides the usual set operators *union, intersection, difference,* and some more exotic ones like *join* and *division.* Discussion here will focus on the *equi-join* operator (here called *join*). The join operator composes two relations, A and B, on some attribute to produce a third relation. For each tuple, ta, in A, the join finds all tuples, tb, in B whose attribute values are equal to that of ta. For each matching pair of tuples, the join operator inserts into the output stream a tuple built by concatenating the pair.

Codd, in a classic paper, showed that the relational data model can represent any form of data, and that these operators are complete [5]. Today, SQL applications are typically a combination of conventional programs and SQL statements. The programs interact with clients, perform data display, and provide high-level direction of the SQL dataflow.

The SQL data model was originally proposed to improve programmer productivity by offering a nonprocedural database language. Data independence was an additional benefit; since the programs do not specify how the query is to be executed, SQL programs continue to operate as the logical and physical database schema evolves.

Parallelism is an unanticipated benefit of the relational model. Since relational queries are really just relational operators applied to very large collections of data, they offer many opportunities for parallelism. Since the queries are presented in a nonprocedural language, they offer considerable latitude in executing the queries.

Relational queries can be executed as a dataflow graph. As mentioned in the first section of this article, these graphs can use both pipelined parallelism and partitioned parallelism. If one operator sends its output to another, the two operators can execute in parallel giving potential speedup of two.

The benefits of pipeline parallelism are limited because of three factors: (1) Relational pipelines are rarely very long—a chain of length ten is unusual. (2) Some relational operators do not emit their first output until they have consumed all their inputs. Aggregate and sort operators have this property. One cannot pipeline these operators. (3) Often, the execution cost of one operator is much greater than the others (this is an example of skew). In such cases, the speedup obtained by pipelining will be very limited.

Partitioned execution offers much better opportunities for speedup and scaleup. By taking the large relational operators and partitioning their inputs and outputs, it is possible to use divide-and-conquer to turn one big job into many independent little ones. This is an ideal situation for speedup and scaleup. Partitioned data is the key to partitioned execution.

Data Partitioning. Partitioning a relation involves distributing its tuples over several disks. Data partitioning has its origins in centralized systems that had to partition files, either because the file was too big for one disk, or because the file access rate could not be supported by a single disk. Distributed databases use data partitioning when they place relation fragments at different network sites [23]. Data par-

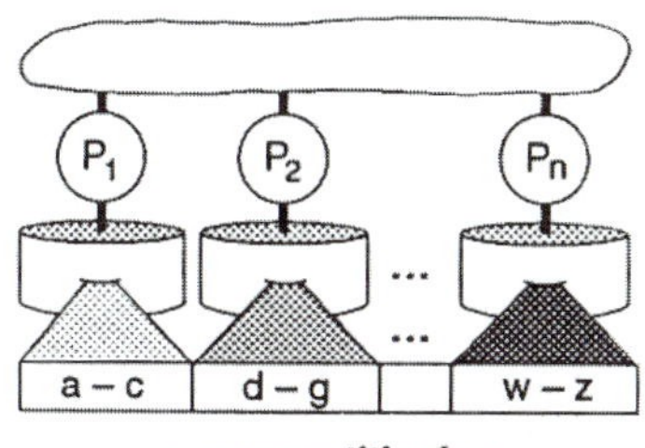

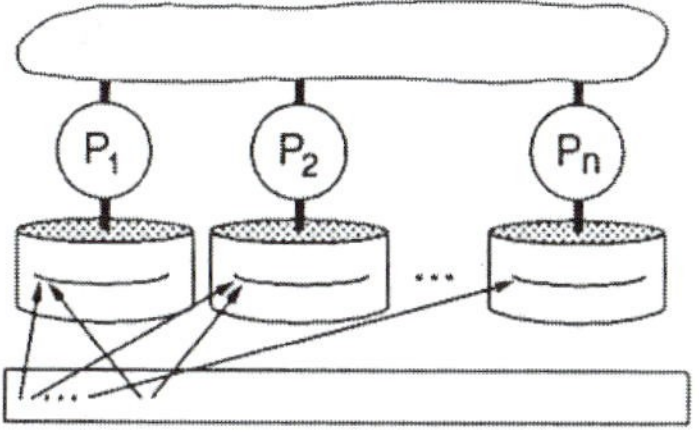

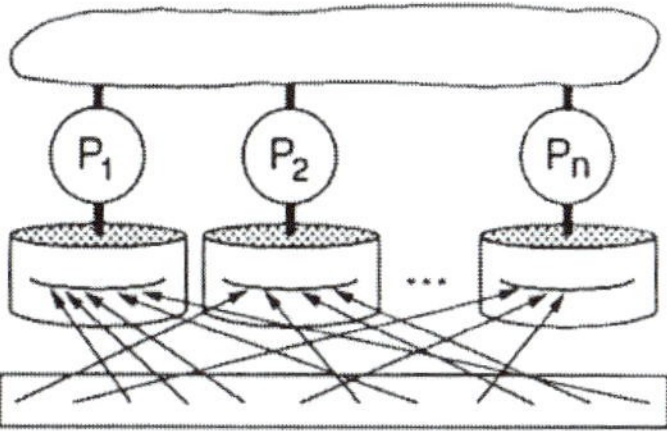

range partitioning round-robin hashing

Figure 7.
The three basic partitioning schemes. Range partitioning maps contiguous attribute ranges of a relation to various disks. Round-robin partitioning maps the i'th tuple to disk i **mod** n. Hashed partitioning maps each tuple to a disk location based on a hash function. Each of these schemes spreads data among a collection of disks, allowing parallel disk access and parallel processing.

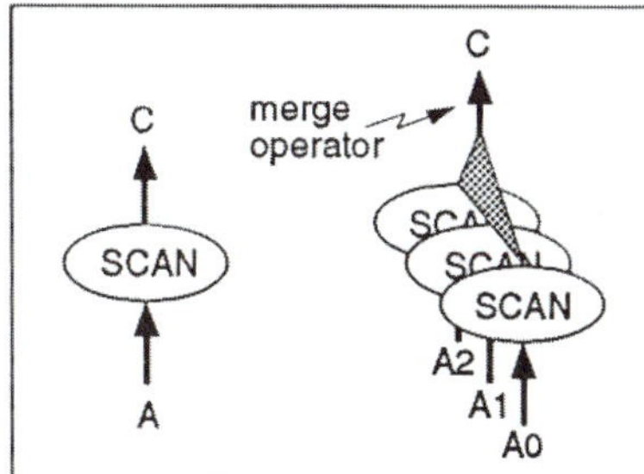

Figure 8.
Partitioned data parallelism. A simple relational dataflow graph showing a relational scan (project and select) decomposed into three scans on three partitions of the input stream or relation. These three scans send their output to a merge node that produces a single data stream.

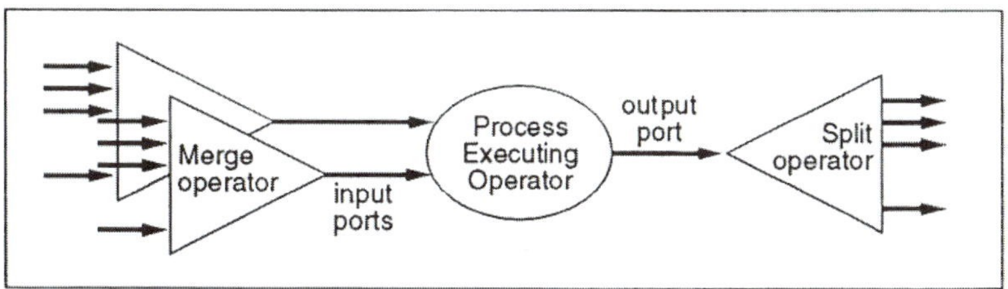

Figure 9.
Merging the inputs and partitioning the output of an operator. A relational dataflow graph showing a relational operator's inputs being merged to a sequential stream per port. The operator's output is being decomposed by a split operator in several independent streams. Each stream may be a duplicate or a partitioning of the operator output stream into many disjoint streams. With the split and merge operators, a web of simple sequential dataflow nodes can be connected to form a parallel execution plan.

titioning allows parallel database systems to exploit the I/O bandwidth of multiple disks by reading and writing them in parallel. This approach provides I/O bandwidth superior to RAID-style systems without needing any specialized hardware [22, 24].

The simplest partitioning strategy distributes tuples among the fragments in a *round-robin* fashion. This is the partitioned version of the classic entry-sequence file. Round-robin partitioning is excellent if all applications want to access the relation by sequentially scanning all of it on each query. The problem with round-robin partitioning is that applications frequently want to associatively access tuples, meaning that the application wants to find all the tuples having a particular attribute value. The SQL query looking for the Smiths in the phone book shown in Figure 6 is an example of an associative search.

Hash partitioning is ideally suited for applications that want only sequential and associative access to the data. Tuples are placed by applying a *hashing* function to an attribute of each tuple. The function specifies the placement of the tuple on a particular disk. Associative access to the tuples with a specific attribute value can be directed to a single disk, avoiding the overhead of starting queries on multiple disks. Hash partitioning mechanisms are provided by Arbre, Bubba, Gamma, and Teradata.

Database systems pay considerable attention to clustering related data together in physical storage. If a set of tuples is routinely accessed together, the database system attempts to store them on the same physical page. For example, if the Smiths of the phone book are routinely accessed in alphabetical order, then they should be stored on pages in that order, these pages should be clustered together on disk to allow sequential prefetching and other optimizations. Clustering is very application-specific. For example, tuples describing nearby streets should be clustered together in geographic databases, tuples describing the line items of an invoice should be clustered with the invoice tuple in an inventory control application.

Hashing tends to randomize data rather than cluster it. *Range partitioning* clusters tuples with similar attributes together in the same partition. It is good for sequential and associative access, and is also good for clustering data. Figure 7 shows range partitioning based on lexicographic order, but any clustering algorithm is possible. Range partitioning derives its name from the typical SQL range queries such as

```
latitude BETWEEN 38° AND 39°
```

Arbre, Bubba, Gamma, Oracle, and Tandem provide range partitioning.

Database Systems **Parallel**

The problem with range partitioning is that it risks *data skew,* where all the data is placed in one partition, and *execution skew* in which all the execution occurs in one partition. Hashing and round-robin are less susceptible to these skew problems. Range partitioning can minimize skew by picking non-uniformly-distributed partitioning criteria. Bubba uses this concept by considering the access frequency *(heat)* of each tuple when creating partitions of a relation; the goal being to balance the frequency with which each partition is accessed (its *temperature*) rather than the actual number of tuples on each disk (its volume) [6].

Table 1.
Sample Split Operators.
Each split operator maps tuples to a set of output streams (ports of other processes) depending on the range value (predicate) of the input tuple. The split operator on the left is for the relation A scan in Figure 10, while the table on the right is for the relation B scan. The tables partition the tuples among three data streams.

Relation A Scan Split Operator		Relation B Scan Split Operator	
Predicate	**Destination Process**	**Predicate**	**Destination Process**
"A-H"	(CPU #5, Process #3, Port #0)	"A-H"	(CPU #5, Process #3, Port #1)
"I-Q"	(CPU #7, Process #8, Port #0)	"I-Q"	(CPU #7, Process #8, Port #1)
"R-Z"	(CPU #2, Process #2, Port #0)	"R-Z"	(CPU #2, Process #2, Port #1)

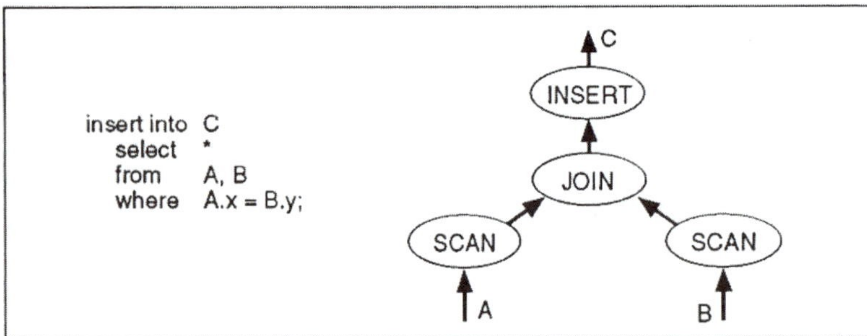
insert into C
select *
from A, B
where A.x = B.y;
C
INSERT
JOIN
SCAN
SCAN
A
B

Figure 10.
A simple SQL query and the associated relational query graph. The query specifies that a join is to be performed between relations A and B by comparing the x attribute of each tuple from the A relation with the y attribute value of each tuple of the B relation. For each pair of tuples that satisfy the predicate, a result tuple is formed from all the attributes of both tuples. This result tuple is then added to the result relation C. The associated logical query graph (as might be produced by a query optimizer) shows a tree of operators, one for the join, one for the insert, and one for scanning each input relation.

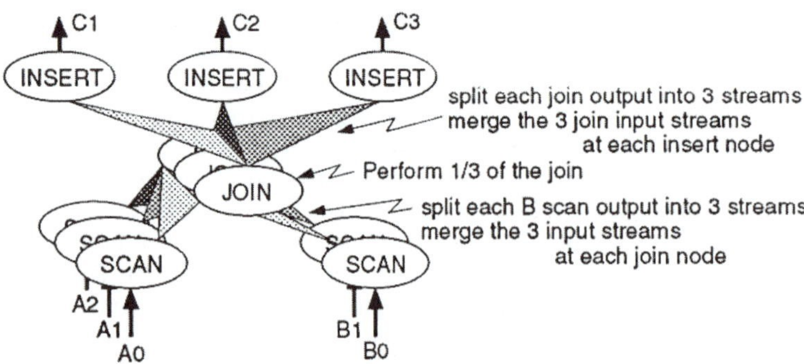
C1
C2
C3
INSERT
INSERT
INSERT
split each join output into 3 streams
merge the 3 join input streams
at each insert node
Perform 1/3 of the join
JOIN
split each B scan output into 3 streams
merge the 3 input streams
at each join node
SCAN
SCAN
A2
A1
A0
B1
B0

Figure 11.
A simple relational dataflow graph. It shows two relational scans (project and select) consuming two input relations, A and B and feeding their outputs to a join operator that in turn produces a data stream C.

While partitioning is a simple concept that is easy to implement, it raises several new physical database design issues. Each relation must now have a partitioning strategy and a set of disk fragments. Increasing the degree of partitioning usually reduces the response time for an individual query and increases the overall throughput of the system. For sequential scans, the response time decreases because more processors and disks are used to execute the query. For associative scans, the response time improves because fewer tuples are stored at each node and hence the size of the index that must be searched decreases.

There is a point beyond which further partitioning actually increases the response time of a query. This point occurs when the cost of starting a query on a node becomes a significant fraction of the actual execution time [6, 11].

Parallelism Within Relational Operators. Data partitioning is the first step in partitioned execution of relational dataflow graphs. The basic idea is to use parallel data streams instead of writing new parallel operators (programs). This approach enables the use of unmodified, existing sequential routines to execute the relational operators in parallel. Each relational operator has a set of *input ports* on which input tuples arrive and an *output* port to which the operator's output stream is sent. The parallel dataflow works by partitioning and merging data streams into these sequential ports. This approach allows the use of existing sequential relational operators to execute in parallel.

Consider a scan of a relation, A, that has been partitioned across three disks into fragments A0, A1, and A2. This scan can be implemented as three scan operators that send their output to a common merge operator. The merge operator produces a single output data stream to the application or to the next relational operator. The parallel query executor creates the three scan processes shown in Figure 8 and directs them to take their inputs from three different sequential input streams (A0, A1, A2). It also directs them to send their outputs to a common merge node. Each scan can run on an independent processor and disk. So the first basic parallelizing operator is a *merge* that can combine several parallel data streams into a single sequential stream.

The merge operator tends to focus data on one spot. If a multistage parallel operation is to be done in parallel, a single data stream must be split into several independent streams. A *split operator* is used to partition or replicate the stream of tuples produced by a relational operator. A split operator defines a mapping from one or more attribute values of the output tuples to a set of destination processes (see Figure 9).

As an example, consider the two split operators shown in Table 1 in conjunction with the SQL query shown in Figure 10. Assume that three processes are used to execute the join operator, and that five other processes execute the two scan operators—three scanning partitions of relation A while two scan partitions of relation B. Each of the three relation A scan nodes will have the same split operator, sending all tuples between "A-H" to port 1 of join process 0, all between "I-Q" to port 1 of join process 1, and all between "R-Z" to port 1 of join process 2. Similarly the two relation B scan nodes have the same split operator except that their outputs are merged by port 1 (not port 0) of each join process. Each join process sees a sequential input stream of A tuples from the port 0 merge (the left-scan nodes) and another sequential stream of B tuples from the port 1 merge (the right-scan nodes). The outputs of each join are, in turn, split into three streams based on the partitioning criterion of relation C.

To clarify this example, consider the first join process in Figure 11 (processor 5, process 3, ports 0 and 1 in Table 1). It will receive all the relation A "A-H" tuples from the three relation A scan operators merged as a single stream on port 0, and will get all the "A-H" tuples from relation B merged as a single stream on port 1. It will join them using a hash-join, sort-merge join, or even a nested join if the tuples arrive in the proper order.

If each of these processes is on an independent processor with an independent disk, there will be little interference among them. Such dataflow designs are a natural application for shared-nothing machine architectures.

The split operator in Table 1 is just an example. Other split operators might duplicate the input stream, or partition it round-robin, or partition it by hash. The partitioning function can be an arbitrary program. Gamma, Volcano, and Tandem use this approach [14]. It has several advantages including the automatic parallelism of any new operator added to the system, plus support for many kinds of parallelism.

The split and merge operators have flow control and buffering built into them. This prevents one operator from getting too far ahead in the computation. When a split-operator's output buffers fill, it stalls the relational operator until the data target requests more output.

For simplicity, these examples have been stated in terms of an operator per process. But it is entirely possible to place several operators within a process to get coarser grained parallelism. The fundamental idea though is to build a self-pacing dataflow graph and distribute it in a shared-nothing machine in a way that minimizes interference.

Specialized Parallel Relational Operators. Some algorithms for relational operators are especially appropriate for parallel execution, either because they minimize data flow, or because they better tolerate data and execution skew. Improved algorithms have been found for most of the relational operators. The evolution of join operator algorithms is sketched here as an example of these improved algorithms.

Recall that the join operator combines two relations, A and B, to produce a third relation containing all tuple pairs from A and B with matching attribute values. The conventional way of computing the join is to sort both A and B into new relations ordered by the join attribute. These two intermediate relations are then compared in sorted order, and matching tuples are inserted in the output stream. This algorithm is called *sort-merge* join.

Many optimizations of sort-merge join are possible, but since sort has execution cost *nlog(n)*, sort-merge join has an *nlog(n)* execution cost. Sort-merge join works well in a parallel dataflow environment unless there is data skew. In case of data skew, some sort partitions may be much larger than others. This in turn creates execution skew and limits speedup and scaleup. These skew problems do not appear in centralized sort-merge joins.

Hash-join is an alternative to sort-merge join. It has linear execution cost rather than *nlog(n)* execution cost, and it is more resistant to data skew. It is superior to sort-merge join unless the input streams are already in sorted order. Hash join works as follows. Each of the relations A and B are first hash partitioned on the join attribute. A hash partition of relation A is hashed into memory. The corresponding partition of table relation B is scanned, and each tuple is compared against the main-memory hash table for the A partition. If there is a match, the pair of tuples are sent to the output stream. Each pair of hash partitions is compared in this way.

The hash join algorithm breaks a big join into many little joins. If the hash function is good and if the data skew is not too bad, then there will be little variance in the hash bucket size. In these cases hash-join is a linear-time join algorithm with linear speedup and scaleup. Many optimizations of the parallel hash-join algorithm have been discovered over the last decade. In pathological skew cases, when many or all tuples have the same attribute value, one bucket may contain all the tuples. In these cases no algorithm is known to speedup or scaleup.

The hash-join example shows that new parallel algorithms can improve the performance of relational operators. This is a fruitful research area [4, 8, 18, 20, 25, 26, 38, 39]. Although parallelism can be obtained from conventional sequential relational algorithms by using split and merge operators, we expect that many new algorithms will be discovered in the future.

The State of the Art

Teradata

Teradata quietly pioneered many of the ideas presented in this article. Since 1978 they have been building shared-nothing highly-parallel SQL systems based on commodity microprocessors, disks, and memories. Teradata systems act as SQL servers to client programs operating on conventional computers.

Teradata systems may have over 1,000 processors and many thousands of disks. The Teradata processors are functionally divided into two groups: Interface Processors (IFPs) and Access Module Processors (AMPs). The IFPs handle communication with the host, query parsing and optimization, and coordination of AMPs during query execution. The AMPs are responsible for executing queries. Each AMP typically has several disks and a large memory cache. IFPs and AMPs are interconnected by a dual redundant, tree-shaped interconnect called the Y-net [33].

Each relation is hash partitioned over a subset of the AMPs. When a tuple is inserted into a relation, a hash function is applied to the primary key of the tuple to select an AMP for storage. Once a tuple arrives at an AMP, a second hash function determines the tuple's placement in its fragment of the relation. The tuples in each fragment are in hash-key order. Given a value for the key attribute, it is possible to locate the tuple in a single AMP. The AMP examines its cache, and if the tuple is not present, fetches it in a single disk read. Hash secondary indices are also supported.

Hashing is used to split the outputs of relational operators into intermediate relations. Join operators are executed using a parallel sort-merge algorithm. Rather than using pipelined parallel execution, during the execution of a query, each operator is run to completion on all participating nodes before the next operator is initiated.

Teradata has installed many systems containing over 100 processors and hundreds of disks. These systems demonstrate near-linear speedup and scaleup on relational queries, and far exceed the speed of traditional mainframes in their ability to process large (terabyte) databases.

Tandem NonStop SQL

The Tandem NonStop SQL system is composed of processor clusters interconnected via 4-plexed fiber-optic rings. Unlike most other systems discussed in this article, the Tandem systems run the applications on the same processors and operating system as the database servers. There is no front-end/back-end distinction between programs and machines. The systems are configured at a disk per MIPS, so each 10-MIPS processor has about 10 disks. Disks are typically duplexed [2]. Each disk is served by a set of processes managing a large shared RAM cache, a set of locks, and log records for the data on that disk pair. Considerable effort is spent on optimizing sequential scans by prefetching large units, and by filtering and manipulating the tuples with SQL predicates at these disk servers. This minimizes traffic on the shared interconnection network.

Relations may be range partitioned across multiple disks. Entry-sequenced, relative, and B-tree organizations are supported. Only B-tree secondary indices are supported. Nested join, sort-merge join, and hash join algorithms are provided. Parallelization of operators in a query plan is achieved by inserting split and merge operators between operator nodes in the query tree. Scans, aggregates, joins, updates, and deletes are executed in parallel. In addition, several utilities use parallelism (e.g., load, reorganize, . . .) [31, 39].

Tandem systems are primary designed for on-line transaction processing (OLTP)—running many simple transactions against a large shared database. Beyond the parallelism inherent in running many independent transactions in parallel, the main parallelism feature for OLTP is parallel index update. SQL relations typically have five indices on them, although it is not uncommon to see 10 indices on a relation. These indices speed reads, but slow down inserts, updates, and deletes. By doing the index maintenance in parallel, the maintenance time for multiple indices can be held almost constant if the indices are spread among many processors and disks.

Overall, the Tandem systems demonstrate near-linear scaleup on transaction processing workloads, and near-linear speedup and scaleup on large relational queries [10, 31].

Gamma

The current version of Gamma runs on a 32-node Intel iPSC/2 Hypercube with a disk attached to each node. In addition to round-robin, range and hash partitioning, Gamma also provides hybrid-range partitioning that combines the best features of the hash and range partitioning strategies [12]. Once a relation has been partitioned, Gamma provides both clustered and nonclustered indices on either the partitioning or nonpartitioning attributes. The indices are implemented as B-trees or hash tables.

Gamma uses split and merge operators to execute relational algebra operators using both parallelism and pipelining [9]. Sort-merge and three different hash join methods are supported [7]. Near-linear speedup and scaleup for relational queries has been measured on this architecture [9, 25, 26].

The Super Database Computer

The Super Database Computer (SDC) project at the University of Tokyo presents an interesting contrast to other database systems [16, 20]. SDC takes a combined hardware and software approach to the performance problem. The basic unit, called a processing module (PM), consists of one or more processors on a shared memory. These processors are augmented by a special-purpose sorting engine that sorts at high speed (3MB/second at present), and by a disk subsystem [19]. Clusters of processing modules are connected via an omega network that provides both nonblocking NxN interconnect and some dynamic routing minimize skewed data distribution during hash joins. The SDC is designed to scale to thousands of PMs, and so considerable attention is paid to the problem of data skew.

Data is partitioned among the PMs by hashing. The SDC software includes a unique operating system, and a relational database query executor. The SDC is a shared-nothing design with a software dataflow architecture. This is consistent with our assertion that current parallel database machines systems use conventional hardware. But the special-purpose design of the omega network and of the hardware sorter clearly contradict the thesis that special-purpose hardware is not a good investment of development resources. Time will tell whether these special-purpose components offer better price performance or peak performance than shared-nothing designs built of conventional hardware.

Bubba

The Bubba prototype was implemented using a 40-node FLEX/32 multiprocessor with 40 disks [4]. Although this is a shared-memory multiprocessor, Bubba was designed as a shared-nothing system and the shared-memory is only used for message passing. Nodes are divided into three groups: Interface Processors for communicating with external host processors and coordinating query execution; Intelligent Repositories for data storage and query execution; and Checkpoint/Logging Repositories. While Bubba also uses partitioning as a storage mechanism (both range and hash partitioning mechanisms are provided) and dataflow processing mechanisms, Bubba is unique in several ways. First, Bubba uses FAD rather than SQL as its interface language. FAD is an extended-relational persistent programming language. FAD provides support for complex objects via several type constructors including shared subobjects, set-oriented data manipulation primitives, and more traditional language constructs. The FAD compiler is responsible for detecting operations that can be executed in parallel according to how the data objects being accessed are partitioned. Program execution is performed using a dataflow execution paradigm. The task of compiling and parallelizing a FAD program is significantly more difficult than parallelizing a relational query. Another Bubba feature is its use of a single-level store mechanism in which the persistent database at each node is mapped to the virtual memory address space of each process executing at the node. This is in contrast to the traditional approach of files and pages. Similar mechanisms are used in IBM's AS400 mapping of SQL databases into virtual memory, HP's mapping of the Image Database into the operating system virtual address space, and Mach's mapped file [34] mechanism. This approach simplified the implementation of the upper levels of the Bubba software.

Other Systems

Other parallel database system prototypes include XPRS [30], Volcano [14], Arbre [21], and the PERSIST project under development at IBM Research Labs in Hawthorne and Almaden. While both Volcano and XPRS are implemented on shared-memory multiprocessors, XPRS is unique in its exploitation of the availability of massive shared-memory in its design. In addition, XPRS is based on several innovative techniques for obtaining extremely high performance and availability.

Recently, the Oracle database system has been implemented atop a 64-node nCUBE shared-nothing system. The resulting system is the first to demonstrate more than 1,000 transactions per second on the industry-standard TPC-B benchmark. This is far in excess of Oracle's performance on conventional mainframe systems—both in peak performance and in price/performance [13].

The NCR Corporation has announced the 3600 and 3700 product lines that employ shared-nothing architectures running System V R4 of Unix on Intel 486 and 586 processors. The interconnection network for the 3600 product line uses an enhanced Y-Net licensed from Teradata while the 3700 is based on a new multistage interconnection network being developed jointly by NCR and Teradata. Two software offerings have been announced. The first, a port of the Teradata software to a Unix environment, is targeted toward the decision-support marketplace. The second, based on a parallelization of the Sybase DBMS, is intended primarily for transaction processing workloads.

Database Machines and Grosch's Law

Today shared-nothing database machines have the best peak performance and best price performance available. When compared to traditional mainframes, the Tandem system scales linearly well beyond the largest reported mainframes on the TPC-A transaction processing benchmark. Its price/performance on these benchmarks is three times cheaper than the comparable mainframe numbers. Oracle on an nCUBE has the highest reported TPC-B numbers, and has very competitive price performance [13, 36]. These benchmarks demonstrate linear scaleup on transaction processing benchmarks.

Gamma, Tandem, and Teradata have demonstrated linear speedup and scaleup on complex relational database benchmarks. They scale well beyond the size of the largest mainframes. Their performance and price performance is generally superior to mainframe systems.

These observations defy Grosch's law. In the 1960s, Herb Grosch observed that there is an economy-of-scale in computing. At that time, expensive computers were much more powerful than inexpensive computers. This gave rise to super-linear speedups and scaleups. The current pricing of mainframes at $25,000/MIPS and $1,000/MB of RAM reflects this view. Meanwhile, microprocessors are selling for $250/MIPS and $100/MB of RAM.

By combining hundreds or thousands of these small systems, one can build an incredibly powerful database machine for much less money than the cost of a modest mainframe. For database problems, the near-linear speedup and scaleup of these shared-nothing machines allows them to outperform current shared-memory and shared disk mainframes.

Grosch's law no longer applies to database and transaction processing problems. There is no economy of scale. At best, one can expect linear speedup and scaleup of performance and price/performance. Fortunately, shared-nothing database architectures achieve this near-linear performance.

Future Directions and Research Problems

Mixing Batch and OLTP Queries

The second section of this article, "Basic Techniques for Parallel Database Machine Implementation", concentrated on the basic techniques used for processing complex relational queries in a parallel database system. Concurrently running a mix of both simple and complex queries concurrently presents several unsolved problems.

One problem is that large relational queries tend to acquire many locks and tend to hold them for a relatively long time. This prevents concurrent updates of the data by simple on-line transactions. Two solutions are currently offered: give the ad-hoc queries a fuzzy picture of the database, not locking any data as they browse it. Such a "dirty-read" solution is not acceptable for some applications. Several systems offer a versioning mechanism that gives readers a consistent (old) version of the database while updators are allowed to create newer versions of objects. Other, perhaps better, solutions for this problem may also exist.

Priority scheduling is another mixed-workload problem. Batch jobs have a tendency to monopolize the processor, flood the memory cache, and make large demands on the I/O subsystem. It is up to the underlying operating system to quantize and limit the resources used by such batch jobs to ensure short response times and low variance in response times for short transactions. A particularly difficult problem is the *priority inversion problem,* in which a low-priority client makes a request to a high-priority server. The server must run at high priority because it is managing critical resources. Given this, the work of the low-priority client is effectively promoted to high priority when the low-priority request is serviced by the high-priority server. There have been several ad-hoc attempts at solving this problem, but considerably more work is needed.

Parallel Query Optimization

Current database query optimizers do not consider all possible plans when optimizing a relational query. While cost models for relational queries running on a single processor are now well-understood [27] they still depend on cost estimators that are a guess at best. Some dynamically select from among several plans at run time depending on, for example, the amount of physical memory actually available and the cardinalities of the intermediate results [15]. To date, no query optimizers consider all the parallel algorithms for each operator and all the query tree organizations. More work is needed in this area.

Another optimization problem relates to highly skewed value distributions. Data skew can lead to high variance in the size of intermediate relations, leading to both poor query plan cost estimates and sub-linear speedup. Solutions to this problem are an area of active research [17, 20, 37, 38].

Application Program Parallelism

The parallel database systems offer parallelism within the database system. Missing are tools to structure application programs to take advantage of parallelism inherent in these parallel systems. While automatic parallelization of applications programs written in COBOL may not be feasible, library packages to facilitate explicitly parallel application programs are needed. Ideally the SPLIT and MERGE operators could be packaged so that applications could benefit from them.

Physical Database Design

For a given database and workload there are many possible indexing and partitioning combinations. Database design tools are needed to help the database administrator select among these many design options. Such tools might accept as input a description of the queries comprising the workload, their frequency of execution, statistical information about the relations in the database, and a description of the processors and disks. The resulting output would suggest a partitioning strategy for each relation plus the indices to be created on each relation. Steps in this direction are beginning to appear.

Current algorithms partition relations using the values of a single attribute. For example, geographic records could be partitioned by longitude or latitude. Partitioning on longitude allows selections for a longitude range to be localized to a limited number of nodes, selections on latitude must be sent to all the nodes. While this is acceptable in a small configuration, it is not acceptable in a system with thousands of processors. Additional research is needed on multidimensional partitioning and search algorithms.

On-line Data Reorganization and Utilities

Loading, reorganizing, or dumping a terabyte database at a megabyte per second takes over 12 days and nights. Clearly parallelism is needed if utilities are to complete within a few hours or days. Even then, it will be essential that the data be available while the utilities are operating. In the SQL world, typical utilities create indices, add or drop attributes, add constraints, and physically reorganize the data, changing its clustering.

One unexplored and difficult problem is how to process database utility commands while the system remains operational and the data remains available for concurrent reads and writes by others. The fundamental properties of such algorithms are that they must be *on-line* (operate without making data unavailable), *incremental* (operate on parts of a large database), *parallel* (exploit parallel processors), and *recoverable* (allow the operation to be canceled and return to the old state).

Summary and Conclusions

Like most applications, database systems want cheap, fast hardware. Today that means commodity processors, memories, and disks. Consequently, the hardware concept of a *database machine* built of exotic hardware is inappropriate for current technology. On the other hand, the availability of fast microprocessors, and small inexpensive disks packaged as standard inexpensive but fast computers is an ideal platform for *parallel database systems*. A shared-nothing architecture is relatively straightforward to implement and, more importantly, has demonstrated both speedup and scaleup to hundreds of processors. Furthermore, shared-nothing architectures actually simplify the software implementation. If the software techniques of data partitioning, dataflow, and intra-operator parallelism are employed, the task of converting an existing database management system to a highly parallel one becomes relatively straightforward. Finally, there are certain applications (e.g., data mining in terabyte databases) that require the computational and I/O resources available only from a parallel architecture.

While the successes of both commercial products and prototypes demonstrate the viability of highly parallel database machines, several research issues remain unsolved including techniques for mixing ad-hoc queries with on-line transaction processing without seriously limiting transaction throughput, improved optimizers for parallel queries, tools for physical database design, on-line database reorganization, and algorithms for handling relations with highly skewed data distributions. Some application domains are not well supported by the relational data model. It appears that a new class of database systems based on an object-oriented data model is needed. Such systems pose a host of interesting research problems that require further examination. ◼

References

1. Alexander, W., et al. Process and dataflow control in distributed data-intensive systems. In *Proceedings of ACM SIGMOD Conference* (Chicago, Ill., June 1988) ACM, NY, 1988.
2. Bitton, D. and Gray, J. Disk shadowing. In *Proceedings of the Fourteenth International Conference on Very Large Data Bases* (Los Angeles, Calif., August, 1988).
3. Boral, H. and DeWitt, D. Database machines: An idea whose time has passed? A critique of the future of database machines. In *Proceedings of the 1983 Workshop on Database Machines.* H.-O. Leilich and M. Missikoff, Eds., Springer-Verlag, 1983.
4. Boral, H. et al. Prototyping Bubba: A highly parallel database system. *IEEE Knowl. Data Eng. 2,* 1, (Mar. 1990).
5. Codd, E.F. A relational model of data for large shared databanks. *Commun. ACM 13,* 6 (June 1970).
6. Copeland, G., Alexander, W., Boughter, E., and Keller, T. Data placement in Bubba. In *Proceedings of ACM-SIGMOD International Conference on Management of Data* (Chicago, May 1988).
7. DeWitt, D.J., Katz, R., Olken, F., Shapiro, D., Stonebraker, M. and Wood, D. Implementation techniques for main memory database systems. In *Proceedings of the 1984 SIGMOD Conference,* (Boston, Mass., June, 1984).
8. DeWitt, D., et al. GAMMA—A high performance dataflow database machine. In *Proceedings of the 1986 VLDB Conference* (Japan, August 1986).
9. DeWitt, D., et al. The Gamma database machine project. *IEEE Knowl. Data Eng. 2,* 1 (Mar. 1990).
10. Engelbert, S, Gray, J., Kocher, T., and Stah, P. A benchmark of non-stop SQL Release 2 demonstrating near-linear speedup and scaleup on large databases. Tandem Computers, Technical Report 89.4, Tandem Part No. 27469, May 1989.
11. Ghandeharizadeh, S., and DeWitt, D.J. Performance analysis of alternative declustering strategies. In *Proceedings of the Sixth International Conference on Data Engineering* (Feb. 1990).
12. Ghandeharizadeh, S., and Dewitt, D.J. Hybrid-range partitioning strategy: A new declustering strategy for multiprocessor database machines. In *Proceedings of the Sixth International Conference on Very Large Data Bases,* (Melbourne, Australia, Aug. 1990).
13. Gibbs, J. Massively parallel systems, rethinking computing for business and science. *Oracle 6,* 1 (Dec. 1991).
14. Graefe, G. Encapsulation of parallelism in the Volcano query processing system. In *Proceedings of 1990*

Parallel Database Systems

ACM-SIGMOD International Conference on Management of Data (May 1990).

15. Graefe, G., and Ward, K. Dynamic query evaluation plans. In *Proceedings of the 1989 SIGMOD Conference*, (Portland, Ore., June 1989).

16. Hirano, M.S. et al. Architecture of SDC, the super database computer. In *Proceedings of JSPP '90*. 1990.

17. Hua, K.A. and Lee, C. Handling data skew in multiprocessor database computers using partition tuning. In *Proceedings of the Seventeenth International Conference on Very Large Data Bases*. (Barcelona, Spain, Sept. 1991).

18. Kitsuregawa, M., Tanaka, H., and Moto-oka, T. Application of hash to data base machine and its architecture. *New Generation Computing 1*, 1 (1983).

19. Kitsuregawa, M., Yang, W., and Fushimi, S. Evaluation of 18-stage pipeline hardware sorter. In *Proceedings of the Third International Conference on Data Engineering* (Feb. 1987).

20. Kitsuregawa, M., and Ogawa, Y. A new parallel hash join method with robustness for data skew in super database computer (SDC). In *Proceedings of the Sixteenth International Conference on Very Large Data Bases*. (Melbourne, Australia, Aug. 1990).

21. Lorie, R., Daudenarde, J., Hallmark, G., Stamos, J., and Young, H. Adding intra-transaction parallelism to an existing DBMS: Early experience. *IEEE Data Engineering Newsletter 12*, 1 (Mar. 1989).

22. Patterson, D. A., Gibson, G. and Katz, R. H. A case for redundant arrays of inexpensive disks (RAID). In *Proceedings of the ACM-SIGMOD International Conference on Management of Data*. (Chicago, May 1988).

23. Ries, D. and Epstein, R. Evaluation of distribution criteria for distributed database systems. UBC/ERL Technical Report M78/22, UC Berkeley, May, 1978.

24. Salem, K. and Garcia-Molina, H. Disk-striping. Department of Computer Science, Princeton University Technical Report EEDS-TR-322-84, Princeton, N.J., Dec. 1984.

25. Schneider, D. and DeWitt, D. A performance evaluation of four parallel join algorithms in a shared-nothing multiprocessor environment. In *Proceedings of the 1989 SIGMOD Conference* (Portland, Ore., June 1989).

26. Schneider, D. and DeWitt, D. Tradeoffs in processing complex join queries via hashing in multiprocessor database machines. In *Proceedings of the Sixteenth International Conference on Very Large Data Bases*. (Melbourne, Australia, Aug., 1990).

27. Selinger P. G., et al. Access path selection in a relational database management system. In *Proceedings of the 1979 SIGMOD Conference* (Boston, Mass., May 1979).

28. Stonebraker, M. Muffin: A distributed database machine. ERL Technical Report UCB/ERL M79/28, University of California at Berkeley, May 1979.

29. Stonebraker, M. The case for shared nothing. *Database Eng. 9*, 1 (1986).

30. Stonebraker, M., Katz, R., Patterson, D., and Ousterhout, J. The design of XPRS. In *Proceedings of the Fourteenth International Conference on Very Large Data Bases*. (Los Angeles, Calif., Aug. 1988).

31. Tandem Database Group. NonStop SQL, a distributed, high-performance, high-reliability implementation of SQL. Workshop on High Performance Transaction Systems, Asilomar, CA, Sept. 1987.

32. Tandem Performance Group. A benchmark of non-stop SQL on the debit credit transaction. In *Proceedings of the 1988 SIGMOD Conference* (Chicago, Ill., June 1988).

33. Teradata Corporation. DBC/1012 Data Base Computer Concepts & Facilities. Document No. C02-0001-00, 1983.

34. Tevanian, A., et al. A Unix interface for shared memory and memory mapped files under Mach. Dept. of Computer Science Technical Report, Carnegie Mellon University, July, 1987.

35. Thakkar, S.S. and Sweiger, M. Performance of an OLTP application on symmetry multiprocessor system. In *Proceedings of the Seventeenth Annual International Symposium on Computer Architecture*. (Seattle, Wash., May, 1990).

36. *The Performance Handbook for Database and Transaction Processing Systems*. J. Gray, Ed., Morgan Kaufmann, San Mateo, Ca., 1991.

37. Walton, C.B., Dale, A.G., and Jenevein, R.M. A taxonomy and performance model of data skew effects in parallel joins. In *Proceedings of the Seventeenth International Conference on Very Large Data Bases*. (Barcelona, Spain, Sept. 1991).

38. Wolf, J.L., Dias, D.M., and Yu, P.S. An effective algorithm for parallelizing sort-merge joins in the presence of data skew. In *Proceedings of the Second International Symposium on Parallel and Distributed Systems*. (Dublin, Ireland, July, 1990).

39. Zeller, H.J. and Gray, J. Adaptive hash joins for a multiprogramming environment. In *Proceedings of the 1990 VLDB Conference* (Australia, Aug. 1990).

CR Categories and Subject Descriptors: B.5.1 [**Register-Transfer-Level Implementation**]: Design-style (e.g., parallel, pipelined, special-purpose); C.1.2 [**Computer Systems Organization**]: Processor Architectures—*Multiple Data Stream Architectures (Multiprocessors)*; F.1.2 [**Computation by Abstract Devices**]: Modes of Computation—*Parallelism*; H.2.1 [**Information Systems**]: Database Management—*Logical design*; H.2.8 [**Information Systems**]: Database Management—*Database Applications*; H.3 [**Information Systems**]: Information Storage and Retrieval

General Terms: Design, Measurement

Additional Keywords and Phrases: Parallelism, parallel database systems, parallel processing systems.

About the Authors:

DAVID DEWITT is a professor in the Computer Sciences Department at the University of Wisconsin. His current research interests include parallel database systems, object-oriented database systems, and database performance evaluation. **Author's Present Address:** Computer Sciences Department, University of Wisconsin, 1210 West Dayton Street, Madison, WI 53706; email: dewitt@cs.wisc.edu

JIM GRAY is a staff member with the Digital Equipment Corporation. His current research interests include databases, transaction processing, and computer architecture. **Author's Present Address:** San Francisco Systems Center, Digital Equipment Corporation, 455 Market Street—7th Floor, San Francisco, CA 94105-2403; email: gray@sfbay.enet.dec.com

This research was partially supported by the Defense Advanced Research Projects Agency under contract N00039-86-C-0578, by the National Science Foundation under grant DCR-8512862, and by research grants from Digital Equipment Corporation, IBM, NCR, Tandem, and Intel Scientific Computers.

Encapsulation of Parallelism in the Volcano Query Processing System

Goetz Graefe

University of Colorado
Boulder, CO 80309-0430
graefe@boulder.colorado.edu

Abstract

Volcano is a new dataflow query processing system we have developed for database systems research and education. The uniform interface between operators makes Volcano extensible by new operators. All operators are designed and coded as if they were meant for a single-process system only. When attempting to parallelize Volcano, we had to choose between two models of parallelization, called here the *bracket* and *operator* models. We describe the reasons for not choosing the bracket model, introduce the novel operator model, and provide details of Volcano's *exchange* operator that parallelizes all other operators. It allows intra-operator parallelism on partitioned datasets and both vertical and horizontal inter-operator parallelism. The exchange operator encapsulates all parallelism issues and therefore makes implementation of parallel database algorithms significantly easier and more robust. Included in this encapsulation is the translation between demand-driven dataflow within processes and data-driven dataflow between processes. Since the interface between Volcano operators is similar to the one used in "real," commercial systems, the techniques described here can be used to parallelize other query processing engines.

1. Introduction

In order to provide a testbed for database systems education and research, we decided to implement an extensible and modular query processing system. One important goal was to achieve flexibility and extensibility without sacrificing efficiency. The result is a small system, consisting of less than two dozen core modules with a total of about 15,000 lines of C code. These modules include a file system, buffer management, sorting, top-down B^+-trees, and two algorithms each for natural join, semi-join, outer join, anti-join, aggregation, duplicate elimination, division, union, intersection, difference, anti-difference, and Cartesian product. Moreover, a single module allows parallel processing of all algorithms listed above.

The last module, called the *exchange* module, is the focus of this paper. It was designed and implemented *after* most of the other query processing modules. The design goal was to parallelize all existing query processing algorithms without modifying their implementations. Equivalently, the goal was to allow parallelizing new algorithms not yet invented without requiring that these algorithms be implemented with concern for parallelism. This goal was met almost entirely, the only change to the existing modules concerned device names and numbers to allow horizontal partitioning over multiple disks, also called disk striping [25].

Parallelizing a query evaluation engine using an operator is a novel idea; earlier research projects used template processes that encompass specific operators. We call the new method of parallelizing the *operator model*. In this paper, we describe this new method and contrast it with the method used in GAMMA and Bubba, which we call the *bracket model*. Since we developed, implemented, and tested the operator model within the framework of the Volcano system, we will describe it as realized in Volcano.

Volcano was designed to be extensible, its design and implementation follows many of the ideas outlined by Batory et al. for the GENESIS design [5]. In this paper, we do not focus on or substantiate the claim to extensibility and instead refer the reader to [17], suffice it to point out that if new operators use and provide Volcano's standard interface between operators, they can easily be included in a Volcano query evaluation plan and parallelized by the exchange operator.

Volcano's mechanism to synchronize multiple operators in complex query trees within a single process and to exchange data items between operators are very similar to many commercial database systems, e.g., Ingres and the System R family of database systems. Therefore, it seems fairly straightforward to apply the techniques developed for Volcano's exchange operator and outlined in this paper to parallelize the query processing engines of such systems.

This paper is organized as follows. In the following section, we briefly review previous work that influenced our design, and introduce the *bracket* model of parallelization. In Section 3, we provide a more detailed description of Volcano. The *operator* model of parallelization and Volcano's *exchange* operator are described in Section 4. We present experimental performance measurements in Section 5 that show the *exchange* operator's low overhead. Section 6 contains a summary and our conclusions from this effort.

2. Previous Work

Since so many different system have been developed to process large dataset efficiently, we only survey the systems that have strongly influenced the design of Volcano

At the start in 1987, we felt that some decisions in WiSS [11] and GAMMA [12] were not optimal for performance or generality For instance, the decisions to protect WiSS's buffer space by copying a data record in or out for each request and to re-request a buffer page for every record during a scan seemed to inflict too much overhead[1] However, many of the design decisions in Volcano were strongly influenced by experiences with WiSS and GAMMA The design of the data exchange mechanism between operators, the focus of this paper, is one of the few radical departures from GAMMA's design

During the design of the EXODUS storage manager [10], many of these issues were revisited Lessons learned and tradeoffs explored in these discussions certainly helped form the ideas behind Volcano The development of E [24] influenced the strong emphasis on iterators for query processing The design of GENESIS [5] emphasized the importance of a uniform iterator interface

Finally, a number of conventional (relational) and extensible systems have influenced our design Without further discussion, we mention Ingres [27], System R [3], Bubba [2], Starburst [26], Postgres [28], and XPRS [29] Furthermore, there has been a large amount of research and development in the database machine area, such that there is an international workshop on the topic Almost all database machine proposals and implementations utilize parallelism in some form We certainly have learned from this work and tried to include its lessons in the design and implementation of Volcano In particular, we have strived for simplicity in the design, *mechanisms* that can support a multitude of *policies*, and efficiency in all details We believe that the query execution engine should provide mechanisms, and that the query optimizer should incorporate and decide on policies

Independently of our work, Tandem Computers has designed an operator called the *parallel operator* which is very similar to Volcano's exchange operator It has proven useful in Tandem's query execution engine [14], but is not yet documented in the open literature We learned about this operator through one of the referees Furthermore, the distributed database system R* used a technique similar to ours to transfer data between nodes [31] However, this operation was used only to effect data transfer and did not support data or intra-operator parallelism

2.1. The Bracket Model of Parallelization

When attempting to parallelize existing single-process Volcano software, we considered two paradigms or models of parallelization The first one, which we call the *bracket model*, has been used in a number of systems, for example GAMMA [12] and Bubba [2] The second one, which we call the *operator model*, is novel and is described in detail in Section 4

[1] This statement only pertains to the original version of WiSS as described in [11] Both decisions were reconsidered for the version of WiSS used in GAMMA

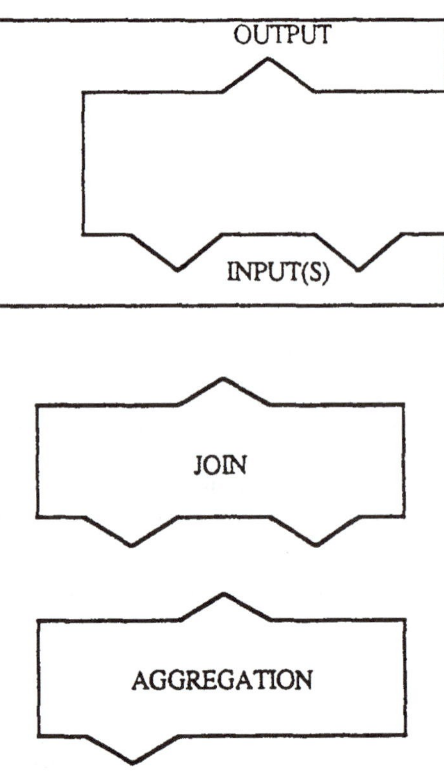

Figure 1 Bracket Model of Parallelization.

In the bracket model, there is a generic process template that can receive and send data and can execute exactly one operator at any point of time A schematic diagram of such a template process is shown in Figure 1 with two possible operators, join and aggregation The code that makes up the generic template invokes the operator which then controls execution, network I/O on the receiving and sending sides are performed as service to the operator on request, implemented as procedures to be called by the operator. The number of inputs that can be active at any point of time is limited to two since there are only unary and binary operators in most database systems The operator is surrounded by generic template code which shields it from its environment, for example the operator(s) that produce its input and consume its output.

One problem with the bracket model is that each locus of control needs to be created This is typically done by a separate scheduler process, requiring software development beyond the actual operators, both initially and for each extension to the set of query processing algorithms Thus, the bracket model seems unsuitable for an extensible system

In a query processing system using the bracket model, operators are coded in such a way that network I/O is their only means of obtaining input and delivering output (with the exception of scan and store operators) The reason is that each operator is its own locus of control and network flow control must be used to coordinate multiple operators, e g , to match two operators' speed in a producer-consumer relationship Unfortunately, this also means that passing a data item from one operator to another always involves expensive inter-process communication (IPC) system calls, even in the cases when an entire query is evaluated on a single machine (and could therefore be evaluated without IPC in a single process) or when data do not need to be repartitioned among nodes in a network An example for the latter is the three-way join query "joinCselAselB" in the Wisconsin Benchmark [6, 9] which uses the same join attribute for both two-way joins Thus, in queries with multiple operators (meaning almost all queries), IPC and its overhead are mandatory rather than optional

In most (single-process) query processing engines, operators schedule each other much more efficiently by means of procedure calls rather the system calls The concepts and methods needed for operators to schedule each other using procedure calls are the subject of the next section

3. Volcano System Design

In this section, we provide an overview of the modules in Volcano Volcano's file system is rather conventional It includes a modules to manage devices, buffer pools, files, records, and B^{+}-trees For a detailed discussion, we refer to [17]

The file system routines are used by the query processing routines to evaluate complex query plans Queries are expressed as complex algebra expressions, the operators of this algebra are query processing algorithms All algebra operators are implemented as *iterators*, i e , they support a simple *open-next-close* protocol similar to conventional file scans

Associated with each algorithm is a *state record* The arguments for the algorithms are kept in the state record All operations on records, e g , comparisons and hashing, are performed by *support functions* which are given in the state records as arguments to the iterators Thus, the query processing modules could be implemented without knowledge or constraint on the internal structure of data objects

In queries involving more than one operator (i e , almost all queries), state records are linked together by means of *input* pointers The input pointers are also kept in the state records They are pointers to a *QEP* structure that consists of four pointers to the entry points of the three procedures implementing the operator (*open*, *next*, and *close*) and a state record All state information for an iterator is kept in its state record, thus, an algorithm may be used multiple times in a query by including more than one state record in the query An operator does not need to know what kind of operator produces its input, and whether its input comes from a complex query tree or from a simple file scan We call this concept *anonymous inputs* or *streams* Streams are a simple but powerful abstraction that allows combining any number of operators to evaluate a complex query Together with the iterator control paradigm, streams represent the most efficient execution model in terms of time (overhead for synchronizing operators) and space (number of records that must reside in memory at any point of time) for single process query evaluation

Calling *open* for the top-most operator results in instantiations for the associated state record, e g , allocation of a hash table, and in *open* calls for all inputs In this way, all iterators in a query are initiated recursively In order to process the query, *next* for the top-most operator is called repeatedly until it fails with an *end of stream* indicator Finally, the *close* call recursively "shuts down" all iterators in the query This model of query execution matches very closely the one being included in the E programming language design [24] and the algebraic query evaluation system of the Starburst extensible relational database system [22]

The tree-structured query evaluation plan is used to execute queries by demand-driven dataflow The return value of *next* is, besides a status value, a structure called *NEXT_RECORD* that consists of a record identifier and a record address in the buffer pool This record is pinned (fixed) in the buffer The protocol about fixing and unfixing records is as follows Each record pinned in the buffer is *owned* by exactly one operator at any point in time After receiving a record, the operator can hold on to it for a while, e g , in a hash table, unfix it, e g , when a predicate fails, or pass it on to the next operator Complex operations like join that create new records have to fix them in the buffer before passing them on, and have to unfix their input records

For intermediate results, Volcano uses *virtual devices* Pages of such a device exist only in the buffer, and are discarded when unfixed. Using this mechanism allows assigning unique RID's to intermediate result records, and allows managing such records in all operators as if they resided on a real (disk) device The operators are not affected by the use of virtual devices, and can be programmed as if all input comes from a disk-resident file and output is written to a disk file

4. The Operator Model of Parallelization

When porting Volcano to a multi-processor machine, we felt it desirable to use the single-process query processing code described above *without any change* The result is very clean, self-scheduling parallel processing We call this novel approach the *operator model* of parallelizing a query evaluation engine In this model, all issues of control are localized in one operator that uses and provides the standard iterator interface to the operators above and below in a query tree

The module responsible for parallel execution and synchronization is called the *exchange* iterator in Volcano Notice that it is an iterator with *open*, *next*, and *close* procedures, therefore, it can be inserted at any one place or at multiple places in a complex query tree Figure 2 shows a complex query execution plan that includes data processing operators, e g file scan and join, and exchange operators

This section describes how the *exchange* iterator implements vertical and horizontal parallelism followed by a detailed example and a discussion of alternative modes of operation of Volcano's *exchange* operator

4.1. Vertical Parallelism

The first function of exchange is to provide *vertical parallelism* or pipelining between processes The *open* procedure creates a new process after creating a data structure in shared memory called a *port* for synchronization and data

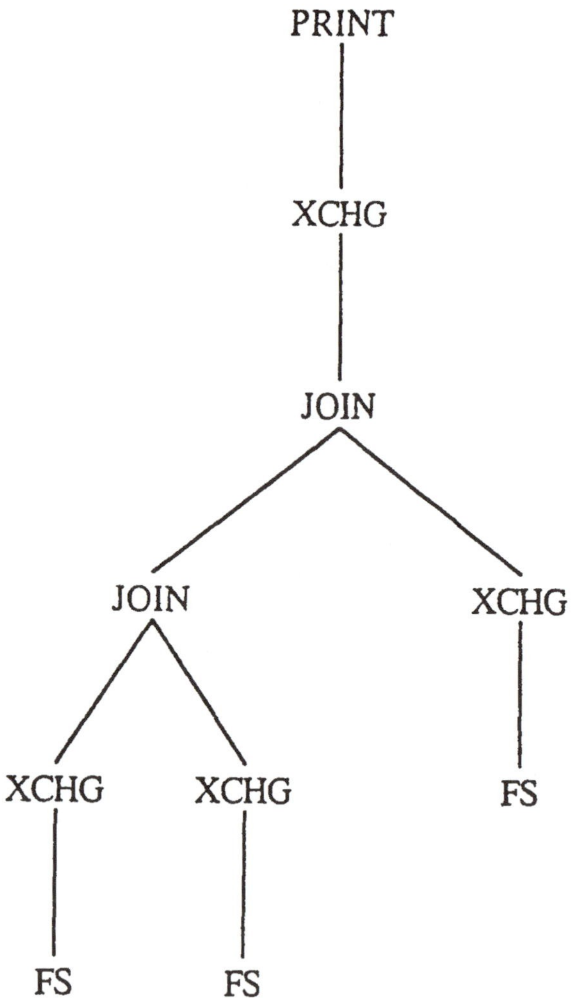

Figure 2 Operator Model of Parallelization

exchange The child process, created using the UNIX *fork* system call, is an exact duplicate of the parent process The exchange operator then takes different paths in the parent and child processes

The parent process serves as the *consumer* and the child process as the *producer* in Volcano. The exchange operator in the consumer process acts as a normal iterator, the only difference from other iterators is that it receives its input via inter-process communication rather than iterator (procedure) calls After creating the child process, *open_exchange* in the consumer is done *Next_exchange* waits for data to arrive via the port and returns them a record at a time *Close_exchange* informs the producer that it can close, waits for an acknowledgement, and returns

The exchange operator in the producer process becomes the *driver* for the query tree below the exchange operator using *open*, *next*, and *close* on its input The output of *next* is collected in *packets*, which are arrays of *NEXT_RECORD* structures The packet size is an argument in the exchange iterator's state record, and can be set between 1 and 32,000 records When a packet is filled, it is inserted into a linked list originating in the *port* and a semaphore is used to inform the consumer about the new packet. Records in packets are fixed in the shared buffer and must be unfixed by a consuming operator

When its input is exhausted, the exchange operator in the producer process marks the last packet with an *end-of-stream* tag, passes it to the consumer, and waits until the consumer allows closing all open files This delay is necessary in Volcano because files on virtual devices must not be closed before all their records are unpinned in the buffer In other words, it is a peculiarity due to other design decisions in Volcano rather than inherent in the exchange iterator or the operator model of parallelization

The alert reader has noticed that the exchange module uses a different dataflow paradigm than all other operators While all other modules are based on demand-driven dataflow (iterators, lazy evaluation), the producer-consumer relationship of exchange uses data-driven dataflow (eager evaluation) There are two reasons for this change in paradigms First, we intend to use the exchange operator also for *horizontal parallelism*, to be described below, which is easier to implement with data-driven dataflow. Second, this scheme removes the need for request messages Even though a scheme with request messages, e g, using a semaphore, would probably perform acceptably on a shared-memory machine, we felt that it creates unnecessary control overhead and delays Since we believe that very high degrees of parallelism and very high-performance query evaluation require a closely tied network, e g, a hypercube, of shared-memory machines, we decided to use a paradigm for data exchange that has has been proven to perform well in a shared-nothing database machine [12, 13]

A run-time switch of exchange enables *flow control* or *back pressure* using an additional semaphore If the producer is significantly faster than the consumer, the producer may pin a significant portion of the buffer, thus impeding overall system performance If flow control is enabled, after a producer has inserted a new packet into the port, it must request the flow control semaphore After a consumer has removed a packet from the port, it releases the flow control semaphore The initial value of the flow control semaphore, e g, 4, determines how many packets the producers may get ahead of the consumers

Notice that flow control and demand-driven dataflow are not the same One significant difference is that flow control allows some "slack" in the synchronization of producer and consumer and therefore truly overlapped execution, while demand-driven dataflow is a rather rigid structure of request and delivery in which the consumer waits while the producer works on its next output The second significant difference is that data-driven dataflow is easier to combine efficiently with horizontal parallelism and partitioning

4.2. Horizontal Parallelism

There are two forms of horizontal parallelism which we call *bushy parallelism* and *intra-operator* parallelism In bushy parallelism, different CPU's execute different subtrees of a complex query tree Bushy parallelism and vertical parallelism are forms of *inter-operator* parallelism Intra-operator parallelism means that several CPU's perform the same operator on different subsets of a stored dataset or an intermediate result[2]

Bushy parallelism can easily be implemented by inserting one or two exchange operators into a query tree For example, in order to sort two inputs into a merge-join in parallel the first or both inputs are separated from the merge-join by an exchange operation[3] The parent process turns to the second sort immediately after forking the child process that will produce the first input in sorted order Thus, the two sort operations are working in parallel

Intra-operator parallelism requires data partitioning Partitioning of stored datasets is achieved by using multiple files, preferably on different devices Partitioning of intermediate results is implemented by including multiple queues in a port If there are multiple consumer processes, each uses its own input queue The producers use a support function to decide into which of the queues (or actually, into which of the packets being filled by the producer) an output record must go Using a support function allows implementing round-robin-, key-range-, or hash-partitioning

If an operator or an operator subtree is executed in parallel by a *group* of processes, one of them is designated the *master* When a query tree is *opened*, only one process is running, which is naturally the master When a master forks a child process in a producer-consumer relationship, the child process becomes the master within its group The first action of the master producer is to determine how many slaves are needed by calling an appropriate support function If the producer operation is to run in parallel, the master producer forks the other producer processes

Gerber pointed out that such a centralized scheme is suboptimal for high degrees of parallelism [15] When we changed our initial implementation from forking all producer processes by the master to using a *propagation tree* scheme, we observed significant performance improvements In such a scheme, the master forks one slave, then both fork a new slave each, then all four fork a new slave each, etc This scheme has been used very effectively for broadcast communication and synchronization in binary hypercubes

Even after optimizing the forking scheme, its overhead is not negligible We have considered using *primed processes*, i e, processes that are always present and wait for work packets Primed processes are used in many commercial database systems Since portable distribution of compiled code (for support functions) is not trivial, we delayed this change and plan on using primed processes only when we move to an environment with multiple shared-memory machines[4] Others have also observed the high cost of process creation and have provided alternatives, in particular "light-weight" processes in various forms, e g, in Mach [1]

After all producer processes are forked, they run without further synchronization among themselves, with two exceptions First, when accessing a shared data structure, e g, the port to the consumers or a buffer table, short-term locks must be acquired for the duration of one linked-list insertion Second, when a producer group is also a consumer group, i e, there are at least two exchange operators and three process groups involved in a vertical pipeline, the processes that are both consumers and producers synchronize twice During the (very short) interval between synchronizations, the master of this group creates a port which serves all processes in its group

When a *close* request is propagated down the tree and reaches the first exchange operator, the master consumer's *close_exchange* procedure informs all producer processes that they are allowed to close down using the semaphore mentioned above in the discussion on vertical parallelism If the producer processes are also consumers, the master of the process group informs its producers, etc. In this way, all operators are shut down in an orderly fashion, and the entire query evaluation is self-scheduling

4.3. An Example

Let us consider an example Assume a query with four operators, A, B, C, and D such that A calls B's, B calls C's, and C calls D's *open*, *close*, and *next* procedures Now assume that this query plan is to be run in three process groups, called A, BC, and D This requires an exchange operator between operators A and B, say X, and one between C and D, say Y B and C continue to pass records via a simple procedure call to the C's *next* procedure without crossing process boundaries Assume further that A runs as a single process, A_0, while BC and D run in parallel in processes BC_0 to BC_2 and D_0 to D_3, for a total of eight processes

A calls X's *open*, *close*, and *next* procedures instead of B's (Figure 2a), without knowledge that a process boundary will be crossed, a consequence of anonymous inputs in Volcano When X is *opened*, it creates a port with one input queue for A_0 and forks BC_0 (Figure 2b), which in turn forks BC_1 and BC_2 (Figure 2c) When the BC group *opens* Y, BC_0 to BC_2 synchronize, and wait until the Y operator in process BC_0 has initialized a port with three input queues BC_0 creates the port and stores its location at an address known only to the BC processes Then BC_0 to BC_2 synchronize again, and BC_1 and BC_2 get the port information from its location Next, BC_0 forks D_0 (Figure 2d) which in turn forks D_1 to D_3 (Figure 2e)

When the D operators have exhausted their inputs in D_0 to D_3, they return an *end-of-stream* indicator to the driver parts of Y In each D process, Y flags its last packets to each of the BC processes (i e, a total of 3x4=12 flagged packets) with an *end-of-stream* tag and then waits on a semaphore for permission to *close* The copies of the

[2] A fourth form of parallelism is inter-query parallelism, i e, the ability of a database management system to work on several queries concurrently In the current version, Volcano does not support inter-query parallelism A fifth and sixth form of parallelism that can be used for database operations involve hardware vector processing [30] and pipelining in the instruction execution Since Volcano is a software architecture and following the analysis in [8], we do not consider hardware parallelism further

[3] In general, sorted streams can be piped directly into the join, both in the single-process and the multi-process case Volcano's sort operator includes a parameter "final merge fan-in" that allows sharing the merge space by two sort operators performing the final merge in an interleaved fashion as requested by the merge join operator

[4] In fact, this work is currently under way

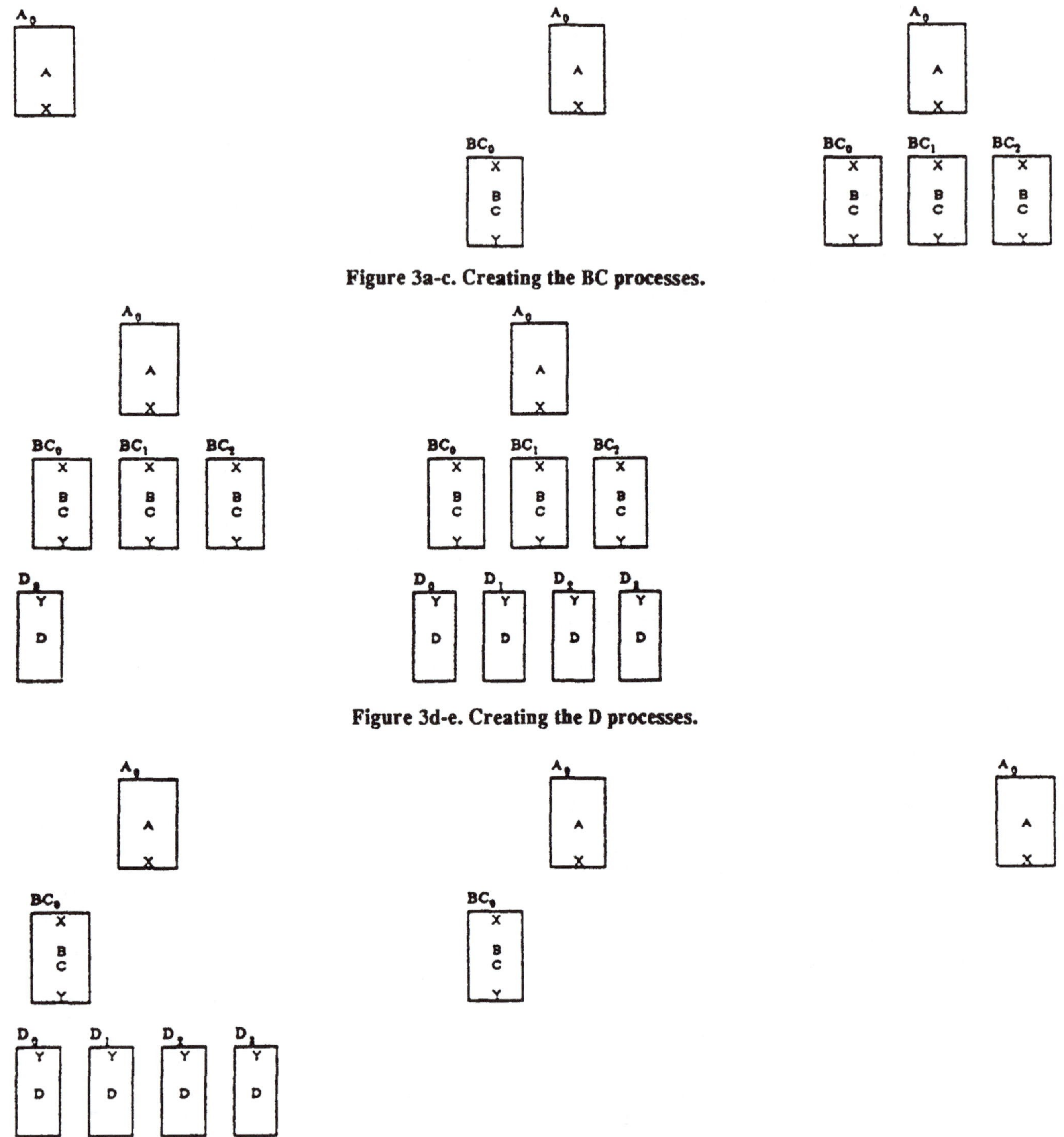

Figure 3a-c. Creating the BC processes.

Figure 3d-e. Creating the D processes.

Figure 3f-h. Closing all processes down.

Y operator in the *BC* processes count the number of tagged packets, after four tags (the number of producers or *D* processes), they have exhausted their inputs, and a call by *C* to *Y*'s ***next*** procedure will return an ***end-of-stream*** indicator In effect, the ***end-or-stream*** indicator has been propagated from the *D* operators to the *C* operators In due turn, C, B, and then the driver part of X will receive an *end-of-stream* indicator After receiving three tagged packets, X's *next* procedure in A_0 will indicate *end-of-stream* to A

When *end-of-stream* reaches the root operator of the query, A, the query tree is *closed* Closing the exchange operator X includes releasing the semaphore that allows the BC processes to shut down (Figure 3f) The X driver in each BC process *closes* its input, operator B B *closes* C, and C *closes* Y Closing Y in BC_1 and BC_2 is an empty operation When the process BC_0 *closes* the exchange operator Y, Y permits the D processes to shut down by releasing a semaphore After the processes of the D group have closed all files and deallocated all temporary data structures, e g, hash tables, they indicate the fact to Y in BC_0 using another semaphore, and Y's *close* procedure returns to its caller, C's *close* procedure, while the D processes terminate (Figure 3g) When all BC processes have *closed* down, X's *close* procedure indicates the fact to A_0 and query evaluation terminates (Figure 3h)

4.4. Variants of the Exchange Operator

There are a number of situations for which the *exchange* operator described so far required some modifications or extensions In this section, we outline additional capabilities implemented in Volcano's exchange operator

For some operations, it is desirable to *replicate* or *broadcast* a stream to *all* consumers For example, one of the two partitioning methods for hash-division [19] requires that the divisor be replicated and used with each partition of the dividend Another example is Baru's parallel join algorithm in which one of the two input relations is not moved at all while the other relation is sent through all processors [4] To support these algorithms, the exchange operator can be directed (by setting a switch in the state record) to send all records to all consumers, after pinning them appropriately multiple times in the buffer pool Notice that it is not necessary to copy the records since they reside in a shared buffer pool, it is sufficient to pin them such that each consumer can unpin them as if it were the only process using them After we implemented this feature, parallelizing our hash-division programs using both divisor partitioning and quotient partitioning [19] took only about three hours and yielded not insignificant speedups

When we implemented and benchmarked parallel sorting [21], we found it useful to add two more features to *exchange* First, we wanted to implement a merge network in which some processors produce sorted streams merge concurrently by other processors Volcano's *sort* iterator can be used to generate a sorted stream A *merge* iterator was easily derived from the sort module It uses a single level merge, instead of the cascaded merge of runs used in sort. The input of a *merge* iterator is an *exchange* Differently from other operators, the merge iterator requires to distinguish the input records by their producer As an example, for a join operation it does not matter where the input records were created, and all inputs can be accumulated in a single input stream For a merge operation, it is crucial to distinguish the input records by their producer in order to merge multiple sorted streams correctly

We modified the *exchange* module such that it can keep the input records separated according to their producers, switched by setting an argument field in the state record A third argument to *next_exchange* is used to communicate the required producer from the *merge* to the *exchange* iterator Further modifications included increasing the number of input buffers used by *exchange*, the number of semaphores (including for flow control) used between producer and consumer part of *exchange*, and the logic for *end-of-stream* All these modifications were implemented in such a way that they support multi-level merge trees, e g, a parallel binary merge tree as used in [7] The merging paths are selected automatically such that the load is distributed as evenly as possible in each level

Second, we implemented a sort algorithm that sorts data randomly partitioned over multiple disks into a range-partitioned file with sorted partitions, i e, a sorted file distributed over multiple disks When using the same number of processors and disks, we used two processes per CPU, one to perform the file scan and partition the records and another one to sort them We realized that creating and running more processes than processors inflicted a significant cost, since these processes competed for the CPU's and therefore required operating system scheduling While the scheduling overhead may not be too significant, in our environment with a central run queue allowing processes to migrate freely and a large cache associated with each CPU, the frequent cache migration adds a significant cost.

In order to make better use of the available processing power, we decided to reduce the number of processes by half, effectively moving to one process per disk This required modifications to the exchange operator Until then, the exchange operator could "live' only at the top or the bottom of the operator tree in a process Since the modification, the exchange operator can also be in the middle of a process' operator tree When the exchange operator is *opened*, it does not fork any processes but establishes a communication port for data exchange The *next* operation requests records from its input tree, possibly sending them off to other processes in the group, until a record for its own partition is found

This mode of operation[5] also makes flow control obsolete A process runs a producer (and produces input for the other processes) only if it does not have input for the consumer Therefore, if the producers are in danger of overrunning the consumers, none of the producer operators gets scheduled, and the consumers consume the available records

In summary, the operator model of parallel query evaluation provides for self-scheduling parallel query evaluation in an extensible database system The most important properties of this novel approach are that the new module implements three forms of parallel processing within a single module, that it makes parallel query processing entirely self-scheduling, and that it did not require any changes in the existing query processing modules, thus leveraging significantly the time and effort spent on them and allowing easy parallel implementation of new algorithms

---

[5] Whether exchange forks new producer processes (the original exchange design describe in Section 4 1) or uses the existing process group to execute the producer operations is a run-time switch

5. Overhead and Performance

From the beginning of the Volcano project, we were very concerned about performance and overhead In this section, we report on experimental measurements of the overhead induced by the exchange operator This is not meant to be an extensive or complete analysis of the operator's performance and overhead, the purpose of this section is to demonstrate that the overhead can be kept in acceptable limits

We measured elapsed times of a program that creates records, fills them with four random integers, passes the records over three process boundaries, and then unfixes the records in the buffer The measurements are elapsed times on a Sequent Symmetry with twelve Intel 16 MHz 80386 CPU's This is a shared-memory machine with a 64 KB cache for each CPU Each CPU delivers about 4 MIPS in this machine The times were measured using the hardware microsecond clock available on such machines Sequent's DYNIX operating system provides exactly the same interface as Berkeley 4 2 BSD or System V UNIX and runs (i e, executes system calls) on all processors

First, we measured the program without any exchange operator Creating 100,000 records and releasing them in the buffer took 20 28 seconds Next, we measured the program with the exchange operator switched to the mode in which it does not create new processes In other words, compared to the last experiment, we added the overhead of three procedure calls for each record For this run, we measured 28 00 seconds Thus, the three exchange operators in this mode added (28 00sec - 20 28sec) / 3 / 100,000 = 25 73μsec overhead per record and exchange operator

When we switched the exchange operator to create new processes, thus creating a pipeline of four processes, we observed an elapsed time of 16 21 seconds with flow control enabled, or 16 16 seconds with flow control disabled The fact that these times ars less than the time for single-process program execution indicates that data transfer using the exchange operator is very fast, and that pipelined multi-process execution is warranted

We were particularly concerned about the granularity of data exchange between processes and its impact on Volcano's performance In a separate experiment, we reran the program multiple times varying the number of records per exchange packet. Table 1 shows the performance for transferring 100,000 records from a producer process group through two intermediate process groups to a single consumer process Each of these three groups included three processes, thus, each of the producer processes created 33,333 records All these experiments were conducted with flow control enabled with three 'slack" packets per exchange We used different partitioning (hash) functions for each exchange iterator to ensure that records were passing along all possible data paths, not only along three independent pipelines

Packet Size [Records]	Elapsed Time [Seconds]
1	176 4
2	97 6
5	45 27
10	27 67
20	20 15
50	15 71
100	13 76
200	12 87
250	12 73

Table 1 Exchange Performance

As can be seen in Table 3, the performance penalty for very small packets was significant The elapsed time was almost cut in half when the packet size was increased from 1 to 2 records, from 176 seconds to 98 seconds As the packet size was increased further, the elapsed time shrank accordingly, to 15 71 seconds for 50 records per packet and 12 73 seconds for 250 records per packet

It seemed reasonable to speculate that for small packets, most of the elapsed time was spent on data exchange To verify this hypothesis, we calculated regression and correlation coefficients of the number of data packets (100,000 divided over the packet size) and the elapsed times We found an intercept (base time) of 12 18 seconds, a slope of 0 001654 seconds per packet, and a correlation of more than 0 99 Considering that we exchanged data over three process boundaries and that on two of those boundaries there were three producers and three consumers, we estimate that the overhead was 1654μsec / 1 667 = 992μsec per packet and process boundary

Two conclusions can be drawn from these experiments First, vertical parallelism can pay off even for very simple query plans if the overhead of data transfer is small Second, since the packet size can be set to any value, the overhead of Volcano's exchange iterator is negligible

6. Summary and Conclusions

We have described Volcano, a new query evaluation system, and how parallel query evaluation is encapsulated in a single module or operator The system is operational on both single- and multi-processor systems, and has been used for a number in database query processing studies [19-21,23]

Volcano utilizes dataflow techniques within processes as well as between processes Within a process, demand-driven dataflow is implemented by means of iterators Between processes, data-driven dataflow is used to exchange data between producers and consumers efficiently If necessary, Volcano's data-driven dataflow can be augmented with flow control or back pressure Horizontal partitioning is used both on stored and intermediate datasets to allow intra-operator parallelism The design of the exchange operator embodies the parallel execution mechanism for vertical, bushy, and intra-operator parallelism, and it performs the transitions from demand-driven to data-driven dataflow and back

Using an operator to encapsulate parallelism as explored in the Volcano project has a number of advantages over the bracket model First, it hides the fact that parallelism is used from all other operators Thus, other operators can be implemented without consideration for parallelism Second, since the exchange operator uses the same interface to its input and output, it can be placed anywhere in a tree and combined with any other operators Hence, it can be used to parallelize new operators, and effectively combines extensibility and parallelism Third, it does not require a separate scheduler process since scheduling (including initialization, flow control, and final clean-up) is part of the operator and therefore performed within the standard *open-next-close* iterator paradigm This turns into an advantage in two situations When a new operator is integrated into the system, the scheduler and the template process would have to be modified, while the exchange operator does not require any modifications When the system is ported to a new environment, only one module requires modifications, the exchange iterator, not two modules, the template process and the scheduler Fourth, it does not require that operators in a parallel query evaluation system use IPC to exchange data. Thus, each process can execute an arbitrary subtree of a complex query evaluation plan. Fifth, a single process can have any number of inputs, not just one or two Finally, the operator can be (and has been) implemented in such a way that it can multiplex a single process between a producer and a consumer In some respects, it efficiently implements application-specific co-routines or threads

We plan on several extensions of the exchange operator First, we plan on extending our design and implementation to support both shared and distributed memory ("shared-nothing architecture") and to allow combining these concepts in a closely tied network of shared-memory multicomputers while maintaining the encapsulation properties. This might require using a pool of "primed" processes and interpreting support functions We believe that in the long run, high-performance database machines, both for transaction and query processing, will employ this architecture Second, we plan on devising a error and exception management scheme that makes exception notification and handling transparent across process and machine boundaries. Third, we plan on using the exchange operator to parallelize query processing in object-oriented database systems [16]. In our model, a complex object is represented in memory by a pointer to the root component (pinned in the buffer) with pointers to the sub-components (also pinned) and passed between operators by passing the root component [18] While the current design already allows passing complex objects in a shared-memory environment, more functionality is needed in a distributed-memory system where objects need to be packaged for network transfer

Volcano is the first implemented query evaluation system that combines extensibility and parallelism. Encapsulating all parallelism issues into one module was essential to making this combination possible The encapsulation of parallelism in Volcano allows for new query processing algorithms to be coded for single-process execution but run in a highly parallel environment without modifications We expect that this will speed parallel algorithm development and evaluation significantly Since the operator model of parallel query processing and Volcano's exchange operator encapsulates parallelism and both uses and provides an iterator interface similar to many existing database systems, the concepts explored and outlined in this paper may very well be useful in parallelizing other database query processing software

Acknowledgements

A number of friends and colleagues were great sounding boards during the design and implementation of parallelism in Volcano, most notably Frank Symonds and Leonard Shapiro Jerry Borgvedt implemented a prototype distributed-memory exchange operator — NSF supported this work with contracts IRI-8805200 and IRI-8912618 Sequent Computer Systems provided machine time for experiments on a large machine.

References

1 M Accetta, R Baron, W. Bolosky, D Golub, R. Rashid, A Tevanian and M Young, "Mach. A New Kernel Foundation for UNIX Development", *Summer Conference Proceedings 1986*,

2 W Alexander and G. Copeland, "Process and Dataflow Control in Distributed Data-Intensive Systems", *Proceedings of the ACM SIGMOD Conference*, Chicago, IL, June 1988, 90-98

3 M M. Astrahan, M W. Blasgen, D. D Chamberlin, K. P. Eswaran, J. N. Gray, P. P. Griffiths, W. F. King, R. A Lorie, P R. McJones, J W Mehl, G. R Putzolu, I L Traiger, B W Wade and V. Watson, "System R· A Relational Approach to Database Management", *ACM Transactions on Database Systems 1*, 2 (June 1976), 97-137.

4. C. K. Baru, O. Frieder, D. Kandlur and M Segal, "Join on a Cube· Analysis, Simulation, and Implementation", *Proceedings of the 5th International Workshop on Database Machines*, 1987.

5 D S. Batory, "GENESIS· A Project to Develop an Extensible Database Management System", *Proceedings of the Int'l Workshop on Object-Oriented Database Systems*, Pacific Grove, CA, September 1986, 207-208.

6. D. Bitton, D. J. DeWitt and C. Turbyfill, "Benchmarking Database Systems: A Systematic Approach", *Proceeding of the Conference on Very Large Data Bases*, Florence, Italy, October-November 1983, 8-19

7 D. Bitton, H. Boral, D. J DeWitt and W. K. Wilkinson, "Parallel Algorithms for the Execution of Relational Database Operations", *ACM Transactions on Database Systems 8*, 3 (September 1983), 324-353

8. H. Boral and D. J DeWitt, "Database Machines. An Idea Whose Time Has Passed? A Critique of the Future of Database Machines", *Proceeding of the International Workshop on Database Machines*, Munich, 1983

9. H. Boral and D J DeWitt, "A Methodology for Database System Performance Evaluation", *Proceedings of the ACM SIGMOD Conference*, Boston, MA, June 1984, 176-185

10 M J Carey, D J DeWitt, J E Richardson and E J. Shekita, "Object and File Management in the EXODUS Extensible Database System", *Proceedings of the Conference on Very Large Data Bases*, Kyoto, Japan, August 1986, 91-100

11 H T. Chou, D J DeWitt, R H Katz and A. C. Klug, "Design and Implementation of the Wisconsin Storage System", *Software - Practice and Experience 15*, 10 (October 1985), 943-962

12. D J DeWitt, R H Gerber, G Graefe, M L. Heytens, K B Kumar and M Muralikrishna,

"GAMMA - A High Performance Dataflow Database Machine", *Proceedings of the Conference on Very Large Data Bases*, Kyoto, Japan, August 1986, 228-237

13 D J DeWitt, S Ghandeharadizeh, D Schneider, A Bricker, H I Hsiao and R Rasmussen, "The Gamma Database Machine Project", *IEEE Transactions on Knowledge and Data Engineering 2*, 1 (March 1990)

14 S Englert, J Gray, R Kocher and P Shah, "A Benchmark of NonStop SQL Release 2 Demonstrating Near-Linear Speedup and Scaleup on Large Databases", *Tandem Computer Systems Technical Report 89 4* (May 1989)

15 R Gerber, "Dataflow Query Processing using Multiprocessor Hash-Partitioned Algorithms", *Ph.D Thesis*, Madison, October 1986

16 G Graefe and D Maier, "Query Optimization in Object-Oriented Database Systems A Prospectus", in *Advances in Object-Oriented Database Systems*, vol 334 , K. R Dittrich (editor), Springer-Verlag, September 1988, 358-363

17 G. Graefe, "Volcano An Extensible and Parallel Dataflow Query Processing System", *Oregon Graduate Center, Computer Science Technical Report*, Beaverton, OR , June 1989

18 G Graefe, "Set Processing and Complex Object Assembly in Volcano and the REVELATION Project", *Oregon Graduate Center, Computer Science Technical Report*, Beaverton, OR , June 1989

19 G. Graefe, "Relational Division. Four Algorithms and Their Performance", *Proceedings of the IEEE Conference on Data Engineering*, Los Angelos, CA, February 1989, 94-101

20 G. Graefe and K Ward, "Dynamic Query Evaluation Plans", *Proceedings of the ACM SIGMOD Conference*, Portland, OR, May-June 1989, 358

21 G Graefe, "Parallel External Sorting in Volcano", *submitted for publication*, February 1990

22 L. M Haas, W F Cody, J C Freytag, G Lapis, B G. Lindsay, G. M Lohman, K Ono and H Pirahesh, "An Extensible Processor for an Extended Relational Query Language", *Computer Science Research Report*, San Jose, CA , April 1988

23 T Keller and G Graefe, "The One-to-One Match Operator of the Volcano Query Processing System", *Oregon Graduate Center, Computer Science Technical Report*, Beaverton, OR , June 1989

24 J E Richardson and M J Carey, "Programming Constructs for Database System Implementation in EXODUS", *Proceedings of the ACM SIGMOD Conference*, San Francisco, CA., May 1987, 208-219

25 K Salem and H Garcia-Molina, "Disk Striping", *Proceedings of the IEEE Conference on Data Engineering*, Los Angeles, CA , February 1986, 336

26 P Schwarz, W Chang, J C Freytag, G Lohman, J McPherson, C Mohan and H Pirahesh, "Extensibility in the Starburst Database System", *Proceedings of the Int'l Workshop on Object-Oriented Database Systems*, Pacific Grove, CA , September 1986, 85-92.

27 M Stonebraker, E. Wong, P. Kreps and G. D. Held, "The Design and Implementation of INGRES", *ACM Transactions on Database Systems 1*, 3 (September 1976), 189-222

28. M. Stonebraker and L A Rowe, "The Design of POSTGRES", *Proceedings of the ACM SIGMOD Conference*, Washington, DC., May 1986, 340-355.

29 M Stonebraker, R. Katz, D. Patterson and J Ousterhout, "The Design of XPRS", *Proceedings of the Conference on Very Large Databases*, Los Angeles, CA, August 1988, 318-330.

30. S. Torii, K. Kojima, Y. Kanada, A. Sakata, S. Yoshizumi and M. Takahashi, "Accelerating Nonnumerical Processing by an Extended Vector Processor", *Proceedings of the IEEE Conference on Data Engineering*, Los Angeles, CA , February 1988, 194-201

31. P. Williams, D. Daniels, L. Haas, G Lapis, B. Lindsay, P. Ng, R. Obermarck, P Selinger, A. Walker, P Wilms and R. Yost, "R*. An Overview of the Architecture", in *Readings in Database Systems*, M. Stonebraker (editor), Morgan-Kaufman, San Mateo, CA , 1988.

AlphaSort: A RISC Machine Sort

Chris Nyberg, Tom Barclay, Zarka Cvetanovic, Jim Gray, Dave Lomet
Digital Equipment Corporation, San Francisco Systems Center
455 Market St, San Francisco, CA. 94105
{Barclay, Gray, Lomet, Nyberg, Zarka} @ SFbay.enet.dec.com

Abstract *A new sort algorithm, called AlphaSort, demonstrates that commodity processors and disks can handle commercial batch workloads. Using Alpha AXP processors, commodity memory, and arrays of SCSI disks, AlphaSort runs the industry-standard sort benchmark in seven seconds. This beats the best published record on a 32-cpu 32-disk Hypercube by 8:1. On another benchmark, AlphaSort sorted more than a gigabyte in a minute.*

AlphaSort is a cache-sensitive memory-intensive sort algorithm. It uses file striping to get high disk bandwidth. It uses QuickSort to generate runs and uses replacement-selection to merge the runs. It uses shared memory multiprocessors to break the sort into subsort chores.

Because startup times are becoming a significant part of the total time, we propose two new benchmarks:
(1) MinuteSort: how much can you sort in a minute, and
(2) DollarSort: how much can you sort for a dollar.

1. Introduction

In 1985, an informal group of 25 database experts from a dozen companies and universities defined three basic benchmarks to measure the transaction processing performance of computer systems.

DebitCredit: a market basket of database reads and writes, terminal IO, and transaction commits to measure on-line transaction processing performance (OLTP). This benchmark evolved to become the TPC-A transactions-per-second and dollars-per-transaction-per-second metrics [12].

Scan: copy a thousand 100-byte records from disk-to-disk with transaction protection. This simple mini-batch transaction measures the ability of a file system or database system to pump data through a user application.

Sort: a disk-to-disk sort of one million, 100-byte records. This has become the standard test of batch and utility performance in the database community [3, 4, 6, 7, 9, 11, 13 18, 21, 22]. Sort tests the processor's, IO subsystem's, and operating system's ability to move data.

SIGMOD 94- 5/94 Minneapolis, Minnesota, USA
© 1994 ACM 0-89791-639-5/94/0005..$3.50

DebitCredit is a simple interactive transaction. Scan is a mini-batch transaction. Sort is an IO-intensive batch transaction. Together they cover a broad spectrum of basic commercial operations.

2. The sort benchmark and prior work on sort

The Datamation article [1] defined the sort benchmark as:

- Input is a disk-resident file of a million 100-byte records.
- Records have 10-byte key fields and can't be compressed.
- The input record keys are in random order.
- The output file must be a permutation of the input file sorted in key ascending order.

The performance metric is the elapsed time of the following seven steps:

(1) launch the sort program.
(2) open the input file and create the output file.
(3) read the input file.
(4) sort the records in key-ascending order.
(5) write the output file.
(6) close the files.
(7) terminate the program

The implementation may use all the "mean tricks" typical of operating systems utilities. It can access the files via low-level interfaces, it can use undocumented interfaces, and it can use as many disks, processors and as much memory as it likes. Sort's price-performance metric normalizes variations in software and hardware configuration. The basic idea is to compute the 5-year cost of the hardware and software, and then prorate that cost for the elapsed time of the sort [1, 12]. A one minute sort on a machine with a 5-year cost of a million dollars would cost 38 cents (0.38$).

In 1985, as reported by Tsukerman, typical systems needed 15 minutes to perform this sort benchmark [1, 6, 21]. As a super-computer response to Tsukerman's efforts, Peter Weinberger of ATT wrote a program to read a disk file into memory, sort it using replacement-selection as records arrived, and then write the sorted data to a file [22]. This code postulated 8-byte keys, a natural size for the Cray, and made some other simplifications. The disks transferred at 8 MB/s, so you might guess that it took 12.5 seconds to read and 12.5 seconds to write for a grand total of 25 seconds. However there was about 1 second worth of overhead in setup, file creation, and file access. The result, 26 seconds, stood as the unofficial sort speed record for seven years. It is much faster than the subsequently reported Hypercube and hardware sorters.

Table 1: Published sort performance on the Datamation 100 MB benchmark in chronological order. Extrapolations marked by (*). Prices are estimated.

System	Time(sec)	$/sort(*)	Cost M$*	CPUs	Disks	Reference
Tandem	3600	4.61	.2.??	2	2	[1, 21]
Beck	6000	1.92	.1	4	4	[7]
Tsukerman + Tandem	980	1.25	.2	3	6	[20]
Weinberger + Cray	26	1.25	7.5	1	1	[22]
Kitsuregawa	320*	0.41	.2	1+	1	[15]
Baugsto	180	0.23	.2	16	16	[4]
Graefe + Sequent	83	0.27	.5	8	4	[11]
Baugsto	40	0.26	1.?	100	100	[4]
DeWitt + Intel iPSC/2	58	0.37	1.0	32	32	[9]
DEC Alpha AXP 7000	9.1	0.022	.4	1	16	1993
DEC Alpha AXP 4000	8.2	0.011	.2	2	14	1993
DEC Alpha AXP 7000	7	0.014	.5	3	28	1993

Since 1986, most sorting effort has focused on multiprocessor sorting, either using shared memory or using partitioned-data designs. DeWitt, Naughton, and Schneider's efforts on an Intel Hypercube is the fastest reported time: 58.3 seconds using 32 processors, 32 disks and 224 MB of memory [9]. Baugsto, Greispland and Kamberbeek mentioned a 40-second sort on a 100-processor 100-disk system [4]. These parallel systems stripe the input and output data across all the disks (30 in the Hypercube case). They read the disks in parallel, performing a preliminary sort of the data at each source, and partition it into equal-sized parts. Each reader-sorter sends the partitions to their respective target partitions. Each target partition processor merges the many input streams into a sorted run that is stored on the local disk. The resulting output file is striped across the 32 disks. The Hypercube sort was two times slower than Weinberger's Cray sort, but it had better price-performance, since the machine is about seven times cheaper.

Table 1 and Graph 2 show that prior to AlphaSort, sophisticated hardware-software combinations were slower than a brute-force one-pass memory intensive sort. Until now, a Cray Y-MP super-computer with a gigabyte of memory, a fast disk, and fast processors was the clear winner. But, the Cray approach was expensive.

Weinberger's Cray-based sort used a fast processor, a fast-parallel-transfer disk, and lots of fast memory. AlphaSort's approach is similar, but it uses commodity products to achieve better price/performance. It uses fast one-chip processors, commodity memory, and commodity disks. It uses file striping to exploit parallel disks, and it breaks the sorting task into subtasks that exploit multi-processors. Using these techniques, AlphaSort beats the Cray YMP in two dimensions: it is about 4x faster and about 100x less expensive.

3. Optimizing for the memory hierarchy

Good external sort programs have always tried to minimize the wait for data transfers between disk and main memory. While this optimization is well known, minimizing cache miss waits is not as widely recognized. AlphaSort has the

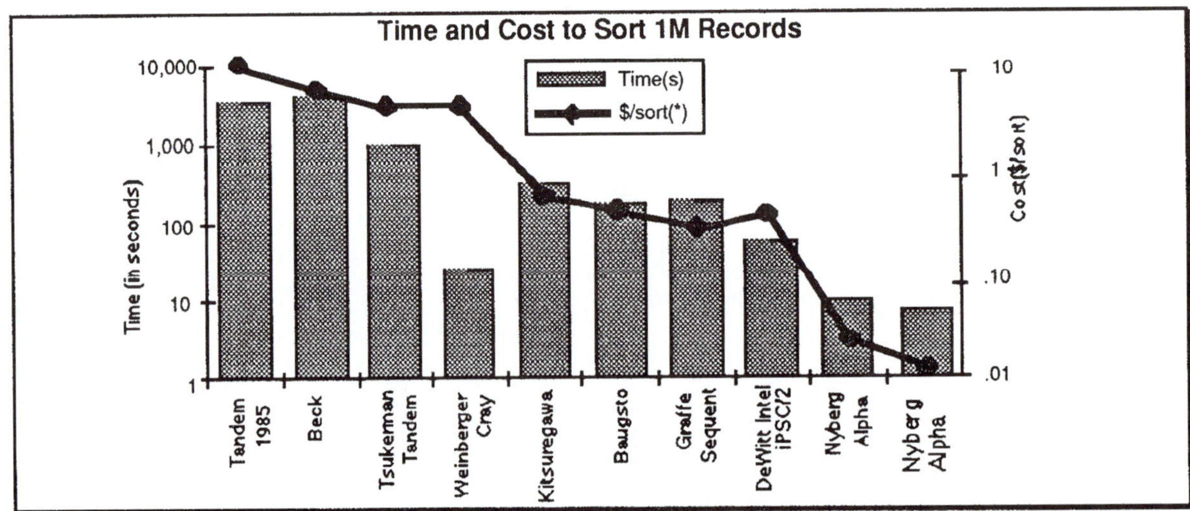

Graph 2: The performance and price-performance trends of sorting displayed in chronological order. Until now, the Cray sort was fastest but the parallel sorts had the best price-performance.

traditional optimizations, but in addition it gets a 4:1 processor-speedup by minimizing cache misses and minimizing the time processors wait for memory transfers. If all cache misses were eliminated, it could get another 3:1 speedup.

AlphaSort is an instance of the new programming style dictated by one-chip RISC architectures. These processors run the SPEC benchmark very well, because most SPEC benchmarks fit in the cache of newer RISC machines [14]. Unfortunately, commercial workloads, like sort and TPC-A, *do not* conveniently fit in cache [5]. These commercial benchmarks stall the processor waiting for memory most of the time. Reducing cache misses has replaced reducing instructions as the most important processor optimization.

The need for algorithms to consider cache behavior is not a transient phenomenon. Processor speeds are projected to increase about 70% per year for many years to come. This trend will widen the speed gap between memory and processor caches. The caches will get larger, but memory speed will not keep pace with processor speeds.

The Alpha AXP memory hierarchy is:
- Registers,
- On-chip instruction and data caches (I-cache & D-cache),
- Unified (program and data) cpu-board cache (B-cache),
- Main memory,
- Disks,
- Tape and other near-line and off-line storage.

To appreciate the issue, consider the whimsical analogy in Figure 3. The scale on the left shows the number of clock ticks to get to various levels of the memory hierarchy (measured in 5ns processor clock ticks). The scale on the right is a more human scale showing time based in human units (minutes). If your body clock ticks in seconds, then divide the times by 60.

AlphaSort is designed to operate within the processor cache ("This Campus" in Figure 3). It minimizes references to memory ("Sacramento" in Figure 3). It performs disk IO asynchronously and in parallel – AlphaSort rarely waits for disks ("Pluto" in Figure 3).

Suppose AlphaSort paid no attention to the cache, suppose rather that it randomly accessed main memory at every instruction. Then the processor would run at memory speed – about 2 million instructions per second – rather than the 200 million instructions per second it is capable of, a 100:1 execution penalty. By paying careful attention to cache behavior, AlphaSort is able to minimize cache misses and to run at 72 million instructions per second.

This careful attention to memory accesses does not suggest that we can ignore disk IO and sorting algorithms. Rather, once the traditional problems are solved, one is faced with achieving speedups by optimizing the use of the memory hierarchy.

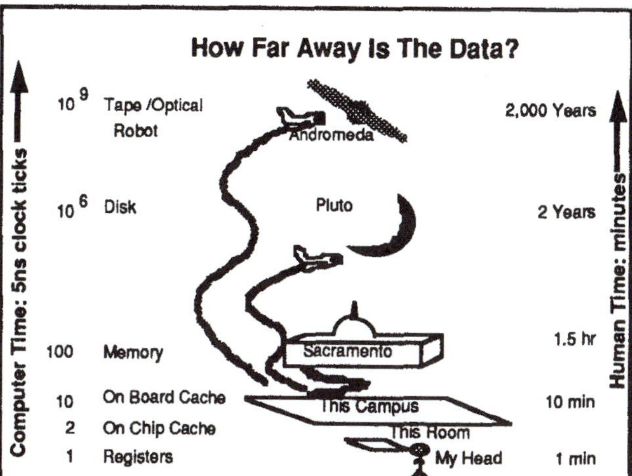

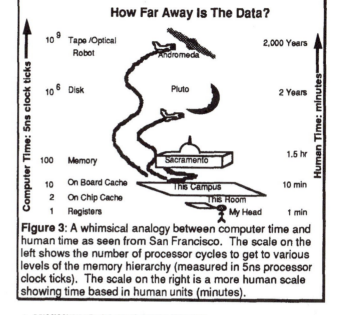

Figure 3: A whimsical analogy between computer time and human time as seen from San Francisco. The scale on the left shows the number of processor cycles to get to various levels of the memory hierarchy (measured in 5ns processor clock ticks). The scale on the right is a more human scale showing time based in human units (minutes).

4. MINIMIZING CACHE-MISS WAITS

AlphaSort uses the following techniques to optimize its use of the processor cache:

1. QuickSort input record groups as they arrive from disk. QuickSort has good cache locality. Dividing into groups allows QuickSorting to be overlapped with file input.
2. Rather than sort records, sort (key-prefix, pointer) pairs. This optimization reduces data movement.
3. The runs generated by QuickSort are merged using a replacement-selection tree. Because the merge tree is small, it has excellent cache behavior. The record pointers emerging from the tree are used to gather (copy) records from where they were read into memory to output buffers. Records are only copied this one time. The copy operation is memory intensive.

By comparison, OpenVMS sort uses a pure replacement-selection sort to generate runs [17]. Replacement-selection is best for a memory constrained environment. On average, replacement-selection generates runs twice as large as memory, while the QuickSort runs are typically smaller than half of memory. However, in a memory-rich environment, QuickSort is faster because it is simpler, makes fewer exchanges on average, and has superior address locality to exploit processor caching.

The worst-case behavior of replacement-selection is very close to its average behavior, while the worst-case behavior of QuickSort is terrible (N^2) – a strong argument in favor of replacement-selection. Despite this risk, QuickSort is widely used because, in practice, it has superior performance. Baugsto, Bitton, Beck, Graefe, and DeWitt used QuickSort [4, 6, 7, 9, 11]. On the other hand, Tsukerman and Weinberger used replacement-selection [21, 22]. IBM's DFsort and (apparently) Syncsort™ use replacement selection in conjunction with a technique called offset-value coding (OVC). We are evaluating OVC[1].

We were reluctant to abandon replacement-selection sort – it has stability and it generates long runs. Our first approach was to improve replacement-selection sort's cache locality. Standard replacement-selection sort has terrible cache behavior unless the tournament fits in cache. The cache thrashes on the bottom levels of the tournament. If you think of the tournament as a tree, each replacement-selection step traverses a path from a pseudo-random leaf of the tree to the root. The upper parts of the tree may be cache resident, but the bulk of the tree is not (see Figure 4).

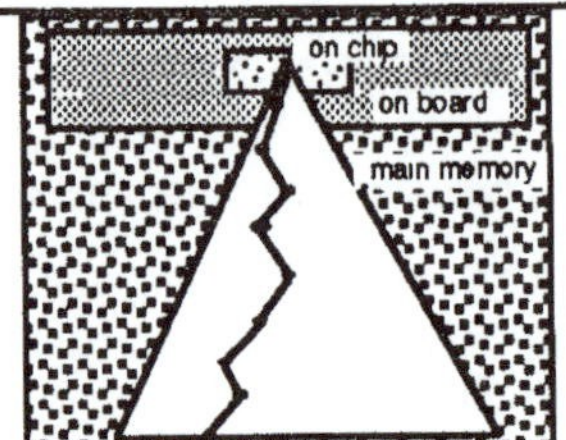

Figure 4. The tournament tree of replacement-selection sort at left has bad cache behavior unless the entire tournament fits in cache. The diagram shows the memory references as a winner is removed and a new element is added to the tournament. Each traversal of the tree has many cache misses at the leaves of the tree. By contrast, the QuickSort diagrammed on the right fits entirely in the on-board cache, and partially in the on-chip cache.

We investigated a replacement-selection sort that clusters tournament nodes so that most parent-child node pairs are contained in the same cache line. That reduces cache misses by a factor of two or three. Nevertheless, replacement-selection sort is still less attractive than QuickSort because:

1. The cache behavior demonstrates less locality than QuickSorts. Even when quicksort runs did not fit entirely in cache, the average compare-exchange time did not increase significantly.
2. Tournament sort is more cpu-intensive than QuickSort. Knuth, [17, page 149] calculated a 2:1 ratio for the programs he wrote. We observed a 2.5:1 speed advantage for QuickSort over the best tournament sort we wrote.

The key to achieving high execution speeds on fast processors is to minimize the number of references that cannot be serviced by the on-board cache (4MB in the case of the DEC 7000 AXP). As mentioned before, QuickSort's memory access patterns are sequential and so have good cache behavior. But, even within the QuickSort algorithm, there are opportunities to improve cache behavior. There are three forms of QuickSort with varying cache behaviors:

Record Sort: the record array is sorted in place. Comparison operators reference the keys in the records and exchange records if appropriate.

Pointer sort: an array of pointers to records is sorted. Comparison operations follow the pointers to reference the record keys, compare the keys and exchange the pointers if appropriate.

Key Sort: an array of (record-key, record-pointer) pairs is sorted. Comparison operators just examine the keys in the array and exchange pairs if appropriate.

To analyze the cache behavior of these three QuickSorts, let R denote the record length (in bytes), K the key length, and P the length of a pointer. For the Datamation sort, these numbers are R=100, K=10, and P=4 .

Record sort has three distinct advantages. (1) It has no setup time, (2) has low storage overhead, and (3) it leaves the records in sorted order. The third issue is important: record sort has about a 30% fewer cache misses during the merge phase. Record sort merges sequential record streams to produce a sorted output stream. Pointer and key sorts must randomly access records to produce the sorted output stream.

If the record is short (e.g., $R \le 16$), record sort has the best cache behavior. If the record is large, then record sort has poor cache behavior. For the Datamation sort parameters (R=100), record sort was 30% slower than pointer sort and 270% slower than key sort (these comparisons are for cpu time). Record sort is slower because each compare (1) references a key from a new record in main memory, (2) compares it to another key, and (3) 25% if the time performs a record exchange. These exchanges are expensive. They move records ($2R$ bytes) rather than moving short pointers ($2P$ bytes) or key-pointer pairs ($2(K+P)$ bytes) and so have significantly more cache faults.

Pointer sort is better than record sort for large records – it moves less data. Pointer sort has poor reference-locality because it accesses records to resolve key comparisons. Even if the pointer array fits in the cache, the records may not. This suggests a detached key sort [19]: storing the key with the pointer in the array: if $K + P << R$., key-pointer sort is a good idea. In the Datamation benchmark case, the key-pointer QuickSort runs three times faster than pointer sort. The later stages of key-pointer QuickSort benefit from running entirely within the 8 KB on chip cache. Even in the early stages, on-chip cache faults get both the pointer (4 bytes) and the key (10-bytes) all in one cache fault. The entire cache line of 32 bytes is brought into the on-chip cache when the pointer or key is accessed. Key-pointer sort runs with at most one on-chip data cache fault per step.

The observation that QuickSort can run in the on-chip data cache (D-cache) suggests an optimization if K is large. The number of entries in the D-cache can be maximized by using

---

1 Offset-value coding of sort keys is a generalization of key-prefix-pointer sorting. It lends itself to a tournament sort [2, 8]. For binary data, like the keys of the Datamation benchmark, offset value coding will not beat AlphaSort's simpler key-prefix sort. A distributive sort that partitions the key-pairs into 256 buckets based on the first byte of the key would eliminate 8 of the 20 compares needed for a 100 MB sort. Such a partition sort might beat AlphaSort's simple QuickSort.

a prefix of the key rather than the full key. The key prefix can also be normalized to an integer type (assuming the key type can be mapped to an integer), allowing most comparisons to be resolved with an integer comparison. AlphaSort employs a key-prefix sort rather than a key sort. For the Datamation benchmark, the QuickSort time improved by 25%.

The risk of using the key-prefix is that it may not be a good discriminator of the key – in that case the comparison must go to the records and key-prefix-sort degenerates to pointer sort. Baer and Lin made similar observations [2]. They recommended keys be prefix compressed into *codewords* so that the (pointer,codeword) QuickSort would fit in cache. We did not to use their version of codewords since they cannot be used to later merge the record pointers.

Traditionally, key sort has been used for complex keys where the cost of key extraction and conditioning is a significant part of the key comparison cost [21]. Key conditioning extracts the sort key from each record, transforms the result to allow efficient byte compares, and stores it with the record as an added field. This is often done for keys involving floating point numbers, signed integers, or character strings with non-standard collating sequences. Comparison operators then do byte-level compares on the conditioned strings. Conditioned keys, or their prefixes can be stored in the pointer-key array.

To summarize, for small records, use record sort. Otherwise, use a key-prefix sort where the prefix is a good discriminator of the keys, and where the pointer and prefix are cache line aligned. Key-prefix sort gives good cache behavior, and for the Datamation benchmark gives more than a 3:1 cpu speedup over record sort.

Once the key-prefix/pointer runs have been QuickSorted, AlphaSort uses a tournament sort to merge the runs. In a one-pass sort there are typically between ten and one hundred runs – the optimal run size balances the time lost waiting for the first run plus time lost QuickSorting the last run, against the time to merge another run during the second phase. The merge results in a stream of in-order record pointers. The pointers are used to gather (copy) the records into the output buffers. Since the records do not fit in the board cache and are referenced in a pseudo-random fashion, the gathering has terrible cache and TLB behavior. More time is spent gathering the records than is consumed in creating, sorting and merging the key-prefix/pointer pairs. When a full buffer of output data is available, it is written to the output file.

5. Shared-memory multiprocessor optimizations

DEC AXP systems may have up to six processors on a shared memory. When running on a multiprocessor, AlphaSort creates a process to use each processor. The first process is called the *root*, the other processes are called *workers*. The root requests affinity to cpu zero, the *i'th* worker process requests affinity to the *i'th* processor. Affinity minimizes the cache faults and invalidation's that occur when a single process migrates among multiple processors.

The root process creates a shared address space, opens the input files, creates the output files and performs all IO operations. The root initiates the worker processes, and coordinates their activities. In its spare time, the root performs sorting chores.

The workers start by requesting processor affinity and attaching to the address space created by the root. With this done, the workers sweep through the address space touching pages. This causes VMS to allocate physical pages for the shared virtual address space. VMS zeroes the allocated pages for security reasons. Zeroing a 1 GB address space takes 12 cpu seconds – this chore has terrible cache behavior. The workers perform it while the root opens and reads the input files.

The root process breaks up the sorting work into independent chores that can be handled by the workers. Chores during the QuickSort phase consist of QuickSorting a data run. Workers generate the arrays of key-prefix pointer pairs and QuickSort them. During the merge phase, the root merges all the (key-prefix, pointer) pairs to produce a sorted string of record pointers. Workers perform the memory-intensive chores of gathering records into output buffers using the record pointer string as a guide. The root writes the sorted record streams to disk.

6. SOLVING THE DISK BOTTLENECK PROBLEM

IO activity for a one-pass sort is purely sequential: sort reads the sequential input file and sequentially creates and writes the output file. The first step in making a fast sort is to use a parallel file system to improve disk read-write bandwidth.

No matter how fast the processor, a 100MB external sort using a single 1993-vintage SCSI disk takes about one minute elapsed time. This one-minute barrier is created by the 3 MB/s sequential transfer rate (bandwidth) of a single commodity disk. We measured both the OpenVMS Sort utility and AlphaSort to take a little under one minute when using one SCSI disk. Both sorts are disk-limited. A faster processor or faster algorithm would not sort much faster because the disk reads at about 4.5 MB/s and writes at about 3.5 MB/s. Thus, it takes about 25 seconds to read the 100 MB, and about 30 seconds to write the 100 MB answer file[2]. Even on mainframes, sort algorithms like SyncSort and DFsort are limited by this one-minute barrier unless disk or file striping is used.

[2] SCSI-II discs support write cache enabled (WCE).that allows the controller to acknowledge a write before the data is on disc. We did not enable WCE because commercial systems demand disk integrity. If WCE were used, 20% fewer discs would be needed.

Disk striping spreads the input and output file across many disks [16]. This allows parallel disk reads and writes to give the sum of the individual disk bandwidths. We investigated both hardware and software approaches to striping.

The Genroco disk array controller allows up to eight disks to be configured as a stripe set. The controller and two fast IPI drives offers a sequential read rate of 15 MB/s (measured). We used three such Genroco controllers each with two fast IPI disk drives in some experiments reported below.

Software file striping spreads the data across commodity SCSI disks that cost about 2000$, hold about 2 GB, read at about 5 MB/s, and write at about 3 MB/s. Eight such disks and their controllers are less expensive than a super-computer disk, and are faster. We implemented a file striping system layered above the OpenVMS file system.. It allows an application to spread (stripe) a file across an array of disks. A striped file is defined by a stripe definition file, a normal file whose name has the suffix, ".str". For every file in the stripe, the definition file includes a line with the file name and number of file blocks per stride for the file. Stripe opens or creates are performed with a call to `StripeOpen()`, which works like a normal open/create except that if the specified file is a stripe definition file then all files in the stripe are opened or created.

The file striping code bandwidth is near-linear as the array grows to nine controllers and thirty-six disks. Bottlenecks appear when a controller saturates; but with enough controllers, the bus, memory, and OS handle the IO load.

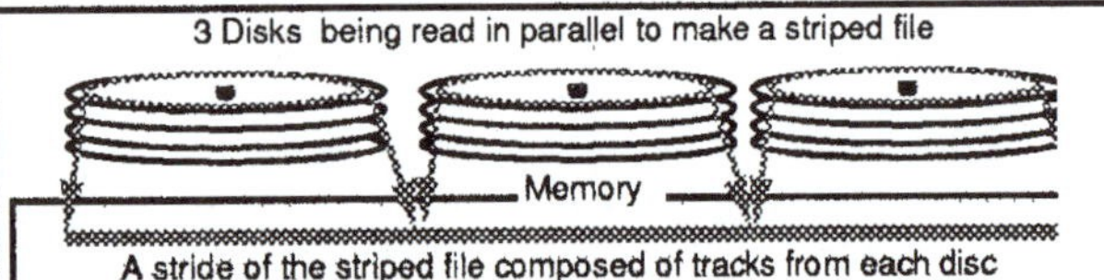

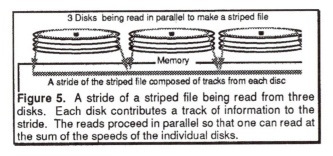

Figure 5. A stride of a striped file being read from three disks. Each disk contributes a track of information to the stride. The reads proceed in parallel so that one can read at the sum of the speeds of the individual disks.

Soft SCSI arrays are less expensive than a special disk array, and they have more bandwidth than a single controller or port. File striping is more flexible than disk striping since the stripe width (number of disks) can be chosen on a file-by-file basis rather than dedicating a set of disks to a fixed stripe set at system generation time. Even with hardware disk arrays, one must stripe across arrays to get bandwidths beyond the limit of a single array. So, software striping must be part of any solution.

Table 6 compares two arrays: (1) a large array of inexpensive disks and controllers, and (2) a smaller array of high-performance disks and controllers. The many-slow array has slightly better performance and price performance for the same storage capacity.

Table 6. Two different disk arrays used in the benchmarks.

	many - slow RAID	**few - fast RAID**
drives	36 RZ26	12 RZ28 + 6 Velocitor
controllers	9 SCSI (kzmsa)	4 SCSI + 3 IPI-Genroco
capacity	36 GB	36 GB
disk speed (measured)	1.8 MB/s	scsi: 4MB/s ipi: 7 MB/s
stripe read rate	64 MB/s	52 MB/s
stripe write rate	49 MB/s	39 MB/s
list price includes cabinets	85 k$	122 k$

It might appear that striping has considerable overhead since opening, creating, or closing a single logical file translates into opening, creating or closing many stripe files. A N-wide striping does introduce overhead and delays. `StripeOpen()` needs to call the operating system once to open the descriptor, and then N times to open the N file stripes. Fortunately, asynchronous operations allow the N steps to proceed in parallel, so there is little increase in elapsed time. With 8-wide striping the fixed overhead for AlphaSort on an 200 Mhz processor is:

Load Sort and process parameters	.11
Open stripe descriptor and eight input stripes	.02
Create and open descriptor and eight output stripes	.01
Close 18 input and output files and descriptors	.01
Return to shell	.05
Total Overhead	**.19 seconds**

This is relatively small overhead.

To summarize, AlphaSort overcomes the IO bottleneck problem by striping data across many disks to get sufficient IO bandwidth. Asynchronous (NoWait) operations open the input files and create the output files in parallel. Triple buffering the reads and writes keeps the disks transferring at their spiral read and write rates. SCSI buffering is especially advantageous in this respect. Striping eight ways provided a read bandwidth of 27 MB/s and a write bandwidth of about 22 MB/s. This put an 8-second limit on our sort speed. Later experiments extended this to 36-way striping and 64 MB/s bandwidth.

A key IO question is when to use a one-pass or two-pass sort. When should the QuickSorted intermediate runs be stored on disk? A two-pass sort uses less memory, but uses twice the disk bandwidth.

Even for surprisingly large sorts it is economic to perform the sort in one pass. A two-pass sort requires twice the disk bandwidth to carry the runs being stored on disk and being read back in during merge phase. The question becomes: What is the relative price of those scratch disks and their controllers versus the price of the memory needed to allow a one-pass sort? Using 1993 prices for Alpha AXP, a disk and it's controller costs about 2400$ (see Table 6). Striping requires 16 such scratch disks dedicated for the entire sort, for a total price of 36k$. A one-pass main memory sort uses a hundred megabytes of RAM. At 100$/MB this is 10k$. It is 360% more expensive to buy the disks for a two-pass sort than to buy 100MB of memory for the one-pass sort. The computation for a 1 GB sort suggests that it would be 15% less expensive to buy 36 extra disks, than to buy the 1 GB of memory needed to do the 1 GB sort (see Table 6).

Multi-gigabyte sorts should be done as two-pass sorts, but for things much smaller than that, one-pass sorts are more economical. In particular, the Datamation sort benchmark should be done in one pass.

Having addressed the IO problem, we now turn to the more interesting problem of minimizing processor waits for transfers among levels of the electronic memory hierarchy.

7. AlphaSort measurements on several platforms

With these ideas in place, let's walk through the 9.11 second AlphaSort of a million hundred-byte records on a uni-processor. The input and output files are striped across sixteen disk drives.

AlphaSort first opens and reads the descriptor file for the input stripe set. Each of the 16 input stripe files is opened asynchronously with a 64 KB stride size. The open call returns indicates a 100MB input file. Asynchronously, AlphaSort requests OpenVMS to create the 100MB striped output file, and to extend the process address space by 110 MB. AlphaSort immediately begins reading the 100MB input file into memory using triple buffering.

It is now 140 milliseconds into the sort. As each stride-read completes, AlphaSort issues the next read. AlphaSort is completely IO limited in this phase.

When the first 1 MB stripe of records arrives in memory, AlphaSort extracts the 8-byte (record address, key-prefix) pairs from each record. These pairs are streamed into an array. When the array grows to 100,000 records, AlphaSort QuickSorts it. This QuickSort is entirely cache resident. When it completes the processor waits for the next array to be built so that it too can be QuickSorted. The pipeline of steps (read-disk array-build then QuickSort) is disk bound at a data rate of about 27 MB/s.

The read of the input file completes at the end of 3.87 seconds. AlphaSort must then sort the last 100,000 record partition (about .12 seconds). During this brief interval, there is no IO activity.

Now AlphaSort has ten sorted runs produced by the ten QuickSort steps. It is now 4 seconds into the sort and can start writing the output to the striped output file. Meanwhile, it issues `Close()` on all stripes of the input file.

AlphaSort runs a tournament scanning the ten QuickSorted runs of the (key-prefix,pointer) pairs in sequential order, picking the minimum key-prefix among the runs. If there is a tie, it examines the full keys in the records. The winning record is gathered (copied) to the output buffer. When a full stripe of output buffer is produced, `StripeWrite()` is called to write the sorted records to the target stripe file in disk. This merge-gather runs more slowly than the QuickSort step because many cache misses are incurred in gathering the records into the output buffers. It takes almost four seconds of processor and memory time (the use of multi-processors speeds this merge step). This phase is also disk limited, taking 4.9 seconds.

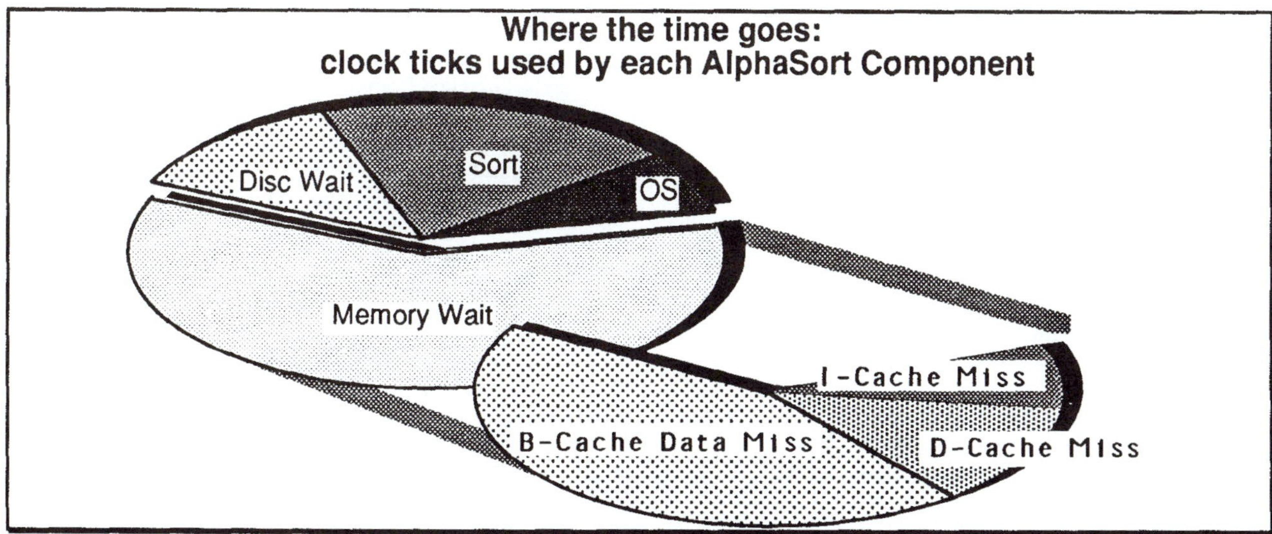

Figure 7. A pie chart showing where the time is going on the DEC 10000 AXP 9-second sort. Even though AlphaSort spends GREAT effort on efficient use of cache, the processor spends most of its time waiting for memory. The vast majority of such waits are for data, and the majority of the time is spent waiting for main memory . The low cost of VMS to launch the sort program, open the files, and move 200 MB through the IO subsystem is impressive. Not shown is the 4% of stalls due to branch mis-predictions.

When the tournament completes 8.8 seconds have elapsed. AlphaSort is ready to close the output files and to return to the shell. Closing takes about 50 milliseconds. AlphaSort then terminates for a total time of 9.1 seconds. Of this 0.3 seconds were consumed loading the program and returning to the command interpreter. The sort time was 8.8 seconds, but the benchmark definition requires that the startup and shutdown time be included

Some interesting statistics about this sort are:

- The cpu time is 7.9 seconds, 1.1 seconds is pure disk wait. Most of the disk wait is in startup and shutdown.
- 6.0 seconds of the cpu time is in the memory-to-memory sort.
- 1.9 seconds are used by OpenVMS AXP to:
  - load the sort program
  - allocate and initialize a 100MB address space
  - open 17 files
  - create and open 17 output files and allocate 100MB of disk on 16 drives.
  - close all these files
  - return to command interpreter and print a time stamp.
- Of the 7.9 seconds of cpu time, the processor is issuing instructions 29% of the time. Most of the rest of the time it is waiting for a cache miss to be serviced from main memory (56%). SPEC benchmarks have much better cache hit ratios because the program and data fit in cache. Database systems executing the TPC-A benchmark have worse cache behavior because they have larger programs (so more I-cache misses).
- The instruction mix is: Integer (51%), Load (15%), Branch (15%), Store (12%) Float (0%). PAL (9%) mostly handling address translation buffer (DTB) misses. 8.4% of the processor time is spent dual issuing.
- The processor chip hardware monitor indicates that 29% of the clocks execute instructions, 4% of the stall time is due to branch mis-predictions, 11% is I-stream misses (4% I-to-B and 7% B-to-main), and 56% are D-stream misses (12% D-to-B and 44% B-to-main).
- The time spent dual-issuing is 8%, compared to 21% spent on single-issues. Over 40% of instuctions are dual issued.

AlphaSort benchmarks on several AXP processors are summarized in Table 8. All of these benchmarks set new performance and price/performance records. The AXP-3000 is the price-performance leader. The DEC AXP 7000 is the performance leader. As spectacular as they are, these numbers are improving. Software is making major performance strides as it adapts to the Alpha AXP architecture. Hardware prices are dropping rapidly.

To summarize, AlphaSort optimizes IO by using host-based file striping to exploit fast but inexpensive disks and disk controllers – no expensive RAID controllers are needed. It uses lots of RAM memory to achieve a one-pass sort. It improves the cache hit ratio by QuickSorting (key-prefix, pointer) pairs if the records are large. If multiprocessors are available, AlphaSort breaks the QuickSort and Merge jobs into smaller chores that are executed by worker processors while the root process performs all IO.

8. New sort metrics: MinuteSort and DollarSort

The original Datamation benchmark has outlived its usefulness. When it was defined, 100MB sorts were taking ten minutes to one hour. More recently, workers have been reporting times near one minute. Now the mark is seven seconds. The next significant step is 1 second. This will give undue weight to startup times. Already, startup and shutdown is over 25% of the cost of the 7-second sort. So, the Datamation Sort benchmark is a startup/shutdown benchmark rather than an IO benchmark.

To maintain its role as an IO benchmark, the sort benchmark needs redefinition. We propose the following:

MinuteSort:

- Sort as much as you can in one minute.
- The input file is resident on external storage (disk).
- The input consists of 100-byte records (incompressible).
- The first ten bytes of each record is a random key.
- The output file is a sorted permutation of the input.
- The input and output files must be readable by a program using conventional tools (a database or a record manager.)

The elapsed time includes the time from calling the sort program to the time that the program returns to the caller – this total time must be less than a minute. If Sort is an operating system utility, then it can be launched from the command shell. If Sort is part of a database system, then it can be launched from the interactive interface of the DBMS. MinuteSort has two metrics:

Size (bytes): the number of gigabytes you can sort in a minute of elapsed time

Price-performance ($/sorted GB): The list price of the hardware and operating system needed to run the benchmark divided by one million. This is the approximate cost of the hardware, software, and maintenance for a minute, if the hardware is depreciated over 3 years. This number reflects the cost (price). To get a price-performance metric, the price is divided by the sort size (in gigabytes).

Table 8. Performance and price/performance of 100MB Datamation sort benchmarks on Alpha AXP systems (October 1993).

System	cpu&clock	controllers	drives	(MB)	time(s)	total price	disk+ctlr	$/sort
DEC-7000-AXP	3x5ns	7 fast-SCSI	28 RZ26	256	**7.0**	312k$	123k$	0.014$
DEC-4000-AXP	2x6.25ns	4 SCSI, 3 IPI	12scsi+6ipi	256	**8.2**	312k$	95k$	0.016$
DEC-7000-AXP	1x5ns	6 fast-SCSI	16 RZ74	256	**9.1**	247k$	65k$	0.014$
DEC-4000-AXP	1x6.25ns	4 fast-SCSI	12 RZ26	384	**11.3**	166k$	48k$	0.014$
DEC-3000-AXP	1x6.6ns	5 SCSI	10 RZ26	256	**13.7**	97k$	48k$	0.009$

This metric includes an *Nlog(N)* term (the number of comparisons) but in the range of interest range ($N > 2^{30}$), *log(N)* grows slowly compared to *N*. As *N* increases by a factor of 1,000, *log(N)* increases by a factor of 1.33.

A three-processor DEC 7000 AXP sorted 1.08 GB in a minute. The 1993 price of this system (36 disks, 1.25 GB of memory, 3 processors, and cabinets) is 512k$. So the 1.1 GB MinuteSort would cost 51 cents (=512k$/1M). The MinuteSort price-performance metric is the cost over the size (.51/1.1) = 0.47$/GB. So, today AlphaSort on a DEC 7000 AXP has a 1.1 GB size and a 0.47$/GB price/performance.

MinuteSort uses a rough 3-year price and omits the price of high-level software because: (1) this is a test of the machine's IO subsystem, and (2) most of the winners will be "special" programs that are written just to win this benchmark – most university software is not for sale (see Table 1). There are 1.58 million minutes in 3 years, so dividing the price by 1M gives a slight (30%) inflator for software and maintenance. Depreciating over 3 years, rather than the 5-year span adopted by the TPC, reflects the new pace of the computer business.

Minute sort is aimed at super-computers. It emphasizes speed rather than price performance – it reports price as an afterthought. This suggests a dual benchmark that is fixed-price rather than fixed-time: DollarSort. DollarSort is just like MinuteSort except that it is limited to using one dollar's worth of computing. Recall that each minute of computer time costs about one millionth of the system list price. So DollarSort would allow a million dollar system to sort for a minute, while a 10,000$ system could sort for 100 minutes. PCs could win the DollarSort benchmark.

Dollar Sort:

- Sort as much as you can for less than a dollar.
- Otherwise, it has the same rules as MinuteSort

The dollar limit price is computed as:

$$1\$ \geq elapsed\ time \times \frac{system\ list\ price}{1000000}$$

Dollar Sort reports two metrics:

Size (bytes): the number of gigabytes you can sort for a dollar.

Elapsed Time: The elapsed time of the sort (reported in to the nearest millisecond).

MinuteSort and DollarSort are an interesting contrast to the Datamation sort benchmark. Datamation sort was fixed size (100MB) and so did not scale with technology. MinuteSort and DollarSort scale with technology because they hold end-user variables constant (time or price) and allow the problem size to vary.

Industrial-strength sorts will always be slower than programs designed to win the benchmarks. There is a big difference between a program like AlphaSort, designed to sort exactly the Datamation test data, and an industrial-strength sort that can deal with many data types, with complex sort keys, and with many sorting options. AlphaSort slowed down as it was productized in Rdb and in OSF/1 HyperSort.

This suggests that there be an additional distinction, a ***street-legal*** sort that restricts entrants to sorts sold and supported by someone. Much as there is an Indianapolis Formula-1 car race run by specially built cars, and a Daytona stock-car race run by production cars, we propose that there be an *Indy* category and a *Daytona* category for both minute-sort and DollarSort. This gives four benchmarks in all:

Indy-MinuteSort: a Formula-1 sort where price is no object.

Daytona-MinuteSort: a stock sort where price is no object.

Indy-Dollar Sort: a Formula-1 biggest-bang-for-the buck sort.

Daytona-Dollar Sort: a stock sort giving the biggest-bang-for-the buck .

Super-computers will probably win the MinuteSort and workstations will win the DollarSort trophies.

The past winners of the Datamation sort benchmark (Barclay, Baugsto, Cvetanovic, DeWitt, Gray, Naughton, Nyberg, Schneider, Tsukerman, and Weinberger) have formed a committee to oversee the recognition of new sort benchmark results. At each annual SIGMOD conference starting in 1994, the committee will grant trophies to the best MinuteSorts and DollarSorts in the Daytona and Indy categories (4 trophies in all). You can enter the contest or poll its status by contacting one of the committee members.

9. Summary and conclusions

AlphaSort is a new algorithm that exploits the cache and IO architectures of commodity processors and disks. It runs the standard sort benchmark in seven seconds. That is four times better than the unpublished record on a Cray Y-MP, and eight times faster than the 32-CPU 32-disk Hypercube record [9, 23]. It can sort 1.1 GB in a minute using multiprocessors. This demonstrates that commodity microprocessors can perform batch transaction processing tasks. It also demonstrates speedup using multiple processors on a shared memory.

The Alpha AXP processor can sort VERY fast. But, the sort benchmark requires reading 100MB from disk and writing 100MB to disk – it is an IO benchmark. The reason for including the Sort benchmark in the Datamation test suite was to measure "how fast the real IO architecture is" [1].

By combining many fast-inexpensive SCSI disks, the Alpha AXP system can read and write disk data at 64 MB/s. AlphaSort implements simple host-based file striping to achieve this bandwidth. With it, one can balance the processor, cache, and IO speed. The result is a breakthrough in both performance and price-performance.

In part, AlphaSort's speed comes from efficient compares, but most of the cpu speedup comes from efficient use of cpu cache. The elapsed-time speedup comes from parallel IO performed by an application-level striped file system.

Our laboratory's focus is on parallel database systems. AlphaSort is part of our work on loading, indexing, and searching terabyte databases. At a gigabyte-per-minute, it takes more than 16 hours to sort a terabyte. We intend to use many processors and many-many disks handle such operations in minutes rather than hours. A terabyte-per-minute parallel sort is our long-term goal (not a misprint!). That will need hundreds of fast processors, gigabytes of memory, thousands of disks, and a 20 GB/s interconnect.. Thus, this goal is five or ten years off.

10. Acknowledgments

Al Avery encouraged us and helped us get access to equipment. Doug Hoeger gave us advice on OpenVMS sort. Ken Bates provided the source code of a file striping prototype he did five years ago. Dave Eiche, Ben Thomas, Rod Widdowson, and Drew Mason gave us good advice on the OpenVMS AXP IO system. Bill Noyce and Dick Sites gave us advice on AXP code sequences. Bruce Fillgate, Richie Lary, and Fred Vasconcellos gave us advice and help on disks and loaned us some RZ74 disks to do the tests. Steve Holmes and Paline Nist gave us access to systems in their labs and helped us borrow hardware. Gary Lidington and Scott Tincher helped get the excellent DEC 4000 AXP results. Joe Nordman of Genroco provided us with fast IPI disks and controllers for the DEC 4000 AXP tests.

11. References

[1] Anon-Et-Al. (1985). "A Measure of Transaction Processing Power." *Datamation*. V.**31**(7): PP. 112-118. also in *Readings in Database Systems,* M.J. Stonebraker ed., Morgan Kaufmann, San Mateo, 1989.

[2] Baer, J.L., Lin, Y.B., "Improving Quicksort Performance with Codeword Data Structure", IEEE Trans. on Software Engineering, **15**(5). May 1989. pp. 622-631.

[3] Baugsto, B.A.W., Greipsland, J.F., "Parallel Sorting Methods for Large Data Volumes on a Hypercube Database Computer", Proc. 6th Int. Workshop on Database Machines, Deauville France, Springer Verlag Lecture Notes No. 368, June 1989, pp.: 126-141.

[4] Baugsto, B.A.W., Greipsland, J.F., Kamerbeek, J. "Sorting Large Data Files on POMA," Proc. CONPAR-90VAPP IV, Springer Verlag Lecture Notes No. 357, Sept. 1990, pp.: 536-547.

[5] Cvetanovic, Z. , D. Bhandarkar, "Characterization of Alpha AXP Performance Using TP and SPEC Workloads", to appear in Proc. Int.Symposium on Computer Architecture, April 1994.

[6] Bitton, D., *Design, Analysis and Implementation of Parallel External Sorting Algorithms*, Ph.D. Thesis, U. Wisconsin, Madison, WI, 1981

[7] Beck, M., Bitton, D., Wilkenson, W.K., "Sorting Large Files on a Backend Multiprocessor", IEEE Transactions on Computers, V. **37**(7), pp. 769-778, July 1988.

[8] Conner, W.M., Offset Value Coding, IBM Technical Disclosure Bulletin, V **20**(7), Dec. 1977, pp. 2832-2837

[9] DeWitt, D.J., Naughton, J.F., Schneider, D.A. "Parallel Sorting on a Shared-Nothing Architecture Using Probabilistic Splitting", Proc. First Int Conf. on Parallel and Distributed Info Systems, IEEE Press, Jan 1992, pp. 280-291

[10] Filgate, Bruce, "SCSI 3.5" 1.05 GB Disk Comparative Performance", Digital Storage Labs, Nov. 10 1992

[11] Graefe, G., "Parallel external sorting in Volcano," U. Colorado Comp. Sci. Tech. Report 459, June 1990.

[12] Graefe, G, S.S. Thakkar, "Tuning a Parallel Sort Algorithm on a Shared-Memory Multiprocessor", Software Practice and Experience, **22**(7), July 1992, pp. 495.

[13] Gray, J. (ed.), *The Benchmark Handbook for Database and Transaction Processing Systems,* Morgan Kaufmann, San Mateo, 1991.

[14] Kaivalya, D., The SPEC Benchmark Suite, Chapter 6 of *The Benchmark Handbook for Database and Transaction Processing Systems, Second Edition, Chapter 6,* Morgan Kaufmann, San Mateo, 1993.

[15] Kitsuregawa, M., Yang, W., Fushimi, S. "Evaluation of an 18-stage Pipeline Hardware Sorter", Proc. 6th Int. Workshop on Database Machines, Deauville France, Springer Verlag Lecture Notes No. 368, June 1989, pp. 142-155.

[16] Kim. M.Y., "Synchronized Disk Interleaving," IEEE TOCS, V. **35**(11), Nov. 1986, pp978-988.

[17] Knuth, E.E., *Sorting and Searching, The Art of Computer Programming,* Addison Wesley, Reading, Ma., 1973.

[18] Lorie, R.A., and Young, H. C., "A Low Communications Sort Algorithm for a Parallel Database Machine," Proc. Fifteenth VLDB, Amsterdam, 1989, pp. 125-134.

[19] Lorin, H. Sorting, Addison Wesley, Englewood Cliffs, NJ, 1974.

[20] Salzberg, B., et al., "FastSort– An External Sort Using Parallel Processing", Proc. SIGMOD 1990, pp. 88-101.

[21] Tsukerman, A., "FastSort– An External Sort Using Parallel Processing" Tandem Systems Review, V **3**(4), Dec. 1986, pp. 57-72.

[22] Weinberger, P.J., Private communication 1986.

[23] Yamane, Y., Take, R. "Parallel Partition Sort for Database Machines", *Database Machines and Knowledge Based Machines*, Kitsuregawa and Tanaka eds., pp.: 1117-130. Klwar Academic Publishers, 1988.

R* Optimizer Validation and Performance Evaluation for Distributed Queries

Lothar F. Mackert [1]
Guy M. Lohman

IBM Almaden Research Center
K55-801, 650 Harry Road, San Jose, CA 95120-6099

Abstract

Few database query optimizer models have been validated against actual performance. This paper extends an earlier optimizer validation and performance evaluation of R* to *distributed* queries, i.e. single SQL statements having tables at multiple sites. Actual R* message, I/O, and CPU resources consumed — and the corresponding costs estimated by the optimizer — were written to database tables using new SQL commands, permitting automated control from application programs for collecting, reducing, and comparing test data. A number of tests were run over a wide variety of dynamically-created test databases, SQL queries, and system parameters. Both high-speed networks (comparable to a local area network) and medium-speed long-haul networks (for linking geographically dispersed hosts) were evaluated. The tests confirmed the accuracy of R*'s message cost model and the significant contribution of local (CPU and I/O) costs, even for a medium-speed network. Although distributed queries consume more resources overall, the response time for some execution strategies improves disproportionately by exploiting both concurrency and reduced contention for buffers. For distributed joins in which a copy of the inner table must be transferred to the join site, shipping the whole inner table dominated the strategy of fetching only those inner tuples that matched each outer-table value, even though the former strategy may require additional I/O. Bloomjoins (hashed semijoins) consistently performed better than semijoins and the best R* strategies.

1. Introduction

One of the most appealing properties of relational data bases is their nonprocedural user interface. Users specify only *what* data is desired, leaving the system optimizer to choose *how* to access that data. The built-in decision capabilities of the optimizer therefore play a central role regarding system performance. Automated selection of optimal access plans is a rather difficult task, because even for simple queries there are many alternatives and factors affecting the performance of each of them.

Optimizers model system performance for some subset of these alternatives, taking into consideration a subset of the relevant factors. As with any other mathematical model, these simplifications — made for modeling and computational efficiency — introduce the potential for errors. The goal of our study was to investigate the performance and to thoroughly validate the optimizer against actual performance of a working experimental database system, R* [LOHM 85], which inherited and extended to a distributed environment [SELI 80, DANI 82] the optimization algorithms of System R [SELI 79]. This paper extends our earlier validation and performance evaluation of local queries [MACK 86] to distributed queries over either (1) a high-speed network having speeds comparable to a local-area network (LAN) or (2) over a medium-speed, long-haul network linking geographically dispersed host machines. For brevity, we assume that the reader is familiar with System R [CHAM 81] and R* [LOHM 85], and with the issues, methodology, and results of that earlier study [MACK 86].

Few of the distributed optimizer models proposed over the last decade [APER 83, BERN 81B, CHAN 82, CHU 82, EPST 78, HEVN 79, KERS 82, ONUE 83, PERR 84, WONG 83, YAO 79, YU 83] have been validated by comparison with actual performance. The only known validations, for Distributed INGRES [STON 82] and the Crystal multicomputer [LU 85], have assumed only a high-speed local-area network linking the distributed systems. Also, the Distributed INGRES study focused primarily on reducing response time by exploiting parallelism using table partitioning and broadcast messages. In contrast, R* seeks to minimize total resources consumed, has not implemented table partitioning[2], and does not presume a network broadcast capability.

There are many important questions that a thorough validation should answer:

- Under what circumstances (regions of the parameter space) does the optimizer choose a suboptimal plan, or, worse, a particularly bad plan?
- To which parameters is the actual performance most sensitive?
- Are these parameters being modeled accurately by the optimizer?
- What is the impact of variations from the optimizer's simplifying assumptions?
- Is it possible to simplify the optimizer's model (by using heuristics, for example) to speed up optimization?
- What are the best database statistics to support optimization?

Performance questions related to optimization include:

- Are there possible improvements in the implementation of distributed join techniques?
- Are there alternative distributed join techniques that are not implemented but look promising?

The next section gives an overview of distributed compilation and optimization in R*. Section 3 discusses how R* was instrumented to collect optimizer estimates and actual performance data at multiple sites in an automated way. Section 4 presents some prerequisite measurements of the cost component weights and the measurement overhead. The results for distributed joins are given in Section 5, and suggestions for improving their performance are discussed in Section 6. Section 7 contains our conclusions.

2. Distributed Compilation and Optimization

The unit of distribution in R* is a table and each table is stored at one and only one site. A ***distributed query*** is any SQL data manipulation statement that references tables at sites other than the ***query site***, the site to which an application program is submitted for compilation. This site serves as the ***master site*** which coordinates the optimization of all SQL statements embedded in that program. For each query, sites other than the master site that store a table referenced in the query are called ***apprentice sites***.

In addition to the parameters chosen for the local case:

---

1 Current address: University of Erlangen-Nürnberg, IMMD-IV, Martensstrasse 3, D-8520 Erlangen, West Germany

2 Published ideas for horizontal and vertical partitioning of tables have not been implemented in R*.

(1) the order in which tables must be joined
(2) the join method (nested-loop or merge-scan), and
(3) the access path for each table (e.g., whether to use an index or not)

optimization of a *distributed* query must also choose for each join[3]:

(4) ***the join site***, i.e. the site at which each join takes place, and,
(5) if the inner table is not stored at the join site chosen in (4), the method for transferring a copy of the inner table to the join site:
(5a) ***ship whole***: ship a copy of the entire table once to the join site, and store it there in a temporary table; or
(5b) ***fetch matches*** (see Figure 1): scan the outer table and sequentially execute the following procedure for each outer tuple:

1. Project the outer table tuple to the join column(s) and ship this value to the site of the inner table.
2. Find those tuples in the inner table that match the value sent and project them to the columns needed.
3. Ship a copy of the projected matching inner tuples back to the join site.
4. Join the matches to the outer table tuple.

Note that this strategy could be characterized as a semijoin for each outer tuple. We will compare it to semijoins in Section 6.

If a copy of an outer (possibly composite) table of a join has to be moved to another site, it is always shipped in its entirety as a blocked pipeline of tuples [LOHM 85].

Compilation, and hence optimization, is truly distributed in R*. The master's optimizer makes all *inter-site* decisions, such as the site at which inter-site joins take place, the method and order for transferring tuples between sites, etc. *Intra-site* decisions (e.g. order and method of join for tables contiguously within a single site) are only *suggested* by the master planner; it delegates to each apprentice the final decision on these choices as well as the generation of an access module to encode the work to be done at that site [DANI 82].

Optimization in R* seeks to minimize a cost function that is a linear combination of four components: CPU, I/O, and two message costs: the number of messages and the total number of bytes transmitted in all messages. I/O cost is measured in number of transfers to or from disk, and CPU cost is measured in terms of number of instructions:

$$\text{R*\_total\_cost} = W_{CPU} * (\#\_\text{instrs}) + W_{I/O} * (\#\_\text{I/Os}) + W_{MSG} * (\#\_\text{msgs}) + W_{BYT} * (\#\_\text{bytes})$$

Unlike System R, R* maintains the four cost components separately, as well as the total cost as a weighted sum of the components [LOHM 85], enabling validation of each of the cost components independently. By assigning (at database generation time) appropriate weights for a given hardware configuration, different optimization criteria can be met. Two of the most common are time (delay) and money cost [SELI 80]. For our study we set these weights so that the R* total cost estimates the total time consumed by all resources, in milliseconds. Since all the sites in our tests had equivalent hardware and software configurations, identical weights were used for each site.

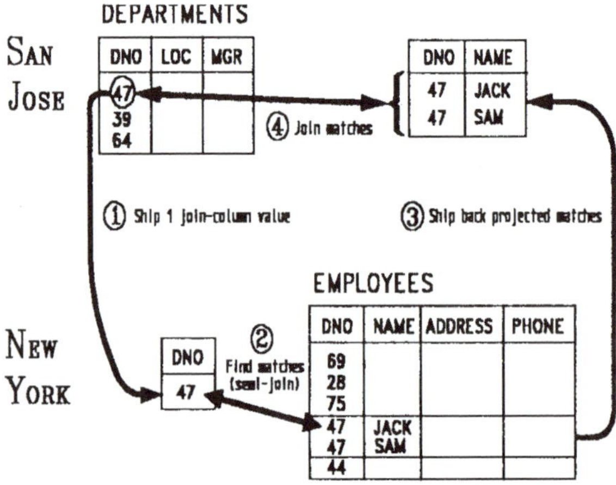

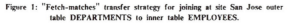

Figure 1: "Fetch-matches" transfer strategy for joining at site San Jose outer table DEPARTMENTS to inner table EMPLOYEES.

3. Instrumentation

An earlier performance study for System R [ASTR 80] demonstrated that extracting performance data using the standard database trace and debugging facilities required substantial manual interaction, severely limiting the number of test cases that could be run. Since we wanted to measure performance under a wide variety of circumstances, we added instrumentation that would automate measurements to a very high degree. The general design of this instrumentation and its application for the evaluation of local queries is described in [MACK 86], so that in this paper we recall only the main ideas and confine our discussion to its distributed aspects. Principals of our design were:

1. Add to the SQL language three statements for test control and performance monitoring which can be executed from an application program as well as interactively.
2. Develop pre-compiled application programs for automatically (a) testing queries using the SQL statements of (1) above, and (b) analyzing the data collected by step (a).
3. Store the output of the SQL statements of (1) and the application programs of (2) in database tables in order to establish a flexible, powerful interface between (1), (2a), and (2b).

We concentrate here on the first item — the SQL-level measurement tools — whose implementation was most complicated by the distribution of tables at different sites.

3.1. Distributed EXPLAIN

The EXPLAIN command writes to user-owned PLAN__TABLEs information describing the access plan chosen by the optimizer for a given SQL statement, and its estimated cost [RDT 84]. For a given distributed query, no single site has the complete access plan: the master site has the inter-site decisions and each apprentice has its local intra-site decisions. Hence the R* EXPLAIN command was augmented to store each apprentice site's plan in a local PLAN__TABLE, and the test application program was altered to retrieve that information from each apprentice's PLAN__TABLE.

3.2. Distributed COLLECT COUNTERS

This new SQL statement collects and stores in a user-owned table the current values of some 40 internal counters in the RSS* component (e.g., counts of disk reads and writes, lookups in the buffer, etc.), which R* inherited from System R, and some newly implemented counters of the communications component DC*. COLLECT COUNTERS automatically collects a (pre-defined) subset of these counters at all sites with which the user currently has open communication sessions, returns those counters to the master site, and inserts into a special user-owned table (COUNTER__TABLE) one tuple for each distinct counter at each site. Each counter value is tagged with its name, the component (RSS* or DC*) and site that maintains the counter, a timestamp, the invoking application program name, and an optional user-supplied sequence number.

The implementation of the COLLECT COUNTERS statement is dependent upon the mechanism for distributed query execution in R* [LIND 83]. The master site establishes communication sessions with all sites with which it has to have direct communication, and spawns children processes at these sites. The children may in turn establish additional sessions and spawn other children processes, creating a tree of processes that may endure through multiple transactions in an application program. Since descendant processes may spawn processes at any site, the tree may contain multiple descendant processes at a single site on behalf of the same master process (***loopback***). For collecting the counters from all sites that are involved in the current computation, we traverse the user's process tree. For each process, counters are collected at that process' site and are

3 The site at which any nested query (***subquery***) is applied must also be determined [LOHM 84], but consideration of subqueries is omitted from this paper to simplify the presentation.

returned to the master site. At the master site, each counter value is handled in the following way:

- If we have not yet inserted a tuple into the COUNTER_TABLE for the given counter from the given site (while executing the COLLECT COUNTERS statement of interest), the counter is inserted into the COUNTER_TABLE.

- RSS* counters from the given site that have already been inserted into the user's COUNTER_TABLE are discarded (loopbacks will cause redundant delivery of certain counters), because RSS* counters are database-site-specific.

- DC* counters are process-specific. If there is already a row in the COUNTER_TABLE for the given DC* counter at the given site, the counter value is added to the counter value in that row.

To be sure that sessions had been established with all sites relevant to a particular test, the test application program was altered to run the test sequence once before the first COLLECT COUNTERS statement.

3.3. FORCE OPTIMIZER

As in the local validation study, we had to be able to overrule the optimizer's choice of plan, to measure the performance of plans that the optimizer thought were suboptimal. This was done with the FORCE OPTIMIZER statement, which was implemented in a special test version of R* only. The FORCE OPTIMIZER statement chooses the plan for the *next* SQL data manipulation (optimizable) statement *only*. The user specifies the desired plan number, a unique positive integer assigned by the master site's optimizer to each candidate plan, by first using the EXPLAIN statement (discussed above) to discover the number of the desired plan. Apprentice optimization can be forced by simply telling each apprentice to utilize the optimization decisions recommended by the master's optimizer in its global plan.

3.4. Conduct of Experiments

Our distributed query tests were conducted in the same way and in the same environment as the local query tests [MACK 86], only with multiple database sites. All measurements were run at night on two totally unloaded IBM 4381's connected via a high-speed channel. Each site was initialized to provide 40 buffer pages of 4K bytes each, which were available exclusively to our test applications. This is approximately equivalent, for example, to a system with each site running 5 simultaneous transactions that are competing for 800K bytes of buffer space. The same effects of buffer size limitations that were investigated in [MACK 86] also apply to distributed queries, and thus are not discussed further in this paper. In order to vary database parameters systematically, synthetic test tables were generated dynamically, inserting tuples whose column values were drawn randomly from separate uniform distributions. For example, the join-columns' values were drawn randomly from a domain of 3000 integer values when generating the tables. All tables had the same schema: four integer and five (fixed) character fields. The tuples were 66 bytes long, and the system stored 50 of them on one page.

Each test was run several times to ensure reproduceability of the results, and to reduce the variance of the average response times. However, the reader is cautioned that these measurements are highly dependent upon numerous factors peculiar to our test environment, including hardware and software configuration, database design, etc. We made no attempt to "tune" these factors to advantage. For example, each test table was assigned to a separate DBSPACE, which tends to favor DBSPACE scans.

What follows is a sample of our results illustrating major trends for distributed queries; space considerations preclude showing all combinations of all parameters that we examined. For example, for joins we tested a matrix of table sizes for the inner and outer tables ranging from 100 to 6000 tuples (3 times the buffer size), varying the projection factor on the joined tables (50% or 100% of both tables) and the availability of totally unclustered indexes on the join columns of the outer and/or inner tables. Since unclustered index scans become very expensive when the buffer is not big enough to hold all the data and index pages of a table, the ratio between the total number of data and index pages of a table to the number of pages in the buffer is more important for the local processing cost than the absolute table size [MACK 85]. Although these tests confirmed the accuracy of the overwhelming majority of the optimizer's predictions, we will concentrate here on those aspects of the R* optimizer that were changed or exhibited anomalous behavior.

4. General Measurements

Several measurements pertaining to the optimizer as a whole were prerequisite to more specific studies. These are discussed briefly below.

4.1. Cost of Measurements

The COLLECT COUNTERS statement, the means by which we measured performance, itself consumes system resources that are tabulated by the R* internal counters. For example, collecting the counters from remote sites itself uses messages whose cost would be reflected in the counters for number of messages and number of bytes transmitted. The resources consumed by the COLLECT COUNTERS instrumentation was determined by running two COLLECT COUNTERS statements with no SQL statements in between, and reducing all other observations by those resources.

4.2. Component Weights

The R* cost component weights for any given cost objective and hardware configuration can be estimated using "back of the envelope" calculations. For example, for converting all components to milliseconds, the weight for CPU is the number of milliseconds per CPU instruction, which can be estimated as just the inverse of the MIP rate, divided by 1000 MIPS/msec. The I/O weight can be estimated as the sum of the average seek, latency, and transfer times for one 4K-byte page of data. The per-message weight can be estimated by dividing the approximate number of instructions to initiate and receive a message by the MIP rate. And the per-byte weight estimate is simply the time to send 8 bits at the *effective* transmission speed of the network, which had been measured as 4M bits/sec for our nominally 24M bit/sec (3M Byte/sec) channel-to-channel connection. These estimates, and the corresponding actual weights for our test configuration, are shown in Figure 2.

$$\text{R*\_total\_cost} = W_{CPU} * (\#\_insts) + W_{I/O} * (\#\_I/O) + W_{MSG} * (\#\_msgs) + W_{BYT} * (\#\_bytes)$$

WEIGHT	UNITS	HARDWARE/SOFTWARE	ESTIMATE	ACTUAL
W_{CPU}	msec/inst.	IBM 4381 CPU	0.0004	0.0004
$W_{I/O}$	msec/I/O	IBM 3380 disk	23.48	17.00[4]
W_{MSG}	msec/msg.	CICS/VTAM	11.54	16.5
W_{BYTE}	msec/byte	24Mbit/sec (nom.), 4Mbit/sec (eff.)	0.002	0.002

Figure 2: Estimated and actual cost component weights.

The actual per-message and per-byte weights were measured by moving to a remote site one table of a two-table query for which the executed plan and the local (I/O and CPU) costs were well known. We chose a query that nested-loop joined a 500-tuple outer table, A, and a 100-tuple inner table, B, having an index on the join column. The plan for the distributed execution of this query had to be one that was executed sequentially (i.e., with no parallelism between sites), so that the response time (which we could measure) equalled the total resource time. By SELECTing all the columns of B, we could require that the large (3500-byte) tuples of B had to be shipped without projection, thereby ensuring that both the number (1000) and size of messages sent was high and that the local processing time was a small part (less than 30%) of the total resource time. We could control the message traffic by varying the number of tuples in B matching values in A: when none matched, only very small messages were transferred (carrying fixed-size R* control information); when each tuple in A matched exactly one tuple in B, 500 small and 500 very large messages were transferred. For a given number

4 The observed per-I/O rate is better than the estimate because the seek time was almost always less than the nominal average seek time, since R* databases are stored by VSAM in clumps of contiguous cylinders called extents.

of matching inner tuples, the query was run 10 times to get the average response (= total resource) time. The message cost was derived by subtracting from the total time the local cost, which was measured by averaging the cost of 10 executions of the same query when both A and B were at the *same* site. Knowing the number and size of the messages (using COLLECT COUNTERS) for that number of matching inner tuples allowed us to compute the per-message and per-byte weights for our test environment: 16.5 msecs. minimal transfer time, and an effective transfer rate of 4M bit/sec. Note that these figures include the instruction and envelope overheads, respectively, of R*, CICS, and VTAM [LIND 83, VTAM 85].

By varying the above per-message and per-byte weights, we could also use the observed number of messages and bytes transmitted on the high-speed channel-to-channel connection to simulate the performance for a medium-speed long-haul network linking geographically dispersed hosts: 50 msecs. minimum transfer time and effective transfer rate of 40K bit/sec (nominal rate of 56K bit/sec, less 30% overhead). The per-message weight differs because of the increased delay due to the speed of light for longer transmissions, routing through relays, etc. Unavailability of resources at remote sites unfortunately precluded validating on a real long-haul network these estimated weights.

5. Distributed Join Results

Having validated the weights used in the R* cost function, and having removed the cost of measuring performance, we were ready to validate the R* optimizer's decisions for distributed queries.

The simplest distributed query accesses a single table at a remote site. However, since partitioning and replication of tables is not supported in R*, accessing a remote table is relatively simple: a process at the remote site accesses the table locally and ships the query result back to the query site as if it were an outer table to a join (i.e., as a blocked pipeline of tuples). Since all of the *distributed* optimization decisions discussed earlier pertain to *joins* of tables at different sites, picking the optimal global plan is solely a local matter: only the access path to the table need be chosen. For this reason, we will not consider single-table distributed queries further, but focus instead entirely upon distributed join methods.

In R*, n-table joins are executed as a sequence of n-1 two-table joins. Hence thorough understanding and correct modeling of distributed two-table joins is a prerequisite to validating n-table distributed joins. Intermediate results of joins are called ***composite*** tables, and may either be returned as a pipeline of tuples or else materialized completely before the succeeding two-table join (e.g., if sorting is required for a merge-scan join). We will therefore limit our discussion in this section to that fundamental operation, the two-table join.

Our discussion will use a simple notation for expressing distributed access plans for joins. There are two different join methods: merge scan joins, denoted by the infix operator "-M-", and nested loop joins, denoted by "-N-". The operand to the left of the join operator specifies the outer table access, the right operand the inner table access. A table access consists of the table name, optionally suffixed with an "I" if we use the index on the join column of this table and/or a "W" or"F" if we ship the table whole or fetch only matching tuples, respectively. For example, AIW-M-B denotes a plan that merge-scan joins tables A and B at B's site, shipping A whole after scanning it with the index on the join column. Since the merge-scan join requires both tables to be in join-column order, this plan implies B has to be sorted to accomplish the join.

5.1. Inner Table Transfer Strategy

The choice of transfer strategy for the inner table involves some interesting trade-offs. Shipping (a copy of) the table whole ("W") transfers the most inner tuples for the least message overhead, but needlessly sends inner tuples that have no matching outer tuples and necessitates additional I/O and CPU for reading the inner at its home site and then storing it in a temporary table at the join site. Any indexes on the inner that might aid a join cannot be shipped with the table, since indexes contain physical addresses that change when tuples are inserted in the temporary table, and R* does not permit dynamic creation of temporary indexes (we will re-visit that design decision in Section 6). However, since the inner is projected and any single-table predicates are applied before it is shipped, the temporary table is potentially much smaller than its permanent version, which might make multiple accesses to it (particularly in a nested-loop join) more cost-effective.

The high-speed channel we were using for communication in our tests imposed a relatively high per-message overhead, thereby emphatically favoring the "W" strategy. Figure 3 compares the actual performance of the best plan for each transfer strategy for both the high-speed channel and the long-haul medium-speed network, when merge-scan joining[5] two indexed 500-tuple tables, C and D, shipping the inner table D and returning the result to C's site. Both tables are projected to 50% of their tuple length, the join column domain has 100 different values, and the ***join cardinality*** — the cardinality of the result of the join — was 2477. If we ship the inner table D as a whole, the best plan is CI-M-DIW, and if we fetch the matching inner tuples ("F"), CI-M-DIF is best.

For the W strategy, the message costs are only 2.9% of the total resource cost, partly due to the relatively high local cost because of the large join cardinality. For the F strategy, we spend 80.9% of the costs for communications, since for each outer tuple we have to send one message containing the outer tuple's value and at least one message containing the matching inner tuples, if any. The total of 1000 messages cannot be reduced, even if there are no matching tuples, since the join site waits for some reply from the inner's site. Note that the number of bytes transmitted as well as the number of messages is much higher for the F strategy, because each message contains relatively little data in proportion to the required R* control information. Another source for the higher number of bytes transmitted is the frequent retransmission of inner table tuples for the large join cardinality of this query. The penalty for this overhead and the discrepancy between the two transfer strategies is exaggerated by slower network speeds. For the medium-speed network in Figure 3, the per-message overhead is 49% of the cost, and the discrepancy between the two strategies increases from a factor of 4.4 to a factor of 11.6.

The importance of per-message costs dictate two sufficient (but not necessary) conditions for the F strategy to be preferred:

1. the cardinality of the outer table must be less than half the number of messages required to ship the inner as a whole, and
2. the join cardinality must be less than the inner cardinality,

after any local (non-join) predicates have been applied and the referenced columns have been projected out. The second condition assures that fewer inner tuples are transferred to the outer's site for F than for W. Since the join cardinality is estimated as the product of the inner cardinality, outer cardinality, and join-predicate selectivity, these two conditions are

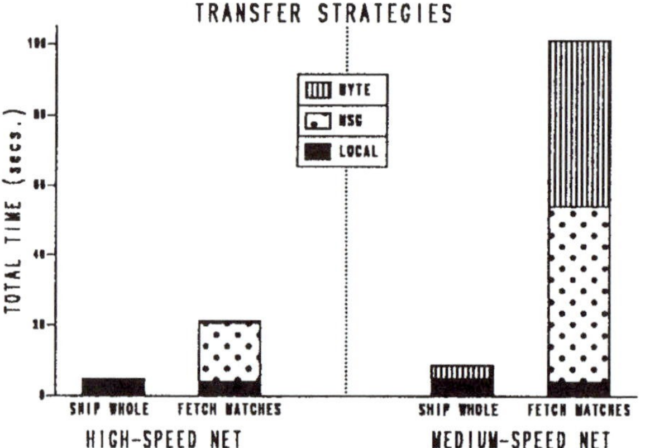

Figure 3: Comparison of the best R* plans, when using the ship-whole ("W") vs. the fetch-matches ("F") strategies for shipping the inner table, when merge-scan joining two indexed 500-tuple tables.

5 Nested loop joins perform very poorly for the "W" strategy, because we can not ship an index on the join column. For a fair comparison, we therefore only consider merge-scan joins.

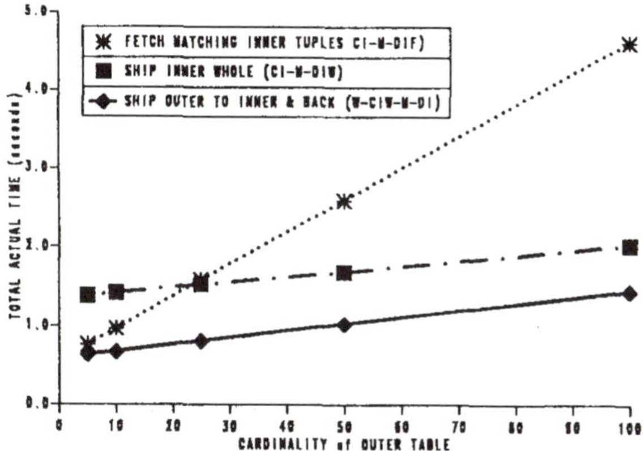

Figure 4: Shipping the outer table (C) to the inner's (D's) site and returning the result dominates both strategies for transferring the inner to the outer's site, even for small outer cardinalities (inner cardinality = 500 tuples).

equivalent to requiring that the outer cardinality be less than the minimum of (a) the inner's size (in bytes) divided by 8K bytes (the size of two messages) and (b) the inverse of the join-predicate's filter factor. Clearly these conditions are sufficiently strict that the F strategy will rarely be optimal.

Even when these conditions hold, it is likely that shipping the outer table to the inner's site and returning the result to the outer's site will be a better plan: by condition (1) the outer will be small, by condition (2) the result returned will be small, and performing the join at the inner's site permits the use of indexes on the inner. This observation is confirmed by Figure 4. The tests of Lu and Carey [LU 85] satisfied condition (2) by having a semijoin selectivity of 10% and condition (1) by cleverly altering the R* F strategy to send the outer-tuple values in one-page batches. Hence they concluded that the F strategy was preferred. Time constraints prevented us from implementing and testing this variation.

We feel that the conditions for the R* fetch-matches strategy to be preferred are so restrictive for both kinds of networks that its implementation without batching the outer-tuple values is not recommended for any future distributed database system. Therefore, henceforth we will consider only joins employing the ship-whole strategy.

5.2. Distributed vs. Local Join

Does distribution of tables improve or diminish performance of a particular query? In terms of total resources consumed, most distributed queries are more expensive than their single-site counterparts. Besides the obvious added communications cost, distributed queries also consume extra CPU processing to insert and retrieve the shipped tuples from communications buffers. In terms of response time, however, distributed queries may outperform equivalent local queries by bringing more resources to bear on a given query and by processing portions of that query in parallel on multiple processing units and I/O channels. Exploiting this parallelism is in fact a major justification for many distributed database systems [EPST 80, APER 83, WONG 83], especially multiprocessor database machines [BABB 79, DEWI 79, VALD 84, MENO 85].

The degree of simultaneity that can be achieved depends on the plan we are executing. Figure 5 compares the total resource time and the response time for some of the better R* access plans for a distributed query that joins two indexed (unclustered) 1000-tuple tables, A and B, at different sites, where the query site is A's site, the join column domain has 3000 different values, and each table is projected by 50%. For the plans shown, the ordering with respect to the total resource time is the same as the response time ordering, although this is not generally true. Plans shipping the outer table enjoy greater simultaneity because the join on the first buffer-full of outer tuples can proceed in parallel with the shipment of the next buffer-full. Plans shipping the inner table (whole) are more sequential: they must wait for the entire table to be received at the join site and inserted into a temporary table (incurring additional local cost) before proceeding with the join. For example, in Figure 5, note the difference between total resource time and response time for BIW-M-AI, as compared to the same difference for AI-M-BIW. Other plans not shown in Figure 5 that ship the inner table exhibit similar relationships to the corresponding plans that ship the outer (e.g., A-M-BW vs. BW-M-A, A-M-BIW vs. BIW-M-A, and AI-M-BW vs. BW-M-AI.). This assymmetry is unknown for local queries.

For merge joins not using indexes to achieve join-column order (e.g., A-M-BW, BW-M-A), R* sorts the two tables sequentially. Although sorting the two tables concurrently would not decrease the total resource time, it would lower the response time for those plans considerably (it should be close to the response time of BIW-M-A).

Comparing the response times for the above set of plans when the query is distributed vs. when it is local (see Figure 6), we notice that the distributed joins are faster. The dramatic differences between distributed and local for BIW-M-AI and AI-M-BIW stem from both simultaneity and the availability of two database buffers in the distributed case. However, by noting that for local joins the response time equals the resource time (since all systems were unloaded) and comparing these to the total resource times for the distributed query in Figure 5, we find that even the total resource costs for BIW-M-AI and AI-M-BIW are less than those for the local joins BI-M-AI and AI-M-BI, so parallelism alone cannot explain the improvement. The other reason is reduced contention: this particular plan is accessing both tables using unclustered indexes, which benefit greatly from larger buffers, and the distributed query enjoys twice as much buffer space as does the local query. However, not all distributed plans have

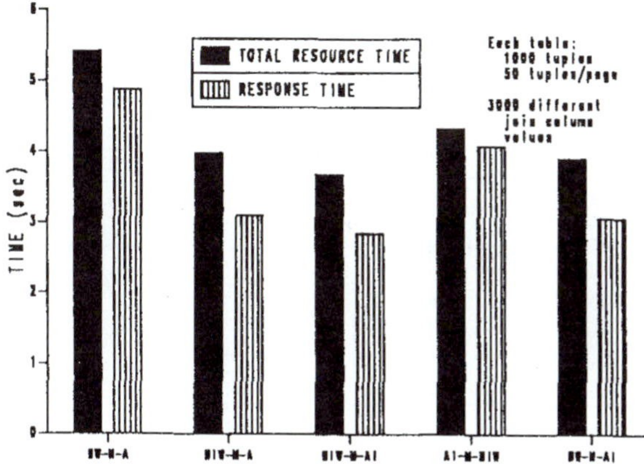

Figure 5: Resource consumption time vs. response time for various access plans, when joining 2 tables (1000 tuples each) distributed across a high-speed network.

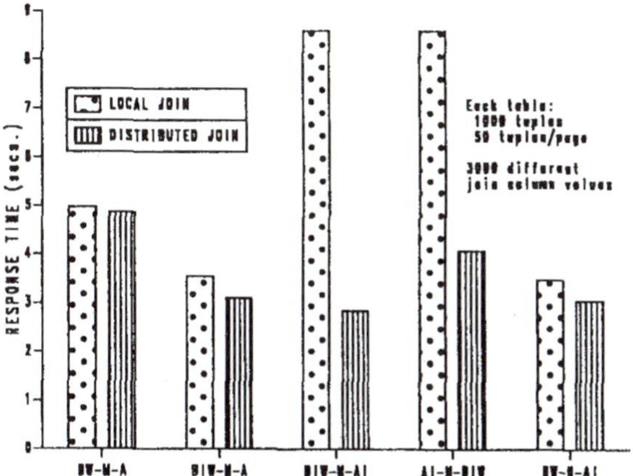

Figure 6: Response times for distributed (across a high-speed network) vs. local execution for various access plans, when joining 2 tables (1000 tuples each).

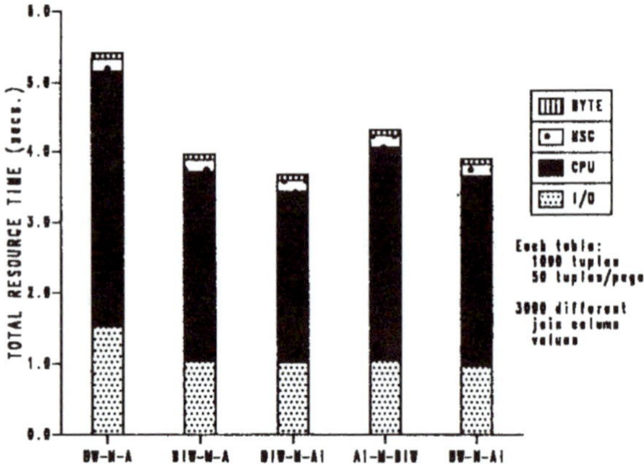

Figure 7: Relative importance of cost components for various access plans when joining 2 tables (of 1000 tuples each) distributed across a high-speed network.

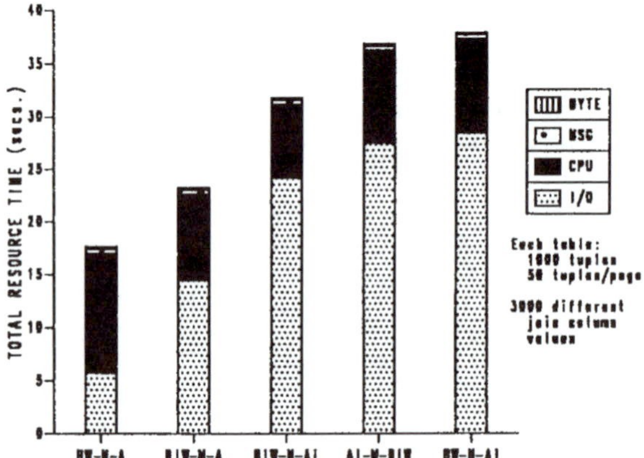

Figure 8: Relative importance of cost components for various access plans when joining 2 tables (of 2500 tuples each) distributed across a high-speed network.

better response times than the corresponding local plan; the increased buffer space doesn't much help the plans that don't access both tables using an index, and most of the distributed plans that ship the inner table to the join site (except for AI-M-BIW) are 15%-30% more expensive than their local counterpart because they exhibit a more sequential execution pattern.

For larger tables (e.g., 2500 tuples each), these effects are even more exaggerated by the greater demands they place upon the local processing resources of the two sites. However, for slower network speeds, the reverse is true; increased communications overhead results in response times for distributed plans being almost twice those of local plans. For a comparison of the resource times see Section 6.

5.3. Relative Importance of Cost Components

Many distributed query optimization algorithms proposed in the literature ignore the *intra*-site costs of CPU and I/O, arguing that those costs get dwarfed by the communication costs for the majority of queries. We have investigated the relative importance of the four cost components when joining two tables at different sites, varying the sizes of the tables and the speeds of the communication lines. Our results confirmed the analysis of Selinger and Adiba [SELI 80], which concluded that local processing costs are relevant and possibly even dominant in modelling the costs of distributed queries.

In a high-speed network such as a local-area network, message costs are of secondary importance, as shown by Figure 7 for the distributed join of two 1000-tuple tables. For our test configuration, message costs usually accounted for less (very often much less) than 10% of the total resource cost. This remained true for joins of larger tables, as shown in Figure 8 for two 2500-tuple tables. Similarly, message costs account for only 9% of the total cost for the optimal plan joining a 1000-tuple table to a 6000-tuple table, delivering the result to the site of the first table. This agrees with the measurements of Lu and Carey [LU 85].

When we altered the weights to simulate a medium-speed long-haul network, local processing costs were still significant, as shown in Figure 9 and Figure 10. In most of the plans, message costs and local processing costs were equally important, neither ever dropping under 30% of the total cost. Hence ignoring local costs might well result in a bad choice of the local parameters whose cost exceeds that of the messages. Also, the relative importance of per-message and per-byte costs reverses for the medium-speed network, because the time spent sending and receiving each message, and the "envelope" bytes appended to each message, are small compared to the much higher cost of getting the same information through a "narrower pipeline" than that of the high-speed network.

5.4. Optimizer Evaluation

How well does the R* optimizer model the costs added by distributed data? For the ship-whole table transfer strategy, for both outer and inner tables, our tests detected only minor differences (<2%) between actual costs and optimizer estimates of the number of messages and the number of bytes transmitted. The additional local cost for storing the inner table shipped whole is also correctly modelled by the optimizer, so that the

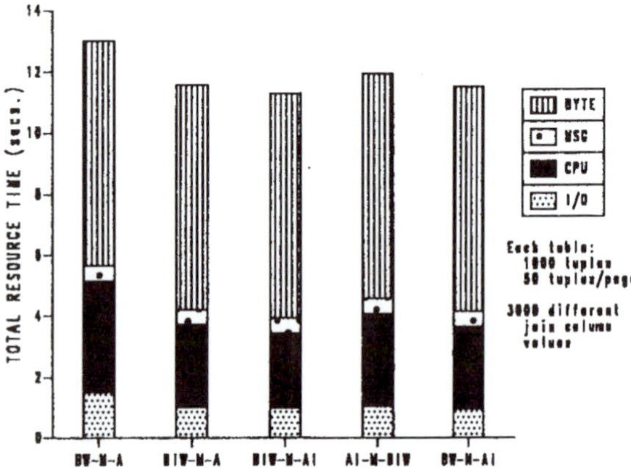

Figure 9: Relative importance of cost components for various access plans when joining 2 tables (of 1000 tuples each) distributed across a (simulated) medium-speed network.

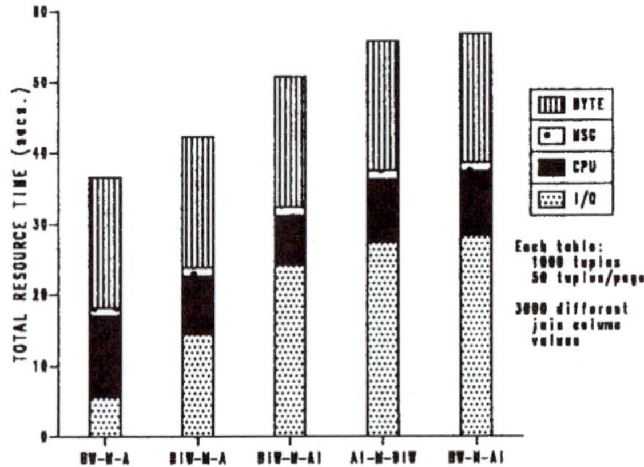

Figure 10: Relative importance of cost components for various access plans when joining 2 tables (of 2500 tuples each) distributed across a (simulated) medium-speed network.

system realizes, for example, that the plan AI-M-BIW is more expensive than BIW-M-AI. For the fetch-matches transfer strategy (for inner tables only), the expected number of messages was equal to the actual number in all cases, and the estimate for the bytes transmitted was never off by more than 25%. Although the number of bytes transferred is somewhat dependent on the join cardinality, the fixed number of bytes shipped with each message typically exceeds the inner-table data in each message, unless the inner's tuples are very wide (after projection) or are highly duplicated on the join-column value.

We encountered more severe problems in estimating the cost of shipping results of a join to the query site, because this cost is directly proportional to the join cardinality, which is difficult to estimate accurately. This problem is a special case of shipping a composite table to any site, so that these errors may be compounded as the number of tables to be joined at different sites increases.

In a high-speed network, where message costs are a small fraction of the total cost and the optimizer's decisions are based more on local processing costs, these errors (assuming that they are less than 50%) are not very crucial. For a given join ordering of tables, the choice of a site at which a particular composite table will be joined with the next inner table will depend mainly upon the indexes available on the inner, the sizes of the two tables, and possibly on the order of the composite's tuples (for a merge-scan join). However, in a medium-speed long-haul communication network, where the communications costs range from 30 to 70% of the total cost, the error in estimating the join cardinality is magnified in the overall cost estimate. In [MACK 86], we have already suggested replacing the current estimates of join cardinality with statistics collected while performing the same join for an earlier SQL statement.

Can we simplify the optimizer for high-speed local-area networks, under the assumption that message costs usually are less than 10% of the total cost? More precisely, can we, starting from the best ***hypothetical local plan*** (assuming all tables are available at the query site) for a given join, construct a distributed plan that is less than 10% more expensive than the optimum? This would considerably facilitate the optimization of distributed queries! Unfortunately the answer is no, because there may be distributed access plans that have a lower local cost than any hypothetical local plan. For example, the plan BIW-M-AI in Figure 5 has a lower local cost than any plan joining the two 1000-tuple tables locally. The corresponding hypothetical local plan BI-M-AI performs very poorly (cf. Figure 6), because the two tables do not fit into one database buffer together.

Estimates of the local processing costs for distributed queries suffered many of the same problems discovered for local queries by our earlier study. In particular, a better model is needed of the re-use of pages in the buffer when performing nested-loop joins using an unclustered index on the inner table [MACK 86]. However, the more distributed the tables participating in a join are, the better the R* optimizer estimates are. The reason for this is that join costs are estimated from the costs for producing the composite table and accessing the inner table, assuming these component costs are independent of each other. This assumption is most likely to be valid when the composite and inner tables are at different sites; tables joined locally compete for the same buffer space. For example, the estimated local costs (CPU and I/O) for joining two 1000-tuple tables locally (BI-M-AI) are the same as the estimated local costs for executing the distributed plan BIW-M-AI, but the first estimate considerably underestimates the actual local cost of BI-M-AI (see Figure 6), whereas it is very accurate for the actual local cost of BIW-M-AI (cf. Figure 5).

6. Alternative Distributed Join Methods

The R* prototype provides an opportunity to compare empirically the actual performance of the distributed join methods that were implemented in R* against some other proposed join methods for equi-joins that were not implemented in R*, but might be interesting candidates for an extension or for future systems:

1. joins using dynamically-created indexes
2. semijoins
3. joins using hashing (Bloom) filters (***Bloomjoins***)

None of these methods are new [BERN 79, DEWI 85, BRAT 85]. Our contribution is the use of performance data on a real system to compare these methods with more traditional methods. We will describe the join algorithms in detail and evaluate their performance using measured R* costs for executing sub-actions such as scans, local joins, sorting of partial results, creating indexes, etc. These costs were adjusted appropriately when necessary: for example, a page does not have to be fetched by a certain sub-action if it already resides in the buffer as a result of a previous sub-action. The alternative methods are presented both in the order in which they were proposed historically and in the order of increasingly more compact data transmission between sites. Although several hash-based join algorithms look promising based upon cost-equation analyses [DEWI 85, BRAT 85], we could not evaluate them adequately using this empirical methodology, simply because we did not have any R* performance figures for the necessary primitives.

Before comparing the methods, we will first analyze the cost for each one for a distributed equi-join of two tables S and T, residing at two different sites 1 and 2, respectively, with site 1 as the query site. Let the equi-predicate be of the form S.a = T.b, where a is a column of S and b is a column of T. For simplicity, we will consider only the two cases where both or neither S and T have an (unclustered) index on their join column(s). To eliminate interference from secondary effects, we further assume that: (1) S and T do not have any indexes on columns other than the join columns, (2) all the columns of S and T are to be returned to the user (no projection), (3) the join predicate is the only predicate specified in the query (no selection), and (4) S and T are in separate DBSPACES that contain no other tables. The extension of the algorithms to the cases excluded by these assumptions is straightforward.

6.1. Dynamically-Created Temporary Index on Inner

R* does not permit the shipment of any access structures such as indexes, since these contain physical addresses (TIDs, which contain page numbers) that are not meaningful outside their home database. Yet earlier studies of local joins have shown how important indexes can be for improving the database performance, and how in some situations creating a temporary index before executing a nested-loop join can be cheaper than executing a merge-scan join without the index [MACK 86]. This is because creating an index requires sorting only key-TID pairs, plus creation of the index structure, whereas a merge-scan join without any indexes on the tables requires sorting the projected tuples of the outer as well as the inner table. The question remains whether dynamically-created temporary indexes are beneficial in a distributed environment. The cost of each step for performing a distributed join using a dynamically-created temporary index is as follows:

1. **Scan table T and ship the whole table to site 1.** The cost for this step is equivalent to our measured cost for a remote access of a single table, subtracting the CPU cost to extract tuples from the message buffers.
2. **Store T and create a temporary index on it at site 1.** Since reading T from a message buffer does not involve any I/O cost, and either reading or writing a page costs one disk I/O, the I/O cost of writing T to a temporary table and creating an index on it will be the same as for reading it from a permanent table via a sequential scan and creating an index on that, except the temporary index is not catalogued. This cost was measured in R* by executing a CREATE INDEX statement, and then adding CPU time for the insert while subtracting the known and fixed number of I/Os to catalog pages.
3. **Execute the best plan for a local join at site 1.** Again, this cost is known from the measurements obtained by our earlier study for local joins. The I/O cost must be reduced by the number of index and data pages of T that remain in the buffer from prior steps.

6.2. Semijoin

Semijoins [BERN 79, BERN 81A, BERN 81B] reduce the tuples of T that are transferred from site 2 to site 1, when only a subset of T matches tuples in S on the join column (i.e., when the ***semijoin selectivity*** < 1), but at the expense of sending all of S.a from site 1 to site 2. The cost of each step for performing a distributed join using a semijoin when neither S.a nor T.b are indexed is as follows:

1. **Sort both S and T on the join column, producing S' and T'.** The costs measured by R* for sorting any table include reading the table initially, sorting it, and writing the sorted result to a temporary table, but not the cost of any succeeding read of the sorted temporary table.

2. **Read S'.a (at site 1), eliminating duplicates, and send the result to site 2.** This cost (and for the sort of S in the previous step) could be measured in R* for a remote "SELECT DISTINCT S.a" query, subtracting the CPU cost to extract tuples from the message buffers. If S' fits into the buffer, the previous step saves us the I/O cost; otherwise all cost components are included.
3. **At site 2, select the tuples of T' that match S'.a, yielding T", and ship them to site 1.** This cost is composed of the costs for scanning S', scanning T', handling matches, and shipping the matching tuples. Reading S'.a from the message buffer incurs no I/O cost, and scanning T' also costs only CPU instructions if T' fits into the buffer. Also, the pages of the matching tuples of T' can be transmitted to site 1 as they are found, and need not be stored, because we are using these tuples as the outer table in later steps. The cost for finding the matching tuples involves only a CPU cost that is roughly proportional to the number of matches found. The cost assessed here was derived from actual R* measurements for local queries, interpolating when the table sizes, projection factors, selection factors, etc. fell between values of those parameters used in the R* experiments.
4. **At site 1, merge-join the (sorted) temporary tables S' and T" and return the resulting tuples to the user.** This cost was measured in the same way as the previous step, less the communications cost. Note that T" inherits the join-column ordering from T'.

If there are indexes on S.a and T.b, we can either use the above algorithm or we can alter each step as follows:

1. This step and its cost can be eliminated.
2. Replace this step with a scan of S.a's index pages only (not touching any data pages) and their transmission to site 2. The cost was measured as in Step (2) above, but with an index existing on S.a; R* can detect that data pages need not be accessed.
3. Using the index on T.b, perform a local merge-scan or a nested-loop join, whichever is faster, at site 2, yielding T". Again, the cost for various local joins was measured in the earlier study; they were reduced by the cost of scanning S that was saved by taking it from the message buffer as pages arrived. Some interpolation between actual experiments was required to save re-running those experiments with the exact join cardinality that resulted here.
4. Join T" with S, using the index on S.a, again choosing between the merge-scan or nested-loop join plans whose costs were measured on R*. A known amount of I/O was subtracted for the index leaf pages that remain in the buffer from step (2).

6.3. Bloomjoin

Hashing techniques are known to be efficient ways of finding matching values, and have recently been applied to database join algorithms [BABB 79, BRAT 84, VALD 84, DEWI 85]. Bloomjoins use Bloom filters [BLOO 70] as a "hashed semijoin" to filter out tuples that have no matching tuples in a join [BABB 79, BRAT 84]. Thus, as with semijoins, Bloomjoins reduce the size of the tables that have to be transferred, sorted, merged, etc. However, the bit tables used in Bloomjoins will typically be smaller than the join-column values transmitted for semijoins. By reducing the size of the inner table at an early stage, Bloomjoins also save local costs. Whereas a semijoin requires executing an extra join for reducing the inner table, Bloomjoins only need an additional scan in no particular order. For simplicity, we use only a single hashing function; further optimization is possible by allowing multiple hashing functions [SEVE 76]. The cost of each step for performing a distributed join using a Bloomjoin when neither S.a nor T.b are indexed is as follows:

1. **Generate a Bloom filter, BfS, from table S.** The Bloom filter, a large vector of bits that are initially all set to "0", is generated by scanning S and hashing each value of column S.a to a particular bit in the vector and setting that bit to "1". As before, the cost of accessing S was measured on R*. We added 200 (machine-level) instructions per tuple (a conservative upper bound for any implementation) for hashing one value and setting the appropriate bit in the vector.
2. **Send BfS to site 2.** We assume that sending a Bloom filter causes the same R* message overhead as if sets of tuples are sent, and the number of bytes is obvious from the size of the Bloom filter.
3. **Scan table T at site 2, hashing the values of T.b using the same hash function as in Step (1). If the bit hashed to is "1", then send that tuple to site 1 as tuple stream T'.** This cost is calculated as in Step (1), but the number of tuples is reduced by the Bloom filtering. We need to estimate the reduced ***Bloomjoin cardinality*** of T, i.e. the cardinality of T'. We know it must be at least the ***semijoin cardinality of T***, SC_T, i.e. the number of tuples in T whose join-column values match a tuple in S. We must add an estimate of the number of non-matching tuples in T that erroneously survive filtration due to collisions. Let F be the size (in bits) of BfS, D_S the number of distinct values of S.a, D_T the number of distinct values of T.b, and C_T the cardinality of T. Then the number of bits set to "1" in BfS is approximated for large D_S by [SEVE 76]:

$$bits_S = F(1 - e^{-(\frac{D_S}{F})})$$

So the expected number of tuples in T', the Bloomjoin cardinality BC_T of table T, is given by

$$BC_T = SC_T + bits_S(1 - e^{-(\frac{\alpha D_T}{F})})$$

where

$$\alpha = (1 - \frac{SC_T}{C_T})$$

is the fraction of non-matching tuples in T.
4. **At site 1, join T' to S and return the result to the user.** This cost was derived as for semijoins, again using the Bloomjoin cardinality estimate for T'.

If there are indexes on S.a and T.b, we can either use the above algorithm or, as with semijoins, use the index on S.a to generate BfS -- thus saving accesses to the data pages in Step (1) — and use the index on both T.b and S.a to perform the join in Step (4).

As with semijoins, filtration can also proceed in the opposite direction: S can also be reduced before the join by sending to site 1 another Bloom filter BfT based upon the values in T. This is usually advantageous if S needs to be sorted for a merge-scan join, because a smaller S will be cheaper to sort. Filtration is maximized by constructing the more selective Bloom filter first, i.e. on the table having the fewer distinct join column values[6], and altering the Bloomjoin procedure accordingly:

- If we first produce BfS, then add step (3.5): while scanning T in step (3), generate BfT, send it to site 1, and use it to reduce S.
- If we first produce BfT, then add step (0.5): generate BfT, send it to site 1, and use it to reduce S while scanning S in step (1).

6.4. Comparison of Alternative Join Methods

Using the actual costs measured by R* as described above, we were able to compare the alternative join methods empirically with the best R* plan, for both the distributed and local join, for a two-table join with no projections and no predicates other than the equi-join on an integer column. The measured cost was total resource time, since response time will vary too much depending upon other applications executing concurrently.

Our experimental parameters for this analysis were identical to those in the previous section. We fixed the size of table A at site 1 at 1000 tuples, and varied the size of table B at site 2 from 100 to 6000 tuples. For the Bloomjoin we chose a filter size (F) of 2K bytes (16384 bits) to ensure that it would fit in one 4K byte page. Again, we assumed the availability of (unclustered) indexes on the join columns. We will discuss the impact of relaxing this and other assumed parameters where appropriate in the following, and at the end of this section.

As in the previous section, we compared the performance of the join methods under two classes of networks:

- a high-speed network (16.5 msecs. minimum transfer time, 4M bit/sec. effective transfer rate); and
- a medium-speed long-haul network (50 msecs. minimum transfer time, 40K bit/sec. effective transfer rate)

by appropriately adjusting the per-message and per-byte weights by which observed numbers of messages and bytes transmitted were multiplied. For each of these classes, we varied the query site between site 1 and site 2.

---

6 If this cannot be determined, simply choose the smaller table [BRAT 84].

6.4.1. High-speed Network

For a high-speed network (Figure 11), the cost of transmission is dominated by local processing costs, as shown by the following table of the average percentage of the total costs for the different join algorithms that are due to local processing costs:

Query Site	*R**	*R* + temp. index*	*Semijoin*	*Bloomjoin*
1 = site of A	88.9%	89.2%	96.5%	93.0%
2 = site of B	86.5%	91.4%	94.7%	90.1%

Temporary indexes generally provided little improvement over R* performance, because the inexpensive shipping costs permit the optimal R* plan to ship B to site 1, there to use the already-existent index on A to perform a very efficient nested-loop join. When there was no index on A, the ability to build temporary indexes improved upon the R* plan by up to 30%: A was shipped to site 2, where a temporary index was dynamically built on it and the join performed. Such a situation would be common in *multi-table* joins having a small composite table that is to be joined with a large inner, so temporary indexes would still be a desirable extension for R*.

Semijoins were advantageous only in the limited case where both the data and index pages of B fit into the buffer ($cardinality(B) \leq 1500$), so that efficient use of the indexes on A and B kept the semijoin's local processing cost only slightly higher than that of the optimal R* plan. Once B no longer fits in the buffer ($cardinality(B) \geq 2000$), the high cost of accessing B with the unclustered index precluded its use, and the added cost of sorting B was not offset by sufficient savings in the transfer cost.

Bloomjoins dominated all other join alternatives, even R* joining local tables! This should not be too surprising, because local Bloomjoins outperform local R* by 20-40%, as already shown in [MACK 86], and transmission costs represent less than 10% of the total costs. The performance gains depend upon the ratios, r_A and r_B, between the Bloomjoin cardinality and the table cardinality of A and B, respectively: r_B is relatively constant (0.31), whereas r_A is varying (e.g., 0.53 for $cardinality(B) = 2000$ and 1.0 for $cardinality(B) = 6000$). But even if those ratios are close to 1, Bloomjoins are still better than R*. For example, when r_A=1.0, r_B=0.8, and $cardinality(B) = 6000$, a Bloomjoin would still be almost two seconds faster than R*. Note that due to a much higher join cardinality in this case, the R* optimum would be more expensive than the plotted one.

Why are Bloomjoins — essentially "hashed semijoins" — so much better than semijoins? The message costs were comparable, because the Bloom filter was relatively large (1 message) compared to the number of distinct join column values, and the number of non-matching tuples not filtered by the Bloom filter was less than 10% of the semijoin cardinality. The answer is that the semijoin incurs higher local processing costs to essentially perform a second join at B's site, compared to a simple scan of B in no particular order to do the hash filtering.

The above results were almost identical when B's site (2) was the query site, because the fast network makes it cheap to ship the results back after performing the join at site 1 (desirable because table A fits in the buffer). The only exception was that temporary indexes have increased advantage over R* when A could be moved to the query site and still have an (dynamically-created temporary) index with which a fast nested-loop join could be done.

We also experimented with combining a temporary index with semijoins and Bloomjoins. Such combinations improved performance only when there were no indexes, and even then by less than 10%.

6.4.2. Medium-speed Network

In a medium-speed network, local processing costs represent a much smaller (but still very significant!) proportion of the cost for each join method:

Query Site	*R**	*R* + temp. index*	*Semijoin*	*Bloomjoin*
1 = site of A	38.5%	22.6%	46.3%	32.3%
2 = site of B	38.5%	36.0%	53.0%	41.6%

Regardless of the choice of query site, Bloomjoins dominated all other distributed join methods by 15-40% for $cardinality(B) > 100$ (compare Figure 12 and Figure 13). The main reason was smaller transmissions: the communications costs for Bloomjoins were 20-40% less than R*'s, and for $cardinality(B) \geq 1500$ shipping the Bloom filter and some non-matching tuples not filtered by the Bloom filter was cheaper than shipping B's join column for semijoins. Because of their compactness, Bloom filters can be shipped equally easily in either direction, whereas R* and R* with temporary indexes always try to perform the join at A's site to avoid shipping table B (which would cost approximately 93.2 seconds when $cardinality(B) = 6000$!).

Also independent of the choice of query site was the fact that temporary indexes improved the R* performance somewhat for bigger tables.

Only R* and semijoins change relative positions depending upon the query site. When the query site is the site of the non-varying 1000-tuple table A, semijoins are clearly better than R* (see Figure 12). When the query

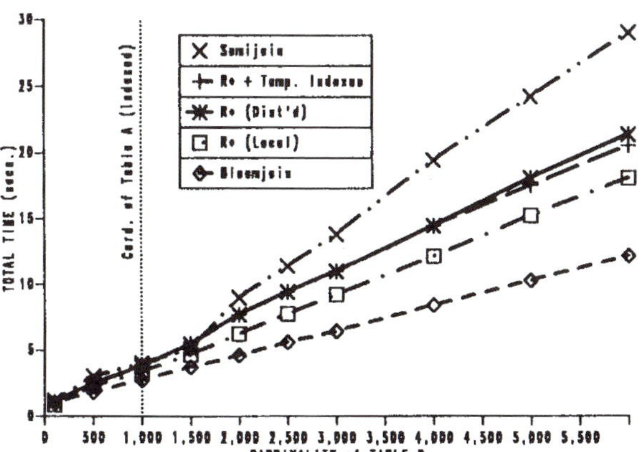

Figure 11: High-speed network; Query Site = 1 (A's site)

R*'s best distributed and local plan (measured) vs. performance of other join strategies (simulated) for a high-speed network, joining an indexed 1000-tuple table A at site 1 with an indexed table B (of increasing size) at site 2, returning the result at site 1.

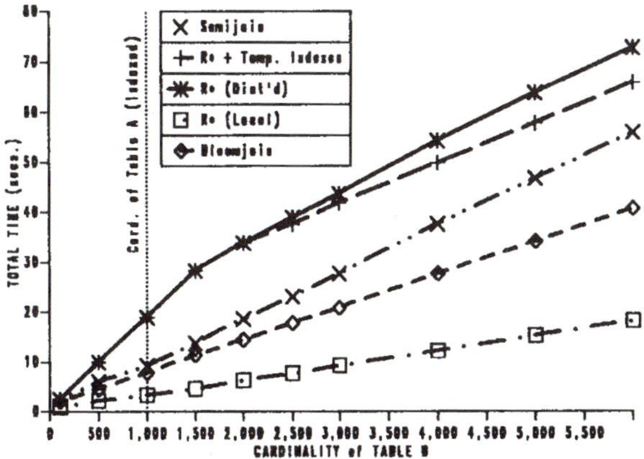

Figure 12: Medium-speed network; Query Site = 1 (A's site)

R*'s best distributed and local plan (measured) vs. performance of other join strategies (simulated) for a medium-speed network, joining an indexed 1000-tuple table A at site 1 with an indexed table B (of increasing size) at site 2, returning the result at site 1.

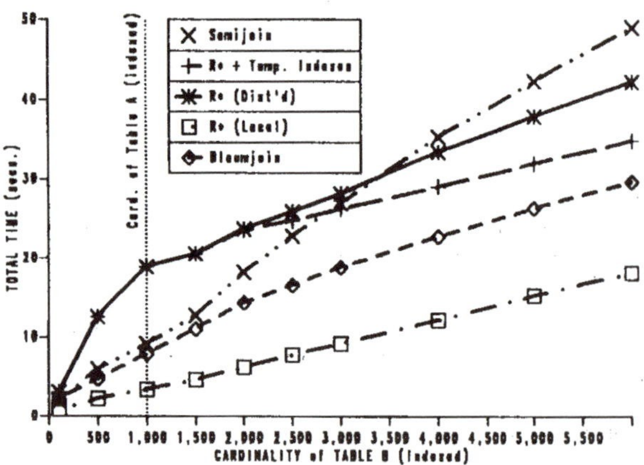

Figure 13: Medium-speed network; Query Site = 2 (B's site)

R*'s best distributed and local plan (measured) vs. performance of other join strategies (simulated) for a medium-speed network, joining an indexed 1000-tuple table A at site 1 with an indexed table B (of increasing size) at site 2, returning the result at site 2.

site is B's site, however, R* still beats semijoins when B is sufficiently large (cf. Figure 13). The reason is straightforward but important for performance on large queries. Since the join columns had a domain of 3000 different values, most of these values had matches in B when *cardinality*(*B*) $\geq$ 3000. Thus, the semijoin cardinality of A was close to its table cardinality, meaning that most of the tuples of A survived the semijoin and were shipped to site 2 anyway (as in the R* plan). With the additional overhead of sending the join column of B to site 1 and the higher local processing cost, semijoins could not compete.

Note that both the R* and the semijoin curves jumped when the index and data pages of table B no longer fit in the buffer (between 1500 and 2000 tuples), because they switched to sorting the tables.

6.4.3. Variation of the Experimental Parameters

Space constraints prevent us from presenting the results of numerous other experiments for different values of our experimental parameters:

- When indexes were clustered (rather than unclustered), semijoins beat R* by at most 10% (except when the query site = B's site and B is very large), but Bloomjoins still dominated all other distributed join techniques.

- Introducing a 50% projection on both tables in our join query did not change the dominance of Bloomjoins, but eliminated any performance advantage that temporary indexes provided over R* and, when the query site was A's site, reduced the local processing cost disadvantage of semijoins sufficiently that they beat R* (but by less than 10%). However, when the query site was B's site, the 50% projection reduced R*'s message costs more than those for semijoins, giving R* an even wider performance margin over semijoins.

- As expected, a wider join column (e.g., a long character column or a multi-column join predicate) decreased the semijoin performance while not affecting the other algorithms.

7. Conclusions

Our experiments on two-table distributed equi-joins found that the strategy of shipping the entire inner table to the join site and storing it there dominates the fetch-matches strategy, which incurs prohibitive per-message costs for each outer tuple even in high-speed networks.

The R* optimizer's modelling of message costs was very accurate, a necessary condition for picking the correct join site. Estimated message costs were within 2% of actual message costs when the cardinality of the table to be shipped was well known. Errors in estimating message costs originated from poor estimates of join cardinalities. This problem is not introduced by distribution, and suggestions for alleviating it by collecting join-cardinality statistics have already been advanced [MACK 86].

The modelling of local costs actually *improves* with greater distribution of the tables involved, because the optimizer's assumption of independence of access is closer to being true when tables do not interfere with each other by competing for the same resource (especially buffer space) within a given site. While more resources are consumed overall by distributed queries, in a high-speed network this results in response times that are actually less than for local queries for certain plans that can benefit from:

- concurrent execution due to pipelining, and/or
- the availability of more key resources — such as buffer space — to reduce contention.

Even for medium-speed, long-haul networks linking geographically dispersed hosts, local costs for CPU and I/O are significant enough to affect the choice of plans. Their relative contribution increases rather than decreases as the tables grow in size, and varies considerably depending upon the access path and join method. Hence no distributed query optimizer can afford to ignore their contribution.

Furthermore, the significance of local costs cannot be ignored when considering alternative distributed join techniques such as semijoins. They are advantageous only when message costs are high (e.g., for a medium-speed network) and any table remote from the join site is quite large. However, we have shown that a Bloomjoin — using Bloom filters to do "hashed semijoins" — dominates the other distributed join methods *in all cases investigated*, except when the semijoin selectivities of the outer and the inner tables are very close to 1. This agrees with the analysis of [BRAT 84].

There remain many open questions which time did not allow us to pursue. We did not test joins for very large tables (e.g., 100,000 tuples), for more than 2 tables, for varying buffer sizes, or for varying tables per DBSPACE. Experimenting with n-table joins, in particular, is crucial to validating the optimizer's selection of join order. We hope to actually test rather than simulate semijoins, Bloomjoins, and medium-speed long-haul networks.

Finally, R* employs a homogeneous model of reality, assuming that all sites have the same processing capabilities and are connected by a uniform network with equal link characteristics. In a real environment, it is very likely that these assumptions are not valid. Adapting the optimizer to this kind of environment is likely to be difficult but important to correctly choosing optimal plans for real configurations.

8. Acknowledgements

We wish to acknowledge the contributions to this work by several colleagues, especially the R* research team, and Lo Hsieh and his group at IBM's Santa Teresa Laboratory. We particularly benefitted from lengthy discussions with — and suggestions by — Bruce Lindsay. Toby Lehman (visiting from the University of Wisconsin) implemented the DC* counters. George Lapis helped with database generation and implemented the R* interface to GDDM that enabled us to graph performance results quickly and elegantly. Paul Wilms contributed some PL/I programs that aided our testing, and assisted in the implementation of the COLLECT COUNTERS and EXPLAIN statements. Christoph Freytag, Laura Haas, Bruce Lindsay, John McPherson, Pat Selinger, and Irv Traiger constructively critiqued an earlier draft of this paper, improving its readability significantly. Finally, Tzu-Fang Chang and Alice Kay provided invaluable systems support and patience while our tests consumed considerable computing resources.

Bibliography

[APER 83] P.M.G. Apers, A.R. Hevner, and S.B. Yao, Optimizing Algorithms for Distributed Queries, *IEEE Trans. on Software Engineering* **SE-9** (January 1983) pp. 57-68.

[ASTR 80] M.M. Astrahan, M. Schkolnick, and W. Kim, Performance of the System R Access Path Selection Mechanism, *Information Processing* **80** (1980) pp. 487-491.

[BABB 79] E. Babb, Implementing a Relational Database by Means of Specialized Hardware, *ACM Trans. on Database Systems* **4,1** (1979) pp. 1-29.

[BERN 79] P.A. Bernstein and N. Goodman, Full reducers for relational queries using multi-attribute semi-joins, *Proc. 1979 NBS Symp. on Comp. Network.* (December 1979).

[BERN 81A] P.A. Bernstein and D.W. Chiu, Using semijoins to solve relational queries, *Journal of the ACM* **28,1** (January 1981) pp. 25-40.

[BERN 81B] P.A. Bernstein, N. Goodman, E. Wong, C.L. Reeve, J. Rothnie, Query Processing in a System for Distributed Databases (SDD-1), *ACM Trans. on Database Systems* **6,4** (December 1981) pp. 602-625.

[BLOO 70] B.H. Bloom, Space/Time Trade-offs in Hash Coding with Allowable Errors, *Communications of the ACM* **13,7** (July 1970) pp. 422-426.

[BRAT 84] K. Bratbergsengen, Hashing Methods and Relational Algebra Operations, *Procs. of the Tenth International Conf. on Very Large Data Bases* (Singapore, 1984) pp. 323-333. Morgan Kaufmann Publishers, Los Altos, CA.

[CHAM 81] D.D. Chamberlin, M.M. Astrahan, W.F. King, R.A. Lorie, J.W. Mehl, T.G. Price, M. Schkolnick, P. Griffiths Selinger, D.R. Slutz, B.W. Wade, and R.A. Yost, Support for Repetitive Transactions and Ad Hoc Queries in System R, *ACM Trans. on Database Systems* **6,1** (March 1981) pp. 70-94.

[CHAN 82] J-M. Chang, A Heuristic Approach to Distributed Query Processing, *Procs. of the Eighth International Conf. on Very Large Data Bases* (Mexico City, September 1982) pp. 54-61. Morgan Kaufmann Publishers, Los Altos, CA.

[CHU 82] W.W. Chu and P. Hurley, Optimal Query Processing for Distributed Database Systems, *IEEE Trans. on Computers* **C-31** (September 1982) pp. 835-850.

[DANI 82] D. Daniels, P.G. Selinger, L.M. Haas, B.G. Lindsay, C. Mohan, A. Walker, and P. Wilms, An Introduction to Distributed Query Compilation in R*, *Procs. Second International Conf. on Distributed Databases* (Berlin, September 1982). Also available as IBM Research Report RJ3497, San Jose, CA, June 1982.

[DEWI 79] D.J. DeWitt, Query Execution in DIRECT, *Procs. of ACM-SIGMOD* (May 1979).

[DEWI 85] D.J. DeWitt and R. Gerber, Multiprocessor Hash-Based Join Algorithms, *Procs. of the Eleventh International Conf. on Very Large Data Bases* (Stockholm, Sweden, September 1985) pp. 151-164. Morgan Kaufmann Publishers, Los Altos, CA.

[EPST 78] R. Epstein, M. Stonebraker, and E. Wong, Distributed Query Processing in a Relational Data Base System, *Procs. of ACM-SIGMOD* (Austin,TX, May 1978) pp. 169-180.

[EPST 80] R. Epstein and M. Stonebraker, Analysis of Distributed Data Base Processing Strategies, *Procs. of the Sixth International Conf. on Very Large Data Bases* (Montreal,IEEE, October 1980) pp. 92-101.

[HEVN 79] A.R. Hevner and S.B. Yao, Query Processing in Distributed Database Systems, *IEEE Trans. on Software Engineering* **SE-5** (May 1979) pp. 177-187.

[KERS 82] L. Kerschberg, P.D. Ting, and S.B. Yao, Query Optimization in Star Computer Networks, *ACM Trans. on Database Systems* **7,4** (December 1982) pp. 678-711.

[LIND 83] B.G. Lindsay, L.M. Haas, C. Mohan, P.F. Wilms, and R.A. Yost, Computation and Communication in R*: A Distributed Database Manager, Proc. 9th ACM Symposium on Principles of Operating Systems (Bretton Woods, October 1983). Also in *ACM Transactions on Computer Systems 2*, 1 (Feb. 1984), pp. 24-38.

[LOHM 84] G.M. Lohman, D. Daniels, L.M. Haas, R. Kistler, P.G. Selinger, Optimization of Nested Queries in a Distributed Relational Database, *Procs. of the Tenth International Conf. on Very Large Data Bases* (Singapore, 1984) pp. 403-415. Morgan Kaufmann Publishers, Los Altos, CA. Also available as IBM Research Report RJ4260, San Jose, CA, April 1984.

[LOHM 85] G.M. Lohman, C. Mohan, L.M. Haas, B.G. Lindsay, P.G. Selinger, P.F. Wilms, and D. Daniels, Query Processing in R*, *Query Processing in Database Systems* (Kim, Batory, & Reiner (eds.), 1985) pp. 31-47. Springer-Verlag, Heidelberg. Also available as IBM Research Report RJ4272, San Jose, CA, April 1984.

[LU 85] H. Lu and M.J. Carey, Some Experimental Results on Distributed Join Algorithms in a Local Network, *Procs. of the Eleventh International Conf. on Very Large Data Bases* (Stockholm, Sweden, August 1985) pp. 292-304. Morgan Kaufmann Publishers, Los Altos, CA.

[MACK 85] L.F. Mackert and G.M. Lohman, Index Scans using a Finite LRU Buffer: A Validated I/O Model, IBM Research Report RJ4836 (San Jose, CA, September 1985).

[MACK 86] L.F. Mackert and G.M. Lohman, R* Optimizer Validation and Performance Evaluation for Local Queries, *Procs. of ACM-SIGMOD* (Washington, DC, May 1986 (to appear)). Also available as IBM Research Report RJ4989, San Jose, CA, January 1986.

[MENO 85] M.J. Menon, Sorting and Join Algorithms for Multiprocessor Database Machines, *NATO-ASI on Relational Database Machine Architecture* (Les Arcs, France, July 1985).

[ONUE 83] E. Onuegbe, S. Rahimi, and A.R. Hevner, Local Query Translation and Optimization in a Distributed System, *Procs. NCC 1983* (July 1983) pp. 229-239.

[PERR 84] W. Perrizo, A Method for Processing Distributed Database Queries, *IEEE Trans. on Software Engineering* **SE-10,4** (July 1984) pp. 466-471.

[RDT 84] *RDT: Relational Design Tool*, IBM Reference Manual SH20-6415. (IBM Corp., June 1984).

[SELI 79] P.G. Selinger, M.M. Astrahan, D.D. Chamberlin, R.A. Lorie, and T.G. Price, Access Path Selection in a Relational Database Management System, *Procs. of ACM-SIGMOD* (1979) pp. 23-34.

[SELI 80] P.G. Selinger and M. Adiba, Access Path Selection in Distributed Database Management Systems, *Procs. International Conf. on Data Bases* (Univ. of Aberdeen, Scotland, July 1980 pp. 204-215. Deen and Hammersly, ed.

[SEVE 76] D.G. Severance and G.M. Lohman, Differential Files: Their Application to the Maintenance of Large Databases, *ACM Trans. on Database Systems* **1,3** (September 1976) pp. 256-267.

[STON 82] M. Stonebraker, J. Woodfill, J. Ranstrom, M. Murphy, J. Kalash, M. Carey, K. Arnold, Performance Analysis of Distributed Data Base Systems, *Database Engineering* **5** (IEEE Computer Society, December 1982) pp. 58-65.

[VALD 84] P. Valduriez and G. Gardarin, Join and Semi-Join Algorithms for a Multiprocessor Database Machine, *ACM Trans. on Database Systems* **9,1** (March 1984) pp. 133-161.

[VTAM 85] *Network Program Products Planning (MVS, VSE, and VM)*, IBM Reference Manual SC23-0110-1 (IBM Corp., April 1985).

[WONG 83] E. Wong, Dynamic Rematerialization: Processing Distributed Queries using Redundant Data, *IEEE Trans. on Software Engineering* **SE-9,3** (May 1983) pp. 228-232.

[YAO 79] S.B. Yao, Optimization of Query Algorithms, *ACM Trans. on Database Systems* **4,2** (June 1979) pp. 133-155.

[YU 83] C.T. Yu, and C.C. Chang, On the Design of a Query Processing Strategy in a Distributed Database Environment, *Proc. SIGMOD 83* (San Jose, CA, May 1983) pp. 30-39.

The VLDB Journal (1996) 5: 48–63

The VLDB Journal

Mariposa: a wide-area distributed database system

Michael Stonebraker, Paul M. Aoki, Witold Litwin[1], Avi Pfeffer[2], Adam Sah, Jeff Sidell, Carl Staelin[3], Andrew Yu[4]

Department of Electrical Engineering and Computer Sciences, University of California, Berkeley, CA 94720-1776, USA

Edited by Henry F. Korth and Amit Sheth. Received November 1994 / Revised June 1995 / Accepted September 14, 1995

Abstract. The requirements of wide-area distributed database systems differ dramatically from those of local-area network systems. In a wide-area network (WAN) configuration, individual sites usually report to different system administrators, have different access and charging algorithms, install site-specific data type extensions, and have different constraints on servicing remote requests. Typical of the last point are production transaction environments, which are fully engaged during normal business hours, and cannot take on additional load. Finally, there may be many sites participating in a WAN distributed DBMS.

In this world, a single program performing global query optimization using a cost-based optimizer will not work well. Cost-based optimization does not respond well to site-specific type extension, access constraints, charging algorithms, and time-of-day constraints. Furthermore, traditional cost-based distributed optimizers do not scale well to a large number of possible processing sites. Since traditional distributed DBMSs have all used cost-based optimizers, they are not appropriate in a WAN environment, and a new architecture is required.

We have proposed and implemented an economic paradigm as the solution to these issues in a new distributed DBMS called Mariposa. In this paper, we present the architecture and implementation of Mariposa and discuss early feedback on its operating characteristics.

Key words: Databases – Distributed systems – Economic site – Autonomy – Wide-area network – Name service

[1] *Present address*: Université Paris IX Dauphine, Section MIAGE, Place de Lattre de Tassigny, 75775 Paris Cedex 16, France

[2] *Present address*: Department of Computer Science, Stanford University, Stanford, CA 94305, USA

[3] *Present address*: Hewlett-Packard Laboratories, M/S 1U-13 P.O. Box 10490, Palo Alto, CA 94303, USA

[4] *Present address*: Illustra Information Technologies, Inc., 1111 Broadway, Suite 2000, Oakland, CA 94607, USA

e-mail: mariposa@postgres.Berkeley.edu

Correspondence to: M. Stonebraker

1 Introduction

The Mariposa distributed database system addresses a fundamental problem in the standard approach to distributed data management. We argue that the underlying assumptions traditionally made while implementing distributed data managers do not apply to today's wide-area network (WAN) environments. We present a set of guiding principles that must apply to a system designed for modern WAN environments. We then demonstrate that existing architectures cannot adhere to these principles because of the invalid assumptions just mentioned. Finally, we show how Mariposa can successfully apply the principles through its adoption of an entirely different paradigm for query and storage optimization.

Traditional distributed relational database systems that offer location-transparent query languages, such as Distributed INGRES (Stonebraker 1986), R* (Williams et al. 1981), SIRIUS (Litwin 1982) and SDD-1 (Bernstein 1981), all make a collection of underlying assumptions. These assumptions include:

– *Static data allocation*: In a traditional distributed DBMS, there is no mechanism whereby objects can quickly and easily change sites to reflect changing access patterns. Moving an object from one site to another is done manually by a database administrator, and all secondary access paths to the data are lost in the process. Hence, object movement is a very "heavyweight" operation and should not be done frequently.

– *Single administrative structure*: Traditional distributed database systems have assumed a query optimizer which decomposes a query into "pieces" and then decides where to execute each of these pieces. As a result, site selection for query fragments is done by the optimizer. Hence, there is no mechanism in traditional systems for a site to refuse to execute a query, for example because it is overloaded or otherwise indisposed. Such "good neighbor" assumptions are only valid if all machines in the distributed system are controlled by the same administration.

– *Uniformity*: Traditional distributed query optimizers generally assume that all processors and network connections are the same speed. Moreover, the optimizer assumes that any join can be done at any site, e.g., all sites have ample disk space to store intermediate results. They further assume that every site has the same collection of data types, functions and operators, so that any subquery can be performed at any site.

These assumptions are often plausible in local-area network (LAN) environments. In LAN worlds, environment uniformity and a single administrative structure are common. Moreover, a high-speed, reasonably uniform interconnect tends to mask performance problems caused by suboptimal data allocation.

In a WAN environment, these assumptions are much less plausible. For example, the Sequoia 2000 project (Stonebraker 1991) spans six sites around the state of California with a wide variety of hardware and storage capacities. Each site has its own database administrator, and the willingness of any site to perform work on behalf of users at another site varies widely. Furthermore, network connectivity is not uniform. Lastly, type extension often is available only on selected machines, because of licensing restrictions on proprietary software or because the type extension uses the unique features of a particular hardware architecture. As a result, traditional distributed DBMSs do not work well in the non-uniform, multi-administrator WAN environments of which Sequoia 2000 is typical. We expect an explosion of configurations like Sequoia 2000 as multiple companies coordinate tasks, such as distributed manufacturing, or share data in sophisticated ways, for example through a yet-to-be-built query optimizer for the World Wide Web.

As a result, the goal of the Mariposa project is to design a WAN distributed DBMS. Specifically, we are guided by the following principles, which we assert are requirements for non-uniform, multi-administrator WAN environments:

– *Scalability to a large number of cooperating sites*: In a WAN environment, there may be a large number of sites which wish to share data. A distributed DBMS should not contain assumptions that will limit its ability to scale to 1000 sites or more.
– *Data mobility*: It should be easy and efficient to change the "home" of an object. Preferably, the object should remain available during movement.
– *No global synchronization*: Schema changes should not force a site to synchronize with all other sites. Otherwise, some operations will have exceptionally poor response time.
– *Total local autonomy*: Each site must have complete control over its own resources. This includes what objects to store and what queries to run. Query allocation cannot be done by a central, authoritarian query optimizer.
– *Easily configurable policies*: It should be easy for a local database administrator to change the behavior of a Mariposa site.

Traditional distributed DBMSs do not meet these requirements. Use of an authoritarian, centralized query optimizer does not scale well; the high cost of moving an object between sites restricts data mobility, schema changes typically require global synchronization, and centralized management designs inhibit local autonomy and flexible policy configuration.

One could claim that these are implementation issues, but we argue that traditional distributed DBMSs *cannot* meet the requirements defined above for fundamental architectural reasons. For example, any distributed DBMS must address distributed query optimization and placement of DBMS objects. However, if sites can refuse to process subqueries, then it is difficult to perform cost-based global optimization. In addition, cost-based global optimization is "brittle" in that it does not scale well to a large number of participating sites. As another example, consider the requirement that objects must be able to move freely between sites. Movement is complicated by the fact that the sending site and receiving site have total local autonomy. Hence the sender can refuse to relinquish the object, and the recipient can refuse to accept it. As a result, allocation of objects to sites cannot be done by a central database administrator.

Because of these inherent problems, the Mariposa design rejects the conventional distributed DBMS architecture in favor of one that supports a microeconomic paradigm for query and storage optimization. All distributed DBMS issues (multiple copies of objects, naming service, etc.) are reformulated in microeconomic terms. Briefly, implementation of an economic paradigm requires a number of entities and mechanisms. All Mariposa clients and servers have an account with a network bank. A user allocates a *budget* in the currency of this bank to each query. The goal of the query processing system is to solve the query within the allotted budget by contracting with various Mariposa processing sites to perform portions of the query. Each query is administered by a *broker*, which obtains bids for pieces of a query from various sites. The remainder of this section shows how use of these economic entities and mechanisms allows Mariposa to meet the requirements set out above.

The implementation of the economic infrastructure supports a large number of sites. For example, instead of using centralized metadata to determine where to run a query, the broker makes use of a distributed advertising service to find sites that might want to bid on portions of the query. Moreover, the broker is specifically designed to cope successfully with very large Mariposa networks. Similarly, a server can join a Mariposa system at any time by buying objects from other sites, advertising its services and then bidding on queries. It can leave Mariposa by selling its objects and ceasing to bid. As a result, we can achieve a highly scalable system using our economic paradigm.

Each Mariposa site makes storage decisions to buy and sell fragments, based on optimizing the revenue it expects to collect. Mariposa objects have no notion of a home, merely that of a current owner. The current owner may change rapidly as objects are moved. Object movement preserves all secondary indexes, and is coded to offer as high performance as possible. Consequently, Mariposa fosters data mobility and the free trade of objects.

Avoidance of global synchronization is simplified in many places by an economic paradigm. Replication is one such area. The details of the Mariposa replication system are contained in a separate paper (Sidell 1995). In short, copy holders maintain the currency of their copies by contracting with other copy holders to deliver their updates. This contract specifies a payment stream for update information delivered within a specified time bound. Each site then runs a "zippering" system to merge update streams in a consistent way. As a result, copy holders serve data which is out of date by varying degrees. Query processing on these divergent copies is resolved using the bidding process. Metadata management is another, related area that benefits from economic processes. Parsing an incoming query requires Mariposa to interact with one or more *name services* to identify relevant metadata about objects referenced in a query, including their location. The copy mechanism described above is designed so that name servers are just like other servers of replicated data. The name servers contract with other Mariposa sites to receive updates to the system catalogs. As a result of this architecture, schema changes do not entail any synchronization; rather, such changes are "percolated" to name services asynchronously.

Since each Mariposa site is free to bid on any business of interest, it has total local autonomy. Each site is expected to maximize its individual profit per unit of operating time and to bid on those queries that it feels will accomplish this goal. Of course, the net effect of this freedom is that some queries may not be solvable, either because nobody will bid on them or because the aggregate of the minimum bids exceeds what the client is willing to pay. In addition, a site can buy and sell objects at will. It can refuse to give up objects, or it may not find buyers for an object it does not want.

Finally, Mariposa provides powerful mechanisms for specifying the behavior of each site. Sites must decide which objects to buy and sell and which queries to bid on. Each site has a *bidder* and a *storage manager* that make these decisions. However, as conditions change over time, policy decisions must also change. Although the bidder and storage manager modules may be coded in any language desired, Mariposa provides a low level, very efficient embedded scripting language and *rule system* called Rush (Sah et al. 1994). Using Rush, it is straightforward to change policy decisions; one simply modifies the rules by which these modules are implemented.

The purpose of this paper is to report on the architecture, implementation, and operation of our current prototype. Preliminary discussions of Mariposa ideas have been previously reported (Stonebraker et al. 1994a, 19994b). At this time (June 1995), we have a complete optimization and execution system running, and we will present performance results of some initial experiments.

In Sect. 2, we present the three major components of our economic system. Section 3 describes the bidding process by which a broker contracts for service with processing sites, the mechanisms that make the bidding process efficient, and the methods by which network utilization is integrated into the economic model. Section 4 describes Mariposa storage management. Section 5 describes naming and name service in Mariposa. Section 6 presents some initial experiments using the Mariposa prototype. Section 7 discusses previous applications of the economic model in computing. Finally, Sect. 8 summarizes the work completed to date and the future directions of the project.

2 Architecture

Mariposa supports transparent fragmentation of tables across sites. That is, Mariposa clients submit queries in a dialect of SQL3; each table referenced in the FROM clause of a

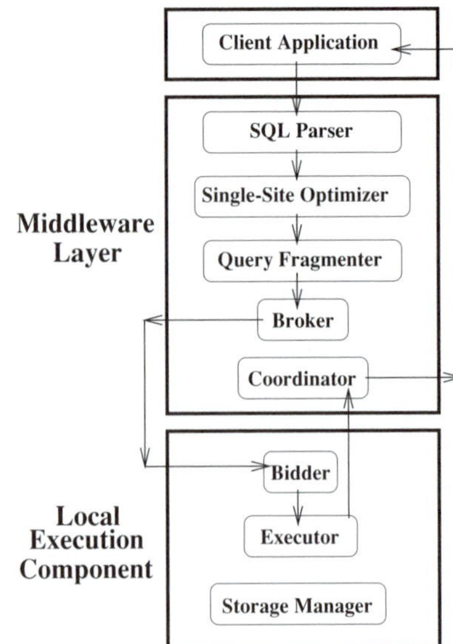

Fig. 1. Mariposa architecture

query could potentially be decomposed into a collection of table *fragments*. Fragments can obey range- or hash-based distribution criteria which logically partition the table. Alternately, fragments can be unstructured, in which case records are allocated to any convenient fragment.

Mariposa provides a variety of fragment operations. Fragments are the units of storage that are bought and sold by sites. In addition, the total number of fragments in a table can be changed dynamically, perhaps quite rapidly. The current owner of a fragment can *split* it into two storage fragments whenever it is deemed desirable. Conversely, the owner of two fragments of a table can *coalesce* them into a single fragment at any time.

To process queries on fragmented tables and support buying, selling, splitting, and coalescing fragments, Mariposa is divided into three kinds of modules as noted in Fig. 1. There is a *client program* which issues queries, complete with bidding instructions, to the Mariposa system. In turn, Mariposa contains a *middleware* layer and a *local execution* component. The middleware layer contains several query preparation modules, and a *query broker*. Lastly, local execution is composed of a *bidder*, a *storage manager*, and a local *execution engine*.

In addition, the broker, bidder and storage manager can be tailored at each site. We have provided a high performance rule system, Rush, in which we have coded initial Mariposa implementations of these modules. We expect site administrators to tailor the behavior of our implementations by altering the rules present at a site. Lastly, there is a low-level utility layer that implements essential Mariposa primitives for communication between sites. The various modules are shown in Fig. 1. Notice that the client module can run anywhere in a Mariposa network. It communicates with a middleware process running at the same or a different site. In turn, Mariposa middleware communicates with local execution systems at various sites.

This section describes the role that each module plays in the Mariposa economy. In the process of describing the modules, we also give an overview of how query processing

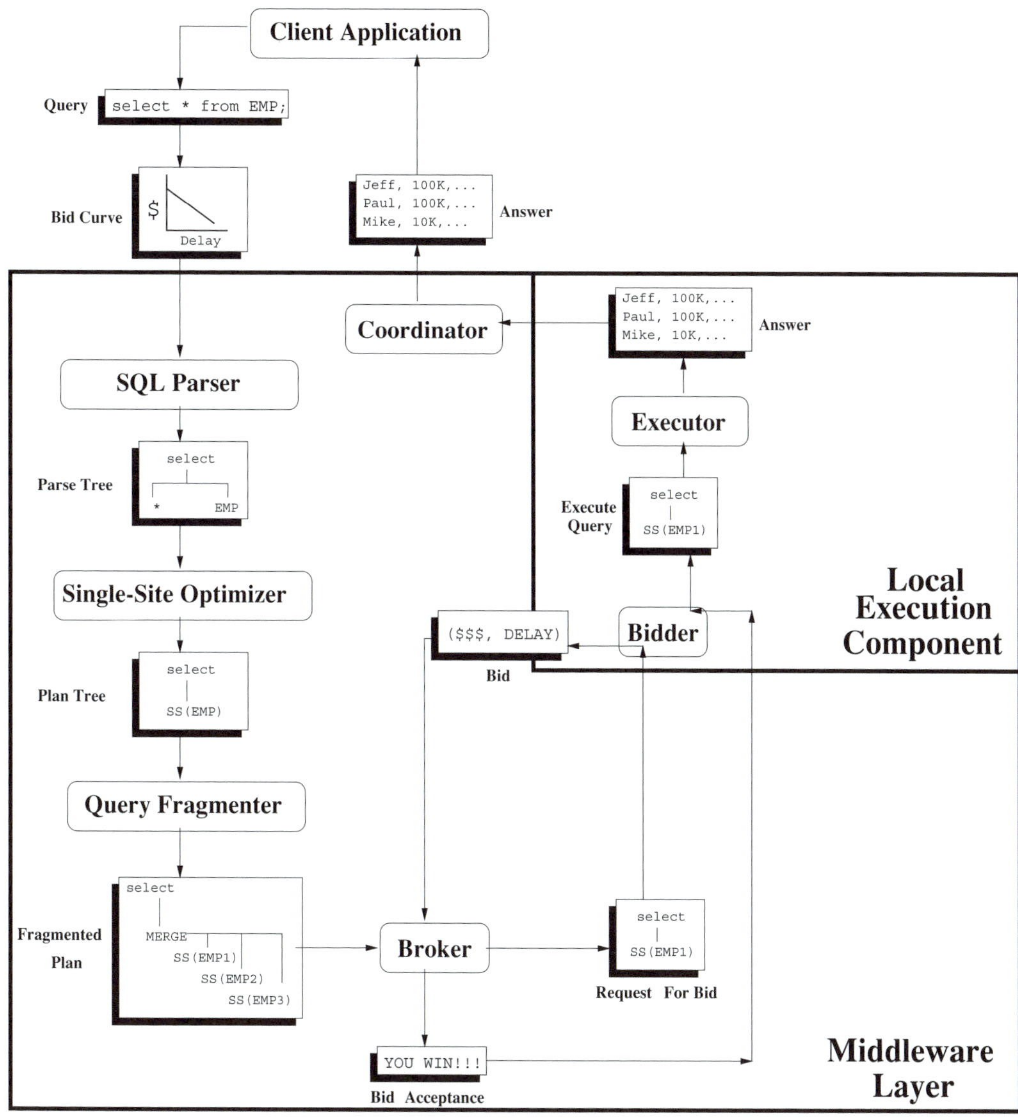

Fig. 2. Mariposa communication

works in an economic framework. Section 3 will explain this process in more detail.

Queries are submitted by the client application. Each query starts with a budget $B(t)$ expressed as a *bid* curve. The budget indicates how much the user is willing to pay to have the query executed within time t. Query budgets form the basis of the Mariposa economy. Figure 2 includes a bid curve indicating that the user is willing to sacrifice performance for a lower price. Once a budget has been assigned (through administrative means not discussed here), the client software hands the query to Mariposa middleware. Mariposa middleware contains an SQL parser, single-site optimizer, query fragmenter, broker, and coordinator module. The broker is primarily coded in Rush. Each of these modules is described below. The communication between modules is shown in Fig. 2.

The parser parses the incoming query, performing name resolution and authorization. The parser first requests *metadata* for each table referenced in the query from some name server. This metadata contains information including the name and type of each attribute in the table, the location of each fragment of the table, and an indicator of the staleness of the information. Metadata is itself part of the economy and has a price. The choice of name server is determined by the desired quality of metadata, the prices offered by the name servers, the available budget, and any local Rush rules defined to prioritize these factors. The parser hands the query, in the form of a parse tree, to the *single-site optimizer*. This is a conventional query optimizer along the lines of Selinger et al. (1979). The single-site optimizer generates a single-site query execution plan. The optimizer ignores data distribution and prepares a plan as if all the fragments were located at a single server site.

The *fragmenter* accepts the plan produced by the single-site optimizer. It uses location information previously obtained from the name server, to decompose the single site plan into a *fragmented query plan*. The fragmenter decomposes each restriction node in the single site plan into subqueries, one per fragment in the referenced table. Joins are decomposed into one join subquery for each pair of fragment joins. Lastly, the fragmenter groups the operations that can proceed in parallel into query *strides*. All subqueries in a stride must be completed before any subqueries in the next stride can begin. As a result, strides form the basis for intraquery synchronization. Notice that our notion of strides does not support *pipelining* the result of one subquery into the execution of a subsequent subquery. This complication would introduce sequentiality within a query stride and complicate the bidding process to be described. Inclusion of pipelining into our economic system is a task for future research.

The *broker* takes the collection of fragmented query plans prepared by the fragmenter and sends out requests for bids to various sites. After assembling a collection of bids, the broker decides which ones to accept and notifies the winning sites by sending out a *bid acceptance*. The bidding process will be described in more detail in Sect. 3.

The broker hands off the task of coordinating the execution of the resulting query strides to a *coordinator*. The coordinator assembles the partial results and returns the final answer to the user process.

At each Mariposa server site there is a local execution module containing a *bidder*, a *storage manager*, and a local execution engine. The *bidder* responds to requests for bids and formulates its bid price and the speed with which the site will agree to process a subquery based on local resources such as CPU time, disk I/O bandwidth, storage, etc. If the bidder site does not have the data fragments specified in the subquery, it may refuse to bid or it may attempt to buy the data from another site by contacting its storage manager. Winning bids must sooner or later be processed. To execute local queries, a Mariposa site contains a number of local execution engines. An idle one is allocated to each incoming subquery to perform the task at hand. The number of executors controls the multiprocessing level at each site, and may be adjusted as conditions warrant. The local executor sends the results of the subquery to the site executing the next part of the query or back to the coordinator process. At each Mariposa site there is also a *storage manager*, which watches the revenue stream generated by stored fragments. Based on space and revenue considerations, it engages in buying and selling fragments with storage managers at other Mariposa sites.

The storage managers, bidders and brokers in our prototype are primarily coded in the rule language Rush. Rush is an embeddable programming language with syntax similar to Tcl (Ousterhout 1994) that also includes rules of the form:

`on <condition> do <action>` Every Mariposa entity embeds a Rush interpreter, calling it to execute code to determine the behavior of Mariposa.

Rush conditions can involve any combination of primitive Mariposa events, described below, and computations on Rush variables. Actions in Rush can trigger Mariposa primitives and modify Rush variables. As a result, Rush can be thought of as a fairly conventional forward-chaining rule system. We chose to implement our own system, rather than use one of the packages available from the AI community, primarily for performance reasons. Rush rules are in the "inner loop" of many Mariposa activities, and as a result, rule interpretation must be very fast. A separate paper (Sah and Blow 1994) discusses how we have achieved this goal.

Mariposa contains a specific inter-site protocol by which Mariposa entities communicate. Requests for bids to execute subqueries and to buy and sell fragments can be sent between sites. Additionally, queries and data must be passed around. The main messages are indicated in Table 1. Typically, the outgoing message is the action part of a Rush rule, and the corresponding incoming message is a Rush event at the recipient site.

Table 1. The main Mariposa primitives

Actions (messages)	Events (received messages)
Request bid	Receive bid request
Bid	Receive bid
Award contract	Contract won
Notify loser	Contract lost
Send query	Receive query
Send data	Receive data

3 The bidding process

Each query Q has a *budget* $B(t)$ that can be used to solve the query. The budget is a non-increasing function of time that represents the value the user gives to the answer to his query at a particular time t. Constant functions represent a willingness to pay the same amount of money for a slow answer as for a quick one, while steeply declining functions indicate that the user will pay more for a fast answer.

The broker handling a query Q receives a query plan containing a collection of subqueries, $Q_1, \ldots, Q_n$, and $B(t)$. Each subquery is a one-variable restriction on a fragment F of a table, or a join between two fragments of two tables. The broker tries to solve each subquery, Q_i, using either an *expensive bid protocol* or a cheaper *purchase order protocol*.

The expensive bid protocol involves two phases: in the first phase, the broker sends out requests for bids to bidder sites. A bid request includes the portion of the query execution plan being bid on. The bidders send back bids that are represented as triples: (C_i, D_i, E_i). The triple indicates that the bidder will solve the subquery Q_i for a cost C_i within a delay $Dsubi$ after receipt of the subquery, and that this bid is only valid until the expiration date, E_i.

In the second phase of the bid protocol, the broker notifies the winning bidders that they have been selected. The broker may also notify the losing sites. If it does not, then the bids will expire and can be deleted by the bidders. This process requires many (expensive) messages. Most queries will not be computationally demanding enough to justify this level of overhead. These queries will use the simpler *purchase order* protocol.

The purchase order protocol sends each subquery to the processing site that would be most likely to win the bidding process if there were one; for example, one of the storage sites of a fragment for a sequential scan. This site receives the query and processes it, returning the answer with a *bill* for services. If the site refuses the subquery, it can either return it to the broker or pass it on to a third processing site. If a broker uses the cheaper purchase order protocol, there is some danger of failing to solve the query within the allotted budget. The broker does not always know the cost and delay which will be charged by the chosen processing site. However, this is the risk that must be taken to use this faster protocol.

3.1 Bid acceptance

All subqueries in each stride are processed in parallel, and the next stride cannot begin until the previous one has been completed. Rather than consider bids for individual subqueries, we consider collections of bids for the subqueries in each stride.

When using the bidding protocol, brokers must choose a winning bid for each subquery with aggregate cost C and aggregate delay D such that the aggregate cost is less than or equal to the cost requirement $B(D)$. There are two problems that make finding the best bid collection difficult: subquery parallelism and the combinatorial search space. The aggregate delay is not the sum of the delays D_i for each subquery Q_i, since there is parallelism within each stride of the query plan. Also, the number of possible bid collections grows exponentially with the number of strides in the query plan. For example, if there are ten strides and three viable bids for each one, then the broker can evaluate each of the 3^{10} bid possibilities.

The estimated delay to process the collection of subqueries in a stride is equal to the highest bid time in the collection. The number of different delay values can be no more than the total number of bids on subqueries in the collection. For each delay value, the optimal bid collection is the least expensive bid for each subquery that can be processed within the given delay. By coalescing the bid collections in a stride and considering them as a single (aggregate) bid, the broker may reduce the bid acceptance problem to the simpler problem of choosing one bid from among a set of aggregated bids for each query stride.

With the expensive bid protocol, the broker receives a collection of zero or more bids for each subquery. If there is no bid for some subquery, or no collection of bids meets the client's minimum price and performance requirements ($B(D)$), then the broker must solicit additional bids, agree to perform the subquery itself, or notify the user that the query cannot be run. It is possible that several collections of bids meet the minimum requirements, so the broker must choose the best collection of bids. In order to compare the bid collections, we define a $difference$ function on the collection of bids: $difference = B(D) - C$. Note that this can have a negative value, if the cost is above the bid curve.

For all but the simplest queries referencing tables with a minimal number of fragments, exhaustive search for the best bid collection will be combinatorially prohibitive. The crux of the problem is in determining the relative amounts of the time and cost resources that should be allocated to each subquery. We offer a heuristic algorithm that determines how to do this. Although it cannot be shown to be optimal, we believe in practice it will demonstrate good results. Preliminary performance numbers for Mariposa are included later in this paper which support this supposition. A more detailed evaluation and comparison against more complex algorithms is planned in the future.

The algorithm is a "greedy" one. It produces a trial solution in which the total delay is the smallest possible, and then makes the greediest substitution until there are no more profitable ones to make. Thus a series of solutions are proposed with steadily increasing delay values for each processing step. On any iteration of the algorithm, the proposed solution contains a collection of bids with a certain delay for each processing step. For every collection of bids with greater delay a *cost gradient* is computed. This cost gradient is the cost decrease that would result for the processing step by replacing the collection in the solution by the collection being considered, divided by the time increase that would result from the substitution.

The algorithm begins by considering the bid collection with the smallest delay for each processing step and computing the total cost C and the total delay D. Compute the cost gradient for each unused bid. Now, consider the processing step that contains the unused bid with the maximum cost gradient, B'. If this bid replaces the current one used in the processing step, then cost will become C' and delay D'. If the resulting $difference$ is greater at D' than at D, then make the bid substitution. That is, if $B(D') - C' > B(D) - C$, then replace B with B'. Recalculate all the cost gradients for the processing step that includes B', and continue making substitutions until there are none that increase the $difference$.

Notice that our current Mariposa algorithm decomposes the query into executable pieces, and then the broker tries to solve the individual pieces in a heuristically optimal way. We are planning to extend Mariposa to contain a second bidding strategy. Using this strategy, the single-site optimizer and fragmenter would be bypassed. Instead, the broker would get the entire query directly. It would then decide whether to decompose it into a collection of two or more "hunks" using heuristics yet to be developed. Then, it would try to find contractors for the hunks, each of which could freely subdivide the hunks and subcontract them. In contrast to our current query processing system which is a "bottom up" algorithm, this alternative would be a "top down" decomposition strategy. We hope to implement this alternative and test it against our current system.

3.2 Finding bidders

Using either the expensive bid or the purchase order protocol from the previous section, a broker must be able to identify one or more sites to process each subquery. Mariposa achieves this through an advertising system. Servers announce their willingness to perform various services by posting *advertisements*. Name servers keep a record of these advertisements in an *Ad Table*. Brokers examine the Ad Table to find out which servers might be willing to perform the tasks they need. Table 2 shows the fields of the Ad Table. In practice, not all these fields will be used in each advertisement. The most general advertisements will specify the fewest number of fields. Table 3 summarizes the valid fields for some types of advertisement.

Using *yellow pages*, a server advertises that it offers a specific service (e.g., processing queries that reference a specific fragment). The date of the advertisement helps a broker decide how timely the yellow pages entry is, and therefore how much faith to put in the information. A server can issue a new yellow pages advertisement at any time without

Table 2. Fields in the Ad Table

Ad Table field	Description
query-template	A description of the service being offered. The query template is a query with parameters left unspecified. For example, `SELECT param-1` `FROM EMP` indicates a willingness to perform any SELECT query on the EMP table, while `SELECT param-1` `FROM EMP` `WHERE NAME = param-2` indicates that the server wants to perform queries that perform an equality restriction on the NAME column.
server-id	The server offering the service.
start-time	The time at which the service is first offered. This may be a future time, if the server expects to begin performing certain tasks at a specific point in time.
expiration-time	The time at which the advertisement ceases to be valid.
price	The price charged by the server for the service.
delay	The time in which the server expects to complete the task.
limit-quantity	The maximum number of times the server will perform a service at the given cost and delay.
bulk-quantity	The number of orders needed to obtain the advertised price and delay.
to-whom	The set of brokers to whom the advertised services are available.
other-fields	Comments and other information specific to a particular advertisement.

explicitly revoking a previous one. In addition, a server may indicate the price and delay of a service. This is a *posted price* and becomes current on the start-date indicated. There is no guarantee that the price will hold beyond that time and, as with yellow pages, the server may issue a new posted price without revoking the old one.

Several more specific types of advertisements are available. If the expiration-date field is set, then the details of the offer are known to be valid for a certain period of time. Posting a *sale price* in this manner involves some risk, as the advertisement may generate more demand than the server can meet, forcing it to pay heavy penalties. This risk can be offset by issuing *coupons*, which, like supermarket coupons, place a limit on the number of queries that can be executed under the terms of the advertisement. Coupons may also limit the brokers who are eligible to redeem them. These are similar to the coupons issued by the Nevada gambling establishments, which require the client to be over 21 years of age and possess a valid California driver's license.

Finally, *bulk purchase contracts* are renewable coupons that allow a broker to negotiate cheaper prices with a server in exchange for guaranteed, pre-paid service. This is analogous to a travel agent who books ten seats on each sailing of a cruise ship. We allow the option of guaranteeing bulk purchases, in which case the broker must pay for the specified queries whether it uses them or not. Bulk purchases are especially advantageous in transaction processing environments, where the workload is predictable, and brokers solve large numbers of similar queries.

Besides referring to the Ad Table, we expect a broker to remember sites that have bid successfully for previous queries. Presumably the broker will include such sites in the bidding process, thereby generating a system that learns over time which processing sites are appropriate for various queries. Lastly, the broker also knows the likely location of each fragment, which was returned previously to the query preparation module by the name server. The site most likely to have the data is automatically a likely bidder.

3.3 Setting the bid price for subqueries

When a site is asked to bid on a subquery, it must respond with a triple (C, D, E) as noted earlier. This section discusses our current bidder module and some of the extensions that we expect to make. As noted earlier, it is coded primarily as Rush rules and can be changed easily.

The *naive* strategy is to maintain a *billing rate* for CPU and I/O resources for each site. These constants are to be set by a site administrator based on local conditions. The bidder constructs an estimate of the amount of each resource required to process a subquery for objects that exist at the local site. A simple computation then yields the required bid. If the referenced object is not present at the site, then the site declines to bid. For join queries, the site declines to bid unless one of the following two conditions are satisfied:

- It possesses one of the two referenced objects.
- It had already bid on a query, whose answer formed one of the two referenced objects.

The time in which the site promises to process the query is calculated with an estimate of the resources required. Under zero load, it is an estimate of the elapsed time to perform the query. By adjusting for the current load on the site, the bidder can estimate the expected delay. Finally, it multiplies by a site-specific safety factor to arrive at a promised delay (the D in the bid). The expiration date on a bid is currently assigned arbitrarily as the promised delay plus a site-specific constant.

This naive strategy is consistent with the behavior assumed of a local site by a traditional global query optimizer. However, our current prototype improves on the naive strategy in three ways. First, each site maintains a billing rate on a per-fragment basis. In this way, the site administrator can bias his bids toward fragments whose business he wants and away from those whose business he does not want. The bidder also automatically declines to bid on queries referencing fragments with billing rates below a site-specific threshold. In this case, the query will have to be processed elsewhere, and another site will have to buy or copy the indicated fragment in order to solve the user query. Hence, this tactic will hasten the sale of low value fragments to somebody else. Our second improvement concerns adjusting bids based on the current site load. Specifically, each site maintains its current load average by periodically running a UNIX utility. It then adjusts its bid, based on its current load average as follows:

$$\textit{actual bid} = \textit{computed bid} \times \textit{load average}$$

In this way, if it is nearly idle (i.e., its load average is near zero), it will bid very low prices. Conversely, it will bid higher and higher prices as its load increases. Notice that this simple formula will ensure a crude form of load balancing

Table 3. Ad Table fields applicable to each type of advertisement

Ad Table field	Type of advertisement				
	Yellow pages	Posted price	Sale price	Coupon	Bulk purchase
query-template	√	√	√	√	√
server-id	√	√	√	√	√
start-date	√	√	√	√	√
expiration-date	–	–	√	√	√
price	–	√	√	√	√
delay	–	√	√	√	√
limit-quantity	–	–	–	√	–
bulk-quantity	–	–	–	–	√
to-whom	–	–	–	*	*
other-fields	*	*	*	*	*

–, null; √, valid; *, optional

among a collection of Mariposa sites. Our third improvement concerns bidding on subqueries when the site does not possess any of the data. As will be seen in the next section, the storage manager buys and sells fragments to try to maximize site revenue. In addition, it keeps a *hot list* of fragments it would like to acquire but has not yet done so. The bidder automatically bids on any query which references a hot list fragment. In this way, if it gets a contract for the query, it will instruct the storage manager to accelerate the purchase of the fragment, which is in line with the goals of the storage manager.

In the future we expect to increase the sophistication of the bidder substantially. We plan more sophisticated integration between the bidder and the storage manager. We view hot lists as merely the first primitive step in this direction. Furthermore, we expect to adjust the billing rate for each fragment automatically, based on the amount of business for the fragment. Finally, we hope to increase the sophistication of our choice of expiration dates. Choosing an expiration date far in the future incurs the risk of honoring lower out-of-date prices. Specifying an expiration date that is too close means running the risk of the broker not being able to use the bid because of inherent delays in the processing engine. Lastly, we expect to consider network resources in the bidding process. Our proposed algorithms are discussed in the next subsection.

3.4 The network bidder

In addition to producing bids based on CPU and disk usage, the processing sites need to take the available network bandwidth into account. The network bidder will be a separate module in Mariposa. Since network bandwidth is a distributed resource, the network bidders along the path from source to destination must calculate an aggregate bid for the entire path and must reserve network resources as a group. Mariposa will use a version of the Tenet network protocols RTIP (Zhang and Fisher 1992) and RCAP (Banerjea and Mah 1991) to perform bandwidth queries and network resource reservation.

A network bid request will be made by the broker to transfer data between source/destination pairs in the query plan. The network bid request is sent to the destination node. The request is of the form: *(transaction-id, request-id, data size, from-node, to-node)*. The broker receives a bid from the network bidder at the destination node of the form: *(transaction-id, request-id, price, time)*. In order to determine the price and time, the network bidder at the destination node must contact each of the intermediate nodes between itself and the source node.

For convenience, call the destination node n_0 and the source node n_k (see Fig. 3.) Call the first intermediate node on the path from the destination to the source n_1, the second such node n_2, etc. Available bandwidth between two adjacent nodes as a function of time is represented as a *bandwidth profile*. The bandwidth profile contains entries of the form *(available bandwidth*, t_1, t_2) indicating the available bandwidth between time t_1 and time t_2. If n_i and n_{i-1} are directly-connected nodes on the path from the source to the destination, and data is flowing from n_i to n_{i-1}, then node n_i is responsible for keeping track of (and charging for) available bandwidth between itself and n_{i-1} and therefore maintains the bandwidth profile. Call the bandwidth profile between node n_i and node n_{i-1} B_i and the price n_i charges for a bandwidth reservation P_i.

The available bandwidth on the entire path from source to destination is calculated step by step starting at the destination node, n_0. Node n_0 contacts n_1 which has B_1, the bandwidth profile for the network link between itself and n_0. It sends this profile to node n_2, which has the bandwidth profile B_2. Node n_2 calculates $\min(B_1, B_2)$, producing a bandwidth profile that represents the available bandwidth along the path from n_2 to n_0. This process continues along each intermediate link, ultimately reaching the source node.

When the bandwidth profile reaches the source node, it is equal to the minimum available bandwidth over all links on the path between the source and destination, and represents the amount of bandwidth available as a function of time on the entire path. The source node, n_k, then initiates a backward pass to calculate the price for this bandwidth along the entire path. Node n_k sends its price to reserve the bandwidth, P_k, to node n_{k-1}, which adds its price, and so on, until the aggregate price arrives at the destination, n_0. Bandwidth could also be reserved at this time. If bandwidth is reserved at bidding time, there is a chance that it will not be used (if the source or destination is not chosen by the broker). If bandwidth is not reserved at this time, then there will be a window of time between bidding and bid award when the available bandwidth may have changed. We are investigating approaches to this problem.

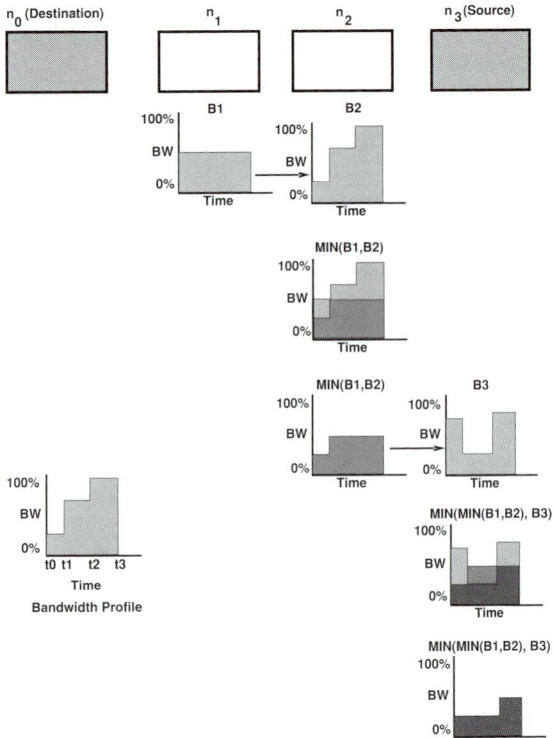

Fig. 3. Calculating a bandwidth profile

In addition to the choice of when to reserve network resources, there are two choices for when the broker sends out network bid requests during the bidding process. The broker could send out requests for network bids at the same time that it sends out other bid requests, or it could wait until the single-site bids have been returned and then send out requests for network bids to the winners of the first phase. In the first case, the broker would have to request a bid from every pair of sites that could potentially communicate with one another. If P is the number of parallelized phases of the query plan, and S_i is the number of sites in phase i, then this approach would produce a total of $\sum_{i=2}^{P} S_i S_{i-1}$ bids. In the second case, the broker only has to request bids between the winners of each phase of the query plan. If $winner_i$ is the winning group of sites for phase i, then the number of network bid requests sent out is $\sum_{i=2}^{P} S_{winner_i} S_{winner_{i-1}}$.

The first approach has the advantage of parallelizing the bidding phase itself and thereby reducing the optimization time. However, the sites that are asked to reserve bandwidth are not guaranteed to win the bid. If they reserve all the bandwidth for each bid request they receive, this approach will result in reserving more bandwidth than is actually needed. This difficulty may be overcome by reserving less bandwidth than is specified in bids, essentially "overbooking the flight."

4 Storage management

Each site manages a certain amount of storage, which it can fill with fragments or copies of fragments. The basic objective of a site is to allocate its CPU, I/O and storage resources so as to maximize its revenue income per unit time. This topic is the subject of the first part of this section. After that, we turn to the splitting and coalescing of fragments into smaller or bigger storage units.

4.1 Buying and selling fragments

In order for sites to trade fragments, they must have some means of calculating the (expected) value of the fragment for each site. Some access history is kept with each fragment so sites can make predictions of future activity. Specifically, a site maintains the *size* of the fragment as well as its *revenue history*. Each record of the history contains the query, number of records which qualified, time-since-last-query, revenue, delay, I/O-used, and CPU-used. The CPU and I/O information is normalized and stored in site-independent units.

To estimate the revenue that a site would receive if it owned a particular fragment, the site must assume that access rates are stable and that the revenue history is therefore a good predictor of future revenue. Moreover, it must convert site-independent resource usage numbers into ones specific to its site through a weighting function, as in Mackert and Lohman (1986). In addition, it must assume that it would have successfully bid on the same set of queries as appeared in the revenue history. Since it will be faster or slower than the site from which the revenue history was collected, it must adjust the revenue collected for each query. This calculation requires the site to assume a shape for the average bid curve. Lastly, it must convert the adjusted revenue stream into a cash value, by computing the net present value of the stream.

If a site wants to bid on a subquery, then it must either *buy* any fragment(s) referenced by the subquery or subcontract out the work to another site. If the site wishes to buy a fragment, it can do so either when the query comes in (*on demand*) or in advance (*prefetch*). To purchase a fragment, a buyer locates the owner of the fragment and requests the revenue history of the fragment, and then places a value on the fragment. Moreover, if it buys the fragment, then it will have to evict a collection of fragments to free up space, adding to the cost of the fragment to be purchased. To the extent that storage is not full, then fewer (or no) evictions will be required. In any case, this collection is called the *alternate fragments* in the formula below. Hence, the buyer will be willing to bid the following price for the fragment:

offer price = *value of fragment*
  −*value of alternate fragments*
  +*price received*

In this calculation, the buyer will obtain the value of the new fragment but lose the value of the fragments that it must evict. Moreover, it will *sell* the evicted fragments, and receive some price for them. The latter item is problematic to compute. A plausible assumption is that *price received* is equal to the value of the alternate fragments. A more conservative assumption is that the price obtained is zero. Note that in this case the offer price need not be positive.

The potential seller of the fragment performs the following calculation: the site will receive the offered price and will lose the value of the fragment which is being evicted. However, if the fragment is not evicted, then a collection of alternate fragments summing in size to the indicated fragment must be evicted. In this case, the site will lose the value of these (more desirable) fragments, but will receive the expected *price received*. Hence, it will be willing to sell the fragment, transferring it to the buyer:

offer price $>$ *value of fragment*
    $-$*value of alternate fragments*
    $+$*price received*

Again, *price received* is problematic, and subject to the same plausible assumptions noted above.

Sites may sell fragments at any time, for any reason. For example, decommissioning a server implies that the server will sell all of its fragments. To sell a fragment, the site conducts a bidding process, essentially identical to the one used for subqueries above. Specifically, it sends the revenue history to a collection of *potential bidders* and asks them what they will offer for the fragment. The seller considers the highest bid and will *accept* the bid under the same considerations that applied when selling fragments on request, namely if:

offered price $>$ *value of fragment*
    $-$*value of alternate fragments*
    $+$*price received*

If no bid is acceptable, then the seller must try to evict another (higher value) fragment until one is found that can be sold. If no fragments are sellable, then the site must lower the value of its fragments until a sale can be made. In fact, if a site wishes to go out of business, then it must find a site to accept its fragments and lower their internal value until a buyer can be found for all of them.

The storage manager is an asynchronous process running in the background, continually buying and selling fragments. Obviously, it should work in harmony with the bidder mentioned in the previous section. Specifically, the bidder should bid on queries for remote fragments that the storage manager would like to buy, but has not yet done so. In contrast, it should decline to bid on queries to remote objects in which the storage manager has no interest. The first primitive version of this interface is the "hot list" mentioned in the the previous section.

4.2 Splitting and coalescing

Mariposa sites must also decide when to split and coalesce fragments. Clearly, if there are too few fragments in a class, then parallel execution of Mariposa queries will be hindered. On the other hand, if there are too many fragments, then the overhead of dealing with all the fragments will increase and response time will suffer, as noted in Copeland et al. (1988). The algorithms for splitting and coalescing fragments must strike the correct balance between these two effects.

At the current time, our storage manager does not have general Rush rules to deal with splitting and coalescing fragments. Hence, this section indicates our current plans for the future.

One strategy is to let market pressure correct inappropriate fragment sizes. Large fragments have high revenue and attract many bidders for copies, thereby diverting some of the revenue away from the owner. If the owner site wants to keep the number of copies low, it has to break up the fragment into smaller fragments, which have less revenue and are less attractive for copies. On the other hand, a small fragment has high processing overhead for queries. Economies of scale could be realized by coalescing it with another fragment in the same class into a single larger fragment.

If more direct intervention is required, then Mariposa might resort to the following tactic. Consider the execution of queries referencing only a single class. The broker can fetch the number of fragments, Num_C, in that class from a name server and, assuming that all fragments are the same size, can compute the expected delay (ED) of a given query on the class if run on all fragments in parallel. The budget function tells the broker the total amount that is available for the entire query under that delay. The amount of the expected feasible bid per site in this situation is:

$$\textit{expected feasible site bid} = \frac{B(ED)}{Num_C}$$

The broker can repeat those calculations for a variable number of fragments to arrive at Num^*, the number of fragments to maximize the expected revenue per site.

This value, Num^*, can be published by the broker, along with its request for bids. If a site has a fragment that is too large (or too small), then in steady state it will be able to obtain a larger revenue per query if it splits (coalesces) the fragment. Hence, if a site keeps track of the average value of Num^* for each class for which it stores a fragment, then it can decide whether its fragments should be split or coalesced.

Of course, a site must honor any outstanding contracts that it has already made. If it discards or splits a fragment for which there is an outstanding contract, then the site must endure the consequences of its actions. This entails either subcontracting to some other site a portion of the previously committed work or buying back the missing data. In either case, there are revenue consequences, and a site should take its outstanding contracts into account when it makes fragment allocation decisions. Moreover, a site should carefully consider the desirable expiration time for contracts. Shorter times will allow the site greater flexibility in allocation decisions.

5 Names and name service

Current distributed systems use a rigid naming approach, assume that all changes are globally synchronized, and often have a structure that limits the scalability of the system. The Mariposa goals of mobile fragments and avoidance of global synchronization require that a more flexible naming service be used. We have developed a decentralized naming facility that does not depend on a centralized authority for name registration or binding.

5.1 Names

Mariposa defines four structures used in object naming. These structures (internal names, full names, common names and name contexts) are defined below.

Internal names are location-dependent names used to determine the physical location of a fragment. Because these are low-level names that are defined by the implementation, they will not be described further.

Full names are completely-specified names that uniquely identify an object. A full name can be resolved to any object regardless of location. Full names are not specific to the querying user and site, and are location-independent, so that when a query or fragment moves the full name is still valid. A name consists of components describing attributes of the containing table, and a full name has all components fully specified.

In contrast, *common names* (sometimes known as synonyms) are user-specific, partially specified names. Using them avoids the tedium of using a full name. Simple rules permit the translation of common names into full names by supplying the missing name components. The binding operation gathers the missing parts either from parameters directly supplied by the user or from the user's environment as stored in the system catalogs. Common names may be ambiguous because different users may refer to different objects using the same name. Because common names are context dependent, they may even refer to different objects at different times. Translation of common names is performed by functions written in the Mariposa rule/extension language, stored in the system catalogs, and invoked by the module (e.g., the parser) that requires the name to be resolved. Translation functions may take several arguments and return a string containing a Boolean expression that looks like a query qualification. This string is then stored internally by the invoking module when called by the name service module. The user may invoke translation functions directly, e.g., `my naming(EMP)`. Since we expect most users to have a "usual" set of name parameters, a user may specify one such function (taking the name string as its only argument) as a default in the `USER` system catalog. When the user specifies a simple string (e.g., `EMP`) as a common name, the system applies this default function.

Finally, a *name context* is a set of affiliated names. Names within a context are expected to share some feature. For example, they may be often used together in an application (e.g., a directory) or they may form part of a more complex object (e.g., a class definition). A programmer can define a name context for global use that everyone can access, or a private name context that is visible only to a single application. The advantage of a name context is that names do not have to be globally registered, nor are the names tied to a physical resource to make them unique, such as the birth site used in Williams et al. (1981). Like other objects, a name context can also be named. In addition, like data fragments, it can be migrated between name servers, and there can be multiple copies residing on different servers for better load balancing and availability. This scheme differs from another proposed decentralized name service (Cheriton and Mann 1989) that avoided a centralized name authority by relying upon each type of server to manage their own names without relying on a dedicated name service.

5.2 Name resolution

A name must be resolved to discover which object is bound to the name. Every client and server has a name cache at the site to support the local translation of common names to full names and of full names to internal names. When a broker wants to resolve a name, it first looks in the local name cache to see if a translation exists. If the cache does not yield a match, the broker uses a rule-driven search to resolve ambiguous common names. If a broker still fails to resolve a name using its local cache, it will query one or more name servers for additional name information.

As previously discussed, names are unordered sets of attributes. In addition, since the user may not know all of an object's attributes, it may be incomplete. Finally, common names may be ambiguous (more than one match) or untranslatable (no matches). When the broker discovers that there are multiple matches to the same common name, it tries to pick one according to the policy specified in its rule base. Some possible policies are "first match," as exemplified by the UNIX shell command search (path), or a policy of "best match" that uses additional semantic criteria. Considerable information may exist that the broker can apply to choose the best match, such as data types, ownership, and protection permissions.

5.3 Name discovery

In Mariposa, a name server responds to metadata queries in the same way as data servers execute regular queries, except that they translate common names into full names using a list of name contexts provided by the client. The name service process uses the bidding protocol of Sect. 3 to interact with a collection of potential bidders. The name service chooses the winning name server based on economic considerations of cost and quality of service. Mariposa expects multiple name servers, and this collection may be dynamic as name servers are added to and removed from a Mariposa environment. Name servers are expected to use advertising to find clients.

Each name server must make arrangements to read the local system catalogs at the sites whose catalogs it serves periodically and build a composite set of metadata. Since there is no requirement for a processing site to notify a name server when fragments change sites or are split or coalesced, the name server metadata may be substantially out of date.

As a result, name servers are differentiated by their *quality of service* regarding their price and the staleness of their information. For example, a name server that is less than one minute out of date generally has better quality information than one which can be up to one day out of date. Quality is best measured by the maximum staleness of the answer to any name service query. Using this information, a broker can make an appropriate tradeoff between price, delay and quality of answer among the various name services, and select the one that best meets its needs.

Quality may be based on more than the name server's polling rate. An estimate of the real quality of the metadata may be based on the observed rate of update. From this we predict the chance that an invalidating update will occur for a time period after fetching a copy of the data into the local

Table 4. Mariposa site configurations

	WAN				LAN			
Site	Host	Location	Model	Memory	Host	Location	Model	Memory
1	huevos	Santa Barbara	3000/600	96 MB	arcadia	Berkeley	3000/400	64 MB
2	triplerock	Berkeley	2100/500	256 MB	triplerock	Berkeley	2100/500	256 MB
3	pisa	San Diego	3000/800	128 MB	nobozo	Berkeley	3000/500X	160 MB

Table 5. Parameters for the experimental test data

Table	Location	Number of tows	Total size
R1	Site 1	50 000	5 MB
R2	Site 2	10 000	1 MB
R3	Site 3	50 000	5 MB

cache. The benefit is that the calculation can be made without probing the actual metadata to see if it has changed. The quality of service is then a measurement of the metadata's rate of update, as well as the name server's rate of update.

6 Mariposa status and experiments

At the current time (June 1995), a complete Mariposa implementation using the architecture described in this paper is operational on Digital Equipment Corp. Alpha AXP workstations running Digital UNIX. The current system is a combination of old and new code. The basic server engine is that of POSTGRES (Stonebraker and Kemnitz 1991), modified to accept SQL instead of POSTQUEL. In addition, we have implemented the fragmenter, broker, bidder and coordinator modules to form the complete Mariposa system portrayed in Fig. 1.

Building a functional distributed system has required the addition of a substantial amount of software infrastructure. For example, we have built a multithreaded network communication package using ONC RPC and POSIX threads. The primitive actions shown in Table 1 have been implemented as RPCs and are available as Rush procedures for use in the action part of a Rush rule. Implementation of the Rush language itself has required careful design and performance engineering, as described in Sah and Blow (1994).

We are presently extending the functionality of our prototype. At the current time, the fragmenter, coordinator and broker are fairly complete. However, the storage manager and the bidder are simplistic, as noted earlier. We are in the process of constructing more sophisticated routines in these modules. In addition, we are implementing the replication system described in Sidell et al. (1995). We plan to release a general Mariposa distribution when these tasks are completed later in 1995.

The rest of this section presents details of a few simple experiments which we have conducted in both LAN and WAN environments. The experiments demonstrate the power, performance and flexibility of the Mariposa approach to distributed data management. First, we describe the experimental setup. We then show by measurement that the Mariposa protocols do not add excessive overhead relative to those in a traditional distributed DBMS. Finally, we show how Mariposa query optimization and execution compares to that of a traditional system.

6.1 Experimental environment

The experiments were conducted on Alpha AXP workstations running versions 2.1 and 3.0 of Digital UNIX. Table 4 shows the actual hardware configurations used. The workstations were connected by a 10 MB/s Ethernet in the LAN case and the Internet in the WAN case. The WAN experiments were performed after midnight in order to avoid heavy daytime Internet traffic that would cause excessive bandwidth and latency variance.

The results in this section were generated using a simple synthetic dataset and workload. The database consists of three tables, R1, R2 and R3. The tables are part of the Wisconsin Benchmark database (Bitton et al. 1983), modified to produce results of the sizes indicated in Table 5. We make available statistics that allow a query optimizer to estimate the size of (R1 join R2), (R2 join R3) and (R1 join R2 join R3) as 1 MB, 3 MB and 4.5 MB, respectively. The workload query is an equijoin of all three tables:

```
SELECT *
FROM R1, R2, R3
WHERE R1.u1 = R2.u1
  AND R2.u1 = R3.u1
```

In the wide area case, the query originates at Berkeley and performs the join over the WAN connecting UC Berkeley, UC Santa Barbara and UC San Diego.

6.2 Comparison of the purchase order and expensive bid protocols

Before discussing the performance benefits of the Mariposa economic protocols, we should quantify the overhead they add to the process of constructing and executing a plan relative to a traditional distributed DBMS. We can analyze the situation as follows. A traditional system plans a query and sends the subqueries to the processing sites; this process follows essentially the same steps as the purchase order protocol discussed in Sect. 3. However, Mariposa can choose between the purchase order protocol and the expensive bid protocol. As a result, Mariposa overhead (relative to the traditional system) is the difference in elapsed time between the two protocols, weighted by the proportion of queries that actually use the expensive bid protocol.

To measure the difference between the two protocols, we repeatedly executed the three-way join query described

Table 6. Elapsed times for various query processing stages

Network	Stage	Time (s)	
		Purchase order protocol	Expensive bid protocol
	Parser	0.18	0.18
LAN	Optimizer	0.08	0.08
	Broker	1.72	6.69
	Parser	0.18	0.18
WAN	Optimizer	0.08	0.08
	Broker	4.52	14.08

in the previous section over both a LAN and a WAN. The elapsed times for the various processing stages shown in Table 6 represent averages over ten runs of the same query. For this experiment, we did not install any rules that would cause fragment migration and did not change any optimizer statistics. The query was therefore executed identically every time. Plainly, the only difference between the purchase order and the expensive bid protocol is in the brokering stage.

The difference in elapsed time between the two protocols is due largely to the message overhead of brokering, but not in the way one would expect from simple message counting. In the purchase order protocol, the single-site optimizer determines the sites to perform the joins and awards contracts to the sites accordingly. Sending the contracts to the two remote sites involves two round-trip network messages (as previously mentioned, this is no worse than the cost in a traditional distributed DBMS of initiating remote query execution). In the expensive bid protocol, the broker sends out request for bid (RFB) messages for the two joins to each site. However, each prospective join processing site then sends out subbids for remote table scans. The whole brokering process therefore involves 14 round-trip messages for RFBs (including subbids), six round-trip messages for recording the bids and two more for notifying the winners of the two join subqueries. Note, however, that the bid collection process is executed in parallel because the broker and the bidder are multithreaded, which accounts for the fact that the additional cost is not as high as might be thought.

As is evident from the results presented in Table 6, the expensive bid protocol is not unduly expensive. If the query takes more than a few minutes to execute, the savings from a better query processing strategy can easily outweigh the small cost of bidding. Recall that the expensive protocol will only be used when the purchase order protocol cannot be. We expect the less expensive protocol to be used for the majority of the time. The next subsection shows how economic methods can produce better query processing strategies.

6.3 Bidding in a simple economy

We illustrate how the economic paradigm works by running the three-way distributed join query described in the previous section, repeatedly in a simple economy. We discuss how the query optimization and execution strategy in Mariposa differs from traditional distributed database systems and how Mariposa achieves an overall performance improvement by adapting its query processing strategy to the environment. We also show how data migration in Mariposa can automatically ameliorate poor initial data placement.

In our simple economy, each site uses the same pricing scheme and the same set of rules. The expensive bid protocol is used for every economic transaction. Sites have adequate storage space and never need to evict alternate fragments to buy fragments. The exact parameters and decision rules used to price queries and fragments are as follows:

Queries: Sites bid on subqueries as described in Sect. 3.3. That is, a bidder will only bid on a join if the criteria specified in Sect. 3.3 are satisfied. The *billing rate* is simply 1.5× *estimated cost*, leading to the following offer price:

$$\textit{actual bid} = (1.5 \times \textit{estimated cost}) \times \textit{load average}$$

load average = 1 for the duration of the experiment, reflecting the fact that the system is lightly loaded. The difference in the bids offered by each bidder is therefore solely due to data placement (e.g., some bidders need to subcontract remote scans).

Fragments: A broker who subcontracts for remote scans also considers buying the fragment instead of paying for the scan. The fragment value discussed in Section 4.1 is set to $\frac{2 \times scan\ cost}{load\ average}$; this, combined with the fact that eviction is never necessary, means that a site will consider selling a fragment whenever

$$offer\ price > \frac{2\ times\ scan\ cost}{load\ average}$$

A broker decides whether to try to buy a fragment or to pay for the remote scan according to the following rule:

```
on (salePrice(frag)
   <= moneySpentForScan(frag))
     do acquire(frag)
```

In other words, the broker tries to acquire a fragment when the amount of money spent scanning the fragment in previous queries is greater than or equal to the price for buying the fragment. As discussed in Sect. 4.1, each broker keeps a hot-list of remote fragments used in previous queries with their associated scan costs. This rule will cause data to move closer to the query when executed frequently.

This simple economy is not entirely realistic. Consider the pricing of selling a fragment as shown above. If *load average* increases, the sale price of the fragment decreases. This has the desirable effect of hastening the sale of fragments to off-load a busy site. However, it tends to cause the sale of hot fragments as well. An effective Mariposa economy will consist of more rules and a more sophisticated pricing scheme than that with which we are currently experimenting.

We now present the performance and behavior of Mariposa using the simple economy described above and the WAN environment shown in Table 4. Our experiments show

Table 7. Execution times, data placement and revenue at each site

		Steps					
		1	2	3	4	5	6
Elapsed time	Brokering	13.06	12.78	18.81	13.97	8.9	10.06
(s)	Total	449.30	477.74	403.61	428.82	394.3	384.04
	R1	1	1	1	1	3	3
Location of	R2	2	2	1	11	13	13
(site)	R3	13	3	3	3	3	3
	Site 1	97.6	97.6	95.5	97.2	102.3	0.0
Revenue	Site 2	2.7	2.7	3.5	1.9	1.9	1.9
(per query)	Site 3	177.9	177.9	177.9	177.9	165.3	267.7

how Mariposa adapts to the environment through the bidding process under the economy and the rules described above.

A traditional query optimizer will use a fixed query processing strategy. Assuming that sites are uniform in their query processing capacity, the optimizer will ultimately differentiate plans based on movement of data. That is, it will tend to choose plans that minimize the amount of base table and intermediate result data transmitted over the network. As a result, a traditional optimizer will construct the following plan:

(1) Move R2 from Berkeley to Santa Barbara. Perform R1 join R2 at Santa Barbara.
(2) Move the answer to San Diego. Perform the second join at San Diego.
(3) Move the final answer to Berkeley.

This plan causes 6.5 MB of data to be moved (1 MB in step 1, 1 MB in step 2, and 4.5 MB in step 3). If the same query is executed repeatedly under identical load conditions, then the same plan will be generated each time, resulting in identical costs.

By contrast, the simple Mariposa economy can adjust the assignment of queries and fragments to reflect the current workload. Even though the Mariposa optimizer will pick the same join order as the traditional optimizer, the broker can change its query processing strategy because it acquires bids for the two joins among the three sites. Examination of Table 7 reveals the performance improvements resulting from dynamic movement of objects. It shows the elapsed time, location of data and revenue generated at each site by running the three-way join query described in Sect. 6.1 repeatedly from site 2 (Berkeley).

At the first step of the experiment, Santa Barbara is the winner of the first join. The price of scanning the smaller table, R2, remotely from Santa Barbara is less than that of scanning R1 remotely from Berkeley; as a result, Santa Barbara offers a lower bid. Similarly, San Diego is the winner of the second join. Hence, for the first two steps, the execution plan resulting from the bidding is identical to the one obtained by a traditional distributed query optimizer.

However, subsequent steps show that Mariposa can generate better plans than a traditional optimizer by migrating fragments when necessary. For instance, R2 is moved to Santa Barbara in step 3 of the experiment, and subsequent joins of R1 and R2 can be performed locally. This eliminates the need to move 1 MB of data. Similarly, R1 and R2 are moved to San Diego at step 5 so that the joins can be performed locally[1]. The cost of moving the tables can be amortized over repeated execution of queries that require the same data.

The experimental results vary considerably because of the wide variance in Internet network latency. Table 7 shows a set of results which best illustrate the beneficial effects of the economic model.

7 Related work

Currently, there are only a few systems documented in the literature that incorporate microeconomic approaches to resource sharing problems. Huberman (1988) presents a collection of articles that cover the underlying principles and explore the behavior of those systems.

Miller and Drexler (1988) use the term "Agoric Systems" for software systems deploying market mechanisms for resource allocation among independent objects. The data-type agents proposed in that article are comparable to our brokers. They mediate between consumer and supplier objects, helping to find the current best price and supplier for a service. As an extension, agents have a "reputation" and their services are brokered by an agent-selection agent. This is analogous to the notion of a quality-of-service of name servers, which also offer their services to brokers.

Kurose and Simha (1989) present a solution to the file allocation problem that makes use of microeconomic principles, but is based on a cooperative, not competitive, environment. The agents in this economy exchange fragments in order to minimize the cumulative system-wide access costs for all incoming requests. This is achieved by having the sites voluntarily cede fragments or portions thereof to other sites if it lowers access costs. In this model, all sites cooperate to achieve a global optimum instead of selfishly competing for resources to maximize their own utility.

Malone et al. describe the implementation of a process migration facility for a pool of workstations connected through a LAN. In this system, a client broadcasts a request for bids that includes a task description. The servers willing to process that task return an estimated completion time, and the client picks the best bid. The time estimate is computed on the basis of processor speed, current system load, a normalized runtime of the task, and the number and length of files to be loaded. The latter two parameters are

[1] Note that the total elapsed time does not include the time to move the fragments. It takes 82 s to move R2 to site 1 at step 3 and 820 s to move R1 and R3 to site 3 at step 5

supplied by the task description. No prices are charged for processing services and there is no provision for a shortcut to the bidding process by mechanisms like posting server characteristics or advertisements of servers.

Another distributed process scheduling system is presented in Waldspurge (1992). Here, CPU time on remote machines is auctioned off by the processing sites, and applications hand in bids for time slices. This is in contrast to our system, where processing sites make bids for servicing requests. There are different types of auctions, and computations are aborted if their funding is depleted. An application is structured into manager and worker modules. The worker modules perform the application processing and several of them can execute in parallel. The managers are responsible for funding their workers and divide the available funds between them in an application-specific way. To adjust the degree of parallelism to the availability of idle CPUs, the manager changes the funding of individual workers.

Wellman (1993) offers a simulation of multicommodity flow that is quite close to our bidding model, but with a bid resolution model that converges with multiple rounds of messages. His clearinghouses violate our constraint against single points of failure. Mariposa name service can be thought of as clearinghouses with only a partial list of possible suppliers. His optimality results are clearly invalidated by the possible exclusion of optimal bidders. This suggests the importance of high-quality name service, to ensure that the winning bidders are usually solicited for bids.

A model similar to ours is proposed by Ferguson et al. (1993), where fragments can be moved and replicated between the nodes of a network of computers, although they are not allowed to be split or coalesced. Transactions, consisting of simple read/write requests for fragments, are given a budget when entering the system. Accesses to fragments are purchased from the sites offering them at the desired price/quality ratio. Sites are trying to maximize their revenue and therefore lease fragments or their copies if the access history for that fragment suggests that this will be profitable. Unlike our model, there is no bidding process for either service purchase or fragment lease. The relevant prices are published at every site in catalogs that can be updated at any time to reflect current demand and system load. The network distance to the site offering the fragment access service is included in the price quote to give a quality-of-service indication. A major difference between this model and ours is that every site needs to have perfect information about the prices of fragment accesses at every other site, requiring global updates of pricing information. Also, it is assumed that a name service, which has perfect information about all the fragments in the network, is available at every site, again requiring global synchronization. The name service is provided at no cost and is hence excluded from the economy. We expect that global updates of metadata will suffer from a scalability problem, sacrificing the advantages of the decentralized nature of microeconomic decisions.

When computer centers were the main source of computing power, several authors studied the economics of such centers' services. The work focussed on the cost of the services, the required scale of the center given user needs, the cost of user delays, and the pricing structure. Several results are reported in the literature, in both computer and management sciences. In particular, Mendelson (1985) proposes a microeconomic model for studies of queueing effects of popular pricing policies, typically not considering the delays. The model shows that when delay cost is taken into account, a low utilization ratio of the center is often optimal. The model is refined by Dewan and Mendelson (1990). The authors assume a nonlinear delay cost structure, and present necessary and sufficient conditions for the optimality of pricing rules that charges out service resources at their marginal capacity cost. Although these and similar results were intended for human decision making, many apply to the Mariposa context as well.

On the other hand, Mendelson and Saharia (1986) propose a methodology for trading off the cost of incomplete information against data-related costs, and for constructing minimum-cost answers to a variety of query types. These results can be useful in the Mariposa context. Users and their brokers will indeed often face a compromise between complete but costly and cheaper but incomplete and partial data and processing.

8 Conclusions

We present a distributed microeconomic approach for managing query execution and storage management. The difficulty in scheduling distributed actions in a large system stems from the combinatorially large number of possible choices for each action, the expense of global synchronization, and the requirement of supporting systems with heterogeneous capabilities. Complexity is further increased by the presence of a rapidly changing environment, including time-varying load levels for each site and the possibility of sites entering and leaving the system. The economic model is well-studied and can reduce the scheduling complexity of distributed interactions because it does not seek globally optimal solutions. Instead, the forces of the market provide an "invisible hand" to guide reasonably equitable trading of resources.

We further demonstrated the power and flexibility of Mariposa through experiments running over a wide-area network. Initial results confirm our belief that the bidding protocol is not unduly expensive and that the bidding process results in execution plans that can adapt to the environment (such as unbalanced workload and poor data placement) in a flexible manner. We are implementing more sophisticated features and plan a general release for the end of 1995.

Acknowledgements. The authors would like to thank Jim Frew and Darla Sharp of the Institute for Computational Earth System Science at the University of California, Santa Barbara and Joseph Pasquale and Eric Anderson of the Department of Computer Science and Engineering of the University of California, San Diego for providing a home for the remote Mariposa sites and their assistance in the initial setup. Mariposa has been designed and implemented by a team of students, faculty and staff that includes the authors as well as Robert Devine, Marcel Kornacker, Michael Olson, Robert Patrick and Rex Winterbottom. The presentation and ideas in this paper have been greatly improved by the suggestions and critiques provided by Sunita Sarawagi and Allison Woodruff. This research was sponsored by the Army Research Office under contract DAAH04-94-G-0223, the Advanced Research Projects Agency under contract DABT63-92-C-0007, the National Science Foundation under grant IRI-9107455, and Microsoft Corp.

References

Banerjea A Mah BA (1991) The real-time channel administration protocol. In: Proc 2nd Int Workshop on Network and Operating System Support for Digital Audio and Video, Heidelberg, Germany, November

Bernstein PA, Goodman N, Wong E, Reeve CL, Rothnie J (1981) Query processing in a system for distributed databases (SDD-1). ACM Trans Database Syst 6:602–625

Bitton D, DeWitt DJ, Turbyfill C (1983) Benchmarking data base systems: a systematic approach. In: Proc 9th Int Conf on Very Large Data Bases, Florence, Italy, November

Cheriton D, Mann TP (1989) Decentralizing a global naming service for improved performance and fault tolerance. ACM Trans Comput Syst 7:147–183

Copeland G, Alexander W, Boughter E, Keller T (1988) Data placement in bubba. In: Proc 1988 ACM-SIGMOD Conf on Management of Data, Chicago, Ill, June, pp 99–108

Dewan S, Mendelson H (1990) User delay costs and internal pricing for a service facility. Management Sci 36:1502–1517

Ferguson D, Nikolaou C, Yemini Y (1993) An economy for managing replicated data in autonomous decentralized systems. Proc Int Symp on Autonomous Decentralized emsSyst (ISADS 93), Kawasaki, Japan, March, pp 367–375

Huberman BA (ed) (1988) The ecology of computation. North-Holland, Amsterdam

Kurose J, Simha R (1989) A microeconomic approach to optimal resource allocation in distributed computer systems. IEEE Trans Comp 38:705–717

Litwin W et al (1982) SIRIUS system for distributed data management. In: Schneider HJ (ed) Distributed data bases. North-Holland, Amsterdam

Mackert LF, Lohman GM (1986) R* Optimizer validation and performance evaluation for distributed queries. Proc 12th Int Conf on Very Large Data Bases, Kyoto, Japan, August, pp 149–159

Malone TW, Fikes RE, Grant KR, Howard MT (1988) Enterprise: a market-like task scheduler for distributed computing environments. In: Huberman BA (ed) The ecology of computation. North-Holland, Amsterdam

Mendelson H (1985) Pricing computer services: queueing effects. Commun ACM 28:312–321

Mendelson H, Saharia AN (1986) Incomplete information costs and database design. ACM Trans Database Syst 11:159–185

Miller MS, Drexler KE (1988) Markets and computation: agoric open systems. In: Huberman BA (ed) The ecology of computation. North-Holland, Amsterdam

Ousterhout JK (1994) Tcl and the Tk Toolkit. Addison-Wesley, Reading, Mass

Sah A, Blow J (1994) A new architecture for the implementation of scripting languages. In: Proc USENIX Symp on Very High Level Languages, Santa Fe, NM, October. pp 21–38

Sah A, Blow J, Dennis B (1994) An introduction to the Rush language. In: In: Proc Tcl'94 Workshop, New Orleans, La, June pp 105–116

Selinger PG, Astrahan MM, Chamberlin DD, Lorie RA, Price TG (1979) Access path selection in a relational database management system. In: Proc 1979 ACM-SIGMOD Conf on Management of Data, Boston, Mass, June

Sidell J, Aoki PM, Barr S, Sah A, Staelin C, Stonebraker M, Yu A (1995) Data replication in Mariposa (Sequoia 2000 Technical Report 95-60) University of California, Berkeley, Calif

Stonebraker M (1986) The design and implementation of distributed INGRES. In: Stonebraker M (ed) The INGRES papers. M. Addison-Wesley, Reading, Mass

Stonebraker M (1991) An overview of the Sequoia 2000 project (Sequoia 2000 Technical Report 91/5), University of California, Berkeley, Calif

Stonebraker M, Kemnitz G (1991) The POSTGRES next-generation database management system. Commun ACM 34:78–92

Stonebraker M, Aoki PM, Devine R, Litwin W, Olson M (1994a) Mariposa: a new architecture for distributed data. In: Proc 10th Int Conf on Data Engineering, Houston, Tex, February, pp 54–65

Stonebraker M, Devine R, Kornacker M, Litwin W, Pfeffer A, Sah A, Staelin C (1994b) An economic paradigm for query processing and data migration in Mariposa. In: Proc 3rd Int Conf on Parallel and Distributed Information Syst, Austin, Tex, September, pp 58–67

Waldspurger CA, Hogg T, Huberman B, Kephart J, Stornetta S (1992) Spawn: a distributed computational ecology. IEEE Trans Software Eng 18:103–117

Wellman MP (1993) A market-oriented programming environment and its applications to distributed multicommodity flow problems. J AI Res 1:1–23

Williams R, Daniels D, Haas L, Lapis G, Lindsay B, Ng P, Obermarck R, Selinger P, Walker A, Wilms P, Yost R (1981) R*: an overview of the architecture. (IBM Research Report RJ3325), IBM Research Laboratory, San Jose, Calif

Zhang H, Fisher T (1992) Preliminary measurement of the RMTP/RTIP. In: Proc Third Int Workshop on Network and Operating System Support for Digital Audio and Video, San Diego, Calif November

Chapter 3
Data Storage and Access Methods

In this section we focus on data storage and access methods, postponing the issues of transactional concurrency and recovery until the next chapter.

Files and indexes are present in most OS file systems, and an age-old controversy surrounds the question of whether database access method services can (or should) be provided by a generic file system. Our first paper in this chapter reflects the frustrations that arose from attempts to use the original UNIX system services for database purposes. This paper is traditionally seen as a harsh critique of the Operating Systems community's work at the time, but the reader should recall that it is a critique born out of good will: the INGRES project took a leap of faith in using UNIX and C in their very early days, and the shortcomings of UNIX that are described here are the result of that experience. After many years of OS research and market pressure from database vendors and customers, one can now work around most of these shortcomings reasonably gracefully in most modern UNIXes and other operating systems. Readers with an interest in the Operating Systems literature are encouraged to survey the various workarounds that have emerged in that community since the time of this paper (kernel threads, scheduler activations, memory mapped files, etc.), and understand the degree to which they help solve these problems. Despite the near-universal understanding of these issues today, it still remains difficult to tightly integrate database needs for storage and buffering into the file system without sacrificing performance on file system workloads. Microsoft is purportedly doing this for their next release of Windows, which will be interesting to watch on two counts: whether it can be done, and whether it is usable for any DBMS other than the one written at Microsoft.

After this introduction, we switch gears to the famous first paper on RAID, which is a low-level storage technique that has become an industry of its own. RAID revisits the industrial-revolution idea of using armies of cheap, replaceable labor instead of using expensive, highly-specialized labor. In the case of RAID, large high-performance disks are replaced by arrays of smaller, cheap disks; the challenge is to do this while maintaining reliability in the face of component disk failures. This paper is well-known for defining five RAID "levels", of which only two are typically remembered: Level 1 (mirroring) and Level 5 ("full" RAID). Mirroring is a very old technique, but is still the recommended storage scheme for database systems, since it provides reliability while keeping the storage system's performance overhead low; moreover, it allows the DBMS to maintain control over disk layout. RAID 5 provides a much more storage-efficient solution while maintaining good reliability, which makes it attractive to storage customers. But in practice it has been observed that the raw performance penalty for writes in RAID 5 is quite high, due to the need to read and update parity bits for every write. (The next paper in this section quotes a 4x performance penalty for RAID writes, quite a bit worse than the back-of-the-envelope predictions here.) This is particularly bad for the On-Line Transaction Processing applications that form the traditional bread and butter of the database industry.

Given this somewhat negative introduction, some notes on RAID are in order. First, since the time of this paper various projects have proposed hybrid RAID schemes to allow for both efficient writes and compact storage. The HP AutoRAID system [WGSS96] is perhaps the best-known of these, using mirroring for frequently-updated items, and RAID 5 for colder data, with policies to "promote" and "demote" between the two. A second note arises from market realities. The storage systems industry is driven by filesystem workloads first, and database workloads second. Hence RAID became an entrenched technology without considering database performance requirements. Despite the inefficiencies of RAID 5 for database workloads, many customers have insisted on using RAID 5 for its storage cost benefits, often blaming the database vendors for the resulting bad performance. As a result, most database systems now have tuning knobs that try to mask the inefficiencies of RAID 5, by tuning buffer replacement and log flushing policies.

Our next paper by Gray and Graefe presents some rules of thumb for buffer replacement policies in a number of settings, including RAID environments. The content of the paper is important, but the style is equally important, since it is an example of one popular approach to systems research. The paper is an exercise in a "scientific" (which is to say "observational") style of systems research, in which developments are viewed over a long period of time to try and extract important technology trends. To their credit, Gray and Graefe avoid calling their observations "laws" (*a la* Moore's "Law") and stick with the more accurate term "rules of thumb". This style of research necessarily glosses over the specific ideas behind technological innovations, in the interest of seeing a bigger picture. Another important aspect of this paper is its stress on choosing appropriate *metrics,* a key feature of good research. It is easy for engineers, researchers and customers to become obsessed with a performance metric like "throughput" without asking whether that metric accurately reflects their actual needs. This paper attempts to re-define storage performance metrics to reflect the shifting *economic cost* of storage systems; as a result it focuses on cost/performance ratios rather than raw performance, and examines both the cost and performance trends of the technologies.

While we are on the topic of buffering, we note that we have not included a paper on buffer replacement *policy* in this edition of the book. Database aficionados should have at least one such scheme in their repertoire, so we discuss them briefly here. In previous editions we included the DBMIN paper by Chou and DeWitt [CD85]; we dropped it in this edition because it is not really a practical scheme. DBMIN is based on the idea that since the buffer replacement policy is sensitive to the query plan, the optimizer can dictate different replacement policies to be used for various blocks depending on the particular query. Unfortunately, in practice systems often run more than one query at a time, and these queries may share blocks but use them in different ways. Planning custom replacement policies for evolving, multi-query workloads becomes messy. However the DBMIN paper remains a worthwhile read because it highlights many of the important database access patterns that drive replacement policy decisions.

Two attractively simple replacement policies that work better than LRU are the LRU-*k* [OOW93] and 2Q [JS94] schemes. Both schemes try to improve on LRU by tracking the *inter-arrival* rate of requests for the same page, and using it to predict which page currently in the buffer pool will be the last to be re-referenced. LRU-*k* is a generalization of LRU, in which instead of just remembering the time of the last reference for each page, you remember the times of the last *k* references. 2Q is an attempt to provide the LRU-2 behavior with a lower-overhead algorithm – LRU-based schemes suffer from the requirement of managing a priority heap to remember what the current "least" is. Unfortunately, inter-arrival time estimations like LRU-k and 2Q do not help with the single-user looping access patterns mentioned at the beginning of this section: the inter-arrival rate is the same for pages, and if ties are broken via LRU than nothing has been gained.

We conclude the chapter by moving up from the storage and buffering layers to discuss access methods. By now, most of the popular access methods (heap files, B+-trees, Linear Hashing) are well covered in the better undergraduate database textbooks. Hence we only discuss the more advanced *multidimensional* access methods, which index data along multiple dimensions simultaneously. These access methods are most often used today for geographic data, to find data within a two-dimensional spatial range. They also have use in advanced applications like image and string searching that are driven by "similar-to" queries (e.g. "find all images similar to this one"). Similarity search is often supported by taking a complex object like an image, and constructing a "signature" or "feature vector" that is an array of numbers. For example, an image can be represented by the histogram of pixel-colors that appear in the image. These signatures can often be in very large numbers of dimensions, but statistical techniques (e.g. the Singular Value Decomposition) can often be used to project them down to 5 or 10 dimensions, often without significantly affecting query results. The resulting low-dimensionality data can often be indexed effectively by a multidimensional access method.

Probably the most-cited multidimensional search structure for databases is the R-tree [Gutt84], which is a generalization of the B+-tree. Numerous variants and improvements to the R-tree have been proposed since then, and we present the R*-tree in this section as a representative of that body of work. The R*-tree is simple and intuitive, and has been shown to out-perform the R-tree in many experiments beyond those presented in this paper. The R*-tree modifies the R-tree in three key ways; two are minor, and one is major. The first two proposals include a different heuristic for choosing leaf nodes during insertion, and a different heuristic for re-apportioning data during page splits. More radically, the R*-tree proposes a "Forced Reinsertion" heuristic that postpones page splits in favor of reinserting data from the top of the tree. The rationale for this is that old insertion decisions in R*-trees can be sub-optimal in the face of subsequent decisions. A disadvantage of this scheme is the impact on concurrency: it turns a single insertion into multiple insertions, which translates into a higher probability of conflicts with other ongoing transactions walking the tree.

The word "heuristic" appears very often in the previous paragraph because most of the practical schemes for multidimensional indexing are heuristics – there are typically no proofs of worst-case or average-case performance (unlike B+-trees, which are well understood both practically and theoretically.) In fact, for most multidimensional indexing schemes it not difficult to construct an "adversarial" workload (a set of insertions and queries) that makes them perform terribly – this is an interesting exercise for the critical reader. Underlying this discussion is a need to understand how well a truly excellent index *could* do if one existed; Indexability Theory [HKM+02] provides an approach to developing such bounds, including tradeoffs between query I/Os and storage. A certain degree of theoretical work has been done to design new multi-dimensional, disk-based indexes that have understandable and even tight bounds (e.g. [ASV99]), but this work has yet to be made practical for real systems.

Readers wanting to become experts in multidimensional indexing have a great deal of reading to do, since the literature is littered with proposals that are hard to weigh against each other. A good survey of multidimensional access methods was written a few years ago [GG98], though it does not include many of the latest structures. We warn the reader to bring a critical eye to multidimensional index papers. When reading these proposals, it is often worth asking (a) whether the access method outperforms sequential scan of a heap file (many do not, due to the overhead of random I/Os!) (b) whether the claims of performance benefits are on a realistic workload (considering both the experimental data and the queries), and (c) whether other natural workloads will result in poor performance. Unfortunately, this large body of work lacks theoretical rigor, standard benchmarks, and industrial "war stories". As a result, most implementations stick with a few of the early structures like R-trees.

There are a number of schemes that attempt to map multi-dimensional data onto one dimension, and translate multi-dimensional queries into B+-tree lookups [Jag90,BBK98,etc.]. These have the attraction that they do not require new access method implementations, with the attendant complexities of index concurrency and recovery that we will discuss in the next chapter. There are also useful extensions to multidimensional index schemes to support similarity search [HS95] and bulk-loading [LLE97]. A difficult challenge in this arena is for an optimizer to estimate the number of disk I/Os that a multidimensional index will perform [BF95,Aok99].

On the practical side, there has been almost no industrial-strength work on multidimensional indexes that includes serious concurrency control and recovery. Most of the commercial database systems do not currently have a multidimensional index tightly integrated into the system; instead they provide "glue" to access remote multidimensional index servers, and/or they provide a table-partitioning scheme instead of true index. Both of these approaches translate either into poor concurrency or the potential for inconsistent indexes. An exception is the work of Kornacker [KMH97, Kor99], whose approach for concurrency and recovery is applicable to many multidimensional database indexes and was implemented in Informix.

We are no longer very optimistic about research into new multidimensional indexing tricks; there have simply been too many proposals with too little evaluation, and new ideas are unlikely to have any impact on real systems. What is needed in this space is either theoretically optimal indexes that are practically useful in real systems, or agreed-upon benchmarks from popular applications that can guide heuristic index designers. In the absence of such developments, system designers are left hedging their bets. They can either minimize their implementation investment by adopting simple but flawed schemes like R-trees, or they can invest in an extensible framework to allow for application-specific index schemes now, and the ability to quickly adopt provably good ideas in the future. We will discuss extensibility in detail in Chapter 5.

References

[Aok99] Paul M. Aoki. How to Avoid Building DataBlades® That Know the Value of Everything and the Cost of Nothing. In *Proc. 11th Int'l Conf. on Scientific and Statistical Database Management (SSDBM)*, Cleveland, OH, July 1999, 122-133.

[ASV99] Lars Arge, Vasilis Samoladas and Jeffrey Scott Vitter. "On Two-Dimensional Indexability and Optimal Range Search Index". In *Proc. ACM SIGACT-SIGMOD-SIGART Symposium on Principles of Database Systems (PODS)*, May-June, 1999.

[BBK98] S. Berchtold, C. Böhm and H.-P. Kriegel. "The Pyramid-Technique: Towards Breaking the Curse of Dimensionality." In *Proc. ACM-SIGMOD International Conference on Management of Data*, 1998.

[BF95] Alberto Belussi and Christos Faloutsos. "Estimating the Selectivity of Spatial Queries Using the 'Correlation' Fractal Dimension." In *Proc. International Conference on Very Large Data Bases (VLDB),* pp. 299-310, 1995.

[CD85] Hong-Tai Chou and David J. DeWitt. An Evaluation of Buffer Management Strategies for Relational Database Systems. In *Proceedings of 11th International Conference on Very Large Data Bases (VLDB),* pages 127-141, Stockholm, Sweden, August 1985.

[GG98] Volker Gaede and Oliver Günther. "Multidimensional Access Methods". *ACM Computing Surveys*, 30(2), 1998.

[Gutt84] Antonin Guttman. R-Trees: A Dynamic Index Structure For Spatial Searching. In *Proc. ACM-SIGMOD International Conference on Management of Data*, pages 47-57, Boston, June 1984.

[HKM+02] Joseph M. Hellerstein, Elias Koutsoupias, Daniel P. Miranker, Christos H. Papadimitriou and Vasilis Samoladas. "On a model of indexability and its bounds for range queries." Journal of the ACM (JACM) 49 (1):35-55, January, 2002.

[HS95] G. Hjaltason and H. Samet. "Ranking in Spatial Databases." In *Proc 4th Int. Symp. on Spatial Databases* (SSD), Portland, USA, pp.83-95, Aug. 1995.

[Jag90] H. V. Jagadish. "Linear Clustering of Objects with Multiple Atributes". In *Proc. ACM-SIGMOD International Conference on Management of Data,* pp. 332-342, 1990.

[JS94] T. Johnson and D. Shasha, "2Q: A low overhead high performance buffer management replacement algorithm," In *Proc. International Conference on Very Large Data Bases (VLDB)*, pp. 297-306, 1994.

[KMH97] Marcel Kornacker, C. Mohan and Joseph M. Hellerstein. "Concurrency and Recovery in Generalized Search Trees". In *Proc. ACM SIGMOD Conf. on Management of Data*, Tucson, AZ, May 1997, 62-72.

[Kor99] Marcel Kornacker. "High-Performance Extensible Indexing."In *Proc. of 25th International Conference on Very Large Data Bases (VLDB)*, Edinburgh, Scotland, September 1999.

[LLE97] S.T. Leutenegger, M.A. Lopez and J.M. Edgington. STR: A Simple and Efficient Algorithm for R-Tree Packing. In *Proc. of the International Conference on Data Engineering* (ICDE), 1997.

[OOW93] Elizabeth J. O'Neil, Patrick E. O'Neil, and Gerhard Weikum. "The LRU-K Page Replacement Algorithm For Database Disk Buffering." In *Proceedings ACM SIGMOD International Conference on Management of Data*, pages 297-306, Washington, D.C., May 1993.

[WGSS96] John Wilkes, Richard Golding, Carl Staelin, and Tim Sullivan. "The HP AutoRAID Hierarchical Storage System." ACM Transactions on Computer Systems, 14(1):108-136, Feb. 1996.

The R*-tree: An Efficient and Robust Access Method for Points and Rectangles+

Norbert Beckmann, Hans-Peter Kriegel
Ralf Schneider, Bernhard Seeger
Praktische Informatik, Universitaet Bremen, D-2800 Bremen 33, West Germany

Abstract

The R-tree, one of the most popular access methods for rectangles, is based on the heuristic optimization of the area of the enclosing rectangle in each inner node By running numerous experiments in a standardized testbed under highly varying data, queries and operations, we were able to design the R*-tree which incorporates a combined optimization of area, margin and overlap of each enclosing rectangle in the directory Using our standardized testbed in an exhaustive performance comparison, it turned out that the R*-tree clearly outperforms the existing R-tree variants Guttman's linear and quadratic R-tree and Greene's variant of the R-tree This superiority of the R*-tree holds for different types of queries and operations, such as map overlay, for both rectangles and multidimensional points in all experiments From a practical point of view the R*-tree is very attractive because of the following two reasons 1 it efficiently supports point and spatial data at the same time and 2 its implementation cost is only slightly higher than that of other R-trees

1.Introduction

In this paper we will consider spatial access methods (SAMs) which are based on the approximation of a complex spatial object by the minimum bounding rectangle with the sides of the rectangle parallel to the axes of the data space

+ This work was supported by grant no Kr 670/4-3 from the Deutsche Forschungsgemeinschaft (German Research Society) and by the Ministry of Environmental and Urban Planning of Bremen

The most important property of this simple approximation is that a complex object is represented by a limited number of bytes Although a lot of information is lost, minimum bounding rectangles of spatial objects preserve the most essential geometric properties of the object, i e the location of the object and the extension of the object in each axis

In [SK 88] we showed that known SAMs organizing (minimum bounding) rectangles are based on an underlying point access method (PAM) using one of the following three techniques clipping, transformation and overlapping regions

The most popular SAM for storing rectangles is the R-tree [Gut 84] Following our classification, the R-tree is based on the PAM B+-tree [Knu 73] using the technique over-lapping regions Thus the R-tree can be easily implemented which considerably contributes to its popularity

The R-tree is based on a heuristic optimization The optimization criterion which it persues, is to minimize the area of each enclosing rectangle in the inner nodes This criterion is taken for granted and not shown to be the best possible Questions arise such as Why not minimize the margin or the overlap of such minimum bounding rectangles Why not optimize storage utilization? Why not optimize all of these criteria at the same time? Could these criteria interact in a negative way? Only an engineering approach will help to find the best possible combination of optimization criteria

Necessary condition for such an engineering approach is the availability of a standardized testbed which allows us to run large volumes of experiments with highly varying data, queries and operations We have implemented such a standardized testbed and used it for performance comparisons particularly of point access methods [KSSS 89]

As the result of our research we designed a new R-tree variant, the R*-tree, which outperforms the known R-tree variants under all experiments For many realistic profiles of data and operations the gain in performance is quite considerable Additionally to the usual point query, rectangle intersection and rectangle enclosure query, we have analyzed our new R*-tree for the map overlay operation, also called spatial join, which is one of the most important operations in geographic and environmental database systems

This paper is organized as follows In section 2, we introduce the principles of R-trees including their optimization criteria In section 3 we present the existing R-tree variants of Guttman and Greene Section 4 describes in detail the design our new R*-tree The results of the comparisons of the R*-tree with the other R-tree variants are reported in section 5 Section 6 concludes the paper

2. Principles of R-trees and possible optimization criteria

An R-tree is a B^+-tree like structure which stores multidimensional rectangles as complete objects without clipping them or transforming them to higher dimensional points before

A non-leaf node contains entries of the form *(cp, Rectangle)* where *cp* is the address of a child node in the R-tree and *Rectangle* is the minimum bounding rectangle of all rectangles which are entries in that child node A leaf node contains entries of the form *(Oid, Rectangle)* where *Oid* refers to a record in the database, describing a spatial object and *Rectangle* is the enclosing rectangle of that spatial object Leaf nodes containing entries of the form *(dataobject, Rectangle)* are also possible This will not affect the basic structure of the R-tree In the following we will not consider such leaf nodes

Let M be the maximum number of entries that will fit in one node and let m be a parameter specifying the minimum number of entries in a node ($2 \le m \le M/2$) An R-tree satisfies the following properties

- The root has at least two children unless it is a leaf
- Every non-leaf node has between m and M children unless it is the root
- Every leaf node contains between m and M entries unless it is the root
- All leaves appear on the same level

An R-tree (R*-tree) is completely dynamic, insertions and deletions can be intermixed with queries and no periodic global reorganization is required Obviously, the structure must allow overlapping directory rectangles Thus it cannot guarantee that only one search path is required for an exact match query For further information we refer to [Gut84]
We will show in this paper that the overlapping-regions-technique does not imply bad average retrieval performance Here and in the following, we use the term directory rectangle, which is geometrically the minimum bounding rectangle of the underlying rectangles

The main problem in R-trees is the following For an arbitrary set of rectangles, dynamically build up bounding boxes from subsets of between m and M rectangles, in a way that arbitrary retrieval operations with query rectangles of arbitrary size are supported efficiently The known parameters of good retrieval performance affect each other in a very complex way, such that it is impossible to optimize one of them without influencing other parameters which may cause a deterioration of the overall performance Moreover, since the data rectangles may have very different size and shape and the directory rectangles grow and shrink dynamically, the success of methods which will optimize one parameter is very uncertain Thus a heuristic approach is applied, which is based on many different experiments carried out in a systematic framework

In this section some of the parameters which are essential for the retrieval performance are considered Furthermore, interdependencies between different parameters and optimization criteria are analyzed

(O1) *The area covered by a directory rectangle should be minimized*, i e the area covered by the bounding rectangle but not covered by the enclosed rectangles, the dead space, should be minimized This will improve performance since decisions which paths have to be traversed, can be taken on higher levels

(O2) *The overlap between directory rectangles should be minimized* This also decreases the number of paths to be traversed

(O3) *The margin of a directory rectangle should be minimized* Here the margin is the sum of the lengths of the edges of a rectangle Assuming fixed area, the object with the smallest margin is the square Thus minimizing the margin instead of the area, the directory rectangles will be shaped more quadratic Essentially queries with large quadratic query rectangles will profit from this optimization More important, minimization of the margin will basically improve the structure Since quadratic objects can be packed easier, the bounding boxes of a level will build smaller directory rectangles in the level above Thus clustering rectangles into bounding boxes with only little variance of the lengths of the edges will reduce the area of directory rectangles

(O4) *Storage utilization should be optimized* Higher storage utilization will generally reduce the query cost as the height of the tree will be kept low Evidently, query types with large query rectangles are influenced more since the concentration of rectangles in several nodes will have a stronger effect if the number of found keys is high

Keeping the area and overlap of a directory rectangle small, requires more freedom in the number of rectangles stored in one node Thus minimizing these parameters will be paid with lower storage utilization. Moreover, when applying (O1) or (O2) more freedom in choosing the shape is necessary Thus rectangles will be less quadratic With (O1) the overlap between directory rectangles may be affected in a positive way since the covering of the data space is reduced As for every geometric optimization, minimizing the margins will also lead to reduced storage utilization However, since more quadratic directory rectangles support packing better, it will be easier to maintain high storage utilization Obviously, the performance for queries with sufficiently large query rectangles will be affected more by the storage utilization than by the parameters of (O1)-(O3)

3. R-tree Variants

The R-tree is a dynamic structure Thus all approaches of optimizing the retrieval performance have to be applied during the insertion of a new data rectangle The insertion algorithm calls two more algorithms in which the crucial decisions for good retrieval performance are made The first is the algorithm ChooseSubtree Beginning in the root, descending to a leaf, it finds on every level the most suitable subtree to accomodate the new entry The second is the algorithm Split It is called, if ChooseSubtree ends in a node filled with the maximum number of entries M Split should distribute M+1 rectangles into two nodes in the most appropriate manner

In the following, the ChooseSubtree- and Split-algorithms, suggested in available R-tree variants are analyzed and discussed We will first consider the original R-tree as proposed by Guttman in [Gut 84]

Algorithm ChooseSubtree

CS1 Set N to be the root
CS2 If N is a leaf,
    return N
  else
    Choose the entry in N whose rectangle needs least area enlargement to include the new data Resolve ties by choosing the entry with the rectangle of smallest area
  end
CS3 Set N to be the childnode pointed to by the childpointer of the chosen entry an repeat from CS2

Obviously, the method of optimization is to minimize the area covered by a directory rectangle, i e (O1) This may also reduce the overlap and the cpu cost will be relatively low

Guttman discusses split-algorithms with exponential, quadratic and linear cost with respect to the number of entries of a node All of them are designed to minimize the area, covered by the two rectangles resulting from the split The exponential split finds the area with the global minimum, but the cpu cost is too high The others try to find approximations In his experiments, Guttman obtains nearly the same retrieval performance for the linear as for the quadratic version We implemented the R-tree in both variants However in our tests with different distributions, different overlap, variable numbers of data-entries and different combinations of M and m, the quadratic R-tree yielded much better performance than the linear version (see also section 5) Thus we will only discuss the quadratic algorithm in detail

Algorithm QuadraticSplit

[Divide a set of M+1 entries into two groups]
QS1 Invoke PickSeeds to choose two entries to be the first entries of the groups
QS2 Repeat
    DistributeEntry
  until
    all entries are distributed or
    one of the two groups has M-m+1 entries
QS3 If entries remain, assign them to the other group such that it has the minimum number m

Algorithm PickSeeds

PS1 For each pair of entries E1 and E2, compose a rectangle R including E1 rectangle and E2 rectangle
  Calculate d = area(R) - area(E1 rectangle) - area(E2 rectangle)
PS2 Choose the pair with the largest d

Algorithm DistributeEntry

DE1 Invoke PickNext to choose the next entry to be assigned
DE2 Add it to the group whose covering rectangle will have to be enlarged least to accommodate it Resolve ties by adding the entry to the group with the smallest area, then to the one with the fewer entries, then to either

Algorithm PickNext

PN1 For each entry E not yet in a group, calculate d_1 = the area increase required in the covering rectangle of Group 1 to include E Rectangle
  Calculate d_2 analogously for Group 2
PN2 Choose the entry with the maximum difference between d_1 and d_2

The algorithm PickSeeds finds the two rectangles which would waste the largest area put in one group In this sense the two rectangles are the most distant ones It is important to mention that the seeds will tend to be small too, if the rectangles to be distributed are of very different size (and) or the overlap between them is high The algorithm DistributeEntry assigns the remaining entries by the criterion of minimum area PickNext chooses the entry with the best area-goodness-value in every situation

If this algorithm starts with small seeds, problems may occur If in d-1 of the d axes a far away rectangle has nearly the same coordinates as one of the seeds, it will be distributed first Indeed, the area and the area enlargement of the created needle-like bounding rectangle will be very small, but the distance is very large This may initiate a very bad split Moreover, the algorithm tends to prefer the bounding rectangle, created from the first assignment of a rectangle to one seed Since it was enlarged, it will be larger than others Thus it needs less area enlargement to include the next entry, it will be enlarged again, and so on Another problem is, that if one group has reached the maximum number of entries M-m+1, all remaining entries are assigned to the other group without considering geometric properties Figure 1 (see section 4 3) gives an example showing all these problems The result is either a split with much overlap (fig 1c) or a split with uneven distribution of the entries reducing the storage utilization (fig 1b)

We tested the quadratic split of our R-tree implementation varying the minimum number of entries m = 20%, 30%, 35% ,40% and 45% relatively to M and obtained the best retrieval performance with m set to 40%

On the occasion of comparing the R-tree with other structures storing rectangles, Greene proposed the following alternative split-algorithm [Gre 89] To determine the appropriate path to insert a new entry she uses Guttman's original ChooseSubtree-algorithm

Algorithm Greene's-Split

[Divide a set of M+1 entries into two groups]

GS1 Invoke ChooseAxis to determine the axis perpendicular to which the split is to be performed

GS2 Invoke Distribute

Algorithm ChooseAxis

CA1 Invoke PickSeeds (see p 5) to find the two most distant rectangles of the current node

CA2 For each axis record the separation of the two seeds

CA3 Normalize the separations by dividing them by the length of the nodes enclosing rectangle along the appropriate axis

CA4 Return the axis with the greatest normalized separation

Algorithm Distribute

D1 Sort the entries by the low value of their rectangles along the chosen axis

D2 Assign the first (M+1) div 2 entries to one group, the last (M+1) div 2 entries to the other

D3 If M+1 is odd, then assign the remaining entry to the group whose enclosing rectangle will be increased least by its addition

Almost the only geometric criterion used in Greene's split algorithm is the choice of the split axis Although choosing a suitable split axis is important, our investigations show that more geometric optimization criteria have to be applied to considerably improve the retrieval performance of the R-tree In spite of a well clustering, in some situations Greene's split method cannot find the "right" axis and thus a very bad split may result Figure 2b (see p 12) depicts such a situation

4. The R*-tree

4.1 Algorithm ChooseSubtree

To solve the problem of choosing an appropriate insertion path, previous R-tree versions take only the area parameter into consideration In our investigations, we tested the parameters area, margin and overlap in different combinations, where the overlap of an entry is defined as follows

Let $E_1, \ldots, E_p$ be the entries in the current node Then

$$\text{overlap}(E_k) = \sum_{i=1, i \neq k}^{p} \text{area}(E_k.\text{Rectangle} \cap E_i.\text{Rectangle}) \quad , 1 \leq k \leq p$$

The version with the best retrieval performance is described in the following algorithm

Algorithm ChooseSubtree

CS1 Set N to be the root

CS2 If N is a leaf,
  return N
 else
  if the childpointers in N point to leaves [determine the minimum overlap cost],
   choose the entry in N whose rectangle needs least overlap enlargement to include the new data rectangle Resolve ties by choosing the entry whose rectangle needs least area enlargement,
  then
   the entry with the rectangle of smallest area
  if the childpointers in N do not point to leaves [determine the minimum area cost],
   choose the entry in N whose rectangle needs least area enlargement to include the new data rectangle Resolve ties by choosing the entry with the rectangle of smallest area
 end

CS3 Set N to be the childnode pointed to by the childpointer of the chosen entry and repeat from CS2

For choosing the best non-leaf node, alternative methods did not outperform Guttman's original algorithm For the leaf nodes, minimizing the overlap performed slightly better

In this version, the cpu cost of determining the overlap is quadratic in the number of entries, because for each entry the overlap with all other entries of the node has to be calculated However, for large node sizes we can reduce the number of entries for which the calculation has to be done, since for very distant rectangles the probability to yield the minimum overlap is very small Thus, in order to reduce the cpu cost, this part of the algorithm might be modified as follows

> [determine the *nearly* minimum overlap cost]
> Sort the rectangles in N in increasing order of their area enlargement needed to include the new data rectangle
> Let A be the group of the first p entries
> From the entries in A, considering all entries in N, choose the entry whose rectangle needs least overlap enlargement Resolve ties as described above

For two dimensions we found that with p set to 32 there is nearly no reduction of retrieval performance to state For more than two dimensions further tests have to be done Nevertheless the cpu cost remains higher than the original version of ChooseSubtree, but the number of disc accesses is reduced for the exact match query preceding each insertion and is reduced for the ChooseSubtree algorithm itself

The tests showed that the ChooseSubtree optimization improves the retrieval performance particulary in the following situation *Queries with small query rectangles on datafiles with non-uniformly distributed small rectangles or points*

In the other cases the performance of Guttman's algorithm was similar to this one Thus principally an improvement of robustness can be stated

4 2 Split of the R*-tree

The R*-tree uses the following method to find good splits Along each axis, the entries are first sorted by the lower value, then sorted by the upper value of their rectangles For each sort M-2m+2 distributions of the M+1 entries into two groups are determined, where the k-th distribution (k = 1, ,(M-2m+2)) is described as follows The first group contains the first (m-1)+k entries, the second group contains the remaining entries

For each distribution goodness values are determined Depending on these goodness values the final distribution of the entries is determined Three different goodness values and different approaches of using them in different combinations are tested experimentally

(i) area-value	area[bb(first group)] + area[bb(second group)]
(ii) margin-value	margin[bb(first group)] + margin[bb(second group)]
(iii) overlap-value	area[bb(first group) ∩ bb(second group)]

Here bb denotes the bounding box of a set of rectangles

Possible methods of processing are to determine

- the minimum over one axis or one sort
- the minimum of the sum of the goodness values over one axis or one sort
- the overall minimum

The obtained values may be applied to determine a split axis or the final distribution (on a chosen split axis) The best overall performance resulted from the following algorithm

Algorithm Split

S1 Invoke ChooseSplitAxis to determine the axis, perpendicular to which the split is performed

S2 Invoke ChooseSplitIndex to determine the best distribution into two groups along that axis

S3 Distribute the entries into two groups

Algorithm ChooseSplitAxis

CSA1 For each axis
  Sort the entries by the lower then by the upper value of their rectangles and determine all distributions as described above Compute S, the sum of all margin-values of the different distributions
 end

CSA2 Choose the axis with the minimum S as split axis

Algorithm ChooseSplitIndex

CSI1 Along the chosen split axis, choose the distribution with the minimum overlap-value Resolve ties by choosing the distribution with minimum area-value

The split algorithm is tested with m = 20%, 30%, 40% and 45% of the maximum number of entries M As ex- periments with several values of M have shown, m = 40% yields the best performance Additionally, we varied m over the life cycle of one and the same R*-tree in order to correlate the storage utilization with geometric paremeters However, even the following method did result in worse retrieval performance Compute a split using m_1 = 30% of M, then compute a split using m_2 =40% If split(m_2)yields overlap and split(m_1) does not, take split(m_1), otherwise take split(m_2)

Concerning the cost of the split algorithm of the R*-tree we will mention the following facts For each axis (dimension) the entries have to be sorted two times which requires O(M log(M)) time As an experimental cost analysis has shown, this needs about half of the cost of the split The remaining split cost is spent as follows For each axis the margin of 2*(2*(M-2m+2)) rectangles and the overlap of 2*(M-2m+2) distributions have to be calculated

4 3 Forced Reinsert

Both, R-tree and R*-tree are nondeterministic in allocating the entries onto the nodes i e different sequences of insertions will build up different trees For this reason the R-tree suffers from its old entries Data rectangles inserted during the early growth of the structure may have introduced directory rectangles, which are not suitable to guarantee a good retrieval performance in the current situation A very local reorganization of the directory rectangles is performend during a split But this is rather poor and therefore it is desirable to have a more powerful and less local instrument to reorganize the structure

The discussed problem would be maintained or even worsened, if underfilled nodes, resulting from deletion of records would be merged under the old parent Thus the known approach of treating underfilled nodes in an R-tree is to delete the node and to reinsert the orphaned entries in the corresponding level [Gut 84] This way the ChooseSubtree algorithm has a new chance of distributing entries into different nodes

Since it was to be expected, that the deletion and reinsertion of old data rectangles would improve the retrieval performance, we made the following simple experiment with the linear R-tree Insert 20000 uniformly distributed rectangles Delete the first 10000 rectangles and insert them again The result was a performance improvement of 20% up to 50%(!) depending on the types of the queries Therefore to delete randomly half of the data and then to insert it again seems to be a very simple way of tuning existing R-tree datafiles But this is a static situation, and for nearly static datafiles the pack algorithm [RL 85] is a more sophisticated approach

To achieve dynamic reorganizations, the R*-tree forces entries to be reinserted during the insertion routine The following algorithm is based on the ability of the insert routine to insert entries on every level of the tree as already required by the deletion algorithm [Gut 84] Except for the overflow treatment, it is the same as described originally by Guttman and therefore it is only sketched here

Algorithm InsertData

ID1 Invoke Insert starting with the leaf level as a parameter, to insert a new data rectangle

Algorithm Insert

I1 Invoke ChooseSubtree, with the level as a parameter, to find an appropriate node N, in which to place the new entry E

I2 If N has less than M entries, accommodate E in N
If N has M entries, invoke OverflowTreatment with the level of N as a parameter [for reinsertion or split]

I3 If OverflowTreatment was called and a split was performed, propagate OverflowTreatment upwards if necessary
If OverflowTreatment caused a split of the root, create a new root

I4 Adjust all covering rectangles in the insertion path such that they are minimum bounding boxes enclosing their children rectangles

Algorithm OverflowTreatment

```
OT1 If the level is not the root level and this is the first
    call of OverflowTreatment in the given level
    during the insertion of one data rectangle, then
        invoke ReInsert
    else
        invoke Split
    end
```

Algorithm ReInsert

RI1 For all M+1 entries of a node N, compute the distance between the centers of their rectangles and the center of the bounding rectangle of N

RI2 Sort the entries in decreasing order of their distances computed in RI1

RI3 Remove the first p entries from N and adjust the bounding rectangle of N

RI4 In the sort, defined in RI2, starting with the maximum distance (= far reinsert) or minimum distance (= close reinsert), invoke Insert to reinsert the entries

If a new data rectangle is inserted, each first overflow treatment on each level will be a reinsertion of p entries This may cause a split in the node which caused the overflow if all entries are reinserted in the same location Otherwise splits may occur in one or more other nodes, but in many situations splits are completely prevented The parameter p can be varied independently for leaf nodes and non-leaf nodes as part of performance tuning, and different values were tested experimentally The experiments have shown that p = 30% of M for leaf nodes as well as for non-leaf nodes yields the best performance Furthermore, for all data files and query files close reinsert outperforms far reinsert Close reinsert prefers the node which included the entries before, and this is intended, because its enclosing rectangle was reduced in size Thus this node has lower probability to be selected by ChooseSubtree again

Summarizing, we can say

- Forced reinsert changes entries between neighboring nodes and thus decreases the overlap
- As a side effect, storage utilization is improved
- Due to more restructuring, less splits occur
- Since the outer rectangles of a node are reinserted, the shape of the directory rectangles will be more quadratic As discussed before, this is a desirable property

Obviously, the cpu cost will be higher now since the insertion routine is called more often This is alleviated, because less splits have to be performed The experiments show that the average number of disc accesses for insertions increases only about 4% (and remains the lowest of all R-tree variants), if Forced Reinsert is applied to the R*-tree This is particularly due to the structure improving properties of the insertion algorithm

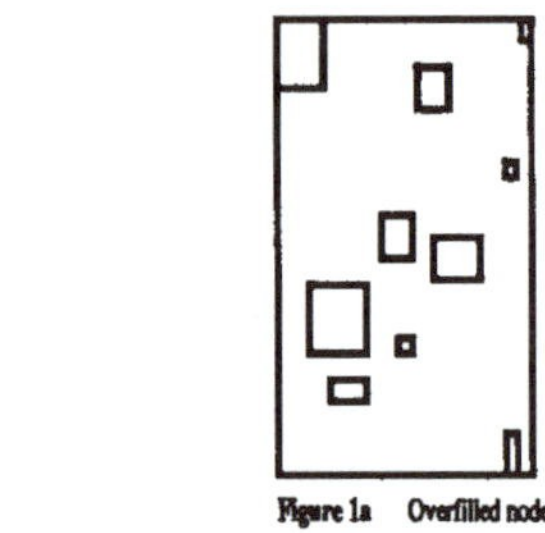

Figure 1a Overfilled node

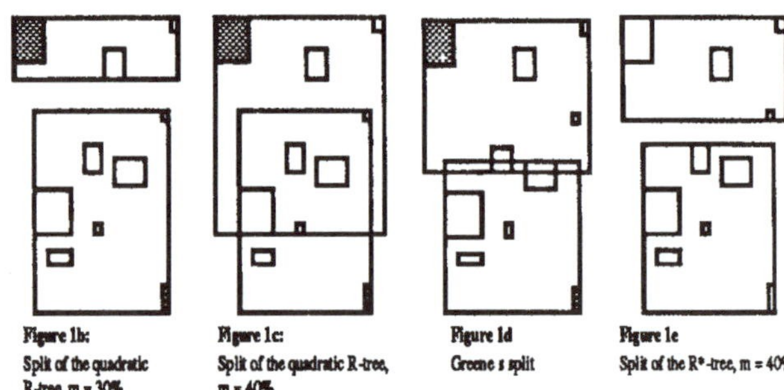

Figure 1b: Split of the quadratic R-tree, m = 30%

Figure 1c: Split of the quadratic R-tree, m = 40%

Figure 1d Greene's split

Figure 1e Split of the R*-tree, m = 40%

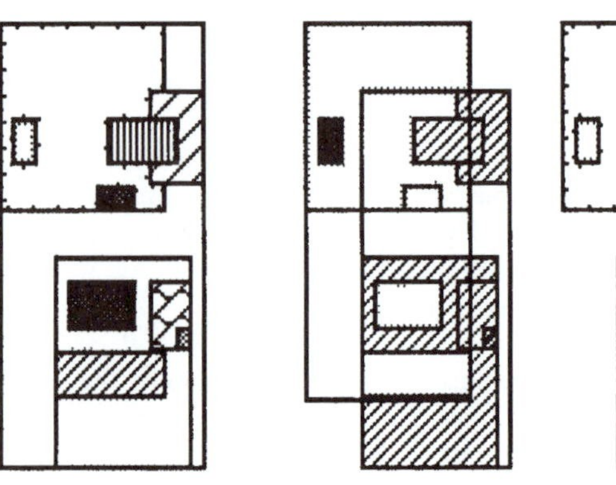

Figure 2a Overfilled node

Figure 2b: Greene's split where the splitaxis is horizontal

Figure 2c: Split of the R* tree where the splitaxis is vertical

5. Performance Comparison

5 1 Experimental Setup and Results of the Experiments

We ran the performance comparison on SUN workstations under UNIX using Modula-2 implementaions of the different R-tree variants and our R*-tree Analogously to our performance comparison of PAM's and SAM's in [KSSS 89] we keep the last accessed path of the trees in main memory If orphaned entries occur from insertions or deletions, they are stored in main memory additionally to the path

In order to keep the performance comparison manageable, we have chosen the page size for data and directory pages to be 1024 bytes which is at the lower end of realistic page sizes Using smaller page sizes, we obtain similar performance results as for much larger file sizes From the chosen page size the maximum number of entries in directory pages is 56 According to our standardized testbed we have restricted the maximum number of entries in a data page to 50

As candidates of our performance comparison we selected the R-tree with quadratic split algorithm (abbre- viation qua Gut), Greene's variant of the R-tree (Greene) and our R*-tree where the parameters of the different structures are set to the best values as described in the previous sections Additionally, we tested the most popular R-tree implementation, the variant with the linear split algorithm (lin Gut) The popularity of the linear R-tree is due to the statement in the original paper [Gut84] that no essential performance gain resulted from the quadratic version vs the linear version For the linear R-tree we found m=20% (of M) to be the variant with the best performance

To compare the performance of the four structures we selected six data files containing about 100,000 2-dimensional rectangle Each rectangle is assumed to be in the unit cube $[0,1)^2$ In the following each data file is described by the distribution of the centers of the rectangles and by the tripel (n, μ_{area} , nv_{area}) Here n denotes the number of rectangles, μ_{area} is the mean value of the area of a rectangle and $nv_{area} = \sigma_{area} / \mu_{area}$ is the normalized variance where σ_{area} denotes the variance of the areas of the rectangles Obviously, the parameter nv_{area} increases independently of the distribution the more the areas of the rectangles differ from the mean value and the average overlap is simply obtained by $n^* \mu_{area}$

(F1) **"Uniform"**

The centers of the rectangles follow a 2-dimensional independent uniform distribution

(n = 100,000, μ_{area} = 0001, nv_{area} = 9505)

(F2) **"Cluster"**

The centers follow a distribution with 640 clusters, each cluster contains about 1600 objects

(n = 99,968, μ_{area} = 00002, nv_{area} = 1 538)

(F3) **"Parcel"**

First we decompose the unit square into 100,000 disjoint rectangles Then we expand the area of each rectangle by the factor 2 5

(n = 100,000, μ_{area} = 00002504, nv_{area} = 30 3458)

(F4) **"Real-data"**

These rectangles are the minimum bounding rectangles of elevation lines from real cartography data

(n = 120,576, μ_{area} = 0000926, nv_{area} = 1 504)

(F5) **"Gaussian"**

The centers follow a 2-dimensional independent Gaussian distribution

(n = 100,000, μ_{area} = 00008, nv_{area} = 89875)

(F6) **"Mixed-Uniform"**

The centers of the rectangles follow a 2-dimensional independent uniform distribution

First we take 99,000 small rectangles with μ_{area} = 0000101 Then we add 1,000 large rectangles with μ_{area} = 001 Finally these two data files are merged to one

(n = 100,000, μ_{area} = 00002, nv_{area} = 6 778)

For each of the files (F1) - (F6) we generated queries of the following three types

- *rectangle intersection query* Given a rectangle S, find all rectangles R in the file with $R \cap S \neq \emptyset$
- *point query* Given a point P, find all rectangles R in the file with $P \in R$
- *rectangle enclosure query* Given a rectangle S, find all rectangles R in the file with $R \supseteq S$

For each of these files (F1) - (F6) we performed 400 rectangle intersection queries where the ratio of the x-extension to the y-extension uniformly varies from 0 25 to 2 25 and the centers of the query rectangles themselves are uniformly distributed in the unit cube In the following, we consider four query files (Q1) - (Q4) of 100 rectangle intersection queries each The area of the query rectangles of each query file (Q1) - (Q4) varies from 1%, 0 1%, 0 01% to 0 001% relatively to the area of the data space For the rectangle enclosure query we consider two query files (Q5) and (Q6) where the corresponding rectangles are the same as in the query files (Q3) and (Q4), respectively Additionally, we analyzed a query file (Q7) of 1,000 point queries where the query points are uniformly distributed

For each query file (Q1) - (Q7) we measured the average number of disc accesses per query In the performance comparison we use the R*-tree as a measuring stick for the other access methods, i e we standardize the number of page accesses for the queries of the R*-tree to 100% Thus we can observe the performance of the R-tree variants relative to the 100% performance of the R*-tree

To analyze the performance for building up the different R-tree variants we measured the parameters insert and stor Here insert denotes the average number of disc accesses per insertion and stor denotes the storage utilization after completely building up the files In the following table we present the results of our experiments depending on the different distributions (data files) For the R*-tree we also depict "# accesses", the average number of disk accesses per query

<u>Uniform</u>

	point	intersection				enclosure		stor	insert
		0.001	0.01	0.1	1.0	0.001	0.01		
lin Gut	225.8	212 6	207 7	183 0	144.5	224.7	248 1	64.1	7 43
qua. Gut	124.8	121.9	124.4	124.1	114.2	116 7	121.9	69 5	4.27
Greene	140 0	136 1	135 4	130 1	115 1	132.8	153.8	70.3	4.67
R*-tree	100 0	100 0	100 0	100 0	100 0	100 0	100 0	75.8	4.42
# accesses	5.26	6 04	7 63	13.29	53 42	4.85	3 66		

<u>Cluster</u>

	point	intersection				enclosure		stor	insert
		0.001	0.01	0.1	1.0	0.001	0.01		
lin Gut	250.9	231 0	219 7	176 6	136.9	247.8	249 4	61 7	6 13
qua Gut	166 1	152.7	160 7	139 1	120.4	155.4	182.9	66.9	4.97
Greene	159 9	151.8	152.2	144.3	116.9	151 6	153.2	69.2	4.32
R*-tree	100 0	100 0	100 0	100 0	100 0	100 0	100 0	72.2	3 77
# accesses	2 00	2.26	2 95	7 13	36 0	1.86	1 58		

<u>Parcel</u>

	point	intersection				enclosure		stor	insert
		0 001	0 01	0 1	1 0	0 001	0 01		
lin Gut	264 1	265 0	258 6	214.3	177.9	269 4	281.0	60.2	23 07
qua Gut	129.5	132.3	129.9	126 1	122 1	131 0	125 6	67 0	13.30
Greene	199.8	196.2	206 9	184 1	156.5	195.8	207.5	68.9	16.02
R*-tree	100 0	100.0	100 0	100 0	100 0	100 0	100 0	72.5	10 73
# accesses	5 67	6.26	7.36	13.29	36 76	5 42	4.96		

<u>Real Data</u>

	point	intersection				enclosure		stor	insert
		0.001	0.01	0.1	1.0	0.001	0.01		
lin Gut	245 6	246 7	220.8	181 6	143.8	268 1	284.1	62.9	7.30
qua Gut	147.3	153 1	143.3	132.5	116 4	158.8	160 1	68 1	5 08
Greene	147.8	144 0	146.5	130.2	115.9	155 1	169.8	69 6	5 05
R*-tree	100 0	100 0	100.0	100 0	100.0	100 0	100 0	70.5	4.22
# accesses	4 78	5.29	7.35	14 65	60.84	4.08	3 08		

<u>Gaussian</u>

	point	intersection				enclosure		stor	insert
		0.001	0.01	0.1	1.0	0.001	0.01		
lin Gut	171 1	165 6	168 1	150 1	143.8	171 1	180.2	63.8	19 12
qua Gut	116.2	108 0	116 0	117 6	119.2	106 4	106.8	68.8	14.0
Greene	123.2	118 7	131.2	122.9	114.2	120 7	130 6	69.9	11 41
R*-tree	100.0	100.0	100 0	100.0	100 0	100.0	100 0	73.8	9 15
# accesses	4.83	5.87	7 69	10.88	46 19	4.39	3.24		

<u>Mixed Uniform</u>

	point	intersection				enclosure		stor	insert
		0.001	0.01	0.1	1.0	0.001	0.01		
lin Gut	354.1	332.5	311 7	233 1	165.9	358 1	401 6	63 4	12 70
qua Gut	127 6	126.3	122.7	119 0	113 0	119 6	124.7	68 2	4 94
Greene	121 4	116 7	116 0	114.5	109.3	114 0	116.3	70 1	4.58
R*-tree	100.0	100 0	100 0	100 0	100 0	100 0	100 0	73 1	4 46
# accesses	4.87	5.51	7.27	13 76	52 06	4.44	3 69		

Additionally to the conventional queries like point query, intersection query and enclosure query we have considered the operation spatial join usually used in applications like map overlay We have defined the spatial join over two rectangle files as the set of all pairs of rectangles where the one rectangle from $file_1$ intersects the other rectangle from $file_2$

For the spatial join operation we performed the following experiments

(SJ1) $file_1$ "Parcel"-distribution with 1000 rectangles randomly selected from file (F3)
$file_2$ data file (F4)

(SJ2) $file_1$ "Parcel"-distribution with 7500 rectangles randomly selected from data file (F3)
$file_2$ 7,536 rectangles generated from elevation lines
(n = 7,536, μ_{area} = 00148, nv_{area} = 1 5)

(SJ3) $file_1$ "Parcel"-distribution with 20,000 rectangles randomly selected from data file (F3)
$file_2$ $file_1$

For these experiments we measured the number of disc accesses per operation The normalized results are presented in the following table

<u>Spatial Join</u>

	(SJ 1)	(SJ 2)	(SJ 3)
lin.Gut	296 6	229.2	257 8
qua.Gut	142 4	154 7	144 8
Greene	187.1	166.3	160 4
R*-tree	100.0	100 0	100.0

5.2 Interpretation of the Results

In table 1 for the parameters *stor* and *insert* we computed the unweighted average over all six distributions (data files) The parameter *spatial join* denotes the average over the three spatial join operations (SJ1) - (SJ3) For the average query performance we present the parameter *query average* which is averaged over all seven query files for each distribution and then averaged over all six distributions

	query average	spatial join	stor	insert
lin Gut	227 5	261 2	62 7	12 63
qua.Gut	130 0	147 3	68 1	7 76
Greene	142 3	171 3	69 7	7 67
R*-tree	100 0	100 0	73 0	6 13

Table 1 unweighted average over all distributions

The loss of information in the parameter ***query average*** is even less in table 2 where the parameter is displayed separately for each data file (F1) - (F6) as an average over all seven query files and in table 3 where the parameter query average is depicted separately for each query (Q1) - (Q7) as an average over all six data files

	gaussian	cluster	mix uni	parcel	real data	uniform
lin Gut	164 3	216 0	308 1	247.2	227.2	206 6
qua Gut	112 9	153 9	121 8	128 1	144.5	121 1
Greene	123 1	147 1	115 5	192 4	144.2	134 8
R*-tree	100 0	100 0	100 0	100 0	100 0	100 0

Table 2 unweighted average over all seven types of queries depending on the distribution

	point	intersection				enclosure		stor	insert
		0.001	0.01	0.1	1.0	0.001	0.01		
lin. Gut	251.9	242.2	231 1	189.8	152 1	256.5	274 1	62.7	12.63
qua. Gut	135.3	132.4	132.8	126.4	117 6	131.3	137.0	68.1	7.76
Greene	148 7	143.9	148 0	137.7	121.3	145.0	155.2	69 7	7 67
R*-tree	100 0	100 0	100.0	100 0	100 0	100 0	100.0	73.0	6.13

Table 3 unweighted average over all six distributions depending on the query type

First of all, the R*-tree clearly outperforms the R-tree variants in all experiments Moreover the most popular variant, the linear R-tree, performs essentially worse than all other R-trees The following remarks emphasize the superiority of the R*-tree in comparison to the R-trees

- The R*-tree is the most robust method which is underligned by the fact that for every query file and every data file less disk acesses are required than by any other variants To say it in other words, there is no experiment where the R*-tree is not the winner

- The gain in efficiency of the R*-tree for smaller query rectangles is higher than for larger query rectangles, because storage utilization gets more important for larger query rectangles This emphasizes the goodness of the order preservation of the R*-tree (i e rectangles close to each other are more likely stored together in one page)

- The maximum performance gain of the R*-tree taken over all query and data files is in comparison to the linear R-tree about 400% (i e it takes four times as long as the R*-tree !!), to Greene's R-tree about 200% and to the quadratic R-tree 180%

- As expected, the R*-tree has the best storage utilization

- Surprisingly in spite of using the concept of Forced Reinsert, the average insertion cost is not increased, but essentially decreased regarding the R-tree variants

- The average performance gain for the spatial join operation is higher than for the other queries The quadratic R-tree, Greene's R-tree and the linear R-tree require 147%, 171% and 261% of the disc accesses of the R*-tree, respectively, averaged over all spatial join operations

5.3 The R*-tree: an efficient point access method

An important requirement for a spatial access method is to handle both spatial objects and point objects efficiently Points can be considered as degenerated rectangles and in most applications rectangles are very small relatively to the data space If a SAM is also an efficient PAM, this would underlign the robustness of the SAM Moreover, in many applications it is desirable to support additionally to the bounding rectangle of an object at least an atomar key with one access method

Therefore we ran the different R-tree variants and our R*-tree against a benchmark proposed and used for point access methods The reader interested in the details of this benchmark is referred to [KSSS 89] In this paper, let us mention that the benchmark incorporates seven data files of highly correlated 2-dimensiuonal points Each data file contains about 100,000 records For each data file we considered five query files each of them containing 20 queries The first query files contain range queries specified by square shaped rectangles of size 0 1%, 1% and 10% relatively to the data space The other two query files contain partial match queries where in the one only the x-value and in the other only the y-value is specified, respectively

Similar to the previous section, we measured the storage utilization (stor), the average insertion cost (insert) and the average query cost averaged over all query and data files The results are presented in table 4 where we included the 2-level grid file ([NHS84], [Hin85]), a very popular point access method

	query average	stor	insert
lin.Gut	233.1	64.1	7 34
qua.Gut	175.9	67.8	4.51
Greene	237.8	69.0	5.20
GRID	127.6	58.3	2.56
R*-tree	100 0	70.9	3.36

Table 4: unweighted average over all seven distributions

We were positively surprised by our results The performance gain of the R*-tree over the R-tree variants is considerably higher for points than for rectangles In particular Greene's R-tree is very inefficient for point data It requires even more accesses than the linear R-tree and 138% more than the R*-tree, whereas the quadratic R-tree requires 75% more disc accesses than the R*-tree Nevertheless, we had expected that PAMs like the 2-level grid file would perform better than the R*-tree However in the over all average the 2-level grid file performs essentially worse than the R*-tree for point data An advantage of the grid file is the low average insertion cost In that sense it might be more suitable in an insertion-intensive application Let us mention that the complexity of the algorithms of the R*-trees is rather low in comparison to highly tuned PAMs

6 Conclusions

The experimental comparison pointed out that the R*-tree proposed in this paper can efficiently be used as an access method in database systems organizing both, multidimensional points and spatial data As demonstrated in an extensive performance comparison with rectangle data, the R*-tree clearly outperforms Greene's R-tree, the quadratic R-tree and the popular linear R-tree in all experiments Moreover, for point data the gain in performance of the R*-tree over the other variants is increased Additionally, the R*-tree performs essentially better than the 2-level grid file for point data

The new concepts incorporated in the R*-tree are based on the reduction of the area, margin and overlap of the directory rectangles Since all three values are reduced, the R*-tree is very robust against ugly data distributions Furthermore, due to the fact of the concept of Forced Reinsert, splits can be prevented, the structure is reorganized dynamically and storage utilization is higher than for other R-tree variants The average insertion cost of the R*-tree is lower than for the well known R-trees Although the R*-tree outperforms its competitors, the cost for the implementation of the R*-tree is only slightly higher than for the other R-trees

In our future work, the we will investigate whether the fan out can be increased by prefixes or by using the grid approximation as proposed in [SK 90] Moreover, we are generalizing the R*-tree to handle polygons efficiently

References:

[Gre 89] D Greene 'An Implementation and Performance Analysis of Spatial Data Access Methods', Proc 5th Int Conf on Data Engineering, 606-615, 1989

[Gut 84] A Guttman 'R-trees a dynamic index structure for spatial searching', Proc ACM SIGMOD Int Conf on Management of Data, 47-57, 1984

[Hin 85] K Hinrichs 'The grid file system implementation and case studies for applications', Dissertation No 7734, Eidgenössische Technische Hochschule (ETH), Zuerich, 1985

[Knu 73] D Knuth 'The art of computer programming', Vol 3 sorting and searching, Addison-Wesley Publ Co , Reading, Mass , 1973

[KSSS 89] H P Kriegel, M Schiwietz, R Schneider, B Seeger 'Performance comparison of point and spatial access methods', Proc Symp on the Design and Implementation of Large Spatial Databases', Santa Barbara, 1989, Lecture Notes in Computer Science

[NHS 84] J Nievergelt, H Hinterberger, K C Sevcik 'The grid file an adaptable, symmetric multikey file structure', ACM Trans on Database Systems, Vol 9, 1, 38-71, 1984

[RL 85] N Roussopoulos, D Leifker 'Direct spatial search on pictorial databases using packed R-trees', Proc ACM SIGMOD Int Conf on Managment of Data, 17-31, 1985

[SK 88] B Seeger, H P Kriegel 'Design and implementation of spatial access methods', Proc 14th Int Conf on Very Large Databases, 360-371, 1988

[SK 90] B Seeger, H P Kriegel 'The design and implementation of the buddy tree', Computer Science Technical Report 3/90, University of Bremen, submitted for publication, 1990

Operating System Support for Database Management

Michael Stonebraker
University of California, Berkeley

SUMMARY: Several operating system services are examined with a view toward their applicability to support of database management functions. These services include buffer pool management; the file system; scheduling, process management, and interprocess communication; and consistency control.

1. Introduction

Database management systems (DBMS) provide higher level user support than conventional operating systems. The DBMS designer must work in the context of the OS he/she is faced with. Different operating systems are designed for different use. In this paper we examine several popular operating system services and indicate whether they are appropriate for support of database management functions. Often we will see that the wrong service is provided or that severe performance problems exist. When possible, we offer some suggestions concerning improvements. In the next several sections we look at the services provided by buffer pool management; the file system; scheduling, process management, and interprocess communication; and consistency control. We then conclude with a discussion of the merits of including all files in a paged virtual memory.

The examples in this paper are drawn primarily from the UNIX operating system [17] and the INGRES relational database system [19, 20] which was designed for use with UNIX. Most of the points made for this environment have general applicability to other operating systems and data managers.

2. Buffer Pool Management

Many modern operating systems provide a main memory cache for the file system. Figure 1 illustrates this service. In brief, UNIX provides a buffer pool whose size is set when the operating system is compiled. Then, all file I/O is handled through this cache. A file read (e.g., read X in Figure 1) returns data directly from a block in the cache, if possible; otherwise, it causes a block to be "pushed" to disk and replaced by the desired block. In Figure 1 we show block Y being pushed to make room for block X. A file write simply moves data into the cache; at some later time the buffer manager writes the block to the disk. The UNIX buffer manager used the popular LRU [15] replacement strategy. Finally, when UNIX detects sequential access to a file, it prefetches blocks before they are requested.

Conceptually, this service is desirable because blocks for which there is so-called *locality of reference* [15, 18] will remain in the cache over repeated reads and writes. However, the problems enumerated in the following subsections arise in using this service for database management.

This research was sponsored by U.S. Air Force Office of Scientific Research Grant 78-3596, U.S. Army Research Office Grant DAAG29-76-G-0245, Naval Electronics Systems Command Contract N00039-78-G-0013, and National Science Foundation Grant MCS75-03839-A01.
Key words and phrases: database management, operating systems, buffer management, file systems, scheduling, interprocess communication
CR Categories: 3.50, 3.70, 4.22, 4.33, 4.34, 4.35
Author's address: M. Stonebraker, Dept. of Electrical Engineering and Computer Sciences, University of California, Berkeley, CA 94720.

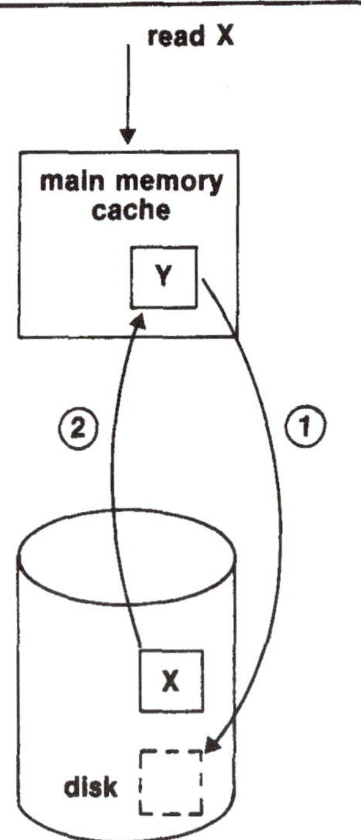

Fig. 1. Structure of a Cache.

2.1 Performance

The overhead to fetch a block from the buffer pool manager usually includes that of a system call and a core-to-core move. For UNIX on a PDP-11/70 the cost to fetch 512 bytes exceeds 5,000 instructions. To fetch 1 byte from the buffer pool requires about 1,800 instructions. It appears that these numbers are somewhat higher for UNIX than other contemporary operating systems. Moreover, they can be cut somewhat for VAX 11/780 hardware [10]. It is hoped that this trend toward lower overhead access will continue.

However, many DBMSs including INGRES [20] and System R [4] choose to put a DBMS managed buffer pool in user space to reduce overhead. Hence, each of these systems has gone to the trouble of constructing its own buffer pool manager to enhance performance.

In order for an operating system (OS) provided buffer pool manager to be attractive, the access overhead must be cut to a few hundred instructions. The trend toward providing the file system as a part of shared virtual memory (e.g., Pilot [16]) may provide a solution to this problem. This topic is examined in detail in Section 6.

2.2 LRU Replacement

Although the folklore indicates that LRU is a generally good tactic for buffer management, it appears to perform only marginally in a database environment. Database access in INGRES is a combination of:

(1) sequential access to blocks which will not be rereferenced;
(2) sequential access to blocks which will be cyclically rereferenced;
(3) random access to blocks which will not be referenced again;
(4) random access to blocks for which there is a nonzero probability of rereference.

Although LRU works well for case 4, it is a bad strategy for other situations. Since a DBMS knows which blocks are in each category, it can use a composite strategy. For case 4 it should use LRU while for 1 and 3 it should use *toss immediately*. For blocks in class 3 the reference pattern is 1, 2, 3, . . . , *n*, 1, 2, 3, ... Clearly, LRU is the worst possible replacement algorithm for this situation. Unless all *n* pages can be kept in the cache, the strategy should be to toss immediately. Initial studies [9] suggest that the miss ratio can be cut 10–15% by a DBMS specific algorithm.

In order for an OS to provide buffer management, some means must be found to allow it to accept "advice" from an application program (e.g., a DBMS) concerning the replacement strategy. Designing a clean buffer management interface with this feature would be an interesting problem.

2.3 Prefetch

Although UNIX correctly prefetches pages when sequential access is detected, there are important instances in which it fails.

Except in rare cases INGRES at (or very shortly after) the beginning of its examination of a block knows exactly which block it will access next. Unfortunately, this block is not necessarily the next one in logical file order. Hence, there is no way for an OS to implement the correct prefetch strategy.

2.4 Crash Recovery

An important DBMS service is to provide recovery from hard and soft crashes. The desired effect is for a unit of work (a transaction) which may be quite large and span multiple files to be either completely done or look like it had never started.

The way many DBMSs provide this service is to maintain an *intentions list*. When the intentions list is complete, a *commit flag* is set. The last step of a transaction is to process the intentions list making the actual updates. The DBMS makes the last operation idempotent (i.e., it generates the same final outcome no matter how many times the intentions list is processed) by careful programming. The general procedure is described in [6, 13]. An alternate process is to do updates as they are found and maintain a log of *before images* so that backout is possible.

During recovery from a crash the commit flag is examined. If it is set, the DBMS recovery utility processes the intentions list to correctly install the changes made by updates in progress at the time of the crash. If the flag is not set, the utility removes the intentions list, thereby backing out the transaction. The impact of crash recovery on the buffer pool manager is the following.

The page on which the commit flag exists must be forced to disk after all pages in the intentions list. Moreover, the transaction is not reliably committed until the commit flag is forced out to the disk, and no response can be given to the person submitting the transaction until this time.

The service required from an OS buffer manager is a *selected force out* which would push the intentions list and the commit flag to disk in the proper order. Such a service is not present in any buffer manager known to us.

2.5 Summary

Although it is possible to provide an OS buffer manager with the required features, none currently exists, at least to our knowledge. Designing such a facility with prefetch advice, block management advice, and selected force out would be an interesting exercise. It would be of interest in the context of both a paged virtual memory and an ordinary file system.

The strategy used by most DBMSs (for example, System R [4] and IMS [8]) is to maintain a separate cache in user space. This buffer pool is managed by a DBMS specific algorithm to circumvent the problems mentioned in this section. The result is a "not quite right" service provided by the OS going unused and a comparable application specific service being provided by the DBMS. Throughout this paper we will see variations on this theme in several service delivery areas.

3. The File System

The file system provided by UNIX supports objects (files) which are character arrays of dynamically varying size. On top of this abstraction, a DBMS can provide whatever higher level objects it wishes.

This is one of two popular approaches to file systems; the second is to provide a record management system inside the OS (e.g., RMS-11 for DEC machines or Enscribe for Tandem machines). In this approach structured files are provided (with or without variable length records). Moreover, efficient access is often supported for fetching records corresponding to a user supplied value (or key) for a designated field or fields. Multilevel directories, hashing, and secondary indexes are often used to provide this service.

The point to be made in this section is that the second service, which is what a DBMS wants, is not always efficient when constructed on top of a character array object. The following subsections explain why.

3.1 Physical Contiguity

The character array object can usually be expanded one block at a time. Often the result is blocks of a given file scattered over a disk volume. Hence, the next logical block in a file is not necessarily physically close to the previous one. Since a DBMS does considerable sequential access, the result is considerable disk arm movement.

The desired service is for blocks to be stored physically contiguous and a whole collection to be read when sequential access is desired. This naturally leads a DBMS to prefer a so-called extent based file system (e.g., VSAM [11]) to one which scatters blocks. Of course, such files must grow an extent at a time rather than a block at a time.

3.2 Tree Structured File Systems

UNIX implements two services by means of data structures which are trees. The blocks in a given file are kept track of in a tree (of indirect blocks) pointed to by a file control block (*i*-node). Second, the files in a given mounted file system have a user visible hierarchical structure composed of directories, subdirectories, etc. This is implemented by a second tree. A DBMS such as INGRES then adds a third tree structure to support keyed access via a multilevel directory structure (e.g., ISAM [7], B-trees [1, 12], VSAM [11], etc.).

Clearly, one tree with all three kinds of information is more efficient than three separately managed trees. The extra overhead for three separate trees is probably substantial.

3.3 Summary

It is clear that a character array is not a useful object to a DBMS. Rather, it is the abstraction presumably desired by language processors, editors, etc. Instead of providing records management on top of character arrays, it is possible to do the converse; the only issue is one of efficiency. Moreover, editors can possibly use records management structures as efficiently as those they create themselves [2]. It is our feeling that OS designers should contemplate providing DBMS facilities as lower level objects and character arrays as higher level ones. This philosophy has already been presented [5].

4. Scheduling, Process Management, and Interprocess Communication

Often, the simplest way to organize a multiuser database system is to have one OS process per user; i.e., each concurrent database user runs in a separate process. It is hoped that all users will share the same copy of the code segment of the database system and perhaps one or more data segments. In particular, a DBMS buffer pool and lock table should be handled as a shared segment. The above structure is followed by System R and, in part, by INGRES. Since UNIX has no shared data segments, INGRES must put the lock table inside the operating system and provide buffering private to each user.

The alternative organization is to allocate one run-time database process which acts as a *server*. All concurrent users send messages to this server with work requests. The one run-time server schedules requests through its own mechanisms and may support its own multitasking system. This organization is followed by Enscribe [21]. Figure 2 shows both possibilities.

Although Lauer [14] points out that the two methods are equally viable in a conceptual sense, the design of most operating systems strongly favors the first approach. For example, UNIX contains a message system (pipes) which is incompatible with the notion of a server process. Hence, it forces the use of the first alternative. There are at least two problems with the process-per-user approach.

4.1 Performance

Every time a run-time database process issues an I/O request that cannot be satisfied by data in the buffer pool, a task switch is inevita-

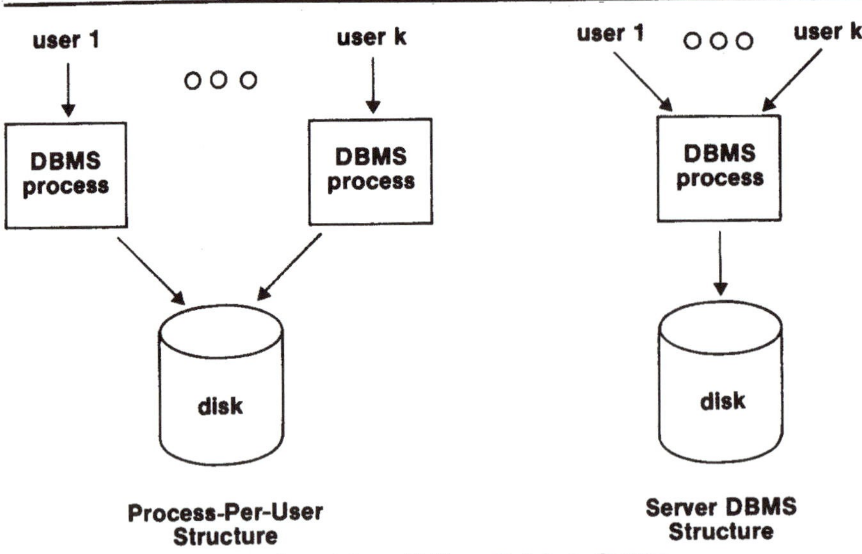

Fig. 2. Two Approaches to Organizing a Multiuser Database System.

ble. The DBMS suspends while waiting for required data and another process is run. It is possible to make task switches very efficiently, and some operating systems can perform a task switch in a few hundred instructions. However, many operating systems have "large" processes, i.e., ones with a great deal of state information (e.g., accounting) and a sophisticated scheduler. This tends to cause task switches costing a thousand instructions or more. This is a high price to pay for a buffer pool miss.

4.2 Critical Sections

Blasgen [3] has pointed out that some DBMS processes have critical sections. If the buffer pool is a shared data segment, then portions of the buffer pool manager are necessarily critical sections. System R handles critical sections by setting and releasing short-term locks which basically simulate semaphores. A problem arises if the operating system scheduler deschedules a database process while it is holding such a lock. All other database processes cannot execute very long without accessing the buffer pool. Hence, they quickly queue up behind the locked resource. Although the probability of this occurring is low, the resulting convoy [3] has a devastating effect on performance.

As a result of these two problems with the process-per-user model, one might expect the server model to be especially attractive. The following subsection explores this point of view.

4.3 The Server Model

A server model becomes viable if the operating system provides a message facility which allows *n* processes to originate messages to a single destination process. However, such a server must do its own scheduling and multitasking. This involves a painful duplication of operating system facilities. In order to avoid such duplication, one must resort to the following tactics.

One can avoid multitasking and a scheduler by a first-come-first-served server with no internal parallelism. A work request would be read from the message system and executed to completion before the next one was started. This approach makes little sense if there is more than one physical disk. Each work request will tend to have one disk read outstanding at any instant. Hence, at most one disk will be active with a non-multitasking server. Even with a single disk, a long work request will be processed to completion while shorter requests must wait. The penalty on average response time may be considerable [18].

To achieve internal parallelism yet avoid multitasking, one could have user processes send work requests to one of perhaps several common servers as noted in Figure 3. However, such servers would have to share a lock table and are only slightly different from the shared code process-per-user model. Alternately, one could have a collection of servers, each of which would send low-level requests to a group of disk processes which actually peform the I/O and handle locking as suggested in Figure 4. A disk process would process requests in first-in-first-out order. Although this organization appears potentially desirable, it still may have the response time penalty mentioned above. Moreover, it results in one message per I/O request. In reality one has traded a task switch per I/O for a message per I/O; the latter may turn out to be more expensive than the former. In the next subsection, we discuss message costs in more detail.

4.4 Performance of Message Systems

Although we have never been offered a good explanation of why messages are so expensive, the fact remains that in most operating systems the cost for a round-trip message is several thousand instructions. For example, in PDP-11/70 UNIX the number is about 5,000. As a result, care must be exercised in a DBMS to avoid overuse of a facility that is not cheap. Consequently, viable DBMS organizations will sometimes be rejected because of excessive message overhead.

4.5 Summary

There appears to be no way out of the scheduling dilemma; both the server model and the individual process model seem unattractive. The basic problem is at least, in part, the overhead in some operating systems of task switches and messages. Either operating system designers must make these facilities cheaper or provide special *fast path* functions for DBMS consumers. If this does not happen, DBMS designers will presumably continue the present practice: implementing their own multitasking, scheduling, and message systems entirely in user space. The result is a "mini" operating system running in user space in addition to a DBMS.

One ultimate solution to task-switch overhead might be for an operating system to create a special scheduling class for the DBMS and other "favored" users. Processes in this class would never be forcibly descheduled but might voluntarily relinquish the CPU at appropriate intervals. This would solve the convoy problem mentioned in Section 4.2. Moreover, such special processes might also be provided with a fast path through the task switch/scheduler loop to pass control to one of their sibling processes. Hence, a DBMS process could pass control to another DBMS process at low overhead.

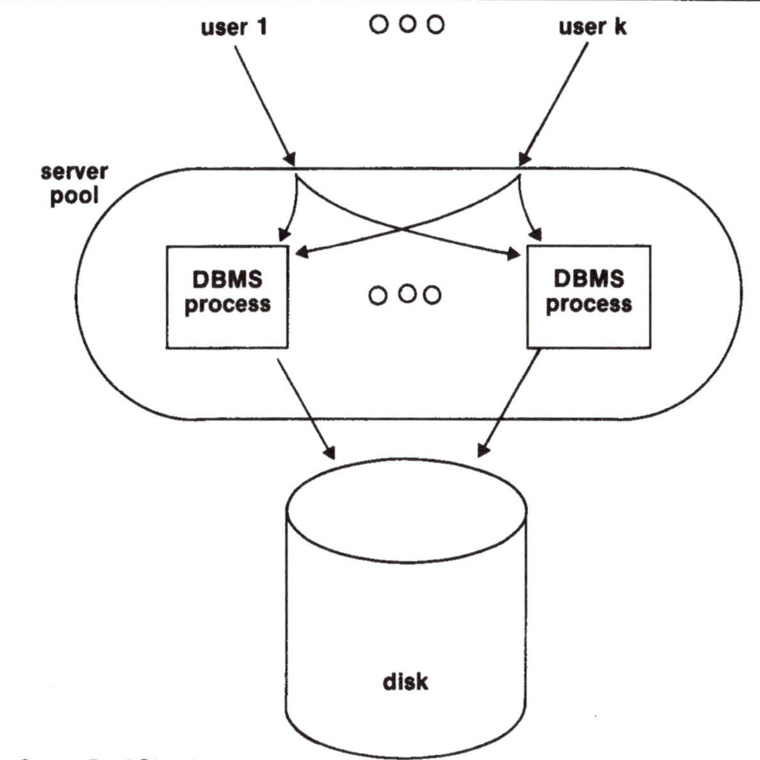

Fig. 3. Server Pool Structure.

5. Consistency Control

The services provided by an operating system in this area include the ability to lock objects for shared or exclusive access and support for crash recovery. Although most operating systems provide locking for files, there are fewer which support finer granularity locks, such as those on pages or records. Such smaller locks are deemed essential in some database environments.

Moreover, many operating systems provide some cleanup after crashes. If they do not offer support for database transactions as discussed in Section 2.4, then a DBMS must provide transaction crash recovery on top of whatever is supplied.

It has sometimes been suggested that both concurrency control and crash recovery for transactions be provided entirely inside the operating system (e.g., [13]). Conceptually, they should be at least as efficient as if provided in user space. The only problem with this approach is buffer management. If a DBMS provides buffer management in addition to whatever is supplied by the operating system, then transaction management by the operating system is impacted as discussed in the following subsections.

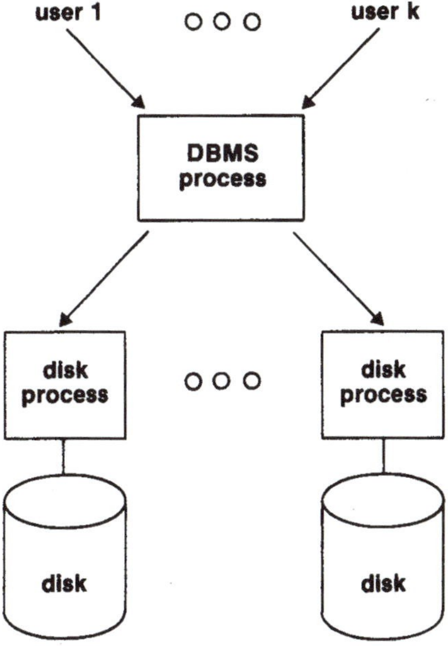

Fig. 4. Disk Server Structure.

5.1 Commit Point

When a database transaction commits, a user space buffer manager must ensure that all appropriate blocks are flushed and a commit delivered to the operating system. Hence, the buffer manager cannot be immune from knowledge of transactions, and operating system functions are duplicated.

5.2 Ordering Dependencies

Consider the following employee data:

Empname	*Salary*	*Manager*
Smith	10,000	Brown
Jones	9,000	None
Brown	11,000	Jones

and the update which gives a 20% pay cut to all employees who earn more than their managers. Presumably, Brown will be the only employee to receive a decrease, although there are alternative semantic definitions.

Suppose the DBMS updates the data set as it finds "overpaid" employees, depending on the operating system to provide backout or recover-forward on crashes. If so,

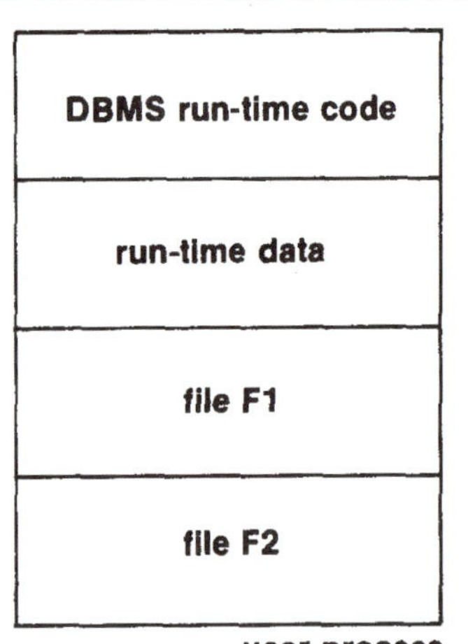

Fig. 5. Binding Files into an Address Space.

Brown might be updated before Smith was examined, and as a result, Smith would also receive the pay cut. It is clearly undesirable to have the outcome of an update depend on the order of execution.

If the operating system maintains the buffer pool and an intentions list for crash recovery, it can avoid this problem [19]. However, if there is a buffer pool manager in user space, it must maintain its own intentions list in order to properly process this update. Again, operating system facilities are being duplicated.

5.3 Summary

It is certainly possible to have buffering, concurrency control, and crash recovery all provided by the operating system. In order for the system to be successful, however, the performance problems mentioned in Section 2 must be overcome. It is also reasonable to consider having all 3 services provided by the DBMS in user space. However, if buffering remains in user space and consistency control does not, then much code duplication appears inevitable. Presumably, this will cause performance problems in addition to increased human effort.

6. Paged Virtual Memory

It is often claimed that the appropriate operating system tactic for database management support is to bind files into a user's paged virtual address space. In Figure 5 we show the address space of a process containing code to be executed, data that the code uses, and the files F1 and F2. Such files can be referenced by a program as if they are program variables. Consequently, a user never needs to do explicit reads or writes; he can depend on the paging facilities of the OS to move his file blocks into and out of main memory. Here, we briefly discuss the problems inherent in this approach.

6.1 Large Files

Any virtual memory scheme must handle files which are large objects. Popular paging hardware creates an overhead of 4 bytes per 4,096-byte page. Consequently, a 100M-byte file will have an overhead of 100K bytes for the page table. Although main memory is decreasing in cost, it may not be reasonable to assume that a page table of this size is entirely resident in primary memory. Therefore, there is the possibility that an I/O operation will induce two page faults: one for the page containing the page table for the data in question and one on the data itself. To avoid the second fault, one must *wire down* a large page table in main memory.

Conventional file systems include the information contained in the page table in a file control block. Especially in extent-based file systems, a very compact representation of this information is possible. A run of 1,000 consecutive blocks can be represented as a starting block and a length field. However, a page table for this information would store each of the 1,000 addresses even though each differs by just one from its predecessor. Consequently, a file control block is usually made main memory resident at the time the file is opened. As a result, the second I/O need never be paid.

The alternative is to bind *chunks* of a file into one's address space. Not only does this provide a multiuser DBMS with a substantial bookkeeping problem concerning whether needed data is currently addressable, but it also may require a number of bind-unbind pairs in a transaction. Since the overhead of a bind is likely to be comparable to that of a file open, this may substantially slow down performance.

It is an open question whether or not novel paging organizations can assist in solving the problems mentioned in this section.

6.2 Buffering

All of the problems discussed in Section 2 concerning buffering (e.g., prefetch, non-LRU management, and selected force out) exist in a paged virtual memory context. How they can be cleanly handled in this context is another unanswered question.

7. Conclusions

The bottom line is that operating system services in many existing systems are either too slow or inappropriate. Current DBMSs usually provide their own and make little or no use of those offered by the operating system. It is important that future operating system designers become more sensitive to DBMS needs.

A DBMS would prefer a small efficient operating system with only desired services. Of those currently available, the so-called *real-time* operating systems which efficiently provide minimal facilities come closest to this ideal. On the other hand, most general-purpose operating systems offer all things to all people at much higher overhead. It is our hope that future operating systems will be able to provide both sets of services in one environment.

References

1. Bayer, R. Organization and maintenance of large ordered indices. Proc. ACM-SIGFIDET Workshop on Data Description and Access, Houston, Texas, Nov. 1970. This paper defines a particular form of a balanced *n*-ary tree, called a B-tree. Algorithms to maintain this structure on inserts and deletes are presented. The original paper on this popular file organization tactic.

2. Birss, E. Hewlett-Packard Corp., General Syst. Div. (private communication).

3. Blasgen, M., et al. The convoy phenomenon. *Operating Systs. Rev. 13*, 2 (April 1979), 20–25. This article points out the problem with descheduling a process which has a short-term lock on an object which other processes require regularly. The impact on performance is noted and possible solutions proposed.

COMPUTING PRACTICES

4. Blasgen, M., et al. System R: An architectural update. Rep. RJ 2581, IBM Res. Ctr., San Jose, Calif., July 1979. Blasgen describes the architecture of System R, a novel full function relational database manager implemented at IBM Research. The discussion centers on the changes made since the original System R paper was published in 1976.

5. Epstein, R., and Hawthorn, P. Design decisions for the Intelligent Database Machine. Proc. Nat. Comptr. Conf., Anaheim, Calif., May 1980, pp. 237–241. An overview of the philosophy of the Intelligent Database Machine is presented. This system provides a database manager on a dedicated "back end" computer which can be attached to a variety of host machines.

6. Gray, J. Notes on operating systems. Report RJ 3120, IBM Res. Ctr., San Jose, Calif., Oct. 1978. A definitive report on locking and recovery in a database system. It pulls together most of the ideas on these subjects including two-phase protocols, write ahead log, and variable granularity locks. Should be read every six months by anyone interested in these matters.

7. IBM Corp. *OS ISAM Logic.* GY28-6618, IBM, White Plains, N.Y., June 1966.

8. IBM Corp. *IMS-VS General Information Manual.* GH20-1260, IBM, White Plains, N.Y., April 1974.

9. Kaplan, J. Buffer management policies in a database system. M.S. Th., Univ. of Calif., Berkeley, Calif., 1980. This thesis simulates various non-LRU buffer management policies on traced data obtained from the INGRES database system. It concludes that the miss rate can be cut 10–15% by a DBMS specific algorithm compared to LRU management.

10. Kashtan, D. UNIX and VMS: Some performance comparisons. SRI Internat., Menlo Park, Calif. (unpublished working paper). Kashtan's paper contains benchmark timings of operating system commands in UNIX and VMS for DEC PDP-11/780 computers. These include timings of file reads, event flags, task switches, and pipes.

11. Keehn, D., and Lacy, J. VSAM data set design parameters. *IBM Systs. J.* (Sept. 1974).

12. Knuth, D. *The Art of Computer Programming, Vol. 3: Sorting and Searching.* Addison Wesley, Reading, Mass., 1978.

13. Lampson, B., and Sturgis, H. Crash recovery in a distributed system. Xerox Res. Ctr., Palo Alto, Calif., 1976 (working paper). The first paper to present the now popular two-phase commit protocol. Also, an interesting model of computer system crashes is discussed and the notion of "safe" storage suggested.

14. Lauer, H., and Needham, R. On the duality of operating system structures. *Operating Systs. Rev. 13*, 2 (April 1979), 3–19. This article explores in detail the "process-per-user" approach to operating systems versus the "server model." It argues that they are inherently dual of each other and that either should be implementable as efficiently as the other. Very interesting reading.

15. Mattson, R., et al. Evaluation techniques for storage hierarchies. *IBM Systs. J.* (June 1970). Discusses buffer management in detail. The paper presents and analyzes serveral policies including FIFO, LRU, OPT, and RANDOM.

16. Redell, D., et al. Pilot: An operating system for a personal computer. *Comm. ACM 23*, 2 (Feb. 1980), 81–92. Redell et al. focus on Pilot, the operating system for Xerox Alto computers. It is closely coupled with Mesa and makes interesting choices in areas like protection that are appropriate for a personal computer.

17. Ritchie, D., and Thompson, K. The UNIX time-sharing system. *Comm. ACM 17*, 7 (July 1974), 365–375. The original paper describing UNIX, an operating system for PDP-11 computers. Novel points include accessing files, physical devices, and pipes in a uniform way and running the command-line interpreter as a user program. Strongly recommended reading.

18. Shaw, A. *The Logical Design of Operating Systetms.* Prentice-Hall, Englewood Cliffs, N.J. 1974.

19. Stonebraker, M., et al. The design and implementation of INGRES. *ACM Trans. Database Systs. 1*, 3 (Sept. 1976), 189–222. The original paper describing the structure of the INGRES database management system, a relational data manager for PDP-11 computers.

20. Stonebraker, M. Retrospection on a database system. *ACM Trans. Database Systs. 5*, 2 (June 1980), 225–240. A self-critique of the INGRES system by one of its designers. The article discusses design flaws in the system and indicates the historical progression of the project.

21. Tandem Computers. *Enscribe Reference Manual.* Tandem, Cupertino, Calif., Aug. 1979.

The Five-Minute Rule Ten Years Later, and Other Computer Storage Rules of Thumb

Jim Gray, Goetz Graefe
Microsoft Research, 301 Howard St. #830, SF, CA 94105
{Gray, GoetzG}@Microsoft.com

Abstract:

Simple economic and performance arguments suggest appropriate lifetimes for main memory pages and suggest optimal page sizes. The fundamental tradeoffs are the prices and bandwidths of RAMs and disks. The analysis indicates that with today's technology, five minutes is a good lifetime for randomly accessed pages, one minute is a good lifetime for two-pass sequentially accessed pages, and 16 KB is a good size for index pages. These rules-of-thumb change in predictable ways as technology ratios change. They also motivate the importance of the new *Kaps, Maps, Scans,* and *$/Kaps, $/Maps, $/TBscan* metrics.

1. The Five-Minute Rule Ten Years Later

All aspects of storage performance are improving, but different aspects are improving at different rates. The charts in Figure 1 roughly characterize the performance improvements of disk systems over time. The caption describes each chart.

In 1986, randomly accessed pages obeyed the *five-minute rule* [1]: pages referenced every five minutes should have been kept in memory rather than reading them from disk each time. Actually, the break-even point was 100 seconds but the rule anticipated that future technology ratios would move the break-even point to five minutes.

The five-minute rule is based on the tradeoff between the cost of RAM (e.g., DRAM) and the cost of disk accesses. The tradeoff is that caching pages in the extra memory can save disk IOs. The break-even point is met when the rent on the extra memory for cache ($/page/sec) exactly matches the savings in disk accesses per second ($/disk_access/sec). The break even time is computed as:

$$BreakEvenReferenceInterval\ (seconds) = \frac{PagesPerMBofRAM}{AccessPerSecondPerDisk} \times \frac{PricePerDiskDrive}{PricePerMBofRAM} \qquad (1)$$

The disk price includes the cost of the cabinets and controllers (typically 30% extra.) The equations in [1] were more complex because they did not realize that you could factor out the depreciation period.

The price and performance from a recent DELL TPC-C benchmark [2] gives the following parameters for Equation 1:

PagesPerMBofRAM = 128 pages/MB (8KB pages)
AccessesPerSecondPerDisk = 64 access/sec/disk
PricePerDiskDrive = 2000 $/disk (9GB + controller)
PricePerMBofRAM = 15 $/MB_DRAM

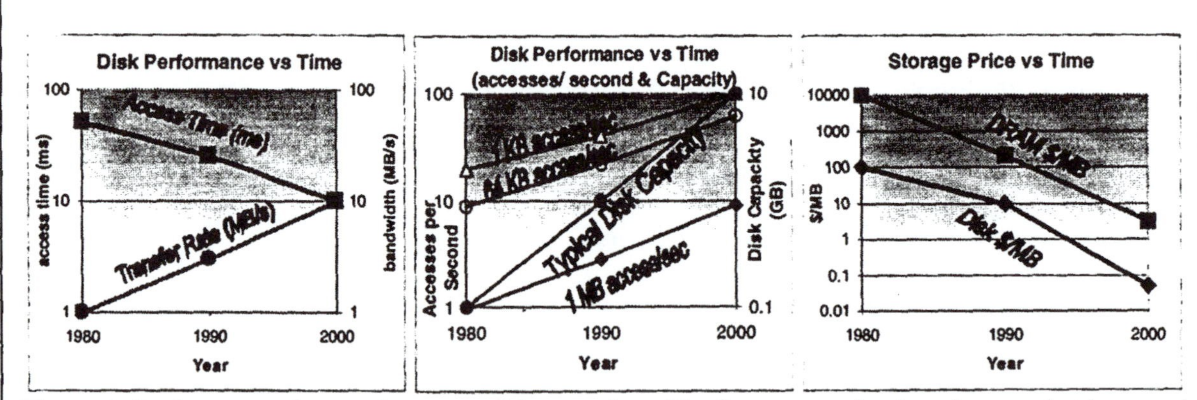

Figure 1: Performance of magnetic storage disks over time. The first two graphs show features that improved 10x or 100x while the third graph shows features that improved 10,000x in the same time. The graphs show that access times have improved relatively little, while prices have dropped by a factor of 10,000; unit capacity and accesses per second have grown by a factor of 100. Higher bandwidth and cheaper DRAM buffers have allowed larger pages. That is one theme of this paper.

Evaluating Equation 1 with these values gives a reference interval of 266 seconds -- about five minutes[1]. So, even in 1997, data referenced every five minutes should be kept in main memory.

Prices for the same equipment vary enormously, but all the categories we have examined follow something like a five-minute rule. Server hardware prices are often three times higher than "street prices" for the same components. DEC Polaris RAM is half the price of DELL. Recent TPC-C Compaq reports have 3x higher RAM prices (47$/MB) and 1.5x higher disk prices (3129$/drive) giving a two-minute rule. The March 1997 SUN+Oracle TPC-C benchmark [3] had prices even better than DELL (13$/MB of RAM and 1690$ per 4GB disk and controllers). These systems all are near the five-minute rule. Mainframes are at 130$/MB for RAM, 10K$/MIPS, and 12k$/disk. Thus, mainframes follow a three-minute rule.

One can think of the first ratio of Equation 1 (*PagesPerMBofRAM/AccessesPerSecondPerDisk*) as a *technology ratio*. The second ratio of Equation 1 (*PriceofDiskDrive/PriceOfMBofRAM*) is an *economic ratio*. Looking at the trend lines in Figure 1, the technology ratio is shifting. Page size has increased with accesses/second so the technology ratio has decreased ten fold (from 512/30 = 17 to 128/64 = 2). Disk drive prices dropped 10x and RAM prices dropped 200x, so that the economic ratio has increased ten fold (20k$/2k$=10 to 2k$/15$=133). The consequent *reference interval* of equation (1) went from 170 seconds (17x10) to 266 seconds (2x133).

These calculations indicate that the *reference interval* of Equation (1) is almost unchanged, despite these 10x, 100x, and 1,000x changes. It is still in the 1-minute to 10-minute range. The 5-minute rule still applies to randomly accessed pages.

The original paper [1] also described the 10-byte rule for trading CPU instructions off against RAM. At the time one instruction cost the same as 10 bytes. Today, PCs follow a 1-byte rule, mini-computers follow a 10 byte rule, while mainframes follow a kilobyte rule because the processors are so overpriced.

[1] The current 2 KB page-size of Microsoft SQL Server 6.5 gives a reference interval of 20 minutes. MS SQL is moving to an 8 KB page size in the 1998 release.

1.2. Sequential Data Access: the One-Minute Sequential Rule

The discussion so far has focused on random access to small (8KB) pages. Sequential access to large pages has different behavior. Modern disks can transfer data at 10 MBps if accessed sequentially (Figure 1a). That is a peak value, the analysis here uses a more realistic 5 MB/s as a disk sequential data rate. Disk bandwidth drops 10x (to 0.5 MBps) if the application fetches random 8KB pages from disk. So, it should not be surprising that sequential IO operations like sort, cube, and join, have different RAM/disk tradeoffs. As shown below, they follow a one-minute-sequential rule.

If a sequential operation reads data and never references it, then there is no need to cache the data in RAM. In such one-pass algorithms, the system needs only enough buffer memory to allow data to stream from disk to main memory. Typically, two or three one-track buffers (~100 KB) are adequate. For one-pass sequential operations, less than a megabyte of RAM per disk is needed to buffer disk operations and allow the device to stream data to the application.

Many sequential operations read a large data-set and then revisit parts of the data. Database join, cube, rollup, and sort operators all behave in this way. Consider the disk access behavior of Sort in particular. Sort uses sequential data access and large disk transfers to optimize disk utilization and bandwidth. Sort ingests the input file, reorganizes the records in sorted order, and then sequentially writes the output file. If the sort cannot fit the file in main memory, it produces sorted runs in a first pass and then merges these runs into a sorted file in the second pass. Hash-join has a similar one-pass two-pass behavior.

The memory demand of a two pass sort is approximately given in equation 2:

$$MemoryForTwoPassSort \approx 6 \times Buffer\_Size + \sqrt{3 \times Buffer\_Size \times File\_Size} \quad ....(2)$$

Equation 2 is derived as follows. The first sort pass produces about *File_Size/Memory_Size* runs while the second pass can merge *Memory_Size/Buffer_Size* runs. Equating these two values and solving for memory size gives the square root term. The constants (3 and 6) depend on the particular sort algorithm. Equation 2 is graphed in Figure 2 for file sizes from megabytes to exabytes.

Sort shows a clear tradeoff of memory and disk IO. A one-pass sort uses half the disk IO but much more memory. When is it appropriate to use a one-pass sort? This is just an application of Equation 1 to compute the break-even reference interval. Use the DEC TPC-C prices [2] and components in the previous section. If sort uses to 64KB transfers then there are 16 pages/MB and it gets 80 accesses per second (about 5 MB/s).

PagesPerMBofRAM = 16 pages/MB
AccessesPerSecondPerDisk = 80 access/sec/disk

Using these parameters, Equation 1 yields a break-even reference interval of 26 seconds (= (16/80) x (2,000/15)). Actually, sort would have to write and then read the pages, so that doubles the IO cost and moves the balance point to 52 seconds. Anticipating higher bandwidths and less expensive RAM, we predict that this value will slowly grow over time.

Consequently, we recommend the ***one-minute-sequential rule****: hash joins, sorts, cubes, and other sequential operations should use main memory to cache data if the algorithm will revisit the data within a minute.*

For example, a one-pass sort is known to run at about 5 GB/minute [4]. Such sorts use many disks and lots of RAM but they use only half the IO bandwidth of a two-pass sort (they pass over the data only once). Applying the one-minute-sequential rule, below 5 GB a one-pass sort is warranted. Beyond that size, a two-pass sort is warranted. With 5GB of RAM a two-pass sort can sort 100 terabytes. This covers ALL current sorting needs.

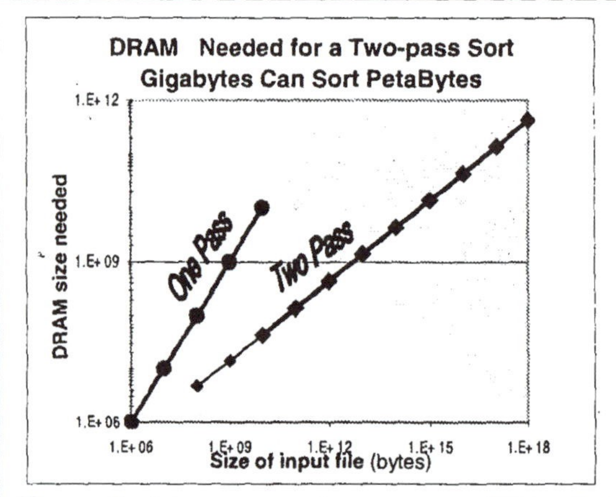

Figure 2: A two-pass sort can process 100 terabyte files with a 5 GB DRAM buffer. The two pass sort balances the run length against the number of runs to merge in the second pass. If it generates a thousand runs of 100 MB each, it can merge them using 100 MB of merge buffers in phase 2. This is a 100 GB sort. With current technology, use a 1-pass sort up to 5GB files. For larger files, do a 2-pass

Similar comments apply to other sequential operations (group by, rollup, cube, hash join, index build, etc...). **In general, sequential operations should use high-bandwidth disk transfers and they should cache data that they will revisit the data within a minute.**

In the limit, for large transfers, sequential access cost degenerates to the cost of the bandwidth. The technology ratio of equation 1 becomes the reciprocal of the bandwidth (in megabytes):

TechnologyRatio
= *(PagesPerMB)/(AccessesPerSecond)*
= *(1E6/TransferSize)/ (DiskBandwidth/TransferSize)*
for purely sequential access
= *1E6/DiskBandwidth.* (3)

This is an interesting result. It gives rise to the asymptote in Figure 3 that shows the reference interval vs. page size. With current disk technology, the reference interval asymptotically approaches 40 seconds as the page size grows.

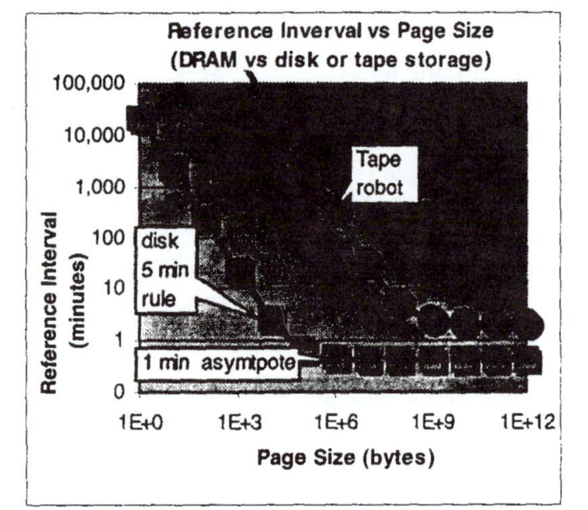

Figure 3: The break-even reference interval for disk vs. DRAM asymptotically approaches something like one minute for current technology. The asymptote is the product of the technology ratio (which becomes 1e6/bandwidth) and the economic ratio. A later section discuses the disk-tape tradeoff. Fundamentally, tape technology is VERY expensive to access. This encourages very large tape page sizes and very cold data on tape. The tape asymptote is approached at 10 GB (tape hardware is described in Table 4).

1.4. RAID and Tape

RAID 0 (striping) spreads IO among disks and so makes the transfer size smaller. Otherwise, RAID 0 does not perturb this analysis. RAID 1 (mirroring) slightly decreases the cost of reads and nearly doubles the cost of writes. RAID 5 increases the cost of writes by up to a factor of 4. In addition RAID5 controllers usually carry a price premium. All these factors tend to increase the economic ratio (making disks more expensive, and raise the technology ratio (lower accesses per second). Overall they tend to increase the random access reference interval by a factor of 2x to 5x.

Tape technology has moved quickly to improve capacity. Today the Quantum DLTstor™ is typical of high performance robots. Table 4 presents the performance of this device.

Table 4: Tape robot price and performance characteristics (source Quantum DLTstor™).

Quantum DLT Tape Robot	9,000$ price
Tape capacity	35 GB
Number of tapes	14
Robot Capacity	490 GB
Mount time (rewind, unmount, put, pick, mount, position)	30 seconds
Transfer rate	5 MBps

Accessing a random data record on a tape requires mounting it, moving to the right spot and then reading the tape. If the next access is on another tape and so one must rewind the current tape, put it away, pick the next one, scan to the correct position, and then read. This can take several minutes, but the specifications above charitably assumed it takes 30 seconds on average.

When should you store data on tape rather than in RAM? Using Equation 1, the break-even reference interval for a 8KB tape block is about two months (keep the page in RAM rather than tape if you will revisit the page within 2 months).

Another alternative is keeping the data on disk. What is the tradeoff of keeping data on disk rather than on tape? The tradeoff is that tape-space rent is 10x less expensive but tape accesses are much more expensive (100,000x more for small accesses and 5x more for large (1GB) accesses). The reference interval balances the lower tape rent against the higher access cost. The resulting curve is plotted in Figure 3.

1.5. Checkpoint Strategies In Light of the 5-minute Rule

Buffer managers typically use an LRU or Clock2 (two round clock) algorithm to manage the buffer pool. In general, they flush (write to disk) pages when (1) there is **contention** for cache space, or (2) the page must be **checkpoint**ed because the page has been dirty for a long time. The checkpoint interval is typically five minutes. Checkpoint limits recovery to redoing the last five or ten minutes of the log.

Hot-standby and remote-disaster-recovery systems reduce the need for checkpoints because they continuously run recovery on their version of the database and can take over within seconds. In these disaster-tolerant systems, checkpoints can be very infrequent and almost all flushes are contention flushes.

To implement the *N*-minute rule for contention flushes and evictions, the buffer manager keeps a list of the names of all pages touched within the last *N* minutes. When a page is re-read from disk, if it is in the *N*-minute list, it is given an *N*-minute lifetime (it will not be evicted for *N*-minutes in the future). This simple algorithm assures that frequently accessed pages are kept in the pool, while pages that are not re-referenced are aggressively evicted.

1.6. Five-Minute Summary

In summary, the five-minute rule still seems to apply to randomly accessed pages, primarily because page sizes have grown from 1KB to 8KB to compensate for changing technology ratios. For large (64KB pages) and two-pass sequential access, a one-minute rule applies today.

2. How Large Should Index Pages Be?

The size of an internal index page determines its retrieval cost and fan-out (*EntriesPerPage*). A B-tree indexing *N* items will have a height (in pages) of:

$$Indexheight \sim \log_2(N)/\log_2(EntriesPerPage) \text{ pages} \quad (4).$$

The *utility* of an index page measures how much closer the index page brings an associative search to the destination data record. It tells how many levels of the binary-tree fit on a page. The utility is the divisor of the Equation 4:

$$IndexPageUtility = \log_2(EntriesPerPage) \quad (5)$$

For example, if each index entry is 20 bytes, then a 2 KB index page that is 70% full will contain about 70 entries. Such a page will have a utility of 6.2, about half the utility of a 128 KB index page (see Table 6).

Reading each index page costs a logical disk access but each page brings us *IndexPageUtility* steps closer to the answer. This cost-benefit tradeoff gives rise to an optimal page size that balances the *IndexPageAccessCost* and the *IndexPageUtility* of each IO.

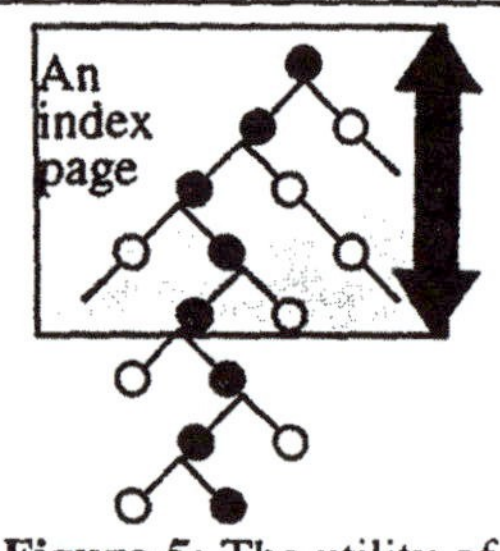

Figure 5: The utility of an index page is the number of levels of the binary tree that it traverses.

The utility rises as the log of the page size. The cost of the access goes up linearly with page sizeConsequently, for a particular disk latency and transfer rate, there is an optimal index page size. The tree at left shows just the search path (it is not balanced because the drawing would be too cluttered).

Reading a 2 KB page from a disk with a 10 ms average access time (seek and rotation) and 10 MB/s transfer rate uses 10.2 ms of disk device time. So the read cost is 10.2 milliseconds. More generally, the cost of accessing an index page is either the storage cost in main memory if the page is cached there, or the access cost if the page is stored on disk. If pages near the index root are cached in main memory, the cache saves a constant number of IOs on average. This constant can be ignored if one is just optimizing the IO subsystem. The index page disk access cost is

IndexPageAccessCost = Disk Latency + PageSize / DiskTransferRate (6)

The benefit-cost ratio of a certain page size and entry size is the ratio of the two quantities.

IndexPageBenefit/Cost = IndexPageUtility / IndexPageAccessCost. (7)

The right column of Table 6 shows this computation for various page sizes assuming 20-byte index entries. It indicates that 8 KB to 32 KB pages are near optimal for these parameters.

Figure 7 graphs the benefit/cost ratios for various entry sizes and page sizes for both current, and next-generation disks. The graphs indicate that, small pages have low benefit because they have low utility and high fixed disk read costs. Very large pages also have low benefit because utility grows only as the log of the page size, but transfer cost grows linearly with page size.

Table 6: Tabulation of index page utility and benefit/cost for 20 byte index entries assuming each page is 70% full and assuming a 10ms latency 10 MBps transfer rate.

page size KB	entries per page Fan-out	Index Page Utility	Index Page Access Cost (ms)	Index Page Benefit/ Cost (20B)
2	68	6.1	10.2	0.60
4	135	7.1	10.4	0.68
8	270	8.1	10.8	0.75
16	541	9.1	11.6	0.78
32	1081	10.1	13.2	0.76
64	2163	11.1	16.4	0.68
128	4325	12.1	22.8	0.53

Table 6 and Figure 7 indicate that for current devices, index page sizes in the range of 8 KB to 32 KB are referable to smaller and larger page sizes. By the year 2005, disks are predicted to have 40 MB/s transfer rates and so 8 KB pages will probably be too small.

Table 6 and Figure 7 indicate that for current devices, index page sizes in the range of 8 KB to 32 KB are preferable to smaller and larger page sizes. By the year 2005, disks are predicted to have 40 MB/s transfer rates and so 8 KB pages will probably be too small.

3. New Storage Metrics

These discussions point out an interesting phenomenon -- the fundamental storage metrics are changing. Traditionally, disks and tapes have been rated by capacity. As disk and tape capacity approach infinity (50 GB disks and 100 GB tapes are in beta test today), the cost/GB goes to zero and the cost/access becomes the dominant performance metric.

The traditional performance metrics are:

GB: storage capacity in gigabytes.

$/GB: device price divided by capacity.

Latency: time between issue of IO and start of data transmission.

Bandwidth: sustained transfer rate from the device.

The latter two are often combined as a single access time metric (time to read a random KB from the device).

Kaps : kilobyte accesses per second.

As device capacities grow, additional metrics become important. Transfers become larger. Indeed, the minimum economical tape transfer is probably a one MB object

Increasingly, applications use a dataflow style of programming and stream the data past the device. Data mining applications and archival applications are the most common example of this today. These suggest the following two new storage metrics.

Maps: Megabyte accesses per second.

Scan: how long it takes to sequentially read or write all the data in the device?

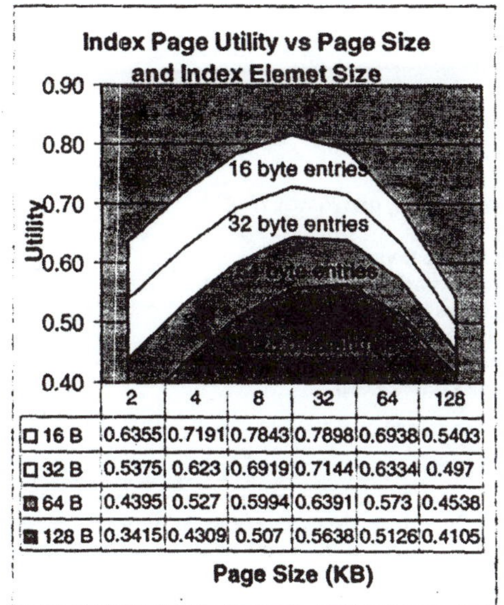

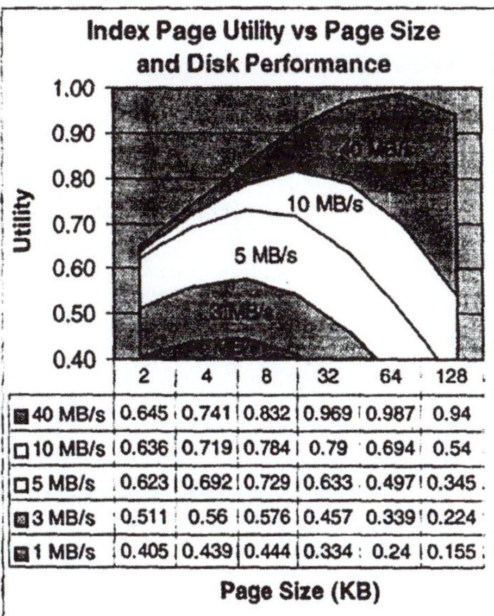

Index Page Utility vs Page Size and Disk Performance
Utility
1.00
0.90
0.80
0.70
0.60
0.50
0.40
10 MB/s
5 MB/s
Page Size (KB)

	2	4	8	32	64	128
40 MB/s	0.645	0.741	0.832	0.969	0.987	0.94
10 MB/s	0.636	0.719	0.784	0.79	0.694	0.54
5 MB/s	0.623	0.692	0.729	0.633	0.497	0.345
3 MB/s	0.511	0.56	0.576	0.457	0.339	0.224
1 MB/s	0.405	0.439	0.444	0.334	0.24	0.155

Figure 7. (a) The left graph shows the utility of index pages versus page size for various index entry sizes using a high-performance disk (10ms latency, 10 MB/s transfer rate). (b) The graphs at right use a fixed-sized 16-byte entry and show the impact of disk performance on optimal page size. For high-performance disks, the optimum index page size grows from 8KB to 64KB.

These metrics become price/performance metrics when combined with the device rent (depreciated over 3 years). The Scan metric becomes a measure of the rent for a terabyte of the media while the media is being scanned. Table 8 displays these metrics for current devices:

Table 8: Performance Metrics of high-performance devices circa 1997.

	RAM	Disk	Tape robot
Unit capacity	1GB	9 GB	14 x 35 GB
Unit price $	15,000$	2,000$	10,000$
$/GB	15,000 $/GB	222$/GB	20 $/GB
Latency (ms)	0.1 micro sec	10 milli sec	30 sec
Bandwidth	500 MBps	5 MBps	5 MBps
Kaps	500,000 Kaps	100 Kaps	.03 Kaps
Maps	500 Maps	4.8 Maps	.03 Maps
Scan time	2 seconds	30 minutes	27 hours
$/Kaps	0.3 nano $	0.2 micro $	3 milli $
$/Maps	.3 micro $	4 micro $	3 milli $
$/TBscan	.32 $	4.23$	296$

4. Summary

The fact that disk access speeds have increased ten-fold in the last twenty years is impressive. But it pales when compared to the hundred-fold increase in disk unit capacity and the ten-thousand-fold decrease in storage costs (Figure 1). In part, growing page sizes sixteen-fold from 512 bytes to 8 KB has ameliorated these differential changes. This growth preserved the five-minute rule for randomly accessed pages. A one- minute rule applies to pages used in two-pass sequential algorithms like sort. As technology advances, secondary storage capacities grow huge. The *Kaps*, *Maps*, and *Scans* metrics that measure access rate and price/access are becoming increasingly important.

5. Acknowledgments

Paul Larson, Dave Lomet, Len Seligman and Catharine Van Ingen helped us clarify our presentation of optimum index page sizes. The *Kaps, Maps,* and *Scans* metrics grew out of discussions with Richie Larry.

6. References

[1] J. Gray & G. F. Putzolu, "The Five-minute Rule for Trading Memory for Disc Accesses, and the 10 Byte Rule for Trading Memory for CPU Time," Proceedings of SIGMOD 87, June 1987, pp. 395-398.

[2] Dell-Microsoft TPC-C Executive summary: http://www.tpc.org/results/individual_results/Dell/dell.6100.es.pdf

[3] Sun-Oracle TPC-C Executive summary: http://www.tpc.org/results/individual_results/Sun/sun.ue6000.oracle.es.pdf

[4] Ordinal Corp. http://www.ordinal.com/

A Case for Redundant Arrays of Inexpensive Disks (RAID)

David A Patterson, Garth Gibson, and Randy H Katz

Computer Science Division
Department of Electrical Engineering and Computer Sciences
571 Evans Hall
University of California
Berkeley, CA 94720
(pattrsn@ginger berkeley edu)

Abstract *Increasing performance of CPUs and memories will be squandered if not matched by a similar performance increase in I/O While the capacity of Single Large Expensive Disks (SLED) has grown rapidly, the performance improvement of SLED has been modest Redundant Arrays of Inexpensive Disks (RAID), based on the magnetic disk technology developed for personal computers, offers an attractive alternative to SLED, promising improvements of an order of magnitude in performance, reliability, power consumption, and scalability This paper introduces five levels of RAIDs, giving their relative cost/performance, and compares RAID to an IBM 3380 and a Fujitsu Super Eagle*

1 Background: Rising CPU and Memory Performance

The users of computers are currently enjoying unprecedented growth in the speed of computers Gordon Bell said that between 1974 and 1984, single chip computers improved in performance by 40% per year, about twice the rate of minicomputers [Bell 84] In the following year Bill Joy predicted an even faster growth [Joy 85]

$$MIPS = 2^{Year-1984}$$

Mainframe and supercomputer manufacturers, having difficulty keeping pace with the rapid growth predicted by "Joy's Law," cope by offering multiprocessors as their top-of-the-line product.

But a fast CPU does not a fast system make Gene Amdahl related CPU speed to main memory size using this rule [Siewiorek 82]

Each CPU instruction per second requires one byte of main memory,

If computer system costs are not to be dominated by the cost of memory, then Amdahl's constant suggests that memory chip capacity should grow at the same rate Gordon Moore predicted that growth rate over 20 years ago

$$transistors/chip = 2^{Year-1964}$$

As predicted by Moore's Law, RAMs have quadrupled in capacity every two [Moore 75] to three years [Myers 86]

Recently the ratio of megabytes of main memory to MIPS has been defined as *alpha* [Garcia 84], with Amdahl's constant meaning alpha = 1 In part because of the rapid drop of memory prices, main memory sizes have grown faster than CPU speeds and many machines are shipped today with alphas of 3 or higher

To maintain the balance of costs in computer systems, secondary storage must match the advances in other parts of the system A key measure of magnetic disk technology is the growth in the maximum number of bits that can be stored per square inch, or the bits per inch in a track times the number of tracks per inch Called M A D , for maximal areal density, the "First Law in Disk Density" predicts [Frank87]

$$MAD = 10^{(Year-1971)/10}$$

Magnetic disk technology has doubled capacity and halved price every three years, in line with the growth rate of semiconductor memory, and in practice between 1967 and 1979 the disk capacity of the average IBM data processing system more than kept up with its main memory [Stevens81]

Capacity is not the only memory characteristic that must grow rapidly to maintain system balance, since the speed with which instructions and data are delivered to a CPU also determines its ultimate performance The speed of main memory has kept pace for two reasons

(1) the invention of caches, showing that a small buffer can be managed automatically to contain a substantial fraction of memory references,

(2) and the SRAM technology, used to build caches, whose speed has improved at the rate of 40% to 100% per year

In contrast to primary memory technologies, the performance of single large expensive magnetic disks (SLED) has improved at a modest rate These *mechanical* devices are dominated by the seek and the rotation delays from 1971 to 1981, the raw seek time for a high-end IBM disk improved by only a factor of two while the rotation time did not change[Harker81] Greater density means a higher transfer rate when the information is found, and extra heads can reduce the average seek time, but the raw seek time only improved at a rate of 7% per year There is no reason to expect a faster rate in the near future

To maintain balance, computer systems have been using even larger main memories or solid state disks to buffer some of the I/O activity This may be a fine solution for applications whose I/O activity has locality of reference and for which volatility is not an issue, but applications dominated by a high rate of random requests for small pieces of data (such as transaction-processing) or by a low number of requests for massive amounts of data (such as large simulations running on supercomputers) are facing a serious performance limitation

2. The Pending I/O Crisis

What is the impact of improving the performance of some pieces of a problem while leaving others the same? Amdahl's answer is now known as Amdahl's Law [Amdahl67]

$$S = \frac{1}{(1-f) + f/k}$$

where

S = the effective speedup,

f = fraction of work in faster mode, and

k = speedup while in faster mode

Suppose that some current applications spend 10% of their time in I/O Then when computers are 10X faster--according to Bill Joy in just over three years--then Amdahl's Law predicts effective speedup will be only 5X When we have computers 100X faster--via evolution of uniprocessors or by multiprocessors--this application will be less than 10X faster, wasting 90% of the potential speedup

While we can imagine improvements in software file systems via buffering for near term I/O demands, we need innovation to avoid an I/O crisis [Boral 83]

3 A Solution: Arrays of Inexpensive Disks

Rapid improvements in capacity of large disks have not been the only target of disk designers, since personal computers have created a market for inexpensive magnetic disks These lower cost disks have lower performance as well as less capacity Table I below compares the top-of-the-line IBM 3380 model AK4 mainframe disk, Fujitsu M2361A "Super Eagle" minicomputer disk, and the Conner Peripherals CP 3100 personal computer disk

Characteristics	*IBM 3380*	*Fujitsu M2361A*	*Conners CP3100*	*3380 v 3100 (>1 means 3100 is better)*	*2361 v 3100*
Disk diameter (inches)	14	10 5	3 5	4	3
Formatted Data Capacity (MB)	7500	600	100	01	2
Price/MB(controller incl)	$18-$10	$20-$17	$10-$7	1-2 5	1 7-3
MTTF Rated (hours)	30,000	20,000	30,000	1	1 5
MTTF in practice (hours)	100,000	?	?	?	?
No Actuators	4	1	1	2	1
Maximum I/O's/second/Actuator	50	40	30	6	8
Typical I/O's/second/Actuator	30	24	20	7	8
Maximum I/O's/second/box	200	40	30	2	8
Typical I/O's/second/box	120	24	20	2	8
Transfer Rate (MB/sec)	3	2 5	1	3	4
Power/box (W)	6,600	640	10	660	64
Volume (cu ft)	24	3 4	03	800	110

Table I *Comparison of IBM 3380 disk model AK4 for mainframe computers, the Fujitsu M2361A "Super Eagle" disk for minicomputers, and the Conners Peripherals CP 3100 disk for personal computers By "Maximum I/O's/second" we mean the maximum number of average seeks and average rotates for a single sector access Cost and reliability information on the 3380 comes from widespread experience [IBM 87] [Gawlick87] and the information on the Fujitsu from the manual [Fujitsu 87], while some numbers on the new CP3100 are based on speculation The price per megabyte is given as a range to allow for different prices for volume discount and different mark-up practices of the vendors (The 8 watt maximum power of the CP3100 was increased to 10 watts to allow for the inefficiency of an external power supply, since the other drives contain their own power supplies)*

One surprising fact is that the number of I/Os per second per actuator in an inexpensive disk is within a factor of two of the large disks In several of the remaining metrics, including price per megabyte, the inexpensive disk is superior or equal to the large disks

The small size and low power are even more impressive since disks such as the CP3100 contain full track buffers *and* most functions of the traditional mainframe controller Small disk manufacturers can provide such functions in high volume disks because of the efforts of standards committees in defining higher level peripheral interfaces, such as the ANSI X3 131-1986 Small Computer System Interface (SCSI) Such standards have encouraged companies like Adeptec to offer SCSI interfaces as single chips, in turn allowing disk companies to *embed* mainframe controller functions at low cost Figure 1 compares the traditional mainframe disk approach and the small computer disk approach The same SCSI interface chip embedded as a controller in every disk can also be used as the direct memory access (DMA) device at the other end of the SCSI bus

Such characteristics lead to our proposal for building I/O systems as arrays of inexpensive disks, either interleaved for the large transfers of supercomputers [Kim 86][Livny 87][Salem86] or independent for the many small transfers of transaction processing Using the information in Table I, 75 inexpensive disks potentially have 12 times the I/O bandwidth of the IBM 3380 and the same capacity, with lower power consumption and cost

4 Caveats

We cannot explore all issues associated with such arrays in the space available for this paper, so we concentrate on fundamental estimates of price-performance and reliability Our reasoning is that if there are no advantages in price-performance or terrible disadvantages in reliability, then there is no need to explore further We characterize a transaction-processing workload to evaluate performance of a collection of inexpensive disks, but remember that such a collection is just one hardware component of a complete tranaction-processing system While designing a complete TPS based on these ideas is enticing, we will resist that temptation in this paper Cabling and packaging, certainly an issue in the cost and reliability of an array of many inexpensive disks, is also beyond this paper's scope

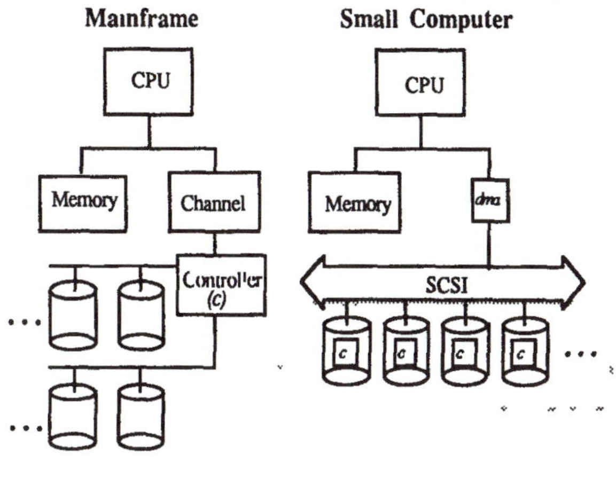

Figure 1 *Comparison of organizations for typical mainframe and small computer disk interfaces Single chip SCSI interfaces such as the Adaptec AIC-6250 allow the small computer to use a single chip to be the DMA interface as well as provide an embedded controller for each disk [Adeptec 87] (The price per megabyte in Table I includes everything in the shaded boxes above)*

5. And Now The Bad News: Reliability

The unreliability of disks forces computer systems managers to make backup versions of information quite frequently in case of failure What would be the impact on reliability of having a hundredfold increase in disks? Assuming a constant failure rate--that is, an exponentially distributed time to failure--and that failures are independent--both assumptions made by disk manufacturers when calculating the Mean Time To Failure (MTTF)--the reliability of an array of disks is

$$MTTF\ of\ a\ Disk\ Array = \frac{MTTF\ of\ a\ Single\ Disk}{Number\ of\ Disks\ in\ the\ Array}$$

Using the information in Table I, the MTTF of 100 CP 3100 disks is 30,000/100 = 300 hours, or less than 2 weeks Compared to the 30,000 hour (> 3 years) MTTF of the IBM 3380, this is dismal If we consider scaling the array to 1000 disks, then the MTTF is 30 hours or about one day, requiring an adjective worse than dismal

Without fault tolerance, large arrays of inexpensive disks are too unreliable to be useful

6. A Better Solution: RAID

To overcome the reliability challenge, we must make use of extra disks containing redundant information to recover the original information when a disk fails Our acronym for these Redundant Arrays of Inexpensive Disks is ***RAID*** To simplify the explanation of our final proposal and to avoid confusion with previous work, we give a taxonomy of five different organizations of disk arrays, beginning with mirrored disks and progressing through a variety of alternatives with differing performance and reliability We refer to each organization as a RAID *level*

The reader should be forewarned that we describe all levels as if implemented in hardware solely to simplify the presentation, for RAID ideas are applicable to software implementations as well as hardware

Reliability Our basic approach will be to break the arrays into reliability groups, with each group having extra "check" disks containing redundant information When a disk fails we assume that within a short time the failed disk will be replaced and the information will be reconstructed on to the new disk using the redundant information This time is called the mean time to repair (MTTR) The MTTR can be reduced if the system includes extra disks to act as "hot" standby spares, when a disk fails, a replacement disk is switched in electronically Periodically a human operator replaces all failed disks Here are other terms that we use

D = total number of disks with data (not including extra check disks),
G = number of data disks in a *group* (not including extra check disks),
C = number of check disks in a group,
$n_G = D/G$ = number of groups,

As mentioned above we make the same assumptions that disk manufacturers make--that failures are exponential and independent (An earthquake or power surge is a situation where an array of disks might not fail independently) Since these reliability predictions will be very high, we want to emphasize that the reliability is only of the the disk-head assemblies with this failure model, and not the whole software and electronic system In addition, in our view the pace of technology means extremely high MTTF are "overkill"--for, independent of expected lifetime, users will replace obsolete disks After all, how many people are still using 20 year old disks?

The general MTTF calculation for single-error repairing RAID is given in two steps First, the group MTTF is

$$MTTF_{Group} = \frac{MTTF_{Disk}}{G+C} * \frac{1}{\textit{Probability of another failure in a group before repairing the dead disk}}$$

As more formally derived in the appendix, the probability of a second failure before the first has been repaired is

$$\textit{Probability of Another Failure} = \frac{MTTR}{MTTF_{Disk}/(No\ Disks\text{-}1)} = \frac{MTTR}{MTTF_{Disk}/(G+C\text{-}1)}$$

The intuition behind the formal calculation in the appendix comes from trying to calculate the average number of second disk failures during the repair time for X single disk failures Since we assume that disk failures occur at a uniform rate, this average number of second failures during the repair time for X first failures is

$$\frac{X * MTTR}{\textit{MTTF of remaining disks in the group}}$$

The average number of second failures for a single disk is then

$$\frac{MTTR}{MTTF_{Disk} / \textit{No of remaining disks in the group}}$$

The MTTF of the remaining disks is just the MTTF of a single disk divided by the number of good disks in the group, giving the result above

The second step is the reliability of the whole system, which is approximately (since $MTTF_{Group}$ is not quite distributed exponentially)

$$MTTF_{RAID} = \frac{MTTF_{Group}}{n_G}$$

Plugging it all together, we get.

$$MTTF_{RAID} = \frac{MTTF_{Disk}}{G+C} * \frac{MTTF_{Disk}}{(G+C\text{-}1)*MTTR} * \frac{1}{n_G} = \frac{(MTTF_{Disk})^2}{(G+C)*n_G * (G+C\text{-}1)*MTTR}$$

$$MTTF_{RAID} = \frac{(MTTF_{Disk})^2}{(D+C*n_G)*(G+C\text{-}1)*MTTR}$$

Since the formula is the same for each level, we make the abstract numbers concrete using these parameters as appropriate D=100 total data disks, G=10 data disks per group, $MTTF_{Disk}$ = 30,000 hours, $MTTR$ = 1 hour, with the check disks per group C determined by the RAID level

Reliability Overhead Cost This is simply the extra check disks, expressed as a percentage of the number of data disks D As we shall see below, the cost varies with RAID level from 100% down to 4%

Useable Storage Capacity Percentage Another way to express this reliability overhead is in terms of the percentage of the total capacity of data disks ***and*** check disks that can be used to store data Depending on the organization, this varies from a low of 50% to a high of 96%

Performance Since supercomputer applications and transaction-processing systems have different access patterns and rates, we need different metrics to evaluate both For supercomputers we count the number of reads and writes per second for large blocks of data, with large defined as getting at least one sector from each data disk in a group During large transfers all the disks in a group act as a single unit, each reading or writing a portion of the large data block in parallel

A better measure for transaction-processing systems is the number of **individual** reads or writes per second Since transaction-processing systems (e g , debits/credits) use a read-modify-write sequence of disk accesses, we include that metric as well Ideally during small transfers each disk in a group can act independently, either reading or writing independent information In summary supercomputer applications need a *high data rate* while transaction-processing need a *high I/O rate*

For both the large and small transfer calculations we assume the minimum user request is a sector, that a sector is small relative to a track, and that there is enough work to keep every device busy Thus sector size affects both disk storage efficiency and transfer size Figure 2 shows the ideal operation of large and small disk accesses in a RAID

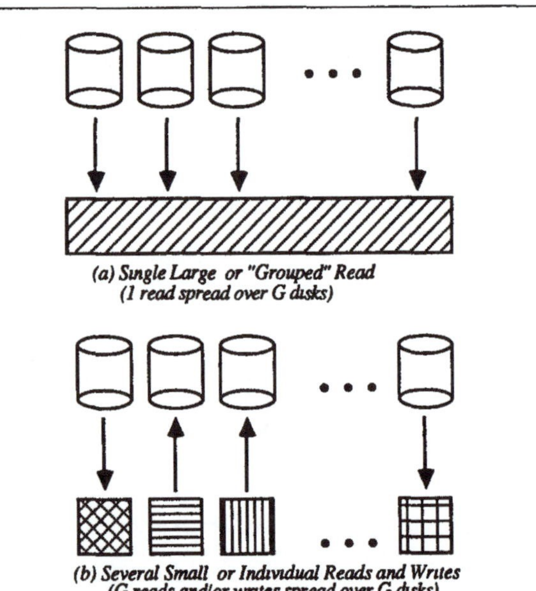

(a) Single Large or "Grouped" Read (1 read spread over G disks)

(b) Several Small or Individual Reads and Writes (G reads and/or writes spread over G disks)

Figure 2. *Large transfer vs small transfers in a group of G disks*

The six performance metrics are then the number of reads, writes, and read-modify-writes per second for both large (grouped) or small (individual) transfers Rather than give absolute numbers for each metric, we calculate efficiency the number of events per second for a RAID relative to the corresponding events per second for a single disk (This is Boral's I/O bandwidth per gigabyte [Boral 83] scaled to gigabytes per disk) In this paper we are after fundamental differences so we use simple, deterministic throughput measures for our performance metric rather than latency

Effective Performance Per Disk The cost of disks can be a large portion of the cost of a database system, so the I/O performance per disk--factoring in the overhead of the check disks--suggests the cost/performance of a system This is the bottom line for a RAID

7. First Level RAID: Mirrored Disks

Mirrored disks are a traditional approach for improving reliability of magnetic disks This is the most expensive option we consider since all disks are duplicated (*G*=1 and *C*=1), and every write to a data disk is also a write to a check disk Tandem doubles the number of controllers for fault tolerance, allowing an optimized version of mirrored disks that lets reads occur in parallel Table II shows the metrics for a Level 1 RAID assuming this optimization

MTTF	Exceeds Useful Product Lifetime (4,500,000 hrs or > 500 years)	
Total Number of Disks	2D	
Overhead Cost	100%	
Useable Storage Capacity	50%	
Events/Sec vs Single Disk	*Full RAID*	*Efficiency Per Disk*
Large (or Grouped) Reads	2D/S	1 00/S
Large (or Grouped) Writes	D/S	50/S
Large (or Grouped) R-M-W	4D/3S	67/S
Small (or Individual) Reads	2D	1 00
Small (or Individual) Writes	D	50
Small (or Individual) R-M-W	4D/3	67

Table II. *Characteristics of Level 1 RAID Here we assume that writes are not slowed by waiting for the second write to complete because the slowdown for writing 2 disks is minor compared to the slowdown S for writing a whole group of 10 to 25 disks Unlike a "pure" mirrored scheme with extra disks that are invisible to the software, we assume an optimized scheme with twice as many controllers allowing parallel reads to all disks, giving full disk bandwidth for large reads and allowing the reads of read-modify-writes to occur in parallel*

When individual accesses are distributed across multiple disks, average queueing, seek, and rotate delays may differ from the single disk case Although bandwidth may be unchanged, it is distributed more evenly, reducing variance in queueing delay and, if the disk load is not too high, also reducing the expected queueing delay through parallelism [Livny 87] When many arms seek to the same track then rotate to the described sector, the average seek and rotate time will be larger than the average for a single disk, tending toward the worst case times This affect should not generally more than double the average access time to a single sector while still getting many sectors in parallel In the special case of mirrored disks with sufficient controllers, the choice between arms that can read any data sector will reduce the time for the average read seek by up to 45% [Bitton 88]

To allow for these factors but to retain our fundamental emphasis we apply a slowdown factor, *S*, when there are more than two disks in a group In general, $1 \leq S \leq 2$ whenever groups of disk work in parallel With synchronous disks the spindles of all disks in the group are synchronous so that the corresponding sectors of a group of disks pass under the heads simultaneously,[Kurzweil 88] so for synchronous disks there is no slowdown and $S = 1$ Since a Level 1 RAID has only one data disk in its group, we assume that the large transfer requires the same number of disks acting in concert as found in groups of the higher level RAIDs 10 to 25 disks

Duplicating all disks can mean doubling the cost of the database system or using only 50% of the disk storage capacity Such largess inspires the next levels of RAID

8 Second Level RAID: Hamming Code for ECC

The history of main memory organizations suggests a way to reduce the cost of reliability With the introduction of 4K and 16K DRAMs, computer designers discovered that these new devices were subject to losing information due to alpha particles Since there were many single bit DRAMs in a system and since they were usually accessed in groups of 16 to 64 chips at a time, system designers added redundant chips to correct single errors and to detect double errors in each group This increased the number of memory chips by 12% to 38%--depending on the size of the group--but it significantly improved reliability

As long as all the data bits in a group are read or written together, there is no impact on performance However, reads of less than the group size require reading the whole group to be sure the information is correct, and writes to a portion of the group mean three steps

1) a read step to get all the rest of the data,

2) a modify step to merge the new and old information,

3) a write step to write the full group, including check information

Since we have scores of disks in a RAID and since some accesses are to groups of disks, we can mimic the DRAM solution by bit-interleaving the data across the disks of a group and then add enough check disks to detect and correct a single error A single parity disk can detect a single error, but to correct an error we need enough check disks to identify the disk with the error For a group size of 10 data disks (*G*) we need 4 check disks (*C*) in total, and if $G = 25$ then $C = 5$ [Hamming50] To keep down the cost of redundancy, we assume the group size will vary from 10 to 25

Since our individual data transfer unit is just a sector, bit- interleaved disks mean that a large transfer for this RAID must be at least G sectors Like DRAMs, reads to a smaller amount implies reading a full sector from each of the bit-interleaved disks in a group, and writes of a single unit involve the read-modify-write cycle to all the disks Table III shows the metrics of this Level 2 RAID

MTTF		Exceeds Useful Lifetime			
		G=10 (494,500 hrs or >50 years)		*G=25* (103,500 hrs or 12 years)	
Total Number of Disks		1 40D		1.20D	
Overhead Cost		40%		20%	
Useable Storage Capacity		71%		83%	
Events/Sec (vs Single Disk)	*Full RAID*	*Efficiency Per Disk*		*Efficiency Per Disk*	
		L2	*L2/L1*	*L2*	*L2/L1*
Large Reads	*D/S*	71/S	71%	86/S	86%
Large Writes	*D/S*	71/S	143%	86/S	172%
Large R-M-W	*D/S*	71/S	107%	86/S	129%
Small Reads	*D/SG*	07/S	6%	03/S	3%
Small Writes	*D/2SG*	04/S	6%	02/S	3%
Small R-M-W	*D/SG*	07/S	9%	03/S	4%

Table III *Characteristics of a Level 2 RAID The L2/L1 column gives the % performance of level 2 in terms of level 1 (>100% means L2 is faster) As long as the transfer unit is large enough to spread over all the data disks of a group, the large I/Os get the full bandwidth of each disk, divided by S to allow all disks in a group to complete Level 1 large reads are faster because data is duplicated and so the redundancy disks can also do independent accesses Small I/Os still require accessing all the disks in a group, so only D/G small I/Os can happen at a time, again divided by S to allow a group of disks to finish Small Level 2 writes are like small R-M-W because full sectors must be read before new data can be written onto part of each sector*

For large writes, the level 2 system has the same performance as level 1 even though it uses fewer check disks, and so on a per disk basis it outperforms level 1 For small data transfers the performance is dismal either for the whole system or per disk, all the disks of a group must be accessed for a small transfer, limiting the maximum number of simultaneous accesses to *D/G* We also include the slowdown factor *S* since the access must wait for all the disks to complete

Thus level 2 RAID is desirable for supercomputers but inappropriate for transaction processing systems, with increasing group size increasing the disparity in performance per disk for the two applications In recognition of this fact, Thinking Machines Incorporated announced a Level 2 RAID this year for its Connection Machine supercomputer called the "Data Vault," with G = 32 and C = 8, including one hot standby spare [Hillis 87]

Before improving small data transfers, we concentrate once more on lowering the cost

9 Third Level RAID: Single Check Disk Per Group

Most check disks in the level 2 RAID are used to determine which disk failed, for only one redundant parity disk is needed to detect an error These extra disks are truly "redundant" since most disk controllers can already detect if a disk failed either through special signals provided in the disk interface or the extra checking information at the end of a sector used to detect and correct soft errors So information on the failed disk can be reconstructed by calculating the parity of the remaining good disks and then comparing bit-by-bit to the parity calculated for the original full group When these two parities agree, the failed bit was a 0, otherwise it was a 1 If the check disk is the failure, just read all the data disks and store the group parity in the replacement disk

Reducing the check disks to one per group (C=1) reduces the overhead cost to between 4% and 10% for the group sizes considered here The performance for the third level RAID system is the same as the Level 2 RAID, but the effective performance per disk increases since it needs fewer check disks This reduction in total disks also increases reliability, but since it is still larger than the useful lifetime of disks, this is a minor point One advantage of a level 2 system over level 3 is that the extra check information associated with each sector to correct soft errors is not needed, increasing the capacity per disk by perhaps 10% Level 2 also allows all soft errors to be corrected "on the fly" without having to reread a sector Table IV summarizes the third level RAID characteristics and Figure 3 compares the sector layout and check disks for levels 2 and 3

MTTF		Exceeds Useful Lifetime					
		G=10			*G=25*		
		(820,000 hrs or >90 years)			(346,000 hrs or 40 years)		
Total Number of Disks		1 10D			1 04D		
Overhead Cost		10%			4%		
Useable Storage Capacity		91%			96%		
Events/Sec (vs Single Disk)	*Full RAID*	*Efficiency Per Disk*			*Efficiency Per Disk*		
		L3	*L3/L2*	*L3/L1*	*L3*	*L3/L2*	*L3/L1*
Large Reads	*D/S*	91/S	127%	91%	96/S	112%	96%
Large Writes	*D/S*	91/S	127%	182%	96/S	112%	192%
Large R-M-W	*D/S*	91/S	127%	136%	96/S	112%	142%
Small Reads	*D/SG*	09/S	127%	8%	04/S	112%	3%
Small Writes	*D/2SG*	05/S	127%	8%	02/S	112%	3%
Small R-M-W	*D/SG*	09/S	127%	11%	04/S	112%	5%

Table IV *Characteristics of a Level 3 RAID The L3/L2 column gives the % performance of L3 in terms of L2 and the L3/L1 column gives it in terms of L1 (>100% means L3 is faster) The performance for the full systems is the same in RAID levels 2 and 3, but since there are fewer check disks the performance per disk improves*

Park and Balasubramanian proposed a third level RAID system without suggesting a particular application [Park86] Our calculations suggest it is a much better match to supercomputer applications than to transaction processing systems This year two disk manufacturers have announced level 3 RAIDs for such applications using synchronized 5 25 inch disks with G=4 and C=1 one from Maxtor and one from Micropolis [Maginnis 87]

This third level has brought the reliability overhead cost to its lowest level, so in the last two levels we improve performance of small accesses without changing cost or reliability

10. Fourth Level RAID Independent Reads/Writes

Spreading a transfer across all disks within the group has the following advantage

- Large or grouped transfer time is reduced because transfer bandwidth of the entire array can be exploited.

But it has the following disadvantages as well

- Reading/writing to a disk in a group requires reading/writing to all the disks in a group, levels 2 and 3 RAIDs can perform only one I/O at a time per group
- If the disks are not synchronized, you do not see average seek and rotational delays, the observed delays should move towards the worst case, hence the S factor in the equations above

This fourth level RAID improves performance of small transfers through parallelism--the ability to do more than one I/O per group at a time We no longer spread the individual transfer information across several disks, but keep each individual unit in a single disk

The virtue of bit-interleaving is the easy calculation of the Hamming code needed to detect or correct errors in level 2 But recall that in the third level RAID we rely on the disk controller to detect errors within a single disk sector Hence, if we store an individual transfer unit in a single sector, we can detect errors on an individual read without accessing any other disk Figure 3 shows the different ways the information is stored in a sector for RAID levels 2, 3, and 4 By storing a whole transfer unit in a sector, reads can be independent and operate at the maximum rate of a disk yet still detect errors Thus the primary change between level 3 and 4 is that we interleave data between disks at the sector level rather than at the bit level

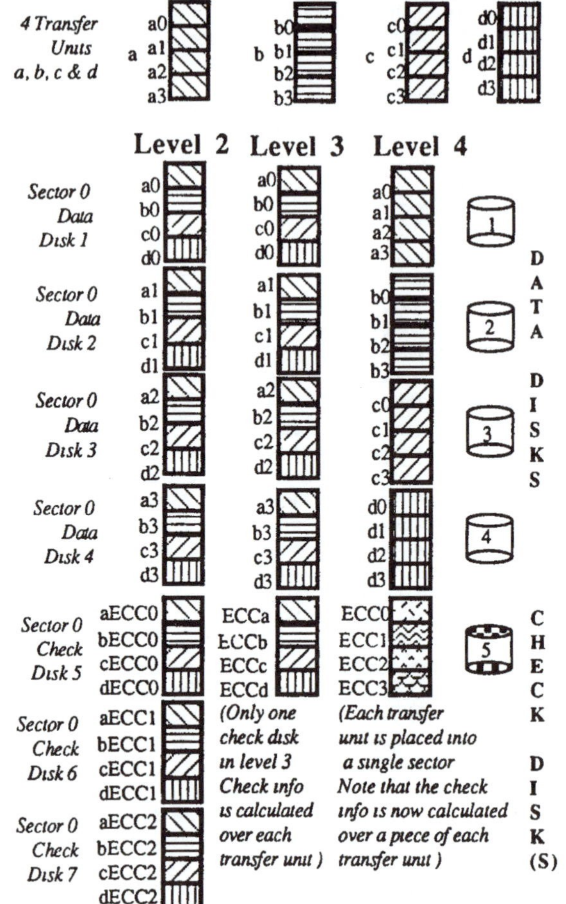

Figure 3 *Comparison of location of data and check information in sectors for RAID levels 2, 3, and 4 for G=4 Not shown is the small amount of check information per sector added by the disk controller to detect and correct soft errors within a sector Remember that we use physical sector numbers and hardware control to explain these ideas but RAID can be implemented by software using logical sectors and disks*

At first thought you might expect that an individual write to a single sector still involves all the disks in a group since (1) the check disk must be rewritten with the new parity data, and (2) the rest of the data disks must be read to be able to calculate the new parity data Recall that each parity bit is just a single exclusive OR of all the corresponding data bits in a group In level 4 RAID, unlike level 3, the parity calculation is much simpler since, if we know the old data value and the old parity value as well as the new data value, we can calculate the new parity information as follows

$$new\ parity = (old\ data\ \mathbf{xor}\ new\ data\ )\ \mathbf{xor}\ old\ parity$$

In level 4 a small write then uses 2 disks to perform 4 accesses--2 reads and 2 writes--while a small read involves only one read on one disk Table V summarizes the fourth level RAID characteristics Note that all small accesses improve--dramatically for the reads--but the small read-modify-write is still so slow relative to a level 1 RAID that its applicability to transaction processing is doubtful Recently Salem and Garcia-Molina proposed a Level 4 system [Salem 86]

Before proceeding to the next level we need to explain the performance of small writes in Table V (and hence small read-modify-writes since they entail the same operations in this RAID) The formula for the small writes divides D by 2 instead of 4 because 2 accesses can proceed in parallel the old data and old parity can be read at the same time and the new data and new parity can be written at the same time The performance of small writes is also divided by *G* because the single check disk in a group must be read and written with every small write in that group, thereby limiting the number of writes that can be performed at a time to the number of groups

The check disk is the bottleneck, and the final level RAID removes this bottleneck

MTTF		Exceeds Useful Lifetime					
		G=10			*G=25*		
		(820,000 hrs or >90 years)			(346,000 hrs or 40 years)		
Total Number of Disks		1 10D			1 04D		
Overhead Cost		10%			4%		
Useable Storage Capacity		91%			96%		
Events/Sec (vs Single Disk)	*Full RAID*	*Efficiency Per Disk*			*Efficiency Per Disk*		
		L4	*L4/L3*	*L4/L1*	*L4*	*L4/L3*	*L4/L1*
Large Reads	*D/S*	91/S	100%	91%	96/S	100%	96%
Large Writes	*D/S*	91/S	100%	182%	96/S	100%	192%
Large R-M-W	*D/S*	91/S	100%	136%	96/S	100%	146%
Small Reads	*D*	91	1200%	91%	96	3000%	96%
Small Writes	*D/2G*	05	120%	9%	02	120%	4%
Small R-M-W	*D/G*	09	120%	14%	04	120%	6%

Table V. *Characteristics of a Level 4 RAID The L4/L3 column gives the % performance of L4 in terms of L3 and the L4/L1 column gives it in terms of L1 (>100% means L4 is faster) Small reads improve because they no longer tie up a whole group at a time Small writes and R-M-Ws improve some because we make the same assumptions as we made in Table II the slowdown for two related I/Os can be ignored because only two disks are involved*

11. Fifth Level RAID: No Single Check Disk

While level 4 RAID achieved parallelism for reads, writes are still limited to one per group since every write must read and write the check disk The final level RAID distributes the data and check information across all the disks--including the check disks Figure 4 compares the location of check information in the sectors of disks for levels 4 and 5 RAIDs

The performance impact of this small change is large since RAID level 5 can support multiple individual writes per group For example, suppose in Figure 4 above we want to write sector 0 of disk 2 and sector 1 of disk 3 As shown on the left Figure 4, in RAID level 4 these writes must be sequential since both sector 0 and sector 1 of disk 5 must be written However, as shown on the right, in RAID level 5 the writes can proceed in parallel since a write to sector 0 of disk 2 still involves a write to disk 5 but a write to sector 1 of disk 3 involves a write to disk 4

These changes bring RAID level 5 near the best of both worlds small read-modify-writes now perform close to the speed per disk of a level 1 RAID while keeping the large transfer performance per disk and high useful storage capacity percentage of the RAID levels 3 and 4 Spreading the data across all disks even improves the performance of small reads, since there is one more disk per group that contains data Table VI summarizes the characteristics of this RAID

Keeping in mind the caveats given earlier, a Level 5 RAID appears very attractive if you want to do just supercomputer applications, or just transaction processing when storage capacity is limited, or if you want to do both supercomputer applications *and* transaction processing

12. Discussion

Before concluding the paper, we wish to note a few more interesting points about RAIDs The first is that while the schemes for disk striping and parity support were presented as if they were done by hardware, there is no necessity to do so We just give the method, and the decision between hardware and software solutions is strictly one of cost and benefit. For example, in cases where disk buffering is effective, there is no extra disks reads for level 5 small writes since the old data and old parity would be in main memory, so software would give the best performance as well as the least cost.

In this paper we have assumed the transfer unit is a multiple of the sector As the size of the smallest transfer unit grows larger than one

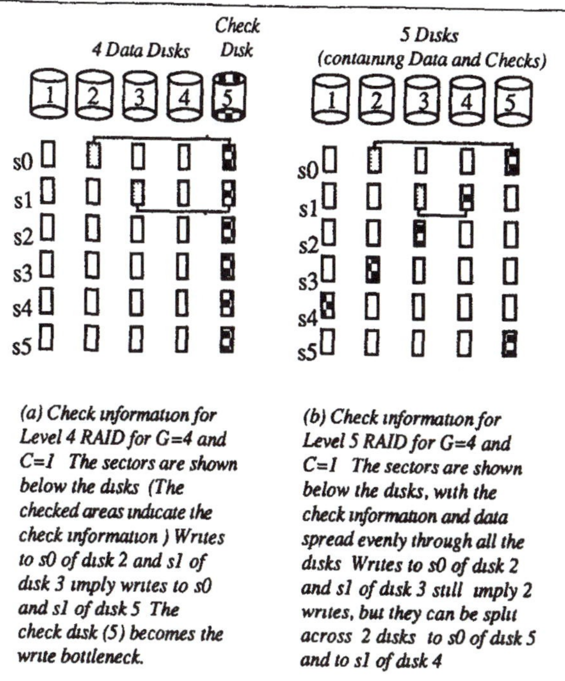

(a) Check information for Level 4 RAID for G=4 and C=1 The sectors are shown below the disks (The checked areas indicate the check information) Writes to s0 of disk 2 and s1 of disk 3 imply writes to s0 and s1 of disk 5 The check disk (5) becomes the write bottleneck.

(b) Check information for Level 5 RAID for G=4 and C=1 The sectors are shown below the disks, with the check information and data spread evenly through all the disks Writes to s0 of disk 2 and s1 of disk 3 still imply 2 writes, but they can be split across 2 disks to s0 of disk 5 and to s1 of disk 4

Figure 4 *Location of check information per sector for Level 4 RAID vs. Level 5 RAID*

MTTF		Exceeds Useful Lifetime					
		G=10			*G=25*		
		(820,000 hrs or >90 years)			(346,000 hrs or 40 years)		
Total Number of Disks		1 10D			1 04D		
Overhead Cost		10%			4%		
Useable Storage Capacity		91%			96%		
Events/Sec (vs Single Disk)	*Full RAID*	*Efficiency Per Disk*			*Efficiency Per Disk*		
		L5	*L5/L4*	*L5/L1*	*L5*	*L5/L4*	*L5/L1*
Large Reads	*D/S*	91/S	100%	91%	96/S	100%	96%
Large Writes	*D/S*	91/S	100%	182%	96/S	100%	192%
Large R-M-W	*D/S*	91/S	100%	136%	96/S	100%	144%
Small Reads	(1+C/G)D	1 00	110%	100%	1 00	104%	100%
Small Writes	(1+C/G)D/4	25	550%	50%	25	1300%	50%
Small R-M-W	(1+C/G)D/2	50	550%	75%	50	1300%	75%

Table VI *Characteristics of a Level 5 RAID The L5/L4 column gives the % performance of L5 in terms of L4 and the L5/L1 column gives it in terms of L1 (>100% means L5 is faster) Because reads can be spread over all disks, including what were check disks in level 4, all small I/Os improve by a factor of 1+C/G Small writes and R-M-Ws improve because they are no longer constrained by group size, getting the full disk bandwidth for the 4 I/O's associated with these accesses We again make the same assumptions as we made in Tables II and V the slowdown for two related I/Os can be ignored because only two disks are involved*

sector per drive--such as a full track with an I/O protocol that supports data returned out-of-order--then the performance of RAIDs improves significantly because of the full track buffer in every disk For example, if every disk begins transferring to its buffer as soon as it reaches the next sector, then *S* may reduce to less than 1 since there would be virtually no rotational delay With transfer units the size of a track, it is not even clear if synchronizing the disks in a group improves RAID performance

This paper makes two separable points the advantages of building I/O systems from personal computer disks and the advantages of five different disk array organizations, independent of disks used in those array The later point starts with the traditional mirrored disks to achieve acceptable reliability, with each succeeding level improving

- *the data rate,* characterized by a small number of requests per second for massive amounts of sequential information (supercomputer applications),

- *the I/O rate*, characterized by a large number of read-modify-writes to a small amount of random information (transaction-processing),
- or *the useable storage capacity*,

or possibly all three

Figure 5 shows the performance improvements per disk for each level RAID The highest performance per disk comes from either Level 1 or Level 5 In transaction-processing situations using no more than 50% of storage capacity, then the choice is mirrored disks (Level 1) However, if the situation calls for using more than 50% of storage capacity, or for supercomputer applications, or for combined supercomputer applications and transaction processing, then Level 5 looks best Both the strength and weakness of Level 1 is that it duplicates data rather than calculating check information, for the duplicated data improves read performance but lowers capacity and write performance,while check data is useful only on a failure

Inspired by the space-time product of paging studies [Denning 78], we propose a single figure of merit called the *space-speed product* the useable storage fraction times the efficiency per event Using this metric, Level 5 has an advantage over Level 1 of 1 7 for reads and 3 3 for writes for G=10

Let us return to the first point, the advantages of building I/O system from personal computer disks Compared to traditional Single Large Expensive Disks (SLED), Redundant Arrays of Inexpensive Disks (RAID) offer significant advantages for the same cost Table VII compares a level 5 RAID using 100 inexpensive data disks with a group size of 10 to the IBM 3380 As you can see, a level 5 RAID offers a factor of roughly 10 improvement in performance, reliability, and power consumption (and hence air conditioning costs) and a factor of 3 reduction in size over this SLED Table VII also compares a level 5 RAID using 10 inexpensive data disks with a group size of 10 to a Fujitsu M2361A "Super Eagle" In this comparison RAID offers roughly a factor of 5 improvement in performance, power consumption, and size with more than two orders of magnitude improvement in (calculated) reliability

RAID offers the further advantage of modular growth over SLED Rather than being limited to 7,500 MB per increase for $100,000 as in the case of this model of IBM disk, RAIDs can grow at either the group size (1000 MB for $11,000) or, if partial groups are allowed, at the disk size (100 MB for $1,100) The flip side of the coin is that RAID also makes sense in systems considerably smaller than a SLED Small incremental costs also makes hot standby spares practical to further reduce MTTR and thereby increase the MTTF of a large system For example, a 1000 disk level 5 RAID with a group size of 10 and a few standby spares could have a calculated MTTF of over 45 years

A final comment concerns the prospect of designing a complete transaction processing system from either a Level 1 or Level 5 RAID The drastically lower power per megabyte of inexpensive disks allows systems designers to consider battery backup for the whole disk array--the power needed for 110 PC disks is less than two Fujitsu Super Eagles Another approach would be to use a few such disks to save the contents of battery

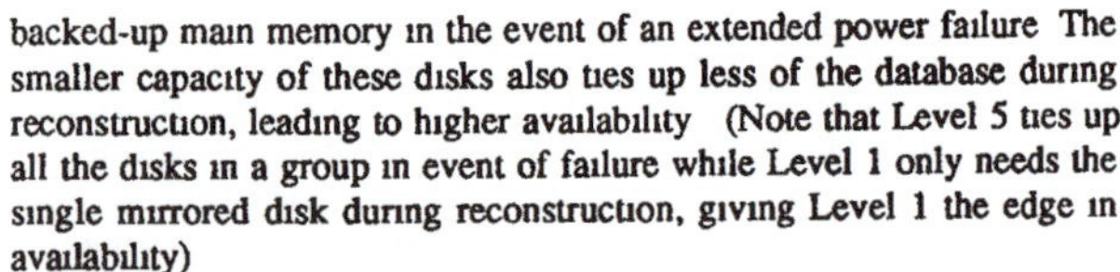

backed-up main memory in the event of an extended power failure The smaller capacity of these disks also ties up less of the database during reconstruction, leading to higher availability (Note that Level 5 ties up all the disks in a group in event of failure while Level 1 only needs the single mirrored disk during reconstruction, giving Level 1 the edge in availability)

13. Conclusion

RAIDs offer a cost effective option to meet the challenge of exponential growth in the processor and memory speeds We believe the size reduction of personal computer disks is a key to the success of disk arrays, just as Gordon Bell argues that the size reduction of microprocessors is a key to the success in multiprocessors [Bell 85] In both cases the smaller size simplifies the interconnection of the many components as well as packaging and cabling While large arrays of mainframe processors (or SLEDs) are possible, it is certainly easier to construct an array from the same number of microprocessors (or PC drives) Just as Bell coined the term "multi" to distinguish a multiprocessor made from microprocessors, we use the term "RAID" to identify a disk array made from personal computer disks

With advantages in cost-performance, reliability, power consumption, and modular growth, we expect RAIDs to replace SLEDs in future I/O systems There are, however, several open issues that may bare on the practicality of RAIDs

- *What is the impact of a RAID on latency?*
- *What is the impact on MTTF calculations of non-exponential failure assumptions for individual disks?*
- *What will be the real lifetime of a RAID vs calculated MTTF using the independent failure model?*
- *How would synchronized disks affect level 4 and 5 RAID performance?*
- *How does "slowdown" S actually behave? [Livny 87]*
- *How do defective sectors affect RAID?*
- *How do you schedule I/O to level 5 RAIDs to maximize write parallelism?*
- *Is there locality of reference of disk accesses in transaction processing?*
- *Can information be automatically redistributed over 100 to 1000 disks to reduce contention?*
- *Will disk controller design limit RAID performance?*
- *How should 100 to 1000 disks be constructed and physically connected to the processor?*
- *What is the impact of cabling on cost, performance, and reliability?*
- *Where should a RAID be connected to a CPU so as not to limit performance? Memory bus? I/O bus? Cache?*
- *Can a file system allow differ striping policies for different files?*
- *What is the role of solid state disks and WORMs in a RAID?*
- *What is the impact on RAID of "parallel access" disks (access to every surface under the read/write head in parallel)?*

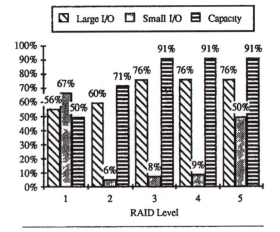

Figure 5 *Plot of Large (Grouped) and Small (Individual) Read-Modify-Writes per second per disk and useable storage capacity for all five levels of RAID (D=100, G=10) We assume a single S factor uniformly for all levels with S=1 3 where it is needed*

Characteristics	*RAID 5L (100 10) (CP3100)*	*SLED (IBM 3380)*	*RAID v SLED (>1 better for RAID)*	*RAID 5L (10,10) (CP3100)*	*SLED (Fujitsu M2361)*	*RAID v SLED (>1 better for RAID)*
Formatted Data Capacity (MB)	10,000	7,500	1 33	1,000	600	1 67
Price/MB (controller incl)	$11-$8	$18-$10	2 2- 9	$11-$8	$20-$17	2 5-1 5
Rated MTTF (hours)	820,000	30,000	27 3	8,200,000	20,000	410
MTTF in practice (hours)	?	100,000	?	?	?	?
No Actuators	110	4	22 5	11	1	11
Max I/O's/Actuator	30	50	6	30	40	8
Max Grouped RMW/box	1250	100	12 5	125	20	6 2
Max Individual RMW/box	825	100	8 2	83	20	4 2
Typ I/O's/Actuator	20	30	7	20	24	8
Typ Grouped RMW/box	833	60	13 9	83	12	6 9
Typ Individual RMW/box	550	60	9 2	55	12	4 6
Volume/Box (cubic feet)	10	24	2 4	1	3 4	3 4
Power/box (W)	1100	6,600	6 0	110	640	5 8
Min Expansion Size (MB)	100-1000	7,500	7 5-75	100-1000	600	0 6-6

Table VII *Comparison of IBM 3380 disk model AK4 to Level 5 RAID using 100 Conners & Associates CP 3100s disks and a group size of 10 and a comparison of the Fujitsu M2361A "Super Eagle" to a level 5 RAID using 10 inexpensive data disks with a group size of 10 Numbers greater than 1 in the comparison columns favor the RAID*

Acknowledgements

We wish to acknowledge the following people who participated in the discussions from which these ideas emerged Michael Stonebraker, John Ousterhout, Doug Johnson, Ken Lutz, Anapum Bhide, Gaetano Borriello Mark Hill, David Wood, and students in SPATS seminar offered at U C Berkeley in Fall 1987 We also wish to thank the following people who gave comments useful in the preparation of this paper Anapum Bhide, Pete Chen, Ron David, Dave Ditzel, Fred Douglis, Dieter Gawlick, Jim Gray, Mark Hill Doug Johnson, Joan Pendleton, Martin Schulze, and Hervé Touati This work was supported by the National Science Foundation under grant # MIP-8715235

Appendix Reliability Calculation

Using probability theory we can calculate the $MTTF_{Group}$ We first assume independent and exponential failure rates Our model uses a biased coin with the probability of heads being the probability that a second failure will occur within the MTTR of a first failure Since disk failures are exponential

$$\text{Probability(at least one of the remaining disks failing in MTTR)} = [\, 1 - (e^{-MTTR/MTTF_{Disk}})^{(G+C-1)} \,]$$

In all practical cases

$$MTTR \ll \frac{MTTF_{Disk}}{G+C}$$

and since $(1 - e^{-X})$ is approximately X for $0 < X \ll 1$

$$\text{Probability(at least one of the remaining disks failing in MTTR)} = MTTR*(G+C-1)/MTTF_{Disk}$$

Then that on a disk failure we flip this coin

heads => a system crash, because a second failure occurs before the first was repaired,

tails => recover from error and continue

Then

$$MTTF_{Group} = \text{Expected[Time between Failures]} * \text{Expected[no of flips until first heads]}$$

$$= \frac{\text{Expected[Time between Failures]}}{\text{Probability(heads)}}$$

$$= \frac{MTTF_{Disk}}{(G+C)*(MTTR*(G+C-1)/MTTF_{Disk})}$$

$$MTTF_{Group} = \frac{(MTTF_{Disk})^2}{(G+C)*(G+C-1)*MTTR}$$

Group failure is not precisely exponential in our model, but we have validated this simplifying assumption for practical cases of $MTTR \ll MTTF/(G+C)$ This makes the MTTF of the whole system just $MTTF_{Group}$ divided by the number of groups, n_G

References

[Bell 84] C G Bell, "The Mini and Micro Industries,' *IEEE Computer* Vol 17 No 10 (October 1984), pp 14-30

[Joy 85] B Joy presentation at ISSCC '85 panel session, Feb 1985

[Siewiorek 82] D P Siewiorek, C G Bell, and A Newell, *Computer Structures Principles and Examples*, p 46

[Moore 75] G E Moore, "Progress in Digital Integrated Electronics," *Proc IEEE Digital Integrated Electronic Device Meeting*, (1975), p 11

[Myers 86] G J Myers A Y C Yu, and D L House, "Microprocessor Technology Trends" *Proc IEEE*, Vol 74, no 12, (December 1986), pp 1605-1622

[Garcia 84] H Garcia Molina, R Cullingford, P Honeyman, R Lipton, "The Case for Massive Memory," Technical Report 326, Dept of EE and CS, Princeton Univ , May 1984

[Myers 86] W Myers, "The Competitiveness of the United States Disk Industry," *IEEE Computer*, Vol 19, No 11 (January 1986), pp 85-90

[Frank 87] P D Frank, "Advances in Head Technology," presentation at *Challenges in Disk Technology Short Course*, Institute for Information Storage Technology, Santa Clara University, Santa Clara, California, December 15-17, 1987

[Stevens 81] L D Stevens, "The Evolution of Magnetic Storage," *IBM Journal of Research and Development*, Vol 25, No 5, Sept 1981, pp 663-675

[Harker 81] J M Harker *et al*, "A Quarter Century of Disk File Innovation," *ibid*, pp 677-689

[Amdahl 67] G M Amdahl, "Validity of the single processor approach to achieving large scale computing capabilities," *Proceedings AFIPS 1967 Spring Joint Computer Conference* Vol 30 (Atlantic City, New Jersey April 1967), pp 483-485

[Boral 83] H Boral and D J DeWitt, "Database Machines An Ideas Whose Time Has Passed? A Critique of the Future of Database Machines," *Proc International Conf on Database Machines*, Edited by H -O Leilich and M Misskoff, Springer-Verlag, Berlin, 1983

[IBM 87] "IBM 3380 Direct Access Storage Introduction," IBM GC 26-4491-0, September 1987

[Gawlick 87] D Gawlick, private communication, Nov , 1987

[Fujitsu 87] "M2361A Mini-Disk Drive Engineering Specifications," (revised) Feb , 1987, B03P-4825-0001A

[Adaptec 87] AIC-6250, *IC Product Guide*, Adaptec, stock # DB0003-00 rev B, 1987, p 46

[Livny 87] Livny, M , S Khoshafian, H Boral, "Multi-disk management algorithms," *Proc of ACM SIGMETRICS*, May 1987

[Kim 86] M Y Kim, "Synchronized disk interleaving," *IEEE Trans on Computers*, vol C-35, no 11, Nov 1986

[Salem 86] K Salem and Garcia-Molina, H , "Disk Striping," *IEEE 1986 Int Conf on Data Engineering*, 1986

[Bitton 88] D Bitton and J Gray, "Disk Shadowing," *in press*, 1988

[Kurzweil 88] F Kurzweil, "Small Disk Arrays - The Emerging Approach to High Performance," presentation at Spring COMPCON 88, March 1, 1988, San Francisco, CA

[Hamming 50] R W Hamming, "Error Detecting and Correcting Codes," *The Bell System Technical Journal*, Vol XXVI, No 2 (April 1950), pp 147-160

[Hillis 87] D Hillis, private communication, October, 1987

[Park 86] A Park and K Balasubramanian, "Providing Fault Tolerance in Parallel Secondary Storage Systems," Department of Computer Science, Princeton University, CS-TR-057-86, Nov 7, 1986

[Maginnis 87] N B Maginnis, "Store More, Spend Less Mid-range Options Abound,"*Computerworld*, Nov 16, 1987, p 71

[Denning 78] P J Denning and D F Slutz, "Generalized Working Sets for Segment Reference Strings," *CACM*, vol 21, no 9, (Sept. 1978) pp 750-759

[Bell 85] Bell, C G , "Multis a new class of multiprocessor computers,"*Science*, vol. 228 (April 26, 1985) 462-467

Chapter 4
Transaction Management

As is well known, transaction management consists of concurrency control and crash recovery. The seminal work in this area is the 1975 paper by Jim Gray and company, which contains a good presentation of **multi-granularity two-phase locking** and **degrees of consistency**. Multi-granularity locking is at the heart of every serious database system's concurrency control scheme. The definitions of the degrees of consistency in this paper are not entirely declarative – they depend upon on a lock-based implementation of concurrency control. This has led to some confusion the SQL standards [BBG+95]. Adya et al. propose a more robust but complex definition [ALO00].

Locking is **pessimistic** in that a transaction is blocked if there is any possibility that a nonserializable schedule could result. On the other hand, a DBMS could use an **optimistic** algorithm that allowed a transaction to continue processing when serializability could be compromised, in the belief that it probably won't be. We have included the original paper on optimistic methods as the second paper in this chapter.

There have been a number of simulation studies that compare dynamic locking to alternate concurrency control schemes including optimistic methods – we include one as the third paper in this chapter. This paper is an example of a category of systems research that is not often covered in collections such as this, namely **performance analysis**. Many system design decisions are too complex to think through analytically, and require detailed simulation to get right. An interesting aspect of this paper is that it not only explores a performance problem, it also explains the contradictory conclusions of previous analyses. The net result of this study is that dynamic locking wins except when unrealistic assumptions are made, such as the existence of an arbitrary number of processors. Hence *all* commercial relational systems use dynamic locking as the mechanism of choice. However in some client-server environments, there is sometimes enough idle time for optimistic techniques to make sense [FCL97]. For a good treatment of the various other concurrency control techniques, the reader is directed to [BHG87].

Only a few embellishments on dynamic locking have been shown to make any sense. First, it is reasonable for read transactions to access the database as of a time in the recent past. This allows such a transaction to set no locks, as explained in [Cha82]. Permitting a reader to set no locks increases parallelism and has been implemented commercial by several vendors. The second embellishment concerns "hot spots" in databases. In high transaction rate systems there are often records that many transactions wish to read and write. The ultimate hot spot is a one-record database. In order to do a large number of transactions per second to a one-record database, some new technique must be used. One possibility is to use some form of *escrow transactions*, as discussed in [One86] and implemented in a variety of IBM products. A third embellishment is that increased parallelism can be obtained in tree-based indexes if a special (non-two-phase) locking protocol is used for index pages. One protocol for these special cases in B+-trees is discussed in the fourth paper in this chapter by Lehman and Yao; this protocol has been extended to other structures like R-trees as well [KMH97]. An alternative family of protocols are described in [Moh96], but only work for B+ trees.

Crash recovery is the second required service performed by any transaction manager, and we have included the very readable paper by Haerder and Reuter as an introduction to this topic. This is universally done via some form of **Write Ahead Log (WAL)** technique in which information is written to a log to assist with recovery. After a crash, this log is processed backward, **undoing** the effect of uncommitted transactions, and then forward, **redoing** the effect of uncommitted transactions.

There are a variety of approaches to the contents of a log. At one extreme, a **physical** log records all physical changes onto secondary storage; that is, the before- and after-image of each changed bit in the database is recorded in the log. In this case, an insert of a new record in a relation will require part of the data page on which it is placed to be logged. In addition, an insert must be performed for each B-tree index defined on the relation in question. Inserting a new key into a B-tree index will cause about half the bits on the corresponding page to be moved and result in a log record on average the size of a page. To perform an insert into a relation with K indexes will generate a collection of log records with combined length in excess of K pages on the average.

The objective of **logical** or **event** logging is to reduce the size of the log. In this case, a log is a collection of events for each of which the system supplies an undo and redo routine. For example, an event might be of the form "a record with values X_1, ..., X_n was inserted into relation *R*." If this event must be undone, then the corresponding undo routine would remove the record from the relation in question and delete appropriate keys from any indexes. Similarly, the redo routine would regenerate the insert and perform index insertions.

It is obvious that logical logging results in a log of reduced size but requires a longer recovery time, because logical undo or redo is presumably slower than physical undo or redo. However there are problems with logical logging. For example, during page splits a B-tree will be physically inconsistent. A concurrency scheme will hide this inconsistency during normal operation, but if a crash happens inopportunely, the B-tree's structure of nodes and pointers may be corrupted. This is no problem with physical logging, because the B-tree will be recovered utilizing the log. However, with logical logging there is no B-tree log, and restoring structural integrity must be guaranteed in another way. One option is to achieve this via careful **ordered writes** to the database: allocate two new pages for the split page and write these pages to disk before updating the parent page. Ordered writes complicate the buffer manager: it requires it to keep track not only of which dirty pages may be replaced, but also of the order in which they can be replaced. Alternatively, one can do **physiological** logging, e.g. physically log structural modifications to an index tree, but logically log the insertion of the tuple. There are a large number of possible systems utilizing combinations of physical and logical logging.

Haerder and Reuter categorize logging techniques as:

- Atomic vs. Not Atomic
- Force vs. No Force
- Steal vs. No Steal

Loosely, atomic means a shadow page recovery scheme, whereas not atomic represents an update-in-place algorithm. Force represents the technique of forcing dirty pages from the buffer pool when a transaction commits. No force is the converse. Last, steal connotes the possibility that dirty data pages will be written to disk prior to the end of the transaction, whereas no steal is the opposite. Any recovery scheme (e.g. some of the ones suggested in the OS literature) should be evaluated by placing it into this taxonomy; it is then easy to decide whether the scheme is suitable without worrying about its details. Although Haerder and Reuter discuss the subject as if there were a collection of reasonable techniques, in fact most commercial database systems use:

- Not Atomic
- No Force
- Steal

The basic reasoning is fairly simple. Atomic writing of pages would require that the DBMS use a shadow page technique. As discussed in [Gra81], use of this technique was one of the major mistakes of System R and had to be corrected in DB2. All commercial systems do "update in place", which essentially entails that writes to the disk not be atomic. Second, a DBMS will go vastly slower if it forces pages at commit time. Hence nobody takes "force" seriously. Also "no steal" requires enough buffer space to hold the updates of the largest transaction. Because "batch" transactions are still quite common, no commercial system is willing to make this assumption. To this taxonomy one can also add Physical vs. Logical log records, though as we discuss above hybrids are common.

As noted above, the conventional wisdom is to recover from crashes for which the disk is intact by processing the log backward, performing undo, and then forward, performing redo. If the disk is not intact, then the system must restore a **dump** and the process the log forward from the dump, performing redo. Last, uncommitted transactions must be undone by processing the log backward, performing undo. Recovering from these two kinds of crashes with different techniques complicates transaction code. The work on ARIES, included as our next paper, shows that a uniform algorithm can be used such that redo is always performed first, followed by undo. The key idea in ARIES is to "repeat history", and reconstruct the database system's state at the time of the crash; after that, the abort of any uncommitted transactions uses the same logic that is used when aborting transactions during normal operation.

In theory, ARIES should result in simpler algorithms, but the ARIES paper is perhaps the most complicated paper in this collection. There are two good overviews of ARIES that the reader might consider before diving into the details: one is in Ramakrishnan and Gehrke's undergraduate textbook, the other is a survey paper by Mike Franklin in the *Handbook of Computer Science* [Fra97].[1] The full ARIES paper here is complicated significantly by its diversionary discussions of the drawbacks of alternative design decisions along the way. On the first pass, the reader is encouraged to ignore this material and focus solely on the ARIES approach; the drawbacks of alternatives are important to understand, but should be saved for a more careful second read. The actual ARIES protocols treat two issues that complicate the presentation further. One issue is the support for efficiently managing internal database state like heap file free-space maps and indexes. This leads to mechanisms for **nested top actions** and **logical undo logging.** Logical undo logging has other uses beyond managing internal state – it is key to exotic concurrency schemes like escrow transactions. The second issue is a set of tricks to minimize system downtime during recovery. In practice, it is important for recovery time to appear as short as possible, since many customers demand so-called 24×7 operation, i.e. continuous availability.

Our last two papers in this section focus on the complications that arise when implementing concurrency and recovery in **distributed** databases, where coordination is done over a network, and **partial failure** of the distributed system can lead to confusion if one machine tries to move forward while disconnected from another.

Unfortunately, most concurrency control techniques discussed in the literature are not very realistic. For a survey of available techniques consult [BG81]. For example, the SDD-1 concurrency control scheme was based on timestamps and conflict graphs [BG80]. This scheme unfortunately does not allow a transaction to abort, assumes that transactions within a single transaction class are sequenced outside the model, and allows a transaction to send only one message to each site. All of these assumptions are unrealistic in a distributed environment, and

---

[1] These overviews are summarized in a slide set available on the website for this book.

timestamp techniques have not enjoyed any measure of success. Moreover, it is clearly difficult to design conflict graphs, as transactions can arbitrarily be assigned to classes. Even CCA, who invented the SDD-1 algorithms, gave up on them in their next prototype, ADAPLEX [Cha83]. The reader is advised to carefully evaluate the reasonableness of the assumptions required in many of the schemes in the literature.

In our opinion, distributed concurrency control is quite simple. In practice, distributed concurrency schemes must allow a heterogeneous set of systems to coordinate via an open, standard API. In an open, interoperable architecture, distributed concurrency control *must* be built on top of local facilities provided by each underlying data manager. At the moment, all commercial products use some variation on locking. Unless there is some sort of global standard that requires a local data manager to send its local "waits-for" graph to somebody else, it will be impossible to do any sort of global deadlock detection because the prerequisite information cannot be assembled from the local data managers. Hence, timeout is the only deadlock detection scheme that will work in this environment. As a result, setting locks at the local sites within the local data manager and using timeout for deadlock detection will be the solution used.

Crash recovery, on the other hand, is a much more complex subject. A distributed transaction must be committed everywhere or aborted everywhere. Since there is a local data manager at each site, it can successfully perform a local commit or abort. The only challenge is for a transaction coordinator to ensure that all local data managers commit or all abort. The main idea is very simple, and has come to be called a **two-phase commit**. When the coordinator is ready to commit a global transaction he cannot simply send out a commit message to each site. The problem is that site *A* must flush all its log pages for the local portion of the transaction and then write a commit record. This could take one or more I/Os for a substantial transaction and consume perhaps hundreds of milliseconds on a busy system. Add perhaps a second of message delay and operating system overhead, and there is perhaps a two second period from the time the coordinator sends out the commit message during which disaster is possible. Specifically, if site *A* crashes then it will not have committed the transaction, and moreover, it will not be able to commit later because the prerequisite log pages were still in main memory at the time of the crash and therefore were lost in the crash. On the other hand, the other sites could have remained up and successfully committed the transaction as directed. In this scenario all sites except *A* have committed the transaction, and site *A* cannot commit. Hence, we have failed to achieve the objective of every site committing. As a result, there is a **window of uncertainty** during the commit process during which a failure will be catastrophic. Such windows of uncertainty have been studied in [Coo82].

The basic solution to this problem is for the coordinator to send out a "prepare" message prior to the commit. This will instruct each local site to force all the log pages for a transaction, so that the transaction can be successfully committed even if there is a site crash. The basic algorithm is described in the paper by Mohan et al., which is our next selection in this book. However the idea seems to have been simultaneously invented by several researchers. With a two-phase commit, a distributed DBMS can successfully recover from all single site failures, all multiple site failures and certain cases of network partitions. The only drawback of a two-phase commit is that it requires another round of messages in the protocol. Hence, this resiliency to crashes does not come for free, and there is a definite "level of service" versus cost tradeoff.

Concerning multiple copies of objects, there are a **large** number of algorithms that have been proposed, e.g. [Tho79, Gif79, Sto79, Her84]. Unfortunately virtually all algorithms are of limited utility, because they fail to deal with constraints imposed by the reality of the commercial marketplace. The first constraint is that a multiple copy algorithm must be optimized for the case that the number of copies is exactly two. There are few DBMS clients interested in 20 copies of a multi-terabyte database. In general they want two, to ensure that they can stay up in the presence of a single failure. The second constraint is that a read request must be satisfied by performing a single physical read to exactly one copy. Any scheme that slows down reads is not likely to win much real-world acceptance. Consequently, schemes which require a transaction to lock a quorum of the copies will fail this litmus test. They will require read locks to be set on both copies in a 2 copy system in order to satisfy a read request. Such an algorithm will lose to a scheme which locks both copies only on writes and one copy on reads. Such a "read-one-write-all" algorithm is presented in [ESC85]. An interesting survey of other algorithms can be found in [BHG87, DGS85].

More recently, the experience of real-world users with replication systems has generated the following unfortunate state of affairs. If one wants to ensure transactional consistency between a data set and its replica, then a two phase commit protocol must be utilized. The extra messages required to commit a transaction entail an overhead and delay in ability to commit the transaction that is unacceptable in the real world – particularly if some of the participants in a transaction are likely to be disconnected frequently. On the other hand, if one implements a scheme that does not include transactional consistency, then there is no semantic guarantee that can be made regarding the relative states of the two replicas. As such, one can either implement an impossibly expensive (but correct) replication scheme, or one that has no consistency guarantees at all. This obvious dilemma has plagued users for some time. Our fourth paper in this chapter by Gray, et al. attempts to quantify the problems that arise with either of these approaches; the analysis is fairly pessimistic, but the point is well taken. It also presents one simple solution to this dilemma by sticking with a "single-mastered" database that allows users to play with copies while they are offline, but without promising that their actions will persist.

References

[ALO00] Atul Adya, Barbara Liskov, and Patrick O'Neil. Generalized Isolation Level Definitions. In 16th *International Conference on Data Engineering (ICDE),* San Diego, CA, February 2000.

[BBG+95] Hal Berenson, Philip A. Bernstein, Jim Gray, Jim Melton, Elizabeth J. O'Neil, and Patrick E. O'Neil. A Critique of ANSI SQL Isolation Levels. In *Proc. ACM SIGMOD International Conference on Management of Data,* pages 1-10, San Jose, CA, May 1995.

[BG80] Philip A. Bernstein and Nathan Goodman. "Timestamp-Based Algorithms for Concurrency Control in Distributed Database Systems". In *Proc. Sixth International Conference on Very Large Data Bases (VLDB).* Montreal, Canada, October, 1980.

[BG81] Philip Bernstein and Nathan Goodman., "Concurrency Control in Distributed Database Systems," *Computing Surveys*, June 1981, p185-222.

[BHG87] Philip Bernstein, Vassos Hadzilacos and Nathan Goodman., *Concurrency Control and Recovery in Database Systems*, Addison-Wesley, Reading, MA, 1987.

[Cha82] Chan, A., et al. "The Implementation of an Integrated Concurrency Control and Recovery Scheme," Proc. 1982 ACM-SIGMOD Conference on Management of Data, Orlando, FL, June 1982.

[Coo82] Eric C. Cooper. "Analysis of Distributed Commit Protocols." In *Proc. ACM-SIGMOD International Conference on Management of Data*. June 2-4, 1982, Orlando, Florida.

[DGS85] Susan B. Davidson, Hector Garcia-Molina and Dale Skeen. "Consistency in Partitioned Networks," *ACM Computing Surveys* 17(3): 341-370, September 1985.

[ESC85] Amr El Abbadi and Dale Skeen and Flaviu Cristian. "An Efficient, Fault-Tolerant Protocol for Replicated Data Management." *In Proceedings of the Fourth ACM SIGACT-SIGMOD Symposium on Principle of Database Systems (PODS)*, March 25-27, 1985, Portland, Oregon, pp. 215-229.

[FCL97] M. Franklin, M, Carey, M. Livny: "Transactional Client-Server Cache Consistency: Alternatives and Performance". *ACM Transactions on Database Systems*, 22(3), September, 1997.

[Fra97] Franklin, M.J., "Concurrency Control and Recovery", in The Handbook of Computer Science and Engineering, A. Tucker, ed., CRC Press, Boca Raton, FL 1997.

[Gif79] Gifford, D., "Weighted Voting for Replicated Data," Proc. 7th Symposium on Operating System Principles, Dec. 1979.

[Gra81] Gray, J., et al., "The Recovery Manager of the System R Database Manager," Computing Surveys, June 1981.

[Her84] Herlihy, M., "General Quorum Consensus: A Replication Method for Abstract Data Types," Dept. of Computer Science, CMU, Pittsburgh, Pa., CMU-CS-84-164, Dec. 1984.

[KMH97] Marcel Kornacker, C. Mohan, and Joseph M. Hellerstein. "Concurrency and Recovery in Generalized Search Trees". In *Proc. ACM SIGMOD International Conference on Management of Data,* pages 62-72, Tucson, AZ, May 1997.

[Moh96] Mohan, C., "Concurrency Control and Recovery Methods for B+-Tree Indexes: ARIES/KVL and ARIES/IM," Performance of Concurrency Control Mechanisms in Centralized Database Systems, Vijay Kumar (ed.), Prentice-Hall, 1996.

[One86] O'Neil, P., "The Escrow Transactional Method," ACM TODS 11(4), Dec. 1986.

[Sto79] Stonebraker, M., "Concurrency Control and Consistency of Multiple Copies in Distributed INGRES," *IEEE Transactions on Software Engineering* 5(3), March 1979.

[Tho79] Thomas, R., "A Majority Consensus Approach to Concurrency Control for Multiple Copy Distributed Database Systems," *ACM Transactions On Database Systems (TODS)* 4(2), June 1979.

Modelling in Data Base Management Systems, G.M. Nijssen, (ed.)
North Holland Publishing Company, 1976

Granularity of Locks and Degrees of Consistency in a Shared Data Base

J.N. Gray, R.A. Lorie, G.R. Putzolu, I.L. Traiger

IBM Research Laboratory
San Jose, California

The problem of choosing the appropriate granularity (size) of lockable objects is introduced and the tradeoff between concurrency and overhead is discussed. A locking protocol which allows simultaneous locking at various granularities by different transactions is presented. It is based on the introduction of additional lock modes besides the conventional share mode and exclusive mode. A proof is given of the equivalence of this protocol to a conventional one.

Next the issue of consistency in a shared environment is analyzed. This discussion is motivated by the realization that some existing data base systems use automatic lock protocols which insure protection only from certain types of inconsistencies (for instance those arising from transaction backup), thereby automatically providing a limited degree of consistency. Four degrees of consistency are introduced. They can be roughly characterized as follows: degree 0 protects others from your updates, degree 1 additionally provides protection from losing updates, degree 2 additionally provides protection from reading incorrect data items, and degree 3 additionally provides protection from reading incorrect relationships among data items (i.e. total protection). A discussion follows on the relationships of the four degrees to locking protocols, concurrency, overhead, recovery and transaction structure.

Lastly, these ideas are compared with existing data management systems.

I. GRANULARITY OF LOCKS:

An important issue which arises in the design of a data base management system is the choice of lockable units, i.e. the data aggregates which are atomically locked to insure consistency. Examples of lockable units are areas, files, individual records, field values, and intervals of field values.

The choice of lockable units presents a tradeoff between concurrency and overhead, which is related to the size or granularity of the units themselves. On the one hand, concurrency is increased if a fine lockable unit (for example a record or field) is chosen. Such unit is appropriate for a "simple" transaction which accesses few records. On the other hand a fine unit of locking would be costly for a "complex" transaction which accesses a large number of records. Such a transaction would have to set and reset a large number of locks, incurring the computational overhead of many invocations of the lock subsystem, and the storage overhead of representing many locks. A coarse lockable unit (for example a file) is probably convenient for a transaction which accesses many records. However, such a coarse unit discriminates against transactions which only want to lock one member of the file. From this discussion it follows that it would be desirable to have lockable units of different granularities coexisting in the same system.

This paper presents a lock protocol satisfying these requirements and discusses the related implementation issues of scheduling, granting and converting lock requests.

Hierarchical locks:

We will first assume that the set of resources to be locked is organized in a hierarchy. Note that this hierarchy is used in the context of a collection of resources and has nothing to do with the data model used in a data base system. The hierarchy of Figure 1 may be suggestive. We adopt the notation that each level of the hierarchy is given a node type which is a generic name for all the node instances of that type. For example, the data base has nodes of type area as its immediate descendants, each area in turn has nodes of type file as its immediate descendants and each file has nodes of type record as its immediate descendants in the hierarchy. Since it is a hierarchy, each node has a unique parent.

Figure 1. A sample lock hierarchy.

Each node of the hierarchy can be locked. If one requests exclusive access (X) to a particular node, then when the request is granted, the requestor has exclusive access to that node and implicitly to each of its descendants. If one requests shared access (S) to a particular node, then when the request is granted, the requestor has shared access to that node and implicitly to each descendant of that node. These two access modes lock an entire subtree rooted at the requested node.

Our goal is to find some technique for implicitly locking an entire subtree. In order to lock a subtree rooted at node R in share or exclusive mode it is important to prevent share or exclusive locks on the ancestors of R which would implicitly lock R and its descendants. Hence a new access mode, intention mode (I), is introduced. Intention mode is used to "tag" (lock) all ancestors of a node to be locked in share or exclusive mode. These tags signal the fact that locking is being done at a "finer" level and thereby prevents implicit or explicit exclusive or share locks on the ancestors.

The protocol to lock a subtree rooted at node R in exclusive or share mode is to first lock all ancestors of R in intention mode and then to lock node R in exclusive or share mode. For example, using Figure 1, to lock a particular file one should obtain intention access to the data base, to the area containing the file and then request exclusive (or share) access to the file itself. This implicitly locks all records of the file in exclusive (or share) mode.

Access modes and compatibility:

We say that two lock requests for the same node by two different transactions are compatible if they can be granted concurrently. The mode of the request determines its compatibility with requests made by other transactions. The three modes X, S and I are incompatible with one another but distinct S requests may be granted together and distinct I requests may be granted together.

The compatibilities among modes derive from their semantics. Share mode allows reading but not modification of the corresponding resource by the requestor and by other transactions. The semantics of exclusive mode is that the grantee may read and modify the resource but no other transaction may read or modify the resource while the exclusive lock is set. The reason for dichotomizing share and exclusive access is that several share requests can be granted concurrently (are compatible) whereas an exclusive request is not compatible with any other request. Intention mode was introduced to be incompatible with share and exclusive mode (to prevent share and exclusive locks). However, intention mode is compatible with itself since two transactions having intention access to a node will explicitly lock descendants of the node in X, S or I mode and thereby will either be compatible with one another or will be scheduled on the basis of their requests at the finer level. For example, two transactions can simultaneously be granted the data base and some area and some file in intention mode. In this case their explicit locks on particular records in the file will resolve any conflicts among them.

The notion of intention mode is refined to intention share mode (IS) and intention exclusive mode (IX) for two reasons: the intention share mode only requests share or intention share locks at the lower nodes of the tree (i.e. never requests an exclusive lock below the intention share node), hence IS is compatible with S mode. Since read only is a common form of access it will be profitable to distinguish this for greater concurrency. Secondly, if a transaction has an intention share lock on a node it can convert this to a share lock at a later time, but one cannot convert an intention exclusive lock to a share lock on a node. Rather to get the combined rights of share mode and intention exclusive mode one must obtain an X or SIX mode lock. (This issue is discussed in the section on rerequests below).

We recognize one further refinement of modes, namely share and intention exclusive mode (SIX). Suppose one transaction wants to read an entire subtree and to update particular nodes of that subtree. Using the modes provided so far it would have the options of: (a) requesting exclusive access to the root of the subtree and doing no further locking or (b) requesting intention exclusive access to the root of the subtree and explicitly locking the lower nodes in intention, share or exclusive mode. Alternative (a) has low concurrency. If only a small fraction of the read nodes are updated then alternative (b) has high locking overhead. The correct access mode would be share access to the subtree thereby allowing the transaction to read all nodes of the subtree without further locking and intention exclusive access to the subtree thereby allowing the transaction to set exclusive locks on those nodes in the subtree which are to be updated and IX or SIX locks on the intervening nodes. Since this is such a common case, SIX mode is introduced for this purpose. It is compatible with IS mode since other transactions requesting IS mode will explicitly lock lower nodes in IS or S mode thereby avoiding any updates (IX or X mode) produced by the SIX mode transaction. However SIX mode is not compatible with IX, S, SIX or X mode requests.

Table 1 gives the compatibility of the request modes, where for completeness we have also introduced the null mode (NL) which represents the absence of requests of a resource by a transaction.

	NL	IS	IX	S	SIX	X
NL	YES	YES	YES	YES	YES	YES
IS	YES	YES	YES	YES	YES	NO
IX	YES	YES	YES	NO	NO	NO
S	YES	YES	NO	YES	NO	NO
SIX	YES	YES	NO	NO	NO	NO
X	YES	NO	NO	NO	NO	NO

Table 1. Compatibilities among access modes.

To summarize, we recognize six modes of access to a resource:

NL: Gives no access to a node, i.e. represents the absence of a request of a resource.

IS: Gives intention share access to the requested node and allows the requestor to lock descendant nodes in S or IS mode. (It does no implicit locking.)

IX: Gives intention exclusive access to the requested node and allows the requestor to explicitly lock descendants in X, S, SIX, IX or IS mode. (It does no implicit locking.)

S: Gives share access to the requested node and to all descendants of the requested node without setting further locks. (It implicitly sets S locks on all descendants of the requested node.)

SIX: Gives share and intention exclusive access to the requested node. (In particular it implicitly locks all descendants of the node in share mode and allows the requestor to explicitly lock descendant nodes in X, SIX or IX mode.)

X: Gives exclusive access to the requested node and to all descendants of the requested node without setting further locks. (It implicitly sets X locks on all descendants. Locking lower nodes in S or IS mode would give no increased access.)

IS mode is the weakest non-null form of access to a resource. It carries fewer privileges than IX or S modes. IX mode allows IS, IX, S, SIX and X mode locks to be set on descendant nodes while S mode allows read only access to all descendants of the node without further locking. SIX mode carries the privileges of S and of IX mode (hence the name SIX). X mode is the most privileged form of access and allows reading and writing of all descendants of a node without further locking. Hence the modes can be ranked in the partial order (lattice) of privileges shown in Figure 2. Note that it is not a total order since IX and S are incomparable.

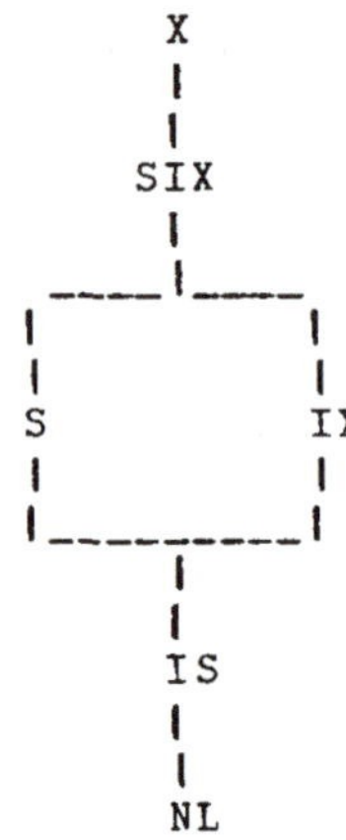

Figure 2. The partial ordering of modes by their privileges.

Rules for requesting nodes:

The implicit locking of nodes will not work if transactions are allowed to leap into the middle of the tree and begin locking nodes at random. The implicit locking implied by the S and X modes depends on all transactions obeying the following protocol:

(a) Before requesting an S or IS lock on a node, all ancestor nodes of the requested node must be held in IX or IS mode by the requestor.

(b) Before requesting an X, SIX or IX lock on a node, all ancestor nodes of the requested node must be held in SIX or IX mode by the requestor.

(c) Locks should be released either at the end of the transaction (in any order) or in leaf to root order. In particular, if locks are not held to end of transaction, one should not hold a lock after releasing its ancestors.

To paraphrase this, *locks are requested root to leaf, and released leaf to root*. Notice that leaf nodes are never requested in intention mode since they have no descendants.

Several examples:

To lock record R for read:

```
 lock data-base              with mode = IS
 lock area containing R      with mode = IS
 lock file containing R      with mode = IS
 lock record R               with mode = S
```

Don't panic, the transaction probably already has the data base, area and file lock.

To lock record R for write-exclusive access:

```
 lock data-base              with mode = IX
 lock area containing R      with mode = IX
 lock file containing R      with mode = IX
 lock record R               with mode = X
```

Note that if the records of this and the previous example are distinct, each request can be granted simultaneously to different transactions even though both refer to the same file.

To lock a file F for read and write access:

```
 lock data-base              with mode = IX
 lock area containing F      with mode = IX
 lock file F                 with mode = X
```

Since this reserves exclusive access to the file, if this request uses the same file as the previous two examples it or the other transactions will have to wait.

To lock a file F for complete scan and occasional update:

```
 lock data-base              with mode = IX
 lock area containing F      with mode = IX
 lock file F                 with mode = SIX
```

Thereafter, particular records in F can be locked for update by locking records in X mode. Notice that (unlike the previous example) this transaction is compatible with the first example. This is the reason for introducing SIX mode.

To quiesce the data base:

```
 lock data base with mode = X.
```

Note that this locks everyone else out.

Directed acyclic graphs of locks:

The notions so far introduced can be generalized to work for directed acyclic graphs (DAG) of resources rather than simply hierarchies of resources. A tree is a simple DAG. The key observation is that to implicitly or explicitly lock a node, one should lock all the parents of the node in the DAG and so by induction lock all ancestors of the node. In particular, to lock a subgraph one must implicitly or explicitly lock all ancestors of the subgraph in the appropriate mode (for a tree there is only one parent). To give an example of a non-hierarchical structure, imagine the locks are organized as in Figure 3.

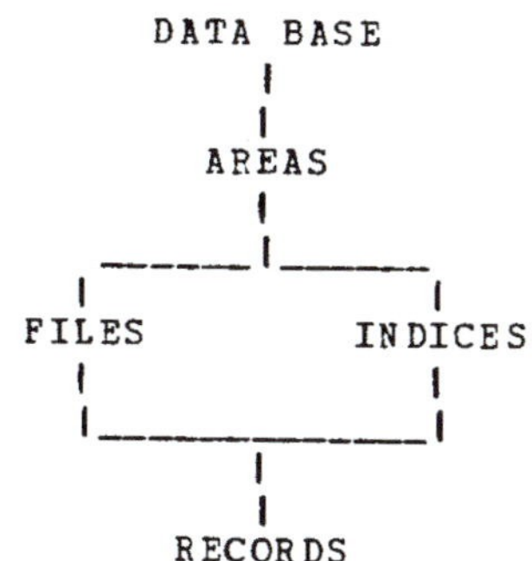

Figure 3. A non-hierarchical lock graph.

We postulate that areas are "physical" notions and that files, indices and records are logical notions. The data base is a collection of areas. Each area is a collection of files and indices. Each file has a corresponding index in the same area. Each record belongs to some file and to its corresponding index. A record is comprised of field values and some field is indexed by the index associated with the file containing the record. The file gives a sequential access path to the records and the index gives an associative access path to the records based on field values. Since individual fields are never locked, they do not appear in the lock graph.

To write a record R in file F with index I:

```
 lock data base            with mode = IX
 lock area containing F    with mode = IX
 lock file F               with mode = IX
 lock index I              with mode = IX
 lock record R             with mode = X
```

Note that <u>all</u> paths to record R are locked. Alternaltively, one could lock F and I in exclusive mode thereby implicitly locking R in exclusive mode.

To give a more complete explanation we observe that a node can be locked <u>explicitly</u> (by requesting it) or <u>implicitly</u> (by appropriate explicit locks on the ancestors of the node) in one of five modes: IS, IX, S, SIX, X. However, the definition of implicit locks and the protocols for setting explicit locks have to be extended for DAG's as follows:

A node is <u>implicitly granted in S</u> mode to a transaction if <u>at least one</u> of its parents is (implicitly or explicitly) granted to the transaction in S, SIX or X mode. By induction that means that at least one of the node's ancestors must be explicitly granted in S, SIX or X mode to the transaction.

A node is <u>implicitly granted in X</u> mode if <u>all</u> of its parents are (implicitly or explicitly) granted to the transaction in X mode. By induction, this is equivalent to the condition that all nodes in some cut set of the collection of all paths leading from the node to the roots of the graph are explicitly granted to the transaction in X mode and all ancestors of nodes in the cut set are explicitly granted in IX or SIX mode.

From Figure 2, a node is implicitly granted in IS mode if it is implicitly granted in S mode, and a node is implicitly granted in IS, IX, S and SIX mode if it is implicitly granted in X mode.

<u>The protocol for explicitly requesting locks on a DAG</u>:

(a) Before requesting an S or IS lock on a node, one should request at least one parent (and by induction a path to a root) in IS (or greater) mode. As a consequence none of the ancestors along this path can be granted to another transaction in a mode incompatible with IS.

(b) Before requesting IX, SIX or X mode access to a node, one should request all parents of the node in IX (or greater) mode. As a consequence all ancestors will be held in IX (or greater mode) and cannot be held by other transactions in a mode incompatible with IX (i.e. S, SIX, X).

(c) Locks should be released either at the end of the transaction (in any order) or in leaf to root order. In particular, if locks are not held to the end of transaction, one should not hold a lower lock after releasing its ancestors.

To give an example using Figure 3, a sequential scan of all records in file F need not use an index so one can get an implicit share lock on each record in the file by:

```
lock data base               with mode = IS
lock area containing F       with mode = IS
lock file F                  with mode = S
```

This gives implicit S mode access to all records in F. Conversely, to read a record in a file via the index I for file F, one need not get an implicit or explicit lock on file F:

```
lock data base               with mode = IS
lock area containing R       with mode = IS
lock index I                 with mode = S
```

This again gives implicit S mode access to all records in index I (in file F). In both these cases, <u>only one path was locked for reading</u>.

But to insert, delete or update a record R in file F with index I one must get an implicit or explicit lock on all ancestors of R.

The first example of this section showed how an explicit X lock on a record is obtained. To get an implicit X lock on all records in a file one can simply lock the index <u>and</u> file in X mode, or lock the area in X mode. The latter examples allow bulk load or update of a file without further locking since all records in the file are implicitly granted in X mode.

<u>Proof of equivalence of the lock protocol</u>.

We will now prove that the described lock protocol is equivalent to a conventional one which uses only two modes (S and X), and which explicitly locks atomic resources (the leaves of a tree or sinks of a DAG).

Let G = (N,A) be a finite (directed acyclic) <u>graph</u> where N is the set of nodes and A is the set of arcs. G is assumed to be without circuits (i.e. there is no non-null path leading from a node n to itself). A node p is a <u>parent</u> of a node n and n is a <u>child</u> of p if there is an arc from p to n. A node n is a <u>source</u> (<u>sink</u>) if n has no parents (no children). Let SI be the set of sinks of G. An <u>ancestor</u> of node n is any node (including n) in a path from a source to n. A <u>node-slice</u> of a sink n is a collection of nodes such that each path from a source to n contains at least one node of the slice.

We also introduce the set of lock modes M = {NL,IS,IX,S,SIX,X} and the compatibility matrix C : MxM->{YES,NO} described in Table 1. Let c : mxm->{YES,NO} be the restriction of C to m = {NL,S,X}.

A lock-graph is a mapping L : N->M such that:

(a) if L(n) ∈ {IS,S} then either n is a source or there exists a parent p of n such that L(p) ∈ {IS,IX,S,SIX,X}. By induction there exists a path from a source to n such that L takes only values in {IS,IX,S,SIX,X} on it. Equivalently L is not equal to NL on the path.

(b) if L(n) ∈ {IX,SIX,X} then either n is a root or for all parents p1...pk of n we have L(pi) ∈ {IX,SIX,X} (i=1...k). By induction L takes only values in {IX,SIX,X} on all the ancestors of n.

The interpretation of a lock-graph is that it gives a map of the explicit locks held by a particular transaction observing the six state lock protocol described above. The notion of projection of a lock-graph is now introduced to model the set of implicit locks on atomic resources acquired by a transaction.

The projection of a lock-graph L is the mapping l: SI->m constructed as follows:

(a) l(n)=X if there exists a node-slice {n1...ns} of n such that L(ni)=X for each node in the slice.

(b) l(n)=S if (a) is not satisfied and there exists an ancestor a of n such that L(a) ∈ {S,SIX,X}.

(c) l(n)=NL if (a) and (b) are not satisfied.

Two lock-graphs L1 and L2 are said to be compatible if C(L1(n),L2(n))=YES for all n ∈ N. Similarly two projections l1 and l2 are compatible if c(l1(n),l2(n))=YES for all n ∈ SI.

Theorem:

If two lock-graphs L1 and L2 are compatible then their projections l1 and l2 are compatible. In other words if the explicit locks set by two transactions do not conflict then also the three-state locks implicitly acquired do not conflict.

Proof: Assume that l1 and l2 are incompatible. We want to prove that L1 and L2 are incompatible. By definition of compatibility there must exist a sink n such that l1(n)=X and l2(n) ∈ {S,X} (or vice versa). By definition of projection there must exist a node-slice {n1...ns} of n such that L1(n1)=...=L1(ns)=X. Also there must exist an ancestor n0 of n such that L2(n0) ∈ {S,SIX,X}. From the definition of lock-graph there is a path P1 from a source to n0 on which L2 does not take the value NL.

If P1 intersects the node-slice at ni then L1 and L2 are incompatible since L1(ni)=X which is incompatible with the non-null value of L2(ni). Hence the theorem is proved.

Alternatively there is a path P2 from n0 to the sink n which intersects the node-slice at ni. From the definition of lock-graph L1 takes a value in {IX,SIX,X} on all ancestors of ni. In particular L1(n0) ∈ {IX,SIX,X}. Since L2(n0) ∈ {S,SIX,X} we have C(L1(n0),L2(n0))=NO. Q.E.D.

Dynamic lock graphs:

Thus far we have pretended that the lock graph is static. However, examination of Figure 3 suggests otherwise. Areas, files and indices are dynamically created and destroyed, and of course records are continually inserted, updated, and deleted. (If the data base is only read, then there is no need for locking at all.)

We introduce the lock protocol for dynamic DAG's by example. Consider the implementation of index interval locks. Rather than being forced to lock entire indices or individual records, we would like to be able to lock all records with a certain contiguous range of index values; for example, lock all records in the bank account file with the location field equal to Napa. Therefore, the index is partitioned into lockable key value intervals. Each indexed record "belongs" to a particular index interval and all records in a file with the same field value on an indexed field will belong to the same key value interval (i.e. all Napa accounts will belong to the same interval). This new structure is depicted in Figure 4. In [1] such locks were called predicate locks and and an alternate (more general but less efficient) implementation was proposed.

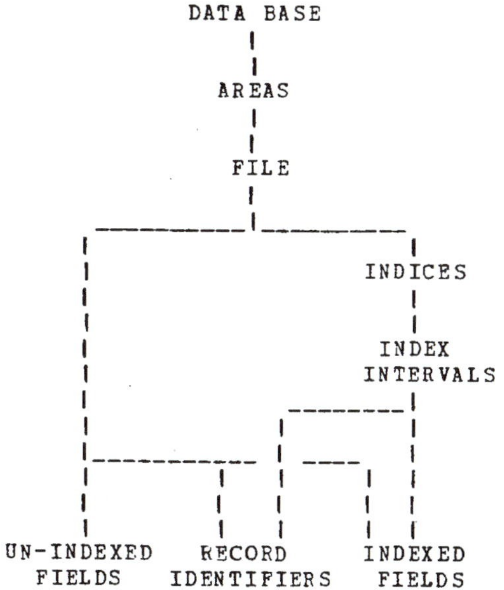

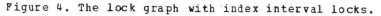

Figure 4. The lock graph with index interval locks.

The only subtle aspect of Figure 4 is the dichotomy between indexed and un-indexed fields. Since the indexed field value and record identifier (logical address) appear in the index, one can read the indexed field directly (i.e. without "touching" the record). Hence an index interval is a parent of the corresponding field values. Further, the index "points" via record identifiers to all records with that value and so is a parent of all such record identifiers. On the other hand, one can read and update un-indexed fields of the record without affecting the index and so the file is the only parent of such fields.

When an indexed field is updated, it and its record identifier move from one index interval to another. For example, when a Napa account is moved to the St. Helena branch, the account record and its location field "leave" the Napa interval of the location index and "join" the St. Helena index interval. When a new record is inserted it "joins" the interval containing the new field value and also it "joins" the file. Deletion removes the record from the index interval and from the file. index is not a lock ancestor of such fields.

Since Figure 4 defines a DAG, albeit a dynamic DAG, the protocol of the previous section can be used to lock the nodes of the DAG. However, the protocol should be extended as follows to handle dynamic changes to the lock graph:

(d) Before moving a node in the lock graph, the node must be implicitly or explicitly granted in X mode in both its old and its new position in the graph. Further, the node must not be moved in such a way as to create a cycle in the graph.

Carrying out the example of this section, to move a Napa bank account to the St. Helena branch:

```
 lock data base                 in mode = IX
 lock area containing accounts  in mode = IX
 lock accounts file             in mode = IX
 lock location index            in mode = IX
 lock Napa interval             in mode = IX
 lock St. Helena interval       in mode = IX
 lock record                    in mode = IX
 lock field                     in mode = X.
```

Alternatively, one could get an implicit lock on the field by requesting explicit X mode locks on the record and index intervals.

Scheduling and granting requests:

Thus far we have described the semantics of the various request modes and have described the protocol which requestors must follow. To complete the discussion we discuss how requests are scheduled and granted.

The set of all requests for a particular resource are kept in a queue sorted by some fair scheduler. By "fair" we mean that no particular transaction will be delayed indefinitely. First-in first-out is the simplest fair scheduler and we adopt such a scheduler for this discussion modulo deadlock preemption decisions.

The group of mutually compatible requests for a resource appearing at the head of the queue is called the granted group. All these requests can be granted concurrently. Assuming that each transaction has at most one request in the queue then the compatibility of two requests by different transactions depends only on the modes of the requests and may be computed using Table 1. Associated with the granted group is a group mode which is the supremum mode of the members of the group which is computed using Figure 2 or Table 3. Table 2 gives a list of the possible types of requests that can coexist in a group and the corresponding mode of the group.

Table 2. Possible request groups and their group mode.
Set brackets indicate that several such requests may be present.

MODES OF REQUESTS	MODE OF GROUP
X	X
SIX, {IS}	SIX
S, {S}, {IS}	S
IX, {IX}, {IS}	IX
IS, {IS}	IS

Figure 5 depicts the queue for a particular resource, showing the requests and their modes. The granted group consists of five requests and has group mode IX. The next request in the queue is for S mode which is incompatible with the group mode IX and hence must wait.

```
*********************************
* GRANTED GROUP: GROUPMODE = IX *
* |IS|--|IX|--|IS|--|IS|--|IS|--*-|S|-|IS|-|X|-|IS|-|IX|
*********************************
```

Figure 5. The queue of requests for a resource.

When a new request for a resource arrives, the scheduler appends it to the end of the queue. There are two cases to consider: either someone is already waiting or all outstanding requests for this resource are granted (i.e. no one is waiting). If no one is waiting and the new request is compatible with the granted group mode then the new request can be granted immediately. Otherwise the new request must wait its turn in the queue and in the case of deadlock it may preempt some incompatible requests in the queue. (Alternatively the new request could be canceled. In Figure 5 all the requests decided to wait.) When a particular request leaves the granted group the group mode of the group may change. If the mode of the first waiting request in the queue is compatible with the new mode of the granted group, then the waiting request is granted. In Figure 5, if the IX request leaves the group, then the group mode becomes IS which is compatible with S and so the S may be granted. The new group mode will be S and since this is compatible with IS mode the IS request following the S request may also join the granted group. This produces the situation depicted in Figure 6:

```
**************************************
* GRANTED GROUP GROUPMODE = S        *
* |IS|--|IS|--|IS|--|IS|--|S|--|IS|--*-|X|-|IS|-|IX|
**************************************
```

Figure 6. The queue after the IX request is released.

The X request of Figure 6 will not be granted until all the requests leave the granted group since it is not compatible with any mode.

Conversions:

A transaction might re-request the same resource for several reasons: Perhaps it has forgotten that it already has access to the record; after all, if it is setting many locks it may be simpler to just always request access to the record rather than first asking itself "have I seen this record before". The lock subsystem has all the information to answer this question and it seems wasteful to duplicate. Alternatively, the transaction may know it has access to the record, but want to increase its access mode (for example from S to X mode if it is in a read, test, and sometimes update scan of a file). So the lock subsystem must be prepared for re-requests by a transaction for a lock. We call such re-requests conversions.

When a request is found to be a conversion, the old (granted) mode of the requestor to the resource and the newly requested mode are compared using Table 3 to compute the new mode which is the supremum of the old and the requested mode (ref. Figure 2).

Table 3. The new mode given the requested and old mode.

	NEW MODE				
	IS	IX	S	SIX	X
IS	IS	IX	S	SIX	X
IX	IX	IX	SIX	SIX	X
S	S	SIX	S	SIX	X
SIX	SIX	SIX	SIX	SIX	X
X	X	X	X	X	X

So for example, if one has IX mode and requests S mode then the new mode is SIX.

If the new mode is equal to the old mode (note it is never less than the old mode) then the request can be granted immediately and the granted mode is unchanged. If the new mode is compatible with the group mode of the other members of the granted group (a requestor is always compatible with himself) then again the request can be granted immediately. The granted mode is the new mode and the group mode is recomputed using Table 2. In all other cases, the requested conversion must wait until the group mode of the other granted requests is compatible with the new mode. Note that this immediate granting of conversions over waiting requests is a minor violation of fair scheduling.

If two conversions are waiting, each of which is incompatible with an already granted request of the other transaction, then a deadlock exists and the already granted access of one must be preempted. Otherwise there is a way of scheduling the waiting conversions: namely, grant a conversion when it is compatible with all other granted modes in the granted group. (Since there is no deadlock cycle this is always possible.)

The following example may help to clarify these points. Suppose the queue for a particular resource is:

```
*******************************
* GROUPMODE = IS              *
*   |IS|---|IS|------------------------------
*******************************
```

Figure 7. A simple queue.

Now suppose the first transaction wants to convert to X mode. It must wait for the second (already granted) request to leave the queue. If it decides to wait then the situation becomes:

```
*******************************
* GROUPMODE = IS              *
*   |IS<-X|---|IS|---------------------------
*******************************
```

Figure 8. A conversion to X mode waits.

No new request may enter the granted group since there is now a conversion request waiting. In general, conversions are scheduled before new requests. If the second transaction now converts to IX, SIX, or S mode it may be granted immediately since this does not conflict with the granted (IS) mode of the first transaction. When the second transaction eventually leaves the queue, the first conversion can be made:

```
*******************************
* GROUPMODE = IS              *
*  |IX|------------------------------------
*******************************
```

Figure 9. One transaction leaves and the conversion is granted.

However, if the second transaction tries to convert to exclusive mode one obtains the queue:

```
*******************************
*   GROUPMODE = IS            *
*  |IS<-X|---|IS<-X|-----------------------
*******************************
```

Figure 10. Two conflicting conversions are waiting.

Since X is incompatible with IS (see Table 1), this situation implies that each transaction is waiting for the other to leave the queue (i.e. deadlock) and so one transaction <u>must</u> be preempted. In all other cases (i.e. when no cycle exists) there is a way to schedule the conversions so that no already granted access is violated.

<u>Deadlock and lock thrashing</u>:

Whenever a transaction waits for a request to be granted, it runs the risk of waiting forever in a deadlock cycle. For the purposes of deadlock detection it is important to know who is waiting for whom. The request queues give this information. Consider any waiting request R by transaction T. There are two cases: If R is a conversion, T is WAITING_FOR all transactions granted incompatible requests to the queue. If R is not a conversion, T is WAITING_FOR all transactions ahead of it in the queue granted or waiting for incompatible requests. Given this WAITING_FOR relation computed for all waiting transactions, there is no deadlock if and only if WAITING_FOR is acyclic.

The WAITING_FOR relation may change whenever a request or release occurs and when a conversion is granted. If a transaction may wait for at most one request at a time, then the deadlock state can only change when some process decides to wait. In this special case (synchronous calls to lock system), only waits require recomputation of the WAITING_FOR relation. If deadlock is improbable, deadlock testing can be done periodically rather than on each wait, further reducing computational overhead.

One new request may form many cycles and each such cycle must be broken. When a cycle is detected, to break the cycle some granted or waiting request must be preempted. The lock scheduler should choose a minimal cost set of victims to preempt, so that all cycles are broken, undo all the changes to the data base made by the victims since the preempted resources were granted, and then preempt the resource and signal the victims that they have been backed up.

The issues discussed so far--lock scheduling, detecting and breaking deadlocks--are low level scheduling decisions. They must be connected with a high level transaction scheduler which regulates the load on the system and regulates the entry and progress of transactions to prevent long waits, high probability of waiting (lock thrashing), and deadlock. By analogy, a page management system with only a low level page frame scheduler, which allocates and preempts page frames in a fairly naive way, is likely to produce page thrashing unless it is coupled with a working set scheduler which regulates the number and character of processes competing for page frames.

II. DEGREES OF CONSISTENCY:

We now focus on how locks can be used to construct transactions out of atomic actions. The data base consists of entities which are related in certain ways. These relationships are best thought of as assertions about the data. Examples of such assertions are:
'Names is an index for Telephone_numbers.'
'The value of Count_of_x gives the number of employees in department x.'

The data base is said to be consistent if it satisfies all its assertions [1]. In some cases, the data base must become temporarily inconsistent in order to transform it to a new consistent state. For example, adding a new employee involves several atomic actions and the updating of several fields. The data base may be inconsistent until all these updates have been completed.

To cope with these temporary inconsistencies, sequences of atomic actions are grouped to form transactions. Transactions are the units of consistency. They are larger atomic actions on the data base which transform it from one consistent state to a new consistent state. Transactions preserve consistency. If some action of a transaction fails then the entire transaction is 'undone' thereby returning the data base to a consistent state. Thus transactions are also the units of recovery. Hardware failure, system error, deadlock, protection violations and program error are each a source of such failure.

If transactions are run one at a time then each transaction will see the consistent state left behind by its predecessor. But if several transactions are scheduled concurrently then locking is required to insure that the inputs to each transaction are consistent.

Responsibility for requesting and releasing locks can either be assumed by the user or be delegated to the system. User controlled locking results in potentially fewer locks due to the user's knowledge of the semantics of the data. On the other hand, user controlled locking requires difficult and potentially unreliable application programming. Hence the approach taken by some data base systems is to use automatic lock protocols which insure protection from general types of inconsistency, while still relying on the user to protect himself against other sources of inconsistencies. For example, a system may automatically lock updated records but not records which are read. Such a system prevents lost updates arising from transaction backup. Still, the user should explicitly lock records in a read-update sequence to insure that the read value does not change before the actual update. In other words, a user is guaranteed a limited automatic degree of consistency. This degree of consistency may be system wide or the system may provide options to select it (for instance a lock protocol may be associated with a transaction or with an entity).

We now present several equivalent definitions of four consistency degrees. The first definition is an operational and intuitive one useful in describing the system behavior to users. The second definition is a procedural one in terms of lock protocols, it is useful in explaining the system implementation. The third definition is in terms of a trace of the system actions, it is useful in formally stating and proving properties of the various consistency degrees.

Informal definition of consistency:

An output (write) of a transaction is committed when the transaction abdicates the right to 'undo' the write thereby making the new value available to all other transactions. Outputs are said to be uncommitted or dirty if they are not yet committed by the writer. Concurrent execution raises the problem that reading or writing other transactions' dirty data may yield inconsistent data.

Using this notion of dirty data, the degrees of consistency may be defined as:

Definition 1:

Degree 3: Transaction T sees degree 3 consistency if:
- (a) T does not overwrite dirty data of other transactions.
- (b) T does not commit any writes until it completes all its writes (i.e. until the end of transaction (EOT)).
- (c) T does not read dirty data from other transactions.
- (d) Other transactions do not dirty any data read by T before T completes.

Degree 2: Transaction T sees degree 2 consistency if:
- (a) T does not overwrite dirty data of other transactions.
- (b) T does not commit any writes before EOT.
- (c) T does not read dirty data of other transactions.

Degree 1: Transaction T sees degree 1 consistency if:
- (a) T does not overwrite dirty data of other transactions.
- (b) T does not commit any writes before EOT.

Degree 0: Transaction T sees degree 0 consistency if:
- (a) T does not overwrite dirty data of other transactions.

Note that if a transaction sees a high degree of consistency then it also sees all the lower degrees.

Degree 0 consistent transactions commit writes before the end of transaction. Hence backing up a degree 0 consistent transaction may require undoing an update to an entity locked by another transaction. In this sense, degree 0 transactions are unrecoverable.

Degree 1 transactions do not committ writes until the end of the transaction. Hence one may undo (back up) an in-progress degree 1 transaction without setting additional locks. This means that transaction backup does not erase other transactions' updates. This is the principal reason one data management system automatically provides degree 1 consistency to all transactions.

Degree 2 consistency isolates a transaction from the uncommitted data of other transactions. With degree 1 consistency a transaction might read uncommitted values which are subsequently updated or are undone. In degree 2 no dirty data values are read.

Degree 3 consistency isolates the transaction from dirty relationships among values. Reads are repeatable. For example, a degree 2 consistent transaction may read two different (committed) values if it reads the same entity twice. This is because a transaction which updates the entity could begin, update and end in the interval of time between the two reads. More elaborate kinds of anomalies due to concurrency are possible if one updates an entity after reading it or if more than one entity is involved (see example below). Degree 3 consistency completely isolates the transaction from inconsistencies due to concurrency [1].

Each transaction can elect the degree of consistency appropriate to its function. When the third definition is given we will be able to state the consistency and recovery properties of such a system more formally.
Briefly:

If one elects degree i consistency then one sees a degree i consistent state (so long as all other transactions run at least degree 0 consistent)

If all transactions run at least degree 1 consistent, system backup (undoing all in-progress transactions) loses no updates of completed transactions.

If all transactions run at least degree 2 consistent, transaction backup (undoing any in-progress transaction) produces a consistent state.

To give an example which demonstrates the application of these several degrees of consistency, imagine a process control system in which some transaction is dedicated to reading a gauge and periodically writing batches of values into a list. Each gauge reading is an individual entity. For performance reasons, this transaction sees degree 0 consistency, committing all gauge readings as soon as they enter the data base. This transaction is not recoverable (can't be undone). A second transaction is run periodically which reads all the recent gauge readings, computes a mean and variance and writes these computed values as entities in the data base. Since we want these two values to be consistent with one another, they must be committed together (i.e. one cannot commit the first before the second is written). This allows transaction undo in the case that it aborts after writing only one of the two values. Hence this statistical summary transaction should see degree 1. A third transaction which reads the mean and writes it on a display sees degree 2 consistency. It will not read a mean which might be 'undone' by a backup. Another transaction which reads both the mean and the variance must see degree 3 consistency to insure that the mean and variance derive from the same computation (i.e. the same run which wrote the mean also wrote the variance).

Lock protocol definition of consistency:

Whether an instantiation of a transaction sees degree 0, 1, 2 or 3 consistency depends on the actions of other concurrent transactions. Lock protocols are used by a transaction to guarantee itself a certain degree of consistency independent of the behavior of other transactions (so long as all transactions at least observe the degree 0 protocol).

The degrees of consistency can be procedurally defined by the lock protocols which produce them. A transaction locks its inputs to guarantee their consistency and locks its outputs to mark them as dirty (uncommitted).

For this section, locks are dichotomized as share mode locks which allow multiple readers of the same entity and exclusive mode locks which reserve exclusive access to an entity. (This is the "two mode" lock protocol. Its generalization to the "six mode" protocol of the previous section should be obvious.) Locks may also be characterized by their duration: locks held for the duration of a single action are called short duration locks while locks held to the end of the transaction are called long duration locks. Short duration locks are used to mark or test for dirty data for the duration of an action rather than for the duration of the transaction.

The lock protocols are:

Definition 2:

Degree 3: transaction T observes degree 3 lock protocol if:
(a) T sets a long exclusive lock on any data it dirties.
(b) T sets a long share lock on any data it reads.

Degree 2: transaction T observes degree 2 lock protocol if:
(a) T sets a long exclusive lock on any data it dirties.
(b) T sets a (possibly short) share lock on any data it reads.

Degree 1: transaction T observes degree 1 lock protocol if:
(a) T sets a long exclusive lock on any data it dirties.

Degree 0: transaction T observes degree 0 lock protocol if:
(a) T sets a (possibly short) exclusive lock on any data it dirties.

The lock protocol definitions can be stated more tersely with the introduction of the following notation. A transaction is well formed with respect to writes (reads) if it always locks an entity in exclusive (shared or exclusive) mode before writing (reading) it. The transaction is well formed if it is well formed with respect to reads and writes.

A transaction is two phase (with respect to reads or updates) if it does not (share or exclusive) lock an entity after unlocking some entity. A two phase transaction has a growing phase during which it acquires locks and a shrinking phase during which it releases locks.

Definition 2 is too restrictive in the sense that consistency will not require that a transaction hold all locks to the EOT (i.e. the EOT is the shrinking phase). Rather, the constraint that the transaction be two phase is adequate to insure consistency. On the other hand, once a transaction unlocks an updated entity, it has committed that entity and so cannot be undone without cascading backup to any transactions which may have subsequently read the entity. For that reason, the shrinking phase is usually deferred to the end of the transaction; thus, the transaction is always recoverable and all updates are committed together. The lock protocols can be redefined as:

Definition 2':

Degree 3: T is well formed
and T is two phase.

Degree 2: T is well formed
and T is two phase with respect to writes.

Degree 1: T is well formed with respect to writes
and T is two phase with respect to writes.

Degree 0: T is well formed with respect to writes.

All transactions are required to observe the degree 0 locking protocol so that they do not update the uncommitted updates of others. Degrees 1, 2 and 3 provide increasing system-guaranteed consistency.

Consistency of schedules:

The definition of what it means for a transaction to see a degree of consistency was given in terms of dirty data. In order to make the notion of dirty data explicit it is necessary to consider the execution of a transaction in the context of a set of concurrently executing transactions. To do this we introduce the notion of a schedule for a set of transactions. A schedule can be thought of as a history or audit trail of the actions performed by the set of transactions. Given a schedule the notion of a particular entity being dirtied by a particular transaction is made explicit and hence the notion of seeing a certain degree of consistency is formalized. These notions may then be used to connect the various definitions of consistency and show their equivalence.

The system directly supports entities and actions. Actions are categorized as begin actions, end actions, share lock actions, exclusive lock actions, unlock actions, read actions, and write actions. An end action is presumed to unlock any locks held by the transaction but not explicitly unlocked by the transaction. For the purposes of the following definitions, share lock actions and their corresponding unlock actions are additionally considered to be read actions and exclusive lock actions and their corresponding unlock actions are additionally considered to be write actions.

A transaction is any sequence of actions beginning with a begin action and ending with an end action and not containing other begin or end actions.

Any (sequence preserving) merging of the actions of a set of transactions into a single sequence is called a schedule for the set of transactions.

A schedule is a history of the order in which actions were executed (it does not record actions which were undone due to backup). The simplest schedules run all actions of one transaction and then all actions of another transaction,... Such one-transaction-at-a-time schedules are called serial because they have no concurrency among transactions. Clearly, a serial schedule has no concurrency induced inconsistency and no transaction sees dirty data.

Locking constrains the set of allowed schedules. In particular, a schedule is legal only if it does not schedule a lock action on an entity for one transaction when that entity is already locked by some other transaction in a conflicting mode.

An initial state and a schedule completely define the system's behavior. At each step of the schedule one can deduce which entity values have been committed and which are dirty: if locking is used, updated data is <u>dirty</u> until it is unlocked.

Since a schedule makes the definition of dirty data explicit, one can apply Definition 1 to define consistent schedules:

<u>Definition 3</u>:

A transaction <u>runs at degree 0 (1, 2 or 3) consistency in schedule S</u> if T sees degree 0 (1, 2 or 3) consistency in S. (Conversely, transaction T sees degree i consistency if all legal schedules run T at degree i consistency.)

If all transactions run at degree 0 (1,2 or 3) consistency in schedule S then S is said to be a <u>degree 0 (1, 2 or 3) consistent schedule</u>.

Given these definitions one can show:

<u>Assertion 1</u>:

(a) If each transaction observes the degree 0 (1, 2 or 3) lock protocol (Definition 2) then any legal schedule is degree 0 (1, 2 or 3) consistent (Definition 3) (i.e, each transaction sees degree 0 (1, 2 or 3) consistency in the sense of Definition 1).

(b) Unless transaction T observes the degree 1 (2 or 3) lock protocol then it is possible to define another transaction T' which does observe the degree 1 (2 or 3) lock protocol such that T and T' have a legal schedule S but T does not run at degree 1 (2 or 3) consistency in S.

In [1] we proved Assertion 1 for degree 3 consistency. That argument generalizes directly to this result.

Assertion 1 says that if a transaction observes the lock protocol definition of consistency (Definition 2) then it is assured of the informal definition of consistency based on committed and dirty data (Definition 1). Unless a transaction actually sets the locks prescribed by degree 1 (2 or 3) consistency one can construct transaction mixes and schedules which will cause the transaction to run at (see) a lower degree of consistency. However, in particular cases such transaction mixes may never occur due to the structure or use of the system. In these cases an apparently low degree of locking may actually provide degree 3 consistency. For example, a data base reorganization usually need do no locking since it is run as an off-line utility which is never run concurrently with other transactions.

<u>Assertion 2</u>:

If each transaction in a set of transactions at least observes the degree 0 lock protocol and if transaction T observes the degree 1 (2 or 3) lock protocol then T runs at degree 1 (2 or 3) consistency (Definitions 1, 3) in any legal schedule for the set of transactions.

Assertion 2 says that each transaction can choose its degree of consistency so long as all transactions observe at least degree 0 protocols. Of course the outputs of degree 0, 1 or 2 consistent transactions may be degree 0, 1 or 2 consistent (i.e. inconsistent) because they were computed with potentially inconsistent inputs. One can imagine that each data entity is tagged with the degree of consistency of its writer: Degree 0 entities are purple, degree 1 entities are red, degree 2 entities are yellow and degree 3 entities are green. The color of the outputs of a transaction is the minimum of the transaction's color and the colors of the entities it reads (because they are potentially inconsistent). Gradually the system will turn purple or red unless everyone runs with a high degree of consistency. If the transaction's author knows something about the systems structure which allows an apparently degree 1 consistent protocol to produce degree 3 consistent results then this color coding is pessimistic. But, in general a transaction must beware of reading entities tagged with degrees lower than the degree of the transaction.

Dependencies among transactions:

One transaction is said to depend on another if the first takes some of its inputs from the second. The notion of dependency is defined differently for each degree of consistency. These dependency relations are completely defined by a schedule and can be useful in discussing consistency and recovery.

Each schedule defines three relations: <, << and <<< on the set of transactions as follows. Suppose that transaction T performs action a on entity e at some step in the schedule and that transaction T' performs action a' on entity e at a later step in the schedule. Further suppose that T does not equal T'. Then:

```
T <<< T' if  a is a write action and a' is a write action
         or  a is a write action and a' is a read  action
         or  a is a read  action and a' is a write action

T << T'  if  a is a write action and a' is a write action
         or  a is a write action and a' is a read  action

T < T'   if  a is a write action and a' is a write action
```

So degree 1 does not care about read dependencies at all. Degree 2 cares only about one kind of read dependency. And degree 3 ignores only read-read dependencies (reads commute). The following table is a notationally convenient way of seeing these definitions:

```
<<<  :  W->W  |  W->R  |  R->W

<<   :  W->W  |  W->R

<    :  W->W
```

meaning that (for example) T <<< T' if T writes (W) something later read (R) by T' or written (W) by T' or T reads (R) something later written (W) by T'.

Let <* be the transitive closure of <, then define:

```
BEFORE1(T) = {T'| T' <* T}
AFTER1(T) = {T'| T <* T'}.
```

The sets BEFORE2, AFTER2, BEFORE3 and AFTER3 are defined analogously from << and <<<.

The obvious interpretation for this is that each BEFORE set is the set of transactions which contribute inputs to T and each AFTER set is the set of transactions which take their inputs from T (where the ordering only considers dependencies induced by the corresponding consistency degree).

If some transaction is both before T and after T in some schedule then no serial schedule could give such results. In this case concurrency has introduced inconsistency. On the other hand, if all relevant transactions are either before or after T (but not both) then T will see a consistent state (of the corresponding degree). If all transactions dichotomize others in this way then the relation <* (<<* or <<<*) will be a partial order and the whole schedule will give degree 1 (2 or 3) consistency. This can be strengthened to:

<u>Assertion 3</u>:

A schedule is degree 1 (2 or 3) consistent if and only if the relation <* (<<* or <<<*) is a partial order.

The <, << and <<< relations are variants of the dependency sets introduced in [1]. In that paper only degree 3 consistency is introduced and Assertion 3 was proved for that case. In particular such a schedule is equivalent to the serial schedule obtained by running the transactions one at a time in <<< order. The proofs of [1] generalize fairly easily to handle assertion 1 in the case of degree 1 or 2 consistency.

Consider the following example:

```
T1 LOCK     A
T1 READ     A
T1 UNLOCK   A
T2 LOCK     A
T2 WRITE    A
T2 LOCK     B
T2 WRITE    B
T2 UNLOCK   A
T2 UNLOCK   B
T1 LOCK     B
T1 WRITE    B
T1 UNLOCK   B
```

In this schedule T2 gives B to T1 and T2 updates A after T1 reads A so T2<T1, T2<<T1, T2<<<T1 and T1<<<T2. The schedule is degree 2 consistent but not degree 3 consistent. It runs T1 at degree 2 consistency and T2 at degree 3 consistency.

It would be nice to define a transaction to see degree 1 (2 or 3) consistency if and only if the BEFORE and AFTER sets are disjoint in some schedule. However, this is not restrictive enough; rather one must require that the before and after sets be disjoint in <u>all</u> schedules in order to state Definition 1 in terms of dependencies. Further, there seems to be no natural way to define the dependencies of degree 0 consistency. Hence the principal application of the dependency definition is as a proof technique and for discussing schedules and recovery issues.

Relationship to transaction backup and system recovery:

A transaction T is said to be *recoverable* if it can be undone before 'EOT' without undoing other transactions' updates. A transaction T is said to be *repeatable* if it will reproduce the original output if rerun following recovery, assuming that no locks were released in the backup process. Recoverability requires system wide degree 1 consistency, repeatibility requires that all other transactions be at least degree 1 and that the repeatable transaction be degree 3.

The *normal* (i.e. trouble free) operation of a data base system can be described in terms of an initial consistent state S0 and a schedule of transactions mapping the data base into a final consistent state S3 (see Figure 11). S1 is a checkpoint state, since transactions are in progress, S1 may be inconsistent. A *system crash* leaves the data base in state S2. Since transactions T3 and T5 were in progress at the time of crash, S2 is potentially inconsistent. *System recovery* amounts to bringing the data base in a new consistent state in one of the following ways:

(a) Starting from state S2, *undo* all actions of transactions in-progress at the time of the crash.

(b) Starting from state S1 first undo all actions of transactions in progress at the time of the crash (i.e. actions of T3 and T4 before S1) and then *redo* all actions of transactions which completed before the crash (i.e. actions of T2 and T3 after S1).

(c) starting at S0 redo all transactions which completed before the crash.

Observe that (a) and (c) are degenerate cases of (b).

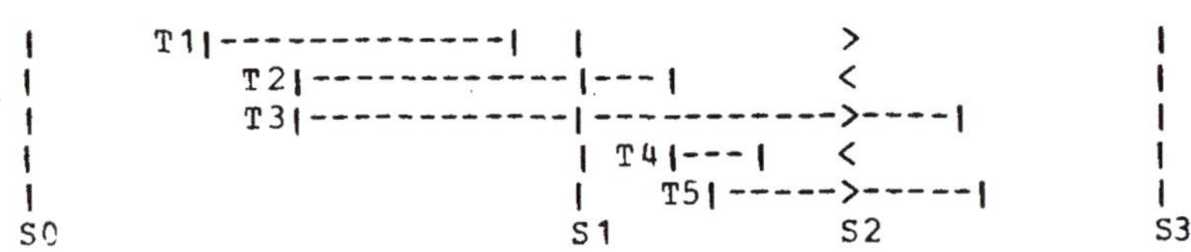

Figure 11. System states, S0 is initial state, S1 is checkpoint state, S2 is a crash and S3 is the state that results in the absence of a crash.

Unless all transactions run at least degree 1 consistency, system recovery may lose updates. If for example, T3 writes a record, r, and then T4 further updates r then undoing T3 will cause the update of T4 to r to be lost. This situation can only arise if some transaction does not hold its write locks to EOT.

(a) If all the transactions run in at least degree 1 consistency then system recovery loses no updates of complete transactions. However there may be no schedule which would give the same result because transactions may have *read* outputs of undone transactions.

(b) If all the transactions run in at least degree 2 then the recovered state is consistent and derives from the schedule obtatined from the original system schedule by deleting incomplete transactions. Note that degree 2 prevents read dependencies on transactions which might be undone by system recovery. of all the completed transactions results in a meaningful schedule.

(c) If a transaction is degree 3 consistent then it is reproducible.

Transaction crash gives rise to transaction backup which has properties analogous to system recovery.

Cost of degrees of consistency:

The only advantage of lower degrees of consistency is performance. If less is locked then less computation and storage is consumed. Further if less is locked, concurrency is increased since fewer conflicts appear. (Note that the granularity lock scheme of the first section was motivated by minimizing the number of explicit locks set.)

We will make some very crude estimates of the storage and computation resources consumed by the locking protocols as a function of the consistency degree. For the remainder of this section assume that all transactions are identical. Also assume that they do R reads and W writes (and hence set approximately R share mode locks and W exclusive mode locks). Further we assume that all the transactions run at the same consistency degree.

Each outstanding lock request consumes a queue element. The maximum per-transaction space for these queue elements as a function of consistency degrees is:

Table 4. Consistency degrees vs storage consumption.

CONSISTENCY DEGREE	STORAGE (in queue elements)
0	1
1	W
2	W+1
3	W+R

Observe that degrees 1 and 2 consume roughly the same amount of storage but that degree 3 consumes substantially more storage. This observation is aggravated by the fact that reads are typically ten times more common than writes.

The estimation of computation (CPU) overhead is much more subtle. We make only a crude estimate here. First one may consider the overhead in requesting and releasing locks. This is shown in Table 5 as a function of consistency degrees.

TABLE 5. Computational overhead vs degrees of consistency.

CONSISTENCY DEGREE	CPU (in calls to lock sys)
0	W
1	W
2	W+R
3	W+R

Table 5 indicates that the computational overhead of degrees 2 and 3 are comparable and are greater than the overhead of degrees 0 or 1. These pairs of degrees set the same locks, they just hold them for different durations.

Table 5 ignores the observation that some lock requests are trivially satisfied (the request is granted immediately) while others require a task switch and hence are quite expensive. The probability that a read lock will have to wait is proportional to the number of conflicting locks (write) currently granted. The probability that a write lock will have to wait is proportional to the number of conflicting (read or write) locks that are currently granted. Table 4 gives a guess of the maximum number of locks of each type held by each transaction. If there are 2*N+1 transactions one can multiply the entries of Table 4 by N to get an average number of locks held by all others. If a wait lock request is C+1 times as expensive as an immediately granted request and if P is the probability that two different requests are for the same resource then the relative computational costs are roughly computed:

```
degree 0 overhead:  W               cost of setting locks
                    P*C*N*W         cost of waits

degree 1 overhead:  W               cost of writes
                    P*C*N*W*W       cost of waits

degree 2 overhead:  W+R             cost of setting locks
                    P*C*N*W*(W+1)   cost of write waits
                    P*C*N*R*W       cost of read waits

degree 3 overhead:  W+R             cost of setting locks
                    P*C*N*W*(W+R)   cost of waiting for writes
                    P*C*N*R*W       cost of waiting for reads
```

TABLE 6. Computational overhead vs degrees of consistency.

CONSISTENCY DEGREE	CPU (in calls to lock sys)
0	W+P*C*N*W*(1)
1	W+P*C*N*W*(W)
2	W+R+P*C*N*W*(W+R+1)
3	W+R+P*C*N*W*(W+2*R)

To consider a specific example, a simple banking transaction does five reads (R=5) and six (W=6) writes. A transaction accesses a random account and there are millions of accounts so the probability of collision, P, is roughly .000001. Suppose there are one hundred transactions per second. A lock takes one hundred instructions and a wait requires five thousand instructions; hence, C=50. So the term P*C*N*W evaluates to 0.015. This implies that Table 5 gave a good estimate of the CPU overhead because the last term in Table 6 is miniscule compared to the term W+R. Of course this analysis is very sensitive to P and one must design the data base so that P takes on a very small value.

The striking thing about these estimates is that degree 2 and degree 3 seem to have similar computational overhead which seems to be substantially larger than the overhead of degree 0 or 1 consistency. We suspect that this conclusion would survive a more careful study of the problem.

ISSUE	DEGREE 0	DEGREE 1	DEGREE 2	DEGREE 3
COMMITTED DATA	WRITES ARE COMMITTED IMMEDIATELY	WRITES ARE COMMITTED AT EOT	SAME AS 1	SAME AS 1
DIRTY DATA	YOU DON'T UPDATE DIRTY DATA	0 AND NO ONE ELSE UPDATES YOUR DIRTY DATA	0,1 AND YOU DON'T READ DIRTY DATA	0,1,2 AND NO ONE ELSE DIRTIES DATA YOU READ
LOCK PROTOCOL	SET SHORT EXCL. LOCKS ON ANY DATA YOU WRITE	SET LONG EXCL. LOCKS ON ANY DATA YOU WRITE	1 AND SET SHORT SHARE LOCKS ON ANY DATA YOU READ	1 AND SET LONG SHARE LOCKS ON ANY DATA YOU READ
TRANSACTION STRUCTURE	WELL FORMED WRT WRITES	(WELL FORMED AND 2 PHASE) WRT WRITES	WELL FORMED (AND 2 PHASE WRT WRITES)	WELL FORMED AND TWO PHASE
CONCURRENCY	GREATEST: ONLY WAIT FOR SHORT WRITE LOCKS	GREAT: ONLY WAIT FOR WRITE LOCKS	MEDIUM: ALSO WAIT FOR READ LOCKS	LOWEST: ANY DATA TOUCHED IS LOCKED TO EOT
OVERHEAD	LEAST: ONLY SET SHORT WRITE LOCKS	SMALL: ONLY SET WRITE LOCKS	MEDIUM: SET BOTH KINDS OF LOCKS BUT NEED NOT STORE SHORT LOCKS	HIGHEST: SET AND STORE BOTH KINDS OF LOCKS
TRANSACT-ION BACKUP	CAN NOT UNDO WITHOUT CASCADING TO OTHERS	UN-DO ALL INCOMPLETE TRANSACTIONS IN ANY ORDER	UN-DO ANY INCOMPLETE TRANSACTIONS IN ANY ORDER	SAME AS 2
PROTECTION PROVIDED	LETS OTHERS RUN HIGHER CONSISTENCY	0 AND CAN'T LOSE WRITES	0,1 AND CAN'T READ BAD DATA ITEMS	0,1,2 AND CAN'T READ BAD DATA RELATIONSHIPS
SYSTEM RECOVERY TECHNIQUE	APPLY LOG IN ORDER OF ARRIVAL	APPLY LOG IN < ORDER	SAME AS 1: BUT RESULT IS SAME AS SOME SCHEDULE	2 AND SCHEDULE IS SERIAL
DEPENDENCIES	NONE	W->W	W->W W->R	W->W W->R R->W
ORDERING	NONE	< IS AN ORDERING OF THE TRANS-ACTIONS	<< IS AN ORDERING OF THE TRANS-ACTIONS	<<< IS AN ORDERING OF THE TRANS-ACTIONS

Table 7. Summary of consistency degrees.

III. LOCK GRANULARITY AND DEGREES OF CONSISTENCY IN EXISTING SYSTEMS:

IMS/VS with the program isolation feature [2] has a two level lock hierarchy: segment types (sets of records), and segment instances (records) within a segment type. Segment types may be locked in EXCLUSIVE (E) mode (which corresponds to our exclusive (X) mode) or in EXPRESS READ (R), RETRIEVE (G), or UPDATE (U) (each of which correspond to our notion of intention (I) mode) [2, pages 3.18-3.27]. Segment instances can be locked in share or exclusive mode. Segment type locks are requested at transaction initiation, usually in intention mode. Segment instance locks are dynamically set as the transaction proceeds. In addition IMS/VS has user controlled share locks on segment instances (the *Q option) which allow other read requests but not other *Q or exclusive requests. IMS/VS has no notion of S or SIX locks on segment types (which would allow a scan of all members of a segment type concurrent with other readers but without the overhead of locking each segment instance). Since IMS/VS does not support S mode on segment types one need not distinguish the two intention modes IS and IX (see the section introducing IS and IX modes). In general, IMS/VS has a notion of intention mode and does implicit locking but does not recognize all the modes described here. It uses a static two level lock tree.

IMS/VS with the program isolation feature basically provides degree 2 consistency. However degree 1 consistency can be obtained on a segment type basis in a PCB (view) by specifying the EXPRESS READ option for that segment. Similarly degree 3 consistency can be obtained by specifying the EXCLUSIVE or UPDATE options. IMS/VS also has the user controlled share locks discussed above which a program can request on selected segment instances to obtain additional consistency over the degree 1 or 2 consistency provided by the system.

IMS/VS without the program isolation feature (and also the previous version of IMS namely IMS/2) doesn't have a lock hierarchy since locking is done only on a segment type basis. It provides degree 1 consistency with degree 3 consistency obtainable for a segment type in a view by specifying the EXCLUSIVE option. User controlled locking is also provided on a limited basis via the HOLD option.

DMS 1100 has a two level lock hierarchy [4]: areas and pages within areas. Areas may be locked in one of seven modes when they are OPENed: EXCLUSIVE RETRIEVAL (which corresponds to our notion of exclusive mode), PROTECTED UPDATE (which corresponds to our notion of share and intention exclusive mode), PROTECTED RETRIEVAL (which we call share mode), UPDATE (which corresponds to our intention exclusive mode), and RETRIEVAL (which is our intention share mode). Given this transliteration, the compatibility matrix displayed in Table 1 is identical to the compatibility matrix of DMS 1100 [3, page 3.59]. However, DMS 1100 sets only exclusive locks on pages within areas (short term share locks are invisibly set during internal pointer following). Further, even if a transaction locks an area in exclusive mode, DMS 1100 continues to set exclusive locks (and internal share locks) on the pages in the area, despite the fact that an exclusive lock on an area precludes reads or updates of the area by other transactions. Similar observations apply to the DMS 1100 implementation of S and SIX modes. In general, DMS 1100 recognizes all the modes described here and uses intention modes to detect conflicts but does not utilize implicit locking. It uses a static two level lock tree.

DMS 1100 provides level 2 consistency by setting exclusive locks on the modified pages and and a temporary lock on the page corresponding to the page which is "current of run unit". The temporary lock is released when the "current of run unit" is moved. In addition a run-unit can obtain additional locks via an explicit KEEP command.

The ideas presented were developed in the process of designing and implementing an experimental data base system at the IBM San Jose Research Laboratory. (We wish to emphasize that this system is a vehicle for research in data base architecture, and does not indicate plans for future IBM products.) A subsystem which provides the modes of locks herein described, plus the necessary logic to schedule requests and conversions, and to detect and resolve deadlocks has been implemented as one component of the data manager. The lock subsystem is in turn used by the data manager to automatically lock the nodes of its lock graph (see Figure 12). Users can be unaware of these lock protocols beyond the verbs "begin transaction" and "end transaction".

The data base is broken into several storage areas. Each area contains a set of relations (files), their indices, and their tuples(records) along with a catalog of the area. Each tuple has a unique tuple identifier (data base key) which can be used to quickly (directly) address the tuple. Each tuple identifier maps to a set of field values. All tuples are stored together in an area-wide heap to allow physical clustering of tuples from different relations. The unused slots in this heap are represented by an area-wide pool of free tuple identifiers (i.e. identifiers not allocated to any relation). Each tuple "belongs" to a unique relation, and all tuples in a relation have the same number and type of fields. One may construct an index on any subset of the fields of a relation. Tuple identifiers give fast direct access to tuples, while indices give fast associative access to field values and to their corresponding tuples. Each key value in an index is made a lockable object in order to solve the problem of "phantoms" [1] without locking the entire index. We do not explicitly lock individual fields or whole indices so those nodes appear in Figure 12 only for pedagogical reasons. Figure 12 gives only the "logical" lock graph; there is also a graph for physical page locks and for other low level resources.

As can be seen, Figure 12 is not a tree. Heavy use is made of the techniques mentioned in the section on locking DAG's. For example, one can read via tuple identifier without setting any index locks but to lock a field for update its tuple identifier and the old and new index key values covering the updated field must be locked in X mode. Further, the tree is not static, since data base keys are dynamically allocated to relations; field values dynamically enter, move around in, and leave index value intervals when records are inserted, updated and deleted; relations and indices are dynamically created and destroyed within areas; and areas are dynamically allocated. The implementation of such operations observes the lock protocol presented in the section on dynamic graphs: when a node changes parents, all old and new parents must be held (explicitly or implicitly) in intention exclusive mode and the node to be moved must be held in exclusive mode.

The described system supports concurrently consistency degrees 1,2 and 3 which can be specified on a transaction basis. In addition share locks on individual tuples can be acquired by the user.

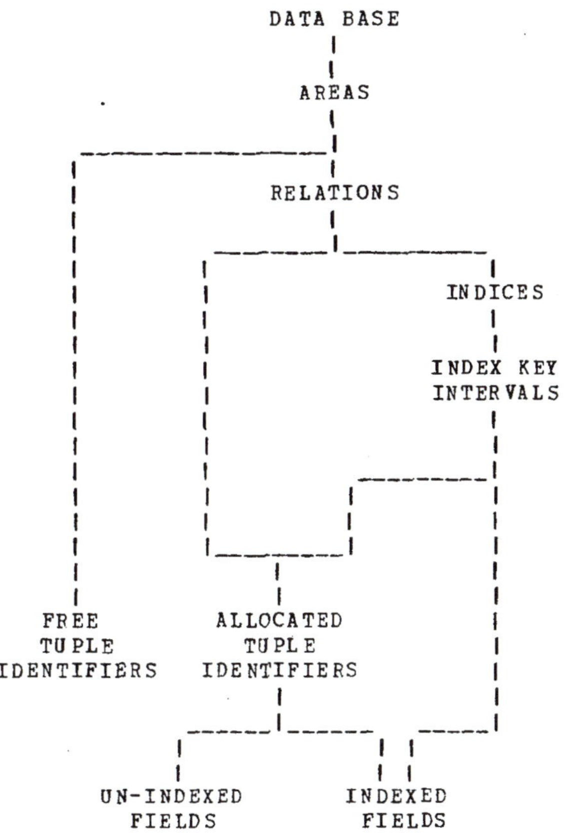

Figure 12. A lock graph.

ACKNOWLEDGMENT

We gratefully acknowledge many helpful discussions with Phil Macri, Jim Mehl and Brad Wade on how locking works in existing systems and how these results might be better presented. We are especially indebted to Paul McJones in this regard.

REFERENCES

[1] K.P. Eswaran, J.N. Gray, R.A. Lorie, I.L. Traiger, On the Notions of Consistency and Predicate Locks, Technical Report RJ.1487, IBM Research Laboratory, San Jose, Ca., Nov. 1974. (to appear CACM).

[2] Information Management System Virtual Storage (IMS/VS). System Application Design Guide, Form No. SH20-9025-2, IBM Corp., 1975.

[3] UNIVAC 1100 Series Data Management System (DMS 1100). ANSI COBOL Field Data Manipulation Language. Order No. UP7908-2, Sperry Rand Corp., May 1973.

On Optimistic Methods for Concurrency Control

H.T. KUNG and JOHN T. ROBINSON
Carnegie-Mellon University

Most current approaches to concurrency control in database systems rely on locking of data objects as a control mechanism. In this paper, two families of nonlocking concurrency controls are presented. The methods used are "optimistic" in the sense that they rely mainly on transaction backup as a control mechanism, "hoping" that conflicts between transactions will not occur. Applications for which these methods should be more efficient than locking are discussed.

Key Words and Phrases: databases, concurrency controls, transaction processing
CR Categories: 4.32, 4.33

1. INTRODUCTION

Consider the problem of providing shared access to a database organized as a collection of objects. We assume that certain distinguished objects, called the roots, are always present and access to any object other than a root is gained only by first accessing a root and then following pointers to that object. Any sequence of accesses to the database that preserves the integrity constraints of the data is called a *transaction* (see, e.g., [4]).

If our goal is to maximize the throughput of accesses to the database, then there are at least two cases where highly concurrent access is desirable.

(1) The amount of data is sufficiently great that at any given time only a fraction of the database can be present in primary memory, so that it is necessary to swap parts of the database from secondary memory as needed.
(2) Even if the entire database can be present in primary memory, there may be multiple processors.

In both cases the hardware will be underutilized if the degree of concurrency is too low.

However, as is well known, unrestricted concurrent access to a shared database will, in general, cause the integrity of the database to be lost. Most current

This research was supported in part by the National Science Foundation under Grant MCS 78-236-76 and the Office of Naval Research under Contract N00014-76-C-0370.
Authors' address: Department of Computer Science, Carnegie-Mellon University, Pittsburgh, PA 15213.

approaches to this problem involve some type of locking. That is, a mechanism is provided whereby one process can deny certain other processes access to some portion of the database. In particular, a lock may be associated with each node of the directed graph, and any given process is required to follow some locking protocol so as to guarantee that no other process can ever discover any lack of integrity in the database temporarily caused by the given process.

The locking approach has the following inherent disadvantages.

(1) Lock maintenance represents an overhead that is not present in the sequential case. Even read-only transactions (queries), which cannot possibly affect the integrity of the data, must, in general, use locking in order to guarantee that the data being read are not modified by other transactions at the same time. Also, if the locking protocol is not deadlock-free, deadlock detection must be considered to be part of lock maintenance overhead.

(2) There are no general-purpose deadlock-free locking protocols for databases that always provide high concurrency. Because of this, some research has been directed at developing special-purpose locking protocols for various special cases. For example, in the case of B-trees [1], at least nine locking protocols have been proposed [2, 3, 9, 10, 13].

(3) In the case that large parts of the database are on secondary memory, concurrency is significantly lowered whenever it is necessary to leave some congested node locked (a congested node is one that is often accessed, e.g., the root of a tree) while waiting for a secondary memory access.

(4) To allow a transaction to abort itself when mistakes occur, locks cannot be released until the end of the transaction. This may again significantly lower concurrency.

(5) Most important for the purposes of this paper, *locking may be necessary only in the worst case.* Consider the following simple example: The directed graph consists solely of roots, and each transaction involves one root only, any root equally likely. Then if there are n roots and two processes executing transactions at the same rate, locking is *really* needed (if at all) every n transactions, on the average.

In general, one may expect the argument of (5) to hold whenever (a) the number of nodes in the graph is very large compared to the total number of nodes involved in all the running transactions at a given time, and (b) the probability of modifying a congested node is small. In many applications, (a) and (b) are designed to hold (see Section 6 for the B-tree application).

Research directed at finding deadlock-free locking protocols may be seen as an attempt to lower the expense of concurrency control by eliminating transaction backup as a control mechanism. In this paper we consider the converse problem, that of eliminating locking. We propose two families of concurrency controls that do not use locking. These methods are "optimistic" in the sense that they rely for efficiency on the hope that conflicts between transactions will not occur. If (5) does hold, such conflict will be rare. This approach also has the advantage that it is completely general, applying equally well to any shared directed graph structure and associated access algorithms. Since locks are not used, it is deadlock-free (however, starvation is a possible problem, a solution for which we discuss).

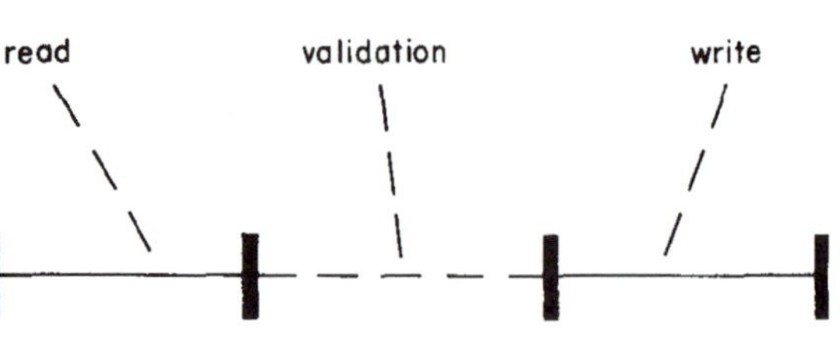

Fig. 1. The three phases of a transaction.

It is also possible using this approach to avoid problems (3) and (4) above. Finally, if the transaction pattern becomes query dominant (i.e., most transactions are read-only), then the concurrency control overhead becomes almost totally negligible (a partial solution to problem (1)).

The idea behind this optimistic approach is quite simple, and may be summarized as follows.

(1) Since reading a value or a pointer from a node can never cause a loss of integrity, reads are completely unrestricted (however, returning a result from a query is considered to be equivalent to a write, and so is subject to validation as discussed below).

(2) Writes are severely restricted. It is required that any transaction consist of two or three phases: a *read phase*, a *validation phase*, and a possible *write phase* (see Figure 1). During the read phase, all writes take place on local copies of the nodes to be modified. Then, if it can be established during the validation phase that the changes the transaction made will not cause a loss of integrity, the local copies are made global in the write phase. In the case of a query, it must be determined that the result the query would return is actually correct. The step in which it is determined that the transaction will not cause a loss of integrity (or that it will return the correct result) is called *validation*.

If, in a locking approach, locking is only necessary in the worst case, then in an optimistic approach validation will fail also only in the worst case. If validation does fail, the transaction will be backed up and start over again as a new transaction. Thus a transaction will have a write phase only if the preceding validation succeeds.

In Section 2 we discuss in more detail the read and write phases of transactions. In Section 3 a particularly strong form of validation is presented. The correctness criteria used for validation are based on the notion of serial equivalence [4, 12, 14]. In the next two sections concurrency controls that rely on the serial equivalence criteria developed in Section 3 for validation are presented. The family of concurrency controls in Section 4 have serial final validation steps, while the concurrency controls of Section 5 have completely parallel validation, at however higher total cost. In Section 6 we analyze the application of optimistic methods to controlling concurrent insertions in B-trees. Section 7 contains a summary and a discussion of future research.

2. THE READ AND WRITE PHASES

In this section we briefly discuss how the concurrency control can support the read and write phases of user-programmed transactions (in a manner invisible to the user), and how this can be implemented efficiently. The validation phase will be treated in the following three sections.

We assume that an underlying system provides for the manipulation of objects of various types. For simplicity, assume all objects are of the same type. Objects are manipulated by the following procedures, where n is the name of an object, i is a parameter to the type manager, and v is a value of arbitrary type (v could be a pointer, i.e., an object name, or data):

create	create a new object and return its name.
delete(n)	delete object n.
read(n, i)	read item i of object n and return its value.
write (n, i, v)	write v as item i of object n.

In order to support the read and write phases of transactions we also use the following procedures:

copy(n)	create a new object that is a copy of object n and return its name.
exchange($n1$, $n2$)	exchange the names of objects $n1$ and $n2$.

The concurrency control is invisible to the user; transactions are written as if the above procedures were used directly. However, transactions are required to use the syntactically identical procedures *tcreate*, *tdelete*, *tread*, and *twrite*. For each transaction, the concurrency control maintains sets of object names accessed by the transaction. These sets are initialized to be empty by a *tbegin* call. The body of the user-written transaction is in fact the read phase mentioned in the introduction; the subsequent validation phase does not begin until after a *tend* call. The procedures *tbegin* and *tend* are shown in detail in Sections 4 and 5. The semantics of the remaining procedures are as follows:

```
tcreate = (
  n := create;
  create set := create set ∪ {n};
  return n)

twrite(n, i, v) = (
  if n ∈ create set
      then write(n, i, v)
  else if n ∈ write set
      then write(copies[n], i, v)
  else (
      m := copy(n);
      copies[n] := m;
      write set := write set ∪ {n};
      write(copies[n], i, v)))

tread(n, i) = (
  read set := read set ∪ {n};
  if n ∈ write set
      then return read(copies[n], i)
```

```
    else
        return read(n, i))

tdelete(n) = (
  delete set := delete set ∪ {n}).
```

Above, *copies* is an associative vector of object names, indexed by object name. We see that in the read phase, no global writes take place. Instead, whenever the first write to a given object is requested, a copy is made, and all subsequent writes are directed to the copy. This copy is potentially global but is inaccessible to other transactions during the read phase by our convention that all nodes are accessed only by following pointers from a root node. If the node is a root node, the copy is inaccessible since it has the wrong name (all transactions "know" the global names of root nodes). It is assumed that no root node is created or deleted, that no dangling pointers are left to deleted nodes, and that created nodes become accessible by writing new pointers (these conditions are part of the integrity criteria for the data structure that each transaction is required to individually preserve).

When the transaction completes, it will request its validation and write phases via a *tend* call. If validation succeeds, then the transaction enters the write phase, which is simply

```
for n ∈ write set do exchange(n, copies[n]).
```

After the write phase all written values become "global," all created nodes become accessible, and all deleted nodes become inaccessible. Of course some cleanup is necessary, which we do not consider to be part of the write phase since it does not interact with other transactions:

```
(for n ∈ delete set do delete(n);
 for n ∈ write set do delete(copies[n])).
```

This cleanup is also necessary if a transaction is aborted.

Note that since objects are virtual (objects are referred to by name, not by physical address), the *exchange* operation, and hence the write phase, can be made quite fast: essentially, all that is necessary is to exchange the physical address parts of the two object descriptors.

Finally, we note that the concept of two-phase transactions appears to be quite valuable for recovery purposes, since at the end of the read phase, all changes that the transaction intends to make to the data structure are known.

3. THE VALIDATION PHASE

A widely used criterion for verifying the correctness of concurrent execution of transactions has been variously called serial equivalence [4], serial reproducibility [11], and linearizability [14]. This criterion may be defined as follows.

Let transactions $T_1, T_2, \ldots, T_n$ be executed concurrently. Denote an instance of the shared data structure by d, and let D be the set of all possible d, so that each T_i may be considered as a function:

$$T_i : D \rightarrow D.$$

If the initial data structure is d_{initial} and the final data structure is d_{final}, the concurrent execution of transactions is correct if some permutation π of $\{1, 2, \ldots, n\}$ exists such that

$$d_{\text{final}} = T_{\pi(n)} \circ T_{\pi(n-1)} \circ \cdots \circ T_{\pi(2)} \circ T_{\pi(1)}(d_{\text{initial}}), \tag{1}$$

where "$\circ$" is the usual notation for functional composition.

The idea behind this correctness criterion is that, first, each transaction is assumed to have been written so as to individually preserve the integrity of the shared data structure. That is, if d satisfies all integrity criteria, then for each T_i, $T_i(d)$ satisfies all integrity criteria. Now, if d_{initial} satisfies all integrity criteria and the concurrent execution of $T_1, T_2, \ldots, T_n$ is serially equivalent, then from (1), by repeated application of the integrity-preserving property of each transaction, d_{final} satisfies all integrity criteria. Serial equivalence is useful as a correctness criterion since it is in general much easier to verify that (a) each transaction preserves integrity and (b) every concurrent execution of transaction is serially equivalent than it is to verify directly that every concurrent execution of transactions preserves integrity. In fact, it has been shown in [7] that serialization is the weakest criterion for preserving consistency of a concurrent transaction system, even if complete syntactic information of the system is available to the concurrency control. However, if semantic information is available, then other approaches may be more attractive (see, e.g., [6, 8]).

3.1 Validation of Serial Equivalence

The use of validation of serial equivalence as a concurrency control is a direct application of eq. (1) above. However, in order to verify (1), a permutation π must be found. This is handled by *explicitly* assigning each transaction T_i a unique integer *transaction number* $t(i)$ during the course of its execution. The meaning of transaction numbers in validation is the following: there must exist a serially equivalent schedule in which transaction T_i comes before transaction T_j whenever $t(i) < t(j)$. This can be guaranteed by the following validation condition: for each transaction T_j with transaction number $t(j)$, and for all T_i with $t(i) < t(j)$; one of the following three conditions must hold (see Figure 2):

(1) T_i completes its write phase before T_j starts its read phase.
(2) The write set of T_i does not intersect the read set of T_j, and T_i completes its write phase before T_j starts its write phase.
(3) The write set of T_i does not intersect the read set *or* the write set of T_j. and T_i completes its read phase before T_j completes its read phase.

Condition (1) states that T_i actually completes before T_j starts. Condition (2) states that the writes of T_i do not affect the read phase of T_j, and that T_i finishes writing before T_j starts writing, hence does not overwrite T_j (also, note that T_j cannot affect the read phase of T_i). Finally, condition (3) is similar to condition (2) but does not require that T_i finish writing before T_j starts writing; it simply requires that T_i not affect the read phase *or* the write phase of T_j (again note that T_j cannot affect the read phase of T_i, by the last part of the condition). See [12] for a set of similar conditions for serialization.

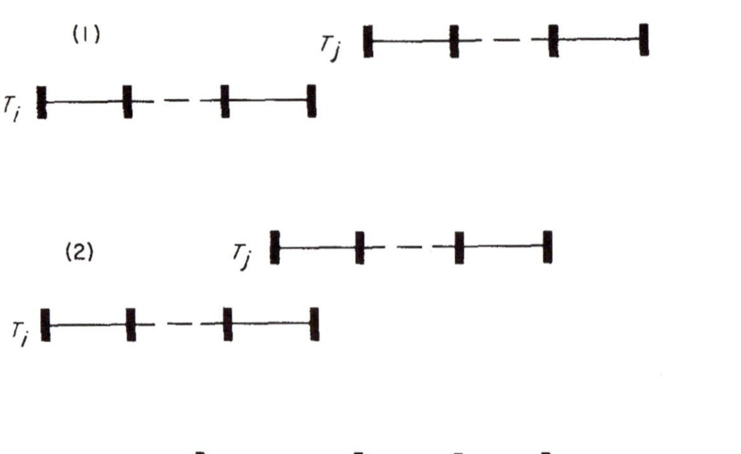

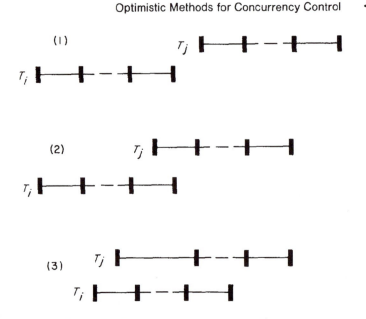

Fig. 2. Possible interleaving of two transactions.

3.2 Assigning Transaction Numbers

The first consideration that arises in the design of concurrency controls that explicitly assign transaction numbers is the question: how should transaction numbers be assigned? Clearly, they should somehow be assigned in order, since if T_i completes before T_j starts, we *must* have $t(i) < t(j)$. Here we use the simple solution of maintaining a global integer counter *tnc* (transaction number counter); when a transaction number is needed, the counter is incremented, and the resulting value returned. Also, transaction numbers must be assigned somewhere before validation, since the validation conditions above require knowledge of the transaction number of the transaction being validated. On first thought, we might assign transaction numbers at the beginning of the read phase; however, this is not optimistic (hence contrary to the philosophy of this paper) for the following reason. Consider the case of two transactions, T_1 and T_2, starting at roughly the same time, assigned transaction number n and $n + 1$, respectively. Even if T_2 completes its read phase much earlier than T_1, before being validated T_2 must wait for the completion of the read phase of T_1, since the validation of T_2 in this case relies on knowledge of the write set of T_1 (see Figure 3). In an optimistic approach, we would like for transactions to be validated immediately if at all possible (in order to improve response time). For these and similar considerations we assign transaction numbers at the end of the read phase. Note that by assigning transaction numbers in this fashion the last part of condition (3), that T_i complete its read phase before T_j completes its read phase if $t(i) < t(j)$, is automatically satisfied.

3.3 Some Practical Considerations

Given this method for assigning transaction numbers, consider the case of a transaction T that has an arbitrarily long read phase. When this transaction is

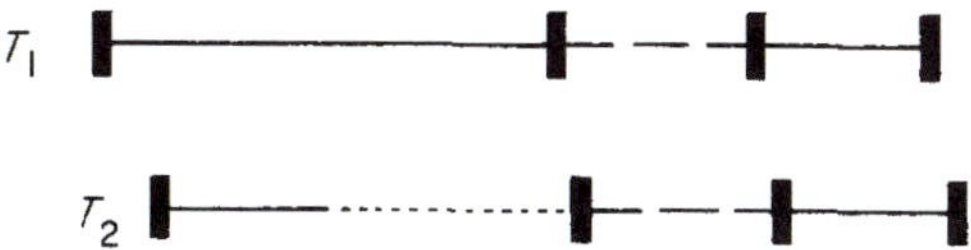

Fig. 3. Transaction 2 waits for transaction 1 in . . . .

validated, the write sets of all transactions that completed their read phase before T but had not yet completed their write phase at the start of T must be examined. Since the concurrency control can only maintain finitely many write sets, we have a difficulty (this difficulty does not arise if transaction numbers are assigned at the beginning of the read phase). Clearly, if such transactions are common, the assignment of transaction numbers described above is unsuitable. Of course, we take the optimistic approach and assume such transactions are very rare; still, a solution is needed. We solve this problem by only requiring the concurrency control to maintain some finite number of the most recent write sets where the number is large enough to validate almost all transactions (we say write set a is more recent than write set b if the transaction number associated with a is greater than that associated with b). In the case of transactions like T, if old write sets are unavailable, validation fails, and the transaction is backed up (probably to the beginning). For simplicity, we present the concurrency controls of the next two sections as if potentially infinite vectors of write sets were maintained; the above convention is understood to apply.

One last consideration must be mentioned at this point, namely, what should be done when validation fails? In such a case the transaction is aborted and restarted, receiving a new transaction number at the completion of the read phase. Now a new difficulty arises: what should be done in the case in which validation repeatedly fails? Under our optimistic assumptions this should happen rarely, but we still need some method for dealing with this problem when it does occur. A simple solution is the following. Later, we will see that transactions enter a short critical section during *tend*. If the concurrency control detects a "starving" transaction (this could be detected by keeping track of the number of times validation for a given transaction fails), the transaction can be restarted, but without releasing the critical section semaphore. This is equivalent to write-locking the entire database, and the "starving" transaction will run to completion.

4. SERIAL VALIDATION

In this section we present a family of concurrency controls that are an implementation of validation conditions (1) and (2) of Section 3.1. Since we are not using condition (3), the last part of condition (2) implies that write phases must be serial. The simplest way to implement this is to place the assignment of a transaction number, validation, and the subsequent write phase all in a critical section. In the following, we bracket the critical section by "⟨" and "⟩." The concurrency control is as follows:

```
tbegin = (
  create set := empty;
  read set := empty;
  write set := empty;
  delete set := empty;
  start tn := tnc)

tend = (
  ⟨finish tn := tnc;
   valid := true;
   for t from start tn + 1 to finish tn do
        if (write set of transaction with transaction number t intersects read set)
          then valid := false;
   if valid
        then ((write phase); tnc := tnc + 1; tn := tnc)⟩;
   if valid
        then (cleanup)
        else (backup)).
```

In the above, the transaction is assigned a transaction number via the sequence *tnc* := *tnc* + 1; *tn* := *tnc*. An optimization has been made in that transaction numbers are assigned only if validation is successful. We may imagine that the transaction is "tentatively" assigned a transaction number of *tnc* + 1 with the statement *finish tn* := *tnc*, but that if validation fails, this transaction number is freed for use by another transaction. By condition (1) of Section 3.1, we need not consider transactions that have completed their write phase before the start of the read phase of the current transaction. This is implemented by reading *tnc* in *tbegin*; since a "real" assignment of a transaction number takes place only after the write phase, it is guaranteed at this point that all transactions with transaction numbers less than or equal to *start tn* have completed their write phase.

The above is perfectly suitable in the case that there is one CPU and that the write phase can usually take place in primary memory. If the write phase often cannot take place in primary memory, we probably want to have concurrent write phases, unless the write phase is still extremely short compared to the read phase (which may be the case). The concurrency controls of the next section are appropriate for this. If there are multiple CPUs, we may wish to introduce more potential parallelism in the validation step (this is only necessary for efficiency if the processors cannot be kept busy with read phases, that is, if validation is not extremely short as compared to the read phase). This can be done by using the solution of the next section, or by the following method. At the end of the read phase, we immediately read *tnc* before entering the critical section and assign this value to *mid tn*. It is then known that at this point the write sets of transactions *start tn* + 1, *start tn* + 2, . . . , *mid tn* must certainly be examined in the validation step, and this can be done outside the critical section. The concurrency control is thus

```
tend := (
   mid tn := tnc;
   valid := true;
```

```
for t from start tn + 1 to mid tn do
if (write set of transaction with transaction number t intersects read set)
    then valid := false;
⟨finish tn := tnc;
 for t from mid tn + 1 to finish tn do
    if (write set of transaction with transaction number t intersects read set)
      then valid := false;
 if valid
    then ((write phase); tnc := tnc + 1; tn := tnc));
 if valid
    then (cleanup)
    else (backup)).
```

The above optimization can be carried out a second time: at the end of the preliminary validation step we read *tnc* a third time, and then, still outside the critical section, check the write sets of those transactions with transaction numbers from *mid tn* + 1 to this most recent value of *tnc*. Repeating this process, we derive a family of concurrency controls with varying numbers of stages of validation and degrees of parallelism, all of which however have a final indivisible validation step and write phase. The idea is to move varying parts of the work done in the critical section outside the critical section, allowing greater parallelism.

Until now we have not considered the question of read-only transactions, or queries. Since queries do not have a write phase, it is unnecessary to assign them transaction numbers. It is only necessary to read *tnc* at the end of the read phase and assign its value to *finish tn*; validation for the query then consists of examining the write sets of the transactions with transaction numbers *start tn* + 1, *start tn* + 2, . . . , *finish tn*. This need not occur in a critical section, so the above discussion on multiple validation stages does not apply to queries. This method for handling queries also applies to the concurrency controls of the next section. Note that for query-dominant systems, validation will often be trivial: It may be determined that *start tn* = *finish tn*, and validation is complete. For this type of system an optimistic approach appears ideal.

5. PARALLEL VALIDATION

In this section we present a concurrency control that uses all three of the validation conditions of Section 3.1, thus allowing greater concurrency. We retain the optimization of the previous section, only assigning transaction numbers after the write phase if validation succeeds. As in the previous solutions, *tnc* is read at the beginning and the end of the read phase; transactions with transactions numbers *start tn* + 1, *start tn* + 2, . . . , *finish tn* all may be checked under condition (2) of Section 3.1. For condition (3), we maintain a set of transaction ids *active* for transactions that have completed their read phase but have not yet completed their write phase. The concurrency control is as follows (*tbegin* is as in the previous section):

```
tend = (
  ⟨finish tn := tnc;
   finish active := (make a copy of active);
   active := active ∪ {id of this transaction}⟩;
   valid := true;
```

```
for t from start tn + 1 to finish tn do
    if (write set of transaction with transaction number t intersects read set)
      then valid := false;
for i ∈ finish active do
    if (write set of transaction T_i intersects read set or write set)
      then valid := false;
if valid
    then (
      (write phase);
      ⟨tnc := tnc + 1;
       tn := tnc;
       active := active—{id of this transaction}⟩;
      (cleanup))
    else (
      ⟨active := active—{id of transaction}⟩;
      (backup))).
```

In the above, at the end of the read phase *active* is the set of transactions that have been assigned "tentative" transaction numbers less than that of the transaction being validated. Note that modifications to *active* and *tnc* are placed together in critical sections so as to maintain the invariant properties of *active* and *tnc* mentioned above. Entry to the first critical section is equivalent to being assigned a "tentative" transaction number.

One problem with the above is that a transaction in the set *finish active* may invalidate the given transaction, even though the former transaction is itself invalidated. A partial solution to this is to use several stages of preliminary validation, in a way completely analogous to the multistage validation described in the previous section. At each stage, a new value of *tnc* is read, and transactions with transaction numbers up to this value are checked. The final stage then involves accessing *active* as above. The idea is to reduce the size of *active* by performing more of the validation before adding a new transaction id to *active*.

Finally, a solution is possible where transactions that have been invalidated by a transaction in *finish active* wait for that transaction to either be invalidated, and hence ignored, or validated, causing backup (this possibility was pointed out by James Saxe). However, this solution involves a more sophisticated process communication mechanism than the binary semaphore needed to implement the critical sections above.

6. ANALYSIS OF AN APPLICATION

We have previously noted that an optimistic approach appears ideal for query-dominant systems. In this section we consider another promising application, that of supporting concurrent index operations for very large tree-structured indexes. In particular, we examine the use of an optimistic method for supporting concurrent insertions in B-trees (see [1]). Similar types of analysis and similar results can be expected for other types of tree-structured indexes and index operations.

One consideration in analyzing the efficiency of an optimistic method is the expected size of read and write sets, since this relates directly to the time spent in the validation phase. For B-trees, we naturally choose the objects of the read and write sets to be the pages of the B-tree. Now even very large B-trees are only a few levels deep. For example, let a B-tree of order m contain N keys. Then if $m = 199$ and $N \leq 2 \times 10^8 - 2$, the depth is at most $1 + \log_{100}(N + 1)/2) < 5$. Since insertions do not read or write more than one already existing node on a given level, this means that for B-trees of order 199 containing up to almost 200 million keys, the size of a read or write set of an insertion will never be more than 4. Since we are able to bound the size of read and write sets by a small constant, we conclude that validation will be fast, the validation time essentially being proportional to the degree of concurrency.

Another important consideration is the time to complete the validation and write phases as compared to the time to complete the read phase (this point was mentioned in Section 4). B-trees are implemented using some paging algorithm, typically least recently used page replaced first. The root page and some of the pages on the first level are normally in primary memory; lower level pages usually need to be swapped in. Since insertions always access a leaf page (here, we call a page on the lowest level a leaf page), a typical insertion to a B-tree of depth d will cause $d - 1$ or $d - 2$ secondary memory accesses. However, the validation and write phases should be able to take place in primary memory. Thus we expect the read phase to be orders of magnitude longer than the validation and write phases. In fact, since the "densities" of validation and write phases are so low, we believe that the serial validation algorithms of Section 4 should give acceptable performance in most cases.

Our final and most important consideration is determining how likely it is that one insertion will cause another concurrent insertion to be invalidated. Let the B-tree be of order m (m odd), have depth d, and let n be the number of leaf pages. Now, given two insertions I_1 and I_2, what is the probability that the write set of I_1 intersects the read set of I_2? Clearly this depends on the size of the write set of I_1, and this is determined by the degree of splitting. Splitting occurs only when an insertion is attempted on an already full page, and results in an insertion to the page on the next higher level. Lacking theoretical results on the distribution of the number of keys in B-tree pages, we make the conservative assumption that the number of keys in any page is uniformly distributed between $(m - 1)/2$ and $m - 1$ (this is a conservative assumption since it predicts storage utilization of 75 percent, but theoretical results do exist for storage utilization [15], which show that storage utilization is about 69 percent—since nodes are on the average emptier than our assumption implies, this suggests that the probability of splitting we use is high). We also assume that an insertion accesses any path from root to leaf equally likely. With these assumptions we find that the write set of I_1 has size i with probability

$$p_s(i) = \left(\frac{2}{m+1}\right)^{i-1}\left(1 - \frac{2}{m+1}\right).$$

Given the size of the write set of I_1, an upper bound on the probability that the read set of I_2 intersects the subtree written by I_1 is easily derived by assuming the maximal number of pages in the subtree, and is

$$p_I(i) < \frac{m^{i-1}}{n}.$$

Combining these, we find the probability of conflict p_C satisfies

$$p_C = \sum_{1 \le i \le d} p_s(i) p_I(i)$$

$$< \frac{1}{n}\left(1 - \frac{2}{m+1}\right) \sum_{1 \le i \le d} \left(\frac{2m}{m+1}\right)^{i-1}.$$

For example, if $d = 3$, $m = 199$, and $n = 10^4$, we have $p_C < 0.0007$. Thus we see that it is very rare that one insertion would cause another concurrent insertion to restart for large B-trees.

7. CONCLUSIONS

A great deal of research has been done on locking approaches to concurrency control, but as noted above, in practice two control mechanisms are used: locking and backup. Here we have begun to investigate solutions to concurrency control that rely almost entirely on the latter mechanism. We may think of the optimistic methods presented here as being orthogonal to locking methods in several ways.

(1) In a locking approach, transactions are controlled by having them wait at certain points, while in an optimistic approach, transactions are controlled by backing them up.

(2) In a locking approach, serial equivalence can be proved by partially ordering the transactions by first access time for each object, while in an optimistic approach, transactions are ordered by transaction number assignment.

(3) The major difficulty in locking approaches is deadlock, which can be solved by using backup; in an optimistic approach, the major difficulty is starvation, which can be solved by using locking.

We have presented two families of concurrency controls with varying degrees of concurrency. These methods may well be superior to locking methods for systems where transaction conflict is highly unlikely. Examples include query-dominant systems and very large tree-structured indexes. For these cases, an optimistic method will avoid locking overhead, and may take full advantage of a multiprocessor environment in the validation phase using the parallel validation techniques presented. Some techniques are definitely needed for determining all instances where an optimistic approach is better than a locking approach, and in such cases, which type of optimistic approach should be used.

A more general problem is the following: Consider the case of a database system where transaction conflict is rare, but not rare enough to justify the use of any of the optimistic approaches presented here. Some type of generalized concurrency control is needed that provides "just the right amount" of locking versus backup. Ideally, this should vary as the likelihood of transaction conflict in the system varies.

REFERENCES

1. BAYER, R., AND MCCREIGHT, E. Organization and maintenance of large ordered indexes. *Acta Inf. 1*, 3 (1972), 173–189.
2. BAYER, R., AND SCHKOLNICK, M. Concurrency of operations on B-trees. *Acta Inf. 9*, 1 (1977), 1–21.

3. ELLIS, C. S. Concurrency search and insertion in 2-3 trees. *Acta Inf. 14*, 1 (1980), 63-86.
4. ESWARAN, K. P., GRAY, J. N., LORIE, R. A., AND TRAIGER, I. L. The notions of consistency and predicate locks in a database system. *Commun. ACM 19*, 11 (Nov. 1976), 624-633.
5. GRAY, J. Notes on database operating systems. In *Lecture Notes in Computer Science* 60: *Operating Systems*, R. Bayer, R. M. Graham, and G. Seegmuller, Eds. Springer-Verlag, Berlin, 1978, pp. 393-481.
6. KUNG, H. T., AND LEHMAN, P. L. Concurrent manipulation of binary search trees. *ACM Trans. Database Syst. 5*, 3 (Sept. 1980), 354-382.
7. KUNG, H. T., AND PAPADIMITRIOU, C. H. An optimality theory of concurrency control for databases. In *Proc. ACM SIGMOD 1979 Int. Conf. Management of Data*, May 1979, pp. 116-126.
8. LAMPORT, L. Towards a theory of correctness for multi-user data base systems. Tech. Rep. CA-7610-0712, Massachusetts Computer Associates, Inc., Wakefield, Mass., Oct. 1976.
9. LEHMAN, P. L., AND YAO, S. B. Efficient locking for concurrent operations on B-trees. Submitted for publication.
10. MILLER, R. E., AND SNYDER, L. Multiple access to B-trees. Presented at Proc. Conf. Information Sciences and Systems, Johns Hopkins Univ., Baltimore, Md., Mar. 1978.
11. PAPADIMITRIOU, C. H., BERNSTEIN, P. A., AND ROTHNIE, J. B. Computational problems related to database concurrency control. In *Conf. Theoretical Computer Science*, Univ. Waterloo, 1977, pp. 275-282.
12. PAPADIMITRIOU, C. H. Serializability of concurrent updates. *J. ACM 26*, 4 (Oct. 1979), 631-653.
13. SAMADI, B. B-trees in a system with multiple users. *Inf. Process. Lett. 5*, 4 (Oct. 1976), 107-112.
14. STEARNS, R. E., LEWIS, P. M., II, AND ROSENKRANTZ, D. J. Concurrency control for database systems. In *Proc. 7th Symp. Foundations of Computer Science*, 1976, pp. 19-32.
15. YAO, A. On random 2-3 trees. *Acta Inf. 2*, 9 (1978), 159-170.

Received May 1979; revised July 1980; accepted September 1980

Concurrency Control Performance Modeling: Alternatives and Implications

RAKESH AGRAWAL
AT&T Bell Laboratories
MICHAEL J. CAREY and MIRON LIVNY
University of Wisconsin

A number of recent studies have examined the performance of concurrency control algorithms for database management systems. The results reported to date, rather than being definitive, have tended to be contradictory. In this paper, rather than presenting "yet another algorithm performance study," we critically investigate the assumptions made in the models used in past studies and their implications. We employ a fairly complete model of a database environment for studying the relative performance of three different approaches to the concurrency control problem under a variety of modeling assumptions. The three approaches studied represent different extremes in how transaction conflicts are dealt with, and the assumptions addressed pertain to the nature of the database system's resources, how transaction restarts are modeled, and the amount of information available to the concurrency control algorithm about transactions' reference strings. We show that differences in the underlying assumptions explain the seemingly contradictory performance results. We also address the question of how realistic the various assumptions are for actual database systems.

Categories and Subject Descriptors: H.2.4 [**Database Management**]: Systems—*transaction processing*; D.4.8 [**Operating Systems**]: Performance—*simulation, modeling and prediction*

General Terms: Algorithms, Performance

Additional Key Words and Phrases: Concurrency control

1. INTRODUCTION

Research in the area of concurrency control for database systems has led to the development of many concurrency control algorithms. Most of these algorithms are based on one of three basic mechanisms: *locking* [23, 31, 32, 44, 48], *timestamps* [8, 36, 52], and *optimistic* concurrency control (also called commit-time validation or certification) [5, 16, 17, 27]. Bernstein and Goodman [9, 10] survey many of

A preliminary version of this paper appeared as "Models for Studying Concurrency Control Performance: Alternatives and Implications," in *Proceedings of the International Conference on Management of Data* (Austin, Tx., May 28–30, 1985).

M. J. Carey and M. Livny were partially supported by the Wisconsin Alumni Research Foundation under National Science Foundation grant DCR-8402818 and an IBM Faculty Development Award.

Authors' addresses: R. Agrawal, AT&T Bell Laboratories, Murray Hill, NJ 07974; M. J. Carey and M. Livny, Computer Sciences Department, University of Wisconsin, Madison, WI 53706.

the algorithms that have been developed and describe how new algorithms may be created by combining the three basic mechanisms.

Given the ever-growing number of available concurrency control algorithms, considerable research has recently been devoted to evaluating the performance of concurrency control algorithms. The behavior of locking has been investigated using both simulation [6, 28, 29, 39–41, 47] and analytical models [22, 24, 26, 35, 37, 50, 51, 53]. A qualitative study that discussed performance issues for a number of distributed locking and timestamp algorithms was presented in [7], and an empirical comparison of several concurrency control schemes was given in [34]. Recently, the performance of different concurrency control mechanisms has been compared in a number of studies. The performance of locking was compared with the performance of basic timestamp ordering in [21] and with basic and multiversion timestamp ordering in [30]. The performance of several alternatives for handling deadlock in locking algorithms was studied in [6]. Results of experiments comparing locking to the optimistic method appeared in [42 and 43], and the performance of several variants of locking, basic timestamp ordering, and the optimistic method was compared in [12 and 15]. Finally, the performance of several integrated concurrency control and recovery algorithms was evaluated in [1 and 2].

These performance studies are informative, but the results that have emerged, instead of being definitive, have been very contradictory. For example, studies by Carey and Stonebraker [15] and Agrawal and DeWitt [2] suggest that an algorithm that uses blocking instead of restarts is preferable from a performance viewpoint, but studies by Tay [50, 51] and Balter et al. [6] suggest that restarts lead to better performance than blocking. Optimistic methods outperformed locking in [20], whereas the opposite results were reported in [2 and 15]. In this paper, rather than presenting "yet another algorithm performance study," we examine the reasons for these apparent contradictions, addressing the models used in past studies and their implications.

The research that led to the development of the many currently available concurrency control algorithms was guided by the notion of *serializability* as the correctness criteria for general-purpose concurrency control algorithms [11, 19, 33]. Transactions are typically viewed as sequences of read and write requests, and the interleaved sequence of read and write requests for a concurrent execution of transactions is called the execution *log*. Proving algorithm correctness then amounts to proving that any log that can be generated using a particular concurrency control algorithm is equivalent to some serial log (i.e., one in which all requests from each individual transaction are adjacent in the log). Algorithm correctness work has therefore been guided by the existence of this widely accepted standard approach based on logs and serializability. Algorithm performance work has not been so fortunate—no analogous standard performance model has been available to guide the work in this area. As we will see shortly, the result is that nearly every study has been based on its own unique set of assumptions regarding database system resources, transaction behavior, and other such issues.

In this paper, we begin by establishing a performance evaluation framework based on a fairly complete model of a database management system. Our model captures the main elements of a database environment, including both *users* (i.e., terminals, the source of transactions) and *physical resources* for storing and processing the data (i.e., disks and CPUs), in addition to the characteristics of the workload and the database. On the basis of this framework, we then show that differences in assumptions explain the apparently contradictory performance results from previous studies. We examine the effects of alternative assumptions, and we briefly address the question of which alternatives seem most reasonable for use in studying the performance of database management systems.

In particular, we critically examine the common assumption of *infinite resources.* A number of studies (e.g., [20, 29, 30, 50, 51]) compare concurrency control algorithms under the assumption that transactions progress at a rate independent of the number of active transactions. In other words, they proceed in *parallel* rather than in an interleaved manner. This is only really possible in a system with enough resources so that transactions *never* have to wait before receiving CPU or I/O service—hence our choice of the phrase "infinite resources." We will investigate this assumption by performing studies with truly infinite resources, with multiple CPU-I/O devices, and with transactions that think while holding locks. The infinite resource case represents an "ideal" system, the multiple CPU-I/O device case models a class of multiprocessor database machines, and having transactions think while executing models an interactive workload.

In addition to these resource-related assumptions, we examine two modeling assumptions related to transaction behavior that have varied from study to study. In each case, we investigate how alternative assumptions affect the performance results. One of the additional assumptions that we address is the *fake restart* assumption, in which it is assumed that a restarted transaction is replaced by a new, independent transaction, rather than running the same transaction over again. This assumption is nearly always used in analytical models in order to make the modeling of restarts tractable. Another assumption that we examine has to do with *write-lock acquisition.* A number of studies that distinguish between read and write locks assume that read locks are set on read-only items and that write locks are set on the items to be updated when they are first read. In reality, however, transactions often acquire a read lock on an item, then examine the item, and only then request that the read lock be upgraded to a write lock—because a transaction must usually examine an item before deciding whether or not to update it [B. Lindsay, personal communication, 1984].

We examine three concurrency control algorithms in this study, two locking algorithms and an optimistic algorithm, which represent extremes as to when and how they detect and resolve conflicts. Section 2 describes our choice of concurrency control algorithms. We use a simulator based on a closed queuing model of a single-site database system for our performance studies. The structure and characteristics of our model are described in Section 3. Section 4 discusses the performance metrics and statistical methods used for the experiments, and it also discusses how a number of our parameter values were chosen. Section 5 presents the resource-related performance experiments and results. Section 6 presents the results of our examination of the other modeling assumptions described above. Finally, in Section 7 we summarize the main conclusions of this study.

2. CONCURRENCY CONTROL STRATEGIES

A transaction T is a sequence of actions $\{a_1, a_2, \ldots, a_n\}$, where a_i is either read or write. Given a concurrent execution of transactions, action a_i of transaction T_i and action a_j of T_j *conflict* if they access the same object and either (1) a_i is read and a_j is write, or (2) a_i is write and a_j is read or write. The various concurrency control algorithms basically differ in the time when they *detect conflicts* and the way that they *resolve conflicts* [9]. For this study we have chosen to examine the following three concurrency control algorithms that represent extremes in conflict detection and resolution:

Blocking. Transactions set read locks on objects that they read, and these locks are later upgraded to write locks for objects that they also write. If a lock request is denied, the requesting transaction is blocked. A waits-for graph of transactions is maintained [23], and deadlock detection is performed each time a transaction blocks.[1] If a deadlock is discovered, the youngest transaction in the deadlock cycle is chosen as the victim and restarted. Dynamic two-phase locking [23] is an example of this strategy.

Immediate-Restart. As in the case of blocking, transactions read-lock the objects that they read, and they later upgrade these locks to write locks for objects that they also write. However, if a lock request is denied, the requesting transaction is aborted and restarted after a restart delay. The delay period, which should be on the order of the expected response time of a transaction, prevents the same conflict from occurring repeatedly. A concurrency control strategy similar to this one was considered in [50 and 51].

Optimistic. Transactions are allowed to execute unhindered and are validated only after they have reached their commit points. A transaction is restarted at its commit point if it finds that any object that it read has been written by another transaction that committed during its lifetime. The optimistic method proposed by Kung and Robinson [27] is based on this strategy.

These algorithms represent two extremes with respect to when conflicts are detected. The blocking and immediate-restart algorithms are based on dynamic locking, so conflicts are detected as they occur. The optimistic algorithm, on the other hand, does not detect conflicts until transaction-commit time. The three algorithms also represent two different extremes with respect to conflict resolution. The blocking algorithm blocks transactions to resolve conflicts, restarting them only when necessary because of a deadlock. The immediate-restart and optimistic algorithms always use restarts to resolve conflicts.

One final note in regard to the three algorithms: In the immediate-restart algorithm, a restarted transaction must be delayed for some time to allow the conflicting transaction to complete; otherwise, the same lock conflict will occur repeatedly. For the optimistic algorithm, it is unnecessary to delay the restarted

[1] Blocking's performance results would change very little if periodic deadlock detection were assumed instead [4].

transaction, since any detected conflict is with an already committed transaction. A restart delay is also unnecessary for the blocking algorithm, since the same deadlock cannot arise repeatedly.

3. PERFORMANCE MODEL

There are three main parts of a concurrency control performance model: a database system model, a user model, and a transaction model. The *database system model* captures the relevant characteristics of the system's hardware and software, including the physical resources (CPUs and disks) and their associated schedulers, the characteristics of the database (e.g., its size and granularity), the load control mechanism for controlling the number of active transactions, and the concurrency control algorithm itself. The *user model* captures the arrival process for users, assuming either an open system or else a closed system with terminals. Also included in the user model is the nature of users' transactions, since they may either be batch-style (noninteractive) or interactive in their behavior. Finally, the *transaction model* captures the reference behavior and processing requirements of the transactions in the workload. A transaction can be thought of as being described via two characteristic strings. There is a logical reference string, which contains concurrency control level read and write requests, and a physical reference string, which contains requests for accesses to physical items on disk and the associated CPU processing time for each item accessed. These strings are typically described in a probabilistic manner for a class of transactions. In addition, if there is more than one class of transactions in the workload, the transaction model must specify the mix of transaction classes. It is our view that a concurrency control performance model that fails to include any of these three major parts is in some sense incomplete. Although our model description is not broken down in exactly this way (it is more transaction-flow oriented), it should become clear to the reader that our model includes all three parts.

Central to our simulation model for studying concurrency control algorithm performance is the closed queuing model of a single-site database system shown in Figure 1. This model is an extended version of the model used in [12 and 15], which in turn had its origins in the model of [39, 40, and 41]. There are a fixed number of terminals from which transactions originate. There is a limit to the number of transactions allowed to be active at any time in the system, the multiprogramming level *mpl*. A transaction is considered active if it is either receiving service or waiting for service inside the database system. When a new transaction originates, if the system already has a full set of active transactions, it enters the *ready queue* where it waits for a currently active transaction to complete or abort. (Transactions in the ready queue are not considered active.) The transaction then enters the *cc queue* (concurrency control queue) and makes the first of its concurrency control requests. If the concurrency control request is granted, the transaction proceeds to the *object queue* and accesses its first object. If more than one object is to be accessed prior to the next concurrency control request, the transaction will cycle through this queue several times. When the next concurrency control request is required, the transaction reenters the concurrency control queue and makes the request. It is assumed for modeling

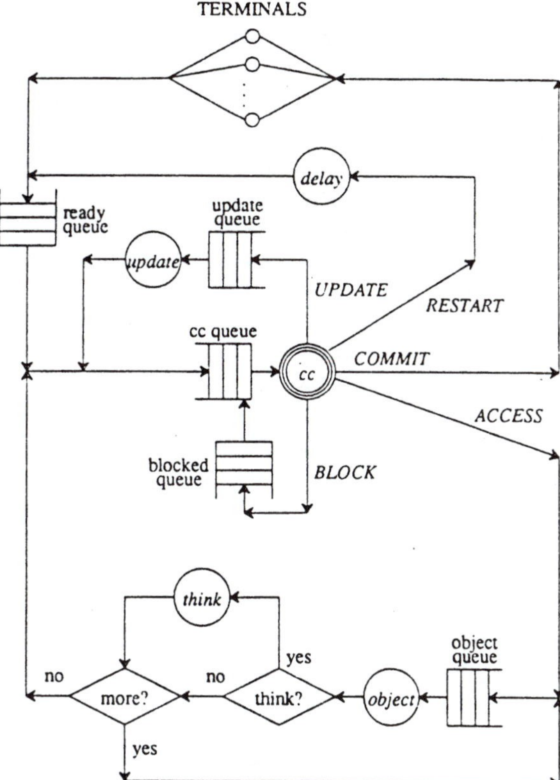

Fig. 1. Logical queuing model.

convenience that a transaction performs all of its reads before performing any writes. In one of the performance studies later in the paper, we examine the performance of concurrency control algorithms under interactive workloads. The think path in the model provides an optional random delay that follows object accesses for this purpose. More will be said about modeling interactive transactions shortly.

If the result of a concurrency control request is that the transaction must block, it enters the *blocked queue* until it is once again able to proceed. If a request leads to a decision to restart the transaction, it goes to the back of the ready queue, possibly after a randomly determined restart delay period of mean *restart_delay* (as in the immediate-restart algorithm). It then begins making all of the *same* concurrency control requests and object accesses over again.[2] Eventually the transaction may complete and the concurrency control algorithm may choose to commit the transaction. If the transaction is read-only, it is finished. If it has written one or more objects during its execution, however, it first enters the *update queue* and writes its deferred updates into the database. Deferred updates are assumed here because our modeling framework is intended to support *any* concurrency control algorithm—all algorithms operate correctly with

[2] The simulator maintains backup copies of transaction read and write sets.

deferred updates, but not all algorithms work with recovery schemes that allow in-place updates prior to transaction-commit time. (Examples of recovery schemes that use some form of deferred updates to minimize the cost of backing out aborted transactions include the Commercial INGRES recovery mechanism [45], the database cache of Elhard and Bayer [18], and the POSTGRES recovery mechanism [49]. Results on the performance of such recovery schemes and their alternatives may be found in [2 and 38]; a study of deferred versus in-place updates and the associated cost of backing out restarted transactions in the presence of limited buffer space is included in [2].)

To further illustrate the flow of transactions in the model, we briefly describe how the locking algorithms and the optimistic algorithm are modeled. For locking, each concurrency control request corresponds to a lock request for an object, and these requests alternate with object accesses. Locks are released together at end-of-transaction (after the deferred updates have been performed). Wait queues for locks and a waits-for graph are maintained by an algorithm-specific portion of the simulator. For optimistic concurrency control, the first concurrency control request is granted immediately (i.e., it is a "no-op"); all object accesses are then performed with no intervening concurrency control requests. Only after the last object access is finished does a transaction return to the concurrency control queue in the optimistic case, at which time its validation test is performed (followed, if successful, by its deferred updates).

Underlying the logical model of Figure 1 are two physical resources, the CPU and the I/O (i.e., disk) resources. Associated with the concurrency control, object access, and deferred update services in Figure 1 are some use of one or both of these two resources. The amounts of CPU and I/O time per logical service are specified as model parameters. The physical queuing model is depicted in Figure 2, and Table I summarizes the associated model parameters. As shown, the physical model is a collection of terminals, multiple CPU servers, and multiple I/O servers. The delay paths for the think and restart delays are also reflected in the physical queuing model. Model parameters specify the number of CPU servers, the number of I/O servers, and the number of terminals for the model. When a transaction needs CPU service, it is assigned a free CPU server; otherwise the transaction waits until one becomes free. Thus, the CPU servers may be thought of as being a pool of servers, all identical and serving one global CPU queue. Requests in the CPU queue are serviced FCFS (first-come, first-served), except that concurrency control requests have priority over all other service requests. Our I/O model is a probabilistic model of a database that is spread out across all of the disks. There is a queue associated with each of the I/O servers. When a transaction needs service, it chooses a disk (at random, with all disks being equally likely) and waits in an I/O queue associated with the selected disk. The service discipline for the I/O queues is also FCFS.

The parameters *obj_io* and *obj_cpu* are the amounts of I/O and CPU time associated with reading or writing an object. Reading an object takes resources equal to *obj_io* followed by *obj_cpu*. Writing an object takes resources equal to *obj_cpu* at the time of the write request and *obj_io* at deferred update time, since it is assumed that transactions maintain deferred update lists in buffers in main memory. These parameters represent constant service time requirements rather than stochastic ones for simplicity. The *ext_think_time* parameter is the mean

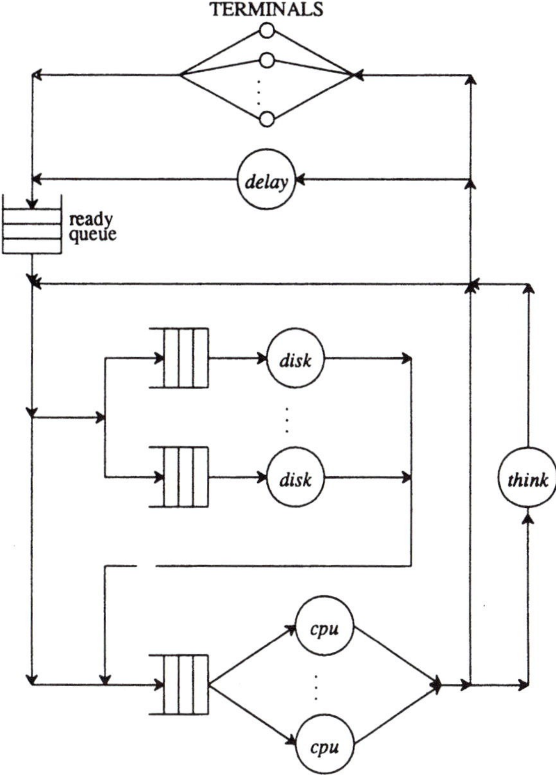

Fig. 2. Physical queuing model.

Table I. Model Parameters

Parameter	Meaning
db_size	Number of objects in database
tran_size	Mean size of transaction
max_size	Size of largest transaction
min_size	Size of smallest transaction
write_prob	Pr(write X | read X)
int_think_time	Mean intratransaction think time
restart_delay	Mean transaction restart delay
num_terms	Number of terminals
mpl	Multiprogramming level
ext_think_time	Mean time between transactions
obj_io	I/O time for accessing an object
obj_cpu	CPU time for accessing an object
num_cpus	Number of cpus
num_disks	Number of disks

time delay between the completion of a transaction and the initiation of a new transaction from a terminal, and the *int_think_time* parameter is the mean intratransaction think time (if any). We assume that both of these think times are exponentially distributed. To model interactive workloads, transactions can be made to undergo a thinking period between finishing their reads and starting their writes.

A transaction is modeled according to the number of objects that it reads and writes. The parameter *tran_size* is the average number of objects read by a transaction, the mean of a uniform distribution between *min_size* and *max_size* (inclusive). These objects are randomly chosen (without replacement) from among all of the objects in the database. The probability that an object read by a transaction will also be written is determined by the parameter *write_prob*. The size of the database is assumed to be *db_size*.

The reader may have noted the absence of explicit concurrency control cost parameters. We assume for the purpose of this study that the cost of performing concurrency control operations is negligible compared to the cost of accessing objects. It has been shown elsewhere that the concurrency control request processing costs for algorithms based on locking and optimistic methods are roughly comparable [13], the main difference being the times at which these costs are incurred; it has also been argued that deadlock detection should not add significantly to the overhead of locking in a centralized database system [3, 13]. Thus, our negligible concurrency control cost assumption should not bias our results. Other sources of overhead that we do not consider in this study are the degradation of operating system and/or database system performance under high multiprogramming levels because of effects such as increased instruction path lengths due to large control structures (e.g., process tables), page thrashing due to memory limitations, increases in context switching, contention for high-traffic semaphores, and so forth. Database operating system issues such as context switching overhead and semaphore contention have been previously addressed by others [25].

4. GENERAL EXPERIMENT INFORMATION

The remainder of this paper presents results from a number of experiments designed to investigate the alternative modeling assumptions discussed in Section 1. Section 5 will describe studies with infinite resources, a small number of resources, various intermediate resource levels, and interactive transactions. Section 6 will describe studies of alternative modeling assumptions regarding restarted transactions and write-lock acquisition. First, however, this section of the paper will discuss the performance metrics and statistical methods used in the rest of the paper, and it will also explain how we chose many of the parameter settings used in the experiments reported here.

4.1 Performance Metrics

The primary performance metric used throughout the paper is the transaction throughput rate, which is the number of transactions completed per second. We employed a modified form of the batch means method [46] for the statistical data analyses of our throughput results, and each simulation was run for 20 batches with a large batch time to produce sufficiently tight 90 percent confidence intervals.[3] The actual batch time varied from experiment to experiment, but our

[3] More information on the details of the modified batch means method may be found in [12].

throughput confidence intervals were typically in the range of plus or minus a few percentage points of the mean value, more than sufficient for our purposes. We omit confidence interval information from our graphs for clarity, but we discuss only the statistically significant performance differences when summarizing our results. Response times, expressed in seconds, are also given in some cases. These are measured as the difference between when a terminal first submits a new transaction and when the transaction returns to the terminal following its successful completion, including any time spent waiting in the ready queue, time spent before (and while) being restarted, and so forth. The response time variance is also examined in a few cases.

Several additional performance-related metrics are used in analyzing the results of our experiments. In analyzing concurrency control activity for the three algorithms, two conflict-related metrics are employed. The first metric is the *blocking ratio*, which gives the average number of times that a transaction has to block per commit (computed as the ratio of the number of transaction-blocking events to the number of transaction commits). The other conflict-related metric is the *restart ratio*, which gives the average number of times that a transaction has to restart per commit (computed similarly). The last set of metrics used in our analysis are the total and useful disk utilizations. The total utilization for a disk gives the fraction of time during which it is busy. The useful utilization indicates the fraction of disk time used to do work that actually completed, excluding the fraction of time used for work that was later undone because of restarts. Note that since disks are uniformly selected when a request arrives, all of the disks have the same utilization over the range of our long simulation times. Disk utilization is used instead of CPU utilization because the disks turn out to be the bottleneck resource with our parameter settings (discussed next).

4.2 Parameter Settings

Table II gives the values of the simulation parameters that all of our experiments have in common (except where otherwise noted). Parameters that vary from experiment to experiment are not listed in Table II and will instead be given with the description of the relevant experiments.

The number of terminals is set to 200 in this study. The multiprogramming level, which limits the number of active transactions, is varied from 5 transactions up to the total number of terminals. This range was chosen for several reasons. First, it includes values that we consider to be reasonable for actual database systems. Second, varying the multiprogramming level in this way provides a wide range of operating conditions with respect to both data contention (conflict probabilities) and resource contention (waiting for CPUs and disks). The object processing costs were chosen on the basis of our notion of roughly what realistic values might be. In varying the number of CPUs and disks, an issue not addressed in Table II, we decided to use 1 CPU and 2 disks as 1 *resource unit*, and then vary the number of resource units assumed. In cases in which we have 1 CPU, we have 2 disks, and in cases in which we have N CPUs, we have $2N$ disks. This balance of CPUs and disks makes the utilization of these resources about equal (i.e., balanced) with our parameter values, as opposed to being either strongly CPU bound or strongly I/O bound; in particular, the system is just slightly I/O

Table II. Simulation Parameter Settings

Parameter	Value
db_size	1,000 pages
tran_size	8-page readset
max_size	12-page readset (maximum)
min_size	4-page readset (minimum)
write_prob	0.25
restart_delay	zero or adaptive (see text)
num_terms	200 terminals
mpl	5, 10, 25, 50, 75, 100, and 200
ext_think_time	1 second
obj_io	35 milliseconds
obj_cpu	15 milliseconds

bound. As for the *restart_delay* parameter, we mentioned in Section 2 that only the immediate-restart algorithm demands a restart delay. Thus, the delay is set to zero for the other two algorithms. For the immediate-restart algorithm we use an exponential delay with a mean equal to the running average of the transaction response time—that is, the duration of the delay is *adaptive*, depending on the observed average response time. We chose to employ an adaptive delay after performing a sensitivity analysis that showed us that the performance of the immediate-restart algorithm is sensitive to the restart delay time, particularly in the infinite resource case. Our preliminary experiments indicated that a delay of about one transaction time is best, and that throughput begins to drop off rapidly when the delay exceeds more than a few transaction times.

In choosing parameter values for our experiments, we wanted to choose database and transaction sizes[4] that would jointly yield a region of operation that would allow the interesting performance effects to be observed without requiring impossibly long simulation times. A preliminary experiment was conducted with an average transaction size of 8 reads and 2 writes, as shown in Table II, but with a database size of 10,000 pages. Due to the large database size and the relatively small transaction size, there were few conflicts in this experiment. The throughput results for a system with infinite resources and a system with limited resources (1 resource unit, meaning 1 CPU and 2 disks) are shown in Figures 3 and 4, respectively. The performance of the three concurrency control strategies was close in both cases, confirming the results reported in [1, 2, 12, and 15] and elsewhere. If conflicts are rare, it makes little difference which concurrency control algorithm is used. In both cases, blocking outperformed the other two algorithms by a small amount. Note also that the throughput curves reach a plateau at a multiprogramming level of 75 in Figure 3 (the infinite resource case). This is due to the fact that with 200 terminals, a 1 second think time, and an expected execution time of 500 milliseconds, increasing the allowed number of active transactions beyond 75 has no effect—all available transactions are already active, and the rest are in the think state. A plateau is reached earlier in Figure 4 (the limited resource case) because the resources are already saturated

[4] These sizes are expressed in pages, as we equate objects and pages in this study.

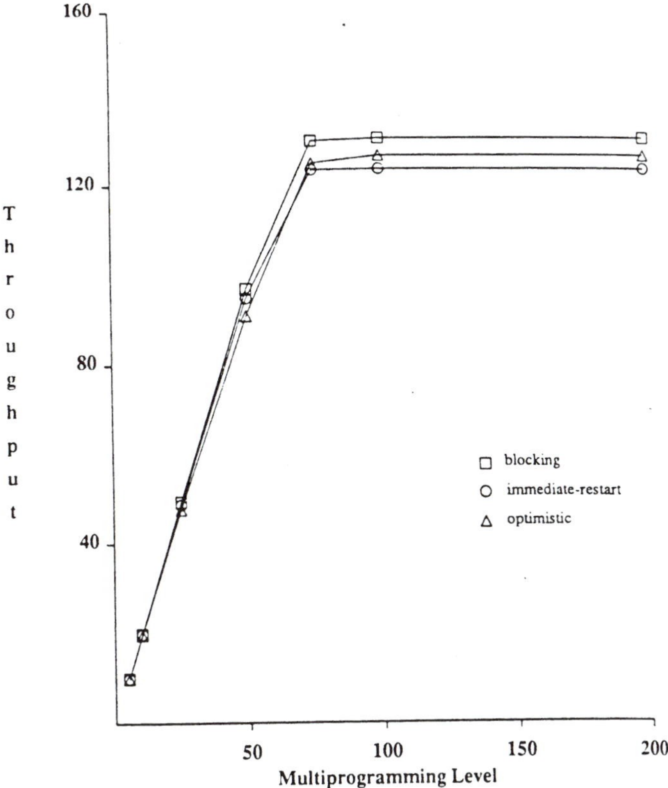

Fig. 3. Throughput (∞ resources).

with 25 concurrently active transactions. Since we are interested in investigating *differences* in concurrency control strategies, we decreased the database size to 1000 objects, as shown in Table II, to create a situation in which conflicts are more frequent. The remainder of our experiments were performed using this smaller database size.

Before closing this section, we should mention that there are a number of parameters that we could have varied but did not. For example, we could have varied the size of transactions, their distribution of sizes, or the granularity of the database; we could have varied the write probability for transactions; we could have investigated workloads containing several classes of transactions, and so forth. We also could have varied our notion of a resource unit, examining systems with less balanced resource utilization characteristics. For the purposes of this study, such variations were not of interest. Our goal was to see how certain basic assumptions affect the results of a concurrency control performance study, not to investigate exactly how performance varies with all possible sets of parameter values. Also, we have reported on the results of experiments with variations such as these elsewhere [12, 14, 15]. Our experience with variations of the first type is that for the most part they are just different ways of varying the probability of conflicts. Results regarding the relative performance of concurrency

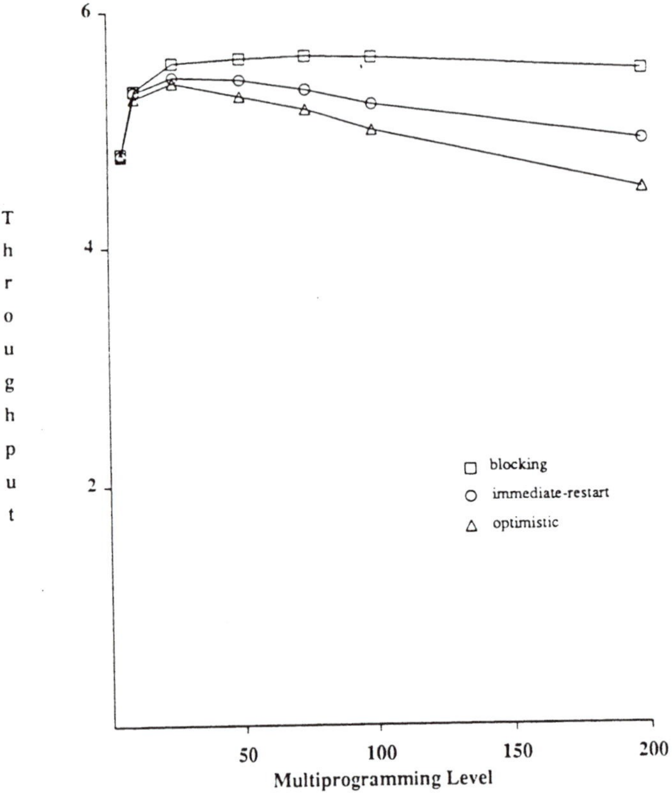

Fig. 4. Throughput (1 resource unit).

control algorithms appear to be insensitive to the particular manner in which this probability is varied, as long as it is indeed varied. (The only significant exception to this statement applies to workloads containing a wide range of transaction sizes or types, where algorithms sometimes display performance biases against a particular transaction class—for example, very large transactions can starve under the immediate-restart and optimistic algorithms, particularly with a workload containing a mix of short and long transactions—but we have studied this effect elsewhere as well [14].) Variations of the second type have been found to be of little or no interest in determining relative algorithm performance, since the primary factor determining the shape of the performance curves for an algorithm is the utilization of the bottleneck resource and not the fact that the bottleneck is the CPU or disk subsystem.

5. RESOURCE-RELATED ASSUMPTIONS

We performed several simulation experiments to study the implications of different resource-related assumptions on the performance of the three concurrency control algorithms described in Section 3. We investigated the performance of the three algorithms under the infinite resources assumption, with limited resources, and with varying numbers of CPUs and disks. To vary the number of

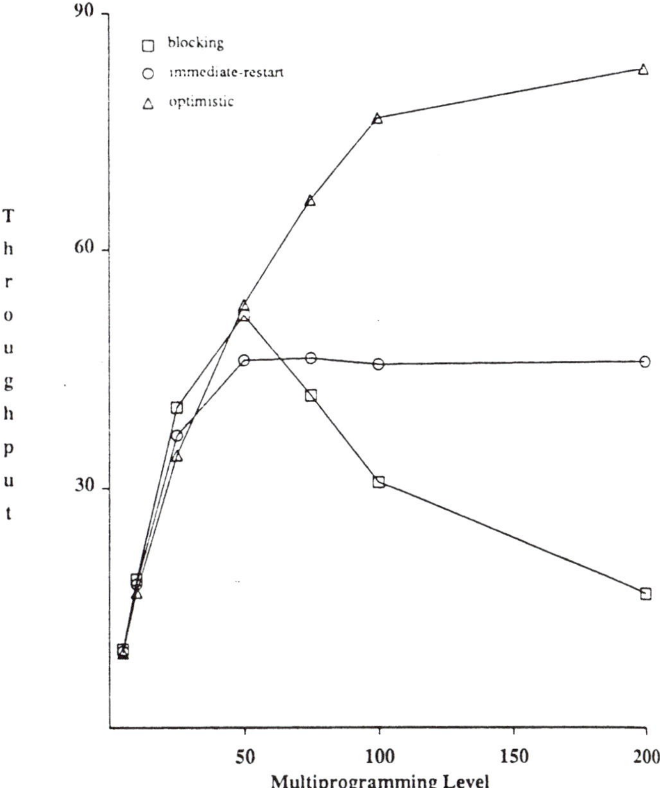

Fig. 5. Throughput (∞ resources).

CPUs and disks, we varied the number of resource units employed (each of which consists of 1 CPU and 2 disks). We also examined the case of an alternative workload type, an interactive workload.

5.1 Experiment 1: Infinite Resources

The first resource-related experiment examined the performance characteristics of the three strategies for a variety of multiprogramming levels, assuming infinite resources. With infinite resources, the throughput should be a nondecreasing function of multiprogramming level in the absence of data contention.[5] However, for a given size database, the probability of conflicts increases as the multiprogramming level increases. For blocking, the increased conflict probability manifests itself in the form of more blocking due to denial of lock requests and an increased number of restarts due to deadlocks. For the restart-oriented strategies, the higher probability of conflicts results in a larger number of restarts.

Figure 5 shows the throughput results for Experiment 1. Blocking starts thrashing as the multiprogramming level is increased beyond a certain level,

[5] We do not attempt to model system overhead phenomena such as the effects of increased operating system and database system control structure sizes on system path lengths.

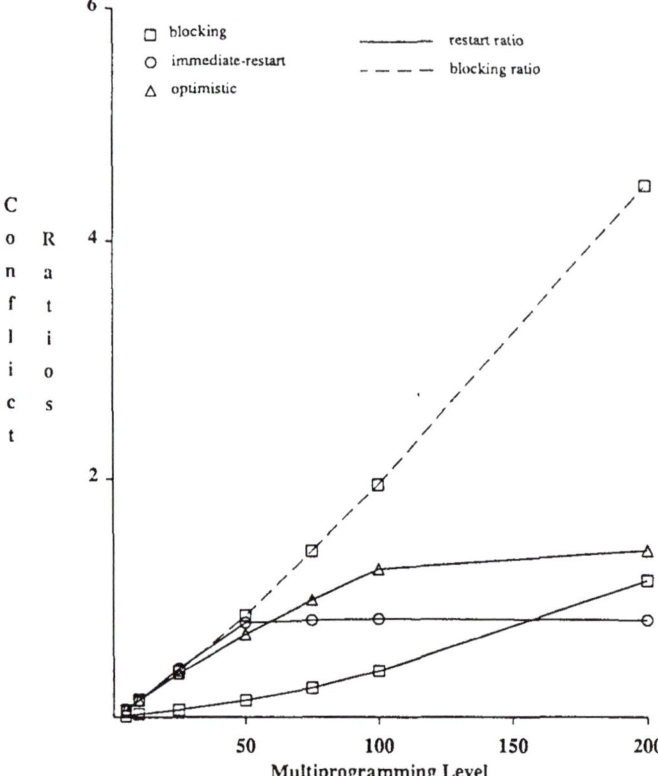

Fig. 6. Conflict ratios (∞ resources).

whereas the throughput keeps increasing for the optimistic algorithm. These results agree with predictions in [20] that were based on similar assumptions. Figure 6 shows the blocking and restart ratios for the three concurrency control algorithms. Note that the thrashing in blocking is due to the large increase in the number of times that a transaction is blocked, which reduces the number of transactions available to run and make forward progress, rather than to an increase in the number of restarts. This result is in agreement with the assertion in [6, 50 and 51] that under low resource contention and a high level of multiprogramming, blocking may start thrashing before restarts do. Although the restart ratio for the optimistic algorithm increases quickly with an increase in the multiprogramming level, new transactions start executing in place of the restarted ones, keeping the effective multiprogramming level high and thus entailing an increase in throughput.

Unlike the other two algorithms, the throughput of the immediate-restart algorithm reaches a plateau. This happens for the following reason: When a transaction is restarted in the immediate-restart strategy, a restart delay is invoked to allow the conflicting transaction to complete before the restarted transaction is placed back in the ready queue. As described in Section 4, the duration of the delay is *adaptive*, equal to the running average of the response

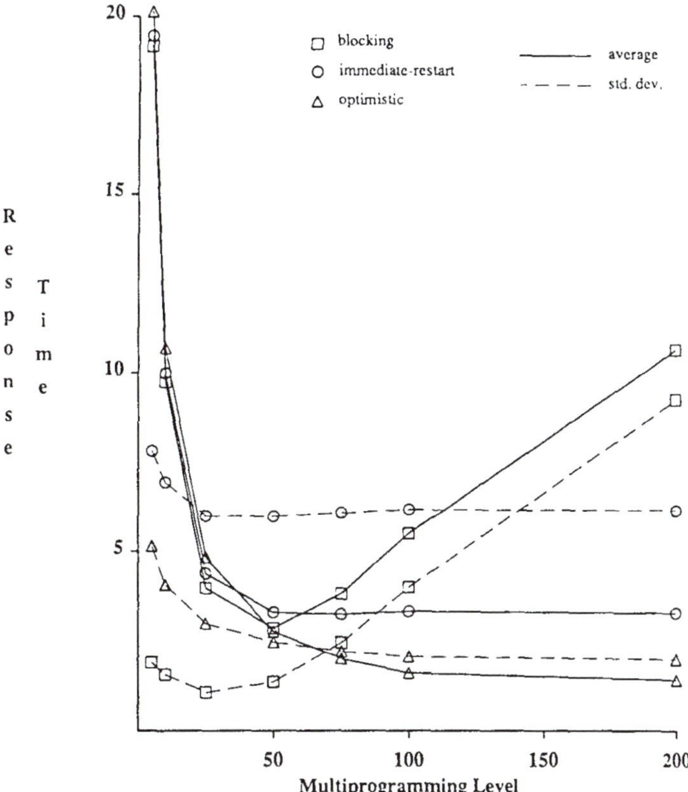

Fig. 7. Response time (∞ resources).

time. Because of this adaptive delay, the immediate-restart algorithm reaches a point beyond which all of the transactions that are not active are either in a restart delay state or else in a terminal thinking state (where a terminal is pausing between the completion of one transaction and submitting a new transaction). This point is reached when the number of active transactions in the system is such that a new transaction is basically sure to conflict with an active transaction and is therefore sure to be quickly restarted and then delayed. Such delays increase the average response time for transactions, which increases their average restart delay time; this has the effect of reducing the number of transactions competing for active status and in turn reduces the probability of conflicts. In other words, the adaptive restart delay creates a negative feedback loop (in the control system sense). Once the plateau is reached, there are simply no transactions waiting in the ready queue, and increasing the multiprogramming level is a "no-op" beyond this point. (Increasing the *allowed* number of active transactions cannot increase the *actual* number if none are waiting anyway.)

Figure 7 shows the mean response time (solid lines) and the standard deviation of response time (dotted lines) for each of the three algorithms. The response times are basically what one would expect, given the throughput results plus the fact that we have employed a closed queuing model. This figure does illustrate one interesting phenomenon that occurred in nearly all of the experiments reported in this paper: The standard deviation of the response time is much smaller for blocking than for the immediate-restart algorithm over most of the multiprogramming levels explored, and it is also smaller than that of the optimistic algorithm for the lower multiprogramming levels (i.e., until blocking's performance begins to degrade significantly because of thrashing). The immediate-restart algorithm has a large response-time variance due to its restart delay. When a transaction has to be restarted because of a lock conflict during its execution, its response time is increased by a randomly chosen restart delay period with a mean of one entire response time, and in addition the transaction must be run all over again. Thus, a restart leads to a large response time increase for the restarted transaction. The optimistic algorithm restarts transactions at the end of their execution and requires restarted transactions to be run again from the beginning, but it does not add a restart delay to the time required to complete a transaction. The blocking algorithm restarts transactions much less often than the other algorithms for most multiprogramming levels, and it restarts them during their execution (rather than at the end) and without imposing a restart delay. Because of this, and because lock waiting times tend to be quite a bit smaller than the additional response time added by a restart, blocking has the lowest response time variance until it starts to thrash significantly. A high variance in response time is undesirable from a user's standpoint.

5.2 Experiment 2: Resource-Limited Situation

In Experiment 2 we analyzed the impact of limited resources on the performance characteristics of the three concurrency control algorithms. A database system with one resource unit (one CPU and two disks) was assumed for this experiment. The throughput results are presented in Figure 8.

Observe that for all three algorithms, the throughput curves indicate thrashing—as the multiprogramming level is increased, the throughput first increases, then reaches a peak, and then finally either decreases or remains roughly constant. In a system with limited CPU and I/O resources, the achievable throughput may be constrained by one or more of the following factors: It may be that not enough transactions are available to keep the system resources busy. Alternatively, it may be that enough transactions are available, but because of data contention, the "useful" number of transactions is less than what is required to keep the resources "usefully" busy. That is, transactions that are blocked due to lock conflicts are not useful. Similarly, the use of resources to process transactions that are later restarted is not useful. Finally, it may be that enough useful, nonconflicting transactions are available, but that the available resources are already saturated.

As the multiprogramming level was increased, the throughput first increased for all three concurrency control algorithms since there were not enough transactions to keep the resources utilized at low levels of multiprogramming. Figure 9 shows the total (solid lines) and useful (dotted lines) disk utilizations for this experiment. As one would expect, there is a direct correlation between the useful utilization curves of Figure 9 and the throughput curves of Figure 8. For blocking, the throughput peaks at mpl = 25, where the disks are being

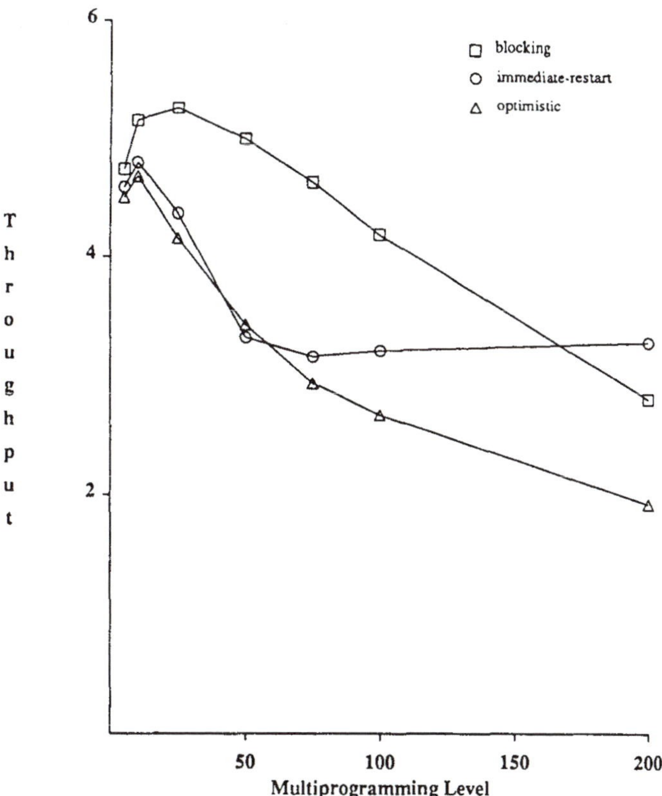

Fig. 8. Throughput (1 resource unit).

97 percent utilized, with a useful utilization of 92 percent.[6] Increasing the multiprogramming level further only increases data contention, and the throughput decreases as the amount of blocking and thus the number of deadlock-induced restarts increase rapidly. For the optimistic algorithm, the useful utilization of the disks peaks at mpl = 10, and the throughput decreases with an increase in the multiprogramming level because of the increase in the restart ratio. This increase in the restart ratio means that a larger fraction of the disk time is spent doing work that will be redone later. For the immediate-restart algorithm, the throughput also peaks at mpl = 10 and then decreases, remaining roughly constant beyond 50. The throughput remains constant for this algorithm for the same reason as described in the last experiment: Increasing the allowable number of transactions has no effect beyond 50, since all of the nonactive transactions are either in a restart delay state or thinking.

With regard to the throughput for the three strategies, several observations are in order. First, the maximum throughput (i.e., the best global throughput) was obtained with the blocking algorithm. Second, immediate-restart performed

[6] The actual throughput peak may of course be somewhere to the left or right of 25, in the 10–50 range, but that cannot be determined from our data.

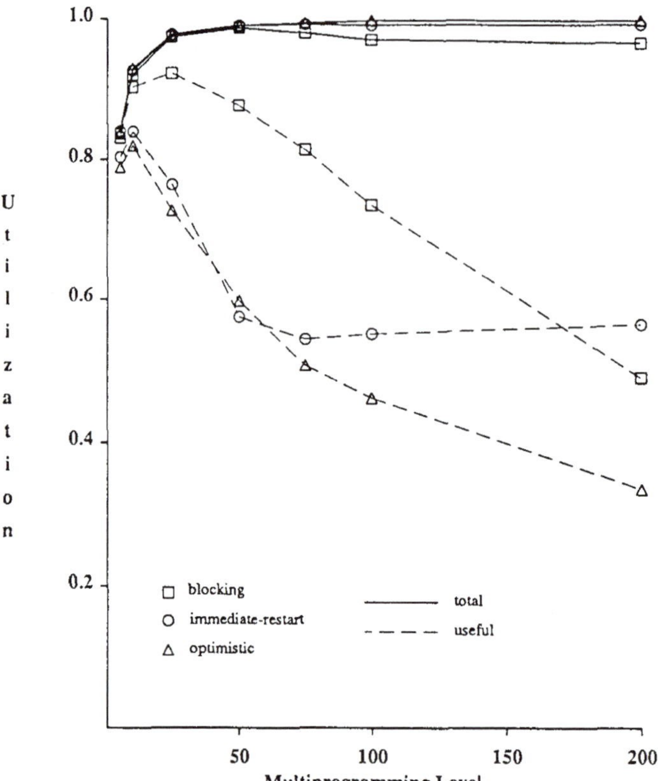

Fig. 9. Disk utilization (1 resource unit).

as well as or better than the optimistic algorithm. There were more restarts with the optimistic algorithm, and each restart was more expensive; this is reflected in the relative useful disk utilizations for the two strategies. Finally, the throughput achieved with the immediate-restart strategy for mpl = 200 was somewhat better than the throughput achieved with either blocking or the optimistic algorithm at this same multiprogramming level.

Figure 10 gives the average and the standard deviation of response time for the three algorithms in the limited resource case. The differences are even more noticeable than in the infinite resource case. Blocking has the lowest delay (fastest response time) over most of the multiprogramming levels. The immediate-restart algorithm is next, and the optimistic algorithm has the worst response time. As for the standard deviations, blocking is the best, immediate-restart is the worst, and the optimistic algorithm is in between the two. As in Experiment 1, the immediate-restart algorithm exhibits a high response time variance.

One of the points raised earlier merits further discussion. Should the performance of the immediate-restart algorithm at mpl = 200 lead us to conclude that immediate-restart is a better strategy at high levels of multiprogramming? We believe that the answer is no, for several reasons. First, the multiprogramming

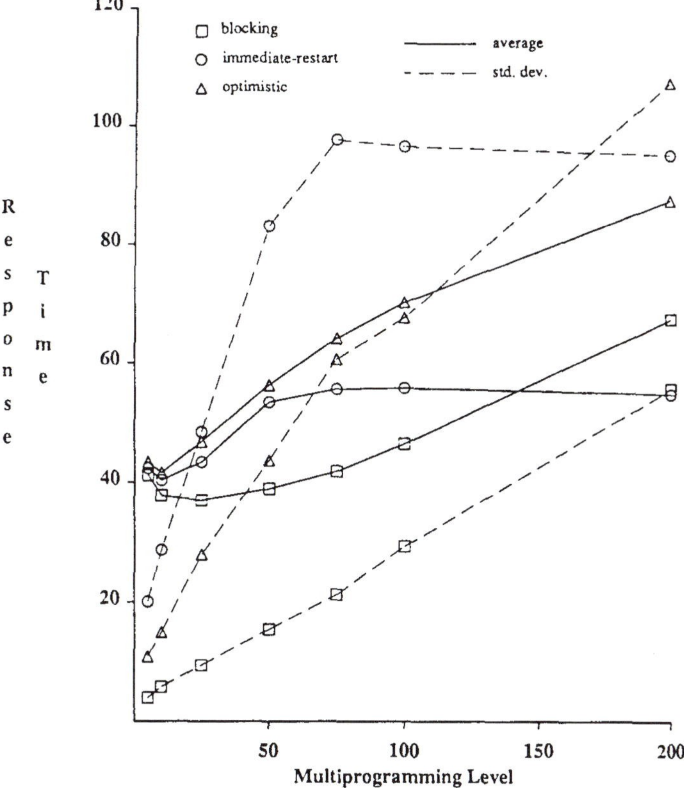

Fig. 10. Response time (1 resource unit).

level is internal to the database system, controlling the number of transactions that may concurrently compete for data and resources, and has nothing to do with the number of users that the database system may support; the latter is determined by the number of terminals. Thus, one should configure the system to keep multiprogramming at a level that gives the best performance. In this experiment, the highest throughput and smallest response time were achieved using the blocking algorithm at mpl = 25. Second, the restart delay in the immediate-restart strategy is there so that the conflicting transaction can complete before the restarted transaction is placed back into the ready queue. However, an unintended side effect of this restart delay in a system with a finite population of users is that it limits the actual multiprogramming level, and hence also limits the number of conflicts and resulting restarts due to reduced data contention. Although the multiprogramming level was increased to the total number of users (200), the actual average multiprogramming level never exceeded about 60. Thus, the restart delay provides a crude mechanism for limiting the multiprogramming level when restarts become overly frequent, and adding a restart delay to the other two algorithms should improve their performance at high levels of multiprogramming as well.

To verify this latter argument, we performed another experiment in which the adaptive restart delay was used for restarted transactions in both the blocking

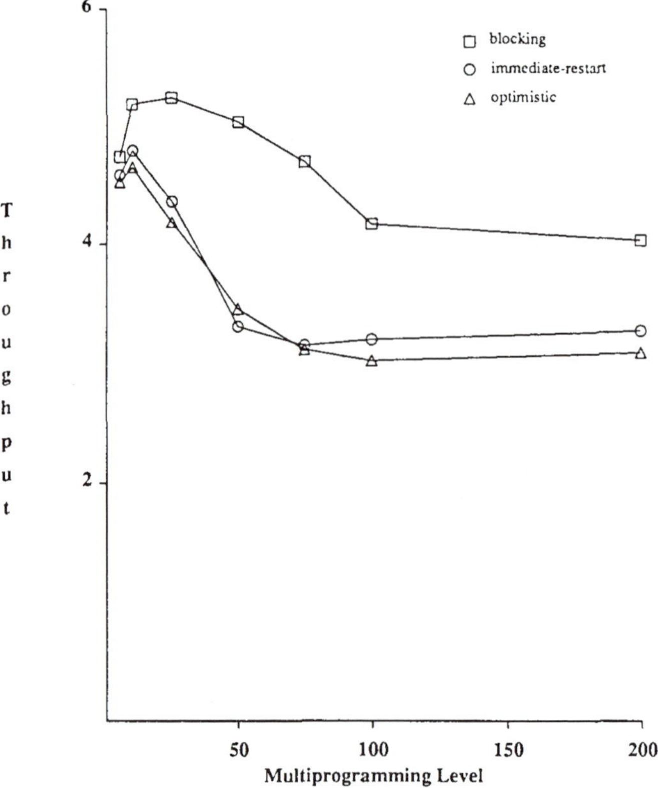

Fig. 11. Throughput (adaptive restart delays).

and optimistic algorithms as well. The throughput results that we obtained are shown in Figure 11. It can be seen that introducing an adaptive restart delay helped to limit the multiprogramming level for the blocking and optimistic algorithms under high conflicts, as it does for immediate-restart, reducing data contention at the upper range of multiprogramming levels. Blocking emerges as the clear winner, and the performance of the optimistic algorithm becomes comparable to the immediate-restart strategy. The one negative effect that we observed from adding this delay was an increase in the standard deviation of the response times for the blocking and optimistic algorithms. Since a restart delay only helps performance for high multiprogramming levels, it seems that a better strategy is to enforce a lower multiprogramming level limit to avoid thrashing due to high contention and to maintain a small standard deviation of response time.

5.3 A Brief Aside

Before discussing the remainder of the experiments, a brief aside is in order. Our concurrency control performance model includes a time delay, *ext_think_time*, between the completion of one transaction and the initiation of the next transaction from a terminal. Although we feel that such a time delay is necessary in a realistic performance model, a side effect of the delay is that it can lead the database system to become "starved" for transactions when the multiprogramming level is increased beyond a certain point. That is, increasing the multiprogramming level has no effect on system throughput beyond this point because the actual number of active transactions does not change. This form of starvation can lead an otherwise increasing throughput to reach a plateau when viewed as a function of the multiprogramming level. In order to verify that our conclusions were not distorted by the inclusion of a think time, we repeated Experiments 1 and 2 with no think time (i.e., with *ext_think_time* = 0).

The throughput results for these experiments are shown in Figures 12 and 13, and the figures to which these results should be compared are Figures 5 and 8. It is clear from these figures that, although the exact performance numbers are somewhat different (because it is now never the case that the system is starved for transactions while one or more terminals is in a thinking state), the relative performance of the algorithms is not significantly affected. The explanations given earlier for the observed performance trends are almost all applicable here as well. In the infinite resource case (Figure 12), blocking begins thrashing beyond a certain point, and the immediate-restart algorithm reaches a plateau because of the large number of restarted transactions that are delaying (due to the restart delay) before running again. The only significant difference in the infinite resource performance trends is that the throughput of the optimistic algorithm continues to improve as the multiprogramming level is increased, instead of reaching a plateau as it did when terminals spent some time in a thinking state (and thus sometimes caused the actual number of transactions in the system to be less than that allowed by the multiprogramming level). Franaszek and Robinson predicted this [20], predicting logarithmically increasing throughput for the optimistic algorithm as the number of active transactions increases under the infinite resource assumption. Still, this result does not alter the general conclusions that were drawn from Figure 5 regarding the relative performance of the algorithms. In the limited resource case (Figure 13), the throughput for each of the algorithms peaks when resources become saturated, decreasing beyond this point as more and more resources are wasted because of restarts, just as it did before (Figure 8). Again, fewer and/or earlier restarts lead to better performance in the case of limited resources. On the basis of the lack of significant differences between the results obtained with and without the external think time, then, we can safely conclude that incorporating this delay in our model has not distorted our results. The remainder of the experiments in this paper will thus be run using a nonzero external think time (just like Experiments 1 and 2).

5.4 Experiment 3: Multiple Resources

In this experiment we moved the system from limited resources toward infinite resources, increasing the level of resources available to 5, 10, 25, and finally 50 resource units. This experiment was motivated by a desire to investigate performance trends as one moves from the limited resource situation of Experiment 2 toward the infinite resource situation of Experiment 1. Since the infinite resource assumption has sometimes been justified as a way of investigating what performance trends to expect in systems with many processors [20], we were interested

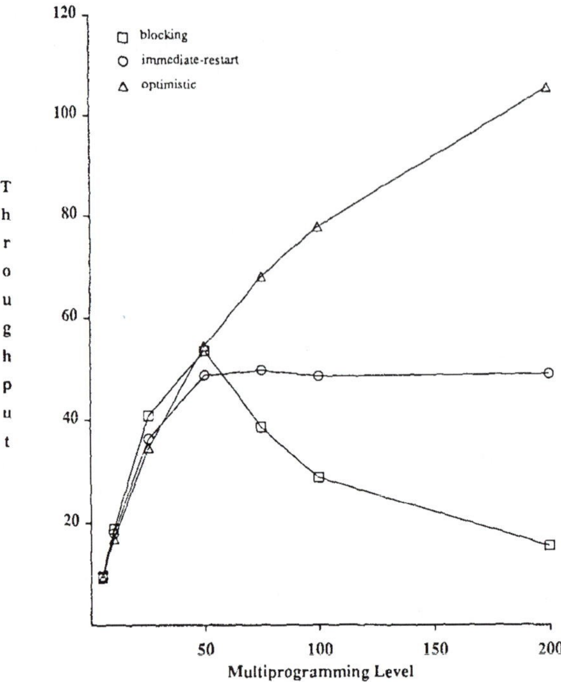

Fig. 12. Throughput (∞ resources, no external think time).

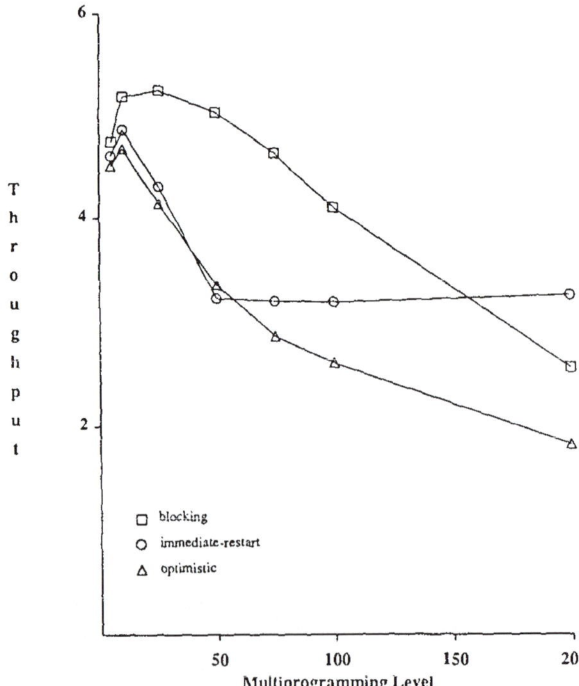

Fig. 13. Throughput (1 resource unit, no external think time).

in determining where (i.e., at what level of resources) the behavior of the system would begin to approach that of the infinite resource case in an environment such as a multiprocessor database machine.

For the cases with 5 and 10 resource units, the relative behavior of the three concurrency control strategies was fairly similar to the behavior in the case of just 1 resource unit. The throughput results for these two cases are shown in Figures 14 and 16, respectively, and the associated disk utilization figures are given in Figures 15 and 17. Blocking again provided the highest overall throughput. For large multiprogramming levels, however, the immediate-restart strategy provided better throughput than blocking (because of its restart delay), but not enough so as to beat the highest throughput provided by the blocking algorithm. With 5 resource units, where the maximum useful disk utilizations for blocking, immediate-restart, and the optimistic algorithm were 72, 60, and 58 percent, respectively, the results followed the same trends as those of Experiment 2. Quite similar trends were obtained with 10 resource units, where the maximum useful utilizations of the disks for blocking, immediate-restart, and optimistic were 56, 45, and 47 percent, respectively. Note that in all cases, the total disk utilizations for the restart-oriented algorithms are higher than those for the blocking algorithm because of restarts; this difference is partly due to wasted resources. By *wasted resources* here, we mean resources used to process objects that were later undone because of restarts—these resources are wasted in the sense that they were consumed, making them unavailable for other purposes such as background tasks.

With 25 resource units, the maximum throughput obtained with the optimistic algorithm beats the maximum throughput obtained with blocking (although not by very much). The throughput results for this case are shown in Figure 18, and the utilizations are given in Figure 19. The total and the useful disk utilizations for the maximum throughput point for blocking were 34 and 30 percent (respectively), whereas the corresponding numbers for the optimistic algorithm were 81 and 30 percent. Thus, the optimistic algorithm has become attractive because a large amount of otherwise unused resources are available, and thus the waste of resources due to restarts does not adversely affect performance. In other words, with useful utilizations in the 30 percent range, the system begins to behave somewhat like it has infinite resources. As the number of available resources is increased still further to 50 resource units, the results become very close indeed to those of the infinite resource case; this is illustrated by the throughput and utilizations shown in Figures 20 and 21. Here, with maximum useful utilizations down in the range of 15 to 25 percent, the shapes and relative positions of the throughput curves are very much like those of Figure 5 (although the actual throughput values here are still not quite as large).

Another interesting observation from these latter results is that, with blocking, resource utilization decreases as the level of multiprogramming increases and hence throughput decreases. This is a further indication that blocking may thrash due to waiting for locks before it thrashes due to the number of restarts [6, 50, 51], as we saw in the infinite resource case. On the other hand, with the optimistic algorithm, as the multiprogramming level increases, the total utilization of resources and resource waste increases, and the throughput decreases

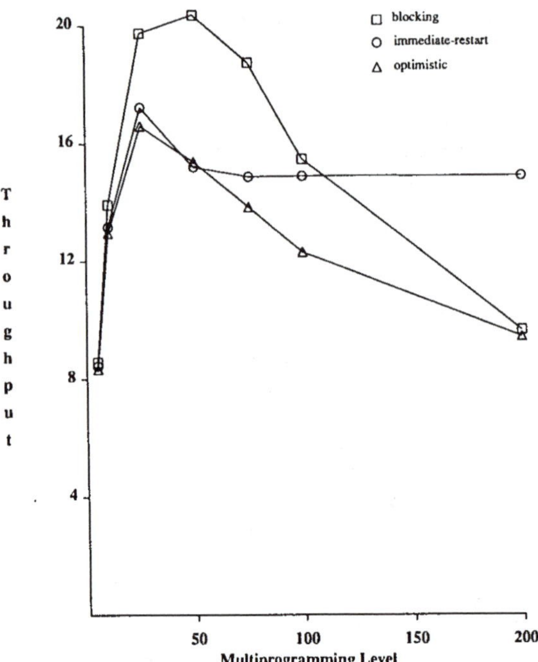

Fig. 14. Throughput (5 resource units).

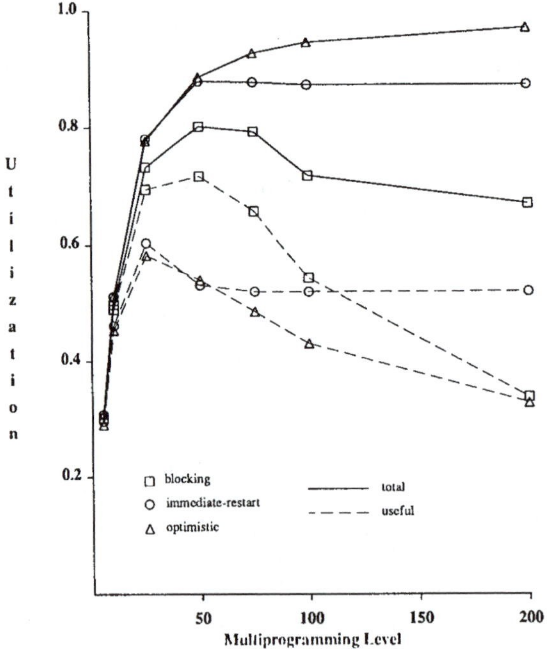

Fig. 15. Disk utilization (5 resource units).

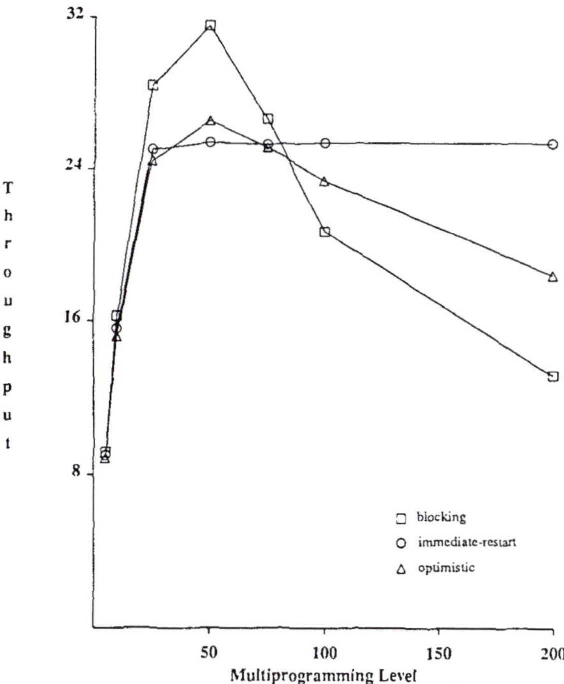

Fig. 16. Throughput (10 resource units).

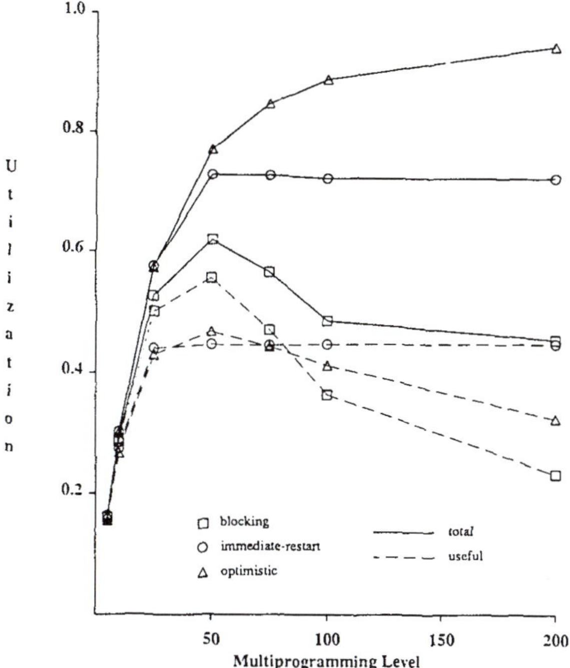

Fig. 17. Disk utilization (10 resource units).

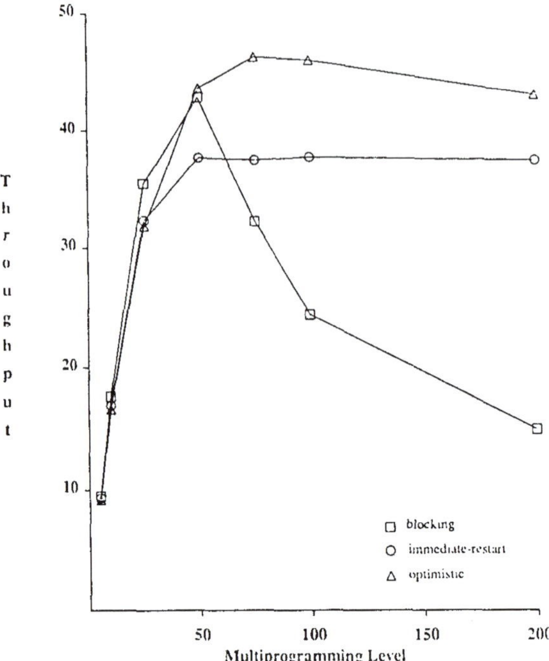

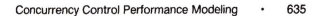

Fig. 18. Throughput (25 resource units).

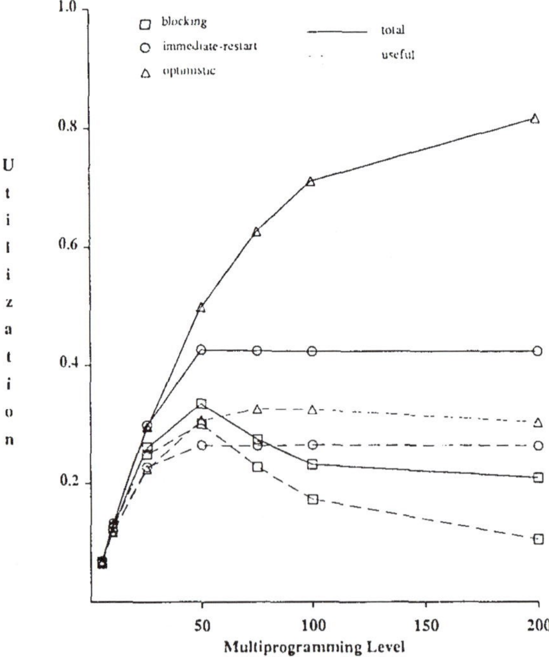

Fig. 19. Disk utilization (25 resource units).

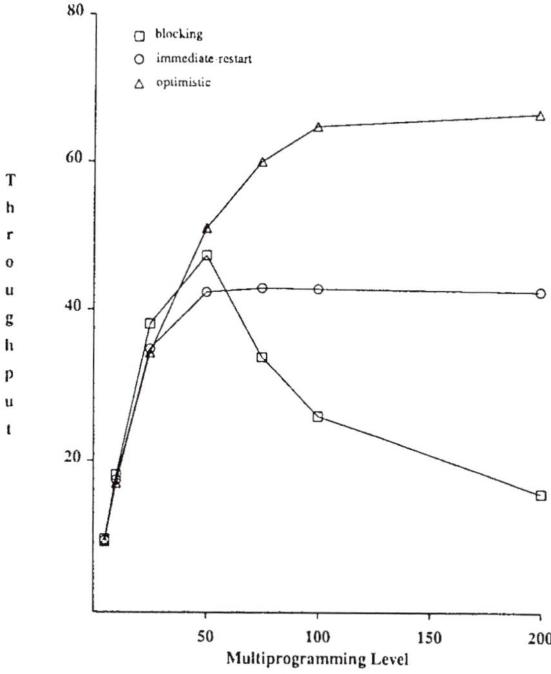

Fig. 20. Throughput (50 resource units).

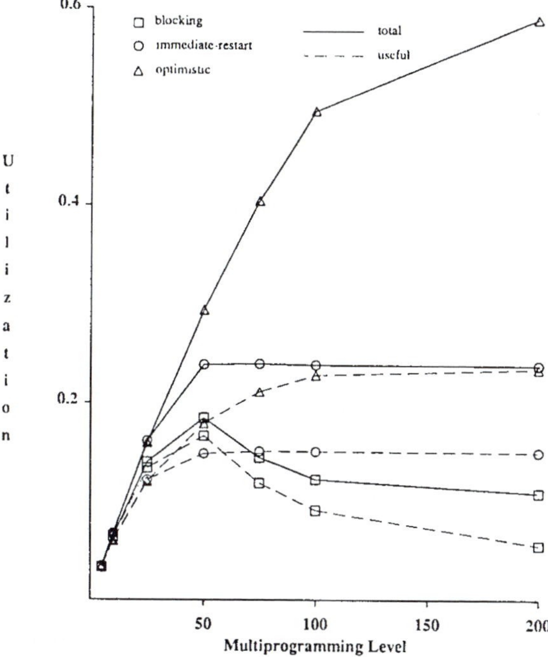

Fig. 21. Disk utilization (50 resource units).

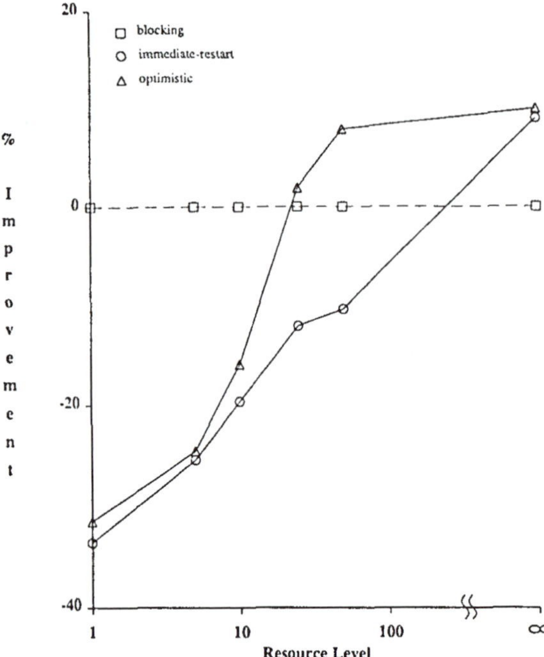

Fig. 22. Improvement over blocking (MPL = 50).

somewhat (except with 50 resource units). Thus, this strategy eventually thrashes because of the number of restarts (i.e., because of resources). With immediate-restart, as explained earlier, a plateau is reached for throughput and resource utilization because the actual multiprogramming level is limited by the restart delay under high data contention.

As a final illustration of how the level of available resources affects the choice of a concurrency control algorithm, we plotted in Figures 22 through 24 the percent throughput improvement of the algorithms with respect to that of the blocking algorithm as a function of the resource level. The resource level axis gives the number of resource units used, which ranges from 1 to infinity (the infinite resource case). Figure 22 shows that, for a multiprogramming level of 50, blocking is preferable with up to almost 25 resource units; beyond this point the optimistic algorithm is preferable. For a multiprogramming level of 100, as shown in Figure 23, the crossover point comes earlier because the throughput for blocking is well below its peak at this multiprogramming level. Figure 24 compares the maximum attainable throughput (over all multiprogramming levels) for each algorithm as a function of the resource level, in which case locking again wins out to nearly 25 resource units. (Recall that useful utilizations were down in the mid-20 percent range by the time this resource level, with 25 CPUs and 50 disks, was reached in our experiments.)

5.5 Experiment 4: Interactive Workloads

In our last resource-related experiment, we modeled interactive transactions that perform a number of reads, think for some period of time, and then perform their

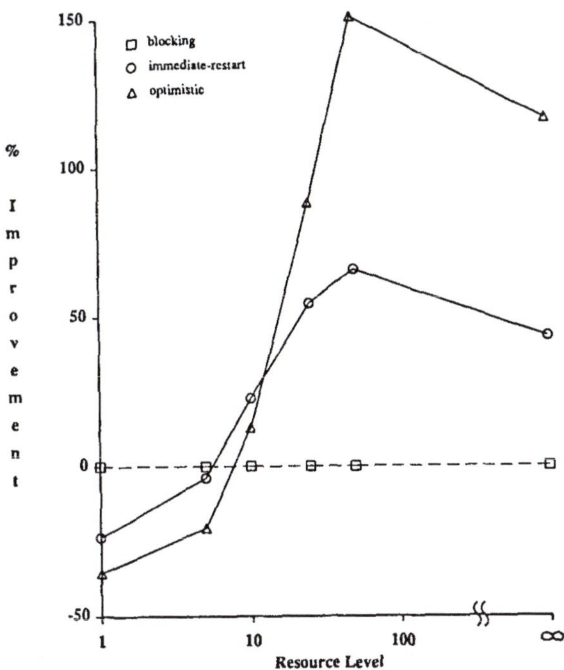

Fig. 23. Improvement over blocking (MPL = 100).

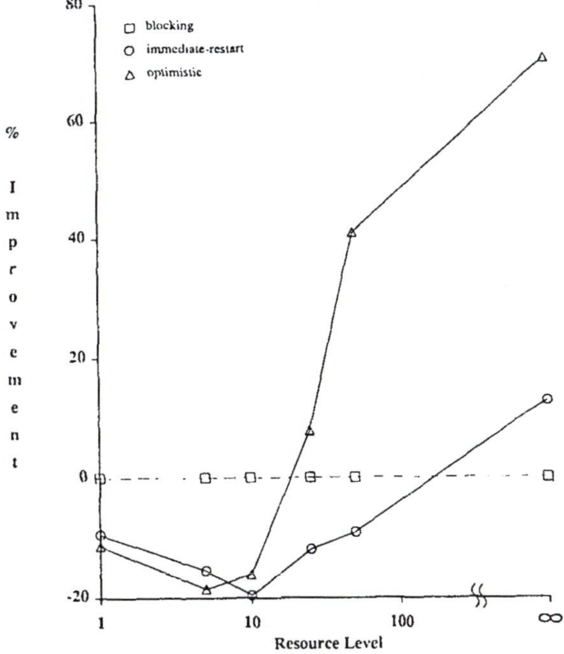

Fig. 24. Improvement over blocking (maximum).

writes. This model of interactive transactions was motivated by a large body of form-screen applications where data is put up on the screen, the user may change some of the fields after staring at the screen awhile, and then the user types "enter," causing the updates to be performed. The intent of this experiment was to find out whether large intratransaction (internal) think times would be another way to cause a system with limited resources to behave like it has infinite resources. Since Experiment 3 showed that low utilizations can lead to behavior similar to the infinite resource case, we suspected that we might indeed see such behavior here. The interactive workload experiment was performed for internal think times of 1, 5, and 10 seconds. At the same time, the external think times were increased to 3, 11, and 21 seconds, respectively, in order to maintain roughly the same ratio of idle terminals (those in an external thinking state) to active transactions. We have assumed a limited resource environment with 1 resource unit for the system in this experiment.

Figure pairs (25, 26), (27, 28), and (29, 30) show the throughput and disk utilizations obtained for the 1, 5, and 10 second intratransaction think time experiments, respectively. On the average, a transaction requires 150 milliseconds of CPU time and 350 milliseconds of disk time, so an internal think time of 5 seconds or more is an order of magnitude larger than the time spent consuming CPU or I/O resources. Even with many transactions in the system, resource contention is significantly reduced because of such think times, and the result is that the CPU and I/O resources behave more or less like infinite resources. Consequently, for large think times, the optimistic algorithm performs better than the blocking strategy (see Figures 27 and 29). For an internal think time of 10 seconds, the useful utilization of resources is much higher with the optimistic algorithm than the blocking strategy, and its highest throughput value is also considerably higher than that of blocking. For a 5-second internal think time, the throughput and the useful utilization with the optimistic algorithm are again better than those for blocking. For a 1-second internal think time, however, blocking performs better (see Figure 25). In this last case, in which the internal think time for transactions is closer to their processing time requirements, the resource utilizations are such that resources wasted because of restarts make the optimistic algorithm the loser.

The highest throughput obtained with the optimistic algorithm was consistently better than that for immediate-restart, although for higher levels of multiprogramming the throughput obtained with immediate-restart was better than the throughput obtained with the optimistic algorithm due to the *mpl*-limiting effect of immediate-restart's restart delay. As noted before, this high multiprogramming level difference could be reversed by adding a restart delay to the optimistic algorithm.

5.6 Resource-Related Conclusions

Reflecting on the results of the experiments reported in this section, several conclusions are clear. First, a blocking algorithm like dynamic two-phase locking is a better choice than a restart-oriented concurrency control algorithm like the immediate-restart or optimistic algorithms for systems with medium to high

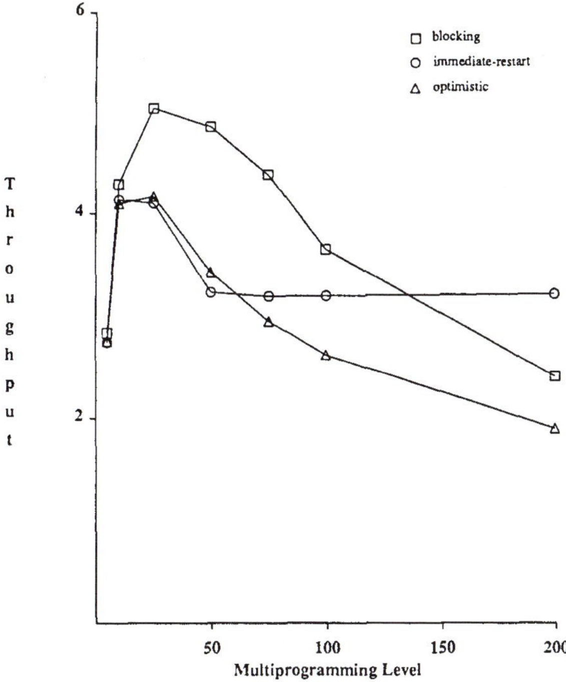

Fig. 25. Throughput (1 second thinking).

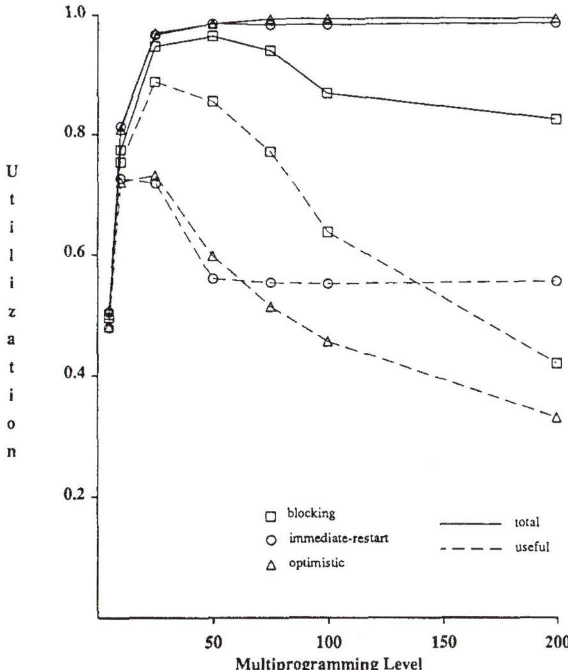

Fig. 26. Disk utilization (1 second thinking).

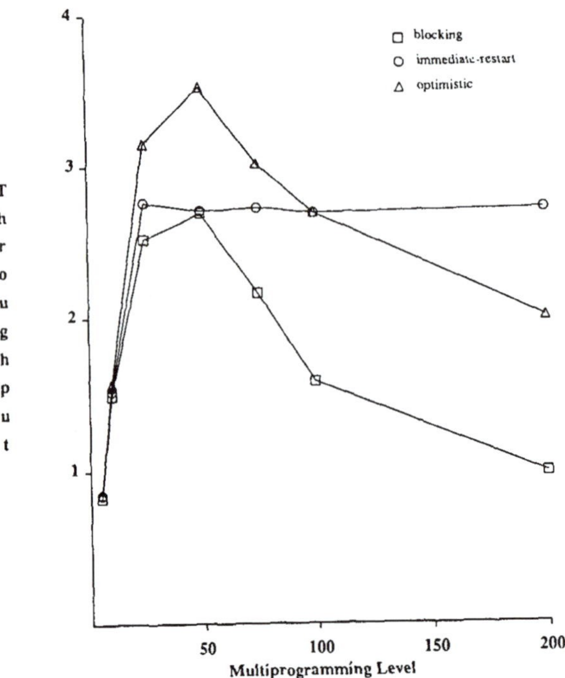

Fig. 27. Throughput (5 seconds thinking).

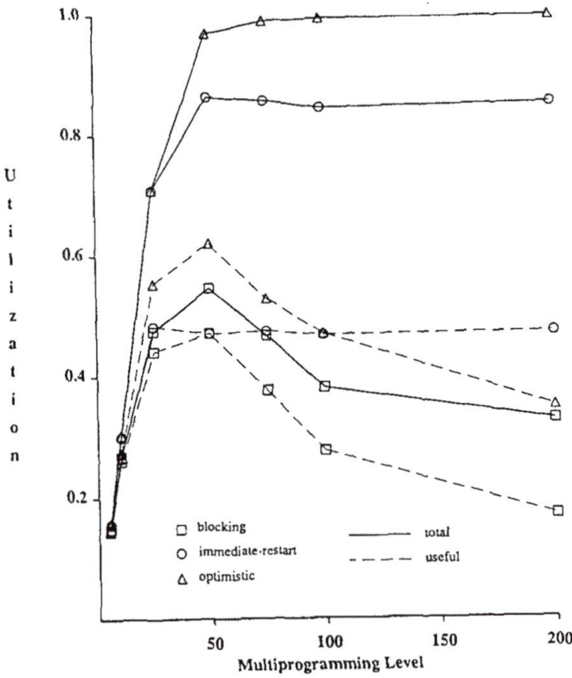

Fig. 28. Disk utilization (5 seconds thinking).

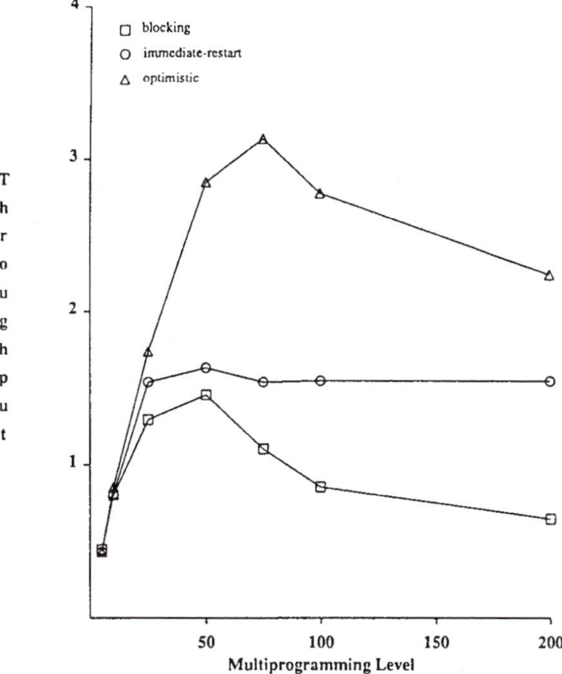

Fig. 29. Throughput (10 seconds thinking).

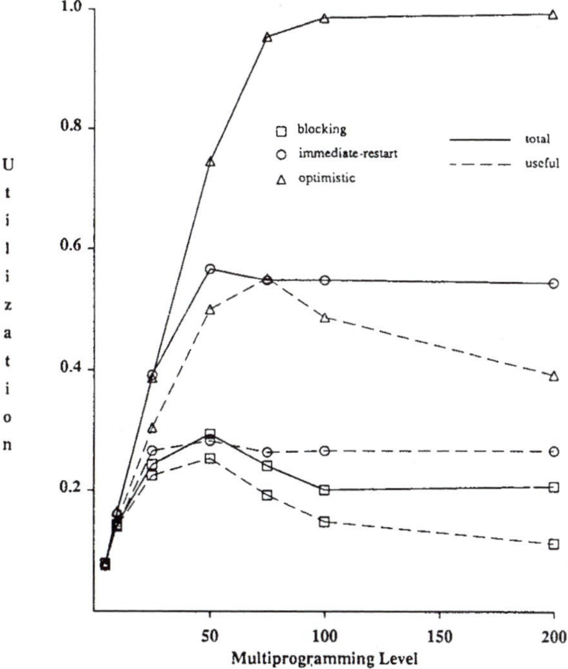

Fig. 30. Disk utilization (10 seconds thinking).

levels of resource utilization. On the other hand, if utilizations are sufficiently low, a restart-oriented algorithm becomes a better choice. Such low resource utilizations arose in our experiments with large numbers of resource units and in our interactive workload experiments with large intratransaction think times. The optimistic algorithm provided the best performance in these cases. Second, the past performance studies discussed in Section 1 were not really contradictory after all: they simply obtained different results because of very different resource modeling assumptions. We obtained results similar to each of the various studies [1, 2, 6, 12, 15, 20, 50, 51] by varying the level of resources that we employed in our database model. Clearly, then, a physically justifiable resource model is a critical component for a reasonable concurrency control performance model. Third, our results indicate that it is important to control the multiprogramming level in a database system for concurrency control reasons. We observed thrashing behavior for locking in the infinite resource case, as did [6, 20, 50, and 51], but in addition we observed that a significant thrashing effect occurs for both locking *and* optimistic concurrency control under higher levels of resource contention. (A similar thrashing effect would also have occurred for the immediate-restart algorithm under higher resource contention levels were it not for the *mpl*-limiting effects of its adaptive restart delay.)

6. TRANSACTION BEHAVIOR ASSUMPTIONS

This section describes experiments that were performed to investigate the performance implications of two modeling assumptions related to transaction behavior. In particular, we examined the impact of alternative assumptions about how restarts are modeled (real versus fake restarts) and how write locks are acquired (with or without upgrades from read locks). Based on the results of the previous section, we performed these experiments under just two resource settings: infinite resources and one resource unit. These two settings are sufficient to demonstrate the important effects of the alternative assumptions, since the results under other settings can be predicted from these two. Except where explicitly noted, the simulation parameters used in this section are the same as those given in Section 4.

6.1 Experiment 6: Modeling Restarts

In this experiment we investigated the impact of transaction-restart modeling on performance. Up to this point, restarts have been modeled by "reincarnating" transactions with their previous read and write sets and then placing them at the end of the ready queue, as described in Section 3. An alternative assumption that has been used for modeling convenience in a number of studies is the *fake restart* assumption, in which a restarted transaction is assumed to be replaced by a new transaction that is independent of the restarted one. In order to model this assumption, we had the simulator reinitialize the read and write sets for restarted transactions in this experiment. The throughput results for the infinite resource case are shown in Figure 31, and Figure 32 shows the associated conflict ratios. Solid lines show the new results obtained using the fake restart assumption, and the dotted lines show the results obtained previously under the real restart model. For the conflict ratio curves, hollow points show restart ratios and

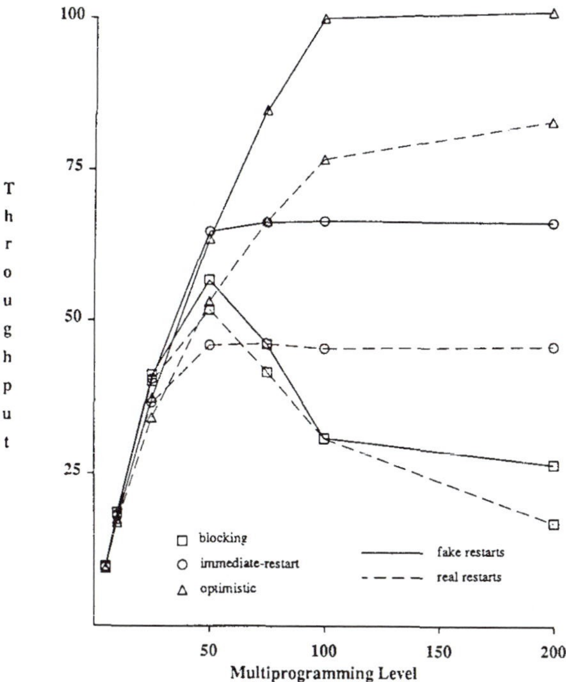

Fig. 31. Throughput (fake restarts, ∞ resources).

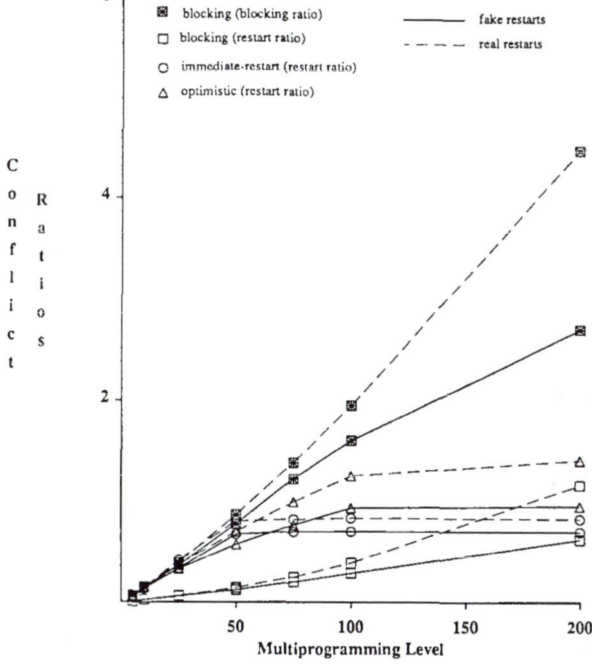

Fig. 32. Conflict ratios (fake restarts, ∞ resources).

solid points show blocking ratios. Figures 33 and 34 show the throughput and conflict ratio results for the limited resource (1 resource unit) case.

In comparing the fake and real restart results for the infinite resource case in Figure 31, several things are clear. The fake restart assumption produces significantly higher throughputs for the immediate-restart and optimistic algorithms. The throughput results for blocking are also higher than under the real restart assumption, but the difference is quite a bit smaller in the case of the blocking algorithm. The restart-oriented algorithms are more sensitive to the fake-restart assumption because they restart transactions much more often. Figure 32 shows how the conflict ratios changed in this experiment, helping to account for the throughput results in more detail. The restart ratios are lower for each of the algorithms under the fake-restart assumption, as is the blocking algorithm's blocking ratio. For each algorithm, if three or more transactions wish to concurrently update an item, repeated conflicts can occur. For blocking, the three transactions will all block and then deadlock when upgrading read locks to write locks, causing two to be restarted, and these two will again block and possibly deadlock. For optimistic, one of the three will commit, which causes the other two to detect readset/writeset intersections and restart, after which one of the remaining two transactions will again restart when the other one commits. A similar problem will occur for immediate-restart, as the three transactions will collide when upgrading their read locks to write locks—only the last of the three will be able to proceed, with the other two being restarted. Fake restarts eliminate this problem, since a restarted transaction comes back as an entirely new transaction. Note that the immediate-restart algorithm has the smallest reduction in its restart ratio. This is because it has a restart delay that helps to alleviate such problems even with real restarts.

Figure 33 shows that, for the limited resource case, the fake-restart assumption again leads to higher throughput predictions for all three concurrency control algorithms. This is due to the reduced restart ratios for all three algorithms (see Figure 34). Fewer restarts lead to better throughput with limited resources, as more resources are available for doing useful (as opposed to wasted) work. For the two restart-oriented algorithms, the difference between fake and real restart performance is fairly constant over most of the range of multiprogramming levels. For blocking, however, fake restarts lead to only a slight increase in throughput at the lower multiprogramming levels. This is expected since its restart ratio is small in this region. As higher multiprogramming levels cause the restart ratio to increase, the difference between fake and real restart performance becomes large. Thus, the results produced under the fake-restart assumption in the limited resource case are biased in favor of the restart-oriented algorithms for low multiprogramming levels. At higher multiprogramming levels, all of the algorithms benefit almost equally from the fake restart assumption (with a slight bias in favor of blocking at the highest multiprogramming level).

6.2 Experiment 7: Write-Lock Acquisition

In this experiment we investigated the impact of write-lock acquisition modeling on performance. Up to now we have assumed that write locks are obtained by upgrading read locks to write locks, as is the case in many real database systems.

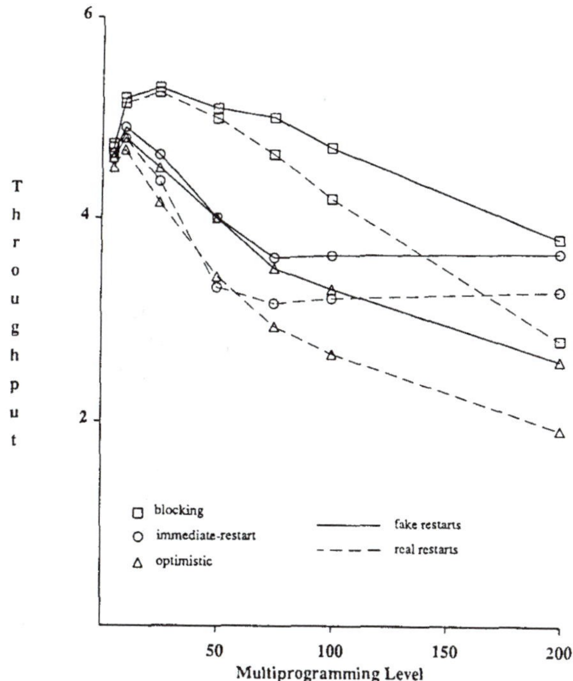

Fig. 33. Throughput (fake restarts, 1 resource unit).

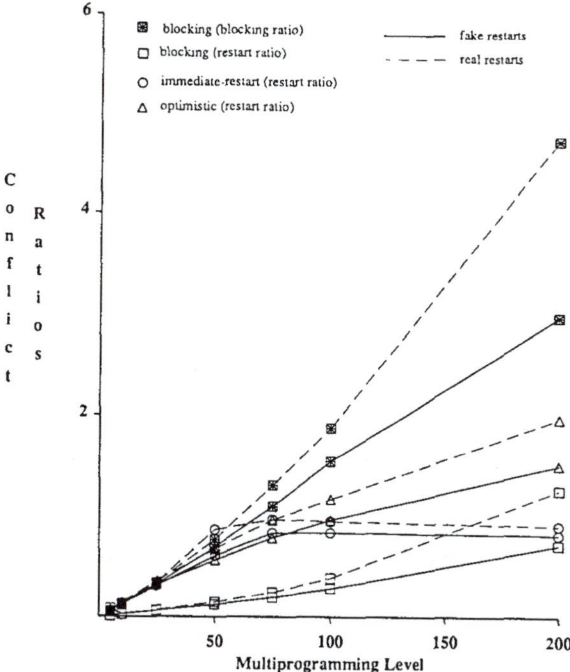

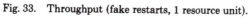

Fig. 34. Conflict ratios (fake restarts, 1 resource unit).

In this section we make an alternative assumption, the *no lock upgrades* assumption, in which a write lock is obtained instead of a read lock on each item that is to eventually be updated the first time the item is read. Figures 35 and 36 show the throughputs and conflict ratios obtained under this new assumption for the infinite resource case, and Figures 37 and 38 show the results for the limited resource case. The line and point-style conventions are the same as those in the previous experiment. Since the optimistic algorithm is (obviously) unaffected by the lock upgrade model, results are only given for the blocking and immediate-restart algorithms.

The results obtained in this experiment are quite easily explained. The upgrade assumption has little effect at the lowest multiprogramming levels, as conflicts are rare there anyway. At higher multiprogramming levels, however, the upgrade assumption does make a difference. The reasons can be understood by considering what happens when two transactions attempt to read and then write the same data item. We consider the blocking algorithm first. With lock upgrades, each transaction will first set a read lock on the item. Later, when one of the transactions is ready to write the item, it will block when it attempts to upgrade its read lock to a write lock; the other transaction will block as well when it requests its lock upgrade. This causes a deadlock, and the younger of the two transactions will be restarted. Without lock upgrades, the first transaction to lock the item will do so using a write lock, and then the other transaction will simply block without causing a deadlock when it makes its lock request. As indicated in Figures 36 and 38, this leads to lower blocking and restart ratios for the blocking algorithm under the no-lock upgrades assumption. For the immediate-restart algorithm, no restart will be eliminated in such a case, since one of the two conflicting transactions must be still restarted. The restart will occur much sooner under the no-lock upgrades assumption, however.

For the infinite resource case (Figures 35 and 36), the throughput predictions are significantly lower for blocking under the no-lock upgrades assumption. This is because write locks are obtained earlier and held significantly longer under this assumption, which leads to longer blocking times and therefore to lower throughput. The elimination of deadlock-induced restarts as described above does not help in this case, since wasted resources are not really an issue with infinite resources. For the immediate-restart algorithm, the no-lock upgrades assumption leads to only a slight throughput increase—although restarts occur earlier, as described above, again this makes little difference with infinite resources.

For the limited resource case (Figures 37 and 38), the throughput predictions for both algorithms are significantly higher under the no-lock upgrades assumption. This is easily explained as well. For blocking, eliminating lock upgrades eliminates upgrade-induced deadlocks, which leads to fewer transactions being restarted. For the immediate-restart algorithm, although no restarts are eliminated, they do occur much sooner in the lives of the restarted transactions under the no-lock upgrades assumption. The resource waste avoided by having fewer restarts with the blocking algorithm or by restarting transactions earlier with the immediate-restart algorithm leads to considerable performance increases for both algorithms when resources are limited.

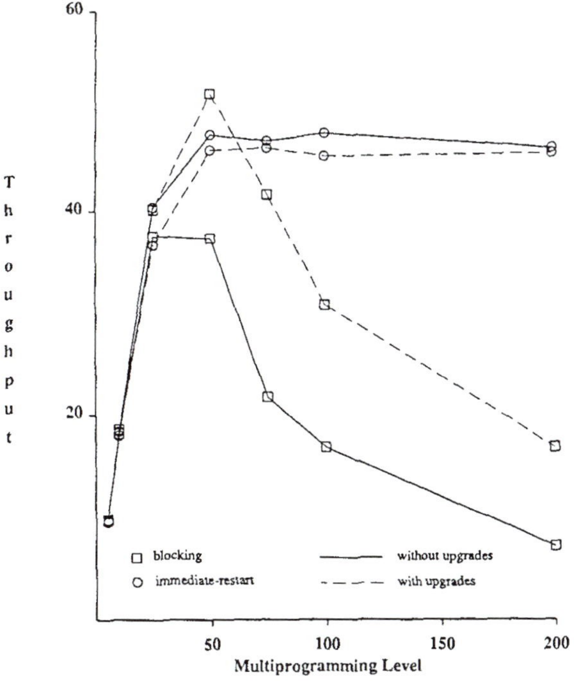

Fig. 35. Throughput (no lock upgrades, ∞ resources).

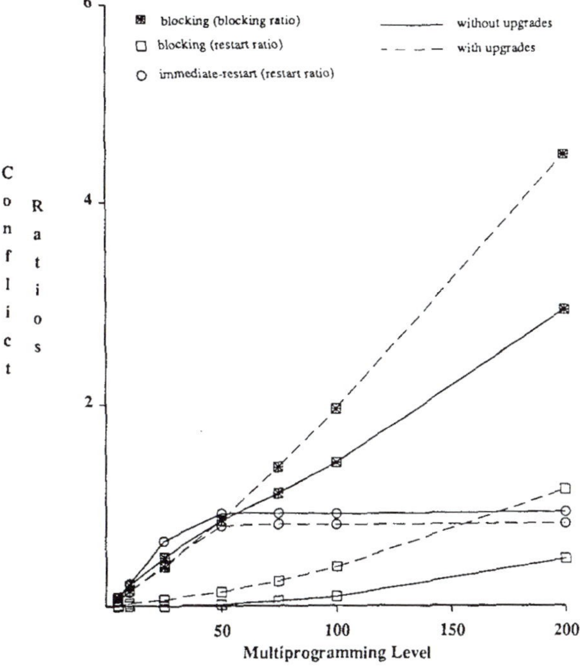

Fig. 36. Conflict ratios (no lock upgrades, ∞ resources).

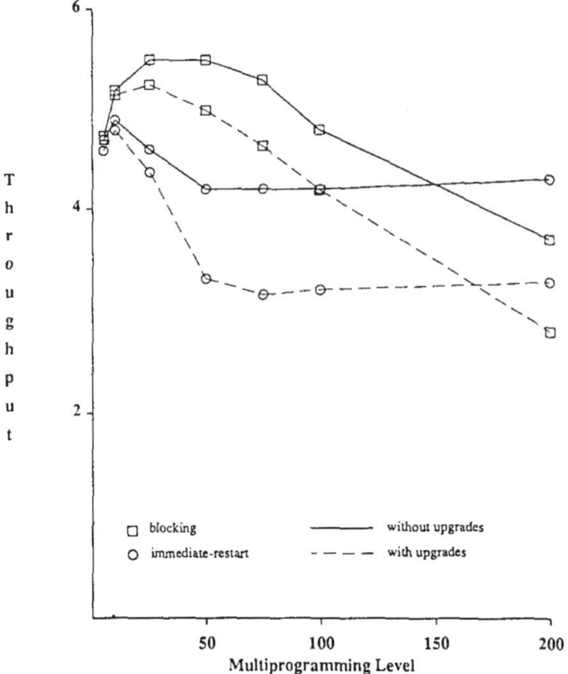

Fig. 37. Throughput (no lock upgrades, 1 resource unit).

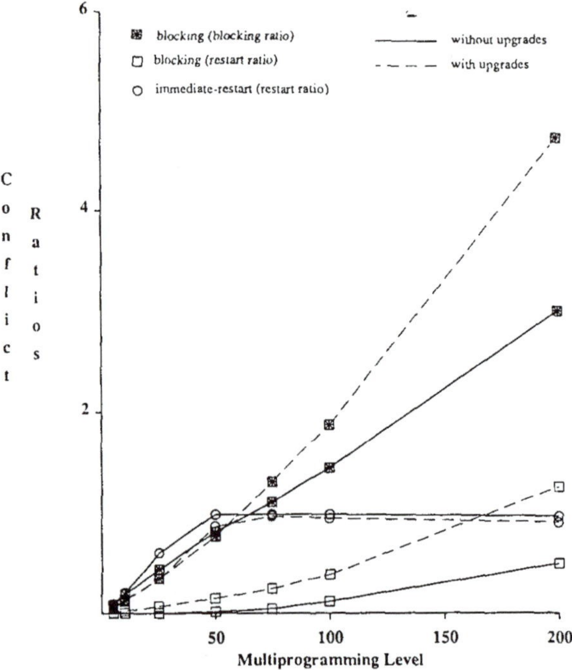

Fig. 38. Conflict ratios (no lock upgrades, 1 resource unit).

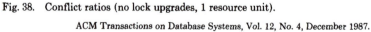

6.3 Transaction Behavior Conclusions

Reviewing the results of Experiments 6 and 7, several conclusions can be drawn. First, it is clear from Experiment 6 that the fake-restart assumption does have a significant effect on predicted throughput, particularly for high multiprogramming levels (i.e., when conflicts are frequent). In the infinite resource case, the fake-restart assumption raises the throughput of the restart-oriented algorithms more than it does for blocking, so fake restarts bias the results against blocking somewhat in this case. In the limited resource case, the results produced under the fake-restart assumption are biased in favor of the restart-oriented algorithms at low multiprogramming levels, and all algorithms benefit about equally from the assumption at higher levels of multiprogramming. In both cases, however, the relative performance results are not all that different with and without fake restarts, at least in the sense that assuming fake restarts does not change which algorithm performs the best of the three. Second, it is clear from Experiment 7 that the no-lock upgrades assumption biases the results in favor of the immediate-restart algorithm, particularly in the infinite resource case. That is, the performance of blocking is significantly underestimated using this assumption in the case of infinite resources, and the throughput of the immediate-restart algorithm benefits slightly more from this assumption than blocking does in the limited resource case.

7. CONCLUSIONS AND IMPLICATIONS

In this paper, we argued that a physically justifiable database system model is a requirement for concurrency control performance studies. We described what we feel are the key components of a reasonable model, including a model of the database system and its resources, a model of the user population, and a model of transaction behavior. We then presented our simulation model, which includes all of these components, and we used it to study alternative assumptions about database system resources and transaction behavior.

One specific conclusion of this study is that a concurrency control algorithm that tends to conserve physical resources by blocking transactions that might otherwise have to be restarted is a better choice than a restart-oriented algorithm in an environment where physical resources are limited. Dynamic two-phase locking was found to outperform the immediate-restart and optimistic algorithms for medium to high levels of resource utilization. However, if resource utilizations are low enough so that a large amount of wasted resources can be tolerated, and in addition there are a large number of transactions available to execute, then a restart-oriented algorithm that allows a higher degree of concurrent execution is a better choice. We found the optimistic algorithm to perform the best of the three algorithms tested under these conditions. Low resource utilizations such as these could arise in a database machine with a large number of CPUs and disks and with a number of users similar to those of today's medium to large timesharing systems. They could also arise in primarily interactive applications in which large think times are common and in which the number of users is such that the utilization of the system is low as a result. It is an open question whether or not such low utilizations will ever actually occur in real systems (i.e., whether or not such operating regions are sufficiently cost-effective). If not, blocking algorithms will remain the preferred method for database concurrency control.

A more general result of this study is that we have reconfirmed results from a number of other studies, including studies reported in [1, 2, 6, 12, 15, 20, 50, and 51]. We have shown that seemingly contradictory performance results, some of which favored blocking algorithms and others of which favored restarts, are not contradictory at all. The studies are all correct within the limits of their assumptions, particularly their assumptions about system resources. Thus, although it is possible to study the effects of data contention and resource contention separately in some models [50, 51], and although such a separation may be useful in iterative approximation methods for solving concurrency control performance models [M. Vernon, personal communication, 1985], it is clear that one cannot select a concurrency control algorithm for a real system on the basis of such a separation—the proper algorithm choice is strongly resource dependent. A reasonable model of database system resources is a crucial ingredient for studies in which algorithm selection is the goal.

Another interesting result of this study is that the level of multiprogramming in database systems should be carefully controlled. We refer here to the multiprogramming level internal to the database system, which controls the number of transactions that may concurrently compete for data, CPU, and I/O services (as opposed to the number of users that may be attached to the system). As in the case of paging operating systems, if the multiprogramming level is increased beyond a certain level, the blocking and optimistic concurrency control strategies start thrashing. We have confirmed the results of [6, 20, 50, and 51] for locking in the low resource contention case, but more important we have also seen that the effect can be significant for both locking and optimistic concurrency control under higher levels of resource contention. We found that when we delayed restarted transactions by an amount equal to the running average response time, it had the beneficial side effect of limiting the actual multiprogramming level, and the degradation in throughput was arrested (albeit a little bit late). Since the use of a restart delay to limit the multiprogramming level is at best a crude strategy, an adaptive algorithm that dynamically adjusts the multiprogramming level in order to maximize system throughput needs to be designed. Some performance indicators that might be used in the design of such an algorithm are useful resource utilization or running averages of throughput, response time, or conflict ratios. The design of such an adaptive load control algorithm is an open problem.

In addition to our conclusions about the impact of resources in determining concurrency control algorithm performance, we also investigated the effects of two transaction behavior modeling assumptions. With respect to fake versus real restarts, we found that concurrency control algorithms differ somewhat in their sensitivity to this modeling assumption; the results with fake restarts tended to be somewhat biased in favor of the restart-oriented algorithms. However, the overall conclusions about which algorithm performed the best relative to the other algorithms were not altered significantly by this assumption. With respect to the issue of how write-lock acquisition is modeled, we found relative algorithm performance to be more sensitive to this assumption than to the fake-restarts assumption. The performance of the blocking algorithm was particularly sensitive to the no-lock upgrades assumption in the infinite resource case, with its throughput being underestimated by as much as a factor of two at the higher multiprogramming levels.

In closing, we wish to leave the reader with the following thoughts about computer system resources and the future, due to Bill Wulf:

> Although the hardware costs will continue to fall dramatically and machine speeds will increase equally dramatically, we must assume that our aspirations will rise even more. Because of this, we are not about to face either a cycle or memory surplus. For the near-term future, the dominant effect will not be machine cost or speed alone, but rather a continuing attempt to increase the return from a finite resource—that is, a particular computer at our disposal. [54, p. 41]

ACKNOWLEDGMENTS

The authors wish to acknowledge the anonymous referees for their many insightful comments. We also wish to acknowledge helpful discussions that one or more of us have had with Mary Vernon, Nat Goodman, and (especially) Y. C. Tay. Comments from Rudd Canaday on an earlier version of this paper helped us to improve the presentation. The NSF-sponsored Crystal multicomputer project at the University of Wisconsin provided the many VAX 11/750 CPU-hours that were required for this study.

REFERENCES

1. AGRAWAL, R. Concurrency control and recovery in multiprocessor database machines: Design and performance evaluation, Ph.D. Thesis, Computer Sciences Department, University of Wisconsin-Madison, Madison, Wisc., 1983.
2. AGRAWAL, R., AND DEWITT, D. Integrated concurrency control and recovery mechanisms: Design and performance evaluation. *ACM Trans. Database Syst. 10*, 4 (Dec. 1985), 529–564.
3. AGRAWAL, R., CAREY, M., AND DEWITT, D. Deadlock detection is cheap. *ACM-SIGMOD Record 13*, 2 (Jan. 1983).
4. AGRAWAL, R., CAREY, M., AND MCVOY, L. The performance of alternative strategies for dealing with deadlocks in database management systems. *IEEE Trans. Softw. Eng.* To be published.
5. BADAL, D. Correctness of concurrency control and implications in distributed databases. In *Proceedings of the COMPSAC '79 Conference* (Chicago, Nov. 1979). IEEE, New York, 1979, pp. 588–593.
6. BALTER, R., BERARD, P., AND DECITRE, P. Why control of the concurrency level in distributed systems is more fundamental than deadlock management. In *Proceedings of the 1st ACM SIGACT SIGOPS Symposium on Principles of Distributed Computing* (Ottawa, Ontario, Aug. 18–20, 1982). ACM, New York, 1982, pp. 183–193.
7. BERNSTEIN, P., AND GOODMAN, N. Fundamental algorithms for concurrency control in distributed database systems. Tech. Rep., Computer Corporation of America, Cambridge, Mass., 1980.
8. BERNSTEIN, P., AND GOODMAN, N. "Timestamp-based algorithms for concurrency control in distributed database systems. In *Proceedings of the 6th International Conference on Very Large Data Bases* (Montreal, Oct. 1980), pp. 285–300.
9. BERNSTEIN, P., AND GOODMAN, N. Concurrency control in distributed database systems. *ACM Comput. Surv. 13*, 2 (June 1981), 185–222.
10. BERNSTEIN, P., AND GOODMAN, N. A sophisticate's introduction to distributed database concurrency control. In *Proceedings of the 8th International Conference on Very Large Data Bases* (Mexico City, Sept. 1982), pp. 62–76.
11. BERNSTEIN, P., SHIPMAN, D., AND WONG, S. Formal aspects in serializability of database concurrency control. *IEEE Trans. Softw. Eng. SE-5*, 3 (May 1979).

12. CAREY, M. Modeling and evaluation of database concurrency control algorithms. Ph.D. dissertation, Computer Science Division (EECS), University of California, Berkeley, Sept. 1983.
13. CAREY, M. An abstract model of database concurrency control algorithms. In *Proceedings of the ACM SIGMOD International Conference on Management of Data* (San Jose, Calif., May 23–26, 1983). ACM, New York, 1983, pp. 97–107.
14. CAREY, M., AND MUHANNA, W. The performance of multiversion concurrency control algorithms. *ACM Trans. Comput. Syst. 4*, 4 (Nov. 1986), 338–378.
15. CAREY, M., AND STONEBRAKER, M. The performance of concurrency control algorithms for database management systems. In *Proceedings of the 10th International Conference on Very Large Data Bases* (Singapore, Aug. 1984), pp. 107–118.
16. CASANOVA, M. The concurrency control problem for database systems. Ph.D. dissertation, Computer Science Department, Harvard University, Cambridge, Mass. 1979.
17. CERI, S., AND OWICKI, S. On the use of optimistic methods for concurrency control in distributed databases. In *Proceedings of the 6th Berkeley Workshop on Distributed Data Management and Computer Networks* (Berkeley, Calif., Feb. 1982), ACM, IEEE, New York, 1982.
18. ELHARD, K., AND BAYER, R. A database cache for high performance and fast restart in database systems. *ACM Trans. Database Syst. 9*, 4 (Dec. 1984), 503–525.
19. ESWAREN, K., GRAY, J., LORIE, R., AND TRAIGER, I. The notions of consistency and predicate locks in a database system. *Commun. ACM 19*, 11 (Nov. 1976), 624–633.
20. FRANASZEK, P., AND ROBINSON, J. Limitations of concurrency in transaction processing. *ACM Trans. Database Syst. 10*, 1 (Mar. 1985), 1–28.
21. GALLER, B. Concurrency control performance issues. Ph.D. dissertation, Computer Science Department, University of Toronto, Ontario, Sept. 1982.
22. GOODMAN, N., SURI, R., AND TAY, Y. A simple analytic model for performance of exclusive locking in database systems. In *Proceedings of the 2nd ACM SIGACT-SIGMOD Symposium on Principles of Database Systems* (Atlanta, Ga., Mar. 21–23, 1983). ACM, New York, 1983 pp. 203–215.
23. GRAY, J. Notes on database operating systems. In *Operating Systems: An Advanced Course*, R. Bayer, R. Graham, and G. Seegmuller, Eds. Springer-Verlag, New York, 1979.
24. GRAY, J., HOMAN, P., KORTH, H., AND OBERMARCK, R. A straw man analysis of the probability of waiting and deadlock in a database system. Tech. Rep. RJ3066, IBM San Jose Research Laboratory, San Jose, Calif., Feb. 1981.
25. HAERDER, T., AND PEINL, P. Evaluating multiple server DBMS in general purpose operating system environments. In *Proceedings of the 10th International Conference on Very Large Data Bases* (Singapore, Aug. 1984).
26. IRANI, K., AND LIN, H. Queuing network models for concurrent transaction processing in a database system. In *Proceedings of the ACM SIGMOD International Conference on Management of Data* (Boston, May 30–June 1, 1979). ACM, New York, 1979.
27. KUNG, H., AND ROBINSON, J. On optimistic methods for concurrency control. *ACM Trans. Database Syst. 6*, 2 (June 1981), 213–226.
28. LIN, W., AND NOLTE, J. Distributed database control and allocation: Semi-annual report. Tech. Rep., Computer Corporation of America, Cambridge, Mass., Jan. 1982.
29. LIN, W., AND NOLTE, J. Performance of two phase locking. In *Proceedings of the 6th Berkeley Workshop on Distributed Data Management and Computer Networks* (Berkeley, Feb. 1982), ACM, IEEE, New York, 1982, pp. 131–160.
30. LIN, W., AND NOLTE, J. Basic timestamp, multiple version timestamp, and two-phase locking. In *Proceedings of the 9th International Conference on Very Large Data Bases* (Florence, Oct. 1983).
31. LINDSAY, B., ET AL. Notes on distributed databases, Tech. Rep. RJ2571, IBM San Jose Research Laboratory, San Jose, Calif., 1979.
32. MENASCE, D., AND MUNTZ, R. Locking and deadlock detection in distributed databases. In *Proceedings of the 3rd Berkeley Workshop on Distributed Data Management and Computer Networks* (San Francisco, Aug. 1978). ACM, IEEE, New York, 1978, pp. 215–232.
33. PAPADIMITRIOU, C. The serializability of concurrent database updates. *J. ACM 26*, 4 (Oct. 1979), 631–653.
34. PEINL, P., AND REUTER, A. Empirical comparison of database concurrency control schemes. In *Proceedings of the 9th International Conference on Very Large Data Bases* (Florence, Oct. 1983), pp. 97–108.

35. POTIER, D., AND LEBLANC, P. Analysis of locking policies in database management systems. *Commun. ACM 23*, 10 (Oct. 1980), 584–593.
36. REED, D. Naming and synchronization in a decentralized computer system. Ph.D. dissertation, Department of Electrical Engineering and Computer Science, Massachusetts Institute of Technology, Cambridge, Mass., 1978.
37. REUTER, A. An analytic model of transaction interference in database systems. IB 68/83, University of Kaiserslautern, West Germany, 1983.
38. REUTER, A. Performance analysis of recovery techniques. *ACM Trans. Database Syst. 9*, 4 (Dec. 1984), 526–559.
39. RIES, D. The effects of concurrency control on database management system performance. Ph.D. dissertation, Department of Electrical Engineering and Computer Science, University of California at Berkeley, Berkeley, Calif., 1979.
40. RIES, D., AND STONEBRAKER, M. Effects of locking granularity on database management system performance. *ACM Trans. Database Syst. 2*, 3 (Sept. 1977), 233–246.
41. RIES, D., AND STONEBRAKER, M. Locking granularity revisited. *ACM Trans. Database Syst. 4*, 2 (June 1979), 210–227.
42. ROBINSON, J. Design of concurrency controls for transaction processing systems. Ph.D. dissertation, Department of Computer Science, Carnegie-Mellon University, Pittsburgh, Pa. 1982.
43. ROBINSON, J. Experiments with transaction processing on a multi-microprocessor. Tech. Rep. RC9725, IBM Thomas J. Watson Research Center, Yorktown Heights, N.Y., Dec. 1982.
44. ROSENKRANTZ, D., STEARNS, R., AND LEWIS, P., II. System level concurrency control for distributed database systems. *ACM Trans. Database Syst. 3*, 2 (June 1978), 178–198.
45. ROWE, L., AND STONEBRAKER, M. The commercial INGRES epilogue. In *The INGRES Papers: Anatomy of a Relational Database System*, M. Stonebraker, Ed. Addison-Wesley, Reading, Mass. 1986.
46. SARGENT, R. Statistical analysis of simulation output data. In *Proceedings of the 4th Annual Symposium on the Simulation of Computer Systems* (Aug. 1976), pp. 39–50.
47. SPITZER, J. Performance prototyping of data management applications. In *Proceedings of the ACM '76 Annual Conference* (Houston, Tx., Oct. 20–22, 1976). ACM, New York, 1976, pp. 287–292.
48. STONEBRAKER, M. Concurrency control and consistency of multiple copies of data in distributed INGRES. *IEEE Trans. Softw. Eng. 5*, 3 (May 1979).
49. STONEBRAKER, M., AND ROWE, L. The Design of POSTGRES. In *Proceedings of the ACM SIGMOD International Conference on Management of Data* (Washington, D.C., May 28–30, 1986). ACM, New York, 1986, pp. 340–355.
50. TAY, Y. A mean value performance model for locking in databases. Ph.D. dissertation, Computer Science Department, Harvard University, Cambridge, Mass. Feb. 1984.
51. TAY, Y., GOODMAN, N., AND SURI, R. Locking performance in centralized databases. *ACM Trans. Database Syst. 10*, 4 (Dec. 1985), 415–462.
52. THOMAS, R. A majority consensus approach to concurrency control for multiple copy databases. *ACM Trans. Database Syst. 4*, 2 (June 1979), 180–209.
53. THOMASIAN, A., AND RYU, I. A decomposition solution to the queuing network model of the centralized DBMS with static locking. In *Proceedings of the ACM-SIGMETRICS Conference on Measurement and Modeling of Computer Systems* (Minneapolis, Minn., Aug. 29–31, 1983). ACM, New York, 1983, pp. 82–92.
54. WULF, W. Compilers and computer architecture. *IEEE Computer* (July 1981).

Received August 1985; revised August 1986; accepted May 1987

Efficient Locking for Concurrent Operations on B-Trees

PHILIP L. LEHMAN
Carnegie-Mellon University
and
S. BING YAO
Purdue University

The B-tree and its variants have been found to be highly useful (both theoretically and in practice) for storing large amounts of information, especially on secondary storage devices. We examine the problem of overcoming the inherent difficulty of concurrent operations on such structures, using a practical storage model. A single additional "link" pointer in each node allows a process to easily recover from tree modifications performed by other concurrent processes. Our solution compares favorably with earlier solutions in that the locking scheme is simpler (no read-locks are used) and only a (small) constant number of nodes are locked by any update process at any given time. An informal correctness proof for our system is given.

Key Words and Phrases: database, data structures, B-tree, index organizations, concurrent algorithms, concurrency controls, locking protocols, correctness, consistency, multiway search trees
CR Categories: 3.73, 3.74, 4.32, 4.33, 4.34, 5.24

1. INTRODUCTION

The B-tree [2] and its variants have been widely used in recent years as a data structure for storing large files of information, especially on secondary storage devices [7]. The guaranteed small (average) search, insertion, and deletion time for these structures makes them quite appealing for database applications.

A topic of current interest in database design is the construction of databases that can be manipulated concurrently and correctly by several processes. In this paper, we consider a simple variant of the B-tree (actually of the B*-tree, proposed by Wedekind [15]) especially well suited for use in a concurrent database system.

Methods for concurrent operations on B*-trees have been discussed by Bayer and Schkolnick [3] and others [6, 12, 13]. The solution given in the current paper

This research was supported by the National Science Foundation under Grant MCS76-16604.
Authors' present addresses: P. L. Lehman, Department of Computer Science, Carnegie-Mellon University, Pittsburgh, PA 15213; S. B. Yao, Department of Computer Science and College of Business and Management, University of Maryland, College Park, MD 20742.

has the advantage that any process for manipulating the tree uses only a small (constant) number of locks at any time. Also, no search through the tree is ever prevented from reading any node (locks only prevent multiple update access). These characteristics do not apply to the previous solution.

A discussion of a similar problem (concurrent binary search trees) has been given by Kung and Lehman [8]. The present paper expands some of the ideas in that paper and applies them to a model in which the concurrent data structure is stored on secondary storage. In addition, a solution for B-trees has the appeal of demonstrated practicality (see, e.g., [1]).

While the analysis is performed for B-trees used as primary indexes, the extension to secondary indexes is straightforward.

2. THE STORAGE MODEL

We consider the database to be stored on some secondary storage device (hereinafter referred to as the "disk"). Many processes are allowed to operate on these data simultaneously. Each process can examine or modify data only by reading those data from the disk into its private primary store (the "memory"). To alter data on the disk, the process must write the data to the disk from its memory.

The disk is partitioned into sections of a fixed size (physical pages; in this paper, these will correspond to logical nodes of the tree). These are the only units that can be read or written by a process. Further, a process is considered to have a fixed amount of primary memory at its disposal, and can therefore only examine a fixed number of pages simultaneously. This primary memory is not shared with other processes.

Finally, a process is allowed to lock and unlock a disk page. This lock gives that process exclusive modification rights to that page; also, a process *must* have a page locked in order to modify that page. Only one process may hold the lock for a given page at any time. Locks *do not* prevent other processes from reading the locked page. (This does not hold for the solutions given, e.g., in [3].)

We assume that some locking discipline is imposed on lock requests, for example, a FIFO discipline or locking administration by a supervisory process.

In the protocol and in the algorithms and proofs given below, we use the following notation. Lowercase symbols (x, t, current, etc.) are used to refer to variables (including pointers) in the primary storage of a process. Uppercase symbols (A, B, C) are used to refer to blocks of primary storage. It is these blocks which are used by the process for reading and writing pages on the disk.

lock(x) denotes the operation of locking the disk page to which x points. If the page is already locked by another process, the operation waits until it is possible to obtain the lock.

unlock(x) similarly denotes the operation of releasing a held lock.

$A \leftarrow get(x)$ denotes the operation of reading into memory block A, the contents of the disk page to which x points.

put(A, x) similarly denotes the operation of writing onto the page to which x points, the contents of memory block A. The procedures must enforce the restriction that a process must hold the lock for that page before performing this operation.

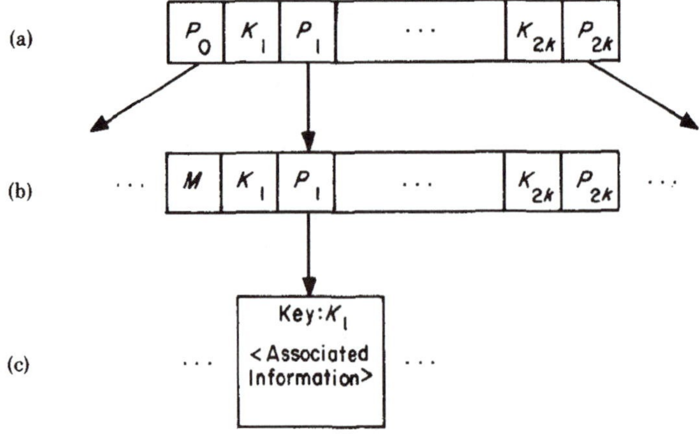

Fig. 1. B*-tree nodes (with no "high key").

To summarize, then, in order to modify a page x, a process must perform essentially the following operations.

```
lock(x);
A ← get(x);                          /* read x into memory from disk*/
modify data in A;
put(A, x);                           /* rewrite memory to disk */
unlock(x);
```

3. THE DATA STRUCTURE

3.1 B*-Trees

In this section we develop the data structure to be used by the concurrent processes. The data structure is a simple variation of the B*-tree described by Wedekind [15] (based on the B-tree defined by Bayer and McCreight [2]).

The definition for a B*-tree is as follows.

3.1.1 *Structure*

(a) Each path from the root to any leaf has the same length, h.
(b) Each node except the root and the leaves has at least $k + 1$ sons. (k is a tree parameter; $2k$ is the maximum number of elements in a node, neglecting the "high key," which is explained below.)
(c) The root is a leaf or has at least two sons.
(d) Each node has at most $2k + 1$ sons.
(e) The keys for all of the data in the B*-tree are stored in the leaf nodes, which also contain pointers to the records of the database. (Each record is associated with a key.) Nonleaf nodes contain pointers and the key values to be used in following those pointers.

B*-trees have nodes that look like those shown in Figure 1. The K_i are instances of the key domain, and the P_i are pointers. The P_i point to other nodes, or—in the case of the P_i in leaf nodes—they may point to records associated with the key values stored in the leaf. This arrangement gives leaf and nonleaf nodes

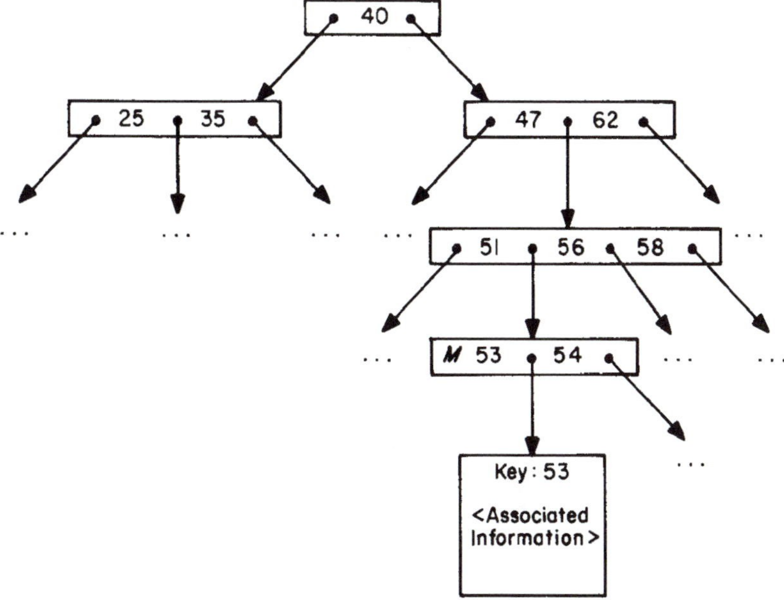

Fig. 2. An example B*-tree (with parameter $k = 2$).

essentially the same structure in our model. M is a marker that indicates a leaf node and occupies the same position as the first pointer in a nonleaf node. An example B*-tree is shown in Figure 2.

3.1.2 *Sequencing*

(a) Within each node, the keys are in ascending order.

(b) In the B*-tree an additional value, called the "high key," is sometimes appended to nonleaf nodes (Figure 3).

(c) In any node, N, each pointer, say P_i, points to a subtree (T_i) (whose root is the node to which P_i points). The values stored in T_i are bounded by the two key values, K_i and K_{i+1}, to the "left" and "right" of P_i in node N. This gives us a set of (pointer, value) pairs in nonleaf nodes, such that the set of values v, stored in subtree T_i, are bounded by

$$K_{i-1} < v \leq K_i,$$

where $k_0 = -\infty$ (or may be considered to be the last k in the node to the left; in any case, k_0 does not *physically* exist in node N), and K_{2k+1} is the high key, if it exists. The high key, then, serves to provide an upper bound on the values that may be stored in the subtree to which P_{2k} points and therefore is an upper bound on values stored in the subtree with root N. Leaf nodes have a similar definition (see Figure 3), with the stipulations that the K_i are the keys stored in the tree, and the P_i are pointers to their associated records.

3.1.3 *Insertion Rule*

(a) If a leaf node has fewer than $2k$ entries, then a new entry and the pointer to the associated record are simply inserted into the node.

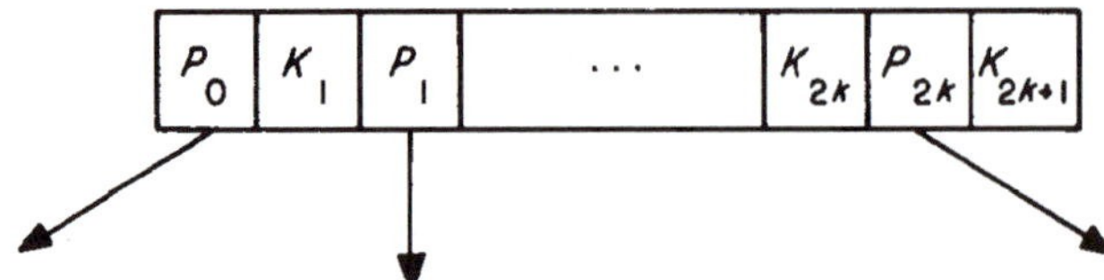

Fig. 3. A B*-tree node with a "high key" (K_{2k+1}).

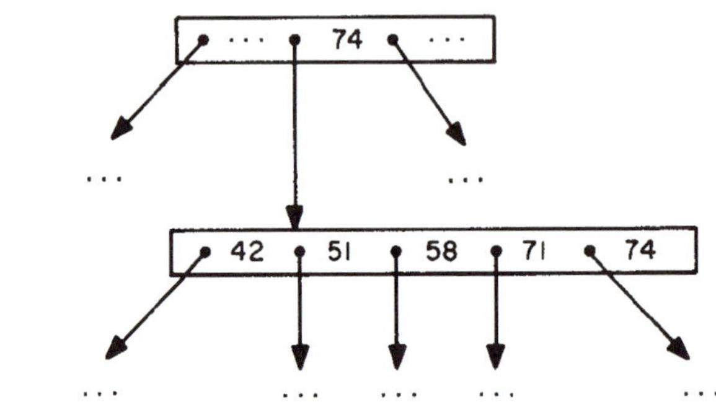

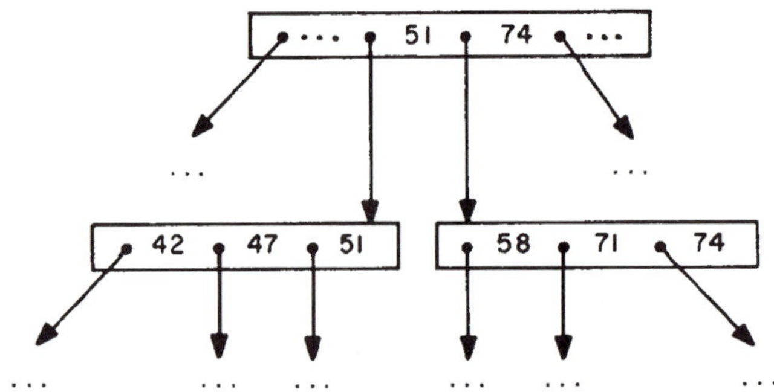

Fig. 4. Splitting a node after adding "47" ($k = 2$).

(b) If a leaf has $2k$ entries, then the new entry is inserted by splitting the node into two nodes, each with half of the entries from the old node. The new entry is inserted into one of these two nodes (in the appropriate position). Since one of the nodes is new, a new pointer must be inserted into the father of the old single node. The new pointer points to the new node; the new key is the key corresponding to the old half-node. In addition, the high key of each of the two new nodes is set.[1] Figure 4 shows an example of the splitting of a node.

(c) Insertion into nonleaf nodes proceeds identically, except that the pointers point to son nodes, rather than to data records.

[1] More specifically, when splitting node a into a' and b', the (new) high key for node a' is inserted into the parent node. The high key for node b' is the same as the old high key for a. A new pointer to b' is also inserted.

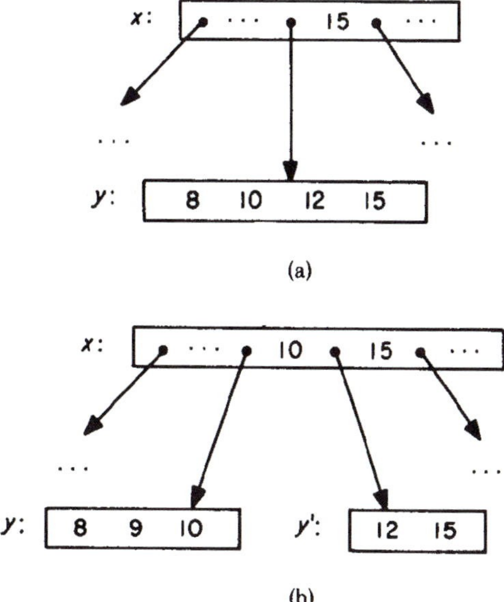

Fig. 5. Counterexample to naive approach.

A node (as in the rules given above) with less than $2k$ entries is said to be "safe" (with respect to insertion), since insertion can be done by a simple operation on the node. Similarly, a node with $2k$ entries is "unsafe," since splitting must occur. A similar definition holds for deletion from a node: a node is "safe" (respectively, "unsafe") if deletion can (cannot) occur in a node without its effects spreading to other nodes, that is, if the node has more than $k + 1$ (exactly $k + 1$) entries.

A simple example suffices to show that the naive approach to concurrent operation on B*-trees is erroneous.

Consider the B*-tree segment shown in Figure 5a. Suppose we have two processes: a search for the value 15 and an insertion of the value 9. The insertion should cause the modification to the tree structure shown in Figure 5b.

Now consider the following sequence of operations:

	search(15)	insert(9)
1.	$C \leftarrow$ read(x)	
2.		$A \leftarrow$ read(x)
3.	examine C; get ptr to y	
4.		examine A; get ptr to y
5.		$A \leftarrow$ read(y)
6.		insert 9 into A; must split into A, B
7.		put(B, y')
8.		put(A, y)
9.		Add to node x a pointer to node y'.
10.	$C \leftarrow$ read(y)	
11.	*error*: 15 not found!	

The problem is that the search first returns a pointer to y (from x) and then reads the page containing y. Between these two operations, the insertion process has altered the tree.

3.2 Previous Approaches

The previous example demonstrates that the naive approach to the concurrent B-tree problem fails: taking no precautions against the pitfalls of concurrency leads to incorrect results due to the operations of several processes. To put the problem in perspective, we briefly outline here some other approaches and solutions that have been proposed.

The first solution to the concurrent B-tree problem was offered by Samadi [13]. His approach is the most straightforward one that considers concurrency at all. The scheme simply uses semaphores (which themselves were first discussed in [5]) to exclusively lock the entire path along which modifications might take place for any given modification to the tree. This effectively locks the entire subtree of the highest affected node.

The algorithm proposed by Bayer and Schkolnick [3] is a substantial improvement to Samadi's method. They propose a scheme for concurrent manipulation of B*-trees; the scheme includes parameters which may be set depending on the degree and type of concurrency desired. First modifiers lock upper sections of the tree with writer-exclusion locks (which only lock out other writers, *not readers*). When the actual modifications must be performed, exclusive locks are applied, mostly in lower sections of the tree. This sparse use of exclusive locks enhances the concurrency of the algorithm.

Miller and Snyder [12] are investigating a scheme which locks a region of the tree of bounded size. The algorithm employs *pioneer* and *follower locks*, to prevent other processes from invading the region of the tree in which a particular process is performing modifications. The locked region moves up the tree, performing appropriate modifications. With the help of a locking discipline that uses a queue, readers moving down the tree "flow over" locked regions, avoiding deadlock. The trade-off between this algorithm and the one presented in the present paper is that the latter locks a substantially smaller section of the tree, but requires a slight modification to the usual B-tree or B*-tree structure, to facilitate concurrency.

Ellis [6] presents a concurrency solution for 2-3 trees. Several methods are used to increase the concurrency possible, and (it is claimed) these are easily extendible to B-trees. The paper includes an application of the idea of reading and writing a set of data in opposite directions (introduced by Lamport [11]), and that of allowing a slight degradation to temporarily occur in the data structure. Also, Ellis uses the idea of relaxing the responsibility of a process to finish its own work: postponing work to a more convenient time.

Guibas and Sedgewick [6a] have proposed a uniform "dichromatic framework" for balanced trees. This is a simplified view for studying balanced trees in general: it reduces all balanced tree schemes to special cases of "colored" binary trees and has the advantage of conceptual clarity. Those authors are using their framework to investigate a *top-down* locking scheme for concurrent operations, which includes splitting "almost-full" nodes on the way down the tree. This contrasts with the *bottom-up* scheme we present below. We project that their scheme will lock somewhat more nodes than ours (decreasing concurrency) and will require slightly more storage.

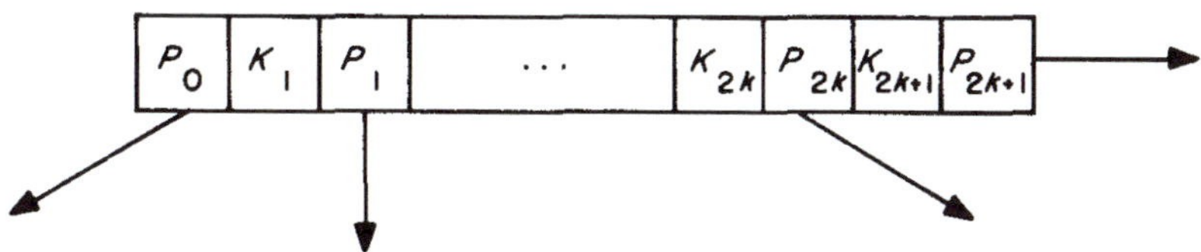

Fig. 6. A $\mathbf{B^{link}}$**-tree** node.

Another approach to concurrent operations on B-trees is currently under investigation by Kwong and Wood [10].

3.3 B^{link}-Tree for Concurrency

The $\mathbf{B^{link}}$**-tree** is a B*-tree modified by adding a single "link" pointer field to each node (P_{2k+1}—see Figure 6). (We pronounce "$\mathbf{B^{link}}$**-tree**" as "B-link-tree.")

This link field points to the next node at the same level of the tree as the current node, except that the link pointer of the rightmost node on a level is a null pointer. This definition for link pointers is consistent, since all leaf nodes lie at the same level of the tree. The $\mathbf{B^{link}}$-tree has all of the nodes at a particular level chained together into a linked list, as illustrated in Figure 7.

The purpose of the link pointer is to provide an additional method for reaching a node. When a node is split because of data overflow, a single node is replaced by two new nodes. The link pointer of the first new node points to the second node; the link pointer of the second node contains the old contents of the link pointer field of the first node. Usually, the first new node occupies the same physical page on the disk as the old single node. The intent of this scheme is that the two nodes, since they are joined by a link pointer, are functionally essentially the same as a single node until the proper pointer from their father can be added. The precise search and insertion algorithms for $\mathbf{B^{link}}$**-trees** are given in the next two sections.

For any given node in the tree (except the first node on any level) there are (usually) two pointers in the tree that point to that node (a "son" pointer from the father of the node and a link pointer from the left twin of the node). One of these pointers must be created first when a node is inserted into the tree. We specify that of these two, the link pointer must exist first; that is, it is legal to have a node in the tree that has no parent, but has a left twin. This is still defined to be a valid tree structure, since the new "right twin" is reachable from the "left twin." (These two twins might still be thought of as a single node.) Of course, the pointer from the father must be added quickly for good search time.

Link pointers have the advantage that they are introduced simultaneously with the splitting of the node. Therefore, the link pointer serves as a "temporary fix" that allows correct concurrent operation, even before all of the usual tree pointers are changed for a new (split) node. If the search key exceeds the highest value in a node (as indicated by the high key), it indicates that the tree structure has been changed, and that the twin node should be accessed using the link pointer. While this is slightly less efficient (we need to do an extra disk read to follow a link pointer), it is still a correct method of reaching a leaf node. The link pointers should be used relatively infrequently, since the splitting of a node is an exceptional case.

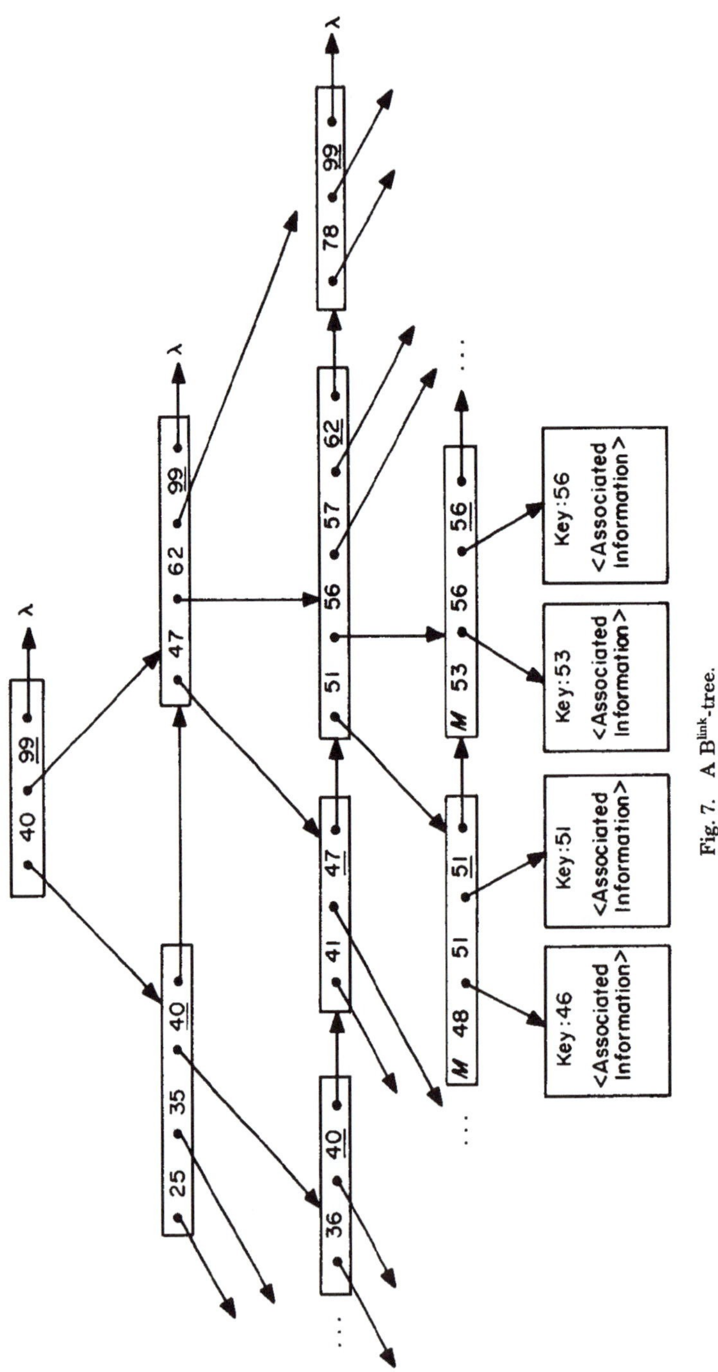

Fig. 7. A B^{link}-tree.

An additional advantage of the B^{link}-tree structure is that when the tree is searched serially, the link pointer is useful for quickly retrieving all of the nodes in the tree in "level-major" order, or, for example, retrieving only leaves.

4. THE SEARCH ALGORITHM

4.1 Algorithm Sketch

To *search* for a value, v, in the tree, the search process begins at the root and proceeds by comparing v with the values in each node in a path down the tree. In each node, the comparisons produce a pointer to follow from that node, whether to the next level, or to a leaf (record) node. If the search process examines a node and finds that the maximum value given by that node is *less* than v, then it infers some change has taken place in the current node that had not been indicated in the father at the time the father was examined by the search. The current node must have been split into two (or more) new nodes. The search must then rectify the error in its position in the tree by following the link pointer of the newly split node instead of by following a son pointer as it would ordinarily do.

The search process eventually reaches the leaf node in which v must reside if it exists. Either this node contains v, or it does not contain v and the maximum value of the node exceeds v. Therefore, the algorithm correctly determines whether v exists in the tree.

4.2 The Algorithm

Search. This procedure searches for a value, v, in the tree. If v exists in the tree, the procedure terminates with the node containing v in A and with t containing a pointer to the record associated with v. Otherwise, A contains the node where v would be if it existed. The notation used in the following algorithm is defined in Section 2. In this procedure, we use an auxiliary operation called *scannode*, defined as follows:

$x \leftarrow$ *scannode*(v, A) denotes the operation of examining the tree node in memory block A for value v and returning the appropriate pointer from A (into x).

```
procedure search(v)
current ← root;                                        /* Get ptr to root node */
A ← get(current);                                    /* Read node into memory */
while current is not a leaf do
begin                                                         /* Scan through tree */
  current ← scannode(v, A);                /* Find correct (maybe link) ptr */
  A ← get(current)                                   /* Read node into memory */
end;
                                                      /* Now we have reached leaves. */
while t ← scannode(v, A) = link ptr of A do
                                                 /* Keep moving right if necessary */
begin
  current ← t;
  A ← get(current)                                                   /* Get node */
end;
                              /* Now we have the leaf node in which v should exist. */
if v is in A then done "success" else done "failure"
```

Note the simplicity of the search, which behaves just as a nonconcurrent search, treating link pointers in exactly the same manner as any other pointer.

Note also that this procedure does no locking of any kind. This contrasts with conventional database search algorithms (e.g., Bayer and Schkolnick [3]), in which all searches read-lock the nodes they examine.

5. THE INSERTION ALGORITHM

5.1 Algorithm Sketch

To *insert* a value, v, in the tree, we perform operations similar to that for *search* above. Beginning at the root, we scan down the tree to the leaf node that should contain the value v. We also keep track of the rightmost node that we examined at each level during the descent through the tree. This descent through the tree constitutes a search for the proper place to insert v (which is, say, node a).

The insertion of the value v into the leaf node may necessitate splitting the node (in the case where it was unsafe). In this case, we split the node (as shown in Figure 8), replacing node a by nodes a' (a new version of a which is written on the same disk page) and b'. The nodes a' and b' have the same contents as a, with the addition of the value v. We then proceed back up the tree (using our "remembered" list of nodes through which we searched) to insert entries for the new node (b') and for the new high key of a' in the parent of the leaf node. This node, too, may need to be split. If so, we backtrack up the tree, splitting nodes and inserting new pointers into their parents, stopping when we reach a safe node—one that does not need to be split. In all cases, we lock a node before modifying it.

Deadlock freedom is guaranteed by the well-ordering of the locking scheme, as shown below. Note the possibility that—as we backtrack up the tree—due to node splitting the node into which we must insert the new pointer may not be the same as that through which we passed on the way to the leaf. Rather, the old node we used during the descent through the tree may have been split; the correct insertion position is now in some node to the right of the one where we expected to insert the pointer. We use link pointers to find this node.

5.2 The Algorithm

In the following algorithms, some procedures are taken as primitives (in the manner of *scannode* above), since they are easily implemented and their operation is not of interest for purposes of this paper. For example,

$A \leftarrow$ *node.insert*(A, w, v) denotes the operation of inserting the pointer w and the value v into the node contained in A.

$u \leftarrow$ *allocate(1 new page for B)* denotes the operation of allocating a new page on the disk. The node contained in B will be written onto this page, using the pointer u.

"*A, B ← rearrange old A, adding ...*" denotes the operation of splitting A into two nodes, A and B, in core.

Insert. This algorithm inserts a value, v (and its associated record), into the tree. When it terminates, this procedure will have inserted v into the tree and will

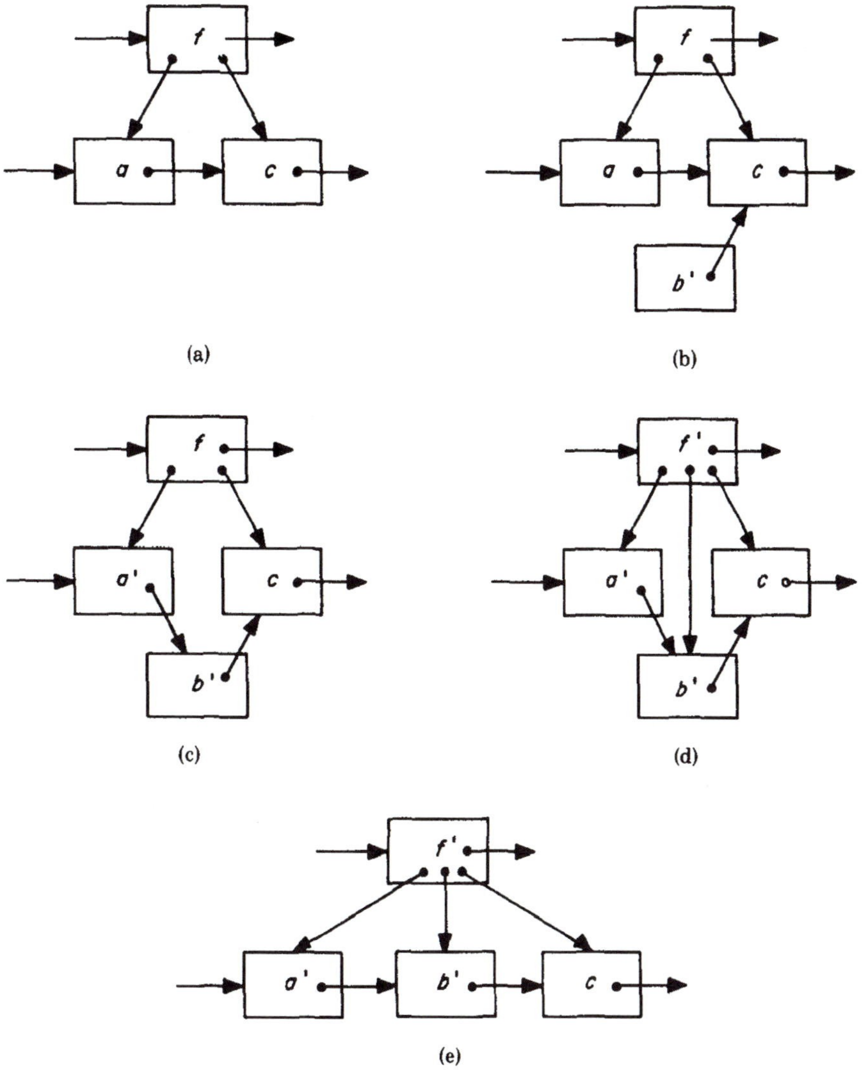

Fig. 8. Splitting node a into nodes a' and b'. (Note that (d) and (e) show identical structures.)

have split nodes, where appropriate, working its way back up the tree.

```
procedure insert(v)
initialize stack;                                  /* For remembering ancestors */
current ← root;
A ← get(current);
while current is not a leaf do
begin                                              /* Scan down tree */
  t ← current;
  current ← scannode(v, A);
  if new current was not link pointer in A then
    push(t);                                       /* Remember node at that level */
  A ← get(current)
end;
```

```
lock(current);                                        /* We have a candidate leaf */
A ← get(current);
move.right;                                           /* If necessary */
if v is in A then stop "v already exists in tree";    /* And t points to its record */
w ← pointer to pages allocated for record associated with v;
Doinsertion:
if A is safe then
begin
  A ← node.insert(A, w, v);        /* Exact manner depends if current is a leaf */
  put(A, current);
  unlock(current);                                /* Success—done backtracking */
end else begin                                    /* Must split node */
  u ← allocate(1 new page for B);
  A, B ← rearrange old A, adding v and w, to make 2 nodes,
    where (link ptr of A, link ptr of B) ← (u, link ptr of old A);
  y ← max value stored in new A;                  /* For insertion into parent */
  put(B, u);                                      /* Insert B before A */
  put(A, current);                         /* Instantaneous change of 2 nodes */
  oldnode ← current;                              /* Now insert pointer in parent */
  v ← y;
  w ← u;
  current ← pop(stack);                           /* Backtrack */
  lock(current);                                  /* Well ordered */
  A ← get(current);
  move.right;                                     /* If necessary */
  unlock(oldnode);
  goto Doinsertion                        /* And repeat procedure for parent */
end
```

Move.right. This procedure, which is called by *insert*, follows link pointers at a given level, if necessary.

```
procedure move.right
while t ← scannode(v, A) is a link pointer of A do
begin                                             /* Move right if necessary */
  lock(t);                                        /* Note left-to-right locking */
  unlock(current);
  current ← t;
A ← get(current);
end
```

Note that this procedure works its way back up the tree one level at a time. Further, at most three nodes are ever locked simultaneously, and this occurs relatively infrequently: only when it is necessary to follow a link pointer while inserting a pointer to a split node. In this case, the locked nodes are: the original half of the split node, and two nodes in the level above the split node, while the insertion is moving to the right. This is a substantial improvement upon the solution of only unlocking a node when it is determined that the node is safe.

The correctness of the algorithm relies on the fact that any change in the tree structure (i.e., any splitting of a node) incorporates a link pointer; a split always moves entries to the right in the tree, where they are reachable by following the link pointer.

In particular, we always have some idea of the correct insertion position for an object (associated with some value) at any level, that is, the "remembered" node through which our search passed at that level. If the correct insertion position has moved, it has done so in a known fashion, that is, via a node splitting to the right, leaving link pointers with which a search (or insertion) can find it. So the correct insertion position for an object is always accessible by a process starting at the old "expected" insertion position.

6. CORRECTNESS PROOF

In order to prove the correctness of our system, we need to prove that the following two propositions hold for each process:

(1) that it will not deadlock (Theorem 1),
(2) that it has correctly performed the desired operation when it terminates. More specifically:
    (a) that all disk operations preserve the correctness of the tree structure (Theorem 2),
    (b) that a consistent tree is seen by all processes other than the process making the modifications (Interaction Theorem 3).

6.1 Freedom from Deadlock

First, we undertake the proof of deadlock freedom of our system.

In order to do so, we impose an order on the nodes: bottom to top across levels and left to right within a given level. This is formalized in the following lemma.

LEMMA 1. *Locks are placed by the inserter according to a well-ordering on the nodes.*

PROOF. Consider the following ordering (<) on the set of nodes in the tree:

(1) At any time, t, if two nodes, a and b, are not at the same distance from the root of the tree (are not on the same level of the tree), then we say "$a < b$" if and only if b is less distant from the root (is at a higher level of the tree) than a.
(2) If a and b are equidistant from the root (are at the same level), then we say "$a < b$" if and only if b is reachable from a by following a chain of one or more link pointers (b is to the right of a).

We see by inspection of the insertion algorithm that if $a < b$ at time t_0, then $a < b$ at all times $t > t_0$, since the node creation procedure simply splits a node, x, into two new nodes, x' and x'', where $x' < x''$, and where

$$\forall_y \, y < x \Leftrightarrow y < x',$$

and

$$\forall_y \, x < y \Leftrightarrow x'' < y.$$

Therefore, the nodes form a well-ordering.

The inserter places locks on nodes, following the well-ordering. Once it places a lock on a node, it never places a lock on any node below it, nor on any node to the left on the same level.

Therefore, the inserter locks the nodes in the given well-order. Q.E.D.

Since the inserter is the only procedure that locks nodes, we immediately have the following theorem.

THEOREM 1: DEADLOCK FREEDOM. *The given system cannot produce a deadlock.*

6.2 Correctness of Tree Modifications

To ensure preservation of the tree structure, we must check all operations that modify that structure. First we note that tree modification can only be performed with a "put" operation. The insertion process has three places in its algorithm where a put is performed.

(1) "put(A, current)" for rewriting a safe node.
(2) "put(B, u)" for unsafe nodes. With this operation, we write the second (rightmost) of the two new nodes that are formed by a node splitting.
(3) "put(A, current)" for unsafe nodes. Here we write the first (leftmost) of the two nodes. We actually rewrite a page (node) that was already in the tree, and modify the link pointer of that page to point to the new node written by "put(B, u)."

Note that in the algorithm (for unsafe nodes), "put(B, u)" immediately precedes "put(A, current)" for unsafe nodes. We show that this ordering reduces the two puts to essentially one operation in the following lemma.

LEMMA 2. *The operation "put(B, u); put(A, current)" is equivalent to one change in the tree structure.*

PROOF. We assume that the two operations write nodes b and a, respectively. At the time "put(B, u)" is performed, no other node contains a pointer to the node (b) being written. Therefore, this put operation has *no effect* on the tree structure.

Now, when "put(A, current)" is performed, this operation modifies the node to which current points (node a). This modification includes changing the link pointer of node a to point to b. At this time, b already exists, and the link pointer of b points to the same node as the link pointer of the old version of a. This has the effect of simultaneously modifying a and introducing b into the tree structure. Q.E.D.

THEOREM 2. *All put operations correctly modify the tree structure.*

PROOF

Case 1. The operation "put(A, current)" for safe nodes. This operation modifies only one locked node in the tree; the correctness of the tree is therefore preserved.

Case 2. The operation "put(B, u)" for unsafe nodes. This operation does not change the tree structure.

Case 3. The operation "put(A, current)" for unsafe nodes. By the lemma, this operation both modifies the current node (say, a) and incorporates an additional node (say, b) into the tree structure: the node written by "put(B, u)." Similarly to case 1, a is locked at the time of "put(A, current)." The difference in this case is that the node is unsafe and must be split. But, by the lemma, we do this with a single operation, preserving the correct tree structure. Q.E.D.

6.3 Correct Interaction

It remains to show that other processes still operate correctly regardless of the action of an insertion process modifying the tree.

THEOREM 3: INTERACTION THEOREM. *Actions of an insertion process do not impair the correctness of the actions of other processes.*

In order to prove the theorem, we first consider the case of a search procedure interacting with an insertion, then of the interaction of two insertion procedures. In general, in order to show that an operation by an inserter does not impair the correctness of another process, we consider the behavior of that process relative to the operation in question. In all cases the operation is atomic.

Assume that the inserter performs a "put" at time t_0 on node a. Consider the time, t', at which the other process reads node a from the disk. Since "get" and "put" operations are assumed to be indivisible, either $t' < t_0$, or $t_0 < t'$. We show that the latter case presents no problem in the following lemma.

LEMMA 3. *If a process P reads node a at some time $t' > t_0$, where t_0 is the time at which a was changed by an insertion process, I, then the correctness of P is not affected by that change.*

PROOF. Consider the path that P follows through node a. The path that P follows *before* it reaches a will not be changed by I. Further, by Theorem 2 above, any change that process I makes in the tree structure will produce a correct tree. Therefore, the path followed by P from a (at time $t > t'$) will proceed correctly regardless of the modification. Q.E.D.

In order to easily break the proof of the theorem into cases, we list here the three possible types of insertion that may be performed for a value on a node.

Type 1. The simple addition of a value and associated pointer to a node. This type of insertion occurs when the node is safe.
Type 2. The splitting of a node where the inserted value is placed in the left half of the split node. The left half is the same node as that which was split.
Type 3. Similarly, the splitting of a node where the inserted value is placed in the right half of the split node. The right half is the newly allocated node.

We now undertake the proof of the theorem. We observe that there are several aspects (cases) to the correctness of the theorem, and we prove these separately.

PROOF. By Lemma 3, it is only necessary to consider the case where the search or insertion process P begins to read the node *before* the change is made by the insertion process I.

Part 1. Consider the interaction between the inserter I—which changes node n at time t_0—and a search process S—which reads node n at time $t' < t_0$. Let n' denote the node after the change. (The argument in this section is also applicable to the case where another inserter (I') is interacting with process I, and I' is performing a search.) The sequence of actions to be considered is: S reads node n; then I modifies node n to n'; then S continues the search based on the contents of n. Consider three types of insertions:

Type 1. Process I performs a simple insertion into node n. For cases where n is a leaf, the inserter does not change any pointer. The result is equivalent to the serial schedule in which S runs before I. If n is a nonleaf node, a pointer/value pair for some node, m', in the next lower level of the tree is inserted in n. Assume that m' is created by splitting I into I' and m'. The only possible interaction is when S obtained the pointer to I prior to the insertion of the pointer to m'. The pointer to I now points to I', and S will use the link pointer in I' to reach m'. Thus the search is correct.

Types 2 and 3. The node n is split into nodes $n1'$ and $n2'$ by the insertion. For the leaf case, the search results on n and on $n1'$ and $n2'$ are the same, except for the newly inserted value which will not be found by S. If n is not a leaf, then a node below it has split, causing a new pointer/value pair to be inserted in node n, which causes n to split. By induction, the split in the level below node n is correct. By Lemma 3, the searching below node n is also correct. Therefore, we must simply show the correctness of the split of node n. Suppose node n splits into nodes $n1'$ and $n2'$ that contain the same set of pointers as node n, with the addition of the newly inserted node. Then starting from node n, the search will reach the same set of nodes in the next level as it would working from $n1'$ with a link pointer to $n2'$. The exceptional case is that in which the search would have followed the newly inserted pointer had it been present when process S read node n. In this case, the pointer followed will be to the left of that new pointer. This will lead the search to a node (say, k) to the left of the node (say, m) to which the new pointer points. Then the link pointer of k will be followed to (eventually) reach m. This is the correct result. (The argument for type 3 is identical to that for type 2, except that the new entry is inserted into the newly created (rather than the old) half of the split node. This makes no difference to the argument, however, since the node is read by S before the split takes place.)

Part 2. We next consider the case where process I interacts with another insertion process, I'. Process I' is either searching for the correct node for an insertion, backtracking to another level, or actually attempting to insert a value/pointer pair into the node n.

In the case where I' is searching for a node into which to insert a value/pointer pair, the search behaves in exactly the same fashion as a search process would. The proof is therefore the same as given above for a search process.

Part 3. In the case where I' is backtracking up the tree, as a result of node split in the level below, I' needed to back up in order to insert a pointer to the new half of the split node. Backtracking is done using the record kept in a stack during the descent through the tree. At each level, the node that is pushed onto the stack is the rightmost node among those that were examined at that level.

Consider what may have happened to a given node, *n*, between the time we inserted it into the stack and the time we return to the node as we backtrack through the tree. The node may have split one or more times. These splits will have caused the formation of new nodes to the "right" of the node *n*. Since all nodes to the right of node *n* are reachable (via link pointers) the appropriate place to insert the value will be reachable by the insertion algorithm.

Part 4. In the case where process *I'* is attempting an insertion into node *n*, it will attempt to lock that node. But the process *I* will already hold the lock on node *n*. Eventually, *I* will release that lock, and *I'* will lock the node and then read it into memory. By the lemma above, the interaction is correct since the reading by *I'* takes place before the insertion by *I*. Either node *n* will be the correct place to make the insertion—in which case it will do so—or the search will have to follow the link pointer from the node to its right twin. Q.E.D.

6.4 Livelock

We wish to point out here that our algorithms do not prevent the possibility of livelock (where one process runs indefinitely). This can happen if a process never terminates because it keeps having to follow link pointers created by other processes. This might happen in the case of a process being run on a (relatively) very slow processor in a multiprocessor system.

We believe, however, that this is extremely unlikely to be a problem in a practical implementation, given the following observations.

(1) In most systems that we know of, processors run with comparable speeds.
(2) Node creation and deletion occur only a small percent of the time in a B-tree, so even a slow processor is likely to encounter little difficulty due to node creation or deletion (that is, it will be required to follow only a small number of link pointers).[2]
(3) Only a fixed number of nodes can be created on any given level of the tree, bounding the amount of "catching up" that a slow processor must do.[3]

We believe that these ideas combine to produce a vanishingly small probability of livelock for a process in a practical system (except perhaps in the case where the speeds of the processes involved are *radically* different). A simulation would enable us to verify that our system does work under "reasonable" conditions, and help us to put bounds on the admissible relative speeds of the processes.

In the case where processes do run at radically different speeds, we might introduce some additional mechanism to prevent livelock. Several alternatives are available for the implementation of such a mechanism. A complete discussion of methods for avoiding livelock is beyond the scope of this paper, but one

[2] It is interesting to note that all of the cases of any difficulty in the present system and in other related systems for concurrency occur only a very small fraction of the time. For example, in a B-tree nodes need be split infrequently compared to the number of insertions performed.

[3] Strictly speaking, this statement ignores the problem of "ghost" nodes created by deletion, which somewhat increases the number of nodes that can be viewed as being on any given level.

example of such a method might be to assign priorities to each process, based, perhaps, on the "age" of the process. This would guarantee that each process would terminate, since it would eventually become the oldest process, and hence the process with the highest priority.

7. DELETION

A simple way of handling deletions is to allow fewer than k entries in a leaf node. This is unnecessary for nonleaf nodes, since deletion only removes keys from a leaf node; a key in a nonleaf node only serves as an *upper bound* for its associated pointer; it is not removed during deletion.

In order, then, to delete an entry from a leaf node, we perform operations on that node quite similar to those described above for case 1 of insertion. In particular, we perform a search for the node in which v should lie. We lock this node, read it into memory, and rewrite the node after removing the value v from the copy in primary memory. Occasionally, this will produce a node with fewer than k entries.

Proofs of the correctness of this algorithm are analogous to the proofs for insertion. For example, the proof of deadlock freedom is trivial, since only one node need be locked by the deleter.

Similarly, correct operation relies on the observation that if a searcher reads the node before the value v is deleted, it will report the presence of v in the node. This reduces to the serial schedule in which the search runs first.

The system we have just sketched is far simpler than one that requires underflows and concatenations. It uses very little extra storage under the assumption that insertions take place more often than deletions. In situations where excessive deletions cause the storage utilization of tree nodes to be unacceptably low, a batch reorganization or an underflow operation which locks the entire tree can be performed.

8. LOCKING EFFICIENCY

Clearly, at least one lock is required in a concurrent scheme, in order to prevent simultaneous update of the same node by distinct processes.

The solution given above for insertion uses at most a constant number of locks (three) for any process at any time. It does this only under the following circumstances: an inserter has just inserted an entry into some node (leaf or nonleaf), and has caused that node to be split. In backing up the tree, in order to insert a pointer to the split half of the new node, the inserter finds that the old father of the split node is no longer the correct place to perform the insertion and begins chaining across the level of nodes containing the father in order to find the correct insertion position for the pointer. Three nodes are locked only for the duration of one operation.

This type of locking occurs rarely in a B^{link}-tree with a large capacity in each node. Therefore, we can expect an extremely small collision probability for this structure unless there are many concurrent processes running.

The behavior of this system could be quantified by simulation, which would be parameterized by the number of concurrent processes, the capacity of each node, and the relative frequencies of search, insert, and delete operations. Such a simulation would also be useful for comparison with other concurrency schemes.

9. SUMMARY AND CONCLUSIONS

The B-tree has been found to be widely useful in maintaining large databases. Concurrent manipulation of such data has the appeal that many users would be able to share data; further, this should be feasible, since there are few cases, in a large database, where the data needs of users will conflict.

We have given an algorithm which performs correct concurrent operations on a variant of the B-tree. The algorithm has the property that only a (small) constant number of locks need be used by any process at any time. The algorithm is straightforward and differs only slightly from the sequential algorithm for the same problem. (The gain in efficiency of the algorithm presented above, as compared with sequential algorithms, or other concurrent algorithms could be quantified by simulation.)

This effect is achieved by a small modification to the data structure that allows recovery in the case where the position of a process is invalidated by the action of another process (cf. [8]).

We hope to expand this work to a more general scheme for concurrent database manipulation. We wish to find a general scheme that entails only a small modification to the data structure and to the sequential algorithm for a database problem. This modification should nevertheless allow a process to recover when its actions have been rendered incorrect by changes to the data structure that have been made by another process.

Another direction for further work is the study of a general method for "parallelizing" algorithms: techniques for converting a (well-understood) sequential algorithm into a concurrent algorithm for the same problem. The goal is to exploit as much as possible the concurrent nature of the problem that the algorithm is designed to solve, without sacrificing the correctness of the algorithm.

REFERENCES

(Note. References [4, 9, 14] are not cited in the text.)

1. Astrahan, M.M., et al. System R: Relational approach to database management. *ACM Trans. Database Syst. 1*, 2 (June 1976), 97-137.
2. Bayer, R., and McCreight, E. Organization and maintenance of large ordered indexes. *Acta Inf. 1* (1972), 173-189.
3. Bayer, R., and Schkolnick, M. Concurrency of operations on B-trees. *Acta Inf. 9* (1977), 1-21.
4. Dijkstra, E.W., et al. On-the-fly garbage collection: An exercise in cooperation. *Commun. ACM 21*, 11 (Nov. 1978), 966-976.
5. Dijkstra, E.W. Cooperating sequential processes. In *Programming Languages*, F. Genuys, Ed. Academic Press, New York, 1968, pp. 43-112.
6. Ellis, C.S. Concurrent search and insertion in 2-3 trees. Tech. Rep. 78-05-01, Dep. Computer Science, Univ. Washington, Seattle, May 1978.

6a. Guibas, L.J., and Sedgewick, R. A dichromatic framework for balanced trees. In *Proc. 19th Ann. Symp. Foundation of Computer Science*, IEEE, 1978.

7. Knuth, D.E. *The Art of Computer Programming*, vol. 3, Sorting and Searching. Addison-Wesley, Reading, Mass., 1973.
8. Kung, H.T., and Lehman, P.L. Concurrent manipulation of binary search trees. *ACM Trans. Database Syst. 5*, 3 (Sept. 1980), 354-382.
9. Kung, H.T., and Song, S.W. A parallel garbage collection algorithm and its correctness proof. In *Proc. 18th Ann. Symp. Foundations of Computer Science*, IEEE, Oct. 1977, pp. 120-131.
10. Kwong, Y.S., and Wood, D. Concurrency in B- and T-trees. In preparation.
11. Lamport, L. Concurrent reading and writing. *Commun. ACM 20*, 11 (Nov. 1977), 806-811.

12. MILLER, R., AND SNYDER, L. Multiple access to B-trees. In *Proc. Conf. Information Sciences and Systems* (preliminary version), Johns Hopkins Univ., Baltimore, March 1978.
13. SAMADI, B. B-trees in a system with multiple users. *Inf. Process. Lett. 5*, 4 (Oct. 1976), 107–112.
14. STEELE, G.L., JR. Multiprocessing compactifying garbage collection. *Commun. ACM 18*, 9 (Sept. 1975), 125–143.
15. WEDEKIND, H. On the selection of access paths in a data base system. In *Data Base Management*, J.W. Klimbie and K.L. Koffeman, Eds. North-Holland, Amsterdam, 1974, pp. 385–397.

Received June 1979; revised May 1980; accepted October 1980

ARIES: A Transaction Recovery Method Supporting Fine-Granularity Locking and Partial Rollbacks Using Write-Ahead Logging

C. MOHAN
IBM Almaden Research Center
and
DON HADERLE
IBM Santa Teresa Laboratory
and
BRUCE LINDSAY, HAMID PIRAHESH and PETER SCHWARZ
IBM Almaden Research Center

In this paper we present a simple and efficient method, called ARIES (*Algorithm for Recovery and Isolation Exploiting Semantics*), which supports partial rollbacks of transactions, fine-granularity (e.g., record) locking and recovery using write-ahead logging (WAL). We introduce the paradigm of *repeating history* to redo all missing updates *before* performing the rollbacks of the loser transactions during restart after a system failure. ARIES uses a log sequence number in each page to correlate the state of a page with respect to logged updates of that page. All updates of a transaction are logged, including those performed during rollbacks. By appropriate chaining of the log records written during rollbacks to those written during forward progress, a bounded amount of logging is ensured during rollbacks even in the face of repeated failures during restart or of nested rollbacks We deal with a variety of features that are very important in building and operating an *industrial-strength* transaction processing system ARIES supports fuzzy checkpoints, selective and deferred restart, fuzzy image copies, media recovery, and high concurrency lock modes (e.g., increment/decrement) which exploit the semantics of the operations and require the ability to perform operation logging. ARIES is flexible with respect to the kinds of buffer management policies that can be implemented. It supports objects of varying length efficiently. By enabling parallelism during restart, page-oriented redo, and logical undo, it enhances concurrency and performance. We show why some of the System R paradigms for logging and recovery, which were based on the shadow page technique, need to be changed in the context of WAL. We compare ARIES to the WAL-based recovery methods of

---

Authors' addresses: C Mohan, Data Base Technology Institute, IBM Almaden Research Center, San Jose, CA 95120; D. Haderle, Data Base Technology Institute, IBM Santa Teresa Laboratory, San Jose, CA 95150; B. Lindsay, H. Pirahesh, and P. Schwarz, IBM Almaden Research Center, San Jose, CA 95120.

ACM Transactions on Database Systems, Vol 17, No. 1, March 1992, Pages 94–162

DB2™, IMS, and Tandem™ systems. ARIES is applicable not only to database management systems but also to persistent object-oriented languages, recoverable file systems and transaction-based operating systems. ARIES has been implemented, to varying degrees, in IBM's OS/2™ Extended Edition Database Manager, DB2, Workstation Data Save Facility/VM, Starburst and QuickSilver, and in the University of Wisconsin's EXODUS and Gamma database machine.

Categories and Subject Descriptors: D.4.5 [**Operating Systems**]: Reliability—*backup procedures, checkpoint/restart, fault tolerance*; E.5. [**Data**]: Files—*backup/recovery*; H.2.2 [**Database Management**]: Physical Design—*recovery and restart*; H.2.4 [**Database Management**]: Systems—*concurrency, transaction processing*; H.2.7 [**Database Management**]: Database Administration—*logging and recovery*

General Terms: Algorithms, Design, Performance, Reliability

Additional Key Words and Phrases: Buffer management, latching, locking, space management, write-ahead logging

1. INTRODUCTION

In this section, first we introduce some basic concepts relating to recovery, concurrency control, and buffer management, and then we outline the organization of the rest of the paper.

1.1 Logging, Failures, and Recovery Methods

The transaction concept, which is well understood by now, has been around for a long time. It encapsulates the *ACID* (Atomicity, Consistency, Isolation and Durability) properties [36]. The application of the transaction concept is not limited to the database area [6, 17, 22, 23, 30, 39, 40, 51, 74, 88, 90, 101]. Guaranteeing the atomicity and durability of transactions, in the face of concurrent execution of multiple transactions and various failures, is a very important problem in transaction processing. While many methods have been developed in the past to deal with this problem, the assumptions, performance characteristics, and the complexity and ad hoc nature of such methods have not always been acceptable. Solutions to this problem may be judged using several metrics: degree of concurrency supported within a page and across pages, complexity of the resulting logic, space overhead on nonvolatile storage and in memory for data and the log, overhead in terms of the number of synchronous and asynchronous I/Os required during restart recovery and normal processing, kinds of functionality supported (partial transaction rollbacks, etc.), amount of processing performed during restart recovery, degree of concurrent processing supported during restart recovery, extent of system-induced transaction rollbacks caused by deadlocks, restrictions placed on stored data (e.g., requiring unique keys for all records, restricting maximum size of objects to the page size, etc.), ability to support novel lock modes which allow the concurrent execution, based on commutativity and other properties [2, 26, 38, 45, 88, 89], of operations like increment/decrement on the same data by different transactions, and so on.

In this paper we introduce a new recovery method, called *ARIES*[1] (*Algorithm for Recovery and Isolation Exploiting Semantics*), which fares very well with respect to all these metrics. It also provides a great deal of flexibility to take advantage of some special characteristics of a class of applications for better performance (e.g., the kinds of applications that IMS Fast Path [28, 42] supports efficiently).

To meet transaction and data recovery guarantees, ARIES records in a *log* the progress of a transaction, and its actions which cause changes to recoverable data objects. The log becomes the source for ensuring either that the transaction's committed actions are reflected in the database despite various types of failures, or that its uncommitted actions are undone (i.e., rolled back). When the logged actions reflect data object content, then those log records also become the source for reconstruction of damaged or lost data (i.e., media recovery). *Conceptually*, the log can be thought of as an ever growing *sequential* file. In the actual implementation, multiple physical files may be used in a serial fashion to ease the job of archiving log records [15]. Every log record is assigned a unique *log sequence number* (*LSN*) when that record is appended to the log. The LSNs are assigned in ascending sequence. Typically, they are the *logical* addresses of the corresponding log records. At times, version numbers or timestamps are also used as LSNs [67]. If more than one log is used for storing the log records relating to *different* pieces of data, then a form of two-phase commit protocol (e.g., the current industry-standard Presumed Abort protocol [63, 64]) must be used.

The nonvolatile version of the log is stored on what is generally called *stable storage*. Stable storage means nonvolatile storage which remains intact and available across system failures. Disk is an example of nonvolatile storage and its stability is generally improved by maintaining synchronously two identical copies of the log on different devices. We would expect the online log records stored on direct access storage devices to be archived to a cheaper and slower medium like tape at regular intervals. The archived log records may be discarded once the appropriate image copies (archive dumps) of the database have been produced and those log records are no longer needed for media recovery.

Whenever log records are written, they are placed first only in the *volatile* storage (i.e., virtual storage) buffers of the log file. Only at certain times (e.g., at commit time) are the log records up to a certain point (LSN) written, in log page sequence, to stable storage. This is called *forcing* the log up to that LSN. Besides forces caused by transaction and buffer manager activi-

[1] The choice of the name ARIES, besides its use as an acronym that describes certain features of our recovery method, is also supposed to convey the relationship of our work to the Starburst project at IBM, since Aries is the name of a constellation.

ties, a system process may, in the background, periodically force the log buffers as they fill up.

For ease of exposition, we assume that each log record describes the update performed to only a single page. This is not a requirement of ARIES. In fact, in the Starburst [87] implementation of ARIES, sometimes a single log record might be written to describe updates to two pages. The *undo* (respectively, *redo*) portion of a log record provides information on how to undo (respectively, redo) changes performed by the transaction. A log record which contains both the undo and the redo information is called an *undo-redo log record*. Sometimes, a log record may be written to contain only the redo information or only the undo information. Such a record is called a *redo-only log record* or an *undo-only log record*, respectively. Depending on the action that is performed, the undo-redo information may be recorded *physically* (e.g., before the update and after the update images or values of specific fields within the object) or *operationally* (e.g., add 5 to field 3 of record 15, subtract 3 from field 4 of record 10). Operation logging permits the use of high concurrency lock modes, which exploit the semantics of the operations performed on the data. For example, with certain operations, the same field of a record could have uncommitted updates of many transactions. These permit more concurrency than what is permitted by the *strict executions* property of the model of [3], which essentially says that modified objects must be locked exclusively (X mode) for commit duration.

ARIES uses the widely accepted write ahead logging (WAL) protocol. Some of the commercial and prototype systems based on WAL are IBM's AS/400™ [9, 21], CMU's Camelot [23, 90], IBM's DB2™ [1, 10, 11, 12, 13, 14, 15, 19, 35, 96], Unisys's DMS/1100 [27], Tandem's Encompass™ [4, 37], IBM's IMS [42, 43, 53, 76, 80, 94], Informix's Informix-Turbo™ [16], Honeywell's MRDS [91], Tandem's NonStop SQL™ [95], MCC's ORION [29], IBM's OS/2 Extended Edition™ Database Manager [7], IBM's QuickSilver [40], IBM's Starburst [87], SYNAPSE [78], IBM's System/38 [99], and DEC's VAX DBMS™ and VAX Rdb/VMS™ [81]. In WAL-based systems, an updated page is written back to the same nonvolatile storage location from where it was read. That is, *in-place updating* is performed on nonvolatile storage. Contrast this with what happens in the shadow page technique which is used in systems such as System R [31] and SQL/DS [5] and which is illustrated in Figure 1. There the updated version of the page is written to a different location on nonvolatile storage and the previous version of the page is used for performing database recovery if the system were to fail before the next checkpoint.

The *WAL protocol* asserts that the log records representing changes to some data must already be on stable storage before the changed data is allowed to replace the previous version of that data on nonvolatile storage. That is, the system is not allowed to write an updated page to the nonvolatile storage version of the database until at least the undo portions of the log records which describe the updates to the page have been written to stable storage. To enable the enforcement of this protocol, systems using the WAL method of recovery store in every page the LSN of the log record that describes the most recent update performed on that page. The reader is

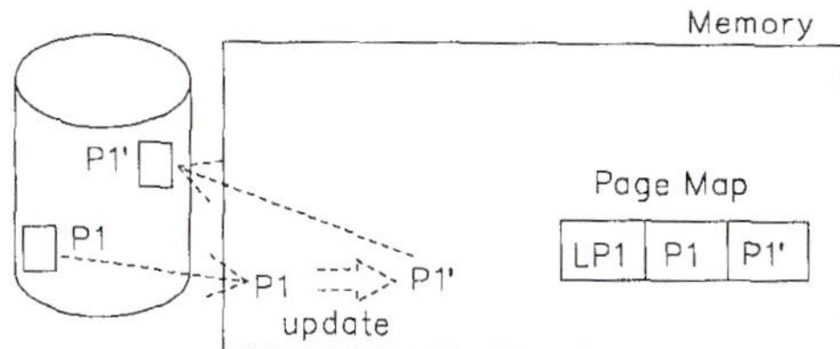

Fig. 1. Shadow page technique.

Logical page LP1 is read from physical page P1 and after modification is written to physical page P1'. P1' is the *current* version and P1 is the *shadow* version. During a checkpoint, the shadow version is discarded and the current version becomes the shadow version also. On a failure, data base recovery is performed using the log and the shadow version of the data base.

referred to [31, 97] for discussions about why the WAL technique is considered to be better than the shadow page technique. [16, 78] discuss methods in which shadowing is performed using a separate log. While these avoid some of the problems of the original shadow page approach, they still retain some of the important drawbacks and they introduce some new ones. Similar comments apply to the methods suggested in [82, 88]. Later, in Section 10, we show why some of the recovery paradigms of System R, which were based on the shadow page technique, are inappropriate in the WAL context, when we need support for high levels of concurrency and various other features that are described in Section 2.

Transaction status is also stored in the log and no transaction can be considered complete until its committed status and all its log data are safely recorded on stable storage by forcing the log up to the transaction's commit log record's LSN. This allows a restart recovery procedure to recover any transactions that completed successfully but whose updated pages were not physically written to nonvolatile storage before the failure of the system. This means that a transaction is not permitted to complete its *commit* processing (see [63, 64]) until the redo portions of all log records of that transaction have been written to stable storage.

We deal with three types of failures: transaction or process, system, and media or device. When a transaction or process failure occurs, typically the transaction would be in such a state that its updates would have to be undone. It is possible that the transaction had corrupted some pages in the buffer pool if it was in the middle of performing some updates when the process disappeared. When a system failure occurs, typically the virtual storage contents would be lost and the transaction system would have to be restarted and recovery performed using the nonvolatile storage versions of the database and the log. When a media or device failure occurs, typically the contents of that media would be lost and the lost data would have to be recovered using an image copy (archive dump) version of the lost data and the log.

Forward processing refers to the updates performed when the system is in normal (i.e., not restart recovery) processing and the transaction is updating the database because of the data manipulation (e.g., SQL) calls issued by the user or the application program. That is, the transaction is not rolling back and using the log to generate the (undo) update calls. *Partial rollback* refers to the ability to set up *savepoints* during the execution of a transaction and later in the transaction request the rolling back of the changes performed by the transaction since the establishment of a previous savepoint [1, 31]. This is to be contrasted with *total rollback* in which all updates of the transaction are undone and the transaction is terminated. Whether or not the savepoint concept is exposed at the application level is immaterial to us since this paper deals only with database recovery. A *nested rollback* is said to have taken place if a partial rollback were to be later followed by a total rollback or another partial rollback whose point of termination is an earlier point in the transaction than the point of termination of the first rollback. *Normal undo* refers to total or partial transaction rollback when the system is in normal operation. A normal undo may be caused by a transaction request to rollback or it may be system initiated because of deadlocks or errors (e.g., integrity constraint violations). *Restart undo* refers to transaction rollback during restart recovery after a system failure. To make partial or total rollback efficient and also to make debugging easier, all the log records written by a transaction are linked via the *PrevLSN* field of the log records in reverse chronological order. That is, the most recently written log record of the transaction would point to the previous most recent log record written by that transaction, if there is such a log record.[2] In many WAL-based systems, the updates performed during a rollback are logged using what are called *compensation log records* (*CLRs*) [15]. Whether a CLR's update is undone, should that CLR be encountered during a rollback, depends on the particular system. As we will see later, in ARIES, a CLR's update is never undone and hence CLRs are viewed as redo-only log records.

Page-oriented redo is said to occur if the log record whose update is being redone describes which page of the database was originally modified during normal processing and if the same page is modified during the redo processing. No internal descriptors of tables or indexes need to be accessed to redo the update. That is, no other page of the database needs to be examined. This is to be contrasted with *logical redo* which is required in System R, SQL/DS and AS/400 for indexes [21, 62]. In those systems, since index changes are not logged separately but are redone using the log records for the data pages, performing a redo requires accessing several descriptors and pages of the database. The index tree would have to be retraversed to determine the page(s) to be modified and, sometimes, the index page(s) modified because of this redo operation may be different from the index page(s) originally modified during normal processing. Being able to perform page-oriented redo allows the system to provide *recovery independence amongst objects*. That is, the recovery of one page's contents does not require accesses to any other

[2] The AS/400, Encompass and NonStop SQL do not explicitly link all the log records written by a transaction. This makes undo inefficient since a *sequential* backward scan of the log must be performed to retrieve all the desired log records of a transaction.

(data or catalog) pages of the database. As we will describe later, this makes media recovery very simple.

In a similar fashion, we can define *page-oriented undo* and *logical undo.* Being able to perform logical undos allows the system to provide higher levels of concurrency than what would be possible if the system were to be restricted only to page-oriented undos. This is because the former, with appropriate concurrency control protocols, would permit uncommitted updates of one transaction to be moved to a different page by another transaction. If one were restricted to only page-oriented undos, then the latter transaction would have had to wait for the former to commit. Page-oriented redo and page-oriented undo permit faster recovery since pages of the database other than the pages mentioned in the log records are not accessed. In the interest of efficiency, ARIES supports page-oriented redo and its supports, in the interest of high concurrency, logical undos. In [62], we introduce the ARIES/IM method for concurrency control and recovery in B^{+}-tree indexes and show the advantages of being able to perform logical undos by comparing ARIES/IM with other index methods.

1.2 Latches and Locks

Normally latches and locks are used to control access to shared information. Locking has been discussed to a great extent in the literature. Latches, on the other hand, have not been discussed that much. *Latches* are like semaphores. Usually, latches are used to guarantee physical consistency of data, while *locks* are used to assure logical consistency of data. We need to worry about physical consistency since we need to support a multiprocessor environment. Latches are usually held for a much shorter period than are locks. Also, the deadlock detector is not informed about latch waits. Latches are requested in such a manner so as to avoid deadlocks involving latches alone, or involving latches and locks.

Acquiring and releasing a latch is much cheaper than acquiring and releasing a lock. In the no-conflict case, the overhead amounts to 10s of instructions for the former versus 100s of instructions for the latter. Latches are cheaper because the *latch control information* is always in virtual memory in a fixed place, and direct addressability to the latch information is possible given the latch name. As the protocols presented later in this paper and those in [57, 62] show, each transaction holds at most two or three latches simultaneously. As a result, the *latch request blocks* can be permanently allocated to each transaction and initialized with transaction ID, etc. right at the start of that transaction. On the other hand, typically, storage for individual locks has to be acquired, formatted and released dynamically, causing more instructions to be executed to acquire and release locks. This is advisable because, in most systems, the number of lockable objects is many orders of magnitude greater than the number of latchable objects. Typically, all information relating to locks currently held or requested by all the transactions is stored in a single, central hash table. Addressability to a particular lock's information is gained by first hashing the lock name to get the address of the hash anchor and then, possibly, following a chain of pointers. Usually, in the process of trying to locate the *lock control block,* because multiple transactions may be simultaneously reading and modifying the contents of the lock table, one or more latches will be acquired and released—one latch on the hash anchor and, possibly, one on the specific lock's chain of holders and waiters.

Locks may be obtained in different *modes* such as S (Shared), X (eXclusive), IX (Intention eXclusive), IS (Intention Shared) and SIX (Shared Intention eXclusive), and at different *granularities* such as record (tuple), table (relation), and file (tablespace) [32]. The S and X locks are the most common ones. S provides the read privilege and X provides the read and write privileges. Locks on a given object can be held simultaneously by different transactions only if those locks' modes are *compatible*. The compatibility relationships amongst the above modes of locking are shown in Figure 2. A check mark ('√') indicates that the corresponding modes are compatible. With *hierarchical locking*, the intention locks (IX, IS, and SIX) are generally obtained on the higher levels of the hierarchy (e.g., table), and the S and X locks are obtained on the lower levels (e.g., record). The nonintention mode locks (S and X), when obtained on an object at a certain level of the hierarchy, *implicitly* grant locks of the corresponding mode on the lower level objects of that higher level object. The intention mode locks, on the other hand, only give the privilege of requesting the corresponding intention or nonintention mode locks on the lower level objects. For example, SIX on a table implicitly grants S on all the records of that table, and it allows X to be requested *explicitly* on the records. Additional, semantically rich lock modes have been defined in the literature [2, 38, 45, 55] and ARIES can accommodate them.

Lock requests may be made with the conditional or the unconditional option. A *conditional* request means that the requestor is not willing to wait if, when the request is processed, the lock is not grantable immediately. An *unconditional* request means that the requestor is willing to wait until the lock becomes grantable. Locks may be held for different durations. An unconditional request for an *instant duration* lock means that the lock is not to be actually granted, but the lock manager has to delay returning the lock call with the success status until the lock becomes grantable. *Manual duration* locks are released some time after they are acquired and, typically, long before transaction termination. *Commit duration* locks are released only when the transaction terminates, i.e., after commit or rollback is completed. The above discussions concerning conditional requests, different modes, and durations, except for commit duration, apply to latches also.

1.3 Fine-Granularity Locking

Fine-granularity (e.g., record) locking has been supported by nonrelational database systems (e.g., IMS [53, 76, 80]) for a long time. Surprisingly, only a few of the commercially available relational systems provide fine-granularity locking, even though IBM's System R [32], S/38 [99] and SQL/DS [5], and Tandem's Encompass [37] supported record and/or key locking from the beginning.[3] Although many interesting problems relating to providing

[3] Encompass and S/38 had only X locks for records and no locks were acquired *automatically* by these systems for reads.

Fig. 2. Lock mode compatability matrix

	S	X	IS	IX	SIX
S	√		√		
X					
IS	√		√	√	√
IX			√	√	
SIX			√		

fine-granularity locking in the context of WAL remain to be solved, the research community has not been paying enough attention to this area [3, 75, 88]. Some of the System R solutions worked only because of the use of the shadow page recovery technique in combination with locking (see Section 10). Supporting fine-granularity locking and variable length records in a flexible fashion requires addressing some interesting storage management issues which have never really been discussed in the database literature. Unfortunately, some of the interesting techniques that were developed for System R and which are now part of SQL/DS did not get documented in the literature. At the expense of making this paper long, we will be discussing here some of those problems and their solutions.

As supporting high concurrency gains importance (see [79] for the description of an application requiring very high concurrency) and as object-oriented systems gain in popularity, it becomes necessary to invent concurrency control and recovery methods that take advantage of the semantics of the operations on the data [2, 26, 38, 88, 89], and that support fine-granularity locking efficiently. Object-oriented systems may tend to encourage users to define a large number of small objects and users may expect object instances to be the appropriate granularity of locking. In the object-oriented logical view of the database, the concept of a page, with its physical orientation as the container of objects, becomes unnatural to think about as the unit of locking during object accesses and modifications. Also, object-oriented system users may tend to have many terminal interactions during the course of a transaction, thereby increasing the lock hold times. If the unit of locking were to be a page, lock wait times and deadlock possibilities will be aggravated. Other discussions concerning transaction management in an object-oriented environment can be found in [22, 29].

As more and more customers adopt relational systems for production applications, it becomes ever more important to handle *hot-spots* [28, 34, 68, 77, 79, 83] and storage management without requiring too much tuning by the system users or administrators. Since relational systems have been welcomed to a great extent because of their ease of use, it is important that we pay greater attention to this area than what has been done in the context of the nonrelational systems. Apart from the need for high concurrency for user data, the ease with which online data definition operations can be performed in relational systems by even ordinary users requires the support for high concurrency of access to, at least, the catalog data. Since a leaf page in an index typically describes data in hundreds of data pages, page-level locking of index data is just not acceptable. A flexible recovery method that allows the support of high levels of concurrency during index accesses is needed.

The above facts argue for supporting semantically rich modes of locking such as increment/decrement which allow multiple transactions to concurrently modify even the same piece of data. In funds-transfer applications, increment and decrement operations are frequently performed on the branch and teller balances by numerous transactions. If those transactions are forced to use only X locks, then they will be serialized, even though their operations commute.

1.4 Buffer Management

The buffer manager (BM) is the component of the transaction system that manages the buffer pool and does I/Os to read/write pages from/to the nonvolatile storage version of the database. The *fix* primitive of the BM may be used to request the buffer address of a logical page in the database. If the requested page is not in the buffer pool, BM allocates a buffer slot and reads the page in. There may be instances (e.g., during a B^+-tree page split, when the new page is allocated) where the current contents of a page on nonvolatile storage are not of interest. In such a case, the *fix_new* primitive may be used to make the BM allocate a *free* slot and return the address of that slot, if BM does not find the page in the buffer pool. The fix_new invoker will then format the page as desired. Once a page is fixed in the buffer pool, the corresponding buffer slot is not available for page replacement until the *unfix* primitive is issued by the data manipulative component. Actually, for each page, BM keeps a fix count which is incremented by one during every fix operation and which is decremented by one during every unfix operation. A page in the buffer pool is said to be *dirty* if the buffer version of the page has some updates which are not yet reflected in the nonvolatile storage version of the same page. The fix primitive is also used to communicate the intention to modify the page. Dirty pages can be written back to nonvolatile storage when no fix with the modification intention is held, thus allowing read accesses to the page while it is being written out. [96] discusses the role of BM in writing in the background, on a continuous basis, dirty pages to nonvolatile storage to reduce the amount of redo work that would be needed if a system failure were to occur and also to keep a certain percentage of the buffer pool pages in the nondirty state so that they may be replaced with other pages without synchronous write I/Os having to be performed at the time of replacement. While performing those writes, BM ensures that the WAL protocol is obeyed. As a consequence, BM may have to force the log up to the LSN of the dirty page before writing the page to nonvolatile storage. Given the large buffer pools that are common today, we would expect a force of this nature to be very rare and most log forces to occur because of transactions committing or entering the prepare state.

BM also implements the support for latching pages. To provide direct addressability to page latches and to reduce the storage associated with those latches, the latch on a logical page is actually the latch on the corresponding buffer slot. This means that a logical page can be latched only after it is fixed in the buffer pool and the latch has to be released before the page is unfixed. These are highly acceptable conditions. The latch control information is stored in the buffer control block (BCB) for the corresponding buffer slot. The BCB also contains the identity of the logical page, what the fix count is, the dirty status of the page, etc.

Buffer management policies differ among the many systems in existence (see Section 11, "Other WAL-Based Methods"). If a page modified by a transaction is allowed to be written to the permanent database on nonvolatile storage before that transaction commits, then the *steal* policy is said to be followed by the buffer manager (see [36] for such terminologies). Otherwise, a *no-steal* policy is said to be in effect. Steal implies that during normal or restart rollback, some undo work might have to be performed on the non-volatile storage version of the database. If a transaction is not allowed to commit until all pages modified by it are written to the permanent version of the database, then a *force* policy is said to be in effect. Otherwise, a *no-force* policy is said to be in effect. With a force policy, during restart recovery, no redo work will be necessary for committed transactions. *Deferred updating* is said to occur if, even in the virtual storage database buffers, the updates are not performed in-place when the transaction issues the corresponding database calls. The updates are kept in a pending list elsewhere and are performed in-place, using the pending list information, only after it is determined that the transaction is definitely committing. If the transaction needs to be rolled back, then the pending list is discarded or ignored. The deferred updating policy has implications on whether a transaction can "see" its own updates or not, and on whether partial rollbacks are possible or not.

For more discussions concerning buffer management, see [8, 15, 24, 96].

1.5 Organization

The rest of the paper is organized as follows. After stating our goals in Section 2 and giving an overview of the new recovery method ARIES in Section 3, we present, in Section 4, the important data structures used by ARIES during normal and restart recovery processing. Next, in Section 5, the protocols followed during normal processing are presented followed, in Section 6, by the description of the processing performed during restart recovery. The latter section also presents ways to exploit parallelism during recovery and methods for performing recovery selectively or postponing the recovery of some of the data. Then, in Section 7, algorithms are described for taking checkpoints during the different log passes of restart recovery to reduce the impact of failures during recovery. This is followed, in Section 8, by the description of how fuzzy image copying and media recovery are supported. Section 9 introduces the significant notion of *nested top actions* and presents a method for implementing them efficiently. Section 10 describes and critiques some of the existing recovery paradigms which originated in the context of the shadow page technique and System R. We discuss the problems caused by using those paradigms in the WAL context. Section 11 describes in detail the characteristics of many of the WAL-based recovery methods in use in different systems such as IMS, DB2, Encompass and NonStop SQL.

Section 12 outlines the many different properties of ARIES. We conclude by summarizing, in Section 13, the features of ARIES which provide flexibility and efficiency, and by describing the extensions and the current status of the implementations of ARIES.

Besides presenting a new recovery method, by way of motivation for our work, we also describe some previously unpublished aspects of recovery in System R. For comparison purposes, we also do a survey of the recovery methods used by other WAL-based systems and collect information appearing in several publications, many of which are not widely available. One of our aims in this paper is to show the intricate and unobvious interactions resulting from the different choices made for the recovery technique, the granularity of locking and the storage management scheme. One cannot make arbitrarily independent choices for these and still expect the combination to function together correctly and efficiently. This point needs to be emphasized as it is not always dealt with adequately in most papers and books on concurrency control and recovery. In this paper, we have tried to cover, as much as possible, all the interesting recovery-related problems that one encounters in building and operating an *industrial-strength* transaction processing system.

2. GOALS

This section lists the goals of our work and outlines the difficulties involved in designing a recovery method that supports the features that we aimed for. The goals relate to the metrics for comparison of recovery methods that we discussed earlier, in Section 1.1.

Simplicity. Concurrency and recovery are complex subjects to think about and program for, compared with other aspects of data management. The algorithms are bound to be error-prone, if they are complex. Hence, we strived for a simple, yet powerful and flexible, algorithm. Although this paper is long because of its comprehensive discussion of numerous problems that are mostly ignored in the literature, the main algorithm itself is quite simple. Hopefully, the overview presented in Section 3 gives the reader that feeling.

Operation logging. The recovery method had to permit operation logging (and value logging) so that semantically rich lock modes could be supported. This would let one transaction modify the same data that was modified earlier by another transaction which has not yet committed, when the two transactions' actions are semantically compatible (e.g., increment/decrement operations; see [2, 26, 45, 88]). As should be clear, recovery methods which always perform *value* or *state logging* (i.e., logging before-images and after-images of modified data), cannot support operation logging. This includes systems that do very physical—byte-oriented—logging of all changes to a page [6, 76, 81]. The difficulty in supporting operation logging is that we need to track precisely, using a concept like the LSN, the exact state of a page with respect to logged actions relating to that page. An undo or a redo of an update should not be performed without being sure that the original update is present or is not present, respectively. This also means that, if one or more transactions that had previously modified a page start rolling back, then we need to know precisely how the page has been affected during the rollbacks and how much of each of the rollbacks had been accomplished so far. This requires that updates performed during rollbacks also be logged via the so-called *compensation log records* (*CLRs*). The LSN concept lets us avoid attempting to redo an operation when the operation's effect is already present in the page. It also lets us avoid attempting to undo an operation when the operation's effect is not present in the page. Operation logging lets us perform, if found desirable, *logical logging*, which means that not everything that was changed on a page needs to be logged explicitly, thereby saving log space. For example, changes of control information, like the amount of free space on the page, need not be logged. The redo and the undo operations can be performed logically. For a good discussion of operation and value logging, see [88].

Flexible storage management. Efficient support for the storage and manipulation of varying length data is important. In contrast to systems like IMS, the intent here is to be able to avoid the need for off-line reorganization of the data to garbage collect any space that might have been freed up because of deletions and updates that caused data shrinkage. It is desirable that the recovery method and the concurrency control method be such that the logging and locking is *logical* in nature so that movements of the data within a page for garbage collection reasons do not cause the moved data to be locked or the movements to be logged. For an index, this also means that one transaction must be able to split a leaf page even if that page currently has some uncommitted data inserted by another transaction. This may lead to problems in performing page-oriented undos using the log; *logical undos* may be necessary. Further, we would like to be able to let a transaction that has freed up some space be able to use, if necessary, that space during its later insert activity [50]. System R, for example, does not permit this in data pages.

Partial rollbacks. It was essential that the new recovery method support the concept of savepoints and rollbacks to savepoints (i.e., partial rollbacks). This is crucial for handling, in a user-friendly fashion (i.e., without requiring a total rollback of the transaction), integrity constraint violations (see [1, 31]), and problems arising from using obsolete cached information (see [49]).

Flexible buffer management. The recovery method should make the least number of restrictive assumptions about the buffer management policies (*steal*, *force*, etc.) in effect. At the same time, the method must be able to take advantage of the characteristics of any specific policy that is in effect (e.g., with a force policy there is no need to perform any redos for committed transactions.) This flexibility could result in increased concurrency, decreased I/Os and efficient usage of buffer storage. Depending on the policies, the work that needs to be performed during restart recovery after a system failure or during media recovery may be more or less complex. Even with large main memories, it must be noted that a steal policy is still very desirable. This is because, with a no-steal policy, a page may never get written to nonvolatile storage if the page always contains *uncommitted* updates due to fine-granularity locking and overlapping transactions' updates to that page. The situation would be further aggravated if there are long-running transactions. Under those conditions, either the system would have to frequently reduce concurrency by quiescing all activities on the page (i.e., by locking all the objects on the page) and then writing the page to nonvolatile storage, or by doing nothing special and then paying a huge restart redo recovery cost if the system were to fail. Also, a no-steal policy incurs additional bookkeeping overhead to track whether a page contains any uncommitted updates. We believe that, given our goal of supporting semantically rich lock modes, partial rollbacks and varying length objects efficiently, in the general case, we need to perform undo logging and in-place updating. Hence, methods like the transaction workspace model of AIM [46] are not general enough for our purposes. Other problems relating to no-steal are discussed in Section 11 with reference to IMS Fast Path.

Recovery independence. It should be possible to image copy (archive dump), and perform media recovery or restart recovery at different granularities, rather than only at the entire database level. The recovery of one object should not force the concurrent or lock-step recovery of another object. Contrast this with what happens in the shadow page technique as implemented in System R, where index and space management information are recovered *lock-step* with user and catalog table (relation) data by starting from an internally consistent state of the *whole* database and redoing changes to all the related objects of the database simultaneously, as in normal processing. Recovery independence means that, during the restart recovery of some object, catalog information in the database cannot be accessed for descriptors of that object and its related objects, since that information itself may be undergoing recovery in parallel with the object being recovered and the two may be out of synchronization [14]. During restart recovery, it should be possible to do selective recovery and defer recovery of some objects to a later point in time to speed up restart and also to accommodate some offline devices. *Page-oriented recovery* means that even if one page in the database is corrupted because of a process failure or a media problem, it should be possible to recover that page alone. To be able to do this efficiently, we need to log every page's change individually, even if the object being updated spans multiple pages and the update affects more than one page. This, in conjunction with the writing of CLRs for updates performed during rollbacks, will make media recovery very simple (see Section 8). This will also permit image copying of different objects to be performed independently and at different frequencies.

Logical undo. This relates to the ability, during undo, to affect a page that is different from the one modified during forward processing, as is needed in the earlier-mentioned context of the split by one transaction of an index page containing uncommitted data of another transaction. Being able to perform logical undos allows higher levels of concurrency to be supported, especially in search structures [57, 59, 62]. If logging is not performed during rollback processing, logical undos would be very difficult to support, if we also desired recovery independence and page-oriented recovery. System R and SQL/DS support logical undos, but at the expense of recovery independence.

Parallelism and fast recovery. With multiprocessors becoming very common and greater data availability becoming increasingly important, the recovery method has to be able to exploit parallelism during the different stages of restart recovery and during media recovery. It is also important that the recovery method be such that recovery can be very fast, if in fact a *hot-standby* approach is going to be used (a la IBM's IMS/VS XRF [43] and Tandem's NonStop [4, 37]). This means that redo processing and, whenever possible, undo processing should be page-oriented (cf. always logical redos and undos in System R and SQL/DS for indexes and space management). It should also be possible to let the backup system start processing new transactions, even before the undo processing for the interrupted transactions completes. This is necessary because undo processing may take a long time if there were long update transactions.

Minimal overhead. Our goal is to have good performance both during normal and restart recovery processing. The overhead (log data volume, storage consumption, etc.) imposed by the recovery method in virtual and nonvolatile storages for accomplishing the above goals should be minimal. Contrast this with the space overhead caused by the shadow page technique. This goal also implied that we should minimize the number of pages that are modified (dirtied) during restart. The idea is to reduce the number of pages that have to be written back to nonvolatile storage and also to reduce CPU overhead. This rules out methods which, during restart recovery, first undo some committed changes that had already reached the nonvolatile storage before the failure and then redo them (see, e.g., [16, 21, 72, 78, 88]). It also rules out methods in which updates that are not present in a page on nonvolatile storage are undone unnecessarily (see, e.g., [41, 71, 88]). The method should not cause deadlocks involving transactions that are already rolling back. Further, the writing of CLRs should not result in an unbounded number of log records having to be written for a transaction because of the undoing of CLRs, if there were nested rollbacks or repeated system failures during rollbacks. It should also be possible to take checkpoints and image copies without quiescing significant activities in the system. The impact of these operations on other activities should be minimal. To contrast, checkpointing and image copying in System R cause major perturbations in the rest of the system [31].

As the reader will have realized by now, some of these goals are contradictory. Based on our knowledge of different developers' existing systems' features, experiences with IBM's existing transaction systems and contacts with customers, we made the necessary tradeoffs. We were keen on learning from the past successes and mistakes involving many prototypes and products.

3. OVERVIEW OF ARIES

The aim of this section is to provide a brief overview of the new recovery method ARIES, which satisfies quite reasonably the goals that we set forth in Section 2. Issues like deferred and selective restart, parallelism during restart recovery, and so on will be discussed in the later sections of the paper.

ARIES guarantees the atomicity and durability properties of transactions in the fact of process, transaction, system and media failures. For this purpose, ARIES keeps track of the changes made to the database by using a log and it does write-ahead logging (WAL). Besides logging, on a per-affected-page basis, update activities performed during forward processing of transactions, ARIES also logs, typically using compensation log records (CLRs), updates performed during partial or total rollbacks of transactions during both normal and restart processing. Figure 3 gives an example of a partial rollback in which a transaction, after performing three updates, rolls back two of them and then starts going forward again. Because of the undo of the two updates, two CLRs are written. In ARIES, CLRs have the property that they are redo-only log records. By appropriate chaining of the CLRs to log records written during forward processing, a bounded amount of logging is ensured during rollbacks, even in the face of repeated failures during restart or of nested rollbacks. This is to be contrasted with what happens in IMS, which may undo the same non-CLR multiple times, and in AS/400, DB2 and NonStop SQL, which, besides undoing the same non-CLR multiple times, may also undo CLRs one or more times (see Figure 4). These have caused severe problems in real-life customer situations.

In ARIES, as Figure 5 shows, when the undo of a log record causes a CLR to be written, the CLR, besides containing a description of the compensating action for redo purposes, is made to contain the *UndoNxtLSN* pointer which points to the *predecessor* of the just undone log record. The predecessor information is readily available since every log record, including a CLR, contains the *PrevLSN* pointer which points to the most recent preceding log record written by the same transaction. The UndoNxtLSN pointer allows us to determine precisely how much of the transaction has not been undone so far. In Figure 5, log record 3′, which is the CLR for log record 3, points to log record 2, which is the predecessor of log record 3. Thus, during rollback, the UndoNxtLSN field of the most recently written CLR keeps track of the progress of rollback. It tells the system from where to continue the rollback of the transaction, if a system failure were to interrupt the completion of the rollback or if a nested rollback were to be performed. It lets the system bypass those log records that had already been undone. Since CLRs are available to describe what actions are actually performed during the undo of an original action, the undo action need not be, in terms of which page(s) is affected, the exact inverse of the original action. That is, logical undo which allows very high concurrency to be supported is made possible. For example,

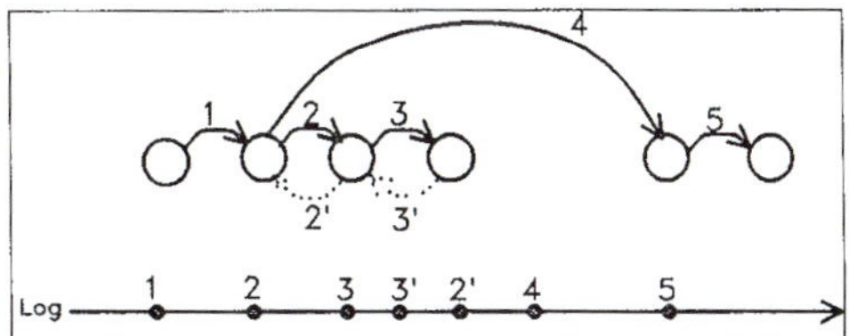

Fig. 3. Partial rollback example.

After performing 3 actions, the transaction performs a partial rollback by undoing actions 3 and 2, writing the compensation log records 3′ and 2′, and then starts going forward again and performs actions 4 and 5

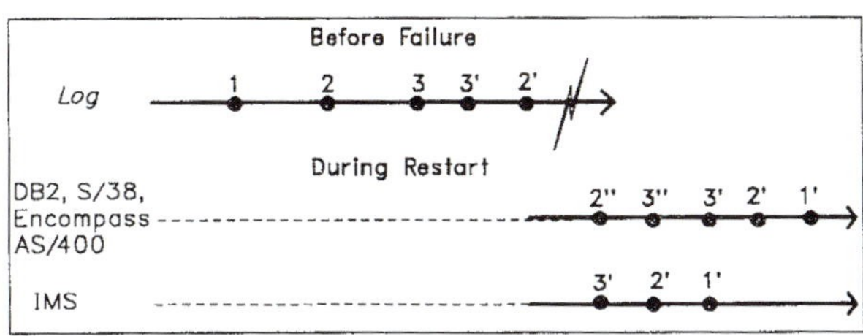

I′ is the CLR for I and I″ is the CLR for I′

Fig. 4 Problem of compensating compensations or duplicate compensations, or both.

a key inserted on page 10 of a B^+-tree by one transaction may be moved to page 20 by another transaction before the key insertion is committed. Later, if the first transaction were to roll back, then the key will be located on page 20 by retraversing the tree and deleted from there. A CLR will be written to describe the key deletion on page 20. This permits page-oriented redo which is very efficient. [59, 62] describe ARIES/LHS and ARIES/IM which exploit this logical undo feature.

ARIES uses a single LSN on each page to track the page's state. Whenever a page is updated and a log record is written, the LSN of the log record is placed in the *page_LSN* field of the updated page. This tagging of the page with the LSN allows ARIES to precisely track, for restart- and media-recovery purposes, the state of the page with respect to logged updates for that page. It allows ARIES to support novel lock modes, using which, before an update performed on a record's field by one transaction is committed, another transaction may be permitted to modify the same data for specified operations.

Periodically during normal processing, ARIES takes checkpoints. The checkpoint log records identify the transactions that are active, their states, and the LSNs of their most recently written log records, and also the modified data (dirty data) that is in the buffer pool. The latter information is needed to determine from where the redo pass of restart recovery should begin its processing.

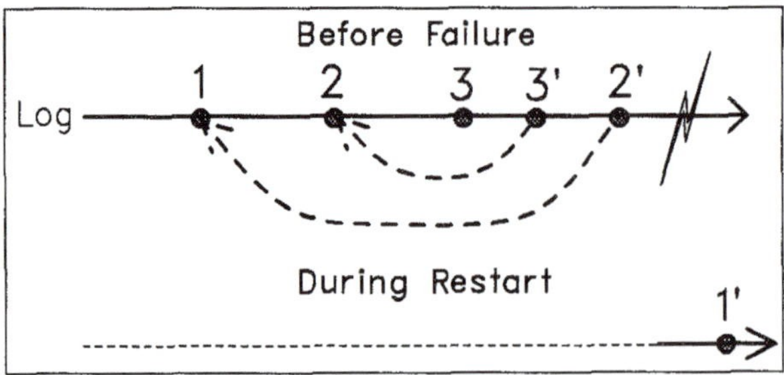

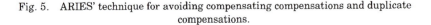

I' is the Compensation Log Record for I
I' points to the predecessor, if any, of I

Fig. 5. ARIES' technique for avoiding compensating compensations and duplicate compensations.

During restart recovery (see Figure 6), ARIES first scans the log, starting from the first record of the last checkpoint, up to the end of the log. During this *analysis pass*, information about dirty pages and transactions that were in progress at the time of the checkpoint is brought up to date as of the end of the log. The analysis pass uses the dirty pages information to determine the starting point (*RedoLSN*) for the log scan of the immediately following redo pass. The analysis pass also determines the list of transactions that are to be rolled back in the undo pass. For each in-progress transaction, the LSN of the most recently written log record will also be determined. Then, during the *redo pass*, ARIES *repeats history*, with respect to those updates logged on stable storage, but whose effects on the database pages did not get reflected on nonvolatile storage before the failure of the system. This is done for the updates of all transactions, including the updates of those transactions that had neither committed nor reached the in-doubt state of two-phase commit by the time of the system failure (i.e., even the missing updates of the so-called *loser* transactions are redone). This essentially reestablishes the state of the database as of the time of the system failure. A log record's update is redone if the affected page's page_LSN is less than the log record's LSN. No logging is performed when updates are redone. The redo pass obtains the locks needed to protect the uncommitted updates of those distributed transactions that will remain in the in-doubt (prepared) state [63, 64] at the end of restart recovery.

The next log pass is the *undo pass* during which all loser transactions' updates are rolled back, in reverse chronological order, in a single sweep of the log. This is done by continually taking the maximum of the LSNs of the next log record to be processed for each of the yet-to-be-completely-undone loser transactions, until no transaction remains to be undone. Unlike during the redo pass, performing undos is not a conditional operation during the undo pass (and during normal undo). That is, ARIES does not compare the page_LSN of the affected page to the LSN of the log record to decide

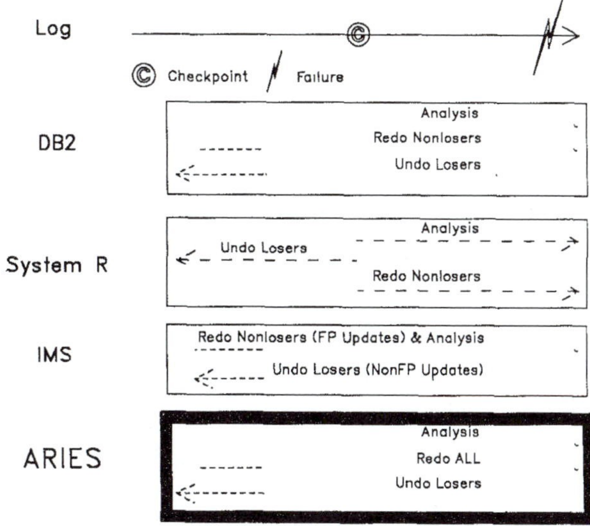

Fig. 6. Restart processing in different methods.

whether or not to undo the update. When a non-CLR is encountered for a transaction during the undo pass, if it is an undo-redo or undo-only log record, then its update is undone. In any case, the next record to process for that transaction is determined by looking at the PrevLSN of that non-CLR. Since CLRs are never undone (i.e., CLRs are not compensated—see Figure 5), when a CLR is encountered during undo, it is used just to determine the next log record to process by looking at the UndoNxtLSN field of the CLR.

For those transactions which were already rolling back at the time of the system failure, ARIES will rollback only those actions that had not already been undone. This is possible since history is repeated for such transactions and since the last CLR written for each transaction points (directly or indirectly) to the next non-CLR record that is to be undone. The net result is that, if only page-oriented undos are involved or logical undos generate only CLRs, then, for rolled back transactions, the number of CLRs written will be exactly equal to the number of undoable) log records written during forward processing of those transactions. This will be the case even if there are repeated failures during restart or if there are nested rollbacks.

4. DATA STRUCTURES

This section describes the major data structures that are used by ARIES.

4.1 Log Records

Below, we describe the important fields that may be present in different types of log records.

LSN. Address of the first byte of the log record in the ever-growing log address space. This is a monotonically increasing value. This is shown here as a field only to make it easier to describe ARIES. The LSN need not actually be stored in the record.

Type. Indicates whether this is a compensation record ('compensation'), a regular update record ('update'), a commit protocol-related record (e.g., 'prepare'), or a nontransaction-related record (e.g., 'OSfile_return').

TransID. Identifier of the transaction, if any, that wrote the log record.

PrevLSN. LSN of the preceding log record written by the same transaction. This field has a value of zero in nontransaction-related records and in the first log record of a transaction, thus avoiding the need for an explicit begin transaction log record.

PageID. Present only in records of type 'update' or 'compensation'. The identifier of the page to which the updates of this record were applied. This PageID will normally consist of two parts: an objectID (e.g., tablespaceID), and a page number within that object. ARIES can deal with a log record that contains updates for multiple pages. For ease of exposition, we assume that only one page is involved.

UndoNxtLSN. Present only in CLRs. It is the LSN of the next log record of this transaction that is to be processed during rollback. That is, UndoNxtLSN is the value of PrevLSN of the log record that the current log record is compensating. If there are no more log records to be undone, then this field contains a zero.

Data. This is the redo and/or undo data that describes the update that was performed. CLRs contain only redo information since they are never undone. Updates can be logged in a logical fashion. Changes to some fields (e.g., amount of free space) of that page need not be logged since they can be easily derived. The undo information and the redo information for the entire object need not be logged. It suffices if the changed fields alone are logged. For increment or decrement types of operations, before and after-images of the field are not needed. Information about the type of operation and the decrement or increment amount is enough. The information here would also be used to determine the appropriate action routine to be used to perform the redo and/or undo of this log record.

4.2 Page Structure

One of the fields in every page of the database is the *page_LSN* field. It contains the LSN of the log record that describes the latest update to the page. This record may be a regular update record or a CLR. ARIES expects the buffer manager to enforce the WAL protocol. Except for this, ARIES does not place any restrictions on the buffer page replacement policy. The steal buffer management policy may be used. In-place updating is performed on nonvolatile storage. Updates are applied immediately and directly to the buffer version of the page containing the object. That is, no deferred updating as in INGRES [86] is performed. If it is found desirable, deferred updating and, consequently, deferred logging can be implemented. ARIES is flexible enough not to preclude those policies from being implemented.

4.3 Transaction Table

A table called the *transaction table* is used during restart recovery to track the state of active transactions. The table is initialized during the analysis pass from the most recent checkpoint's record(s) and is modified during the analysis of the log records written after the beginning of that checkpoint. During the undo pass, the entries of the table are also modified. If a checkpoint is taken during restart recovery, then the contents of the table will be included in the checkpoint record(s). The same table is also used during normal processing by the transaction manager. A description of the important fields of the transaction table follows:

TransID. Transaction ID.

State. Commit state of the transaction: prepared ('P'—also called in-doubt) or unprepared ('U').

LastLSN. The LSN of the latest log record written by the transaction.

UndoNxtLSN. The LSN of the next record to be processed during rollback. If the most recent log record written or seen for this transaction is an undoable non-CLR log record, then this field's value will be set to LastLSN. If that most recent log record is a CLR, then this field's value is set to the UndoNxtLSN value from that CLR.

4.4 Dirty_Pages Table

A table called the *dirty_pages table* is used to represent information about dirty buffer pages during normal processing. This table is also used during restart recovery. The actual implementation of this table may be done using hashing or via the deferred-writes queue mechanism of [96]. Each entry in the table consists of two fields: PageID and *RecLSN* (recovery LSN). During normal processing, when a nondirty page is being fixed in the buffers with the intention to modify, the buffer manager records in the *buffer pool* (BP) dirty_pages table, as RecLSN, the current end-of-log LSN, which will be the LSN of the next log record to be written. The value of RecLSN indicates from what point in the log there may be updates which are, possibly, not yet in the nonvolatile storage version of the page. Whenever pages are written back to nonvolatile storage, the corresponding entries in the BP dirty_pages table are removed. The contents of this table are included in the checkpoint record(s) that is written during normal processing. The *restart* dirty_pages table is initialized from the latest checkpoint's record(s) and is modified during the analysis of the other records during the analysis pass. The minimum RecLSN value in the table gives the starting point for the redo pass during restart recovery.

5. NORMAL PROCESSING

This section discusses the actions that are performed as part of normal transaction processing. Section 6 discusses the actions that are performed as part of recovering from a system failure.

5.1 Updates

During normal processing, transactions may be in forward processing, partial rollback or total rollback. The rollbacks may be system- or application-initiated. The causes of rollbacks may be deadlocks, error conditions, integrity constraint violations, unexpected database state, etc.

If the granularity of locking is a record, then, when an update is to be performed on a record in a page, after the record is locked, that page is fixed in the buffer and latched in the X mode, the update is performed, a log record is appended to the log, the LSN of the log record is placed in the page_LSN field of the page and in the transaction table, and the page is unlatched and unfixed. The page latch is held during the call to the logger. This is done to ensure that the order of logging of updates of a page is the same as the order in which those updates are performed on the page. This is very important if some of the redo information is going to be logged physically (e.g., the amount of free space in the page) and repetition of history has to be guaranteed for the physical redo to work correctly. The page latch must be held during read and update operations to ensure physical consistency of the page contents. This is necessary because inserters and updaters of records might move records around within a page to do garbage collection. When such garbage collection is going on, no other transaction should be allowed to look at the page since they might get confused. Readers of pages latch in the S mode and modifiers latch in the X mode.

The data page latch is not held while any necessary index operations are performed. At most two page latches are held simultaneously (also see [57, 62]). This means that two transactions, T1 and T2, that are modifying different pieces of data may modify a particular data page in one order (T1, T2) and a particular index page in another order (T2, T1).[4] This scenario is impossible in System R and SQL/DS since in those systems, locks, instead of latches are used for providing physical consistency. Typically, all the (physical) page locks are released only at the end of the RSS (data manager) call. A single RSS call deals with modifying the data and all relevant indexes. This may involve waiting for many I/Os and locks. This means that deadlocks involving (physical) page locks alone or (physical) page locks and

[4] The situation gets very complicated if operations like increment/decrement are supported with high concurrency lock modes and indexes are allowed to be defined on fields on which such operations are supported. We are currently studying those situations.

(logical) record/key locks are possible. They have been a major problem in System R and SQL/DS.

Figure 7 depicts a situation at the time of a system failure which followed the commit of two transactions. The dotted lines show how up to date the states of pages P1 and P2 are on nonvolatile storage with respect to logged updates of those pages. During restart recovery, it must be realized that the most recent log record written for P1, which was written by a transaction which later committed, needs to be redone, and that there is nothing to be redone for P2. This situation points to the need for having the LSN to relate the state of a page on nonvolatile storage to a particular position in the log and the need for knowing where restart redo pass should begin by noting some information in the checkpoint record (see Section 5.4). For the example scenario, the restart redo log scan should begin at least from the log record representing the most recent update of P1 by T2, since that update needs to be redone.

It is not assumed that a single log record can always accommodate all the information needed to redo or undo the update operation. There may be instances when more than one record needs to be written for this purpose. For example, one record may be written with the undo information and another one with the redo information. In such cases, (1) the undo-only log record should be written before the redo-only log record is written, and (2) it is the LSN of the *redo-only log record* that should be placed in the page_LSN field. The first condition is enforced to make sure that we do not have a situation in which the redo-only record and not the undo-only record gets written to stable storage before a failure, and that during restart recovery, the redo of that redo-only log record is performed (because of the repeating history feature) only to realize later that there isn't an undo-only record to undo the effect of that operation. Given that the undo-only record is written before the redo-only record, the second condition ensures that we do not have a situation in which even though the page in nonvolatile storage already contains the update of the redo-only record, that same update gets redone unnecessarily during restart recovery because the page contained the LSN of the undo-only record instead of that of the redo-only record. This unnecessary redo could cause integrity problems if operation logging is being performed.

There may be some log records written during forward processing that cannot or should not be undone (prepare, free space inventory update, etc. records). These are identified as *redo-only* log records. See Section 10.3 for a discussion of this kind of situation for free space inventory updates.

Sometimes, the identity of the (data) record to be modified or read may not be known before a (data) page is examined. For example, during an insert, the record ID is not determined until the page is examined to find an empty slot. In such cases, the record lock must be obtained after the page is latched. To avoid waiting for a lock while holding a latch, which could lead to an undetected deadlock, the lock is requested *conditionally*, and if it is not granted, then the latch is released and the lock is requested *unconditionally*. Once the unconditionally requested lock is granted, the page is latched again, and any previously verified conditions are rechecked. This rechecking is

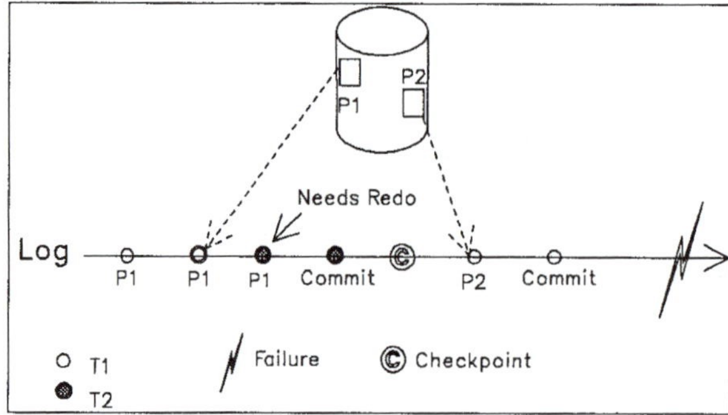

Fig. 7. Database state as a failure.

required because, after the page was unlatched, the conditions could have changed. The page_LSN value at the time of unlatching could be remembered to detect quickly, on relatching, if any changes could have possibly occurred. If the conditions are still found to be satisfied for performing the update, it is performed as described above. Otherwise, corrective actions are taken. If the conditionally requested lock is granted immediately, then the update can proceed as before.

If the granularity of locking is a page or something coarser than a page, then there is no need to latch the page since the lock on the page will be sufficient to isolate the executing transaction. Except for this change, the actions taken are the same as in the record-locking case. But, if the system is to support unlocked or *dirty* reads, then, even with page locking, a transaction that is updating a page should be made to hold the X latch on the page so that readers who are not acquiring locks are assured physical consistency if they hold an S latch while reading the page. Unlocked reads may also be performed by the image copy utility in the interest of causing the least amount of interference to normal transaction processing.

Applicability of ARIES is not restricted to only those systems in which locking is used as the concurrency control mechanism. Even other concurrency control schemes that are similar to locking, like the ones in [2], could be used with ARIES.

5.2 Total or Partial Rollbacks

To provide flexibility in limiting the extent of transaction rollbacks, the notion of a *savepoint* is supported [1, 31]. At any point during the execution of a transaction, a savepoint can be established. Any number of savepoints could be outstanding at a point in time. Typically, in a system like DB2, a savepoint is established before every SQL data manipulation command that might perform updates to the data. This is needed to support SQL statement-level atomicity. After executing for a while, the transaction or the system can request the undoing of all the updates performed after the establishment of a still outstanding savepoint. After such a partial rollback, the transaction can continue execution and start going forward again (see Figure 3). A particular savepoint is no longer outstanding if a rollback has been performed to that savepoint or to a preceding one. When a savepoint is established, the LSN of the latest log record written by the transaction, called *SaveLSN*, is remembered in virtual storage. If the savepoint is being established at the beginning of the transaction (i.e., when it has not yet written a log record) SaveLSN is set to zero. When the transaction desires to roll back to a savepoint, it supplies the remembered SaveLSN. If the savepoint concept were to be exposed at the user level, then we would expect the system not to expose the SaveLSNs to the user but use some symbolic values or sequence numbers and do the mapping to LSNs internally, as is done in IMS [42] and INGRES [18].

Figure 8 describes the routine *ROLLBACK* which is used for rolling back to a savepoint. The input to the routine is the SaveLSN and the TransID. No locks are acquired during rollback, even though a latch is acquired during undo activity on a page. Since we have always ensured that latches do not get involved in deadlocks, a rolling back transaction cannot get involved in a deadlock, as in System R and R* [31, 64] and in the algorithms of [100]. During the rollback, the log records are undone in reverse chronological order and, for each log record that is undone, a CLR is written. For ease of exposition, assume that all the information about the undo action will fit in a single CLR. It is easy to extend ARIES to the case where multiple CLRs need to be written. It is possible that, when a logical undo is performed, some non-CLRs are sometimes written, as described in [59, 62]. As mentioned before, when a CLR is written, its UndoNxtLSN field is made to contain the PrevLSN value in the log record whose undo caused this CLR to be written. Since CLRs will never be undone, they don't have to contain undo information (e.g., before-images). Redo-only log records are ignored during rollback. When a non-CLR is encountered, after it is processed, the next record to process is determined by looking up its PrevLSN field. When a CLR is encountered during rollback, the UndoNxtLSN field of that record is looked up to determine the next log record to be processed. Thus, the UndoNxtLSN pointer helps us skip over already undone log records. This means that if a nested rollback were to occur, then, because of the UndoNxtLSN in CLRs, during the second rollback none of the log records that were undone during the first rollback would be processed again. Even though Figures 4, 5, and 13 describe partial rollback scenarios in conjunction with restart undos in the various recovery methods, it should be easy to see how nested rollbacks are handled efficiently by ARIES.

Being able to describe, via CLRs, the actions performed during undo gives us the flexibility of not having to force the undo actions to be the exact inverses of the original actions. In particular, the undo action could affect a page which was not involved in the original action. Such logical undo situations are possible in, for example, index management [62] and space management (see Section 10.3).

ARIES' guarantee of a bounded amount of logging during undo allows us to deal safely with small computer systems situations in which a circular online

```
ROLLBACK(SaveLSN,TransID);
UndoNxt := Trans_Table[TransID].UndoNxtLSN;                   /* addr of 1st record to undo    */
WHILE SaveLSN < UndoNxt DO;                              /* loop thru all relevant records      */
  LogRec := Log_Read(UndoNxt);                           /* read record to be processed         */
  SELECT (LogRec.Type)
    WHEN('update') DO;
      IF LogRec is undoable THEN DO;
        Page := fix&latch(LogRec.PageID,'X');
        Undo_Update(Page,LogRec);
        Log_Write('compensation',LogRec.TransID,Trans_Table[TransID].LastLSN,
                LogRec.PageID,LogRec.PrevLSN, ...,LgLSN,Data);                /* write CLR */
        Page.LSN := LgLSN;
        Trans_Table[TransID].LastLSN := LgLSN;
        unfix&unlatch(Page);
      END;
      UndoNxt := LogRec.PrevLSN;
    END; /* WHEN('update') */
    WHEN('compensation')  UndoNxt := LogRec.UndoNxtLSN;          /* a CLR - nothing to undo */
    OTHERWISE  UndoNxt := LogRec.PrevLSN              /* skip record and go to previous one */
  END; /* SELECT */
  Trans_Table[TransID].UndoNxtLSN := UndoNxt;
END;   /* WHILE  */
RETURN;
```

Fig. 8. Pseudocode for rollback.

log might be used and log space is at a premium. Knowing the bound, we can keep in reserve enough log space to be able to roll back all currently running transactions under critical conditions (e.g., log space shortage). The implementation of ARIES in the OS/2 Extended Edition Database Manager takes advantage of this.

When a transaction rolls back, the locks obtained after the establishment of the savepoint which is the target of the rollback may be released after the partial or total rollback is completed. In fact, systems like DB2 do not and cannot release any of the locks after a partial rollback because, after such a lock release, a later rollback may still cause the same updates to be undone again, thereby causing data inconsistencies. System R does release locks after a partial rollback completes. But, because ARIES never undoes CLRs nor ever undoes a particular non-CLR more than once, because of the chaining of the CLRs using the UndoNxtLSN field, during a (partial) rollback, when the transaction's very first update to a particular object is undone and a CLR is written for it, the system can release the lock on that object. This makes it possible to consider resolving deadlocks using partial rollbacks rather than always resorting to total rollbacks.

5.3 Transaction Termination

Assume that some form of two-phase commit protocol (e.g., Presumed Abort or Presumed Commit (see [63, 64])) is used to terminate transactions and that the *prepare* record which is *synchronously* written to the log as part of the protocol includes the list of update-type locks (IX, X, SIX, etc.) held by the transaction. The logging of the locks is done to ensure that if a system failure were to occur after a transaction enters the in-doubt state, then those locks could be reacquired, during restart recovery, to protect the uncommitted updates of the in-doubt transaction.[5] When the prepare record is written, the read locks (e.g., S and IS) could be released, if no new locks would be acquired later as part of getting into the prepare state in some other part of the distributed transaction (at the same site or a different site). To deal with actions (such as the dropping of objects) which may cause files to be erased, for the sake of avoiding the logging of such objects' complete contents, we postpone performing actions like erasing files until we are sure that the transaction is definitely committing [19]. We need to log these *pending actions* in the prepare record.

Once a transaction enters the in-doubt state, it is committed by writing an *end* record and releasing its locks. Once the end record is written, if there are any pending actions, they they must be performed. For each pending action which involves erasing or returning a file to the operating system, we write an *OSfile_return* redo-only log record. For ease of exposition, we assume that this log record is not associated with any particular transaction and that this action does not take place when a checkpoint is in progress.

[5] Another possibility is not to log the locks, but to regenerate the lock names during restart recovery by examining all the log records written by the in-doubt transaction—see Sections 6.1 and 6 4, and item 18 (Section 12) for further ramifications of this approach

A transaction in the *in-doubt* state is rolled back by writing a *rollback* record, rolling back the transaction to its beginning, discarding the pending actions list, releasing its locks, and then writing the end record. Whether or not the rollback and end records are *synchronously* written to stable storage will depend on the type of two-phase commit protocol used. Also, the writing of the prepare record may be avoided if the transaction is not a distributed one or is read-only.

5.4 Checkpoints

Periodically, checkpoints are taken to reduce the amount of work that needs to be performed during restart recovery. The work may relate to the extent of the log that needs to be examined, the number of data pages that have to be read from nonvolatile storage, etc. Checkpoints can be taken asynchronously (i.e., while transaction processing, including updates, is going on). Such a *fuzzy checkpoint* is initiated by writing a *begin_chkpt* record. Then the *end_chkpt* record is constructed by including in it the contents of the normal transaction table, the BP dirty_pages table, and any file mapping information for the objects (like tablespace, indexspace, etc.) that are "open" (i.e., for which BP dirty_pages table has entries). Only for simplicity of exposition, we assume that all the information can be accommodated in a single end_chkpt record. It is easy to deal with the case where multiple records are needed to log this information. Once the end_chkpt record is constructed, it is written to the log. Once that record reaches stable storage, the LSN of the begin_chkpt record is stored in the *master record* which is in a well-known place on stable storage. If a failure were to occur before the end_chkpt record migrates to stable storage, but after the begin_chkpt record migrates to stable storage, then that checkpoint is considered an *incomplete checkpoint*. Between the *begin_chkpt* and *end_chkpt* log records, transactions might have written other log records. If one or more transactions are likely to remain in the *in-doubt* state for a long time because of prolonged loss of contact with the commit coordinator, then it is a good idea to include in the end_chkpt record information about the update-type locks (e.g., X, IX and SIX) held by those transactions. This way, if a failure were to occur, then, during restart recovery, those locks could be reacquired without having to access the prepare records of those transactions.

Since latches may need to be acquired to read the dirty_pages table correctly while gathering the needed information, it is a good idea to gather the information a little at a time to reduce contention on the tables. For example, if the dirty_pages table has 1000 rows, during each latch acquisition 100 entries can be examined. If the already examined entries change before the end of the checkpoint, the recovery algorithms remain correct (see Figure 10). This is because, in computing the restart redo point, besides taking into account the minimum of the RecLSNs of the dirty pages included in the end_chkpt record, ARIES also takes into account the log records that were written by transactions since the beginning of the checkpoint. This is important because the effect of some of the updates that were performed since the initiation of the checkpoint might not be reflected in the dirty page list that is recorded as part of the checkpoint.

ARIES does not require that any dirty pages be forced to nonvolatile storage during a checkpoint. The assumption is that the buffer manager is, on a continuous basis, writing out dirty pages in the background using system processes. The buffer manager can batch the writes and write multiple pages in one I/O operation. [96] gives details about how DB2 manages its buffer pools in this fashion. Even if there are some hot-spot pages which are frequently modified, the buffer manager has to ensure that those pages are written to nonvolatile storage reasonably often to reduce restart redo work, just in case a system failure were to occur. To avoid the prevention of updates to such hot-spot pages during an I/O operation, the buffer manager could make a copy of each of those pages and perform the I/O from the copy. This minimizes the data unavailability time for writes.

6. RESTART PROCESSING

When the transaction system restarts after a failure, recovery needs to be performed to bring the data to a consistent state and ensure the atomicity and durability properties of transactions. Figure 9 describes the *RESTART* routine that gets invoked at the beginning of the restart of a failed system. The input to this routine is the LSN of the master record which contains the pointer to the begin_chkpt record of the last complete checkpoint taken before site failure or shutdown. This routine invokes the routines for the analysis pass, the redo pass and the undo pass, in that order. The buffer pool dirty_pages table is updated appropriately. At the end of restart recovery, a checkpoint is taken.

For high availability, the duration of restart processing must be as short as possible. One way of accomplishing this is by exploiting parallelism during the redo and undo passes. Only if parallelism is going to be employed is it necessary to latch pages before they are modified during restart recovery. Ideas for improving data availability by allowing new transaction processing during recovery are explored in [60].

6.1 Analysis Pass

The first pass of the log that is made during restart recovery is the *analysis pass*. Figure 10 describes the *RESTART_ANALYSIS* routine that implements the analysis pass actions. The input to this routine is the LSN of the *master* record. The outputs of this routine are the transaction table, which contains the list of transactions which were in the *in-doubt* or unprepared state at the time of system failure or shutdown; the dirty_pages table, which contains the list of pages that were potentially dirty in the buffers when the system failed or was shut down; and the *RedoLSN*, which is the location on the log from which the redo pass must start processing the log. The only log records that may be written by this routine are end records for transactions that had totally rolled back before system failure, but for whom end records are missing.

```
RESTART(Master_Addr);
Restart_Analysis(Master_Addr,Trans_Table, Dirty_Pages, RedoLSN);
Restart_Redo(RedoLSN, Trans_Table, Dirty_Pages);
buffer pool Dirty_Pages table := Dirty_Pages;
remove entries for non-buffer-resident pages from the buffer pool Dirty_Pages table;
Restart_Undo(Trans_Table);
reacquire locks for prepared transactions;
checkpoint();
RETURN;
```

Fig. 9. Pseudocode for restart.

During this pass, if a log record is encountered for a page whose identity does not already appear in the dirty_pages table, then an entry is made in the table with the current log record's LSN as the page's RecLSN. The transaction table is modified to track the state changes of transactions and also to note the LSN of the most recent log record that would need to be undone if it were determined ultimately that the transaction had to be rolled back. If an OSfile_return log record is encountered, then any pages belonging to that file which are in the dirty_pages table are removed from the latter in order to make sure that no page belonging to that version of that file is accessed during the redo pass. The same file may be recreated and updated later, once the original operation causing the file erasure is committed. In that case, some pages of the recreated file will reappear in the dirty_pages table later with RecLSN values greater than the end_of_log LSN when the file was erased. The RedoLSN is the minimum RecLSN from the dirty_pages table at the end of the analysis pass. The redo pass can be skipped if there are no pages in the dirty_pages table.

It is not necessary that there be a separate analysis pass and, in fact, in the ARIES implementation in the OS/2 Extended Edition Database Manager there is no analysis pass. This is especially because, as we mentioned before (see also Section 6.2), in the redo pass, ARIES unconditionally redoes all missing updates. That is, it redoes them irrespective of whether they were logged by loser or nonloser transactions, unlike System R, SQL/DS and DB2. Hence, redo does not need to know the loser or nonloser status of a transaction. That information is, strictly speaking, needed only for the undo pass. This would not be true for a system (like DB2) in which for in-doubt transactions their update locks are reacquired by inferring the lock names from the log records of the in-doubt transactions, as they are encountered during the redo pass. This technique for reacquiring locks forces the RedoLSN computation to consider the Begin_LSNs of in-doubt transactions which in turn requires that we know, before the start of the redo pass, the identities of the in-doubt transactions.

Without the analysis pass, the transaction table could be constructed from the checkpoint record and the log records encountered during the redo pass. The RedoLSN would have to be the minimum(minimum(RecLSN from the dirty_pages table in the end_chkpt record), LSN(begin_chkpt record)). Suppression of the analysis pass would also require that other methods be used to

```
RESTART_ANALYSIS(Master_Addr, Trans_Table, Dirty_Pages, RedoLSN);
initialize the tables Trans_Table and Dirty_Pages to empty;
Master_Rec := Read_Disk(Master_Addr);
Open_Log_Scan(Master_Rec.ChkptLSN);                    /* open log scan at Begin_Chkpt record */
LogRec := Next_Log();                                        /* read in the Begin_Chkpt record */
LogRec := Next_Log();                                /* read log record following Begin_Chkpt */
WHILE NOT(End_of_Log) DO;
  IF trans related record & LogRec.TransID NOT in Trans_Table THEN /* not chkpt/OSfile_return*/
    insert (LogRec.TransID,'U',LogRec.LSN,LogRec.PrevLSN) into Trans_Table;     /* log record */
  SELECT(LogRec.Type)
    WHEN('update' | 'compensation') DO;
      Trans_Table[LogRec.TransID].LastLSN := LogRec.LSN;
      IF LogRec.Type = 'update' THEN
        IF LogRec is undoable THEN Trans_Table[LogRec.TransID].UndoNxtLSN := LogRec.LSN;
      ELSE Trans_Table[LogRec.TransID].UndoNxtLSN := LogRec.UndoNxtLSN;
                                /* next record to undo is the one pointed to by this CLR */
      IF LogRec is redoable & LogRec.PageID NOT IN Dirty_Pages THEN
        insert (LogRec.PageID, LogRec.LSN) into Dirty_Pages;
    END; /* WHEN('update' | 'compensation') */
    WHEN('Begin_Chkpt') ;  /* found an incomplete checkpoint's Begin_Chkpt record. ignore it */
    WHEN('End_Chkpt') DO;
      FOR each entry in LogRec.Tran_Table DO;
        IF TransID NOT IN Trans_Table THEN DO;
          insert entry(TransID,State,LastLSN,UndoNxtLSN) in Trans_Table;
        END;
      END; /* FOR */
      FOR each entry in LogRec.Dirty_PagLst DO;
        IF PageID NOT IN Dirty_Pages THEN insert entry(PageID,RecLSN) in Dirty_Pages;
        ELSE set RecLSN of Dirty_Pages entry to RecLSN in Dirty_PagLst;
      END; /* FOR */
    END; /* WHEN('End_Chkpt') */
    WHEN('prepare' | 'rollback') DO;
      IF LogRec.Type = 'prepare' THEN Trans_Table[LogRec.TransID].State := 'P';
      ELSE Trans_Table[LogRec.TransID].State := 'U';
      Trans_Table[LogRec.TransID].LastLSN := LogRec.LSN;
    END; /* WHEN('prepare' | 'rollback') */
    WHEN('end') delete Trans_Table entry for which TransID = LogRec.TransID;
    WHEN('OSfile_return') delete from Dirty_Pages all pages of returned file;
  END; /* SELECT */
  LogRec := Next_Log();
END; /* WHILE */
FOR EACH Trans_Table entry with (State = 'U') & (UndoNxtLSN = 0) DO; /* rolled back trans    */
  write end record and remove entry from Trans_Table;            /* with missing end record */
END; /* FOR */
RedoLSN := minimum(Dirty_Pages.RecLSN);                   /* return start position for redo */
RETURN;
```

Fig. 10. Pseudocode for restart analysis.

avoid processing updates to files which have been returned to the operating system. Another consequence is that the dirty_pages table used during the redo pass cannot be used to filter update log records which occur after the begin_chkpt record.

6.2 Redo Pass

The second pass of the log that is made during restart recovery is the *redo pass*. Figure 11 describes the *RESTART_REDO* routine that implements

```
RESTART_REDO(RedoLSN, Dirty_Pages);
Open_Log_Scan(RedoLSN);                        /* open log scan and position at restart pt */
LogRec := Next_Log();                          /* read log record at restart redo point    */
WHILE NOT(End_of_Log) DO;                         /* look at all records till end of log */
  IF LogRec.Type = ('update'|'compensation') & LogRec is redoable &
     LogRec.PageID IN Dirty_Pages & LogRec.LSN >= Dirty_Pages[LogRec.PageID].RecLSN
    THEN DO;            /* a redoable page update. updated page might not have made it to */
                        /* disk before sys failure. need to access page and check its LSN */
      Page := fix&latch(LogRec.PageID,'X');
      IF Page.LSN < LogRec.LSN THEN DO            /* update not on page. need to redo it */
        Redo_Update(Page,LogRec);                                      /* redo update */
        Page.LSN := LogRec.LSN;
      END;                                                             /* redid update */
      ELSE Dirty_Pages[LogRec.PageID].RecLSN := Page.LSN+1;      /* update already on page */
                  /* update dirty page list with correct info. this will happen if this */
                  /* page was written to disk after the checkpt but before sys failure  */
      unfix&unlatch(Page);
    END;                                                /* LSN on page has to be checked */
  LogRec := Next_Log();                                              /* read next log record */
END;                                                              /* reading till end of log */
RETURN;
```

Fig. 11. Pseudocode for restart redo.

the redo pass actions. The inputs to this routine are the RedoLSN and the dirty_pages table supplied by the restart_analysis routine. No log records are written by this routine. The redo pass starts scanning the log records from the RedoLSN point. When a redoable log record is encountered, a check is made to see if the referenced page appears in the dirty_pages table. If it does and if the log record's LSN is greater than or equal to the RecLSN for the page in the table, then it is suspected that the page state might be such that the log record's update might have to be redone. To resolve this suspicion, the page is accessed. If the page's LSN is found to be less than the log record's LSN, then the update is redone. Thus, the RecLSN information serves to limit the number of pages which have to be examined. This routine reestablishes the database state as of the time of system failure. Even updates performed by loser transactions are redone. The rationale behind this repeating of history is explained in Section 10.1. It turns out that some of that redo of loser transactions' log records may be unnecessary. In [69] we have explored further the idea of restricting the repeating of history to possibly reduce the number of pages which get dirtied during this pass.

Since redo is page-oriented, only the pages with entries in the dirty_pages table may get modified during the redo pass. Only the pages listed in the dirty_pages table will be read and examined during this pass. Not all the pages that are read may require redo. This is because some of the pages that were dirty at the time of the last checkpoint or which became dirty later might have been written to nonvolatile storage before the system failure. Because of reasons like reducing log volume and saving some CPU overhead, we do not expect systems to write log records that identify the dirty pages that were written to nonvolatile storage, although that option is available and such log records can be used to eliminate the corresponding pages from the dirty_pages table when those log records are encountered during the analysis pass. Even if such records were always to be written after I/Os complete, a system failure in a narrow window could prevent them from being written. The corresponding pages will not get modified during this pass.

For brevity, we do not discuss here as to how, if a failure were to occur after the logging of the end record of a transaction, but before the execution of all the pending actions of that transaction, the remaining pending actions are redone during the redo pass.

For exploiting parallelism, the availability of the information in the dirty_pages table gives us the possibility of initiating asynchronous I/Os in parallel to read all these pages so that they may be available in the buffers possibly before the corresponding log records are encountered in the redo pass. Since updates performed during the redo pass are not logged, we can also perform sophisticated things like building in-memory queues of log records which potentially need to be reapplied (as dictated by the information in the dirty_pages table) on a per page or group of pages basis and, as the asynchronously initiated I/Os complete and pages come into the buffer pool, processing the corresponding log record queues using multiple processes. This requires that each queue be dealt with by only one process. Updates to *different* pages may get applied in different orders from the order represented in the log. This does not violate any correctness properties since for a given page all its missing updates are reapplied in the same order as before. These parallelism ideas are also applicable to the context of supporting disaster recovery via remote backups [73].

6.3 Undo Pass

The third pass of the log that is made during restart recovery is the *undo pass*. Figure 12 describes the *RESTART_UNDO* routine that implements the undo pass actions. The input to this routine is the restart transaction table. The dirty_pages table is not consulted during this undo pass. Also, since history is repeated before the undo pass is initiated, the LSN on the page is not consulted to determine whether an undo operation should be performed or not. Contrast this with what we describe in Section 10.1 for systems like DB2 that do not repeat history but perform selective redo.

The restart_undo routine rolls back losers transactions, in reverse chronological order, in a single sweep of the log. This is done by continually taking the maximum of the LSNs of the next log record to be processed for each of the yet-to-be-completely-undone loser transactions, until no loser transaction remains to be undone. The next record to process for each transaction to be rolled back is determined by an entry in the transaction table for each of those transactions. The processing of the encountered log records is exactly as we described before in Section 5.2. In the process of rolling back the transactions, this routine writes CLRs. The buffer manager follows the usual WAL protocol while writing dirty pages to nonvolatile storage during the undo pass.

```
RESTART_UNDO(Trans_Table);
WHILE EXISTS(Trans with State = 'U' in Trans_Table) DO;
  UndoLSN := maximum(UndoNxtLSN) from Trans_Table entries with State = 'U';
                          /* pick up UndoNxtLSN of unprepared trans with maximum UndoNxtLSN */
  LogRec := Log_Read(UndoLSN);                     /* read log record to be undone or a CLR */
  SELECT(LogRec.Type)
    WHEN('update') DO;
      IF LogRec is undoable THEN DO;         /* record needs undoing (not redo-only record) */
        Page := fix&latch(LogRec.PageID,'X');
        Undo_Update(Page,LogRec);
        Log_Write('compensation',LogRec.TransID,Trans_Table[LogRec.TransID].LastLSN,
               LogRec.PageID,LogRec.PrevLSN, ...,LgLSN,Data);                   /* write CLR */
        Page.LSN := LgLSN;                                        /* store LSN of CLR in page */
        Trans_Table[LogRec.TransID].LastLSN := LgLSN;            /* store LSN of CLR in table */
        unfix&unlatch(Page);
      END;                                                            /* undoable record case */
      ELSE;                                              /* record cannot be undone - ignore it */
      Trans_Table[LogRec.TransID].UndoNxtLSN := LogRec.PrevLSN; /* next record to process is */
                                        /* the one preceding this record in its backward chain */
      IF LogRec.PrevLSN = 0 THEN DO;                /* have undone completely - write end */
        Log_Write('end',LogRec.TransID,Trans_Table[LogRec.TransID].LastLSN,...);
        delete Trans_Table entry where TransID = LogRec.TransID;  /* delete trans from table */
      END;                                                            /* trans fully undone */
    END; /* WHEN('update') */
    WHEN('compensation') Trans_Table[LogRec.TransID].UndoNxtLSN := LogRec.UndoNxtLSN;
                                                     /* pick up addr of next record to examine */
    WHEN('rollback'|'prepare') Trans_Table[LogRec.TransID].UndoNxtLSN := LogRec.PrevLSN;
                                                     /* pick up addr of next record to examine */
  END; /* SELECT */
END;   /* WHILE */
RETURN;
```

Fig. 12. Pseudocode for estart undo.

To exploit parallelism, the undo pass can also be performed using multiple processes. It is important that each transaction be dealt with completely by a single process because of the UndoNxtLSN chaining in the CLRs. This still leaves open the possibility of writing the CLRs first, without applying the undos to the pages (see Section 6.4 for problems in accomplishing this for objects that may require logical undos), and then redoing the CLRs in parallel, as explained in Section 6.2. In this fashion, the undo work of actually applying the changes to the pages can be performed in parallel, even for a single transaction.

Figure 13 depicts an example restart recovery scenario using ARIES. Here, all the log records describe updates to the same page. Before the failure, the page was written to disk after the second update. After that disk write, a partial rollback was performed (undo of log records 4 and 3) and then the transaction went forward (updates 5 and 6). During restart recovery, the missing updates (3, 4, 4′, 3′, 5 and 6) are first redone and then the undos (of 6, 5, 2 and 1) are performed. Each update log record will be matched with at most one CLR, regardless of how many times restart recovery is performed.

With ARIES, we have the option of allowing the continuation of loser transactions after restart recovery is completed. Since ARIES repeats history and supports the savepoint concept, we could, in the undo pass, roll back each

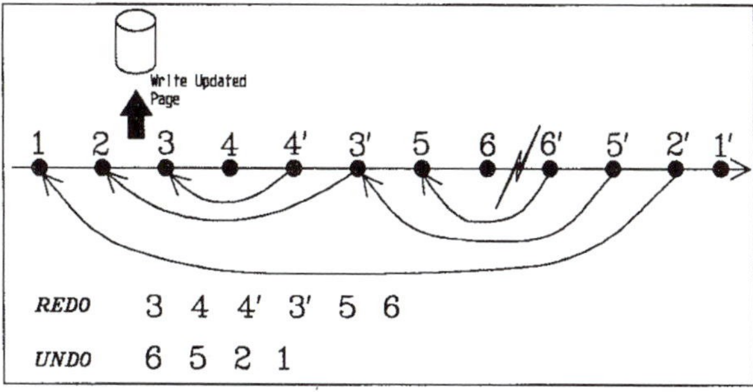

Fig. 13. Restart recovery example with ARIES.

loser only to its latest savepoint, instead of totally rolling back the loser transactions. Later, we could resume the transaction by invoking its application at a special entry point and passing enough information about the savepoint from which execution is to be resumed. Doing this correctly would require (1) the ability to generate lock names from the transaction's log records for its uncommitted, not undone updates, (2) reacquiring those locks before completing restart recovery, and (3) logging enough information whenever savepoints are established so that the system can restore cursor positions, application program state, and so on.

6.4 Selective or Deferred Restart

Sometimes, after a system failure, we may wish to restart the processing of new transactions as soon as possible. Hence, we may wish to defer doing some recovery work to a later point in time. This is usually done to reduce the amount of time during which some critical data is unavailable. It is accomplished by recovering such data first and then opening the system for the processing of new transactions. In DB2, for example, it is possible to perform restart recovery even when some of the objects for which redo and/or undo work needs to be performed are offline when the system is brought up. If some undo work needs to be performed for some loser transactions on those offline objects, then DB2 is able to write the CLRs alone and finish handling the transactions. This is possible because the CLRs can be generated based solely on the information in the non-CLR records written during the forward processing of the transactions [15]. Because page (or minipage, for indexes) is the smallest granularity of locking, the undo actions will be exact inverses of the original actions. That is, there are no logical undos in DB2. DB2 remembers, in an exceptions table (called the database allocation (DBA) table) that is maintained in the log and in virtual storage, the fact that those offline objects need to be recovered when they are brought online, before they are made accessible to other transactions [14]. The LSN ranges of log records to be applied are also remembered. Unless there are some in-doubt transactions with uncommitted updates to those objects, no locks need to be acquired to protect those objects since accesses to those objects will not be permitted until recovery is completed. When those objects are brought online, then recovery is performed efficiently by rolling forward using the log records in the remembered ranges. Even during normal rollbacks, CLRs may be written for offline objects.

In ARIES also, we can take similar actions, provided none of the loser transactions has modified one or more of the offline objects that may require logical undos. This is because logical undos are based on the current state of the object. Redos are not at all a problem, since they are always page-oriented. For logical undos involving space management (see Section 10.3), generally we can take a conservative approach and generate the appropriate CLRs. For example, during the undo of an insert record operation, we can write a CLR for the space-related update stating that the page is 0% full. But for the high concurrency, index management methods of [62] this is not possible, since the effect of the logical undo (e.g., retraversing the index tree to do a key deletion), in terms of which page may be affected, is unpredictable; in fact, we cannot even predict when page-oriented undo will not work and hence logical undo is necessary.

It is not possible to handle the undos of some of the records of a transaction during restart recovery and handle the undos (possibly, logical) of the rest of the records at a later point in time, if the two sets of records are interspersed. Remember that in all the recovery methods, undo of a transaction is done in reverse chronological order. Hence, it is enough to remember, for each transaction, the next record to be processed during the undo; from that record, the PrevLSN and/or the UndoNxtLSN chain leads us to all the other records to be processed.

Even under the circumstances where one or more of the loser transactions have to perform, potentially logical, undos on some offline objects, if deferred restart needs to be supported, then we suggest the following algorithm:

1. Perform the repeating of history for the *online* objects, as usual; postpone it for the *offline* objects and remember the log ranges.
2. Proceed with the undo pass as usual, but stop undoing a loser transaction when one of its log records is encountered for which a CLR cannot be generated for the above reasons. Call such a transaction a *stopped transaction*. But continue undoing the other, unstopped transactions.
3. For the stopped transactions, acquire locks to protect their updates which have not yet been undone. This could be done as part of the undo pass by continuing to follow the pointers, as usual, even for the stopped transactions and acquiring locks based on the encountered non-CLRs that were written by the stopped transactions.
4. When restart recovery is completed and later the previously offline objects are made online, first repeat history based on the remembered log ranges and then continue with the undoing of the stopped transactions. After each of the stopped transactions is totally rolled back, release its still held locks.
5. Whenever an offline object becomes online, when the repeating of history is completed for that object, new transactions can be allowed to access that object in parallel with the further undoing of all of the stopped transactions that can make progress.

The above requires the ability to generate lock names based on the information in the update (non-CLR) log records. DB2 is doing that already for in-doubt transactions.

Even if none of the objects to be recovered is offline, but it is desired that the processing of new transactions start before the rollbacks of the loser transactions are completed, then we can accommodate it by doing the following: (1) first repeat history and reacquire, based on their log records, the locks for the uncommitted updates of the loser and in-doubt transactions, and (2) then start processing new transactions even as the rollbacks of the loser transactions are performed in parallel. The locks acquired in step (1) are released as each loser transaction's rollback completes. Performing step (1) requires that the restart RedoLSN be adjusted appropriately to ensure that all the log records of the loser transactions are encountered during the redo pass. If a loser transaction was already rolling back at the time of the system failure, then, with the information obtained during the analysis pass for such a transaction, it will be known as to which log records remain to be undone. These are the log records whose LSNs are less than or equal to the UndoNxtLSN of the transaction's last CLR. Locks need to be obtained during the redo pass only for those updates that have not yet been undone.

If a long transaction is being rolled back and we would like to release some of its locks as soon as possible, then we can mark specially those log records which represent the first update by that transaction on the corresponding object (e.g., record, if record locking is in effect) and then release that object's lock as soon as the corresponding log record is undone. This works only because we do not undo CLRs and because we do not undo the same non-CLR more than once; hence, it will not work in systems that undo CLRs (e.g., Encompass, AS/400, DB2) or that undo a non-CLR more than once (e.g., IMS). This early release of locks can be performed in ARIES during normal transaction undo to possibly permit resolution of deadlocks using partial rollbacks.

7. CHECKPOINTS DURING RESTART

In this section, we describe how the impact of failures on CPU processing and I/O can be reduced by, optionally, taking checkpoints during different stages of restart recovery processing.

Analysis pass. By taking a checkpoint at the end of the analysis pass, we can save some work if a failure were to occur during recovery. The entries of the transaction table of this checkpoint will be the same as the entries of the transaction table at the end of the analysis pass. The entries of the dirty_pages list of this checkpoint will be the same as the entries that the *restart* dirty_pages table contains at the end of the analysis pass. This is different from what happens during a normal checkpoint. For the latter, the dirty_pages list is obtained from the buffer pool (BP) dirty_pages table.

Redo pass. At the beginning of the redo pass, the buffer manager (BM) is notified so that, whenever it writes out a modified page to nonvolatile storage during the redo pass, it will change the restart dirty_pages table entry for that page by making the RecLSN be equal to the LSN of that log record such that all log records up to that log record had been processed. It is enough if BM manipulates the restart dirty_pages table in this fashion. BM does not have to maintain its own dirty_pages table as it does during normal processing. Of course, it should still be keeping track of what pages are currently in the buffers. The above allow checkpoints to be taken any time during the redo pass to reduce the amount of the log that would need to be redone if a failure were to occur before the end of the redo pass. The entries of the dirty_pages list of this checkpoint will be the same as the entries of the *restart* dirty_pages table at the time of the checkpoint. The entries of the transaction table of this checkpoint will be the same as the entries of the transaction table at the end of the analysis pass. This checkpointing is not affected by whether or not parallelism is employed in the redo pass.

Undo pass. At the beginning of the undo pass, the restart dirty_pages table becomes the BP dirty_pages table. At this point, the table is cleaned up by removing those entries for which the corresponding pages are no longer in the buffers. From then onward, the BP manager manipulates this table as it does during normal processing—removing entries when pages are written to nonvolatile storage, adding entries when pages are about to become dirty, etc. During the undo pass, the entries of the transaction table are modified as during normal undo. If a checkpoint is taken any time during the undo pass, then the entries of the dirty_pages list of that checkpoint are the same as the entries of the BP dirty_pages table at the time of the checkpoint. The entries of the transaction table of this checkpoint will be the same as the entries of the transaction table at that time.

In System R, during restart recovery, sometimes it may be required that a checkpoint be taken to free up some physical pages (the shadow pages) for more undo or redo work to be performed. This is another consequence of the fact that history cannot be repeated in System R. This complicates the restart logic since the view depicted in Figure 17 would no longer be true after a restart checkpoint completes. The restart checkpoint logic and its effect on a restart following a system failure during an earlier restart were considered too complex to be describable in [31]. ARIES is able to easily accommodate checkpoints during restart. While these checkpoints are optional in our case, they may be forced to take place in System R.

8. MEDIA RECOVERY

We will assume that media recovery will be required at the level of a file or some such (like DBspace, tablespace, etc.) entity. A *fuzzy image copy* (also called a *fuzzy archive dump*) operation involving such an entity can be performed concurrently with modifications to the entity by other transactions. With such a high concurrency image copy method, the image copy might contain some uncommitted updates, in contrast to the method of [52]. Of course, if desired, we could also easily produce an image copy with no uncommitted updates. Let us assume that the image copying is performed directly from the nonvolatile storage version of the entity. This means that more recent versions of some of the copied pages may be present in the transaction system's buffers. Copying directly from the nonvolatile storage version of the object would usually be much more efficient since the device geometry can be exploited during such a copy operation and since the buffer manager overheads will be eliminated. Since the transaction system does not have to be up for the direct copying, it may also be more convenient than copying via the transaction system's buffers. If the latter is found desirable (e.g., to support incremental image copying, as described in [13]), then it is easy to modify the presented method to accommodate it. Of course, in that case, some minimal amount of synchronization will be needed. For example, latching at the page level, but no locking will be needed.

When the fuzzy image copy operation is initiated, the location of the begin_chkpt record of the most recent complete checkpoint is noted and remembered along with the image copy data. Let us call this checkpoint the *image copy checkpoint*. The assertion that can be made based on this checkpoint information is that all updates that had been logged in log records with LSNs less than minimum(minimum(RecLSNs of dirty pages of the image-copied entity in the image copy checkpoint's end_chkpt record), LSN(begin_chkpt record of the image copy checkpoint)) would have been externalized to nonvolatile storage by the time the fuzzy image copy operation began. Hence, the image-copied version of the entity would be at least as up to date as of that point in the log. We call that point the *media recovery redo point*. The reason for taking into account the LSN of the begin_chkpt record in computing the media recovery redo point is the same as the one given in Section 5.4 while discussing the computation of the restart redo point.

When media recovery is required, the image-copied version of the entity is reloaded and then a redo scan is initiated starting from the media recovery redo point. During the redo scan, all the log records relating to the entity being recovered are processed and the corresponding updates are applied, unless the information in the image copy checkpoint record's dirty_pages list or the LSN on the page makes it unnecessary. Unlike during *restart* redo, if a log record refers to a page that is not in the dirty_pages list and the log record's LSN is greater than the LSN of the begin_chkpt log record of the image copy checkpoint, then that page must be accessed and its LSN compared to the log record's LSN to check if the update must be redone. Once the end of the log is reached, if there are any in-progress transactions, then those transactions that had made changes to the entity are undone, as in the undo pass of restart recovery. The information about the identities, etc. of such transactions may be kept separately somewhere (e.g., in an exceptions table such as the DBA table in DB2—see Section 6.4) or may be obtained by performing an analysis pass from the last complete checkpoint in the log until the end of the log.

Page-oriented logging provides recovery independence amongst objects. Since, in ARIES, every database page's update is logged separately, even if an arbitrary database page is damaged in the nonvolatile storage and the page needs recovery, the recovery can be accomplished easily by extracting an earlier copy of that page from an image copy and rolling forward that version of the page using the log as described above. This is to be contrasted with systems like System R in which, since for some pages' updates (e.g., index and space management pages') log records are not written, recovery from damage to such a page may require the expensive operation of reconstructing the entire object (e.g., rebuilding the complete index even when only one page of an index is damaged). Also, even for pages for which logging is performed explicitly (e.g., data pages in System R), if CLRs are not written when undo is performed, then bringing a page's state up to date by starting from the image copy state would require paying attention to the log records representing the transaction state (commit, partial or total rollback) to determine what actions, if any, should be undone. If any transactions had rolled back partially or totally, then backward scans of such transactions would be required to see if they made any changes to the page being recovered so that they are undone. These backward scans may result in useless work being performed, if it turns out that some rolled back transaction had not made any changes to the page being recovered. An alternative would be to preprocess the log and place forward pointers to skip over rolled back log records, as it is done in System R during the analysis pass of restart recovery (see Section 10.2 and Figure 18).

Individual pages of the database may be corrupted not only because of media problems but also because of an abnormal process termination while the process is actively making changes to a page in the buffer pool and before the process gets a chance to write a log record describing the changes. If the database code is executed by the application process itself, which is what performance-conscious systems like DB2 implement, such abnormal terminations may occur because of the user's interruption (e.g., by hitting the *attention* key) or due to the operating system's action on noting that the process had exhausted its CPU time limit. It is generally an expensive operation to put the process in an uninterruptable state before every page update. Given all these circumstances, an efficient way to recover the corrupted page is to read the uncorrupted version of the page from the nonvolatile storage and bring it up to date by rolling forward the page state using all relevant log records for that page. The roll-forward redo scan of the log is started from the RecLSN remembered for the buffer by the buffer manager. DB2 does this kind of internal recovery operation automatically [15]. The corruption of a page is detected by using a bit in the page header. The bit is set to '1' after the page is fixed and X-latched. Once the update operation is complete (i.e., page updated, update logged and page LSN modified), the bit is reset to '0'. Given this, whenever a page is latched, for read or write, first this bit is tested to see if its value is equal to '1', in which case automatic page recovery is initiated. From an availability viewpoint, it is unacceptable to bring down the entire transaction system to recover from such a *broken page* situation by letting restart recovery redo all those logged updates that were in the corrupted page but were missing in the uncorrupted version of the page on nonvolatile storage. A related problem is to make sure that for those pages that were left in the fixed state by the abnormally terminating process, unfix calls are issued by the transaction system. By leaving enough *footprints* around before performing operations like fix, unfix and latch, the user process aids system processes in performing the necessary clean-ups.

For the variety of reasons mentioned in this section and elsewhere, writing CLRs is a very good idea even if the system is supporting only page locking. This is to be contrasted with the no-CLRs approach, suggested in [52], which supports only page locking.

9. NESTED TOP ACTIONS

There are times when we would like some updates of a transaction to be committed, irrespective of whether the transaction ultimately commits or not. We do need the atomicity property for these updates themselves. This is illustrated in the context of file extension. After a transaction extends a file which causes updates to some system data in the database, other transactions may be allowed to use the extended area prior to the commit of the extending transaction. If the extending transaction were to roll back, then it would not be acceptable to undo the effects of the extension. Such an undo might very well lead to a loss of updates performed by the other committed transactions. On the other hand, if the extension-related updates to the system data in the database were themselves interrupted by a failure before their completion, it is necessary to undo them. These kinds of actions have been traditionally performed by starting independent transactions, called *top actions* [51]. A transaction initiating such an independent transaction waits until that independent transaction commits before proceeding. The independent transaction mechanism is, of course, vulnerable to lock conflicts between the initiating transaction and the independent transaction, which would be unacceptable.

In ARIES, using the concept of a *nested top action*, we are able to support the above requirement very efficiently, without having to initiate independent transactions to perform the actions. A nested top action, for our purposes, is taken to mean any subsequence of actions of a transaction which should not be undone once the sequence is complete and some later action which is dependent on the nested top action is logged to stable storage, irrespective of the outcome of the enclosing transaction.

A transaction execution performing a sequence of actions which define a nested top action consists of the following steps:

(1) ascertaining the position of the current transaction's last log record;

(2) logging the redo and undo information associated with the actions of the nested top action; and

(3) on completion of the nested top action, writing a *dummy CLR* whose UndoNxtLSN points to the log record whose position was remembered in step (1).

We assume that the effects of any actions like creating a file and their associated updates to system data normally resident outside the database are externalized, before the dummy CLR is written. When we discuss redo, we are referring to only the system data that is resident in the database itself.

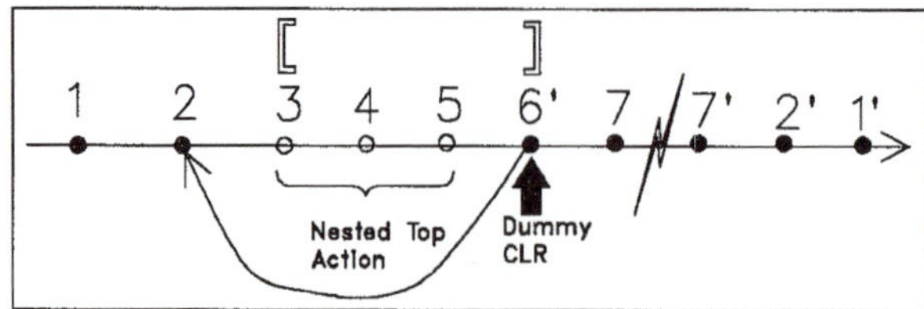

Fig. 14. Nested top action example.

Using this nested top action approach, if the enclosing transaction were to roll back after the completion of the nested top action, then the dummy CLR will ensure that the updates performed as part of the nested top action are not undone. If a system failure were to occur before the dummy CLR is written, then the incomplete nested top action will be undone since the nested top action's log records are written as undo-redo (as opposed to redo-only) log records. This provides the desired atomicity property for the nested top action. Unlike for the normal CLRs, there is nothing to redo when a dummy CLR is encountered during the redo pass. The dummy CLR in a sense can be thought of as the commit record for the nested top action. The advantage of our approach is that the enclosing transaction need not wait for this record to be forced to stable storage before proceeding with its subsequent actions.[6] Also, we do not pay the price of starting a new transaction. Nor do we run into lock conflict problems. Contrast this approach with the costly independent-transaction approach.

Figure 14 gives an example of a nested top action consisting of the actions 3, 4 and 5. Log record 6′ acts as the dummy CLR. Even though the enclosing transaction's activity is interrupted by a failure and hence it needs to be rolled back, 6′ ensures that the nested top action is not undone.

It should be emphasized that the nested top action implementation relies on repeating history. If the nested top action consists of only a single update, then we can log that update using a single *redo-only* log record and avoid writing the dummy CLR. Applications of the nested top action concept in the context of a hash-based storage method and index management can be found in [59, 62].

10. RECOVERY PARADIGMS

This section describes some of the problems associated with providing fine-granularity (e.g., record) locking and handling transaction rollbacks. Some additional discussion can be found in [97]. Our aim is to show how certain features of the existing recovery methods caused us difficulties in accomplishing our goals and to motivate the need for certain features which we had to include in ARIES. In particular, we show why some of the recovery paradigms of System R, which were developed in the context of the shadow page

[6] The dummy CLR may have to be forced if some *unlogged* updates may be performed later by other transactions which depended on the nested top action having completed.

technique, are inappropriate when WAL is to be used and there is a need for high levels of concurrency. In the past, one or more of those System R paradigms have been adopted in the context of WAL, leading to the design of algorithms with limitations and/or errors [3, 15, 16, 52, 71, 72, 78, 82, 88]. The System R paradigms that are of interest are:

—selective redo during restart recovery.

—undo work preceding redo work during restart recovery.

—no logging of updates performed during transaction rollback (i.e., no CLRs).

—no logging of index and space management information changes.

—no tracking of page state on page itself to relate it to logged updates (i.e., no LSNs on pages).

10.1 Selective Redo

The goal of this subsection is to introduce the concept of selective redo that has been implemented in many systems and to show the problems that it introduces in supporting fine-granularity locking with WAL-based recovery. The aim is to motivate why ARIES repeats history.

When transaction systems restart after failures, they generally perform database recovery updates in 2 passes of the log: a redo pass and an undo pass (see Figure 6). System R first performs the undo pass and then the redo pass. As we will show later, the System R paradigm of *undo preceding redo is incorrect with WAL and fine-granularity locking*. The WAL-based DB2, on the other hand, does just the opposite. During the redo pass, System R redoes only the actions of committed and prepared (i.e., in-doubt) transactions [31]. We call this *selective redo*. While the selective redo paradigm of System R intuitively seems to be the efficient approach to take, it has many pitfalls, as we discuss below.

Some WAL-based systems, such as DB2, support only page locking and perform selective redo [15]. This approach will lead to data inconsistencies in such systems, if record locking were to be implemented. Let us consider a WAL technique in which each page contains an LSN as described before. During the redo pass, the page LSN is compared to the LSN of a log record describing an update to the page to determine whether the log record's update needs to be reapplied to the page. If the page LSN is less than the log record's LSN, then the update is redone and the page's LSN is set to the log record's LSN (see Figure 15). During the undo pass, if the page LSN is less than the LSN of the log record to be undone, then no undo action is performed on the page. Otherwise, undo is performed on the page. Whether or not undo needs to be actually performed on the page, a CLR describing the updates that would have been performed as part of the undo operation is always written, when the transaction's actions are being rolled back. The CLR is written, even when the page does not contain the update, just to make media recovery simpler and not force it to handle rolled back updates in a special way. Writing the CLR when an undo is not actually performed on the page turns out to be necessary also when handling a failure of the system

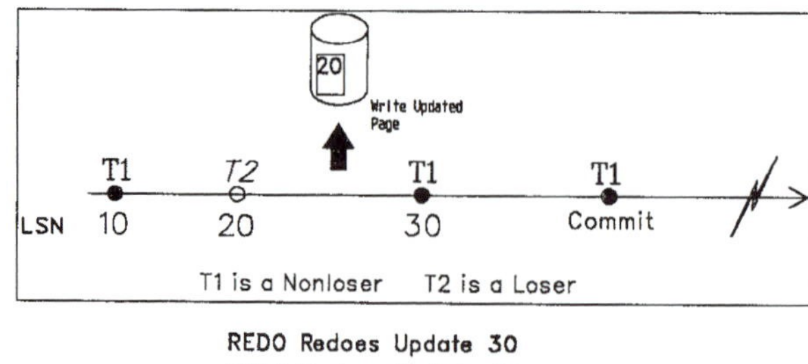

REDO Redoes Update 30
UNDO Undoes Update 20

Fig. 15. Selective redo with WAL—problem-free scenario.

during restart recovery. This will happen, if there was an update U2 for page P1 which did not have to be undone, but there was an earlier update U1 for P1 which had to be undone, resulting in U1′ (CLR for U1) being written and P1's LSN being changed to the LSN of U1′ (> LSN of U2). After that, if P1 were to be written to nonvolatile storage before a system failure interrupts the completion of this restart, then, during the next restart, it would appear as if P1 contains the update U2 and an attempt would be made to undo it. On the other hand, if U2′ had been written, then there would not be any problem. It should be emphasized that this problem arises even when only page locking is used, as is the case with DB2 [15].

Given these properties of the selective redo WAL-based method under discussion, we would lose track of the state of a page with respect to a losing (in-progress or in-rollback) transaction in the situation where the page modified first by the losing transaction (say, update with LSN 20 by T2) was subsequently modified by a nonloser transaction's update (say, update with LSN 30 by T1) which had to be redone. The latter would have pushed the LSN of the page beyond the value established by the loser. So, when the time comes to undo the loser, we would not know if its update needs to be undone or not. Figures 15 and 16 illustrate this problem with selective redo and fine-granularity locking. In the latter scenario, not redoing the update with LSN 20 since it belongs to a loser transaction, but redoing the update with LSN 30 since it belongs to a nonloser transaction, causes the undo pass to perform the undo of the former update even though it is not present in the page. This is because the undo logic relies on the page_LSN value to determine whether or not an update should be undone (undo if page_LSN is greater than or equal to log record's LSN). By not repeating history, the page_LSN is no longer a true indicator of the current state of the page.

Undoing an action even when its effect is not present in a page will be harmless only under certain conditions; for example, with physical/byte-oriented locking and logging, as they are implemented in IMS [76], VAX DBMS and VAX Rdb/VMS [81], and other systems [6], there is no automatic reuse of freed space, and unique keys for all records. With operation logging, data inconsistencies will be caused by undoing an original operation whose effect is not present in the page.

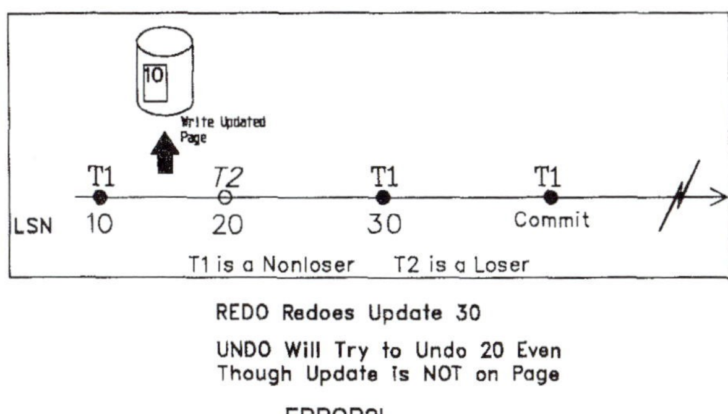

Fig. 16. Selective redo with WAL—problem scenario.

Reversing the order of the selective redo and the undo passes will not solve the problem either. This *incorrect* approach is suggested in [3]. If the undo pass were to precede the redo pass, then we might lose track of which actions need to be redone. In Figure 15, the undo of 20 would make the page LSN become greater than 30, because of the writing of a CLR and the assignment of that CLR's LSN to the page. Since, during the redo pass, a log record's update is redone only if the page_LSN is less than the log record's LSN, we would not redo 30 even though that update is not present on the page. Not redoing that update would violate the durability and atomicity properties of transactions.

The use of the shadow page technique by System R makes it unnecessary to have the concept of page_LSN in that system to determine what needs to be undone and what needs to be redone. With the shadow page technique, during a checkpoint, an action consistent version of the database, called the *shadow version*, is saved on nonvolatile storage. Updates between two checkpoints create a new version of the updated page, thus constituting the *current version* of the database (see Figure 1). During restart, recovery is performed from the *shadow* version, and shadowing is done even during restart recovery. As a result, there is no ambiguity about which updates are in the database and which are not. All updates logged after the last checkpoint are not in the database, and all updates logged before the checkpoint are in the database.[7] This is one reason the System R recovery method functions correctly even with selective redo. The other reason is that index and space management changes are not logged, but are redone or undone logically.[8]

[7] This simple view, as it is depicted in Figure 17, is not completely accurate—see Section 10.2.

[8] In fact, if index changes had been logged, then selective redo would not have worked. The problem would have come from structure modifications (like page split) which were performed after the last checkpoint by *loser* transactions which were taken advantage of later by transactions which ultimately committed. Even if logical undo were performed (if necessary), if redo was page oriented, selective redo would have caused problems. To make it work, the structure modifications could have been performed using separate transactions. Of course, this would have been very expensive. For an alternate, efficient solution, see [62].

As was described before, ARIES does not perform selective redo, but *repeats history*. Apart from allowing us to support fine-granularity locking, repeating history has another beneficial side effect. It gives us the ability to commit some actions of a transaction irrespective of whether the transaction ultimately commits or not, as was described in Section 9.

10.2 Rollback State

The goal of this subsection is to discuss the difficulties introduced by rollbacks in tracking their progress and how writing CLRs that describe updates performed during rollbacks solves some of the problems. While the concept of writing CLRs has been implemented in many systems and has been around for a long time, there has not really been, in the literature, a significant discussion of CLRs, problems relating to them and the advantages of writing them. Their utility and the fundamental role that they play in recovery have not been well recognized by the research community. In fact, whether undone actions could be undone and what additional problems these would present were left as open questions in [56]. In this section and elsewhere in this paper, in the appropriate contexts, we try to note all the known advantages of writing CLRs. We summarize these advantages in Section 13.

A transaction may totally or partially roll back its actions for any number of reasons. For example, a unique key violation will cause only the rollback of the update statement causing the violation and not of the entire transaction. Figure 3 illustrates a partial roll back. Supporting partial rollback [1, 31], at least internally, if not also at the application level, is a very important requirement for present-day transaction systems. Since a transaction may be rolling back when a failure occurs and since some of the effects of the updates performed during the rollback might have been written to nonvolatile storage, we need a way to keep track of the state of progress of transaction rollback. It is relatively easy to do this in System R. The only time we care about the transaction state in System R is at the time a checkpoint is taken. So, the checkpoint record in System R keeps track of the next record to be undone for each of the active transactions, some of which may already be rolling back. The rollback state of a transaction at the time of a system failure is unimportant since the database changes performed after the last checkpoint are not *visible* in the database during restart. That is, restart recovery starts from the state of the database as of the last checkpoint before the system failure—this is the shadow version of the database at the time of system failure. Despite this, since CLRs are never written, System R needs to do some special processing to handle those committed or in-doubt transactions which initiated and completed partial rollbacks after the last checkpoint. The special handling is to avoid the need for multiple passes over the log during the redo pass. The designers wanted to avoid redoing some actions only to have to undo them a little later with a backward scan, when the information about a partial rollback having occurred is encountered.

Figure 18 depicts an example of a restart recovery scenario for System R. All log records are written by the same transaction, say T1. In the checkpoint

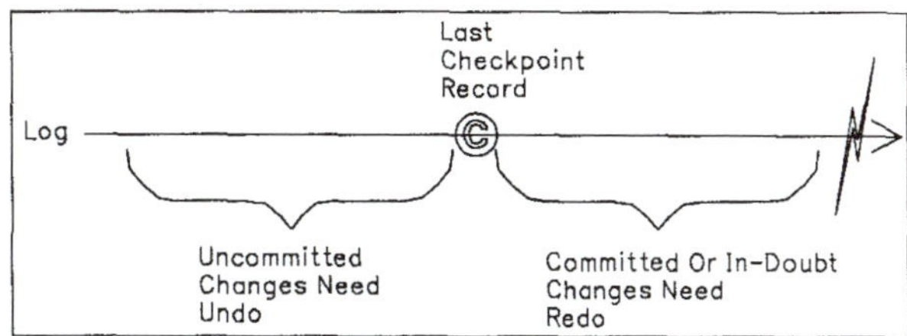

Fig. 17. Simple view of recovery processing in System R

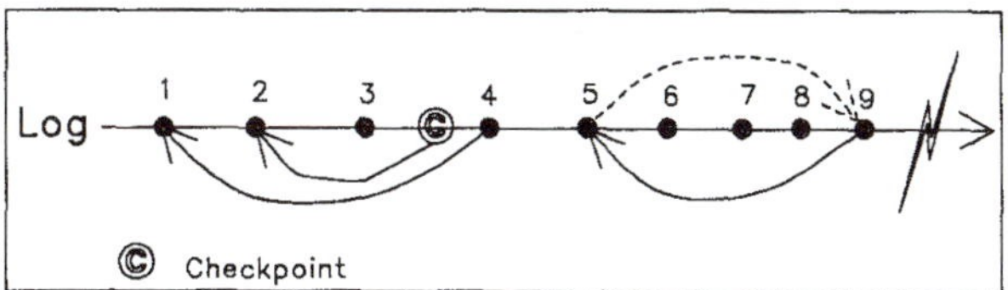

Fig. 18. Partial rollback handling in System R.

record, the information for T1 points to log record 2 since by the time the checkpoint was taken log record 3 had already been undone because of a partial rollback. System R not only does not write CLRs, but it also does not write a separate log record to say that a partial rollback took place. Such information must be inferred from the breakage in the chaining of the log records of a transaction. Ordinarily, a log record written by a transaction points to the record that was most recently written by that transaction via the PrevLSN pointer. But the first forward processing log record written after the completion of a partial rollback does not follow this protocol. When we examine, as part of the analysis pass, log record 4 and notice that its Prev_LSN pointer is pointing to 1, instead of the immediately preceding log record 3, we conclude that the partial rollback that started with the undo of 3 ended with the undo of 2. Since, during restart, the database state from which recovery needs to be performed is the state of the database as of the last checkpoint, log record 2 definitely needs to be undone. Whether 1 needs to be undone or not will depend on whether T1 is a losing transaction or not.

During the analysis pass it is determined that log record 9 points to log record 5 and hence it is concluded that a partial rollback had caused the undo of log records 6, 7, and 8. To ensure that the rolled back records are not redone during the redo pass, the log is patched by putting a forward pointer during the analysis pass in log record 5 to make it point to log record 9.

If log record 9 is a commit record then, during the undo pass, log record 2 will be undone and during the redo pass log records 4 and 5 will be redone. Here, the same transaction is involved both in the undo pass and in the redo pass. To see why the undo pass has to precede the redo pass in System R,[9]

[9] In the other systems, because of the fact that CLRs are written and that, sometimes, page LSNs are compared with log record's LSNs to determine whether redo needs to be performed or not, the redo pass *precedes* the undo pass—see the Section "10.1. Selective Redo" and Figure 6.

consider the following scenario: Since a transaction that deleted a record is allowed to reuse that record's ID for a record inserted later by the same transaction, in the above case, a record might have been deleted because of the partial rollback, which had to be dealt with in the undo pass, and that record's ID might have been reused in the portion of the transaction that is dealt with in the redo pass. To repeat history with respect to the original sequence of actions be fore the failure, the undo must be performed before the redo is performed.

If 9 is neither a commit record nor a prepare record, then the transaction will be determined to be a loser and during the undo pass log records 2 and 1 will be undone. In the redo pass, none of the records will be redone.

Since CLRs are not written in System R and hence the exact way in which one transaction's undo operations were interspersed with other transactions' forward processing or undo actions is not known, the processing, for a given page as well as across different pages during restart may be quite different from what happened during normal processing (i.e., *repeating history* is impossible to guarantee). Not logging index changes in System R also further contributes to this (see footnote 8). These could potentially cause some space management problems such as a split that did not occur during normal processing being required during the restart redo or undo processing (see also Section 5.4). Not writing CLRs also prevents logging of redo information from being done physically (i.e., the operation performed on an object has to be logged—not the after-image created by the operation). Let us consider an example: A piece of data has value 0 after the last checkpoint. Then, transaction T1 adds 1, T2 adds 2, T1 rolls back, and T2 commits. If T1 and T2 had logged the after-image for redo and the operation for undo, then there will be a data integrity problem because after recovery the data will have the value 3 instead of 2. In this case, in System R, undo for T1 is being accomplished by not redoing its update. Of course, System R did not support the fancy lock mode which would be needed to support 2 concurrent updates by different transactions to the same object. Allowing the logging of redo information physically will let redo recovery be performed very efficiently using *dumb* logic. This does not necessarily mean byte-oriented logging; that will depend on whether or not flexible storage management is used (see Section 10.3). Allowing the logging of undo information logically will permit high concurrency to be supported (see [59, 62] for examples). ARIES supports these.

WAL-based systems handle this problem by logging actions performed during rollbacks using CLRs. So, as far as recovery is concerned, the state of the data is always "marching" forward, even if some original actions are being rolled back. Contrast this with the approach, suggested in [52], in which the state of the data, as denoted by the LSN, is "pushed" back during rollbacks. That method works only with page level (or coarser granularity) locking. The immediate consequence of writing CLRs is that, if a transaction were to be rolled back, then some of its original actions are undone more than once and, worse still, the compensating actions are also undone, possibly more than once. This is illustrated in Figure 4, in which a transaction had started rolling back even before the failure of the system. Then, during recovery, the previously written CLRs are undone and already undone non-CLRs are undone again. ARIES avoids such a situation, while still retaining the idea of writing CLRs. Not undoing CLRs has benefits relating to deadlock management and early release of locks on undone objects also (see item 22, Section 12, and Section 6.4). Additional benefits of CLRs are discussed in the next section and in [69]. Some were already discussed in the Section 8.

Unfortunately, recovery methods like the one suggested in [92] do not support partial rollbacks. We feel that this is an important drawback of such methods.

10.3 Space Management

The goal of this subsection is to point out the problems involved in space management when finer than page level granularity of locking and varying length records are to be supported efficiently.

A problem to be dealt with in doing record locking with flexible storage management is to make sure that the space released by a transaction during record deletion or update on a data page is not consumed by another transaction until the space-releasing transaction is committed. This problem is discussed briefly in [76]. We do not deal with solutions to this space reservation problem here. The interested reader is referred to [50]. For index updates, in the interest of increasing concurrency, we do not want to prevent the space released by one transaction from being consumed by another before the commit of the first transaction. The way undo is dealt with under such circumstances using a logical undo approach is described in [62].

Since flexible storage management was a goal, it was not desirable to do physical (i.e., byte-oriented) locking and logging of data within a page, as some systems do (see [6, 76, 81]). That is, we did not want to use the address of the first byte of a record as the lock name for the record. We did not want to identify the specific bytes that were changed on the page. The logging and locking have to be logical within a page. The record's lock name looks something like (page #, slot #) where the slot # identifies a location on the page which then points to the actual location of the record. The log record describes how the contents of the data record got changed. The consequence is that garbage collection that collects unused space on a page does not have to lock or log the records that are moved around within the page. This gives us the flexibility of being able to move records around within a page to store and modify variable length records efficiently. In systems like IMS, utilities have to be run quite frequently to deal with storage fragmentation. These reduce the availability of data to users.

Figure 19 shows a scenario in which not keeping track of the actual page state (by, e.g., storing the LSN in the nonvolatile storage version of the page) and attempting to perform redo from an earlier point in the log leads to problems when flexible storage management is used. Assuming that all updates in Figure 19 involve the same page and the same transaction, an insert requiring 200 bytes is attempted on a page which has only 100 bytes of free space left in it. This shows the need for exact tracking of page state

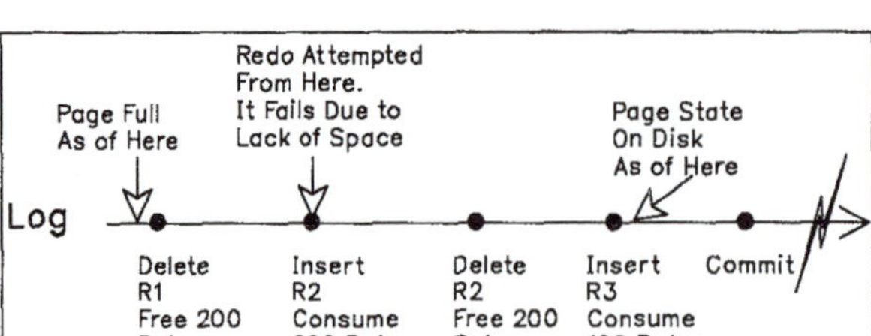

Fig. 19. Wrong redo point-causing problem with space for insert.

using an LSN to avoid attempting to redo operations which are already applied to the page.

Typically, each file containing records of one or more relations has a few pages called free space inventory pages (FSIPs). They are called space map pages (SMPs) in DB2. Each FSIP describes the space information relating to many data or index pages. During a record insert operation, possibly based on information obtained from a clustering index about the location of other records with the same key (or closely related keys) as that of the new record, one or more FSIPs are consulted to identify a data page with enough free space in it for inserting the new record. The FSIP keeps only approximate information (e.g., information such as that at least 25% of the page is full, at least 50% is full, etc.) to make sure that not every space-releasing or -consuming operation to a data page requires an update to the space information in the corresponding FSIP. To avoid special handling of the recovery of the FSIPs during redo and undo, and also to provide recovery independence, updates to the FSIPs must also be logged.

Transaction T1 might cause the space on the page to change from 23% full to 27% full, thereby requiring an update to the FSIP to change it from 0% full to 25% full. Later, T2 might cause the space to go to 35% full, which does not require an update to the FSIP. Now, if T1 were to roll back, then the space would change to 31% full and this should not cause an update to the FSIP. If T1 had written its FSIP change log record as a redo/undo record, then T1's rollback would cause the FSIP entry to say 0% full, which would be wrong, given the *current* state of the data page. This scenario points to the need for logging the changes to the FSIP as *redo-only* changes and for the need to do logical undos with respect to the free space inventory updates. That is, while undoing a data page update, the system has to determine whether that operation causes the free space information to change and if it does cause a change, then update the FSIP and write a CLR which describes the change to the FSIP. We can easily construct an example in which a transaction does not perform an update to the FSIP during forward processing, but needs to perform an update to the FSIP during rollback. We can also construct an example in which the update performed during forward processing is not the exact inverse of the update during the rollback.

10.4 Multiple LSNs

Noticing the problems caused by having one LSN per page when trying to support record locking, it may be tempting to suggest that we track each object's state precisely by assigning a separate LSN to each object. Next we explain why it is not a good idea.

DB2 already supports a granularity of locking that is less than a page. This happens in the case of indexes where the user has the option of requiring DB2 to physically divide up each *leaf* page of the index into 2 to 16 minipages and do locking at the granularity of a minipage [10, 12]. The way DB2 does recovery properly on such pages, despite not redoing actions of loser transactions during the redo pass, is as follows. DB2 tracks each minipage's state separately by associating an LSN with each minipage, besides having an LSN for the leaf page as a whole. Whenever a minipage is updated, the corresponding log record's LSN is stored in the minipage LSN field. The page LSN is set equal to the *maximum* of the minipage LSNs. During undo, it is the minipage LSN and not the page LSN that is compared to the log record's LSN to determine if that log record's update needs to be actually undone on the minipage. This technique, besides incurring too much space overhead for storing the LSNs, tends to fragment (and therefore waste) space available for storing keys. Further, it does not carry over conveniently to the case of record and key locking, especially when varying length objects have to be supported efficiently. Maintaining LSNs for deleted objects is cumbersome at best. We desired to have a *single* state variable (LSN) for each page, even when minipage locking is being done, to make recovery, especially media recovery, very efficient. The simple technique of repeating history during restart recovery before performing the rollback of loser transactions turns out to be sufficient, as we have seen in ARIES. Since DB2 *physically* divides up a page into a fixed number of minipages, no special technique is needed to handle the space reservation problem. Methods like the one proposed in [61] for fine-granularity locking do not support varying length objects (*atoms* in the terminology of that paper).

11. OTHER WAL-BASED METHODS

In the following, we summarize the properties of some other significant recovery methods which also use the WAL protocol. Recovery methods based on the shadow page technique (like that of System R) are not considered here because of their well-known disadvantages, e.g., very costly checkpoints, extra nonvolatile storage space overhead for the shadow copies of data, disturbing the physical clustering of data, and extra I/Os involving page map blocks (see the previous sections of this paper and [31] for additional discussions). First, we briefly introduce the different systems and recovery methods which we will be examining in this section. Next, we compare the different methods along various dimensions. We have been informed that the DB-cache recovery method of [25] has been implemented with significant modifications by Siemens. But, because of lack of information about the implementation, we are unable to include it here.

IBM's IMS/VS [41, 42, 43, 48, 53, 76, 80, 94], which is a hierarchical database system, consists of two parts: IMS Full Function (FF), which is relatively flexible, and IMS Fast Path [28, 42, 93], which is more efficient but has many restrictions (e.g., no support for secondary indexes). A single IMS transaction can access both FF and Fast Path (FP) data. The recovery and buffering methods used by the two parts have many differences. In FF, depending on the database types and the operations, the granularities of the locked objects vary. FP supports two kinds of databases: main storage databases (MSDBs) and data entry databases (DEDBs). MSDBs support only fixed length records, but FP provides the mechanisms (i.e., *field calls*) to make the lock hold times be the minimum possible for MSDB records. Only page locking is supported for DEDBs. But, DEDBs have many high-availability and parallelism features and large database support. IMS, with XRF, provides *hot-standby* support [43]. IMS, via global locking, also supports data sharing across two different systems, each with its own buffer pools [80, 94].

DB2 is IBM's relational database system for the MVS operating system. Limited distributed data access functions are available in DB2. The DB2 recovery algorithm has been presented in [1, 13, 14, 15, 19]. It supports different locking granularities (tablespace, table and page for data, and minipage and page for indexes) and consistency levels (*cursor stability*, *repeatable read*) [10, 11, 12]. DB2 allows logging to be turned off temporarily for tables and indexes only during utility operations like loading and reorganizing data. A single transaction can access both DB2 and IMS data with atomicity. The Encompass recovery algorithm [4, 37] with some changes has been incorporated in Tandem's NonStop SQL [95]. With NonStop, Tandem provides hot-standby support for its products. Both Encompass and NonStop SQL support distributed data access. They allow multisite updates within a single transaction using the Presumed Abort two-phase commit protocol of [63, 64]. NonStop SQL supports different locking granularities (file, key prefix and record) and consistency levels (cursor stability, repeatable read, and unlocked or dirty read). Logging can be turned off temporarily or permanently even for nonutility operations on files.

Schwarz [88] presents two different recovery methods based on value logging (a la IMS) and operation logging. The two methods have several differences, as will be outlined below. The value logging method (VLM), which is much less complex than the operation logging method (OLM), has been implemented in CMU's Camelot [23, 90].

Buffer management. Encompass, NonStop SQL, OLM, VLM and DB2 have adopted the steal and no-force policies. During normal processing, VLM and OLM write a *fetch* record whenever a page is read from nonvolatile storage and an *end-write* record every time a dirty page is successfully written back to nonvolatile storage. These are written during restart processing also in OLM alone. These records help in identifying the super set of dirty pages that might have been in the buffer pool at the time of system failure. DB2 has a sophisticated buffer manager [10, 96], and writes a log record whenever a tablespace or an indexspace is opened, and another record whenever such a space is closed. The close operation is performed only after all the dirty pages of the space have been written back to nonvolatile storage. DB2's analysis pass uses these log records to bring the dirty objects information up to date as of the failure.

For MSDBs, IMS FP does deferred updating. This means that a transaction does not see its own MSDB updates. For DEDBs, a no-steal policy is used. FP writes, at commit time, all the log records for a given transaction in a single call to the log manager. After placing the log records in the *log buffers* (not on stable storage), the MSDB updates are applied and the MSDB record locks are released. The MSDB locks are released even before the commit log record is placed on stable storage. This is how FP minimizes the amount of time locks are held on the MSDB records. The DEDB locks are transferred to system processes. The log manager is given time to let it force the log records to stable storage ultimately (i.e., group commit logic is used—see [28]). After the logging is completed (i.e., *after* the transaction has been committed), all the pages of the DEDBs that were modified by the transaction are forced to nonvolatile storage using system processes which, on completion of the I/Os, release the DEDB locks. This does not result in any uncommitted updates being forced to nonvolatile storage since page locking with a no-steal policy is used for DEDBs. The use of separate processes for writing the DEDB pages to nonvolatile storage is intended to let the user process go ahead with the next transaction's processing as soon as possible and also to gain parallelism for the I/Os. IMS FF follows the steal and force policies. *Before* committing a transaction, IMS FF forces to nonvolatile storage all the pages that were modified by that transaction. Since finer than page locking is supported by FF, this may result in some uncommitted data being placed on nonvolatile storage. Of course, all the recovery algorithms considered in this section force the log during commit processing.

Normal checkpointing. Normal checkpoints are the ones that are taken when the system is not in the restart recovery mode. OLM and VLM quiesce all activity in the system and take, similar to System R, an operation consistent (not necessarily transaction consistent) checkpoint. The contents of the checkpoint record are similar to those of ARIES. DB2, IMS, NonStop SQL, and Encompass do take (fuzzy) checkpoints even when update and logging activities are going on concurrently. DB2's checkpoint actions are similar to what we described for ARIES. The major difference is that, instead of writing the dirty_pages table, it writes the dirty objects (tablespaces, indexspaces, etc.) list with a RecLSN for each object [96]. For MSDBs alone, IMS writes their complete contents alternately on one of two files on nonvolatile storage during a checkpoint. Since deferred updating is performed for MSDBs, no uncommitted changes will be present in their checkpointed version. Also, it is ensured that no partial committed changes of a transaction are present. Care is needed since the updates are applied after the commit record is written. For DEDBs, any *committed* updated pages which have not yet been written to nonvolatile storage are included in the checkpoint records. These together avoid the need for examining, during restart recovery, any log records written before the checkpoint for FP data recovery. Encompass and NonStop SQL might force some dirty pages to nonvolatile storage during a checkpoint. They enforce the policy that requires that a page once dirtied must be written to nonvolatile storage before the completion of the second checkpoint following the dirtying of the page. Because of this policy, the completion of a checkpoint may be delayed waiting for the completion of the writing of the old dirty pages.

Partial rollbacks. Encompass, NonStop SQL, OLM and VLM do not support partial transaction rollback. From Version 2 Release 1, IMS supports partial rollbacks. In fact, the savepoint concept is exposed at the application program level. This support is available only to those applications that do not access FP data. The reason FP data is excluded is because FP does not write undo data in its log records and because deferred updating is performed for MSDBs. DB2 supports partial rollbacks for internal use by the system to provide statement-level atomicity [1].

Compensation log records. Encompass, NonStop SQL, DB2, VLM, OLM and IMS FF write CLRs during normal rollbacks. During a normal rollback, IMS FP does not write CLRs since it would not have written any log records for changes to such data until the decision to rollback is made. This is because FP is always the coordinator in two-phase commit and hence it never needs to get into the prepared state. Since deferred updating is performed for MSDBs, the updates kept in pending (to-do) lists are discarded at rollback time. Since a no-steal policy is followed and page locking is done for DEDBs, the modified pages of DEDBs are simply purged from the buffer pool at rollback time. Encompass, NonStop SQL, DB2 and IMS (FF and FP) write CLRs during restart rollbacks also. During restart recovery, IMS FP might find some log records written by (at the most) one in-progress transaction. This transaction must have been in commit processing—i.e., about to commit, with some of its log records already having been written to nonvolatile storage—when the system went down. Even though, because of the no-steal policy, none of the corresponding FP updates would have been written to nonvolatile storage and hence there would be nothing to be undone, IMS FP writes CLRs for such records to simplify media recovery [93]. Since the FP log records contain only redo information, just to write these CLRs, for which the undo information is needed, the corresponding unmodified data on nonvolatile storage is accessed during restart recovery. This should illustrate to the reader that even with a no-steal policy and without supporting partial rollbacks, there are still some problems to be dealt with at restart for FP. Too often, people assume that no-steal eliminates many problems. Actually, it has many shortcomings.

VLM does not write CLRs during restart rollbacks. As a result, a bounded amount of logging will occur for a rolled back transaction, even in the face of repeated failures during restart. In fact, CLRs are written only for normal rollbacks. Of course, this has some negative implications with respect to media recovery. OLM writes CLRs for undos *and redos* performed during restart (called *undomodify* and *redomodify* records, respectively). This is done to deal with failures during restart. OLM might write multiple undomodify and redomodify records for a given update record if failures interrupt restart processing. No CLRs are generated for CLRs themselves. During restart recovery, Encompass and DB2 undo changes of CLRs, thus causing the writing of CLRs for CLRs and the writing of multiple, identical CLRs for a given record written during forward or restart processing. In the worst case, the number of log records written during repeated restart failures grows exponentially. Figure 5 shows how ARIES avoids this problem. IMS ignores CLRs during the undo pass and hence does not write CLRs for them. The net result is that, because of multiple failures, like the others, IMS might wind up writing multiple times the same CLR for a given record written during forward processing. In the worst case, the number of log records written by IMS and OLM grows linearly. Because of its force policy, IMS will need to redo the CLR's updates only during media recovery.

Log record contents. IMS FP writes only redo information (i.e., after-image of records) because of its no-steal policy. As mentioned before, IMS does value (or state) logging and physical (i.e., byte-range) locking (see [76]). IMS FF logs both the undo information and the redo information. Since IMS does not undo CLRs' updates, CLRs need to have only the redo information. For providing the XRF hot-standby support, IMS includes enough information in its log records for the backup system to track the lock names of updated objects. IMS FP also logs the address of the buffer occupied by a modified page. This information is used during a backup's takeover or restart recovery to reduce the amount of redo work of DEDBs' updates. Encompass and VLM also log complete undo and redo information of updated records. DB2 and NonStop SQL log only the before- and after-images of the updated fields. OLM logs the description of the update operation. The CLRs of Encompass and DB2 need to contain both the redo and the undo information since their CLRs might be undone. OLM periodically logs an operation consistent *snapshot* of each object. OLM's undomodify and redomodify records contain no redo or undo information but only the LSNs of the corresponding modify records. But OLM's modify, redomodify and undomodify records also contain a page map which specifies the set of pages where parts of the modified object reside.

Page overhead. Encompass and NonStop SQL use one LSN on each page to keep track of the state of the page. VLM uses no LSNs, but OLM uses one LSN. DB2 uses one LSN and IMS FF no LSN. Not having the LSN in IMS FF and VLM to know the exact state of a page does not cause any problems because of IMS' and VLM's value logging and physical locking attributes. It is acceptable to redo an already present update or undo an absent update. IMS FP uses a field in the pages of DEDBs as a version number to correctly handle redos after all the data sharing systems have failed [67]. When DB2 divides an index leaf page into minipages then it uses one LSN for each minipage, besides one LSN for the page as a whole.

Log passes during restart recovery. Encompass and NonStop SQL make two passes (redo and then undo), and DB2 makes three passes (analysis, redo, and then undo—see Figure 6). Encompass and NonStop SQL start their redo passes from the beginning of the penultimate successful checkpoint. This is sufficient because of the buffer management policy of writing to disk a dirty page within two checkpoints after the page became dirty. They also seem to repeat history before performing the undo pass. They do not seem to repeat history if a backup system takes over when a primary system fails [4]. In the case of a takeover by a hot-standby, locks are first reacquired for the losers' updates and then the rollbacks of the losers are performed in parallel with the processing of new transactions. Each loser transaction is rolled back using a separate process to gain parallelism. DB2 starts its redo scan from that point, which is determined using information recorded in the last successful checkpoint, as modified by the analysis pass. As mentioned before, DB2 does selective redo (see Section 10.1).

VLM makes one backward pass and OLM makes three passes (analysis, undo, and then redo). Many lists are maintained during OLM's and VLM's passes. The undomodify and redomodify log records of OLM are used only to modify these lists, unlike in the case of the CLRs written in the other systems. In VLM, the one backward pass is used to undo uncommitted changes on nonvolatile storage and also to redo missing committed changes. No log records are written during these operations. In OLM, during the undo pass, for each object to be recovered, if an operation consistent version of the object does not exist on nonvolatile storage, then it restores a snapshot of the object from the snapshot log record so that, starting from a consistent version of the object, (1) in the remainder of the undo pass any to-be-undone updates that precede the snapshot log record can be undone logically, and (2) in the redo pass any committed or in-doubt updates (modify records only) that follow the snapshot record can be redone logically. This is similar to the shadowing performed in [16, 78] using a separate log—the difference is that the database-wide checkpointing is replaced by object-level checkpointing and the use of a single log instead of two logs.

IMS first reloads MSDBs from the file that received their contents during the latest successful checkpoint before the failure. The dirty DEDB buffers that were included in the checkpoint records are also reloaded into the same buffers as before. This means that, during the restart after a failure, the number of buffers cannot be altered. Then, it makes just one forward pass over the log (see Figure 6). During that pass, it accumulates log records in memory on a per-transaction basis and redoes, if necessary, completed transactions' FP updates. Multiple processes are used in parallel to redo the DEDB updates. As far as FP is concerned, only the updates starting from the last checkpoint before the failure are of interest. At the end of that one pass, in-progress transactions' FF updates are undone (using the log records in memory), in parallel, using one process per transaction. If the space allocated in memory for a transaction's log records is not enough, then a backward scan of the log will be performed to fetch the needed records during that transaction's rollback. In the XRF context, when a hot-standby IMS takes over, the handling of the loser transactions is similar to the way Tandem does it. That is, rollbacks are performed in parallel with new transaction processing.

Page forces during restart. OLM, VLM and DB2 force all dirty pages at the end of restart. Information on Encompass and NonStop SQL is not available.

Restart checkpoints. IMS, DB2, OLM and VLM take a checkpoint only at the end of restart recovery. Information on Encompass and NonStop SQL is not available.

Restrictions on data. Encompass and NonStop SQL require that every record have a unique key. This unique key is used to guarantee that if an attempt is made to undo a logged action which was never applied to the nonvolatile storage version of the data, then the latter is realized and the undo fails. In other words, idempotence of operations is achieved using the unique key. IMS in effect does byte-range locking and logging and hence does not allow records to be moved around freely within a page. This results in the fragmentation and the less efficient usage of free space. IMS imposes some additional constraints with respect to FP data. VLM requires that an object's representation be divided into fixed length (less than one page sized), unrelocatable quanta. The consequences of these restrictions are similar to those for IMS.

[2, 26, 56] do not discuss recovery from system failures, while the theory of [33] does not include semantically rich modes of locking (i.e., operation logging). In other sections of this paper, we have pointed out the problems with some of the other approaches that have been proposed in the literature.

12. ATTRIBUTES OF ARIES

ARIES makes few assumptions about the data or its model and has several advantages over other recovery methods. While ARIES is simple, it possesses several interesting and useful properties. Each of most of these properties has been demonstrated in one or more existing or proposed systems, as summarized in the last section. However, we know of no single system, proposed or real, which has all of these properties. Some of these properties of ARIES are:

(1) *Support for finer than page-level concurrency control and multiple granularities of locking.* ARIES supports page-level and record-level locking in a uniform fashion. Recovery is not affected by what the granularity of locking is. Depending on the expected contention for the data, the appropriate level of locking can be chosen. It also allows multiple granularities of locking (e.g., record, table, and tablespace-level) for the same object (e.g., tablespace). Concurrency control schemes other than locking (e.g., the schemes of [2]) can also be used.

(2) *Flexible buffer management during restart and normal processing.* As long as the write-ahead logging protocol is followed, the buffer manager is

free to use any page replacement policy. In particular, dirty pages of incomplete transactions can be written to nonvolatile storage before those transactions commit (*steal* policy). Also, it is not required that all pages dirtied by a transaction be written back to nonvolatile storage before the transaction is allowed to commit (i.e., *no-force* policy). These properties lead to reduced demands for buffer storage and fewer I/Os involving frequently updated (*hot-spot*) pages. ARIES does not preclude the possibilities of using deferred-updating and force-at-commit policies and benefiting from them. ARIES is quite flexible in these respects.

(3) *Minimal space overhead—only one LSN per page.* The permanent (excluding log) space overhead of this scheme is limited to the storage required on each page to store the LSN of the last logged action performed on the page. The LSN of a page is a monotonically increasing value.

(4) *No constraints on data to guarantee idempotence of redo or undo of logged actions.* There are no restrictions on the data with respect to unique keys, etc. Records can be of variable length. Data can be moved around within a page for garbage collection. Idempotence of operations is ensured since the LSN on each page is used to determine whether an operation should be redone or not.

(5) *Actions taken during the undo of an update need not necessarily be the exact inverses of the actions taken during the original update.* Since CLRs are being written during undos, any differences between the inverses of the original actions and what actually had to be done during undo can be recorded in the former. An example of when the inverse might not be correct is the one that relates to the free space information (like at least 10% free, 20% free) about data pages that are maintained in space map pages. Because of finer than page-level granularity locking, while no free space information change takes place during the initial update of a page by a transaction, a free space information change might occur during the undo (from 20% free to 10% free) of that original change because of intervening update activities of other transactions (see Section 10.3).

Other benefits of this attribute in the context of hash-based storage methods and index management can be found in [59, 62].

(6) *Support for operation logging and novel lock modes.* The changes made to a page can be logged in a logical fashion. The undo information and the redo information for the entire object need not be logged. It suffices if the changed fields alone are logged. Since history is repeated, for increment or decrement kinds of operations before- and after-images of the field are not needed. Information about the type of operation and the decrement or increment amount is enough. Garbage collection actions and changes to some fields (e.g., amount of free space) of that page need not be logged. Novel lock modes based on commutativity and other properties of operations can be supported [2, 26, 88].

(7) *Even redo-only and undo-only records are accommodated.* While it may be efficient (single call to the log component) sometimes to include the undo and redo information about an update in the same log record, at other

times it may be efficient (from the original data, the undo record can be constructed and, after the update is performed *in-place* in the data record, from the updated data, the redo record can be constructed) and/or necessary (because of log record size restrictions) to log the information in two different records. ARIES can handle both situations. Under these conditions, the undo record must be logged before the redo record.

(8) *Support for partial and total transaction rollback.* Besides allowing transactions to be rolled back totally, ARIES allows the establishment of savepoints and the partial rollback of transactions to such savepoints. Without the support for partial rollbacks, even logically recoverable errors (e.g., unique key violation, out-of-date cached catalog information in a distributed database system) will require total rollbacks and result in wasted work.

(9) *Support for objects spanning multiple pages.* Objects can span multiple pages (e.g., an IMS "record" which consists of multiple segments may be scattered over many pages). When an object is modified, if log records are written for every page affected by that update, ARIES works fine. ARIES itself does not treat multipage objects in any special way.

(10) *Allows files to be acquired or returned, any time, from or to the operating system.* ARIES provides the flexibility of being able to return files dynamically and permanently to the operating system (see [19] for the detailed description of a technique to accomplish this). Such an action is considered to be one that cannot be undone. It does not prevent the same file from being reallocated to the database system. Mappings between objects (tablespaces, etc.) and files are not required to be defined statically as in System R.

(11) *Some actions of a transaction may be committed even if the transaction as a whole is rolled back.* This refers to the technique of using the concept of a dummy CLR to implement nested top actions. File extension has been given as an example situation which could benefit from this. Other applications of this technique, in the context of hash-based storage methods and index management, can be found in [59, 62].

(12) *Efficient checkpoints (including during restart recovery).* By supporting fuzzy checkpointing, ARIES makes taking a checkpoint an efficient operation. Checkpoints can be taken even when update activities and logging are going on concurrently. Permitting checkpoints even during restart processing will help reduce the impact of failures during restart recovery. The dirty_pages information written during checkpointing helps reduce the number of pages which are read from nonvolatile storage during the redo pass.

(13) *Simultaneous processing of multiple transactions in forward processing and/or in rollback accessing same page.* Since many transactions could simultaneously be going forward or rolling back on a given page, the level of concurrent access supported could be quite high. Except for the short duration latching which has to be performed any time a page is being

physically modified or examined, be it during forward processing or during rollback, rolling back transactions do not affect one another in any unusual fashion.

(14) *No locking or deadlocks during transaction rollback.* Since no locking is required during transaction rollback, no deadlocks will involve transactions that are rolling back. Avoiding locking during rollbacks simplifies not only the rollback logic, but also the deadlock detector logic. The deadlock detector need not worry about making the mistake of choosing a rolling back transaction as a victim in the event of a deadlock (cf. System R and R* [31, 49, 64]).

(15) *Bounded logging during restart in spite of repeated failures or of nested rollbacks.* Even if repeated failures occur during restart, the number of CLRs written is unaffected. This is also true if partial rollbacks are nested. The number of log records written will be the same as that written at the time of transaction rollback during normal processing. The latter again is a fixed number and is, usually, equal to the number of undoable records written during the forward processing of the transaction. No log records are written during the redo pass of restart.

(16) *Permits exploitation of parallelism and selective/deferred processing for faster restart.* Restart can be made faster by not doing all the needed I/Os synchronously one at a time while processing the corresponding log record. ARIES permits the early identification of the pages needing recovery and the initiation of asynchronous parallel I/Os for the reading in of those pages. The pages can be processed concurrently as they are brought into memory during the redo pass. Undo parallelism requires complete handling of a given transaction by a single process. Some of the restart processing can be postponed to speed up restart or to accommodate offline devices. If desired, undo of loser transactions can be performed in parallel with new transaction processing.

(17) *Fuzzy image copying (archive dumping) for media recovery.* Media recovery and image copying of the data are supported very efficiently. To take advantage of device geometry, the actual act of copying can even be performed outside the transaction system (i.e., without going through the buffer pool). This can happen even while the latter is accessing and modifying the information being copied. During media recovery only one forward traversal of the log is made.

(18) *Continuation of loser transactions after a system restart.* Since ARIES repeats history and supports the savepoint concept, we could, in the undo pass, instead of totally rolling back the loser transactions, roll back each loser only to its latest savepoint. Locks must be acquired to protect the transaction's uncommitted, not undone updates. Later, we could resume the transaction by invoking its application at a special entry point and passing enough information about the savepoint from which execution is to be resumed.

(19) *Only one backward traversal of log during restart or media recovery.*

Both during media recovery and restart recovery one backward traversal of the log is sufficient. This is especially important if any portion of the log is likely to be stored in a slow medium like tape.

(20) *Need only redo information in compensation log records.* Since compensation records are never undone they need to contain only redo information. So, on the average, the amount of log space consumed during a transaction rollback will be half the space consumed during the forward processing of that transaction.

(21) *Support for distributed transactions.* ARIES accommodates distributed transactions. Whether a given site is a coordinator or a subordinate site does not affect ARIES.

(22) *Early release of locks during transaction rollback and deadlock resolution using partial rollbacks.* Because ARIES never undoes CLRs and because it never undoes a particular non-CLR more than once, during a (partial) rollback, when the transaction's very first update to a particular object is undone and a CLR is written for it, the system can release the lock on that object. This makes it possible to consider resolving deadlocks using partial rollbacks.

It should be noted that ARIES does not prevent the shadow page technique from being used for selected portions of the data to avoid logging of only undo information or both undo and redo information. This may be useful for dealing with long fields, as is the case in the OS/2 Extended Edition Database Manager. In such instances, for such data, the modified pages would have to be forced to nonvolatile storage before commit. Whether or not media recovery and partial rollbacks can be supported will depend on what is logged and for which updates shadowing is done.

13. SUMMARY

In this paper, we presented the ARIES recovery method and showed why some of the recovery paradigms of System R are inappropriate in the WAL context. We dealt with a variety of features that are very important in building and operating an *industrial-strength* transaction processing system. Several issues regarding operation logging, fine-granularity locking, space management, and flexible recovery were discussed. In brief, ARIES accomplishes the goals that we set out with by logging all updates on a per-page basis, using an LSN on every page for tracking page state, repeating history during restart recovery before undoing the loser transactions, and chaining the CLRs to the predecessors of the log records that they compensated. Use of ARIES is not restricted to the database area alone. It can also be used for implementing persistent object-oriented languages, recoverable file systems and transaction-based operating systems. In fact, it is being used in the QuickSilver distributed operating system [40] and in a system designed to aid the backing up of workstation data on a host [44].

In this section, we summarize as to which specific features of ARIES lead to which specific attributes that give us flexibility and efficiency.

Repeating history exactly, which in turn implies using LSNs and writing CLRs during undos, permits the following, irrespective of whether CLRs are chained using the UndoNxtLSN field or not:

(1) Record level locking to be supported and records to be moved around within a page to avoid storage fragmentation without the moved records having to be locked and without the movements having to be logged.
(2) Use only one state variable, a log sequence number, per page.
(3) Reuse of storage released by one transaction for the same transaction's later actions or for other transactions' actions once the former commits, thereby leading to the preservation of clustering of records and the efficient usage of storage.
(4) The inverse of an action origianlly performed during forward processing of a transaction to be different from the action(s) performed during the undo of that original action (e.g., class changes in the space map pages). That is, logical undo with recovery independence is made possible.
(5) Multiple transactions may undo on the same page concurrently with transactions going forward.
(6) Recovery of each page independently of other pages or of log records relating to transaction state, especially during media recovery.
(7) If necessary, the continuation of transactions which were in progress at the time of system failure.
(8) Selective or deferred restart, and undo of losers concurrently with new transaction processing to improve data availability.
(9) Partial rollback of transactions.
(10) Operation logging and logical logging of changes within a page. For example, decrement and increment operations may be logged, rather than the before- and after-images of modified data.

Chaining, using the UndoNxtLSN field, CLRs to log records written during forward processing permits the following, provided the protocol of repeating history is also followed:

(1) The avoidance of undoing CLRs' actions, thus avoiding writing CLRs for CLRs. This also makes it unnecessary to store undo information in CLRs.
(2) The avoidance of the undo of the same log record written during forward processing more than once.
(3) As a transaction is being rolled back, the ability to release the lock on an object when all the updates to that object had been undone. This may be important while rolling back a long transaction or while resolving a deadlock by partially rolling back the victim.
(4) Handling partial rollbacks without any special actions like patching the log, as in System R.
(5) Making permanent, if necessary via nested top actions, some of the

changes made by a transaction, irrespective of whether the transaction itself subsequently rolls back or commits.

Performing the analysis pass before repeating history permits the following:

(1) Checkpoints to be taken any time during the redo and undo passes of recovery.
(2) Files to be returned to the operating system dynamically, thereby allowing dynamic binding between database objects and files.
(3) Recovery of file-related information concurrently with the recovery of user data, without requiring special treatment for the former.
(4) Identifying pages possibly requiring redo, so that asynchronous parallel I/Os could be initiated for them even before the redo pass starts.
(5) Exploiting opportunities to avoid redos on some pages by eliminating those pages from the dirty_pages table on noticing, e.g., that some empty pages have been freed.
(6) Exploiting opportunities to avoid reading some pages during redo, e.g., by writing end_write records after dirty pages have been written to non-volatile storage and by eliminating those pages from the dirty_pages table when the end_write records are encountered.
(7) Identifying the transactions in the in-doubt and in-progress states so that locks could be reacquired for them during the redo pass to support selective or deferred restart, the continuation of loser transactions after restart, and undo of loser transactions in parallel with new transaction processing.

13.1 Implementations and Extensions

ARIES forms the basis of the recovery algorithms used in the IBM Research prototype systems Starburst [87] and QuickSilver [40], in the University of Wisconsin's EXODUS and Gamma database machine [20], and in the IBM program products OS/2 Extended Edition Database Manager [7] and Workstation Data Save Facility/VM [44]. One feature of ARIES, namely *repeating history*, has been implemented in DB2 Version 2 Release 1 to use the concept of nested top action for supporting segmented tablespaces. A simulation study of the performance of ARIES is reported in [98]. The following conclusions from that study are worth noting: "Simulation results indicate the success of the ARIES recovery method in providing fast recovery from failures, caused by long intercheckpoint intervals, efficient use of page LSNs, log LSNs, and RecLSNs avoids redoing updates unnecessarily, and the actual recovery load is reduced skillfully. Besides, the overhead incurred by the concurrency control and recovery algorithms on transactions is very low, as indicated by the negligibly small difference between the mean transaction response time and the average duration of a transaction if it ran alone in a never failing system. This observation also emerges as evidence that the recovery method goes well with concurrency control through fine-granularity locking, an important virtue."

We have extended ARIES to make it work in the context of the nested transaction model (see [70, 85]). Based on ARIES, we have developed new methods, called ARIES/KVL, ARIES/IM and ARIES/LHS, to efficiently provide high concurrency and recovery for B^+-tree indexes [57, 62] and for hash-based storage structures [59]. We have also extended ARIES to restrict the amount of repeating of history that takes place for the loser transactions [69]. We have designed concurrency control and recovery algorithms, based on ARIES, for the N-way data sharing (i.e., shared disks) environment [65, 66, 67, 68]. *Commit_LSN*, a method which takes advantage of the page_LSN that exists in every page to reduce the locking, latching and predicate reevaluation overheads, and also to improve concurrency, has been presented in [54, 58, 60]. Although messages are an important part of transaction processing, we did not discuss message logging and recovery in this paper.

ACKNOWLEDGMENTS

We have benefited immensely from the work that was performed in the System R project and in the DB2 and IMS product groups. We have learned valuable lessons by looking at the experiences with those systems. Access to the source code and internal documents of those systems was very helpful. The Starburst project gave us the opportunity to begin from scratch and design some of the fundamental algorithms of a transaction system, taking into account experiences with the prior systems. We would like to acknowledge the contributions of the designers of the other systems. We would also like to thank our colleagues in the research and product groups that have adopted our research results. Our thanks also go to Klaus Kuespert, Brian Oki, Erhard Rahm, Andreas Reuter, Pat Selinger, Dennis Shasha, and Irv Traiger for their detailed comments on the paper.

REFERENCES

1. Baker, J., Crus, R., and Haderle, D. Method for assuring atomicity of multi-row update operations in a database system. U.S. Patent 4,498,145, IBM, Feb. 1985.
2. Badrinath, B. R., and Ramamritham, K. Semantics-based concurrency control: Beyond commutativity. In *Proceedings 3rd IEEE International Conference on Data Engineering* (Feb. 1987).
3. Bernstein, P., Hadzilacos, V., and Goodman, N. *Concurrency Control and Recovery in Database Systems*. Addison-Wesley, Reading, Mass., 1987.
4. Borr, A. Robustness to crash in a distributed database: A non-shared-memory multiprocessor approach. In *Proceedings 10th International Conference on Very Large Data Bases* (Singapore, Aug. 1984).
5. Chamberlin, D., Gilbert, A., and Yost, R. A history of System R and SQL/Data System. In *Proceedings 7th International Conference on Very Large Data Bases* (Cannes, Sept. 1981).
6. Chang, A., and Mergen, M. 801 storage: Architecture and programming. *ACM Trans. Comput. Syst., 6,* 1 (Feb. 1988), 28–50.
7. Chang, P. Y., and Myre, W. W. OS/2 EE database manager: Overview and technical highlights. *IBM Syst. J. 27*, 2 (1988).
8. Copeland, G., Khoshafian, S., Smith, M., and Valduriez, P. Buffering schemes for permanent data. In *Proceedings International Conference on Data Engineering* (Los Angeles, Feb. 1986).

9. CLARK, B. E., AND CORRIGAN, M. J. Application System/400 performance characteristics. *IBM Syst. J. 28*, 3 (1989).
10. CHENG, J., LOOSELY, C., SHIBAMIYA, A., AND WORTHINGTON, P. IBM Database 2 performance: Design, implementation, and tuning. *IBM Syst. J. 23*, 2 (1984).
11. CRUS, R , HADERLE, D., AND HERRON, H. Method for managing lock escalation in a multiprocessing, multiprogramming environment. U.S. Patent 4,716,52 8, IBM, Dec. 1987.
12. CRUS, R., MALKEMUS, T., AND PUTZOLU, G. R. Index mini-pages *IBM Tech. Disclosure Bull. 26*, 4 (April 1983), 5460-5463.
13. CRUS, R., PUTZOLU, F., AND MORTENSON, J. A Incremental data base log image copy *IBM Tech. Disclosure Bull. 25*, 7B (Dec. 1982), 3730-373 2.
14. CRUS, R., AND PUTZOLU, F. Data base allocation table. *IBM Tech. Disclosure Bull. 25*, 7B (Dec. 1982), 3722-2724.
15. CRUS, R. Data recovery in IBM Database 2. *IBM Syst. J. 23*, 2 (1984).
16. CURTIS, R. Informix-Turbo, In *Proceedings IEEE Compcon Spring '88* (Feb.-March 1988).
17. DASGUPTA, P., LEBLANC, R., JR., AND APPELBE, W. The Clouds distributed operating system. In *Proceedings 8th International Conference on Distributed Computing Systems* (San Jose, Calif., June 1988).
18. DATE, C. *A Guide to INGRES*. Addison-Wesley, Reading, Mass., 1987.
19. DEY, R., SHAN, M., AND TRAIGER, I. Method for dropping data sets. *IBM Tech. Disclosure Bull. 25*, 11A (April 1983), 5453-5455.
20. DEWITT, D., GHANDEHARIZADEH, S., SCHNEIDER, D., BRICKER, A., HSIAO, H.-I., AND RASMUSSEN, R. The Gamma database machine project. *IEEE Trans. Knowledge Data Eng. 2*, 1 (March 1990).
21. DELORME, D., HOLM, M., LEE, W., PASSE, P., RICARD, G., TIMMS, G., JR., AND YOUNGREN, L. Database index journaling for enhanced recovery. U.S. Patent 4 ,819,156, IBM, April 1989
22. DIXON, G. N., PARRINGTON, G. D., SHRIVASTAVA, S., AND WHEATER, S. M. The treatment of persistent objects in Arjuna. *Comput. J. 32*, 4 (1989).
23. DUCHAMP, D. Transaction management. Ph.D. dissertation, Tech. Rep. CMU-CS-88-192, Carnegie-Mellon Univ., Dec. 1988.
24. EFFELSBERG, W., AND HAERDER, T. Principles of database buffer management. *ACM Trans. Database Syst. 9*, 4 (Dec. 1984).
25. ELHARDT, K , AND BAYER, R. A database cache for high performance and fast restart in database systems. *ACM Trans Database Syst. 9*, 4 (Dec. 1984).
26. FEKETE, A., LYNCH, N., MERRITT, M., AND WEIHL, W. Commutativity-based locking for nested transactions. Tech. Rep. MIT/LCS/TM-370.b, MIT, July 1989.
27. FOSSUM, B Data base integrity as provided for by a particular data base management system. In *Data Base Management*, J. W. Klimbie and K. L. Koffeman, Eds., North-Holland, Amsterdam, 1974.
28. GAWLICK, D., AND KINKADE, D. Varieties of concurrency control in IMS/VS Fast Path. *IEEE Database Eng. 8*, 2 (June 1985).
29. GARZA, J., AND KIM, W. Transaction management in an object-oriented database system. In *Proceedings ACM-SIGMOD International Conference on Management of Data* (Chicago, June 1988).
30. GHEITH, A., AND SCHWAN, K. CHAOS^{art}: Support for real-time atomic transactions. In *Proceedings 19th International Symposium on Fault-Tolerant Computing* (Chicago, June 1989).
31. GRAY, J., MCJONES, P., BLASGEN, M., LINDSAY, B., LORIE, R., PRICE, T., PUTZOLU, F., AND TRAIGER, I. The recovery manager of the System R database manager. *ACM Comput. Surv. 13*, 2 (June 1981).
32. GRAY, J. Notes on data base operating systems. In *Operating Systems—An Advanced Course*, R. Bayer, R. Graham, and G. Seegmuller, Eds., LNCS Vol. 60, Springer-Verlag, New York, 1978.
33. HADZILACOS, V. A theory of reliability in database systems. *J. ACM 35*, 1 (Jan. 1988), 121-145.
34. HAERDER, T. Handling hot spot data in DB-sharing systems. *Inf. Syst. 13*, 2 (1988), 155-166.

35. HADERLE, D., AND JACKSON, R. IBM Database 2 overview. *IBM Syst. J. 23,* 2 (1984).
36. HAERDER, T., AND REUTER, A. Principles of transaction oriented database recovery—A taxonomy. *ACM Comput. Surv. 15,* 4 (Dec. 1983).
37. HELLAND, P. The TMF application programming interface: Program to program communication, transactions, and concurrency in the Tandem NonStop system. Tandem Tech. Rep. TR89.3, Tandem Computers, Feb. 1989.
38. HERLIHY, M., AND WEIHL, W. Hybrid concurrency control for abstract data types. In *Proceedings 7th ACM SIGACT-SIGMOD-SIGART Symposium on Principles of Database Systems* (Austin, Tex., March 1988).
39. HERLIHY, M., AND WING, J. M. Avalon: Language support for reliable distributed systems. In *Proceedings 17th International Symposium on Fault-Tolerant Computing* (Pittsburgh, Pa., July 1987).
40. HASKIN, R., MALACHI, Y., SAWDON, W., AND CHAN, G. Recovery management in QuickSilver. *ACM Trans. Comput. Syst. 6,* 1 (Feb. 1988), 82–108.
41. *IMS/VS Version 1 Release 3 Recovery/Restart.* Doc. GG24-1652, IBM, April 1984.
42. *IMS/VS Version 2 Application Programming.* Doc. SC26-4178, IBM, March 1986.
43. *IMS/VS Extended Recovery Facility (XRF): Technical Reference.* Doc. GG24-3153, IBM, April 1987.
44. *IBM Workstation Data Save Facility/VM: General Information.* Doc. GH24-5232, IBM, 1990.
45. KORTH, H. Locking primitives in a database system. *JACM 30,* 1 (Jan. 1983), 55–79.
46. LUM, V., DADAM, P., ERBE, R., GUENAUER, J., PISTOR, P., WALCH, G., WERNER, H., AND WOODFILL, J. Design of an integrated DBMS to support advanced applications. In *Proceedings International Conference on Foundations of Data Organization* (Kyoto, May 1985).
47. LEVINE, F., AND MOHAN, C. Method for concurrent record access, insertion, deletion and alteration using an index tree. U.S. Patent 4,914,569, IBM, April 1990.
48. LEWIS, R. Z. *IMS Program Isolation Locking.* Doc. GG66-3193, IBM Dallas Systems Center, Dec. 1990.
49. LINDSAY, B., HAAS, L., MOHAN, C., WILMS, P., AND YOST, R. Computation and communication in R*: A distributed database manager. *ACM Trans. Comput. Syst. 2,* 1 (Feb. 1984). Also in *Proceedings 9th ACM Symposium on Operating Systems Principles* (Bretton Woods, Oct. 1983). Also available as IBM Res. Rep. RJ3740, San Jose, Calif., Jan. 1983.
50. LINDSAY, B., MOHAN, C., AND PIRAHESH, H. Method for reserving space needed for "rollback" actions. *IBM Tech. Disclosure Bull. 29,* 6 (Nov. 1986).
51. LISKOV, B., AND SCHEIFLER, R. Guardians and actions: Linguistic support for robust, distributed programs. *ACM Trans. Program. Lang. Syst. 5,* 3 (July 1983).
52. LINDSAY, B., SELINGER, P., GALTIERI, C., GRAY, J., LORIE, R., PUTZOLU, F., TRAIGER, I., AND WADE, B. Notes on distributed databases. IBM Res. Rep. RJ2571, San Jose, Calif., July 1979.
53. MCGEE, W. C. The information management system IMS/VS—Part II: Data base facilities; Part V: Transaction processing facilities. *IBM Syst. J. 16,* 2 (1977).
54. MOHAN, C., HADERLE, D., WANG, Y., AND CHENG, J. Single table access using multiple indexes: Optimization, execution, and concurrency control techniques. In *Proceedings International Conference on Extending Data Base Technology* (Venice, March 1990). An expanded version of this paper is available as IBM Res. Rep. RJ7341, IBM Almaden Research Center, March 1990.
55. MOHAN, C., FUSSELL, D., AND SILBERSCHATZ, A. Compatibility and commutativity of lock modes. *Inf. Control 61,* 1 (April 1984). Also available as IBM Res. Rep. RJ3948, San Jose, Calif., July 1983.
56. MOSS, E., GRIFFETH, N., AND GRAHAM, M. Abstraction in recovery management. In *Proceedings ACM SIGMOD International Conference on Management of Data* (Washington, D.C., May 1986).
57. MOHAN, C. ARIES/KVL: A key-value locking method for concurrency control of multiaction transactions operating on B-tree indexes. In *Proceedings 16th International Conference on Very Large Data Bases* (Brisbane, Aug. 1990). Another version of this paper is available as IBM Res. Rep. RJ7008, IBM Almaden Research Center, Sept. 1989.

58. MOHAN, C. Commit–LSN: A novel and simple method for reducing locking and latching in transaction processing systems In *Proceedings 16th International Conference on Very Large Data Bases* (Brisbane, Aug. 1990). Also available as IBM Res. Rep. RJ7344, IBM Almaden Research Center, Feb. 1990.
59 MOHAN, C. ARIES/LHS: A concurrency control and recovery method using write-ahead logging for linear hashing with separators. IBM Res. Rep., IBM Almaden Research Center, Nov. 1990.
60. MOHAN, C. A cost-effective method for providing improved data availability during DBMS restart recovery after a failure In *Proceedings of the 4th International Workshop on High Performance Transaction Systems* (Asilomar, Calif., Sept. 1991). Also available as IBM Res. Rep. RJ8114, IBM Almaden Research Center, April 1991.
61. MOSS, E., LEBAN, B., AND CHRYSANTHIS, P. Fine grained concurrency for the database cache. In *Proceedings 3rd IEEE International Conference on Data Engineering* (Los Angeles, Feb. 1987).
62. MOHAN, C., AND LEVINE, F. ARIES/IM: An efficient and high concurrency index management method using write-ahead logging. IBM Res. Rep. RJ6846, IBM Almaden Research Center, Aug. 1989.
63. MOHAN, C., AND LINDSAY, B. Efficient commit protocols for the tree of processes model of distributed transactions. In *Proceedings 2nd ACM SIGACT/SIGOPS Symposium on Principles of Distributed Computing* (Montreal, Aug. 1983). Also available as IBM Res. Rep. RJ3881, IBM San Jose Research Laboratory, June 1983.
64. MOHAN, C., LINDSAY, B., AND OBERMARCK, R. Transaction management in the R* distributed database management system. *ACM Trans. Database Syst. 11*, 4 (Dec. 1986).
65. MOHAN, C., AND NARANG, I. Recovery and coherency-control protocols for fast intersystem page transfer and fine-granularity locking in a shared disks transaction environment. In *Proceedings 17th International Conference on Very Large Data Bases* (Barcelona, Sept. 1991). A longer version is available as IBM Res. Rep. RJ8017, IBM Almaden Research Center, March 1991.
66. MOHAN, C., AND NARANG, I. Efficient locking and caching of data in the multisystem shared disks transaction environment. In *Proceedings of the International Conference on Extending Database Technology* (Vienna, Mar. 1992). Also available as IBM Res. Rep. RJ8301, IBM Almaden Research Center, Aug. 1991.
67. MOHAN, C., NARANG, I., AND PALMER, J. A case study of problems in migrating to distributed computing: Page recovery using multiple logs in the shared disks environment. IBM Res. Rep. RJ7343, IBM Almaden Research Center, March 1990.
68. MOHAN, C., NARANG, I., SILEN, S. Solutions to hot spot problems in a shared disks transaction environment. In *Proceedings of the 4th International Workshop on High Performance Transaction Systems* (Asilomar, Calif., Sept. 1991). Also available as IBM Res Rep. 8281, IBM Almaden Research Center, Aug. 1991.
69. MOHAN, C., AND PIRAHESH, H. ARIES-RRH: Restricted repeating of history in the ARIES transaction recovery method. In *Proceedings 7th International Conference on Data Engineering* (Kobe, April 1991). Also available as IBM Res. Rep. RJ7342, IBM Almaden Research Center, Feb. 1990
70. MOHAN, C , AND ROTHERMEL, K. Recovery protocol for nested transactions using write-ahead logging. *IBM Tech. Disclosure Bull. 31*, 4 (Sept 1988).
71. MOSS, E. Checkpoint and restart in distributed transaction systems. In *Proceedings 3rd Symposium on Reliability in Distributed Software and Database Systems* (Clearwater Beach, Oct. 1983).
72. MOSS, E Log-based recovery for nested transactions. In *Proceedings 13th International Conference on Very Large Data Bases* (Brighton, Sept. 1987).
73. MOHAN, C., TRIEBER, K., AND OBERMARCK, R. Algorithms for the management of remote backup databases for disaster recovery. IBM Res. Rep. RJ7885, IBM Almaden Research Center, Nov. 1990.
74. NETT, E., KAISER, J., AND KROGER, R. Providing recoverability in a transaction oriented distributed operating system. In *Proceedings 6th International Conference on Distributed Computing Systems* (Cambridge, May 1986).

75. Noe, J., Kaiser, J., Kroger, R., and Nett, E. The commit/abort problem in type-specific locking. GMD Tech. Rep. 267, GMD mbH, Sankt Augustin, Sept. 1987.
76. Obermarck, R. IMS/VS program isolation feature. IBM Res. Rep. RJ2879, San Jose, Calif., July 1980.
77. O'Neill, P. The Escrow transaction method. *ACM Trans. Database Syst. 11*, 4 (Dec. 1986).
78. Ong, K. SYNAPSE approach to database recovery. In *Proceedings 3rd ACM SIGACT-SIGMOD Symposium on Principles of Database Systems* (Waterloo, April 1984).
79. Peinl, P., Reuter, A., and Sammer, H. High contention in a stock trading database: A case study. In *Proceedings ACM SIGMOD International Conference on Management of Data* (Chicago, June 1988).
80. Peterson, R. J., and Strickland, J. P. Log write-ahead protocols and IMS/VS logging. In *Proceedings 2nd ACM SIGACT-SIGMOD Symposium on Principles of Database Systems* (Atlanta, Ga., March 1983).
81. Rengarajan, T. K., Spiro, P., and Wright, W. High availability mechanisms of VAX DBMS software. *Digital Tech. J. 8* (Feb. 1989).
82. Reuter, A. A fast transaction-oriented logging scheme for UNDO recovery. *IEEE Trans. Softw. Eng. SE-6*, 4 (July 1980).
83. Reuter, A. Concurrency on high-traffic data elements. In *Proceedings ACM SIGACT-SIGMOD Symposium on Principles of Database Systems* (Los Angeles, March 1982).
84. Reuter, A. Performance analysis of recovery techniques. *ACM Trans. Database Syst. 9*, 4 (Dec. 1984), 526–559.
85. Rothermel, K., and Mohan, C. ARIES/NT: A recovery method based on write-ahead logging for nested transactions. In *Proceedings 15th International Conference on Very Large Data Bases* (Amsterdam, Aug. 1989). A longer version of this paper is available as IBM Res. Rep. RJ6650, IBM Almaden Research Center, Jan. 1989.
86. Rowe, L., and Stonebraker, M. The commercial INGRES epilogue. Ch. 3 in *The INGRES Papers*, Stonebraker, M., Ed., Addson-Wesley, Reading, Mass., 1986.
87. Schwarz, P., Chang, W., Freytag, J., Lohman, G., McPherson, J., Mohan, C., and Pirahesh, H. Extensibility in the Starburst database system. In *Proceedings Workshop on Object-Oriented Data Base Systems* (Asilomar, Sept. 1986). Also available as IBM Res. Rep. RJ5311, San Jose, Calif., Sept. 1986.
88. Schwarz, P. Transactions on typed objects. Ph.D. dissertation, Tech. Rep. CMU-CS-84-166, Carnegie Mellon Univ., Dec. 1984.
89. Shasha, D., and Goodman, N. Concurrent search structure algorithms. *ACM Trans. Database Syst. 13*, 1 (March 1988).
90. Spector, A., Pausch, R., and Bruell, G. Camelot: A flexible, distributed transaction processing system. In *Proceedings IEEE Compcon Spring '88* (San Francisco, Calif., March 1988).
91. Spratt, L. The transaction resolution journal: Extending the before journal. *ACM Oper. Syst. Rev. 19*, 3 (July 1985).
92. Stonebraker, M. The design of the POSTGRES storage system. In *Proceedings 13th International Conference on Very Large Data Bases* (Brighton, Sept. 1987).
93. Stillwell, J. W., and Rader, P. M. *IMS/VS Version 1 Release 3 Fast Path Notebook*. Doc. G320-0149-0, IBM, Sept. 1984.
94. Strickland, J., Uhrowczik, P., and Watts, V. IMS/VS: An evolving system. *IBM Syst. J. 21*, 4 (1982).
95. The Tandem Database Group. NonStop SQL: A distributed, high-performance, high-availability implementation of SQL. In *Lecture Notes in Computer Science Vol. 359*, D. Gawlick, M. Haynie, and A. Reuter, Eds., Springer-Verlag, New York, 1989.
96. Teng, J., and Gumaer, R. Managing IBM Database 2 buffers to maximize performance. *IBM Syst. J. 23*, 2 (1984).
97. Traiger, I. Virtual memory management for database systems. *ACM Oper. Syst. Rev. 16*, 4 (Oct. 1982), 26–48.
98. Vural, S. A simulation study for the performance analysis of the ARIES transaction recovery method. M.Sc. thesis, Middle East Technical Univ., Ankara, Feb. 1990.

99 Watson, C. T., and Aberle, G. F System/38 machine database support. In *IBM Syst. 38/Tech. Dev.*, Doc. G580-0237, IBM July 1980.

100. Weikum, G. Principles and realization strategies of multi-level transaction management. *ACM Trans. Database Syst. 16*, 1 (Mar. 1991).

101. Weinstein, M., Page, T., Jr , Livezey, B., and Popek, G. Transactions and synchronization in a distributed operating system. In *Proceedings 10th ACM Symposium on Operating Systems Principles* (Orcas Island, Dec. 1985).

Received January 1989; revised November 1990; accepted April 1991

Transaction Management in the R* Distributed Database Management System

C. MOHAN, B. LINDSAY, and R. OBERMARCK
IBM Almaden Research Center

This paper deals with the transaction management aspects of the R* distributed database system. It concentrates primarily on the description of the R* commit protocols, Presumed Abort (PA) and Presumed Commit (PC). PA and PC are extensions of the well-known, two-phase (2P) commit protocol. PA is optimized for read-only transactions and a class of multisite update transactions, and PC is optimized for other classes of multisite update transactions. The optimizations result in reduced intersite message traffic and log writes, and, consequently, a better response time. The paper also discusses R*'s approach toward distributed deadlock detection and resolution.

Categories and Subject Descriptors: C.2.4 [**Computer-Communication Networks**]: Distributed Systems—*distributed databases*; D.4.1 [**Operating Systems**]: Process Management—*concurrency; deadlocks; synchronization*; D.4.7 [**Operating Systems**]: Organization and Design—*distributed systems*; D.4.5 [**Operating Systems**]: Reliability—*fault tolerance*; H.2.0 [**Database Management**]: General—*concurrency control*; H.2.2 [**Database Management**]: Physical Design—*recovery and restart*; H.2.4 [**Database Management**]: Systems—*distributed systems; transaction processing*; H.2.7 [**Database Management**]: Database Administration—*logging and recovery*

General Terms: Algorithms, Design, Reliability

Additional Key Words and Phrases: Commit protocols, deadlock victim selection

1. INTRODUCTION

R* is an experimental, distributed database management system (DDBMS) developed and operational at the IBM San Jose Research Laboratory (now renamed the IBM Almaden Research Center) [18, 20]. In a distributed database system, the actions of a transaction (an atomic unit of consistency and recovery [13]) may occur at more than one site. Our model of a transaction, unlike that of some other researchers' [25, 28], permits multiple data manipulation and definition statements to constitute a single transaction. When a transaction execution starts, its actions and operands are not constrained. Conditional execution and ad hoc SQL statements are available to the application program. The whole transaction need not be fully specified and made known to the system in advance. A distributed transaction commit protocol is required in order to ensure either that *all* the effects of the transaction persist or that *none* of the

Authors' address: IBM Almaden Research Center, K55/801, 650 Harry Road, San Jose, CA 95120.

effects persist, despite intermittent site or communication link failures. In other words, a commit protocol is needed to guarantee the uniform commitment of distributed transaction executions.

Guaranteeing uniformity requires that certain facilities exist in the distributed database system. We assume that each process of a transaction is able to *provisionally* perform the actions of the transaction in such a way that they can be undone if the transaction is or needs to be aborted. Also, each database of the distributed database system has a *log* that is used to recoverably record the state changes of the transaction during the execution of the commit protocol and the transaction's changes to the database (the UNDO/REDO log [14, 15]). The log records are carefully written sequentially in a file that is kept in *stable* (nonvolatile) *storage* [17].

When a log record is written, the write can be done synchronously or asynchronously. In the former case, called *forcing* a log record, the forced log record *and* all preceding ones are *immediately* moved from the virtual memory buffers to stable storage. The transaction writing the log record is not allowed to continue execution until this operation is completed. This means that, if the site crashes (assuming that a crash results in the loss of the contents of the virtual memory) after the force-write has completed, then the forced record and the ones preceding it will have survived the crash and will be available, from the stable storage, when the site recovers. It is important to be able to "batch" force-writes for high performance [11]. R* does rudimentary batching of force-writes.

On the other hand, in the asynchronous case, the record gets written to virtual memory buffer storage and is allowed to migrate to the stable storage later on (due to a subsequent force or when a log page buffer fills up). The transaction writing the record is allowed to continue execution before the migration takes place. This means that, if the site crashes after the log write, then the record may not be available for reading when the site recovers. An important point to note is that a synchronous write increases the response time of the transaction compared to an asynchronous write. Hereafter, we refer to the latter as simply a write and the former as a force-write.

Several commit protocols have been proposed in the literature, and some have been implemented [8, 16, 17, 19, 23, 26, 27]. These are variations of what has come to be known as the two-phase (2P) commit protocol. These protocols differ in the number of messages sent, the time for completion of the commit processing, the level of parallelism permitted during the commit processing, the number of state transitions that the protocols go through, the time required for recovery once a site becomes operational after a failure, the number of log records written, and the number of those log records that are force-written to stable storage. In general, these numbers are expressed as a function of the number of sites or processes involved in the execution of the distributed transaction.

Some of the desirable characteristics in a commit protocol are (1) guaranteed transaction atomicity always, (2) ability to "forget" outcome of commit processing after a short amount of time, (3) minimal overhead in terms of log writes and message traffic, (4) optimized performance in the no-failure case, (5) exploitation of completely or partially read-only transactions, and (6) maximizing the ability to perform unilateral aborts.

This paper concentrates on the performance aspects of commit protocols, especially the logging and communication performance during no-failure situations. We have been careful in describing when and what type of log records are written. The discussions of commit protocols in the literature are very vague, if there is any mention at all, about this crucial (for correctness and performance) aspect of the protocols. We also exploit the read-only property of the complete transaction or some of its processes. In such instances, one can benefit from the fact that for such processes of the transaction it does not matter whether the transaction commits or aborts, and hence they can be excluded from the second phase of the commit protocol. This also means that the (read) locks acquired by such processes can be released during the first phase. No a priori assumptions are made about the read-only nature of transactions. Such information is discovered only during the first phase of the commit protocol.

Here, we suggest that complicated protocols developed for dealing with rare kinds of failures during commit coordination are not worth the costs that they impose on the processing of distributed transactions during normal times (i.e., when no failures occur). Multilevel hierarchical commit protocols are also suggested to be more natural than the conventional two-level (one coordinator and a set of subordinates) protocols. This stems from the fact that the distributed query processing algorithms are efficiently implemented as a tree of cooperating processes.

With these goals in mind, we extended the conventional 2P commit protocol to support a tree of processes [18] and defined the Presumed Abort (PA) and the Presumed Commit (PC) protocols to improve the performance of distributed transaction commit.

R*, which is an evolution of the centralized DBMS System R [5], like its predecessor, supports transaction serializability and uses the two-phase locking (2PL) protocol [10] as the concurrency control mechanism. The use of 2PL introduces the possibility of deadlocks. R*, instead of preventing deadlocks, allows them (even distributed ones) to occur and then resolves them by deadlock detection and victim transaction abort.

Some of the desirable characteristics in a distributed deadlock detection protocol are (1) all deadlocks are resolved in spite of site and link failures, (2) each deadlock is detected only once, (3) overhead in terms of messages exchanged is small, and (4) once a distributed deadlock is detected the time taken to resolve it (by choosing a victim and aborting it) is small.

The general features of the global deadlock detection algorithm used in R* are described in [24]. Here we concentrate on the specific implementation of that distributed algorithm in R* and the solution adopted for the global deadlock victim selection problem. In general, as far as global deadlock management is concerned, we suggest that if distributed detection of global deadlocks is to be performed then, in the event of a global deadlock, it makes sense to choose as the victim a transaction that is local to the site of detection of that deadlock (in preference to, say, the "youngest" transaction which may be a nonlocal transaction), assuming that such a local transaction exists.

The rest of this paper is organized as follows. First, we give a careful presentation of 2P. Next, we derive from 2P in a stepwise fashion the two new protocols, namely, PA and PC. We then present performance comparisons, optimizations, and extensions of PA and PC. Next, we present the R* approach to global deadlock detection and resolution. We then conclude by outlining the current status of R*.

2. THE TWO-PHASE COMMIT PROTOCOL

In 2P, the model of a distributed transaction execution is such that there is one process, called the *coordinator,* that is connected to the user application and a set of other processes, called the *subordinates.* During the execution of the commit protocol the subordinates communicate only with the coordinator, not among themselves. Transactions are assumed to have globally unique names. The processes are assumed to have globally unique names (which also indicate the locations of the corresponding processes; the processes do not migrate from site to site).[1] All the processes together accomplish the actions of a distributed transaction.

2.1 2P Under Normal Operation

First, we describe the protocol without considering failures. When the user decides to commit a transaction, the coordinator, which receives a commit-transaction command from the user, initiates the first phase of the commit protocol by sending *PREPARE* messages, in parallel, to the subordinates to determine whether they are willing to commit the transaction.[2] Each subordinate that is willing to let the transaction be committed *first* force-writes a *prepare* log record and then sends a *YES VOTE* to the coordinator and waits for the final decision (commit/abort) from the coordinator. The process is then said to be in the **prepared** state, and it cannot unilaterally commit or abort the transaction. Each subordinate that wants to have the transaction aborted force-writes an *abort* record and sends a *NO VOTE* to the coordinator. Since a *NO VOTE* acts like a veto, the subordinate knows that the transaction will definitely be aborted by the coordinator. Hence the subordinate does not need to wait for a coordinator response before aborting the local effects of the transaction. Therefore, the subordinate aborts the transaction, releases its locks, and "forgets" it (i.e., no information about this transaction is retained in virtual storage).

After the coordinator receives the votes from all its subordinates, it initiates the second phase of the protocol. If all the votes were *YES VOTE*s, then the coordinator moves to the **committing** state by force-writing a *commit* record and sending *COMMIT* messages to all the subordinates. The completion of the force-write takes the transaction to its **commit point.** Once this point is passed the user can be told that the transaction has been committed. If the coordinator had received even one *NO VOTE,* then it moves to the **aborting** state by force-writing an *abort* record and sends *ABORT*s to (only) all the subordinates that are in the **prepared** state or have not responded to the *PREPARE.* Each subordinate, after receiving a *COMMIT,* moves to the **committing** state,

[1] For ease of exposition, we assume that each site participating in a distributed transaction has only one process of that transaction. However, the protocols presented here have been implemented in R*, where this assumption is relaxed to permit more than one such process per site.

[2] In cases where the user or the coordinator wants to abort the transaction, the latter sends an *ABORT* message to each of the subordinates. If a transaction is resubmitted after being aborted, it is given a new name.

force-writes a *commit* record, sends an acknowledgment (*ACK*) message to the coordinator, and then commits the transaction and "forgets" it. Each subordinate, after receiving an *ABORT*, moves to the **aborting** state, force-writes an *abort* record, sends an *ACK* to the coordinator, and then aborts the transaction and "forgets" it. The coordinator, after receiving the *ACK*s from all the subordinates that were sent a message in the second phase (remember that subordinates who voted *NO* do not get any *ABORT*s in the second phase), writes an *end* record and "forgets" the transaction.

By requiring the subordinates to send *ACK*s, the coordinator ensures that all the subordinates are aware of the final outcome. By forcing their *commit/abort* records before sending the *ACK*s, the subordinates make sure that they will *never* be required (while recovering from a processor failure) to ask the coordinator about the final outcome after having acknowledged a *COMMIT/ABORT*. The general principle on which the protocols described in this paper are based is that if a subordinate acknowledges the receipt of any particular message, then it should make sure (by forcing a log record with the information in that message *before* sending the *ACK*) that it will never ask the coordinator about that piece of information. If this principle is not adhered to, transaction atomicity may not be guaranteed.

The log records at each site contain the type (*prepare*, *end*, etc.) of the record, the identity of the process that writes the record, the name of the transaction, the identity of the coordinator, the names of the exclusive locks held by the writer in the case of *prepare* records, and the identities of the subordinates in the case of the *commit/abort* records written by the coordinator.

To summarize, for a committing transaction, during the execution of the protocol, each subordinate writes two records (*prepare* and *commit*, both of which are forced) and sends two messages (*YES VOTE* and *ACK*). The coordinator sends two messages (*PREPARE* and *COMMIT*) to each subordinate and writes two records (*commit*, which is forced, and *end*, which is not).

Figure 1 shows the message flows and log writes for an example transaction following 2P.

2.2 2P and Failures

Let us now consider site and communication link failures. We assume that at each active site a *recovery process* exists and that it processes all messages from recovery processes at other sites and handles all the transactions that were executing the commit protocol at the time of the last failure of the site. We assume that, as part of recovery from a crash, the recovery process at the recovering site reads the log on stable storage and accumulates in *virtual storage* information relating to transactions that were executing the commit protocol at the time of the crash.[3] It is this information in virtual storage that is used to answer queries from other sites about transactions that had their coordinators at this site and to send unsolicited information to other sites that had subordinates for transactions that had their coordinators at this site. Having the

[3] The extent of the log that has to be read on restart can be controlled by taking *checkpoints* during normal operation [14, 15]. The log is scanned forward starting from the last checkpoint before the crash until the end of the log.

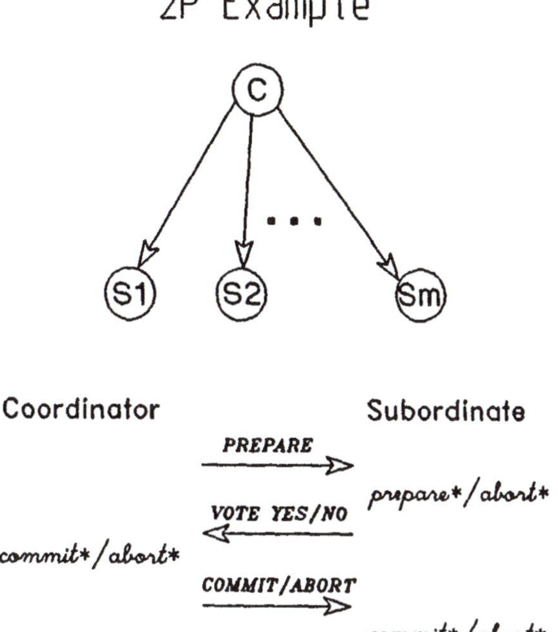

Fig. 1. Message flows and log writes in 2P. The names in italics indicate the types of log records written. An * next to the record type means that the record is forced to stable storage.

information in virtual storage allows remote site inquiries to be answered quickly. There will be no need to consult the log to answer the queries.

When the recovery process finds that it is in the **prepared** state for a particular transaction, it *periodically* tries to contact the coordinator site to find out how the transaction should be resolved. When the coordinator site resolves a transaction and lets this site know the final outcome, the recovery process takes the steps outlined before for a subordinate when it receives an *ABORT/COMMIT*. If the recovery process finds that a transaction was executing at the time of the crash and that no commit protocol log record had been written, then the recovery process neither knows nor cares whether it is dealing with a subordinate or the coordinator of the transaction. It aborts that transaction by "undoing" its actions, if any, using the UNDO log records, writing an *abort* record, and "forgetting" it.[4] If the recovery process finds a transaction in the **committing** (respectively, **aborting**) state, it periodically tries to send the *COMMIT* (*ABORT*) to all the subordinates that have not acknowledged and awaits their *ACK*s. Once all the

[4] It should be clear now why a subordinate cannot send a *YES VOTE* first and then write a *prepare* record, and why a coordinator cannot send a *COMMIT* first and then write the *commit* record. If such actions were permitted, then a failure after the message sending but before the log write may result in the wrong action being taken at restart; some sites might have committed and others may abort.

ACKs are received, the recovery process writes the *end* record and "forgets" the transaction.

In addition to the workload that the recovery process accumulates by reading the log during restart, it may be handed over some transactions during normal operation by local coordinator and subordinate processes that notice some link or remote site failures during the commit protocol (see [18] for information relating to how such failures are noticed). We assume that all failed sites ultimately recover.

If the coordinator process notices the failure of a subordinate while waiting for the latter to send its vote, then the former aborts the transaction by taking the previously outlined steps. If the failure occurs when the coordinator is waiting to get an *ACK*, then the coordinator hands the transaction over to the recovery process.

If a subordinate notices the failure of the coordinator before the former sent a *YES VOTE* and moved into the **prepared** state, then it aborts the transaction (this is called the *unilateral abort* feature). On the other hand, if the failure occurs after the subordinate has moved into the **prepared** state, then the subordinate hands the transaction over to the recovery process.

When a recovery process receives an inquiry message from a **prepared** subordinate site, it looks at its information in virtual storage. If it has information that says the transaction is in the **aborting** or **committing** state, then it sends the appropriate response. The natural question that arises is what action should be taken if **no information** is found in virtual storage about the transaction. Let us see when such a situation could arise. Since both *COMMITs* and *ABORTs* are being acknowledged, the fact that the inquiry is being made means that the inquirer had not received and processed a *COMMIT/ABORT* before the inquiree "forgot" the transaction. Such a situation comes about when (1) the inquiree sends out *PREPAREs*, (2) it crashes before receiving all the votes and deciding to commit/abort, and (3) on restart, it aborts the transaction and does not inform any of the subordinates. As mentioned before, on restart, the recipient of an inquiry cannot tell whether it is a coordinator or subordinate, if no commit protocol log records exist for the transaction. Given this fact, the correct response to an inquiry in the **no information** case is an *ABORT*.

2.3 Hierarchical 2P

2P as described above is inadequate for use in systems where the transaction execution model is such that multilevel (>2) trees of processes are possible, as in R* and ENCOMPASS [8]. Each process communicates directly with only its immediate neighbors in the tree, that is, parent and children. In fact, a process would not even know about the existence of its nonneighbor processes. There is a simple extension of 2P that would work in this scenario. In the hierarchical version of 2P, the root process that is connected to the user/application acts only as a coordinator, the leaf processes act only as subordinates, and the nonleaf, nonroot processes act as both coordinators (for their child processes) and subordinates (for their parent processes). The root process and the leaf processes act as in nonhierarchical 2P. A nonroot, nonleaf process after receiving a *PREPARE* propagates it to its subordinates and only after receiving their votes does it send its combined (i.e., subtree) vote to its coordinator. The type of the subtree vote is determined by the types of the votes of the subordinates and the type of the vote of the subtree's root process. If any vote is a *NO VOTE*, then the subtree vote is a *NO VOTE* also (in this case, the subtree root process, after sending the subtree vote to its coordinator, sends *ABORT*s to all those subordinates that voted *YES*). If none of the votes is a *NO VOTE*, then the subtree vote is a *YES VOTE*. A nonroot, nonleaf process in the **prepared** state, on receiving an *ABORT* or a *COMMIT*, propagates it to its subordinates after force-writing its *commit* record and sending the *ACK* to its coordinator.

3. THE PRESUMED ABORT PROTOCOL

In Section 2.2 we noticed that, in the absence of any information about a transaction, the recovery process orders an inquiring subordinate to abort. A careful examination of this scenario reveals the fact that it is safe for a coordinator to "forget" a transaction immediately after it makes the decision to abort it (e.g., by receiving a *NO VOTE*) and to write an *abort* record.[5] This means that the *abort* record need not be forced (both by the coordinator and each of the subordinates), and no *ACK*s need to be sent (by the subordinates) for *ABORT*s. Furthermore, the coordinator need not record the names of the subordinates in the *abort* record or write an *end* record after an *abort* record. Also, if the coordinator notices the failure of a subordinate while attempting to send an *ABORT* to it, the coordinator does *not* need to hand the transaction over to the recovery process. It will let the subordinate find out about the abort when the recovery process of the subordinate's site sends an inquiry message. Note that the changes that we have made so far to the 2P protocol have not changed the performance (in terms of log writes and message sending) of the protocol with respect to committing transactions.

Let us now consider completely or partially *read-only* transactions and see how we can take advantage of them. A transaction is partially read-only if some processes of the transaction do not perform any updates to the database while the others do. A transaction is (completely) read-only if no process of the transaction performs any updates. We do not need to know before the transaction starts whether it is read-only or not.[6] If a leaf process receives a *PREPARE* and it finds that it has not done any updates (i.e., no UNDO/REDO log records have been written), then it sends a *READ VOTE*, releases its locks, and "forgets" the transaction. The subordinate writes **no** log records. As far as it is concerned, it does not matter whether the transaction ultimately gets aborted or committed. So the subordinate, who is now known to the coordinator to be read-only, does not need to be sent a *COMMIT/ABORT* by the coordinator. A nonroot, nonleaf sends a *READ VOTE* only if its own vote and those of its subordinates' are also *READ VOTE*s. Otherwise, as long as none of the latter is a *NO VOTE*, it sends a *YES VOTE*.

[5] Remember that in 2P the coordinator (during normal execution) "forgets" an abort only after it is sure that all the subordinates are aware of the abort decision.

[6] If the program contains conditional statements, the same program during different executions may be either read-only or update depending on the input parameters and the database state.

Root Process

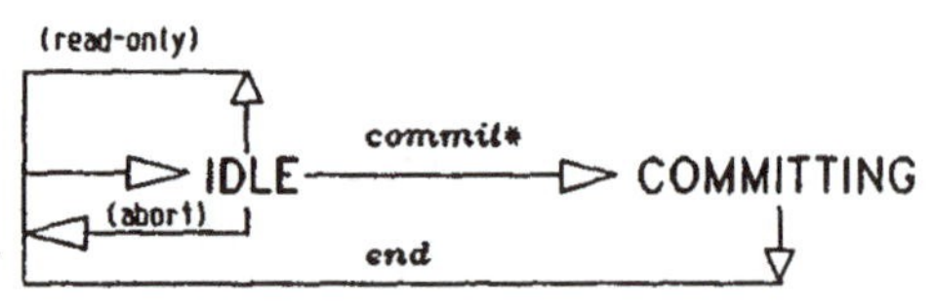

Leaf Process

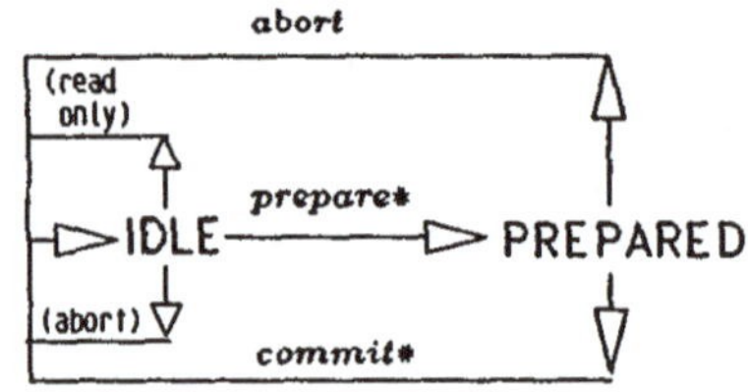

Non-Root, Non-Leaf Process

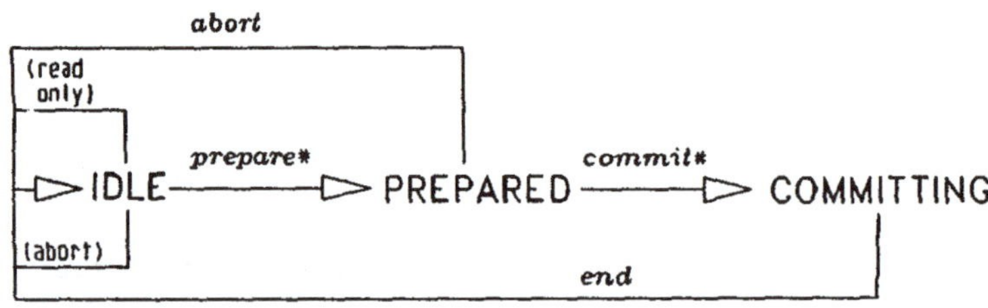

State Changes and Log Writes
for Presumed Abort

Fig. 2. The names in italics on the arcs of the state-transition diagrams indicate the types of log records written. An * next to the record type means that the record is forced to stable storage. No log records are written during some transitions. In such cases, information in parentheses indicates under what circumstances such transitions take place. IDLE is the initial and final state for each process.

There will not be a second phase of the protocol if the root process is read-only and it gets only *READ VOTE*s. In this case the root process, just like the other processes, writes **no** log records for the transaction. On the other hand, if the root process or one of its subordinates votes *YES* and none of the others vote *NO*, then the root process behaves as in 2P. But note that it is sufficient for a nonleaf process to include in the *commit* record only the identities of those subordinates (if any) that voted *YES* (only those processes will be in the **prepared** state, and hence only they will need to be sent *COMMIT*s). If a nonleaf process or one of its subordinates votes *NO*, then the former behaves as described earlier in this section.

To summarize, for a (completely) read-only transaction, none of the processes write any log records, but each one of the nonleaf processes sends one message (*PREPARE*) to each subordinate and each one of the nonroot processes sends one message (*READ VOTE*).

For a committing partially read-only transaction, the root process sends two messages (*PREPARE* and *COMMIT*) to each update subordinate and one message (*PREPARE*) to each of the read-only subordinates. Each one of the nonleaf,

Presumed Commit Example

A B C

collecting* PREPARE collecting* PREPARE VOTE READ VOTE YES prepare* commit* COMMIT commit

TIME

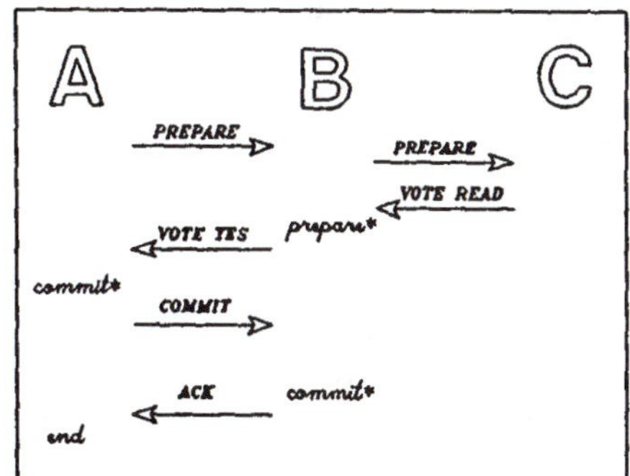

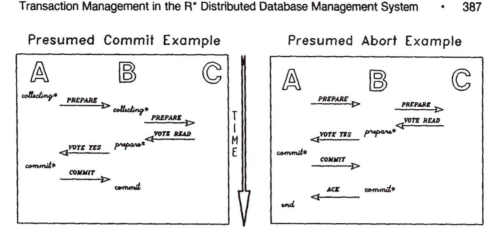

Fig. 3. Message flows and log writes in PA and PC. *A* (update/read-only) is the root of the process tree with *B* (update) as its child. *C* (read-only) is the leaf of the tree and the child of *B*.

nonroot processes that is the root of an update subtree sends two messages (*PREPARE* and *COMMIT*) to each update subordinate, one message (*PREPARE*) to each of the other subordinates, and two messages (*YES VOTE* and *ACK*) to its coordinator. Each one of the nonleaf, nonroot processes that is the root of a read-only subtree behaves just like the corresponding processes in a completely read-only transaction following PA. Each one of the nonleaf processes writes three records (*prepare* and *commit*, which are forced, and *end*, which is not) if there is at least one update subordinate, and only two records (*prepare* and *commit*, which are forced) if the nonleaf process itself is an update one and it does not have any update subordinates. A read-only leaf process behaves just like the one in a completely read-only transaction following PA, and an update leaf process behaves like a subordinate of a committing transaction in 2P.

By making the above changes to hierarchical 2P, we have generated the PA protocol. The name arises from the fact that in the **no information** case the transaction is presumed to have aborted, and hence the recovery process's response to an inquiry is an *ABORT*. Figure 2 shows the state transitions and log writes performed by the different processes following PA. Figure 3 shows the message flows and log writes for an example transaction following PA.

4. THE PRESUMED COMMIT PROTOCOL

Since most transactions are expected to commit, it is only natural to wonder if, by requiring *ACK*s for *ABORT*s, commits could be made cheaper by eliminating the *ACK*s for *COMMIT*s. A simplistic idea that comes to mind is to require that *ABORT*s be acknowledged, while *COMMIT*s need not be, and also that *abort* records be forced while *commit* records need not be by the subordinates. The consequences are that, in the **no information** case, the recovery process responds with a *COMMIT* when a subordinate inquiries. There is, however, a problem with this approach.

Consider the situation when a root process has sent the *PREPARE*s, one subordinate has gone into the **prepared** state, and before the root process is able to collect all the votes and make a decision, the root process crashes. Note that so far the root process would not have written *any* commit protocol log records. When the crashed root process's site recovers, its recovery process will abort this transaction and "forget" it without informing anyone, since **no** information is available about the subordinates. When the recovery process of the **prepared** subordinate's site then inquires the root process's site, the latter's recovery process would respond with a *COMMIT*,[7] causing an unacceptable inconsistency.

The way out of this problem is for each coordinator (i.e., nonleaf process) to record the names of its subordinates safely *before* any of the latter could get into the **prepared** state. Then, when the coordinator site aborts on recovery from a crash that occurred after the sending of the *PREPARE*s (but before the coordinator moved into the **prepared** state, in the case of the nonroot coordinators), the restart process will know who to inform (and get *ACK*s) about the abort. These modifications give us the PC protocol. The name arises from the fact that in the **no information** case the transaction is presumed to have committed and hence the response to an inquiry is a *COMMIT*.

In PC, a nonleaf process behaves as in PA except (1) at the start of the first phase (i.e., before sending the *PREPARE*s) it force-writes a *collecting* record, which contains the names of all the subordinates, and moves into the **collecting** state; (2) it force-writes only *abort* records (except in the case of the root process, which force-writes *commit* records also); (3) it requires *ACK*s only for *ABORT*s and not for *COMMIT*s; (4) it writes an *end* record only after an *abort* record (if the abort is done after a *collecting* record is written) and not after a *commit* record; (5) only when in the **aborting** state will it, on noticing a subordinate's failure, hand over the transaction to the restart process; and (6) in the case of a (completely) read-only transaction, it would not write any records at the end of the first phase in PA, but in PC it would write a *commit* record and then "forget" the transaction.

The subordinates behave as in PA except that now they force-write only *abort* records and not *commit* records, and they *ACK* only *ABORT*s and not *COMMIT*s. On restart, if the recovery process finds, for a particular transaction, a *collecting* record and no other records following it, then it force-writes an *abort* record, informs all the subordinates, gets *ACK*s from them, writes the *end* record, and "forgets" the transaction. In the **no information** case, the recovery process responds to an inquiry with a *COMMIT*.

To summarize, for a (completely) read-only transaction, each one of the nonleaf processes writes two records (*collecting*, which is forced, and *commit*, which is not) and sends one message (*PREPARE*) to each subordinate. Furthermore, each one of the nonleaf, nonroot processes sends one more message (*READ VOTE*). The leaf processes write no log records, but each one of them sends one message (*READ VOTE*) to its coordinator.

[7] Note that, as far as the recovery process is concerned, this situation is the same as when a root process, after force-writing a *commit* record (which now will not contain the names of the subordinates), tries to inform a *prepared* subordinate, finds it has crashed, and therefore "forgets" the transaction (i.e., does not hand it to the recovery process). Later on, when the subordinate inquires, the recovery process would find no information and hence would respond with a *COMMIT*.

Root Process

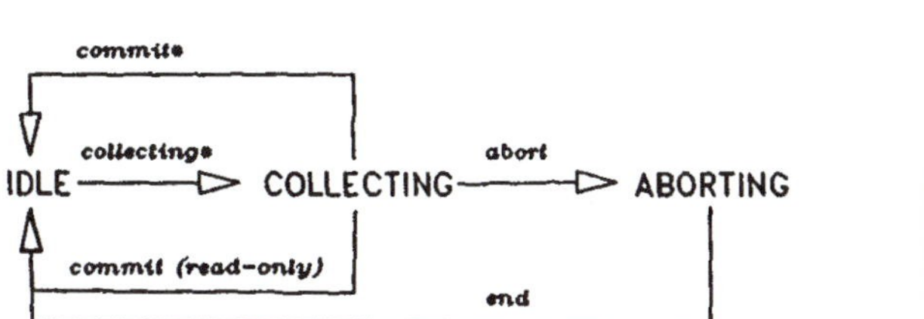

Leaf Process

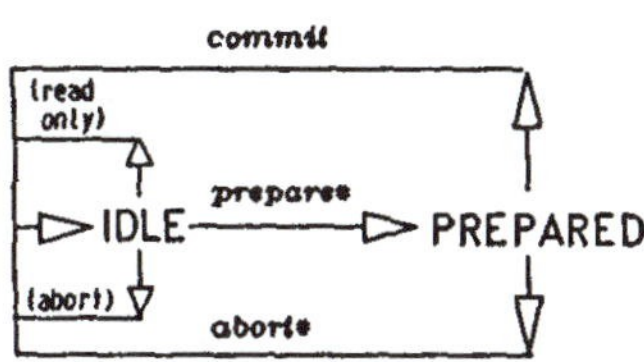

Non-Root, Non-Leaf Process

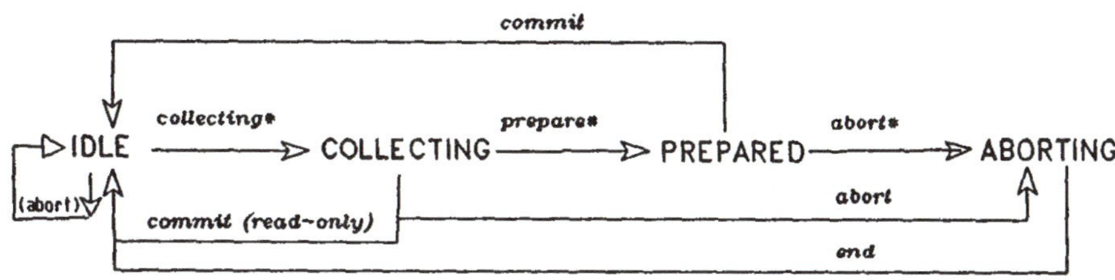

State Changes and Log Writes
for Presumed Commit

Figure 4

For a committing partially read-only transaction, the root process writes two records (*collecting* and *commit*, both of which are forced) and sends two messages (*PREPARE* and *COMMIT*) to each subordinate that sent a *YES VOTE* and one message (*PREPARE*) to each one of the other subordinates. Each one of the nonleaf, nonroot processes that is the root of an update subtree sends two messages (*PREPARE* and *COMMIT*) to each subordinate that sent a *YES VOTE*, one message (*PREPARE*) to each one of the other subordinates, and one message (*YES VOTE*) to its coordinator, and it writes three records (*collecting* and *prepared*, which are forced, and *commit*, which is not). Read-only leaf processes, and processes that are roots of read-only subtrees, behave just like the corresponding processes in a completely read-only transaction. An update leaf process sends one message (*YES VOTE*) and writes two records (*prepare*, which is forced, and *commit*, which is not).

Figure 4 shows the state transitions and log writes performed by the different processes following PC. Figure 3 shows the message flows and log writes for an example transaction following PC.

Protocol Type \ Process Type	Coordinator			Subordinate	
	U Yes US	U No US	R	US	RS
Standard 2P	2,1,-,2	-	-	2,2,2	-
Presumed Abort	2,1,1,2	1,1,1	0,0,1	2,2,2	0,0,1
Presumed Commit	2,2,1,2	2,2,1	2,1,1	2,1,1	0,0,1

U - Update Transaction
R - Read-Only Transaction
RS - Read-Only Subordinate
US - Update Subordinate
m,n,o,p - m Records Written, n of Them Forced
o For a Coordinator: # of Messages Sent to Each RS
For a Subordinate: # of Messages Sent to Coordinator
p # of Messages Sent to Each US

Fig. 5. Comparison of log I/O and messages for committing two-level process tree transactions with 2P, PA, and PC.

5. DISCUSSION

In the table of Figure 5 we summarize the performance of 2P, PA, and PC with respect to committing update and read-only transactions that have two-level process trees. Note that as far as 2P is concerned all transactions appear to be completely update transactions and that under all circumstances PA is better than 2P. It is obvious that PA performs better than PC in the case of (completely) read-only transactions (saving the coordinator two log writes, including a force) and in the case of partially read-only transactions in which only the coordinator does any updates (saving the coordinator a force-write). In both cases, PA and PC require the same number of messages to be sent. In the case of a transaction with only one update subordinate, PA and PC are equal in terms of log writes, but PA requires an extra message (*ACK* sent by the update subordinate). For a transaction with $n > 1$ update subordinates, both PA and PC require the same number of records to be written, but PA will force $n - 1$ times when PC will not. These correspond to the forcing of the *commit* records by the subordinates. In addition, PA will send n extra messages (*ACKs*).

Depending on the transaction mix that is expected to be run against a particular distributed database, the choice between PA and PC can be made. It should also be noted that the choice could be made on a transaction-by-transaction basis (instead of on a systemwide basis) at the time of the start of the first phase by the root process.[8] At the time of starting a transaction, the user could give a *hint* (*not* a guarantee) that it is likely to be read-only, in which case PA could be chosen; otherwise PC could be chosen.

It should be pointed out that our commit protocols are blocking [26] in that they require a **prepared** process that has noticed the failure of its coordinator to wait until it can reestablish communication with its coordinator's site to determine the final outcome (commit or abort) of the commit processing for that transaction. We have extended, but not implemented, PA and PC to reduce the probability of blocking by allowing a **prepared** process that encounters a coordinator failure to ask its peers about the transaction outcome. The extensions require an additional phase in the protocols and result in more messages and/or synchronous log writes even during normal times. In [23] we have proposed an approach to dealing with the blocking problem in the context of the Highly Available Systems project in our laboratory. This approach makes use of Byzantine Agreement protocols. To some extent the results of [9] support our conclusion that blocking commit protocols are not undesirable.

To handle the rare situation in which a blocked process holds up too many other transactions from gaining access to its locked data, we have provided an interface that allows the operator to find out the identities of the **prepared** processes and to forcibly commit or abort them. Of course, the misuse of this facility could lead to inconsistencies caused by parts of a transaction being committed while the rest of the transaction is aborted. In cases where a link failure is the cause of blocking, the operator at the blocked site could use the telephone to find out the coordinator site's decision and force the same decision at his or her site.

Given that we have our efficient commit protocols PA and PC, and the fact that remote updates are expected or postulated to be infrequent, the time spent executing the commit protocol is going to be small compared to the total time spent executing the whole transaction. Furthermore, site and link failures cannot be frequent or long-duration events in a well-designed and well-managed distributed system. So the probability of the failure of a coordinator happening after it sent *PREPARE*s, thereby blocking the subordinates that vote *YES* in the **prepared** state until its recovery, is going to be very low.

In R*, each site has one transaction manager (TM) and one or more database managers (DBMs). Each DBM is very much like System R [5] and performs similar functions. TM is a new (to R*) component and its function is to manage the commit protocol, perform local and global deadlock detection, and assign transaction IDs to new transactions originating at that site. So far we have pretended that there is only one log file at each site. In fact, the TM and the

[8] If this approach is taken (as we have done in R*), then the nonleaf processes should include the name of the protocol chosen in the *PREPARE* message, and all processes should include this name in the first commit protocol log record that each one writes. The name should also be included in the inquiry messages sent by restart processes, and this information is used by a recovery process in responding to an inquiry in the *no information* case.

DBMs each have their own log files. A transaction process executes both the TM code and one DBM's code (for each DBM accessed by a transaction, one process is created). The DBM incarnation of the process should be thought of as the child of the (local) TM incarnation of the same process. When the process executes the TM code, it behaves like a nonleaf node in the process tree, and it writes only commit-protocol-related records in the TM log. When the process executes the DBM code, it behaves like a leaf node in the process tree, and it writes both UNDO/REDO records and commit-protocol-related records. When different processes communicate with each other during the execution of the commit protocol, it is actually the TM incarnations of those processes, not the DBM incarnations, that communicate. The leaf nodes of the process tree in this scenario are always DBM incarnations of the processes, and the nonleaf nodes are always TM incarnations of the processes.

In cases where the TM and the DBMs at a given site make use of the same file for inserting log information of all the transactions at that site (i.e., a common log), we wanted to benefit from the fact that the log records inserted during the execution of the commit protocol by the TM and the DBMs would be in a certain order, thereby avoiding some synchronous log writes (currently, in R*, the commit protocols have been designed and implemented to take advantage of the situation when the DBMs and the TM use the same log). For example, a DBM need not force-write its *prepare* record since the subsequent force-write of the TM's *prepare* record into the same log will force the former to disk. Another example is in the case of PC, when a process and all its subordinates are at the same site. In this case, the former does not have to force-write its *collecting* record since the force of the *collecting/prepared* record by a subordinate will force it out.

With a common log, in addition to explicitly avoiding some of the synchronous writes, one can also benefit from the batching effect of more log records being written into a single file. Whenever a log page in the virtual memory buffers fills up, we write it out immediately to stable storage.

If we assume that processes of a transaction communicate with each other using virtual circuits (as in R* [20]), and that new subordinate processes may be created even at the time of receipt of a *PREPARE* message by a process (e.g., to install updates at the sites of replicated copies), then it seems reasonable to use the tree structure to send the commit-protocol-related messages also (i.e., not flatten the multilevel tree into a two-level tree just for the purposes of the commit protocol). This approach avoids the need to set up any new communication channels just for use by the commit protocol. Furthermore, there is no need to make one process in each site become responsible for dealing with commit-related messages for different transactions (as in ENCOMPASS [8]).

Just as the R* DBMs take checkpoints periodically to bound DBM restart recovery time [14], the R* TM also takes its own checkpoints. The TM's checkpoint records contain the list of active processes that are currently executing the commit protocol and those processes that are in recovery (i.e., processes in the **prepared/collecting** state and processes waiting to receive *ACK*s from subordinates). Note that we do not have to include those transactions that have not yet started executing the commit protocol. TM checkpoints are taken without completely stopping all TM activity (this is in contrast with what happens in the R* DBMs). During site restart recovery, the last TM checkpoint record is read by a recovery process, and a transaction table is initialized with its contents. Then the TM log is scanned forward and, as necessary, new entries are added to the transaction table or existing entries are modified/deleted. Unlike in the case of the DBM log (see [14]), there is no need to examine the portion of the TM log before the last checkpoint. The time of the next TM checkpoint depends on the number of transactions initiated since the last checkpoint, the amount of log consumed since the last checkpoint, and the amount of space still available in the circular log file on disk.

6. DEADLOCK MANAGEMENT IN R*

The distributed 2PL concurrency control protocol is used in R*. Data are locked where they are stored. There is no separate lock manager process. All locking-related information is maintained in shared storage where it is accessible to the processes of transactions. The processes themselves execute the locking-related code and synchronize one another. Since many processes of a transaction might be concurrently active in one or more sites, more than one lock request might be made concurrently by a transaction. It is still the case that each process of a transaction will be requesting only one lock at a time. A process might wait for one of two reasons: (1) to obtain a lock and (2) to receive a message from a cohort process of the same transaction.[9] In this scenario, deadlocks, including distributed/global ones, are a real possibility. Once we chose to do deadlock detection instead of deadlock avoidance/prevention, it was only natural, for reliability reasons, to use a distributed algorithm for global deadlock detection.[10]

In R*, there is one deadlock detector (DD) at each site. The DDs at different sites operate asynchronously. The frequencies at which local and global deadlock detection searches are initiated can vary from site to site. Each DD wakes up periodically and looks for deadlocks after gathering the wait-for information from the local DBMs and the communication manager. If the DD is looking for multisite deadlocks during a detection phase, then any information about Potential Global (i.e., multisite) Deadlock Cycles (PGDCs) received earlier from other sites is combined with the local information. No information gathered/generated during a deadlock detection phase is retained for use during a subsequent detection phase of the same DD. Information received from a remote DD is consumed by the recipient, at the most, during one deadlock detection phase. This is necessary in order to make sure that false information sent by a remote DD, which during many subsequent deadlock detection phases may not have anything to send, is not consumed repeatedly by a DD, resulting in the repeated detection of, possibly, false deadlocks. If, due to the different deadlock detection frequencies of the different DDs, information is received from multiple phases of a particular remote DD before it is consumed by the recipient, then only that remote DD's last phase's information is retained for consumption by the recipient. This is because the latest information is the best information.

The result of analyzing the wait-for information could be the discovery of some local/global deadlocks and some PGDCs. Each PGDC is a list of transactions

[9] All other types of waits are not dealt with by the deadlock detector.

[10] We refer the reader to other papers for discussions concerning deadlock detection versus other approaches [3, 4, 24].

(*not* processes) in which each transaction, except the last one, is on a lock wait on the next transaction in the list. In addition, the first transaction's one local process is known to be expected to send response data to its cohort at another site, and the last transaction's one local process is known to be waiting to receive response data from its cohort at another site. This PGDC is sent to the site on which the last transaction's local process is waiting if the first transaction's name is lexicographically less than the last transaction's name; otherwise, the PGDC is discarded. Thus wait-for information travels only in the direction of the real/potential deadlock cycle, and on the average, only half the sites involved in a global deadlock send information around the cycle. In general, in this algorithm only one site will detect a given global deadlock.

Once a global deadlock is detected, the interesting question is how to choose a victim. While one could use detailed cost measures for transactions and choose as the victim the transaction with the least cost (see [4] for some performance comparisons), the problem is that such a transaction might not be in execution at the site where the global deadlock is detected. Then, the problem would be in identifying the site that has to be informed about the victim so that the latter could be aborted. Even if information about the locations of execution of every transaction in the wait-for graph were to be sent around with the latter, or if we pass along the cycle the identity of the victim, there would still be a delay and cost involved in informing remote sites about the nonlocal victim choice. This delay would cause an increase in the response times of the other transactions that are part of the deadlock cycle. Hence, in order to expedite the breaking of the cycle, one can choose as the victim a transaction that is executing locally, assuming that the wait-for information transmission protocol guarantees the existence of such a local transaction. The latter is the characteristic of the deadlock detection protocol of R* [6, 24], and hence we choose a local victim. If more than one local transaction could be chosen as the victim, then an appropriate cost measure (e.g., elapsed time since transaction began execution) is used to make the choice. If one or more transactions are involved in more than one deadlock, no effort is made to choose as the victim a transaction that resolves the maximum possible number of deadlocks.

Depending on whether or not (1) the wait-for information transmission among different sites is synchronized and (2) the nodes of the wait-for graph are transactions or individual processes of a transaction, false deadlocks might be detected. In R* transmissions are not synchronized and the nodes of the graph are transactions. Since we do not expect false deadlocks to occur frequently, we treat every detected deadlock as a true deadlock.

Even though the general impression might be that our database systems release all locks of a transaction only at the end of the transaction, in fact, some locks (e.g., short duration page-level locks when data are being locked at the tuple-level and locks on nonleaf nodes of the indices) are released before all the locks are acquired. This means that when a transaction is aborting it will have to reacquire those locks to perform its undo actions. Since a transaction could get into a deadlock any time it is requesting locks, if we are not careful we could have a situation in which we have a deadlock involving only aborting transactions. It would be quite messy to resolve such a deadlock. To avoid this situation, we permit, at any time, only one aborting transaction to be actively reacquiring locks in a given DBM. While the above-mentioned potential problem had to be dealt with even in System R, it is somewhat complicated in R*. We have to ensure that in a global deadlock cycle there is at least one local transaction that is not already aborting and that could be chosen as the victim.

This reliable, distributed algorithm for detecting global deadlocks is operational now in R*.

7. CURRENT STATUS

The R* implementation has reached a mature state, providing support for snapshots [1, 2], distributed views [7], migration of tables, global deadlock detection, distributed query compilation and processing [20], and crash recovery. Currently there is no support for replicated or fragmented data. The prototype is undergoing experimental evaluations [21].

REFERENCES

1. ADIBA, M. Derived relations: A unified mechanism for views, snapshots and distributed data. Res. Rep. RJ2881, IBM, San Jose, Calif., July 1980.
2. ADIBA, M., AND LINDSAY, B. Database snapshots. In *Proceedings of the 6th International Conference on Very Large Data Bases* (Montreal, Oct. 1980). IEEE Press, New York, 1980, 86–91.
3. AGRAWAL, R., AND CAREY, M. The performance of concurrency control and recovery algorithms for transaction-oriented database systems. *Database Eng. 8*, 2 (June 1985), 58–67.
4. AGRAWAL, R., CAREY, M., AND MCVOY, L. The performance of alternative strategies for dealing with deadlocks in database management systems. Tech. Rep. 590, Dept. of Computer Sciences, Univ. of Wisconsin, Madison, Mar. 1985.
5. ASTRAHAN, M., BLASGEN, M., CHAMBERLIN, D., GRAY, J., KING, F., LINDSAY, B., LORIE, R., MEHL, J., PRICE, T., PUTZOLU, F., SCHKOLNICK, M., SELINGER, P., SLUTZ, D., STRONG, R., TIBERIO, P., TRAIGER, I., WADE, B., AND YOST, R. System R: A relational data base management system. *Computer 12*, 5 (May 1979), 43–48.
6. BEERI, C., AND OBERMARCK, R. A resource class-independent deadlock detection algorithm. In *Proceedings of the 7th International Conference on Very Large Data Bases* (Cannes, Sept. 1981). IEEE Press, New York, 1981, 166–178.
7. BERTINO, E., HAAS, L., AND LINDSAY, B. View management in distributed data base systems. In *Proceedings of the 9th International Conference on Very Large Data Bases* (Florence, Oct. 1983) VLDB Endowment, 1983, 376–378. Also available as Res. Rep. RJ3851, IBM, San Jose, Calif., Apr. 1983.
8. BORR, A. Transaction monitoring in ENCOMPASS: Reliable distributed transaction processing. In *Proceedings of the 7th International Conference on Very Large Data Bases* (Cannes, Sept. 1981). IEEE Press, New York, 1981, 155–165.
9. COOPER, E. Analysis of distributed commit protocols. In *Proceedings of the ACM SIGMOD International Conference on Management of Data* (Orlando, Fla., June 1982). ACM, New York, 1982, 175–183.
10. ESWARAN, K. P., GRAY, J. N., LORIE, R., A., AND TRAIGER, I. L. The notions of consistency and predicate locks in a database system. *Commun. ACM 19*, 11 (Nov. 1976), 624–633.
11. GAWLICK, D., AND KINKADE, D. Varieties of concurrency control in IMS/VS fast path. *Database Eng. 8*, 2 (June 1985), 3–10.
12. GRAY, J. Notes on data base operating systems. In *Operating Systems—An Advanced Course*. Lecture Notes in Computer Science, vol. 60. Springer-Verlag, New York, 1978.
13. GRAY, J. The transaction concept: Virtues and limitations. In *Proceedings of the 7th International Conference on Very Large Data Bases* (Cannes, Oct. 1981). IEEE Press, New York, 1981, 144–154.

14. GRAY, J., MCJONES, P., BLASGEN, M., LINDSAY, B., LORIE, R., PRICE, T., PUTZOLU, F., AND TRAIGER, I. The recovery manager of the system R database manager. *ACM Comput. Surv. 13*, 2 (June 1981), 223–242.
15. HAERDER, T., AND REUTER, A. Principles of transaction oriented database recovery—A taxonomy. *ACM Comput. Surv. 15*, 4 (Dec. 1983), 287–317.
16. HAMMER, M., AND SHIPMAN, D. Reliability mechanisms for SDD-1: A system for distributed databases. *ACM Trans. Database Syst. 5*, 4 (Dec. 1980), 431–466.
17. LAMPSON, B. Atomic transactions. In *Distributed Systems—Architecture and Implementation*. Lecture Notes in Computer Science, vol. 100, B. Lampson, Ed. Springer-Verlag, New York, 1980, 246–265.
18. LINDSAY, B. G., HAAS, L. M., MOHAN, C., WILMS, P. F., AND YOST, R. A. Computation and communication in R*: A distributed database manager. *ACM Trans. Comput. Syst. 2*, 1 (Feb. 1984), 24–38. Also Res. Rep. RJ3740, IBM, San Jose, Calif., Jan. 1983.
19. LINDSAY, B., SELINGER, P., GALTIERI, C., GRAY, J., LORIE, R., PUTZOLU, F., TRAIGER, I., AND WADE, B. Single and multi-site recovery facilities. In *Distributed Data Bases*, I. W. Draffan and F. Poole, Eds. Cambridge University Press, New York, 1980. Also available as Notes on distributed databases. Res. Rep. RJ2571, IBM, San Jose, Calif., July 1979.
20. LOHMAN, G., MOHAN, C., HAAS, L., DANIELS, D., LINDSAY, B., SELINGER, P., AND WILMS, P. Query processing in R*. In *Query Processing in Database Systems*, W. Kim, D. Reiner, and D. Batory, Eds. Springer-Verlag, New York, 1984. Also Res. Rep. RJ4272, IBM, Apr. 1984.
21. MACKERT, L., AND LOHMAN, G. Index scans using a finite LRU buffer: A validated I/O model. Res. Rep. RJ4836, IBM, San Jose, Calif., Sept. 1985.
22. MOHAN, C. *Tutorial: Recent Advances in Distributed Data Base Management*. IEEE catalog number EH0218-8, IEEE Press, New York, 1984.
23. MOHAN, C., STRONG, R., AND FINKELSTEIN, S. Method for distributed transaction commit and recovery using Byzantine agreement within clusters of processors. In *Proceedings of the 2nd ACM SIGACT/SIGOPS Symposium on Principles of Distributed Computing* (Montreal, Aug. 1983). ACM, New York, 1983, 89–103. Reprinted in ACM/SIGOPS Operating Systems Review, July 1985. Also Res. Rep. RJ3882, IBM, San Jose, Calif., June 1983.
24. OBERMARCK, R. Distributed deadlock detection algorithm. *ACM Trans. Database Syst. 7*, 2 (June 1982), 187–208.
25. ROTHNIE, J. B., JR., BERNSTEIN, P. A., FOX, S., GOODMAN, N., HAMMER, M., LANDERS, T. A., REEVE, C., SHIPMAN, D. W., AND WONG, E. Introduction to a system for distributed databases (SDD-1). *ACM Trans. Database Syst. 5*, 1 (Mar. 1980), 1–17.
26. SKEEN, D. Nonblocking commit protocols. In *Proceedings of the ACM/SIGMOD International Conference on Management of Data* (Ann Arbor, Mich., May 1981). ACM, New York, 1981, 133–142.
27. SKEEN, D. A quorum-based commit protocol. In *Proceedings of the 6th Berkeley Workshop on Distributed Data Management and Computer Networks* (May 1982). Lawrence Berkeley Laboratories, 1982, 69–90.
28. STONEBRAKER, M. Concurrency control and consistency of multiple copies of data in distributed INGRES. *IEEE Trans. Softw. Eng. 5*, 3 (May 1979), 235–258.

Received September 1985; revised July 1986; accepted July 1986

The Dangers of Replication and a Solution

Jim Gray (Gray@Microsoft.com)
Pat Helland (PHelland@Microsoft.com)
Patrick O'Neil (POneil@cs.UMB.edu)
Dennis Shasha (Shasha@cs.NYU.edu)

Abstract: *Update anywhere-anytime-anyway transactional replication has unstable behavior as the workload scales up: a ten-fold increase in nodes and traffic gives a thousand fold increase in deadlocks or reconciliations. Master copy replication (primary copy) schemes reduce this problem. A simple analytic model demonstrates these results. A new two-tier replication algorithm is proposed that allows mobile (disconnected) applications to propose tentative update transactions that are later applied to a master copy. Commutative update transactions avoid the instability of other replication schemes.*

1. Introduction

Data is replicated at multiple network nodes for performance and availability. ***Eager replication*** keeps all replicas exactly synchronized at all nodes by updating all the replicas as part of one atomic transaction. Eager replication gives serializable execution -- there are no concurrency anomalies. But, eager replication reduces update performance and increases transaction response times because extra updates and messages are added to the transaction.

Eager replication is not an option for mobile applications where most nodes are normally disconnected. Mobile applications require ***lazy replication*** algorithms that asynchronously propagate replica updates to other nodes after the updating transaction commits. Some continuously connected systems use lazy replication to improve response time.

Lazy replication also has shortcomings, the most serious being stale data versions. When two transactions read and write data concurrently, one transaction's updates should be serialized after the other's. This avoids concurrency anomalies. Eager replication typically uses a locking scheme to detect and regulate concurrent execution. Lazy replication schemes typically use a multi-version concurrency control scheme to detect non-serializable behavior [Bernstein, Hadzilacos, Goodman], [Berenson, et. al.]. Most multi-version isolation schemes provide the transaction with the most recent committed value. Lazy replication may allow a transaction to see a very old committed value. Committed updates to a local value may be "in transit" to this node if the update strategy is "lazy".

SIGMOD '96 6/96 Montreal, Canada

Eager replication delays or aborts an uncommitted transaction if committing it would violate serialization. Lazy replication has a more difficult task because some replica updates have already been committed when the serialization problem is first detected. There is usually no automatic way to reverse the committed replica updates, rather a program or person must ***reconcile*** conflicting transactions.

To make this tangible, consider a joint checking account you share with your spouse. Suppose it has $1,000 in it. This account is replicated in three places: your checkbook, your spouse's checkbook, and the bank's ledger.

Eager replication assures that all three books have the same account balance. It prevents you and your spouse from writing checks totaling more than $1,000. If you try to overdraw your account, the transaction will fail.

Lazy replication allows both you and your spouse to write checks totaling $1,000 for a total of $2,000 in withdrawals. When these checks arrived at the bank, or when you communicated with your spouse, someone or something reconciles the transactions that used the virtual $1,000.

It would be nice to automate this reconciliation. The bank does that by rejecting updates that cause an overdraft. This is a master replication scheme: the bank has the master copy and only the bank's updates really count. Unfortunately, this works only for the bank. You, your spouse, and your creditors are likely to spend considerable time reconciling the "extra" thousand dollars worth of transactions. In the meantime, your books will be inconsistent with the bank's books. That makes it difficult for you to perform further banking operations.

The database for a checking account is a single number, and a log of updates to that number. It is the simplest database. In reality, databases are more complex and the serialization issues are more subtle.

The theme of this paper is that update-anywhere-anytime-anyway replication is unstable.

1. *If the number of checkbooks per account increases by a factor of ten, the deadlock or reconciliation rates rises by a factor of a thousand.*
2. *Disconnected operation and message delays mean lazy replication has more frequent reconciliation.*

Figure 1: When replicated, a simple single-node transaction may apply its updates remotely either as part of the same transaction (*eager*) or as separate transactions (*lazy*). In either case, if data is replicated at *N* nodes, the transaction does *N* times as much work

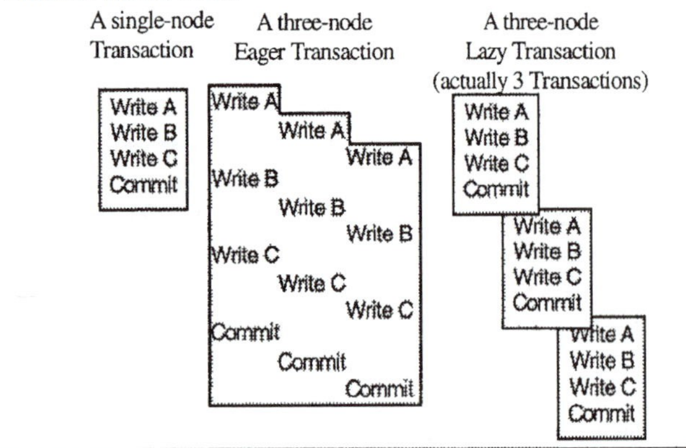

Simple replication works well at low loads and with a few nodes. This creates a ***scaleup pitfall***. A prototype system demonstrates well. Only a few transactions deadlock or need reconciliation when running on two connected nodes. But the system behaves very differently when the application is scaled up to a large number of nodes, or when nodes are disconnected more often, or when message propagation delays are longer. Such systems have higher transaction rates. Suddenly, the deadlock and reconciliation rate is astronomically higher (cubic growth is predicted by the model). The database at each node diverges further and further from the others as reconciliation fails. Each reconciliation failure implies differences among nodes. Soon, the system suffers ***system delusion*** — the database is inconsistent and there is no obvious way to repair it [Gray & Reuter, pp. 149-150].

This is a bleak picture, but probably accurate. Simple replication (transactional update-anywhere-anytime-anyway) cannot be made to work with global serializability.

In outline, the paper gives a simple model of replication and a closed-form average-case analysis for the probability of waits, deadlocks, and reconciliations. For simplicity, the model ignores many issues that would make the predicted behavior even worse. In particular, it ignores the message propagation delays needed to broadcast replica updates. It ignores "true" serialization, and assumes a weak multi-version form of committed-read serialization (no read locks) [Berenson]. The paper then considers object master replication. Unrestricted lazy master replication has many of the instability problems of eager and group replication.

A restricted form of replication avoids these problems: ***two-tier replication*** has ***base nodes*** that are always connected, and ***mobile nodes*** that are usually disconnected.

1. Mobile nodes propose tentative update transactions to objects owned by other nodes. Each mobile node keeps two object versions: a local version and a best known master version.
2. Mobile nodes occasionally connect to base nodes and propose tentative update transactions to a master node. These proposed transactions are re-executed and may succeed or be rejected. To improve the chances of success, tentative transactions are designed to commute with other transactions. After exchanges the mobile node's database is synchronized with the base nodes. Rejected tentative transactions are reconciled by the mobile node owner who generated the transaction.

Our analysis shows that this scheme supports lazy replication and mobile computing but avoids system delusion: tentative updates may be rejected but the base database state remains consistent.

2. Replication Models

Figure 1 shows two ways to propagate updates to replicas:

1. ***Eager***: Updates are applied to all replicas of an object as part of the original transaction.
2. ***Lazy:*** One replica is updated by the originating transaction. Updates to other replicas propagate asynchronously, typically as a separate transaction for each node.
3.

Figure 2: Updates may be controlled in two ways. Either all updates emanate from a master copy of the object, or updates may emanate from any. Group ownership has many more chances for conflicting updates.

Object Master

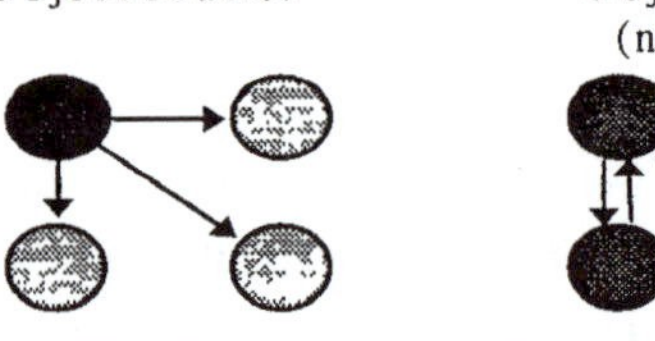

Object Group (no master)

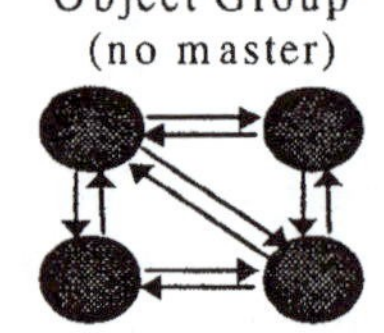

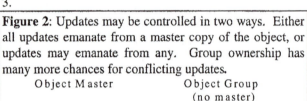

Figure 2 shows two ways to regulate replica updates:

1. ***Group***: Any node with a copy of a data item can update it. This is often called *update anywhere.*
2. ***Master***: Each object has a master node. Only the master can update the *primary copy* of the object. All other replicas are read-only. Other nodes wanting to update the object request the master do the update.
3.

Table 1: A taxonomy of replication strategies contrasting propagation strategy (eager or lazy) with the ownership strategy (master or group).

Propagation vs. Ownership	Lazy	Eager
Group	N transactions N object owners	one transaction N object owners
Master	N transactions one object owner	one transaction one object owner
Two Tier	N+1 transactions, one object owner tentative local updates, eager base updates	

Table 2. Variables used in the model and analysis	
DB_Size	number of distinct objects in the database
Nodes	number of nodes; each node replicates all objects
Transactions	number of concurrent transactions at a node. This is a derived value.
TPS	number of transactions per second originating at this node.
Actions	number of updates in a transaction
Action_Time	time to perform an action
Time_Between_ Disconnects	mean time between network disconnect of a node.
Disconnected_ time	mean time node is disconnected from network
Message_Delay	time between update of an object and update of a replica (ignored)
Message_cpu	processing and transmission time needed to send a replication message or apply a replica update (ignored)

The analysis below indicates that group and lazy replication are more prone to serializability violations than master and eager replication

The model assumes the database consists of a fixed set of objects. There are a fixed number of nodes, each storing a replica of all objects. Each node originates a fixed number of transactions per second. Each transaction updates a fixed number of objects. Access to objects is equi-probable (there are no hotspots). Inserts and deletes are modeled as updates. Reads are ignored. Replica update requests have a transmit delay and also require processing by the sender and receiver. These delays and extra processing are ignored; only the work of sequentially updating the replicas at each node is modeled. Some nodes are mobile and disconnected most of the time. When first connected, a mobile node sends and receives deferred replica updates. Table 2 lists the model parameters.

One can imagine many variations of this model. Applying eager updates in parallel comes to mind. Each design alternative gives slightly different results. The design here roughly characterizes the basic alternatives. We believe obvious variations will not substantially change the results here.

Each node generates *TPS* transactions per second. Each transaction involves a fixed number of actions. Each action requires a fixed time to execute. So, a transaction's duration is *Actions x Action_Time*. Given these two observations, the number of concurrent transactions originating at a node is:

$$Transactions = TPS \times Actions \times Action\_Time \qquad (1)$$

A more careful analysis would consider that fact that, as system load and contention rises, the time to complete an action increases. In a scaleable server system, this *time-dilation* is a second-order effect and is ignored here.

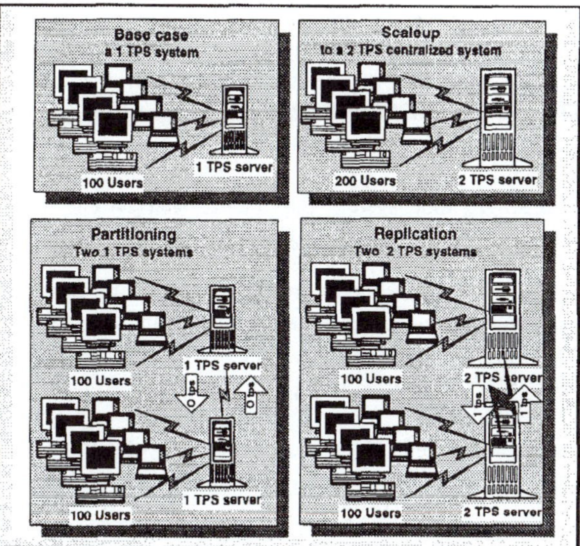

Figure 3: Systems can grow by (1) *scaleup*: buying a bigger machine, (2) *partitioning*: dividing the work between two machines, or (3) *replication*: placing the data at two machines and having each machine keep the data current. This simple idea is key to understanding the N^2 growth. Notice that each of the replicated servers at the lower right of the illustration is performing 2 TPS and the aggregate rate is 4 TPS. Doubling the users increased the total workload by a factor of four. Read-only transactions need not generate any additional load on remote nodes.

In a system of *N* nodes, *N* times as many transactions will be originating per second. Since each update transaction must replicate its updates to the other *(N-1)* nodes, it is easy to see that the transaction size for eager systems grows by a factor of *N* and the node update rate grows by N^2. In lazy systems, each *user* update transaction generates *N-1* lazy replica updates, so there are *N* times as many concurrent transactions, and the node update rate is N^2 higher. This non-linear growth in node update rates leads to unstable behavior as the system is scaled up.

3. Eager Replication

Eager replication updates all replicas when a transaction updates any instance of the object. There are no serialization anomalies (inconsistencies) and no need for reconciliation in eager systems. Locking detects potential anomalies and converts them to waits or deadlocks.

With eager replication, reads at connected nodes give current data. Reads at disconnected nodes may give stale (out of date) data. Simple eager replication systems prohibit updates if any node is disconnected. For high availability, eager replication systems allow updates among members of the quorum or cluster [Gifford], [Garcia-Molina]. When a node joins the quorum, the quorum sends the new node all replica updates since the node was disconnected. We assume here that a quorum or fault tolerance scheme is used to improve update availability.

Even if all the nodes are connected all the time, updates may fail due to deadlocks that prevent serialization errors. The following simple analysis derives the wait and deadlock rates of an eager replication system. We start with wait and deadlock rates for a single-node system.

In a single-node system the "other" transactions have about $\frac{Tranascations \times Actions}{2}$ resources locked (each is about half way complete). Since objects are chosen uniformly from the database, the chance that a request by one transaction will request a resource locked by any other transaction is: $\frac{Transactions \times Actions}{2 \times DB\_size}$. A transaction makes *Actions* such requests, so the chance that it will wait sometime in its lifetime is approximately [Gray et. al.], [Gray & Reuter pp. 428]:

$$PW \approx 1 - (1 - \frac{Transactions \times Actions}{2 \times DB\_size})^{Acctions} \approx \frac{Transactions \times Actions^2}{2 \times DB\_Size} \quad (2)$$

A deadlock consists of a cycle of transactions waiting for one another. The probability a transaction forms a cycle of length two is PW^2 divided by the number of transactions. Cycles of length j are proportional to PW^j and so are even less likely if $PW << 1$. Applying equation (1), the probability that the transaction deadlocks is approximately:

$$PD \approx \frac{PW^2}{Transactions} = \frac{Transactions \times Actions^4}{4 \times DB\_Size^2} = \frac{TPS \times Action\_Time \times Actions^5}{4 \times DB\_Size^2} \quad (3)$$

Equation (3) gives the deadlock hazard for a transaction. The deadlock rate for a transaction is the probability it deadlock's in the next second. That is PD divided by the transaction lifetime (*Actions x Action_Time*).

$$Trans\_Deadlock\_rate \approx \frac{TPS \times Actions^4}{4 \times DB\_Size^2} \quad (4)$$

Since the node runs *Transactions* concurrent transactions, the deadlock rate for the whole node is higher. Multiplying equation (4) and equation (1), the node deadlock rate is:

$$Node\_Deadlock\_Rate \approx \frac{TPS^2 \times Action\_Time \times Actions^5}{4 \times DB\_Size^2} \quad (5)$$

Suppose now that several such systems are replicated using eager replication — the updates are done immediately as in Figure 1. Each node will initiate its local load of *TPS* transactions per second[1]. The transaction size, duration, and aggregate transaction rate for eager systems is:

$$\begin{aligned} &Transaction\_Size = Actions \times Nodes \\ &Transaction\_Duration = Actions \times Nodes \times Action\_Time \\ &Total\_TPS = TPS \times Nodes \end{aligned} \quad (6)$$

Each node is now doing its own work and also applying the updates generated by other nodes. So each update transaction actually performs many more actions (*Nodes x Actions*) and so has a much longer lifetime — indeed it takes at least *Nodes* times longer[2]. As a result the total number of transactions in the system rises quadratically with the number of nodes:

$$Total\_Transactions = TPS \times Actions \times Action\_Time \times Nodes^2 \quad (7)$$

This rise in active transactions is due to eager transactions taking *N*-Times longer and due to lazy updates generating *N*-times more transactions. The action rate also rises very fast with *N*. Each node generates work for all other nodes. The eager work rate, measured in actions per second is:

$$\begin{aligned} Action\_Rate &= Total\_TPS \times Transaction\_Size \\ &= TPS \times Actions \times Nodes^2 \end{aligned} \quad (8)$$

It is surprising that the action rate and the number of active transactions is the same for eager and lazy systems. Eager systems have fewer-longer transactions. Lazy systems have more and shorter transactions. So, although equations (6) are different for lazy systems, equations (7) and (8) apply to both eager and lazy systems.

Ignoring message handling, the probability a transaction waits can be computed using the argument for equation (2). The transaction makes *Actions* requests while the other Total_Transactions have *Actions/2* objects locked. The result is approximately:

$$\begin{aligned} PW\_eager &\approx Total\_Transactions \times Actions \times \frac{Actions}{2 \times DB\_Size} \\ &= \frac{TPS \times Action\_Time \times Actions^3 \times Nodes^2}{2 \times DB\_Size} \end{aligned} \quad (9)$$

This is the probability that one transaction waits. The wait rate (waits per second) for the entire system is computed as:

$$\begin{aligned} &Total\_Eager\_Wait\_Rate \\ &\approx \frac{PW\_eager}{Transaction\_Duration} \times Total\_Transactions \quad (10) \\ &= \frac{TPS^2 \times Action\_Time \times (Actions \times Nodes)^3}{2 \times DB\_Size} \end{aligned}$$

As with equation (4), The probability that a particular transaction deadlocks is approximately:

$$\begin{aligned} PD\_eager &\approx \frac{Total\_Transactions \times Actions^4}{4 \times DB\_Size^2} \\ &= \frac{TPS \times Action\_Time \times Actions^5 \times Nodes^2}{4 \times DB\_Size^2} \end{aligned} \quad (11)$$

[1] The assumption that transaction arrival rate per node stays constant as nodes are replicated assumes that nodes are lightly loaded. As the replication workload increases, the nodes must grow processing and IO power to handle the increased load. Growing power at an N^2 rate is problematic.

[2] An alternate model has eager actions broadcast the update to all replicas in one instant. The replicas are updated in parallel and the elapsed time for each action is constant (independent of *N*). In our model, we attempt to capture message handing costs by serializing the individual updates. If one follows this model, then the processing at each node rises quadraticly, but the number of concurrent transactions stays constant with scaleup. This model avoids the polynomial explosion of waits and deadlocks if the total TPS rate is held constant.

The equation for a single-transaction deadlock implies the total deadlock rate. Using the arguments for equations (4) and (5), and using equations (7) and (11):

$$Total\_Eager\_Deadlock\_Rate$$

$$\approx Total\_Transactions \times \frac{PD\_eager}{Transaction\_Duration} \quad (12)$$

$$\approx \frac{TPS^2 \times Action\_Time \times Actions^5 \times Nodes^3}{4 \times DB\_Size^2}$$

If message delays were added to the model, then each transaction would last much longer, would hold resources much longer, and so would be more likely to collide with other transactions. Equation (12) also ignores the "second order" effect of two transactions racing to update the same object at the same time (it does not distinguish between *Master* and *Group* replication). If *DB_Size* >> *Node*, such conflicts will be rare.

This analysis points to some serious problems with eager replication. Deadlocks rise as the third power of the number of nodes in the network, and the fifth power of the transaction size. Going from one-node to ten nodes increases the deadlock rate a thousand fold. A ten-fold increase in the transaction size increases the deadlock rate by a factor of 100,000.

To ameliorate this, one might imagine that the database size grows with the number of nodes (as in the checkbook example earlier, or in the TPC-A, TPC-B, and TPC-C benchmarks). More nodes, and more transactions mean more data. With a scaled up database size, equation (12) becomes:

$$Eager\_Deadlock\_Rate\_Scaled\_DB$$

$$\approx \frac{TPS^2 \times Action\_Time \times Actions^5 \times Nodes}{4 \times DB\_Size^2} \quad (13)$$

Now a ten-fold growth in the number of nodes creates *only* a ten-fold growth in the deadlock rate. This is still an unstable situation, but it is a big improvement over equation (12)

Having a master for each object helps eager replication avoid deadlocks. Suppose each object has an owner node. Updates go to this node first and are then applied to the replicas. If, each transaction updated a single replica, the object-master approach would eliminate all deadlocks.

In summary, eager replication has two major problems:

1. Mobile nodes cannot use an eager scheme when disconnected.
2. The probability of deadlocks, and consequently failed transactions rises very quickly with transaction size and with the number of nodes. A ten-fold increase in nodes gives a thousand-fold increase in failed transactions (deadlocks).

We see no solution to this problem. If replica updates were done concurrently, the action time would not increase with N then the growth rate would *only* be quadratic.

4. Lazy Group Replication

Lazy group replication allows any node to update any local data. When the transaction commits, a transaction is sent to every other node to apply the root transaction's updates to the replicas at the destination node (see Figure 4). It is possible for two nodes to update the same object and race each other to install their updates at other nodes. The replication mechanism must detect this and reconcile the two transactions so that their updates are not lost.

Timestamps are commonly used to detect and reconcile lazy-group transactional updates. Each object carries the timestamp of its most recent update. Each replica update carries the new value and is tagged with the old object timestamp. Each node detects incoming replica updates that would overwrite earlier committed updates. The node tests if the local replica's timestamp and the update's old timestamp are equal. If so, the update is safe. The local replica's timestamp advances to the new transaction's timestamp and the object value is updated. If the current timestamp of the local replica does not match the old timestamp seen by the root transaction, then the update may be "dangerous". In such cases, the node rejects the incoming transaction and submits it for *reconciliation*.

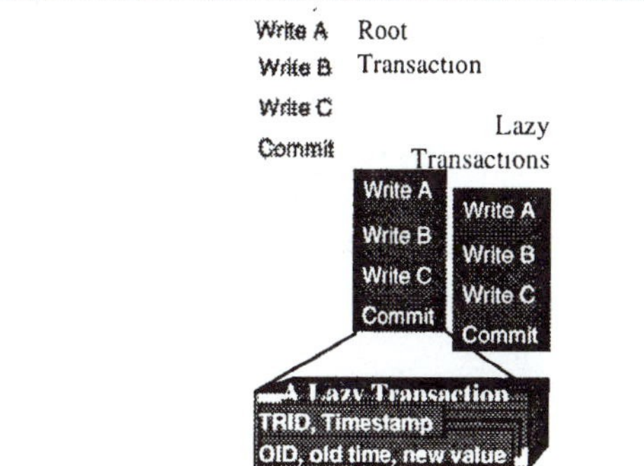

Figure 4: A lazy transaction has a root execution that updates either master or local copies of data. Then subsequent transactions update replicas at remote nodes — one lazy transaction per remote replica node. The lazy updates carry timestamps of each original object. If the local object timestamp does not match, the update may be dangerous and some form of reconciliation is needed.

Transactions that would wait in an eager replication system face reconciliation in a lazy-group replication system. Waits are much more frequent than deadlocks because it takes two waits to make a deadlock. Indeed, if waits are a rare event, then deadlocks are very rare *(rare²)*. Eager replication waits cause delays while deadlocks create application faults. With lazy replication, the much more frequent waits are what determines the reconciliation frequency. So, the system-wide lazy-group reconciliation rate follows the transaction wait rate equation (Equation 10):

$$Lazy\_Group\_Reconciliation\_Rate \approx \frac{TPS^2 \times Action\_Time \times (Actions \times Nodes)^3}{2 \times DB\_Size} \quad (14)$$

As with eager replication, if message propagation times were added, the reconciliation rate would rise. Still, having the reconciliation rate rise by a factor of a thousand when the system scales up by a factor of ten is frightening.

The really bad case arises in mobile computing. Suppose that the typical node is disconnected most of the time. The node accepts and applies transactions for a day. Then, at night it connects and downloads them to the rest of the network. At that time it also accepts replica updates. It is as though the message propagation time was 24 hours.

If any two transactions at any two different nodes update the same data during the disconnection period, then they will need reconciliation. What is the chance of two disconnected transactions colliding during the *Disconnected_Time*?

If each node updates a small fraction of the database each day then the number of distinct *outbound* pending object updates at reconnect is approximately:

$$Outbound\_Updates \approx Disconnect\_Time \times TPS \times Actions \quad (15)$$

Each of these updates applies to all the replicas of an object. The pending *inbound updates* for this node from the rest of the network is approximately *(Nodes-1)* times larger than this.

$$Inbound\_Updates \approx (Nodes - 1) \times Disconnect\_Time \times TPS \times Actions \quad (16)$$

If the inbound and outbound sets overlap, then reconciliation is needed. The chance of an object being in both sets is approximately:

$$P(collision) \approx \frac{Inbound\_Updates \times Outbound\_Updates}{DB\_Size} \approx \frac{Nodes \times (Disconnect\_Time \times TPS \times Actions)^2}{DB\_Size} \quad (17)$$

Equation (17) is the chance one node needs reconciliation during the *Disconnect_Time* cycle. The rate for all nodes is:

$$Lazy\_Group\_Reconciliation\_Rate \approx P(collision) \times \frac{Nodes}{Disconnect\_Time} \approx \frac{Disconnect\_Time \times (TPS \times Actions \times Nodes)^2}{DB\_Size} \quad (18)$$

The quadratic nature of this equation suggests that a system that performs well on a few nodes with simple transactions may become unstable as the system scales up.

5. Lazy Master Replication

Master replication assigns an owner to each object. The owner stores the object's correct current value. Updates are first done by the owner and then propagated to other replicas. Different objects may have different owners.

When a transaction wants to update an object, it sends an RPC (remote procedure call) to the node owning the object. To get serializability, a read action should send read-lock RPCs to the masters of any objects it reads.

To simplify the analysis, we assume the node originating the transaction broadcasts the replica updates to all the slave replicas after the master transaction commits. The originating node sends one slave transaction to each slave node (as in Figure 1). Slave updates are timestamped to assure that all the replicas converge to the same final state. If the record timestamp is newer than a replica update timestamp, the update is "stale" and can be ignored. Alternatively, each master node sends replica updates to slaves in sequential commit order.

Lazy-Master replication is not appropriate for mobile applications. A node wanting to update an object must be connected to the object owner and participate in an atomic transaction with the owner.

As with eager systems, lazy-master systems have no reconciliation failures; rather, conflicts are resolved by waiting or deadlock. Ignoring message delays, the deadlock rate for a lazy-master replication system is similar to a single node system with much higher transaction rates. Lazy master transactions operate on master copies of objects. But, because there are *Nodes* times more users, there are *Nodes* times as many concurrent master transactions and approximately $Nodes^2$ times as many replica update transactions. The replica update transactions do not really matter, they are background housekeeping transactions. They can abort and restart without affecting the user. So the main issue is how frequently the master transactions deadlock. Using the logic of equation (4), the deadlock rate is approximated by:

$$Lazy\_Master\_Deadlock\_Rate \approx \frac{(TPS \times Nodes)^2 \times Actions^4}{4 \times DB\_Size^2} \quad (19)$$

This is better behavior than lazy-group replication. Lazy-master replication sends fewer messages during the base transaction and so completes more quickly. Nevertheless, all of these replication schemes have troubling deadlock or reconciliation rates as they grow to many nodes.

In summary, lazy-master replication requires contact with object masters and so is not useable by mobile applications. Lazy-master replication is slightly less deadlock prone than eager-group replication primarily because the transactions have shorter duration.

6. Non-Transactional Replication Schemes

The equations in the previous sections are facts of nature — they help explain another fact of nature. They show why there are no high-update-traffic replicated databases with globally serializable transactions.

Certainly, there are replicated databases: bibles, phone books, check books, mail systems, name servers, and so on. But updates to these databases are managed in interesting ways — typically in a lazy-master way. Further, updates are not record-value oriented; rather, updates are expressed as transactional transformations such as "Debit the account by $50" instead of "change account from $200 to $150".

One strategy is to abandon serializabilty for the ***convergence property***: if no new transactions arrive, and if all the nodes are connected together, they will all converge to the same replicated state after exchanging replica updates. The resulting state contains the committed appends, and the most recent replacements, but updates may be lost.

Lotus Notes gives a good example of convergence [Kawell]. Notes is a lazy group replication design (update anywhere, anytime, anyhow). Notes provides convergence rather than an ACID transaction execution model. The database state may not reflect any particular serial execution, but all the states will be identical. As explained below, timestamp schemes have the lost-update problem.

Lotus Notes achieves convergence by offering lazy-group replication at the transaction level. It provides two forms of update transaction:

1. ***Append*** adds data to a Notes file. Every appended note has a timestamp. Notes are stored in timestamp order. If all nodes are in contact with all others, then they will all converge on the same state.
2. ***Timestamped replace a value*** replaces a value with a newer value. If the current value of the object already has a timestamp greater than this update's timestamp, the incoming update is discarded.

If convergence were the only goal, the timestamp method would be sufficient. But, the timestamp scheme may lose the effects of some transactions because it just applies the most recent updates. Applying a timestamp scheme to the checkbook example, if there are two concurrent updates to a checkbook balance, the highest timestamp value wins and the other update is discarded as a "stale" value. Concurrency control theory calls this the *lost update problem*. Timestamp schemes are vulnerable to lost updates.

Convergence is desirable, but the converged state should reflect the effects of all committed transactions. In general this is not possible unless global serialization techniques are used.

In certain cases transactions can be designed to commute, so that the database ends up in the same state no matter what transaction execution order is chosen. Timestamped Append is a kind of commutative update but there are others (e.g., adding and subtracting constants from an integer value). It would be possible for Notes to support a third form of transaction:

3. ***Commutative updates*** that are incremental transformations of a value that can be applied in any order.

Lotus Notes, the Internet name service, mail systems, Microsoft Access, and many other applications use some of these techniques to achieve convergence and avoid delusion.

Microsoft Access offers convergence as follows. It has a single design master node that controls all schema updates to a replicated database. It offers update-anywhere for record instances. Each node keeps a version vector with each replicated record. These version vectors are exchanged on demand or periodically. The most recent update wins each pairwise exchange. Rejected updates are reported [Hammond].

The examples contrast with a simple update-anywhere-anytime-anyhow lazy-group replication offered by some systems. If the transaction profiles are not constrained, lazy-group schemes suffer from unstable reconciliation described in earlier sections. Such systems degenerate into system delusion as they scale up.

Lazy group replication schemes are emerging with specialized reconciliation rules. Oracle 7 provides a choice of twelve reconciliation rules to merge conflicting updates [Oracle]. In addition, users can program their own reconciliation rules. These rules give priority certain sites, or time priority, or value priority, or they merge commutative updates. The rules make some transactions commutative. A similar, transaction-level approach is followed in the two-tier scheme described next.

7. Two-Tier Replication

An ideal replication scheme would achieve four goals:

Availability and scaleability: Provide high availability and scaleability through replication, while avoiding instability.

Mobility: Allow mobile nodes to read and update the database while disconnected from the network.

Serializability: Provide single-copy serializable transaction execution.

Convergence: Provide convergence to avoid system delusion.

The safest transactional replication schemes, (ones that avoid system delusion) are the eager systems and lazy master systems. They have no reconciliation problems (they have no reconciliation). But these systems have other problems. As shown earlier:

1. Mastered objects cannot accept updates if the master node is not accessible. This makes it difficult to use master replication for mobile applications.
2. Master systems are unstable under increasing load. Deadlocks rise quickly as nodes are added.
3. Only eager systems and lazy master (where reads go to the master) give ACID serializability.

Circumventing these problems requires changing the way the system is used. We believe a scaleable replication system must function more like the check books, phone books, Lotus Notes, Access, and other replication systems we see about us.

Lazy-group replication systems are prone to reconciliation problems as they scale up. Manually reconciling conflicting transactions is unworkable. One approach is to *undo* all the work of any transaction that needs reconciliation — backing out all the updates of the transaction. This makes transactions atomic, consistent, and isolated, but not durable — or at least not durable until the updates are propagated to each node. In such a lazy group system, every transaction is tentative until all its replica updates have been propagated. If some mobile replica node is disconnected for a very long time, all transactions will be tentative until the missing node reconnects. So, an undo-oriented lazy-group replication scheme is untenable for mobile applications.

The solution seems to require a modified mastered replication scheme. To avoid reconciliation, each object is mastered by a node — much as the bank owns your checking account and your mail server owns your mailbox. Mobile agents can make tentative updates, then connect to the base nodes and immediately learn if the tentative update is acceptable.

The ***two-tier replication*** scheme begins by assuming there are two kinds of nodes:

Mobile nodes are disconnected much of the time. They store a replica of the database and may originate tentative transactions. A mobile node may be the master of some data items.

Base nodes are always connected. They store a replica of the database. Most items are mastered at base nodes.

Replicated data items have two versions at mobile nodes:

Master Version: The most recent value received from the object master. The version at the object master is *the* master version, but disconnected or lazy replica nodes may have older versions.

Tentative Version: The local object may be updated by tentative transactions. The most recent value due to local updates is maintained as a tentative value.

Similarly, there are two kinds of transactions:

Base Transaction: Base transactions work only on master data, and they produce new master data. They involve at most one connected-mobile node and may involve several base nodes.

Tentative Transaction: Tentative transactions work on local tentative data. They produce new tentative versions. They also produce a base transaction to be run at a later time on the base nodes.

Tentative transactions must follow a ***scope rule***: they may involve objects mastered on base nodes and mastered at the mobile node originating the transaction (call this the transaction's *scope*). The idea is that the mobile node and all the base nodes will be in contact when the tentative transaction is processed as a "real" base transaction — so the real transaction will be able to read the master copy of each item in the scope.

Local transactions that read and write *only* local data can be designed in any way you like. They cannot read-or write any tentative data because that would make them tentative.

Figure 5: The two-tier-replication scheme. Base nodes store replicas of the database. Each object is mastered at some node. Mobile nodes store a replica of the database, but are usually disconnected. Mobile nodes accumulate tentative transactions that run against the tentative database stored at the node. Tentative transactions are reprocessed as base transactions when the mobile node reconnects to the base. Tentative transactions may fail when reprocessed.

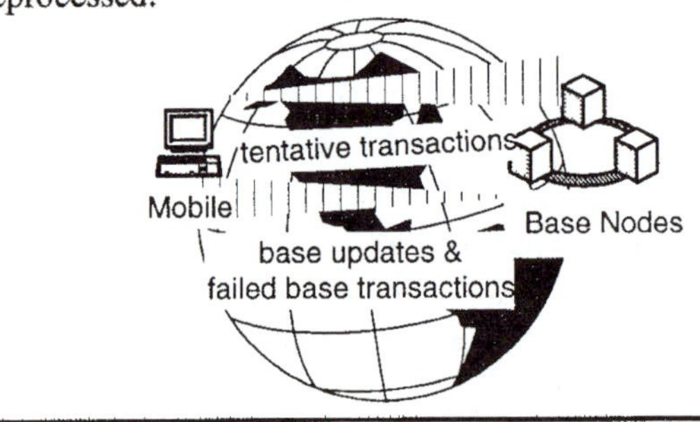

The base transaction generated by a tentative transaction may fail or it may produce different results. The base transaction has an ***acceptance criterion***: a test the resulting outputs must pass for the slightly different base transaction results to be acceptable. To give some sample acceptance criteria:

- The bank balance must not go negative.
- The price quote can not exceed the tentative quote.
- The seats must be aisle seats.

If a tentative transaction fails, the originating node and person who generated the transaction are informed it failed and why it failed. Acceptance failure is equivalent to the reconciliation mechanism of the lazy-group replication schemes. The differences are (1) the master database is always converged — there is no system delusion, and (2) the originating node need only contact a base node in order to discover if a tentative transaction is acceptable.

To continue the checking account analogy, the bank's version of the account is the master version. In writing checks, you and your spouse are creating tentative transactions which result in tentative versions of the account. The bank runs a base transaction when it clears the check. If you contact your bank and it clears the check, then you know the tentative transaction is a real transaction.

Consider the two-tier replication scheme's behavior during connected operation. In this environment, a two-tier system operates much like a lazy-master system with the additional restriction that no transaction can update data mastered at more than one mobile node. This restriction is not really needed in the connected case.

Now consider the disconnected case. Imagine that a mobile node disconnected a day ago. It has a copy of the base data as of yesterday. It has generated tentative transactions on that base data and on the local data mastered by the mobile node. These transactions generated tentative data versions at the mobile node. If the mobile node queries this data it sees the tentative values. For example, if it updated documents, produced contracts, and sent mail messages, those tentative updates are all visible at the mobile node.

When a mobile node connects to a base node, the mobile node:
1. Discards its tentative object versions since they will soon be refreshed from the masters,
2. Sends replica updates for any objects mastered at the mobile node to the base node "hosting" the mobile node,
3. Sends all its tentative transactions (and all their input parameters) to the base node to be executed in the order in which they committed on the mobile node,
4. Accepts replica updates from the base node (this is standard lazy-master replication), and
5. Accepts notice of the success or failure of each tentative transaction.

The "host" base node is the other tier of the two tiers. When contacted by a mobile note, the host base node:
1. Sends delayed replica update transactions to the mobile node.
2. Accepts delayed update transactions for mobile-mastered objects from the mobile node.
3. Accepts the list of tentative transactions, their input messages, and their acceptance criteria. Reruns each tentative transaction in the order it committed on the mobile node. During this reprocessing, the base transaction reads and writes object master copies using a lazy-master execution model. The scope-rule assures that the base transaction only accesses data mastered by the originating mobile node and base nodes. So master copies of all data in the transaction's scope are available to the base transaction. If the base transaction fails its acceptance criteria, the base transaction is aborted and a diagnostic message is returned to the mobile node. If the acceptance criteria requires the base and tentative transaction have identical outputs, then subsequent transactions reading tentative results written by T will fail too. On the other hand, weaker acceptance criteria are possible.
4. After the base node commits a base transaction, it propagates the lazy replica updates as transactions sent to all the other replica nodes. This is standard lazy-master.
5. When all the tentative transactions have been reprocessed as base transactions, the mobile node's state is converged with the base state.

The key properties of the two-tier replication scheme are:
1. Mobile nodes may make tentative database updates.
2. Base transactions execute with single-copy serializability so the master base system state is the result of a serializable execution.
3. A transaction becomes durable when the base transaction completes.
4. Replicas at all connected nodes converge to the base system state.
5. If all transactions commute, there are no reconciliations.

This comes close to meeting the four goals outlined at the start of this section.

When executing a base transaction, the two-tier scheme is a lazy-master scheme. So, the deadlock rate for base transactions is given by equation (19). This is still an N^2 deadlock rate. If a base transaction deadlocks, it is resubmitted and reprocessed until it succeeds, much as the replica update transactions are resubmitted in case of deadlock.

The reconciliation rate for base transactions will be zero if all the transactions commute. The reconciliation rate is driven by the rate at which the base transactions fail their acceptance criteria.

Processing the base transaction may produce results different from the tentative results. This is acceptable for some applications. It is fine if the checking account balance is different when the transaction is reprocessed. Other transactions from other nodes may have affected the account while the mobile node was disconnected. But, there are cases where the changes may not be acceptable. If the price of an item has increased by a large amount, if the item is out of stock, or if aisle seats are no longer available, then the salesman's price or delivery quote must be reconciled with the customer.

These acceptance criteria are application specific. The replication system can do no more than detect that there is a difference between the tentative and base transaction. This is probably too pessimistic a test. So, the replication system will simply run the tentative transaction. If the tentative transaction completes successfully and passes the acceptance test, then the replication system assumes all is well and propagates the replica updates as usual.

Users are aware that all updates are tentative until the transaction becomes a base transaction. If the base transaction fails, the user may have to revise and resubmit a transaction. The programmer must design the transactions to be commutative and to have acceptance criteria to detect whether the tentative transaction agrees with the base transaction effects.

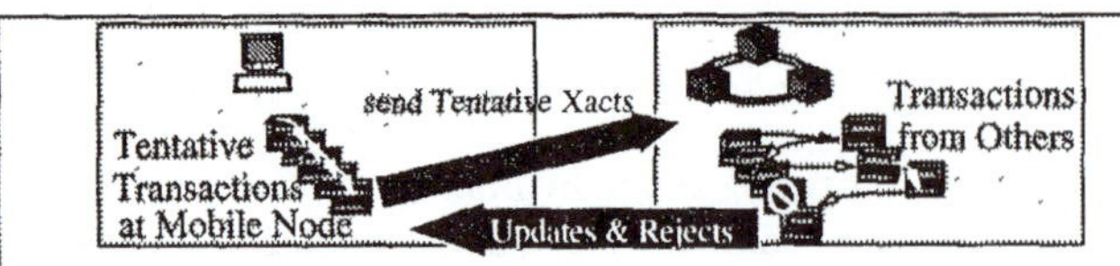

Figure 6: Executing tentative and base transactions in two-tier replication.

Thinking again of the checkbook example of an earlier section. The check is in fact a tentative update being sent to the bank. The bank either honors the check or rejects it. Analogous mechanisms are found in forms flow systems ranging from tax filing, applying for a job, or subscribing to a magazine. It is an approach widely used in human commerce.

This approach is similar to, but more general than the Data Cycle architecture [Herman] which has a single master node for all objects.

The approach can be used to obtain pure serializability if the base transaction only reads and writes master objects (current versions).

8. Summary

Replicating data at many nodes and letting anyone update the data is problematic. Security is one issue, performance is another. When the standard transaction model is applied to a replicated database, the size of each transaction rises by the degree of replication. This, combined with higher transaction rates means dramatically higher deadlock rates.

It might seem at first that a lazy replication scheme will solve this problem. Unfortunately, lazy-group replication just converts waits and deadlocks into reconciliations. Lazy-master replication has slightly better behavior than eager-master replication. Both suffer from dramatically increased deadlock as the replication degree rises. None of the master schemes allow mobile computers to update the database while disconnected from the system.

The solution appears to be to use semantic tricks (timestamps, and commutative transactions), combined with a two-tier replication scheme. Two-tier replication supports mobile nodes and combines the benefits of an eager-master-replication scheme and a local update scheme.

9. Acknowledgments

Tanj (John G.) Bennett of Microsoft and Alex Thomasian of IBM gave some very helpful advice on an earlier version of this paper. The anonymous referees made several helpful suggestions to improve the presentation.

10. References

Bernstein, P.A., V. Hadzilacos, N. Goodman, Concurrency Control and Recovery in Database Systems, Addison Wesley, Reading MA., 1987.

Berenson, H., Bernstein, P.A., Gray, J., Jim Melton, J., O'Neil, E., O'Neil, P., "A Critique of ANSI SQL Isolation Levels," Proc. ACM SIGMOD 95, pp. 1-10, San Jose CA, June 1995.

Garcia Molina, H. "Performance of Update Algorithms for Replicated Data in a Distributed Database," TR STAN-CS-79-744, CS Dept., Stanford U., Stanford, CA., June 1979.

Garcia Molina, H., Barbara, D., "How to Assign Votes in a Distributed System," J. ACM, 32(4). Pp. 841-860, October, 1985.

Gifford, D. K., "Weighted Voting for Replicated Data," Proc. ACM SIGOPS SOSP, pp: 150-159, Pacific Grove, CA, December 1979.

Gray, J., Reuter, A., *Transaction Processing: Concepts and Techniques,* Morgan Kaufmann, San Francisco, CA. 1993.

Gray, J., Homan, P, Korth, H., Obermarck, R., "A Strawman Analysis of the Probability of Deadlock," IBM RJ 2131, IBM Research, San Jose, CA., 1981.

Hammond, Brad, "Wingman, A Replication Service for Microsoft Access and Visual Basic", Microsoft White Paper, bradha@microsoft.com

Herman, G., Gopal, G, Lee, K., Weinrib, A., "The Datacycle Architecture for Very High Throughput Database Systems," Proc. ACM SIGMOD, San Francisco, CA. May 1987.

Kawell, L.., Beckhardt, S., Halvorsen, T., Raymond Ozzie, R., Greif, I.,"Replicated Document Management in a Group Communication System," Proc. Second Conference on Computer Supported Cooperative Work, Sept. 1988.

Oracle, "Oracle7 Server Distributed Systems: Replicated Data," Oracle part number A21903.March 1994, Oracle, Redwood Shores, CA. Or http://www.oracle.com/products/oracle7/server/whitepapers/replication/html/index

Chapter 5
Extensibility

An *extensible* system is one that allows components to be added to the system's core in the field. It usually implies that such components can be written by third-party developers ("extenders") who are not experts in the system's internals. The system designers publish an *extensibility API* that exposes the relevant system interfaces, and this should be sufficient information for extenders to add their application-specific code.

Extensibility is one of the major challenges in system architecture. Of course, any system can be extended with sufficient effort by hacking the source code. But a good extensibility interface should expose *just enough* of the system's needs to make the extender's application logic run fast. Database systems research dealt with extensibility relatively early on, because (a) other than database systems, most shared servers at the time were already general-purpose timesharing systems with Turing-complete interfaces (i.e. programming shells), and (b) since database applications are data-intensive, there were major performance benefits available in moving application logic into the system, rather than copying large amounts of the database out of the system into application space. There is a sizeable literature on extensible operating systems [RTY+87, HC92, EKO95, SESS96, etc.], but this largely emerged later than the DBMS work, and in part as a result of lessons from the database community (e.g. the Stonebraker paper on "Operating System Support for Data Management" in this book.)

The unifying theme of extensible system research is to cleanly factor out components of a system, identify the fundamental interactions among the components, and share components whenever possible. The goal of achieving a "separation of concerns" is a part of system architecture religion, but extensibility work really forces designers to observe the religion. A typical characteristic of good extensible designs is that they teach something new about what were thought to be well-understood ideas. When reading the papers in this chapter, it is important to go beyond the specifics of the designs, and think about how the designs shed light on the problem at hand: what are the key issues and how do they interact; what techniques are available to address each issue; how can techniques be mixed and matched to achieve new points in the design space?

Theoreticians often have a hard time appreciating these kinds of system architecture issues, but there is an analogous exercise in mathematics: capturing a complex system via a minimal set of simple axioms. Extensibility research is an effort to "axiomatize" system architectures. Complex software systems are never as clean as mathematical axiom systems, but the spirit of the exercise and the insights to be gained are analogous.

The Need to Extend Early Relational Systems

Codd's relational model is admirably succinct; it takes a strong stand on the key issue of normalization ("flat" relations with no pointers), but says very little else. In particular, it makes no restrictions on the set of data types that can be used in the columns of the system, and no restriction on the predicates that are applied to such data types. The initial relational systems were thus free to choose whatever type systems and predicates they saw fit. However, neither of the two famous prototype DBMSs focused on elaborate type systems. Both INGRES and System R implemented a fixed, fairly traditional set of possible column types: basically numeric types of various sorts, character types, and fixed- and variable-length strings – with lengths limited by a constant upper bound (in order to ensure that each tuple would fit on a disk page.) The predicates were those that were natural to the types: arithmetic comparisons over arithmetic expressions, and simple string matching.

The INGRES project was the first to run across the limitations of their fixed type system first. The initial work on INGRES was funded under an urban planning grant, and geographic data (roads, land boundaries, etc.) was always a scenario of interest in the project. Unfortunately, the natural queries in a Geographic Information System (GIS) are geometric, and these are clumsy to express using a relational language with simple types and predicates (an example is given in the first paper in this section). Moreover, even if one can express these queries, the features of a typical DBMS are not designed to make these specialized queries run fast. Special indexes and optimizations can improve performance of these queries by orders of magnitude.

GIS is a specialized application, and one could build a special data model and DBMS for it. However very similar problems arise in Computer Aided Design (CAD), which has circuit and chip diagrams that are not unlike road data in GIS systems. And as time progresses there seem to be more and more unusual kinds of information that do not mesh well with simple data types: time-series data (e.g. stock histories), network layouts, multimedia, marked-up documents, and so on. Each of these applications has its own idiosyncratic data types and predicates, but all of them also shared traditional database modeling needs for many of their attributes. Given the difficulty of designing and implementing a DBMS, the market cannot support a specialized database system for every class of application. Some kind of more flexible system is required.

Extensibility in POSTGRES

ADT-INGRES was an early incremental effort to address type extensibility in a database system. That effort morphed into the POSTGRES project at Berkeley, which discarded the INGRES code base and began anew. Both systems attempted to build a relational database that allowed Abstract Data Types (ADTs) to be used in column declarations for tables, and in the comparisons and expressions in predicates.

The initial paper in this section was a "first strike" in that agenda. It proposes metadata that a system must manage in order to allow post-hoc additions of ADTs to the system. All the type and predicate information in the system is table-driven from the database catalog, and commands are introduced to the data definition language to define new ADTs and associated functions. In addition to language and catalog issues, the paper outlines some of the challenges in making such a system provide respectable performance for queries over ADTs. In particular, it highlights the need for an Extensible Access Method Interface (EAMI) for ADTs, and the ability for the optimizer to reason about these access methods. The POSTGRES system was an almost direct incarnation of this design, including the table-driven ADTs and the EAMI interface for new access methods.

By any measure, the POSTGRES design was extremely influential. POSTGRES was commercialized as the Illustra system, which was purchased by Informix, which marketed the technology heavily. In response, IBM and Oracle stepped up their efforts to include ADT features in their systems. Microsoft is finally catching up on this front as well. Thus essentially all modern relational systems support ADTs in a manner analogous to the one proposed here. In hindsight, the biggest extensibility issue that POSTGRES missed was *security*; although the problem was mentioned in the paper included here, it was never addressed in the system or the research. The possibility of server crashes and data corruption due to extensions eventually became a big issue in the commercial marketplace. The canonical solution today is to use a Java Virtual Machine, or a script language interpreter (PERL, Python, etc.) Of course hindsight is always 20-20. There was no Java in the days of POSTGRES, interpreted languages were too slow on the hardware of the day, and the world of computing was quite a bit more idealistic and cooperative than it is today. Still, security is an important theme in extensibility, and it's one that has seen more focus in the OS and language communities than in the DB community.

GiST

To demonstrate the benefits of extensible access methods, the POSTGRES group implemented R-trees in the system; this gave POSTGRES a distinct performance advantage over traditional systems for a variety of non-traditional applications.

However, history shows that nobody outside the POSTGRES group ever added another access method to POSTGRES, largely because the EAMI proposed in the paper is at too low a level. Users with extensibility needs were simply incapable of writing their own access methods – that task required not only inventing and implementing such an access method, but also coding the access method so that it interacted correctly with the DBMS' pre-existing concurrency control and recovery system. This was essentially impossible without becoming an expert on the POSTGRES internals.

Our second paper on Generalized Search Trees (GiST) raises the level of abstraction for an access method extensibility interface. It begins with the observation that most of the application-specific indexing schemes posed in the database literature behave structurally very much like B+-trees. It then attempts to design a minimalist extensibility API that removes all data semantics from B+-trees, leaving only the structure of a balanced tree with data at the leaves that grows by splitting upwards. By leaving all the structure modification logic opaque to the extender, the GiST can be made to handle all the tricky concurrency and recovery logic internally [KMH97], with no need for any application-specific knowledge. The result is a far more approachable extensibility interface than the EAMI, with no sacrifice in performance. Many research groups have implemented custom indexing schemes over GiST, something that never occurred with the POSTGRES EAMI. In terms of performance, the flexibility of GiST often allows it to be tuned to run faster than traditional "built-in" indexes. Informix had one of the only commercial R-tree implementations in a DBMS. They implemented GiST in their engine as well, but discovered that their R-tree extension over GiST ran faster than their "native" R-tree implementation [Kor00]. The open-source PostGIS system, a GIS built over the open-source PostgreSQL system, also uses GiST rather than the native POSTGRES R-trees (GiST was added to PostgreSQL – via the EAMI interface – in the late 1990's).

We include the first GiST paper here since it is a good introduction, but we note that the interface was actually simplified over time. In particular, the reader should ignore the special-case interfaces for simulating B+-trees efficiently. Cleaner versions of the standard interface appear in Kornacker's work on concurrency and recovery [KMH97], and tricks for special traversals (including B+-tree traversal as well as nearest-neighbor traversals) are generalized and clarified by Aoki [Aok98]. Theoretically-minded readers are also referred to [HKMPS02] for exposition of the idea of *indexability theory* that is raised at the end of the paper included here.

Extensible Optimizers

As noted in our first paper, extensibility in the query language has to be supported by the query optimizer, or efficiency suffers enormously. POSTGRES addressed this issue to some extent; for example, the EAMI allowed the optimizer to know about relevant indexes, and subsequent research showed how the system could be made to efficiently optimize queries with time-consuming code embedded in the ADTs [Hel98,CS99,Aok99].

Other extensibility projects were even more aggressive in exploring the possibilities of an extensible query optimizer. The Starburst project at IBM had an optimizer was designed to generalize the System R optimizer, and make it extensible in two ways. First, the set of physical operators in the query executor could be extended, and it was important to be able to easily "teach" the optimizer to use new operators intelligently. Second, the set of logical operators in the query language could be extensible, in order to support new query language features. Our next paper by Guy Lohman describes the Starburst design for an extensible query optimizer. Essentially it abstracts the dynamic programming and pruning of the Selinger algorithm, and exposes the expansions done during dynamic programming as grammar-like rules. This approach is particularly attractive given the popularity of Selinger's optimizer. A competing scheme was proposed by Graefe and DeWitt in the Exodus project at Wisconsin, and was refined over the years by Graefe in the Volcano [GM93], Cascades [Gra95], and MS SQL Server systems. The Graefe/DeWitt approach generates a complete initial plan based on heuristics and explores the search space from there, making simple local modifications to algebraic plans (e.g. replacing a logical algebra operator with a physical operator, swapping physical operators, flipping the two inputs to a join, reordering a pair of adjacent joins, etc.), until all legal physical plans are considered. The legal modifications are expressed in Exodus as rules, somewhat similar to Starburst, but the Exodus rules *transform* plans, while the Starburst rules *generate* them. The subsequent work by Graefe is an interesting alternative to the Selinger approach with both pros and cons, and anyone aspiring to be an expert on query optimization should know this work well.

Extensible query optimization is particularly interesting because it points the way to a very general future for database optimization and execution architectures. If the details of the relational algebra can be abstracted away from a query optimizer, then it should be possible to apply database-like optimization schemes to any dataflow-oriented programming model, of which there are many [KMC+00,LP95, AYKJ00, etc.]

Historical Context

Before we leave this topic, some context is useful for readers who wish to pursue more of the literature in this area. Historically, database extensibility research was undertaken in system prototypes that were exploring enhanced data models, in particular *object-oriented* data models. In retrospect, it is very useful to separate the contributions of those systems into architectural issues involving extensibility, and data modeling issues involving language and schema design. Unfortunately there is no systematic paper that lays out all the various ideas in extensible database systems and the data models that went with them, and tries to show which of the architectural ideas can be combined with which of the modeling and language features. Two systems with reasonable overview papers are Postgres [PGCACM] and O2 [D90]. Designers of systems for new data models and languages (XML-based approaches come to mind, but there will be others in future) are encouraged to read the prior work carefully, to tease apart the architectural ideas from the specifics of the data model research, and consider mixing and matching the ideas to solve current needs.

As an alternative to extensible systems, there was also research into so-called "toolkits" for generating app-specific DBMSs – notably the EXODUS project at Wisconsin, and the Genesis project at UT-Austin. The toolkit idea was to decompose a DBMS cleanly into subsystems, so that a collection of subsystems and extensions could be cobbled together easily to build an application-specific DBMS. In these systems, the components had to be extensible to support general reuse. For example, the optimizer in EXODUS had to support "any" query language and "any" set of execution operators. In practice, neither EXODUS nor Genesis was seriously used in any configurations other than the default. However, as noted above, the EXODUS optimizer was influential, both as a precursor of the Cascades work [Cascades] now used in MS SQL Server, and as the main point of contrast to the Starburst work (which lives on in IBM DB2).

References

[AYKJ00] Danielle Argiro, Mark Young, Steve Kubica, and Steve Jorgensen. "Khoros: An Integrated Development Environment for Scientific Computing and Visualization." In *Enabling Technologies for Computational Science: Frameworks, Middleware and Environments*, Kluwer Academic Publishers, March 2000, pp. 147-157.

[Aok98] P.M. Aoki. "Generalizing 'Search' in Generalized Search Trees". In *Proc. 14th IEEE Int'l Conf. on Data Engineering* (ICDE '98), Orlando, FL, Feb. 1998, 380-389.

[Aok99] P.M. Aoki. "How to Avoid Building DataBlades® That Know the Value of Everything and the Cost of Nothing". *Proc. 11th IEEE Int'l Conf. on Scientific and Statistical Database Mgmt.* (SSDBM '99), Cleveland, OH, July 1999, 122-133.

[CS99] Surajit Chaudhuri and Kyuseok Shim. Optimization of Queries with User- Defined Predicates. *ACM Transactions on Database Systems (TODS),* 24(2):177- 228, 1999.

[D90] O. Deux et al. "The Story of O2." *IEEE Trans. Knowledge and Data Eng.* 2(1):91–108, March, 1990.

[EKO95] Dawson R. Engler, M. Frans Kaashoek, and James O'Toole Jr. "Exokernel: an operating system architecture for application-level resource management." In *Proceedings of the 15th ACM Symposium on Operating Systems Principles (SOSP),* Copper Mountain Resort, Colorado, December 1995.

[GM93] Goetz Graefe and William J. McKenna. The Volcano Optimizer Generator: Extensibility and Efficient Search. In *Proc. 9th International Conference on Data Engineering (ICDE),* pages 209-218, Vienna, Austria, April 1993.

[Gra95] Goetz Graefe. The Cascades Framework for Query Optimization. *IEEE Data Engineering Bulletin,* 18(3):19-29, 1995.

[HC92] K. Harty and D. Cheriton. "Application controlled physical memory using external page cache management." In *Fifth International Conference on Architectural Support for Programming Languages and Operating Systems (ASPLOS),* October 1992.

[Hel98] Joseph M. Hellerstein. Optimization Techniques for Queries with Expensive Methods. *ACM Transactions on Database Systems (TODS),* 23(2):113-157, 1998.

[HKMPS02] J. M. Hellerstein, E. Koutsoupias, D. P. Miranker, C. H. Papadimitriou, and V. Samoladas. "On a model of indexability and its bounds for range queries". *Journal of the ACM (JACM)* 49(1):35--55, 2002.

[KMC+00] Eddie Kohler, Robert Morris, Benjie Chen, John Jannotti and M. Frans Kaashoek. *ACM Transactions on Computer Systems (TOCS)* 18(3): 263--297, August, 2000.

[KMH97] Marcel Kornacker, C. Mohan and Joseph M. Hellerstein. "Concurrency and Recovery in Generalized Search Trees". In *Proc. ACM SIGMOD Conf. on Management of Data*, Tucson, AZ, May 1997, 62-72.

[Kor99] Marcel Kornacker. High-Performance Extensible Indexing. In *Proceedings of 25th International Conference on Very Large Data Bases (VLDB)*, September 7-10, 1999, Edinburgh, Scotland.

[LP95] Edward A. Lee and Thomas M. Parks. "Dataflow Process Networks." *Proceedings of the IEEE*, 83(5):773-801, May, 1995.

[RTY+87] Richard Rashid, Avadis Tevanian, Jr., Michael Young, David Golub, Robert Baron, David Black, William Bolosky, and Jonathan Chew. "Machine-Independent Virtual Memory Management for Paged Uniprocessor and Multiprocessor Architectures". In *Proceedings of the 2nd Symposium on Architectural Support for Programming Languages and Operating Systems (ASPLOS)*, October, 1987.

[SESS96] Margo Seltzer, Yasuhiro Endo, Christopher Small, and Keith A. Smith. "Dealing with Disaster: Surviving Misbehaved Kernel Extensions". In *Proceedings of the 1996 Symposium on Operating Systems Design and Implementation (OSDI)*, Seattle, WA, October 1996.

[SK91] Michael Stonebraker and Greg Kemnitz. "The POSTGRES next generation database management system." *Communications of the ACM* 34 (10): 78 – 92, October 1991.

INCLUSION OF NEW TYPES IN RELATIONAL DATA BASE SYSTEMS

Michael Stonebraker
EECS Dept.
University of California, Berkeley

Abstract

This paper explores a mechanism to support user-defined data types for columns in a relational data base system. Previous work suggested how to support new operators and new data types. The contribution of this work is to suggest ways to allow query optimization on commands which include new data types and operators and ways to allow access methods to be used for new data types.

1. INTRODUCTION

The collection of built-in data types in a data base system (e.g. integer, floating point number, character string) and built-in operators (e.g. +, -, *, /) were motivated by the needs of business data processing applications. However, in many engineering applications this collection of types is not appropriate. For example, in a geographic application a user typically wants points, lines, line groups and polygons as basic data types and operators which include intersection, distance and containment. In scientific application, one requires complex numbers and time series with appropriate operators. In such applications one is currently required to simulate these data types and operators using the basic data types and operators provided by the DBMS at substantial inefficiency and complexity. Even in business applications, one sometimes needs user-defined data types. For example, one system [RTI84] has implemented a sophisticated date and time data type to add to its basic collection. This implementation allows subtraction of dates, and returns "correct" answers, e.g.

"April 15" - "March 15" = 31 days

This definition of subtraction is appropriate for most users; however, some applications require all months to have 30 days (e.g. programs which compute interest on bonds). Hence, they require a definition of subtraction which yields 30 days as the answer to the above computation. Only a user-defined data type facility allows such customization to occur.

Current data base systems implement hashing and B-trees as fast access paths for built-in data types. Some user-defined data types (e.g. date and time) can use existing access methods (if certain extensions are made); however other data types (e.g. polygons) require new access methods. For example R-trees [GUTM84], KDB trees [ROBI81] and Grid files are appropriate for spatial objects. In addition, the introduction of new access methods for conventional business applications (e.g. extendible hashing [FAGI79, LITW80]) would be expeditied by a facility to add new access methods.

This research was sponsored by the U.S. Air Force Office of Scientific Research Grant 83-0254 and the Naval Electronics Systems Command Contract N39-82-C-0235

A complete extended type system should allow:

1) the definition of user-defined data types
2) the definition of new operators for these data types
3) the implementation of new access methods for data types
4) optimized query processing for commands containing new data types and operators

The solution to requirements 1 and 2 was described in [STON83]; in this paper we present a complete proposal. In Section 2 we begin by presenting a motivating example of the need for new data types, and then briefly review our earlier proposal and comment on its implementation. Section 3 turns to the definition of new access methods and suggests mechanisms to allow the designer of a new data type to use access methods written for another data type and to implement his own access methods with as little work as possible. Then Section 4 concludes by showing how query optimization can be automatically performed in this extended environment.

2. ABSTRACT DATA TYPES

2.1. A Motivating Example

Consider a relation consisting of data on two dimensional boxes. If each box has an identifier, then it can be represented by the coordinates of two corner points as follows:

```
create box (id = i4, x1 = f8, x2 = f8, y1 = f8, y2 = f8)
```

Now consider a simple query to find all the boxes that overlap the unit square, ie. the box with coordinates (0, 1, 0, 1). The following is a compact representation of this request in QUEL:

```
retrieve (box.all) where not
  (box.x2 <= 0 or box.x1 >= 1
  or box.y2 <= 0 or box.y1 >= 1)
```

The problems with this representation are:

The command is too hard to understand.

The command is too slow because the query planner will not be able to optimize something this complex.

The command is too slow because there are too many clauses to check.

The solution to these difficulties is to support a box data type whereby the box relation can be defined as:

```
create box (id = i4, desc = box)
```

and the resulting user query is:

```
retrieve (box.all) where box.desc !! "0, 1, 0, 1"
```

Here "!!" is an overlaps operator with two operands of data type box which returns a boolean. One would want a substantial collection of operators for user defined types. For example, Table 1 lists a collection of useful operators for the box data type.

Fast access paths must be supported for queries with qualifications utilizing new data types and operators. Consequently, current access methods must be extended to operate in this environment. For example, a reasonable collating sequence for boxes would be on ascending area, and a B-tree storage structure could be built for boxes using this sequence. Hence, queries such as

retrieve (box.all) where box.desc AE "0,5,0,5"

Binary operator	symbol	left operand	right operand	result
overlaps	!!	box	box	boolean
contained in	<<	box	box	boolean
is to the left of	<L	box	box	boolean
is to the right of	>R	box	box	boolean
intersection	??	box	box	box
distance	"	box	box	float
area less than	AL	box	box	boolean
area equals	AE	box	box	boolean
area greater	AG	box	box	boolean

Unary operator	symbol	operand	result
area	AA	box	float
length	LL	box	float
height	HH	box	float
diagonal	DD	box	line

Operators for Boxes

Table 1

should use this index. Moreover, if a user wishes to optimize access for the !! operator, then an R-tree [GUTM84] may be a reasonable access path. Hence, it should be possible to add a user defined access method. Lastly, a user may submit a query to find all pairs of boxes which overlap, e.g:

range of b1 is box
range of b2 is box
retrieve (b1.all, b2.all) where b1.desc !! b2.desc

A query optimizer must be able to construct an access plan for solving queries which contains user defined operators.

We turn now to a review of the prototype presented in [STON83] which supports some of the above function.

2.2. DEFINITION OF NEW TYPES

To define a new type, a user must follow a registration process which indicates the existence of the new type, gives the length of its internal representation and provides input and output conversion routines, e.g:

```
define type-name length = value,
                 input = file-name
                 output = file-name
```

The new data type must occupy a fixed amount of space, since only fixed length data is allowed by the built-in access methods in INGRES. Moreover, whenever new values are input from a program or output to a user, a conversion routine must be called. This routine must convert from character string to the new type and back. A data base system calls such routines for built-in data types (e.g. ascii-to-int, int-to-ascii) and they must be provided for user-defined data types. The input conversion routine must accept a pointer to a value of type character string and return a pointer to a value of the new data type. The output routine must perform the converse transformation.

Then, zero or more operators can be implemented for the new type. Each can be defined with the following syntax:

```
define operator token = value,
                left-operand = type-name,
                right-operand = type-name,
                result = type-name,
                precedence-level like operator-2,
                file = file-name
```

For example:

```
define operator token = !!,
                left-operand = box,
                right-operand = box,
                result = boolean,
                precedence like *,
                file = /usr/foobar
```

All fields are self explanatory except the precedence level which is required when several user defined operators are present and precedence must be established among them. The file /usr/foobar indicates the location of a procedure which can accept two operands of type box and return true if they overlap. This procedure is written in a general purpose programming language and is linked into the run-time system and called as appropriate during query processing.

2.3. Comments on the Prototype

The above constructs have been implemented in the University of California version of INGRES [STON76]. Modest changes were required to the parser and a dynamic loader was built to load the required user-defined routines on demand into the INGRES address space. The system was described in [ONG84].

Our initial experience with the system is that dynamic linking is not preferable to static linking. One problem is that initial loading of routines is slow. Also, the ADT routines must be loaded into data space to preserve sharability of the DBMS code segment. This capability requires the construction of a non-trivial loader. An "industrial strength" implementation might choose to specify the user types which an installation wants at the time the DBMS is installed. In this case, all routines could be linked into the run time system at system installation time by the linker provided by the operating system. Of course, a data base system implemented as a single server process with internal multitasking would not be subject to any code sharing difficulties, and a dynamic loading solution might be reconsidered.

An added difficulty with ADT routines is that they provide a serious safety loophole. For example, if an ADT routine has an error, it can easily crash the DBMS by overwriting DBMS data structures accidentally. More seriously, a malicious ADT routine can overwrite the entire data base with zeros. In addition, it is unclear whether such errors are due to bugs in the user routines or in the DBMS, and finger-pointing between the DBMS implementor and the ADT implementor is likely to result.

ADT routines can be run in a separate address space to solve both problems, but the performance penalty is severe. Every procedure call to an ADT operator must be turned into a round trip message to a separate address space. Alternately, the DBMS can interpret the ADT procedure and guarantee safety, but only by building a language processor into the run-time system and paying the performance penalty of interpretation. Lastly, hardware support for protected procedure calls (e.g. as in Multics) would also solve the problem.

However, on current hardware the prefered solution may be to provide two environments for ADT procedures. A protected environment would be provided for debugging purposes. When a user was confident that his routines worked correctly, he could install them in the unprotected DBMS. In this way, the DBMS implementor could refuse to be concerned unless a bug could be produced in the safe version.

We now turn to extending this environment to support new access methods.

3. NEW ACCESS METHODS

A DBMS should provide a wide variety of access methods, and it should be easy to add new ones. Hence, our goal in this section is to describe how users can add new access methods that will efficiently support user-defined data types. In the first subsection we indicate a registration process that allows implementors of new data types to use access methods written by others. Then, we turn to designing lower level DBMS interfaces so the access method designer has minimal work to perform. In this section we restrict our attention to access methods for a single key field. Support for composite keys is a straight forward extension. However, multidimensional access methods that allow efficient retrieval utilizing subsets of the collection of keys are beyond the scope of this paper.

3.1. Registration of a New Access Method

The basic idea which we exploit is that a properly implemented access method contains only a small number of procedures that define the characteristics of the access method. Such procedures can be replaced by others which operate on a different data type and allow the access method to "work" for the new type. For example, consider a B-tree and the following generic query:

retrieve (target-list) where relation.key OPR value

A B-tree supports fast access if OPR is one of the set:

{=, <, <=, >=, >}

and includes appropriate procedure calls to support these operators for a data type (s). For example, to search for the record matching a specific key value, one need only descend the B-tree at each level searching for the minimum key whose value exceeds or equals the indicated key. Only calls on the operator "<=" are required with a final call or calls to the

TEMPLATE-1	AM-name	condition
	B-tree	P1
	B-tree	P2
	B-tree	P3
	B-tree	P4
	B-tree	P5
	B-tree	P6
	B-tree	P7

TEMPLATE-2	AM-name	opr-name	opt	left	right	result
	B-tree	=	opt	fixed	type1	boolean
	B-tree	<	opt	fixed	type1	boolean
	B-tree	<=	req	fixed	type1	boolean
	B-tree	>	opt	fixed	type1	boolean
	B-tree	>=	opt	fixed	type1	boolean

Templates for Access Methods

Table 2

AM	class	AM-name	opr	generic name	opr-id opr	Ntups	Npages
	int-ops	B-tree	=	=	id1	N / Ituples	2
	int-ops	B-tree	<	<	id2	F1 * N	F1 * NUMpages
	int-ops	B-tree	<=	<=	id3	F1 * N	F1 * NUMpages
	int-ops	B-tree	>	>	id4	F2 * N	F2 * NUMpages
	int-ops	B-tree	>=	>=	id5	F2 * N	F2 * NUMpages
	area-op	B-tree	AE	=	id6	N / Ituples	3
	area-op	B-tree	AL	<	id7	F1 * N	F1 * NUMpages
	area-op	B-tree	AG	>	id8	F1 * N	F1 * NUMpages

The AM Relation

Table 3

routine supporting "=".

Moreover, this collection of operators has the following properties:

P1) key-1 < key-2 and key-2 < key-3 then key-1 < key-3
P2) key-1 < key-2 implies not key-2 < key-1
P3) key-1 < key-2 or key-2 < key-1 or key-1 = key-2
P4) key-1 <= key-2 if key-1 < key-2 or key-1 = key-2
P5) key-1 = key-2 implies key-2 = key-1
P6) key-1 > key-2 if key-2 < key-1
P7) key-1 >= key-2 if key-2 <= key-1

In theory, the procedures which implement these operators can be replaced by any collection of procedures for new operators that have these properties and the B-tree will "work" correctly. Lastly, the designer of a B-tree access method may disallow variable length keys. For example, if a binary search of index pages is performed, then only fixed length keys are possible. Information of this restriction must be available to a type designer who wishes to use the access method.

The above information must be recorded in a data structure called an access method **template**. We propose to store templates in two relations called TEMPLATE-1 and TEMPLATE-2 which would have the composition indicated in Table 2 for a B-tree access method. TEMPLATE-1 simply documents the conditions which must be true for the operators provided by the access method. It is included only to provide guidance to a human wishing to utilize the access method for a new data type and is not used internally in the system. TEMPLATE-2, on the other hand, provides necessary information on the data types of operators. The column "opt" indicates whether the operator is required or optional. A B-tree must have the operator "<=" to build the tree; however, the other operators are optional. Type1, type2 and result are possible types for the left operand, the right operand, and the result of a given operator. Values for these fields should come from the following collection;

a specific type, e.g. int, float, boolean, char
fixed, i.e. any type with fixed length
variable, i.e. any type with a
 prescribed varying length format
fix-var, i.e. fixed or variable
type1, i.e. the same type as type1
type2, i.e. the same as type2

After indicating the template for an access method, the designer can propose one or more collections of operators which satisfy the template in another relation, AM. In Table 3 we have shown an AM containing the original set of integer operators provided by the access method designer along with a collection added later by the designer of the box data type. Since operator names do not need to be unique, the field opr-id must be included to specify a unique identifier for a given operator. This field is present in a relation which contains the operator specific information discussed in Section 2. The fields, Ntups and Npages are query processing parameters which estimate the number of tuples which satisfy the qualification and the number of pages touched when running a query using the operator to compare a key field in a relation to a constant. Both are formulas which utilize the variables found in Table 4, and values reflect approximations to the computations found in [SELI79] for the case that each record set occupies an individual file. Moreover, F1 and F2 are surogates for the following quantities:

F1 = (value - low-key) / (high-key - low-key)
F2 = (high-key - value) / (high-key - low-key)

With these data structures in place, a user can simply modify relations to B-tree using any class of operators defined in the AM relation. The only addition to the modify command

Variable	Meaning
N	number of tuples in a relation
NUMpages	number of pages of storage used by the relation
Ituples	number of index keys in an index
Ipages	number of pages in the index
value	the constant appearing in: rel-name.field-name OPR value
high-key	the maximum value in the key range if known
low-key	the minimum value in the key range if known

Variables for Computing Ntups and Npages

Table 4

is a clause "using class" which specifies what operator class to use in building and accessing the relation. For example the command

modify box to B-tree on desc using area-op

will allow the DBMS to provide optimized access on data of type box using the operators {AE,AL,AG}. The same extension must be provided to the index command which constructs a secondary index on a field, e.g:

index on box is box-index (desc) using area-op

To illustrate the generality of these constructs, the AM and TEMPLATE relations are shown in Tables 5 and 6 for both a hash and an R-tree access method. The R-tree is assumed to support three operators, contained-in (<<), equals (==) and contained-in-or-equals (<<=). Moreover, a fourth operator (UU) is required during page splits and finds the box which is the union of two other boxes. UU is needed solely for maintaining the R-tree data structure, and is not useful for search purposes. Similarly, a hash access method requires a hash function, H, which accepts a key as a left operand and an integer number of buckets as a right operand to produce a hash bucket as a result. Again, H cannot be used for searching purposes. For compactness, formulas for Ntups and Npages have been omitted from Table 6.

3.2. Implementing New Access Methods

In general an access method is simply a collection of procedure calls that retrieve and update records. A generic abstraction for an access method could be the following:

open (relation-name)

This procedure returns a pointer to a structure containing all relevant information about a relation. Such a "relation control block" will be called a descriptor. The effect is to make the relation accessible.

close (descriptor)

This procedure terminates access to the relation indicated by the descriptor.

get-first (descriptor, OPR, value)

This procedure returns the first record which satisfies the qualification

..where key OPR value

get-next (descriptor, OPR, value, tuple-id)

TEMPLATE-1	AM-name	condition
	hash	Key-1 = Key-2 implies H(key1) = H(key-2)
	R-tree	Key-1 << Key-2 and Key-2 << Key-2 implies Key-1 << key-3
	R-tree	Key-1 << Key-2 implies not Key-2 << Key-1
	R-tree	Key-1 <<= Key-2 implies Key-1 << Key-2 or Key-1 == Key-2
	R-tree	Key-1 == Key-2 implies Key-2 == Key-1
	R-tree	Key-1 << Key-1 UU Key-2
	R-tree	Key-2 << Key-1 UU Key-2

TEMPLATE-2	AM-name	opr-name	opt	left	right	result
	hash	=	opt	fixed	type1	boolean
	hash	H	req	fixed	int	int
	R-tree	<<	req	fixed	type1	boolean
	R-tree	==	opt	fixed	type1	boolean
	R-tree	<<=	opt	fixed	type1	boolean
	R-tree	UU	req	fixed	type1	boolean

Templates for Access Methods

Table 5

AM	class	AM-name	opr name	generic opr	opr-id	Ntups	Npages
	box-ops	R-tree	==	==	id10		
	box-ops	R-tree	<<	<<	id11		
	box-ops	R-tree	<<=	<<=	id12		
	box-ops	R-tree	UU	UU	id13		
	hash-op	hash	=	=	id14		
	hash-op	hash	H	H	id15		

The AM Relation

Table 6

This procedure gets the next tuple following the one indicated by tuple-id which satisfies the qualification.

get-unique (descriptor, tuple-id)

This procedure gets the tuple which corresponds to the indicated tuple identifier.

insert (descriptor, tuple)

This procedure inserts a tuple into the indicated relation

delete (descriptor, tuple-id)

This procedure deletes a tuple from the indicated relation.

replace (descriptor, tuple-id, new-tuple)

This procedure replaces the indicated tuple by a new one.

build (descriptor, keyname, OPR)

Of course it is possible to build a new access method for a relation by successively inserting tuples using the insert procedure. However, higher performance can usually be obtained by a bulk loading utility. Build is this utility and accepts a descriptor for a relation along with a key and operator to use in the build process.

There are many different (more or less similar) access method interfaces; see [ASTR76, ALLC80] for other proposals. Each DBMS implementation will choose their own collection of procedures and calling conventions.

If this interface is publicly available, then it is feasible to implement these procedures using a different organizing principle. A clean design of open and close should make these routines universally usable, so an implementor need only construct the remainder. Moreover, if the designer of a new access method chooses to utilize the same physical page layout as some existing access method, then replace and delete do not require modification, and additional effort is spared.

The hard problem is to have a new access method interface correctly to the transaction management code. (One commercial system found this function to present the most difficulties when a new access method was coded.) If a DBMS (or the underlying operating system) supports transactions by physically logging pages and executing one of the popular concurrency control algorithms for page size granules, (e.g. [BROW81, POPE81, SPEC83, STON85] then the designer of a new access method need not concern himself with transaction management. Higher level software will begin and end transactions, and the access method can freely read and write pages with a guarantee of atomicity and serializability. In this case the access method designer has no problems concerning transactions, and this is a significant advantage for transparent transactions. Unfortunately, much higher performance will typically result if a different approach is taken to both crash recovery and concurrency control. We now sketch roughly what this alternate interface might be.

With regard to crash recovery, most current systems have a variety of special case code to perform logical logging of events rather than physical logging of the changes of bits. There are at least two reasons for this method of logging. First, changes to the schema (e.g. create a relation) often require additional work besides changes to the system catalogs (e.g. creating an operating system file in which to put tuples of the relation). Undoing a create command because a transaction is aborted will require deletion of the newly created file. Physical backout cannot accomplish such extra function. Second, some data base updates are extremely inefficient when physically logged. For example, if a relation is modified from B-tree to hash, then the entire relation will be written to the log (perhaps more than once depending on the implementation of the modify utility). This costly extra I/O can be avoided by simply logging the command that is being performed. In the unlikely event that this event in the log must be undone or redone, then the modify utility can be rerun to make the changes anew. Of course, this sacrifices performance at recovery time for a compression of the log by several orders of magnitude.

If such logical logging is performed, then a new access method must become involved in logging process and a clean event-oriented interface to logging services should be provided. Hence, the log should be a collection of **events**, each having an event-id, an associated **event type** and an arbitrary collection of data. Lastly, for each event type, T, two procedures, REDO(T) and UNDO(T) are required which will be called when the log manager is rolling forward redoing log events and rolling backward undoing logged events respectively. The system must also provide a procedure,

LOG (event-type, event-data)

which will actually insert events into the log. Moreover, the system will provide a collection of **built-in event types**. For each such event, UNDO and REDO are available in system libraries. Built-in events would include:

replace a tuple
insert a tuple at a specific tuple identifier address
delete a tuple
change the storage structure of a relation
create a relation
destroy a relation

A designer of a new access method could use the built-in events if they were appropriate to his needs. Alternately, he could specify new event types by writing UNDO and REDO procedures for the events and making entries in a system relation holding event information. Such an interface is similar to the one provided by CICS [IBM80].

We turn now to discussing the concurrency control subsystem. If this service is provided transparently and automatically by an underlying module, then special case concurrency control for the system catalogs and index records will be impossible. This approach will severely impact performance as noted in [STON85]. Alternately, one can follow the standard scheduler model [BERN81] in which a module is callable by code in the access methods when a concurrency control decision must be made. The necessary calls are:

read (object-identifier)
write (object-identifier)
begin
abort
commit
savepoint

and the scheduler responds with yes, no or abort. The calls to begin, abort, commit and savepoint are made by higher level software, and the access methods need not be concerned with them. The access method need only make the appropriate calls on the scheduler when it reads or writes an object. The only burden which falls on the implementor is to choose the appropriate size for objects.

The above interface is appropriate for data records which are handled by a conventional algorithm guaranteeing serializability. To provide special case parallelism on index or system catalog records, an access method requires more control over concurrency decisions. For example, most B-tree implementations do not hold write locks on index pages which are split until the end of the transaction which performed the insert. It appears easiest to provide specific lock and unlock calls for such special situations, i.e:

lock (object, mode)
unlock (object)

These can be used by the access method designer to implement special case parallelism in his data structures.

The last interface of concern to the designer of an access method is the one to the buffer manager. One requires five procedures:

get (system-page-identifier)
fix (system-page-identifier)
unfix (system-page-identifier)
put (system-page-identifier)
order (system-page-identifier,
  event-id or system-page-identifier)

The first procedure accepts a page identifier and returns a pointer to the page in the buffer pool. The second and third procedures pin and unpin pages in the buffer pool. The last call specifies that the page holding the given event should be written to disk prior to the indicated data page. This information is necessary in write-ahead log protocols. More generally, it allows two data pages to be forced out of memory in a specific order.

An access method implementor must code the necessary access method procedures utilizing the above interfaces to the log manager, the concurrency control manager and the buffer manager. Then, he simply registers his access method in the two TEMPLATE relations.

3.3. Discussion

A transparent interface to the transaction system is clearly much preferred to the complex collection of routines discussed above. Moreover, the access method designer who utilizes these routines must design his own events, specify any special purpose concurrency control in his data structures, and indicate any necessary order in forcing pages out of the buffer pool. An open research question is the design of a simpler interface to these services that will provide the required functions.

In addition, the performance of the crash recovery facility will be inferior to the recovery facilities in a conventional system. In current transaction managers, changes to indexes are typically not logged. Rather, index changes are recreated from the corresponding update to the data record. Hence, if there are n indexes for a given object, a single log entry for the data update will result in n+1 events (the data update and n index updates) being undone or redone in a conventional system. Using our proposed interface all n+1 events will appear in the log, and efficiency will be sacrificed.

The access method designer has the least work to perform if he uses the same page layout as one of the built-in access methods. Such an access method requires get-first, get-next, and insert to be coded specially. Moreover, no extra event types are required, since the built-in ones provide all the required functions. R-trees are an example of such an access method. On the other hand, access methods which do not use the same page layout will require the designer to write considerably more code.

4. QUERY PROCESSING AND ACCESS PATH SELECTION

To allow optimization of a query plan that contains new operators and types, only four additional pieces of information are required when defining an operator. First, a selectivity factor, Stups, is required which estimates the expected number of records satisfying the clause:

...where rel-name.field-name OPR value

A second selectivity factor, S, is the expected number of records which satisfy the clause

...where relname-1.field-1 OPR relname-2.field-2

Stups and S are arithmetic formulas containing the predefined variables indicated earlier in Table 4. Moreover, each variable can have a suffix of 1 or 2 to specify the left or right operand respectively.

Notice that the same selectivity appears both in the definition of an operator (Stups) and in the entry (Ntups) in AM if the operator is used in an index. In this case, Ntups from AM should be used first, and supports an if-then-else specification used for example in the [SELI79] for the operator "=" as follows:

selectivity = (1 / Ituples) ELSE 1/10

In this example selectivity is the reciprocal of the number of index tuples if an index exists else it is 1/10. The entry for Ntups in AM would be (N / Ituples) while Stups in the operator definition would be N / 10.

The third piece of necessary information is whether merge-sort is feasible for the operator being defined. More exactly, the existence of a second operator, OPR-2 is required such that OPR and OPR-2 have properties P1-P3 from Section 3 with OPR replacing "=" and OPR-2 replacing "<". If so, the relations to be joined using OPR can be sorted using OPR-2 and then merged to produce the required answer.

The last piece of needed information is whether hash-join is a feasible joining strategy for this operator. More exactly, the hash condition from Table 6 must be true with OPR replacing "=".

An example of these pieces of information for the operator, AE, would be:

```
define operator token = AE,
                left-operand = box,
                right-operand = box,
                result = boolean,
                precedence like *,
                file = /usr/foobar,
                Stups = 1,
                S = min (N1, N2),
                merge-sort with AL,
                hash-join
```

We now turn to generating the query processing plan. We assume that relations are stored keyed on one field in a single file and that secondary indexes can exist for other fields. Moreover, queries involving a single relation can be processed with a scan of the relation, a scan of a portion of the primary index, or a scan of a portion of one secondary index. Joins can be processed by iterative substitution, merge-sort or a hash-join algorithm. Modification to the following rules for different environments appears straigth-forward.

Legal query processing plans are described by the following statements.

1) Merge sort is feasible for a clause of the form:

relname-1.field-1 OPR relname-2.field-2

if field-1 and field-2 are of the same data type and OPR has the merge-sort property. Moreover, the expected size of the result is S. The cost to sort one or both relations is a built-in computation.

2) Iterative substitution is always feasible to perform the join specified by a clause of the form:

relname-1.field-1 OPR relname-2.field-2

The expected size of the result is calculated as above. The cost of this operation is the cardinality of the outer relation multiplied by the expected cost of the one-variable query on the inner relation.

3) A hash join algorithm can be used to perform a join specified by:

relname-1.field-1 OPR relname-2.field-2

if OPR has the hash-join property. The expected size of the result is as above, and the cost to hash one or both relations is another built-in computation.

4) An access method, A for relname can be used to restrict a clause of the form

relname.field-name OPR value

only if relname uses field-name as a key and OPR appears in the class used in the modify command to organize relname. The expected number of page and tuple accesses are given by the appropriate row in AM.

5) A secondary index, I for relname can be used to restrict a clause of the form:

relname.field-name OPR value

only if the index uses field-name as a key and OPR appears in the class used to build the index. The expected number of index page and tuple accesses is given by the appropriate row in AM. To these must be added 1 data page and 1 data tuple per index tuple.

6) A sequential search can always be used to restrict a relation on a clause of the form:

relname.field-name OPR value

One must read NUMpages to access the relation and the expected size of the result is given by Stups from the definition of OPR.

A query planner, such as the one discussed in [SELI79] can now be easily modified to compute a best plan using the above rules to generate legal plans and the above selectivities rather than the current hard-wired collection of rules and selectivities. Moreover, a more sophisticated optimizer which uses statistics (e.g. [KOOI82, PIAT84] can be easily built that uses the above information.

5. CONCLUSIONS

This paper has described how an abstract data type facility can be extended to support automatic generation of optimized query processing plans, utilization of existing access methods for new data types, and coding of new access methods. Only the last capability will be difficult to use, and a cleaner high performance interface to the transaction manager would be highly desirable. Moreover, additional rules in the query optimizer would probably be a useful direction for evolution. These could include when to cease investigating alternate plans, and the ability to specify one's own optimizer parameters, e.g. the constant W relating the cost of I/O to the cost of CPU activity in [SELI79].

REFERENCES

[ALLC80] Allchin, J. et. al., "FLASH: A Language Independent Portable File Access Method," Proc. 1980 ACM-SIGMOD Conference on Management of Data, Santa Monica, Ca., May 1980.

[ASTR76] Astrahan, M. et. al., "System R: A Relational Approach to Data," ACM-TODS, June 1976.

[BERN81] Bernstein, P. and Goodman, N., "Concurrency Control in Distributed Database Systems," ACM Computing Surveys, June 1981.

[BROW81] Brown, M. et. al., "The Cedar DBMS: A Preliminary Report," Proc. 1981 ACM-SIGMOD Conference on Management of Data, Ann Arbor, Mich., May 1981.

[FAGI79] Fagin, R. et. al., "Extendible Hashing: A Fast Access Method for Dynamic Files," ACM-TODS, Sept. 1979.

[GUTM84] Gutman, A., "R-trees: A Dynamic Index Structure for Spatial Searching," Proc. 1984 ACM-SIGMOD Conference on Management of Data, Boston, Mass. June 1984.

[IBM80] IBM Corp, "CICS System Programmers Guide," IBM Corp., White Plains, N.Y., June 1980.

[KOOI82] Kooi, R. and Frankfurth, D., "Query Optimization in INGRES," IEEE Database Engineering, September 1982.

[LITW80] Litwin, W., "Linear Hashing: A New Tool for File and Table Addressing," Proc. 1980 VLDB Conference, Montreal, Canada, October 1980.

[ONG84] Ong, J. et. al., "Implementation of Data Abstraction in the Relational System, INGRES," ACM SIGMOD Record, March 1984.

[PIAT84] Piatetsky-Shapiro, G. and Connell, C., "Accurate Estimation of the Number of Tuples Satisfying a Condition," Proc. 1984 ACM-SIGMOD Conference on Management of Data, Boston, Mass. June 1984.

[POPE81] Popek, G., et. al., "LOCUS: A Network Transparent, High Reliability Distributed System," Proc. Eighth Symposium on Operating System Principles, Pacific Grove, Ca., Dec. 1981.

[RTI84] Relational Technology, Inc., "INGRES Reference Manual, Version 3.0," November 1984.

[ROBI81] Robinson, J., "The K-D-B Tree: A Search Structure for Large Multidimensional Indexes," Proc. 1981 ACM-SIGMOD Conference on Management of Data, Ann Arbor, Mich., May 1981.

[SELI79] Selinger, P. et. al., "Access Path Selection in a Relational Database Management System," Proc. 1979 ACM-SIGMOD Conference on Management of Data, Boston, Mass., June 1979.

[SPEC83] Spector, A. and Schwartz, P., "Transactions: A Construct for Reliable Distributed Computing," Operating Systems Review, Vol 17, No 2, April 1983.

[STON76] Stonebraker, M. et al., "The Design and Implementation of INGRES," TODS 2, 3, September 1976.

[STON83] Stonebraker, M. et. al., "Application of Abstract Data Types and Abstract Indices to CAD Data," Proc. Engineering Applications Stream of Database Week/83, San Jose, Ca., May 1983.

[STON85] Stonebraker, M. et. al., "Interfacing a Relational Data Base System to an Operating System Transaction Manager," SIGOPS Review, January 1985.

Generalized Search Trees for Database Systems

(Extended Abstract)

Joseph M. Hellerstein
University of Wisconsin, Madison
jmh@cs.berkeley.edu

Jeffrey F. Naughton*
University of Wisconsin, Madison
naughton@cs.wisc.edu

Avi Pfeffer
University of California, Berkeley
avi@cs.berkeley.edu

Abstract

This paper introduces the Generalized Search Tree (GiST), an index structure supporting an extensible set of queries and data types. The GiST allows new data types to be indexed in a manner supporting queries natural to the types; this is in contrast to previous work on tree extensibility which only supported the traditional set of equality and range predicates. In a single data structure, the GiST provides all the basic search tree logic required by a database system, thereby unifying disparate structures such as B+-trees and R-trees in a single piece of code, and opening the application of search trees to general extensibility.

To illustrate the flexibility of the GiST, we provide simple method implementations that allow it to behave like a B+-tree, an R-tree, and an *RD-tree*, a new index for data with set-valued attributes. We also present a preliminary performance analysis of RD-trees, which leads to discussion on the nature of tree indices and how they behave for various datasets.

1 Introduction

An efficient implementation of search trees is crucial for any database system. In traditional relational systems, B+-trees [Com79] were sufficient for the sorts of queries posed on the usual set of alphanumeric data types. Today, database systems are increasingly being deployed to support new applications such as geographic information systems, multimedia systems, CAD tools, document libraries, sequence databases, fingerprint identification systems, biochemical databases, etc. To support the growing set of applications, search trees must be extended for maximum flexibility. This requirement has motivated two major research approaches in extending search tree technology:

1. *Specialized Search Trees:* A large variety of search trees has been developed to solve specific problems. Among the best known of these trees are spatial search trees such as R-trees [Gut84]. While some of this work has had significant impact in particular domains, the approach of developing domain-specific search trees is problematic. The effort required to implement and maintain such data structures is high. As new applications need to be supported, new tree structures have to be developed from scratch, requiring new implementations of the usual tree facilities for search, maintenance, concurrency control and recovery.

2. *Search Trees For Extensible Data Types:* As an alternative to developing new data structures, existing data structures such as B+-trees and R-trees can be made *extensible* in the data types they support [Sto86]. For example, B+-trees can be used to index any data with a linear ordering, supporting equality or linear range queries over that data. While this provides extensibility in the data that can be indexed, it does not extend the set of queries which can be supported by the tree. Regardless of the type of data stored in a B+-tree, the only queries that can benefit from the tree are those containing equality and linear range predicates. Similarly in an R-tree, the only queries that can use the tree are those containing equality, overlap and containment predicates. This inflexibility presents significant problems for new applications, since traditional queries on linear orderings and spatial location are unlikely to be apropos for new data types.

In this paper we present a third direction for extending search tree technology. We introduce a new data structure called the Generalized Search Tree (GiST), which is easily extensible both in the data types it can index and in the queries it can support. Extensibility of queries is particularly important, since it allows new data types to be indexed in a manner that supports the queries natural to the types. In addition to providing extensibility for new data types, the GiST unifies previously disparate structures used for currently common data types. For example, both B+-trees and R-trees can be implemented as extensions of the GiST, resulting in a single code base for indexing multiple dissimilar applications.

The GiST is easy to configure: adapting the tree for different uses only requires registering six *methods* with the database system, which encapsulate the structure and behavior of the object class used for keys in the tree. As an illustration of this flexibility, we provide method implementations that allow the GiST to be used as a B+-tree, an R-tree, and an *RD-tree*, a new index for data with set-valued attributes. The GiST can be adapted to work like a variety of other known search tree structures, *e.g.* partial sum trees

* Hellerstein and Naughton were supported by NSF grant IRI-9157357.

Proceedings of the 21st VLDB Conference
Zurich, Switzerland, 1995

[WE80], k-D-B-trees [Rob81], Ch-trees [KKD89], Exodus large objects [CDG+90], hB-trees [LS90], V-trees [MCD94], TV-trees [LJF94], etc. Implementing a new set of methods for the GiST is a significantly easier task than implementing a new tree package from scratch: for example, the POSTGRES [Gro94] and SHORE [CDF+94] implementations of R-trees and B+-trees are on the order of 3000 lines of C or C++ code each, while our method implementations for the GiST are on the order of 500 lines of C code each.

In addition to providing an unified, highly extensible data structure, our general treatment of search trees sheds some initial light on a more fundamental question: if any dataset can be indexed with a GiST, does the resulting tree always provide efficient lookup? The answer to this question is "no", and in our discussion we illustrate some issues that can affect the efficiency of a search tree. This leads to the interesting question of how and when one can build an efficient search tree for queries over non-standard domains — a question that can now be further explored by experimenting with the GiST.

1.1 Structure of the Paper

In Section 2, we illustrate and generalize the basic nature of database search trees. Section 3 introduces the Generalized Search Tree object, with its structure, properties, and behavior. In Section 4 we provide GiST implementations of three different sorts of search trees. Section 5 presents some performance results that explore the issues involved in building an effective search tree. Section 6 examines some details that need to be considered when implementing GiSTs in a full-fledged DBMS. Section 7 concludes with a discussion of the significance of the work, and directions for further research.

1.2 Related Work

A good survey of search trees is provided by Knuth [Knu73], though B-trees and their variants are covered in more detail by Comer [Com79]. There are a variety of multidimensional search trees, such as R-trees [Gut84] and their variants: R*-trees [BKSS90] and R+-trees [SRF87]. Other multidimensional search trees include quad-trees [FB74], k-D-B-trees [Rob81], and hB-trees [LS90]. Multidimensional data can also be transformed into unidimensional data using a space-filling curve [Jag90]; after transformation, a B+-tree can be used to index the resulting unidimensional data.

Extensible-key indices were introduced in POSTGRES [Sto86, Aok91], and are included in Illustra [Ill94], both of which have distinct extensible B+-tree and R-tree implementations. These extensible indices allow many types of data to be indexed, but only support a fixed set of query predicates. For example, POSTGRES B+-trees support the usual ordering predicates ($<, \leq, =, \geq, >$), while POSTGRES R-trees support only the predicates Left, Right, OverLeft, Overlap, OverRight, Right, Contains, Contained and Equal [Gro94].

Extensible R-trees actually provide a sizable subset of the GiST's functionality. To our knowledge this paper represents the first demonstration that R-trees can index data that has

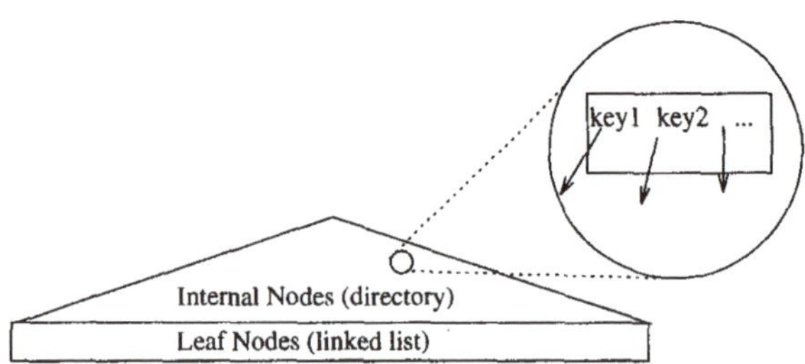

Figure 1: Sketch of a database search tree.

not been mapped into a spatial domain. However, besides their limited extensibility R-trees lack a number of other features supported by the GiST. R-trees provide only one sort of key predicate (Contains), they do not allow user specification of the PickSplit and Penalty algorithms described below, and they lack optimizations for data from linearly ordered domains. Despite these limitations, extensible R-trees are close enough to GiSTs to allow for the initial method implementations and performance experiments we describe in Section 5.

Analyses of R-tree performance have appeared in [FK94] and [PSTW93]. This work is dependent on the spatial nature of typical R-tree data, and thus is not generally applicable to the GiST. However, similar ideas may prove relevant to our questions of when and how one can build efficient indices in arbitrary domains.

2 The Gist of Database Search Trees

As an introduction to GiSTs, it is instructive to review search trees in a simplified manner. Most people with database experience have an intuitive notion of how search trees work, so our discussion here is purposely vague: the goal is simply to illustrate that this notion leaves many details unspecified. After highlighting the unspecified details, we can proceed to describe a structure that leaves the details open for user specification.

The canonical rough picture of a database search tree appears in Figure 1. It is a balanced tree, with high fanout. The internal nodes are used as a directory. The leaf nodes contain pointers to the actual data, and are stored as a linked list to allow for partial or complete scanning.

Within each internal node is a series of keys and pointers. To search for tuples which match a query predicate q, one starts at the root node. For each pointer on the node, if the associated key is *consistent* with q, *i.e.* the key does not rule out the possibility that data stored below the pointer may match q, then one traverses the subtree below the pointer, until all the matching data is found. As an illustration, we review the notion of consistency in some familiar tree structures. In B+-trees, queries are in the form of range predicates (*e.g.* "find all i such that $c_1 \leq i \leq c_2$"), and keys logically delineate a range in which the data below a pointer is contained. If the query range and a pointer's key range overlap, then the two are consistent and the pointer is traversed. In R-trees, queries are in the form of region predicates (*e.g.* "find all i such that (x_1, y_1, x_2, y_2) overlaps i"), and keys delineate the bounding box in which the data below a pointer is contained. If the query region and the pointer's key box overlap, the pointer is traversed.

Note that in the above description the only restriction on a key is that it must logically match each datum stored below it, so that the consistency check does not miss any valid data. In B+-trees and R-trees, keys are essentially "containment" predicates: they describe a contiguous region in which all the data below a pointer are contained. Containment predicates are not the only possible key constructs, however. For example, the predicate "elected_official(i) $\wedge$ has_criminal_record(i)" is an acceptable key if every data item i stored below the associated pointer satisfies the predicate. As in R-trees, keys on a node may "overlap", *i.e.* two keys on the same node may hold simultaneously for some tuple.

This flexibility allows us to generalize the notion of a search key: *a search key may be any arbitrary predicate that holds for each datum below the key.* Given a data structure with such flexible search keys, a user is free to form a tree by organizing data into arbitrary nested sub-categories, labelling each with some characteristic predicate. This in turn lets us capture the essential nature of a database search tree: *it is a hierarchy of partitions of a dataset, in which each partition has a categorization that holds for all data in the partition.* Searches on arbitrary predicates may be conducted based on the categorizations. In order to support searches on a predicate q, the user must provide a Boolean method to tell if q is consistent with a given search key. When this is so, the search proceeds by traversing the pointer associated with the search key. The grouping of data into categories may be controlled by a user-supplied node splitting algorithm, and the characterization of the categories can be done with user-supplied search keys. Thus by exposing the key methods and the tree's split method to the user, arbitrary search trees may be constructed, supporting an extensible set of queries. These ideas form the basis of the GiST, which we proceed to describe in detail.

3 The Generalized Search Tree

In this section we present the abstract data type (or "object") *Generalized Search Tree* (GiST). We define its structure, its invariant properties, its extensible methods and its built-in algorithms. As a matter of convention, we refer to each indexed datum as a "tuple"; in an Object-Oriented or Object-Relational DBMS, each indexed datum could be an arbitrary data object.

3.1 Structure

A GiST is a balanced tree of variable fanout between kM and M, $\frac{2}{M} \leq k \leq \frac{1}{2}$, with the exception of the root node, which may have fanout between 2 and M. The constant k is termed the *minimum fill factor* of the tree. Leaf nodes contain $(p, \mathtt{ptr})$ pairs, where p is a predicate that is used as a search key, and ptr is the identifier of some tuple in the database. Non-leaf nodes contain $(p, \mathtt{ptr})$ pairs, where p is a predicate used as a search key and ptr is a pointer to another tree node. Predicates can contain any number of free variables, as long as any single tuple referenced by the leaves of the tree can instantiate all the variables. Note that by using "key compression", a given predicate p may take as little as zero bytes of storage. However, for purposes of exposition we will assume that entries in the tree are all of uniform size. Discussion of variable-sized entries is deferred to Section 6. We assume in an implementation that given an entry $E = (p, \mathtt{ptr})$, one can access the node on which E currently resides. This can prove helpful in implementing the key methods described below.

3.2 Properties

The following properties are invariant in a GiST:

1. Every node contains between kM and M index entries unless it is the root.

2. For each index entry $(p, \mathtt{ptr})$ in a leaf node, p is true when instantiated with the values from the indicated tuple (*i.e.* p *holds* for the tuple.)

3. For each index entry $(p, \mathtt{ptr})$ in a non-leaf node, p is true when instantiated with the values of any tuple reachable from ptr. Note that, unlike in R-trees, for some entry $(p', \mathtt{ptr}')$ reachable from ptr, we do not require that $p' \to p$, merely that p and p' both hold for all tuples reachable from $\mathtt{ptr}'$.

4. The root has at least two children unless it is a leaf.

5. All leaves appear on the same level.

Property 3 is of particular interest. An R-tree would require that $p' \to p$, since bounding boxes of an R-tree are arranged in a containment hierarchy. The R-tree approach is unnecessarily restrictive, however: the predicates in keys above a node N must hold for data below N, and therefore one need not have keys on N restate those predicates in a more refined manner. One might choose, instead, to have the keys at N characterize the sets below based on some entirely orthogonal classification. This can be an advantage in both the information content and the size of keys.

3.3 Key Methods

In principle, the keys of a GiST may be arbitrary predicates. In practice, the keys come from a user-implemented object class, which provides a particular set of methods required by the GiST. Examples of key structures include ranges of integers for data from $\mathbb{Z}$ (as in B+-trees), bounding boxes for regions in $\mathbb{R}^n$ (as in R-trees), and bounding sets for set-valued data, *e.g.* data from $\mathcal{P}(\mathbb{Z})$ (as in RD-trees, described in Section 4.3.) The key class is open to redefinition by the user, with the following set of six methods required by the GiST:

- **Consistent**(E,q): given an entry $E = (p, \mathtt{ptr})$, and a query predicate q, returns false if $p \wedge q$ can be guaranteed unsatisfiable, and true otherwise. Note that an accurate test for satisfiability is not required here: Consistent may return true incorrectly without affecting the correctness of the tree algorithms. The penalty for such errors is in performance, since they may result in exploration of irrelevant subtrees during search.

- **Union**(P): given a set P of entries $(p_1, \texttt{ptr}_1)$, ... $(p_n, \texttt{ptr}_n)$, returns some predicate r that holds for all tuples stored below $\texttt{ptr}_1$ through $\texttt{ptr}_n$. This can be done by finding an r such that $(p_1 \vee \ldots \vee p_n) \rightarrow r$.

- **Compress**(E): given an entry $E = (p, \texttt{ptr})$ returns an entry $(\pi, \texttt{ptr})$ where π is a compressed representation of p.

- **Decompress**(E): given a compressed representation $E = (\pi, \texttt{ptr})$, where π = Compress(p), returns an entry $(r, \texttt{ptr})$ such that $p \rightarrow r$. Note that this is a potentially "lossy" compression, since we do not require that $p \leftrightarrow r$.

- **Penalty**(E_1, E_2): given two entries $E_1 = (p_1, \texttt{ptr}_1)$, $E_2 = (p_2, \texttt{ptr}_2)$, returns a domain-specific penalty for inserting E_2 into the subtree rooted at E_1. This is used to aid the Split and Insert algorithms (described below.) Typically the penalty metric is some representation of the increase of size from $E_1.p_1$ to Union($\{E_1, E_2\}$). For example, Penalty for keys from $\mathbb{R}^2$ can be defined as area(Union($\{E_1, E_2\}$)) − area($E_1.p_1$) [Gut84].

- **PickSplit**(P): given a set P of $M + 1$ entries $(p, \texttt{ptr})$, splits P into two sets of entries P_1, P_2, each of size at least kM. The choice of the minimum fill factor for a tree is controlled here. Typically, it is desirable to split in such a way as to minimize some badness metric akin to a multi-way Penalty, but this is left open for the user.

The above are the only methods a GiST user needs to supply. Note that Consistent, Union, Compress and Penalty have to be able to handle any predicate in their input. In full generality this could become very difficult, especially for Consistent. But typically a limited set of predicates is used in any one tree, and this set can be constrained in the method implementation.

There are a number of options for key compression. A simple implementation can let both Compress and Decompress be the identity function. A more complex implementation can have Compress((p, ptr)) generate a valid but more compact predicate r, $p \rightarrow r$, and let Decompress be the identity function. This is the technique used in SHORE's R-trees, for example, which upon insertion take a polygon and compress it to its bounding box, which is itself a valid polygon. It is also used in prefix B+-trees [Com79], which truncate split keys to an initial substring. More involved implementations might use complex methods for both Compress and Decompress.

3.4 Tree Methods

The key methods in the previous section must be provided by the designer of the key class. The tree methods in this section are provided by the GiST, and may invoke the required key methods. Note that keys are Compressed when placed on a node, and Decompressed when read from a node. We consider this implicit, and will not mention it further in describing the methods.

3.4.1 Search

Search comes in two flavors. The first method, presented in this section, can be used to search any dataset with any query predicate, by traversing as much of the tree as necessary to satisfy the query. It is the most general search technique, analogous to that of R-trees. A more efficient technique for queries over linear orders is described in the next section.

Algorithm Search(R, q)

Input: GiST rooted at R, predicate q

Output: all tuples that satisfy q

Sketch: Recursively descend all paths in tree whose keys are consistent with q.

S1: [Search subtrees] If R is not a leaf, check each entry E on R to determine whether Consistent(E, q). For all entries that are Consistent, invoke Search on the subtree whose root node is referenced by $E.\texttt{ptr}$.

S2: [Search leaf node] If R is a leaf, check each entry E on R to determine whether Consistent(E, q). If E is Consistent, it is a qualifying entry. At this point $E.\texttt{ptr}$ could be fetched to check q accurately, or this check could be left to the calling process.

Note that the query predicate q can be either an exact match (equality) predicate, or a predicate satisfiable by many values. The latter category includes "range" or "window" predicates, as in B+ or R-trees, and also more general predicates that are not based on contiguous areas (*e.g.* set-containment predicates like "all supersets of $\{6, 7, 68\}$".)

3.4.2 Search In Linearly Ordered Domains

If the domain to be indexed has a linear ordering, and queries are typically equality or range-containment predicates, then a more efficient search method is possible using the FindMin and Next methods defined in this section. To make this option available, the user must take some extra steps when creating the tree:

1. The flag **IsOrdered** must be set to true. IsOrdered is a static property of the tree that is set at creation. It defaults to false.

2. An additional method **Compare**(E_1, E_2) must be registered. Given two entries $E_1 = (p_1, \texttt{ptr}_1)$ and $E_2 = (p_2, \texttt{ptr}_2)$, Compare reports whether p_1 precedes p_2, p_1 follows p_2, or p_1 and p_2 are ordered equivalently. Compare is used to insert entries in order on each node.

3. The PickSplit method must ensure that for any entries E_1 on P_1 and E_2 on P_2, Compare(E_1, E_2) reports "precedes".

4. The methods must assure that no two keys on a node overlap, *i.e.* for any pair of entries E_1, E_2 on a node, Consistent($E_1, E_2.p$) = false.

If these four steps are carried out, then equality and range-containment queries may be evaluated by calling FindMin and repeatedly calling Next, while other query predicates may still be evaluated with the general Search method. FindMin/Next is more efficient than traversing the tree using Search, since FindMin and Next only visit the non-leaf nodes along one root-to-leaf path. This technique is based on the typical range-lookup in B+-trees.

Algorithm FindMin(R, q)

Input: GiST rooted at R, predicate q

Output: minimum tuple in linear order that satisfies q

Sketch: descend leftmost branch of tree whose keys are Consistent with q. When a leaf node is reached, return the first key that is Consistent with q.

FM1: [Search subtrees] If R is not a leaf, find the first entry E in order such that Consistent(E, q)[1]. If such an E can be found, invoke FindMin on the subtree whose root node is referenced by E.ptr. If no such entry is found, return NULL.

FM2: [Search leaf node] If R is a leaf, find the first entry E on R such that Consistent(E, q), and return E. If no such entry exists, return NULL.

Given one element E that satisfies a predicate q, the Next method returns the next existing element that satisfies q, or NULL if there is none. Next is made sufficiently general to find the next entry on non-leaf levels of the tree, which will prove useful in Section 4. For search purposes, however, Next will only be invoked on leaf entries.

[1] The appropriate entry may be found by doing a binary search of the entries on the node. Further discussion of intra-node search optimizations appears in Section 6.

Algorithm Next(R, q, E)

Input: GiST rooted at R, predicate q, current entry E

Output: next entry in linear order that satisfies q

Sketch: return next entry on the same level of the tree if it satisfies q. Else return NULL.

N1: [next on node] If E is not the rightmost entry on its node, and N is the next entry to the right of E in order, and Consistent(N, q), then return N. If ¬Consistent(N, q), return NULL.

N2: [next on neighboring node] If E is the righmost entry on its node, let P be the next node to the right of R on the same level of the tree (this can be found via tree traversal, or via sideways pointers in the tree, when available [LY81].) If P is non-existent, return NULL. Otherwise, let N be the leftmost entry on P. If Consistent(N, q), then return N, else return NULL.

3.4.3 Insert

The insertion routines guarantee that the GiST remains balanced. They are very similar to the insertion routines of R-trees, which generalize the simpler insertion routines for B+-trees. Insertion allows specification of the level at which to insert. This allows subsequent methods to use Insert for reinserting entries from internal nodes of the tree. We will assume that level numbers increase as one ascends the tree, with leaf nodes being at level 0. Thus new entries to the tree are inserted at level $l = 0$.

Algorithm Insert(R, E, l)

Input: GiST rooted at R, entry $E = (p, \texttt{ptr})$, and level l, where p is a predicate such that p holds for all tuples reachable from ptr.

Output: new GiST resulting from insert of E at level l.

Sketch: find where E should go, and add it there, splitting if necessary to make room.

I1. [invoke ChooseSubtree to find where E should go] Let L = ChooseSubtree(R, E, l)

I2. If there is room for E on L, install E on L (in order according to Compare, if IsOrdered.) Otherwise invoke Split(R, L, E).

I3. [propagate changes upward] AdjustKeys(R, L).

ChooseSubtree can be used to find the best node for insertion at any level of the tree. When the IsOrdered property holds, the Penalty method must be carefully written to assure that ChooseSubtree arrives at the correct leaf node in order. An example of how this can be done is given in Section 4.1.

Algorithm ChooseSubtree(R, E, l)

Input: subtree rooted at R, entry $E = (p, \mathtt{ptr})$, level l

Output: node at level l best suited to hold entry with characteristic predicate $E.p$

Sketch: Recursively descend tree minimizing Penalty

CS1. If R is at level l, return R;

CS2. Else among all entries $F = (q, \mathtt{ptr}')$ on R find the one such that Penalty(F, E) is minimal. Return ChooseSubtree$(F.\mathtt{ptr}', E, l)$.

The Split algorithm makes use of the user-defined PickSplit method to choose how to split up the elements of a node, including the new tuple to be inserted into the tree. Once the elements are split up into two groups, Split generates a new node for one of the groups, inserts it into the tree, and updates keys above the new node.

Algorithm Split(R, N, E)

Input: GiST R with node N, and a new entry $E = (p, \mathtt{ptr})$.

Output: the GiST with N split in two and E inserted.

Sketch: split keys of N along with E into two groups according to PickSplit. Put one group onto a new node, and Insert the new node into the parent of N.

SP1: Invoke PickSplit on the union of the elements of N and $\{E\}$, put one of the two partitions on node N, and put the remaining partition on a new node N'.

SP2: [Insert entry for N' in parent] Let $E_{N'} = (q, \mathtt{ptr}')$, where q is the Union of all entries on N', and $\mathtt{ptr}'$ is a pointer to N'. If there is room for $E_{N'}$ on Parent(N), install $E_{N'}$ on Parent(N) (in order if IsOrdered.) Otherwise invoke Split$(R, \text{Parent}(N), E_{N'})$[2].

SP3: Modify the entry F which points to N, so that $F.p$ is the Union of all entries on N.

---

[2]We intentionally do not specify what technique is used to find the Parent of a node, since this implementation interacts with issues related to concurrency control, which are discussed in Section 6. Depending on techniques used, the Parent may be found via a pointer, a stack, or via re-traversal of the tree.

Step SP3 of Split modifies the parent node to reflect the changes in N. These changes are propagated upwards through the rest of the tree by step I3 of the Insert algorithm, which also propagates the changes due to the insertion of N'.

The AdjustKeys algorithm ensures that keys above a set of predicates hold for the tuples below, and are appropriately specific.

Algorithm AdjustKeys(R, N)

Input: GiST rooted at R, tree node N

Output: the GiST with ancestors of N containing correct and specific keys

Sketch: ascend parents from N in the tree, making the predicates be accurate characterizations of the subtrees. Stop after root, or when a predicate is found that is already accurate.

PR1: If N is the root, or the entry which points to N has an already-accurate representation of the Union of the entries on N, then return.

PR2: Otherwise, modify the entry E which points to N so that $E.p$ is the Union of all entries on N. Then AdjustKeys(R, Parent(N).)

Note that AdjustKeys typically performs no work when IsOrdered = true, since for such domains predicates on each node typically partition the entire domain into ranges, and thus need no modification on simple insertion or deletion. The AdjustKeys routine detects this in step PR1, which avoids calling AdjustKeys on higher nodes of the tree. For such domains, AdjustKeys may be circumvented entirely if desired.

3.4.4 Delete

The deletion algorithms maintain the balance of the tree, and attempt to keep keys as specific as possible. When there is a linear order on the keys they use B+-tree-style "borrow or coalesce" techniques. Otherwise they use R-tree-style reinsertion techniques. The deletion algorithms are omitted here due to lack of space; they are given in full in [HNP95].

4 The GiST for Three Applications

In this section we briefly describe implementations of key classes used to make the GiST behave like a B+-tree, an R-tree, and an RD-tree, a new R-tree-like index over set-valued data.

4.1 GiSTs Over $\mathbb{Z}$ (B+-trees)

In this example we index integer data. Before compression, each key in this tree is a pair of integers, representing the interval contained below the key. Particularly, a key $<a, b>$ represents the predicate Contains$([a, b), v)$ with variable v.

The query predicates we support in this key class are Contains(interval, v), and Equal(number, v). The interval in the Contains query may be closed or open at either end. The boundary of any interval of integers can be trivially converted to be closed or open. So without loss of generality, we assume below that all intervals are closed on the left and open on the right.

The implementations of the Contains and Equal query predicates are as follows:

- **Contains**($[x, y), v$) If $x \leq v < y$, return true. Otherwise return false.
- **Equal**(x, v) If $x = v$ return true. Otherwise return false.

Now, the implementations of the GiST methods:

- **Consistent**(E, q) Given entry $E = (p, \texttt{ptr})$ and query predicate q, we know that $p = $ Contains($[x_p, y_p), v$), and either $q = $ Contains($[x_q, y_q), v$) or $q = $ Equal(x_q, v). In the first case, return true if $(x_p < y_q) \wedge (y_p > x_q)$ and false otherwise. In the second case, return true if $x_p \leq x_q < y_p$, and false otherwise.
- **Union**($\{E_1, \ldots, E_n\}$) Given $E_1 = ([x_1, y_1), \texttt{ptr}_1), \ldots, E_n = ([x_n, y_n), \texttt{ptr}_n)$), return $[\text{MIN}(x_1, \ldots, x_n), \text{MAX}(y_1, \ldots, y_n))$.
- **Compress**($E = ([x, y), \texttt{ptr})$) If E is the leftmost key on a non-leaf node, return a 0-byte object. Otherwise return x.
- **Decompress**($E = (\pi, \texttt{ptr})$) We must construct an interval $[x, y)$. If E is the leftmost key on a non-leaf node, let $x = -\infty$. Otherwise let $x = \pi$. If E is the rightmost key on a non-leaf node, let $y = \infty$. If E is any other key on a non-leaf node, let y be the value stored in the next key (as found by the Next method.) If E is on a leaf node, let $y = x + 1$. Return $([x, y), \texttt{ptr})$.
- **Penalty**($E = ([x_1, y_1), \texttt{ptr}_1), F = ([x_2, y_2), \texttt{ptr}_2)$) If E is the leftmost pointer on its node, return $\text{MAX}(y_2 - y_1, 0)$. If E is the rightmost pointer on its node, return $\text{MAX}(x_1 - x_2, 0)$. Otherwise return $\text{MAX}(y_2 - y_1, 0) + \text{MAX}(x_1 - x_2, 0)$.
- **PickSplit**(P) Let the first $\lfloor \frac{|P|}{2} \rfloor$ entries in order go in the left group, and the last $\lceil \frac{|P|}{2} \rceil$ entries go in the right. Note that this guarantees a minimum fill factor of $\frac{M}{2}$.

Finally, the additions for ordered keys:

- **IsOrdered** = true
- **Compare**($E_1 = (p_1, \texttt{ptr}_1), E_2 = (p_2, \texttt{ptr}_2)$) Given $p_1 = [x_1, y_1)$ and $p_2 = [x_2, y_2)$, return "precedes" if $x_1 < x_2$, "equivalent" if $x_1 = x_2$, and "follows" if $x_1 > x_2$.

There are a number of interesting features to note in this set of methods. First, the Compress and Decompress methods produce the typical "split keys" found in B+-trees, *i.e.* $n - 1$ stored keys for n pointers, with the leftmost and rightmost boundaries on a node left unspecified (*i.e.* $-\infty$ and ∞). Even though GiSTs use key/pointer pairs rather than split keys, this GiST uses no more space for keys than a traditional B+-tree, since it compresses the first pointer on each node to zero bytes. Second, the Penalty method allows the GiST to choose the correct insertion point. Inserting (*i.e.* Unioning) a new key value k into a interval $[x, y)$ will cause the Penalty to be positive only if k is not already contained in the interval. Thus in step CS2, the ChooseSubtree method will place new data in the appropriate spot: any set of keys on a node partitions the entire domain, so in order to minimize the Penalty, ChooseSubtree will choose the one partition in which k is already contained. Finally, observe that one could fairly easily support more complex predicates, including disjunctions of intervals in query predicates, or ranked intervals in key predicates for supporting efficient sampling [WE80].

4.2 GiSTs Over Polygons in $\mathbb{R}^2$ (R-trees)

In this example, our data are 2-dimensional polygons on the Cartesian plane. Before compression, the keys in this tree are 4-tuples of reals, representing the upper-left and lower-right corners of rectilinear bounding rectangles for 2d-polygons. A key $(x_{ul}, y_{ul}, x_{lr}, y_{lr})$ represents the predicate $\text{Contains}((x_{ul}, y_{ul}, x_{lr}, y_{lr}), v)$, where (x_{ul}, y_{ul}) is the upper left corner of the bounding box, (x_{lr}, y_{lr}) is the lower right corner, and v is the free variable. The query predicates we support in this key class are Contains(box, v), Overlap(box, v), and Equal(box, v), where box is a 4-tuple as above.

The implementations of the query predicates are as follows:

- **Contains**($(x^1_{ul}, y^1_{ul}, x^1_{lr}, y^1_{lr}), (x^2_{ul}, y^2_{ul}, x^2_{lr}, y^2_{lr})$) Return true if
$$(x^1_{lr} \geq x^2_{lr}) \wedge (x^1_{ul} \leq x^2_{ul}) \wedge (y^1_{lr} \leq y^2_{lr}) \wedge (y^1_{ul} \geq y^2_{ul}).$$
Otherwise return false.
- **Overlap**($(x^1_{ul}, y^1_{ul}, x^1_{lr}, y^1_{lr}), (x^2_{ul}, y^2_{ul}, x^2_{lr}, y^2_{lr})$) Return true if
$$(x^1_{ul} \leq x^2_{lr}) \wedge (x^2_{ul} \leq x^1_{lr}) \wedge (y^1_{lr} \leq y^2_{ul}) \wedge (y^2_{lr} \leq y^1_{ul}).$$
Otherwise return false.
- **Equal**($(x^1_{ul}, y^1_{ul}, x^1_{lr}, y^1_{lr}), (x^2_{ul}, y^2_{ul}, x^2_{lr}, y^2_{lr})$) Return true if
$$(x^1_{ul} = x^2_{ul}) \wedge (y^1_{ul} = y^2_{ul}) \wedge (x^1_{lr} = x^2_{lr}) \wedge (y^1_{lr} = y^2_{lr}).$$
Otherwise return false.

Now, the GiST method implementations:

- **Consistent**((E, q) Given entry $E = (p, \texttt{ptr})$, we know that p = Contains$((x^1_{ul}, y^1_{ul}, x^1_{lr}, y^1_{lr}), v)$, and q is either Contains, Overlap or Equal on the argument $(x^2_{ul}, y^2_{ul}, x^2_{lr}, y^2_{lr})$. For any of these queries, return true if Overlap$((x^1_{ul}, y^1_{ul}, x^1_{lr}, y^1_{lr}), (x^2_{ul}, y^2_{ul}, x^2_{lr}, y^2_{lr}))$, and return false otherwise.

- **Union**$(\{E_1, \ldots, E_n\})$ Given $E_1 = ((x^1_{ul}, y^1_{ul}, x^1_{lr}, y^1_{lr}), \texttt{ptr}_1), \ldots, E_n = (x^n_{ul}, y^n_{ul}, x^n_{lr}, y^n_{lr}))$, return (MIN$(x^1_{ul}, \ldots, x^n_{ul})$, MAX$(y^1_{ul}, \ldots, y^n_{ul})$, MAX$(x^1_{lr}, \ldots, x^n_{lr})$, MIN$(y^1_{lr}, \ldots, y^n_{lr})$).

- **Compress**$(E = (p, \texttt{ptr}))$ Form the bounding box of polygon p, *i.e.*, given a polygon stored as a set of line segments $l_i = (x^i_1, y^i_1, x^i_2, y^i_2)$, form $\pi = (\forall_i \text{MIN}(x^i_{ul}), \forall_i \text{MAX}(y^i_{ul}), \forall_i \text{MAX}(x^i_{lr}), \forall_i \text{MIN}(y^i_{lr}))$. Return $(\pi, \texttt{ptr})$.

- **Decompress**$(E = ((x_{ul}, y_{ul}, x_{lr}, y_{lr}), \texttt{ptr}))$ The identity function, *i.e.*, return E.

- **Penalty**(E_1, E_2) Given $E_1 = (p_1, \texttt{ptr}_1)$ and $E_2 = (p_2, \texttt{ptr}_2)$, compute q = Union$(\{E_1, E_2\})$, and return area(q) − area$(E_1.p)$. This metric of "change in area" is the one proposed by Guttman [Gut84].

- **PickSplit**(P) A variety of algorithms have been proposed for R-tree splitting. We thus omit this method implementation from our discussion here, and refer the interested reader to [Gut84] and [BKSS90].

The above implementations, along with the GiST algorithms described in the previous chapters, give behavior identical to that of Guttman's R-tree. A series of variations on R-trees have been proposed, notably the R*-tree [BKSS90] and the R+-tree [SRF87]. The R*-tree differs from the basic R-tree in three ways: in its PickSplit algorithm, which has a variety of small changes, in its ChooseSubtree algorithm, which varies only slightly, and in its policy of reinserting a number of keys during node split. It would not be difficult to implement the R*-tree in the GiST: the R*-tree PickSplit algorithm can be implemented as the PickSplit method of the GiST, the modifications to ChooseSubtree could be introduced with a careful implementation of the Penalty method, and the reinsertion policy of the R*-tree could easily be added into the built-in GiST tree methods (see Section 7.) R+-trees, on the other hand, cannot be mimicked by the GiST. This is because the R+-tree places duplicate copies of data entries in multiple leaf nodes, thus violating the GiST principle of a search tree being a hierarchy of *partitions* of the data.

Again, observe that one could fairly easily support more complex predicates, including n-dimensional analogs of the disjunctive queries and ranked keys mentioned for B+-trees, as well as the *topological relations* of Papadias, *et al.* [PTSE95] Other examples include arbitrary variations of the usual overlap or ordering queries, *e.g.* "find all polygons that overlap more than 30% of this box", or "find all polygons that overlap 12 to 1 o'clock", which for a given point p returns all polygons that are in the region bounded by two rays that exit p at angles 90° and 60° in polar coordinates. Note that this infinite region cannot be defined as a polygon made up of line segments, and hence this query cannot be expressed using typical R-tree predicates.

4.3 GiSTs Over $\mathcal{P}(\mathbb{Z})$ (RD-trees)

In the previous two sections we demonstrated that the GiST can provide the functionality of two known data structures: B+-trees and R-trees. In this section, we demonstrate that the GiST can provide support for a new search tree that indexes set-valued data.

The problem of handling set-valued data is attracting increasing attention in the Object-Oriented database community [KG94], and is fairly natural even for traditional relational database applications. For example, one might have a university database with a table of students, and for each student an attribute courses_passed of type setof(integer). One would like to efficiently support containment queries such as "find all students who have passed all the courses in the prerequisite set {101, 121, 150}."

We handle this in the GiST by using sets as containment keys, much as an R-tree uses bounding boxes as containment keys. We call the resulting structure an RD-tree (or "Russian Doll" tree.) The keys in an RD-tree are sets of integers, and the RD-tree derives its name from the fact that as one traverses a branch of the tree, each key contains the key below it in the branch. We proceed to give GiST method implementations for RD-trees.

Before compression, the keys in our RD-trees are sets of integers. A key S represents the predicate Contains(S, v) for set-valued variable v. The query predicates allowed on the RD-tree are Contains(set, v), Overlap(set, v), and Equal(set, v).

The implementation of the query predicates is straightforward:

- **Contains**(S, T) Return true if $S \supseteq T$, and false otherwise.

- **Overlap**(S, T) Return true if $S \cap T \neq \emptyset$, false otherwise.

- **Equal**(S, T) Return true if $S = T$, false otherwise.

Now, the GiST method implementations:

- **Consistent**$(E = (p, \texttt{ptr}), q)$ Given our keys and predicates, we know that p = Contains(S, v), and either q = Contains(T, v), q = Overlap(T, v) or q = Equal(T, v). For all of these, return true if Overlap(S, T), and false otherwise.

- **Union**$(\{E_1 = (S_1, \texttt{ptr}_1), \ldots, E_n = (S_n, \texttt{ptr}_n)\})$ Return $S_1 \cup \ldots \cup S_n$.

- **Compress**$(E = (S, \texttt{ptr}))$ A variety of compression techniques for sets are given in [HP94]. We briefly describe one of them here. The elements of S are sorted, and then converted to a set of n disjoint ranges $\{[l_1, h_1], [l_2, h_2], \ldots, [l_n, h_n]\}$ where $l_i \leq h_i$, and $h_i < l_{i+1}$. The conversion uses the following algorithm:

```
Initialize:  consider each element a_m ∈ S
              to be a range [a_m, a_m].
while (more than n ranges remain) {
        find the pair of adjacent ranges
            with the least interval
            between them;
        form a single range of the pair;
}
```

The resulting structure is called a *rangeset*. It can be shown that this algorithm produces a rangeset of n items with minimal addition of elements not in S [HP94].

- **Decompress(**E = (rangeset, ptr)**)** Rangesets are easily converted back to sets by enumerating the elements in the ranges.
- **Penalty(**$E_1 = (S_1, \texttt{ptr}_1), E_2 = (S_2, \texttt{ptr}_2)$**)** Return $|E_1.S_1 \cup E_2.S_2| - |E_1.S_1|$. Alternatively, return the change in a weighted cardinality, where each element of $\mathbb{Z}$ has a weight, and $|S|$ is the sum of the weights of the elements in S.
- **PickSplit(**P**)** Guttman's quadratic algorithm for R-tree split works naturally here. The reader is referred to [Gut84] for details.

This GiST supports the usual R-tree query predicates, has containment keys, and uses a traditional R-tree algorithm for PickSplit. As a result, we were able to implement these methods in Illustra's extensible R-trees, and get behavior identical to what the GiST behavior would be. This exercise gave us a sense of the complexity of a GiST class implementation (c.500 lines of C code), and allowed us to do the performance studies described in the next section. Using R-trees did limit our choices for predicates and for the split and penalty algorithms, which will merit further exploration when we build RD-trees using GiSTs.

5 GiST Performance Issues

In balanced trees such as B+-trees which have non-overlapping keys, the maximum number of nodes to be examined (and hence I/O's) is easy to bound: for a point query over duplicate-free data it is the height of the tree, *i.e.* $O(\log n)$ for a database of n tuples. This upper bound cannot be guaranteed, however, if keys on a node may overlap, as in an R-tree or GiST, since overlapping keys can cause searches in multiple paths in the tree. The performance of a GiST varies directly with the amount that keys on nodes tend to overlap.

There are two major causes of key overlap: data overlap, and information loss due to key compression. The first issue is straightforward: if many data objects overlap significantly, then keys within the tree are likely to overlap as well. For

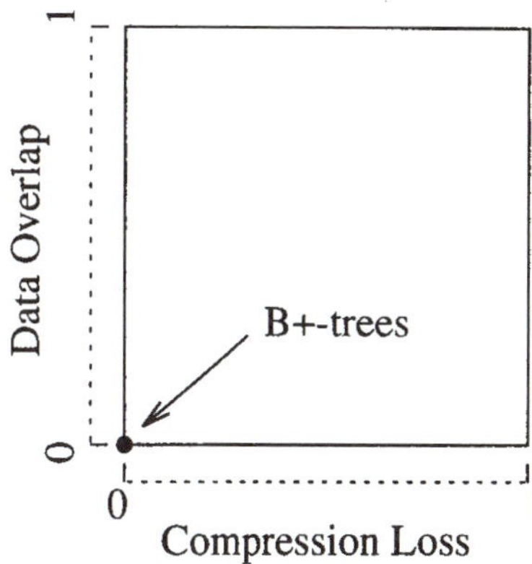

Figure 2: Space of Factors Affecting GiST-Performance

example, any dataset made up entirely of identical items will produce an inefficient index for queries that match the items. Such workloads are simply not amenable to indexing techniques, and should be processed with sequential scans instead.

Loss due to key compression causes problems in a slightly more subtle way: even though two sets of data may not overlap, the keys for these sets may overlap if the Compress/Decompress methods do not produce exact keys. Consider R-trees, for example, where the Compress method produces bounding boxes. If objects are not box-like, then the keys that represent them will be inaccurate, and may indicate overlaps when none are present. In R-trees, the problem of compression loss has been largely ignored, since most spatial data objects (geographic entities, regions of the brain, etc.) tend to be relatively box-shaped.[3] But this need not be the case. For example, consider a 3-d R-tree index over the dataset corresponding to a plate of spaghetti: although no single spaghetto intersects any other in three dimensions, their bounding boxes will likely all intersect!

The two performance issues described above are displayed as a graph in Figure 2. At the origin of this graph are trees with no data overlap and lossless key compression; which have the optimal logarithmic performance described above. Note that B+-trees over duplicate-free data are at the origin of the graph. As one moves towards 1 along either axis, performance can be expected to degrade. In the worst case on the x axis, keys are consistent with any query, and the whole tree must be traversed for any query. In the worst case on the y axis, all the data are identical, and the whole tree must be traversed for any query consistent with the data.

In this section, we present some initial experiments we have done with RD-trees to explore the space of Figure 2. We chose RD-trees for two reasons:

1. We were able to implement the methods in Illustra R-trees.
2. Set data can be "cooked" to have almost arbitrary over-

[3]Better approximations than bounding boxes have been considered for doing spatial joins [BKSS94]. However, this work proposes using bounding boxes in an R*-tree, and only using the more accurate approximations in main memory during post-processing steps.

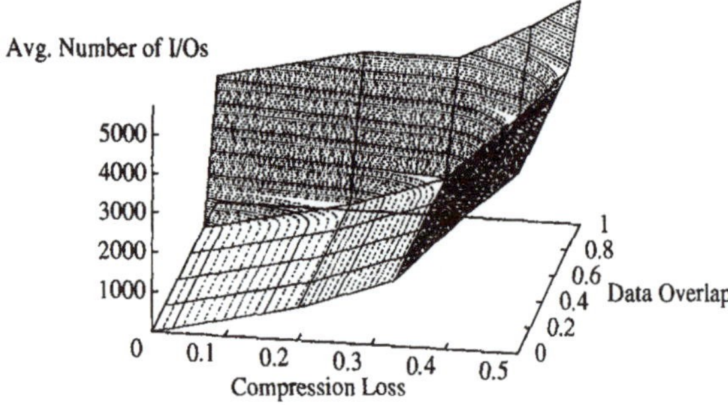

Figure 3: Performance in the Parameter Space

This surface was generated from data presented in [HNP95]. Compression loss was calculated as (numranges − 20)/numranges, while data overlap was calculated as overlap/10.

lap, as opposed to polygon data which is contiguous within its boundaries, and hence harder to manipulate. For example, it is trivial to construct n distant "hot spots" shared by all sets in an RD-tree, but is geometrically difficult to do the same for polygons in an R-tree. We thus believe that set-valued data is particularly useful for experimenting with overlap.

To validate our intuition about the performance space, we generated 30 datasets, each corresponding to a point in the space of Figure 2. Each dataset contained 10000 set-valued objects. Each object was a regularly spaced set of ranges, much like a comb laid on the number line (*e.g.* $\{[1, 10], [100001, 100010], [200001, 200010], \ldots\}$). The "teeth" of each comb were 10 integers wide, while the spaces between teeth were 99990 integers wide, large enough to accommodate one tooth from every other object in the dataset. The 30 datasets were formed by changing two variables: *numranges*, the number of ranges per set, and *overlap*, the amount that each comb overlapped its predecessor. Varying numranges adjusted the compression loss: our Compress method only allowed for 20 ranges per rangeset, so a comb of $t > 20$ teeth had $t - 20$ of its inter-tooth spaces erroneously included into its compressed representation. The amount of overlap was controlled by the left edge of each comb: for overlap 0, the first comb was started at 1, the second at 11, the third at 21, etc., so that no two combs overlapped. For overlap 2, the first comb was started at 1, the second at 9, the third at 17, etc. The 30 datasets were generated by forming all combinations of numranges in $\{20, 25, 30, 35, 40\}$, and overlap in $\{0, 2, 4, 6, 8, 10\}$.

For each of the 30 datasets, five queries were performed. Each query searched for objects overlapping a different tooth of the first comb. The query performance was measured in number of I/Os, and the five numbers averaged per dataset. A chart of the performance appears in [HNP95]. More illustrative is the 3-d plot shown in Figure 3, where the x and y axes are the same as in Figure 2, and the z axis represents the average number of I/Os. The landscape is much as we expected: it slopes upwards as we move away from 0 on either axis.

While our general insights on data overlap and compression loss are verified by this experiment, a number of performance variables remain unexplored. Two issues of concern are *hot spots* and the *correlation factor* across hot spots. Hot spots in RD-trees are integers that appear in many sets. In general, hot spots can be thought of as very specific predicates satisfiable by many tuples in a dataset. The correlation factor for two integers j and k in an RD-tree is the likelihood that if one of j or k appears in a set, then both appear. In general, the correlation factor for two hot spots p, q is the likelihood that if $p \vee q$ holds for a tuple, $p \wedge q$ holds as well. An interesting question is how the GiST behaves as one denormalizes data sets to produce hot spots, and correlations between them. This question, along with similar issues, should prove to be a rich area of future research.

6 Implementation Issues

In previous sections we described the GiST, demonstrated its flexibility, and discussed its performance as an index for secondary storage. A full-fledged database system is more than just a secondary storage manager, however. In this section we point out some important database system issues which need to be considered when implementing the GiST. Due to space constraints, these are only sketched here; further discussion can be found in [HNP95].

- **In-Memory Efficiency:** The discussion above shows how the GiST can be efficient in terms of disk access. To streamline the efficiency of its in-memory computation, we open the implementation of the Node object to extensibility. For example, the Node implementation for GiSTs with linear orderings may be overloaded to support binary search, and the Node implementation to support hB-trees can be overloaded to support the specialized internal structure required by hB-trees.

- **Concurrency Control, Recovery and Consistency:** High concurrency, recoverability, and degree-3 consistency are critical factors in a full-fledged database system. We are considering extending the results of Kornacker and Banks for R-trees [KB95] to our implementation of GiSTs.

- **Variable-Length Keys:** It is often useful to allow keys to vary in length, particularly given the Compress method available in GiSTs. This requires particular care in implementation of tree methods like Insert and Split.

- **Bulk Loading:** In unordered domains, it is not clear how to efficiently build an index over a large, pre-existing dataset. An extensible BulkLoad method should be implemented for the GiST to accommodate bulk loading for various domains.

- **Optimizer Integration:** To integrate GiSTs with a query optimizer, one must let the optimizer know which query predicates match each GiST. The question of estimating the cost of probing a GiST is more difficult, and will require further research.

- **Coding Details:** We propose implementing the GiST in two ways. The Extensible GiST will be runtime-extensible like POSTGRES or Illustra for maximal convenience; the Template GiST will compilation-extensible like SHORE for maximal efficiency. With a little care, these two implementations can be built off of the same code base, without replication of logic.

7 Summary and Future Work

The incorporation of new data types into today's database systems requires indices that support an extensible set of queries. To facilitate this, we isolated the essential nature of search trees, providing a clean characterization of how they are all alike. Using this insight, we developed the Generalized Search Tree, which unifies previously distinct search tree structures. The GiST is extremely extensible, allowing arbitrary data sets to be indexed and efficiently queried in new ways. This flexibility opens the question of when and how one can generate effective search trees.

Since the GiST unifies B+-trees and R-trees into a single structure, it is immediately useful for systems which require the functionality of both. In addition, the extensibility of the GiST also opens up a number of interesting research problems which we intend to pursue:

- *Indexability:* The primary theoretical question raised by the GiST is whether one can find a general characterization of workloads that are amenable to indexing. The GiST provides a means to index arbitrary domains for arbitrary queries, but as yet we lack an "indexability theory" to describe whether or not trying to index a given data set is practical for a given set of queries.

- *Indexing Non-Standard Domains:* As a practical matter, we are interested in building indices for unusual domains, such as sets, terms, images, sequences, graphs, video and sound clips, fingerprints, molecular structures, etc. Pursuit of such applied results should provide an interesting feedback loop with the theoretical explorations described above. Our investigation into RD-trees for set data has already begun: we have implemented RD-trees in SHORE and Illustra, using R-trees rather than the GiST. Once we shift from R-trees to the GiST, we will also be able to experiment with new PickSplit methods and new predicates for sets.

- *Query Optimization and Cost Estimation:* Cost estimates for query optimization need to take into account the costs of searching a GiST. Currently such estimates are reasonably accurate for B+-trees, and less so for R-trees. Recently, some work on R-tree cost estimation has been done [FK94], but more work is required to bring this to bear on GiSTs in general. As an additional problem, the user-defined GiST methods may be time-consuming operations, and their CPU cost should be registered with the optimizer [HS93]. The optimizer must then correctly incorporate the CPU cost of the methods into its estimate of the cost for probing a particular GiST.

- *Lossy Key Compression Techniques:* As new data domains are indexed, it will likely be necessary to find new lossy compression techniques that preserve the properties of a GiST.

- *Algorithmic Improvements:* The GiST algorithms for insertion are based on those of R-trees. As noted in Section 4.2, R*-trees use somewhat modified algorithms, which seem to provide some performance gain for spatial data. In particular, the R*-tree policy of "forced reinsert" during split may be generally beneficial. An investigation of the R*-tree modifications needs to be carried out for non-spatial domains. If the techniques prove beneficial, they will be incorporated into the GiST, either as an option or as default behavior. Additional work will be required to unify the R*-tree modifications with R-tree techniques for concurrency control and recovery.

Finally, we believe that future domain-specific search tree enhancements should take into account the generality issues raised by GiSTs. There is no good reason to develop new, distinct search tree structures if comparable performance can be obtained in a unified framework. The GiST provides such a framework, and we plan to implement it in an existing extensible system, and also as a standalone C++ library package, so that it can be exploited by a variety of systems.

Acknowledgements

Thanks to Praveen Seshadri, Marcel Kornacker, Mike Olson, Kurt Brown, Jim Gray, and the anonymous reviewers for their helpful input on this paper. Many debts of gratitude are due to the staff of Illustra Information Systems — thanks to Mike Stonebraker and Paula Hawthorn for providing a flexible industrial research environment, and to Mike Olson, Jeff Meredith, Kevin Brown, Michael Ubell, and Wei Hong for their help with technical matters. Thanks also to Shel Finkelstein for his insights on RD-trees. Simon Hellerstein is responsible for the acronym GiST. Ira Singer provided a hardware loan which made this paper possible. Finally, thanks to Adene Sacks, who was a crucial resource throughout the course of this work.

References

[Aok91] P. M. Aoki. Implementation of Extended Indexes in POSTGRES. *SIGIR Forum*, 25(1):2–9, 1991.

[BKSS90] Norbert Beckmann, Hans-Peter Kriegel, Ralf Schneider, and Bernhard Seeger. The R*-tree: An Efficient and Robust Access Method

For Points and Rectangles. In *Proc. ACM-SIGMOD International Conference on Management of Data*, pages 322–331, Atlantic City, May 1990.

[BKSS94] Thomas Brinkhoff, Hans-Peter Kriegel, Ralf Schneider, and Bernhard Seeger. Multi-Step Processing of Spatial Joins. In *Proc. ACM-SIGMOD International Conference on Management of Data*, Minneapolis, May 1994, pages 197–208.

[CDF+94] Michael J. Carey, David J. DeWitt, Michael J. Franklin, Nancy E. Hall, Mark L. McAuliffe, Jeffrey F. Naughton, Daniel T. Schuh, Marvin H. Solomon, C. K. Tan, Odysseas G. Tsatalos, Seth J. White, and Michael J. Zwilling. Shoring Up Persistent Applications. In *Proc. ACM-SIGMOD International Conference on Management of Data*, Minneapolis, May 1994, pages 383–394.

[CDG+90] M.J. Carey, D.J. DeWitt, G. Graefe, D.M. Haight, J.E. Richardson, D.H. Schuh, E.J. Shekita, and S.L. Vandenberg. The EXODUS Extensible DBMS Project: An Overview. In Stan Zdonik and David Maier, editors, *Readings In Object-Oriented Database Systems*. Morgan-Kaufmann Publishers, Inc., 1990.

[Com79] Douglas Comer. The Ubiquitous B-Tree. *Computing Surveys*, 11(2):121–137, June 1979.

[FB74] R. A. Finkel and J. L. Bentley. Quad-Trees: A Data Structure For Retrieval On Composite Keys. *ACTA Informatica*, 4(1):1–9, 1974.

[FK94] Christos Faloutsos and Ibrahim Kamel. Beyond Uniformity and Independence: Analysis of R-trees Using the Concept of Fractal Dimension. In *Proc. 13th ACM SIGACT-SIGMOD-SIGART Symposium on Principles of Database Systems*, pages 4–13, Minneapolis, May 1994.

[Gro94] The POSTGRES Group. POSTGRES Reference Manual, Version 4.2. Technical Report M92/85, Electronics Research Laboratory, University of California, Berkeley, April 1994.

[Gut84] Antonin Guttman. R-Trees: A Dynamic Index Structure For Spatial Searching. In *Proc. ACM-SIGMOD International Conference on Management of Data*, pages 47–57, Boston, June 1984.

[HNP95] Joseph M. Hellerstein, Jeffrey F. Naughton, and Avi Pfeffer. Generalized Search Trees for Database Systems. Technical Report #1274, University of Wisconsin at Madison, July 1995.

[HP94] Joseph M. Hellerstein and Avi Pfeffer. The RD-Tree: An Index Structure for Sets. Technical Report #1252, University of Wisconsin at Madison, October 1994.

[HS93] Joseph M. Hellerstein and Michael Stonebraker. Predicate Migration: Optimizing Queries With Expensive Predicates. In *Proc. ACM-SIGMOD International Conference on Management of Data*, Minneapolis, May 1994, pages 267–276.

[Ill94] Illustra Information Technologies, Inc. *Illustra User's Guide, Illustra Server Release 2.1*, June 1994.

[Jag90] H. V. Jagadish. Linear Clustering of Objects With Multiple Attributes. In *Proc. ACM-SIGMOD International Conference on Management of Data*, Atlantic City, May 1990, pages 332–342.

[KB95] Marcel Kornacker and Douglas Banks. High-Concurrency Locking in R-Trees. In *Proc. 21st International Conference on Very Large Data Bases*, Zurich, September 1995.

[KG94] Won Kim and Jorge Garza. Requirements For a Performance Benchmark For Object-Oriented Systems. In Won Kim, editor, *Modern Database Systems: The Object Model, Interoperability and Beyond*. ACM Press, June 1994.

[KKD89] Won Kim, Kyung-Chang Kim, and Alfred Dale. Indexing Techniques for Object-Oriented Databases. In Won Kim and Fred Lochovsky, editors, *Object-Oriented Concepts, Databases, and Applications*, pages 371–394. ACM Press and Addison-Wesley Publishing Co., 1989.

[Knu73] Donald Ervin Knuth. *Sorting and Searching*, volume 3 of *The Art of Computer Programming*. Addison-Wesley Publishing Co., 1973.

[LJF94] King-Ip Lin, H. V. Jagadish, and Christos Faloutsos. The TV-Tree: An Index Structure for High-Dimensional Data. *VLDB Journal*, 3:517–542, October 1994.

[LS90] David B. Lomet and Betty Salzberg. The hB-Tree: A Multiattribute Indexing Method. *ACM Transactions on Database Systems*, 15(4), December 1990.

[LY81] P. L. Lehman and S. B. Yao. Efficient Locking For Concurrent Operations on B-trees. *ACM Transactions on Database Systems*, 6(4):650–670, 1981.

[MCD94] Maurício R. Mediano, Marco A. Casanova, and Marcelo Dreux. V-Trees — A Storage Method For Long Vector Data. In *Proc. 20th International Conference on Very Large Data Bases*, pages 321–330, Santiago, September 1994.

[PSTW93] Bernd-Uwe Pagel, Hans-Werner Six, Heinrich Toben, and Peter Widmayer. Towards an Analysis of Range Query Performance in Spatial Data Structures. In *Proc. 12th ACM SIGACT-SIGMOD-SIGART Symposium on Principles of Database Systems*, pages 214–221, Washington, D. C., May 1993.

[PTSE95] Dimitris Papadias, Yannis Theodoridis, Timos Sellis, and Max J. Egenhofer. Topological Relations in the World of Minimum Bounding Rectangles: A Study with R-trees. In *Proc. ACM-SIGMOD International Conference on Management of Data*, San Jose, May 1995.

[Rob81] J. T. Robinson. The k-D-B-Tree: A Search Structure for Large Multidimensional Dynamic Indexes. In *Proc. ACM-SIGMOD International Conference on Management of Data*, pages 10–18, Ann Arbor, April/May 1981.

[SRF87] Timos Sellis, Nick Roussopoulos, and Christos Faloutsos. The R+-Tree: A Dynamic Index For Multi-Dimensional Objects. In *Proc. 13th International Conference on Very Large Data Bases*, pages 507–518, Brighton, September 1987.

[Sto86] Michael Stonebraker. Inclusion of New Types in Relational Database Systems. In *Proceedings of the IEEE Fourth International Conference on Data Engineering*, pages 262–269, Washington, D.C., February 1986.

[WE80] C. K. Wong and M. C. Easton. An Efficient Method for Weighted Sampling Without Replacement. *SIAM Journal on Computing*, 9(1):111–113, February 1980.

Grammar-like Functional Rules for Representing Query Optimization Alternatives

Guy M. Lohman
IBM Almaden Research Center
San Jose, CA 95120

Abstract

Extensible query optimization requires that the "repertoire" of alternative strategies for executing queries be represented as data, not embedded in the optimizer code Recognizing that query optimizers are essentially expert systems, several researchers have suggested using strategy rules to transform query execution plans into alternative or better plans Though extremely flexible, these systems can be very inefficient at any step in the processing, many rules may be eligible for application and complicated conditions must be tested to determine that eligibility during unification We present a constructive, "building blocks" approach to defining alternative plans, in which the rules defining alternatives are an extension of the productions of a grammar to resemble the definition of a function in mathematics The extensions permit each token of the grammar to be parametrized and each of its alternative definitions to have a complex condition The terminals of the grammar are base-level database operations on tables that are interpreted at run-time The non-terminals are defined declaratively by production rules that combine those operations into meaningful plans for execution Each production produces a set of alternative plans, each having a vector of properties, including the estimated cost of producing that plan Productions can require certain properties of their inputs, such as tuple order and location, and we describe a "glue" mechanism for augmenting plans to achieve the required properties We give detailed examples to illustrate the power and robustness of our rules and to contrast them with related ideas

1. Introduction

Ever since the first query optimizers [WONG 76, SELI 79] were built for relational databases, revising the "repertoire" of ways to construct a procedural execution plan from a non-procedural query has required complicated and costly changes to the optimizer code itself This has limited the repertoire of any one optimizer by discouraging or slowing experimentation with — and implementation of — all the new advances in relational technology, such as improved join methods [BABB 79, BRAT 84, DEWI 85], distributed query optimization [EPST 78, CHU 82, DANI 82, LOHM 85], semijoins [BERN 81], Bloomjoins [BABB 79, MACK 86], parallel joins on fragments [WONG 83], join indexes [HAER 78, VALD 87], dynamic creation of indexes [MACK 86], and many other variations of traditional processing strategies The recent surge in interest in extensible database systems [STON 86, CARE 86, SCHW 86, BATO 86] has only exacerbated the burden on optimizers, adding the need to customize a database system for a particular class of applications, such as geographic [LOHM 83], CAD/CAM, or expert systems Now optimizers must adapt to new access methods, storage managers, data types, user-defined functions, etc , all combined in novel ways Clearly the traditional specification of all feasible strategies in the optimizer code cannot support such fluidity

Perhaps the most challenging aspect of extensible query optimization is the representation of alternative execution strategies Ideally, this representation should be readily understood and modified by the Database Customizer (DBC)[1] Recognizing that query optimizers are expert systems, several authors have observed that rules show great promise for this purpose [ULLM 85, FREY 87, GRAE 87a] Rules provide a high-level, *declarative* (i e , non-procedural), and compact specification of legal alternatives, which may be input *as data* to the optimizer and traced to explain the origin of any execution plan This makes it easy to modify the strategies without impacting the optimizer, and to encapsulate the strategies executable by a particular processor in a heterogeneous network But how should rules represent alternative strategies? The EXODUS project [GRAE 87a, GRAE 87b] and Freytag [FREY 87] use rules to transform a given execution plan into other feasible plans The NAIL! project [ULLM 85, MORR 86] employs "capture rules" to determine which of a set of available plans can be used to execute a query

In this paper, we use rules to describe how to *construct* — rather than to *alter* or to *match* — plans Our rules "compose" low-level database operations on tables (such as ACCESS, JOIN, and SORT) into higher-level operations that can be re-used in other definitions These constructive, "building blocks" rules, which resemble the productions of a grammar, have two major advantages over plan transformation rules

- **They are more readily understood**, because they enable the DBC to build increasingly complex plans from common building blocks, the details of which may be transparent to him, and
- **They can be processed more efficiently** during optimization, by simply finding the definition of any building block that is referenced, using a simple dictionary search, much as is done in macro expanders By contrast, plan transformation rules usually must

1 We feel this term more accurately describes the role of adapting an implemented but extensible database system than does the term *Database Implementor (DBI)*, coined by Carey et al [CARE 86]

examine a large set of rules and apply complicated conditions on each of a large set of plans generated thus far, in order to determine if that plan matches the pattern to which that rule applies As new rules create new patterns, existing rules may have to add conditions that deal with those new patterns

Our grammar-like approach is founded upon a few fundamental observations about query optimization

- **All database operators consume and produce a common object — a table,** viewed as a stream of tuples that is generated by accessing a table [BATO 87a] The output of one operation becomes the input of the next Streams from individual tables are merged by joins, eventually into a single stream [FREY 87, GRAE 87a]

- **Optimizers construct legal sequences of such operators that are understood by an interpreter, the *query evaluator*** In other words, the repertoire of legal plans is a *language* that might well be defined by a grammar

- **Decisions made by the optimizer have an inherent sequence dependency** that limits the scope of subsequent decisions [BATO 87a, FREY 87] For example, for a given plan, the order in which a given set of tables are joined must be determined before the access path for any of those tables is chosen, because the table order determines which predicates are eligible and hence might be applied by the access path of any table (commonly referred to as "pushing down the selection") Thus, for any set of tables, the rules for ordering table accesses must precede those for choosing the access path of each table, and the former serve to limit significantly which of the latter rules are applicable

- **Alternative plans may incorporate the same plan fragment,** whose alternatives need be evaluated only once This further limits the rules generating alternatives to just the *new* portions of the plan

- Unlike the simple pattern-matching of tokens to determine the applicability of productions in grammars, in query optimization **specifying the *conditions* under which a rule is applicable is usually harder than specifying the rule's *transformation*** For example, a multi-column index can apply one or more predicates only if the columns referenced in the predicates form a prefix of the columns in the index Assigning the predicates to be applied by the index is far easier to express than the condition that permits that assignment

These observations prompted us to use "strategy" rules to construct legal nestings of database operators declaratively, much as the productions of a grammar construct legal sequences of tokens However, our rules resemble more the definition of a function in mathematics or a rule in Prolog, in that the "tokens" of our grammar may be parametrized and their definition alternatives may have complex conditions The reader is cautioned that the *application* — not the representation — is our claim to novelty Logic programming uses rules to construct new relations from base relations [ULLM 85], whereas we are using rules to construct new operators from base operators that operate on tables

Our approach is a general one, but we will present it in the context of its intended use the Starburst prototype extensible database system, which is under development at the IBM Almaden Research Center [SCHW 86, LIND 87]

The paper is organized as follows Section 2 first defines the end-product of optimization — plans We describe what they're made of, what they look like, how our rules are used to construct all of them for a query In Section 3, we associate properties with plans, and allow rules to impose requirements on the properties of their input plans A set of possible rules for joins is given in Section 4 to illustrate the power of our rules to specify some of the most complicated strategies of existing systems, including several not addressed by other authors Section 5 outlines how the DBC can make extensions to rules, properties, and database operators Having thoroughly described our approach, we contrast it with related work in Section 6, and conclude in Section 7

2. Plan Generation

In this section, we describe the form of our rules We must first define what we want to produce with these rules, namely a query evaluation plan, and its constituents

2.1. Plans

The basic object to be manipulated — and the class of "terminals" in our grammar — is a ***LOw-LEvel Plan OPerator (LOLEPOP)*** that will be interpreted by the query evaluator at run-time LOLEPOPs are a variation of the relational algrebra (e g , **JOIN, UNION**, etc), supplemented with low-level operators such as **ACCESS, SORT, SHIP**, etc [FREY 87] Each LOLEPOP is viewed as a function that operates on 1 or 2 tables[2], which are parameters to that function, and produces a single table as output A ***table*** can be either a table stored on disk or a "stream of tuples" in memory or a communication pipe The **ACCESS** LOLEPOP converts a stored table to a stream of tuples, and the **STORE** LOLEPOP does the reverse In addition to input tables, a LOLEPOP may have other parameters that control its operation For example, one parameter of the **SORT** LOLEPOP is the set of columns on which to sort Parameters may also specify a ***flavor*** of LOLEPOP For example, different join methods having the same input parameter structure are represented by different flavors of the **JOIN** LOLEPOP, differences in input parameters would necessitate a distinct LOLEPOP Parameters may be optional, for example, the **ACCESS** LOLEPOP may optionally apply a set of predicates

A ***query evaluation plan*** (***QEP***, or ***plan***) is a directed graph of LOLEPOPs An example plan is shown in Figure 1 Note that arrows point toward the source of the stream, not the direction in which tuples flow This plan shows a sort-merge **JOIN** of DEPT as the outer table and **EMP** as the inner table The **DEPT** stream is generated by an **ACCESS** to the stored table DEPT, then **SORT**ed into the order of column DNO for the merge-join The EMP stream is generated by an **ACCESS** to the stored index on column EMP DNO[3] that includes as one "column" the ***tuple identifier (TID)*** For each tuple in the stream, the **GET** LOLEPOP then uses the TID to get additional columns from its stored table columns NAME and ADDRESS from EMP in this example

Another way of representing this plan is as a nesting of functions [BATO 87a, FREY 87]

```
JOIN (sort merge, DEPT DNO=EMP DNO,
      SORT(ACCESS(DEPT, {DNO,MGR}, {MGR='Haas'}), DNO),
      GET(ACCESS(Index on EMP DNO,{TID,DNO}, φ),
          EMP, {NAME,ADDRESS}, φ                    )       )
```

This representation would be a lot more readable, and easier to construct, if we were to define intermediate functions D and E for the last two parameters to JOIN

```
JOIN (sort merge, D DNO=E DNO, D, E)
```

where

---

2 Nothing in the structure of our rules prevents LOLEPOPs from operating on any number of tables

3 Actually, ACCESSes to base tables and to access methods such as this index use different flavors of ACCESS

/

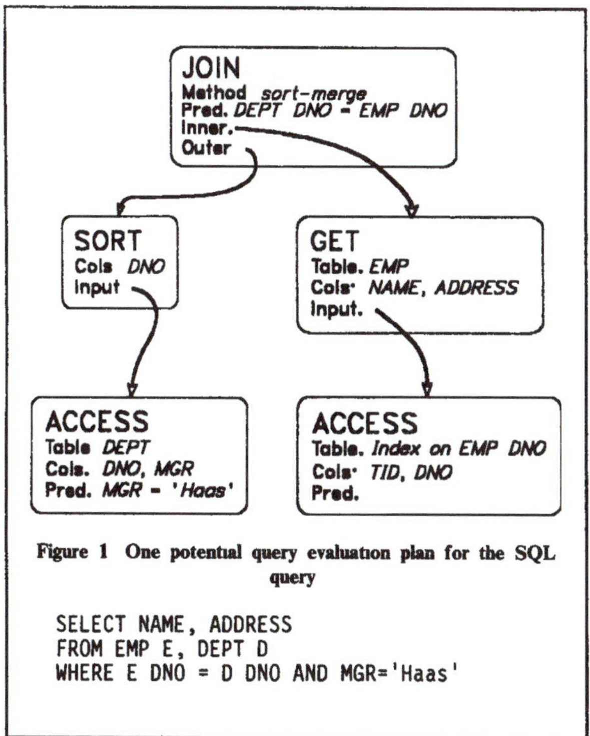

Figure 1 One potential query evaluation plan for the SQL query

```
SELECT NAME, ADDRESS
FROM EMP E, DEPT D
WHERE E DNO = D DNO AND MGR='Haas'
```

D = **SORT**(**ACCESS**(*DEPT*, {*DNO*, *MGR*}, {*MGR*='*Haas*'}), *DNO*)

and

E = **GET**(**ACCESS**(*Index onEMP DNO*, {*TID*, *DNO*}, ϕ),
EMP, {*NAME*, *ADDRESS*}, ϕ)

If properly parametrized, these intermediate functions could be re-used for creating an ordered stream for *any* table, e g

OrderedStream1(*T*, C, *P*, *order*) = **SORT**(**ACCESS**(*T*, C, *P*), *order*)

and

OrderedStream2(*T*, C, *P*, *order*) =
GET(**ACCESS**(*a*, {*TID*}, ϕ), *T*, C, *P*) IF *order* $\sqsubseteq$ *a*

where *T* is the stored table (base table or base tables represented in a stored intermediate result) to be accessed, *C* is the set of columns to be accessed, *P* is the set of predicates to be applied, and "*order* $\sqsubseteq$ *a*" means "the ordered list of columns of *order* are a prefix of those of access path *a* of *T*" Now it becomes apparent that OrderedStream1 and OrderedStream2 provide two alternative definitions for a single concept, an OrderedStream, in which the second definition depends upon the existence of a suitable access path

OrderedStream(*T*, C, *P*, *order*) =

[**SORT**(**ACCESS**(*T*, C, *P*), *order*)
[**GET**(**ACCESS**(*a*, {*TID*}, ϕ), *T*, C, *P*) IF *order* $\sqsubseteq$ *a*

This higher-level construct can now be nested within other functions needing an ordered stream, without having to worry about the details of how the ordered stream was created [BATO 87a] It is precisely this train of reasoning that inspired the grammar-like design of our rules for constructing plans

2 2 Rules

Executable plans are defined using a grammar-like set of parametrized production rules called ***STrategy Alternative Rules (STARs)*** that define higher-level constructs from lower-level constructs, in a way resembling common mathematical functions or a functional programming language [BACK 78] A STAR defines a named, parametrized object (the "nonterminals" in our grammar) in terms of one or more ***alternative definitions***, each of which

- may have a ***condition of applicability***, and
- defines a plan by referencing one or more LOLEPOPs or other STARs, specifying ***arguments*** for their parameters

Arguments and conditions of applicability may reference constants, parameters of the STAR being defined, or other LOLEPOPs or STARs For example, the intermediate functions OrderedStream1 and OrderedStream2, defined above, are examples of STARs with only one alternative definition, but OrderedStream has two alternative definitions The first of these references the SORT LOLEPOP, whose first argument is a reference to the ACCESS LOLEPOP and whose second argument is the parameter ***order*** The conditions of applicability for all the alternatives may either overlap or be exclusive If they overlap, as they do for OrderedStream, then the STAR may return more than one plan

In addition, we may wish to apply the function to every element of a set For example, in OrderedStream2 above, any other index on EMP having DNO as its major column could achieve the desired order So we need a STAR to generate an ACCESS plan *for each index i in that set I*

IndexAccess(*T*) = $\forall i \in I$ **ACCESS**(*i*, {*TID*}, ϕ)

Using rule IndexAccess in rule OrderedStream2 as the first argument should apply the GET LOLEPOP to each such plan, i e , for each alternative plan returned by IndexAccess, the **GET** function will be referenced with that plan as its first argument So **GET** (IndexAccess(***EMP***), *C*, *P*) will also return multiple plans Therefore any STAR having overlapping conditions or referencing a multi-valued STAR will itself be multi-valued It is easiest to treat all STARs as operations on the abstract data type ***Set of Alternative Plans for a stream (SAP)***, which consume one or two SAPs and are mapped (in the LISP sense [FREY 87]) onto each element of those SAPs to produce an output SAP Set-valued parameters other than SAPs (such as the sets of columns *C* and predicates *P* above) are treated as a single parameter unless otherwise designated by the $\forall$ clause, as was done in the definition of IndexAccess

2.3. Use and Implementation

As our functional notation suggests, the rule mechanism starts with the ***root STAR***, which is the "starting state" of our grammar The root STAR has one or more alternative definitions, each of which may reference other STARs, which in turn may reference other STARs, and so on top down until a STAR is defined totally in terms of "terminals", i e LOLEPOPs operating on constants Each reference of a STAR is evaluated by replacing the reference with its alternative definitions that satisfy the condition of applicability, and replacing the parameters of those definitions with the arguments of the reference Unlike transformational rules, this substitution process is remarkably simple and fast, the fanout of any reference of a STAR is limited to just those STARs referenced in its definition, and alternative definitions may be evaluated in parallel Therein lies the real advantage of STARs over transformational rules The implementation of a prototype interpreter for STARs, including a very general mechanism for controlling the order in which STARs are evaluated, is described in [LEE 88]

Thus far in Starburst, we have sets of STARs for accessing individual tables and joins, but STARs may be defined for any new operation, e g outer join, and may reference any other STAR The root STAR for joins is called JoinRoot, a possible definition of which appears in Section "4 Example Join STARs", along with the STARs that it references Simplified definitions of the single-table access STARs are given in [LEE 88] For any given SQL query, we build plans bottom up, first referencing the AccessRoot STAR to build plans to access individual tables, and then repeatedly referencing the JoinRoot STAR to join plans that were generated earlier, until all tables have been joined What constitutes a joinable pair of streams depends upon a compile-time parameter The default is to give preference to those streams having an eligible join predicate linking them, as did System R and R*, but this can be overridden to also consider Cartesian products between two streams of small estimated cardinality In addition, in Starburst we exploit all predicates that reference more than one table as join predicates This generalization of System R's and R*'s "col1 = col2" join predicates, plus allowing plans to have composite inners (e g , (A*B)*(C*D)) and Cartesian products (when the appropriate parameters are specified), significantly complicates the generation of legal join pairs and increases their number However, a cheaper plan is more likely to be discovered among this expanded repertoire[1] We will address this aspect of query optimization in a forthcoming paper on join enumeration

3. Properties of Plans

The concept of cost has been generalized to include all properties a plan might have We next present how properties are defined and changed, and how they interact with STARs

3.1. Description

Every table (either base table or result of a plan) has a set of ***properties*** that summarize the work done on the table thus far (as in [GRAE 87b], [BATO 87a],and [ROSE 87]) and hence are important to the cost model These properties are of three types

relational the relational content of the plan, e g due to joins, projections, and selections

physical the physical aspects of the tuples, which affect the cost but not the relational content, e g the order of the tuples

estimated properties derived from the previous two as part of the cost model, e g estimated cardinality of the result and cost to produce it

Examples of these properties are summarized in Figure 2 All properties are handled uniformly as elements of a ***property vector***, which can easily be extended to add more properties (see section 5)

Initially, the properties of stored objects such as tables and access methods are determined from the system catalogs For example, for a table, the catalogs contain its constituent columns (COLS), the SITE at which it is stored [LOHM 85], and the access PATHS defined on it No predicates (PREDS) have been applied yet, it is not a TEMPorary table, and no COST has been incurred in the query The ORDER is "unknown" unless the table is known to store tuples in some order, in which case the order is defined by the ordered set of columns on which the tuples are ordered

Each LOLEPOP changes selected properties, including adding cost, in a way determined by the arguments of its reference and the properties of any arguments that are plans For example, **SORT** changes the ORDER of tuples to the order specified in a parameter **SHIP** changes the SITE property to the specified site Both LOLEPOPs add to the COST property of their input stream additional cost that depends upon the size of that stream, which is a function of its properties CARD and COLS **ACCESS** changes a stored table to a memory-resident stream of tuples, but optionally can also subset columns (relational project) and apply predicates (relational select) that may be enumerated as arguments The latter option will of course change the CARD property as well These changes, including the appropriate cost and cardinality estimates, are defined in Starburst by a ***property function*** for each LOLEPOP Each property function is passed the arguments of the LOLEPOP, including the property vector for arguments that are STARs or LOLEPOPs, and returns the revised property vector Thus, once STARs are reduced to LOLEPOPs, the cost of any plan can be assessed by invoking the property function for successive LOLEPOPs These cost functions are well established and validated [MACK 86], so will not be discussed further here

```
• Relational (WHAT)

  TABLES   Set of tables accessed
  COLS     Set of columns accessed
  PREDS    Set of predicates applied

• Physical (HOW)

  ORDER    Ordering of tuples
           (an ordered list of columns)
  SITE     Site to which tuples delivered
  TEMP     "True" if materialized in a tempo-
           rary table
  PATHS    Set of available access paths on
           (set of) tables, each element an
           ordered list of columns

• Estimated (HOW MUCH)

  CARD     Estimated number of tuples result-
           ing
  COST     Estimated cost (total resources, a
           linear combination of I/O, CPU, and
           communications costs [LOHM 85])
```

Figure 2 Example properties of a plan.

3.2. Required vs. Available Properties

A reference of a STAR or LOLEPOP, especially for certain join methods, may require certain properties for its arguments For example, the merge-join requires its input table streams to be ordered by the join columns, and the nested-loop join requires the inner table's access method to apply the join predicate as though it were a single-table predicate ("pushes the selection down") Dyadic LOLEPOPs such as **GET**, **JOIN**, and **UNION** require that the SITE of both input streams be the same

In the previous section, we constructed a STAR for an OrderedStream, where the desired order was a parameter of that STAR Clearly we could require a particular order by referencing OrderedStream with the required order as the corresponding argument The problem is that we may simultaneously require values for any of the 2^n combinations of n properties, and hence would have to have a differently-named STAR for each combination For example, if the sort-merge **JOIN** in the example is to take place

SITE = x then we need to define a SitedOrderedStream that has parameters for SITE and ORDER and references in its definition **SHIP** LOLEPOPs to send any stream to SITE x, as well as a SitedStream, an OrderedStream, and a STREAM. Actually, SitedOrderedStream subsumes the others, since we can pass nulls for the properties not required. But in general, every STAR will need this same capability to specify some or all of the properties that might be required by referencing STARs as parameters. Much of the definition of each of these STARs would be redundant, because these properties really are orthogonal to what the stream produces. In addition, we often want to find the *cheapest* plan that satisfies the required properties, even if there is a plan that naturally produces the required properties. For example, even though there is an index EMP.DNO by which we can access EMP in the required DNO order, it might be cheaper, if EMP were not ordered by DNO, to access EMP sequentially and sort it into DNO order.

We therefore factor out a separate mechanism called ***Glue***, which can be referenced by any STAR and which

1. checks if any plans exist for the required relational properties (TABLES, COLS, and PREDS), referencing the top-most STAR with those parameters if not,
2. adds to any existing plan "Glue" operators as a "veneer" to achieve the required properties (for example, a SORT LOLEPOP can be added to change the tuple ORDER, or a **SHIP** LOLEPOP to change the SITE), and
3. either returns the cheapest plan satisfying the requirments or (optionally) all plans satisfying the requirements.

In fact, Glue can be specified using STARs, and Glue operators can be STARs as well as LOLEPOPs, as described in [LEE 88].

Required properties in the STAR reference are enclosed in square brackets next to the affected SAP argument, to associate the required properties with the stream on which they are imposing requirements. Different properties may be required by references in different STARs, the requirements are accumulated until Glue is referenced. This will be illustrated in the next section.

An example of this Glue mechanism is shown in Figure 3. In this example, we assume that table DEPT is stored at SITE=N.Y., but the STAR requires DEPT to be delivered to SITE=L.A. in DNO order. None of the available plans meets those requirements. The first available plan must be augmented with a **SHIP** LOLEPOP to change the SITE property from N.Y. to L.A. The second plan, a simple **ACCESS** of DEPT, must be both **SORT**ed and **SHIP**ped. The third plan, perhaps created by an earlier reference of Glue that didn't have the ORDER requirement, has already added a **SHIP** to plan 2 to get it to L.A., but still needs a **SORT** to achieve the ORDER requirement.

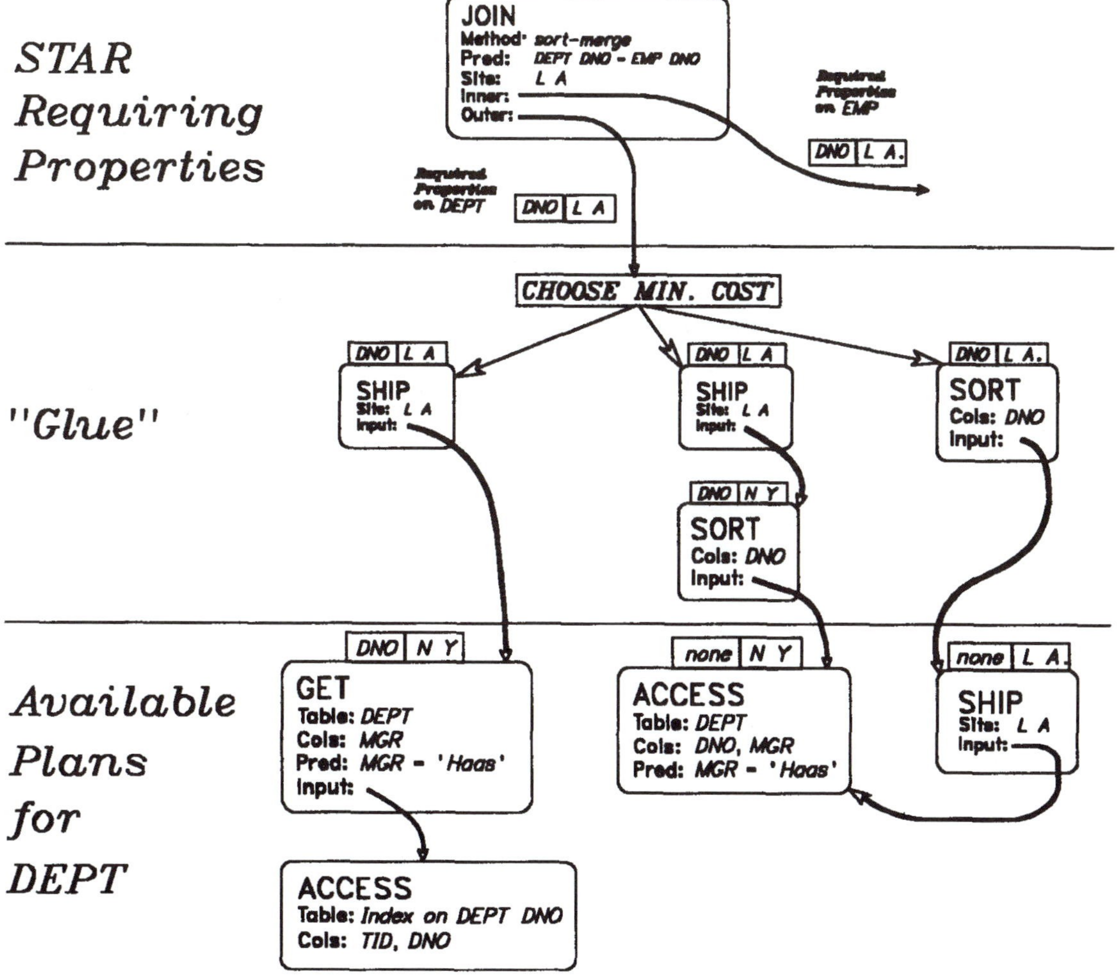

Figure 3. Example of "Glue" mechanism injecting "Glue" operators to match plans to required properties, and choosing the cheapest. Only two properties, order and site, are shown here, as "ears" on top of the top-most LOLEPOP for each plan.

4. Example: Join STARs

To illustrate the power of STARs in this section we discuss one possible set of STARs for generating the join strategies of the R* optimizer (in Sections 4 1 - 4 4), plus several additional strategies such as

- composite inners (Sections 4 1 and 4 3),
- new access methods (Section 4 5 2),
- new join methods (Section 4 4),
- dynamic creation of indexes on intermediate results (Section 4 5 3),
- materialization of inner streams of nested-loop joins to force projection (Section 4 5 2)

Although there may be better ways within our STAR structure to express the same set of strategies, the purpose of this section is to illustrate the full power of STARs Some of the strategies (e g , hash joins) have not yet been implemented in Starburst, they are included merely for illustrating what is involved in adding these strategies to the optimizer

These STARs are by no means complete we have intentionally simplified them by removing parameters and STARs that deal with subqueries treated as joins, for example The reader is cautioned against construing this omission as an inability to handle other cases, on the contrary, it illustrates the flexibility of STARs! We can construct, but have omitted for brevity, additional STARs for

- sorting TIDs taken from an unordered index in order to order I/O accesses to data pages,
- ANDing and ORing of multiple indexes for a single table,
- treating subqueries as joins having different quantifier types (i e , generalizing the predicate calculus quantifiers of ALL and EXISTS to include the FOR EACH quantifier for joins and the UNIQUE quantifier for scalar ("=") subqueries),
- filtration methods such as semi-joins and Bloom-joins

We believe that any desired strategy for non-recursive queries will be expressible using STARs, and are currently investigating what difficulties, if any, arise with recursive queries and multiple execution streams resulting from table partitioning [BATO 87a]

In these definitions, for readability we denote ***exclusive alternative definitions*** by a left *curly brace* and ***inclusive alternative definitions*** by a left *square bracket* In practice, no distinction is necessary In all examples, we will write non-terminals (STAR names) in RegularMixedCase, parameters in *italics* (those which may be sets are denoted by capital letters), and terminals in bold, with LOLEPOPs distinguished by **BOLD CAPITAL LETTERS** Required properties are written in **small bold letters** and surrounded by a pair of [square brackets] For brevity, we have had to shorten names, e g , "JMeth" should read "JoinMethod" The function "$\chi(\cdot)$" denotes "columns of $(\cdot)$", where $\cdot$ can be a set of tables, an index, etc We assume the existence of the basic set functions of $\in, \cap, \subseteq, -$ (set difference), etc

STARs are defined here top down (i e , a STAR referenced by any STAR is defined after its reference), which is also the order in which they will be referenced We start with the root STAR, JoinRoot, which is referenced for a given set of parameters

- table (quantifier) sets *T1* and *T2* (with no order implied)
- the set of (newly) eligible predicates, *P*

Suppose, for example, that plans for joining tables X and Y and for accessing table Z had already been generated, so we were ready to construct plans for joining X*Y with Z Then JoinRoot would be referenced with *T1* = {X,Y}, *T2* = {Z}, and *P* = {X g = Z m, Y h = Z n}

4.1. Join Permutation Alternatives

```
                       [ PermutedJoin(T1, T2, P)
JoinRoot(T1, T2, P) =  [
                       [ PermutedJoin(T2, T1, P)
```

The meaning of this STAR should be obvious either table-set *T1* or table-set *T2* can be the outer stream, with the other table-set as the inner stream Both are possible alternatives, denoted by an inclusive (square) bracket Note that we have no conditions on either alternative, to exclude a ***composite inner*** (i e , an inner that is itself the result of a join), we could add a condition restricting the inner table-set to be one table

This simple STAR fails to adequately tax the power of STARs, and thus resembles the comparable rule of transformational approaches However, note that since none of the STARs referenced by JoinRoot or any of its descendants will reference JoinRoot, there is no danger of this STAR being invoked again and "undoing" its effect, as there is in transformational rules [GRAE 87a]

4.2. Join-Site Alternatives

```
PermutedJoin(T1, T2, P) =

      { SitedJoin(T1, T2, P)                     IF local query
      { ∀s∈σ  RemoteJoin(T1, T2, P, s)           OTHERWISE

RemoteJoin(T1, T2, P, s) =
                     SitedJoin(T1[site = s], T2[site = s], P)

where
      σ ≡ set of sites at which tables of the query
                are stored, plus the query site
```

This STAR generates the same join-site alternatives as R* [LOHM 84], and illustrates the specification of a required property Note that Glue is not referenced yet, so the required **site** property accumulates on each alternative until it is The interpretation is

1 If all tables (of the query) are located at the query site, go on to SitedJoin, i e , bypass the RemoteJoin STAR which dictates the join site
2 Otherwise, require that the join take place at one of the sites at which tables are stored or the query originated

If a site with a particularly efficient join engine were available, then that site could easily be added to the definition of σ

4.3 Store Inner Stream?

```
                        { JMeth(T1, T2[temp], P)        IF C1
SitedJoin(T1, T2, P) =  {
                        { JMeth(T1, T2, P)              OTHERWISE

where

       C1 ≡ IF |T2| >1 OR T2[site] ≠ T2'[site]
```

Again, this simple STAR has an obvious interpretation, although the condition C1 is a bit complicated

1 IF the inner stream (*T2*) is a composite, or its site is not the same as its required site ('[**site**]), then dictate that it be stored as a temp and call JMeth
2 OTHERWISE, reference JMeth with no additional requirements

Note that if the second disjunct of condition C1 were absent, there would be no reason that this STAR couldn't be the parent (reference) of the previous STAR, instead of vice versa As written, SitedJoin exploits decisions made in its parent STAR, PermutedJoin A transformational rule would either have to test if the site decision were made yet, or else inject the temp requirement redundantly in every transformation that dictated a site

4.4. Alternative Join Methods

```
JMeth(T1, T2, P) =

 [ JOIN (NL, Glue(T1, φ), Glue(T2, JP ∪ IP), JP, P-(JP ∪ IP))
 [ JOIN ( MG, Glue(T1[order = χ(SP) ∩ χ(T1)], φ),
 [             Glue(T2[order = χ(SP) ∩ χ(T2)], IP),
 [             SP, P-(IP ∪ SP)                         ) IF SP ≠ φ
where

P  ≡   all eligible predicates
JP ≡   join predicates (multi-table, no ORs or
       subqueries, etc , but expressions OK)
SP ≡   sortable predicates
   =   { p ∈ JP of form 'col1 op col2', where
       col1 ∈ χ(T1) & col2 ∈ χ(T2) or vice versa }
IP ≡   predicates eligible on the inner only,
       i e , predicates p such that χ(p) ⊆ χ(T2)
```

This STAR references two alternative join methods, both represented as references of the **JOIN** LOLEPOP with different parameters

1 the join method (flavor of **JOIN**),
2 the outer stream and any required properties on that stream,
3 the inner stream and any required properties on that stream,
4 the join predicate(s) applicable by that join method (needed for the cost equations),
5 any residual predicates to apply *after* the join

The two join methods here are

1 **Nested-Loop (NL) Join,** which can always be done For each outer tuple instance, columns of the join predicates (JP) in the outer are instantiated to convert each JP to a single-table predicate on the inner stream[4] These and any predicates on just the inner (IP) are "pushed down" to be applied by the inner stream, if possible Any multi-table predicates that don't qualify as join predicates must be applied as residual predicates Note that the predicates to be applied by the inner stream are *parameters, not required attributes* This forces Glue to re-reference the single-table STARs to generate plans that *exploit* the converted JP predicates rather than *retrofitting* a **FILTER** LOLEPOP to existing plans that applied only the IP predicates

2 **Merge (MG) Join** If there are sortable predicates (SP), dictate that both inner and outer be sorted on their columns of SP Note that the merge join, unlike the nested-loop join, applies the sortable predicates as part of the join itself, pushing down to the inner stream only the single-table predicates on the inner (IP) The JOIN LOLEPOP in Figure 1, for example, would be generated by this alternative As before, remaining multi-table predicates must be applied by JOIN as residuals after the join

Glue will first reference the STARs for accessing the given table(s), applying the given predicate(s), if no plans exist for those parameters In Starburst, a data structure hashed on the tables and predicates facilitates finding all such plans, if they exist Glue then adds the necessary operators to each of these plans, as described in the previous section Simplified STARs for Glue, which this STAR references, and for accessing stored tables, which Glue references, are given in [LEE 88]

4.5. Additional Join Methods

Suppose now we wanted to augment the above alternatives with additional join methods All of the following alternative definitions would be added to the right-hand side of the above STAR (JMeth)

4 5 1 Hash Join Alternative

The hash join has shown promising performance [BABB 79, BRAT 84, DEWI 85] We assume here a hash-join flavor **(HA)** that atomically bucketizes both input streams and does the join on the buckets

```
JOIN (HA, Glue(T1, φ), Glue(T2, IP), HP, P-IP)     IF HP ≠ φ
where
    HP ≡ hashable predicates
       ≡ { p ∈ JP of form 'expr(χ(T1)) = expr(χ(T2))' }
```

As in the merge join, only single-table predicates can be pushed down to the inner Note that all multi-table predicates (P-IP) — even the hashable predicates (HP) — remain as residual predicates, since there may be hash collisions Also note that the set of hashable predicates HP contains some predicates not in the set of sortable predicates SP (expressions on any number of columns in the same table), and vice versa (inequalities)

An alternate (and probably preferable) approach would be to add a **bucketized** property to the property vector and a LOLEPOP to achieve that property, so that any join method in the JMeth STAR could perform the join in parallel on each of the bucketized streams, with appropriate adjustments to its cost

4.5 2. Forcing Projection Alternative

To avoid expensive in-memory copying, tuples are normally retained as pages in the buffer just as they were **ACCESSed**, until they are materialized as a temp or **SHIPped** to another site Therefore, in nested-loop joins it may be advantageous to materialize **(STORE)** the selected and projected inner and re-**ACCESS** it before joining, whenever a very small percentage of the inner table results (i e , when the predicates on the inner table are quite selective and/or only a few columns are referenced) Batory suggests the same strategy whenever the inner "is generated by a complex expression" [BATO 87a] The following forces that alternative

```
JOIN ( NL, Glue(T1, φ),
           TableAccess(Glue(T2[temp], IP), *, JP),
           JP, P-(IP ∪ JP)                          )
```

This JMeth alternative accesses the inner stream (*T2*), applying only the single-table predicates (IP), and forcing Glue to **STORE** the result in a temp (permanently stored tables are not considered temps initially) All columns (*) of the temp are then re-accessed, re-using the STAR for accessing any stored table, TableAccess Note that the STAR structure allows us to specify that the join predicates (JP) can be pushed down only to this access, to prevent the temp from being re-materialized *for each outer tuple!*

4 Ullman has coined the term "sideways information passing" [ULLM 85] for this conversion of join predicates to single-table predicates by instantiating one side of the predicate which was done in System R [SELI 79]

```
TableAccess(T, C, P) =

  { ACCESS(Heap, T, C, P)        IF StMgr(T) = 'heap'
  { ACCESS(BTree, T, C, P)       IF StMgr(T) = 'B-tree'
```

A TableAccess can be one (and only one) of the following flavors of **ACCESS**, depending upon the type of storage manager (StMgr) used, as described in [LIND 87]

1 A physically-sequential **ACCESS** of the pages of table *T*, if the storage manager type of *T* is 'heap', or
2 A B-Tree type **ACCESS** of table *T*, if the storage manager type of *T* is 'B-tree',

retrieving columns *C* and applying predicates *P* By now it should be apparent how easily alternatives for additional storage manager types could be added to this STAR alone, and affect all STARs that reference TableAccess

4 5 3 Dynamic Indexes Alternative

The nested-loop join works best when an index on the inner table can be used to limit the search of the inner to only those tuples satisfying the join and/or single-table predicates on the inner Such an index may not have been created by the user, or the inner may be an intermediate result, in which case no auxiliary access paths such as an index are normally created However, we can force Glue to create the index as another alternative Although this sounds more expensive than sorting for a merge join, it saves sorting the outer for a merge join, and will pay for itself when the join predicate is selective [MACK 86]

```
JOIN ( NL, Glue(T1, φ),
            Glue(T2[paths ⊇ IX], XP∪IP), XP - IP, P-(XP ∪ IP) )
where
    XP ≡ indexable multi-table predicates
       = { p ∈ JP of form 'expr(χ(T1)) op T2 col' }
    IX ≡ columns of indexable predicates
       = (χ(IP) ∪ χ(XP)) ∩ χ(T2), '=' predicates first
```

This alternative forces Glue to make sure that the access paths property of the inner contains an index on the columns that have either single-table (IP) or indexable (XP) predicates, ordered so that those involved in equality predicates are applied first If this index needs to be created, the STARs implementing Glue will add **[order]** and **[temp]** requirements to ensure the creation of a compact index on a stored table As in the nested-loop alternative, the indexable multi-table predicates "pushed down" to the inner are effectively converted to single-table predicates that change for each outer tuple

5. Extensibility – What's Really Involved

Here we discuss briefly the steps required to change various aspects of the optimizer strategies, in order to demonstrate the extensibility and modularity of our STAR mechanism

Easiest to change are the STARs themselves, when an existing set of LOLEPOPs suffices If the STARs are treated as input data to a rule interpreter, then new STARs can be added to that file without impacting the Starburst system code at all [LEE 88] If STARs are compiled to generate an optimizer (as in [GRAE 87a, GRAE 87b]), then updates of the STARs would be followed by a re-generation of the optimizer In either case, any STAR having a condition not yet defined would require defining a C function for that condition, compiling that function, and relinking that part of the optimizer to Starburst Note that we assume that the DBC specifies the STARs correctly, i e without infinite cycles or meaningless sequences of LOLEPOPs An open issue is how to verify that any given set of STARs is correct

Less frequently, we may wish to add a new LOLEPOP, e g **OUTERJOIN** This necessitates defining and compiling two C functions a run-time execution routine that will be invoked by the query evaluator, and a property function for the optimizer to specify the changes to plan properties (including cost) made by that LOLEPOP In addition, STARs must be added and/or modified, as described above, to reference the LOLEPOP under the appropriate circumstances

Probably the least likely and most serious alterations occur when a property is added (or changed in any way) in the property vector Since the default action of any LOLEPOP on any property is to leave the input property unchanged, only those property functions that reference the new property would have to be updated, recompiled, and relinked to Starburst By representing the property vector as a self-defining record having a variable number of fields, each of which is a property, we can insulate unaffected property functions from any changes to the structure of the property vector STARs would be affected only if the new property were required or produced by that STAR

6. Related Work

Some aspects of our STARs resemble features of earlier work, but there are some important differences As we mentioned earlier, our STARs are inspired by functional programming concepts [BACK 78] A major difference is that our "functions" (STARs) can be multi-valued, i e a *set* of alternative objects (plans) The other major inspiration, a production of a grammar, does not permit a condition upon alternative expansions of a non-terminal it either matches or it doesn't (and the alternatives must be exclusive) Hoping to use a standard compiler generator to compile our STARs, we investigated the use of partially context-sensitive W-grammars [CLEA 77] for enforcing the "context" of required properties, but were discouraged by the same combinatorial explosion of productions described above when many properties are possible Koster [KOST 71] has solved this using a technique similar to ours, in which a predicate called an "affix" (comparable to our condition of applicability) may be associated with each alternative definition He has shown affix grammars to be Turing complete In addition, grammars are typically used in a parser to find ***just one*** expansion to terminals, whereas our goal is to construct ***all*** such expansions Although a grammar can be used to construct all legal sequences, this set may be infinite [ULLM 85]

The transformational approach of the EXODUS optimizer [GRAE 87a, GRAE 87b] uses C functions for the IF conditions and expresses the alternatives in rules, as do we, but then compiles those rules and conditions using an "optimizer generator" into executable code Given one initial plan, this code generates all legal variations of that plan using two kinds of rules transformation rules to define alternative transformations of a plan, and implementation rules to define alternative methods for implementing an operator (e g , nested-loop and sort-merge algorithms for implementing the JOIN operator) Our approach does not require an initial plan, and has only one type of rule, which permits us to express interactions between transformations and methods Our property functions are indistinguishable from Graefe's property and functions, although we have identified more properties than any other author to date Graefe does not deal with the need of some rules (e g merge join) to require certain properties, as discussed in Section 3 2 and illustrated in Sections 4 2 - 4 4, 4 5 2, and 4 5 3 Although Graefe re-uses common subplans in alternative plans, transformational rules may subsequently generate alternatives and pick a new optimal plan for the subplan, forcing re-estimation of the cost of every plan that has already incorporated that subplan Our building blocks approach avoids this problem by generating all plans for the subplan before incorporating that subplan in other plans, although Glue may generate some new plans having different properties and/or parameters And while the structure of our STARs does not preclude compilation by an optimizer generator, it also permits interpreting the STARs by a simple yet efficient interpreter during optimization, as was done in our prototype Interpretation saves re-compiling the optimizer component every time a strategy is added or changed, and also allows greater control of the order of evaluation For example, depending upon the value of a STAR's parameter, we may never have to construct entire subtrees within the decision tree, but a compiled optimizer must contain a completely general decision tree for all queries

Freytag [FREY 87] proposes a more LISP-like set of transformational rules that starts from a non-procedural set of parameters from the query, as do we, and transforms them into all alternative plans He points to the EXODUS optimizer generator as a possible implementation, but does not address several key implementation issues such as his ellipsis ("   ") operator, which denotes any number of expressions, e g

$$((\text{JOIN}\ T_1 (\quad T_2 \quad)) \rightarrow (\text{JOIN}\ T_1 (\qquad) T_2))$$

And the ORDER and SITE properties (only) are expressed as functions, which presumably would have to be re-derived each time they were referenced in the conditions Freytag does not exploit the structure of query optimization to limit what rules are applicable at any time and to prevent re-application of the same rules to common subplans shared by two alternative plans, although he suggests the need to do so

Rosenthal and Helman [ROSE 87] suggest specifications for "well-formed" plans, so that transformational rules can be verified as valid if they transform well-formed plans to well-formed plans Like Graefe, they associate properties with plans, viewed as predicates that are true about the plan Alternative plans producing the same intermediate result with the same properties converge on "data nodes", on which "transformations that insert unary operators are more naturally applied" An operator is then well-formed if any input plan satisfying the required input properties produces an output plan that satisfies the output properties The paper emphasizes representations for verifiability and search issues, rather than detailing mechanisms (1) to construct well-formed transformations, (2) to match input data nodes to output data nodes (corresponding to our Glue), and (3) to recalculate the cost of all plans that share (through a common data node) a common subplan that is altered by a transformation

Probably the closest work to ours is Batory's "synthetic" architecture for the entire GENESIS extensible database system (not just the query optimizer [BATO 87b]), in which "atoms" of "primitive algorithms" are composed by functions into "molecules", in layers that successively add implementation details [BATO 87a] Developed concurrently and independently, Batory's functional notation closely resembles STARs, but is presented and implemented as rewrite (transformational) rules that are used to construct and compile the complete set of alternatives *a priori* for a given optimizer, after first selecting from a catalog of available algorithms those desired to implement operators for each layer At the highest layer, for example, the DBC chooses from many optimization algorithms (e g depth-first vs breadth-first), while the choices at the lowest layers correspond to our flavors of LOLEPOPs or Graefe's methods The functions that compose these operations do not explicitly permit conditions on the alternative definitions, as do we Batory considers them unnecessary when rules are constructed properly but alludes to them in comments next to some alternatives and in a footnote Inclusive alternatives automatically become arguments of a CHOOSE_CHEAPEST function during the composition process The rewrite rules include rules to match properties (which he calls characteristics) even if they are unneeded e g a SORT may be applied to a stream that is already ordered appropriately by an index, as well as rules to simplify the resulting compositions and eliminate any such unnecessary operations By treating the stored vs in-memory distinction as a property of streams, and by having a general-purpose Glue mechanism, we manage to factor out most of these redundancies in our STARs Although clearly relevant to query optimization, Batory s larger goal was to incorporate an encyclopedic array of known query processing algorithms within his framework, including operators for splitting, processing in parallel, and assembling horizontal partitions of tables

7. Conclusions

We have presented a grammar for specifying the set of legal strategies that can be executed by the query evaluator The grammar composes low-level database operators (LOLEPOPs) into higher-level constructs using rules (STARs) that resemble the definition of functions they may have alternative definitions that have IF conditions, and these alternative definitions may, in turn, reference other functions that have already been defined The functions are parametrized objects that produce one or more alternative plans Each plan has a vector of properties, including the cost to produce that plan, which may be altered only by LOLEPOPs When an alternative definition requires certain properties of an input, "Glue" can be referenced to do "impedance matching" between the plans created thus far and the required properties by injecting a veneer of Glue operators

We have shown the power of STARs by specifying some of the strategies considered by the R* system and several additional ones, and believe that any desired extension can be represented using STARs We find our constructive, "building-blocks" grammar to be a more natural paradigm for specifying the "language" of legal sequences of database operators than plan transformational rules, because they allow the DBC to build higher levels of abstraction from lower-level constructs, without having to be aware of how those lower-level constructs are defined And unlike plan transformational rules, which consider all rules applicable at every iteration and which must do complicated unification to determine applicability, referencing a STAR triggers in an obvious way only those STARs referenced in its definition, just like a macro expander This limited fanout of STARs should make it possible to achieve our goal of expressing alternative optimizer strategies as data and still use these rules to generate and evaluate the cost of a large number of plans within a reasonable amount of time

8. Acknowledgements

We wish to acknowledge the contributions to this work by several colleagues, especially the Starburst project team We particularly benefitted from lengthy discussions with — and suggestions by — Johann Christoph Freytag (now at the European Community Research Center in Munich), Laura Haas, and Kiyoshi Ono (visiting from the IBM Tokyo Research Laboratory) Laura Haas, Bruce Lindsay, Tim Malkemus (IBM Entry Systems Division in Austin, TX), John McPherson, Kiyoshi Ono, Hamid Pirahesh, Irv Traiger, and Paul Wilms constructively critiqued an earlier draft of this paper, improving its readability significantly We also thank the referees for their helpful suggestions

Bibliography

[BABB 79] E Babb, Implementing a Relational Database by Means of Specialized Hardware, *ACM Trans on Database Systems* **4,1** (1979) pp 1-29

[BATO 86] D S Batory et al , GENESIS An Extensible Database Management System, *Tech Report TR-86-07* (Dept of Comp Sci , Univ of Texas at To appear in IEEE Trans on Software Engineering

[BATO 87a] D S Batory, A Molecular Database Systems Technology, *Tech Report TR-87-23* (Dept of Comp Sci , Univ of Texas at

[BATO 87b] D Batory, Extensible Cost Models and Query Optimization in GENESIS, *IEEE Database Engineering* **10,4** (Nov 1987)

[BACK 78] J Backus, Can programming be liberated from the von Neumann style? A functional style and its algebra of programs", *Comm ACM* **21,8** (Aug 1978)

[BERN 81] P Bernstein and D -H Chiu, Using Semi-Joins to Solve Relational Queries, *Journal ACM* **28,1** (Jan 1981) pp 25-40

[BRAT 84] K Bratbergsengen, Hashing Methods and Relational Algebra Operations, *Procs of the Tenth International Conf on Very Large Data Bases (Singapore),* **Morgan Kaufmann Publishers** (Los Altos, CA, 1984) pp 323-333

[CARE 86] M J Carey, D J DeWitt, D Frank, G Graefe, J E Richardson, E J Shekita, and M Muralikrishna, The Architecture of the EXODUS Extensible DBMS a Preliminary Report, *Procs of the International Workshop on Object-Oriented Database Systems* (Asilomar, CA, Sept 1986)

[CHU 82] W W Chu and P Hurley, Optimal Query Processing for Distributed Database Systems, *IEEE Trans on Computers* **C-31,9** (Sept 1982) pp 835-850

[CLEA 77] J C Cleaveland and R C Uzgalis, *Grammars for Programming Languages,* **Elsevier North-Holland** (New York, 1977)

[DANI 82] D Daniels, P G Selinger, L M Haas, B G Lindsay, C Mohan, A Walker, and P Wilms, An Introduction to Distributed Query Compilation in R*, *Procs Second International Conf on Distributed Databases* (Berlin, September 1982) Also available as IBM Research Report RJ3497, San Jose, CA, June 1982

[DEWI 85] D J DeWitt and R Gerber, Multiprocessor Hash-Based Join Algorithms, *Procs of the Eleventh International Conf on Very Large Data Bases (Stockholm, Sweden),* **Morgan Kaufmann Publishers** (Los Altos, CA, September 1985) pp 151-164

[EPST 78] R Epstein, M Stonebraker, and E Wong, Distributed Query Processing in a Relational Data Base System, *Procs of ACM-SIGMOD* (Austin, TX, May 1978) pp 169-180

[FREY 87] J C Freytag, A Rule-Based View of Query Optimization, *Procs of ACM-SIGMOD* (San Francisco, CA, May 1987) pp 173-180

[GRAE 87a] G Graefe and D J DeWitt, The EXODUS Optimizer Generator, *Procs of ACM-SIGMOD* (San Francisco, CA, May 1987) pp 160-172

[GRAE 87b] G Graefe, Software Modularization with the EXODUS Optimizer Generator, *IEEE Database Engineering* **10,4** (Nov 1987)

[HAER 78] T Haerder, Implementing a Generalized Access Path Structure for a Relational Database System, *ACM Trans on Database Systems* **3,3** (Sept 1978) pp 258-298

[KOST 71] C H A Koster, Affix Grammars, *ALGOL 68 Implementation* **Elsevier North-Holland** (J E L Peck (ed), Amsterdam, 1971) pp 95-109

[LEE 88] M K Lee, J C Freytag, and G M Lohman, Implementing an Interpreter for Functional Rules in a Query Optimizer, *IBM Research Report RJ6125* **IBM Almaden Research Center** (San Jose, CA, March 1988)

[LIND 87] B Lindsay, J McPherson, and H Pirahesh, A Data Management Extension Architecture, *Procs of ACM-SIGMOD* (San Francisco, CA, May 1987) pp 220-226 Also available as IBM Res Report RJ5436, San Jose, CA, Dec 1986

[LOHM 83] G M Lohman, J C Stoltzfus, A N Benson, M D Martin, and A F Cardenas, Remotely-Sensed Geophysical Databases Experience and Implications for Generalized DBMS, *Procs of ACM-SIGMOD* (San Jose, CA, May 1983) pp 146-160

[LOHM 84] G M Lohman, D Daniels, L M Haas, R Kistler, P G Selinger, Optimization of Nested Queries in a Distributed Relational Database, *Procs of the Tenth International Conf on Very Large Data Bases (Singapore),* **Morgan Kaufmann Publishers** (Los Altos, CA, 1984) pp 403-415 Also available as IBM Research Report RJ4260, San Jose, CA, April 1984

[LOHM 85] G M Lohman, C Mohan, L M Haas, B G Lindsay, P G Selinger, P F Wilms, and D Daniels, Query Processing in R*, *Query Processing in Database Systems, Springer-Verlag* (Kim, Batory, & Reiner (eds), 1985) pp 31-47 Also available as IBM Research Report RJ4272, San Jose, CA, April 1984

[MACK 86] L F Mackert and G M Lohman, R* Optimizer Validation and Performance Evaluation for Distributed Queries, *Procs of the Twelfth International Conference on Very Large Data Bases (Kyoto)* **Morgan Kaufmann Publishers** (Los Altos, CA, August 1986) pp 149-159 Also available as IBM Research Report RJ5050, San Jose, CA, April 1986

[MORR 86] K Morris, J D Ullman, and A Van Gelder, Design Overview of the NAIL! System, *Report No STAN-CS-86-1108* **Stanford University** (Stanford, CA, May 1986)

[ROSE 87] A Rosenthal and P Helman, Understanding and Extending Transformation-Based Optimizers, *IEEE Database Engineering* **10,4** (Nov 1987)

[SCHW 86] P M Schwarz, W Chang, J C Freytag, G M Lohman, J McPherson, C Mohan, and H Pirahesh, Extensibility in the Starburst Database System, *Procs of the International Workshop on Object-Oriented Database Systems (Asilomar, CA),* **IEEE** (Sept 1986)

[SELI 79] P G Selinger, M M Astrahan, D D Chamberlin, R A Lorie, and T G Price, Access Path Selection in a Relational Database Management System *Procs of ACM-SIGMOD* (May 1979) pp 23-34

[STON 86] M Stonebraker and L Rowe, The Design of Postgres *Procs of ACM-SIGMOD* (May 1986) pp 340-355

[ULLM 85] J D Ullman, Implementation of Logical Query Languages for Databases, *ACM Trans on Database Systems* **10,3** (September 1985) pp 289-321

[VALD 87] P Valduriez, Join Indices, *ACM Trans on Database Systems* **12,2** (June 1987) pp 219-246

[WONG 76] E Wong and K Youssefi, Decomposition — a Strategy for Query Processing, *ACM Trans on Database Systems* **1,3** (Sept 1976) pp 223-241

[WONG 83] E Wong and R Katz, Distributing a Database for Parallelism, *Procs of ACM-SIGMOD* (San Jose CA May 1983) pp 23-29

Chapter 6
Database Evolution

A common adage of the IT world says that "there is no such thing as a static database." Generally speaking, a schema is developed for one application, and then over time that schema must be modified as a result of a variety of factors, including:

- Changing business conditions (your bank buys another bank, and the IT systems must be merged)
- Changing requirements (the government changes the rules)
- Changing application mix (the collection of access paths previously thought best are no longer a good choice)
- The Web (you now need to exchange information with your customers and suppliers)

This is undoubtedly only a partial list of the reasons why schemas must be altered over time.

Whenever the schema must change, there are several issues to confront. These include physical schema evolution, logical schema evolution, and change management. We discuss these three topics in the rest of this introduction.

Physical Schema Evolution

Physical schema evolution includes modifying the tuning parameters of a DBMS as well as changing the access paths to data. Current commercial DBMSs have scores of tuning parameters. These include such esoterica as the size of the log buffer, how many fragments to horizontally partition a table into, how big a scratch space to use for sorting tables, how many virtual processes the system should allocate, and so on. Whenever the application mix changes, these parameters must be reevaluated. In current systems, this task falls to a human data base administrator.

Our personal experience is that there are not nearly enough competent DBAs to go around. Moreover, in a desire to keep costs down enterprises always want to minimize the number of DBAs they employ. As a result, when performance starts to degrade, the customer typically calls the vendor who sold them the system. The vendor dispatches one of his system engineers (SEs) to fix the problem. Hence, the complex tuning parameters typically get set by the SEs. Having talked to many SEs, it is our opinion that most do not understand the complex interactions of performance parameters. Therefore, many maintain a "crib sheet" of values that have worked in other installations. A common practice is to start with the parameters that worked well in some other installation that appears similar to this one. As a result, tuning parameters are often set by a combination of folklore and what seemed to work elsewhere.

Obviously, it would be a good idea to set tuning parameters automatically using some sort of automated logic, and all of the vendors are moving aggressively in this direction. Our first paper in this section by Chaudhuri deals with choosing indexes with the help of a training set of queries and special query evaluation calls to the optimizer. This technology has been added to the SQL Server DBMS by Microsoft. Over time, we expect essentially all physical performance parameters to be set automatically using this sort of technology.

Of course, this capability will have to be optional, since there are expert DBAs who demand access to the tuning knobs. In the early days of query optimization, an expert human could usually beat an automatic program. Over time, it has become harder and harder for a human to beat the query optimizer. Hence, few humans demand the capability to override the optimizer. In the long run, we expect this evolution to occur in physical performance tuning; i.e. it will become totally automatic.

Logical Schema Evolution

When the logical schema changes, the DBA has the problem of converting his existing application from the old schema to the new schema. The view mechanisms in relational DBMSs were designed to minimize or eliminate the need for program maintenance in this situation. Hence, the old schema is defined as a view on top of the new schema, and in theory all of the applications, which used to work on real tables, should continue to work on virtual tables. Unfortunately, it is difficult to process update commands against views, as noted in the first paper of this book. Hence, the possibility of isolating applications from change by using views is not universal.

If views do not work, then the DBA faces two problems. She must evolve the schema through more complex transformations, and application program maintenance will be inevitable. It is not clear how to design applications that make such program maintenance as easy to accomplish as possible.

In addition, some sort of schema evolution tool is required that will provide assistance with more complex transformations. The design of such a tool is an incredibly important (and incredibly hard) problem. A start at such a tool is documented in the second paper in this section by Bernstein.

Online Change Management

An obvious goal is to perform physical schema changes without taking the DBMS offline. There is a clear trend toward "7 X 24" operation, and to the extent possible physical changes should be accomplished while the system is running.

Hence, it should be possible to add or drop indexes, changing the number of disks over which a table is horizontally partitioned, and alter the size of the buffer pool while a DBMS system is running. More challenging, but seemingly possible, would be to change an existing access path from one implementation to another, for example from hash to B-tree.

To include such capabilities in a DBMS requires substantial changes to the code. For example, the size of the buffer pool is usually a static array. To change the size of the buffer pool in many systems requires that the system be taken down and rebooted. Obviously, a dynamic array implementation is required to alleviate this issue.

For changes in storage structures, more complex data structures are required to support on-line changes. The third paper in this section discusses the sort of data structures that designers must think about to accomplish this goal. Hopefully, additional work will be done in this important area that will improve the technology in this area.

The "holy grail" in this area would be to move from Version I to Version I+1 of a vendor's DBMS software without taking the data base offline.

Cut-Over

In the absence of truly online change facilities, DBMS installations must be occasionally taken (partially or completely) offline by the DBA. When program maintenance is required, there is the old code line and the new code line, and testing and cutover must be considered. Today's information systems have serious uptime requirements. Hence, it is often not practical to take a system down for several days to reorganize the schema or install a new version of the DBMS.

As a result, it is common practice to have a second development and test system. The revised application is built on this machine using the new configuration, and exhaustive testing is performed. Once, the system administrator is comfortable with the reliability of the new system, he must **cut over** to the new system. Often, there is not enough "dead time" in the application to dump the data out of the old system and load it into the new on. Hence, cut over is a daunting problem in applications, such as airline reservations, where little or no downtime can be tolerated. Techniques must be developed to make this procedure much more seamless. The "holy of holy grails" would be to change the logical schema without taking the data base offline.

A second cutover issue is what to do if the new system fails. Although exhaustive testing is usually performed on the development system, there are cases where the new system fails when put into production. In this case, one can only restore the old system and go back to the drawing board. System availability, of course, suffers in this situation. Again more seamless cutover and cut back would be very helpful.

AutoAdmin "What-if" Index Analysis Utility

Surajit Chaudhuri
Microsoft Research
surajitc@microsoft.com

Vivek Narasayya
Microsoft Research
viveknar@microsoft.com

Abstract

As databases get widely deployed, it becomes increasingly important to reduce the overhead of database administration. An important aspect of data administration that critically influences performance is the ability to select indexes for a database. In order to decide the right indexes for a database, it is crucial for the database administrator (DBA) to be able to perform a *quantitative analysis* of the existing indexes. Furthermore, the DBA should have the ability to propose hypothetical ("what-if") indexes and quantitatively analyze their impact on performance of the system. Such impact analysis may consist of analyzing workloads over the database, estimating changes in the cost of a workload, and studying index usage while taking into account projected changes in the sizes of the database tables. In this paper we describe a novel index analysis utility that we have prototyped for Microsoft SQL Server 7.0. We describe the interfaces exposed by this utility that can be leveraged by a variety of front-end tools and sketch important aspects of the user interfaces enabled by the utility. We also discuss the implementation techniques for efficiently supporting "what-if" indexes. Our framework can be extended to incorporate analysis of other aspects of physical database design.

1. Introduction

Enterprise-class databases require database administrators who are responsible for performance tuning. Database Administrators (DBAs) need to take into account resources on the database system, application requirements, and characteristics of the workload and DBMS. With large-scale deployment of databases, minimizing database administration function becomes important. The AutoAdmin project at Microsoft Research [1] is investigating new techniques to make it easy to tune external and internal database system parameters to achieve competitive performance. One important area where tuning is required is in determining physical database design and specifically in the choice of indexes to build for a database.

The index selection problem has been studied since the early 70's and the importance of this problem is well recognized. Despite a long history of work in this area, there are two fundamental reasons why this problem has not been addressed. First, index selection is intrinsically a hard search problem. For an enterprise class database, there are a large number of possible single and multi-column indexes. Moreover, since modern query processors use indexes in several innovative ways (e.g., index intersection, indexed-only access), it is hard to enumerate the search space efficiently. Next, the problem of picking the right of set of indexes cannot be simply solved by a good search algorithm. Enterprise databases are simply too complex for the DBA to hit the "accept " button on the recommendations of an index selection tool until he/she has been able to perform an *impact analysis* of the suggested index recommendations. Some examples of impact analysis are: (1) Which queries and updates that we executed in the last 3 days will slow down because of the changes? (2) Which queries will benefit from the index that you are proposing to add and to what extent? To the best of our knowledge, no adequate utility exists that allows DBAs to undertake an impact analysis study. Indeed, even in the absence of an index selection tool, such an index analysis utility is of great importance since it allows the DBA to propose hypothetical ("what-if") indexes and quantitatively analyze their impact on performance of the system. In this paper we use the terms hypothetical and "what-if" interchangeably. Such a utility also provides a natural back-end for an index selection tool to enumerate and pick an appropriate set of indexes by using the index analysis utility as the "probe" to determine the goodness of the set of indexes. In the context of the AutoAdmin project, we have built an index selection tool as well as an index analysis utility. The index selection tool has been described in [4] and it leverages off the index analysis component. This paper focuses on the index analysis utility. We now provide an overview of the "what-if" index analysis utility and the system architecture for index selection in AutoAdmin.

SIGMOD '98 Seattle, WA, USA

1.1 Overview of Architecture

Figure 1 illustrates the related system components for the task of index selection. We use Microsoft SQL Server 7.0 as the database server. In this paper, we use the term *configuration* to mean a set of indexes, and the sizes of each table in the database. *A hypothetical configuration* may consist of existing ("real") indexes as well as hypothetical ("what-if") indexes. We define a *workload* to be a set of SQL statements. The hypothetical configuration analysis (HCA) engine supports two sets of interfaces for (a) simulating a hypothetical configuration (b) summary analysis on the data resulting from the simulation. The HCA engine can be implemented either as a library that client tools can link to, as a middle-ware process that serves multiple clients or directly as server extensions. In our prototype, we have implemented the HCA engine as a dynamic linked library (DLL).

Using the hypothetical configuration simulation interfaces, client tools can define workloads, define hypothetical configurations, and evaluate a workload for a hypothetical configuration. By evaluating a workload for a configuration, we can *estimate* the cost of queries in the workload *if* the configuration were made "real" (i.e. the indexes in the configuration were materialized). In addition, we can tell for each query, which indexes in the configuration would be used to answer that query. The dotted line in Figure 1 shows that the interfaces for hypothetical configuration simulation are available directly as SQL Server extensions. However, for software engineering reasons, the HCA engine encapsulates this functionality and provides the complete set of interfaces for index analysis to client tools. In this paper, we will discuss the HCA interfaces and discuss its implementation over a SQL Database, describing the necessary extensions to server interfaces.

The summary analysis interface makes it possible to perform sophisticated summarization of workloads, configurations, performance of the current configuration and projected changes for a new configuration. Examples of such analysis are: (a) Analyze a workload by counting each type of query – SELECT, INSERT, UPDATE, DELETE. (b) Estimate the storage space of a hypothetical configuration. (c) Identify queries in the workload that are most affected by the addition (or removal) of indexes.

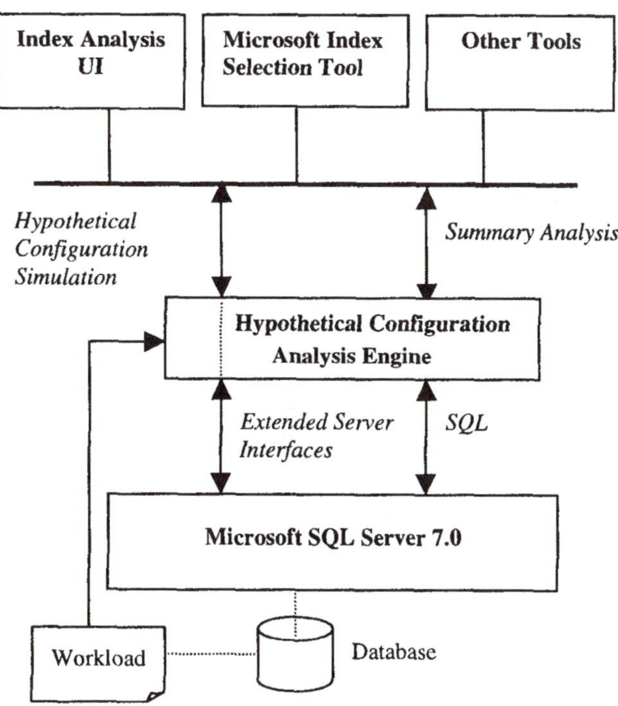

Figure 1. Architecture Overview

The rest of the paper is organized as follows. In Section 2, we review the related work in this area. Section 3 presents the interfaces for hypothetical configuration simulation, and describes their implementation on Microsoft SQL Server. Section 4 describes the summary analysis interfaces and their implementation, and provides an example "session" that illustrates how the synergy among different summary analysis components can assist the DBA in selecting the right indexes for a database. We discuss future work and conclude in Section 5.

2. Related Work

There is a substantial body of literature on physical database design dating back to the early 70's. Nonetheless, to the best of our knowledge, no previous work has addressed the problem of estimating the impact of possible changes to the index configurations and database size in a comprehensive manner. Stonebraker [12] discusses the use of views in simulating hypothetical databases. His approach creates a query to "simulate the hypothetical database" and therefore relies on actual execution. This is very computation intensive. Our approach is based on relative estimation of the cost that enables a large class of analysis at low cost. Furthermore, we have provided an efficient mechanism to implement hypothetical structures using sampling based techniques.

The index selection algorithms in [4,6] can exploit the infrastructure presented in this paper for exploring the space of alternatives to pick an optimal index configuration. Those papers focus on efficiently searching the space of alternatives. In addition to the above, there is a significant body of work in index selection, including [2,5,7,9,11]. Most of the other work in index selection has the serious shortcoming that the index selection tools do not stay in step with the optimizer (see [3] for a discussion). In any case, these papers do not discuss support for hypothetical configurations.

3. Simulating Hypothetical Configurations

In this section we present the interfaces for hypothetical configuration simulation and describe how these interfaces are implemented efficiently. We first present the foundational concepts supported by the HCA engine that set the context for the rest of the section.

(a) Workload. A workload consists of a set of SQL statements. Most modern databases support the ability to generate a representative workload for the system by logging activity on the server over a specified period of time. For example, in Microsoft SQL Server, the SQL Server Profiler provides this functionality.

(b) Hypothetical Configuration. A configuration consists of a set of indexes that are consistent with schema constraints. For example, if a table has a uniqueness constraint on a column C, then an index on C must be part of every configuration. Likewise, a table can have at most one clustering index. A configuration may also have a ***database scaling value*** associated with it. A database scaling value is a set of multipliers that captures the *size* of the database. A multiplier m_j is associated with each table T_j. A hypothetical configuration with a database scaling value represents a database where each table T_j in the database has m_j times the number of rows in the current database. Thus, the scaling factor can be used to represent not only a database that is significantly larger or smaller than the current database, but also a database where the relative sizes of the tables are different from

today's database. As a result, the HCA engine makes it possible able to project changes to the current database along two dimensions: changes in configuration as well as changes in database size.

(c) *Estimation of projected changes.* The *effect* of the projected changes to the current database is captured in two ways. First, the HCA engine supports the ability to estimate the *cost* of a query in the workload with respect to a hypothetical configuration. Second, the HCA engine can estimate the *index usage* since it can project which indexes in the hypothetical configuration would be used to answer a query in the workload.

3.1 Interfaces for Hypothetical Configuration Simulation

Our approach to designing the interfaces for hypothetical configuration simulation is influenced by the observation that simulating a hypothetical configuration consists of estimating (a) the *cost* of queries in the workload and (b) *usage* of indexes. In presenting these interfaces, we focus on their functionality, and not on syntax.

A) Define Workload < workload_name > [From <file> | As $(Q_1, f_1), (Q_2, f_2), \ldots (Q_n, f_n)]$
B) Define Configuration <configuration_name> As $(Table_1, column\_list_1), \ldots, (Table_i, column\_list_i)$
C) Set Database Size of <configuration_name> As $(Table_1, rowcount), \ldots, (Table_i, row\_count_i)$
D) Estimate Configuration of <workload_name> for <configuration_name>
E) Remove [Workload <workload_name>| Configuration <configuration_name> | Cost-Usage <workload_name>, <configuration_name>]

For each command (A)-(E), we now describe the semantics of the command, and the information generated when the command is executed . We refer to this information as *analysis data.* For simplicity, we present the analysis data as relations in non-first-normal form). In our implementation, we use multiple (normalized) tables to store analysis data.

The *Create Workload* command associates a name with a set of queries. These queries can be specified from a file or can be passed in directly through the command. The workload information generated as a result of executing the command is shown in Table 1. A *frequency* value f_i, which is associated with query Q_i in the workload. The frequency is interpreted by the HCA engine to mean that the workload consists of f_i copies of query Q_i. In addition, the HCA engine uses extended server interfaces that expose the parsed information of a query to associate a set of properties with a query. Some examples of query properties are: (a) The SQL Text (b) Set of tables referenced in the query (c) Columns in the query with conditions on them.

The *Define Configuration* command has the effect of registering a new configuration and associating a set of indexes with that configuration. The indexes may be existing ("real") indexes or hypothetical indexes. If the index exists, then the index name can optionally be substituted for (Table, column_list). The *Set Database Size* command sets the scaling values for each table in the database. Table 2 shows the information associated with a configuration by the HCA engine. The information associated with each index is shown in Table 3. Since indexes (real and hypothetical) are entities supported by the database, this information is available in the system catalogs. (In Section 3.2 we describe how a *hypothetical* index is created). We note that the syntax of the *Define Configuration* is general enough to include other features of physical database design (e.g. materialized views) in addition to indexes. However, the main challenge in adding new hypothetical features arises not from having to extend the syntax of *Define Configuration*, but because the creation and use of these hypothetical features must be supported efficiently.

Workload name	Query ID	Frequency	Query Properties
Wrkld_A	1	1	<SQL Text>, $\{T_1, T_2\}$, etc.

Table 1. Workload information

Configuration Name	Indexes in Configuration	Scaling values
Current_Conf	Ind_A, Ind_B, Ind_D	$(T_1, 1), (T_2, 5)$

Table 2. Configuration Information

Index Name	Table Name	Num Rows	Num. Pages	Cols.	Index Statistics
Ind_A	R	100,000	1865	R.a	<histogram>

Table 3. Index Information

Config name	Query ID	Cost	Indexes Used
New_Config	1	0.02	Ind_A, Ind_D
New_Config	2	0.11	Ind_B

Table 4. Information generated by *Estimate Configuration*

The result of executing *Estimate Configuration* for a given workload and configuration is a relation that has the format shown in Table 4. Conceptually, the relation has as many rows as there are queries in the workload. The unit of *Cost* is relative to the total cost of the workload in the current configuration. The attribute *Indexes-Used* for a query represents the indexes that are expected to be used by the server to answer the query if the hypothetical configuration existed.

The *Remove* command provides the ability to remove analysis data generated by commands (A)-(D). We observe that when *Remove Workload* (respectively *Configuration*) is invoked, all information about the Workload (Configuration) is removed, including any cost and usage information. However, when *Remove Cost-Usage* is invoked, only the cost-usage information for the specified workload and configuration is removed, but the workload and configuration information is retained.

Finally, we note that user interfaces in the AutoAdmin index analysis utility makes it easy to define a workload and configuration. In Microsoft SQL Server, a representative workload for the system can be generated by logging events at the server over a specified period of time using the SQL Server Profiler to a file. In addition, filters can be specified so that only relevant events are logged. Alternatively, a workload can be dynamically created from the Query Analyzer interface. In this approach, a highlighted buffer of queries is used to define a workload dynamically. While defining the configuration, the user-interface presents successive screens to set the indexes and the table sizes. In each of the screens, the user (typically the DBA) is presented with the list of objects for the current ("true") configuration and can create a new configuration by adding (or removing) indexes to the current configuration.

3.2 Implementing the Hypothetical Configuration Simulation Interface

The commands (A)-(C) are primarily definitional and do not pose implementation challenges. Likewise command (E) involves deleting rows from the analysis data tables corresponding to the workload, configuration or cost-usage specified in the command. Therefore, in this section we focus on the issue of efficiently implementing the core functionality of the hypothetical configuration simulation interface: the *Estimate Configuration* command.

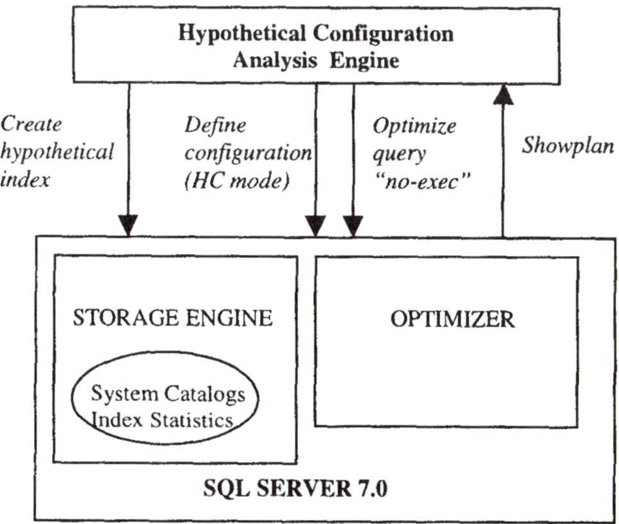

Figure 2. Interfaces between HCA Engine and SQL Server

The simplest option of simulating a hypothetical configuration by *physically* altering the current configuration is not viable since it incurs the serious overhead of dropping and creating indexes. Perhaps, even more seriously, such an approach is flawed since changing indexes affects operational queries and can seriously degrade the performance of the system. Likewise, updating the system tables with the database scaling value can lead to error in optimizer's estimates of operational queries. Therefore, we need an alternative where indexes in the hypothetical configuration do not need to be constructed and where changes in the database scaling value does not affect the system tables directly.

The solution to this problem relies on the observation that the *cost* metric of a query that we are interested in is the optimizer-estimated cost and *not* the actual execution cost. This metric is justified since the "consumer" of a configuration is the optimizer. In other words, unless the optimizer finds a hypothetical index useful, it is unlikely to make use of that index when it is made "real" (see [4] for additional justification). An optimizer's decision on whether or not use an index is solely based on the statistical information on the column(s) in the index. Such information consists of (a) a histogram on the column values on which the index is defined (b) density. Moreover, to gather these statistics it is not necessary to scan all rows in the table. These statistical measures can be efficiently gathered via sampling, without significantly compromising accuracy [3]. Once these statistics have been collected, it is possible for the optimizer to consider the hypothetical index for plan generation (although execution of that plan is not possible). We will discuss our approach to collecting the statistics in Section 3.2.1.

The steps in executing *Estimate Configuration* for a query are illustrated in Figure 2.

1. Create all needed hypothetical indexes in the configuration.
2. Request the optimizer to: (a) Restrict its choice of indexes to those in the given configuration. (b) Consider the table and index sizes in the database to be as adjusted by the scaling values.
3. Request the optimizer to produce the optimal execution plan for the query and gather the results: (a) the cost of the query (b) indexes (if any) used to answer the query.

These steps are repeated for each query in the workload. We now discuss implementation details of each of these steps (1) – (3) on SQL Server and provide an example that illustrates the operation of the hypothetical configuration simulation module.

Sample-table = Sample **m** pages
New-Sample = { }
While not (*convergence-of-measures*) **do**
Sample-Table = *Sample-Table* Union *New-Sample*
New-sample = Sample another m pages
Convergence-of-measures = check_for_convergence (*Sample-Table*, *New-Sample*)
End do

Figure 3. Adaptive page-level sampling algorithm for histogram construction.

3.2.1 Creation of Hypothetical Indexes

We extend the CREATE INDEX statement in SQL with the qualifier WITH STATISTICS_ONLY [= <fraction>]. It is optionally possible to specify the fraction of the table to be scanned when gathering sample data on columns of the index. If <fraction> is not specified, the system determines the appropriate fraction of rows to be scanned. For example:

CREATE INDEX supplier_stats on ON Orders (supplier) WITH STATISTICS_ONLY

This command creates a hypothetical index on the *supplier* column of the *Orders* table.

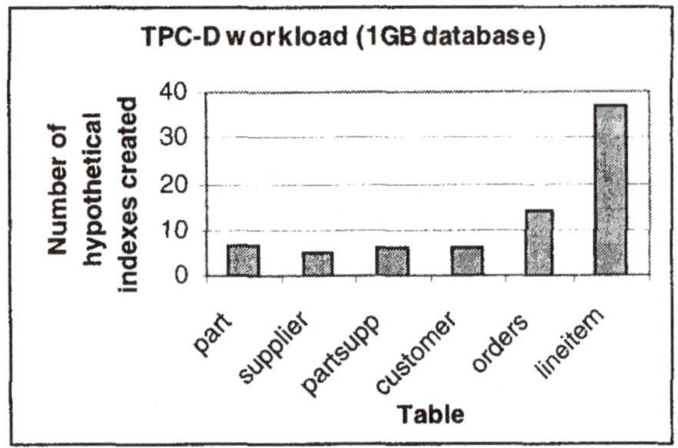

Figure 4. Number of hypothetical indexes for each table.

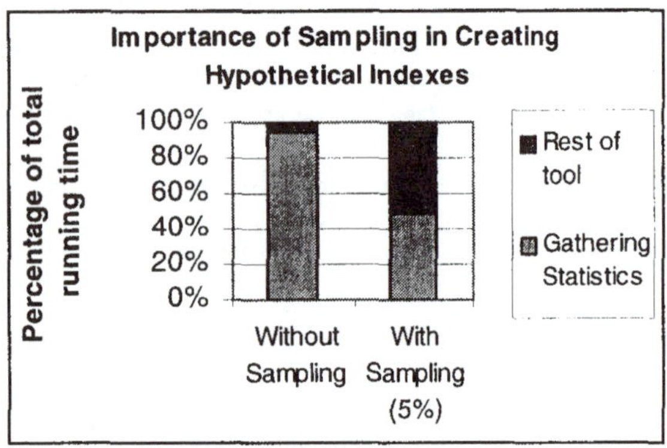

Figure 5. Fraction of running time spent creating hypothetical indexes by index selection tool.

We now describe the sampling strategy used for creating hypothetical indexes. We use an adaptive page-level sampling algorithm to efficiently gather statistical measures relevant to query optimization. The algorithm, shown in Figure 3, starts with a "seed" sample of **m** pages. In our current implementation we set $\mathbf{m} = \sqrt{\mathbf{n}}$ where **n** is the number of pages in the table. At any given time in the algorithm, the server maintains the sorted list of values in the *Sample-Table* and the set of statistical measures based on *Sample-Table*. In SQL Server, these statistical measures consist of (1) density of the data set and (2) Equi-Depth histograms (characterized by the step boundaries). The data in *New-Sample* is used for cross-validation purposes. In other words, it is checked if the values in *New-Sample* are divided approximately in equal numbers in each bin of the histogram (2). Our empirical results indicate that when the above test is true, the density measure also reaches convergence. If the test for the convergence fails, then the new sample is added to *Sample-Table*. This addition is done via a merge algorithm to build a new *Sample-Table* that is in sorted order. In the absence of convergence, the above step is repeated. The technical details of the algorithm and its behavior on varying data distributions are presented elsewhere [3].

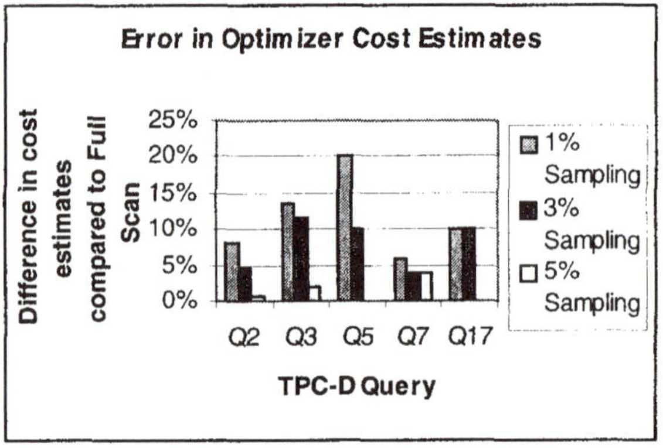

Figure 6. Effect of sampling on optimizer cost estimates.

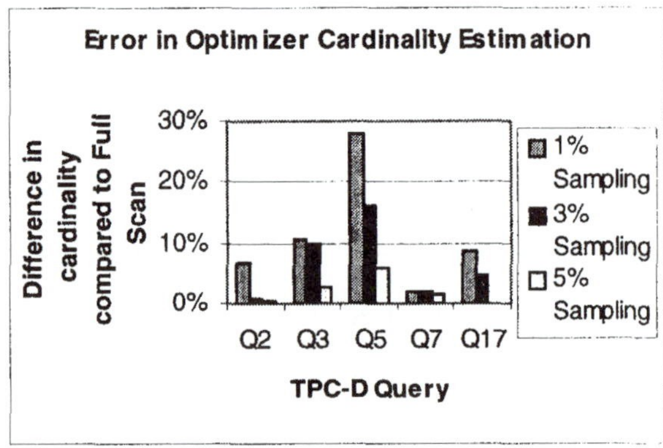

Figure 7. Effect of sampling on estimated number of rows.

As an example of the effectiveness of this server extension, we present the requests made by an index selection tool [4] to the HCA engine to create hypothetical indexes. Figure 4 shows the distribution of hypothetical indexes explored by the tool over tables of the TPC-D 1GB database. Figure 5 confirms our expectation that sampling can significantly reduce the cost of creating a hypothetical index. In fact, the total running time was reduced by a factor of 16. In both cases, the index selection tool recommended the *same* final set of indexes.

We now present an example to show that using sampling to create hypothetical indexes does not adversely affect the optimizer's estimates. We ran an index selection tool [4] on a workload consisting of the five most expensive queries on the TPC-D 1GB database. The adaptive sampling algorithm sampled about 5% of the data for hypothetical indexes on largest table (*lineitem*). We then ran the tool with fixed sampling rates of 1%, 3%, 5% and full table scan, and recorded the optimizer cost estimates and the estimated number of rows in each case. Figure 6 shows that the maximum error in cost estimation when using a 5% sample was only 4% when compared to a full table scan. Figure 7 shows that similar results hold for the maximum error in the estimated number of rows.

3.2.2 Defining a Hypothetical Configuration

A key issue in supporting hypothetical configurations and database scaling value is ensuring that operational queries can run concurrently on the real database while queries on a hypothetical configuration are being optimized. The optimizer obtains information on tables, indexes and their sizes from system catalogs. Therefore, a hypothetical configuration *cannot* be supported by updating system catalogs. Instead, the information for the hypothetical configuration must be conveyed to the optimizer in a connection-specific manner. This is achieved by augmenting the server with a connection-specific *HC mode* call using extensible interfaces in Microsoft SQL Server. The HC mode call takes as arguments: (1) Set of indexes corresponding to the hypothetical configuration to be used in generating a query plan. (2) The "base index" for each table in the configuration. The base index for a table is either the clustered index on the table or the heap structure for the table (if no clustered index is present). In SQL Server, the leaf node of a non-clustered B+-tree index contains the keys of the clustered index (if any) on that table. Since the plan chosen by the optimizer depends on the columns available in the index, it is necessary to indicate the base index to the optimizer. (3) Sizes of tables and indexes in the database. The HCA engine projects the size of each index in the configuration based on the database scaling value. In addition, it accounts for the fact that in SQL Server, the *size* of a non-clustered index depends on the clustered index (if any) on that table. For example, if there is a clustered index is on column A, and a non-clustered index is on column B, then the size of the index on B is proportional to the Width(column B) + Width(column A). Thus, if I_1 and I_2 are hypothetical clustered indexes, and I_3 is a non-clustered index, when simulating a hypothetical configuration $\{I_1, I_3\}$, the HCA engine computes a different value for the size of I_3 than when simulating the configuration $\{I_2, I_3\}$.

3.2.3 Obtaining Optimizer Estimates

Once the hypothetical configuration is defined via the HC mode, the task of obtaining the optimizer estimates uses the traditional SQL Server API to optimize queries in the "no-execution" mode. Such a mode is supported in Microsoft SQL Server and other database systems. The results of query optimization are obtained through the Showplan interface. In addition to providing the optimizer's cost estimate, Showplan also provides the execution plan for the query, including the indexes used to answer the query.

Example: Consider a database whose current configuration consists of a table T with indexes I_1 and I_2, where I_1 is the clustered index for T. The table T has 1 million rows. For a given workload W, we wish to simulate a hypothetical configuration $\{I_1, I_3\}$ when the table T has 10 million rows. To simulate the proposed configuration for W, the HCA engine would execute the following sequence of steps:

- Since the index on I_3 does not exist, the HCA engine first calls the CREATE INDEX command with the "WITH STATISTICS_ONLY" clause to create the hypothetical index I_3.
- The HCA engine computes the new sizes of the indexes I_1 and I_3, when the number of rows is scaled to 10,000,000 taking into account the fact that I_1 is the clustered index. Let these sizes be S_1 and S_3 respectively.
- HC-mode((I_1,I_3), (1,0), (S_1,S_3)) This first argument indicates that I_1 and I_3 are to be considered by the optimizer for plan generation. The second argument indicates that I_1 is the "base index" for table T in the proposed configuration. The third argument passes the sizes of each index in the configuration.
- The HCA engine then executes each query in the W in the "no-execute" mode and obtains the cost and index usage information via *Showplan*.

3.3 Maintaining Analysis Data Tables

In Section 3.1 we described the schema of each analysis data table and discussed how the data is generated. We now address the issue of maintaining the analysis data tables in the system. We observe that once the properties of entities supported by HCA engine (queries, indexes etc.) are determined, the schema of the analysis data tables can be assumed to be fixed. Therefore, the important issues are: (a) How are these tables named? (b) Where are they stored? We now propose two alternatives to this problem.

3.3.1 Analysis Data in System Catalogs

In this approach, each analysis data table is a system catalog. This solves the naming issue since system catalog names are fixed a-priori. When any of the server interfaces to simulate a hypothetical configuration is invoked, the server writes the resulting data to the appropriate system catalog. These tables can be accessed (a) directly by the user using SQL (b) via the summary analysis interfaces of the HCA engine.

3.3.2 Analysis Data in User Specified Tables

In this approach, the HCA engine writes the analysis data returned by the server into temporary tables that are connection specific. When an index analysis session with the HCA engine is complete, the user is provided the option of saving the analysis data generated during the session into user specified tables. This approach requires the hypothetical configuration simulation interfaces to be augmented with a *Save* command. Subsequently, the user can name the saved tables to the HCA engine and perform summary analysis on the data, or can directly post arbitrary SQL queries against these tables. In our current implementation, we have adopted this approach.

4. Summary Analysis

The ability to simulate hypothetical configurations provides the foundation for summary analysis. In this section, we show how the AutoAdmin index analysis utility builds on that infrastructure to provide sophisticated analyses of proposed changes. Figures 8 through 10 provide some examples of summary analysis that a database administrator finds useful. Figure 8 shows a breakdown of the workload by the type of queries. Figure 9 "drills-down" on the queries of type selection and provides a breakdown of selection conditions in queries by table. Such summary analysis provides the DBA with a better grasp of the workload that the system is facing. Figure 10 is an example where the DBA can view the relative frequencies of usage of indexes in the current configuration. The DBA may use this information to identify indexes that are rarely used and perhaps are good candidates for dropping. Indeed, one can think of many useful ways to analyze the information gathered during hypothetical configuration simulation (Tables 1-4 in Section 3.1). (We refer to this information as analysis data).

One option for producing summary statistics on analysis data is to allow the DBA as well as other tools to directly use the SQL interface to query the information collected during the process of hypothetical configuration simulation. Unfortunately, the approach of generating SQL queries is a relatively low-level interface for performing summary analysis, since it shifts the burden of analysis to the consumer of the information. The other option is to provide a set of "canned" queries that support a set of predetermined summary analyses. However useful, the canned queries do not provide an extensible framework for generating new summary statistics from the available analysis data. What is needed is an interface that retains the flexibility of formulating ad-hoc requests for summary analysis, but without the overhead of manually generating complex SQL queries over the analysis data. In the next section, we describe a query-like interface that the HCA engine supports to fulfil this need. The interface that we describe was used in AutoAdmin for a principled design of a powerful user interface that can invoke the HCA summary analysis interfaces in a rich way.

We begin in Section 4.1 with a description of a generic summary analysis interface that captures the structure of questions that can be posed against the analysis data. In Section 4.2, we present the summary analysis interfaces and describe the properties of query, index and cost-usage analysis objects that are used to formulate queries. Section 4.3 provides examples of interesting queries that can be posed using the analysis interfaces, and gives a flavor of user interfaces. We discuss the implementation of the summary analysis interface in Section 4.4. In Section 4.5 we present a sample session that a database administrator might have with the index analysis utility.

4.1 Conceptual Model for Summary Analysis

Our model for summary analysis recognizes that the three foundational objects for analysis are:

- *Workload Analysis,* which consists of *queries* and their structural properties
- *Configuration Analysis*, which consists of *indexes* and their structural properties
- *Cost and Index Usage Analysis*, which represent relationship properties between a query and a configuration

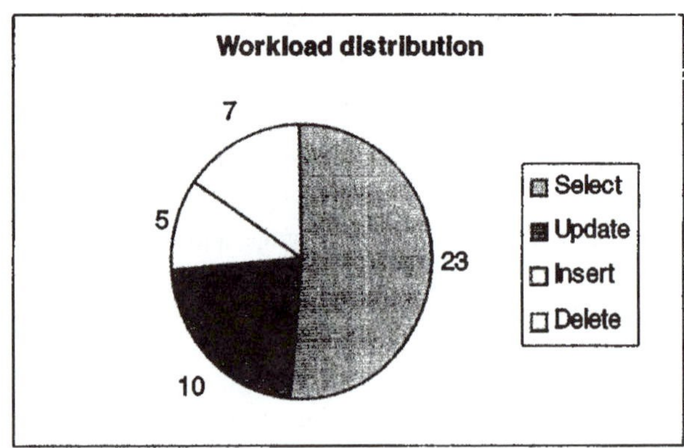

Figure 8. Distribution of workload by SQL Type.

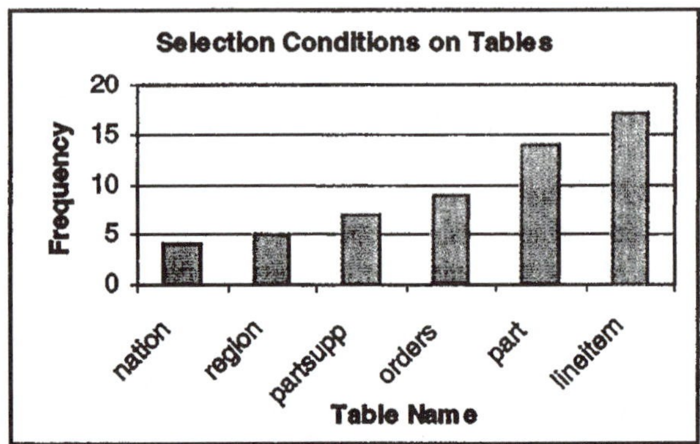

Figure 9. Distribution of conditions over tables.

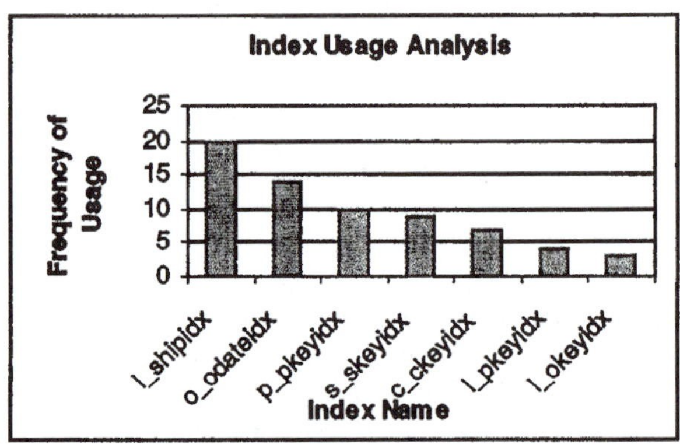

Figure 10. Analyzing the frequency of index usage for a given configuration and workload.

While the specific summary questions that are of interest relate to one of the above three objects, the HCA summary analysis interface provides a generic querying model. Such a generic analysis interface has the advantage that as we extend the framework into more complex physical database design, it exploits the common thread that runs through each kind of analysis.

4.1.1 Objects and Properties

Any summary analysis is over a *set of objects*. For example, for workload analysis, it is a set of queries. In configuration analysis, the objects in question are indexes. For cost and index-usage analysis, the objects are relationship objects that capture the interaction between a specific configuration and queries in a workload. In each case, the set of objects for summary analysis can be implicitly identified. For workload analysis, the workload name uniquely identifies the queries in the workload. Likewise the configuration name identifies the indexes in the hypothetical configuration being analyzed. For Cost and Index Usage Analysis, the combination of the workload name and configuration name uniquely identifies the set of objects to be analyzed.

Each object has *properties* associated with it. These properties can be classified as follows: (a) *Properties with an atomic value*, e.g. the number of tables in a query. A special case of atomic value is Boolean (e.g., whether or not an index is clustered). (b) *Properties with a list (or set) value*, e.g. the *list* of columns in an index or the *set* of tables referenced in a query. For each of the three types of objects we now list the properties of that object that are gathered by the HCA engine in AutoAdmin.

4.1.1.1 Properties of Queries

For workload analysis, the object in consideration is a query. Below, we list properties that are currently parsed by the HCA engine for a query. The properties with *atomic value* are query type (Insert/Delete/Update/Select), whether the query has a Group By clause (Boolean), whether the query has an Order By clause (Boolean), whether the query has nested subqueries (Boolean). The *properties with list values* are tables referenced in query, required columns from each table, columns on which selection conditions exist, columns on which join conditions exist, Equi-join conditions. We note that above list of properties can be easily extended by collecting additional interesting parsed query information.

Example: Consider the query:
SELECT R.a, S.c FROM R, S WHERE R.a = S.c AND R.b = v_1
The properties are: (1) SQL Type: Select. (2) The required tables are {R, S}. (3) The required columns are: {R.a, R.b, S.c} (4) Columns on which selection conditions exist: {R.b} (5) Equi-join conditions: {(R.a = S.c)}

4.1.1.2 Properties of Indexes

For configuration analysis, the objects of interest are indexes. The properties of indexes with *atomic value* are table on which index is built, width of index (number of columns), storage space, time of creation, whether or not the index is clustered (Boolean). The property with list values is the list of columns in the index (in major to minor order).

Example: Consider a clustered index I_1 on columns (C_1, C_2) of table T. The properties of I_1 are (1) Table = T (2) Width = 2 (3) Clustered = True (4) list of columns = $\{C_1, C_2\}$. The storage space and time of creation properties would also be filled appropriately.

4.1.1.3 Properties of Relationship Object of Query and Configuration

For the relationship object of a query and a configuration, the property with *atomic value* is cost of the query for the configuration. The property with *list value* is the list of indexes in the configuration used to answer the query. We note that the properties of the relationship object between a query and a configuration can be augmented with other information about the query execution plan (e.g. operators used in the plan).

4.1.2 Measures and Aggregate Measures

Objects and properties form the fundamental primitives for summary analysis. However, derived measures are useful for posing queries against analysis data. With each property of an object, we can derive one or more numerical *measures*. For an atomic property this measure could be the value of the property itself (e.g. storage for an index) or a user defined function of the value. For a list or set property, the measure may be the *count* of the number of elements in the list or set, e.g., the number of tables referenced in a query. A measure for a list/set property may be derived also by applying one of the *aggregate functions* (e.g., SUM, AVERAGE) on the values in the list/set. For example, the aggregate functions may be used on measures to obtain a derived measure for a set of objects. Thus the specification of a numerical measure consists of (a) a property name (b) an expression that derives a numerical measure from the property value. For list/set valued property p, the aggregate measure is f (p), where f is an aggregation function. In our current implementation, f can be *Count, Min, Max, Sum, Average.*

We lift the notion of a numerical measure to a list/set of objects to derive an *aggregate measure* in the obvious way. Given a measure **m** for each object, we derive a corresponding measure f(**m**) over a set of objects by applying an aggregate function f. For example, given a workload (a set of queries), we can compute the average number of tables referenced per query in the workload.

4.2 Summary Analysis Interfaces

Although simple, the abstractions of objects, properties and measures provide an approach to the problem of defining a convenient and yet powerful query-like interface for summary analysis. The generic analysis interface that we present in this section is geared towards supporting the following paradigm of analyzing information from hypothetical configuration simulation:

1. Determine a **class of analysis** (workload analysis, configuration analysis, cost/index usage analysis)
2. Specify necessary information to uniquely **identify** the set of **objects** of analysis. E.g., specify workload name to identify associated queries.
3. **Filter** a subset of objects (based on their properties) to focus on objects of interest, e.g., consider queries that reference a table "Orders". There may be successive filtering operation, supported through "drill-down" using user interfaces, e.g., consider queries that reference the column "Supplier" in "Orders".

4. **Partition** the filtered objects in a set of classes by a measure. For example, the queries that survive the filter in (3), maybe partitioned by their query type (Insert/Delete/Update/Select). The partitions need not be disjoint.
5. **Rank or Summarize** the objects. Ranking is achieved by associating a measure with each object (e.g. for a query, the number of tables referenced in the query) and using the measure to order the objects. Thus the interface supports picking the top **k** objects ranked by the measure. The interface also supports summarizing the objects based on an aggregate measure (e.g., average number of tables referenced in queries). If no partitioning is mentioned, then the ranking and summarization is done for all objects that qualify the filter. Otherwise, it is done for each partition but all partitions share the same ranking/summarization criteria.

The Filter and Partition steps described above are optional. Thus the simplest form of analysis is to rank objects by a given measure or summarize all objects through an aggregation function. We now present the "query-like" summary analysis interface and explain the syntax and semantics of this interface using a series of examples to highlight each aspect. As with the interfaces for hypothetical configuration simulation, our focus is on the functionality enabled by this interface rather than the syntax.

ANALYZE[WORKLOAD|CONFIGURATION|COST-USAGE]
WITH *<parameter-list>*
[TOP *<number>|* ***SUMMARIZE USING*** *<aggregation-function>]* ***BY*** *<measure>*
WHERE *<filter-expression >*
{PARTITION BY *<partition-parameter>* ***IN*** *<number>* ***STEPS}***

4.3.1 Format of Output

The format of the results produced depends on whether ranking or summarize output is desired. If the query uses SUMMARIZE, then the output consists of one row for each partition. Each row has two columns, one has the value of the partitioning parameter and the other has the summarized value for that partition. For example, **Q1** counts the number of queries in the workload of each type (Select/Update/Insert/Delete).

Q1: ANALYZE WORKLOAD WITH Workload_A
SUMMARIZE USING Count
PARTITION BY Query_Type

If the partitioning clause is omitted, then the output is a scalar, representing the summarized value for all objects selected. For example, **Q2** counts the total number of indexes in a configuration.

Q2: ANALYZE CONFIGURATION WITH *Current_Config*
SUMMARIZE USING *Count*

When the ranking option is used (i.e., TOP is used), the output format has three columns: the first column has the partitioning attribute, the second column has the object itself (e.g., the query string), and the third column specifies the rank of the object within the partition. If no partitioning clause is present, then there will be altogether <number> of 3-column tuples. For example, **Q3** returns the 20 most expensive queries in Wkld_B for the current configuration. Each tuple in the output for **Q3** is of the form (Workload-name, Query, Rank).

Q3: ANALYZE COST_USAGE WITH *Wkld_B, Current_Config*
TOP 20 BY *Cost*

4.3.2 Measures

As described earlier, measures can be useful for posing interesting queries on the analysis data. Measures can be specified in the BY *<measure>* clause and the PARTITION BY *<partition-parameter>* clause. A measure has one of the following two forms: (a) an atomic property of an object. For example **Q4** returns the top 3 indexes in *New_Config* ranked by storage. (b) *<aggregation-function>(<list/set property>)*. **Q5** counts the number of queries in *Wrkld_A* where a given number of tables are referenced. In our current implementation, we support Count, Max, Min, Sum, and Average for *<aggregation-function>*. We note that when *Count* is used in the SUMMARIZE USING clause, the *<measure>* specification is not required (e.g. **Q1, Q2, Q5**).

Q4: ANALYZE CONFIGURATION *New_Config*
TOP 3 BY *Storage*

Q5: ANALYZE WORKLOAD WITH *Wkld_A*
SUMMARIZE USING *Count*
PARTITION BY *Count (Tables)*

4.3.3 Filter Expressions

The syntax of *<filter-expression>* is a Boolean expression where base predicates are composed using Boolean connectors. For atomic properties, the base predicates have the form: *<property> <operator> <value>*. The operator can be any comparison operator, e.g., *storage > 50.* However, for Boolean properties only equality check is legal. For example, **Q6** counts the number of two-column, non-clustered indexes in *Current_Config.*

Q6: ANALYZE CONFIGURATION WITH Current_Config
SUMMARIZE USING *Count*
WHERE (*Num-Columns* = 2) AND (*Is-Clustered* = FALSE)

For set-valued properties base predicates have one of the following three forms:

- *<set property > [SUBSET-OF| SUPERSET-OF |=] <set>.* For example, **Q7** returns the 10 most expensive queries in Wkld_A for the current configuration such that the query references at least the tables *part* and *supplier.*
- *f (<set property>) <operator> <value>*, where f is an aggregation function and <operator> is any comparison operator, e.g., the following filter is satisfied for queries that reference at least two tables: *Count(Tables) > 1.*

- For list valued properties, all base predicates as for set valued predicates apply by interpreting the list as the corresponding set. However, in addition, the following predicate based on prefix matching is allowed: *<list property> [SUBLIST-OF| SUPERLIST-OF|=] <list* >. For example, **Q8** counts the number of indexes in Config_A that have part.size as their leading column. Here, *Columns* is the list property of an index that contains the columns in the index.

Q7: ANALYZE COST_USAGE WITH *Wkld_A, Current_Config*
TOP 10 BY *Cost*
WHERE *Tables* SUPERSET-OF {part, supplier}

Q8: ANALYZE CONFIGURATION WITH *Wrkld_A, Config_A*
SUMMARIZE USING *Count*
WHERE *Columns* SUPERLIST-OF *(part.size)*

4.3.4 Partitioning the Results

The objects being analyzed may be partitioned either by a property (need not be numeric, e.g. **Q1**) or by a numeric measure (e.g. **Q5**). An important special case is when *<partition-parameter>* is the name of a list or a set valued property. In such a case, there is a separate partition for each distinct value of the list or set. A set valued object S belongs to the partition for d if and only d is a member of the set S. For example, in **Q9**, a query belongs to the partition of each table that is referenced in that query. **Q9** computes the average number of indexes used for queries on each table (but eliminating join queries). Finally, when the partitioning domain is numeric, the number of steps allows partitions to be coalesced into fewer steps.

Q9: ANALYZE COST_USAGE WITH *Workload-A, Current*
SUMMARIZE USING *Average* BY *Count (Indexes-Used)*
WHERE *Count (Join-Columns)* = 0
PARTITION BY *Tables*

4.3.5 Specifying Objects for Analysis

In each of the examples **Q1-Q9**, depending on the class of analysis, the *<parameter-list>* can contain a (a) workload name (b) configuration name or (c) workload name and configuration name. In general, it is possible to specify multiple workloads and configurations in the *<parameter-list>*, making it possible to *compare* workloads or configurations. We do not discuss details of possible formats of *<parameter-list>* due to lack of space. However, to illustrate the idea, we present **Q10**, which compares the cost of two configurations for queries that reference table Orders.

Q10: ANALYZE COST-USAGE WITH *Workload-A, (Current_Config, Proposed_Config)*
SUMMARIZE USING *Sum* BY *cost*
WHERE *Tables* SUPERSET-OF *Order*

4.3 Examples of Summary Analysis and User Interfaces

The summary analysis interface is expressive and can be used to perform a rich set of analyses. We now provide examples of each *class* of summary analysis and the user interfaces that make it easy for a database administrator to visualize the results of summary analysis. All examples presented below can be expressed using the summary analysis interface.

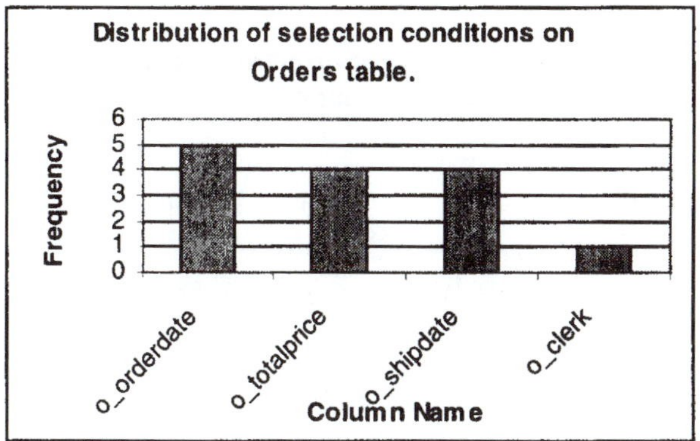

Figure 11. Distribution of selection conditions on a given table.

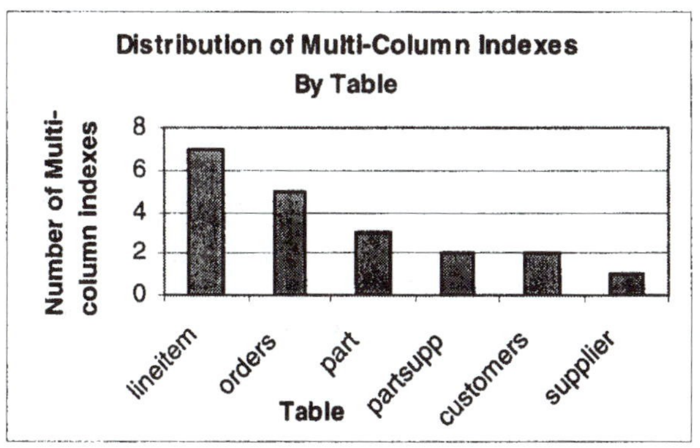

Figure 12. Analyzing distribution of multi-column indexes over tables.

4.3.1 Workload Analysis

(1) An example of application of partitioning is to count the number of queries by SQL Type (see Figure 8).
(2) List the top 5 tables on which most queries are posted.
(3) Comparing summary statistics from two workloads.
(4) Drilling-down at a table level to find which columns of the table that have most conditions posted on them (see Figure 11).

4.3.2 Configuration Analysis

(1) An example of application of partitioning is to count the number of indexes for each table.
(2) List the top 6 tables ranked by the count of the multi-column indexes on those tables. (See Figure 12)

4.3.3 Cost-Usage Analysis

(1) Analyzing the frequency of usage of each index in the configuration for the workload (Figure 10).

(2) Analyzing the cost of each query in the workload for the proposed configurations (relative to the current configuration). (Figure 13).

(3) Comparing the cost of two configurations for a given workload by SQL Type. (Figure 14).

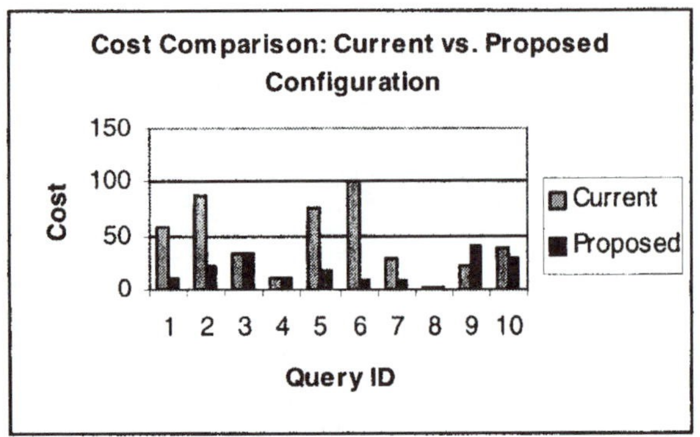

Figure 13. Comparing cost of the 10 most expensive queries for two configurations.

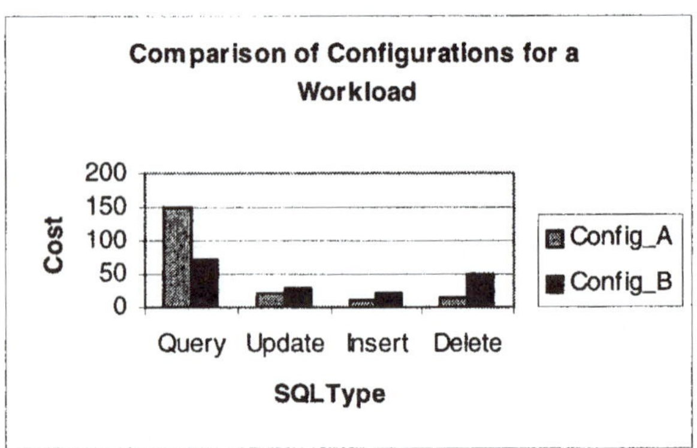

Figure 14. Comparing cost of workload for two configurations by SQL Type of query.

4.4 Implementation of Summary Analysis Interfaces

In this section, we briefly describe the issues involved in implementing the summary analysis interface. As described in Section 3.3, the data generated during hypothetical configuration simulation are stored in tables at the server. When a query is posed using the summary analysis interface, the HCA engine maps the query into an equivalent SQL query over the analysis data tables. In addition, the HCA engine may further process the results of the SQL query before completing the analysis (e.g. bucketizing results). The fact that the summary analysis interface resembles SQL makes it easier for the HCA engine to map the input into a SQL query. In addition, the implementation of the summary analysis engine also exploits the ability to compose operations using table expressions in the FROM clause of a SQL query.

The kind of analysis (Workload, Configuration, or Cost-Usage) specified in the summary analysis query determines the superset of analysis data tables that need to be joined to answer the query. For example, for Workload analysis, we only need to access the workload information tables (see Table 1). The HCA engine then generates a table expression (T_1) that joins the required analysis data tables, only retrieving objects that are specified in the *<parameter-list>*. In addition, the *<filter-expression>* (if any) specified in the query is included in T_1. The HCA engine then generates a table expression T_2 that partitions T_1 using the *<partition-parameter>* (if any), using the GROUP BY construct, and the *<aggregation-function>* is applied to the attribute specified by *<measure>*. If instead, the query requests the TOP *<number>* of rows BY *<measure>*, then T_2 is generated by applying an ORDER BY clause on the *<measure>* attribute of T_1. A cursor is opened for T_2 to return the first *<number>* rows.

4.5 Example of a Session

In this section we provide an example of a typical session by a DBA using the impact analysis utility.

4.5.1. Analyzing the workload

As mentioned earlier, in AutoAdmin, evaluation of the current or a proposed design is always done with respect to a workload. Therefore, DBA begins by specifying a workload for the session. This may be a log of queries that have run against the system over the past week. The DBA tries to understand the workload mix and asks for a breakdown of the queries by SQL Type. The result of this analysis looks like Figure 8. The DBA may then decide to focus on the most expensive queries in the workload for the existing configuration, by requesting the top 25 queries ordered by cost. To decide which tables are good candidates for indexing, the DBA may wish to see the distribution of conditions in queries on tables (Figure 9). Having picked a table that has many conditions on it, the DBA may decide to further "drill-down" and look at the distribution of conditions in queries over columns of that table (Figure 11). This gives a good idea of which columns on the table are likely candidates for indexes. The DBA finds that columns A and B of table T_2 look promising.

4.5.2 Analyzing the current configuration

The DBA may then wish to see if indexes on A and B of table T_2 already exist in the current configuration. He does this by requesting to see all indexes on T_2 in the current configuration ordered by their storage requirement. In this case, there is an index on A, but no index on B. So the DBA decides to explore hypothetical configuration scenarios that include an index on B.

4.5.3 Exploring "what-if" scenarios

The DBA then decides to explore two "what-if" scenarios and evaluate each relative to the current configuration. He first proposes a hypothetical configuration consisting of the current configuration with an additional non-clustered single-column index on column B of T_2. For this configuration he compares the cost of the workload with the cost of the workload in the current configuration. Adding a single-column index on B produces a 5% improvement in total cost of the workload (Figure 13). By studying index usage in the proposed configuration (Figure 10), the DBA sees that the new index was used in three queries. Not being impressed with the improvement in performance, the DBA decides to explore a different hypothetical configuration. This time he proposes a two-column index (B, A) on table T_2 in addition to the current configuration. Once again, the DBA compares the cost of this configuration with the current configuration and sees an 18% improvement for the workload. He then looks at the top five queries in the workload that are affected by adding the index and notices that two of the most expensive queries under the current configuration were positively affected and that there were no queries that were negatively affected. He then decides to build the two-column index (B,A) and schedules the index to be built at midnight.

5. Conclusion

In this paper we have shown how an index analysis utility can help the DBA of an enterprise-class database to select indexes for the database. We have presented the interfaces supported by a hypothetical configuration analysis engine and shown how this functionality can be used to conduct interesting and powerful analysis studies. We have described the implementation of the hypothetical configuration analysis engine for Microsoft SQL Server 7.0, including the necessary server extensions. In the future, we will extend our current framework to incorporate other aspects of physical database design.

6. Acknowledgments

We would like to acknowledge Nigel Ellis from the SQL Server relational engine group for helping incorporate our extensions into the server.

7. References

[1] AutoAdmin Project, Database Group, Microsoft Research, http://www.research.microsoft.com/db.

[2] Choenni S., Blanken H. M., Chang T., "Index Selection in Relational Databases", Proceedings of 5th IEEE ICCI 1993.

[3] Chaudhuri, S., Motwani, R., Narasayya, V., "Random Sampling for Histogram Construction: How Much Is Enough?". Proceedings of ACM SIGMOD '98.

[4] Chaudhuri, S., Narasayya, V., "An Efficient, Cost-Driven Index Selection Tool for Microsoft SQL Server. ". Proceedings of the 23rd VLDB Conference, Greece, 1997.

[5] Frank M., Omiecinski E., Navathe S., "Adaptive and Automative Index Selection in RDBMS", Proceedings of EDBT 92.

[6] Finkelstein S, Schkolnick M, Tiberio P."Physical Database Design for Relational Databases", ACM TODS, Mar 1988.

[7] Gupta H., Harinarayan V., Rajaramana A., Ullman J.D., "Index Selection for OLAP", Proceedings of ICDE97.

[8] Harinarayan V., Rajaramana A., Ullman J.D., "Implementing Data Cubes Efficiently", Proceedings of ACM SIGMOD 96.

[9] Labio W.J., Quass D., Adelberg B., "Physical Database Design for Data Warehouses", Proceedings of ICDE97.

[10] Olken F., "Random Sampling in Databases", Technical Report, 1993.

[11] Rozen S., Shasha D. "A Framework for Automating Physical Database Design", Proceedings of VLDB 1991.

[12] Stonebraker M., Hypothetical Data Bases as Views. Proceedings of ACM SIGMOD 1981.

Applying Model Management to Classical Meta Data Problems

Philip A. Bernstein

Microsoft Research
One Microsoft Way
Redmond, WA 98052-6399
philbe@microsoft.com

Abstract

Model management is a new approach to meta data management that offers a higher level programming interface than current techniques. The main abstractions are models (e.g., schemas, interface definitions) and mappings between models. It treats these abstractions as bulk objects and offers such operators as Match, Merge, Diff, Compose, Apply, and ModelGen. This paper extends earlier treatments of these operators and applies them to three classical meta data management problems: schema integration, schema evolution, and round-trip engineering.

1 Introduction

Many information system problems involve the design, integration, and maintenance of complex application artifacts, such as application programs, databases, web sites, workflow scripts, formatted messages, and user interfaces. Engineers who perform this work use tools to manipulate formal descriptions, or *models*, of these artifacts, such as object diagrams, interface definitions, database schemas, web site layouts, control flow diagrams, XML schemas, and form definitions. This manipulation usually involves designing transformations between models, which in turn requires an explicit representation of *mappings*, which describe how two models are related to each other. Some examples are:

- mapping between class definitions and relational schemas to generate object wrappers,
- mapping between XML schemas to drive message translation,
- mapping between data sources and a mediated schema to drive heterogeneous data integration,
- mapping between a database schema and its next release to guide data migration or view evolution,
- mapping between an entity-relationship (ER) model and a SQL schema to navigate between a database design and its implementation,
- mapping source makefiles into target makefiles, to drive the transformation of make scripts from one programming environment to another, and
- mapping interfaces of real-time devices to the interfaces required by a system management environment to enable it to communicate with the device.

Following conventional usage, we classify these as *meta data management* applications, because they mostly involve manipulating descriptions of data, rather than the data itself.

Today's approach to implementing such applications is to translate the given models into an object-oriented representation and manipulate the models and mappings in that representation. The manipulation includes designing mappings between the models, generating a model from another model along with a mapping between them, modifying a model or mapping, interpreting a mapping, and generating code from a mapping. Database query languages offer little help for this kind of manipulation. Therefore, most of it is programmed using object-at-a-time primitives.

We have proposed to avoid this object-at-a-time programming by treating models and mappings as abstractions that can be manipulated by model-at-a-time and mapping-at-a-time operators [6]. We believe that an implementation of these abstractions and operators, called a *model management system*, could offer an order-of-magnitude improvement in programmer productivity for meta data applications.

The approach is meant to be *generic* in the sense that a single implementation is applicable to all of the data models in the above examples. This is possible because the same modeling concepts are used in virtually all modeling environments, such as UML, extended ER (EER), and XML Schema. Thus, an implementation that uses a representation of models that includes most of those concepts would be applicable to all such environments.

There are many published approaches to the list of meta data problems above and others like them. We borrow from these approaches by abstracting their algorithms into a small set of operators and generalizing them across applications and, to some extent, across data models. We

Proceedings of the 2003 CIDR Conference

thereby hope to offer a more powerful database platform for such applications than is available today.

In a model management system, models and mappings are syntactic structures. They are expressed in a type system, but do not have additional semantics based on a constraint language or query language. Despite this limited expressiveness, model management operators are powerful enough to avoid most object-at-a-time programming in meta data applications. And it is precisely this limited expressiveness that makes the semantics and implementation of the operators tractable.

Still, for a complete solution, meta data problems often require some semantic processing, typically the manipulation of formulas in a mathematical system, such as logic or state machines. To cope with this, model management offers an extension mechanism to exploit the power of an inferencing engine for any such mathematical system.

Before diving into details, we offer a short preview to see what model management consists of and how it can yield programmer productivity improvements. First, we summarize the main model management operators:

- Match – takes two models as input and returns a mapping between them
- Compose – takes a mapping between models A and B and a mapping between models B and C, and returns a mapping between A and C
- Diff – takes a model A and mapping between A and some model B, and returns the sub-model of A that does not participate in the mapping
- ModelGen – takes a model A, and returns a new model B based on A (typically in a different data model than A's) and a mapping between A and B
- Merge – takes two models A and B and a mapping between them, and returns the union C of A and B along with mappings between C and A, and C and B.

Second, to see how the operators might be used, consider the following example [7]: Suppose we are given a mapping map_1 from a data source S_1 to a data warehouse S_W, and want to map a second source S_2 to S_W, where S_2 is similar to S_1. See Figure 1. (We use S_1, S_W, and S_2 to name both the schemas and databases.) First we call Match(S_1, S_2) to obtain a mapping map_2 between S_1 and S_2, which shows where S_2 is the same as S_1. Second, we call Compose(map_1, map_2) to obtain a mapping map_3 between S_2 and S_W, which maps to S_W those objects of S_2 that correspond to objects of S_1. To map the other objects of S_2 to S_W, we call Diff(S_2, map_3) to find the sub-model S_3 of S_2 that is not mapped by map_3 to S_W, and map_4 to identify corresponding objects of S_2 and S_3. We can then call other operators to generate a warehouse schema for S_3 and merge it into S_W. The latter details are omitted, but we will see similar operator sequences later in the paper.

The main purpose of this paper is to define the semantics of the operators in enough detail to make the above sketchy example concrete, and to present additional examples to demonstrate that model management is a credible approach to solving problems of this type. Although this paper is not the first overview of model management, it is the most complete proposal to date. Past papers presented a short vision [5,6], an example of applying model management to a data warehouse loading scenario [7], an application of Merge to mediated schemas [22], and an initial mathematical semantics for model management [1]. We also studied the match operator [23], which has developed into a separate research area. This paper offers the following new contributions to the overall program:

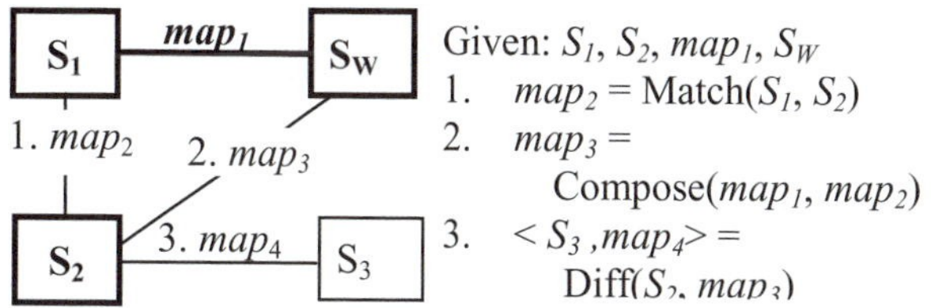
S1
map1
SW
1. map2
2. map3
S2
3. map4
S3
Given: S_1, S_2, map_1, S_W
1. map_2 = Match(S_1, S_2)
2. map_3 = Compose(map_1, map_2)
3. < S_3 ,map_4> = Diff(S_2, map_3)

Figure 1 Using model management to help generate a data warehouse loading script

- The first full description of all of the model management operators.
- New details about two of the operators, Diff and Compose, and a new proposed operator, ModelGen.
- Applications of model management to three well known meta data problems: schema integration, schema evolution, and round-trip engineering.

We regard the latter as particularly important, since they offer the first detailed demonstration that model management can help solve a wide range of meta data problems.

The paper is organized as follows: Section 2 describes the two main structures of model management, models and mappings. Section 3 describes the operators on models and mappings. Section 4 presents walkthroughs of solutions to schema integration, schema evolution, and round-trip engineering. Section 5 gives a few thoughts about implementing model management. Section 6 discusses related work. Section 7 is the conclusion.

2 Models and Mappings

2.1 Models

For the purposes of this paper, the exact choice of model representation is not important. However, there are several technical requirements on the representation of models, which the definitions of mappings and model management operators depend on.

First, a model must contain a set of objects, each of which has an identity. A model needs to be a set so that its content is well-defined (i.e., some objects are in the set while others are not). By requiring that objects have identity, we can define a mapping between models in terms of mappings between objects or combinations of objects.

Second, we want the expressiveness of the representation of models to be comparable to that of EER models. That is, objects can have attributes (i.e., properties), and can be related by is-a (i.e., generalization) relationships, has-a (i.e., aggregation or part-of) relationships, and associations (i.e., relationships with no special semantics). As well, there may be some built-in types of constraints, such as the min and max cardinality of set-valued properties.

Third, since a model is an object structure, it needs to support the usual object-at-a-time operations to create or delete an object, read or write a property, and add or remove a relationship.

Fourth, we expect objects, properties and relationships to have types. Thus, there are (at least) three meta-levels in the picture. Using conventional meta data terminology, we have: instances, which are models; a meta-model that consists of the type definitions for the objects of models; and the meta-meta-model, which is the representation language in which models and meta-models are expressed. We avoid using the term "data model," because it is ambiguous in the meta data world. In some contexts, it means the meta-meta-model, e.g., in a relational database system, the relational data model is the meta-meta-model. In other contexts, it means the meta-model; for example, in a model management system, a relational schema (such as the personnel schema) is a model, which is an instance of the relational meta-model (which says that a relational schema consists of table definitions, columns definitions, etc.), where both the model and meta-model are represented in the meta-meta-model (such as an EER model).

Since a goal of model management is to be as generic as possible, a rich representation is desirable so that when a model is imported from another data model, little or no semantics is lost. However, to ensure model management operators are implementable, some compromises are inevitable between expressiveness and tractability.

To simplify the discussion in this paper, we define a *model* to be a set objects, each of which has properties, has-a relationships, and associations. We assume that a model is identified by its root object and includes exactly the set of objects reachable from the root by paths of has-a relationships. In an implementation, we would expect a richer model comparable to EER models.

2.2 Mappings

Given two models M_1 and M_2, a *morphism* over M_1 and M_2 is a binary relation over the objects of the two models. That is, it is a set of pairs $<o_1, o_2>$ where o_1 and o_2 are in M_1 and M_2 respectively. A *mapping* between models M_1 and M_2 is a model, map_{12}, and two morphisms, one between map_{12} and M_1 and another between map_{12} and M_2. Thus, each object m in mapping map_{12} can relate a set of objects in M_1 to a set of objects in M_2, namely the objects that are related to m via the morphisms. For example, in Figure 2, Map_{ee} is a mapping between models Emp and Employee, where has-a relationships are represented by solid lines and morphisms by dashed lines.

In effect, a mapping reifies the concept of a relationship between models. That is, instead of representing the relationship as a set of pairs (of objects), a mapping repre-

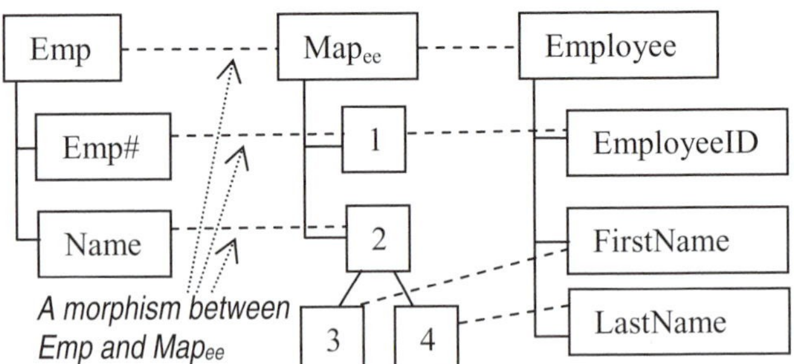

Figure 2 An example of a mapping

sents it as a set of objects (each of which can relate objects in the two models). In our experience, this reification is often needed for satisfactory expressiveness. For example, if the mapping in Figure 2 were represented as a relationship, it would presumably include the pairs <Name, FirstName> and <Name, LastName>, which loses the structure in Map_{ee} that shows FirstName and LastName as components of Name.

In addition to enabling more structural expressiveness, reifying a mapping also allows us to attach custom semantics to it. We can do this by having a property called *Expression* for each object m in a mapping, which is an expression whose variables include the objects that m directly or indirectly references in M_1 and M_2. For example, in Figure 2 we could associate an expression with object 2 that says Name equals the concatenation of FirstName and LastName. We will have more to say about the nature of these expressions at the end of Section 3.

Despite these benefits of reifying mappings as models, we expect there is value in specializing model management operators to operate directly on morphisms, rather than mappings. However, such a specialization is outside the scope of this paper. Thus, the operators discussed here work on models and mappings, but not on morphisms (separately from the mappings that contain them).

3 Model Management Algebra

3.1 Match

The operator Match takes two models as input and returns a mapping between them. The mapping identifies combinations of objects in the input models that are either equal or similar, based on some externally provided definition of equality and similarity. In some cases, the definition is quite simple. For example, the equality of two objects may be based on equality of their identifiers or names. In other cases, it is quite complex and perhaps subjective. For example, the equality of database schema objects for databases that were independently developed by different enterprises may depend on different terminologies used to name objects.

This range of definitions of equality leads to two versions of the match operator: Elementary Match and Complex Match. Elementary Match is based on the simple definition of equality. It is used where that simple definition is likely to yield an accurate mapping, e.g., when one model is known to be an incremental modification of another model.

Complex Match is based on complex definitions of equality. Although it need not set the Expression property on mapping objects, it should at least distinguish sets of objects that are equal (=) from those that are only similar (≅). By similar, we mean that they are related but we do not express exactly how. For example, in Figure 3, object 1 says that Emp# and EmployeeID are equal, while object 2 says that Name is similar to a combination of FirstName and LastName. A human mapping designer might update object 2's Expression property to say that Name equals the concatenation of FirstName and LastName.

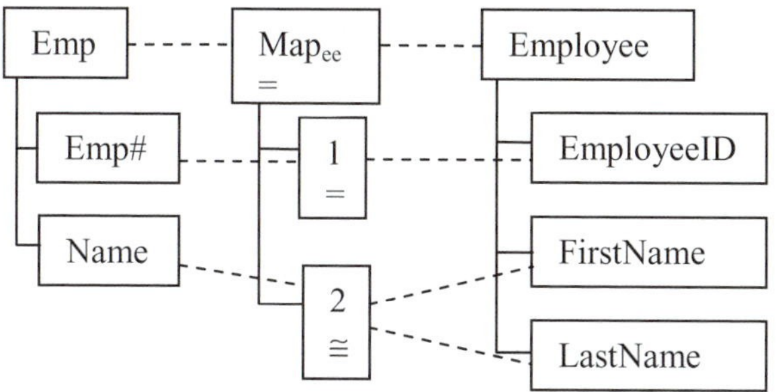

Figure 3 A mapping output from Complex Match

In practice, Complex Match is not an algorithm that returns a mapping but rather is a design environment to help a human designer develop a mapping. It potentially benefits from using technology from a variety of fields: graph isomorphism to identify structural similarity in large models; natural language processing to identify similarity of names or to analyze text documentation of a model; domain-specific thesauri; and machine learning and data mining to use similarity of data instances to infer the equality of model objects. A recent survey of approaches to Complex Match is [23].

3.2 Diff

Intuitively, the difference between two models is the set of objects in one model that do not correspond to any object in the other model. One part of computing a difference is determining which objects do correspond. This is the main function of Match. Rather than repeating this semantics as part of the diff operator, we compute a difference relative to a given mapping, which may have been computed by an invocation of Match. Thus, given a mapping map_1 between models M_1 and M_2, the operator Diff(M_1, map_1) returns the objects of M_1 that are not referenced in map_1's morphism between M_1 and map_1.

There are three problems with this definition of Diff, which require changing it a bit. First, the root of map_1 always references an object (often the root) of M_1, so the result of Diff(M_1, map_1) would not include that object. This is inconvenient, because it makes it hard to align the result of Diff with M_1 in subsequent operations. We will see examples of this in Section 4. Therefore, we alter the definition of Diff to require that the result includes the object of M_1 referenced by map_1's root.

Second, recall that a model is the set of objects reachable by paths of has-a relationships from the root. Since the result of Diff may equal any subset of the objects of M_1, some of those objects may not be connected to the Diff result's root. If they are not, the result of Diff is not a model. For example, consider Diff(Employee, Map$_{ee}$) on the models and mapping in Figure 4. Since FirstName and LastName are not referenced by Map$_{ee}$'s morphism between Employee and Map$_{ee}$, they are in the result. However, Name is not in the result, so FirstName and LastName are not connected to the root, Employee, of the result and therefore are not in that model. This is undesirable, since such objects cannot be subsequently processed by other operators, all of which expect a model as input. Therefore, to ensure that the result of Diff is a well-formed model, for every object o in the result, we require the result to include all objects O on a path of has-a relationships from the M_1 object referenced by map_1's root to o. Objects in O that are referenced in map_1's morphism to M_1 are called *support objects*, because they are added only to support the structural integrity of the model. For example, in Figure 5, Name is a support object in the result of Diff(Employee, Map$_{ee}$).

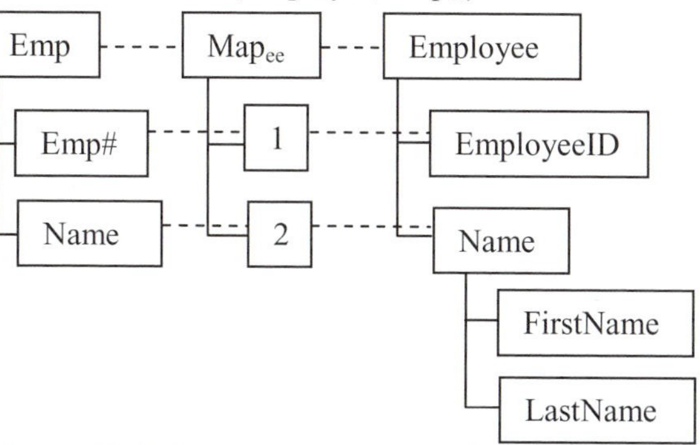

Figure 4 Diff(Employee, map$_{ee}$) includes FirstName and LastName but not Name

Having made this decision, we now have a third problem, namely, in the model that is returned by Diff, how to distinguish support objects from objects that are meant to be in the result of Diff (i.e., that do not participate in map_1)? We could simply mark support objects in the result. But this introduces another structure, namely a marked model. To avoid this complication, we use our two existing structures to represent the result, namely, model and mapping. That is, the result of Diff is a pair <M_1', map_2>, where

- M_1' includes a copy of: the M_1 object r referenced by map_1's root; the set S of objects in M_1 that are not referenced by map_1's morphism between map_1 and M_1; all support objects, i.e., those on a path of has-a relationships from r to an object in S that are not otherwise required in M_1'; every has-a relationship between two objects of M_1 that are also in M_1'; and every association between two objects in S or between an object in S and an object outside of M_1.

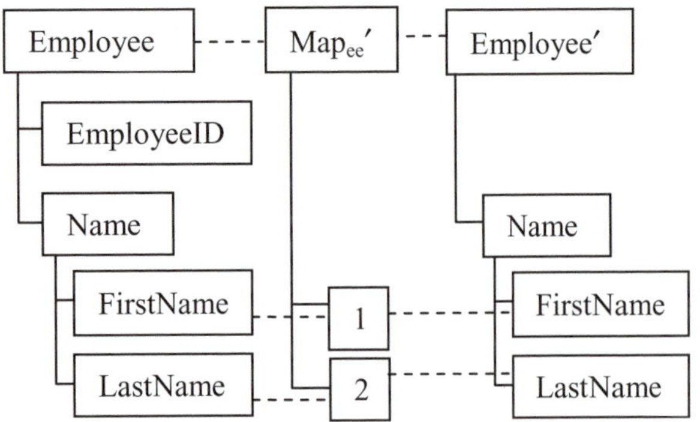

Figure 5 The result of Diff(Employee, Map$_{ee}$) is <Employee′, Map$_{ee}$′>

- map_2 connects the root of M_1' to r in M_1 and connects each object of S to the corresponding object of M_1'.

For example, given Employee and Map$_{ee}$ in Figure 4, the result of Diff(Employee, Map$_{ee}$) is <Employee′, Map$_{ee}$′> as shown in Figure 5.

3.3 Merge

The merge operation returns a copy of all of the objects of the input models, except that objects of the input models that are equal are collapsed into a single object in the output. Stating this more precisely, given two models M_1 and M_2 and a mapping map_1 between them, Merge(M_1, M_2, map_1) returns a model M_3 such that

- M_3 includes a copy of all of the objects of M_1, M_2, and map_1, except that for each object m of map_1 that declares objects of M_1 and M_2 to be equal, those equal objects are dropped from M_3 and their properties and relationships are added to m. The root of map_1 must declare the roots of M_1 and M_2 to be equal.
- All relationships in M_1, M_2, and map_1 are copied to the corresponding objects in M_3. For example, in Figure 6 Emp′ is the result of Merge(Emp, Employee, Map$_{ee}$) on the models and mappings of Figure 2.
- Merge also returns two mappings, map_{13} between M_1 and M_3 and map_{23} between M_2 and M_3, which relate each object of M_3 to the objects from which it was derived. Thus, the output of Merge is a triple <M_3, map_{13}, map_{23}>. For example, Figure 7 shows the map pings between the merge result in Figure 6 and the two input models of the merge, Emp and Employee.

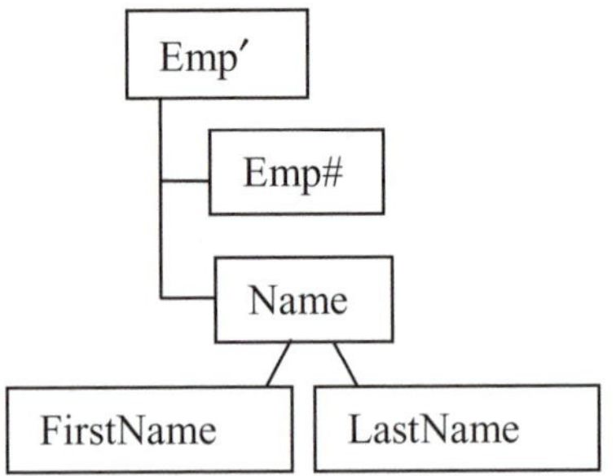

Figure 6 The result of Merge applied to Figure 2

The effect of collapsing objects into a single object can cause the output of Merge to violate basic constraints that models must satisfy. For example, suppose map_1 declares objects m_1 of M_1 and m_2 of M_2 to be equal, and suppose m_1 is of type integer and m_2 is of type image. The type of the merged object m_3 is both integer and image. If a constraint on models is that each object is allowed to have at most one type, then m_3 manifests a constraint violation that must be repaired, either as part of Merge or in a post-processing step. A solution to this specific problem appears in [9]. A more general discussion of constraint violations in merge results appears in [15].

3.4 Compose

The composition operator, represented by •, creates a mapping by combining two other mappings. If map_1 relates models M_1 and M_2, and map_2 relates M_2 and M_3, then the composition $map_3 = map_2 \bullet map_1$ is a mapping that relates M_1 and M_3 (i.e., $map_3(M_1) \equiv map_2(map_1(M_1))$.

To explain the semantics of composition, we will use mathematical function terminology: For each object m_1 in map_1, we refer to the objects that m_1 references in M_1 as its *domain*, and those that m_1 references in M_2 as its *range*. That is, domain(m_1) $\subseteq M_1$ and range(m_1) $\subseteq M_2$. Similarly, for each object m_2 in map_2, domain(m_2) $\subseteq M_2$ and range(m_2) $\subseteq M_3$.

In principle, a composition can be driven by either the left mapping (map_1) or right mapping (map_2). However, in this paper we restrict our attention to right compositions, since that is enough for the examples in Section 4. In a right composition, the structure of map_2 determines the structure of the output mapping.

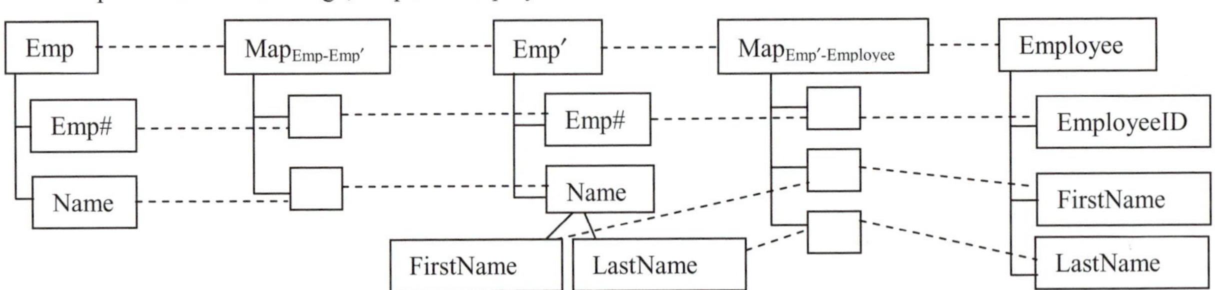

Figure 7 The merge result, Emp′, of Figure 2 with its mappings to the input models Emp and Employee

To compute the composition, for each object m_2 in map_2, we identify each object m_1 in map_1 where range(m_1) ∩ domain(m_2) ≠ ∅, which means that range(m_1) can supply at least one object to domain(m_2). For example, in Figure 8, the ranges of 4, 5, and 6 in map_1 can each supply one object to domain(11) in map_2. Suppose objects m_{11}, …, m_{1n} in map_1 together supply all of domain(m_2), and each m_{1i} (1≤i≤n) supplies at least one object to domain(m_2). That is, $\bigcup_{1 \le i \le n} range(m_{1i}) \supseteq domain(m_2)$ and (range(m_{1i}) ∩ domain(m_2)) ≠ ∅ for 1≤i≤n. Then m_2 should generate an output object m_3 in map_3 such that range(m_3) = range(m_2) and domain(m_3) = $\bigcup_{1 \le i \le n} domain(m_{1i})$.

For example, in Figure 8, range(4) and range(5) can supply all of domain(11). That is, range(4) ∪ range(5) = {7, 8, 9} ⊇ domain(11) = {7, 9}. Then object 11 should generate an output object m_3 in map_3 (not shown in the figure), such that range(m_3) = range(m_2) = {13} and domain(m_3) = domain(4) ∪ domain(5) = {1,2}.

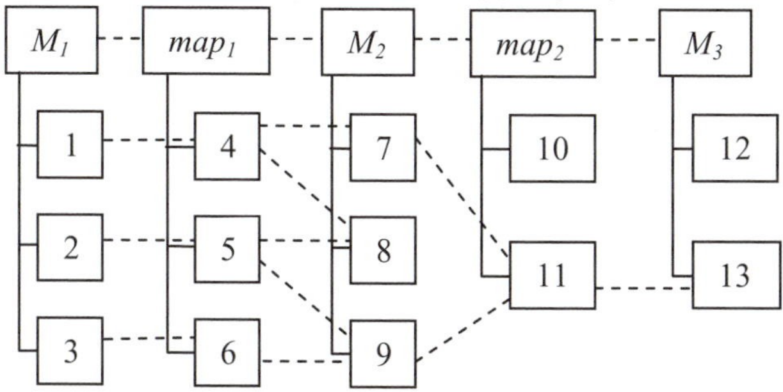

Figure 8 Mappings map₁ and map₂ can be composed

There is a problem, though: for a given m_2 in map_2, there may be more than one set of objects m_{11}, …, m_{1n} in map_1 that can supply all of domain(m_2). For example, in Figure 8, {4, 5} and {4, 6} can each supply all of domain(11). When defining composition, which set do we choose? In this paper, rather than choosing among them, we use all of them. That is, we compose each m_2 in map_2 with the union of all objects m_1 in map_1 where range(m_1) ∩ domain(m_2) ≠ ∅ ({4,5,6} in the example). This semantics supports all of the application scenarios in Section 4.

Given this decision, we define the right composition map_3 of map_1 and map_2 constructively as follows:

1. (Copy) Create a copy map_3 of map_2. Note that map_3 has the same morphisms to M_2 and M_3 as map_2 and, therefore, the same domains and ranges.
2. (Precompute Input) For each object m_3 in map_3, let Input(m_3) be the set of all objects m_1 in map_1 such that range(m_1) ∩ domain(m_2) ≠ ∅.
3. (Define domains) For each m_3 in map_3,
   a. if $\bigcup_{m_{1i} \in Input(m_3)} range(m_{1i}) \supseteq domain(m_3)$, then set domain($m_3$) = $\bigcup_{m_{1i} \in Input(m_3)} domain(m_{1i})$.
   b. else if m_3 is not needed as a support object (because none of its descendants satisfies (3a)), then delete it, else set domain(m_3) = range(m_3) = ∅.

Step 3 defines the domain of each object m_3 in map_3. Input(m_3) is the set of all objects in map_1 whose range intersects the domain of m_3. If the union of the ranges of Input(m_3) contains the domain of m_3, then the union of the domains of Input(m_3) becomes the domain of m_3. Otherwise, m_3 is not in the composition, so it is either deleted (if it is not a support object, required to maintain the well-formed-ness of map_3), or its domain and range are cleared (since it does not compose with objects in map_1).

Sometimes it is useful to keep every object of map_2 in map_3 even though its Input set does not cover its domain. This is called a *right outer composition*, because all objects of the right operand, map_2, are retained. Its semantics is the same as right composition, except that step 3b is replaced by "else set domain(m_3) = ∅."

A definition of composition that allows a more flexible choice of inputs to m_2 is in [7]. It is more complex than the one above and is not required for the examples in Section 4, so we omit it here.

3.5 Apply

The operator Apply takes a model and an arbitrary function *f* as inputs and applies *f* to every object of the model. In many cases, *f* modifies the model, for example, by modifying certain properties and relationships of each object. The purpose of Apply is to reduce the need for application programs to do object-at-a-time navigation over a model. There can be variations of the operator for different traversal strategies, such as pre-order or post-order over has-a relationships with the proviso that it does not visit any object twice (in the event of cycles).

3.6 Copy

The operator Copy takes a model as input and returns a copy of that model. The returned model includes all of the relationships of the input model, including those that connect its objects to objects outside the model.

One variation of Copy is of special interest to us, namely DeepCopy. It takes a model and mapping as input, where the mapping is incident to the model. It returns a copy of both the model and mapping as output. In essence, DeepCopy treats the input model and mapping as a single model, creating a copy of both of them together. To see the need for DeepCopy, consider how complicated it would be to get its effect without it, by copying the model and mapping independently. Several other variations of Copy are discussed in [6].

3.7 ModelGen

Applications of model management usually involve the generation of a model in one meta-model from a model in another meta-model. Examples are the generation of a SQL schema from an ER diagram, interface definitions from a UML model, or HTML links from a web site map. A model generator is usually meta-model specific. For example, the behavior of an ER-to-SQL generator very much depends on the source and target being ER and SQL models respectively. Therefore, one would not expect model generation to be a generic, i.e., meta-model-independent, operator.

Still, there is some common structure across all model generators worth abstracting. One is that the generation step should produce not only the output model but also a mapping from the input model to the output model. This allows later operators to propagate changes from one model to the other. For example, if an application developer modifies a SQL schema, it helps to know how the modified objects relate to the ER model, so the ER model can be made consistent with the revised SQL schema. This scenario is developed in some detail in Section 4.3.

A second common structure is that most model generators simply traverse the input model in a predetermined order, much like Apply, and generate output model objects based on the type of input object it is visiting. For example, a SQL generator might generate a table definition for each entity type, a column definition for each attribute type, a foreign key for each 1:n relationship type, and so on. In effect, the generator is a case-statement, where the case-statement variable is the type of the object being visited. If the case-statement is encapsulated as a function, it can be executed using the operator Apply.

Since the case-statement is driven by object types, one can go a step further in automating model generation by tagging each meta-model object (which is a type definition) by the desired generation behavior for model objects of that type, as proposed in [10]. Using it, model generation could be encapsulated as a model management operator, which we call *ModelGen*.

3.8 Enumerate

Although our goal is to capture as much model manipulation as possible in model-at-a-time operators, there will be times when iterative object-at-a-time code is needed. To simplify application programming in this case, we offer an operator called Enumerate, which takes a model as input and returns a "cursor" as output. The operator Next, when applied to a cursor, returns an object in the model that was the input to Enumerate, or null when it hits the end of the cursor. Like Apply, Enumerate may offer variations for different traversal orderings.

3.9 Other Data Manipulation Operators

Since models are object structures, they can be manipulated by the usual object-at-a-time operators: read an attribute; traverse a relationship, create an object, update an attribute, add or remove a relationship, etc. In addition, there are two other bulk database operators of interest:

- Select – Return the subset of a model that satisfies a qualification formula. The returned subset includes additional support objects, as in Diff. Like Diff, it also returns a mapping between the returned model and the input model, to identify the non-support objects.
- Delete – This deletes all of the objects in a given model, except for those that are reachable by paths of has-a relationships from other models.

3.10 Semantics

The model management operators defined in Section 3 are purely syntactic. That is, they treat models and mappings as graph structures, not as schemas that are templates for instances. The syntactic orientation is what enables model and mapping manipulation operators to be relatively generic. Still, in most applications, to be useful, models and mappings must ultimately be regarded as templates for instances. That is, they must have semantics. Thus, there is a semantic gap between model management and applications that needs to be filled.

The gap can be partially filled by making the meta-meta-model described in Sections 2.1 more expressive and extending the behavior of the operators to exploit that extra expressiveness. So, rather than knowing only about has-a and association relationships, the meta-meta-model should be extended to include is-a, data types, keys, etc.

Another way to introduce semantics is to use the Expression property in each mapping object *m*. Recall that such an expression's variables are the objects referenced by *m* in the two models being related. To exploit these expressions, the model management operators that generate mappings should be extended to produce expressions for any mapping objects they generate. For example, when Compose combines several objects from the two input mappings into an output mapping object *m*, it would also generate an expression for *m* based on the expressions on the input mapping objects. Similarly, for Diff and Merge.

The expression language is meta-model-specific, e.g., for the relational data model, it could be conjunctive queries. Therefore, the extensions to model management operators that deal with expressions must be meta-model-specific too and should be performed by a meta-model-specific expression manipulation engine. For example, the expression language extension for Compose would call this engine to generate an expression for each output mapping object it creates [16]. Some example walk-throughs of these extensions for SQL queries are given in [7]. However, a general-purpose interface between model management operators and expression manipulation engines has not yet been worked out.

Another approach to adding semantics to mappings is to develop a design tool for the purpose, such as Clio [17,27].

4 Application Scenarios

In this section, we discuss three common meta data management problems that involve the manipulation of models and mappings: schema integration, schema evolution, and round-trip engineering. We describe each problem in terms of models and mappings and show how to use model management operators to solve it.

4.1 Schema Integration

The problem is to create: a schema S_3 that represents all of the information expressed in two given database schemas, S_1 and S_2; and mappings between S_1 and S_3 and between S_2 and S_3 (see Figure 9). The schema integration literature offers many algorithms for doing this [1,8,23]. They all consist of three main activities: identifying overlapping information in S_1 and S_2; using the identified overlaps to guide a merge of S_1 and S_2; and resolving conflict situations (i.e., where the same information was represented differently in S_1 and S_2) during or after the merge. The main differentiator between these algorithms is in the conflict resolution approaches.

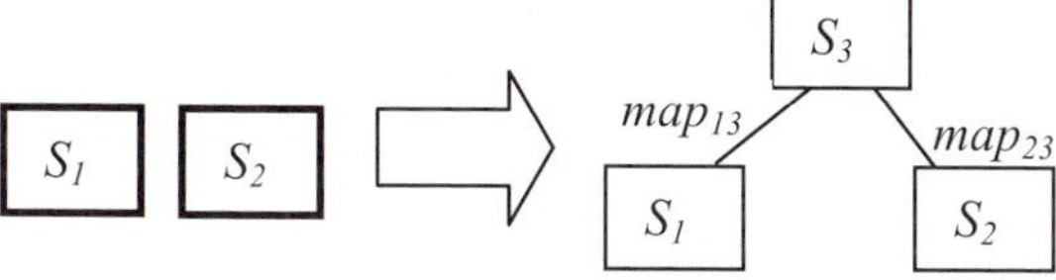

Figure 9 The schema integration problem

If each schema is regarded as a model, then we can express the first two activities using model management operators as follows:

1. map_{12} = Match(S_1, S_2). This step identifies the equal and similar objects in S_1 and S_2. Since Match is creating a mapping between two independently developed schemas, this is best done with a Complex Match operator (rather than Elementary Match).
2. <S_3, map_{13}, map_{23}> = Merge(S_1, S_2, map_{12}). Given the mapping created in the previous step, Merge produces the integrated schema S_3 and the desired mappings.

For example, in Figure 10, Map_{ee} could be the result of Match(Emp, Employee). Notice that this is similar to Figure 3, except that Emp has an additional object Address and Employee has an additional object Phone, neither of which are mapped to objects in the other model.

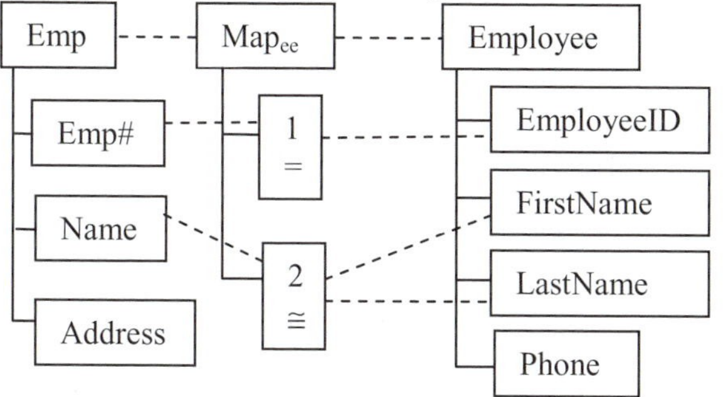

Figure 10 The result of matching Emp and Employee

Figure 11 shows the result of merging Emp and Employee with respect to Map_{ee}. (The mappings between Emp′ and Emp and between Emp′ and Employee are omitted, to avoid cluttering the figure.) Since Map_{ee} says that the Emp# and EmployeeID objects are equal, they are collapsed into a single object Emp#. The two objects have different names; Merge chose the name of the left object, Emp#, one of the many details to nail down in a complete specification of Merge's semantics. Since Address and Phone are not referenced by Map_{ee}, they are simply copied to the output. Since Map_{ee} says that Name is similar to FirstName and LastName, these objects are partially integrated in S_{12} under an object labeled ≅, which is a placeholder for an expression that relates Name to FirstName and LastName.

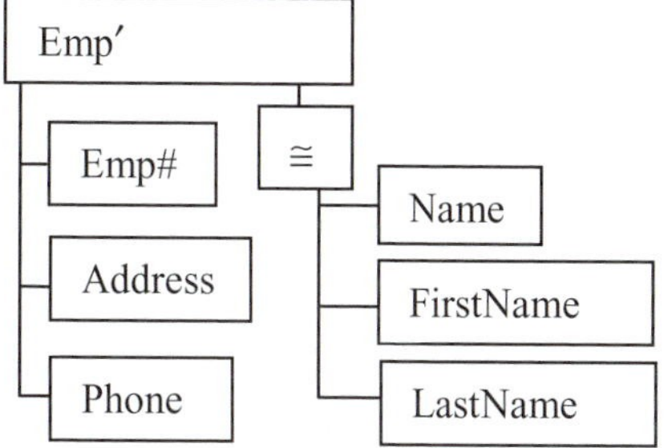

Figure 11 The result of merging Emp and Employee based on Map_{ee} in Figure 10

The sub-structure rooted by "≅" represents a conflict between the two input schemas. A schema integration algorithm needs rules to cope with such conflicts. In this case it could consult a knowledge base that explains that first name concatenated with last name is a name. It could use this knowledge to replace the sub-structure rooted by ≅ either by FirstName and LastName, since together they subsume Name, or by a nested structure Name with sub-objects FirstName and LastName. The latter is probably preferable in a data model that allows nested structures, such as XML Schema. The former is probably necessary when nested structures are not supported, as in SQL. Overall, the resolution strategy depends on the capabilities of the knowledge base and on the expressiveness of the output data model. So this activity is not captured by the generic model management operators. Instead, it should be expressed in an application-specific function.

When application-specific conflict resolution functions are used, the apply operator can help by executing a conflict resolution rule on all objects of the output of Merge. The rule tests for an object that is marked by ≅, and if so applies its action to that object and its sub-structure (knowledge-base lookup plus meta-model-specific merge). This avoids the need for the application-specific code to include logic to navigate the model.

To finish the job, the mappings map_{12} and map_{13} that are returned by Merge must be translated into view definitions. To do this, the models and mappings can no longer be regarded only as syntactic structures. Rather, they need semantics. Thus, creating view definitions requires semantic reasoning: the manipulation of expressions that explain the semantics of mappings. In Section 3.10 we explained in broad outline how to do this, though as we said there, the details are beyond the scope of this paper.

4.2 Schema Evolution

The schema evolution problem arises when a change to a database schema breaks views that are defined on it [3, 12]. Stated more precisely, we are given a base schema S_1, a set of view schemas V_1 over S_1, and a mapping map_1 that maps objects of S_1 to objects of V_1. (See Figure 12.)

For example, if S_1 and V_1 are relational schemas, then we would expect each object m of map_1 to contain a relational view definition that tells how to derive a view relation in V_1 from some of the relations in S_1; the morphisms of m would refer to the objects of S_1 and V_1 that are mentioned in m's view definition. Then, given a new version S_2 of S_1, the problem is to define a new version V_2 of V_1 that is consistent with S_2 and a mapping map_2 from S_2 to V_2.

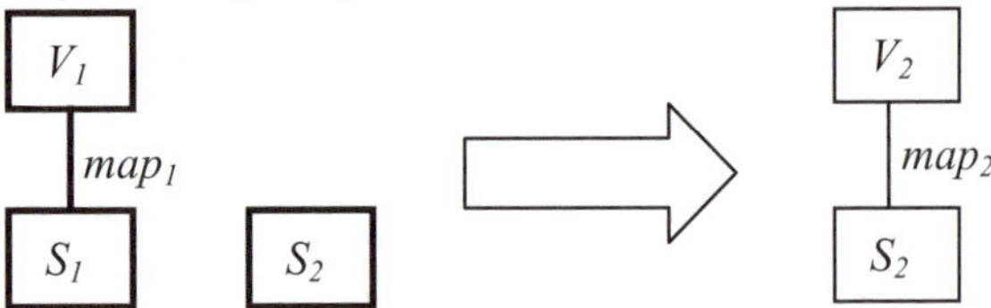

Figure 12 The schema evolution problem

We can solve this problem using model management operators as follows (Figure 13):

1. map_3 = Match(S_1, S_2). This returns a mapping between S_1 and S_2 that identifies what is unchanged in S_2 relative to S_1. If we know that S_2 is an incremental modification of S_1, then this can be done by Elementary Match. If not, then Complex Match is required.

2. $map_4 = map_1 \bullet map_3$. This is a right composition. Intuitively, each mapping object in map_4 describes a part of map_1 that is unaffected by the change from S_1 to S_2. A mapping object m in map_1 survives the composition (i.e., becomes an object of map_4) if every object in S_1 that is connected to m is also connected to some object of S_2 via map_3. If so, then m is transformed into m' in map_4 by replacing each reference from m to an object of S_1 by a reference to the corresponding objects in S_2.

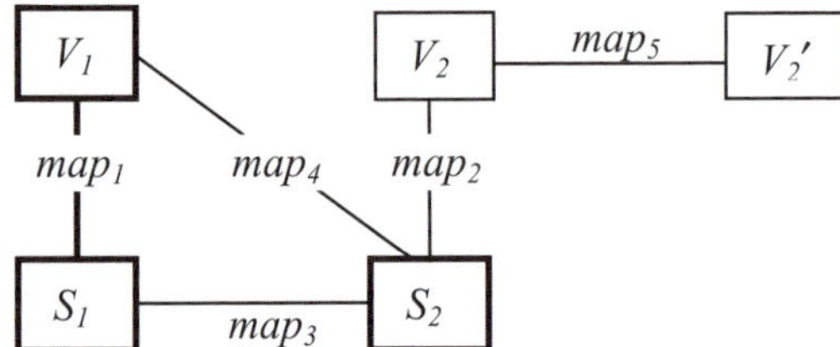

Figure 13 Result of schema evolution solution

Some objects of V_1 may now be "orphans" in the sense that they are not incident to map_4. An orphan arises because it maps via map_1 to an object in S_1 that has no corresponding object in S_2 via map_3. One way to deal with orphans is to eliminate them. Since doing this would corrupt map_1, we first make a copy of V_1 and then delete the orphans from the copy:

3. <V_2, map_2> = DeepCopy(V_1, map_4). This makes a copy V_2 of V_1 along with a copy map_2 of map_4.

4. <V_2', map_5> = Diff(V_2, map_2). Identify the orphans.

5. For each e in Enumerate(map_5), delete *domain(e)* from V_2. This enumerates the orphans and deletes them. Notice that we are treating map_5 as a model.

At this point we have successfully completed the task. An alternative to steps 4 and 5 is to be more selective in deleting view objects, based on knowledge about the syntax and semantics of the mapping expressions. For example, suppose the schemas and views are in the relational data model and S_2 is missing an attribute that is used to populate an attribute of a view in V_2. In the previous approach, if each view is defined by one object in map_1, then the entire view would be an orphan and deleted. Instead, we could drop the attribute from the view without dropping the entire view relation that contains it. To get this effect, we could replace Step 2 above by a right outer composition, so that all objects of map_1 are copied to map_4, even if they connect to S_1 objects that have no counterpart in S_2. Then we can write a function f that encapsulates the semantic knowledge necessary to strip out parts of a view definition and replace steps 4 and 5 by Apply(f, map_2). Thus, f gives us a way of exploiting non-generic model semantics while still working within the framework of the model management algebra.

4.3 Round-Trip Engineering

Consider a design tool that generates a compiled version of a high-level specification, such as an ER modeling tool that generates SQL DDL or a UML modeling tool that generates C++ interfaces. After a developer modifies the generated version of such a specification (e.g., SQL DDL), the modified generated version is no longer consistent with its specification. Repairing the specification is called round-trip engineering, because the tool forward-engineers the specification into a generated version after which the modified generated version is reverse-engineered back to a specification.

Stating this scenario more precisely, we are given a specification S_1, a generated model G_1 that was derived from S_1, a mapping map_1 from S_1 to G_1, and a modified version G_2 of G_1. The problem is to produce a revised specification S_2 that is consistent with G_2 and a mapping map_2 between S_2 and G_2. See Figure 14. Notice that diagrammatically, this is isomorphic to the schema evolution problem; it is exactly like Figure 12, with S_1 and S_2 replacing V_1 and V_2, and G_1 and G_2 replacing S_1 and S_2.

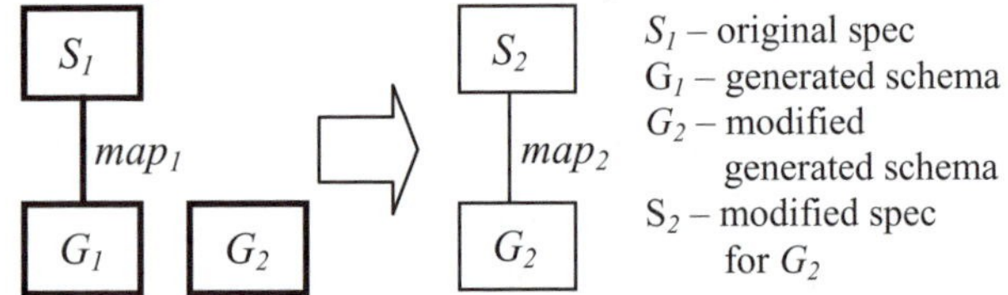

Figure 14 The round-trip engineering problem

As in schema evolution, we start by matching G_1 and G_2, composing the resulting mapping with map_1, and doing a deep copy of the mapping produced by Compose:

1. map_3 = Match(G_1, G_2). This returns a mapping that identifies what is unchanged in G_2 relative to G_1. Since G_2 is an incremental modification of G_1, Elementary Match should suffice. See Figure 15a.

2. $map_4 = map_1 \bullet map_3$. Mapping map_4, between S_1 and G_2, includes a copy of each object in map_1 all of whose incident G_1 objects are still present in G_2.
3. $<S_3, map_5> =$ DeepCopy(S_1, map_4). This makes a copy S_3 of S_1 along with a copy map_5 of map_4.

Steps 2 and 3 eliminate from the specification S_3 all objects that do not correspond to generated objects in G_2. One could retain these objects by replacing the composition in step 2 by outer composition. The remaining steps in this section would then proceed without modification.

Next, we need to reverse engineer the new objects that were introduced in G_2 and merge them with S_3. Here is one way to do it (see Figure 15a):

4. $<G_2', map_6> =$ Diff(G_2, map_3). This produces a model G_2' that includes objects of G_2 that do not participate in the mapping map_3, which are exactly the new objects of G_2, plus support objects O that are needed to keep G_2' well-formed. Mapping map_6 maps each object of G_2' not in O to the corresponding object of G_2.

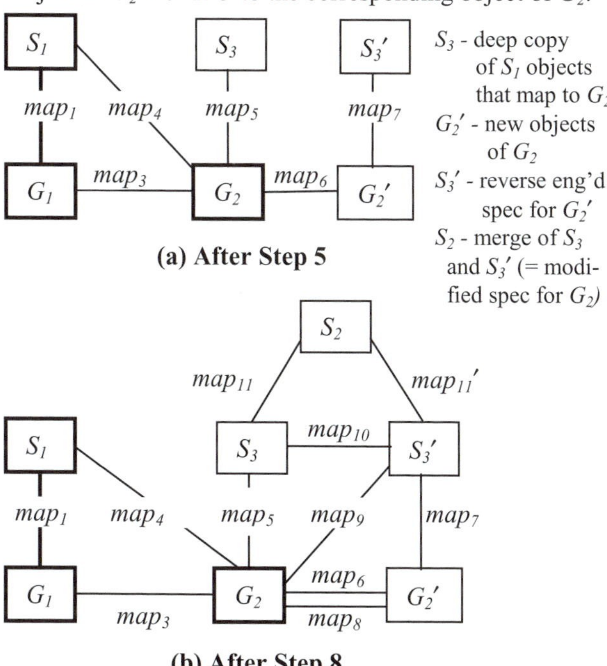

Figure 15 Result of round-trip engineering solution

For example, suppose G_2 and G_2' are SQL schemas, and G_2' introduced a new column C into table T. In the model management representation G_2 of the schema, C is an object that is a child of object T. Since C is new, it is not connected via map_3 to G_1, so it is in the result of Diff. However, to keep G_2' connected, since C is a child of T, T is also in the result of Diff as a support object, though it is not connected to G_2 via map_6.

5. $<S_3', map_7> =$ ModelGen(G_2'). In this case, ModelGen is customized to reverse engineer each object of G_2' into an object of the desired form for integration into S_2. For example, if G_2' is a SQL schema and the S_i's are ER models, then ModelGen maps each SQL column into an ER attribute, each table into either an entity type or relationship type (depending on the key structure of the table), etc.

We need to merge S_3 and S_3' into a single model S_2, which is half of the desired result. (The other half is map_2, coming soon.) To do this, we need to create a mapping between S_3 and S_3' that connects objects of S_3 and S_3' that represent the same thing. Continuing the example after step 4 above, where G_2' introduces a new column C into table T, the desired mapping should connect the reverse engineered object for T in S_3' (e.g., an entity type) with the original object for T in S_3 (e.g., the entity type that was used to generate T in G_2 in the first place). By contrast, the reverse engineered object for C in S_3' will not map to any object in S_3 because it is a new object that was introduced in G_2', and therefore was not present S_3. We can create the desired mapping by a Match followed by two compositions, after which we can do the merge, as follows (see Figure 15b):

6. $map_8 =$ Match(G_2, G_2'). This matches every object in G_2' with its corresponding copy in G_2. Unlike map_6, map_8 connects to all objects in G_2', including support objects.
7. $map_9 = map_7 \bullet map_8$. This right composition creates a mapping map_9 between the objects of G_2 that are also in G_2' and their corresponding objects of S_3'. Since map_8 is incident to all objects of G_2', every object of map_7 generates a map_9 object that connects to G_2.
8. $map_{10} = map_5 \bullet map_9$. If there are mapping objects of map_5 and map_9 that connect an object of G_2 (e.g., T) to both S_3 and S_3', then those mapping objects compose and the corresponding objects of S_3 and S_3' are related by map_{10}. This should be an "inner" Compose, which only returns objects that connect to both S_3 and S_3'.
9. $<S_2, map_{11}, map_{11}'> =$ Merge(S_3, S_3', map_{10}). This merges the reverse engineered objects of S_3' (which came from the new objects introduced in G_2) with S_3, producing the desired model S_2 (cf. Figure 14).

Finally, we need to produce the desired mapping map_2 between G_2 and S_2. This is the union (i.e., merge) of $map_{11} \bullet map_5$ and $map_{11}' \bullet map_9$. To see why this is what we want, recall that G_2' contains the objects of G_2 that do not map to S_3 via map_5. Mapping map_7 connects those objects to S_3', as does map_9, except on the original objects in G_2 rather than on the copies in G_2'. Hence, every object in G_2 connects to a mapping object in either map_5 or map_9.

So to start, we need to compute these compositions:

10. $map_2' = map_{11} \bullet map_5$
11. $map_2'' = map_{11}' \bullet map_9$

Next, we need the union of map_2' and map_2''. But there is a catch: an object of G_2 could be connected to objects in both map_5 and map_9. Continuing our example, table T is such an object because it is mapped to S_3 as well as reverse engineered to S_3'. Such objects have two mappings to G_2 via the union of the compositions, which is probably not what is desired. Getting rid of the duplicates is a bit of effort. One way is to merge the mappings. To do this, we need to match map_2' and map_2'' from steps 10 and 11 to find the duplicates (which we can do because mappings are models), and then merge the mappings based on the match result. Here are the steps (not shown in Figure 15):

12. map_{12} = Match(map_2', map_2''). Objects m_2' in map_2' and m_2'' in map_2'' match if they connect to exactly the same objects of G_2 and S_2. To use this matching condition, one needs to regard the morphisms of map_2' and map_2'' as parts of each map's model; e.g., the morphisms could be available as relationships on each map's model. Using this simple match criterion, Elementary Match suffices.
13. map_2 = Merge(map_2', map_2'', map_{12}). The morphisms of map_2' and map_2'' should be merged like ordinary relationships. That is, if map_{12} connects m_2' in map_2' and m_2'' in map_2'', then Merge collapses m_2' and m_2'' into a single object m_2. Object m_2 should have only one copy of the mapping connections that m_2' and m_2'' had to G_2 and S_2.

We now have map_2 and S_2, so we're done! Cf. Figure 14.

5 Implementation

We envision an implementation of models, mappings, and model management operators on a persistent object-oriented system. Given technology trends, an object-relational system is likely to be the best choice, but an XML database system might also be suitable. The system consists of four layers:

Models and mappings – This layer supports the model and mapping abstractions, each implemented as an object-oriented structure, both on disk and heavily cached for fast navigation. The representation of models should be extensible, so that the system can be specialized to more expressive meta-meta-models. And it should be semi-structured, so that models can be imported from more expressive representations without loss of information. This layer supports:

- Models – We need the usual object-at-a-time operations on objects in models, plus GetSubmodels (of a given model) and DeleteSubmodel, where a submodel is a model rooted by an object in another model. Also Copy (deep and shallow) is supported here.
- Mappings - CreateMapping returns a model and two morphisms. GetSource and GetTarget return the morphisms of a given mapping.
- Morphisms – These are accessible and updatable like normal relationships.

Algebraic operators – This layer implements Match, Merge, Diff, Compose, Apply, ModelGen, and Enumerate. It should have an extension mechanism for handling semantics, such as an expression manipulation engine as discussed in Section 3.10.

Model-driven generator of user interface – Much like an advanced drawing tool, one can tag meta-model objects with descriptions of objects and their behavior (e.g., a table definition is a blue rectangle and a column definition is a line within its table's rectangle).

Generic tools over models and mappings – browser, editor, catalog, import/export, scripting.

6 Related Work

Although the model management approach is new, much of the existing literature on meta data management offers either algorithms that can be generalized for use in model management or examples that can be studied as challenges for the model management operators. This literature is too large to cite here, but we can highlight a few areas where there is obvious synergy worth exploring. Some of them were mentioned earlier: schema matching (see the survey in [23]); schema integration [1,8,15,25], which is both an example and a source of algorithms for Match and Merge; and adding semantics to mappings [7,17,21,27]. Others include:

- Data translation [24];
- Differencing [11,19,26]; and
- EER-style representations and their expressive power, which may help select the best representation for models and mappings [2,14,15,18,20].

7 Conclusion

In this paper, we described model management — a new approach to manipulating models (e.g., schemas) and mappings as bulk objects using operators such as Match, Merge, Diff, Compose, Apply, Copy, Enumerate, and ModelGen. We showed how to apply these operators to three classical meta data management problems: schema integration, schema evolution, and round-trip engineering. We believe these example solutions strongly suggest that an implementation of model management would provide major programming productivity gains for a wide variety of meta data management problems. Of course, to make this claim compelling, an implementation is needed. If successful, such an implementation could be the prototype for a new category of database system products.

In addition to implementation, there are many other areas where work is needed to fully realize the potential of this approach. Some of the more pressing ones are:

- Choosing a representation that captures most of the constructs of models and mappings of interest, yet is tractable for model management operators.
- More detailed semantics of model management operators. There is substantial work on Match. Merge, Compose, and ModelGen are less well developed.
- A mathematical semantics of model management. The beginnings of a category-theoretic approach appears in [1], but there is much left to do. A less abstract analysis that can speak to the completeness of the set

of operators would help define the boundary of useful model management computations.

- Mechanisms are needed to fill the gap between models and mappings, which are syntactic structures, and their semantics, which treat models as templates for instances and mappings as transformations of instances. Various theories of conjunctive queries are likely to be helpful.
- Trying to apply model management to especially challenging meta data management problems, to identify limits to the approach and opportunities to extend it.

This is a broad agenda that will take many years and many research groups to develop. Although it will be a lot of work, we believe the potential benefits of the approach make the agenda well worth pursuing.

Acknowledgments

The ideas in this paper have benefited greatly from my ongoing collaborations with Suad Alagi , Alon Halevy, Renée Miller, Rachel Pottinger, and Erhard Rahm. I also thank the many people whose discussions have stimulated me to extend and sharpen these ideas, especially Kajal Claypool, Jayant Madhavan, Sergey Melnik, Peter Mork, John Mylopoulos, Arnie Rosenthal, Elke Rundensteiner, Aamod Sane, and Val Tannen.

8 References

1. Alagic, S. and P.A. Bernstein, "A Model Theory for Generic Schema Management," Proc. DBPL 2001, Springer Verlag LNCS.
2. Atzeni, Paolo and Riccardo Torlone: Management of Multiple Models in an Extensible Database Design Tool. EDBT 1996: 79-95
3. Banerjee, Jay, Won Kim, Hyoung-Joo Kim, Henry F. Korth: Semantics and Implementation of Schema Evolution in Object-Oriented Databases. SIGMOD Conference 1987: 311-322
4. Beeri, C. and T. Milo: Schemas for integration and translation of structured and semi-structured data. ICDT, 1999: 296-313,.
5. Bernstein, P.A.: Generic Model Management – A Database Infrastructure for Schema Manipulation. Springer Verlag LNCS 2172, CoopIS 2001: 1-6.
6. Bernstein, Philip A., Alon Y. Halevy, and Rachel A. Pottinger. A vision of management of complex models. SIGMOD Record 29(4):55-63 (2000).
7. Bernstein, Philip A., Erhard Rahm: Data Warehouse Scenarios for Model Management. ER 2000: 1-15.
8. Biskup, J. and B. Convent. A formal view integration method. SIGMOD 1986: 398-407.
9. Buneman, P., S.B. Davidson, A. Kosky. Theoretical aspects of schema merging. EDBT 1992: 152-167.
10. Cattell, R.G.G., D. K. Barry, M. Berler, J. Eastman, D. Jordan, D. Russell, O. Schadow, T. Stanienda, and F. Velez, editors: *The Object Database Standard: ODMG 3.0*. Morgan Kaufmann Publishers, 2000.
11. Chawathe, Sudarshan S. and Hector Garcia-Molina: Meaningful Change Detection in Structured Data. SIGMOD 1997: 26-37.
12. Claypool, K. T., J. Jin, E. A. Rundensteiner: SERF: Schema Evolution through an Extensible, Re-usable and Flexible Framework. CIKM 1998: 314-321.
13. Claypool, K.T., E.A. Rundensteiner, X. Zhang, H. Su, H.A. Kuno, W-C Lee, G. Mitchell: Gangam - A Solution to Support Multiple Data Models, their Mappings and Maintenance. SIGMOD 2001
14. Hull, Richard and Roger King: Semantic Database Modeling:Survey, Applications, and Research Issues. ACM Computing Surveys 19(3): 201-260 (1987)
15. Larson, James A., Shamkant B. Navathe, and Ramez Elmasri. A theory of attribute equivalence in databases with application to schema integration. Trans. on Soft. Eng. 15(4):449-463 (April 1989).
16. Madhavan, J., P. A. Bernstein, P. Domingos, A.Y. Halevy: Representing and Reasoning About Mappings between Domain Models. 18th National Conference on Artificial Intelligence (AAAI 2002).
17. Miller, R.J., L. M. Haas, M. A. Hernández: Schema Mapping as Query Discovery. VLDB 2000: 77-88.
18. Miller, R. J., Y. E. Ioannidis, Raghu Ramakrishnan: Schema equivalence in heterogeneous systems: bridging theory and practice. Information Systems 19(1): 3-31 (1994)
19. Myers, E.: An O(ND) Difference Algorithm and its Variations. Algorithmica 1(2): 251-266 (1986).
20. Mylopoulos, John, Alexander Borgida, Matthias Jarke, Manolis Koubarakis: Telos: Representing Knowledge About Information Systems. TOIS 8(4): 325-362 (1990).
21. Popa, Lucian, Val Tannen: An Equational Chase for Path-Conjunctive Queries, Constraints, and Views. ICDT 1999: 39-57.
22. Pottinger, Rachel A. and Philip A. Bernstein. Creating a Mediated Schema Based on Initial Correspondences. IEEE Data Engineering Bulletin, Sept. 2002.
23. Rahm, Erhard and Philip A. Bernstein. A survey of approaches to automatic schema matching. VLDB J. 10(4):334-350 (2001).
24. Shu, Nan C., Barron C. Housel, R. W. Taylor, Sakti P. Ghosh, Vincent Y. Lum: EXPRESS: A Data EXtraction, Processing, amd REStructuring System. TODS 2(2): 134-174 (1977).
25. Spaccapietra, Stefano and Christine Parent. View integration: A step forward in solving structural conflicts. TKDE 6(2): 258-274 (April 1994).
26. J. T-L. Wang, D. Shasha, G. J-S. Chang, L. Relihan, K. Zhang, G. Patel: Structural Matching and Discovery in Document Databases. SIGMOD 1997: 560-563
27. Yan, Ling-Ling, Renée J. Miller, Laura M. Haas, Ronald Fagin: Data-Driven Understanding and Refinement of Schema Mappings. SIGMOD 2001.

Algorithms for Creating Indexes for Very Large Tables Without Quiescing Updates

C. Mohan
Inderpal Narang

Data Base Technology Institute, IBM Almaden Research Center, San Jose, CA 95120, USA
{mohan, narang}@almaden.ibm.com

Abstract As relational DBMSs become more and more popular and as organizations grow, the sizes of individual tables are increasing dramatically. Unfortunately, current DBMSs do not allow updates to be performed on a table while an index (e.g., a B^+-tree) is being built for that table, thereby decreasing the systems' availability. This paper describes two algorithms in order to relax this restriction. Our emphasis has been to maximize concurrency, minimize overheads and cover all aspects of the problem. Builds of both unique and nonunique indexes are handled correctly. We also describe techniques for making the index-build operation restartable, without loss of all work, in case a system failure were to interrupt the completion of the creation of the index. In this connection, we also present algorithms for making a long sort operation restartable. These include algorithms for the sort and merge phases of sorting.

1. Introduction

This paper describes two algorithms which would allow a data base management system (DBMS) to support the building of an index (e.g., a B^+-tree) on a table concurrently with changes being made to that data by (ordinary) transactions. Current DBMSs do not allow updates to a table while building an index on it. Eliminating this restriction in the context of very large tables has been identified as an open problem [DeGr90, SiSU91]. As sizes of individual tables get larger and larger (e.g., petabytes, 10**15 bytes), it may take several days to just scan all the pages of a table to build an index on such a table [DeGr90]! Even though a large table may be partitioned into smaller pieces with each piece having its own primary index, still building a global secondary index would require a scan of *all* the partitions [Moha92]. We are already aware of customers who would like to store more than 100 gigabytes of data in a single table! Disallowing updates while building an index may become unacceptable for several reasons. Relational DBMSs with their promise and ability to support simultaneously both *transaction* and query workloads have aggravated the situation with respect to availability by not supporting index build with concurrent updates.[1]

1.1. General Assumptions

Data Storage Model We assume that the records of a table are stored in one or more files whose pages are called ***data pages***. The indexes contain ***keys*** of the form *<key value, RID>*, where ***RID*** is the record ID of the record containing the associated key value. ***Key value*** is the concatentation of the values of the columns (fields) of the table over which the index is defined. We can handle both unique and nonunique indexes. In a ***unique index***, there can be at most only one key with a particular key value. Without loss of generality, we assume that the keys are stored in the ascending order. The section "6.2. Extensions" discusses how our algorithms can be adapted to work in the context of a storage model in which all the records of a table are stored in the primary index (*<primary key value, record data>*) and the secondary indexes contain entries of the form *<key value, primary key value>*, where the primary key value is required to be unique.

Recovery We assume that write-ahead logging (WAL) [Gray78, MHLPS92] is being used for recovery. The ***undo*** (respectively, ***redo***) portion of a log record provides information on how to undo (respectively, redo) changes performed by the transaction. A log record which contains both the undo and the redo information is called an ***undo-redo log record.*** Sometimes, a log record may be written to contain only the redo information or only the undo information. Such a record is called a ***redo-only log record*** or an ***undo-only log record***, respectively.

Execution Model The term ***index-builder (IB)*** is used to refer to the process which scans the data pages, builds index keys and inserts them into the index tree. Regular user transactions can be making updates to the table while IB is performing its tasks. IB does *not lock the data* while extracting keys, but it latches[2] each page as it is accessed in the share mode. Transactions do their usual latching and locking [MHLPS92, Moha90a, MoLe92]. This execution model permits very high concurrency and decreases CPU overhead.

1.2. Problems

This section discusses the problems introduced by the execution model that we have assumed. These problems stem from the fact that IB does not lock the data.

- **Duplicate-Key-Insert Problem** An attempt may be made to insert a duplicate key (i.e., two identical <key value, RID> entries) as a result of competing actions by IB and an insert from a transaction. This is because, to avoid deadlocks involving latches, neither the transactions nor IB holds a latch on the data page while inserting keys in the index [MHLPS92, Moha90a, MoLe92]. A page's latch is held only during the time of extraction of the keys from the records in that page. Also, as we will see later, there is a long time gap between the time IB extracts a key and the time when it inserts that key into the index.
- **Delete-Key Problem** A key which was deleted by a committed transaction could be inserted later by IB because of race conditions between the two processes. The race condition can occur for the same reason as the one described above for the insert case.

1992 ACM SIGMOD - 6/92/CA, USA
© 1992 ACM 0-89791-522-4/92/0005/0361...$1.50

1.3. Overview

In this paper, we present two algorithms, called ***NSF*** (*No Side-File*) and ***SF*** (*Side-File*). They allow index builds concurrently with inserts and deletes of keys by transactions. NSF allows IB to *tolerate* interference by transactions. That is, while IB is inserting keys into the index, transactions could be inserting and deleting keys from the same index tree. SF does not allow transactions to interfere with IB's insertion of keys into the index. In SF, key inserts and deletes relating to the index still being constructed are maintained by the transactions in a side-file as long as IB is active. A ***side-file*** is an append-only (sequential) table in which the transactions insert tuples of the form <*operation, key*>, where *operation* is insert or delete. Transactions append entries without doing any locking of the appended entries. At the end, IB processes the side-file to bring the index up to date.

In this paper, we also describe techniques for making the index-build operation restartable so that, in case a system failure were to interrupt the completion of the index-build operation, not all the so-far-accomplished work is lost. For this purpose, we present algorithms for making a long sort operation restartable. These include algorithms for the sort and merge phases of sorting. The algorithms relating to sort have very general applicability, apart from their use in the current context of sorting keys for index creation.

The rest of the paper is organized as follows. In sections 2 and 3, we present the details of the NSF and SF algorithms, respectively. We cover in detail the mainline and recovery operations, and restarting of the index-build utility. Our emphasis has been to maximize concurrency, minimize overheads and cover all aspects of the problem. In section 4, we compare the two algorithms and discuss their performance qualitatively. Algorithms for making the sort operation restartable are presented in section 5. Finally, in section 6, we summarize our work. We also discuss extensions of our algorithms to allow multiple indexes to be built in one scan of the data and to support a different storage model.

2. Algorithm NSF: Index Build Without Side-File

In this section, we present the NSF (*No Side-File*) algorithm. First, we give a brief overview of the solutions to the problems described in the section "1.2. Problems". Then, we describe the NSF algorithm in detail. For ease of explanation, we pretend that only one index is being created at any given time for a table. Later, in the section "6.2. Extensions", we discuss how both NSF and SF can easily create multiple indexes simultaneously in one scan of the data.

2.1. Overview of NSF

Assumptions

- Both IB and the transactions write log records (e.g., as in ARIES/IM [MoLe92]) for the changes that they make to the index being built.

2.1.1. Solution to the Duplicate-Key-Insert Problem

In NSF, the IB or the transaction inserter, whichever attempts to insert the *same* key *later*, avoids inserting the duplicate key in the index when the key is already found to be present in the index. The transaction always writes a log record saying that it inserted the key even though sometimes it may not actually insert the key since IB had already inserted it. The log record is written to ensure that in case this transaction were to roll back, then the key, which was inserted earlier by IB, would be deleted by the transaction from the index. Without that log record, the transaction will not remove the key from the index and that would be wrong since it would introduce an inconsistency between the table and the index data.

2.1.2. Solution to the Delete-Key Problem

If a transaction needs to delete a key and the key is *not* found in the index, then the deleter inserts a *pseudo-deleted* key. A key present in the index is said to be ***pseudo deleted*** if the key is logically, as opposed to physically, deleted from the index (this is done, for example, in the case of IMS indexes [Ober80]). Obviously, keys deleted in such a fashion take up room in the index. A 1-bit flag is associated with every key in the index to indicate whether the key is pseudo deleted or not. There are other motivations for keeping a deleted key as a pseudo-deleted key for as long as the deleting transaction is uncommitted (see [Moha90b] for details). For example, the deleter of a key does not have to do *next key locking* (see [Moha90a, MoLe92]) which saves an exclusive (X) lock call and improves concurrency. Next key locking prevents any key inserts in the key range spanning from the currently existing key which is previous to (i.e., smaller than) the deleted key to the next key (i.e., next higher key currently in the index). The transaction, by leaving a trail in the form of a pseudo-deleted key, lets IB avoid inserting that key later on, in case IB had picked up the key before the transaction deleted or updated the corresponding data. During the insert of the pseudo-deleted key, the transaction writes a log record so that in case the transaction were to roll back, then the key will be reactivated (i.e., put in the inserted state) in the index.

2.2. Details of the NSF Algorithm

When an index is being created on a table, IB will take the following actions.

1. Create the descriptor for the index
2. Extract the keys and sort them
3. Insert the keys into the index while periodically committing the inserts
4. Make the index available for read
5. Optionally, schedule cleanup of the pseudo-deleted keys

Below, we describe most of the above actions in detail.

2.2.1. Index Descriptor Creation

After the descriptor is created, the new index is visible for key insert and delete operations by transactions. The index is still not available to the transactions to use it as an access path for retrievals. Such usage has to be delayed until

1 In parallel with our work, some solutions to this problem were independently proposed in [SrCa91].

2 A latch is like a semaphore and it is very cheap in terms of instructions executed [Moha90a, Moha90b]. It provides physical consistency of the data when a page is being examined. Readers of the page acquire a share (S) latch, while updaters acquire an exclusive (X) latch.

the entire index is built.[3] For key inserts and deletes into the new index, it is assumed that these operations start at transaction boundaries after the index descriptor is created. That is, there will be no uncommitted updates against the table when the descriptor is being created. This is a short term quiesce of updates against the table. This can be achieved, for example, by IB acquiring a share (S) lock on the table and holding it for the duration of the index descriptor create operation. After the descriptor is built, the update transactions are allowed to start execution. Note that this quiesce lasts for a much shorter duration than the time interval between the start and end of the complete index build operation.

The following scenario illustrates the need for quiescing the update transactions before the descriptor is built. A transaction T1 inserted a record prior to creation of the descriptor for an index I1. Therefore, T1 did not write a log record for I1. Now, IB starts and inserts the key for T1's record into I1 (note that IB does not check for uncommitted records by locking). If later T1 were to roll back, then it would not delete the key from the index, thereby leaving a key in the index which points to a deleted record. The alternative is that the IB does locking to check whether the record is uncommitted. Due to the enormous locking overhead that this might entail, we did not take that approach (of course, we would have used the Commit_LSN idea [Moha90b] to avoid the locking when the circumstances were right). Instead, we chose to quiesce the update transactions just to create the descriptor. The SF algorithm does not require this quiescing. As explained later (see the section "3.2.3. Inserts and Deletes by Transactions While IB is Active"), in NSF also we can avoid the quiescing by logging, in the data page log record, the number of visible indexes and by performing, if necessary, logical undos to indexes during transaction rollback.

2.2.2. Extraction of Keys

IB reads the data pages sequentially to extract the keys. To make the CPU processing and I/Os efficient, multiple pages may be read in one I/O by employing sequential prefetch [TeGu84]. Also, the data pages may be read in parallel using multiple processes [PMCLS90] to speed up the key create and sort operations. As IB scans all the data pages, it extracts the keys and sorts them in a pipelined fashion. It completes that processing *before* it inserts any key into the index. This approach is adopted to make the index update operation very efficient (i.e., all the keys will be handled in key sequence). Note that the final merge phase of sort can be performed as keys are being inserted into the index. Doing all of the above may involve, depending on the size of the table, a considerable amount of processing. Therefore, to guard against loss of too much work in case of a system failure, NSF would employ a restartable sort like the one described in the section "5. Restartable Sort".

When accessing a data page, IB latches the page to extract keys from the records in that page. IB does **not** lock records when it extracts keys from them. Therefore, it is possible that IB will insert or attempt to insert a key for a record that has been inserted or updated by an uncommitted transaction. The uncommitted transaction may have already inserted that key or it may attempt to insert that key later on. The uncommitted transaction may also try to roll back its insert and, in that process, delete that key later on. In the next section, we explain the actions that must be taken as a consequence of IB possibly competing with transactions' uncommitted operations.

2.2.3. Inserting Keys into the Index by IB

Keys are inserted into the index while holding latches on index pages, as described in [Moha90a, MoLe92]. To make IB's insert processing efficient, the index manager will accept multiple keys in a single call. For transactions, the index is traversed from the root to insert or delete a key. For IB, tree traversals are avoided most of the time by remembering the path from the root to the leaf, as in ARIES/IM [MoLe92], and by exploiting that information during a subsequent call (see [CHHIM91] for a discussion of how this is done for retrievals). The proper amount of desired free space (for future inserts during normal processing) is left in the leaf pages as multiple keys are inserted.

It is assumed that an *undo-redo* log record is written as IB's keys are inserted into a leaf page. The log record can contain multiple keys. Page splits are also logged as in ARIES/IM. Logging by IB ensures that (1) the index tree would be in a structurally consistent state after restart or process recovery, and (2) media recovery can be supported without the user being forced to take an image (dump) copy of the index immediately after the index build completes. If the strategy is to restart the index build all over in case of a failure, then log writes by IB can be avoided. This strategy is probably unacceptable for large tables.

Next, we explain the actions that must be taken as a consequence of IB possibly competing with transactions' key insert and delete operations.

IB and Insert Operations

NSF deals with the problems caused by IB competing with a transaction's insert operation by extending the index management logic to reject insertion of a duplicate key. If the *transaction* actually inserts the key, then it writes an *undo-redo* log record. If the transaction does not insert the key because it had already been inserted by IB, then it writes an *undo-only* log record. In this case, the undo-only log record is needed so that, if the transaction were to roll back later, then that key will be deleted from the index by the transaction even though the key was originally inserted by IB. If the transaction were to commit, then the undo-redo log record written by IB or the transaction would ensure that the insert operation would be reflected in the index even if that index page were not written to disk due to a system failure. However, if IB's insert is rejected because of duplication, then no log record is written by IB.

We distinguish inserts of a duplicate key *value* for a nonunique index and for a unique index. This is because, for a unique index, *unique key value violation* needs to be detected and appropriate action taken. For a nonunique index, the key must match completely (<*key value, RID*>) for rejection. For a unique index, *transactions* use the current approach to detect the duplicate key value. That is, if the key value part of the key is found to be already present, then the transaction ensures that the found key, which may be a pseudo-deleted key, belongs to a committed record (or that the key is its own uncommitted insert) before it

3 Actually, if we are ambitious, then we could make the index gradually available for a range of key values starting from the smallest possible key value in the index as the index is being continuously modified by IB to include higher and higher key values.

determines whether a unique key value violation error needs to be returned. This is normally done by locking the key. The lock may be avoidable using the Commit_LSN technique of [Moha90b].

A similar approach is used by IB except that IB has to check that (1) the record on whose behalf IB is inserting the key is committed and (2) the record whose identical key value already exists in the index is also committed. Therefore, IB would lock both records in share mode, and then access the index page and the corresponding data page(s) to verify whether the duplicate key value condition still exists. If it does, then the index-build operation is abnormally terminated since a unique index cannot be built on this table.

No *next key locking* is done during key inserts into the new index while index build is still in progress. This locking, which is done to guarantee serializability by handling the *phantom problem* [Moha90a, MoLe92], is not needed since no readers are allowed to access the index while it is still being created. For a unique index, normally, next key locking is also done to ensure that one transaction does not insert a key with a particular key value when another *still-uncommitted* transaction had earlier deleted another key with the same key value. If next key locking is not done by both transactions, then the former will be able to do its insert and commit, and later the other transaction might roll back, causing a situation from which we cannot recover correctly. Here, the pseudo deletion of keys allows the transactions to keep out of such trouble without doing next key locking (see also [Moha90b]).

IB and Delete Operations

The following extensions to the index management logic are needed to deal with the race conditions between transactions' key deletes and IB's operations. The actions performed by a transaction trying to delete a key (*deleter*) are based on whether the key exists in the index at the time the transaction looks for it in the index. The key delete may be happening as a result of a forward processing action (record delete or update) or a rollback action (undo of an earlier key insert).

If the key exists in the index, then the deleter (1) modifies the key to be a pseudo-deleted key and (2) writes the usual log record.[4] IB's attempt to insert a key which is currently present in the index in the pseudo-deleted state is rejected. Note that the deleter will **not** physically delete the key since it may not be aware if IB had already extracted that key from the data page for subsequent insert into the index. Even if NSF were to maintain some information about IB's data page accesses (as is done in SF), which may let the deleter determine whether IB has already extracted the key, NSF cannot physically delete the key in the case of a *unique* index. This is to avoid the problem discussed earlier with reference to next key locking and a unique key value violation scenario which involved two transactions.

If the key does *not* exist in the index, then the deleter (1) **inserts** the key with an indicator that it is pseudo deleted and (2) writes the usual log record.[4] Again, the reason for inserting the pseudo-deleted key is to correctly deal with a race condition between the deleter and IB. For example, the key might have already been extracted by IB and IB may try to insert the key after the deleter commits. By leaving a *tombstone* in the form of a pseudo-deleted key and later rejecting IB's insert, NSF correctly deals with the race condition.

Note that if a key is not inserted by IB because an uncommitted transaction had deleted the data record by the time IB's scan reaches the corresponding data page, then the key would reappear in the index if that transaction were to roll back. This is because the rollback processing of the deleter would process the undo portion of its log record for the index and that would place the key in the inserted state. This is the reason for writing an *undo-redo* log record, as opposed to a redo-only log record, when the key is not found by the deleter. Such a log record is guaranteed to exist since the deleting transaction must have begun only after the index descriptor was created. The latter will be true because of the quiescing of update transactions at the time of descriptor creation.

Next, we give examples of insert and delete operations which can happen while IB is active.

1. Transaction T1 inserts a record with RID R and key value K for a nonunique index which is being concurrently built.
2. T1 inserts the key (<K, R>) into the index being constructed.
3. IB reads the new record and tries to insert its key.
4. Since IB finds the duplicate key, it does not insert the key.
5. T1 rolls back.
6. T1 marks the key as being pseudo-deleted and deletes the record in the data page.
7. T2 inserts a record at the same location (RID R) and the same key value (K).
8. T2 inserts the key (<K, R>) which would result in resetting the pseudo-deleted flag (that is, placing the key in the inserted state).
9. T2 commits which would result in <K,R> in the index and a valid record at RID R.

If, instead, T2 had inserted the same record with RID R1, then the index would have <K, R> as a pseudo-deleted key and <K, R1> as a normal key. In this case, if the index had been a unique index, then T2 would have (1) determined that the inserter of the pseudo-deleted version of <K, R> had terminated and (2) reset the pseudo-deleted flag in the existing entry and replaced R with R1.

Periodic Checkpointing by IB

For assuring the restartability of the key insert phase of index build, IB can periodically checkpoint the *highest* key that it has so far inserted into the index. This involves IB recording on stable storage the highest key and issuing a *commit* call. For restart of IB, this key can be used to determine the keys in the sorted list which remain to be inserted into the index. Though there is no integrity problem in IB trying to insert keys which were already inserted prior to the failure (since those attempted reinsertions would be rejected as a result of the previously explained duplicate keys handling logic and hence no log records would be written), it does avoid unnecessary work after restart. Note that, since log records for the index updates are written by the transactions and IB, the index would be in a structurally

4 With ARIES/IM, for a forward processing action, it would be a redo-undo log record, and for a rollback action, it would be a compensation (redo-only) log record.

consistent state after restart recovery is completed [MoLe92].

2.2.4. Cleanup of Pseudo-Deleted Keys

After IB completes its processing, garbage collection of the pseudo-deleted keys in the index can be scheduled as a background activity. If the index is created when the table has low delete activity, then this cleanup may not be worthwhile. Otherwise, pseudo-deleted keys can cause unnecessary page splits and cause more pages to be allocated for the index than are actually required. We would expect that an index-build operation would not be scheduled during a period of time when a significant portion of the table is expected to be updated. The garbage collection of pseudo-deleted keys involves the following steps: Scan the leaf pages. For each page, latch the page and check if there are any pseudo-deleted keys. If there are, then apply the Commit_LSN check [Moha90b]. If it is successful, then garbage collect those keys; otherwise, for each pseudo-deleted key, request a conditional instant share lock on it. If the lock is granted, then delete the key; otherwise, skip it since the key's deletion is probably uncommitted.

2.3. Discussion of the NSF Algorithm

2.3.1. Performance

In NSF, IB does not have complete control over the index tree when it is inserting keys into it since transactions are allowed to concurrently insert and delete keys directly in the tree. As a result, NSF cannot build the tree in a bottom-up fashion. In a ***bottom-up index build***, the keys are sorted in key sequence and then inserted into the first index page which acts as a root as well as a leaf. When this leaf becomes full, the next two index pages are allocated with one of them becoming the new root and the other one a leaf which will be used to insert the subsequent keys in the input stream. The old root is made into a leaf. Note that this is a special form of the page split operation in which no keys are moved from the splitting page to the new page. In a normal page split, usually, half the keys in the page being split are moved to the new page [Moha90a, MoLe92].

The above process is repeated until all the keys are inserted by the index builder. Note that the new keys are always added to the rightmost leaf in the tree without a tree traversal from the root and without the cost of latching pages and comparing keys. The result of this method of inserting keys is that the tree grows in a bottom-up, left to right fashion. Needed new pages are always allocated from the end of the index file which keeps growing. The resultant tree would be such that if a range scan of all the keys in ascending sequence were to be done at the leaf level, then pages in the index file would be accessed in *ascending* order of page numbers. That is, a ***clustered index scan*** would be possible. This would enable prefetching of index pages in *physical* sequence to be quite effective [TeGu84].

In NSF, to compensate for its inability to build the index tree bottom-up and to help range scanners, we can perform prefetch of index leaf pages effectively by using an idea suggested in [CHHIM91]. The idea is to perform prefetch of leaf pages by looking up their page-IDs in their parent pages, instead of prefetching pages in physical sequence. To avoid a tree traversal for inserting each key, NSF can (1) remember the path from the root to the leaf, as in ARIES/IM [MoLe92], and exploit that information during a subsequent call (see [CHHIM91] for a discussion of how this is done for retrievals), and (2) pass multiple keys for insertion in one call to the index manager. If splits caused by IB's key inserts were handled just like splits during normal processing, then those keys that were inserted by *transactions* before IB starts adding keys to the index may be moved through a large number of leaf pages. To avoid the unnecessary CPU and logging overhead that this would cause, IB's splits can be specialized as follows: During a split, if there are any keys on the leaf which are higher than the key that IB is attempting to insert (these keys must have been inserted earlier by transactions), then IB can move those higher keys alone to a new leaf page and try to insert the new key.[5] If there are no such keys, then IB allocates a new leaf and inserts the new key there. This approach tries to mimic what happens in a bottom-up build. As a consequence, if the concurrent update activities by transactions are not significant, then the trees generated by NSF and by bottom-up build should be close in terms of clustering and the cost of tree creation.

The following additional points are worth noting regarding the performance of IB:

- During IB's scan of the records for extraction of keys, multiple *data* pages can be read in one disk I/O because of sequential access. Data pages could also be read in parallel. We believe that I/O time to scan the data pages would be a significant portion of the total elapsed time to build the index. Therefore, parallel reads would be required.
- The last page to be processed by the data page scan can be noted before starting IB's data scan so that if there are any extensions of the file after IB starts, IB does not have to process the new pages. Transactions would insert directly into the index the keys of records belonging to those new pages.
- During extraction of keys, each data page is only latched and no locking is performed. This saves the pathlength of lock and unlock, and it supports high concurrency by reducing interferences with transactions.
- One log record for multiple keys would save the pathlength of a log call for each key and reduce the number of log records written.
- The index leaf pages are only latched and no locking is done. These have concurrency advantages [Moha90a, MoLe92].

2.3.2. Restarting or Cancelling Index Build

By using a restartable sort (see the section "5. Restartable Sort"), if a system failure were to occur when IB is still scanning the data pages, then IB can be restarted without it having to rescan the data pages from the beginning. By periodically checkpointing the highest key inserted by IB, insertion of keys needs to be resumed only from the last checkpoint onwards, rather than all the way from the beginning. The reason the index itself cannot be used to determine the highest key inserted by IB after restart is because there is interference by transactions. Hence, IB has to track its position in the list of sorted keys.

5 If we are very ambitious about attaining close to perfect clustering, then we could collect statistics about key value distributions during the sorting of the keys by IB and estimate what the ideal page would be, in terms of its physical location in the index file, for the higher valued keys that are moved out.

Since cancelling an in-progress index build requires that the descriptor of the index be deleted, we need to quiesce update transactions by acquiring a share lock on the table. Quiescing is required so that the transactions which roll back can process their log records against the index without running into any abnormal situations. The rest of the processing for cancelling an index build is the same as what is normally required for the dropping of an index.

3. Algorithm SF: Bottom-Up Index Build with Side-File

In this section, we present the SF (*Side-File*) algorithm. First, we give a brief overview of the solutions to the problems described in the section "1.2. Problems". Then, we describe the SF algorithm in detail.

3.1. Overview of SF

The SF algorithm has the following features:

- IB first builds the index tree bottom-up without any interference being caused by direct key inserts or deletes in the index by transactions.
- Transactions' key inserts and deletes for the index under construction are appended in a side-file while IB is active *and* the index is "visible" to the transactions (details about when the index becomes visible to a particular transaction are given later). A side-file is an append-only (sequential) table in which the transactions insert tuples of the form *<operation, key>*, where *operation* is insert or delete. Transactions append entries without doing any locking of the appended entries.
- After inserting into the tree all the keys that it extracted from the records in the data pages, IB processes the side-file. When this is happening, transactions continue to append to the side-file.
- On completing the processing of the side-file, IB signals that from then on transactions must directly insert or delete keys in the new index.

Assumptions

- IB does **not** write log records for the inserts of keys that it extracts from the records in the data pages. It does write *redo-undo* log records for the key inserts and deletes that it performs while processing the side-file.
- Transactions write *redo-only* log records for the appends that they make to the side-file.

SF and NSF are different with respect to when they make the existence of the new index *visible* to update transactions. In NSF, the index is made visible when the index descriptor is created and from then on update transactions start making key inserts and deletes directly in the new index. In SF, the index is made visible based on IB's current position in its scan of the data pages. IB maintains a ***Current-RID*** position as it scans records from page to page. The index becomes ***visible*** to an update transaction if it modifies (inserts, deletes or updates) a record with a record ID, call it the ***Target-RID***, which is *less than* Current-RID. The Current-RID and Target-RID cannot be the same because of the page latching protocol used by update transactions and IB when they access a page. As mentioned before, as long as IB is active, only when a new index is visible to a transaction does the transaction make an entry in the side-file based on its record operation in the data page.

Next, we discuss how SF avoids the Duplicate-insert-key problem and the Delete-key problem. Even though a side-file is being used, these problems still need to be taken into account.

3.1.1. Duplicate-Key-Insert Problem

SF avoids the race condition between IB and a transaction attempting to insert the same key in the index by ensuring that the transaction will generate a key insert entry in the side-file only if the index is visible to it. That is, if the record is being inserted *behind* IB's scan position (i.e., target-RID < Current-RID), then IB will not be aware of that key and hence it will not insert that key into the index. If the index is not visible to the transaction (i.e., target-RID > Current-RID), then the transaction will not make any entries in the side-file and IB will insert that key into the index. Considerations relating to the rollback of the inserter are described later.

3.1.2. Delete-Key Problem

SF ensures that if a key were to be first extracted by IB for subsequent insert into the index and later a transaction were to perform an action on the corresponding record which necessitates the deletion of that key, then that transaction will append a key delete entry to the side-file. The latter action will occur because, by the time the transaction performs its record operation, Current-RID will be greater than Target-RID. Since IB first inserts into the index tree those keys that it extracted from the data pages and only after that it processes the side-file, SF guarantees that ultimately the key of the above example will be deleted.

We now consider the impact of the rollback of a transaction with respect to the *visibility* of an index. The question is, what would happen if during the forward processing of a transaction the index was *not* visible, but by the time the transaction rolls back the index becomes visible. What this implies is that (1) for a forward processing operation necessitating a key insert (i.e, a record insert or a record update involving key columns), IB would have inserted the new key in the index, and (2) for a forward processing operation necessitating a key delete (i.e, a record delete or a record update involving key columns), IB would have missed the old key and hence would not have attempted deleting it. For both cases, we must undo those actions. That is, in the first case, the new key must be eliminated from the index and in the second case, the old key must be inserted into the index. SF's approach to dealing with this problem is to make the transaction include information, such as the count of visible indexes, in the log record for the **data page update**. From this information, it would be possible to infer that the index was not visible during forward processing, but became visible during rollback. In such a case, if the index build is not yet completed, then an entry will be appended to the side-file when the log record for the data page is undone; for a completely built index, the index would be traversed to perform the necessary undo action.

To summarize, SF requires the following changes in the transaction forward processing and undo logic:

- The record management component has to be aware whether IB is active or not and if it is, then what the current scan position of IB is. This is because, if IB is active, then an append to the side-file of the index needs to be performed only if Current-RID is greater than Target-RID.

- Maintenance of a side-file which is an append-only table to make entries for insert or delete key actions. These appends are logged. New entries may be appended during the rollback of a transaction.
- Additional information is required in the log record for a data page operation. This will be the count of the visible indexes at the time the data page update was performed.[6]
- During undo processing, the count of visible indexes recorded in the log record of the data page is compared with the current count of visible indexes. If the former is smaller, then it implies that IB's action(s) needs to be compensated as follows: (1) if the index build for the last index is not complete, by making an entry (of key delete or insert) in the side-file; (2) for the newly visible indexes for which index build has been completed, by performing a logical undo (i.e., by traversing the tree from the root).

3.2. Details of the SF Algorithm

In this section, we describe the details of SF in the same manner that we described them for NSF.

3.2.1. Index Descriptor Creation

The descriptor for the new index is created and appended to the list of descriptors for the preexisting indexes of the table without quiescing (update) transactions. IB sets a flag (*Index_Build = '1'*) which indicates that an index-build operation is in progress. This flag is examined by a transaction as it performs a record insert, delete or update operation while holding the data page latch.

3.2.2. Extraction of Keys

Like NSF, SF also reads multiple pages with one I/O and employs parallelism for reads. Keys of the records in a data page are extracted while holding a share latch on the page. As in NSF, IB does not lock records when it extracts keys. A current scan position called Current-RID is maintained as each record is processed to extract the key. This scan position determines whether the index is visible to the transactions or not, as was described earlier (see also Figure 1 and Figure 2). When IB finishes processing the last data page, it sets Current-RID to *infinity*. This ensures that, if the file were to be subsequently extended for the addition of records, then transactions which perform those actions will make entries in the side-file. As the data pages are scanned and keys are extracted, the keys are sorted. Like NSF, SF also uses a restartable sort algorithm.

3.2.3. Inserts and Deletes by Transactions While IB is Active

Transactions take actions based on the *Index_Build* flag and the current scan position of IB. In Figure 1 and Figure 2, we give the pseudo-code for index updates during forward processing and rollback of transactions. The pseudo-code with the comments should be self-explanatory to the reader.[7] It should be observed that SF is **not** quiescing all update transactions at any time. The one point that may need some explanation is that, in the case of the pseudo-code for rollback, it is possible for the difference between the numbers of indexes visible at the time of the original data page operation and during rollback to be even greater than one. This can happen, for example, because of the following sequence of events: T1 updates data page P10; index build for I3 begins and completes; index build for I4 begins and causes IB to process P10 and move Target-RID past P10; T1 rolls back its change to P10. In this scenario, while undoing its change to P10, T1 has to make an entry in the side-file for the index undo to be performed in I4 and it should perform a logical undo (by traversing the tree) in I3.

3.2.4. Inserting Keys into the Index by IB

The keys are completely sorted before their insertion into the index. Like NSF, SF also can pipeline the output of the last merge pass into the key insert logic. When IB is active, only IB inserts keys into the index. Because of these reasons, the index is built in a bottom-up fashion which is very efficient, as explained in the section "2.3.1. Performance". IB does not traverse the index from the root to insert keys as long as it has not started processing the side-file. IB does not write log records for its index operations until it starts processing the side-file. IB can check for unique-key violation in the same way as it does in NSF.

Periodic Checkpointing by IB

Until IB starts processing the side-file, periodically, IB can checkpoint the highest key inserted into the index and the page-IDs of the rightmost branch of the index. This checkpointing to stable storage is done after all the dirty pages of the index have been written to disk. In case of a failure, the index pages can be reset in such a way that the keys higher than the checkpointed key disappear from the index.

```
Target_Page := Data page for record
     Insert/Delete/Update operation
X-latch(Target_Page)
Target_RID := RID of affected record
IF Index_Build = '1' THEN /* index being built */
| IF Target_RID < Current_RID THEN /* New Index
| |        is VISIBLE; need to make entry in SF */
| | Modify target record, log action and count of
| |          visible indexes, and Update Page_LSN
| | Unlatch(Target_Page)
| | Make entry in side-file for insert key or
| |              delete key for index being built
| | Update all other indexes directly
| ELSE     /* Target_RID >= IB's scan position */
| |  /* New index INVISIBLE; no SF entry made */
| | Modify target record, log action and count of
| |          visible indexes, and Update Page_LSN
| | Unlatch(Target_Page)
| | Update all other indexes directly, completely
| |                   ignoring index being built
ELSE          /* No index creation in progress */
| Modify target record, log action and count of
| all indexes, and Update Page_LSN
| Unlatch(Target_Page)
| Update all indexes
Return
```

Figure 1: Pseudo-Code for Index Updates by Transactions During Forward Processing in SF

6 As a result, a minor restriction is that an index cannot be dropped while update transactions are active. That is, the number of indexes can only increase while update transactions are active. Hence, a drop index operation must acquire a share lock on the table before doing the drop. NSF also has this locking requirement since it cannot make the index descriptor disappear while update transactions are active.

7 While the pseudo-code is written, for brevity, as if only one index is being created at any given time for a table, as we discuss in the section "6.2. Extensions", creation of multiple indexes simultaneously in one scan of the data can be easily accomplished.

```
Target_Page := Data page for undo of record
               Insert/Delete/Update operation
X-latch(Target_Page)
Target_RID := RID of affected record
IF Index_Build = '1' THEN /* index being built */
| IF Target_RID < Current_RID THEN  /* IB will
| |   reflect in new index old state of record */
| | Current_Count := Count of all indexes,
| |                          including new one
| ELSE /* IB will not reflect in new index old
| |                          state of record */
| | Current_Count := Count of all indexes,
| |                          excluding new one
| Modify target record, log action and
|                            Update Page_LSN
| Unlatch(Target_Page)
| IF data page log record's count < Current_Count
|        THEN
| | undo logically index change on those indexes
| |      made visible since original data change
| | /* i.e., make entry in SF for index under
| |    construction and for others, if any,
| |    traverse the trees to reflect effect of
| |    record's undo on index key           */
ELSE          /* No index creation in progress */
| Current_Count := Count of all indexes
| Modify target record, log action and
|                            Update Page_LSN
| Unlatch(Target_Page)
| IF data page log record's count < Current_Count
|                              THEN
|   undo logically index change on those indexes
|     made visible since original data change by
|     retraversing their tree
Return
```

Figure 2: Pseudo-Code for Index Updates by Transactions During Rollback Processing in SF

Also, the pages which keep track of index page allocation-deallocation status will be updated to indicate that the index pages allocated after the latest index checkpoint are in the deallocated state (i.e., they are available for allocation). This is easy to do since, with a bottom-up index build, as more keys are added and new pages are needed, the pages will be allocated to the index sequentially from the beginning of the file (see the section "2.3.1. Performance").

3.2.5. Processing of the Side-File

After building the index in a bottom-up fashion, IB processes the side-file from the beginning to end. While doing so, IB traverses the index from the root and, based on the entry in the side-file, inserts or deletes the key in the index as a normal transaction would do. That is, IB writes undo-redo log records which describe its actions. In order to avoid losing too much work if a failure were to occur when the side-file is being processed, periodically IB can checkpoint its progress in processing the side-file and issue a commit call. Until IB reaches the last entry in the side-file, transactions may still be appending new entries to the side-file. After processing the last entry in the side-file, IB resets the Index_Build flag so that subsequently transactions would modify the index directly. For improved performance, IB could sort the entries of the side-file, without modifying the relative positions of the identical keys, before applying those updates to the index. The sorting and processing of the sort stream must be done carefully to make them restartable. Also, by the time the application of the sorted entries to the index is completed, some more pages might have been added to the side-file. They could be processed sequentially (i.e., without sorting).

4. Comparison of the Algorithms

The main difference between NSF and SF is the maintenance of a side-file. The other differences between SF and NSF are:

- In SF, IB is able to build the index more efficiently than in NSF for the following reasons:
  - No log records are written by IB for inserting keys until side-file processing begins. In NSF, log records are written for all key inserts by IB. NSF reduces this overhead by logging all the keys inserted on a particular index page using a single log record.
  - Tree traversal from the root page of the index tree is not required to insert keys until side-file processing begins. In NSF, most of the time, IB would avoid tree traversals by remembering the path from the root to the leaf and exploiting that information during a subsequent call.
- In SF, no quiescing of table updates by transactions is required at any time. NSF quiesces all update transactions while creating the index descriptor.
- SF does not require the support of the concept of pseudo deletion of keys. This means that no changes are required for the existing index page and key formats.

It is expected that the index built by SF would be more clustered (i.e., consecutive keys being on consecutive pages on disk) than the one built by NSF. Deviations from the perfect clustering achievable without concurrent updates would be a function of the transactions' key insert and delete activities during the time of index build. These deviations need to be quantified for both algorithms.

5. Restartable Sort

In this section, we describe algorithms for making the different phases of the sort operation restartable. The two phases to be considered are: the sort phase and the merge phase. We discuss each one in turn next. We assume that a tournament tree sort [Knut73] is used. Without loss of generality, we assume that the keys are being sorted in ascending order.

5.1. Sort Phase

We assume that the sort is being performed, using a tournament tree, in a pipelined fashion as the data is being scanned by IB and the keys are being extracted from records. Periodically, we checkpoint the sorted streams as of certain scan position up to which the IB has scanned data pages of the table. This is so that, in case of a failure, IB would not have to rescan those data pages up to which the corresponding sorted streams were checkpointed. While taking a checkpoint, we wait for the tournament tree to output all the keys that have so far been extracted. We force to disk all those keys. We checkpoint the information (file names, etc.) relating to the already output sorted streams and the position of the IB data scan up to which keys have already been extracted and sorted. For the last sorted stream that was produced, we also record the value of the highest key that was output.

When we have to restart after a failure, we take the following steps:

- Read in the information from the latest checkpoint before the failure.
- Reposition the IB scan to the position indicated in the checkpoint.
- Discard any output sorted streams that did not exist as of the last checkpoint.
- Reposition the last sorted output stream that existed during the last checkpoint to the end of file position recorded in the checkpoint.
- Restart the tournament tree by inputting from the IB scan. If the smallest key produced during this sort phase is higher than the checkpointed value (i.e., highest key output at the time of the last checkpoint before the failure), then the output keys can still be sent to the same sorted stream in which we performed repositioning in the previous step. Otherwise, a new sorted output stream must be created.

5.2. Merge Phase

At different points during the merge phase, we need to write to disk all the keys that have been output so far from the merge operation. Let's call this a checkpoint operation. When we take such a checkpoint, we need to also record enough information so that we know how to repopulate the tournament tree with keys from the different input sorted streams correctly, in case we have to later on restart from this checkpoint. We should ensure that no key is left out from the merge and that no key is output more than once. This requires that we know precisely, for each input stream, the position of the highest key which has already been output by the merge operation. This tracking can be done as follows:

- Associate with the tournament tree a vector of N counters, where each counter is associated with one input stream and N is the number of leaf nodes in the tournament tree. All the counters are initialized to 1.
- Since, in a tournament sort, during the merge phase, a particular leaf node of the tree is always fed from the same input stream and a particular input stream is associated with only one leaf node, as we produce an output from the root of the tree, we know exactly which input stream that value came from. Consequently, while outputting a value from the tree, we increment by one the counter associated with the input stream from which that value came.
- During a checkpoint operation, we record the contents of the vector of counters and the descriptions (file names, etc.) of the input streams associated with those counters. Essentially, we are checkpointing the input streams' scan positions. We also record the information relating to the output stream (the position of the end of file on the output file, etc.).

When we have to resume the merge operation after a system failure, we look at the latest checkpoint information for the merge and do the following:

- Truncate the tail of the output file so that its end of file position corresponds to the checkpointed information.
- Read in the contents of the vector of counters and use the associated input file descriptions to reposition the input files to the positions indicated by the counters' values. If the counter value for a file is k, then that file should be positioned so that the next key to be input into the merge from that file would be the key at position k.
- Restart the merge operation by initializing the counters to the checkpointed values and reading from the input files at their current positions as set up in the previous step.

6. Conclusions

As the sizes of the tables to be stored in DBMSs grow and several indexes may need to be created long after the tables were created, disallowing updates to a table while creating an index for it will not always be acceptable. Higher availability of data is becoming more and more important as many companies expand towards world-wide operations and as users' expectations about data availability increase [Moha92]. The so-called *batch window* is rapidly shrinking. As more and more companies merge, and automation of various operations become common place, the volume of data to be handled grows enormously. As disk storage prices drop and the disks' storage capacities increase, users tend to keep more and more of their data online. These trends have necessitated a new approach to the construction of indexes.

6.1. Summary

We described two efficient algorithms, called NSF (No Side-File) and SF (Side File), which allow concurrent update operations by transactions during index build. Our emphasis has been to maximize concurrency, minimize overheads and cover all aspects of the problem, including recovering from failures without complete loss of work. The efficiency of these algorithms comes from the following: (1) When data is scanned, no locks are acquired on the data pages or the records. (2) The index is built bottom up in SF and a multiple-keys interface is used in NSF. (3) Parallel reads and bulk I/Os (i.e., read of multiple pages in one I/O) are used to shorten the time to scan data. SF first builds the index bottom up and maintains a side-file for updates which occur while it is constructing the index. SF and NSF can create correctly both unique and nonunique indexes, without giving spurious unique-key-value-violation error messages in the case of unique indexes.

We also presented algorithms for making the sort operation and the tree building operation restartable. The algorithms relating to sort have very general applicability, apart from their use in the current context of sorting for index creation.

We did not consider using the log, instead of the side-file, to bring the index up to date for reasons like the following:

- The log records written for the data page updates may not contain enough information to determine how the index should be updated. For example, the new index being built may be defined on columns C1 and C2, and the log record for the data page update may contain only the before and after values of the modified column, say C2, of the updated record. Given only C2's before and after values from the log record, there is no cost-effective way to determine what key has to be deleted from the index and what key has to be inserted into the index since C1's value is not known. Extracting that information by examining the record in the data page would not be possible if the record had already advanced to a future state where the C1 value is no longer what it used to be.
- Even if the DBMS were to be inefficient enough to log even unmodified columns and hence the above is not a problem, the amount of log that would have to be scanned may be too much to make this a viable approach. Also, the system must ensure that the relevant portion of the

log is not discarded before the index build operation completes.[8]

6.2. Extensions

Since the cost of accessing all the data pages may be a significant part of the overall cost of index build, it would be very beneficial to build multiple indexes in one data scan. Our algorithms are flexible enough to accommodate that. The functions of scanning data and extracting keys for all the indexes being built simultaneously must be separated from the functions of sorting the keys, inserting them into the index and processing the side-file for each of those indexes. A process can be spawned for each index to sort the keys, insert them and process the side-file.

Our algorithms can also be easily extended to the storage model in which the records are stored in the primary index and the primary key is required to be unique. We would perform a complete range scan of the primary index to construct the keys for the new index. In SF, in the place of Current-RID, we would use the current-key as the scan position in the primary index. Since the primary key has to be unique, this position also would be a unique one in the index.

We assumed that the index manager does *data-only locking*, as in ARIES/IM [MoLe92]. In data-only locking, the lock names for the locks on the keys are the same as the names for the locks on the data from which those keys are derived. For example, with record locking, the lock on a key is the same as the lock on the corresponding record and, with page locking, it is the lock on the data page containing the corresponding record. Consequently, even if IB were to insert into the index a key of an *uncommitted* record, the transaction which performed that record operation (insert or update) does not have to acquire a new lock to protect the uncommitted key in the new index. It is because of this reason that IB, once it finishes building the index, can make available the new index for reads by transactions without the danger of exposing those transactions performing *index-only* read accesses to uncommitted keys. If the index locks were different from data locks, as in ARIES/KVL [Moha90a], then IB, on finishing building the index, would have to quiesce all update transactions before allowing reads of the new index.

Additional work needs to be done to permit concurrent index build when the DBMS supports transient versioning of index data to avoid locking by read-only transactions [MoPL92].

7. References

CHHIM91 Cheng, J., Haderle, D., Hedges, R., Iyer, B., Messinger, T., Mohan, C., Wang, Y. *An Efficient Hybrid Join Algorithm: a DB2 Prototype*, **Proc. 7th International Conference on Data Engineering**, Kobe, April 1991. An expanded version of this paper is available as **IBM Research Report RJ7884**, IBM Almaden Research Center, December 1990.

DeGr90 DeWitt, D., Gray, J. *Parallel Database Systems: The Future of Database Processing or a Passing Fad?*, **ACM SIGMOD Record**, Volume 19, Number 4, Decemeber 1990.

Gray78 Gray, J. *Notes on Data Base Operating Systems*, In **Operating Systems - An Advanced Course**, R. Bayer, R. Graham, and G. Seegmuller (Eds.), LNCS Volume 60, Springer-Verlag, 1978.

Knut73 Knuth, D. **The Art of Computer Programming: Volume 3**, Addison-Wesley Publishing Co., 1973.

MHLPS92 Mohan, C., Haderle, D., Lindsay, B., Pirahesh, H., Schwarz, P. *ARIES: A Transaction Recovery Method Supporting Fine-Granularity Locking and Partial Rollbacks Using Write-Ahead Logging*, **ACM Transactions on Database Systems**, Vol. 17, No. 1, March 1992. Also available as **IBM Research Report RJ6649**, IBM Almaden Research Center, January 1989.

Moha90a Mohan, C. *ARIES/KVL: A Key-Value Locking Method for Concurrency Control of Multiaction Transactions Operating on B-Tree Indexes*, **Proc. 16th International Conference on Very Large Data Bases**, Brisbane, August 1990. A different version of this paper is available as **IBM Research Report RJ7008**, IBM Almaden Research Center, September 1989.

Moha90b Mohan, C. *Commit_LSN: A Novel and Simple Method for Reducing Locking and Latching in Transaction Processing Systems*, **Proc. 16th International Conference on Very Large Data Bases**, Brisbane, August 1990. Also available as **IBM Research Report RJ7344**, IBM Almaden Research Center, February 1990.

Moha92 Mohan, C. *Supporting Very Large Tables*, **Proc. 7th Brazilian Symposium on Database Systems**, Porto Alegre, May 1992.

MoLe92 Mohan, C., Levine, F. *ARIES/IM: An Efficient and High Concurrency Index Management Method Using Write-Ahead Logging*, **Proc. ACM SIGMOD International Conference on Management of Data**, San Diego, June 1992. A longer version of this paper is available as **IBM Research Report RJ6846**, IBM Almaden Research Center, August 1989.

MoPL92 Mohan, C., Pirahesh, H., Lorie, R. *Efficient and Flexible Methods for Transient Versioning of Records to Avoid Locking by Read-Only Transactions*, **Proc. ACM SIGMOD International Conference on Management of Data**, San Diego, June 1992.

Ober80 Obermarck, R. *IMS/VS Program Isolation Feature*, **IBM Research Report RJ2879**, IBM San Jose Research Laboratory, July 1980.

PMCLS90 Pirahesh, H., Mohan, C., Cheng, J., Liu, T.S., Selinger, P. *Parallelism in Relational Data Base Systems: Architectural Issues and Design Approaches*, **Proc. 2nd International Symposium on Databases in Parallel and Distributed Systems**, Dublin, July 1990. An expanded version of this paper is available as **IBM Research Report RJ7724**, IBM Almaden Research Center, October 1990.

SiSU91 Silberschatz, A., Stonebraker, M., Ullman, J. (Eds.) *Database Systems: Achievements and Opportunities*, **Communications of the ACM**, Vol. 34, No. 10, October 1991.

SrCa91 Srinivasan, V., Carey, M. *On-Line Index Construction Algorithms*, **Proc. 4th International Workshop on High Performance Transaction Systems**, Asilomar, September 1991.

TeGu84 Teng, J., Gumaer, R. *Managing IBM Database 2 Buffers to Maximize Performance*, **IBM Systems Journal**, Vol. 23, No. 2, 1984.

8 Log records may be discarded if image copies of the data have been taken and the log records are not needed for restart recovery, normal undo or media recovery using such image copies.

Chapter 7
Data Warehousing

This section of the book deals with data warehousing techniques and practices. Because this topic largely originated in industrial practice and was more recently studied by the research community, it is widely misunderstood. Hence, we spend some of this introduction explaining the issues involved and also include a survey paper by Chaudhuri and Dayal that goes into more detail.

A typical large enterprise has a multitude of mission-critical operational systems, typically numbering in the tens or even the hundreds. The reason for this number of important computer systems is the decentralization practiced by most large enterprises. A (typically self-contained) business unit is set up and charged with moving the enterprise into some new area. This business unit often sets up its own computer system, so it can be in charge of its own destiny, rather than be at the mercy of some other group's computer system and priorities. Over a couple of decades, this leads to a proliferation of systems. These days it is also leading to a serious initiative in many enterprises aimed at server consolidation.

Each operational system is run by a system administrator (SA) who lives (and dies) by his ability to keep the system up and functioning during appropriate business hours and by his ability to provide good response time to the users of the system (who are typically entering transactions). To accomplish his goals, the SA will invariably jealously guard his computing resources and refuse to make modifications to his system, unless essential to the business unit. This creates a self-contained "island of information", and a typical enterprise has hundreds of such islands. Each island refuses to provide access to others in the enterprise (since this would degrade response time) and refuses to change the system to accommodate the needs of others (since this will lead to instability and lower system availability).

In this sort of world, a given customer of the enterprise will appear in the operational system of each business unit with which he has a relationship. There are obvious business opportunities if the islands of information can be integrated. A typical scenario is called "cross-selling": offering a customer additional products and services that may be of interest based on their history. An example of this nirvana would be to respond to a customer, who called his bank to discuss his checking account, with a suggestion that he investigate a refinance of his home since his rate of X% is enough above the current rate of Y% to make it worthwhile. This cross selling situation requires the checking account clerk to know that the customer on the phone has a home loan with the same bank.

To perform this information integration without changing every operational system (a no-no), an obvious strategy is to buy a large machine and then periodically copy relevant data from each operational system (typically during "dead" time) to the big machine. On this machine, the required data integration can be performed.

A second situation that arises frequently in retail applications is exemplified by the following example. An international chain store has a few hundred stores around North America. Each in-store system records every item that passes through a checkout lane. The data from each store is sent to a central place, and kept for (say) a year. Corporate buyers interrogate this system to see what is selling and what is not. For "hot" items, the buyer submits a large order to the manufacturer to tie up his production capability, and deny merchandise to his competitor. "Cold" items are put on sale or returned to the supplier, if possible. Hence, this integration of historical data can be used to help with stock rotation and purchasing.

Every large enterprise we know of has set up a central **data warehouse** to perform information integration like our first example or historical data integration like our second example. Such warehouses invariably have a collection of common characteristics to which we now turn.

Warehousing projects are typically way over budget and way behind schedule. The problem is always **semantic heterogeneity**. The various operational systems store data elements in different ways and with different semantics. For example, there are many different meanings for "two day delivery". Also, one of us is Mike Stonebraker in one system, and M. R. Stonebraker in another. Figuring out the exact semantics of data elements and then writing the conversion routines to change them to a common representation is very tedious, time consuming and expensive. Furthermore, there are cases where this conversion is near impossible. If you call an item "rubber hand protectors" and I call them "latex gloves", who is to say whether they are the same or different products?

Essentially all warehouses are loaded periodically and otherwise are read-only. The only exception is cleaning operations to remove errors. For historical warehouses, which record transactional data that has happened in past months, the correct way to organize such data is invariably to have a large **fact** table that records each transaction (who bought what, where, when, for how much, etc). The fact table is then joined to a collection of **dimension** tables, which record information about each customer, store, product, time period, etc. The fact table usually contains a huge number of rows, each of which is filled mostly with ID numbers (foreign keys to dimension table tuples). The number of rows in the dimension tables is usually tiny in comparison. Hence, the size of the warehouse is determined by the size of the fact table.

If one imagines the fact table in the center of a picture and the dimensions on the periphery, then the reasonable joins between the dimension tables and the fact table form a star. Hence, the name **star schema** is used to describe the logical data base design used in most warehouses. Sometimes, dimensions have multiple levels. For example, time period can be composed of quarters, made up of months, and then days. If there is a table for each level of a dimension, then a **snowflake schema** results.

Warehouse queries from business analysts are often **very** complex. They typically entail computing some aggregate over the fact table after joining it to a couple of dimension tables, filtered according to some other data elements in the dimension tables, and grouping the elements in the fact table by yet other elements of the dimension tables. An example query would be to compute the sales volume of the jewelry department for each store in the retail chain for each month for the last year. The result of this query often inspires the business analyst to ask a different query, which is some other aggregate grouping on different data elements in the same or different dimensions.

As a result, it is essentially impossible to choose a good primary key for the fact table. One would like to have it sorted in the order of the filtering attribute(s) (which is in some other table), but this attribute changes from query to query. Hence, the best tactic for improving warehouse performance is to materialize views, which sort the fact table in the order required by popular queries.

Warehouse queries are usually run on large multi-processors. It is sometimes important to utilize intra-query parallelism in order to run especially hard queries in parallel using multiple disks and multiple CPUs.

Many of the data elements have small cardinality. For example, there are only 50 states and less than 100,000 cities in the USA. Therefore, it is often desirable to code data elements in the warehouse. Instead of storing "state" as two ASCII characters consuming 16 bits, one can store it as a 6 bit code. Also, it is invariably true that **bit map indexes** outperform traditional B-tree indexes. For example, in an N record table the data element "state" can be indexed by 50 bit strings of length N, one per state. Since each bit string is sparse, it can be run-length encoded to further reduce space by at least a factor of 2. In contrast, a B-tree requires more than 32 bits per record. Also, bit map indexes can be intersected and unioned very efficiently to deal with Boolean combinations of predicates. B-trees are much less efficient in this kind of processing. In many practical warehousing scenarios, bit map indexes take up far less space and are far more efficient than B-tree ones. Since a warehouse is updated in batch, the maintenance cost of updating bitmap indexes is tolerable. Hence, bit map indexes are a key indexing technology in data warehouses

In the early 1990's the term **on line analytical processing** (OLAP) was coined to loosely stand for the functionality in the Arbor product, Essbase. This system allowed one to define a collection of hierarchical dimension similar to the ones discussed above. Then, for display purposes, any two dimensions could be chosen for the X and Yaxes, and an aggregate could be shown in the cells for each pair of dimension values. This multidimensional structure was called a **data cube**, because two dimensions of an N-dimensional cube could be displayed at any one time. Also, for the hierarchical dimensions found in snowflake schemas, one could zoom in and out of a dimension that was displayed. Hence OLAP became synonymous with a data visualization system for N-dimensional data. **Drill-down** was the term used for getting more detail from a hierarchical dimension, **Roll-up** the term used for aggregating data up to a higher level of the hierarachy.

Arbor's product contained special (non-tabular) data structures to efficiently compute and maintain data cubes. Hence, Essbase was a cube-oriented data visualization system written for specialized data storage structures, and this architecture became synonymous with OLAP. A data cube interface can also be put on top of a relational product, and these were called **relational OLAP** products (or ROLAP). The advantage of ROLAP products is that one could subset the data, and then investigate data cubes for ad-hoc data sets. This capability was difficult in the original OLAP products, which came to be known as Multidimensional OLAP (MOLAP) to distinguish them from ROLAP solutions.

Most newer warehouse-oriented products have been called business intelligence (BI) tools. They allow one to form ad-hoc queries and then visualize the result in a variety of ways. They are invariably built on top of relational DBMSs. In this environment, data cubes are merely one of several visualization techniques.

Business analysts interact with most warehouses using BI tools and submit ad-hoc queries for visualization. Some business analysts also run data mining code against a warehouse.

The periodic loading required for all warehouses is a complex task. The data must be extracted from various operational systems, transformed to a common schema, cleaned (if there are errors present), and then loaded into the warehouse. Products which assist in this extract-transform-load process have been called **ETL** tools. Transformations are often quite complex, and are typically described in an ETL tool using some sort of workflow representation.

We begin this section with a detailed survey by Chaudhuri and Dayal that describes the warehouse environment in greater detail than what was presented above. Following this survey article, we include a paper by O'Neill and Quass on bitmap indexes as well a variety of extensions. This paper further explains why bit-oriented indexes are especially valuable in a warehouse environment.

Because materialized views are so valuable in a warehouse environment, we have included two papers on this topic. When the underlying tables used in the materialized view are updated, the MV is rendered invalid. One can discard and then recreate the MV, a costly operation, or one can attempt to update the MV in place. Research on updating MVs is represented by the next paper of this chapter by Ceri and Widom. Our commercial experience with warehouse applications is that most MVs are relatively easy to update in place because of their simple structure (e.g. all joins between a dimension table and the fact table are 1-n). Hence, the updating of real world MVs is well within the state of the art.

However, the more difficult problem is to decide which MVs to keep in the first place. Essentially all of the major DBMS vendors have patents on algorithms that examine a collection of queries (the training set) and then create a carefully-chosen set of MVs that provide good performance on the training queries subject to some space limitation. The interested reader is directed to the on-line patent repository to explore these algorithms. From the open literature we have chosen a representative, relatively practical paper on the choice of MVs, by Kotidis and Roussopoulos.

Data cubes are one of the popular interfaces for BI users. Hence, we have included two papers on cubes in this section. The first one deals with a collection of query language extensions that will "slice and dice" data into cubes. This paper by Gray et. al. brings the traditionally non-standard data cube model into traditional SQL environments. The second paper deals with the simultaneous computation of cube elements in both MOLAP and ROLAP systems and is written by Zhao, Deshpande and Naughton.

Warehouse queries are often long-running, and it is clear that parallel query processing is desirable to lower response times. The obvious technique is to horizontally partition each table, and then perform the query on each partition in parallel. This is a well known technique exploited by the "software data base machines", such as Gamma [DEWI86] and Bubba [BORA90]. The survey paper on parallel query processing by Dewitt and Gray in Chapter 2 provides good coverage of this topic.

Even with parallelism, some queries take a very long time. In such cases, it is sometimes sensible to trade off result accuracy for better response time. Since most long-running warehouse queries compute summary statistics (i.e. aggregates), statistical techniques can approximate the query results very effectively. Various schemes have been proposed for approximate query answering, including sampling (e.g. [HOT88, OLK93]), as well as precomputed "synopses" including wavelets (e.g. [CHAK00]) and "sketches" based on random projections [AMS96] and probabilistic counting [FM85]. There are two practical problems with this work. First, the synopsis work typically ignores the systems issues in doing full-featured query processing; most of the synopsis schemes are not arbitrarily composable with an algebra for multi-operator queries (e.g. two or more joins with selection and projection). Second, there is a problem trying to sell this kind of technology to customers. If you ask the typical BI customer whether they are willing to use an approximate answer, they will typically say no, regardless of what you may tell them about the statistical validity of the answer. This is an end-user issue that cannot be neglected.

The CONTROL project at Berkeley and IBM took a more user-centric approach to approximation, starting with the work on *online aggregation* that is the focus of our last paper in this section. With online or progressive approximations, the user is given a running, easily visualized estimate of the query results during execution, and can "stop early" when they see fit, or let the query run to completion if they prefer. Most users are quite comfortable with this approach even if they are generally uncomfortable with approximation schemes, because it provides intuitive feedback and gives the user *control* of the tradeoff between accuracy and time, This work also focused on end-to-end systems solutions for sampling-based approximation of a large class of SQL queries. While attractive, these ideas have been tough to translate to products. To deliver online query processing functionality, one has to change not only the DBMS, but also the BI applications that run over the engine – *everything* must become interactive. The applications are often provided by a family of vendors different from the DBMS vendor, so any changes to the engine require significant buy-in from an entire sub-industry in order to be worth the DBMS vendor's investment. Similarly, a lightweight startup company has a tough time pushing this agenda, since it requires support from the core DBMS engine.

The state of the art today in commercial query approximation is still painfully crude. Despite IBM's expertise in the area, both IBM and Oracle only support "Bernoulli" (coin-toss) sampling of base tables – for every tuple from a given table in the FROM clause, a weighted coin is flipped to decide whether to look at that tuple in the query. Bernoulli sampling of base tables does not provide any way to characterize the quality of the answers returned from join queries, for example, nor any way to make the sampling progressive and interactive a la online aggregation. In short, query approximation is a technique where the research is well ahead of the marketplace.

We close this introduction with a disturbing prediction. Warehouses have found near universal acceptance in large enterprises. However, most warehouse administrators have quickly discovered a serious flaw, namely that the warehouse is stale by half the refresh interval on average. This staleness is not an issue for historical queries, but it becomes very problematic in other circumstances. One warehouse user confided to us that he was frustrated because he could not compare yesterday against today, because yesterday was in the warehouse but today was still in the operational system. When one wants analyses closer to real time, staleness becomes an issue. In addition, some users want "real time warehouses". By this they often mean the ability to use data warehouse data to decide what to do with an operational transaction. For example, one might want to make a credit decision in a current transaction based on the transactions that the customer had executed in the recent past.

Put differently, business intelligence applications can be performed on historical data or on a mix of historical and current data. As enterprises strive to make decisions based on timely information (the so-called real time enterprise), then warehouses will have to become more current.

Although one can run the ETL process more often (say every hour) and thereby get the warehouse to be less stale, this will call into question some of the performance tactics currently used such as bitmap indexes and materialized views. Moreover, such a warehouse is still stale by an average of 30 minutes. Getting more current than this will require a fundamental rethinking of the way enterprises deal with operational systems and BI systems, and hence a rethinking of the basic architecture of major enterprise systems.

References

[AMS96] N. Alon, Y. Matias and M. Szegedy, "The Space Complexity of Approximating the Frequency Moments". In *Proceedings of the 28th Annual ACM Symposium on Theory of Computing (STOC)*, pp. 20-29, May, 1996.

[BORA90] Boral, H. et. al: Prototyping Bubba: A Highly Parallel Database System, *IEEE Knowledge and Data Engineering*, 2(1), (March 1990).

[CHAK00] Kaushik Chakrabarti , Minos Garofalakis, Rajeev Rastogi , and Kyuseok Shim ."Approximate Query Processing Using Wavelets" In *Proc. International Conference on Very Large Data Bases (VLDB)*, Cairo, Egypt, September 2000, pp. 111-122.

[DEWI86] Dewitt, D. et. al: Gamma – A High Performance Dataflow Machine. In *Proc. International Conference on Very Large Data Bases (VLDB)*, Tokyo, Japan, Sept. 1986.

[FM85] Philippe Flajolet and G. Nigel Martin. Probabilistic Counting Algorithms for Data Base Applications. *Journal of Computing System Science*, 31(2):182-209, 1985.

[HOT88] Wen-Chi Hou , Gultekin Özsoyoglu, Baldeo K. Taneja : Statistical Estimators for Relational Algebra Expressions. In *Proc. ACM SIGACT-SIGMOD-SIGART Symposium on Principles of Database Systems (PODS),* 1988, pp. 276-287,

[OLK93] Olken, F., Random Sampling from Databases. PhD. dissertation, Lawrence Berkeley Laboratory Tech. Report LBL-32883, April, 1993.

An Overview of Data Warehousing and OLAP Technology

Surajit Chaudhuri
Microsoft Research, Redmond
surajitc@microsoft.com

Umeshwar Dayal
Hewlett-Packard Labs, Palo Alto
dayal@hpl.hp.com

Abstract

Data warehousing and on-line analytical processing (OLAP) are essential elements of decision support, which has increasingly become a focus of the database industry. Many commercial products and services are now available, and all of the principal database management system vendors now have offerings in these areas. Decision support places some rather different requirements on database technology compared to traditional on-line transaction processing applications. This paper provides an overview of data warehousing and OLAP technologies, with an emphasis on their new requirements. We describe back end tools for extracting, cleaning and loading data into a data warehouse; multidimensional data models typical of OLAP; front end client tools for querying and data analysis; server extensions for efficient query processing; and tools for metadata management and for managing the warehouse. In addition to surveying the state of the art, this paper also identifies some promising research issues, some of which are related to problems that the database research community has worked on for years, but others are only just beginning to be addressed. This overview is based on a tutorial that the authors presented at the VLDB Conference, 1996.

1. Introduction

Data warehousing is a collection of *decision support* technologies, aimed at enabling the *knowledge worker* (executive, manager, analyst) to make better and faster decisions. The past three years have seen explosive growth, both in the number of products and services offered, and in the adoption of these technologies by industry. According to the *META Group*, the data warehousing market, including hardware, database software, and tools, is projected to grow from $2 billion in 1995 to $8 billion in 1998. Data warehousing technologies have been successfully deployed in many industries: manufacturing (for order shipment and customer support), retail (for user profiling and inventory management), financial services (for claims analysis, risk analysis, credit card analysis, and fraud detection), transportation (for fleet management), telecommunications (for call analysis and fraud detection), utilities (for power usage analysis), and healthcare (for outcomes analysis). This paper presents a roadmap of data warehousing technologies, focusing on the special requirements that data warehouses place on database management systems (DBMSs).

A data warehouse is a "subject-oriented, integrated, time-varying, non-volatile collection of data that is used primarily in organizational decision making."[1] Typically, the data warehouse is maintained separately from the organization's operational databases. There are many reasons for doing this. The data warehouse supports on-line analytical processing (OLAP), the functional and performance requirements of which are quite different from those of the on-line transaction processing (OLTP) applications traditionally supported by the operational databases.

OLTP applications typically automate clerical data processing tasks such as order entry and banking transactions that are the bread-and-butter day-to-day operations of an organization. These tasks are structured and repetitive, and consist of short, atomic, isolated transactions. The transactions require detailed, up-to-date data, and read or update a few (tens of) records accessed typically on their primary keys. Operational databases tend to be hundreds of megabytes to gigabytes in size. Consistency and recoverability of the database are critical, and maximizing transaction throughput is the key performance metric. Consequently, the database is designed to reflect the operational semantics of known applications, and, in particular, to minimize concurrency conflicts.

Data warehouses, in contrast, are targeted for decision support. Historical, summarized and consolidated data is more important than detailed, individual records. Since data warehouses contain consolidated data, perhaps from several operational databases, over potentially long periods of time, they tend to be orders of magnitude larger than operational databases; enterprise data warehouses are projected to be hundreds of gigabytes to terabytes in size. The workloads are query intensive with mostly ad hoc, complex queries that can access millions of records and perform a lot of scans, joins, and aggregates. Query throughput and response times are more important than transaction throughput.

To facilitate complex analyses and visualization, the data in a warehouse is typically modeled *multidimensionally*. For example, in a sales data warehouse, time of sale, sales district, salesperson, and product might be some of the dimensions of interest. Often, these dimensions are hierarchical; time of sale may be organized as a day-month-quarter-year hierarchy, product as a product-category-industry hierarchy. Typical

OLAP operations include *rollup* (increasing the level of aggregation) and *drill-down* (decreasing the level of aggregation or increasing detail) along one or more dimension hierarchies, *slice_and_dice* (selection and projection), and *pivot* (re-orienting the multidimensional view of data).

Given that operational databases are finely tuned to support known OLTP workloads, trying to execute complex OLAP queries against the operational databases would result in unacceptable performance. Furthermore, decision support requires data that might be missing from the operational databases; for instance, understanding trends or making predictions requires historical data, whereas operational databases store only current data. Decision support usually requires consolidating data from many heterogeneous sources: these might include external sources such as stock market feeds, in addition to several operational databases. The different sources might contain data of varying quality, or use inconsistent representations, codes and formats, which have to be reconciled. Finally, supporting the multidimensional data models and operations typical of OLAP requires special data organization, access methods, and implementation methods, not generally provided by commercial DBMSs targeted for OLTP. It is for all these reasons that data warehouses are implemented separately from operational databases.

Data warehouses might be implemented on standard or extended relational DBMSs, called Relational OLAP (ROLAP) servers. These servers assume that data is stored in relational databases, and they support extensions to SQL and special access and implementation methods to efficiently implement the multidimensional data model and operations. In contrast, multidimensional OLAP (MOLAP) servers are servers that directly store multidimensional data in special data structures (e.g., arrays) and implement the OLAP operations over these special data structures.

There is more to building and maintaining a data warehouse than selecting an OLAP server and defining a schema and some complex queries for the warehouse. Different architectural alternatives exist. Many organizations want to implement an integrated enterprise warehouse that collects information about all subjects (e.g., customers, products, sales, assets, personnel) spanning the whole organization. However, building an enterprise warehouse is a long and complex process, requiring extensive business modeling, and may take many years to succeed. Some organizations are settling for *data marts* instead, which are departmental subsets focused on selected subjects (e.g., a marketing data mart may include customer, product, and sales information). These data marts enable faster roll out, since they do not require enterprise-wide consensus, but they may lead to complex integration problems in the long run, if a complete business model is not developed.

In Section 2, we describe a typical data warehousing architecture, and the process of designing and operating a data warehouse. In Sections 3-7, we review relevant technologies for loading and refreshing data in a data warehouse, warehouse servers, front end tools, and warehouse management tools. In each case, we point out what is different from traditional database technology, and we mention representative products. In this paper, we do not intend to provide comprehensive descriptions of all products in every category. We encourage the interested reader to look at recent issues of trade magazines such as *Databased Advisor*, *Database Programming and Design*, *Datamation*, and *DBMS Magazine*, and vendors' Web sites for more details of commercial products, white papers, and case studies. The OLAP Council[2] is a good source of information on standardization efforts across the industry, and a paper by Codd, et al.[3] defines twelve rules for OLAP products. Finally, a good source of references on data warehousing and OLAP is the Data Warehousing Information Center[4].

Research in data warehousing is fairly recent, and has focused primarily on query processing and view maintenance issues. There still are many open research problems. We conclude in Section 8 with a brief mention of these issues.

2. Architecture and End-to-End Process

Figure 1 shows a typical data warehousing architecture.

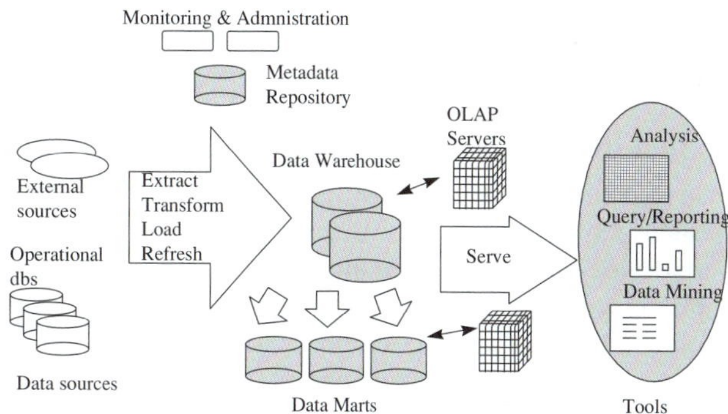

Figure 1. Data Warehousing Architecture

It includes tools for extracting data from multiple operational databases and external sources; for cleaning, transforming and integrating this data; for loading data into the data warehouse; and for periodically refreshing the warehouse to reflect updates at the sources and to purge data from the warehouse, perhaps onto slower archival storage. In addition to the main warehouse, there may be several departmental data marts. Data in the warehouse and data marts is stored and managed by one or more warehouse servers, which present multidimensional views of data to a variety of front end tools: query tools, report writers, analysis tools, and data mining tools. Finally, there is a repository for storing and managing metadata, and tools for monitoring and administering the warehousing system.

The warehouse may be distributed for load balancing, scalability, and higher availability. In such a distributed architecture, the metadata repository is usually replicated with each fragment of the warehouse, and the entire warehouse is administered centrally. An alternative architecture, implemented for expediency when it may be too expensive to construct a single logically integrated enterprise warehouse, is a federation of warehouses or data marts, each with its own repository and decentralized administration.

Designing and rolling out a data warehouse is a complex process, consisting of the following activities[5].

- Define the architecture, do capacity planning, and select the storage servers, database and OLAP servers, and tools.
- Integrate the servers, storage, and client tools.
- Design the warehouse schema and views.
- Define the physical warehouse organization, data placement, partitioning, and access methods.
- Connect the sources using gateways, ODBC drivers, or other wrappers.
- Design and implement scripts for data extraction, cleaning, transformation, load, and refresh.
- Populate the repository with the schema and view definitions, scripts, and other metadata.
- Design and implement end-user applications.
- Roll out the warehouse and applications.

3. Back End Tools and Utilities

Data warehousing systems use a variety of data extraction and cleaning tools, and load and refresh utilities for populating warehouses. Data extraction from "foreign" sources is usually implemented via gateways and standard interfaces (such as Information Builders EDA/SQL, ODBC, Oracle Open Connect, Sybase Enterprise Connect, Informix Enterprise Gateway).

Data Cleaning

Since a data warehouse is used for decision making, it is important that the data in the warehouse be correct. However, since large volumes of data from multiple sources are involved, there is a high probability of errors and anomalies in the data.. Therefore, tools that help to detect data anomalies and correct them can have a high payoff. Some examples where data cleaning becomes necessary are: inconsistent field lengths, inconsistent descriptions, inconsistent value assignments, missing entries and violation of integrity constraints. Not surprisingly, optional fields in data entry forms are significant sources of inconsistent data.

There are three related, but somewhat different, classes of data cleaning tools. *Data migration* tools allow simple transformation rules to be specified; e.g., "replace the string *gender* by *sex*". Warehouse Manager from Prism is an example of a popular tool of this kind. *Data scrubbing* tools use domain-specific knowledge (e.g., postal addresses) to do the scrubbing of data. They often exploit parsing and fuzzy matching techniques to accomplish cleaning from multiple sources. Some tools make it possible to specify the "relative cleanliness" of sources. Tools such as Integrity and Trillum fall in this category. *Data auditing* tools make it possible to discover rules and relationships (or to signal violation of stated rules) by scanning data. Thus, such tools may be considered variants of data mining tools. For example, such a tool may discover a suspicious pattern (based on statistical analysis) that a certain car dealer has never received any complaints.

Load

After extracting, cleaning and transforming, data must be loaded into the warehouse. Additional preprocessing may still be required: checking integrity constraints; sorting; summarization, aggregation and other computation to build the derived tables stored in the warehouse; building indices and other access paths; and partitioning to multiple target storage areas. Typically, batch load utilities are used for this purpose. In addition to populating the warehouse, a load utility must allow the system administrator to monitor status, to cancel, suspend and resume a load, and to restart after failure with no loss of data integrity.

The load utilities for data warehouses have to deal with much larger data volumes than for operational databases. There is only a small time window (usually at night) when the warehouse can be taken offline to refresh it. Sequential loads can take a very long time, e.g., loading a terabyte of data can take weeks and months! Hence, pipelined and partitioned parallelism are typically exploited [6]. Doing a full load has the advantage that it can be treated as a long batch transaction that builds up a new database. While it is in progress, the current database can still support queries; when the load transaction commits, the current database is replaced with the new one. Using periodic checkpoints ensures that if a failure occurs during the load, the process can restart from the last checkpoint.

However, even using parallelism, a full load may still take too long. Most commercial utilities (e.g., RedBrick Table Management Utility) use incremental loading during refresh to reduce the volume of data that has to be incorporated into the warehouse. Only the updated tuples are inserted. However, the load process now is harder to manage. The incremental load conflicts with ongoing queries, so it is treated as a sequence of shorter transactions (which commit periodically, e.g., after every 1000 records or every few seconds), but now this sequence of transactions has to be coordinated to ensure consistency of derived data and indices with the base data.

Refresh
Refreshing a warehouse consists in propagating updates on source data to correspondingly update the base data and derived data stored in the warehouse. There are two sets of issues to consider: *when* to refresh, and *how* to refresh. Usually, the warehouse is refreshed periodically (e.g., daily or weekly). Only if some OLAP queries need current data (e.g., up to the minute stock quotes), is it necessary to propagate every update. The refresh policy is set by the warehouse administrator, depending on user needs and traffic, and may be different for different sources.

Refresh techniques may also depend on the characteristics of the source and the capabilities of the database servers. Extracting an entire source file or database is usually too expensive, but may be the only choice for legacy data sources. Most contemporary database systems provide replication servers that support incremental techniques for propagating updates from a primary database to one or more replicas. Such replication servers can be used to incrementally refresh a warehouse when the sources change. There are two basic replication techniques: data shipping and transaction shipping.

In data shipping (e.g., used in the Oracle Replication Server, Praxis OmniReplicator), a table in the warehouse is treated as a remote snapshot of a table in the source database. *After_row* triggers are used to update a snapshot log table whenever the source table changes; and an automatic refresh schedule (or a manual refresh procedure) is then set up to propagate the updated data to the remote snapshot.

In transaction shipping (e.g., used in the Sybase Replication Server and Microsoft SQL Server), the regular transaction log is used, instead of triggers and a special snapshot log table. At the source site, the transaction log is sniffed to detect updates on replicated tables, and those log records are transferred to a replication server, which packages up the corresponding transactions to update the replicas. Transaction shipping has the advantage that it does not require triggers, which can increase the workload on the operational source databases. However, it cannot always be used easily across DBMSs from different vendors, because there are no standard APIs for accessing the transaction log.

Such replication servers have been used for refreshing data warehouses. However, the refresh cycles have to be properly chosen so that the volume of data does not overwhelm the incremental load utility.

In addition to propagating changes to the base data in the warehouse, the derived data also has to be updated correspondingly. The problem of constructing logically correct updates for incrementally updating derived data (materialized views) has been the subject of much research [7 8 9 10]. For data warehousing, the most significant classes of derived data are summary tables, single-table indices and join indices.

4. Conceptual Model and Front End Tools

A popular conceptual model that influences the front-end tools, database design, and the query engines for OLAP is the *multidimensional* view of data in the warehouse. In a multidimensional data model, there is a set of *numeric measures* that are the objects of analysis. Examples of such measures are sales, budget, revenue, inventory, ROI (return on investment). Each of the numeric measures depends on a set of *dimensions,* which provide the context for the measure. For example, the dimensions associated with a sale amount can be the city, product name, and the date when the sale was made. The dimensions together are assumed to *uniquely* determine the measure. Thus, the multidimensional data views a measure as a value in the multidimensional space of dimensions. Each dimension is described by a set of attributes. For example, the Product dimension may consist of four attributes: the category and the industry of the product, year of its introduction, and the average profit margin. For example, the soda Surge belongs to the category beverage and the food industry, was introduced in 1996, and may have an average profit margin of 80%. The attributes of a dimension may be related via a hierarchy of relationships. In the above example, the product name is related to its category and the industry attribute through such a hierarchical relationship.

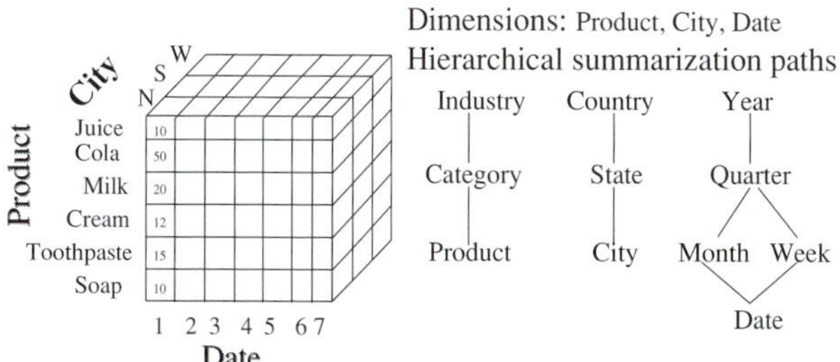

Figure 2. Multidimensional data

Another distinctive feature of the conceptual model for OLAP is its stress on *aggregation* of measures by one or more dimensions as one of the key operations; e.g., computing and ranking the *total* sales by each county (or by each year). Other popular operations include *comparing* two measures (e.g., sales and budget) aggregated by the same dimensions. Time is a dimension that is of particular significance to decision support (e.g., trend analysis). Often, it is desirable to have built-in knowledge of calendars and other aspects of the time dimension.

Front End Tools

The multidimensional data model grew out of the view of business data popularized by PC spreadsheet programs that were extensively used by business analysts. The spreadsheet is still the most compelling front-end application for OLAP. The challenge in supporting a query environment for OLAP can be crudely summarized as that of supporting spreadsheet operations efficiently over large multi-gigabyte databases. Indeed, the Essbase product of Arbor Corporation uses Microsoft Excel as the front-end tool for its multidimensional engine.

We shall briefly discuss some of the popular operations that are supported by the multidimensional spreadsheet applications. One such operation is *pivoting*. Consider the multidimensional schema of Figure 2 represented in a spreadsheet where each row corresponds to a sale . Let there be one column for each dimension and an extra column that represents the amount of sale. The simplest view of pivoting is that it selects two dimensions that are used to aggregate a measure, e.g., sales in the above example. The aggregated values are often displayed in a grid where each value in the (x,y) coordinate corresponds to the aggregated value of the measure when the first dimension has the value x and the second dimension has the value y. Thus, in our example, if the selected dimensions are city and year, then the x-axis may represent all values of city and the y-axis may represent the years. The point (x,y) will represent the aggregated sales for city x in the year y. Thus, what were values in the original spreadsheets have now become row and column headers in the pivoted spreadsheet.

Other operators related to pivoting are *rollup* or *drill-down*. Rollup corresponds to taking the current data object and doing a further group-by on one of the dimensions. Thus, it is possible to roll-up the sales data, perhaps already aggregated on city, additionally by product. The drill-down operation is the converse of rollup. *Slice_and_dice* corresponds to reducing the dimensionality of the data, i.e., taking a projection of the data on a subset of dimensions for selected values of the other dimensions. For example, we can slice_and_dice sales data for a specific product to create a table that consists of the dimensions city and the day of sale. The other popular operators include *ranking* (sorting), *selections* and defining *computed* attributes.

Although the multidimensional spreadsheet has attracted a lot of interest since it empowers the end user to analyze business data, this has not replaced traditional analysis by means of a *managed query environment*. These environments use stored procedures and predefined complex queries to provide packaged analysis tools. Such tools often make it possible for the end-user to query in terms of domain-specific business data. These applications often use raw data access tools and optimize the access patterns depending on the back end database server. In addition, there are query environments (e.g., Microsoft Access) that help build *ad hoc* SQL queries by "pointing-and-clicking". Finally, there are a variety of data mining tools that are often used as front end tools to data warehouses.

5. Database Design Methodology

The multidimensional data model described above is implemented directly by MOLAP servers. We will describe these briefly in the next section. However, when a relational ROLAP server is used, the multidimensional model and its operations have to be mapped into relations and SQL queries. In this section, we describe the design of relational database schemas that reflect the multidimensional views of data.

Entity Relationship diagrams and normalization techniques are popularly used for database design in OLTP environments. However, the database designs recommended by ER diagrams are inappropriate for decision support systems where efficiency in querying and in loading data (including incremental loads) are important.

Most data warehouses use a *star schema* to represent the multidimensional data model. The database consists of a single fact table and a single table for each dimension. Each tuple in the fact table consists of a pointer (foreign key - often uses a generated key for efficiency) to each of the dimensions that provide its multidimensional coordinates, and stores the numeric measures for those coordinates. Each dimension table consists of columns that correspond to attributes of the dimension. Figure 3 shows an example of a star schema.

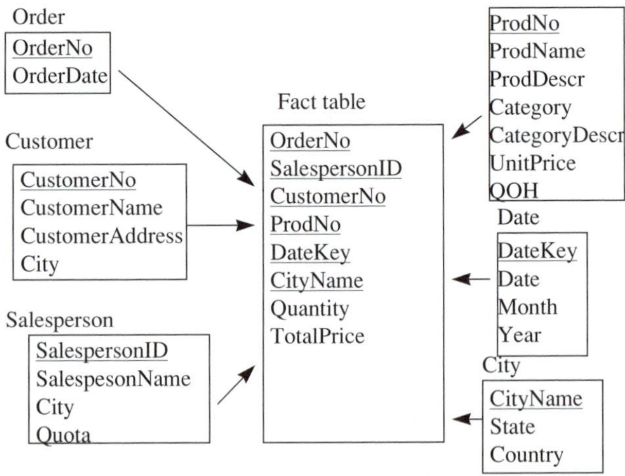

Figure 3. A Star Schema.

Star schemas do not explicitly provide support for attribute hierarchies. *Snowflake schemas* provide a refinement of star schemas where the dimensional hierarchy is explicitly represented by normalizing the dimension tables, as shown in Figure 4. This leads to advantages in maintaining the dimension tables. However, the denormalized structure of the dimensional tables in star schemas may be more appropriate for browsing the dimensions.

Fact constellations are examples of more complex structures in which multiple fact tables share dimensional tables. For example, projected expense and the actual expense may form a fact constellation since they share many dimensions.

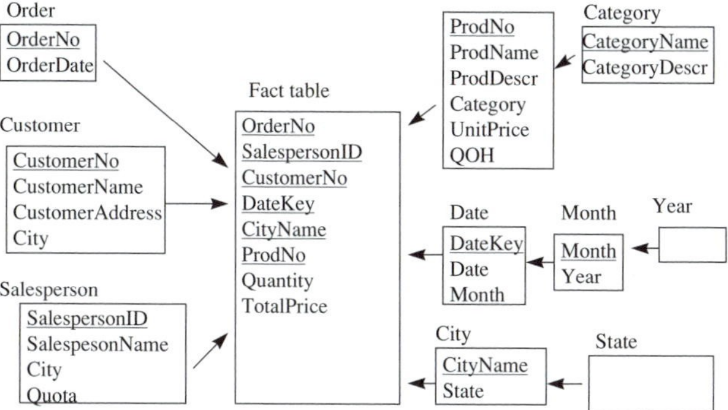

Figure 4. A Snowflake Schema.

In addition to the fact and dimension tables, data warehouses store selected summary tables containing pre-aggregated data. In the simplest cases, the pre-aggregated data corresponds to aggregating the fact table on one or more selected dimensions. Such pre-aggregated summary data can be represented in the database in at least two ways. Let us consider the example of a summary table that has total sales by product by year in the context of the star schema of Figure 3. We can represent such a summary table by *a separate fact table* which shares the dimension Product and also *a separate shrunken dimension table* for time, which consists of only the attributes of the dimension that make sense for the summary table (i.e., year). Alternatively, we can represent the summary table by encoding the aggregated tuples in the *same fact table* and the *same dimension tables* without adding new tables. This may be accomplished by adding a new *level* field to each dimension and using *nulls*: We can encode a day, a month or a year in the Date dimension table as follows: (id0, 0, 22, 01, 1960) represents a record for Jan 22, 1960, (id1, 1, NULL, 01, 1960) represents the month Jan 1960 and (id2, 2, NULL, NULL, 1960) represents the year 1960. The second attribute represents the new attribute *level*: 0 for days, 1 for months, 2 for years. In the fact table, a record containing the foreign key id2 represents the aggregated sales for a Product in the year 1960. The latter method, while reducing the number of tables, is often a source of operational errors since the level field needs be carefully interpreted.

6. Warehouse Servers

Data warehouses may contain large volumes of data. To answer queries efficiently, therefore, requires highly efficient access methods and query processing techniques. Several issues arise. First, data warehouses use redundant structures such as indices and materialized views. Choosing which indices to build and which views to materialize is an important physical design problem. The next challenge is to effectively use the existing indices and materialized views to answer queries. Optimization of complex queries is another important problem. Also, while for data-selective queries, efficient index scans may be very effective, data-intensive queries need the use of sequential scans. Thus, improving the efficiency of scans is important. Finally, parallelism needs to be exploited to reduce query response times. In this short paper, it is not possible to elaborate on each of these issues. Therefore, we will only briefly touch upon the highlights.

Index Structures and their Usage

A number of query processing techniques that exploit indices are useful. For instance, the selectivities of multiple conditions can be exploited through *index intersection*. Other useful index operations are union of indexes. These index operations can be used to significantly reduce and in many cases eliminate the need to access the base tables.

Warehouse servers can use *bit map indices*, which support efficient index operations (e.g., union, intersection). Consider a leaf page in an index structure corresponding to a domain value *d*. Such a leaf page traditionally contains a list of the record ids (RIDs) of records that contain the value *d*. However, bit map indices use an alternative representation of the above RID list as a bit vector that has one bit for each record, which is set when the domain value for that record is *d*. In a sense, the bit map index is not a new index structure, but simply an alternative representation of the RID list. The popularity of the bit map index is due to the fact that the bit vector representation of the RID lists can speed up index intersection, union, join, and aggregation[11]. For example, if we have a query of the form column1 = d & column2 = d', then we can identify the qualifying records by taking the AND of the two bit vectors. While such representations can be very useful for low cardinality domains (e.g., gender), they can also be effective for higher cardinality domains through compression of bitmaps (e.g., run length encoding). Bitmap indices were originally used in Model 204, but many products support them today (e.g., Sybase IQ). An interesting question is to decide on which attributes to index. In general, this is really a question that must be answered by the physical database design process.

In addition to indices on single tables, the specialized nature of star schemas makes *join indices* especially attractive for decision support. While traditionally indices map the value in a column to a list of rows with that value, a join index maintains the relationships between a foreign key with its matching primary keys. In the context of a star schema, a join index can relate the values of one or more attributes of a dimension table to matching rows in the fact table. For example, consider the schema of Figure 3. There can be a join index on City that maintains, for each city, a list of RIDs of the tuples in the fact table that correspond to sales in that city. Thus a join index essentially precomputes a binary join. Multikey join indices can represent precomputed n-way joins. For example, over the Sales database it is possible to construct a multidimensional join index from (Cityname, Productname) to the fact table. Thus, the index entry for (Seattle, jacket) points to RIDs of those tuples in the Sales table that have the above combination. Using such a multidimensional join index can sometimes provide savings over taking the intersection of separate indices on Cityname and Productname. Join indices can be used with bitmap representations for the RID lists for efficient join processing[12].

Finally, decision support databases contain a significant amount of descriptive text and so indices to support text search are useful as well.

Materialized Views and their Usage

Many queries over data warehouses require summary data, and, therefore, use aggregates. Hence, in addition to indices, materializing summary data can help to accelerate many common queries. For example, in an investment environment, a large majority of the queries may be based on the performance of the most recent quarter and the current fiscal year. Having summary data on these parameters can significantly speed up query processing.

The challenges in exploiting materialized views are not unlike those in using indices: (a) identify the views to materialize, (b) exploit the materialized views to answer queries, and (c) efficiently update the materialized views during load and refresh. The currently adopted industrial solutions to these problems consider materializing views that have a relatively simple structure. Such views consist of joins of the fact table with a subset of dimension tables (possibly after some selections on those dimensions), with the aggregation of one or more measures grouped by a set of attributes from the dimension tables. The structure of these views is a little more complex when the underlying schema is a snowflake.

Despite the restricted form, there is still a wide choice of views to materialize. The selection of views to materialize must take into account workload characteristics, the costs for incremental update, and upper bounds on storage requirements. Under simplifying assumptions, a greedy algorithm was shown to have good performance[13]. A related problem that underlies optimization as well as choice of materialized views is that of estimating the effect of aggregation on the cardinality of the relations.

A simple, but extremely useful, strategy for using a materialized view is to use *selection* on the materialized view, or *rollup* on the materialized view by grouping and aggregating on additional columns. For example, assume that a materialized view contains the total sales by quarter for each product. This materialized view can be used to answer a query that requests the total sales of Levi's jeans for the year by first applying the selection and then rolling up from quarters to years. It should be emphasized that the ability to do roll-up from a partially aggregated result, relies on algebraic properties of the aggregating functions (e.g., *Sum* can be rolled up, but some other statistical function may not be).

In general, there may be several candidate materialized views that can be used to answer a query. If a view V has the same set of dimensions as Q, if the selection clause in Q implies the selection clause in V, and if the group-by columns in V are a subset of the group-by columns in Q, then view V can act as a *generator* of Q. Given a set of materialized views M, a query Q, we can define a set of *minimal generators* M' for Q (i.e., smallest set of generators such that all other generators generate some member of M'). There can be multiple minimal generators for a query. For example, given a query that asks for total sales of clothing in Washington State, the following two views are both generators: (a) total sales by each state for each product (b) total sales by each city for each category. The notion of minimal generators can be used by the optimizer to narrow the search for the appropriate materialized view to use. On the commercial side, HP Intelligent Warehouse pioneered the use of the minimal generators to answer queries. While we have defined the notion of a generator in a restricted way, the general problem of optimizing queries in the presence of multiple materialized views is more complex. In the special case of Select-Project-Join queries, there has been some work in this area.[14 15 16]

Transformation of Complex SQL Queries

The problem of finding efficient techniques for processing complex queries has been of keen interest in query optimization. In a way, decision support systems provide a testing ground for some of the ideas that have been studied before. We will only summarize some of the key contributions.

There has been substantial work on "unnesting" complex SQL queries containing *nested subqueries* by translating them into single block SQL queries when certain syntactic restrictions are satisfied[17 18 19 20]. Another direction that has been pursued in optimizing nested subqueries is reducing the number of invocations and batching invocation of inner subqueries by semi-join like techniques[21 22]. Likewise, the problem of flattening queries containing views has been a topic of interest. The case where participating views are SPJ queries is well understood. The problem is more complex when one or more of the views contain aggregation[23]. Naturally, this problem is closely related to the problem of commuting group-by and join operators. However, commuting group-by and join is applicable in the context of single block SQL queries as well.[24 25 26] An overview of the field appears in a recent paper[27].

Parallel Processing

Parallelism plays a significant role in processing massive databases. Teradata pioneered some of the key technology.

All major vendors of database management systems now offer data partitioning and parallel query processing technology. The article by Dewitt and Gray provides an overview of this area[28] . One interesting technique relevant to the read-only environment of decision support systems is that of piggybacking scans requested by multiple queries (used in Redbrick). Piggybacking scan reduces the total work as well as response time by overlapping scans of multiple concurrent requests.

Server Architectures for Query Processing

Traditional relational servers were not geared towards the intelligent use of indices and other requirements for supporting multidimensional views of data. However, all relational DBMS vendors have now moved rapidly to support these additional requirements. In addition to the traditional relational servers, there are three other categories of servers that were developed specifically for decision support.

- *Specialized SQL Servers:* Redbrick is an example of this class of servers. The objective here is to provide advanced query language and query processing support for SQL queries over star and snowflake schemas in read-only environments.
- *ROLAP Servers:* These are intermediate servers that sit between a relational back end server (where the data in the warehouse is stored) and client front end tools. Microstrategy is an example of such servers. They extend traditional relational servers with specialized middleware to efficiently support multidimensional OLAP queries, and they typically optimize for specific back end relational servers. They identify the views that are to be materialized, rephrase given user queries in terms of the appropriate materialized views, and generate multi-statement SQL for the back end server. They also provide additional services such as scheduling of queries and resource assignment (e.g., to prevent runaway queries). There has also been a trend to tune the ROLAP servers for domain specific ROLAP tools. The main strength of ROLAP servers is that they exploit the scalability and the transactional features of relational systems. However, intrinsic mismatches between OLAP-style querying and SQL (e.g., lack of sequential processing, column aggregation) can cause performance bottlenecks for OLAP servers.
- *MOLAP Servers:* These servers directly support the multidimensional view of data through a multidimensional storage engine. This makes it possible to implement front-end multidimensional queries on the storage layer through direct mapping. An example of such a server is Essbase (Arbor). Such an approach has the advantage of excellent indexing properties, but provides poor storage utilization, especially when the data set is sparse. Many MOLAP servers adopt a 2-level storage representation to adapt to sparse data sets and use compression extensively. In the two-level storage representation, a set of one or two dimensional subarrays that are likely to be dense are identified, through the use of design tools or by user input, and are represented in the array format. Then, the traditional indexing structure is used to index onto these "smaller" arrays. Many of the techniques that were devised for statistical databases appear to be relevant for MOLAP servers.

SQL Extensions

Several extensions to SQL that facilitate the expression and processing of OLAP queries have been proposed or implemented in extended relational servers. Some of these extensions are described below.

- *Extended family of aggregate functions:* These include support for *rank* and *percentile* (e.g., all products in the top 10 percentile or the top 10 products by total Sale) as well as support for a variety of functions used in financial analysis (*mean, mode, median*).
- *Reporting Features:* The reports produced for business analysis often requires aggregate features evaluated on a *time window*, e.g., *moving average*. In addition, it is important to be able to provide breakpoints and running totals. Redbrick's SQL extensions provide such primitives.
- *Multiple Group-By:* Front end tools such as multidimensional spreadsheets require grouping by different sets of attributes. This can be simulated by a set of SQL statements that require scanning the same data set multiple times, but this can be inefficient. Recently, two new operators, *Rollup* and *Cube,* have been proposed to augment SQL to address this problem[29]. Thus, *Rollup* of the list of attributes (*Product, Year, City*) over a data set results in answer sets with the following applications of group by: (a) group by (Product, Year, City) (b) group by (Product, Year), and (c) group by Product. On the other hand, given a list of k columns, the *Cube* operator provides a group-by for each of the 2^k combinations of columns. Such multiple group-by operations can be executed efficiently by recognizing

commonalties among them[30]. Microsoft SQL Server supports Cube and Rollup.

- *Comparisons:* An article by Ralph Kimball and Kevin Strehlo provides an excellent overview of the deficiencies of SQL in being able to do comparisons that are common in the business world, e.g., compare the difference between the total projected sale and total actual sale by each quarter, where projected sale and actual sale are columns of a table[31]. A straightforward execution of such queries may require multiple sequential scans. The article provides some alternatives to better support comparisons. A recent research paper also addresses the question of how to do comparisons among aggregated values by extending SQL[32].

7. Metadata and Warehouse Management

Since a data warehouse reflects the business model of an enterprise, an essential element of a warehousing architecture is metadata management. Many different kinds of metadata have to be managed. *Administrative* metadata includes all of the information necessary for setting up and using a warehouse: descriptions of the source databases, back-end and front-end tools; definitions of the warehouse schema, derived data, dimensions and hierarchies, predefined queries and reports; data mart locations and contents; physical organization such as data partitions; data extraction, cleaning, and transformation rules; data refresh and purging policies; and user profiles, user authorization and access control policies. *Business* metadata includes business terms and definitions, ownership of the data, and charging policies. *Operational* metadata includes information that is collected during the operation of the warehouse: the lineage of migrated and transformed data; the currency of data in the warehouse (active, archived or purged); and monitoring information such as usage statistics, error reports, and audit trails.

Often, a metadata repository is used to store and manage all the metadata associated with the warehouse. The repository enables the sharing of metadata among tools and processes for designing, setting up, using, operating, and administering a warehouse. Commercial examples include Platinum Repository and Prism Directory Manager.

Creating and managing a warehousing system is hard. Many different classes of tools are available to facilitate different aspects of the process described in Section 2. Development tools are used to design and edit schemas, views, scripts, rules, queries, and reports. Planning and analysis tools are used for what-if scenarios such as understanding the impact of schema changes or refresh rates, and for doing capacity planning. Warehouse management tools (e.g., HP Intelligent Warehouse Advisor, IBM Data Hub, Prism Warehouse Manager) are used for monitoring a warehouse, reporting statistics and making suggestions to the administrator: usage of partitions and summary tables, query execution times, types and frequencies of drill downs or rollups, which users or groups request which data, peak and average workloads over time, exception reporting, detecting runaway queries, and other quality of service metrics. System and network management tools (e.g., HP OpenView, IBM NetView, Tivoli) are used to measure traffic between clients and servers, between warehouse servers and operational databases, and so on. Finally, only recently have workflow management tools been considered for managing the extract-scrub-transform-load-refresh process. The steps of the process can invoke appropriate scripts stored in the repository, and can be launched periodically, on demand, or when specified events occur. The workflow engine ensures successful completion of the process, persistently records the success or failure of each step, and provides failure recovery with partial roll back , retry, or roll forward.

8. Research Issues

We have described the substantial technical challenges in developing and deploying decision support systems. While many commercial products and services exist, there are still several interesting avenues for research. We will only touch on a few of these here.

Data cleaning is a problem that is reminiscent of heterogeneous data integration, a problem that has been studied for many years. But here the emphasis is on *data* inconsistencies instead of schema inconsistencies. Data cleaning, as we indicated, is also closely related to data mining, with the objective of suggesting possible inconsistencies.

The problem of physical design of data warehouses should rekindle interest in the well-known problems of index selection, data partitioning and the selection of materialized views. However, while revisiting these problems, it is important to recognize the special role played by aggregation. Decision support systems already provide the field of query optimization with increasing challenges in the traditional questions of selectivity estimation and cost-based algorithms that can exploit transformations without exploding the search space (there are plenty of transformations, but few reliable cost estimation techniques and few smart cost-based algorithms/search strategies to exploit them). Partitioning the functionality of the query engine between the middleware (e.g., ROLAP layer) and the back end server is also an interesting problem.

The management of data warehouses also presents new challenges. Detecting runaway queries, and managing and scheduling resources are problems that are important but have not been well solved. Some work has been done on the logical correctness of incrementally updating materialized views, but the performance, scalability, and recoverability properties of these techniques have not been investigated. In particular, failure and checkpointing issues in load and refresh in the presence of many indices and materialized views needs further research. The adaptation and use of workflow technology might help, but this needs further investigation.

Some of these areas are being pursued by the research community[33 34], but others have received only cursory attention, particularly in relationship to data warehousing.

Acknowledgement

We thank Goetz Graefe for his comments on the draft.

References

[1] Inmon, W.H., *Building the Data Warehouse*. John Wiley, 1992.

[2] http://www.olapcouncil.org

[3] Codd, E.F., S.B. Codd, C.T. Salley, "Providing OLAP (On-Line Analytical Processing) to User Analyst: An IT Mandate." Available from Arbor Software's web site http://www.arborsoft.com/OLAP.html.

[4] http://pwp.starnetinc.com/larryg/articles.html

[5] Kimball, R. *The Data Warehouse Toolkit*. John Wiley, 1996.

[6] Barclay, T., R. Barnes, J. Gray, P. Sundaresan, "Loading Databases using Dataflow Parallelism." *SIGMOD Record*, Vol. 23, No. 4, Dec.1994.

[7] Blakeley, J.A., N. Coburn, P. Larson. "Updating Derived Relations: Detecting Irrelevant and Autonomously Computable Updates." *ACM TODS*, Vol.4, No. 3, 1989.

[8] Gupta, A., I.S. Mumick, "Maintenance of Materialized Views: Problems, Techniques, and Applications." *Data Eng. Bulletin*, Vol. 18, No. 2, June 1995.

[9] Zhuge, Y., H. Garcia-Molina, J. Hammer, J. Widom, "View Maintenance in a Warehousing Environment, *Proc. of SIGMOD Conf.*, 1995.

[10] Roussopoulos, N., et al., "The Maryland ADMS Project: Views R Us." *Data Eng. Bulletin*, Vol. 18, No.2, June 1995.

[11] O'Neil P., Quass D. "Improved Query Performance with Variant Indices", To appear in *Proc. of SIGMOD Conf.*, 1997.

[12] O'Neil P., Graefe G. "Multi-Table Joins through Bitmapped Join Indices" *SIGMOD Record*, Sep 1995.

[13] Harinarayan V., Rajaraman A., Ullman J.D. " Implementing Data Cubes Efficiently" *Proc. of SIGMOD Conf.*, 1996.

[14] Chaudhuri S., Krishnamurthy R., Potamianos S., Shim K. "Optimizing Queries with Materialized Views" *Intl. Conference on Data Engineering*, 1995.

[15] Levy A., Mendelzon A., Sagiv Y. "Answering Queries Using Views" *Proc. of PODS*, 1995.

[16] Yang H.Z., Larson P.A. "Query Transformations for PSJ Queries", *Proc. of VLDB*, 1987.

[17] Kim W. "On Optimizing a SQL-like Nested Query" *ACM TODS*, Sep 1982.

[18] Ganski,R., Wong H.K.T., "Optimization of Nested SQL Queries Revisited " *Proc. of SIGMOD Conf.*, 1987.

[19] Dayal, U., "Of Nests and Trees: A Unified Approach to Processing Queries that Contain Nested Subqueries, Aggregates and Quantifiers" *Proc. VLDB Conf.*, 1987.

[20] Murlaikrishna, "Improved Unnesting Algorithms for Join Aggregate SQL Queries" *Proc. VLDB Conf.*, 1992.

[21] Seshadri P., Pirahesh H., Leung T. "Complex Query Decorrelation" *Intl. Conference on Data Engineering*, 1996.

[22] Mumick I.S., Pirahesh H. "Implementation of Magic Sets in Starburst" *Proc.of SIGMOD Conf.*, 1994.

[23] Chaudhuri S., Shim K. "Optimizing Queries with Aggregate Views", *Proc. of EDBT*, 1996.

[24] Chaudhuri S., Shim K. "Including Group By in Query Optimization", *Proc. of VLDB*, 1994.

[25] Yan P., Larson P.A. "Eager Aggregation and Lazy Aggregation", *Proc. of VLDB*, 1995.

[26] Gupta A., Harinarayan V., Quass D. "Aggregate-Query Processing in Data Warehouse Environments", *Proc. of VLDB*, 1995.

[27] Chaudhuri S., Shim K. "An Overview of Cost-based Optimization of Queries with Aggregates" *IEEE Data Enginering Bulletin*, Sep 1995.

[28] Dewitt D.J., Gray J. "Parallel Database Systems: The Future of High Performance Database Systems" *CACM*, June 1992.

[29] Gray J. et.al. "Data Cube: A Relational Aggregation Operator Generalizing Group-by, Cross-Tab and Sub Totals" *Data Mining and Knowledge Discovery Journal*, Vol 1, No 1, 1997.

[30] Agrawal S. et.al. "On the Computation of Multidimensional Aggregates" *Proc. of VLDB Conf.*, 1996.

[31] Kimball R., Strehlo., "Why decision support fails and how to fix it", reprinted in *SIGMOD Record*, 24(3), 1995.

[32] Chatziantoniou D., Ross K. "Querying Multiple Features in Relational Databases" *Proc. of VLDB Conf.*, 1996.

[33] Widom, J. "Research Problems in Data Warehousing." *Proc. 4th Intl. CIKM Conf.*, 1995.

[34] Wu, M-C., A.P. Buchmann. "Research Issues in Data Warehousing." Submitted for publication.

Improved Query Performance with Variant Indexes

Patrick O'Neil
Department of Mathematics and Computer Science
University of Massachusetts at Boston
Boston, MA 02125-3393
poneil@cs.umb.edu

Dallan Quass
Department of Computer Science
Stanford University
Stanford, CA 94305
quass@cs.stanford.edu

Abstract: The read-mostly environment of data warehousing makes it possible to use more complex indexes to speed up queries than in situations where concurrent updates are present. The current paper presents a short review of current indexing technology, including row-set representation by Bitmaps, and then introduces two approaches we call Bit-Sliced indexing and Projection indexing. A Projection index materializes all values of a column in RID order, and a Bit-Sliced index essentially takes an orthogonal bit-by-bit view of the same data. While some of these concepts started with the MODEL 204 product, and both Bit-Sliced and Projection indexing are now fully realized in Sybase IQ, this is the first rigorous examination of such indexing capabilities in the literature. We compare algorithms that become feasible with these variant index types against algorithms using more conventional indexes. The analysis demonstrates important performance advantages for variant indexes in some types of SQL aggregation, predicate evaluation, and grouping. The paper concludes by introducing a new method whereby multi-dimensional group-by queries, reminiscent of OLAP/Datacube queries but with more flexibility, can be very efficiently performed.

1. Introduction

Data warehouses are large, special-purpose databases that contain data integrated from a number of independent sources, supporting clients who wish to analyze the data for trends and anomalies. The process of analysis is usually performed with queries that aggregate, filter, and group the data in a variety of ways. Because the queries are often complex and the warehouse database is often very large, processing the queries quickly is a critical issue in the data warehousing environment.

Data warehouses are typically updated only periodically, in a batch fashion, and during this process the warehouse is unavailable for querying. This means a batch update process can *reorganize* data and indexes to a new optimal clustered form, in a manner that would not work if the indexes were in use. In this simplified situation, it is possible to use specialized indexes and materialized aggregate views (called *summary tables* in data warehousing literature), to speed up query evaluation.

This paper reviews current indexing technology, including row-set representation by Bitmaps, for speeding up evaluation of complex queries. It then introduces two indexing structures, which we call Bit-Sliced indexes and Projection indexes. We show that these indexes each provide significant performance advantages over traditional Value-List indexes for certain classes of queries, and argue that it may be desirable in a data warehousing environment to have more than one type of index available on a column, so that the best index can be chosen for the query at hand. The Sybase IQ product currently provides both variant index types [EDEL95, FREN95], and recommends multiple indexes per column in some cases.

Late in the paper, we introduce a new indexing approach to support OLAP-type queries, commonly used in Data Warehouses. Such queries are called *Datacube* queries in [GBLP96]. OLAP query performance depends on creating a set of summary tables to efficiently evaluate an expected set of queries. The summary tables pre-materialize needed aggregates, an approach that is possible only when the expected set of queries is known in advance. Specifically, the OLAP approach addresses queries that group by different combinations of columns, known as *dimensions*.

Example 1.1. Assume that we are given a star-join schema, consisting of a central fact table Sales, containing sales data, and dimension tables known as Stores (where the sales are made), Time (when the sales are made), Product (involved in the sales), and Promotion (method of promotion being used). (See [KIMB96], Chapter 2, for a detailed explanation of this schema. A comparable Star schema is pictured in Figure 5.1.) Using precalculated summary tables based on these dimensions, OLAP systems can answer some queries quickly, such as the total dollar sales that were made for a brand of products in a store on the East coast during the past 4 weeks with a sales promotion based on price reduction. The dimensions by which the aggregates are "sliced and diced" result in a multi-dimensional crosstabs calculation (Datacube) where some or all of the cells may be precalculated and stored in summary tables. But if we want to perform some selection criterion that has not been precalculated, such as repeating the query just given, but only for sales that occurred on days where the temperature reached 90, the answer could not be supplied quickly if summary tables with dimensions based upon temperature did not exist. And there is a limit to the number of dimensions that can be represented in precalculated summary tables, since all combinations of such dimensions must be precalculated in order to achieve good performance at runtime. This suggests that queries requiring rich selection criteria must be evaluated by accessing the base data, rather than precalculated summary tables. ◊

The paper explores indexes for efficient evaluation of OLAP-style queries with such rich selection criteria.

Paper outline: We define Value-List, Projection, and Bit-Sliced indexes and their use in query processing in Section 2. Section 3 presents algorithms for evaluating aggregate functions using the index types presented in Section 2. Algorithms for evaluating Where Clause conditions, specifically range predicates, are presented in Section 4. In Section 5, we introduce an index method whereby OLAP-style queries that permit non-dimensional selection criteria can be efficiently performed. The method combines Bitmap indexing and physical row clustering, two features which provide important advantage for OLAP-style queries. Our conclusions are given in Section 6.

SIGMOD '97 AZ,USA
© 1997 ACM 0-89791-911-4/97/0005...$3.50

2. Indexing Definitions

In this section we examine traditional Value-List indexes and show how Bitmap representations for RID-lists can easily be used. We then introduce Projection and Bit-Sliced indexes.

2.1 Traditional Value-List Indexes

Database indexes provided today by most database systems use B^+-tree[1] indexes to retrieve rows of a table with specified values involving one or more columns (see [COMER79]). The leaf level of the B-tree index consists of a sequence of entries for index keyvalues. Each keyvalue reflects the value of the indexed column or columns in one or more rows in the table, and each keyvalue entry references the set of rows with that value. Since all rows of an indexed relational table are referenced exactly once in the B-tree, the rows are partitioned by keyvalue. However, object-relational databases allow rows to have multi-valued attributes, so that in the future the same row may appear under many keyvalues in the index. We therefore refer to this type of index simply as a Value-List index.

Traditionally, Value-List (B-tree) indexes have referenced each row individually as a RID, a *Row IDentifier*, specifying the disk position of the row. A sequence of RIDs, known as a RID-list, is held in each distinct keyvalue entry in the B-tree. In indexes with a relatively small number of keyvalues compared to the number of rows, most keyvalues will have a large number of associated RIDs and the potential for compression arises by listing a keyvalue once, at the head of what we call a ***RID-list Fragment***, containing a long list of RIDs for rows with this keyvalue. For example, MVS DB2 provides this kind of compression, (see [O'NEI96], Figure 7.19). Keyvalues with RID-lists that cross leaf pages require multiple Fragments. We assume in what follows that RID-lists (and Bitmaps, which follow) are read from disk in multiples of Fragments. With this amortization of the space for the keyvalue over multiple 4-byte RIDs of a Fragment, the length in bytes of the leaf level of the B-tree index can be approximated as 4 times the number of rows in the table, divided by the average fullness of the leaf nodes. In what follows, we assume that we are dealing with data that is updated infrequently, so that B-tree leaf pages can be completely filled, reorganized during batch updates. Thus the length in bytes of the leaf level of a B-tree index with a small number of keyvalues is about 4 times the number of table rows.

2.1.1 Bitmap Indexes

Bitmap indexes were first developed for database use in the Model 204 product from Computer Corporation of America (see [O'NEI87]). A Bitmap is an alternate form for representing RID-lists in a Value-List index. Bitmaps are more space-efficient than RID-lists when the number of keyvalues for the index is low. Furthermore, we will show that Bitmaps are usually more CPU-efficient as well, because of the simplicity of their representation. To create Bitmaps for the n rows of a table $T = \{r_1, r_2, \ldots r_n\}$, we start with a 1-1 mapping m from rows of T to Z[M], the first M positive integers. In what follows we avoid frequent reference to the mapping m. When we speak of the *row number* of a row r of T, we will mean the value m(r).

Note that while there are n rows in $T = \{r_1, r_2, \ldots r_n\}$, it is not necessarily true that the maximum row number M is the same as n, since a method is commonly used to associate a fixed number of rows p with each disk page for fast lookup. Thus for a given row r with row number j, the table page number accessed to retrieve row r is j/p and the page slot is (in C terms) j%p. This means that rows will be assigned row numbers in disk clustered sequence, a valuable property. Since the rows might have variable size and we may not always be able to accommodate an equal number of rows on each disk page, the value p must be a chosen as a maximum, so some integers in Z[M] might be wasted. They will correspond to non-existent slots on pages that cannot accommodate the full set of p rows. (And we may find that $m^{-1}(j)$ for some row numbers j in Z[M] is undefined.)

A "Bitmap" B is defined on T as a sequence of M bits. If a Bitmap B is meant to list rows in T with a given property P, then for each row r with row number j that has the property P, we set bit j in B to one; all other bits are set to zero. A Bitmap index for a column C with values $v_1, v_2, \ldots, v_k$, is a B-tree with entries having these keyvalues and associated data portions that contain Bitmaps for the properties $C = v_1, \ldots, C = v_k$. Thus Bitmaps in this index are just a new way to specify lists of RIDs for specific column values. See Figure 2.1 for an Example. Note that a series of successive Bitmap Fragments make up the entry for "department = 'sports'".

B-tree Root Node for department

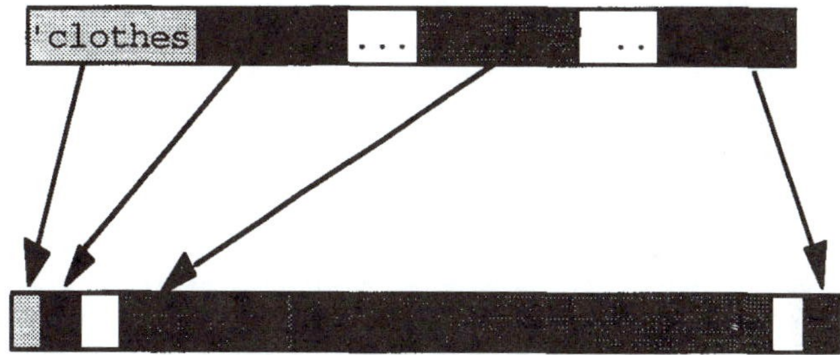

Figure 2.1. Example of a Bitmap Index on department, a column of the SALES table

We say that Bitmaps are *dense* if the proportion of one-bits in the Bitmap is large. A Bitmap index for a column with 32 values will have Bitmaps with average density of 1/32. In this case the disk space to hold a Bitmap column index will be comparable to the disk space needed for a RID-list index (which requires about 32 bits for each RID present). While the uncompressed Bitmap index size is proportional to the number of column values, a RID-list index is about the same size for any number of values (as long as we can continue to amortize the keysize with a long block of RIDs). For a column index with a very small number of values, the Bitmaps will have high densities (such as 50% for predicates such as GENDER = 'M' or GENDER = 'F'), and the disk savings is enormous. On the other hand, when average Bitmap density for a Bitmap index becomes too low, methods exist for compressing a Bitmap. The simplest of these is to translate the Bitmap back to a RID list, and we will assume this in what follows.

2.1.2 Bitmap Index Performance

An important consideration for database query performance is the fact that Boolean operations, such as AND, OR, and NOT are

[1]B^+-trees are commonly referred to simply as B-trees in database documentation, and we will follow this convention.

extremely fast for Bitmaps. Given Bitmaps B1 and B2, we can calculate a new Bitmap B3, B3 = B1 AND B2, by treating all bitmaps as arrays of long ints and looping through them, using the & operation of C:

```
for (i = 0; i < len(B1); i++)
        /* Note: len(B1)=len(B2)=len(B3)     */
   B3[i] = B1[i] & B2[i];
        /* B3 = B1 AND B2                    */
```

We would not normally expect the entire Bitmap to be memory resident, but would perform a loop to operate on Bitmaps by reading them in from disk in long Fragments. We ignore this loop here. Using a similar approach, we can calculate B3 = B1 OR B2. But calculating B3 = NOT(B1) requires an extra step. Since some bit positions can correspond to non-existent rows, we postulate an *Existence Bitmap* (designated *EBM*) which has exactly those 1 bits corresponding to existing rows. Now when we perform a NOT on a Bitmap B, we loop through a long int array performing the ~ operation of C, then AND the result with the corresponding long int from EBM.

```
for (i = 0; i < len(B1); i++)
   B3[i] = ~B1[i] & EBM[i];
        /* B3 = NOT(B1)for rows that exist  */
```

Typical Select statements may have a number of predicates in their Where Clause that must be combined in a Boolean manner. The resulting set of rows, which is then retrieved or aggregated in the Select target-list, is called a *Foundset* in what follows. Sometimes, the rows filtered by the Where Clause must be further grouped, due to a group-by clause, and we refer to the set of rows restricted to a single group as a *Groupset*.

Finally, we show how the COUNT function for a Bitmap of a Foundset can be efficiently performed. First, a short int array shcount[ ] is declared, with entries initialized to contain *the number of bits set to one in the entry subscript*. Given this array, we can loop through a Bitmap as an array of short int values, to get the count of the total Bitmap as shown in Algorithm 2.1. Clearly the shcount[ ] array is used to provide parallelism in calculating the COUNT on many bits at once.

Algorithm 2.1. Performing COUNT with a Bitmap

```
/* Assume B1[ ] is a short int array
   overlaying a Foundset Bitmap                */
count = 0;
for (i = 0; i < SHNUM; i++)
   count += shcount[B1[i]];
/* add count of bits for next short int        */
```

◊

Loops for Bitmap AND, OR, NOT, or COUNT are extremely fast compared to loop operations on RID lists, where several operations are required for each RID, so long as the Bitmaps involved have reasonably high density (down to about 1%).

Example 2.1. In the Set Query benchmark of [O'NEI91], the results from one of the SQL statements in Query Suite Q5 gives a good illustration of Bitmap performance. For a table named BENCH of 1,000,000 rows, two columns named K10 and K25 have cardinalities 10 and 25, respectively, with all rows in the table equally likely to take on any valid value for either column. Thus the Bitmap densities for indexes on this column are 10% and 4% respectively. One SQL statement from the Q5 Suite is:

```
[2.1] SELECT K10, K25, COUNT(*) FROM BENCH
         GROUP BY K10, K25;
```

A 1995 benchmark on a 66 MHz Power PC of the Praxis Omni Warehouse, a C language version of MODEL 204, demonstrated an elapsed time of 19.25 seconds to perform this query. The query plan was to read Bitmaps from the indexes for all values of K10 and K25, perform a double loop through all 250 pairs of values, AND all pairs of Bitmaps, and COUNT the results. The 250 ANDs and 250 COUNTs of 1,000,000 bit Bitmaps required only 19.25 seconds on a relatively weak processor. By comparison, MVS DB2 Version 2.3, running on an IBM 9221/170 used an algorithm that extracted and wrote out all pairs of (K10, K25) values from the rows, sorted by value pair, and counted the result in groups, taking 248 seconds of elapsed time and 223 seconds of CPU. (See [O'NEI96] for more details.) ◊

2.1.3 Segmentation

To optimize Bitmap index access, Bitmaps can be broken into Fragments of equal sizes to fit on single fixed-size disk pages. Corresponding to these Fragments, the rows of a table are partitioned into *Segments*, with an equal number of row slots for each segment. In MODEL 204 (see [M204, O'NEI87]), a Bitmap Fragment fits on a 6 KByte page, and contains about 48K bits, so the table is broken into segments of about 48K rows each. This segmentation has two important implications.

The first implication involves RID-lists. When Bitmaps are sufficiently sparse that they need to be converted to RID-lists, the RID-list for a segment is guaranteed to fit on a disk page (1/32 of 48K is about 1.5K; MODEL 204 actually allows sparser Bitmaps than 1/32, so several RID lists might fit on a single disk page). Furthermore, RIDs need only be two bytes in length, because they only specify the row position within the segment (the 48K rows of a segment can be counted in a short int). At the beginning of each RID-list, the segment number will specify the higher order bits of a longer RID (4 bytes or more), but the segment-relative RIDs only use two bytes each. This is an important form of prefix RID compression, which greatly speeds up index range search.

The second implication of segmentation involves combining predicates. The B-tree index entry for a particular value in MODEL 204 is made up of a number of pointers by segment to Bitmap or RID-list Fragments, but there are no pointers for segments that have no representative rows. In the case of a clustered index, for example, each particular index value entry will have pointers to only a small set of segments. Now if several predicates involving different column indexes are ANDed, the evaluation takes place segment-by-segment. If one of the predicate indexes has no pointer to a Bitmap Fragment for a segment, then the segment Fragments for the other indexes can be ignored as well. Queries like this can turn out to be very common in a workload, and the I/O saved by ignoring I/O for these index Fragments can significantly improve performance.

Bitmap representations and RID-list representations are interchangeable: both provide a way to list all rows with a given index value or range of values. It is simply the case that, when the Bitmap representations involved are relatively dense, Bitmaps are much more efficient than RID-lists, both in storage use and efficiency of Boolean operations. Indeed a Bitmap index can contain RID-lists for some entry values or even for some Segments within a value entry, whenever the number of rows with a given keyvalue would be too sparse in the segment for a

Bitmap to be efficiently used. In what follows, we will assume that a Bitmapped index combines Bitmap and RID-list representations where appropriate, and continue to refer to the hybrid form as a *Value-List Index.* When we refer to the *Bitmap* for a given value v in the index, this should be understood to be a generic name: it may be a Bitmap or it may be a RID-list, or a segment-by-segment combination of the two forms.

2.2 Projection Indexes

Assume that C is a column of a table T; then the Projection index on C consists of a stored sequence of column values from C, in order by the row number in T from which the values are extracted. (Holes might exist for unused row numbers.) If the column C is 4 bytes in length, then we can fit 1000 values from C on each 4 KByte disk page (assuming no holes), and continue to do this for successive column values, until we have constructed the Projection index. Now for a given row number n = m(r) in the table, we can access the proper disk page, p, and slot, s, to retrieve the appropriate C value with a simple calculation: p = n/1000 and s = n%1000. Furthermore, given a C value in a given position of the Projection index, we can calculate the row number easily: n = 1000*p + s.

If the column values for C are variable length instead of fixed length, there are two alternatives. We can set a maximum size and place a fixed number of column value on each page, as before, or we can use a B-tree structure to access the column value C by a lookup of the row number n. The case of variable-length values is obviously somewhat less efficient than fixed-length, and we will assume fixed-length C values in what follows.

The Projection index turns out to be quite efficient in certain cases where column values must be retrieved for all rows of a Foundset. For example, if the density of the Foundset is 1/50 (no clustering, so the density is uniform across all table segments), and the column values are 4 bytes in length, as above, then 1000 values will fit on a 4 KByte page, and we expect to pick up 20 values per Projection index page. In contrast, if the rows of the table were retrieved, then assuming 200-byte rows only 20 rows will fit on a 4 KByte page, and we expect to pick up only 1 row per page. Thus reading the values from a Projection index requires only 1/20 the number of disk page access as reading the values from the rows. The Sybase IQ product is the first one to have utilized the Projection index heavily, under the name of "Fast Projection Index" [EDEL95, FREN95].

The definition of a Projection index is reminiscent of vertically partitioning the columns of a table. Vertical partitioning is a good strategy for workloads where small numbers of columns are retrieved by most Select statements, but it is a bad idea when most queries retrieve many most of the columns. Vertical partitioning is actually forbidden by the TPC-D benchmark, presumably on the theory that the queries chosen have not been sufficiently tuned to penalize this strategy. But Projection indexes are not the same as vertical partitioning. We assume that rows of the table are still stored in contiguous form (the TPC-D requirement) and the Projection indexes are auxiliary aids to retrieval efficiency. Of course this means that column values will be duplicated in the index, but in fact all traditional indexes duplicate column values in this same sense.

2.3 Bit-Sliced Indexes

A Bit-Sliced index stores a set of "Bitmap slices" which are "orthogonal" to the data held in a Projection index. As we will see, they provide an efficient means to calculate aggregates of Foundsets. We begin our definition of Bit-Sliced indexes with an example.

Example 2.2. Consider a table named SALES which contains rows for all sales that have been made during the past month by individual stores belonging to some large chain. The SALES table has a column named dollar_sales, which represents for each row the dollar amount received for the sale.

Now interpret the dollar_sales column as an integer number of pennies, represented as a binary number with N+1 bits. We define a function D(n, i), i = 0, . . . , N, for row number n in SALES, to have value 0, except for rows with a non-null value for dollar_sales, where the value of D(n, i) is defined as follows:

D(n, 0) = 1 if the 1 bit for dollar_sales in row number n is on
D(n, 1) = 1 if the 2 bit for dollar_sales in row number n is on
. . .
D(n, i) = 1 if the 2^i bit for dollar_sales in row number n is on

Now for each value i, i = 0 to N, such that D(n, i) > 0 for *some* row in SALES, we define a Bitmap B_i on the SALES table so that bit n of Bitmap B_i is set to D(n, i). Note that by requiring that D(n, i) > 0 for some row in SALES, we have guaranteed that we do not have to represent any Bitmap of all zeros. For a real table such as SALES, the appropriate set of Bitmaps with non-zero bits can easily be determined at Create Index time. ◊

The definitions of Example 2.1 generalize to any column C in a table T, where the column C is interpreted as a sequence of bits, from least significant (i = 0) to most significant (i = N).

Definition 2.1: Bit-Sliced Index. The Bit-Sliced index on the C column of table T is the set of all Bitmaps B_i as defined analogously for dollar_sales in Example 2.2. Since a null value in the C column will not have any bits set to 1, it is clear that only rows with non-null values appear as 1-bits in any of these Bitmaps. Each individual Bitmap B_i is called a *Bit-Slice* of the column. We also define the Bit-Sliced index to have a Bitmap B_{nn} representing the set of rows with non-null values in column C, and a Bitmap B_n representing the set of rows with null values. Clearly B_n can be derived from B_{nn} and the Existence Bitmap EBM, but we want to save this effort in algorithms below. In fact, the Bitmaps B_{nn} and B_n are so useful that we assume from now on that B_{nn} exists for Value-List Bitmap indexes (clearly B_n already exists, since null is a particular value). ◊

In the algorithms that follow, we will normally be assuming that the column C is numeric, either an integer or a floating point value. In using Bit-Sliced indexes, it is necessary that different values have matching decimal points in their binary representations. Depending on the variation in size of the floating point numbers, this could lead to an exceptionally large number of slices when values differ by many orders of magnitude. Such an eventuality is unlikely in business applications, however.

A user-defined method to bit-slice aggregate quantities was used by some MODEL 204 customers and is defined on page 48 of [O'NEI87]. Sybase IQ currently provides a fully realized Bit-Sliced index, which is known to the query optimizer and transparent to SQL users. Usually, a Bit-Sliced index for a quantity of the kind in Example 2.2 will involve a relatively small number of Bitmaps (less than the maximum significance), although there is no real limit imposed by the definition. Note that 20

Bitmaps, 0 . . .19, for the dollar_sales column will represent quantities up to 2^{20} - 1 pennies, or $10,485.75, a large sale by most standards. If we assume normal sales range up to $100.00, it is very likely that nearly all values under $100.00 will occur for some row in a large SALES table. Thus, a Value-List index would have nearly 10,000 different values, and row-sets with these values in a Value-List index would almost certainly be represented by RID-lists rather than Bitmaps. The efficiency of performing Boolean Bitmap operations would be lost with a Value-List index, but not with a Bit-Sliced index, where all values are represented with about 20 Bitmaps.

It is important to realize that these index types are all basically equivalent.

Theorem 2.1. For a given column C on a table T, the information in a Bit-sliced index, Value-List index, or Projection index can each be derived from either of the others.

Proof. With all three types of indexes, we are able to determine the values of columns C for all rows in T, and this information is sufficient to create any other index. ◊

Although the three index types contain the same information, they provide different performance advantages for different operations. In the next few sections of the paper we explore this.

3. Comparing Index types for Aggregate Evaluation

In this section we give algorithms showing how Value-List indexes, Projection indexes, and Bit-Sliced indexes can be used to speed up the evaluation of aggregate functions in SQL queries. We begin with an analysis evaluating SUM on a single column. Other aggregate functions are considered later.

3.1 Evaluating Single-Column Sum Aggregates

Example 3.1. Assume that the SALES table of Example 2.2 has 100 million rows which are each 200 bytes in length, stored 20 to a 4 KByte disk page, and that the following Select statement has been submitted:

```
[3.1]  SELECT SUM(dollar_sales) FROM SALES
           WHERE condition;
```

The condition in the Where clause that restricts rows of the SALES table will result in a Foundset of rows. We assume in what follows that the Foundset has already been determined, and is represented by a Bitmap B_f, it contains 2 million rows and the rows are not clustered in a range of disk pages, but are spread out evenly across the entire table. We vary these assumptions later. The most likely case is that determining the Foundset was easily accomplished by performing Boolean operations on a few indexes, so the resources used were relatively insignificant compared to the aggregate evaluation to follow.

Query Plan 1: Direct access to rows to calculate SUM. Each disk page contains only 20 rows, so there must be a total of 5,000,000 disk pages occupied by the SALES table. Since 2,000,000 rows in the Foundset B_f represent only 1/50 of all rows in the SALES table, the number of disk pages that the Foundset occupies can be estimated (see [O'NEI96], Formula [7.6.4]) as:

$$5{,}000{,}000(1 - e^{-2{,}000{,}000/5{,}000{,}000}) = 1{,}648{,}400 \text{ disk pages}$$

The time to perform such a sequence of I/Os, assuming one disk arm retrieves 100 disk pages per second in relatively close sequence on disk, is 16,484 seconds, or more than 4 hours of disk arm use. We estimate 25 instructions needed to retrieve the proper row and column value from each buffer resident page, and this occurs 2,000,000 times, but in fact the CPU utilization associated with reading the proper page into buffer is much more significant. Each disk page I/O is generally assumed to require several thousand instructions to perform (see, for example, [PH96], Section 6.7, where 10,000 instructions are assumed).

Query Plan 2: Calculating SUM with a Projection index. We can use the Projection index to calculate the sum by accessing each dollar_sales value in the index corresponding to a row number in the Foundset; these row numbers will be provided in increasing order. We assume as in Example 2.2 that the dollar_sales Projection index will contain 1000 values per 4 KByte disk page. Thus the Projection index will require 100,000 disk pages, and we can expect all of these pages to be accessed in sequence when the values for the 2,000,000 row Foundset are retrieved. This implies we will have 100,000 disk page I/Os, with elapsed time 1000 seconds (roughly 17 minutes), given the same I/O assumptions as in Query Plan 1. In addition to the I/O, we will use perhaps 10 instructions to convert the Bitmap row number into a disk page offset, access the appropriate value, and add this to the SUM.

Query Plan 3: Calculating SUM with a Value-List index. Assuming we have a Value-List index on dollar_sales, we can calculate SUM(dollar_sales) for our Foundset by ranging through all possible values in the index and determining the rows with each value, then determining how many rows with each value are in the Foundset, and finally multiplying that count by the value and adding to the SUM. In pseudo code, we have Algorithm 3.1 below.

Algorithm 3.1. Evaluating SUM(C) with Value-List Index

```
If (COUNT(Bf AND Bnn) == 0)      /* no non-null values   */
    Return null;
SUM = 0.00;
For each non-null value v in the index for C {
    Designate the set of rows with the value v as Bv
    SUM += v * COUNT(Bf AND Bv);
}
Return SUM;
```

◊

Our earlier analysis counted about 10,000 distinct values in this index, so the Value-List index evaluation of SUM(C) requires 10,000 Bitmap ANDs and 10,000 COUNTs. If we make the assumption that the Bitmap B_f is held in memory (100,000,000 bits, or 12,500,000 bytes) while we loop through the values, and that the sets B_v for each value v are actually RID-lists, this will entail 3125 I/Os to read in B_f, 100,000 I/Os to read in the index RID-lists for all values (100,000,000 RIDs of 4 bytes each, assuming all pages are completely full), and a loop of several instructions to translate 100,000,000 RIDs to bit positions and test if they are on in B_f.

Note that this algorithm gains an enormous advantage by assuming B_f is a Bitmap (rather than a RID-list), and that it can be held in memory, so that RIDs from the index can be looked up quickly. If B_f were held as a RID-list instead, the lookup would be a good deal less efficient, and would probably entail a sort by RID value of values from the index, followed by a merge-intersect with the RID-list B_f. Even with the assumption that B_f is a Bitmap in memory, the loop through 100,000,000 RIDs is extremely CPU intensive, especially if the translation from RID to bit ordinal entails a complex lookup in a memory-resident tree to determine the extent containing the disk page of the RID and the corresponding RID number within the extent. With optimal assumptions, Plan 3 seems to require 103,125 I/Os and a loop of length 100,000,000, with a loop body of perhaps 10 instructions. Even so, Query Plan 3 is probably superior to Query Plan 1, which requires I/O for 1,340,640 disk pages.

Query Plan 4: Calculating SUM with a Bit-Sliced index. Assuming we have a Bit-Sliced index on dollar_sales as defined in Example 2.2, we can calculate SUM(dollar_sales) with the pseudo code of Algorithm 3.2.

Algorithm 3.2. Evaluating SUM(C) with a Bit-Sliced Index

```
/* We are given a Bit-Sliced index for C, containing bitmaps
   B_i, i = 0 to N (N = 19), B_n and B_nn, as in Example 2.2
   and Definition 2.1.                                  */
   If (COUNT(B_f AND B_nn) == 0)
       Return null;
   SUM = 0.00
   For i = 0 to N
       SUM += 2^i * COUNT(B_i AND B_f);
   Return SUM;
◊
```

With Algorithm 3.2, we can calculate a SUM by performing 21 ANDs and 21 COUNTs of 100,000,000 bit Bitmaps. Each Bitmap is 12.5 MBytes in length, requiring 3125 I/Os, but we assume that B_f can remain in memory after the first time it is read. Therefore, we need to read a total of 22 Bitmaps from disk, using 22*3125 = 68,750 I/Os, a bit over half the number needed in Query Plan 2. For CPU, we need to AND 21 pairs of Bitmaps, which is done by looping through the Bitmaps in long int chunks, a total number of loop passes on a 32-bit machine equal to: 21*(100,000,000/32) = 65,625,000. Then we need to perform 21 COUNTs, looping through Bitmaps in half-word chunks, with 131,250,000 passes. However, all these 196,875,000 passes to perform ANDs and COUNTs are single instruction loops, and thus presumably take a good deal less time than the 100,000,000 multi-instruction loops of Plan 2.

3.1.1 Comparing Algorithm Performance

Table 3.1 compares the above four Query Plans to calculate SUM, in terms of I/O and factors contributing to CPU.

Method	I/O	CPU contributions
Add from Rows	1,341K	I/O + 2M*(25 ins)
Projection index	100K	I/O + 2M *(10 ins)
Value-List index	103K	I/O + 100M *(10 ins)
Bit-Sliced index	69K	I/O + 197M *(1 ins)

Table 3.1. I/O and CPU factors for the four plans

We can compare the four query plans in terms of dollar cost by converting I/O and CPU costs to dollar amounts, as in [GP87]. In 1997, a 2 GB hard disk with a 10 ms access time costs roughly $600. With the I/O rate we have been assuming, this is approximately $6.00 per I/O per second. A 200 MHz Pentium computer, which processes approximately 150 MIPS (million instructions per second), costs roughly $1800, or approximately $12.00 per MIPS. If we assume that each of the plans above is submitted at a rate of once each 1,000 seconds, the most expensive plan, "Add from rows", will keep 13.41 disks busy at a cost of $8046 purchase. We calculate the number of CPU instructions needed for I/O for the various plans, with the varying assumptions in Table 3.2 of how many instructions are needed to perform an I/O. Adding the CPU cost for algorithmic loops to the I/O cost, we determine the total dollar cost ($Cost) to support the method. For example, for the "Add from Rows" plan, assuming one submission each 1000 seconds, if an I/O uses (2K, 5K, 10K) instructions, the CPU cost is ($32.78, $81.06, $161.52). The cost for disk access ($8046) clearly swamps the cost of CPU in this case, and in fact the relative cost of I/O compared to CPU holds for all methods. Table 3.2 shows that the Bit-sliced index is the most efficient for this problem, with the Projection index and Value-List index a close second and third. The Projection index is so much better than the fourth ranked plan of accessing the rows that one would prefer it even if thirteen different columns were to be summed, notwithstanding the savings to be achieved by summing all the different columns from the same memory-resident row.

Method	$Cost for 2K ins per I/O	$Cost for 5K ins per I/O	$Cost for 10K ins per I/O
Add from Rows	$8079	$8127	$8207
Projection index	$603	$606	$612
Value-List index	$632	$636	$642
Bit-Sliced index	$418	$421	$425

Table 3.2. Dollar costs of four plans for SUM

3.1.2 Varying Foundset Density and Clustering

Changing the number of rows in the Foundset has little effect on the Value-List index or Bit-Sliced index algorithms, because the entire index must still be read in both cases. However, the algorithms Add from rows and using a Projection index entail work proportional to the number of rows in the foundset. We stop considering the plan to Add from rows in what follows.

Suppose the Foundset contains kM (k million) rows, clustered on a fraction f of the disk space. Both the Projection and Bit-Sliced index algorithms can take advantage of the clustering. The table below shows the comparison between the three index algorithms.

Method	I/O	CPU contributions
Projection index	f · 100K	I/O + kM · (10 ins)
Value-List index	103K	I/O + 100M · (10 ins)
Bit-Sliced index	f · 69K	I/O + f · 197M · (1 ins)

Table 3.3. Costs of four plans, I/O and CPU factors, with kM rows and clustering fraction f

Clearly there is a relationship between k and f in Table 3.3, since for k = 100, 100M rows sit on a fraction f = 1.0 of the table, we must have $k \le f \cdot 100$. Also, if f becomes very small compared to k/100, we will no longer pick up every page in the Projection or Bit-Sliced index. In what follows, we assume that f is sufficiently large that the I/O approximations in Table 3.3 are valid.

The dollar cost of I/O continues to dominate total dollar cost of the plans when each plan is submitted once every 1000 seconds.

For the Projection index, the I/O cost is f·$600. The CPU cost, assuming that I/O requires 10K instructions is: ((f·100·10,000+k·1000·10)/1,000,000)·$12. Since $k \leq f·100$, the formula $f·100·10,000 + k·1000·10 \leq f·100·10,000 + f·100·1000·10 = f·2,000,000$. Thus, the total CPU cost is bounded above by f·$24, which is still cheap compared to an I/O cost of f·$600. Yet this is the highest cost we assume for CPU due to I/O, which is the dominant CPU term. In Table 3.4, we give the maximum dollar cost for each index approach.

Method	$Cost for 10K ins per I/O
Projection index	f·$624
Value-List index	$642
Bit-Sliced index	f·$425

Table 3.4. Costs of the four plans in dollars, with kM rows and clustering fraction f

The clustered case clearly affects the plans by making the Projection and Bit-Sliced indexes more efficient compared to the Value-List index.

3.2 Evaluating Other Column Aggregate Functions

We consider aggregate functions of the form in [3.2], where AGG is an aggregate function, such as COUNT, MAX, MIN, etc.

[3.2] SELECT AGG(C) FROM T WHERE condition;

Table 3.5 lists a group of aggregate functions and the index types to evaluate these functions. We enter the value "Best" in a cell if the given index type is the most efficient one to have for this aggregation, "Slow" if the index type works but not very efficiently, etc. Note that Table 3.5 demonstrates how different index types are optimal for different aggregate situations.

Aggregate	Value-List Index	Projection Index	Bit-Sliced Index
COUNT	Not needed	Not needed	Not needed
SUM	Not bad	Good	**Best**
AVG (SUM/COUNT)	Not bad	Good	**Best**
MAX and MIN	**Best**	Slow	Slow
MEDIAN, N-TILE	Usually Best	Not Useful	Sometimes Best[2]
Column-Product	Very Slow	**Best**	Very Slow

Table 3.5. Tabulation of Performance by Index Type for Evaluating Aggregate Functions

The COUNT and SUM aggregates have already been covered. COUNT requires no index, and AVG can be evaluated as SUM/COUNT, with performance determined by SUM.

The MAX and MIN aggregate functions are best evaluated with a Value-List index. To determine MAX for a Foundset B_f, one loops from the largest value in the Value-List index down to the smallest, until finding a row in B_f. To find MAX and MIN using a Projection index, one must loop through all values stored. The algorithm to evaluate MAX or MIN using a Bit-Sliced index is given in our extended paper, [O'NQUA], together with other algorithms not detailed in this Section.

To calculate MEDIAN(C) with C a keyvalue in a Value-List index, one loops through the non-null values of C in decreasing (or increasing) order, keeping a count of rows encountered, until for the first time with some value v the number of rows encountered so far is greater than COUNT(B_f AND B_{nn})/2. Then v is the MEDIAN. Projection indexes are not useful for evaluating MEDIAN, unless the number of rows in the Foundset is very small, since all values have to be extracted and sorted. Surprisingly, a Bit-Sliced index can also be used to determine the MEDIAN, in about the same amount of time as it takes to determine SUM (see [O'NQUA]).

The N-TILE aggregate function finds values $v_1, v_2, \ldots, v_{N-1}$, which partition the rows in B_f into N sets of (approximately) equal size based on the interval in which their C value falls: $C \le v_1$, $v_1 < C \le v_2, \ldots, v_{N-1} < C$. MEDIAN equals 2-TILE.

An example of a COLUMN-PRODUCT aggregate function is one which involves the product of different columns. In the TPC-D benchmark, the LINEITEM table has columns L_EXTENDEDPRICE and L_DISCOUNT. A large number of queries in TPC-D retrieve the aggregate: SUM(L_EXTENDEDPRICE*(1-L_DISCOUNT)), usually with the column alias "REVENUE". The most efficient method for calculating Column-Product Aggregates uses Projection indexes for the columns involved. It is possible to calculate products of columns using Value-List or Bit-Sliced indexes, with the sort of algorithm that was used for SUM, but in both cases, Foundsets of all possible cross-terms of values must be formed and counted, so the algorithm are terribly inefficient.

4. Evaluating Range Predicates

Consider a Select statement of the following form:

[4.1] SELECT target-list FROM T
WHERE C-range AND <condition>;

Here, C is a column of T, and <condition> is a general search-condition resulting in a Foundset B_f. The C-range represents a range predicate, {C > c1, C >= c1, C = c1, C >= c1, C > c1, C between c1 and c2}, where c1 and c2 are constant values. We will demonstrate below how to further restrict the Foundset B_f, creating a new Foundset B_F, so that the compound predicate "C-range AND <condition>" holds for exactly those rows contained in B_F. We do this with varying assumptions regarding index types on the column C.

Evaluating the Range using a Projection Index. If there is a Projection index on C, we can create B_F by accessing each C value in the index corresponding to a row number in B_f and testing whether it lies within the specified range.

Evaluating the Range using a Value-List Index. With a Value-List index, evaluation the C-range restriction of [4.1] uses an algorithm common in most database products, looping through the index entries for the range of values. We vary slightly by accumulating a Bitmap B_r as an OR of all row sets in the index for values that lie in the specified range, then AND this result with B_f to get B_F. See Algorithm 4.1.

[2]Best only if there is a clustering of rows in B in a local region, a fraction f of the pages, $f \leq 0.755$.

Note that for Algorithm 4.1 to be efficiently performed, we must find some way to guarantee that the Bitmap B_r remains in memory at all times as we loop through the values v in the range. This requires some forethought in the Query Optimizer if the table T being queried is large: 100 million rows will mean that a Bitmap B_r of 12.5 MBytes must be kept resident.

Algorithm 4.1. Range Predicate Using a Value-List Index
B_r = the empty set
For each entry v in the index for C that satisfies the range specified
Designate the set of rows with the value v as B_v
$B_r = B_r$ OR B_v
$B_F = B_f$ AND B_r
◊

Evaluating the Range using a Bit-Sliced Index. Rather surprisingly, it is possible to evaluate range predicates efficiently using a Bit-Sliced index. Given a Foundset B_f, we demonstrate in Algorithm 4.2 how to evaluate the set of rows B_{GT} such that C > c1, B_{GE} such that C >= c1, B_{EQ} such that C = c1, B_{LE} such that C <= c1, B_{LT} such that C < c1.

In use, we can drop Bitmap calculations in Algorithm 4.2 that do not evaluate the condition we seek. If we only need to evaluate C >= c1, we don't need steps that evaluate B_{LE} or B_{LT}.

Algorithm 4.2. Range Predicate Using a Bit-Sliced Index
$B_{GT} = B_{LT}$ = the empty set; $B_{EQ} = B_{nn}$
For each Bit-Slice B_i for C in decreasing significance
If bit i is on in constant c1
$B_{LT} = B_{LT}$ OR (B_{EQ} AND NOT(B_i))
$B_{EQ} = B_{EQ}$ AND B_i
else
$B_{GT} = B_{GT}$ OR (B_{EQ} AND B_i)
$B_{EQ} = B_{EQ}$ AND NOT(B_i)
$B_{EQ} = B_{EQ}$ AND B_f;
$B_{GT} = B_{GT}$ AND B_f; $B_{LT} = B_{LT}$ AND B_f
$B_{LE} = B_{LT}$ OR B_{EQ}; $B_{GE} = B_{GT}$ OR B_{EQ}
◊

Proof that B_{EQ} B_{GT} and B_{GE} are properly evaluated. The method to evaluate B_{EQ} clearly determines all rows with C = c1, since it requires that all 1-bits on in c1 be on and all 0-bits 0 in c1 be off for all rows in B_{EQ}. Next, note that B_{GT} is the OR of a set of Bitmaps with certain conditions, which we now describe.

Assume that the bit representation of c1 is $b_N b_{N-1} \ldots b_1 b_0$, and that the bit representation of C for some row r in the database is $r_N r_{N-1} \ldots r_1 r_0$. For each bit position i from 0 to N with bit b_i off in c1, a row r will be in B_{GT} if bit r_i is on and bits $r_N r_{N-1} \ldots r_1 r_{i+1}$ are all equal to bits $b_N b_{N-1} \ldots b_{i+1}$. It is clear that C > c1 for any such row r in B_{GT}. Furthermore for any value of C > c1, there must be some bit position i such that the i-th bit position in c1 is off, the i-th bit position of C is on, and all more-significant bits in the two values are identical. Therefore, Algorithm 4.2 properly evaluates B_{GT}. ◊

4.1 Comparing Algorithm Performance

Now we compare performance of these algorithms to evaluate a range predicate, "C between c1 and c2". We assume that C values are not clustered on disk. The cost of evaluating a range predicate using a Projection index is similar to evaluating SUM using a Projection index, as seen in Fig. 3.2. We need the I/O to access each of the index pages with C values plus the CPU cost to test each value and, if the row passes the range test, to turn on the appropriate bit in a Foundset.

As we have just seen, it is possible to determine the Foundset of rows in a range using Bit-Sliced indexes. We can calculate the range predicate c2 >= C >= c1 using a Bit-Sliced index by calculating B_{GE} for c1 and B_{LE} for c2, then ANDing the two. Once again the calculation is generally comparable in cost to calculating a SUM aggregate, as seen in Fig. 3.2.

With a Value-List index, algorithmic effort is proportional to the width of the range, and for a wide range, it is comparable to the effort needed to perform SUM for a large Foundset. Thus for wide ranges the Projection and Bit-Sliced indexes have a performance advantage. For short ranges the work to perform the Projection and Bit-Sliced algorithms remain nearly the same (assuming the range variable is not a clustering value), while the work to perform the Value-List algorithm is proportional to the number of rows found in the range. Eventually as the width of the range decreases the Value-List algorithm is the better choice. These considerations are summarized in Table 4.1.

Range Evaluation	**Value-List Index**	**Projection Index**	**Bit-Sliced Index**
Narrow Range	**Best**	Good	Good
Wide Range	Not bad	Good	**Best**

Table 4.1. Range Evaluation Performance by Index Type

4.2 Range Predicate with Base > 2 Bit-Sliced Index

Sybase IQ was the first product to demonstrate in practice that the same Bit-Sliced index, called the "High NonGroup Index" [EDEL95], could be used both for evaluating range predicates (Algorithm 4.2) and performing Aggregates (Algorithm 3.2, et al). For many years, MODEL 204 has used a form of indexing to evaluate range predicates, known as "Numeric Range" [M204]. Numeric Range evaluation is similar to Bit-Sliced Algorithm 4.2, except that numeric quantities are expressed in a larger base (base 10). It turns out that the effort of performing a range retrieval can be reduced if we are willing to store a larger number of Bitmaps. In [O'NQUA] we show how Bit-Sliced Algorithm 4.2 can be generalized to base 8, where the Bit-Slices represent sets of rows with octal digit $O_i \geq c$, c a non-zero octal digit. This is a generalization of Binary Bit-Slices, which represent sets of rows with binary digit $B_i \geq 1$.

5. Evaluating OLAP-style Queries

Figure 5.1 pictures a star-join schema with a central fact table, SALES, containing sales data, together with dimension tables known as TIME (when the sales are made), PRODUCT (product sold), and CUSTOMER (purchaser in the sale). Most OLAP products do not express their queries in SQL, but much of the work of typical OLAP queries *could* be represented in SQL [GBLP96] (although more than one query might be needed).

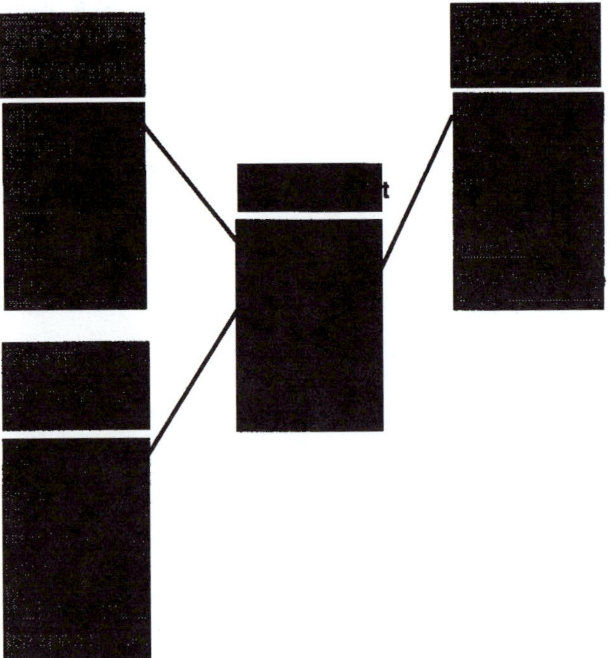

Figure 5.1. Star Join Schema of SALES, CUSTOMER, PRODUCT, and TIME

Query [5.1] retrieves total dollar sales that were made for a product brand during the past 4 weeks to customers in New England.

```
[5.1] SELECT P.brand, T.week, C.city, SUM(S.dollar_sales)
  FROM SALES S, PRODUCT P, CUSTOMER C, TIME T
      WHERE S.day = T.day and S.cid = C.cid
        and S.pid = P.pid and P.brand = :brandvar
        and T.week >= :datevar and C.state in
           ('Maine', 'New Hampshire', 'Vermont',
            'Massachusetts', 'Connecticut', 'Rhode Island')
        GROUP BY P.brand, T.week, C.city;
```

An important advantage of OLAP products is evaluating such queries quickly, even though the fact tables are usually very large. The OLAP approach precalculates results of some Grouped queries and stores them in what we have been calling *summary tables*. For example, we might create a summary table where sums of Sales.dollar_sales and sums of Sales.unit_sales are precalculated for all combination of values at the lowest level of granularity for the dimensions, e.g., for C.cid values, T.day values, and P.pid values. Within each dimension there are also hierarchies sitting above the lowest level of granularity. A week has 7 days and a year has 52 weeks, and so on. Similarly, a customer exists in a geographic hierarchy of city and state. When we precalculate a summary table at the lowest dimensional level, there might be many rows of detail data associated with a particular cid, day, and pid (a busy product reseller customer), or there might be none. A summary table, at the lowest level of granularity, will usually save a lot of work, compared to detailed data, for queries that group by attributes at higher levels of the dimensional hierarchy, such as city (of customers), week, and brand. We would typically create many summary tables, combining various levels of the dimensional hierarchies. The higher the dimensional levels, the fewer elements in the summary table, but there are a lot of possible combinations of hierarchies. Luckily, we don't need to create all possible summary tables in order to speed up the queries a great deal. For more details, see [STG95, HRU96].

By doing the aggregation work beforehand, summary tables provide quick response to queries, so long as all selection conditions are restrictions on dimensions that have been foreseen in advance. But, as we pointed out in Example 1.1, if some restrictions are non-dimensional, such as temperature, then summary tables sliced by dimensions will be useless. And since the size of data in the summary tables grows as the product of the number of values in the independent dimensions (counting values of hierarchies within each dimension), it soon becomes impossible to provide dimensions for all possible restrictions. The goal of this section is to describe and analyze a variant indexing approach that is useful for evaluating OLAP-style queries quickly, even when the queries cannot make use of preaggregation. To begin, we need to explain Join indexes.

5.1 Join Indexes

Definition 5.1. Join Index. A Join index is an index on one table for a quantity that involves a column value of a different table through a commonly encountered join ◊

Join indexes can be used to avoid actual joins of tables, or to greatly reduce the volume of data that must be joined, by performing restrictions in advance. For example, the Star Join index — invented a number of years ago — concatenates ordinal encodings of column values from different dimension tables of a Star schema, and lists RIDs in the central fact table for each concatenated value. The Star Join index was the best approach known in its day, but there is a problem with it, comparable to the problem with summary tables. If there are numerous columns used for restrictions in each dimension table, then the number of Star Join indexes needed to be able to combine arbitrary column restrictions from each dimension table is a product of the number of columns in each dimension. Thus, there will be a "combinatorial explosion" of Join Indexes in terms of the number of independent columns.

The Bitmap join index, defined in [O'NGG95], addresses this problem. In its simplest form, this is an index on a table T based on a single column of a table S, where S commonly joins with T in a specified way. For example, in the TPC-D benchmark database, the O_ORDERDATE column belongs to the ORDER table, but two TPC-D queries need to join ORDER with LINEITEM to restrict LINEITEM rows to a range of O_ORDERDATE. This can better be accomplished by creating an index for the value ORDERDATE on the LINEITEM table. This doesn't change the design of the LINEITEM table, since the index on ORDERDATE is for a virtual column through a join. The number of indexes of this kind increases linearly with the number of useful columns in all dimension tables. We depend on the speed of combining Bitmapped indexes to create ad-hoc combinations, and thus the explosion of Star Join indexes because of different combinations of dimension columns is not a problem. Another way of looking at this is that Bitmap join indexes are *Recombinant*, whereas Star join indexes are not.

The variant indexes of the current paper lead to an important point, that Join indexes can be of any type: Projection, Value-List, or Bit-Sliced. To speed up Query [5.1], we use Join indexes on the SALES fact table for columns in the dimensions. If appropriate join indexes exist for all dimension table columns mentioned in the queries, then explicit joins with dimension tables may no longer be necessary at all. Using Value-List or Bit-

Sliced join indexes we can evaluate the selection conditions in the Where Clause to arrive at a Foundset on SALES, and *using Projection join indexes we can then retrieve the dimensional values for the Query [5.1] target-list, without any join needed.*

5.2 Calculating Groupset Aggregates

We assume that in star-join queries like [5.1], an aggregation is performed on columns of the central fact table, F. There is a Foundset of rows on the fact table, and the group-by columns in the Dimension tables D1, D2, . . . (they might be primary keys of the Dimension tables, in which case they will also exist as foreign keys on F). Once the Foundset has been computed from the Where Clause, the bits in the Foundset must be partitioned into groups, which we call *Groupsets*, again sets of rows from F. Any aggregate functions are then evaluated separately over these different Groupsets. In what follows, we describe how to compute Groupset aggregates using our different index types.

Computing Groupsets Using Projection Indexes. We assume Projection indexes exist on F for each of the group-by columns (these are Join Indexes, since the group-by columns are on the Dimension tables), and also for all columns of F involved in aggregates. If the number of group cells is small enough so that all grouped aggregate values in the target list will fit into memory, then partitioning into groups and computing aggregate functions for each group can usually be done rather easily.

For each row of the Foundset returned by the Where clause, classify the row into a group-by cell by reading the appropriate Projection indexes on F. Then read the values of the columns to be aggregated from Projection indexes on these columns, and aggregate the result into the proper cell of the memory-resident array. (This approach can be used directly for functions such a SUM(C); for functions such as AVG(C), it can be done by accumulating a "handle" of results, SUM(C) and COUNT(C), to calculate the final aggregate.)

If the total set of cells in the group-by cannot be retained in a memory-resident array, then the values to be aggregated can be tagged with their group cell values, and then values with identical group cell values brought together using a disk sort (this is a common method used today, not terribly efficient).

Computing Groups Using Value-List Indexes. The idea of using Value-List indexes to compute aggregate groups is not new. As mentioned in Example 2.1, Model 204 used them years ago. In this section we formally present this approach.

Algorithm 5.1. Grouping by columns D1.A, D2.B using a Value-List Index

```
For each entry v1 in the Value-List index for D1.A
    For each entry v2 in the Value-List index for D2.B
        Bg = Bv1 AND Bv2 AND Bf
        Evaluate AGG(F.C) on Bg
        /* We would do this with a Projection index      */
◊
```

Algorithm 5.1 presents an algorithm for computing aggregate groups that works for queries with two group-by columns (with Bitmap Join Value-List indexes on Dimension tables D1 and D2). The generalization of Algorithm 5.1 to the case of n group-by attributes is straightforward. Assume the Where clause condition already performed resulted in the Foundset B_f on the fact table F. The algorithm generates a set of Groupsets, B_g, one for each (D1.A, D2.B) group. The aggregate function AGG(F.C) is evaluated for each group using B_g in place of B_f.

Algorithm 5.1 can be quite inefficient when there are a lot of Groupsets and rows of table F in each Groupset are randomly placed on disk. The aggregate function must be re-evaluated for each group and, when the Projection index for the column F.C is too large to be cached in memory, we must revisit disk pages for each Groupset. With many Groupsets, we would expect there to be few rows in each, and evaluating the Grouped AGG(F.C) in Algorithm 5.1 might require an I/O for each individual row.

5.3 Improved Grouping Efficiency Using Segmentation and Clustering

In this section we show how segmentation and clustering can be used to accelerate a query with one or more group-by attributes, using a generalization of Algorithm 5.1. We assume that the rows of the table F are partitioned into Segments, as explained in Section 2.1. Query evaluation is performed on one Segment at a time, and the results from evaluating each Segment are combined at the end to form the final query result. Segmentation is most effective when the number of rows per Segment is the number of bits that will fit on a disk page. With this Segment size, we can read the bits in an index entry that correspond to a segment by performing a single disk I/O.

As pointed out earlier, if a Segment s_1 of the Foundset (or Groupset) is completely empty (i.e., all bits are 0), then ANDing s_1 with any other Segment s_2 will also result in an empty Segment. As explained in [O'NEI87], the entry in the B-tree leaf level for a column C that references an all-zeros Bitmap Segment is simply missing, and a reasonable algorithm to AND Bitmaps will test this before accessing any Segment Bitmap pages. Thus neither s_1 nor s_2 will need be read from disk after an early phase of evaluation. This optimization becomes especially useful when rows are clustered on disk by nested dimensions used in grouping, as we will see.

Consider a Star Join schema with a central fact table F and a set of three dimension tables, D_1, D_2, D_3. We can easily generalize the analysis that follows to more than three dimensions. Each dimension D_m, $1 \le m \le 3$, has a primary key, d_m, with a domain of values having an order assigned by the DBA. We represent the number of values in the domain of d_m by n_m, and list the values of d_m in increasing order, differentiated by superscript, as: $d_m^1, d_m^2, \ldots, d_m^{n_m}$. For example, the primary key of the TIME dimension of Figure 5.1 would be days and have a natural temporal order. The DBA would probably choose the order of values in the PRODUCT dimension so that the most commonly used hierarchies, such as product_type or category, consist of contiguous sets of values in the dimensional order. See Figure 5.2.

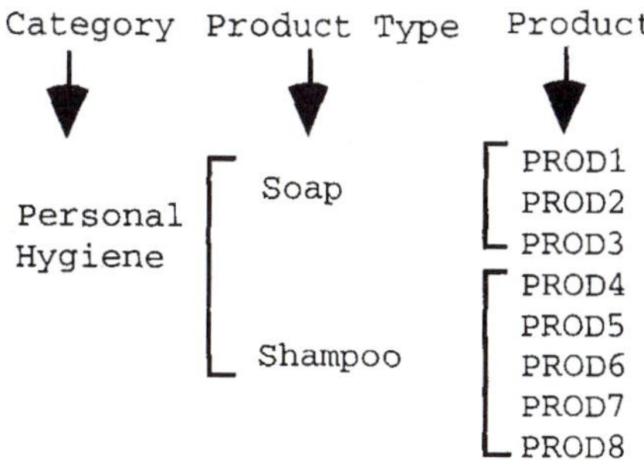

Figure 5.2. Order of Values in PRODUCT Dimensions

In what follows, we will consider a workload of OLAP-type queries which have group-by clauses on some values in the dimension tables (not necessarily the primary key values). The fact table F contains foreign key columns that match the primary keys of the various dimensions. We will assume indexes on these foreign keys for table F and make no distinction between these and these and the primary keys of the Dimensions. We intend to demonstrate how these indexes can be efficiently used to perform group-by queries using Algorithm 5.1.

We wish to cluster the fact table F to improve performance of the most finely divided group-by possible (grouping by primary key values of the dimensions rather than by any hierarchy values above these). It will turn out that this clustering is also effective for arbitrary group-by queries on the dimensions. To evaluate the successive Groupsets by Algorithm 5.1, we consider performing the nested loop of Figure 5.3.

```
For each key-value v1 in order from D1
    For each key-value v2 in order from D2
        For each key-value v3 in order from D3
            <calculate aggregates for cell v1, v2, v3>
        End For v3
    End For v2
End For v1
```

Figure 5.3. Nested Loop to Perform a Group-By

In the loop of Figure 5.3, we assume the looping order for dimensions (D_1, D_2, D_3) is determined by the DBA (this order has long-term significance; we give an example below). The loop on dimension values here produces conjoint cells (v_1, v_2, v_3), of the group-by. Each cell may contain a large number of rows from table F or none. The set of rows in a particular cell is what we have been referring to as a Groupset.

It is our intent to *cluster the rows of the fact table F* so that all the rows with foreign keys matching the dimension values in each cell (v_1, v_2, v_3) *are placed together on disk,* and furthermore that the successive cells fall in the same order on disk as the nested loop above on (D_1, D_2, D_3).

Given this clustering, the Bitmaps for each Groupset will have 1-bits in a limited contiguous range. Furthermore, as the loop is performed to calculate a group-by, successive cells will have rows in Groupset Bitmaps that are contiguous one to another and increase in row number. Figure 5.4 gives a schematic representation of the Bitmaps for index values of three dimensions.

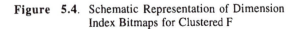

```
D1  = d1^1   1111111111111111110000000000000000000...
    = d1^2   0000000000000000011111111111111111000...
     . . .
D2  = d2^1   1111110000000000011111100000000000111...
    = d2^2   0000000111111100000000001111111000000...
     . . .
D3  = d3^1   1100000011000000001100000000000000110...
    = d3^2   0011000001100000000110000000000000001...
     . . .
    = d3^n3  0000011000001100000000110000000000001...
```

Figure 5.4. Schematic Representation of Dimension Index Bitmaps for Clustered F

The Groupset Bitmaps are calculated by ANDing the appropriate index Bitmaps for the given values. Note that as successive Groupset Bitmaps in loop order are generated from ANDing, the 1-bits in each Groupset move from left to right. In terms of Figure 5.4, the Groupset for the first cell (d_1^1, d_2^1, d_3^1) calculated by a Bitmap AND of the three index Bitmaps $D_1 = d_1^1$, $D_2 = d_2^1$, and $D_3 = d_3^1$, is as follows.

```
1100000000000000000000000000000000000...
```

The Groupset for the next few cells will have Bitmaps:

```
0011000000000000000000000000000000000...
0000110000000000000000000000000000000...
```

And so on, moving from left to right.

To repeat: as the loop to perform the most finely divided group-by is performed, and Groupset Bitmaps are generated, successive blocks of 1-bits by row number will be created, and successive row values from the Projection index will be accessed to evaluate an aggregate. Because of Segmentation, no unnecessary I/Os are ever performed to AND the Bitmaps of the individual dimensions. Indeed, due to clustering, it is most likely that Groupset Bitmaps for successive cells will have 1-bits that move from left to right on each Segment Bitmap page of the Value index, and the column values to aggregate will move from left to right in each Projection index page, only occasionally jumping to the next page. This is tremendously efficient, since relevant pages from the Value-list dimension indexes and Projection indexes on the fact table *need be read only once from left to right to perform the entire group-by.*

If we consider group-by queries where the Groupsets are less finely divided than in the primary key loop given, grouping instead by higher hierarchical levels in the dimensions, this approach should still work. We materialize the grouped Aggregates in memory, and aggregate in nested loop order by the primary keys of the dimensions as we examine rows in F. Now for each cell, (v_1, v_2, v_3) in the loop of Figure 5.3, we determine the higher order hierarchy values of the group-by we are trying to compute. Corresponding to each dimension primary key value of the current cell, $v_i = d_i^m$, there is a value in the dimension hierarchy we are grouping by h_i^r; thus, as we loop through the finely divided cells, we aggregate the results for ($d_1^{m_1}$, $d_2^{m_2}$, $d_3^{m_3}$) into the aggregate cell for ($h_1^{r_1}$, $h_2^{r_2}$, $h_3^{r_3}$). As long as we can hold all aggregates for the higher hierarchical levels in memory at once, we have lost none of the nested loop efficiency. This is why we attempted to order the lowest level dimension values by higher level aggregates, so the cells here can be materialized, aggregated, and stored on disk in a streamed fashion. In a similar manner, if we were to group by only a subset of dimensions, we would be able to treat all dimensions not named as the highest hierarchical level for that dimension, which we refer to as ALL, and continue to use this nested loop approach.

5.4 Groupset Indexes

While Bitmap Segmentation permits us to use normal Value-List indexing, ANDing Bitmaps (or RID-lists) from individual indexes to find Groupsets, there is some inefficiency associated with calculating which Segments have no 1-bits for a particular Cell to save ANDing segment Bitmaps. In Figure 5.1, for example, the cell ($d_1{}^1$, $d_2{}^1$, $d_3{}^1$) has only the leftmost 2 bits on, but the Value-List index Bitmaps for these values have many other segments with bits on, as we see in Figure 5.4, and Bitmaps for individual index values might have 1-bits that span many Segments.

To reduce this overhead, we can create a *Groupset index*, whose keyvalues are a concatenation of the dimensional primary-key values. Since the Groupset Bitmaps in nested loop order are represented as successive blocks of 1-bits in row number, the Groupset index value can be represented by a simple integer, which represents the starting position of the first 1-bit in the Groupset, and the ending position of that Bitmap can be determined as one less than the starting position for the following index entry. Some cells will have no representative rows, and this will be most efficiently represented in the Groupset index by the fact that there is no value representing a concatenation of the dimensional primary-key values.

We believe that the Groupset index makes the calculation of a multi-dimensional group-by as efficient as possible when precalculating aggregates in summary tables isn't appropriate.

6. Conclusion

The read-mostly environment of data warehousing has made it feasible to use more complex index structures to speed up the evaluation of queries. This paper has examined two new index structures: Bit-Sliced indexes and Projection indexes. Indexes like these were used previously in commercial systems, Sybase IQ and MODEL 204, but never examined in print.

As a new contribution, we have shown how ad-hoc OLAP-style queries involving aggregation and grouping can be efficiently evaluated using indexing and clustering, and we have introduced a new index type, Groupset indexes, that are especially well-suited for evaluating this type of query.

References

[COMER79] Comer, D. The Ubiquitous B-tree. Comput. Surv. 11 (1979), pp. 121-137.

[EDEL95] Herb Edelstein. Faster Data Warehouses. Information Week, Dec. 4, 1995, pp. 77-88. Give title and author on http://www.techweb.com/search/advsearch.html.

[FREN95] Clark D. French. "One Size Fits All" Database Architectures Do Not Work for DSS. Proceedings of the 1995 ACM SIGMOD Conference, pp. 449-450.

[GBLP96] Jim Gray, Adam Bosworth, Andrew Layman, and Hamid Pirahesh. Data Cube: A Relational Operator Generalizing Group-By, Cross-Tab, and Sub-Totals. Proc. 12th Int. Conf. on Data Eng., pp. 152-159, 1996.

[GP87] Jim Gray and Franco Putzolu. The Five Minute Rule for Trading Memory for Disk Accesses and The 10 Byte Rule for Trading Memory for CPU Time. Proc. 1987 ACM SIGMOD, pp. 395-398.

[HRU96] Venky Harinarayan, Anand Rajaraman, and Jeffrey D. Ullman. Implementing Data Cubes Efficiently. Proc. 1996 ACM SIGMOD, pp. 205-216.

[KIMB96] Ralph Kimball. The Data Warehouse Toolkit. John Wiley & Sons, 1996.

[M204] MODEL 204 File Manager's Guide, Version 2, Release 1.0, April 1989, Computer Corporation of America.

[O'NEI87] Patrick O'Neil. Model 204 Architecture and Performance. Springer-Verlag Lecture Notes in Computer Science 359, 2nd Int. Workshop on High Performance Transactions Systems (HPTS), Asilomar, CA, 1987, pp. 40-59.

[O'NEI91] Patrick O'Neil. The Set Query Benchmark. The Benchmark Handbook for Database and Transaction Processing Systems, Jim Gray (Ed.), Morgan Kaufmann, 2nd Ed. 1993, pp. 359-395.

[O'NEI96] Patrick O'Neil. Database: Principles, Programming, and Performance. Morgan Kaufmann, 3rd printing, 1996.

[O'NGG95] Patrick O'Neil and Goetz Graefe. Multi-Table Joins Through Bitmapped Join Indices. SIGMOD Record, September, 1995, pp. 8-11,

[O'NQUA] Patrick O'Neil and Dallan Quass. Improved Query Performance with Variant Indexes. Extended paper, available on http:/www.cs.umb.edu/~poneil/varindexx.ps

[PH96] D. A. Patterson and J. L. Hennessy. Computer Architecture, A Quantitative Approach. Morgan Kaufmann, 1996.

[STG95] Stanford Technology Group, Inc., An INFORMIX Co.. Designing the Data Warehouse on Relational Databases. Informix White Paper, 1995, http://www.informix.com.

[TPC] TPC Home Page. Descriptions and results of TPC benchmarks, including the TPC-C and TPC-D benchmarks. http://www.tpc.org.

Data Mining and Knowledge Discovery 1, 29–53 (1997)

Data Cube: A Relational Aggregation Operator Generalizing Group-By, Cross-Tab, and Sub-Totals*

JIM GRAY Gray@Microsoft.com
SURAJIT CHAUDHURI SurajitC@Microsoft.com
ADAM BOSWORTH AdamB@Microsoft.com
ANDREW LAYMAN AndrewL@Microsoft.com
DON REICHART DonRei@Microsoft.com
MURALI VENKATRAO MuraliV@Microsoft.com
Microsoft Research, Advanced Technology Division, Microsoft Corporation, One Microsoft Way, Redmond, WA 98052

FRANK PELLOW Pellow@vnet.IBM.com
HAMID PIRAHESH Pirahesh@Almaden.IBM.com
IBM Research, 500 Harry Road, San Jose, CA 95120

Editor: Usama Fayyad

Received July 2, 1996; Revised November 5, 1996; Accepted November 6, 1996

Abstract. Data analysis applications typically aggregate data across many dimensions looking for anomalies or unusual patterns. The SQL aggregate functions and the `GROUP BY` operator produce zero-dimensional or one-dimensional aggregates. Applications need the N-dimensional generalization of these operators. This paper defines that operator, called the **data cube** or simply **cube**. The cube operator generalizes the histogram, cross-tabulation, roll-up, drill-down, and sub-total constructs found in most report writers. The novelty is that cubes are relations. Consequently, the cube operator can be imbedded in more complex non-procedural data analysis programs. The cube operator treats each of the N aggregation attributes as a dimension of N-space. The aggregate of a particular set of attribute values is a point in this space. The set of points forms an N-dimensional cube. Super-aggregates are computed by aggregating the N-cube to lower dimensional spaces. This paper (1) explains the cube and roll-up operators, (2) shows how they fit in SQL, (3) explains how users can define new aggregate functions for cubes, and (4) discusses efficient techniques to compute the cube. Many of these features are being added to the SQL Standard.

Keywords: data cube, data mining, aggregation, summarization, database, analysis, query

1. Introduction

Data analysis applications look for unusual patterns in data. They categorize data values and trends, extract statistical information, and then contrast one category with another. There are four steps to such data analysis:

formulating a query that extracts relevant data from a large database,
extracting the aggregated data from the database into a file or table,

*An extended abstract of this paper appeared in Gray et al. (1996).

visualizing the results in a graphical way, and
analyzing the results and formulating a new query.

Visualization tools display data trends, clusters, and differences. Some of the most exciting work in visualization focuses on presenting new graphical metaphors that allow people to discover data trends and anomalies. Many of these visualization and data analysis tools represent the dataset as an N-dimensional space. Visualization tools render two and three-dimensional sub-slabs of this space as 2D or 3D objects.

Color and time (motion) add two more dimensions to the display giving the potential for a 5D display. A spreadsheet application such as Excel is an example of a data visualization/analysis tool that is used widely. Data analysis tools often try to identify a subspace of the N-dimensional space which is "interesting" (e.g., discriminating attributes of the data set).

Thus, visualization as well as data analysis tools do "dimensionality reduction", often by summarizing data along the dimensions that are left out. For example, in trying to analyze car sales, we might focus on the role of model, year and color of the cars in sale. Thus, we ignore the differences between two sales along the dimensions of date of sale or dealership but analyze the totals sale for cars by model, by year and by color only. Along with summarization and dimensionality reduction, data analysis applications extensively use constructs such as histogram, cross-tabulation, subtotals, roll-up and drill-down.

This paper examines how a relational engine can support efficient extraction of information from a SQL database that matches the above requirements of the visualization and data analysis. We begin by discussing the relevant features in Standard SQL and some vendor-specific SQL extensions. Section 2 discusses why `GROUP BY` fails to adequately address the requirements. The `CUBE` and the `ROLLUP` operators are introduced in Section 3 and we also discuss how these operators overcome some of the shortcomings of `GROUP BY`. Sections 4 and 5 discuss how we can address and compute the Cube.

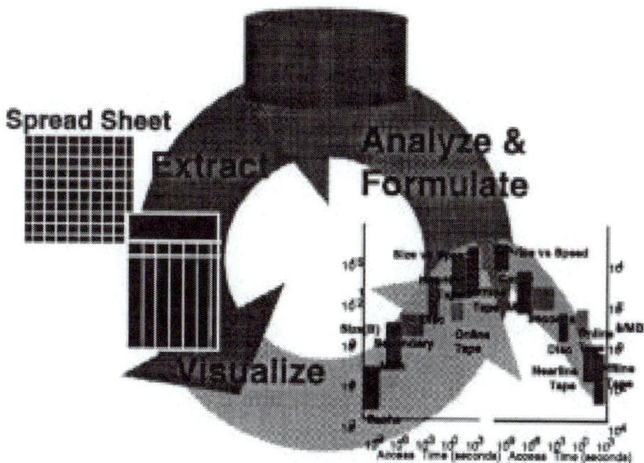

Figure 1. Data analysis tools facilitate the Extract-Visualize-Analyze loop. The cube and roll-up operators along with system and user-defined aggregates are part of the extraction process.

Table 1.

Weather					
Time (UCT)	Latitude	Longitude	Altitude (m)	Temp. (c)	Pres. (mb)
96/6/1:1500	37:58:33N	122:45:28W	102	21	1009
Many more rows like the ones above and below					
96/6/7:1500	34:16:18N	27:05:55W	10	23	1024

1.1. Relational and SQL data extraction

How do traditional relational databases fit into this multi-dimensional data analysis picture? How can 2D flat files (SQL tables) model an N-dimensional problem? Furthermore, how do the relational systems support operations over N-dimensional representations that are central to visualization and data analysis programs?

We address two issues in this section. The answer to the first question is that relational systems model N-dimensional data as a relation with N-attribute domains. For example, 4-dimensional (4D) earth temperature data is typically represented by a `Weather` table (Table 1). The first four columns represent the four dimensions: latitude, longitude, altitude, and time. Additional columns represent measurements at the 4D points such as temperature, pressure, humidity, and wind velocity. Each individual weather measurement is recorded as a new row of this table. Often these measured values are aggregates over time (the hour) or space (a measurement area centered on the point).

As mentioned in the introduction, visualization and data analysis tools extensively use dimensionality reduction (aggregation) for better comprehensibility. Often data along the other dimensions that are not included in a “2-D” representation are summarized via aggregation in the form of histogram, cross-tabulation, subtotals etc. In the SQL Standard, we depend on aggregate functions and the `GROUP BY` operator to support aggregation.

The SQL standard (*IS 9075 International Standard for Database Language SQL*, 1992) provides five functions to aggregate the values in a table: `COUNT()`, `SUM()`, `MIN()`, `MAX()`, and `AVG()`. For example, the average of all measured temperatures is expressed as:

```
SELECT   AVG(Temp)
FROM     Weather;
```

In addition, SQL allows aggregation over distinct values. The following query counts the distinct number of reporting times in the `Weather` table:

```
SELECT   COUNT(DISTINCT Time)
FROM     Weather;
```

Aggregate functions return a single value. Using the `GROUP BY` construct, SQL can also create a table of many aggregate values indexed by a set of attributes. For example, the

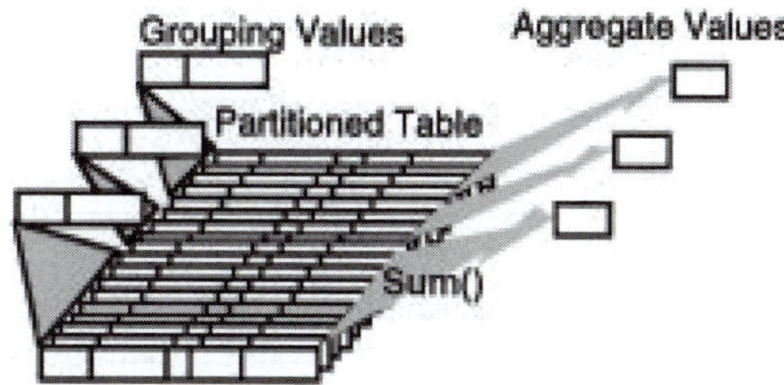

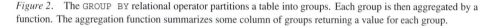

Figure 2. The GROUP BY relational operator partitions a table into groups. Each group is then aggregated by a function. The aggregation function summarizes some column of groups returning a value for each group.

following query reports the average temperature for each reporting time and altitude:

```
SELECT   Time, Altitude, AVG(Temp)
FROM     Weather
GROUP BY Time, Altitude;
```

GROUP BY is an unusual relational operator: It partitions the relation into disjoint tuple sets and then aggregates over each set as illustrated in figure 2.

SQL's aggregation functions are widely used in database applications. This popularity is reflected in the presence of aggregates in a large number of queries in the decision-support benchmark TPC-D (*The Benchmark Handbook for Database and Transaction Processing Systems*, 1993). The TPC-D query set has one 6D GROUP BY and three 3D GROUP BYs. One and two dimensional GROUP BYs are the most common. Surprisingly, aggregates appear in the TPC online-transaction processing benchmarks as well (TPC-A, B and C). Table 2 shows how frequently the database and transaction processing benchmarks use aggregation and GROUP BY. A detailed description of these benchmarks is beyond the scope of the paper (see (Gray, 1991) and (*The Benchmark Handbook for Database and Transaction Processing Systems*, 1993).

Table 2. SQL aggregates in standard benchmarks.

Benchmark	Queries	Aggregates	GROUP BYs
TPC-A, B	1	0	0
TPC-C	18	4	0
TPC-D	16	27	15
Wisconsin	18	3	2
AS^3AP	23	20	2
SetQuery	7	5	1

1.2. Extensions in some SQL systems

Beyond the five standard aggregate functions defined so far, many SQL systems add statistical functions (median, standard deviation, variance, etc.), physical functions (center of mass, angular momentum, etc.), financial analysis (volatility, Alpha, Beta, etc.), and other domain-specific functions.

Some systems allow users to add new aggregation functions. The Informix Illustra system, for example, allows users to add aggregate functions by adding a program with the following three callbacks to the database system (*DataBlade Developer's Kit*):

`Init``(&handle)`: Allocates the handle and initializes the aggregate computation.
`Iter``(&handle, value)`: Aggregates the next value into the current aggregate.
`value =` **`Final`**`(&handle)`: Computes and returns the resulting aggregate by using data saved in the handle. This invocation deallocates the handle.

Consider implementing the `Average()` function. The `handle` stores the `count` and the `sum` initialized to `zero`. When passed a new non-null value, `Iter()` increments the count and adds the `sum` to the value. The `Final()` call deallocates the `handle` and returns `sum` divided by `count`. IBM's DB2 Common Server (Chamberlin, 1996) has a similar mechanism. This design has been added to the Draft Proposed standard for SQL (1997).

Red Brick systems, one of the larger UNIX OLAP vendors, adds some interesting aggregate functions that enhance the `GROUP BY` mechanism (*RISQL Reference Guide, Red Brick Warehouse VPT*, 1994):

`Rank``(expression)`: Returns the expressions rank in the set of all values of this domain of the table. If there are N values in the column, and this is the highest value, the rank is N, if it is the lowest value the rank is 1.
`N_tile``(expression, n)`: The range of the expression (over all the input values of the table) is computed and divided into `n` value ranges of approximately equal population. The function returns the number of the range containing the expression's value. If your bank account was among the largest 10% then your `rank(account.balance,10)` would return 10. Red Brick provides just `N_tile(expression,3)`.
`Ratio_To_Total``(expression)`: Sums all the expressions. Then for each instance, divides the expression instance by the total sum.

To give an example, the following SQL statement

```
SELECT    Percentile, MIN(Temp), MAX(Temp)
FROM      Weather
GROUP BY  N_tile(Temp,10) as Percentile
HAVING    Percentile = 5;
```

returns one row giving the minimum and maximum temperatures of the middle 10% of all temperatures.

Red Brick also offers three **cumulative aggregates** that operate on ordered tables.

`Cumulative``(expression)`: Sums all values so far in an ordered list.
`Running_Sum``(expression,n)`: Sums the most recent `n` values in an ordered list. The initial `n-1` values are `NULL`.
`Running_Average``(expression,n)`: Averages the most recent `n` values in an ordered list. The initial `n-1` values are `NULL`.

These aggregate functions are optionally reset each time a grouping value changes in an ordered selection.

2. Problems with `GROUP BY`

Certain common forms of data analysis are difficult with these SQL aggregation constructs. As explained next, three common problems are: (1) Histograms, (2) Roll-up Totals and Sub-Totals for drill-downs, (3) Cross Tabulations.

The standard SQL `GROUP BY` operator does not allow a direct construction of **histograms** (aggregation over computed categories). For example, for queries based on the `Weather` table, it would be nice to be able to group times into days, weeks, or months, and to group locations into areas (e.g., US, Canada, Europe,...). If a `Nation()` function maps latitude and longitude into the name of the country containing that location, then the following query would give the daily maximum reported temperature for each nation.

```
SELECT    day, nation, MAX(Temp)
FROM      Weather
GROUP BY  Day(Time) AS day,
          Nation(Latitude, Longitude) AS nation;
```

Some SQL systems support histograms directly but the standard does not[1]. In standard SQL, histograms are computed indirectly from a table-valued expression which is then aggregated. The following statement demonstrates this SQL92 construct using nested queries.

```
SELECT day, nation, MAX(Temp)
FROM (SELECT Day(Time)              AS day,
             Nation(Latitude, Longitude)  AS nation,
             Temp
       FROM Weather
     ) AS foo
GROUP BY day, nation;
```

A more serious problem, and the main focus of this paper, relates to roll-ups using totals and sub-totals for drill-down reports. Reports commonly aggregate data at a coarse level, and then at successively finer levels. The car sales report in Table 3 shows the idea (this and other examples are based on the sales summary data in the table in figure 4). Data is aggregated by Model, then by Year, then by Color. The report shows data aggregated at three levels. Going up the levels is called **rolling-up** the data. Going down is called **drilling-down** into the data. Data aggregated at each distinct level produces a sub-total.

Table 3a suggests creating 2^N aggregation columns for a roll-up of N elements. Indeed, Chris Date recommends this approach (Date, 1996). His design gives rise to Table 3b.

The representation of Table 3a is not relational because the empty cells (presumably `NULL` values), cannot form a key. Representation 3b is an elegant solution to this problem, but we rejected it because it implies enormous numbers of domains in the resulting tables.

Table 3a. Sales Roll Up by Model by Year by Color.

Model	Year	Color	Sales by Model by Year by Color	Sales by Model by Year	Sales by Model
Chevy	1994	Black	50		
		White	40		
				90	
	1995	Black	85		
		White	115		
				200	
					290

Table 3b. Sales Roll-Up by Model by Year by Color as recommended by Chris Date (Date, 1996).

Model	Year	Color	Sales	Sales by Model by Year	Sales by Model
Chevy	1994	Black	50	90	290
Chevy	1994	White	40	90	290
Chevy	1995	Black	85	200	290
Chevy	1995	White	115	200	290

Table 4. An Excel pivot table representation of Table 3 with Ford sales data included.

Sum sales	Year/Color						
	1994			1995			
Model	Black	White	1994 total	Black	White	1995 total	Grand total
Chevy	50	40	90	85	115	200	290
Ford	50	10	60	85	75	160	220
Grand total	100	50	150	170	190	360	510

We were intimidated by the prospect of adding 64 columns to the answer set of a 6D TPCD query. The representation of Table 3b is also not convenient—the number of columns grows as the power set of the number of aggregated attributes, creating difficult naming problems and very long names. The approach recommended by Date is reminiscent of pivot tables found in Excel (and now all other spreadsheets) (*Microsoft Excel*, 1995), a popular data analysis feature of Excel[2].

Table 4 an alternative representation of Table 3a (with Ford Sales data included) that illustrates how a pivot table in Excel can present the Sales data by Model, by Year, and then by Color. The pivot operator transposes a spreadsheet: typically aggregating cells based on values in the cells. Rather than just creating columns based on subsets of column names, pivot creates columns based on subsets of column *values*. This is a *much* larger set. If one pivots on two columns containing N and M values, the resulting pivot table has $N \times M$ values. We cringe at the prospect of so many columns and such obtuse column names.

Rather than extend the result table to have many new columns, a more conservative approach prevents the exponential growth of columns by overloading column values. The idea is to introduce an ALL value. Table 5a demonstrates this relational and more convenient representation. The dummy value "ALL" has been added to fill in the super-aggregation items:

Table 5a is not really a completely new representation or operation. Since Table 5a is a relation, it is not surprising that it can be built using standard SQL. The SQL statement to build this SalesSummary table from the raw Sales data is:

```
SELECT 'ALL', 'ALL', 'ALL', SUM(Sales)
   FROM      Sales
   WHERE     Model = 'Chevy'
UNION
SELECT Model, 'ALL', 'ALL', SUM(Sales)
   FROM      Sales
   WHERE     Model = 'Chevy'
   GROUP BY  Model
UNION
SELECT Model, Year, 'ALL', SUM(Sales)
   FROM      Sales
   WHERE     Model = 'Chevy'
   GROUP BY  Model, Year
UNION
SELECT Model, Year, Color, SUM(Sales)
   FROM      Sales
   WHERE     Model = 'Chevy'
   GROUP BY  Model, Year, Color;
```

This is a simple 3-dimensional roll-up. Aggregating over N dimensions requires N such unions.

Table 5a. Sales summary.

Model	Year	Color	Units
Chevy	1994	Black	50
Chevy	1994	White	40
Chevy	1994	ALL	90
Chevy	1995	Black	85
Chevy	1995	White	115
Chevy	1995	ALL	200
Chevy	ALL	ALL	290

Roll-up is asymmetric—notice that Table 5a aggregates sales by year but not by color. These missing rows are shown in Table 5b.

Table 5b. Sales summary rows missing form Table 5a to convert the roll-up into a cube.

Model	Year	Color	Units
Chevy	ALL	Black	135
Chevy	ALL	White	155

These additional rows could be captured by adding the following clause to the SQL statement above:

```
UNION
SELECT Model, 'ALL', Color, SUM(Sales)
    FROM      Sales
    WHERE     Model = 'Chevy'
    GROUP BY  Model, Color;
```

The symmetric aggregation result is a table called a **cross-tabulation**, or **cross tab** for short. Tables 5a and 5b are the relational form of the crosstabs, but crosstab data is routinely displayed in the more compact format of Table 6.

This cross tab is a two-dimensional aggregation. If other automobile models are added, it becomes a 3D aggregation. For example, data for Ford products adds an additional cross tab plane.

The cross-tab-array representation (Tables 6a and b) is equivalent to the relational representation using the ALL value. Both generalize to an N-dimensional cross tab. Most report writers build in a cross-tabs feature, building the report up from the underlying tabular data such as Table 5. See for example the TRANSFORM-PIVOT operator of Microsoft Access (*Microsoft Access Relational Database Management System for Windows, Language Reference*, 1994).

Table 6a. Chevy sales cross tab.

Chevy	1994	1995	Total (ALL)
Black	50	85	135
White	40	115	155
Total (ALL)	90	200	290

Table 6b. Ford sales cross tab.

Ford	1994	1995	Total (ALL)
Black	50	85	135
White	10	75	85
Total (ALL)	60	160	220

The representation suggested by Table 5 and unioned `GROUP BY`s "solve" the problem of representing aggregate data in a relational data model. The problem remains that expressing roll-up, and cross-tab queries with conventional SQL is daunting. A six dimension cross-tab requires a 64-way union of 64 different `GROUP BY` operators to build the underlying representation.

There is another very important reason why it is inadequate to use GROUP BYs. The resulting representation of aggregation is too complex to analyze for optimization. On most SQL systems this will result in 64 scans of the data, 64 sorts or hashes, and a long wait.

3. CUBE and ROLLUP operators

The generalization of group by, roll-up and cross-tab ideas seems obvious: Figure 3 shows the concept for aggregation up to 3-dimensions. The traditional `GROUP BY` generates the N-dimensional data cube *core*. The $N - 1$ lower-dimensional aggregates appear as points, lines, planes, cubes, or hyper-cubes hanging off the data cube core.

The data cube operator builds a table containing all these aggregate values. The total aggregate using function `f()` is represented as the tuple:

```
ALL, ALL, ALL,..., ALL, f(*)
```

Points in higher dimensional planes or cubes have fewer `ALL` values.

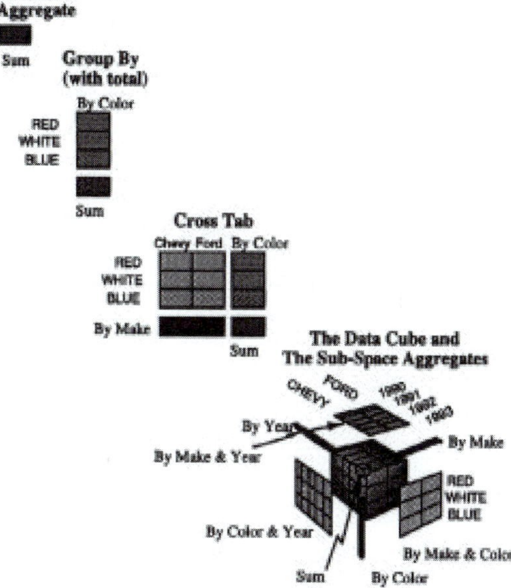

Figure 3. The `CUBE` operator is the N-dimensional generalization of simple aggregate functions. The 0D data cube is a point. The 1D data cube is a line with a point. The 2D data cube is a cross tabulation, a plane, two lines, and a point. The 3D data cube is a cube with three intersecting 2D cross tabs.

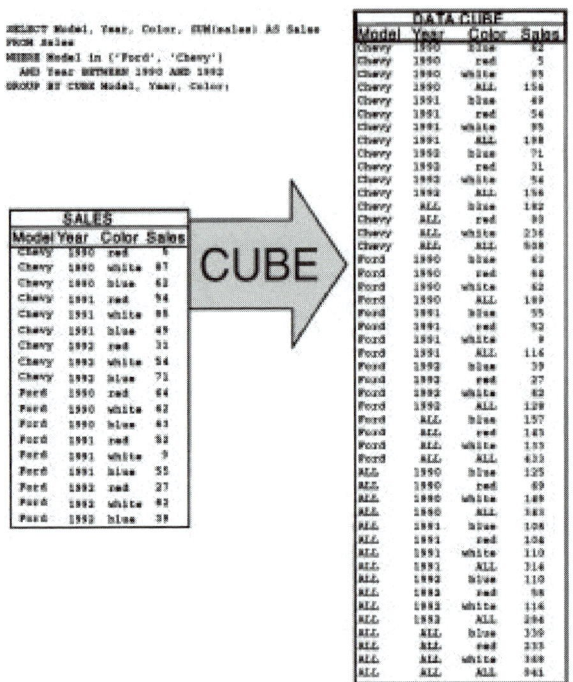

Figure 4. A 3D data cube (right) built from the table at the left by the CUBE statement at the top of the figure.

Creating a data cube requires generating the power set (set of all subsets) of the aggregation columns. Since the CUBE is an aggregation operation, it makes sense to externalize it by overloading the SQL GROUP BY operator. In fact, the cube is a relational operator, with GROUP BY and ROLL UP as degenerate forms of the operator. This can be conveniently specified by overloading the SQL GROUP BY[3].

Figure 4 has an example of the cube syntax. To give another, here follows a statement to aggregate the set of temperature observations:

```
SELECT     day, nation, MAX(Temp)
FROM       Weather
GROUP BY CUBE
           Day(Time) AS day,
           Country(Latitude, Longitude)
                                AS nation;
```

The semantics of the CUBE operator are that it first aggregates over all the <select list> attributes in the GROUP BY clause as in a standard GROUP BY. Then, it UNIONs in each super-aggregate of the global cube—substituting ALL for the aggregation columns. If there are N attributes in the <select list>, there will be $2^N - 1$ super-aggregate values. If the cardinality of the N attributes are $C_1, C_2, \ldots, C_N$ then the cardinality of the resulting cube relation is $\Pi(C_i + 1)$. The extra value in each domain is `ALL`. For example, the SALES table has $2 \times 3 \times 3 = 18$ rows, while the derived data cube has $3 \times 4 \times 4 = 48$ rows.

If the application wants only a roll-up or drill-down report, similar to the data in Table 3a, the full cube is overkill. Indeed, some parts of the full cube may be meaningless. If the answer set is not is not normalized, there may be functional dependencies among columns. For example, a date functionally defines a week, month, and year. Roll-ups by year, week, day are common, but a cube on these three attributes would be meaningless.

The solution is to offer `ROLLUP` in addition to `CUBE`. `ROLLUP` produces just the super-aggregates:

```
(v1 ,v2 ,...,vn,  f()),
(v1 ,v2 ,...,ALL, f()),

          ...
(v1 ,ALL,...,ALL, f()),
(ALL,ALL,...,ALL, f()).
```

Cumulative aggregates, like running sum or running average, work especially well with `ROLLUP` because the answer set is naturally sequential (linear) while the `full data cube` is naturally non-linear (multi-dimensional). `ROLLUP` and `CUBE` must be ordered for cumulative operators to apply.

We investigated letting the programmer specify the exact list of super-aggregates but encountered complexities related to collation, correlation, and expressions. We believe `ROLLUP` and `CUBE` will serve the needs of most applications.

3.1. The GROUP, CUBE, ROLLUP algebra

The `GROUP BY`, `ROLLUP`, and `CUBE` operators have an interesting algebra. The `CUBE` of a `ROLLUP` or `GROUP BY` is a `CUBE`. The `ROLLUP` of a `GROUP BY` is a `ROLLUP`. Algebraically, this operator algebra can be stated as:

```
CUBE(ROLLUP) = CUBE
ROLLUP(GROUP BY) = ROLLUP
```

So it makes sense to arrange the aggregation operators in the compound order where the "most powerful" cube operator at the core, then a roll-up of the cubes and then a group by of the roll-ups. Of course, one can use any subset of the three operators:

```
GROUP BY <select list>
       ROLLUP <select list>
              CUBE <select list>
```

The following SQL demonstrates a compound aggregate. The "shape" of the answer is diagrammed in figure 5:

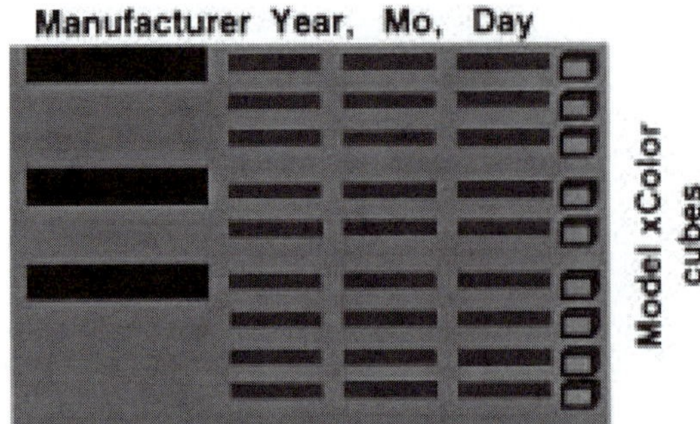

Figure 5. The combination of a GROUP BY on Manufacture, ROLLUP on year, month, day, and CUBE on some attributes. The aggregate values are the contents of the cube.

```
SELECT Manufacturer, Year, Month, Day,  Color, Model,
                  SUM(price) AS Revenue
FROM    Sales
GROUP BY Manufacturer,
   ROLLUP    Year(Time) AS Year,
             Month(Time) AS Month,
             Day(Time) AS Day,
        CUBE Color, Model;
```

3.2. A syntax proposal

With these concepts in place, the syntactic extension to SQL is fairly easily defined. The current SQL GROUP BY syntax is:

```
GROUP BY
       {<column name> [collate clause] ,...}
```

To support histograms and other function-valued aggregations, we first extend the GROUP BY syntax to:

```
GROUP BY <aggregation list>
<aggregation list> ::=
    { ( <column name> | <expression> )
           [ AS <correlation name>    ]
           [ <collate clause>         ]
             ,...}
```

These extensions are independent of the CUBE operator. They remedy some pre-existing problems with GROUP BY. Many systems already allow these extensions.

Now extend SQL's GROUP BY operator:

```
GROUP BY [ <aggregation list> ]
      [ ROLLUP <aggregation list> ]
         [ CUBE <aggregation list> ]
```

3.3. A discussion of the ALL value

Is the ALL value really needed? Each ALL value really represents a set—the set over which the aggregate was computed[4]. In the Table 5 SalesSummary data cube, the respective sets are:

```
Model.ALL = ALL(Model) = {Chevy, Ford}
Year.ALL  = ALL(Year)  = {1990,1991,1992}
Color.ALL = ALL(Color) = {red,white,blue}
```

In reality, we have stumbled in to the world of nested relations—relations can be values. This is a major step for relational systems. There is much debate on how to proceed. In this section, we briefly discuss the semantics of ALL in the context of SQL. This design may be eased by SQL3's support for set-valued variables and domains.

We can interpret each ALL value as a context-sensitive token representing the set it represents. Thinking of the ALL value as the corresponding set defines the semantics of the relational operators (e.g., equals and IN). A function ALL() generates the set associated with this value as in the examples above. ALL() applied to any other value returns NULL.

The introduction of ALL creates substantial complexity. We do not add it lightly—adding it touches many aspects of the SQL language. To name a few:

- ALL becomes a new keyword denoting the set value.
- ALL [NOT] ALLOWED is added to the column definition syntax and to the column attributes in the system catalogs.
- The set interpretation guides the meaning of the relational operators {=, IN}.

There are more such rules, but this gives a hint of the added complexity. As an aside, to be consistent, if ALL represents a set then the other values of that domain must be treated as singleton sets in order to have uniform operators on the domain.

It is convenient to know when a column value is an aggregate. One way to test this is to apply the ALL() function to the value and test for a non-NULL value. This is so useful that we propose a Boolean function GROUPING() that, given a select list element, returns TRUE if the element is an ALL value, and FALSE otherwise.

3.4. Avoiding the ALL value

Veteran SQL implementers will be terrified of the ALL value—like NULL, it will create many special cases. Furthermore, the proposal in Section 3.3. requires understanding of sets as values. If the goal is to help report writer and GUI visualization software, then it may be simpler to adopt the following approach[5]:

- Use the NULL value in place of the ALL value.
- Do not implement the ALL() function.
- Implement the GROUPING() function to discriminate between NULL and ALL.

In this minimalist design, tools and users can simulate the ALL value as by for example:

```
SELECT  Model,Year,Color,SUM(sales),
                    GROUPING(Model),
                    GROUPING(Year),
                    GROUPING(Color)
FROM Sales
GROUP BY CUBE Model, Year, Color;
```

Wherever the ALL value appeared before, now the corresponding value will be NULL in the data field and TRUE in the corresponding grouping field. For example, the global sum of figure 4 will be the tuple:

```
(NULL,NULL,NULL,941,TRUE,TRUE,TRUE)
```

rather than the tuple one would get with the "real" cube operator:

```
(ALL, ALL, ALL, 941).
```

Using the limited interpretation of ALL as above excludes expressing some meaningful queries (just as traditional relational model makes it hard to handle disjunctive information). However, the proposal makes it possible to express results of CUBE as a single relation in the current framework of SQL.

3.5. Decorations

The next step is to allow *decorations*, columns that do not appear in the GROUP BY but that are functionally dependent on the grouping columns. Consider the example:

```
SELECT    department.name, sum(sales)
FROM      sales JOIN department USING (department_number)
GROUP BY  sales.department_number;
```

The department.name column in the answer set is not allowed in current SQL, since it is neither an aggregation column (appearing in the GROUP BY list) nor is it an aggregate. It is just there to decorate the answer set with the name of the department. We recommend the rule that *if a decoration* column (or column value) is functionally dependent on the aggregation columns, then it may be included in the SELECT answer list.

Decoration's interact with aggregate values. If the aggregate tuple functionally defines the decoration value, then the value appears in the resulting tuple. Otherwise the decoration field is NULL. For example, in the following query the continent is not specified unless nation is.

```
SELECT  day,nation,MAX(Temp),
         continent(nation) AS continent
FROM    Weather
GROUP BY CUBE
         Day(Time) AS day,
         Country(Latitude, Longitude)
                           AS nation
```

The query would produce the sample tuples:

Table 7. Demonstrating decorations and ALL.

day	**nation**	**max**(temp)	**continent**
25/1/1995	USA	28	North America
ALL	USA	37	North America
25/1/1995	ALL	41	NULL
ALL	ALL	48	NULL

3.6. *Dimensions star, and snowflake queries*

While strictly not part of the CUBE and ROLLUP operator design, there is an important database design concept that facilitates the use of aggregation operations. It is common to record events and activities with a detailed record giving all the ***dimensions*** of the event. For example, the sales item record in figure 6 gives the id of the buyer, seller, the product purchased, the units purchased, the price, the date and the sales office that is credited with the sale. There are probably many more dimensions about this sale, but this example gives the idea.

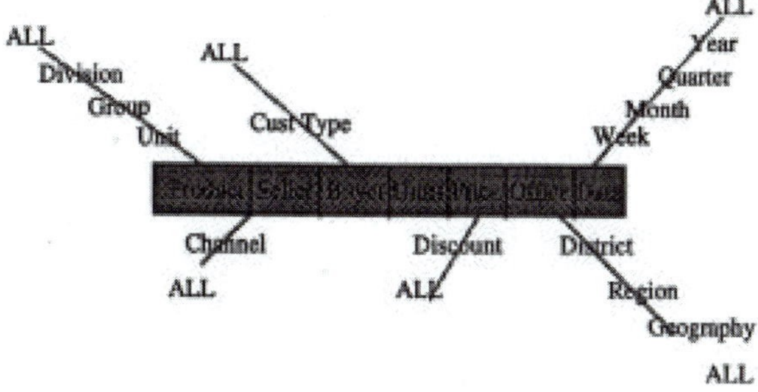

Figure 6. A snowflake schema showing the core fact table and some of the many aggregation granularities of the core dimensions.

There are side tables that for each dimension value give its attributes. For example, the San Francisco sales office is in the Northern California District, the Western Region, and the US Geography. This fact would be stored in a dimension table for the Office[6]. The dimension table may also have decorations describing other attributes of that Office. These dimension tables define a spectrum of aggregation granularities for the dimension. Analysists might want to cube various dimensions and then aggregate or roll-up the cube up at any or all of these granularities.

The general schema of figure 6 is so common that it has been given a name: a **snowflake schema**. Simpler schemas that have a single dimension table for each dimension are called a **star schema**. Queries against these schemas are called **snowflake queries** and **star queries** respectively.

The diagram of figure 6 suggests that the granularities form a pure hierarchy. In reality, the granularities typically form a lattice. To take just a very simple example, days nest in weeks but weeks do not nest in months or quarters or years (some weeks are partly in two years). Analysts often think of dates in terms of weekdays, weekends, sale days, various holidays (e.g., Christmas and the time leading up to it). So a fuller granularity graph of figure 6 would be quite complex. Fortunately, graphical tools like pivot tables with pull down lists of categories hide much of this complexity from the analyst.

4. Addressing the data cube

Section 5 discusses how to compute data cubes and how users can add new aggregate operators. This section considers extensions to SQL syntax to easily access the elements of a data cube—making it recursive and allowing aggregates to reference sub-aggregates.

It is not clear where to draw the line between the reporting-visualization tool and the query tool. Ideally, application designers should be able to decide how to split the function between the query system and the visualization tool. Given that perspective, the SQL system must be a Turing-complete programming environment.

SQL3 defines a Turing-complete procedural programming language. So, anything is possible. But, many things are not easy. Our task is to make simple and common things easy.

The most common request is for percent-of-total as an aggregate function. In SQL this is computed as a nested SELECT SQL statements.

```
SELECT Model,Year,Color,SUM(Sales),
       SUM(Sales)/
          (SELECT SUM(Sales)
           FROM Sales
       WHERE Model IN {'Ford','Chevy'}
       AND Year BETWEEN 1990 AND 1992
          )
FROM   Sales
WHERE  Model IN { 'Ford', 'Chevy' }
  AND  Year BETWEEN 1990 AND 1992
GROUP BY CUBE Model, Year, Color;
```

It seems natural to allow the shorthand syntax to name the global aggregate:

```
SELECT Model, Year, Color
                SUM(Sales) AS total,
     SUM(Sales) / total(ALL,ALL,ALL)
FROM Sales
WHERE Model IN {'Ford', 'Chevy'}
  AND Year BETWEEN 1990 AND 1992
GROUP BY CUBE Model, Year, Color;
```

This leads into deeper water. The next step is a desire to compute the *index* of a value—an indication of how far the value is from the expected value. In a set of N values, one expects each item to contribute one Nth to the sum. So the 1D index of a set of values is:

$$index(v_i) = v_i/(\Sigma_j v_j)$$

If the value set is two dimensional, this commonly used financial function is a nightmare of indices. It is best described in a programming language. The current approach to selecting a field value from a 2D `cube` would read as:

```
SELECT v
FROM    cube
WHERE   row    = :i
  AND   column = :j
```

We recommend the simpler syntax:

```
cube.v(:i, :j)
```

as a shorthand for the above selection expression. With this notation added to the SQL programming language, it should be fairly easy to compute super-super-aggregates from the base cube.

5. Computing cubes and roll-ups

`CUBE` and `ROLLUP` generalize aggregates and `GROUP BY`, so all the technology for computing those results also apply to computing the core of the cube (Graefe, 1993). The basic technique for computing a `ROLLUP` is to sort the table on the aggregating attributes and then compute the aggregate functions (there is a more detailed discussion of the kind of aggregates in a moment.) If the `ROLLUP` result is small enough to fit in main memory, it can be computed by scanning the input set and applying each record to the in-memory `ROLLUP`. A cube is the union of many rollups, so the naive algorithm computes this union.

As Graefe (1993) points out, the basic techniques for computing aggregates are:

- To minimize data movement and consequent processing cost, compute aggregates at the lowest possible system level.

- If possible, use arrays or hashing to organize the aggregation columns in memory, storing one aggregate value for each array or hash entry.
- If the aggregation values are large strings, it may be wise to keep a hashed symbol table that maps each string to an integer so that the aggregate values are small. When a new value appears, it is assigned a new integer. With this organization, the values become dense and the aggregates can be stored as an N-dimensional array.
- If the number of aggregates is too large to fit in memory, use sorting or hybrid hashing to organize the data by value and then aggregate with a sequential scan of the sorted data.
- If the source data spans many disks or nodes, use parallelism to aggregate each partition and then coalesce these aggregates.

Some innovation is needed to compute the "ALL" tuples of the cube and roll-up from the GROUP BY core. The ALL value adds one extra value to each dimension in the CUBE. So, an N-dimensional cube of N attributes each with cardinality C_i, will have $\Pi(C_i + 1)$ values. If each $C_i = 4$ then a 4D CUBE is 2.4 times larger than the base GROUP BY. We expect the C_i to be large (tens or hundreds) so that the CUBE will be only a little larger than the GROUP BY. By comparison, an N-dimensional roll-up will add *only N* records to the answer set.

The cube operator allows many aggregate functions in the aggregation list of the GROUP BY clause. Assume in this discussion that there is a single aggregate function $F()$ being computed on an N-dimensional cube. The extension to computing a list of functions is a simple generalization.

Figure 7 summarizes how aggregate functions are defined and implemented in many systems. It defines how the database execution engine initializes the aggregate function, calls the aggregate functions for each new value and then invokes the aggregate function to get the final value. More sophisticated systems allow the aggregate function to declare a computation cost so that the query optimizer knows to minimize calls to expensive functions. This design (except for the cost functions) is now part of the proposed SQL standard.

The simplest algorithm to compute the cube is to allocate a handle for each cube cell. When a new tuple: $(x_1, x_2, \ldots, x_N, v)$ arrives, the `Iter(handle, v)` function is called 2^N times—once for each handle of each cell of the cube matching this value. The 2^N comes from the fact that each coordinate can either be x_i or ALL. When all the input tuples

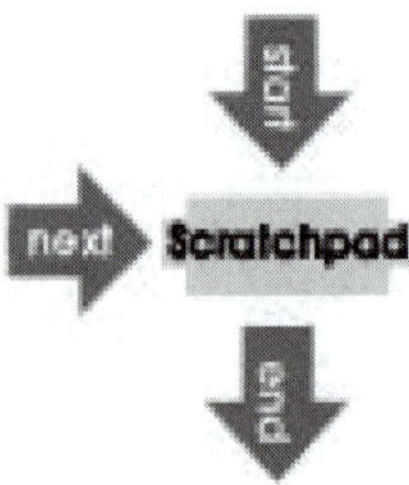

Figure 7. System defined and user defined aggregate functions are initialized with a start() call that allocates and initializes a scratchpad cell to compute the aggregate. Subsequently, the next() call is invoked for each value to be aggregated. Finally, the end() call computes the aggregate from the scratchpad values, deallocates the scratchpad and returns the result.

have been computed, the system invokes the `final(&handle)` function for each of the $\Pi(C_i + 1)$ nodes in the cube. Call this the ***2^N-algorithm***. There is a corresponding order-N algorithm for roll-up.

If the base table has cardinality T, the 2^N-*algorithm* invokes the `Iter()` function $T \times 2^N$ times. It is often faster to compute the super-aggregates from the core `GROUP BY`, reducing the number of calls by approximately a factor of T. It is often possible to compute the cube from the core or from intermediate results only M times larger than the core. The following trichotomy characterizes the options in computing super-aggregates.

Consider aggregating a two dimensional set of values $\{X_{ij} \mid i = 1, \ldots, I;\ j = 1, \ldots, J\}$. Aggregate functions can be classified into three categories:

Distributive: Aggregate function $F()$ is distributive if there is a function $G()$ such that $F(\{X_{i,j}\}) = G(\{F(\{X_{i,j} \mid i = 1, \ldots, I\}) \mid j = 1, \ldots J\})$. `COUNT()`, `MIN()`, `MAX()`, `SUM()` are all distributive. In fact, $F = G$ for all but `COUNT()`. $G =$ `SUM()` for the `COUNT()` function. Once order is imposed, the cumulative aggregate functions also fit in the distributive class.

Algebraic: Aggregate function $F()$ is algebraic if there is an M-tuple valued function $G()$ and a function $H()$ such that $F(\{X_{i,j}\}) = H(\{G(\{X_{i,j} \mid i = 1, \ldots, I\}) \mid j = 1, \ldots, J\})$. Average(), standard deviation, MaxN(), MinN(), center_of_mass() are all algebraic. For Average, the function $G()$ records the sum and count of the subset. The $H()$ function adds these two components and then divides to produce the global average. Similar techniques apply to finding the N largest values, the center of mass of group of objects, and other algebraic functions. The key to algebraic functions is that a fixed size result (an M-tuple) can summarize the sub-aggregation.

Holistic: Aggregate function $F()$ is holistic if there is no constant bound on the size of the storage needed to describe a sub-aggregate. That is, there is no constant M, such that an M-tuple characterizes the computation $F(\{X_{i,j} \mid i = 1, \ldots, I\})$. Median(), MostFrequent() (also called the Mode()), and Rank() are common examples of holistic functions.

We know of no more efficient way of computing super-aggregates of holistic functions than the 2^N-algorithm using the standard `GROUP BY` techniques. We will not say more about cubes of holistic functions.

Cubes of distributive functions are relatively easy to compute. Given that the core is represented as an N-dimensional array in memory, each dimension having size $C_i + 1$, the $N - 1$ dimensional slabs can be computed by projecting (aggregating) one dimension of the core. For example the following computation aggregates the first dimension.

$$\texttt{CUBE}(\texttt{ALL}, x_2, \ldots, x_N) = F(\{\texttt{CUBE}(i, x_2, \ldots, x_N) \mid i = 1, \ldots C_1\}).$$

N such computations compute the $N - 1$ dimensional super-aggregates. The distributive nature of the function $F()$ allows aggregates to be aggregated. The next step is to compute the next lower dimension—an (...`ALL`,..., `ALL`...) case. Thinking in terms of the cross tab, one has a choice of computing the result by aggregating the lower row, or aggregating the right column (aggregate (`ALL`, $*$) or ($*$, `ALL`)). Either approach will give the same answer. The algorithm will be most efficient if it aggregates the smaller of the two (pick the $*$ with the smallest C_i). In this way, the super-aggregates can be computed dropping one dimension at a time.

Algebraic aggregates are more difficult to compute than distributive aggregates. Recall that an algebraic aggregate saves its computation in a handle and produces a result in the end—at the `Final()` call. `Average()` for example maintains the count and sum values in its handle. The super-aggregate needs these intermediate results rather than just the raw sub-aggregate. An algebraic aggregate must maintain a handle (M-tuple) for each element of the cube (this is a standard part of the group-by operation). When the core `GROUP BY` operation completes, the CUBE algorithm passes the set of handles to each $N - 1$ dimensional super-aggregate. When this is done the handles of these super-aggregates are passed to the super-super aggregates, and so on until the (`ALL`, `ALL`, ..., `ALL`) aggregate has been computed. This approach requires a new call for distributive aggregates:

```
Iter_super(&handle, &handle)
```

which folds the sub-aggregate on the right into the super aggregate on the left. The same ordering idea (aggregate on the smallest list) applies at each higher aggregation level.

Interestingly, the distributive, algebraic, and holistic taxonomy is very useful in computing aggregates for parallel database systems. In those systems, aggregates are computed for each partition of a database in parallel. Then the results of these parallel computations are combined. The combination step is very similar to the logic and mechanism used in figure 8.

If the data cube does not fit into memory, array techniques do not work. Rather one must either partition the cube with a hash function or sort it. These are standard techniques for computing the `GROUP BY`. The super-aggregates are likely to be orders of magnitude smaller than the core, so they are very likely to fit in memory. Sorting is especially convenient for `ROLLUP` since the user often wants the answer set in a sorted order—so the sort must be done anyway.

It is possible that the core of the cube is sparse. In that case, only the non-null elements of the core and of the super-aggregates should be represented. This suggests a hashing or a B-tree be used as the indexing scheme for aggregation values (*Method and Apparatus for Storing and Retrieving Multi-Dimensional Data in Computer Memory*, 1994).

6. Maintaining cubes and roll-ups

SQL Server 6.5 has supported the CUBE and ROLLUP operators for about a year now. We have been surprised that some customers use these operators to compute and store the cube. These customers then define triggers on the underlying tables so that when the tables change, the cube is dynamically updated.

This of course raises the question: how can one incrementally compute (user-defined) aggregate functions after the cube has been materialized? Harinarayn et al. (1996) have interesting ideas on pre-computing a sub-cubes of the cube assuming all functions are holistic. Our view is that users avoid holistic functions by using approximation techniques. Most functions we see in practice are distributive or algebraic. For example, medians and quartiles are approximated using statistical techniques rather than being computed exactly.

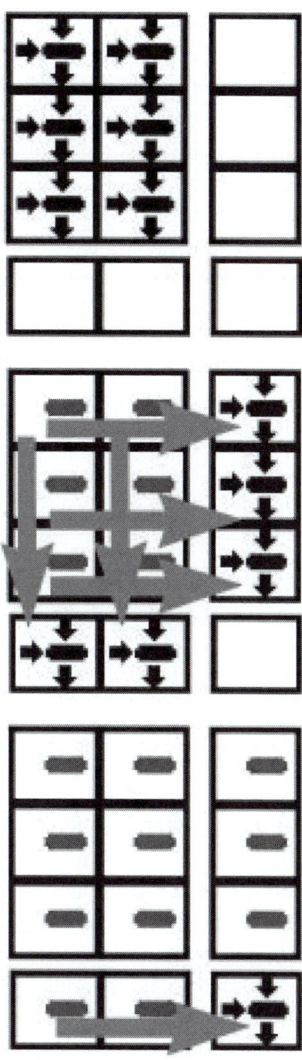

Figure 8. (Top) computing the cube with a minimal number of calls to aggregation functions. If the aggregation operator is algebraic or distributive, then it is possible to compute the core of the cube as usual. (Middle) then, the higher dimensions of the cube are computed by calling the super-iterator function passing the lower-level scratch-pads. (Bottom) once an N-dimensional space has been computed, the operation repeats to compute the $N-1$ dimensional space. This repeats until $N = 0$.

The discussion of distributive, algebraic, and holistic functions in the previous section was completely focused on SELECT statements, not on UPDATE, INSERT, or DELETE statements.

Surprisingly, the issues of maintaining a cube are quite different from computing it in the first place. To give a simple example: it is easy to compute the maximum value in a cube—max is a distributive function. It is also easy to propagate inserts into a "max"

N-dimensional cube. When a record is inserted into the base table, just visit the $2N$ super-aggregates of this record in the cube and take the max of the current and new value. This computation can be shortened—if the new value "loses" one competition, then it will lose in all lower dimensions. Now suppose a delete or update changes the largest value in the base table. Then 2^N elements of the cube must be recomputed. The recomputation needs to find the global maximum. This seems to require a recomputation of the entire cube. So, max is a distributive for `SELECT` and `INSERT`, but it is holistic for `DELETE`.

This simple example suggests that there are orthogonal hierarchies for `SELECT`, `INSERT`, and `DELETE` functions (update is just delete plus insert). If a function is algebraic for insert, update, and delete (count() and sum() are such a functions), then it is easy to maintain the cube. If the function is distributive for insert, update, and delete, then by maintaining the scratchpads for each cell of the cube, it is fairly inexpensive to maintain the cube. If the function is delete-holistic (as max is) then it is expensive to maintain the cube. These ideas deserve more study.

7. Summary

The cube operator generalizes and unifies several common and popular concepts:

> aggregates,
> group by,
> histograms,
> roll-ups and drill-downs and,
> cross tabs.

The cube operator is based on a relational representation of aggregate data using the `ALL` value to denote the set over which each aggregation is computed. In certain cases it makes sense to restrict the cube operator to just a roll-up aggregation for drill-down reports.

The data cube is easy to compute for a wide class of functions (distributive and algebraic functions). SQL's basic set of five aggregate functions needs careful extension to include functions such as rank, N_tile, cumulative, and percent of total to ease typical data mining operations. These are easily added to SQL by supporting user-defined aggregates. These extensions require a new super-aggregate mechanism to allow efficient computation of cubes.

Acknowledgments

Joe Hellerstein suggested interpreting the `ALL` value as a set. Tanj Bennett, David Maier and Pat O'Neil made many helpful suggestions that improved the presentation.

Notes

1. These criticisms led to a proposal to include these features in the draft SQL standard (ISO/IEC DBL:MCI-006, 1996).
2. It seems likely that a relational pivot operator will appear in database systems in the near future.

3. An earlier version of this paper (Gray et al., 1996) and the Microsoft SQL Server 6.5 product implemented a slightly different syntax. They suffix the `GROUP BY` clause with a `ROLLUP` or `CUBE` modifier. The SQL Standards body chose an infix notation so that `GROUP BY` and `ROLLUP` and `CUBE` could be mixed in a single statement. The improved syntax is described here.
4. This is distinct from saying that ALL represents *one* of the members of the set.
5. This is the syntax and approach used by Microsoft's SQL Server (version 6.5).
6. Database normalization rules (Date, 1995) would recommend that the California District be stored once, rather than storing it once for each Office. So there might be an office, district, and region tables, rather than one big denormalized table. Query users find it convenient to use the denormalized table.

References

Agrawal, R., Deshpande, P., Gupta, A., Naughton, J.F., Ramakrishnan, R., and Sarawagi, S. 1996. On the Computation of Multidimensional Aggregates. Proc. 21st VLDB, Bombay.

Chamberlin, D. 1996. *Using the New DB2—IBM's Object-Relational Database System.* San Francisco, CA: Morgan Kaufmann.

DataBlade Developer's Kit: Users Guide 2.0. Informix Software, Menlo Park, CA, 1996.

Date, C.J. 1995. *Introduction to Database Systems.* 6th edition, N.Y.: Addison Wesley.

Date, C.J. 1996. Aggregate functions. *Database Programming and Design*, 9(4): 17–19.

Graefe, C.J. 1993. Query evaluation techniques for large databases. *ACM Computing Surveys*, 25.2, pp. 73–170.

Gray, J. (Ed.) 1991. *The Benchmark Handbook.* San Francisco, CA: Morgan Kaufmann.

Gray, J., Bosworth, A., Layman, A., and Pirahesh, H. 1996. Data cube: A relational operator generalizing group-by, cross-tab, and roll-up. Proc. International Conf. on Data Engineering. New Orleans: IEEE Press.

Harinarayn, V., Rajaraman, A., and Ullman, J.D. 1996. Implementing data cubes efficiently. Proc. ACM SIGMOD. Montreal, pp. 205–216.

1992. IS 9075 International Standard for Database Language SQL, document ISO/IEC 9075:1992, J. Melton (Ed.).

1996. ISO/IEC DBL:MCI-006 (ISO Working Draft) Database Language SQL—Part 4: Persistent Stored Modules (SQL/PSM), J. Melton (Ed.).

Melton, J. and Simon, A.R. 1993. *Understanding the New SQL: A Complete Guide.* San Francisco, CA: Morgan Kaufmann.

1994. Method and Apparatus for Storing and Retrieving Multi-Dimensional Data in Computer Memory. Inventor: Earle; Robert J., Assignee: Arbor Software Corporation, US Patent 05359724.

1994. Microsoft Access Relational Database Management System for Windows, Language Reference—Functions, Statements, Methods, Properties, and Actions, DB26142, Microsoft, Redmond, WA.

1995. Microsoft Excel—User's Guide. Microsoft. Redmond, WA.

1996. Microsoft SQL Server: Transact-SQL Reference, Document 63900. Microsoft Corp. Redmond, WA.

1994. RISQL Reference Guide, Red Brick Warehouse VPT Version 3, Part no.: 401530, Red Brick Systems, Los Gatos. CA.

Shukla, A., Deshpande, P., Naughton, J.F., and Ramaswamy, K. 1996. Storage estimation for multidimensional aggregates in the presence of hierarchies. Proc. 21st VLDB, Bombay.

1993. The Benchmark Handbook for Database and Transaction Processing Systems—2nd edition, J. Gray (Ed.), San Francisco, CA: Morgan Kaufmann. Or http://www.tpc.org/

Jim Gray is a specialist in database and transaction processing computer systems. At Microsoft his research focuses on scaleable computing: building super-servers and workgroup systems from commodity software and hardware. Prior to joining Microsoft, he worked at Digital, Tandem, IBM and AT&T on database and transaction processing systems including Rdb, ACMS, NonStopSQL, Pathway, System R, SQL/DS, DB2, and IMS-Fast Path. He is editor of the *Performance Handbook for Database and Transaction Processing Systems*, and coauthor of *Transaction Processing Concepts and Techniques*. He holds doctorates from Berkely and Stuttgart, is a Member of the National Academy of Engineering, Fellow of the ACM, a member of the National Research council's computer Science and Telecommunications Board, Editor in Chief of the VLDB Journal, Trustee of the VLDB Foundation, and Editor of the Morgan Kaufmann series on Data Management.

Surajit Chaudhuri is a researcher in the Database research Group of Microsoft Research. From 1992 to 1995, he was a Member of the Technical Staff at Hewlett-Packard Laboratories, Palo Alto. He did his B.Tech from Indian Institute of Technology, Kharagpur and his Ph.D. from Stanford University. Surajit has published in SIGMOD, VLDB and PODS in the area of optimization of queries and multimedia systems. He served in the program committees for VLDB 1996 and International Conference on Database Theory (ICDT), 1997. He is a vice-chair of the Program Committee for the upcoming International Conference on Data Engineering (ICDE), 1997. In addition to query processing and optimization, Surajit is interested in the areas of data mining, database design and uses of databases for nontraditional applications.

Adam Bosworth is General Manager (co-manager actually) of Internet Explorer 4.0. Previously General Manager of ODBC for Microsoft and Group Program Manager for Access for Microsoft; General Manager for Quattro for Borland.

Andrew Layman has been a Senior Program Manager at Microsoft Corp. since 1992. He is currently working on language integration for Internet Explorer. Before that, he designed and built a number of high-performance, data-bound Active-X controls for use across several Microsoft products and worked on the original specs for Active-X controls (nee "OLE Controls"). Formerly he was Vice-President of Symantec.

Don Reichart is currently a software design engineer at Microsoft working in the SQL Server query engine area. He holds a B.Sc. degree in computer science from the University of Southern California.

Murali Venkatrao is a program manager at Microsoft Corp. Currently he is working on multi-dimensional databases and the use of relational DBMS for OLAP type applications. During his 5 years at Microsoft, he has mainly worked on designing interfaces for heterogeneous database access. Murali's graduate work was in the area of computational complexity theory and its applications to real time scheduling.

Frank Pellow is a senior development analyst at the IBM Laboratory in Toronto. As an external software architect, Frank is part of the small team responsible for the SQL language in the DB2 family of products. Most recently, he has focused on callable SQL (CLI, ODBC) as well as on object extensions to the relational model both within IBM and within the SQL standards bodies. Frank wrote the ANSI and ISO proposals to have the SQL standards extended with many of the capabilities outlined in this paper.

Hamid Pirahesh, Ph.D., has been a Research Staff Member at IBM Almaden Research Center in San Jose, California since 1985. He has been involved in research, design and implementation of Starburst extensible database system. Dr. Pirahesh has close cooperations with IBM Database Technology Institute and IBM product division. He also has direct responsibilities in development of IBM DB2 CS product. He has been active in several areas of database management systems, computer networks, and object oriented systems, and has served on many program committees of major computer conferences. His recent research activities cover various aspects of database management systems, including extensions for Object Oriented systems, complex query optimization, deductive databases, concurrency control, and recovery. Before joining IBM, he worked at Citicorp/TTI in the areas of distributed transaction processing systems amd computer networks. Previous to that, he was active in the design and implementation of computer applications and electronic hardware systems. Dr. Pirahesh is an associate editor of ACM Computing Surveys Journal. He received M.S. and Ph.D. degrees in computer science from University of California at Los Angeles and a B.S. degree in Electrical Engineering from Institute of Technology, Tehran.

An Array-Based Algorithm for Simultaneous Multidimensional Aggregates *

Yihong Zhao
Computer Sciences Department
University of Wisconsin-Madison
zhao@cs.wisc.edu

Prasad M. Deshpande
Computer Sciences Department
University of Wisconsin-Madison
pmd@cs.wisc.edu

Jeffrey F. Naughton
Computer Sciences Department
University of Wisconsin-Madison
naughton@cs.wisc.edu

Abstract

Computing multiple related group-bys and aggregates is one of the core operations of On-Line Analytical Processing (OLAP) applications. Recently, Gray et al. [GBLP95] proposed the "Cube" operator, which computes group-by aggregations over all possible subsets of the specified dimensions. The rapid acceptance of the importance of this operator has led to a variant of the Cube being proposed for the SQL standard. Several efficient algorithms for Relational OLAP (ROLAP) have been developed to compute the Cube. However, to our knowledge there is nothing in the literature on how to compute the Cube for Multidimensional OLAP (MOLAP) systems, which store their data in sparse arrays rather than in tables. In this paper, we present a MOLAP algorithm to compute the Cube, and compare it to a leading ROLAP algorithm. The comparison between the two is interesting, since although they are computing the same function, one is value-based (the ROLAP algorithm) whereas the other is position-based (the MOLAP algorithm.) Our tests show that, given appropriate compression techniques, the MOLAP algorithm is significantly faster than the ROLAP algorithm. In fact, the difference is so pronounced that this MOLAP algorithm may be useful for ROLAP systems as well as MOLAP systems, since in many cases, instead of cubing a table directly, it is faster to first convert the table to an array, cube the array, then convert the result back to a table.

1 Introduction

Computing multiple related group-bys and aggregates is one of the core operations of On-Line Analytical Processing (OLAP) applications. Recently, Gray et al. [GBLP95] proposed the "Cube" operator, which computes group-by aggregations over all possible subsets of the specified dimensions. The rapid acceptance of the importance of this operator has led to a variant of the Cube being proposed for the SQL standard. Several efficient algorithms for Relational OLAP (ROLAP) have been developed to compute the Cube. However, to our knowledge there is nothing to date in the literature on how to compute the Cube for Multidimensional OLAP (MOLAP) systems.

For concreteness, consider a very simple multidimensional model, in which we have the dimensions *product*, *store*, *time*, and the "measure" (data value) sales. Then to compute the "cube" we will compute sales grouped by all subsets of these dimensions. That is, we will have sales by product, store, and date; sales by product and store; sales by product and date; sales by store and date; sales by product; sales by store; sales by date; and overall sales. In multidimensional applications, the system is often called upon to compute all of these aggregates (or at least a large subset of them), either in response to a user query, or as part of a "load process" that precomputes these aggregates to speed later queries. The challenge, of course, is to compute the cube with far more efficiency than the naive method of computing each component aggregate individually in succession.

MOLAP systems present a different sort of challenge in computing the cube than do ROLAP systems. The main reason for this is the fundamental difference in the data structures in which the two systems store their data. ROLAP systems (for example, MicroStrategy [MS], Informix's Metacube [MC], and Information Advantage [IA]) by definition use relational tables as their data structure. This means that a "cell" in a logically multidimensional space is represented in the system as a tuple, with some attributes that identify the location of the tuple in the multidimensional space, and other attributes that contain the data value corresponding to that data cell. Returning to our example, a cell of the array might be represented by the tuple `(shoes, WestTown, 3-July-96, $34.00)`. Computing the cube over such a table requires a generalization of standard relational aggregation operators [AADN96]. In prior work, three main ideas have been used to make ROLAP computation efficient:

1. Using some sort of grouping operation on the dimension attributes to bring together related tuples (e.g., sorting or hashing),
2. Using the grouping performed on behalf of one of the sub-aggregates as a partial grouping to speed the computation another sub-aggregate, and
3. To compute an aggregate from another aggregate, rather than from the (presumably much larger) base table.

By contrast, MOLAP systems (for example, Essbase from Arbor Software [CCS93, RJ, AS], Express from Oracle [OC],

*This work supported by NSF grant IRI-9157357, a grant under the IBM University Partnership Program, and ARPA contract DAAB07-91-C-Q518

SIGMOD '97 AZ,USA
© 1997 ACM 0-89791-911-4/97/0005...$3.50

and LightShip from Pilot [PSW]) store their data as sparse arrays. Returning to our running example, instead of storing the tuple `(shoes, WestTown, 3-July-1996, $34.00)`, a MOLAP system would just store the data value `$34.00`; the position within the sparse array would encode the fact that this is a sales volume for shoes in the West Town store on July 3, 1996. When we consider computing the cube on data stored in arrays, one can once again use the ROLAP trick of computing one aggregate from another. However, none of the other techniques that have been developed for ROLAP cube computations apply. Most importantly, there is no equivalent of "reordering to bring together related tuples" based upon their dimension values. The data values are already stored in fixed positions determined by those dimension values; the trick is to visit those values in the right order so that the computation is efficient. Similarly, there is no concept of using an order generated by one subaggregate in the computation of another; rather, the trick is to simultaneously compute spatially-delimited partial aggregates so that a cell does not have to be revisited for each sub-aggregate. To do so with minimal memory requires a great deal of care and attention to the size of the dimensions involved. Finally, all of this is made more complicated by the fact that in order to store arrays efficiently on disk, one must "chunk" them into small memory-sized pieces, and perform some sort of "compression" to avoid wasting space on cells that contain no valid data.

In this paper, we present a MOLAP algorithm incorporating all of these ideas. The algorithm succeeds in overlapping the computation of multiple subaggregates, and makes good use of available main memory. We prove a number of theorems about the algorithm, including a specification of the optimal ordering of dimensions of the cube for reading chunks of base array, and an upper bound on the memory requirement for a one-pass computation of the cube that it is in general much smaller than the size of the original base array.

We have implemented our algorithm and present performance results for a wide range of dimension sizes, data densities, and buffer-pool sizes. We show that the algorithm performs significantly faster than the naive algorithm of computing aggregates separately, even when the "naive" algorithm is smart about computing sub-aggregates from superaggregates rather than from the base array. We also compared the algorithm with an implementation of a previously-proposed ROLAP cube algorithm, and found that the MOLAP algorithm was significantly faster.

Clearly, this MOLAP cube algorithm can be used by a multidimensional database system. However, we believe it may also have some applicability within relational database systems as part of support for multidimensional database applications, for two reasons. First, as relational database systems provide richer and richer type systems, it is becoming feasible to implement arrays as a storage device for RDBMS data. In another paper [ZTN], we explored the performance implications of such an approach for "consolidation" operations; the study in this paper adds more weight to the conclusion that including array storage in relational systems can significantly enhance RDBMS performance for certain workloads.

The second application of this algorithm to ROLAP systems came as a surprise to us, although in retrospect perhaps we should have foreseen this result. Simply put, one can always use our MOLAP algorithm in a relational system by the following three-step procedure:

1. Scan the table, and load it into an array.
2. Compute the cube on the resulting array.
3. Dump the resulting cubed array into tables.

The result is the same as directly cubing the table; what was surprising to us was that this three-step approach was actually faster than the direct approach of cubing the table. In such a three-step approach, the array is being used as an internal data structure, much like the hash table in a hash join in standard relational join processing.

The rest of the paper is organized as follows. In Section 2, we introduce the chunked array representation, and then discuss how we compressed these arrays and our algorithm for loading chunked, compressed arrays from tables. We then present a basic array based algorithm in Section 3. Our new algorithm, the *Multi-Way* Array method, is described in Section 4, along with some theorems that show how to predict and minimize the memory requirements for the algorithm. We present the performance results in Section 5, and we conclude in Section 6.

2 Array Storage Issues

In this section we discuss the basic techniques we used to load and store large, sparse arrays efficiently. There are three main issues to resolve. First, it is highly likely in a multidimensional application that the array itself is far too large to fit in memory. In this case, the array must be split up into "chunks", each of which is small enough to fit comfortably in memory. Second, even with this "chunking", it is likely that many of the cells in the array are empty, meaning that there is no data for that combination of coordinates. To efficiently store this sort of data we need to compress these chunks. Third, in many cases an array may need to be loaded from data that is not in array format (e.g., from a relational table or from an external load file.) We conclude this section with a description of an efficient algorithm for loading arrays in our compressed, chunked format.

2.1 Chunking Arrays

As we have mentioned, for high performance large arrays must be stored broken up into smaller chunks. The standard programming language technique of storing the array in a row major or column major order is not very efficient. Consider a row major representation of a two-dimensional array, with dimensions *Store* and *Date*, where *Store* forms the row and *Date* forms the column. Accessing the array in the row order (order of *Stores*) is efficient with this representation, since each disk page that we read will contain several *Stores*. However, accessing in the order of columns (*Dates*) is inefficient. If the *Store* dimension is big, each disk page read will only contain data for one *Date*. Thus to get data for the next *Date* will require another disk access; in fact there will be one disk access for each *Date* required. The simple row major layout creates an asymmetry among the dimensions, favoring one over the other. This is because data is accessed from disk in units of pages.

To have a uniform treatment for all the dimensions, we can chunk the array, as suggested by Sarawagi [SM94]. Chunking is a way to divide an n-dimensional array into small size n-dimensional chunks and store each chunk as one object on disk. Each array chunk has n dimensions and will correspond to the blocking size on the disk. We will be using chunks which have the same size on each dimension.

2.2 Compressing Sparse Arrays

For dense chunks, which we define as those in which more than 40% of the array cells have a valid value, we do not compress the array, simply storing all cells of the array as-is but assigning a null value to invalid array cells. Each chunk therefore has a fixed length. Note that storing a dense multidimensional data set in an array is already a significant compression over storing the data in a relational table, since we do not store the dimension values. For example, in our running example we do not store product, store, or date values in the array.

However, for a sparse chunk, that is one with data density less than 40%, storing the array without compression is wasteful, since most of the space is devoted to invalid cells. In this case we use what we call "chunk-offset compression." In chunk-offset compression, for each valid array entry, we store a pair, (offsetInChunk,data). The offsetInChunk integer can be computed as follows: consider the chunk as a normal (uncompressed) array. Each cell c in the chunk is defined by a set of indices; for example, if we are working with a three-dimensional chunk, a given cell will have an "address" (i, j, k) in the chunk. To access this cell in memory, we would convert the triple (i, j, k) into an offset from the start of the chunk, typically by assuming that the chunk is laid out in memory in some standard order. This offset is the "offsetInChunk" integer we store.

Since in this representation chunks will be of variable length, we use some meta data to hold the length of each chunk and store the meta data at the beginning of the data file.

We also experimented with compressing the array chunks using a lossless compression algorithm (LZW compression [Wel84]) but this was far less effective for a couple of reasons. First, the compression ratio itself was not as good as the "chunk-offset compression." Intuitively, this is because LZW compression uses no domain knowledge, whereas "chunk-offset compression" can use the fact that it is storing array cells to minimize storage. Second, and perhaps most important, using LZW compression it is necessary to materialize the (possibly very sparse) full chunk in memory before it can be operated on. By contrast, with chunk-offset compression we can operate directly on the compressed chunk.

2.3 Loading Arrays from Tables

We have designed and implemented a partition-based loading algorithm to convert a relational table or external load file to a (possibly compressed) chunked array. As input the algorithm takes the table, along with each dimension size and a predefined chunk size. Briefly, the algorithm works as follows.

Since we know the size of the full array and the chunk size, we know how many chunks are in the array to be loaded. If the available memory size is less than the size of the resulting array, we partition the set of chunks into partitions so that the data in each partition fits in memory. (This partitioning is logical at this phase. For example, if we have 8 chunks 0 - 7, and we need two partitions, we would put tuples corresponding to cells that map to chunks 0-3 in partition one, and those that map to chunks 4-7 in partition two.)

Once the partitions have been determined, the algorithm scans the table. For each tuple, the algorithm calculates the tuple's chunk number and the offset from the first element of its chunk. This is possible by examining the dimension values in the tuple. The algorithm then stores this chunk number and offset, along with the data element, into a tuple, and inserts the tuple into the buffer page of the corresponding partition. Once any buffer page for a partition is full, the page is written to the disk resident file for this partition. In the second pass, for each partition, the algorithm reads in each partition tuple and assigns it to a bucket in memory according to its chunk number. Each bucket corresponds to a unique chunk. Once we assign all tuples to buckets, the algorithm constructs array chunks for each bucket, compresses them if necessary using chunk-offset compression, and writes those chunks to disk. One optimization is to compute the chunks of the first partition in the first pass. After we allocate each partition a buffer page, we allocate the rest of available memory to the buckets for the first partition. This is similar to techniques used in the Hybrid Hash Join algorithm [DKOS84] to keep the "first bucket" in memory.

3 A Basic Array Cubing Algorithm

We first introduce an algorithm to compute the cube of a chunked array in multiple passes by using minimum memory. The algorithm makes no attempt to overlap any computation, computing each "group by" in a separate pass. In the next section, we modify this simple algorithm to minimize the I/O cost and to overlap the aggregation of related group-bys.

First consider how to compute a group-by from a simple non-chunked array. Suppose we have a three dimensional array, with dimensions A, B, and C. Suppose furthermore that we want to compute the aggregate AB, that is, we want to project out C and aggregate together all these values. This can be seen as projecting onto the AB plane; logically, this can be done by sweeping a plane through the C dimension, aggregating as we go, until the whole array has been swept.

Next suppose that this ABC array is stored in a number of chunks. Again the computation can be viewed as sweeping through the array, aggregating away the C dimension. But now instead of sweeping an entire plane of size $|A||B|$, where $|A|$ and $|B|$ are the sizes of the A and B dimensions, we do it on a chunk by chunk basis. Suppose that the A dimension in a chunk has size A_c, and the B dimension in a chunk has size B_c. If we think of orienting the array so that we are looking at the AB face of the array (with C going back into the paper) we can begin with the chunk in the upper left-hand portion of the array, and sweep a plane of size A_cB_c back through that chunk, aggregating away the C values as we go. Once we have finished this upper left-hand chunk, we continue to sweep this plane through the chunk immediately behind the one on the front of the array in the upper left corner. We continue in this fashion until we have swept all the way through the array. At this point we have computed the portion of the AB aggregate corresponding to the upper-left hand sub-plane of size A_cB_c. We can store this plane to disk as the first part of the AB aggregate, and move on to compute the sub-plane corresponding to another chunk, perhaps the one immediately to the right of the initial chunk.

Note that in this way each chunk is read only once, and that at the end of the computation the AB aggregate will be on disk as a collection of planes of size A_cB_c. The memory used by this computation is only enough to hold one chunk, plus enough to hold the A_cB_c plane as it is swept through the chunks. This generalization of this algorithm to higher dimensions is straight-forward; instead of sweeping planes through arrays, in higher dimensions, say k dimensional arrays, one sweeps $k-1$ dimensional subarrays through the array.

Up to now we have discussed only computing a single aggregate of an array. But, as we have mentioned in the introduction, to "cube" an array requires computing all aggregates of the array. For example, if the array has dimensions ABC, we need to compute AB, BC, AC, and A, B, C, as well as the overall total aggregate. The most naive approach would be to compute all of these aggregates from the initial ABC array. A moment's thought shows that this is a very bad idea; it is far more efficient to compute A from AB than it is to compute A from ABC. This idea has been explored in the ROLAP cube computation literature [AADN96]. If we look at an entire cube computation, the aggregates to be computed can be viewed as a lattice, with ABC as the root. ABC has children AB, BC, and AC; AC has children A and C, and so forth. To compute the cube efficiently we embed a tree in this lattice, and compute each aggregate from its parent in this tree.

One question that arises is which tree to use for this computation? For ROLAP cube computations this is a difficult question, since the sizes of the tables corresponding to the nodes in the lattice are not known until they are computed, so heuristics must be used. For our chunk-based array algorithm we are more fortunate, since by knowing the dimension sizes of the array and the size of the chunks used to store the array, we can compute exactly the size of the array corresponding to each node in the lattice, and also how much storage will be needed to use one of these arrays to compute a child. Hence we can define the "minimum size spanning tree" for the lattice. For each node n in the lattice, its parent in the minimum size spanning tree is the node n' which has the minimum size and from which n can be computed.

We can now state our basic array cubing algorithm. We first construct the minimum size spanning tree for the group-bys of the Cube. We compute any group-by $D_{i_1}D_{i_2}..D_{i_k}$ of a Cube from the "parent" $D_{i_1}D_{i_2}..D_{i_{k+1}}$, which has the minimum size. We read in each chunk of $D_{i_1}D_{i_2}..D_{i_{k+1}}$ along the dimension $D_{i_{k+1}}$ and aggregate each chunk to a chunk of $D_{i_1}D_{i_2}..D_{i_k}$. Once the chunk of $D_{i_1}D_{i_2}..D_{i_k}$ is complete, we output the chunk to disk and use the memory for the next chunk of $D_{i_1}D_{i_2}..D_{i_k}$. Note that we need to keep only one $D_{i_1}D_{i_2}..D_{i_k}$ chunk in memory at any time.

In this paper, we will use a three dimensional array as an example. The array ABC is a $16 \times 16 \times 16$ array with $4 \times 4 \times 4$ array chunks laid out in the dimension order ABC (see Figure 1). The order of layout is indicated by the chunk numbers shown in the figure. The chunks are numbered from 1 to 64. The Cube of the array consists of the group-bys AB, AC, BC, B, C, A, and ALL. For example, to compute the BC group-by, we read in the chunk number order from 1 to 64, aggregate each four ABC chunks to a BC chunk, output the BC chunk to disk, and reuse the memory for the next BC chunk.

While this algorithm is fairly careful about using a hierarchy of aggregates to compute the cube and using minimal memory for each step, it is somewhat naive in that it computes each subaggregate independently. In more detail, suppose we are computing AB, AC, and BC from ABC in our example. This basic algorithm will compute AB from ABC, then will re-scan ABC to compute AC, then will scan it a third time to compute BC. In the next few sections we discuss how to modify this algorithm to compute all the children of a parent in a single pass of the parent.

4 The Multi-Way Array Algorithm

We now present our multi-way array cubing algorithm. This algorithm overlaps the computations of the different group-bys, thus avoiding the multiple scans required by the naive algorithm. Recall that a data Cube for a n-dimensional array contains multiple related group-bys. Specifically, it consists of 2^n group-bys, one for each subset of the dimensions. Each of these group-bys will also be represented as arrays. Ideally, we need memory large enough to hold all these group-bys so that we can overlap the computation of all those group-bys and finish the Cube in one scan of the array. Unfortunately, the total size of the group-bys is usually much larger than the buffer pool size. Our algorithm tries to minimize the memory needed for each computation, so that we can achieve maximum overlap. We will describe our algorithm in two steps. Initially we will assume that there is sufficient memory to compute all the group-bys in one scan. Later we will extend it to the other case where memory is insufficient.

4.1 A Single-pass Multi-way Array Cubing Algorithm

As we showed in the naive algorithm, it is not necessary to keep the entire array in memory for any group-by — keeping only the relevant part of the array in memory at each step will suffice. Thus we will be reducing memory requirements by keeping only parts of the group-by arrays in memory. When computing multiple group-bys simultaneously, the total memory required depends critically on the order in which the input array is scanned. In order to reduce this total amount of memory our algorithm makes use of a special logical order called "dimension order".

4.1.1 Dimension Order

A dimension order of the array chunks is a row major order of the chunks with the n dimensions $D_1, D_2, .., D_n$ in some order $\mathcal{O} = (D_{j_1}, D_{j_2}, .., D_{j_n})$. Different dimension orders $\mathcal{O}'$ lead to different orders of reading the array chunks. Note that this logical order of reading is independent of the actual physical layout of the chunks on the disk. The chunks of array may be laid out on the disk in an order different from the dimension order. We will now see how the dimension order determines the amount of memory needed for the computation.

4.1.2 Memory Requirements

Assuming that we read in the array chunks in a dimension order, we can formulate a general rule to determine what chunks of each group-by of the cube need to stay in memory in order to avoid rescanning a chunk of the input array. We use the above 3-D array to illustrate the rule with an example.

The array chunks are read in the dimension order ABC, i.e., from chunk 1 to chunk 64. Suppose chunk 1 is read in. For group-by AB, this chunk is aggregated along the C dimension to get a chunk of AB. Similarly for AC and BC, this chunk is aggregated along B and A dimensions respectively. Thus the first chunk's AB group-by is aggregated to the chunk a_0b_0 of AB; the first chunk's AC is aggregated to the chunk a_0c_0 of AC; the first chunk's BC is aggregated to the chunk b_0c_0 of BC. As we read in new chunks, we aggregate the chunk's AB, AC and BC group-by to the corresponding chunks of group-bys AB, AC and BC. To compute each chunk of AB, AC, and BC group-by, we may

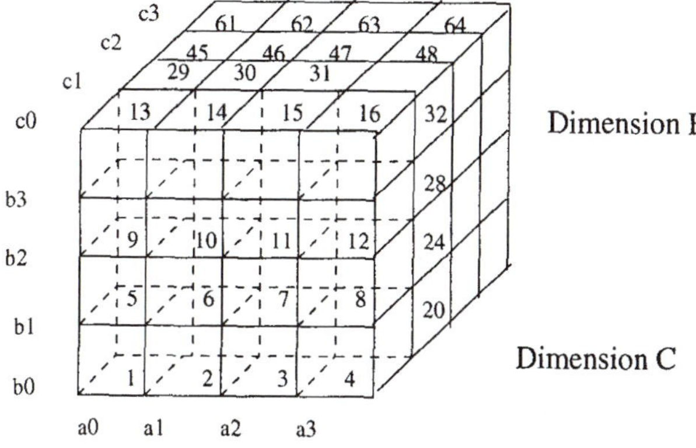

Dimension A

Figure 1: 3 D array

naively allocate memory to each chunk of those group-bys in memory. However, we can exploit the order in which each chunk is brought in memory to reduce the memory required by each group-by to the minimum so that we can compute the group-bys AC, AB, and BC in one scan of the array ABC.

Let us look into how we compute each chunk of those group-bys in detail. Notice that we read the chunks in dimension order (A, B, C) layout, which is a linear order from chunk 1 to chunk 64. For the chunk 1 to chunk 4, we complete the aggregation for the chunk b_0c_0 of BC after aggregating each chunk's BC group-by to the chunk b_0c_0 of BC. Once the b_0c_0 chunk is completed, we write out the chunk and reassign the chunk memory to the chunk b_1c_0, which is computed from the next 4 chunks of ABC i.e. the chunk 4 to chunk 8. So we allot only one chunk of BC in memory to compute the entire BC group-by. Similarly, we allocate memory to the chunks a_0c_0, a_1c_0, a_2c_0, and a_3c_0 of the AC group-by while scanning the first 16 chunks of ABC. To finish the aggregation for the chunk a_0c_0, we aggregate the AC of the chunks 1, 5, 9, and 13, to the chunk a_0c_0. After we aggregate the first 16 chunks of AC to those chunks of AC, the aggregation for those AC chunks are done. We output those AC chunks to disk in order of (A, C) and reassign those chunks' memory to the a_0c_1, a_1c_1,a_2c_1, and a_3c_1 of the AC group-by. To compute the AB group-by in one scan of the array ABC, we need to allocate memory to each of the 16 chunks of AB. For the first 16 chunks of ABC, we aggregate each chunk's AB to the corresponding AB chunks. The aggregation for those AB is not complete until we aggregate all 64 chunks' AB to those AB chunks. Once the aggregation for AB chunks is done, we output those chunks in (A, B) order.

Notice that we generate each BC chunk in the dimension order (B, C). So, before we write each BC chunk to disk, we use the BC chunks to compute the chunks of B or C as if we read in each BC chunk in the dimension order (B, C). Generally, the chunks of each group-bys of the Cube are generated in a proper dimension order. In fact, this is the key to apply our general memory requirement rule recursively to the nodes of the minimum memory spanning tree (MMST) and overlap computation for the Cube group-bys. We will explain this idea in detail when we discuss the MMST.

In this example, for computing BC we need memory to hold 1 chunk of BC, for AC we need memory to hold 4 chunks of AC and for AB we need memory to hold $4*4 = 16$ chunks of AB. Generalizing, we allocate $|B_c||C_c|u$ memory to BC group-by, $|A_d||C_c|u$ to AC group-by, and $|A_d||B_d|u$ to AB group-by, where $|X_d|$ stands for the size of dimension X, $|Y_c|$ stands for the chunk size of dimension Y, and u stands for the size of each chunk element. The size of the chunk element is same as the array element size which depends on the type of the array. For an integer array, each array element takes four bytes. There is a pattern for allocating memory to AB, AC, and BC group-bys for the dimension order (A, B, C). If XY contains a prefix of ABC with the length p, then we allocate $16^p \times 4^{2-p} \times u$ memory to XY group-bys. This is because each dimension is of size 16 and each chunk dimension has size 4. To generalize this for all group-bys of a n-dimensional array, we have the following rule.

Rule 1 *For a group-by* $(D_{j_1}, .., D_{j_{n-1}})$ *of the array* $(D_1, .., D_n)$ *read in the dimension order* $\mathcal{O} = (D_1, .., D_n)$, *if* $(D_{j_1}, .., D_{j_{n-1}})$ *contains a prefix of* $(D_1, .., D_n)$ *with length* p, $0 \leq p \leq n-1$, *we allocate* $\prod_{i=1}^{p} |D_i| \times \prod_{i=p+1}^{n-1} |C_i|$ *units of array element to* $(D_{j_1}, .., D_{j_{n-1}})$ *group-by, where* $|D_i|$ *is the size of dimension* i *and* $|C_i|$ *is the chunk size of dimension* i.

$|C_i|$ is much smaller than $|D_i|$ for most dimensions. Thus, according to the **Rule 1**, we allocate an amount of memory less than the size of the group-by for many of the group-bys. The benefit of reducing the memory allocated to each group-by is to compute more group-bys of the Cube simultaneously and overlap the computation of those group-bys to a higher degree. We need some kind of structure to coordinate the overlapped computation. A spanning tree on the lattice of group-bys can be used for this purpose. For a given dimension order, different spanning trees will require different amounts of memory. We define a minimum memory spanning tree in the next section.

4.1.3 Minimum Memory Spanning Tree

A MMST for a Cube $(D_1, .., D_n)$ in a dimension order $\mathcal{O} = (D_{j_1}, .., D_{j_n})$ has $n + 1$ levels with the root $(D_{j_1}, .., D_{j_n})$ at level n. Any tree node N at level i below the level n may be computed from those nodes at one level up whose dimensions contain the dimensions of node N. For any node N at level i, there may be more than one node at level $i + 1$ from which it can be computed. We choose the node that makes the node N require the minimum memory according to the **Rule 1**. In other words, the prefix of the parent node contained in node N has the minimum length. So a MMST, for a given dimension order, is minimum in terms of the total memory requirement for that dimension order. If node N contains the minimum prefix for several upper level nodes, we use the size of those nodes to break the tie and choose the node with the minimum size as the parent of the node N.

Once we build the MMST for the Cube in a dimension order $\mathcal{O}$ we can overlap the computation of the MMST subtrees. We use the same example, the array ABC, to explain how to do it. Let us assume that we have enough memory to allocate each node's required memory. The MMST for the array ABC in a dimension order (A, B, C) is shown in Figure 2. As mentioned before, chunks of BC, AC, and AB are calculated in dimension orders (B, C), (A, C), and (A, B) in memory since we read ABC chunks in dimension order (A, B, C) to produce each chunk of BC, AC, and AB. To each node A, B,and C, this is equivalent to reading in chunks of group-by AB and AC in the dimension order (A, B) and

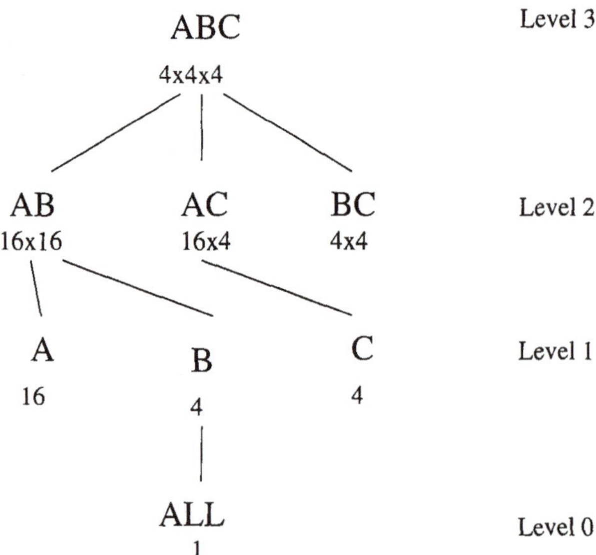

Figure 2: 3-D array MMST in dimension order (A, B, C)

(A, C). Similar to the nodes of the level 2, the chunks of the nodes A, B, and C are generated in the proper dimension orders. To generalize for any MMST, the nodes from the level n to the level 0, the chunks of each tree node are generated in a proper dimension order. Therefore, we can recursively apply the **Rule** 1 to the nodes from the level n to the level 0 so that we allocate minimum number of chunks to each nodes instead of all chunks. Furthermore, we can compute the chunks of each tree node simultaneously. For example, we can aggregate the chunk a_0c_0 of AC along C dimension to compute the chunk c_0 of C after we aggregate the chunk 1, 5, 9, 13 of ABC to the chunk a_0c_0 and before we write the chunk a_0c_0 to disk. Generally, if we allocate each MMST node its required memory we can compute the chunks of the tree nodes from the top level to the level 0 simultaneously.

We now give a way of calculating the memory required for the MMST of any given dimension order $\mathcal{O} = (D_1, D_2, \dots, D_n)$. We will assume that each array element takes u bytes. In addition, all the numbers used for the memory size in the following sections are in units of the array element size.

Memory requirements for the MMST

Let us assume that the chunk size is the same for each dimension, i.e., for all i, $|C_i| = c$. We can calculate the memory required by each tree node at each level of the MMST using **Rule** 1. We have the root of the MMST at the level n and allocate c^n to the root $D_1..D_n$. At the level $n-1$, which is one level down from the root $D_1..D_n$, we have the nodes: $D_1..D_{n-2}D_{n-1}$, $D_1..D_{n-2}D_n$, $\cdots$, and $D_2D_3..d_n$. Each node omits one dimension of the root dimensions $D_1..D_n$. So each node contains a prefix of the root $(D_1..D_n)$. The length of the prefix for each above node is $n-1$, $n-2$, $\cdots$, and 0. According to the **Rule** 1, the sum of memory required by those nodes is

$$\prod_{i=1}^{n-1}|D_i| + (\prod_{i=1}^{n-2}|D_i|)c + (\prod_{i=1}^{n-3}|D_i|)c^2 + \cdots + c^{n-1}.$$

At level $n-2$, we classify the tree nodes into the following types according to the length of the prefix of the root contained in those nodes: $D_1..D_{n-2}$, $D_1..D_{n-3}W_1$, $\cdots$, $D_1W_1W_2..W_{n-2}$, and $W_1W_2..W_{n-2}$. For the type $D_1..D_k$-$W_1..W_{n-2-k}$, the nodes start with the prefix $D_1..D_k$ of the root and followed by W_i, which are those dimensions not included in $D_1, D_2, \cdots, D_k$ and D_{k+1}. So there are $C(n-(k+1), n-2-k)$ nodes belonging to this type, i.e. we are choosing $n-2-k$ dimensions from $n-(k+1)$ dimensions. We use $n-(k+1)$ since we should not choose the dimension D_{k+1} for W_i. If we do so, the node will become the type of $D_1..D_{k+1}W_1..W_{n-2-(k+1)}$ instead of the type of $D_1..D_kW_1..W_{n-2-k}$. Hence the sum of the memory required by the nodes at this level is:

$$\prod_{i=1}^{n-2}|D_i| + C(2,1)(\prod_{i=1}^{n-3}|D_i|)c + C(3,2)(\prod_{i=1}^{n-4}|D_i|)c^2 + \cdots + C(n-1, n-2)c^{n-2}.$$

Similarly, we calculate the total memory required by the nodes at the level $n-3$. We have the sum:

$$\prod_{i=1}^{n-3}|D_i| + C(3,1)(\prod_{i=1}^{n-4}|D_i|)c + C(4,2)(\prod_{i=1}^{n-5}|D_i|)c^2 + \cdots + C(n-1, n-3)c^{n-3}.$$

In general we get the following rule.

Rule 2 *The total memory requirement for level j of the MMST for a dimension order $\mathcal{O} = (D_1, .., D_n)$ is given by :*

$$\prod_{i=1}^{n-j}|D_i| + C(j,1)(\prod_{i=1}^{n-j-1}|D_i|)c + C(j+1,2)(\prod_{i=1}^{n-j-2}|D_i|)c^2 + \cdots + C(n-1, n-j)c^{n-j}.$$

As a further example, the sum of the memory for level 1 nodes is $D_1 + C(n-1, 1)c$. At the level 0, there is one node "ALL" and it requires c amount of memory.

For different dimension orders of the array $(D_1, .., D_n)$, we may generate different MMSTs, which may have profoundly different memory requirements. To illustrate this, we use a four dimension array $ABCD$ which has 10x10x10x10 chunks. The sizes of dimensions A, B, C, and D are 10, 100, 1000, and 10000. The MMSTs for the dimension order (A, B, C, D) and for the dimension order (D, B, C, A) are shown in Figures 3 and 4. The number below each group-by node in the figures is the number of units of array element required by the node. Adding up those numbers for each MMST, we find the MMST for the order (D, B, C, A) requires approximately 4GB for a one-pass computation, whereas the tree for the order (A, B, C, D) requires only 4MB. On investigating the reason for this difference between the two trees, we find that switching the order of A and D changes the amount of memory required by each tree node. Clearly, it is important to determine which dimension order will require the least memory.

4.1.4 Optimal Dimension Order

The optimal dimension order is the dimension order whose MMST requires the least amount of memory. We prove that the optimal dimension order $\mathcal{O}$ is $(D_1, D_2, \dots, D_n)$, where $|D_1| \le |D_2| \le \cdots \le |D_n|$. Here, $|D_i|$ denotes size of the dimension D_i. So the dimensions are ordered incrementally in the dimension order $\mathcal{O}$.

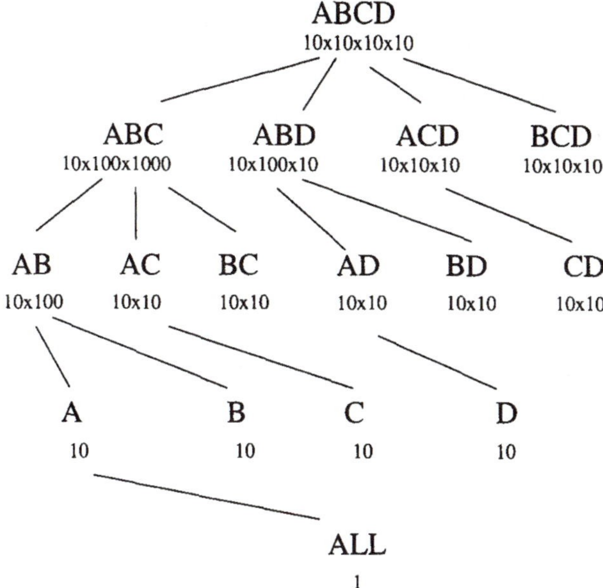

Figure 3: MMST for Dimension Order ABCD (Total Memory Required 4 MB)

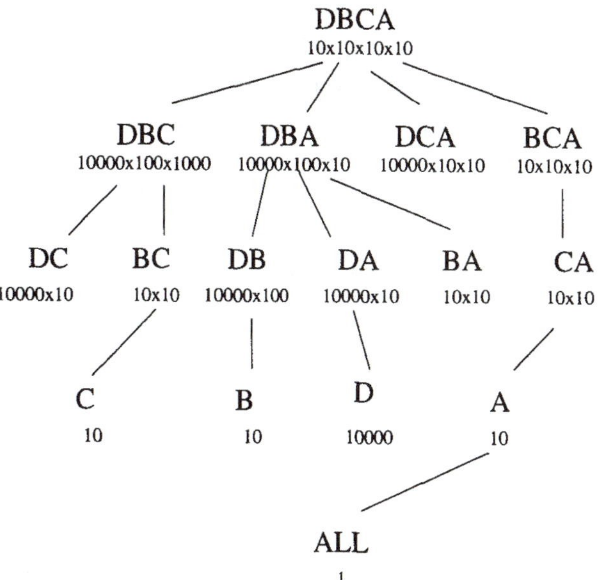

Figure 4: MMST for Dimension Order DBCA (Total Memory Required 4 GB)

Theorem 1 *Consider a chunked multidimensional array A of size $\prod_{i=1}^{n} |D_i|$ and having chunks of size $\prod_{i=1}^{n} |C_i|$, where $|C_i| = c$ for all $i (1 \le i \le n)$. If we read the chunks in logical order $\mathcal{O}$, where $\mathcal{O} = (D_1, D_2,,, D_n)$ and $|D_1| \le |D_2| \le |D_3| \cdots \le |D_n|$, the total amount of memory required to compute the Cube of the array in one scan of A is minimum.*

The question that naturally follows is "What is the upper bound for the total amount of memory required by MMST $\mathcal{T}_{\mathcal{O}}$?" The next theorem and corollary answer this question.

Theorem 2 *For a chunked multidimensional array A with the size $\prod_{i=1}^{n} |D_i|$, where $|D_i| = d$ for all i, and each array chunk has the size $\prod_{i=1}^{n} |C_i|$, where $|C_i| = c$ for all i, the total amount of memory to compute the Cube of the array in one scan of A is less than $c^n + (d+1+c)^{n-1}$.*

Corollary 1 *For a chunked multidimensional array with the size $\prod_{i=1}^{n} |D_i|$, where $|D_1| \le |D_2| \cdots \le |D_n|$, and each array chunk has the size $\prod_{i=1}^{n} |C_i|$, where $|C_i| = c$ for all i, the total amount of memory to compute the Cube of the array in one scan is less than $c^n + (d+1+c)^{n-1}$, where $d = (\prod_{i=1}^{n-1} |D_i|)^{1/(n-1)}$.*

Note that this indicates that the bound is independent of the size of the largest dimension D_n. The single-pass multi-way algorithm assumes that we have the memory required by the MMST of the optimal dimension order. If we have this memory, all the group-bys can be computed recursively in a single scan of the input array (as described previously in the example for ABC). But if the memory is insufficient we need multiple passes. We need a multi-pass algorithm to handle this case, as described in the next section.

4.2 Multi-pass Multi-way Array Algorithm

Let $\mathcal{T}$ be the MMST for the optimal dimension ordering $\mathcal{O}$ and $M_{\mathcal{T}}$ be the memory required for $\mathcal{T}$, calculated using Rule 1. If $M \le M_{\mathcal{T}}$, we cannot allocate the required memory for some of the subtrees of the MMST. We call these subtrees "incomplete subtrees." We need to use some extra steps to compute the group-bys included in the incomplete subtrees.

The problem of allocating memory optimally to the different subtrees is similar to the one described in [AADN96] and is likely to be NP-hard. We use a heuristic of allocating memory to subtrees of the root from the right to left order. For example, in Figure 1, the order in which the subtrees are considered is BC, AC and then AB. We use this heuristic since BC will be the largest array and we want to avoid computing it in multiple passes. The multi-pass algorithm is listed below:

```
(1)       Create the MMST T for a dimension order O
(2)       Add T to the Tobecomputed list.
(3)       For each tree T' in Tobecomputed list
          {
(3.1)         Create the working subtree W and
                  incomplete subtrees Is
(3.2)         Allocate memory to the subtrees
(3.3)         Scan the array chunk of the root of T'
                  in the order O
              {
(3.3.1)           aggregate each chunk to the groupbys
                      in W
(3.3.2)           generate intermediate results for Is
(3.3.3)           write complete chunks of W to disk
(3.3.4)           write intermediate results to the
                      partitions of Is
              }
(3.4)         For each I
              {
(3.4.1)           generate the chunks from the
                      partitions of I
(3.4.2)           write the completed chunks of I to disk
(3.4.3)           Add I to Tobecomputed
              }
          }
```

The incomplete subtrees Is exist in the the case where $M \leq M_{\mathcal{T}}$. To compute the Cube for this case, we need multiple passes. We divide $\mathcal{T}$ into a working subtree and a set of incomplete subtrees. We allocate each node of the working subtree the memory required by it and finish aggregation for the group-bys contained in the working subtree during the scan of the array. For each incomplete subtree $D_{j_1}, D_{j_2}, .., D_{j_{n-1}}$, we allocate memory equal to a chunk size of the group-by $D_{j_1}, D_{j_2}, .., D_{j_{n-1}}$, aggregate each input array chunk to the group-by $D_{j_1}, D_{j_2}, .., D_{j_{n-1}}$ and write the intermediate result to disk. Each intermediate result is aggregation of the $D_{j_1}, D_{j_2}, .., D_{j_{n-1}}$ group-by for each chunk of $D_1, D_2, .., D_n$. But, each of the intermediate result is incomplete since the intermediate results for different $D_1, D_2, .., D_n$ chunks map to the same chunk of the $D_{j_1}, D_{j_2}, .., D_{j_{n-1}}$ group-by.

We need to aggregate these different chunks to produce one chunk of the $D_{j_1}, D_{j_2}, .., D_{j_{n-1}}$ group-by. It is possible that the amount of memory required by the $D_{j_1}, D_{j_2}, .., D_{j_{n-1}}$ group-by is larger than M. Therefore, we have to divide the chunks of the $D_{j_1}, D_{j_2}, .., D_{j_{n-1}}$ group-by into partitions according to the dimension order so that the chunks in each partition fit in memory. When we output the intermediate chunks of $D_{j_1}, D_{j_2}, .., D_{j_{n-1}}$, we write them to the partition to which they belong to. For example, the partition may be decided by the values of $D_{j_{n-1}}$ in the chunk. Different ranges of values of $D_{j_{n-1}}$ will go to different partitions. In step (3.4.1), for each partition, we read each intermediate result and aggregate them to the corresponding chunk of the $D_{j_1}, D_{j_2}, .., D_{j_{n-1}}$ group-by. After we finish processing each intermediate result, each chunk of the $D_{j_1}, D_{j_2}, .., D_{j_{n-1}}$ group-by in memory is complete and we output them in the dimension order $D_{j_1}, D_{j_2}, .., D_{j_{n-1}}$. Once we are done for each partition, we complete the computation for the group-by $D_{j_1}, D_{j_2}, .., D_{j_{n-1}}$. To compute the subtrees of the $D_{j_1}, D_{j_2}, .., D_{j_{n-1}}$ node, we repeat loop 3 until we finish the aggregation for each node of the subtree.

5 Performance Results

In this section, we present the performance results of our MOLAP Cube algorithm and a previously published ROLAP algorithm. All experiments were run on a Sun SPARC 10 machine running SunOS 3.4. The workstation has a 32 MB memory and a 1 GB local disk with a sequential read speed 2.5 MB/second. The implementation uses the unix file system provided by the OS.

5.1 Data Sets

We used synthetic data sets to study the algorithms' performance. There are a number of factors that affect the performance of a cubing algorithm. These include:

- Number of valid data entries.

  That is, what fraction of the cells in a multidimensional space actually contain valid data? Note that the number of valid data entries is just the number of tuples in a ROLAP table implementing the multidimensional data set.

- Dimension size.

  That is, how many elements are there in each dimension? Note that for a MOLAP array implementation, the dimension size determines the size of the array. For a ROLAP implementation, the table size remains constant as we vary dimension size, but the range from which the values in the dimension attributes are drawn changes.

- Number of dimensions.

  This is obvious; here we just mention that by keeping the number of valid data cells constant, varying the number of dimensions impacts ROLAP and MOLAP implementations differently. Adding dimensions on MOLAP causes the shape of the array to change; adding dimensions in ROLAP adds or subtracts attributes from the tuples in the table.

Since the data density, number of the array dimensions, and the array size affect the algorithm performance, we designed three data sets.

Data Set 1: Keep the number of valid data elements constant, vary the dimension sizes. The data set consists of three 4-dimension arrays. For those arrays, three of the four dimensions sizes are fixed at 40, while the fourth dimension is either 40 (for the first array), or 100 (for the second), or 1000 (for the third). Every array has the 640000 valid elements. This results in the data density of the arrays (fraction of valid cells) ranging from 25%, to 10%, to 1%. The size of the input compressed array for the Array method turned out to be 5.1MB. The input table size for the ROLAP method was 12.85MB.

Data Set 2: Keep dimension sizes fixed, vary number of valid data elements.

All members of this data set are logically 4-dimensional arrays, with size 40x40x40x100. We varied the number of valid data elements so that the array data density ranges from 1% to 40%. The input compressed array size varied from 0.5MB, to 5.1MB, to 12.2MB, to 19.9MB. The corresponding table sizes for the ROLAP tables were 1.28MB, 12.8MB, 32.1MB, 51.2MB.

Data Set 3: this data set contains three arrays, with the number of dimensions ranging from 3, to 4, to 5. Our goal was to keep the density and number of valid cells constant throughout the data set, so the arrays have the following sizes: $40 \times 400 \times 4000$, $40 \times 40 \times 40 \times 1000$, and $10 \times 40 \times 40 \times 40 \times 100$. For each array, it has the same data density 1%. Hence, each array has 640000 valid array cells. The size of the input array was 5.1MB. The table size for ROLAP changed from 10.2MB, to 12.8MB, to 15.6MB, due to added attributes in the tuples.

We generated uniform data for all three data sets. Since these data sets are small, we used a proportionately small buffer pool, 0.5 MB, for most experiments. We will indicate the available memory size for those tests not using the same memory size.

5.2 Array-Based Cube Algorithms

In this section, we compare the naive and the *Multi-way* Array algorithms, study the effect of the compression algorithm to the performance of the *Multi-way* algorithm, investigate its behaviour as the buffer pool size decreases, and test its scale up as the number of dimensions increases.

5.2.1 Naive vs. Multi-way Array Algorithm

We ran the tests for the naive and the *Multi-way* Array algorithm on three 4-dimension arrays. Three of the four dimension sizes are fixed at 40, while the fourth dimension is varied from 100, to 200, to 300. Each array has the same data density 10%. In Figure 5, we see that the naive array algorithm is more than 40% slower than the *Multi-way* Array algorithm, due to multiple scans of the parent group-bys.

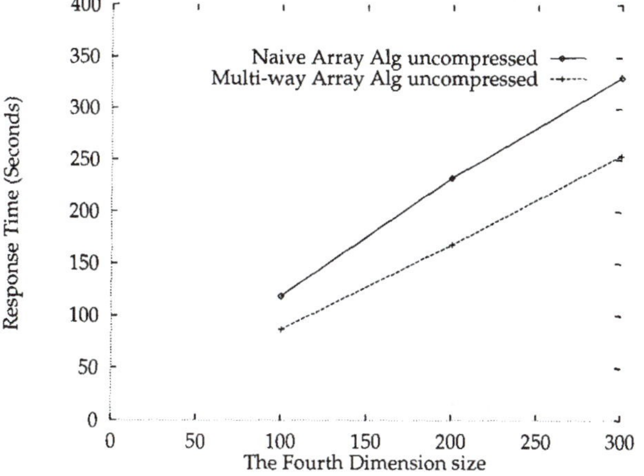

Figure 5: Naive vs. Multi-way Array Alg.

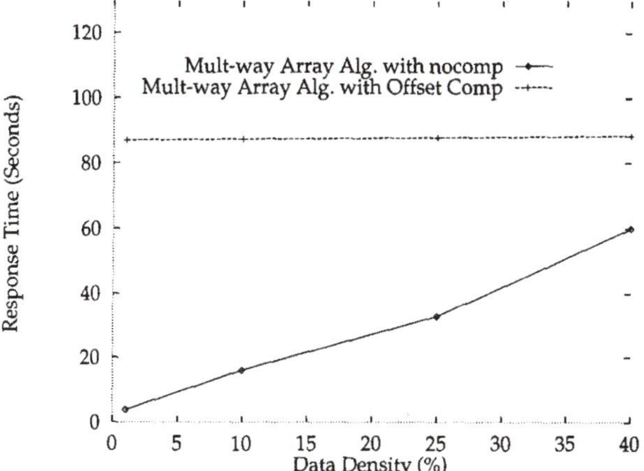

Figure 6: Two Compression Methods

5.2.2 Compression Performance

In Figure 6, we compare the array with no compression to the array with offset compression for **Data Set 2**. It shows that for data density less than 40% the *Multi-way* Array algorithm performed on the input array compressed by the offset algorithm is much faster than on uncompressed input array. There are two reasons for this. At lower densities, the compressed array size is much smaller. Hence, it reduces the I/O cost for reading the input array. The other is that the *Multi-way* Array algorithm only processes the valid array cells of the input array during computing the data Cube if the input array is compressed by the offset algorithm. For the uncompressed input array the *Multi-way* Array algorithm has to handle invalid array cells as well.

5.2.3 The Multi-way Array with Different Buffer Sizes

We ran experiments for **Data Set 2** at 10% density by varying the buffer pool size. In Figure 7, we see that the performance of *Multi-way* Array algorithm becomes a step function of the available memory size. In this test, we increased the available memory size from 52 KB to 0.5 MB. The first step on the right is caused by generating two incomplete subtrees in the first scan of the input array due to insufficient memory to hold the required chunks for the two subtrees. The algorithm goes through the second pass to produce each incomplete subtree and computes the group-bys contained in the two subtrees. As the available memory size increases to 300KB, only one incomplete subtree is generated, which causes the second step on the right. With the available memory more than 400 KB, the algorithm allocates memory to the entire MMST and computes the Cube in one scan of the input array. We flushed the OS cache before we process each working subtrees from their partitions. Theorem 2 predicts a bound of 570KB for the memory required for this data. The graph shows that above 420KB the entire MMST fits in memory. Thus the bound is quite close to the actual value.

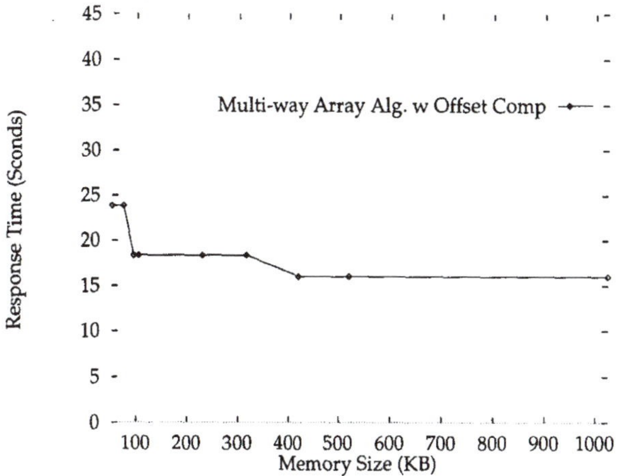

Figure 7: Multi-way Array Alg. with Various Memory Size

5.2.4 Varying Number of Dimensions

We discuss varying the number of dimensions when we compare the array algorithm with the ROLAP algorithm below.

5.3 The ROLAP vs. the Multi-Way Array Algorithms

In this section, we investigate the performance of our MOLAP algorithm with a previously published sort-based ROLAP algorithm in three cases. We used the *Overlap* method from [AADN96] as a benchmark for this comparison. In ROLAP the data is stored as tables. Computing the cube on a table produces a set of result tables representing the group-bys. On the other hand, in MOLAP data is stored as sparse multidimensional arrays. The cube of an array will produce a array for each of the group-bys. Since there are different formats (Table and Array) possible for the input and output data, there could be several ways of comparing the two methods. These are described in the following sections.

5.3.1 Tables vs. Arrays

One way to compare the array vs. table-based algorithms is to examine how they could be expected to perform in their "native" systems. That is, we consider how the multi-way array algorithm performs in a system that stores its data in array format, and how the table based algorithm performs in a system that stores its data in tables.

One might argue that arrays already order the data in such a way as to facilitate cube computation, whereas tables may not do so. Accordingly, in our tests we began with the table already sorted in the order desired by the table-based algorithm. This is perhaps slightly unfair to the array-based algorithm, since unless the table is stored in this specific order, the table based cube algorithm will begin with a large sort.

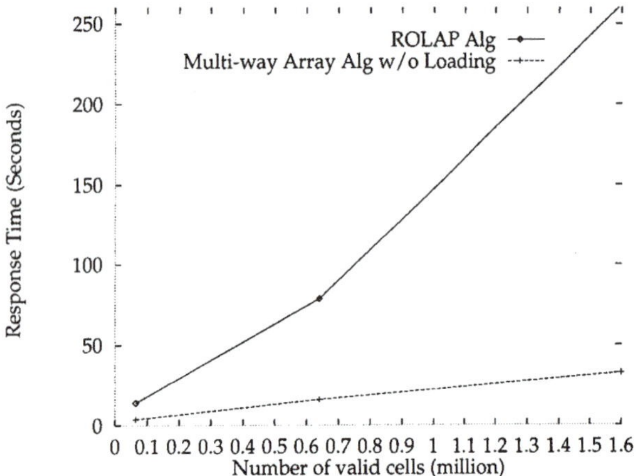

Figure 8: ROLAP vs. Multi-way Array for Data Set 2

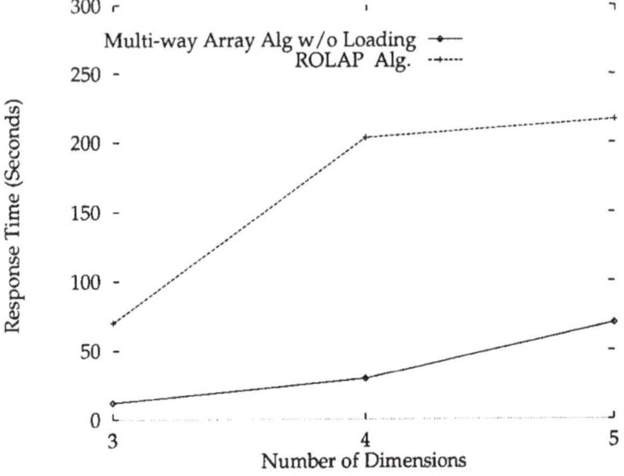

Figure 9: ROLAP vs. Multi-way Array for Data Set 3

The graphs in Figures 8, 9 and 10 compare the two methods for **Data Sets 2, 3** and **1**. For **Data Set 2**, as the density increases, the size of the input table increases. This also leads to bigger group-bys, i.e. the result table sizes also increase. The ROLAP method will need more memory due to this increase in size. Since the memory is kept constant at 0.5M, the ROLAP method has to do multiple passes and thus the performance becomes progressively worse. (As we shall see below, it is the growing CPU cost due to these multiple passes that dominates rather than the I/O cost.) For the array method, the array dimension sizes are not changing. Since the memory requirement for a single pass computation for the array method depends only on the dimension sizes, and not on the number of valid data cells, in all cases the array method can finish the computation in one pass. Thus we see a smaller increase in the time required for the array method.

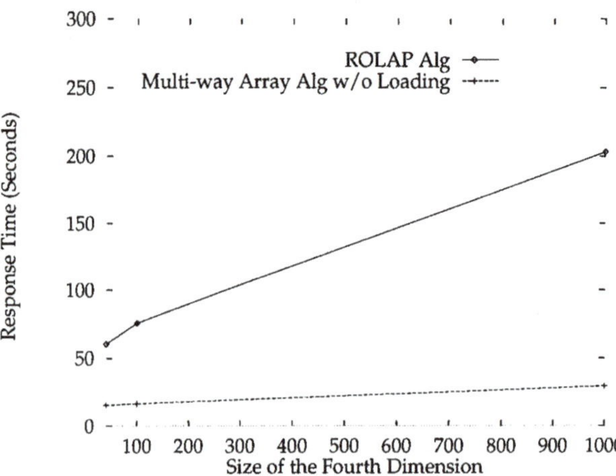

Figure 10: ROLAP vs. Multi-way Array w/o Loading for Data Set 1

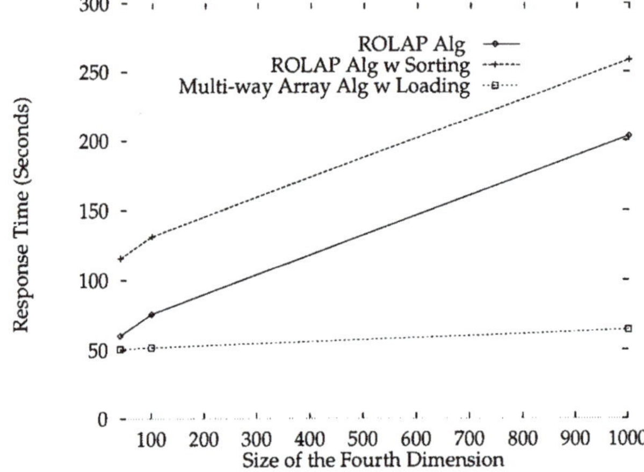

Figure 11: ROLAP vs. Multi-way Array with Loading for Data Set 1

Similarly for **Data Set 1**, as the size of the fourth dimension is increased, the sizes of the group-bys containing the fourth dimension in the ROLAP computation grow. Though the input table size is constant, the increase in the size of the group-bys leads to greater memory requirements. But due to the memory available being constant at 0.5MB, once again the ROLAP method reverts to multiple passes and its performance suffers. Turning to the array algorithm, the array sizes also increase due to increase in the size of the fourth dimension. But in the optimal dimension order, as given by Theorem 4.1.4, the biggest (fourth) dimension is kept last. Furthermore, by Corollary 4.1.4, the size of this last dimension does not affect the memory required fo ra single pass computation. Thus the memory requirements of the array algorithm remains constant at 0.5MB and it always computes everything in one pass. Thus the running time of the array method does not increase significantly.

In **Data Set 3**, we vary the number of dimensions from 3 to 5. The number of group-bys to be computed is exponential in the number of dimensions. Since both algorithms compute all of these group-bys, the running time of both the methods increases with the number of dimensions.

5.3.2 The MOLAP Algorithm for ROLAP Systems

Although it was designed for MOLAP systems, the array method could also be applied to any ROLAP system. Since the array method is much faster than the table method, it might be viable to convert the input table first into an array, cube the array, and then convert back the resulting arrays into tables. In this approach, rather than being used as a persistent storage structure, the array is used as a query evaluation data structure, like a hash table in a join. We did two experiments to study the performance of this approach.

In the first comparison, the *Multi-way* Array method loads data from an input table into an array as a first step. The ROLAP method just computes the cube from the input table as in the previous case. The input table is unsorted, so the ROLAP method has to specifically sort the input. The times for **Data Set 1** are shown in Figure 11. It can be seen that the array method with loading is much faster than the ROLAP method. We then repeated the experiments with a sorted input table for the ROLAP method, so that the initial sorting step can be avoided. The times are shown in the same graph. It turns out that even in this case, the *Multi-way* Array method turns out to be faster.

5.4 Drilling Down on Performance

In this section, we try to explain why the *Multi-way* Array method performs much better than the ROLAP method. Our experiments showed for the ROLAP method, about 70% of the time is spent on CPU computations and the remaining is I/O. The ROLAP method reads and writes data into tables. These table sizes are significantly bigger than the compressed arrays used by the *Multi-way* Array method. Thus the ROLAP method reads and writes more data, meaning that the 30% of the running time due to I/O dominates the I/O time used in the MOLAP algorithm.

Turning to the CPU usage, on profiling the code we found that a significant percentage of time (about 55-60%) is spent in sorting intermediate results while about (10-12%) time is spent in copying data. These sorts are costly, largely due to a large number of tuple comparisons. Tuple comparisons incur a lot of cost, since there are multiple fields to be compared. The copying arises because the ROLAP method has to copy data to generate the result tuples. This copying is also expensive since the tuples are bigger than the array cells used in the MOLAP algorithm.

On the other hand, the *Multi-way* Array method is a position based method. Different cells of the array are aggregated together based on their position, without incurring the cost of multiple sorts (the multidimensional nature of the array captures the relationships among all the dimensions.) Thus once an array has been built, computing different group-bys from it incurs very little cost. One potential problem with the array could be sparsity, since the array size will grow as the data becomes sparse. However, we found that the offset compression method is very effective. It not only compresses the array, but different compressed chunks can be directly aggregated without having to decompress them. This leads to much better performance for the array. It turns out that the *Multi-way* Array method is even more CPU intensive than the ROLAP algorithm (about 88% CPU time). Most of this time (about 70%) is spent in doing the aggregation, while 10% is spent in converting the offset to the index values while processing the compressed chunks.

6 Conclusion

In this paper we presented the Multi-Way Array based method for cube computation. This method overlaps the computation of different group-bys, while using minimal memory for each group-by. We have proven that the dimension order used by the algorithm minimizes the total memory requirement for the algorithm.

Our performance results show that that the Multi-Way Array method performs much better than previously published ROLAP algorithms. In fact, we found that the performance benefits of the Multi-Way Array method are so substantial that in our tests it was faster to load an array from a table, cube the array, then dump the cubed array into tables, than it was to cube the table directly. This suggests that this algorithm could be valuable in ROLAP as well as MOLAP systems — that is, it is not necessary that the system support arrays as a persistent storage type in order to obtain performance benefits from this algorithm.

References

[AADN96] S. Agarwal, R. Agrawal, P. Deshpande, J. Naughton, S. Sarawagi and R. Ramakrishnan. "On the Computation of Multidimensional Aggregates". In *Proceedings of the 22nd International Conference on Very Large Databases*, Mumbai (Bombay), 1996.

[AS] Arbor Software. "The Role of the Multidimensional Database in a Data Warehousing Solution". White Paper, Arbor Software. http://www.arborsoft.com/papers/wareTOC.html

[CCS93] E.F. Codd, S.B. Codd, and C.T. Salley. "Providing OLAP (On-line Analytical Processing) to User-Analysts: An IT Mandate", White Paper, E.F. Codd and Associates. http://www.arborsoft.com/papers/coddTOC.html

[DKOS84] D. Dewitt, R. Katz, G. Olken, L. Shapiro, M. Stonebraker, D. Wood. "Implementation Techniques for Main Memory Database Systems". In Proceedings of SIGMOD, Boston, 1984.

[GBLP95] J. Gray, A. Bosworth, A.Layman, and H.Pirahesh. "Data Cube: A relational aggregation operator generalizing group-by, cross-tabs and sub-totals. Technical Report MSR-TR-95-22, Microsoft Research, Advance Technology Division, Microsoft Corporation, Redmond, 1995.

[GC96] G. Colliad. "OLAP, Relational, and Multidimensional Database Systems". SIGMOD Record, Vol. 25. No. 3, September 1996.

[IA] Information Advantage. "OLAP - Scaling to the Masses". White Paper, Information Advantage. http://www.infoadvan.com/

[MC] Stanford Technology Group, Inc. "INFORMIX-MetaCube". Product Brochure. http://www.informix.com/informix/products/new_plo/stgbroch/brochure.html

[MS] MicroStrategy Incorporated. "The Case For Relational OLAP". White Paper, MicroStrategy Incorporated. http://www.strategy.com/dwf/wp_b_al.html

[OC] Oracle Corporation. "Oracle OLAP Products". White Paper, Oracle Corporation. http://www.oracle.com/products/collatrl/olapwp.pdf

[PSW] Pilot Software. "An Introduction to OLAP". White Paper, Pilot Software. http://www.pilotsw.com/r_and_t/whtpaper/olap/olap.htm

[RJ] Arbor Software Corporation, Robert J. Earle, U.S.Patent # 5359724

[SM94] Sunita Sarawagi, Michael Stonebraker, "Efficient Organization of Large Multidimensional Arrays". In *Proceedings of the Eleventh International Conference on Data Engineering*, Houston, TX, February 1994.

[Wel84] T. A. Welch. "A Technique for High-Performance Data Compression". IEEE Computer, 17(6), 1984.

[ZTN] Y.H. Zhao, K. Tufte, and J.F. Naughton. "On the Performance of an Array-Based ADT for OLAP Workloads". Technical Report CS-TR-96-1313, University of Wisconsin-Madison, CS Department, May 1996.

Deriving Production Rules for Incremental View Maintenance

Stefano Ceri *
Jennifer Widom

IBM Almaden Research Center
650 Harry Road
San Jose, CA 95120
ceri@cs.stanford.edu, widom@ibm.com

Abstract. It is widely recognized that production rules in database systems can be used to automatically maintain derived data such as views. However, writing a correct set of rules for efficiently maintaining a given view can be a difficult and ad-hoc process. We provide a facility whereby a user defines a view as an SQL **select** expression, from which the system automatically derives set-oriented production rules that maintain a materialization of that view.

The maintenance rules are triggered by operations on the view's base tables. Generally, the rules perform incremental maintenance: the materialized view is modified according to the sets of changes made to the base tables, which are accessible through logical tables provided by the rule language. However, for some operations substantial recomputation may be required. We give algorithms that, based on key information, perform syntactic analysis on a view definition to determine when efficient maintenance is possible.

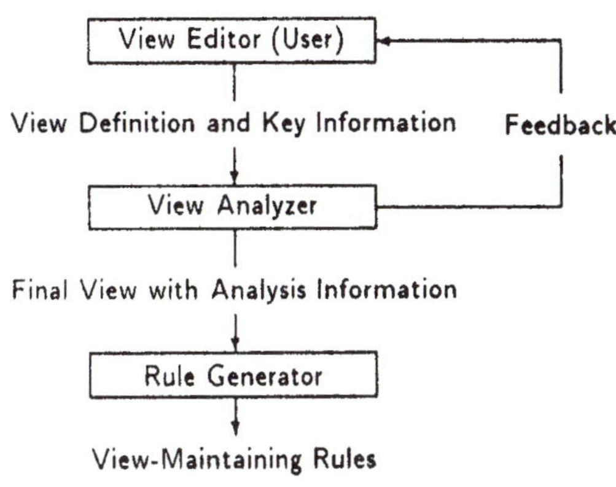

Figure 1: *Rule derivation system*

1 Introduction

In relational database systems, a *view* is a logical table derived from one or more physical (*base*) tables. Views are useful for presenting different levels of abstraction or different portions of a database to different users. Typically, a view is specified as an SQL **select** expression. A retrieval query over a view is written as if the view were a physical table; the query's answer is logically equivalent to evaluating the view's **select** expression, then performing the query using the result. There are two well-known approaches to implementing views. In the first approach, views are *virtual*: queries over views are modified into queries over base tables [Sto75]. In the second approach, views are *materialized*: they are computed from the base tables and stored in the database [BLT86,KP81,SI84]. Different applications favor one or the other approach. In this paper we consider the problem of view materialization.

Production rules in database systems allow specification of data manipulation operations that are executed automatically when certain events occur or conditions are met, e.g. [DE89, MD89, SJGP90, WF90]. Clearly, production rules can be used to maintain materialized views: when base tables change, rules are triggered that modify the view.[1] Writing a correct set of rules for efficiently maintaining a given view can be a difficult process, however. The rules could simply rematerialize the view from the base tables, but this can be very inefficient. Efficiency is achieved by *incremental* maintenance, in which the changed portions of the base tables are propagated to the view, without full recomputation. We have developed a method that automatically derives incremental maintenance rules for a wide class of views. The rules produced are executable using the rule language of the Starburst database system at the IBM Almaden Research Center [WCL91].

Figure 1 shows the structure of our system, which is invoked at compile-time when a view is created. Initially, the user enters the view as an SQL **select** expression, along with information about keys for the view's base tables.[2] Our system then performs syntactic analysis on the view definition; this analysis determines two things: (1) whether the view may contain duplicates (2) for each base table referenced in the view, whether efficient view maintenance rules are possible for operations on that table. The user is provided with the results of this analysis. The results may indicate that, in order to improve the efficiency of view maintenance, further interaction with the system is necessary prior to rule generation. In particular:

*Permanent address: Dip. di Elettronica, Politecnico di Milano, Piazza L. Da Vinci 32, 20133 Milano, Italy

[1] Production rules also can be used to implement virtual views, as shown in [SJGP90].

[2] Key information is essential for view analysis, as we will show. Functional dependencies could be specified as well, but we assume that keys are more easily understood and specified by the user; in normalized tables, functional dependencies are captured by keys anyway.

- Views with duplicates cannot be maintained efficiently, as explained in Section 4.3. Hence, if the system detects that the view may contain duplicates, then the user should add **distinct** to the view definition. (In SQL, **distinct** eliminates duplicates.)
- If the system detects that efficient maintenance rules are not possible for some base table operations, this may indicate to the user that not all key information has been included, or the user may choose to modify the view definition.

If changes are made, view analysis is repeated. In practice, we have discovered that efficient rules are possible for most views and operations once all key information is provided. However, there are cases when certain base table operations cannot be supported efficiently. If these operations are expected to occur frequently, view materialization may be inappropriate. The responsibility for considering these trade-offs lies with the user; our system provides all necessary information.

Once the user is satisfied with the view definition and its properties, the system generates the set of view-maintaining rules. Rules are produced for **insert**, **delete**, and **update** operations on each base table referenced in the view. The rule language we use is *set-oriented*, meaning that rules are triggered after arbitrary sets of changes to the database (Section 3). For those operations for which the system has determined that efficiency is possible, the maintenance rules modify the view incrementally according to the changes made to the base tables. These changes are accessible using the rule system's *transition table* mechanism (Section 3). For those operations for which efficiency is not possible, rematerialization is performed.

Note that the view must be computed in its entirety once, after which it is maintained automatically. The frequency of view maintenance depends on the frequency of rule invocation, which is flexible; see Section 3. Our method is directly applicable for simultaneous maintenance of multiple views; see Section 9.

1.1 Related Work

Most other work in incremental view maintenance differs from ours in two ways: (1) It takes an algebraic approach, considering a restricted class of views and operations. In contrast, we consider a practical class of views specified using a standard query language, and we consider arbitrary database operations. (2) It suggests view maintenance mechanisms that must be built into the database system. In contrast, we propose view maintenance as an application of an existing mechanism. In addition, our system provides interaction whereby the user can modify a view so the system will guarantee efficient maintenance.

In [BLT86], views are specified as relational algebra expressions. Algorithms are given for determining when base table changes are irrelevant to the view and for differentially reevaluating a view after a set of insert and delete operations. [Han87] extends this work to exploit common subexpressions and proposes an alternative approach using RETE networks; [Han87] also includes algorithms for incremental aggregate maintenance. In [RCBB89], an algebra of "delta relations" is described, including a "changes" operator that can be applied to views. There is a suggested connection to the production rules of HiPAC [MD89], but rule derivation is not included. In [SP89], incremental maintenance of single-table views is considered, with emphasis on issues of distribution.

Our work here is loosely related to that reported in [CW90], where we gave a method for deriving production rules that maintain integrity constraints. Our solutions to the two problems differ considerably, but the approaches are similar: In both cases we describe a general compile-time facility in which the user provides a high-level declarative specification, then the system uses syntactic analysis to produce a set of lower-level production rules with certain properties relative to the user's specification.

1.2 Outline

Section 2 defines our SQL-based syntax for view definition and Section 3 provides an overview of our production rule language. Section 4 motivates our approach: it gives an informal overview of view analysis, explains incremental maintenance, and describes certain difficulties encountered with duplicates and updates.[3] Subsequent sections contain the core technical material, formally describing our methods for view analysis and rule generation. We consider *top-level* table references in Section 5, *positively nested* subqueries in Section 6, *negatively nested* subqueries in Section 7, and *set operators* in Section 8. In each of these sections we describe how view analysis can guarantee certain properties, and we show how these properties are used to determine if efficient maintenance is possible. Section 9 addresses system execution, showing that the generated rules behave correctly at run-time. Finally, in Section 10 we conclude and discuss future work.

Due to space constraints, some details have been omitted. For further details and additional examples see [CW91].

2 View Definition Language

Views are defined using a subset of the SQL syntax for select expressions. The grammar is given in Figure 2 and should be self-explanatory to readers familiar with SQL [IBM88].[4] Several examples are given in subsequent sections. Our view definition language is quite powerful, but, for brevity and to make our approach more presentable, the language does include certain restrictions:

[3] Note that we are not dealing with the *view update problem*, which addresses how updates on views are propagated to updates on base tables. We are considering how updates on base tables are propagated to updates on views.

[4] We include multi-column **in** (grammar productions 12 and 16), which is not standard in all SQL implementations.

1.	*View-Def*	::=	**define view** *V*(*Col-List*): *View-Exp*
2.	*View-Exp*	::=	*Select-Exp* | *Set-Exp*
3.	*Select-Exp*	::=	**select** [**distinct**] *Col-List* **from** *Table-List* [**where** *Predicate*]
4.	*Set-Exp*	::=	$Select\text{-}Exp_1$ **union distinct** $Select\text{-}Exp_2$ **union distinct** ... $Select\text{-}Exp_n$
5.		|	$Select\text{-}Exp_1$ **intersect** $Select\text{-}Exp_2$ **intersect** ... $Select\text{-}Exp_n$
6.	*Col-List*	::=	$Col_1, \ldots, Col_n$ | *
7.	*Col*	::=	[*T*.]*C* | [*Var*.]*C*
8.	*Table-List*	::=	T_1 [Var_1], ..., T_n [Var_n]
9.	*Predicate*	::=	*Item Comp Item*
10.		|	**exists** (*Simple-Select*)
11.		|	**not exists** (*Simple-Select*)
12.		|	*Item* **in** (*Simple-Select*)
13.		|	*Item* **not in** (*Simple-Select*)
14.		|	*Item Comp* **any** (*Simple-Select*)
15.		|	*Predicate* **and** *Predicate*
16.	*Item*	::=	*Col* | (*Col-List*) | constant
17.	*Comp*	::=	= | < | <= | > | >= | !=
18.	*Simple-Select*	::=	**select** *Col-List* **from** *Table-List* [**where** *Simple-Pred*]
19.	*Simple-Pred*	::=	*Item Comp Item*
20.		|	*Simple-Pred* **and** *Simple-Pred*

Figure 2: *Grammar for View Definitions*

- Disjunction in predicates is omitted. (There is little loss of expressive power since **or** usually can be simulated using **union**.)
- Subqueries are limited to one level of nesting.
- Set operators **union** and **intersect** may not be mixed; set operator **minus** is omitted.
- Comparison operators using **all** are omitted.

The reader will see that our method could certainly be extended to eliminate these restrictions, but the details are lengthy. Note also that we have omitted aggregates. Incremental methods for maintaining aggregates have been presented elsewhere [Han87]; these techniques can be adapted for our framework.

3 Production Rule Language

We provide a brief but self-contained overview of the set-oriented, SQL-based production rule language used in the remainder of the paper. Further details and numerous examples appear in [WF90, WCL91]. Here we describe only the subset of the rule language used by the view maintenance rules.

Our rule facility is fully integrated into the Starburst database system. Hence, all the usual database functionality is available; in addition, a set of rules may be defined. Rules are based on the notion of *transitions*, which are database state changes resulting from execution of a sequence of data manipulation operations. We consider only the net effect of transitions, as in [BLT86, WF90]. The syntax for defining production rules is:[5]

```
create rule name
when transition predicate
then action
[ precedes rule-list ]
```

Transition predicates specify one or more operations on tables: **inserted into T**, **deleted from T**, or **updated T**. A rule is *triggered* by a given transition if at least one of the specified operations occurred in the net effect of the transition. The action part of a rule specifies an arbitrary sequence of SQL data manipulation operations to be executed when the rule is triggered. The optional **precedes** clause is used to induce a partial ordering on the set of defined rules. If a rule R_1 specifies R_2 in its **precedes** list, then R_1 is higher than R_2 in the ordering. When no ordering is specified between two rules, their order is arbitrary but deterministic [ACL91].

A rule's action may refer to the current state of the database through top-level or nested SQL **select** operations. In addition, rule actions may refer to *transition tables*. A transition table is a logical table reflecting changes that have occurred during a transition. At the end of a given transition, transition table "**inserted T**" refers to those tuples of table **T** in the current state that were inserted by the transition, transition table "**deleted T**" refers to those tuples of table **T** in the pre-transition state that were deleted by the transition, transition table "**old updated T**" refers to those tuples of table **T** in the pre-transition state that were updated by the transition, and transition table "**new updated T**" refers to the current values of the same tuples. Transition tables may be referenced in place of tables in the **from** clauses of **select** operations.

Rules are activated at *rule assertion points*. There is an assertion point at the end of each transaction, and there may be additional user-specified assertion points within a transaction.[6] We describe the semantics of rule execution at an arbitrary assertion point. The state change resulting from the user-generated database operations executed since the last assertion point (or start of the transaction) create the first relevant transition, and some set of rules are triggered by this transition. A triggered rule *R* is chosen from this set such that no other triggered rule is higher in the ordering. *R*'s action is executed. After execution of *R*'s action, all other rules are triggered only if their transition predicate holds with respect to the composite transition created by the initial transaction and subsequent execution of *R*'s action. That is, these rules consider *R*'s action as if it were executed as part of the initial transition. Rule *R*, however,

[5] Rules also may contain *conditions* in **if** clauses, but these are not needed for view maintenance.

[6] Currently, assertion points are at transaction commit only. We will soon extend the system with a flexible mechanism that supports additional points [WCL91].

has already "processed" the initial transition; thus, R is triggered again only if its transition predicate holds with respect to the transition created by its action. From the new set of triggered rules, a rule is chosen such that no other triggered rule is higher in the ordering, and its action is executed. At an arbitrary time in rule processing, a given rule is triggered if its transition predicate holds with respect to the (composite) transition since the last time at which its action was executed; if its action has not yet been executed, it is considered with respect to the transition since the last rule assertion point or start of the transaction. When the set of triggered rules is empty, rule processing terminates.

For view maintenance, it sometimes is necessary for a rule to consider the entire pre-transition value of a table (see, e.g., Section 5.4). Currently there is no direct mechanism in the rule language for obtaining this value, but it can be derived from transition tables. In the action part of view maintenance rules, we use "**old T**" to refer to the value of table **T** at the start of the transition triggering the rule. **old T** is translated to:

```
(T minus inserted T minus new updated T)
union deleted T union old updated T
```

This expression may seem rather complex, but one should observe that in most cases the transition tables are small or empty.

4 Motivation

4.1 View Analysis

Initially, the user defines a view using the language of Section 2, and the user specifies a set of (single- or multi-column) keys for the view's base tables. All known keys for each table should be specified, since this provides important information for view analysis. Using the key information, during view analysis the system considers each list of table references in the view definition. For each list, it first computes the "bound columns" of the table references. Based on the bound columns, it then determines for each table reference whether the reference is "safe". When a table reference is safe, incremental view maintenance rules can be generated for operations on that table, as described in Section 4.2. The system also uses the bound columns for the top-level tables to determine if the view may contain duplicates. Formal definitions for bound columns and safety are based on the context of table references and are given in Sections 5–7.

4.2 Incremental Maintenance

The definition of a view V can be interpreted as an expression mapping base tables to table V. That is, $V = V_{exp}(T_1, .., T_n)$, where $T_1, .., T_n$ are the base tables appearing in V's definition. Efficient maintenance of V is achieved when changes to $T_1, .., T_n$ can be propagated incrementally to V, without substantial recomputation. Consider any table reference T_i in V, and assume for the moment that T_i appears only once in V's definition. If view analysis determines that T_i is safe, then changes to T_i can be propagated incrementally to V. More formally, changes to T_i (sets of insertions, deletions, or updates), denoted ΔT_i, produce changes to V, denoted ΔV, that can be computed using only ΔT_i and the other base tables: $\Delta V = V'_{exp}(T_1, .., \Delta T_i, .., T_n)$, where V'_{exp} is an expression derived from V_{exp}. Table V is then modified by inserting or deleting tuples from ΔV as appropriate. We assume that ΔT_i is small with respect to T_i and ΔV is small with respect to V; hence, safe table references result in efficient maintenance rules. If T_i appears more than once in V's definition, we separately analyze each reference. If all references are safe, then changes to T_i can be propagated incrementally to V. If any reference is unsafe, changes to T_i may cause rematerialization.

4.3 Duplicates

Our method does not support efficient maintenance of views with duplicates. The main difficulty lies in generating rule actions in SQL that can manipulate exact numbers of duplicates. As an example, the SQL **delete** operation is based on truth of a predicate; hence, if a table contains four copies of a tuple (say), there is no SQL operation that can delete exactly two copies. To correctly maintain views with duplicates, such partial deletions can be necessary. [BLT86] also considers the problem of duplicates in views, proposing two solutions. In the first solution, an extra column is added in the view table to count the number of occurrences of each tuple. We choose not to use this approach because rule generation can become quite complex and the result is not transparent to the user. (The user must reference duplicates in the view through the extra column.) The second solution proposed in [BLT86] ensures that a view will not contain duplicates by requiring it to include key columns for each of the base tables. We have essentially taken this approach, however we have devised algorithms that allow us to loosen the key requirement considerably, yet still guarantee that a view will not contain duplicates.

4.4 Update Operations

When update operations are performed on a view's base tables, we would like to consequently perform an update operation on the view. In many cases, however, this is not the semantic effect. As a simple example, consider two tables `T1(A,B)` and `T2(C,D)` where `T1` contains tuples `(x,y)`, `(z,y)`, and `(u,v)`, and `T2` contains tuples `(x,z)` and `(v,x)`. Consider the following view:

```
define view V(A): select T1.A from T1, T2
                  where T1.B = T2.C
```

Initially, `V` contains only one tuple, `(u)`. Now suppose the following two update operations are performed on table `T2`:

```
update T2 set C = u where D = x ;
update T2 set C = y where D = z
```

The effect of the first update is to remove tuple `(u)` from view `V`, while the effect of the second update is to add tuples `(x)` and `(z)` to `V`. There is no way to reflect the update operations on base table `T2` as an update operation on view `V`; rather, the updates must be reflected as delete and insert operations on V. There do exist some cases in which update operations on base tables can be reflected as updates on views. However, for general and automatic rule derivation, in our approach update operations on base tables always result in delete and/or insert operations on the view.

5 Top-Level Table References

Assume now that the user has defined a view and has specified key information for the view's base tables. Assume that the view does not include set operators **union** or **intersect**; views with set operators are covered in Section 8. The system first analyzes the top-level table references, i.e., those references generated from the *Table-List* in grammar production 3 of Figure 2. This analysis reveals both whether the view may contain duplicates and whether efficient maintenance rules are possible for operations on the top-level tables. Consider a view V with the general form:[7]

> **define view** V(*Col-List*):
> **select** $C_1, .., C_n$ **from** $T_1, .., T_m$ **where** P

where $T_1, .., T_m$ are the top-level table references, $C_1, .., C_n$ are columns of $T_1, .., T_m$, and P is a predicate.

5.1 Bound Columns

View analysis relies on the concept of *bound columns*. The bound columns of the top-level table references in view V are denoted $B(V)$ and are computed as follows:

Definition 5.1 (Bound Columns for Top-Level Table References)

1. Initialize $B(V)$ to contain the columns $C_1, .., C_n$ projected in the view definition.
2. Add to $B(V)$ all columns of $T_1, .., T_m$ such that predicate P includes an equality comparison between the column and a constant.
3. Repeat until $B(V)$ is unchanged:
   (a) Add to $B(V)$ all columns of $T_1, .., T_m$ such that predicate P includes an equality comparison between the column and a column in $B(V)$.
   (b) Add to $B(V)$ all columns of any table T_i, $1 \leq i \leq m$, if $B(V)$ includes a key for T_i. □

Bound columns can be computed using syntactic analysis and guarantee the following useful property (Lemma 5.2 below): If two tuples in the cross-product of top-level tables $T_1, .., T_m$ satisfy predicate P and differ in their bound columns, then the tuples also must differ in view columns $C_1, .., C_m$. Let $Proj(t, C_1, .., C_j)$ denote the projection of a tuple t onto a set of columns $C_1, .., C_j$.

Lemma 5.2 (Bound Columns Lemma for Top-Level Tables) Let t_1 and t_2 be tuples in the cross-product of $T_1, .., T_m$ such that t_1 and t_2 both satisfy P. By definition, columns $C_1, .., C_n$ are in $B(V)$. If $D_1, .., D_k$ are additional columns in $B(V)$ such that t_1 and t_2 are guaranteed to differ in $C_1, .., C_n, D_1, .., D_k$, i.e. $Proj(t_1, C_1, .., C_n, D_1, .., D_k) \neq Proj(t_2, C_1, .., C_n, D_1, .., D_k)$, then t_1 and t_2 also are guaranteed to differ in $C_1, .., C_n$, i.e. $Proj(t_1, C_1, .., C_n) \neq Proj(t_2, C_1, .., C_n)$.

Proof: Suppose, for the sake of a contradiction, that $Proj(t_1, C_1, .., C_n) = Proj(t_2, C_1, .., C_n)$. Then there must be some D_i in $D_1, .., D_k$ such that $Proj(t_1, D_i) \neq Proj(t_2, D_i)$. We show that this is impossible. Consider any column D_i in $D_1, .., D_k$. Since D_i is in $B(V)$, by the recursive definition of $B(V)$ and since t_1 and t_2 both satisfy predicate P, the value of column D_i in both t_1 and t_2 must either

1. satisfy an equality with a constant k, or
2. satisfy an equality with a column C_j in $C_1, .., C_n$, or
3. be functionally dependent on a constant k or column C_j. (This is the case where D_i was added to $B(V)$ because a key for D_i's table was present; recall that all columns of a table are functionally dependent on any key for that table.)

In the case of a constant, $Proj(t_1, D_i)$ and $Proj(t_2, D_i)$ are both equal to or functionally dependent on the same constant, so $Proj(t_1, D_i) = Proj(t_2, D_i)$. In the case of a column C_j, $Proj(t_1, C_j) = Proj(t_2, C_j)$ by our supposition, so $Proj(t_1, D_i) = Proj(t_2, D_i)$. □

5.2 Duplicate Analysis

If V's definition does not include **distinct**, then our system performs duplicate analysis. If this analysis reveals that V may contain duplicates, then the user is notified that maintenance rules cannot be generated for V unless V's definition is modified to include **distinct**. (The system does not add **distinct** automatically since it may change the view's semantics.) Once the bound columns for top-level table references have been computed, duplicate analysis is straightforward:

Theorem 5.3 (Duplicates) If $B(V)$ includes a key for every top-level table, then V will not contain duplicates.

Proof: Let t_1 and t_2 be two different tuples in the cross-product of the top-level tables in V such that t_1 and t_2 both satisfy predicate P. We must show that t_1 and t_2 cannot produce duplicate tuples in V, i.e. $Proj(t_1, C_1, .., C_n) \neq Proj(t_2, C_1, .., C_n)$. By the theorem's assumption, there must be additional columns $D_1, .., D_k$ in $B(V)$ such that $C_1, .., C_n, D_1, .., D_k$ include a key for every top-level table. Then t_1 and t_2 must differ in $C_1, .., C_n, D_1, .., D_k$. Consequently, by Lemma 5.2, $Proj(t_1, C_1, .., C_n) \neq Proj(t_2, C_1, .., C_n)$. □

5.3 Safety Analysis

Safety of top-level table references is similar to duplicate analysis:

Definition 5.4 (Safety of Top-Level Table References) Top-level table reference T_i is *safe* in V if $B(V)$ includes a key for T_i. □

The following three theorems show that if table reference T_i is safe, then **insert**, **delete**, and **update** operations on T_i can be reflected by incremental changes to V.

[7] For clarity and without loss of generality, we omit the use of table variables here.

Theorem 5.5 (Insertion Theorem for Top-Level Tables) Let T_i be a safe top-level table reference in V and suppose a tuple t is inserted into T_i. If v is a tuple in the cross-product of the top-level tables using tuple t from T_i, and v satisfies predicate P so that $Proj(v, C_1, .., C_n)$ is in view V after the insertion, then $Proj(v, C_1, .., C_n)$ was not in V before the insertion.

Proof: Suppose, for the sake of a contradiction, that there was a tuple v' in V before the insertion such that $Proj(v', C_1, .., C_n) = Proj(v, C_1, .., C_n)$. Let $D_1, .., D_k$ be additional bound columns so that $C_1, .., C_n, D_1, .., D_k$ includes a key for T_i. (We know such columns exist since T_i is safe.) Since v and v' include different tuples from T_i, then $Proj(v, C_1, .., C_n, D_1, .., D_k) \neq Proj(v', C_1, .., C_n, D_1, .., D_k)$. Hence, by Lemma 5.2, $Proj(v, C_1, .., C_n) \neq Proj(v', C_1, .., C_n)$. □

The practical consequence of this theorem is that if a set of tuples ΔT_i are inserted into T_i, then the tuples ΔV that should be inserted into V can be derived from the cross-product of the top-level tables using ΔT_i instead of T_i. This exactly corresponds to the definition of incremental maintenance in Section 4.2, and is implemented in the rules given below.

Similar theorems with similar consequences apply for delete and update operations. The proofs are omitted since they also are similar [CW91].

Theorem 5.6 (Deletion Theorem for Top-Level Tables) Let T_i be a safe top-level table reference in V and suppose a tuple t is deleted from T_i. If v is a tuple in the cross-product of the top-level tables using tuple t from T_i, and v satisfies predicate P so that $Proj(v, C_1, .., C_n)$ was in view V before the deletion, then $Proj(v, C_1, .., C_n)$ is not in V after the deletion. □

Theorem 5.7 (Update Theorem for Top-Level Tables) Let T_i be a safe top-level table reference in V and suppose a tuple t is updated in T_i. Let v_O be a tuple in the cross-product of the top-level tables using the old value of tuple t from T_i, where v_O satisfies P so that $Proj(v_O, C_1, .., C_n)$ was in view V before the update. Let v_N be a tuple in the cross-product of the top-level tables using the new value of tuple t from T_i, where v_N satisfies P so that $Proj(v_N, C_1, .., C_n)$ is in V after the update. Finally, let v be a tuple in the cross-product of the top-level tables not using t, where v satisfies P so v is in V both before and after the update. Then $Proj(v_O, C_1, .., C_n) \neq Proj(v, C_1, .., C_n)$ and $Proj(v_N, C_1, .., C_n) \neq Proj(v, C_1, .., C_n)$. □

5.4 Rule Generation

We describe how maintenance rules are generated for the top-level tables. We first consider safe table references, then unsafe references. Initially, for each table reference we generate four rules—one triggered by **inserted**, one by **deleted**, and two by **updated**. Subsequently we explain how some rules can be combined and how the entire rule set is ordered.

Let T_i be a safe top-level table reference in view V defined as above. If tuples are inserted into T_i, then we want to insert into V those tuples produced by the view definition using **inserted Ti** instead of **Ti** in the top-level table list. By Theorem 5.5, these insertions cannot create duplicates in the view. However, if a similar rule is applied because tuples also were inserted into a different top-level table, then duplicates could appear. Hence, before inserting a new tuple, the rule must ensure that the tuple has not already been inserted by a different rule. This is checked efficiently using transition table **inserted V**. The rule for **inserted** is:

```
create rule ins-Ti-V
when inserted into Ti
then insert into V
        (select C1,..,Cn
         from T1,..,inserted Ti,..,Tm
         where P and <C1,..,Cn> not in inserted V)
```

If tuples are deleted from T_i, then we want to delete from V those tuples produced by the view definition using **deleted Ti** instead of **Ti** in the top-level table list. By Theorem 5.6, we know that these tuples should no longer be in the view. Again, however, we must remember that other tables in the top-level table list may have been modified. Hence, to identify the correct tuples to delete from V, we must consider the pre-transition value of all other tables, obtained using the **old** feature described in Section 3. For predicate P, let *P-old* denote P with all table references **T** replaced by **old T**. The rule for **deleted** is:

```
create rule del-Ti-V
when deleted from Ti
then delete from V
      where <C1,..,Cn> in
        (select C1,..,Cn
         from old T1,..,deleted Ti,..,old Tm
         where P-old)
```

As explained in Section 4.4, update operations on base tables always cause delete and/or insert operations on views. In fact, we generate two separate rules triggered by **updated**—one to perform deletions and the other to perform insertions. They are similar to the rules for **deleted** and **inserted**, and their correctness follows from Theorem 5.7:

```
create rule old-upd-Ti-V
when updated Ti
then delete from V
      where <C1,..,Cn> in
        (select C1,..,Cn
         from old T1,..,old updated Ti,..,old Tm
         where P-old)

create rule new-upd-Ti-V
when updated Ti
then insert into V
        (select C1,..,Cn
         from T1,..,new updated Ti,..,Tm
         where P and <C1,..,Cn> not in inserted V)
```

If a table appears more than once in the top-level table list, then rules are generated for each reference. Rules with identical triggering operations whose actions perform the same operation (either insert or delete) are merged into one rule by sequencing or combining their actions. Once the entire set of rules is generated (including those for nested table references, described below), they are ordered by adding **precedes** clauses so that all rules performing deletions precede all rules performing insertions.[8]

Now consider the case when a top-level table reference T_i is unsafe, so the properties guaranteed by the theorems may not hold. For insertions, incremental maintenance is still possible; the only difference from the safe case is that all new tuples must be checked against V itself to guarantee that duplicates are not produced. If V is indexed, this can be performed efficiently.

```
create rule ins-Ti-V
when inserted into Ti
then insert into V
        (select C1,..,Cn
         from T1,..,inserted Ti,..,Tm
         where P and <C1,..,Cn> not in V)
```

Delete and update operations are more difficult, and this is where recomputation must occur. If a tuple is deleted from T_i, without Theorem 5.6 we cannot determine whether corresponding tuples should be deleted from V—those tuples still may be produced by other base table tuples that have not been deleted; a similar problem occurs with update. The only solution is to reevaluate the view expression itself. Since this is equivalent to rematerializing the view, we choose to create a single distinguished rule that performs rematerialization. This rule will be triggered by all operations for which efficient maintenance is impossible. (As mentioned above, if these operations are expected to occur frequently, then materialization may be inappropriate for this view.) The rematerialization rule with triggering operations for T_i is:

```
create rule rematerialize-V
when deleted from Ti,
     updated Ti
then delete from V;
     insert into V
       (select C1,..,Cn from T1,..,Tm where P);
     deactivate-rules(V)
```

This rule will have precedence over all other rules for V. Since execution of the first two rule actions entirely rematerializes V, the rule's final action, **deactivate-rules(V)**, deactivates all other rules for V until the next rule assertion point.[9] Note that when a triggering operation appears in the rematerialization rule, any other rules triggered by that operation can be eliminated.

5.5 Examples

We draw examples from a simple airline reservations database with the following schema:

```
flight (FLIGHT-ID, flight-no, date)
res (RES-ID, psgr-id, flight-id, seat)
psgr (PSGR-ID, name, phone, meal, ffn)
ff (FFN, miles)
```

Most of the schema is self-explanatory, with **res** denoting reservation, **ff** denoting frequent flier, and **ffn** denoting frequent flier number. Primary keys for each table are capitalized; other keys are **<flight-no,date>** for table **flight**, **<psgr-id,flight-id>** or **<flight-id, seat>** for table **res**, and **ffn** for table **psgr**.

Consider the following view, which provides the seat numbers and meal preferences of all passengers on a given flight (**FID**) who have ordered special meals:

```
define view special-meals(seat, meal):
  select res.seat, psgr.meal
  from res, psgr
  where res.flight-id = FID
  and res.psgr-id = psgr.psgr-id
  and psgr.meal != null
```

Using Definition 5.1, we determine that the bound columns of top-level table references **res** and **psgr** are: projected columns **res.seat** and **psgr.meal**, column **res.flight-id** since it is equated to a constant in the predicate, all remaining columns of **res** since **<flight-id,seat>** is a key, and **psgr.psgr-id** since it is equated to bound column **res.psgr-id**. Since the bound columns include keys for both top-level tables, the view will not contain duplicates, and incremental maintenance rules can be generated for both tables. The rules triggered by operations on table **res** are given here; the rules for table **psgr** are similar:

```
create rule ins-res-special-meals
when inserted into res
then insert into special-meals
       (select res.seat, psgr.meal
        from inserted res, psgr
        where res.flight-id = FID
        and res.psgr-id = psgr.psgr-id
        and psgr.meal != null
        and <seat,meal> not in
              inserted special-meals)

create rule del-res-special-meals
when deleted from res
then delete from special-meals
     where <seat,meal> in
       (select res.seat, psgr.meal
        from deleted res, old psgr
        where res.flight-id = FID
        and res.psgr-id = psgr.psgr-id
        and psgr.meal != null)

create rule old-upd-res-special-meals
when updated res
then delete from special-meals
where <seat,meal> in
        (select res.seat, psgr.meal
         from old updated res, old psgr
         where res.flight-id = FID
         and res.psgr-id = psgr.psgr-id
         and psgr.meal != null)
```

[8] This is why we merge only rules with the same action operation and why we create two separate rules for **updated**—for ordering, we cannot generate rule actions that perform both deletions and insertions.

[9] This feature is not included in the current rule system but can easily be simulated using rule conditions; see [Wid91]. We intend to add this feature in the near future.

```
create rule new-upd-res-special-meals
when updated res
then insert into special-meals
       (select res.seat, psgr.meal
        from new updated res, psgr
        where res.flight-id = FID
        and res.psgr-id = psgr.psgr-id
        and psgr.meal != null
        and <seat,meal> not in
              inserted special-meals)
```

As a second example, consider the following view, which provides the frequent flier numbers of all passengers currently holding reservations:

```
define view ff-res(ffn):
  select psgr.ffn
  from psgr, res
  where psgr.psgr-id = res.psgr-id
```

The bound columns are all columns of table psgr (since ffn is a key) and column res.psgr-id. Since the bound columns do not include a key for table res, the view may contain duplicates, and **distinct** must be added. Table reference psgr is safe, so the rules for operations on psgr are similar to those in the previous example. Table reference res is unsafe, however, so the following rules are generated:

```
create rule ins-res-ff-res
when inserted into res
then insert into ff-res
       (select distinct psgr.ffn
        from psgr, inserted res
        where psgr.psgr-id = res.psgr-id
        and ffn not in ff-res)

create rule rematerialize-ff-res
when deleted from res,
        updated res
then delete from ff-res;
        insert into ff-res
          (select distinct psgr.ffn from psgr, res
           where psgr.psgr-id = res.psgr-id);
        deactivate-rules(ff-res)
```

6 Positively Nested Subqueries

A *positively nested* subquery is a nested **select** expression preceded by **exists**, **in**, or *Comp* **any**, where *Comp* is any comparison operator except !=. We first describe safety analysis and rule generation for table references in **exists** subqueries. Similar methods apply for the other positively nested subqueries and are explained in Section 6.3. Consider a view V as follows, where $N_1, .., N_l$ are the table references under consideration:

> define view V(*Col-List*):
> select $C_1, .., C_n$ from $T_1, .., T_m$
> where P' and exists
> (select *Cols* from $N_1, .., N_l$ where P)

6.1 Bound Columns and Safety Analysis

To analyze nested table references we introduce the concept of columns that are *bound by correlation* to the bound columns of the top-level tables. We assume that set $B(V)$ of top-level bound columns already has been computed. Correlated bound columns are denoted $C(V)$, and for **exists** they are computed as follows:

Definition 6.1 (Correlated Bound Columns for Exists)

1. Initialize $C(V)$ to contain all columns of $N_1, .., N_l$ such that predicate P includes an equality comparison between the column and a column in $B(V)$.
2. Add to $C(V)$ all columns of $N_1, .., N_l$ such that predicate P includes an equality comparison between the column and a constant.
3. Repeat until $C(V)$ is unchanged:
   (a) Add to $C(V)$ all columns of $N_1, .., N_l$ such that predicate P includes an equality comparison between the column and a column in $C(V)$.
   (b) Add to $C(V)$ all columns of any table N_i, $1 \leq i \leq l$, if $C(V)$ includes a key for N_i. □

Correlated bound columns for **exists** guarantee the following property:

Lemma 6.2 (Bound Columns Lemma for Exists) Consider four tuples, t_1 and t_2 in the cross-product of $T_1, .., T_m$ and n_1 and n_2 in the cross-product of $N_1, .., N_l$, such that t_1 and t_2 satisfy predicate P', n_1 satisfies nested predicate P using t_1 for the top-level cross-product, and n_2 satisfies P using t_2 for the top-level cross-product. Let $D_1, .., D_k$ be columns of $N_1, .., N_l$ in $C(V)$ such that n_1 and n_2 are guaranteed to differ in $D_1, .., D_k$, i.e. $Proj(n_1, D_1, .., D_k) \neq Proj(n_2, D_1, .., D_k)$. Then t_1 and t_2 are guaranteed to differ in $C_1, .., C_n$, i.e. $Proj(t_1, C_1, .., C_n) \neq Proj(t_2, C_1, .., C_n)$.

Proof: Suppose, for the sake of a contradiction, that $Proj(t_1, C_1, .., C_n) = Proj(t_2, C_1, .., C_n)$. By supposition there is some D_i in $D_1, .., D_k$ such that $Proj(n_1, D_i) \neq Proj(n_2, D_i)$. D_i is in $C(V)$, so by the recursive definitions of $C(V)$ and $B(V)$, since t_1 and t_2 satisfy P', and since n_1 with t_1 and n_2 with t_2 both satisfy predicate P, the value of column D_i in both n_1 and n_2 must either

1. satisfy an equality with a constant k, or
2. satisfy an equality with a column C_j in $C_1, .., C_n$, or
3. be functionally dependent on a constant k or column C_j.

As in Bound Columns Lemma 5.2, in all cases $Proj(n_1, D_i) = Proj(n_2, D_i)$. □

Safety analysis and rule generation for positively nested subqueries is similar to top-level tables:

Definition 6.3 (Safety of Table References for Exists) Table reference N_i in an **exists** subquery is *safe* in V if $C(V)$ includes a key for N_i. □

The following three theorems show that if N_i is safe, then insert, delete, and update operations on N_i can be reflected by incremental changes to V. We include a proof for the insertion theorem only; the other proofs follow by analogy.

Theorem 6.4 (Insertion Theorem for Exists) Let N_i be a safe table reference in an **exists** subquery in V and suppose a tuple n_i is inserted into N_i. Let v be a tuple in the cross-product of the top-level tables such that v satisfies P' and there is a tuple n in the cross-product of the nested tables using n_i such that n satisfies P using v, so $Proj(v, C_1,..,C_n)$ is in view V after the insertion. Then $Proj(v, C_1,..,C_n)$ was not in V before the insertion.

Proof: Suppose, for the sake of a contradiction, that $Proj(v, C_1,..,C_n)$ was in V before the insertion. Then there must have been a tuple n' in the cross-product of the nested tables before the insertion and a tuple v' in the top-level cross-product such that $Proj(v', C_1,..,C_n) = Proj(v, C_1,..,C_n)$, v' satisfies P', and n' satisfies P using v'. Let $D_1,..,D_k$ be correlated bound columns of $N_1,..,N_l$ such that $D_1,..,D_k$ includes a key for N_i. Since n and n' use different tuples from N_i, $Proj(n, D_1,..,D_k) \neq Proj(n', D_1,..,C_k)$. Then, by Lemma 6.2, $Proj(v', C_1,..,C_n) \neq Proj(v, C_1,..,C_n)$. □

Theorem 6.5 (Deletion Theorem for Exists) Let N_i be a safe table reference in an **exists** subquery in V and suppose a tuple n_i is deleted from N_i. Let v be a tuple in the cross-product of the top-level tables such that v satisfies P' and there is a tuple n in the cross-product of the nested tables using n_i such that n satisfies P using v, so $Proj(v, C_1,..,C_n)$ was in view V before the deletion. Then $Proj(v, C_1,..,C_n)$ is not in V after the deletion. □

Theorem 6.6 (Update Theorem for Exists) Let N_i be a safe table reference in an **exists** subquery in V and suppose a tuple n_i is updated in N_i. Let v_O be a tuple in the cross-product of the top-level tables such that v_O satisfies P' and there is a tuple n_O in the cross-product of the nested tables using the old value of n_i such that n_O satisfies P using v_O, so $Proj(v_O, C_1,..,C_n)$ was in view V before the update. Let v_N be a tuple in the cross-product of the top-level tables such that v_N satisfies P' and there is a tuple n_N in the cross-product of the nested tables using the new value of n_i such that n_N satisfies P using v_N, so $Proj(v_N, C_1,..,C_n)$ is in V after the update. If $Proj(v_O, C_1,..,C_n) \neq Proj(v_N, C_1,..,C_n)$, then $Proj(v_O, C_1,..,C_n)$ is not in V after the update and $Proj(v_N, C_1,..,C_n)$ was not in V before the update. □

6.2 Rule Generation

First consider safe table references. The properties guaranteed by Theorems 6.4–6.6 allow incremental maintenance to be performed just as for safe top-level table references: N_i is replaced by **inserted Ni** in the **inserted** rule, by **deleted Ni** in the **deleted** rule, and by **old updated Ni** and **new updated Ni** in the two **updated** rules. In the rules that perform insertions, we must check that tuples have not already been inserted by another rule; in the rules that perform deletions we must use the **old** value of other tables. If a table appears more than once in $N_1,..,N_l$, or if a table in $N_1,..,N_l$ also appears elsewhere in the view definition, then rules are merged as previously described. Unsafe table references also are handled similarly to top-level tables: If nested table reference N_i is unsafe, triggering operations **deleted from Ni** and **updated Ni** are included in the distinguished rematerialization rule for V. The **inserted** rule is similar to the safe rule, except "**not in V**" is added to the predicate rather than "**not in inserted V**".

6.3 Other Positively Nested Subqueries

Safety analysis and rule generation for subqueries preceded by **< any**, **<= any**, **> any**, and **>= any** is identical to **exists**. The method for **= any** and **in** (which are equivalent) also is identical to **exists**, except the set of correlated bound columns may be larger. Consider a view V of the form:

> **define view** V(*Col-List*):
> **select** $C_1,..,C_n$ **from** $T_1,..,T_m$
> **where** P' **and** $\langle D_1,..,D_j \rangle$ **in**
> (select $E_1,..,E_j$ **from** $N_1,..,N_l$ **where** P)

Definition 6.1 of correlated bound columns is modified to include the case:

- Add to $C(V)$ every column E_i such that corresponding column D_i is in $B(V)$, $1 \leq i \leq j$.

The reader may note that view V above is equivalent to view V':

> **define view** V'(*Col-List*):
> **select** $C_1,..,C_n$ **from** $T_1,..,T_m$
> **where** P' **and exists**
> (**select** * **from** $N_1,..,N_l$ **where** P
> **and** $D_1 = E_1$ **and** ... **and** $D_j = E_j$)

As expected, the correlated bound columns of view V' using Definition 6.1 for **exists** are equivalent to the correlated bound columns of V using the extended definition for **in**.[10]

6.4 Example

Using the airline reservations database introduced in Section 5.5, the following view provides the ID's of all passengers with more than 50,000 frequent flier miles:

```
define view many-miles(id):
  select psgr-id from psgr
  where psgr.ffn in
    (select ffn from ff where miles > 50,000)
```

All columns of top-level table **psgr** are bound since psgr-id is a key. Using our extended definition for **in**, ff.ffn is a correlated bound column. Since **ffn** is a key, nested table reference **ff** is safe. The **inserted** and **deleted** rules for table **ff** follow; the **updated** rules are similar.

[10] The reader may also note that select expressions with positive subqueries often can be transformed into equivalent select expressions without subqueries, as in [CG85,Kim82]. By considering the actual transformations, we see that the maintenance rules produced for any transformed view are equivalent to the maintenance rules produced for the original view.

```
create rule ins-ff-many-miles
when inserted into ff
then insert into many-miles
       (select psgr-id from psgr
        where psgr.ffn in
          (select ffn from inserted ff
           where miles > 50,000)
        and psgr-id not in inserted many-miles)

create rule del-ff-many-miles
when deleted from ff
then delete from many-miles
      where psgr-id in
              (select psgr-id from old psgr
               where psgr.ffn in
                 (select ffn from deleted ff
                  where miles > 50,000))
```

7 Negatively Nested Subqueries

A *negatively nested* subquery is a nested **select** expression preceded by **not exists**, **not in**, or **!=any**. We describe safety analysis and rule generation for table references in **not exists** subqueries. Similar methods apply for the other negatively nested subqueries; see [CW91]. Consider a view V of the form:

> **define view** V(*Col-List*):
> **select** $C_1, .., C_n$ **from** $T_1, .., T_m$
> **where** P' **and not exists**
> (**select** *Cols* **from** $N_1, .., N_l$ **where** P)

With negatively nested subqueries, insert operations on nested tables result in delete operations on the view, while delete operations on nested tables result in insert operations on the view.

7.1 Safety Analysis

For a negatively nested table reference N_i, we define two notions of safety: *I-safety* indicates that insert operations on N_i can be reflected by incremental changes to V, and *DU-safety* indicates that delete and update operations on N_i can be reflected by incremental changes to V. The definition of I-safety is somewhat different from previous safety definitions—correlated bound columns are not used, and all nested table references are considered together. Assume that set $B(V)$ of top-level bound columns already has been computed.

Definition 7.1 (I-Safety of Table References for Not Exists) Table references $N_1, .., N_l$ in a **not exists** subquery are *I-safe* in V if predicate P refers only to columns of N_i, $1 \leq i \leq l$, columns in $B(V)$, and constants. □

Using this notion of safety, we prove the following theorem for insertions:

Theorem 7.2 (Insertion Theorem for Not Exists) Let N_i be an I-safe table reference in a **not exists** subquery in V and suppose a tuple n_i is inserted into N_i. Let v be a tuple in the cross-product of the top-level tables such that v satisfies top-level predicate P' and there is a tuple n in the cross-product of the nested tables using n_i such that n satisfies nested predicate P using v. Then $Proj(v, C_1, .., C_n)$ is not in V after the insertion.

Proof: Suppose, for the sake of a contradiction, that $Proj(v, C_1, .., C_n)$ is in V after the insertion. Then there must be a tuple v' other than v in the cross-product of the top-level tables such that $Proj(v', C_1, .., C_n) = Proj(v, C_1, .., C_n)$, v' satisfies P', and there is no tuple n' in the cross-product of the nested tables such that n' satisfies P using v'. We show that there is such an n', namely n. By Definition 5.1 of $B(V)$, since v and v' both satisfy P' and $Proj(v', C_1, .., C_n) = Proj(v, C_1, .., C_n)$, v and v' are equivalent in all columns of $B(V)$. Since N_i is I-safe and since n satisfies P using v, by Definition 7.1 of safety, n also satisfies P using v'. □

For deletes and updates, we combine our new notion of I-safety with the previous notion of safety using keys. Correlated bound columns for negatively nested table references are defined as for positive references (Definition 6.1), and Bound Columns Lemma 6.2 still holds.

Definition 7.3 (DU-Safety of Table References for Not Exists) Table reference N_i in a **not exists** subquery is *DU-safe* in V if it is I-safe and $C(V)$ includes a key for N_i. □

Theorem 7.4 (Deletion Theorem for Not Exists) Let N_i be a DU-safe table reference in a **not exists** subquery in V and suppose a tuple n_i is deleted from N_i. Let v be a tuple in the cross-product of the top-level tables such that v satisfies P' and there is a tuple n in the cross-product of the nested tables using n_i such that n satisfies P using v. Then: (1) $Proj(v, C_1, .., C_n)$ was not in V before the deletion. (2) $Proj(v, C_1, .., C_n)$ is in V after the deletion.

Proof: The proof of (1) is analogous to the proof of Insertion Theorem 7.2. For (2), suppose, for the sake of a contradiction, that $Proj(v, C_1, .., C_n)$ is not in V after the deletion. Then there must be a tuple n' in the cross-product of the nested tables such that n' satisfies P using v. Let $D_1, .., D_k$ be correlated bound columns of $N_1, .., N_l$ such that $D_1, .., D_k$ includes a key for N_i. Since n and n' use different tuples from N_i, $Proj(n, D_1, .., D_k) \neq Proj(n', D_1, .., C_k)$. Then, by Lemma 6.2, $Proj(v, C_1, .., C_n) \neq Proj(v, C_1, .., C_n)$, which is impossible. □

Theorem 7.5 (Update Theorem for Not Exists) Let N_i be a DU-safe table reference in a **not exists** subquery in V and suppose a tuple n_i is updated in N_i. Let v_O be a tuple in the cross-product of the top-level tables such that v_O satisfies P' and there is a tuple n_O in the cross-product of the nested tables using the old value of n_i such that n_O satisfies P using v. Let v_N be a tuple in the cross-product of the top-level tables such that v_N satisfies P' and there is a tuple n_N in the cross-product of the nested tables using the new value of n_i such that n_N satisfies P using v. If $Proj(v_O, C_1, .., C_n) \neq Proj(v_N, C_1, .., C_n)$ then: (1) $Proj(v_N, C_1, .., C_n)$ is not in V after the update. (2) $Proj(v_O, C_1, .., C_n)$ was not in V before the update. (3) $Proj(v_O, C_1, .., C_n)$ is in V after the update.

Proof: Analogous to Theorems 7.2 and 7.4. □

7.2 Rule Generation

If nested table reference N_i is I-safe, then, using Theorem 7.2, the following incremental rule is generated:

```
create rule ins-Ni-V
when inserted into Ni
then delete from V
     where <C1,..,Cn> in
        (select C1,..,Cn from T1,..,Tm
         where P' and exists
           (select Cols
            from N1,..,inserted Ni,..,Nl
            where P))
```

Notice that the subquery's "not exists" is converted to "exists"; this conversion occurs in the **deleted** and **updated** rules as well. If N_i is not I-safe, then the view expression would need to be reevaluated to determine which tuples should be deleted. Hence in the unsafe case, **inserted into Ni** is included in the rematerialization rule for V.

If N_i is DU-safe, then, using Theorems 7.4 and 7.5, the following incremental rule for **deleted** is generated. The rules for **updated** correspond to the **inserted** and **deleted** rules as previously.

```
create rule del-Ni-V
when deleted from Ni
then insert into V
        (select C1,..,Cn from T1,..,Tm
         where P' and exists
           (select Cols
            from old N1,..,deleted Ni,..,old Nl
            where P)
         and <C1,..Cn> not in inserted V)
```

If table reference N_i is not DU-safe, **updated Ti** is included in the rematerialization rule for V. For **deleted**, however, incremental maintenance still can be performed—as previously, for the unsafe case the rule above is modified to use "not in V" rather than "not in inserted V".

7.3 Example

Using the airline reservations database introduced in Section 5.5, the following view provides the ID's of all reservations whose flight-id is not in table flight:

```
define view bad-flight(res-id):
  select res-id from res
  where not exists
    (select * from flight
     where flight.flight-id = res.flight-id)
```

By Definitions 7.1 and 7.3, nested table reference flight is both I-safe and DU-safe. The **inserted** and **deleted** rules for table flight follow; the **updated** rules are similar.

```
create rule ins-flight-bad-flight
when inserted into flight
then delete from bad-flight
     where res-id in
        (select res-id from res
         where exists
           (select * from inserted flight
            where flight.flight-id =
                  res.flight-id))

create rule del-flight-bad-flight
when deleted from flight
then insert into bad-flight
        (select res-id from res
         where exists
           (select * from deleted flight
            where flight.flight-id =
                  res.flight-id)
         and res-id not in inserted bad-flight)
```

8 Set Operators

Finally, consider views with *set operators*. A view definition may include either **union distinct** or **intersect**. For these views, view analysis and rule generation initially is performed independently on each component **select** expression. The rules are then modified to incorporate the set operators.

8.1 Union Views

Consider a view V of the form:

> **define view** V(*Col-List*):
> **select** $Cols_1$ **from** $Tables_1$ **where** P_1
> **union distinct** ...
> **union distinct select** $Cols_k$ **from** $Tables_k$ **where** P_k

First, duplicate analysis is performed on each **select** expression as in Section 5.2; if any **select** expression may contain duplicates, the user is required to add **distinct** to that **select** expression. For each **select** expression, an initial set of view-maintaining rules is generated using the methods of the preceding sections. The rules' actions are then modified to incorporate **union**. In actions that perform **insert** operations, if "not in inserted V" has been added to predicate P_i due to a safe table reference, it is changed to "not in V"; this ensures that duplicates are not added by different **select** expressions. If the rule already includes "not in V" due to an unsafe table reference, it remains unchanged. Modifications for **delete** operations are more complicated. If a tuple no longer is produced by one of the **select** expressions, it should be deleted from V only if it is not produced by any of the other **select** expressions. Without loss of generality, consider a **delete** operation in the action of a rule generated from the first **select** expression in V. The following conjunct must be added to the **delete** operation's **where** clause:

```
and <Cols> not in
      (select Cols2 from Tables2 where P2)
and ...
and <Cols> not in
      (select Colsk from Tablesk where Pk)
```

Clearly, such conjuncts may cause considerable recomputation, depending on the complexity of the **select** expressions. For rules in which the recomputation cost appears large, the user may choose to move the triggering operation to the rematerialization rule for V.

As usual, rules with common triggering and action operations are merged, and rules whose triggering operations also appear in the rematerialization rule are eliminated.

8.2 Intersect Views

A view V with **intersect** operators is handled similarly to views with **union** operators. In rule modification, however, all rules performing **delete** operations remain unchanged. (If a tuple is deleted from any **select** expression, then it always should be deleted from V.) Modifications for **insert** operations are similar to the modifications for **delete** operations in **union** views: If a tuple is newly produced by one of the **select** expressions, it should be inserted into V only if it also is produced by all the other **select** expressions. Consider an **insert** operation in the action of a rule generated from the first **select** expression in V. The following conjunct must be added to the **where** clause of the **insert** operation's **select** expression:

```
and <Cols> in
      (select Cols2 from Tables2 where P2)
and ...
and <Cols> in
      (select Colsk from Tablesk where Pk)
```

Again, if the **select** expressions are sufficiently complex, the user may decide that rematerialization is more appropriate.

9 System Execution

So far, we have described only the compile-time aspects of our facility. View definition, view analysis, and rule generation all occur prior to database system execution. We still must ensure that, at run-time, derived rules will behave as desired, i.e., views will be maintained correctly. Suppose our facility has been used to derive sets of maintenance rules for several views. The system orders the set of rules for each view so that all **delete** operations in rule actions precede all **insert** operations. No ordering is necessary between rules for different views—the action part of each rule modifies only the view itself, so rules for different views have no effect on each other.

Consider the set of rules for a given view V, and suppose an arbitrary set of changes has been made to V's base tables. If the rematerialization rule for V is triggered, the view certainly is maintained correctly: V is recomputed from its base tables; all other rules for V are deactivated, so V cannot be modified until the base tables change again. Suppose the rematerialization rule is not triggered. During rule processing, first some rules delete tuples from V, then other rules insert tuples into V. Consider the deletions. For each type of table reference, our theorems guarantee that the generated **delete** operations never delete tuples that should remain in V. Furthermore, these operations always delete all tuples that should no longer be in V. Consider the insertions. First, notice that all generated **insert** operations use nested **select** expressions based on the view definition itself. Since we know the view definition cannot produce duplicates, the set of tuples in **insert** operations never includes duplicates. Furthermore, our theorems (along with the "`not in inserted V`" clauses) guarantee that tuples already in V are never inserted. Finally, in each case the **insert** operations produce all tuples that should be added to V.

We must consider that other production rules in addition to view-maintaining rules may be defined in the system. Although these rules cannot modify views, they can modify base tables. Our view-maintaining rules behave correctly even in the presence of other rules, and no additional rule ordering is necessary. Recall the semantics of rule execution (Section 3): a rule is considered with respect to the transition since the last time its action was executed; if its action has not yet been executed, it is considered with respect to the transition since the last rule assertion point (or start of the transaction). Hence, the first time a view-maintaining rule R is triggered during rule processing, it processes all base table changes since the last assertion point. Suppose that, subsequently during rule processing, the base tables are changed by a non-view-maintaining rule. Then R will be triggered again and will modify the view according to the new set of changes. When rule processing terminates, no rules are triggered, so all view-maintaining rules will have processed all relevant changes to base tables.

10 Conclusions and Future Work

We have described a facility that automatically derives a set of production rules to maintain a materialization of a user-defined view. This approach both frees the view definer from handling view maintenance and guarantees that the view remains correct. Through analysis techniques based on key information, incremental maintenance rules are generated whenever possible. Our facility allows the user to interact with the system: view definitions and key information can be modified to guarantee that the system produces efficient maintenance rules for frequent base table operations. In practice, efficient rules are possible for a wide class of views—efficiency relies on safe table references, and it can be seen from our criteria for safety that table references routinely fall into this class. In those cases where efficiency is not possible for the user's desired view, our system provides recognition of this fact; the user either may use the rules produced for automatic rematerialization or may decide that query modification is more appropriate.

We plan to implement our facility using the Starburst Rule System, then conduct experiments to evaluate the run-time efficiency of our approach on a variety of views. Meanwhile, we want to extend view analysis and rule generation so that the full power of SQL **select** statements can be used in view definitions. (We have started this and expect it to be tedious but not difficult.) Currently, the biggest drawback of our approach is that views with duplicates are not handled; we will consider ways to remove this restriction. We would like to add automatic rule optimization as a post-rule-generation component in our system. The rules produced by our method have a standard form, and in some cases can be optimized as in [CW90]. In addition, rules for different views could be merged and common subexpressions could be exploited as in [Han87]. Finally, the properties guaranteed by our algorithms are useful in other areas (such as query optimization), and we intend to explore this connection.

Acknowledgements

Thanks to Guy Lohman and Laura Haas for helpful comments on an initial draft.

References

[ACL91] R. Agrawal, R.J. Cochrane, and B. Lindsay. On maintaining priorities in a production rule system. In *Proceedings of the Seventeenth International Conference on Very Large Data Bases*, Barcelona, Spain, September 1991.

[BLT86] J.A. Blakeley, P.-A. Larson, and F.W. Tompa. Efficiently updating materialized views. In *Proceedings of the ACM SIGMOD International Conference on Management of Data*, pages 61–71, Washington, D.C., June 1986.

[CG85] S. Ceri and G. Gottlob. Translating SQL into relational algebra: Optimization, semantics, and equivalence of SQL queries. *IEEE Transactions on Software Engineering*, 11(4):324–345, April 1985.

[CW90] S. Ceri and J. Widom. Deriving production rules for constraint maintenance. In *Proceedings of the Sixteenth International Conference on Very Large Data Bases*, pages 566–577, Brisbane, Australia, August 1990.

[CW91] S. Ceri and J. Widom. Deriving production rules for incremental view maintenance. IBM Research Report RJ 8027, IBM Almaden Research Center, March 1991.

[DE89] L.M.L. Delcambre and J.N. Etheredge. The Relational Production Language: A production language for relational databases. In L. Kerschberg, editor, *Expert Database Systems—Proceedings from the Second International Conference*, pages 333-351. Benjamin/Cummings, Redwood City, California, 1989.

[Han87] E. Hanson. *Efficient Support for Rules and Derived Objects in Relational Database Systems*. PhD thesis, University of California, Berkeley, August 1987.

[IBM88] IBM Form Number SC26-4348-1. *IBM Systems Application Architecture, Common Programming Interface: Database Reference*, October 1988.

[Kim82] W. Kim. On optimizing an SQL-like nested query. *ACM Transactions on Database Systems*, 7(3):443–469, September 1982.

[KP81] S. Koenig and R. Paige. A transformational framework for the automatic control of derived data. In *Proceedings of the Seventh International Conference on Very Large Data Bases*, pages 306–318, Cannes, France, September 1981.

[MD89] D.R. McCarthy and U. Dayal. The architecture of an active database management system. In *Proceedings of the ACM SIGMOD International Conference on Management of Data*, pages 215–224, Portland, Oregon, May 1989.

[RCBB89] A. Rosenthal, S. Chakravarthy, B. Blaustein, and J. Blakeley. Situation monitoring for active databases. In *Proceedings of the Fifteenth International Conference on Very Large Data Bases*, pages 455–464, Amsterdam, The Netherlands, August 1989.

[SI84] O. Shmueli and A. Itai. Maintenance of views. In *Proceedings of the ACM SIGMOD International Conference on Management of Data*, pages 240–255, Boston, Massachusetts, May 1984.

[SJGP90] M. Stonebraker, A. Jhingran, J. Goh, and S. Potamianos. On rules, procedures, caching and views in data base systems. In *Proceedings of the ACM SIGMOD International Conference on Management of Data*, pages 281–290, Atlantic City, New Jersey, May 1990.

[SP89] A. Segev and J. Park. Updating distributed materialized views. *IEEE Transactions on Knowledge and Data Engineering*, 1(2):173–184, June 1989.

[Sto75] M. Stonebraker. Implementation of integrity constraints and views by query modification. In *Proceedings of the ACM SIGMOD International Conference on Management of Data*, pages 65–78, San Jose, California, May 1975.

[WCL91] J. Widom, R.J. Cochrane, and B.G. Lindsay. Implementing set-oriented production rules as an extension to Starburst. In *Proceedings of the Seventeenth International Conference on Very Large Data Bases*, Barcelona, Spain, September 1991.

[WF90] J. Widom and S.J. Finkelstein. Set-oriented production rules in relational database systems. In *Proceedings of the ACM SIGMOD International Conference on Management of Data*, pages 259–270, Atlantic City, New Jersey, May 1990.

[Wid91] J. Widom. Deduction in the Starburst production rule system. *Submitted for publication*, 1991.

Data Mining and Knowledge Discovery, 12, 281–314, 2000

Informix under CONTROL: Online Query Processing

JOSEPH M. HELLERSTEIN jmh@cs.berkeley.edu
RON AVNUR ronathan@cs.berkeley.edu
VIJAYSHANKAR RAMAN rshankar@cs.berkeley.edu
Computer Science Division, U.C. Berkeley, USA

Editors: Fayyad, Mannila, Ramakrishnan

Abstract. The goal of the CONTROL project at Berkeley is to develop systems for interactive analysis of large data sets. We focus on systems that provide users with iteratively refining answers to requests and online control of processing, thereby tightening the loop in the data analysis process. This paper presents the database-centric subproject of CONTROL: a complete *online* query processing facility, implemented in a commercial Object-Relational DBMS from Informix. We describe the algorithms at the core of the system, and detail the end-to-end issues required to bring the algorithms together and deliver a complete system.

Keywords: online query processing, interactive, informix, control, data analysis, ripple joins, online reordering

1. Introduction

Of all men's miseries, the bitterest is this: to know so much and have control over nothing.
–Herodotus

Data analysis is a complex task. Many tools can been brought to bear on the problem, from user-driven SQL and OLAP systems, to machine-automated data mining algorithms, with hybrid approaches in between. All the solutions on this spectrum share a basic property: analyzing large amounts of data is a time-consuming task. Decision-support SQL queries often run for hours or days before producing output; so do data mining algorithms (Agrawal, 1997). It has recently been observed that user appetite for online data storage is growing faster than what Moore's Law predicts for the growth in hardware performance (Papadopoulos, 1997; Winter and Auerbach, 1998), suggesting that the inherent sluggishness of data analysis will only worsen over time.

In addition to slow performance, non-trivial data analysis techniques share a second common property: they require thoughtful deployment by skilled users. It is well-known that composing SQL queries requires sophistication, and it is not unusual today to see an SQL query spanning dozens of pages (Walter, 1998). Even for users of graphical front-end tools, generating the correct query for a task is very difficult. Perhaps less well-appreciated is the end-user challenge of deploying the many data mining algorithms that have been developed. While data mining algorithms are typically free of complex input languages, using them effectively depends on a judicious choice of algorithm, and on the careful tuning of various algorithm-specific parameters (Fayyad, 1996).

A third common property of data analysis is that it is a multi-step process. Users are unlikely to be able to issue a single, perfectly chosen query that extracts the "desired information" from a database; indeed the idea behind data analysis is to extract heretofore unknown information. User studies have found that information seekers very naturally work in an iterative fashion, starting by asking broad questions, and continually refining them based on feedback and domain knowledge (O'day and Jeffries, 1993). This iteration of analyses is a natural human mode of interaction, and not clearly an artifact of current software, interfaces, or languages.

Taken together, these three properties result in a near-pessimal human-computer interaction: data analysis today is a complex process involving multiple time-consuming steps. A poor choice or erroneous query at a given step is not caught until the end of the step when results are available. The long delay and absolute lack of control between successive queries disrupts the concentration of the user and hampers the process of data analysis. Therefore many users eschew sophisticated techniques in favor of cookie-cutter reports, significantly limiting the impact of new data analysis technologies. In short, the mode of human-computer interaction during data analysis is fundamentally flawed.

1.1. CONTROL: Interactive data analysis

The CONTROL[1] project attempts to improve the interaction between users and computers during data analysis. Traditional tools present *black box* interfaces: users provide inputs, the system processes silently for a significant period, and returns outputs. Because of the long processing times, this interaction is reminiscent of the *batch* processing of the 1960's and '70's. By contrast, CONTROL systems have an *online* mode of interaction: users can control the system at all times, and the system continuously provides useful output in the form of approximate or partial results. Rather than a black box, online systems are intended to operate like a *crystal ball*: the user "sees into" the online processing, is given a glimpse of the final results, and can use that information to change the results by changing the processing. This significantly tightens the loop for asking multiple questions: users can quickly sense if their question is a useful one, and can either refine or halt processing if the question was not well-formed. We describe a variety of interactive online systems in Section 2.

Though the CONTROL project's charter was to solve interface problems, we quickly realized that the solutions would involve fundamental shifts in system performance goals (Hellerstein, 1997). Traditional algorithms are optimized to complete as quickly as possible. By contrast, online data analysis techniques may never complete; users halt them when answers are "good enough". So instead of optimizing for completion time, CONTROL systems must balance two typically conflicting performance goals: minimizing uneventful "dead time" between updates for the user, while simultaneously maximizing the rate at which partial or approximate answers approach a correct answer. Optimizing only one of these goals is relatively easy: traditional systems optimize the second goal (they quickly achieve a correct answer) by pessimizing the first goal (they provide no interactivity). Achieving both goals simultaneously requires redesigning major portions of a data analysis system, employing a judicious mix of techniques from data delivery, query processing, statistical estimation and user interfaces. As we will see, these techniques can interact in non-trivial ways.

1.2. Online query processing in informix

In this paper we focus on systems issues for implementing online query processing—i.e., CONTROL for SQL queries. Online query processing enables a user to issue an SQL query, see results immediately, and adjust the processing as the query runs. In the case of an online *aggregation* query, the user sees refining estimates of the final aggregation results. In the case of an online *enumeration* query (i.e., a query with no aggregation), the user receives an ever-growing collection of result records, which are available for browsing via user interface tools. In both cases, users should be able to provide feedback to the system while the query is running, to control the flow of estimates or records. A common form of control is to terminate delivery of certain classes of estimates or records; more generally, users might express a preference for certain classes of estimates or records over others.

Online query processing algorithms are designed to produce a steady stream of output records, which typically serve as input to statistical estimators and/or intelligent user interfaces. Our discussion here focuses mostly on the pipelined production of records and the control of that data flow; statistical and interface issues are considered in this paper only to the extent that they drive the performance goals, or interact with implementation issues. The interested reader is referred to Section 1.4 for citations on the statistical and interface aspects of online query processing.

As a concrete point of reference, we describe our experience implementing online query processing in a commercial object-relational database management system (DBMS): Informix's Dynamic Server with Universal Data Option (UDO) (Informix, 1998). The pedigree of UDO is interesting: formerly known as Informix Universal Server, it represents the integration of Informix's original high-performance relational database engine with the object-relational facilities of Illustra (Illustra, 1994), which in turn was the commercialization of the Postgres research system (Stonebraker and Kemnitz, 1991). Informix Corporation made its source code and development environment available to us for this research, enabling us to test our ideas within a complete SQL database engine.

Working with UDO represented a significant challenge and opportunity. UDO is a large and complex system developed (in its various ancestral projects) over more than 15 years. As we describe in Hellerstein et al. (1997), online query processing cannot simply be implemented as a "plug-in" module for an existing system. Most of the work described in this paper involved adding significant new features to the UDO database engine itself. In a few cases—particularly in crafting an API for standard client applications—we were able to leverage the object-relational extensibility of UDO to our advantage, as we describe below.

In addition to adding new algorithms to the system, a significant amount of effort went into architecting a complete end-to-end implementation. Our implementation allows the various algorithms to be pipelined into complex query plans, and interacts effectively with a wide variety of client tools. This paper describes both the core algorithms implemented in UDO, as well as the architectural issues required to provide a usable system.

1.3. Structure of the paper

We discuss related work in Section 1.4. In Section 2 we describe a number of application scenarios for CONTROL-based systems. Section 3 describes the core algorithms used in online query processing including access methods, data delivery algorithms, and join algorithms. Section 4 describes the end-to-end challenges of putting these algorithms together in the context of a commercial object-relational database management system. Section 5 demonstrates the performance of the system, in terms both of interactivity and rate of convergence to accurate answers. In Section 6 we conclude with a discussion of future work.

1.4. Related work

The CONTROL project began by studying online aggregation, which was motivated in (Hellerstein (1997a) and Hellerstein et al. (1997). The idea of online processing has been expanded upon within the project (Hellerstein, 1997b; Hellerstein, 1998a; Hellerstein et al., 1999; Hidber, 1997) a synopsis of these thrusts is given in Section 2. Recently we have presented the details of two of our core query processing algorithms: ripple joins (Haas and Hellerstein, 1999) and online reordering (Raman et al., 1999). Estimation and confidence interval techniques for online aggregation are presented in Haas (1996, 1997) and Haas and Hellerstein (1999). To our knowledge, the earliest work on approximate answers to decision-support queries appears in Morgenstein's dissertation from Berkeley (Morgenstein, 1980), in which he presents motivation quite similar to ours, along with proposed techniques for sampling from relations and from join results.

Our work on online aggregation builds upon earlier work on estimation and confidence intervals in the database context (Hou et al., 1988; Haas et al., 1996; Lipton et al., 1993). The prior work has been concerned with methods for producing a confidence interval with a width that is specified prior to the start of query processing (e.g. "get within 2% of the actual answer with 95% probability"). The underlying idea in most of these methods is to effectively maintain a running confidence interval (not displayed to the user) and stop sampling as soon as the length of this interval is sufficiently small. Hou, et al. (1989) consider the related problem of producing a confidence interval of minimal length, given a real-time stopping condition (e.g. "run for 5 minutes only"). The drawback with using sampling to produce approximate answers is that the end-user needs to understand the statistics. Moreover, making the user specify statistical stopping conditions at the beginning reduces the execution time but does not make the execution interactive; for instance there is no way to dynamically control the rate of processing—or the desired accuracy—for individual groups of records.

More recent work has focused on maintaining precomputed summary statistics for approximately answering queries (Gibbons and Matias, 1998; Gibbons et al., 1998); Olken also proposed the construction of sample views (Olken, 1993). In a similar though simpler vein, Informix has included simple precomputed samples for approximate results to ROLAP queries (Informix, 1998). These techniques are to online query processing what materialized views are to *ad hoc* queries: they enhance performance by precomputing results, but are inapplicable when users ask queries that cannot exploit the precomputed results. In the context of approximate query answers, *ad hoc* specification applies both to queries and to the stopping criteria for sampling: a user may specify any query, and want to see answers with differing accuracies. Unlike general materialized views, most precomputed summaries are on single tables, so many of the advantages of precomputed samples can be achieved in an online query processing system via simple buffer management techniques. In short, work on precomputed summaries is complementary to the techniques of this paper; it seems viable to automate the choice and construction of precomputed summaries as an aid to online query processing, much as Hybrid OLAP chooses queries to precompute to aid OLAP processing (Shukla et al., 1998; Harinarayan et al., 1996; Pilot Software, 1998; SQL, 1998).

A related but quite different notion of precomputation for online query processing involves semantically modeling data at multiple resolutions (Silberschatz et al., 1992). A version of this idea was implemented in a system called APPROXIMATE (Vrbsky and Liu, 1993). This system defines an approximate relational algebra which it uses to process standard relational queries in an iteratively refined manner. If a query is stopped before completion, a superset of the exact answer is returned in a combined extensional/intensional format. This model is different from the type of data browsing we address with online query processing: it is dependent on carefully designed metadata and does not address aggregation or statistical assessments of precision.

There has been some initial work on "fast-first" query processing, which attempts to quickly return the first few tuples of a query. Antoshenkov and Ziauddin report on the Oracle Rdb (formerly DEC Rdb/VMS) system, which addresses the issues of fast-first processing by running multiple query plans simultaneously; this intriguing architecture requires some unusual query processing support (Antoshenkov and Ziauddin, 1996). Bayardo and Miranker propose optimization and execution techniques for fast-first processing using nested-loops joins (Bayardo and Miranker, 1996). Carey and Kossman (1997, 1998), Chaudhuri and Gravano (1996, 1999), and Donjerkovic and Ramakrishnan (1999) discuss techniques for processing ranking and "top-N" queries, which have a "fast-first" flavor as well. Much of this work seems applicable to online query optimization, though integration with online query processing algorithms has yet to be considered. Fagin (1998) proposes an interesting algorithm for the execution of ranking queries over multiple sources that optimizes for early results. This algorithm has a similar flavor to the Ripple Join algorithm we discuss in Section 3.3.

2. Application scenarios and performance requirements

The majority of data analysis solutions are architected to provide black-box, batch behavior for large data sets: this includes software for the back-office (SQL decision-support systems), the desktop (spreadsheets and OLAP tools), and statistical analysis techniques (statistics packages and data mining). The result is that either the application is frustratingly slow (discouraging its use), or the user interface prevents the application from entering batch states (constraining its use.) The applications in this section are being handled by current tools with one or both of these approaches. In this section we describe online processing scenarios, including online aggregation and enumeration, and online visualization. We also briefly mention some ideas in online data mining.

2.1. Online aggregation

Aggregation queries in relational database systems often require scanning and analyzing a significant portion of a database. In current relational systems such query execution has batch behavior, requiring a long wait for the user. Online query processing can make aggregation an interactive process.

Consider the following simple relational query:

```
  SELECT college, AVG(grade)
    FROM enroll
GROUP BY college;
```

This query requests that all records in the `enroll` table be partitioned into groups by college, and then for each college its name and average grade should be returned. The output of this query in an online aggregation system can be a set of interfaces, one per output group, as in figure 1. For each output group, the user is given a current estimate of the final answer. In addition, a graph is drawn showing these estimates along with a description of their accuracy: each estimate is drawn with bars that depict a *confidence interval*, which says that

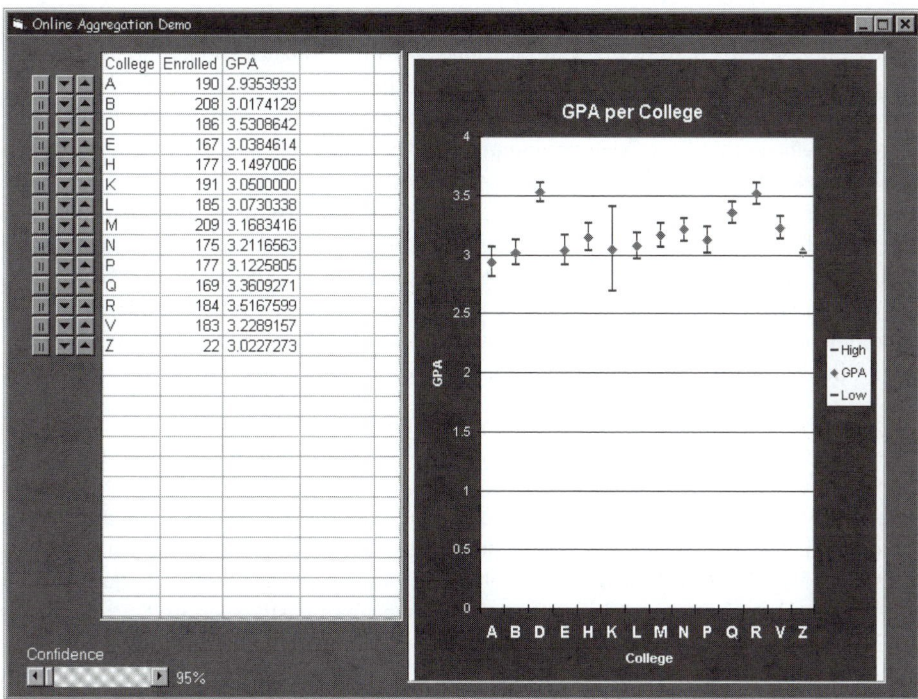

Figure 1. An online aggregation interface.

with $X\%$ probability, the current estimate is within an interval of $\pm\epsilon$ from the final answer (X is set to 95% in the figure). The "Confidence" slider on the lower left allows the user to control the percentage probability, which in turn affects the $2 \cdot \epsilon$ width of the bars. In addition, controls on the upper left of the screen are provided to stop processing on a group, or to speed up or slow down one group relative to others. These controls allow the user to devote more processing to groups of particular interest. These interfaces require the support of significant modifications to a DBMS, which we describe in this paper. We have developed estimators and corresponding implementation techniques for the standard SQL aggregates `AVG, COUNT,` and `STDDEV`[2] (Hellerstein et al., 1997; Hass and Hellerstein, 1999).

Online aggregation is particularly useful in "drill-down" scenarios: a user may ask for aggregates over a coarse-grained grouping of records, as in the query above. Based on a quick online estimate of the coarse-grained results, the user may choose to issue another query to "drill down" into a set of particularly anomalous groups. Alternatively the user may quickly find that their first query shows no interesting groups, and they may issue an alternate query, perhaps grouping on different attributes, or requesting a different aggregate computation. The interactivity of online aggregation enables users to explore their data in a relatively painless fashion, encouraging data browsing.

The obvious alternative to online aggregation is to precompute aggregation results before people use the system—this is the solution of choice in the *multidimensional* OLAP (MOLAP) tools (e.g., Hypersion Essbase OLAP Server, 1999). Note that the name OLAP ("OnLine Analytic Processing") is something of a misnomer for these systems. The analytic processing in many OLAP tools is in fact done "off line" in batch mode; the user merely navigates the stored results on line. This solution, while viable in some contexts, is an example of the constrained usage mentioned at the beginning of this section: the only interactive queries are those that have been precomputed. This constraint is often disguised with a graphical interface that allows only precomputed queries to be generated. A concomitant and more severe constraint is that these OLAP systems have trouble scaling beyond a few dozen gigabytes because of both the storage costs of precomputed answers, and the time required to periodically "refresh" those answers. Hybrids of precomputation and online aggregation are clearly possible, in the same way that newer systems provide hybrids of precomputation and batch query processing (e.g., Shukla et al., 1998; Harinarayan et al., 1996; Pilot Software, 1998; Maier and Stein, 1986).

2.2. *Online enumeration: Scalable spreadsheets*

Database systems are often criticized as being hard to use. Many data analysts are experts in a domain other than computing, and hence prefer simple *direct-manipulation* interfaces like those of spreadsheets (Shneiderman, 1982), in which the data is at least partially visible at all times. Domain-specific data patterns are often more easily seen by "eyeballing" a spreadsheet than by attempting to formulate a query. For example, consider analyzing a table of student grades. By sorting the output by GPA and scrolling to the top, middle, and bottom, an analyst may notice a difference in the ethnic mix of names in different GPA quantiles; this may be evidence of discrimination. By contrast, imagine trying to write an

SQL aggregation query asking for the average grade per apparent ethnicity of the name column—there is no way to specify the ethnicity of a name declaratively. The difficulty is that the (rough) name-to-ethnicity mapping is domain knowledge in the analyst's head, and not captured in the database.

Unfortunately, spreadsheets do not scale gracefully to large datasets. An inherent problem is that many spreadsheet behaviors are painfully slow on large datasets—if the spreadsheet allows large data sets at all. Microsoft Excel, for example, restricts table size to 64K rows or fewer, presumably to ensure interactive behavior. The difficulty of guaranteeing acceptable spreadsheet performance on large datasets arises from the "speed of thought" response time expected of spreadsheet operations such as scrolling, sorting on different columns, pivoting, or jumping to particular cells in the table (by address or cell-content prefix). Thus traditional spreadsheets are not useful for analyzing large amounts of data.

We are building *A-B-C*, a scalable spreadsheet that allows online interaction with individual records (Raman et al., 1999a). As records are enumerated from a large file or a database query returning many rows, A-B-C allows the user to view example rows and perform typical spreadsheet operations (scroll, sort, jump) at any time. A-B-C provides interactive (sub-second) responses to all these operations via the access methods and reordering techniques of Sections 3.1 and 3.2.

Hypotheses formed via online enumeration can be made concrete in A-B-C by grouping records "by example": the user can highlight example rows, and use them to interactively develop a regular expression or other group identity function. Groups are then "rolled up" in a separate panel of the spreadsheet, and users can interactively specify aggregation functions to compute on the groups online. In this case, the online enumeration features of A-B-C are a first step in driving subsequent online aggregation.

2.3. Aggregation + enumeration: Online data visualization

Data visualization is an increasingly active research area, with rather mature prototypes in the research community (e.g. Tioga Datasplash (Aiken et al., 1996), DEVise (Livny et al., 1997), Pad (Perlin and Fox, 1993)), and products emerging from vendors (Ohno, 1998). These systems are interactive data exploration tools, allowing users to "pan" and "zoom" over visual "canvases" representing a data set, and derive and view new visualizations quickly.

An inherent challenge in architecting a data visualization system is that it must present large volumes of information efficiently. This involves scanning, aggregating and rendering large datasets at point-and-click speeds. Typically these visualization systems do not draw a new screen until its image has been fully computed. Once again, this means batch-style performance for large datasets. This is particularly egregious for visualization systems that are expressly intended to support browsing of large datasets.

Related work in the CONTROL project involves the development of online visualization techniques we call CLOUDS (Hellerstein et al., 1999), which can be thought of as *visual* aggregations and enumerations for an online query processing system. CLOUDS performs both enumeration and aggregation simultaneously: it renders records as they are fetched, and also uses those records to generate an overlay of shaded rectangular regions of color

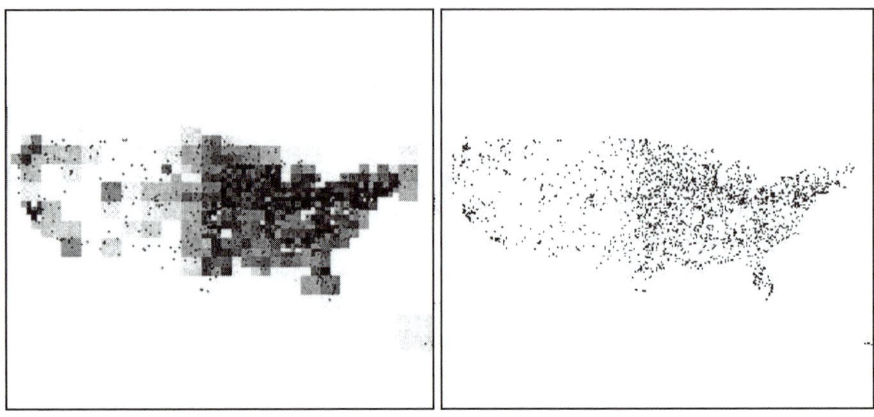

Figure 2. Snapshots of an online visualization of cities in the United States, with and without CLOUDS.

("clouds"), corresponding to nodes in a carefully constructed quad tree. The combination of the clouds and the rendered sample is intended to approximate the final image. This means that the clouds are not themselves an approximation of the image, but rather a *compensatory* shading that accounts for the difference between the rendered records and the projected final outcome. During processing, the user sees the picture improve much the way that images become refined during network transmission. This can be particularly useful when a user pans or zooms over the results of an *ad hoc* query: in such scenarios the accuracy of what is seen is not as important as the rough sense of the moving picture. Figure 2 shows a snapshot of an online visualization of cities in the United States, with and without CLOUDS. Note how the CLOUDS version contains shading that approximates the final density of areas better than the non-CLOUDS version; note also how the CLOUDS visualization renders both data points and shading.

As with the Scalable Spreadsheet, our data visualization techniques tie into data delivery, and benefit directly from the access methods and reordering techniques described in Sections 3.1 and 3.2. For DBMS-centric visualization tools like DEVise and Tioga, the full power of an online query processing system—including joins, aggregations, and so on—is needed in the back end.

2.4. Online data mining

Many data mining algorithms make at least one complete pass over a database before producing answers. In addition, most mining algorithms have a number of parameters to tune, which are not adjustable while the algorithm is running. While we do not focus on data mining algorithms in this paper, we briefly consider them here to highlight analogies to online query processing.

As a well-known example, consider the oft-cited *apriori* algorithm for finding "association rules" in market-basket data (Agrawal and Srikant, 1994). To use an association rule application, a user specifies values for two variables: one that sets a minimum threshold on the amount of evidence required for a set of items to be produced (*minsupport*) and another which sets a minimum threshold on the correlation between the items in the set (*minconfidence*). These algorithms can run for hours without output, before producing association rules that passed the minimum support and confidence thresholds. Users who set those thresholds incorrectly typically have to start over. Setting thresholds too high means that few rules are returned. Setting them too low means that the system (a) runs even more slowly, and (b) returns an overwhelming amount of information, most of which is useless. Domain experts may also want to explicitly prune irrelevant correlations during processing.

The traditional algorithm for association rules is a sequence of aggregation queries, and can be implemented in an online fashion using techniques for online query processing described in this paper. An alternative association rule algorithm called CARMA was developed in the CONTROL project (Hidber, 1997). While not clearly applicable to SQL query processing, CARMA is worthy of mention here for two reasons. First, it very efficiently provides online interaction and early answers. Second—and somewhat surprisingly—CARMA often produces a final, accurate answer faster than the traditional "batch" algorithms, both because it makes fewer passes of the dataset and because it manages less memory-resident state. So in at least one scenario, inventing an algorithm for online processing resulted in a solution that is also better for batch processing!

Most other data mining algorithms (clustering, classification, pattern-matching) are similarly time-consuming. CONTROL techniques seem worth considering for these algorithms, and the development of such techniques seems to be a tractable research challenge. Note that CONTROL techniques tighten loops in the knowledge-discovery process (Fayyad et al., 1996), bringing mining algorithms closer in spirit to data visualization and browsing. Such synergies between user-driven and automated techniques for data analysis seem like a promising direction for cross-pollenation between research areas.

3. Algorithms for online query processing

Relational systems implement a relatively small set of highly tuned query processing operators. Online query processing is driven by online analogs of the standard relational query processing operators, along with a few new operators. In this section we discuss our implementation in Informix of online query processing operators, including randomized data access, preferential data delivery, relational joins, and grouping of result records. Of these, randomized data access was the simplest to address, and our solution required no additions to the Informix SQL engine. It does, however, have an impact on the *physical design* of a database, i.e., the layout of tables and indexes on disk.

3.1. *Randomized data access and physical database design*

In most scenarios, it is helpful if the output of a partially-completed online query can be treated as a random sample. In online aggregation queries, the estimators for aggregates like AVG and SUM require random sampling in order to allow for confidence intervals or other statements about accuracy. This requirement is less stringent for online enumeration, but still beneficial: in most scenarios a user would prefer to see a representative sample of the data at any given time. Hence we begin our discussion of query operators by considering techniques for randomized data access.

In order to guarantee random data delivery, we need *access methods*—algorithms for data access—that produce ever-larger random samples of tables. This can be accomplished in a number of ways. Random sampling is the same as simply scanning a table in certain scenarios: particularly, when the rows have been randomly permuted prior to query processing or when, as verified by statistical testing, the storage order of the rows on disk is independent of the values of the attributes involved in the aggregation query. Alternatively, it may be desirable to actually sample a table during query processing, or to materialize a small random sample of each base relation during an initialization step, and then subsequently scan the sample base relations during online processing. Olken (1993) surveys techniques for sampling from databases and for maintaining materialized sample views.

We chose to guarantee random delivery in Informix by storing tables in random order. This approach is already available in any DBMS that supports user-defined functions: we *cluster*[3] tables randomly by clustering records on a user-defined function $f(\ )$ that generates pseudo-random numbers.[4] Scans of the table produce ever-larger random samples at full disk bandwidth. To make this scheme work in the face of updates, new tuples should be inserted to random positions in the table, with the tuples formerly in those positions being appended to the end of the table. While not difficult, we have not added random insertion functionality to our Informix prototype.

There are two potential drawbacks to this approach. The first is that every scan of the table generates the same random sample; over time the random but static properties of the order could be misinterpreted as representative of all possible orderings. This can be alleviated somewhat by starting scans at an arbitrary points in the file (as is done in the "shared scans" of some DBMSs (Red Brick Systems, Inc., 1998)), though of course the properties of the fixed order are still reflected. A better solution is to periodically force some random shuffling in the table; this is analogous to the "reorganization" steps common in database administration, and it easily could be made automatic and incremental.

The second problem with this approach is that a relation stored in random order is by definition not stored in some other order. This has ramifications for database design, since it is typical for a database administrator to cluster a table on an attribute frequently referenced in range queries, rather than on a random function. This can be solved in a manner analogous to that of traditional database design: if one has a clustering on some column, and a secondary random clustering is desired, one can generate a secondary random ordering via an index on a random-valued attribute. This can be done without modification in any object-relational system like Informix that supports *functional* indexes (Maier and Stein, 1986; Lynch and Stonebrakere, 1988). One simply constructs a functional index on $f(R \cdot x)$, where $f(\ )$ is a random-number generator, and x is any column of R. The resulting index on R serves as a secondary random ordering structure. Note that scanning a secondary index requires a random I/O per record; this is a performance drawback of secondary random indexes as well. As with most physical database design decisions, there are no clear rules of thumb here: the choice of which clustering to use depends on whether online queries or traditional range queries are more significant to the workload performance. These kinds of decision can be aided or even automated by workload analysis tools (e.g., Chaudhuri and Narasayya, 1998)).

3.2. *Preferential data delivery: Online reordering*

It is not sufficient for data delivery in an online query processing system to be random. It also must be user-controllable. This requirement was not present in traditional batch systems, and hence the techniques we discuss in this section do not have direct analogs in traditional systems.

A key aspect of an online query processing system is that users perceive data being processed *over time*. Hence an important performance goal for these systems is to present data of interest early on in the processing, so that users can get satisfactory results quickly, halt processing early, and move on to their next request. The "speed" buttons shown in the Online Aggregation interface in figure 1 are one interface for specifying preferences: they allow users to request preferential delivery for particular groups. The scrollbar of a spreadsheet is another interface: items that can be displayed at the current scrollbar position are of greatest interest, and the likelihood of navigation to other scrollbar positions determines the relative preference of other items.

To support preferential data delivery, we developed an *online reordering* operator that reorders data on the fly based on user preferences—it attempts to ensure that *interesting* items get processed first (Raman et al., 1999b). We allow users to dynamically change their definition of "interesting" during the course of a query; the reordering operator alters the data delivery to try and meet the specification at any time.

In order to provide user control, a data processing system must accept user preferences for different items and use them to guide the processing. These preferences are specified in a value-based, application-specific manner, usually based on values in the data items. The mapping from user preferences to the rates of data delivery depends on the performance goals of the application. This is derived for some typical applications in Raman et al. (1999b). Given a statement of preferences, the reorder operator should permute the data items at the source so as to make an application-specific *quality of feedback* function rise as fast as possible.

Since our goal is interactivity, the reordering must not involve pre-processing or other overheads that will increase runtime. Instead, we do a "best effort" reordering *without* slowing down the processing, by making the reordering concurrent with the processing. Figure 3 illustrates our scheme of inserting a reorder operator into a data flow. We can

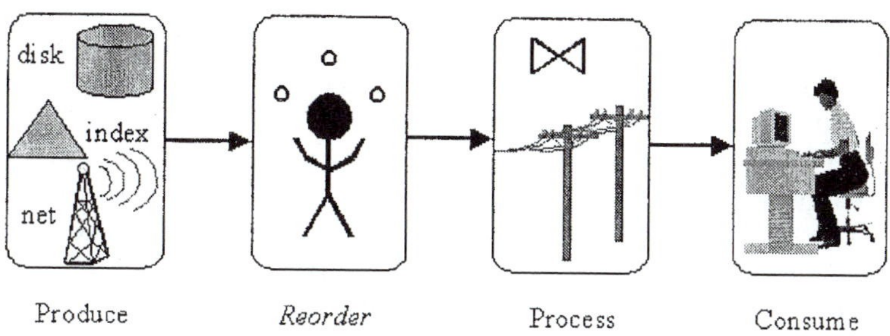

Figure 3. The reordering operator in context.

divide any data flow into four stages: the `produce` stage, the `reorder` stage, the `process` stage, and the `consume` stage. In the context of query processing, `Produce` represents an access method generating records. `Reorder` reorders the items according to the dynamically changing preferences of the consumer. `Process` is the set of operations that are applied "downstream" to the records—this could involve query plan operators like joins, shipping data across a slow network, rendering data onto the screen in data visualization, etc. `Consume` captures the user think-time, if any—this is mainly for interactive interfaces such as spreadsheets or data visualization. Since all these operations can go on concurrently, we exploit the difference in throughput between the `produce` stage and the `process` or `consume` stages to permute the items. For disk-based data sources, `Produce` can run as fast as the sequential read bandwidth, whereas `process` may involve several random I/Os which are much slower (Gray and Graefe, 1997). While the items sent out so far are being processed/consumed, `reorder` can take more items from `produce` and permute them.

The `reorder` operator tries to `put` as many interesting items as possible onto a main-memory buffer, and the `process` operator issues requests to `get` items from the buffer. `Process` decides which item to `get` based on its performance goals. `Reorder` uses the time gap between successive `gets` from the buffer (which may arise due to processing or consumption time) to populate the buffer with more interesting items. It does this either by using an index to fetch interesting items, or by aggressively prefetching from the input, spooling uninteresting items onto an auxiliary disk. Policies for management of the buffer and organization of the auxiliary disk are described in more detail in Raman et al. (1999b); the basic idea is to evict least-interesting items from the buffer, and place them into chunks on disk of records from the same group.

If the reorder operator can `get` records much faster than they can be `processed`, then the reordering has two phases. In the first phase, reorder continually `gets` data, and tries to keep the buffer full of interesting items in the appropriate ratios, carefully spooling uninteresting items to chunks on the side disk. The second phase occurs when there is no more data to `get`; at this point, reorder simply *enriches* the buffer by fetching chunks of interesting tuples of interest from the side disk.

3.2.1. Index stride and database design issues. The Index Stride access method was first presented in Hellerstein et al. (1997); it works as follows. Given a B-tree index on the grouping columns,[5] on the first request for a tuple we open a scan on the leftmost edge of the index, where we find a key value k_1. We assign this scan a search key of the form $[=k_1]$. After fetching the first tuple with key value k_1, on a subsequent request for a tuple we open a second index scan with search key $[>k_1]$, in order to quickly find the next group in the table. When we find this value, k_2, we change the second scan's search key to be $[=k_2]$, and return the tuple that was found. We repeat this procedure for subsequent requests until we have a value k_n such that a search key $[>k_n]$ returns no tuples. At this point, we satisfy requests for tuples by fetching from the scans $[=k_1], \ldots, [=k_n]$ in a round-robin fashion. In order to capture user preference for groups, we do not actually use round-robin scheduling among the groups; rather we use lottery scheduling (Waldspurger and Weihl, 1995), assigning more "tickets" to groups of greater interest.

Index Stride can be used to support online reordering, because the reorder operator can `get` tuples in the appropriate ratios by simply passing its weighting of groups to the Index Stride access method. A drawback of using an index is that it involves many random I/Os. For many scenarios, Index Stride is significantly less efficient than simply running an online reordering operator over a table-scan. However for groups of very low cardinality Index Stride can be extremely beneficial. A hybrid of Index Stride and table-scan can be achieved via *partial indexes* (Seshadri and Swami, 1995; Stonebraker, 1989): an index is built over the small groups, and the reorder operator is run over a union of the small groups (in the index) and the larger groups (in the heap file). In a system without partial indexes like UDO, the hybrid scheme can be effected by explicitly partitioning the table into its rare and common groups, storing the rare groups in a separate table. Performance tradeoffs between Index Stride and online reordering of table-scans are presented in Raman et al. (1999b).

3.3. Ripple join algorithms

Up to this point, our discussion has focused on algorithms for delivering data from individual tables. These techniques are appropriate for SQL queries on single tables; they are also appropriate for simple spreadsheet-like systems built on files, as sketched in Section 2.2. In general, however, SQL queries often combine data from multiple tables—this requires relational join operators.

The fastest classical join algorithms (see, e.g., Graefe (1993)) are inappropriate for online query processing. Sort-merge join is blocking: it generates no output until it has consumed its entire input. Hybrid hash join (DeWitt et al., 1984) does produce output from the beginning of processing, but at a fraction of the rate at which it consumes its input. Moreover most commercial systems use Grace hash join (Fushimi et al., 1986) which is a blocking algorithm.

The only classical algorithm that is completely pipelining is nested-loops join, but it is typically quite slow unless an index is present to speed up the inner loop. Using nested-loops join in an online fashion is often more attractive than using a blocking algorithm like sort-merge join. But the absolute performance of the online nested-loops join is often unacceptably slow even for producing partial results—this is particularly true for estimating aggregates.

To see this, consider an online aggregation query over two tables, R and S. When a sample of R is joined with a sample of S, an estimate of the aggregate function can be produced, along with a confidence interval (Haas, 1997). We call this scenario the end of a *sampling step*—at the end of each sampling step in a join, the running estimate can be updated and the confidence interval tightened. In nested loops join, a sampling step completes only at the end of each inner loop. If S is the relation in the outer loop of the join in our example, then a sampling step completes after each full scan of R. But if R is of non-trivial size (as is often the case for decision-support queries), then the amount of time between successive sampling steps—and hence successive updates to the running estimate and confidence interval—can be excessive.

In addition to having large pauses between estimation updates, nested-loops join has an additional problem: it "samples" more quickly from one relation (the inner loop) than from

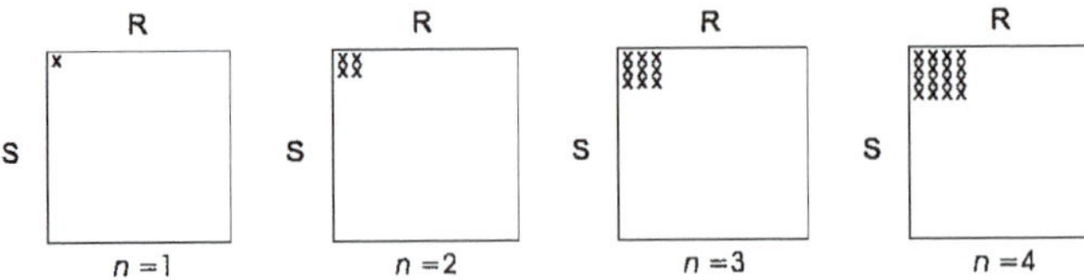

Figure 4. The elements of $R \times S$ that have been seen after n steps of a "square" ripple join.

the other. If the relation in the outer loop contributes significantly to the variance of inputs to the aggregation function, it can be beneficial to more carefully balance the rates of reading from the two relations.

To address these problems, we developed a new join algorithm for online query processing, called the *ripple join* (Haas and Hellerstein, 1999). In the simplest version of the two-table ripple join (figure 6), one previously-unseen random tuple is retrieved from each of R and S at each sampling step; these new tuples are joined with the previously-seen tuples and with each other. Thus, the Cartesian product $R \times S$ is swept out as depicted in the "animation" of figure 4. In each matrix in the figure, the R axis represents tuples of R, the S axis represents tuples of S, each position (r, s) in each matrix represents a corresponding tuple in $R \times S$, and each "x" inside the matrix corresponds to an element of $R \times S$ that has been seen so far. In the figure, the tuples in each of R and S are displayed in the order provided by the access methods; this order is assumed to be random.

The "square" version of the ripple join described above draws samples from R and S at the same rate. As discussed in Haas and Hellerstein (1999), it is often beneficial to sample one relation (the "more variable" one) at a higher rate in order to provide the shortest possible confidence intervals for a given aggregation query. This requirement leads to the general "rectangular" version of the ripple join[6] depicted in figure 5. The general algorithm with K ($\geq$2) base relations $R_1, R_2, \ldots, R_K$ retrieves β_k previously-unseen random tuples from R_k at each sampling step for $1 \leq k \leq K$. (figure 5 corresponds to the special case in which $K = 2$, $\beta_1 = 3$, and $\beta_2 = 2$.) Note the tradeoff between interactivity of the display and estimation accuracy. When, for example, $\beta_1 = 1$ and $\beta_2 = 2$, more I/O's are required per sampling step than when $\beta_1 = 1$ and $\beta_2 = 1$, so that the time between updates to the confidence intervals is longer; on the other hand, after each sampling step the confidence interval typically is shorter when $\beta_1 = 1$ and $\beta_2 = 2$.

In Haas and Hellerstein (1999) we provide full details of ripple joins, and their interaction with aggregation estimators. We also include detailed discussion on the statistics behind

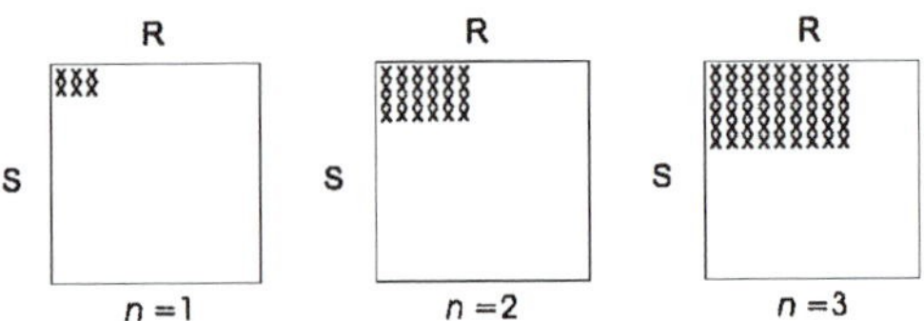

Figure 5. The elements of $R \times S$ that have been seen after n sampling steps of a "rectangular" ripple join with aspect ratio 3×2.

```
for (max = 1 to infinity) {
  for (i = 1 to max-1)
    if (predicate(R[i],S[max]))
      output(R[i],S[max]);
  for (i = 1 to max)
    if (predicate(R[max],S[i]))
      output(R[max],S[i]);
}
```

Figure 6. A simple square ripple join. The tuples within each relation are referred to in array notation.

tuning the aspect ratios to shrink the confidence intervals as fast as possible, while still attempting to meet a user's goal for interactivity. In addition, we demonstrate that ripple join generalizes pipelining nested-loops and hash joins. That leads to descriptions of higher-performance algorithmic variants on figure 6 based on blocking (analogous to blocked nested loops join), hashing (generalizing the pipelined hash join of Wilschut and Apers (1991), and indexes (identical to index nested loops).

The benefits of ripple join for enumeration (non-aggregation) queries are akin to the benefits of sampling for these queries: the running result of a ripple join arguably represents a "representative" subset of the final result, since it is made from sizable random samples from each input relation. In an enumerative query, the ripple join aspect ratio can be tuned to maximize the size of the output, rather than a statistical property.

3.4. Hash-based grouping

SQL aggregation queries can contain a GROUP BY clause, which partitions tuples into groups. This process can be done via sorting or hashing; in either case, the stream of tuples resulting from selections, projections and joins are grouped into partitions such that within a partition all tuples match on the GROUP BY columns. Sorting is a blocking operation and hashing is not (at least not for a reasonable number of groups), so it is important that an online aggregation system implement GROUP BY via hashing. Further discussion of unary hashing and sorting appears in Hellerstein and Naughton (1996).

4. End-to-end issues in online query processing

A collection of algorithms does not make a system; the various building blocks must be made to interact correctly, and consideration must be given to the end-to-end issues required to deliver useful behavior to users. In this section we discuss our experience implementing online query processing in Informix UDO. This implementation is more than a simple "plug-in": the various algorithms must be incorporated inside the server alongside their traditional counterparts, and must be made to work together correctly. In addition, interfaces must be added to the system to handle interactive behaviors that are not offered by a traditional system. In this section we describe interfaces to the system, and implementation details in composing query execution plans. We also discuss some of remaining challenges in realizing a completely online query processing system. There were some issues in implementing the estimators in a DBMS that are not clear from an algorithmic standpoint. We discuss these in Appendix A.

4.1. Client-server interfaces

A traditional database Application Programming Interface (API) accepts SQL queries as input, and returns a *cursor* as output; the cursor is a handle with which the client can request output tuples one at a time. A batch system may process for a long time before the cursor is available for fetching output, while an online system will make the cursor available almost immediately. Beyond this minor change in interaction lie more significant changes in the client-server API: online query processing allows for ongoing interaction between a client application and database server. Two basic issues need to be handled. First, the system needs to provide output beyond relational result records. Second, users can provide many kinds of input to the system while a query is running.

Before actually deciding on functions to add, we had to decide how applications would invoke our functions. We took two approaches to this problem. Our first solution was to extend Informix's Embedded SQL (ESQL) API, which is a library of routines that can be called from C programs. This was problematic, however, because implementing clients in C is an unpleasant low-level task.

We preferred to use a combination of Windows-based tools to build our application: the interface of figure 1 consists of a few hundred lines of Visual Basic code that invoke Informix's MetaCube client tool, and also utilize a Microsoft Excel spreadsheet that provides the table and graph widgets. These Windows-based tools do not work over ESQL; instead they communicate with the DBMS via the standard Open Database Connectivity (ODBC) protocol. Unfortunately ODBC is part of the MS Windows operating systems, and its API is not extensible by third parties. Hence we developed a second architecture that conforms to the traditional ODBC paradigm: all input is done via SQL queries, and output via cursors. Sticking to this restricted interface has a number of advantages: it enables the use of ODBC and similar connectivity protocols (such as Java's JDBC), and it also allows standard client tools to be deployed over an online query processing system.

Given this architecture, we proceed to discuss our CONTROL API for output and input in turn.

4.1.1. Output API. Online enumeration queries provide the same output as traditional database queries; the only distinction is that they make a cursor available for fetching almost instantly. Online aggregation queries provide a form of output not present in traditional systems: running estimates and confidence intervals for results. We chose to have these running outputs appear as regular tuples, with the same attributes as the actual output tuples. This means that a single SQL query is issued, which returns a stream of tuples that includes both estimates and results. For example, the query of Section 2.1 can be issued as:

```
  SELECT ONLINE AVG(grade), CONFIDENCE_AVG(grade, 95)
    FROM enroll
GROUP BY college;
```

The addition of the ONLINE keyword and the CONFIDENCE_AVG function to the query can be done automatically by the client application, or explicitly by a user. In this example, CONFIDENCE_AVG is a user-defined aggregate function (UDA) that returns a confidence interval "half-width" ϵ corresponding to the probability given by the second argument to the aggregate (i.e., the estimate is $\pm\epsilon$ of the correct average with 95% probability). The interface of figure 1 shows the ϵ values displayed as "error bars" in a graph. Immediately after issuing this query, a cursor is available for fetching results. In a traditional system, this query would produce one tuple per `college`. In our system, the query produces multiple tuples per `college`, each representing an estimate of the average `grade` along with a confidence interval half-width. If the query is run to completion, the *last* tuple fetched per `college` represents the accurate final answer.

Any ODBC client application can handle this sequence of tuples. In particular, a standard text-based client works acceptably for online aggregation—estimates stream across the screen, and the final results remain on the last lines of the output. This proved to be our client of choice while developing the system. Our new interfaces (e.g., figure 1) overwrite old estimates with updated ones by assigning groups to positions in a tabular display.

4.1.2. Input API. Users should be able to control a running query by interacting with a client, which passes user input on to the server. As a concrete example from our implementation, the user should be able to speed up, slow down, or stop groups in an online aggregation query. Similarly, the spreadsheet widget should be able to express a preference for records that are in the range currently being shown on screen.

For clients implemented in C over our enhanced ESQL, input to the server is direct: the client simply invokes API functions that we have added to ESQL, such as `pause_group(x)`, `speed_up_group(x)`, etc. Such invocations can be interleaved arbitrarily with requests to fetch data from a cursor. For clients communicating via ODBC rather than ESQL, direct invocation of API functions is not an option. For this scenario, we were able to leverage the Object-Relational features of UDO in a non-standard manner. In an object-relational system, an SQL query can invoke user-defined functions (UDFs) in the SELECT statement. We added UDFs to our database that invoke each of our API functions. Hence the client can issue a query of the form

```
SELECT PAUSE_GROUP(x);
```

and get the same effect as a client using ESQL. Clients can interleave such "control" queries with requests to fetch tuples from the main query running on the database. Originally we considered this an inelegant design (Hellerstein et al., 1997), because it significantly increases the code path for each gesture a user makes. In practice, however, the performance of this scheme has been acceptable, and the ease of use afforded by ODBC and Windows-based 4GLs has been beneficial.

4.1.3. Pacing. Online aggregation queries can return updated estimates quite frequently—for a single-table aggregation query like that of Section 2.1, a new estimate is available for every tuple scanned from the table. However, many clients use complex graphical interfaces or slow network connections, and are unable to fetch and display updates as fast as the database can generate them. In these scenarios it is preferable for the system to produce a new estimate once for every $k \gg 1$ tuples. This prevents overburdening the client. There is a second reason to avoid producing too many updated estimates. Typically, SQL query output is synchronized between the server and client: after the client fetches a tuple, the server is idle until the next request for a tuple from the client. This architecture is an artifact of batch system design, in which most of the server processing is done before the first tuple can be fetched. In an online aggregation query, time spent handling updated estimates at the client is time lost at the server. Hence it pays to amortize this lost time across a significant amount of processing at the server—i.e., one does not want to incur such a loss too often.

A solution to this problem would be to reimplement the threading model for online aggregation so that the query processing could proceed in parallel with the delivery of estimates. To achieve this, the aggregation query could run as one thread, and a separate request-handling thread could process fetch requests by "peeking" at the state of the query thread and returning an estimate. Rather than rearchitecting Informix's structure in this way, we chose to maintain Informix's single-thread architecture, and simply return an output tuple for every k tuples that are aggregated. We refer to the number k as the *skip factor*. The skip factor is set by the user in terms of time units (seconds), and we translate those time units into a skip factor via a dynamic feedback technique that automatically calibrates the throughput of client fetch-handling.

4.2. *Implementing online query operators*

The algorithms of Section 3 were designed in isolation, but a number of subtleties arise when integrating them into a complete system. In this section, we discuss issues in implementing online query processing operators in Informix.

4.2.1. Online reordering. Like the early System R DBMS prototype (Astrahan et al., 1976), Informix UDO is divided into two parts: a storage manager called RSAM, and a query optimization/execution engine implemented on top of RSAM. In our prototype, we decided to implement all our algorithms entirely above RSAM. This decision was motivated by considerations of programming complexity, and by the fact that RSAM has a well-defined, published API that we did not want to modify (Informix, 1998).

Implementing Index Stride above RSAM resulted in some compromises in performance. RSAM presents interfaces for scanning relations, and for fetching tuples from indexes. The index-based interface to RSAM takes as arguments a relation R, an index I, and a predicate p, and returns tuples from R that match p. To amortize I/O costs, an efficient implementation of Index Stride would fetch tuples a disk block at a time: one block of tuples from the first group, then one from the second, and so on. Since the RSAM interface is tuple-at-a-time, there is no way to explicitly request a block of tuples. In principle the buffer manager could solve this problem by allocating a buffer per group: then when fetching the first tuple from a block it would put the block in the buffer pool, and it would be available on the next fetch. Unfortunately this buffering strategy does not correspond naturally to the replacement policies in use in a traditional DBMS. The performance of Index Stride could be tuned up by either implementing a page-based Index Stride in RSAM, or enhancing the buffer manager to recognize and optimize Index Stride-style access.

4.2.2. Ripple join. Performance is not the only issue that requires attention in a complete implementation; we also encountered correctness problems resulting from the interaction of ripple join and our data delivery algorithms. As described in figure 6, ripple join rescans each relation multiple times. Upon each scan, it expects tuples to be fetched in the same order. Traditional scans provide this behavior, delivering tuples in the same order every time. However, sampling-based access methods may not return the same order when restarted. Moreover, the online reordering operator does not guarantee that its output is the same when it is restarted, particularly because users can change its behavior dynamically.

To address this problem, we introduce a cache above non-deterministic operators like the reorder operator, which keeps a copy of incoming tuples so that downstream ripple join operators can "replay" their inputs accurately. This cache also prevents ripple join from actually repeating I/Os when it rescans a table—in this sense the cache is much like the "building" hash table of a hash join.

In ordinary usage, we expect online queries to be terminated quickly. However, if a query is allowed to run for a long period of time, the ripple caches can consume more than the available memory. At that point two options are available. The first alternative is to allow the cache to become larger than available memory, spilling some tuples to disk, and recovering them as necessary—much as is done in hash join algorithms. The second alternative is to stop caching at some point, but ensure that the data delivery algorithms output the same tuples each time they are restarted. For randomized access methods this can be achieved by storing the seed of the random number generator. For user-controllable reordering, this requires remembering previous user interactions and "replaying" them internally when restarting the delivery. We implemented the latter technique in Informix.

An additional issue arises when trying to provide aggregation estimates over ripple joins. As noted in Section 3.3, estimates and confidence intervals over ripple joins can be refreshed when a sample of R has been joined with sample of S—this corresponds to a "corner" in the pictures of figure 4. It therefore makes sense for the estimates in a join query to be updated at every k'th corner for skip-factor k. However it is possible that the tuple corresponding to a corner may not satisfy the WHERE clause; in this case, the system does not pass a tuple up the plan tree, and the estimators are not given the opportunity to produce a refined output tuple. To avoid this loss of interactivity, when a ripple join operator reaches a "corner", it returns a dummy, "null tuple" to the aggregation code. These null tuples are handled specially: they are not counted as part of the aggregation result, but serve as a trigger for the aggregation code to update estimates and confidence intervals. Null tuples were easy to implement in UDO as generalizations of tuples in *outer join* operators: an outer join tuple has null columns from a proper subset of its input relations, whereas a null tuple has null columns from all of its input relations.

4.3. Constructing online query plans

Like any relational database system, an online query processing system must map declarative SQL queries to explicit query plans: this process is typically called *query optimization*. Online processing changes the optimization task in two ways: the performance goals of an online system are non-traditional, and there are interactive aspects to online query processing

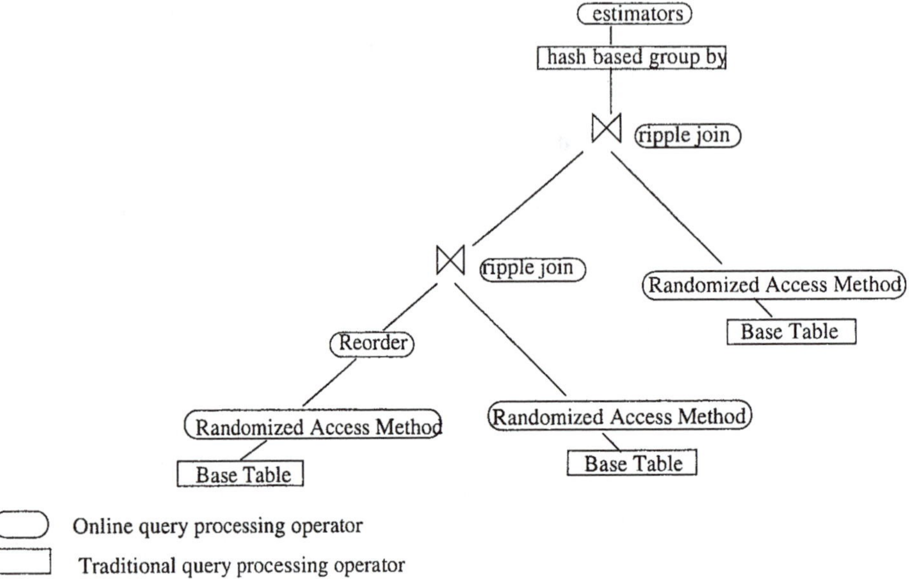

Figure 7. An online query plan tree.

that are not present in traditional databases. For example, for any given query we want to minimize not the time to completion but rather the time to "reasonable" accuracy. Online query optimization is an open research area we have only begun to address in the CONTROL project. In our first prototype we modified Informix UDO's optimizer and query executor to produce reasonable online query plans, without worrying about optimality. In this section we describe our implementation, and raise issues for future research. As motivation, figure 7 shows a complete online query plan, including a number of online query processing operators.

4.3.1. Access method selection. The choice of access methods dictates the extent to which a user can control data delivery. The choices of access methods lie on a spectrum of controllability. At one extreme, sequential scan provides no control, but it is fast and does not require indexes. At the other extreme, Index Stride provides complete control over the processing rates from different groups in a GROUP BY query, but it is slow because it performs many random I/Os. Online reordering lies between these two extremes. It runs almost as fast as a sequential scan (except for a small CPU overhead), but only does a best-effort reordering: if the user has a high preference for extremely rare groups, online reordering can deliver tuples only as fast as it scans them. In our implementation, we modified the UDO optimizer to handle SELECT ONLINE queries with a simple heuristic: if there is a clustered index on the GROUP BY column we use an Index Stride access method, and otherwise we use a sequential scan access method and follow it with online reordering.

An open issue is to allow for reordering when there are GROUP BY clauses over columns from multiple tables: in this case the reordering operators must work in concert with ripple join to produce groups in the appropriate ratio. Currently, we add a reordering operator to only the leftmost table in the query plan that has a GROUP BY. We intend to address this issue in future work.

4.3.2. Join ordering. Unlike most traditional join algorithms, ripple joins are essentially symmetric: there is no distinction between the "outer" and "inner" relations. Hence for a tree of ripple joins, the join ordering problem is quite simple: all that is required is to tune the aspect ratios described in Section 3.3; this is done dynamically as described in Haas and Hellerstein (1999). This view of the problem is overly simplistic, since there is a choice of ripple join variants (block, index or hash), and the join order can affect this choice. For example, in a query over relations R, S and T, there may be equality join clauses connecting R to S, and S to T, but no join clause connecting R to T. In this case the join order $(R \bowtie T) \bowtie S$ cannot use a hash- or index-ripple join since we need to form the cross-product of R and T; by contrast, the join order $(R \bowtie S) \bowtie T$ can use two hash joins.

In our current prototype, we let UDO decide on the join ordering and join algorithms in its usual fashion, optimizing for batch performance. We then post-process the plan, inserting reorder operators above access methods, converting hash joins to hash-ripple joins, index nested-loops joins to index-ripple joins, and nested-loops joins to block-ripple joins.

In ongoing related work, we are studying query optimization in the online context. We have developed a prototype of a continuous optimization scheme based on the notion of an *eddy* (Avnur and Hellerstein, 2000). An eddy is an n-ary query operator interposed between n input tables and $n - 1$ joins, which adaptively routes tuples through the joins. The output of each join is sent back to the eddy for further processing by other joins. By interposing an eddy in the data flow, we change the join order of the query for every tuple as it passes through the query plan. Eddies hold promise not only for online query processing, but for any pipelined set of operations that operate in an uncertain environment—any scenario where user preferences, selectivities or costs are unpredictable and dynamic.

4.4. Beyond select-project-join

The majority of our discussion up to this point has concentrated on simple SQL query blocks—consisting of selection, projection and join—followed by grouping and aggregation. A complete online SQL system must handle other variations of SQL queries as well. We have not implemented all of SQL in an online fashion: some of it is best done by the user interface, and some is future research. We detail these issues here.

4.4.1. Order by, Having. The ORDER BY clause in SQL sorts output tuples based on the values in some column(s). Implementing an online ORDER BY at the server is somewhat pointless: at any time the server could construct an ordered version of the output so far, but re-shipping it to the client for each update would be wasteful. Instead, we believe that ORDER BY is best implemented at the client, using an interface like those described in Section 2.2. Note that the ORDER BY clause is often used to get a "ranking", where a few representative rows near the top will suffice (Carey and Kossmann, 1997; Chaudhuri and Gravano, 1996). In this case an online spreadsheet interface may be more appropriate to get a typical smattering of the top few rows; the strict total ordering of SQL's ORDER BY may over-constrain the request at the expense of performance.

SQL's HAVING clause filters out groups in a GROUP BY query, based on per-group values—either aggregation functions or grouping columns. Consider a version of the query of Section 2.1 that contains an additional clause at the end, `HAVING AVG(grade) > 3.0`; this is an example of a HAVING clause with an aggregate in it. Over time, some college's estimated average grade may go from a value greater than 3.0 to one less than 3.0. In that case, the client *must* handle the deletion of the group from the display; the server does not control how the client displays previously-delivered tuples. Since the HAVING clause has to be handled appropriately by clients, we did not implement a HAVING-clause update scheme at the server.

4.4.2. Subqueries and other expensive predicates. SQL allows queries to be nested in the FROM, WHERE and HAVING clauses. Queries containing such *subqueries* can sometimes be rewritten into single-level queries (see Leung et al. (1998) or Cherniack (1998) for an overview), but there are cases where such subqueries are unavoidable. The problem with such subqueries is that they force batch-style processing: the outer query cannot produce output until the subquery is fully processed. For *correlated* subqueries, the problem is exacerbated: the outer query must complete processing (at least!) one subquery before each tuple of output. A similar problem arises with *expensive* user-defined functions in an object-relational system (Hellerstein, 1998b; Chaudhuri and Shim, 1996): at least one expensive computation must be completed before each tuple is passed to the output.

To date, we have not addressed the online processing of SQL queries with subqueries. One perspective on subqueries in an online system is to view them as the composition of two online systems: the subquery Q_0 is an input to the outer query Q, and the goal is to produce running estimates for $Q(Q_0(\,))$. The optimization of such compositions has been studied in the AI community as *anytime algorithms* (Zilberstein and Russell, 1996), but it is not immediately clear whether that body of work is applicable to multiset-based operators like SQL queries. Recently (Tan et al., 1999) have suggested that queries with subqueries be executed as two threads, one each for the outer and inner query blocks, with the outer block executing based on estimated results from the inner block. The user controls the rate of execution of these two threads, and thereby the accuracy of the answers. While this approach is promising, it works only when the subquery simply computes an aggregate, and the predicate linking the outer block to the inner block is a comparison predicate; it will be interesting to see if this approach can be extended to other predicates. Various techniques are available for efficiently executing correlated subqueries and expensive functions during processing (Rao and Ross, 1998; Hellerstein and Naughton, 1996); these ameliorate but do not solve the batch-style performance.

5. A Study of CONTROL in action

In this section, we illustrate the performance of interactive data analysis in Informix UDO via a sample usage scenario. Our goal is to demonstrate the benefits of online query processing: continually improving feedback on the final result, and interactive control of the processing. We also give an example which combines a ripple join and online reordering to show the completeness of our system against all "select-project-join" queries. Note that this is not intended as an robust analytic study of performance; comparisons of online algorithms

```
Query 1:  SELECT ONLINE avg(o_totalprice), confidence_avg(o_totalprice)
          FROM order;

Query 2:  SELECT ONLINE avg(o_totalprice), o_orderpriority, confidence_avg(o_totalprice)
          FROM order
          WHERE NOT EXISTS (SELECT * FROM lineitem WHERE o_orderkey = l_orderkey
                            AND l_shipmode = 'AIR')
          GROUP BY o_orderpriority;

Query 3:  SELECT ONLINE avg(l_extendedprice), l_shipmode, confidence_avg(o_totalprice)
          FROM order, lineitem
          WHERE o_orderkey = l_orderkey
          GROUP BY o_orderpriority;
```

Figure 8. Queries used in our data analysis session.

under different distributions and parameter settings are given in Hellerstein et al. (1997), Haas and Hellerstein (1999) and Raman et al. (1999).

We scale up all numbers by an undisclosed factor to honor privacy commitments to Informix Corporation while still allowing comparative analysis (hence time is expressed in abstract "chronons"). We give rough figures for the actual wall-clock times in order to show the interactivity of CONTROL.[7] We run each of our experiments only until reaonable accuracy is reached and the analyst switches to the next query.

Our data analysis session uses three queries (see figure 8) against the TPC-D database with a scale factor of 1 (about 1 Gb of data) (Transaction Processing Council). Since online reordering is more difficult for skewed distributions of group values, we use a Zipfian distribution ($1{:}\frac{1}{2}{:}\frac{1}{3}{:}\frac{1}{4}{:}\frac{1}{5}$) of tuples across different order priorities in the `Order` table. In Queries 2 and 3 we group by `o_orderpriority`, to demonstrate the effectiveness of online reordering even in the presence of the skewed distributions commonly found in real data.

Our scenario begins with an analyst issuing Query 1, to find the average price of various orders. Although the base table takes a while to scan (it is about 276MB), the analyst immediately starts getting estimates of the final average. Figure 9 shows the decrease in the

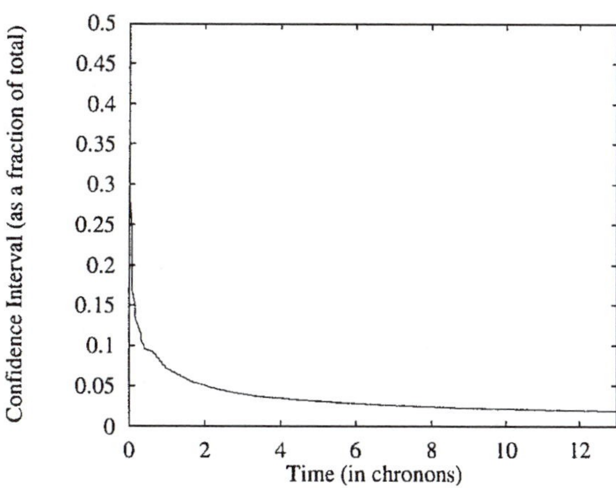

Figure 9. Decrease in the confidence interval for Query 1.

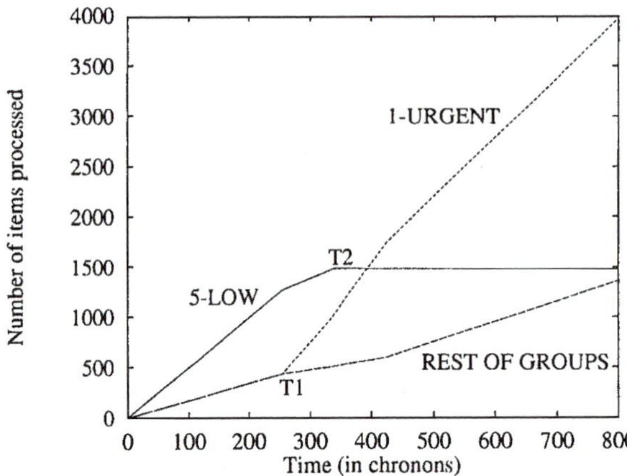

Figure 10. Number of tuples processed for different groups for Query 2.

confidence interval for the average as a function of time. We see that very accurate results are obtained within 12 chronons. On the other hand, a non-online version of the same query took 1490 chronons to complete, or over two orders of magnitude higher! To give an idea of the interactivity, the online version took about a second to reach reasonable (confidence interval <2%) accuracy whereas the non-online version took on the order of a few minutes to complete.

After 12 chronons, the analyst looks at the estimates and feels (based on domain knowledge) that they "are not quite right". Wondering what is happening, the analyst hypothesizes that the prices may be skewed by the presence of some expensive air shipments. Hence the next query issued is Query 2, which finds the average price of orders that do not have any item shipped by air. Notice that with a traditional DBMS, the analyst would not be able to try out this alternative until the first query had completed and returned a result.

Since Query 2 involves a non-flattenable subquery, Informix cannot pick a ripple join. It instead scans `Order`, using the index on `Lineitem` to evaluate the subquery condition. It chooses online reordering to permit user control over the processing from different groups of `Order`. Almost immediately after Query 2 starts running, the analyst decides, from the estimates, that the group with `o_orderpriority` as 5-LOW is more interesting than others, and presses the "speed up" button (see figure 1) to give 5-LOW a preference of 5, compared to 1 for the rest of the groups. Figure 10 shows the number of tuples processed for different groups as a function of time. After some time (point T1 in the figure), 5-LOW's confidence interval has narrowed sufficiently, and the analyst shifts interest to group 1-URGENT, giving it a preference of 5, and reducing that of all other groups to 1.[8] We see that online reordering is able to meet user preferences quite well, despite the interesting groups being rare. In contrast, a sequential scan will actually process the interesting group 5-LOW more slowly than others, because it is uncommon.

Figure 11 shows the rate at which the confidence intervals for the estimates decrease for the same query. We see that the reorder operator automatically adjusts the rates of processing so as to decrease confidence intervals based on user preferences. Also note that at T1 when

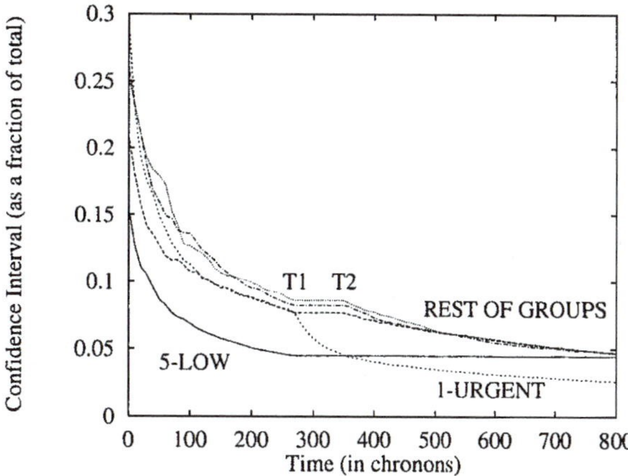

Figure 11. Decrease in confidence interval for different groups for Query 2 with online reordering. Note that the confidence interval for 5-LOW decreases sharply at the beginning, and that the preference for 1-URGENT drops sharply at T1.

the preference for 1-URGENT is increased, the other groups stop for a while (until T2) (in fact 5-LOW plateaus for so long after T2 that the analyst sees no further updates for this group before quitting at 800 chronons; this same behavior is also seen in Figure 10). Likewise, there is a sudden spurt in the processing of tuples from 1-URGENT from T1 until T2. This happens because, reorder realizes that it has processed very few tuples from 1-URGENT with respect to the new preferences, and starts to compensate for it. After T2, the different groups get processed according to their preferences. This compensation arises because of the performance goal that we use: we view the preferences as a weight on the importance of a group, and try to make the weighted average confidence interval across all groups decrease as fast as possible. The motivation for this goal, as well as performance for several other goals, is given in greater detail in Raman et al. (1999).

The mechanism for doing the reordering to decrease the confidence intervals in an optimal manner is explained in Raman et al. (1999). In that paper we also present results that show that online reordering performs well against a variety of data distributions, processing costs, and user preference change scenarios. We also show its efficacy in reordering for an online enumeration application, and for speeding up traditional batch query processing.

After seeing the estimates for 800 chronons, the query does not seem to exhibit any interesting trends. Hence the analyst decides to proceed in a different direction, and submits a new query (Query 3), which drills down on the average lineitem prices, grouping by the `o_order_priority`. Online reordering has helped the analyst to narrow down the estimates for the group of interest and drill down much before Query 2 completes; the entire query takes 58730 chronons to run.

Query 3 needs to access the `Order` *and* `Lineitem` tuples, and since the join predicate is equality it can be evaluated with a hash ripple join. Again, we use online reordering on `Order` to allow user control over the processing of tuples from different order priorities. This query involves running a hash-ripple join over a reorder operator.

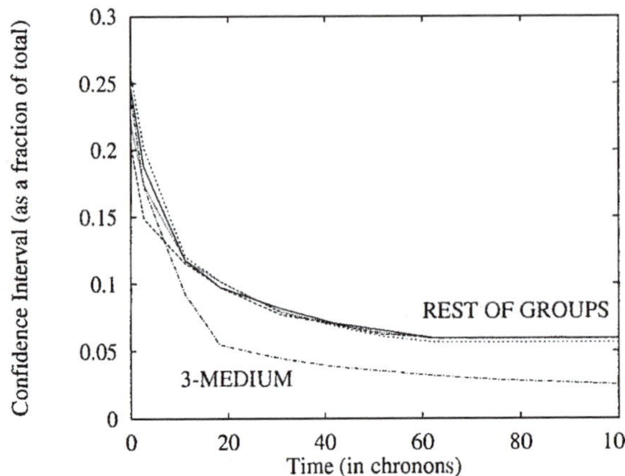

Figure 12. Decrease in confidence interval for different groups for Query 3 with online reordering. Note that the confidence interval for 3-MEDIUM decreases much faster than the others.

Figure 12 shows the decrease in confidence intervals for different groups over time. The analyst increases the preference for group 3-MEDIUM to 20 at the beginning of the processing, and this is reflected in the faster decrease in its confidence interval. We see that within 100 chronons, a reasonably accurate picture emerges, especially for 3-MEDIUM. In contrast, a regular hash join took 68210 chronons to execute this query, which is about three orders of magnitude slower! Notice that this query involves running a hash ripple join over a reorder operator. Hence the join replays tuples from `Lineitem` using a cache of the previous results from reorder as explained in Section 4.2.2. Further comparisons of ripple joins are presented in Haas and Hellerstein (1999) including a comparison of hash, index, and block ripple joins with batch algorithms, and a study of the importance of tuning join aspect ratios for shrinking confidence intervals.

6. Conclusions and future work

We have implemented a prototype online query processing system in Informix UDO, which supports *ad-hoc* select-project-join queries with grouping and aggregation. Our prototype cannot be considered "shippable" software, but it is fairly complete. The set of algorithms we developed provides interactive processing for a large family of SQL queries, and we were able to address most of the details required to implement a usable general-purpose system. We have been able to interface our system with 4GL-based client tools with little difficulty, resulting in quite serviceable online data analysis applications.

A number of lessons emerged in our work. Most significantly, we found that extending an SQL engine to provide online query processing is neither trivial nor overly daunting. A full implementation does require extending the database engine from within, and extensions are required from the access methods through the query operators, optimizer, and client API. But most of the changes are analogous to facilities already present in a complete SQL engine, and are therefore relatively simple to add.

We believe that many of our lessons in extending the system are pertinent outside the specific domain of online query processing. For example, any extension of a database system to handle new interactions will require some of the same API considerations mentioned in this paper. Similarly, additions of new access methods entail new considerations in database design. In addition, the issues raised by *composing* algorithms into large query plans are generally important, and perhaps too often neglected outside the context of relational database systems. Because these kinds of issues are often ignored in initial publications, new data analysis techniques are often passed over by practitioners. On occasion these pragmatic issues can also become rather interesting research problems, which would not naturally arise outside the context of a full implementation.

The most significant lesson for us resulted from the leverage we got from cross-disciplinary synergy: in our case, the mixture of statistics, computer systems and user interfaces. Our work was motivated by user interface goals; these mapped to system performance requirements, which were in turn clarified by optimizing for statistical metrics. Ripple join is perhaps the clearest example of this synergy: in order to achieve a balance between interactivity and output quality for multi-table queries, we developed a new query processing algorithm, which led to a very non-standard dynamic optimization paradigm (adjusting aspect ratios) based on variance of input to statistical estimators. We believe that this kind of cross-disciplinary synthesis is a fertile approach for developing future computer systems.

A number of issues remain as future work in online query processing. We have barely begun to study the user interface issues involved in online data analysis; much work remains to be done in understanding and constructing usable applications, especially for online enumeration and visualization. In the systems arena, we are extending our results to work in a parallel context, which entails algorithmic work as well as statistical work—e.g., parallel ripple joins are akin to stratified sampling techniques, which affects the estimators and confidence intervals for online aggregation. It would also be helpful to find general techniques for handling subqueries—many typical decision-support queries contain subqueries (e.g. the TPC-D benchmark queries (Transaction Processing Council)), and some of those cannot be rewritten away.

More generally, we are interested in the way that interactive techniques change the process of data analysis and knowledge discovery: when long-running operations become more interactive, the distinction between so-called "automated" techniques (e.g., data mining) and user-driven techniques (data visualization, SQL) are significantly blurred. The implications are likely to go beyond the obvious issues of faster interaction, to suggest new and more natural human-computer interactions for data analysis.

Appendix: A. Issues in implementing aggregate estimation

Online aggregation queries raise additional complications, since query processing must be integrated with estimation techniques. While this paper does not dwell on the statistics involved in our estimators, we do describe some of the system implementation issues that they raise.

A.1. Choice of confidence intervals

Three different classes of confidence intervals for online aggregation are detailed in (Haas, 1997). *Deterministic* confidence intervals give strict bounds on the error of an estimator, using bounds on the cardinalities of the tables and on the values of the input to the aggregation function. *Conservative* estimators are based on Hoeffding's inequality (Hoeffding, 1963), and can be used for samples of any size, but appear inapplicable to certain aggregation functions like STDDEV. *Large sample* estimators are based on Central Limit Theorems, and can be used on large samples (where large can be as small as 20–30 tuples) to provide quite tight confidence intervals. All three of these estimators can be extended to work on the cross-product samples provided by ripple joins (Haas and Hellerstein, 1999). We prefer to use large-sample confidence intervals because they are typically much tighter than deterministic or conservative estimates (Haas, 1997) and apply to a wider range of aggregate functions. However, there are two scenarios in which large-sample confidence intervals are inappropriate.

First, large sample confidence intervals fluctuate wildly at the beginning of a query, until a "large enough" sample has been processed. In order to avoid misleading the user, conservative confidence intervals should be used at first, until a large sample has been obtained. A reasonable choice might be to switch to large-sample confidence intervals only after 40 or 50 tuples have passed the query's WHERE clause. For those aggregates that cannot use conservative confidence intervals, it makes sense to simply postpone producing confidence intervals for that period. In general it is difficult to robustly decide when the Central Limit Theorem "kicks in" and one can switch estimators; in practice the sample sizes resulting from "big picture" database queries become large enough very quickly. Second, towards the end of processing a query large-sample confidence intervals are too conservative. Even after all tuples have been processed, a large-sample confidence interval will have a finite, although small, width. Thus towards the end of a query it is appropriate to switch to using deterministic confidence intervals. This switch can be done as soon as the deterministic interval is tighter than the large-sample interval.

In most situations, we expect user to stop processing online queries well before they complete, so the issue of deterministic confidence intervals may seem irrelevant. However deterministic confidence intervals can get used quite often because of reordering in GROUP BY queries. If a user is especially interested in a particular group, they will speed up that group's delivery to the point where it all tuples from the group will get fetched quickly; this is analogous to the "end-of-query" scenario for that group. If large-sample confidence intervals were used, that group could have a wide confidence interval even though it was finished.

A.2. Interaction of reordering and aggregate estimation

Reordering the data delivery biases the order in which tuples are read from different groups; in this sense it does not produce unbiased random samples. However, a key property of our reordering methods is that, *within* a group, reordering does not affect the order of tuples produced, and hence unbiased random samples are guaranteed per group. Since the aggregate function for each group in a GROUP BY query is estimated independently, no bias is involved in the estimation.

A.3. Calculation of quantities for estimation

A number of quantities are required as inputs to our estimators and confidence-interval computations. We briefly describe how we derive these in our implementation.

First, the estimators we use require knowledge of the actual number of tuples read from each table *before* any selections are applied. Obtaining this information required us to modify the RSAM layer slightly, since RSAM only returns tuples that satisfy relevant selections in the query's WHERE clause. This was the only situation where we added code in the RSAM layer.

Second, a few of our estimators and confidence interval computations require knowledge of the cardinalities of individual groups in a table (Haas, 1997; Hass and Hellerstein, 1999). To obtain this information for an Index Stride, we require a histogram on the GROUP BY column; a more natural solution would be to use a *ranked* index (Knuth, 1973; Antoshenkov, 1992; Aoki, 1998), but this is not available in most commercial databases. In the first phase of the reordering operator described at the end of 3.2, we can estimate a group's cardinality as the fraction of tuples from that group in the currently scanned sample. The statistics in the confidence intervals need to take the error of this estimation into account (Haas, 1997; Hass and Hellerstein, 1999); the statistical details remain as future work. In the second phase of the reordering operator, the exact cardinalities of all groups are known, so our usual estimation techniques apply.

Third, deterministic confidence intervals also require upper and lower bounds on the inputs to the aggregation functions. If the input to the function is a column (e.g. `AVG(enroll.grade)`), these bounds are typically available from the system catalogs. If the input is more complex (e.g. `AVG(f(enroll.grade)` for some UDF `f`) the only bounds available are those of the data type of the input (e.g. MAXINT is an upper bound for integers).

Acknowledgments

Bruce Lo implemented our user interface for online aggregation, and was involved in early development of our Informix extensions. Chris Olston and Andy Chou developed the CLOUDS system we describe in Section 2.3, and Christian Hidber developed the CARMA data mining algorithm described in Section 2.4. We are indebted to the CONTROL group at Berkeley for many interesting discussions: Andy Chou, Christian Hidber, Bruce Lo, Chris Olston, Tali Roth and Kirk Wylie. We are also grateful to Peter Haas of IBM Almaden Research for his many contributions to this work. Our relationship with Informix was made possible by Mike Stonebraker and Cristi Garvey; this kind of close academic/industrial collaboration is all too rare. At Informix, we received great help from Chih-Po Wen, Robyn Chan, Paul Friedman, Kathey Marsden, and Satheesh Bandaram. Helen Wang and Andrew MacBride contributed to an earlier Postgres-based prototype of online query processing. This work was supported by a grant from Informix Corporation, a California MICRO grant, NSF grant IIS-9802051, and a Sloan Foundation Fellowship. Computing and network resources for this research were provided through NSF RI grant CDA-9401156.

Notes

1. Continuous Output and Navigation Technology with Refinement On Line.
2. The other SQL aggregates, `MIN` and `MAX`, are "needle-in-a-haystack" scenarios that cannot be satisfied via sampling schemes like online aggregation: the minimum or maximum value may not appear until the last tuple is fetched. However, related user-defined-aggregates are amenable to online aggregation: e.g., `99-percentile`, which displays a tuple that can be said to be within ϵ of the 99'th percentile with some confidence.
3. The term *clustering* in relational databases is distinct from the statistical notion of clustering. A table in a database is said to be clustered on a column (or list of columns) if it is stored on disk in ascending order of that column (or ascending lexicographic order of the list of columns).
4. In order for this scheme to work, one must declare the function $f(\ )$ to SQL as being "NOT VARIANT". This informs the system that the value of $f(\ )$ for a tuple will not change over time, and the index can serve as a cache of the $f(\ )$ value for each tuple. This might seem counterintuitive since $f(\ )$ generates random numbers, but the point is that the *use* of the random numbers is static: once they define an initial random ordering of the table, that ordering is static until the table is reclustered.
5. Index Stride is naturally applicable to other types of indices as well, but we omit discussion here.
6. The name "ripple join" has two sources. One is shown in the pictures in figures 4 and 5—the algorithm sweeps out the plane like ripples spreading in a pond. The other source is the rectangular version of the algorithm, which produces "Rectangles of Increasing Perimeter Length".
7. We ran all experiments on a lightly-loaded dual-processor 200 MHz UltraSPARC machine running SunOS 5.5.1 with 256MB RAM. We used the INFORMIX Dynamic Server with Universal Data Option version 9.14 which we enhanced with online aggregation and reordering features. We used a separate disk for the side-disk for online reordering. We used a statistical confidence parameter (Haas, 1997) of 95% for our large sample confidence intervals. Note that we did not bother to tune our Informix installation carefully, since our online results were already performing sufficiently well. The performance of online and batch results presented here are not necessarily indicative of the peak performance available in a well-tuned installation, and readers should not use this study to extrapolate about the performance of Informix UDO.
8. To ensure that preferences are changed at a fixed, repeatable point in our experiments, we modified the *reorder* operator to read in the preference change points from a configuration file instead of from the GUI of figure 1.

References

Agrawal, R. 1997. Personal communication.

Agrawal, R. and Srikant, R. 1994. Fast algorithms for mining association rules. In Proc. 20th International Conference on Very Large Data Bases, Santiago de Chile, September 1994.

Aiken, A., Chen, J., Stonebraker, M., and Woodruff, A. 1996. Tioga-2: A direct-manipulation database visualization environment. In Proc. 12th IEEE International Conference on Data Engineering, New Orleans, February 1996.

Antoshenkov, G. 1992. Random sampling from pseudo-ranked B+ trees. In Proc. 18th International Conference on Very Large Data Bases, Vancouver, August 1992.

Antoshenkov, G. and Ziauddin, M. 1996. Query processing and optimization in Oracle Rdb. VLDB Journal, 5(4):229–237.

Aoki, P.M. 1998. Generalizing "search" in generalized search trees. In IEEE International Conference on Data Engineering, Orlando, February 1998.

Astrahan, M., Blasgen, M., Chamberlin, D., Eswaran, K., Gray, J., Griffiths, P., King, W., Lorie, R., McJones, P., Mehl, J., Putzolu, G., Traiger, I., Wade, B., and Watson, V. 1976. System R: Relational approach to database management. ACM Transactions on Database Systems, 1(2):97–137.

Avnur, R. and Hellerstein, J.M. 2000. Eddies: Continuously adaptive query processing. In Proc. ACM-SIGMOD International Conference on Management of Data, Dallas, May 2000.

Bayardo Jr., R.J. and Miranker, D.P. 1996. Processing queries for first-few answers. In Fifth Intl. Conf. Information and Knowledge Management, Rockville, MD.

Carey, M.J. and Kossmann, D. 1997. On saying "Enough Already!" in SQL. In Proc. ACM-SIGMOD International Conference on Management of Data, Tucson, May 1997.

Carey, M.J. and Kossmann, D. 1998. Reducing the braking distance of an SQL query engine. In Proc. 24th International Conference on Very Large Data Bases, New York City.

Chaudhuri, S. and Gravano, L. 1996. Optimizing queries over multimedia repositories. In Proc. ACM-SIGMOD International Conference on Management of Data, Montreal, June 1996.

Chaudhuri, S. and Gravano, L. 1999. Evaluating top-k selection queries. In Proc. International Conference on Very Large Data Bases, Edinburgh.

Chaudhuri, S. and Narasayya, V. 1998. AutoAdmin "What-If" index analysis utility. In Proc. ACM-SIGMOD International Conference on Management of Data, Seattle, June 1998.

Chaudhuri, S. and Shim, K. 1996. Optimization of queries with user-defined predicates. In Proc. 24th International Conference on Very Large Data Bases, Bombay (Mumbai), September 1996.

Cherniack, M. 1998. Building query optimizers with combinators. PhD Thesis, Brown University.

DeWitt, D.J., Katz, R.H., Olken, Frank, Shapiro, L.D., Stonebraker, R.M., and Wood, D. 1984. Implementation techniques for main memory database systems. In Proc. ACM-SIGMOD International Conference on Management of Data, Boston, June 1984.

Donjerkovic, D. and Ramakrishnan, R. 1999. Probabilistic optimization of Top N queries. In Proc. International Conference on Very Large Data Bases, Edinburgh.

Fagin, R. 1998. Fuzzy queries in multimedia database systems. In Proc. ACM SIGACT-SIGMOD-SIGART Symposium on Principles of Database Systems, Seattle, June 1998.

Fayyad, U., Piatetsky-Shapiro, G., and Smyth, P. 1996. The kdd process for extracting useful knowledge from volumes of data. Communications of the ACM, 39(11).

Fushimi, S., Kitsuregawa, M., and Tanaka, H. 1986. An overview of the system software of a parallel relational database machine GRACE. In Proc. 24th International Conference on Very Large Data Bases, Kyoto, August 1986.

Gibbons, P.B. and Matias, Y. 1998. New sampling-based summary statistics for improving approximate query answers. In Proc. ACM-SIGMOD International Conference on Management of Data, Seattle.

Gibbons, P.B., Poosala, V., Acharya, S., Bartal, Y., Matias, Y., Muthukrishnan, S., Ramaswamy, S., and Suel, T. 1998. Aqua: System and techniques for approximate query answering. Technical Report, Bell Laboratories.

Graefe, G. 1993. Query evaluation techniques for large databases. ACM Computing Surveys, 25(2):73–170.

Gray, J. and Graefe, G. 1997. The five-minute rule ten years later, and other computer storage rules of thumb. SIGMOD Record, 26(4).

Haas, P.J. 1996. Hoeffding inequalities for join-selectivity estimation and online aggregation. IBM Research Report RJ 10040, IBM Almaden Research Center.

Haas, P.J. 1997. Large-sample and deterministic confidence intervals for online aggregation. In Proc. 9th International Conference on Scientific and Statistical Database Management, Olympia, WA, August 1997.

Haas, P.J. and Hellerstein, J.M. 1999. Ripple algorithms for online aggregation. In Proc. ACM-SIGMOD International Conference on Management of Data, Philadelphia, May 1999.

Haas, P.J., Naughton, J.F., Seshadri, S., and Swami, A.N. 1996. Selectivity and cost estimation for joins based on random sampling. Journal of Computer System Science, 52:550–569.

Harinarayan, V., Rajaraman, A., and Ullman, J.D. 1996. Implementing data cubes efficiently. In Proc. ACM-SIGMOD International Conference on Management of Data, Montreal, June 1996.

Hellerstein, J.M. 1997a. The case for online aggregation. Computer Science Technical Report CSD-97-958, University of California, Berkeley.

Hellerstein, J.M. 1997b. Online processing redux. IEEE Data Engineering Bulletin, 20(3).

Hellerstein, J.M. 1998a. Looking forward to interactive queries. Database Programming and Design, 11(8):28–33.

Hellerstein, J.M. 1998b. Optimization techniques for queries with expensive predicates. ACM Transactions on Database Systems, 23(2).

Hellerstein, J.M., Avnur, R., Chou, A., Hidber, C., Olston, C., Raman, V., and Roth, T. 1999. Interactive Data Analysis with CONTROL. IEEE Computer 32(9):51–59.

Hellerstein, J.M., Haas, P.J., and Wang, H.J. 1997. Online aggregation. In Proc. ACM-SIGMOD International Conference on Management of Data, Tucson, May 1997.

Hellerstein, J.M. and Naughton, J.F. 1996. Query execution techniques for caching expensive methods. In Proc. ACM-SIGMOD International Conference on Management of Data, Montreal, June 1996.

Hidber, C. 1997. Online association rule mining. In Proc. ACM-SIGMOD International Conference on Management of Data, Tucson, May 1997.

Hoeffding, W. 1963. Probability inequalities for sums of bounded random variables. Journal of the American Statistical Association, 58.

Hou, W.C., Ozsoyoglu, G., and Taneja, B.K. 1988. Statistical estimators for relational algebra expressions. In Proc. 7th ACM SIGACT-SIGMOD-SIGART Symposium on Principles of Database Systems, Austin, March 1998.

Hou, W.C., Ozsoyoglu, G., and Taneja, B.K. 1989. Processing aggregate relational queries with hard time constraints. In Proc. ACM-SIGMOD International Conference on Management of Data, Portland, May–June 1989.

Hyperion Essbase OLAP Server, 1998. URL http://www.hyperion.com/essbaseolap.cfm.

Illustra Information Technologies, Inc. 1994. Illustra User's Guide, Illustra Server Release 2.1.

Informix Corp. 1998a. Sampling: The latest breakthrough in decision support technology. Informix White Paper 000-21681-70.

Informix Corp. 1998b. C-ISAM Version 7.24 for the UNIX Operating System.

Informix Corp. 1998c. Informix Dynamic Server with Universal Data Option 9.1x.

Knuth, D.E. 1973. The Art of Computer Programming: Vol. 3, Sorting and Searching. Addison-Wesley.

Leung, T.Y.C., Pirahesh, H., Seshadri, P., and Hellerstein, J.M. 1998. Query rewrite optimization rules in IBM DB/2 universal database. In Readings in Database Systems, 3rd ed., M. Stonebraker and J.M. Hellerstein (Eds.). San Francisco: Morgan-Kaufmann.

Lipton, R.J., Naughton, J.F., Schneider, D.A., and Seshadri, S. 1993. Efficient sampling strategies for relational database operations. Theoretical Computer Science, 116:195–226.

Livny, M., Ramakrishnan, R., Beyer, K.S., Chen, G., Donjerkovic, D., Lawande, S., and Myllymaki, J. 1997. DEVise: Integrated querying and visualization of large datasets. In Proc. ACM-SIGMOD International Conference on Management of Data, Tucson, May 1997.

Lynch, C. and Stonebraker, M. 1988. Extended user-defined indexing with application to textual databases. In Proc. 14th International Conference on Very Large Data Bases, Los Angeles, August–Septeber 1998.

Maier, D. and Stein, J. 1986. Indexing in an object-oriented DBMS. In Proc. 1st Workshop on Object-Oriented Database Systems, Asilomar, September 1986.

Morgenstein, J.P. 1980. Computer based management information systems embodying answer accuracy as a user parameter. PhD Thesis, U.C. Berkeley.

O'day, V. and Jeffries, R. 1993. Orienteering in an information landscape: How information seekers get from here to there. In INTERCHI.

Ohno, P. 1998. Visionary. Informix Magazine.

Olken, F. 1993. Random sampling from databases. PhD Thesis, University of California, Berkeley.

Papadopoulos, G. Chief Technology Officer. 1997. Sun Microsystems. Untitled talk. Berkeley NOW Retreat, July 1997.

Perlin, K. and Fox, D. 1993. Pad: An alternative approach to the computer interface. In Proc. ACM SIGGRAPH, Anaheim, pp. 57–64.

Pilot Software 1998. Announces release of PDSS 6.0. URL http://www.pilotsw.com/about/pressrel/pr72998.htm.

Raman, V., Chou, A., and Hellerstein, J.M. 1999a. Scalable spreadsheets for interactive data analysis. In DMKD Workshop.

Raman, V., Raman, B., and Hellerstein, J.M. 1999b. Online dynamic reordering for interactive data processing. In Proc. International Conference on Very Large Data Bases, Edinburgh.

Rao, J. and Ross, K.A. 1998. Reusing invariants: A new strategy for correlated queries. In Proc. ACM-SIGMOD International Conference on Management of Data, Seattle, June 1998.

Red Brick Systems, Inc. 1998. Red brick warehouse. URL http://www.redbrick.com/products/rbw/rbw.html.

Seshadri, P. and Swami, A. 1995. Generalized partial indexes. In Proc. 11th IEEE International Conference on Data Engineering, Taipei, March 1995.

Shneiderman, B. 1982. The future of interactive systems and the emergence of direct manipulation. Behavior and Information Technology, 1(3):237–256.

Shukla, A., Deshpande, P., and Naughton, J.F. 1998. Materialized view selection for multidimensional datasets. In Proc. 24th International Conference on Very Large Data Bases, New York City.

Silberschatz, A., Read, R.L., and Fussell, D.S. 1992. A multi-resolution relational data model. In Proc. 18th International Conference on Very Large Data Bases, Vancouver, August 1992.

QL 1998. Server 7.0 OLAP services. URL http://www.microsoft.com/backoffice/sql/70/whpprs/olapoverview.htm.

Stonebraker, M. 1989. The case for partial indexes. SIGMOD Record, 18(4):4–11.

Stonebraker, M. and Kemnitz, G. 1991. The POSTGRES Next-Generation database management system. Communications of the ACM, 34(10):78–92.

Tan, K., Goh, C.H., and Ooi, B.C. 1999. Online feedback for nested aggregate queries with multi-threading. In Prov. International Conference on Very Large Data Bases, Edinburgh.

Transaction Processing Council. TPC-D Rev. 1.2.3 Benchmark Specification. URL http://www.tpc.org/dspec.html.

Vrbsky, S.V. and Liu, J.W.S. 1993. APPROXIMATE—A query processor that produces monotonically improving approximate answers. IEEE Transactions on Knowledge and Data Engineering, 5(6):1056–1068.

Waldspurger, C.A. and Weihl, W.E. 1995. Lottery scheduling: Flexible proportional-share resource management. In First Symposium on Operating Systems Design and Implementation (OSDI).

Walter, T., Chief Technical Officer. 1998. NCR parallel systems. Complex queries. NSF Database Systems Industrial/Academic Workshop, October 1998.

Wilschut, A.N. and Apers, P.M.G. 1991. Dataflow query execution in a parallel main-memory environment. In Proc. First Intl. Conf. Parallel and Distributed Info. Sys. (PDIS), pages 68–77, Miami Beach, December 1991.

Winter, R. and Auerbach, K. 1998. The big time: 1998 winter VLDB survey. Database Programming and Design.

Zilberstein, S. and Russell, S.J. 1996. Optimal composition of real-time systems. Artificial Intelligence, 82(1/2):181–213.

DynaMat: A Dynamic View Management System for Data Warehouses*

Yannis Kotidis
Department of Computer Science
University of Maryland
kotidis@cs.umd.edu

Nick Roussopoulos
Department of Computer Science
University of Maryland
nick@cs.umd.edu

Abstract

Pre-computation and materialization of views with aggregate functions is a common technique in Data Warehouses. Due to the complex structure of the warehouse and the different profiles of the users who submit queries, there is need for tools that will automate the selection and management of the materialized data. In this paper we present DynaMat, a system that dynamically materializes information at multiple levels of granularity in order to match the demand (workload) but also takes into account the maintenance restrictions for the warehouse, such as down time to update the views and space availability. DynaMat unifies the view selection and the view maintenance problems under a single framework using a novel "goodness" measure for the materialized views. DynaMat constantly monitors incoming queries and materializes the best set of views subject to the space constraints. During updates, DynaMat reconciles the current materialized view selection and refreshes the most beneficial subset of it within a given maintenance window. We compare DynaMat against a system that is given all queries in advance and the pre-computed optimal static view selection. The comparison is made based on a new metric, the Detailed Cost Savings Ratio introduced for quantifying the benefits of view materialization against incoming queries. These experiments show that DynaMat's dynamic view selection outperforms the optimal static view selection and thus, any sub-optimal static algorithm that has appeared in the literature.

1 Introduction

Materialized views represent a set of redundant entities in a data warehouse that are used to accelerate On-Line Analytical Processing (OLAP). A substantial effort of the academic community in the last years [HRU96, GHRU97, Gup97, BPT97, SDN98] has been for a given workload, to select an appropriate set of views that would provide the best performance benefits. The amount of redundancy added is controlled by the data warehouse administrator who specifies the space that is willing to allocate for the materialized data. Given this space restriction and, if available, some description of the workload, these algorithms return a suggested set of views that can be materialized for better performance.

This static selection of views however, contradicts the dynamic nature of decision support analysis. Especially for add-hoc queries where the expert user is looking for interesting trends in the data repository, the query pattern is difficult to predict. In addition, as the data and these trends are changing overtime, a static selection of views might very quickly become outdated. This means that the administrator should monitor the query pattern and periodically "re-calibrate" the materialized views by re-running these algorithms. This task for a large warehouse where many users with different profiles submit their queries is rather complicated and time consuming. Microsoft's [Aut] is a step towards automated management of system resources and shows that vendors have realized the need to simplify the life of the data warehouse administrator.

Another inherit drawback of the static view selection is that the system has no way of tuning a wrong selection, i.e use results of queries that couldn't be answered by the materialized set. Notice that although OLAP queries take an enormous amount of disk I/O and CPU processing time to be completed, their output is, in many cases, relatively small. `Find the total volume of sales for the last 10 years` is a fine example of that. Processing this query might take hours of scanning vast tables and aggregating, while the result is just an 8-byte float value that can be easily "cached" for future use. Moreover, during *roll−up* operations, when we access data at a progressively coarser granularity, future queries are likely to be totally computable out of the results of previous operations, without accessing the base tables at all. Thus, we expect a great amount of inter-dependency among a set of OLAP queries.

Furthermore, selecting a view set to materialize is just the tip of the iceberg. Clearly, query performance is

*This research was sponsored partially by NASA under grant NAG 5-2926, by NSA/Lucite under contract CG9815, by a gift from Advanced Communication Technology, Inc., and by the University of Maryland Institute for Advanced Computer Studies (UMIACS).

tremendously improved as more views are materialized. With the ratio $$/disk-volume constantly dropping, disk storage constraint is no longer the limiting factor in the view selection but the window to refresh the materialized set during updates. More materialization implies a larger maintenance window. This update window is the major data warehouse parameter, constraining over-materialization. Some view selection algorithms [Gup97, BPT97] take into account the maintenance cost of the views and try to minimize both query-response time and the maintenance overhead under a given space restriction. In [TS97] the authors define the Data Warehouse configuration problem as a state-space optimization problem where the maintenance cost of the views needs to be minimized, while all the queries can be answered by the selected views. The trade-off between space of pre-computed results and maintenance time is also discussed in [DDJ+98]. However, none of these publications considers the dynamic nature of the view selection problem, nor they propose a solution that can adapt on the fly to changes in the workload.

Our philosophy starts with the premise that a result is a terrible thing to waste and that its generation cost should be amortized over multiple uses of the result. This philosophy goes back to our earlier work on caching of query results on the client's database $ADMS+$ architecture [RK86, DR92], the work on prolonging their useful life through incremental updates [Rou91] and their re-use in the ADMS optimizer [CR94]. This philosophy is a major departure from the static paradigm of pre-selecting a set of views to be materialized and run all queries against this static set.

In this paper we present DynaMat, a system that dynamically materializes information at multiple levels of granularity in order to match the demand (workload) but also takes into account the maintenance restrictions for the warehouse, such as down time to update the views and space availability. DynaMat unifies the view selection and the view maintenance problems under a single framework using a novel "goodness" measure for the materialized views. DynaMat constantly monitors incoming queries and materializes the best set of views subject to the space constraints. During updates, DynaMat reconciles the current materialized view selection and refreshes the most beneficial subset of it within a given maintenance window. The critical performance issue is how fast we can incorporate the updates to the warehouse. Clearly if naive re-computation is assumed for refreshing materialized views, then the number of views will be minimum and this will lessen the value of DynaMat. On the other hand, efficient computation of these views using techniques like [AAD+96, HRU96, ZDN97, GMS93, GL95, JMS95, MQM97] and/or bulk incremental updates [RKR97] tremendously enhances the overall performance of the system. In DynaMat any of these techniques can be applied. In section 2.4.2 we propose a novel algorithm that based on the goodness measure, computes an update plan for the data stored in the system.

The main benefit of DynaMat, is that it represents a complete self-tunable solution that relieves the warehouse administrator from having to monitor and calibrate the system constantly. In our experiments, we compare DynaMat against a system that is given all queries in advance and the pre-computed optimal static view selection. These experiments show that the dynamic view selection outperforms the optimal static view selection and thus, any sub-optimal static algorithm proposed in the literature [HRU96, GHRU97, Gup97, BPT97].

The rest of the paper is organized as follows: Section 2 gives an overview of the system's architecture. Subsections 2.2 and 2.3 discuss how stored results are being reused for answering a new query, whereas in section 2.4 we address the maintenance problem for the stored data. Section 3 contains the experiments and in section 4 we draw the conclusions.

2 System overview

DynaMat is designed to operate as a complete view management system, tightly coupled with the rest of the data warehouse architecture. This means that DynaMat can co-exist and co-operate with caching architectures that operate at the client site like [DFJ+96, KB96]. Figure 1 depicts the architecture of the system. *View Pool* $\mathcal{V}$ is the information repository that is used for storing materialized results. We distinguish two operational phases of the system. The first one is the "on-line" during which DynaMat answers queries posed to the warehouse using the *Fragment Locator* to determine whether or not already materialized results can be efficiently used to answer the query. This decision is based upon a cost model that compares the cost of answering a query through the repository with the cost of running the same query against the warehouse. A *Directory Index* is maintained in order to support sub-linear search in $\mathcal{V}$ for finding candidate materialized results. This structure will be described in detail in the following sections. If the search fails to reveal an efficient way to use data stored in $\mathcal{V}$ for answering the query then the system follows the conventional approach where the warehouse infrastructure (fact table+indices) is queried. Either-way, after the result is computed and given to the user, it is tested by the *Admission Control Entity* which decides whether or not it is beneficial to store it in the Pool.

During the on-line phase, the goal of the system is to answer as many queries as possible from the pool, because most of them will be answered a lot faster from $\mathcal{V}$ than from the conventional methods. At the same time DynaMat will quickly adapt to new query patterns and efficiently utilize the system resources.

The second phase of DynaMat is the update phase, during which updates received from the data sources get stored in the warehouse and materialized results in the Pool get refreshed. In this paper we assume, but we are not restricted to, that the update phase is "off-line" and queries are not

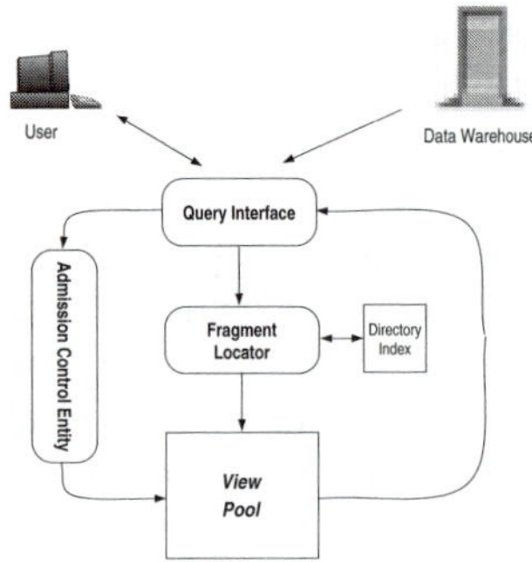

Figure 1: DynaMat's architecture

permitted during this phase. The maximum length of the update window W is specified by the administrator and would probably lead us to evict some of the data stored in the pool as not update-able within this time constraint.

2.1 View Pool organization

The View Pool utilizes a dedicated disk storage for managing materialized data. An important design parameter is the type of secondary storage organization that will be used. DynaMat can support any underling storage structure, as long as we can provide a cost model for querying and updating the views.

Traditionally summary data are stored as relational tables in most ROLAP implementations, e.g [BDD$^+$98]. However, tables alone are not enough to guarantee reasonable query performance. Scanning a large summary table to locate an interesting subset of tuples can be wasteful and in some cases slower than running the query against the warehouse itself, if there are no additional indices to support random access to the data. Moreover, relational tables and traditional indexing schemes, are in most cases space wasteful and inadequate for efficiently supporting bulk incremental update operations. More eligible candidate structures include multidimensional arrays like chunked files [SS94, DRSN98] and also Cubetrees [RKR97]. Cubetrees are multidimensional data structures that provide both storage and indexing in a single organization. In [KR98] we have shown that Cubetrees, when used for storing summary data, provide extremely fast update rates, better overall query performance and better disk space utilization compared to relational tables and conventional indexes.

During the "on-line" phase of the warehouse, results from incoming queries are being added in the Pool. If the pool had unlimited disk space, the size of the materialized data would grow monotonically overtime. During an update phase u_i, some of the materialized results may not be update-able within the time constraint of W and thus, will be evicted from the pool. This is the update **time bound** case shown in Figure 2 with the size of the pool increasing between the two update phases u_1 and u_2. The two local minimums correspond to the amount of materialized data that can be updated within W and the local maximums to the pool size at the time of the updates.

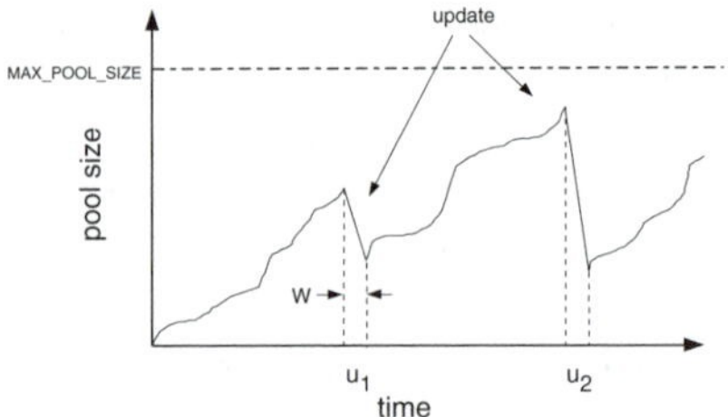

Figure 2: The **time bound** case

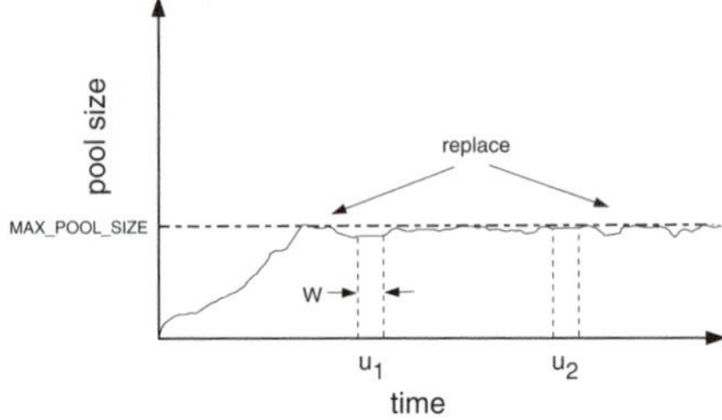

Figure 3: The **space bound** case

The **space bound** case is when the size of the pool is the constraining factor and not W. In this case, when the pool becomes full, we have to use some *replacement* policy. This can vary from simply not admitting more materialized results to the pool, to known techniques like LRU, FIFO etc, or to using heuristics for deciding whether or not a new result is more beneficial for the system than an older one. Figure 3 shows the variations in the pool size in this case. Since we assumed a sufficiently large update window W, the stored results are always update-able and the actual content of the pool is now controlled by the replacement policy.

Depending on the workload, the disk space and the update window, the system will in some cases act as in time bound and in others as in space bound, or both. In such cases views are evicted from the pool, either because there is no more space or they can not be updated within the update window.

2.2 Using MRFs as the basic logical unit of the pool

A multidimensional data warehouse (MDW) is a data repository in which data is organized along a set of dimensions $\mathcal{D} = \{d_1, d_2, \ldots, d_n\}$. A possible way to design a MDW is the star-schema [Kim96] which, for each dimension it stores a *dimension table* D_i that has d_i as its primary key and also uses a *fact table* F that correlates the information stored in these tables through the keys $d_1, \ldots, d_n$. The Data Cube operator [GBLP96] performs the computation of one or more aggregate functions for all possible combinations of grouping attributes (which are actually attributes selected from the dimension tables D_i). The lattice [HRU96] representation of the Data Cube in Figure 4 shows an example for three dimensions, namely a, b and c. Each node in the lattice represents a view that aggregates data over the attributes present in that node. For example (ab) in an aggregate view over the a and b grouping attributes.[1]

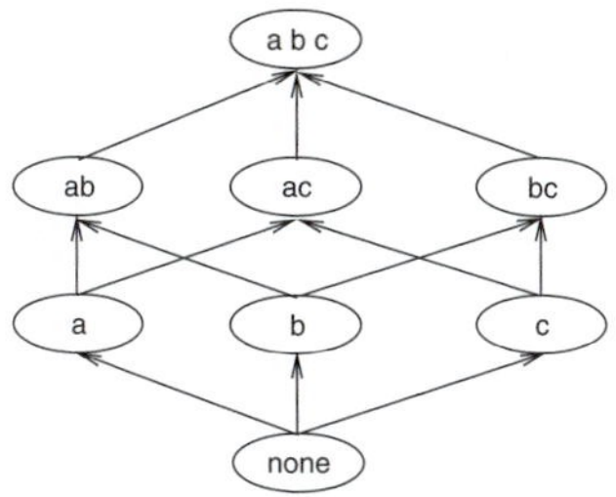

Figure 4: The Data Cube lattice for dimensions a, b and c

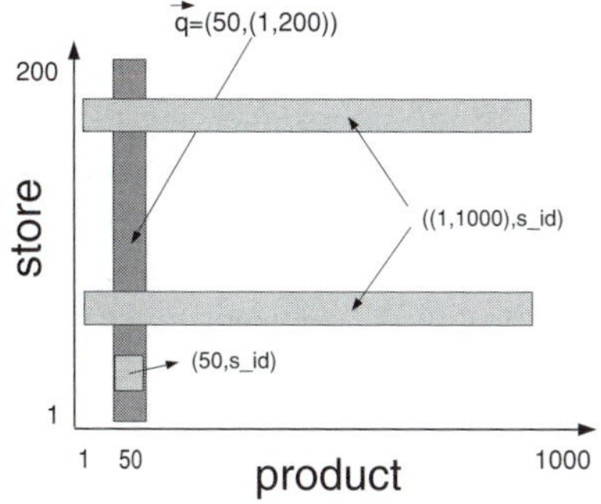

Figure 5: Querying stored MRFs

The lattice is frequently used by view selection algorithms [HRU96, GHRU97, SDN98] because it captures the computational dependencies among the elements of the Data Cube. Such dependencies are shown in Figure 4 as directed edges that connect two views, if the pointed view computes the other one. In Figure 4 we show only dependencies between adjacent views and not those in the transitive closure of this lattice. For example, view (a) can be computed from view (ab), while view (abc) can be used to derive any other view.

In this context, we assume that the warehouse workload is a collection of *Multidimensional Range queries* (MR-queries) each of which can be visualized as a *hyper-plane* in the Data Cube space using a n-dimensional "vector" $\vec{q}$:

$$\vec{q} = \{R_1, R_2, \ldots, R_n\} \quad (1)$$

where R_i is a range in the dimension's d_i domain. We restrict each range to be one of the followings:

- a full range: $R_i = (min_{d_i}, max_{d_i})$, where min_{d_i} and max_{d_i} are the minimum and maximum values for key d_i.
- a single value for d_i
- an empty range which denotes a dimension that is not present in the query.

[1] For simplicity in the notation, in this paper we do not consider the case where the grouping is done over attributes other than the dimension keys d_i. However our framework is still applicable in the presence of more grouping attributes and hierarchies, using the extensions of [HRU96] for the lattice.

For instance, suppose that $D = \{product, store\}$ is the set of dimensions in the MDW, with values $1 \leq product \leq 1000$ and $1 \leq store \leq 200$ respectively. The hyper-plane $\vec{q} = \{50, (1, 200)\}$ corresponds to the SQL query:

```
select product, store, aggregate_list
from F
where product=50
group by product, store
```

where *aggregate_list* is a list of aggregate functions (e.g sum,count). If the grouping was done on attributes different than the dimension keys then the actual SQL description would include joins between some dimension tables and the fact table. This type of queries are called *slice queries* [GHRU97, BPT97, KR98]. We prefer the MR notation over the SQL description because it describes the workload in the Data Cube space independent of the actual schema of the MDW.

The same notation permits us to represent the materialized results of MR queries which we call Multidimensional Range Fragments (MRFs). DynaMat maps each SQL query to one, or more, MR queries. Given such a MR-query and a cost model for accessing the stored MRFs, we want to find the "best" subset of them in $\mathcal{V}$ to answer q. Based on the definition of MRFs, we argue that is doesn't pay to check for combinations of materialized results for answering q. With extremely high probability, q is best computable out of a single fragment f or not computable at all. We will try to demonstrate this with the following example: Suppose that the previous query $\vec{q} = \{50, (1, 200)\}$ is given. If no single MRF in the pool computes q, then a stored MRF that partially computes q is of the form $\{50, s\_id\}$ or $\{(1, 1000), s\_id\}$, where s_id is some store value, see Figure 5. In order to answer q there should be at least one such fragment for all values of s_id between 1 and 200. Even if such a combination exists, it is highly unlikely that querying 200 different fragments to get the complete result provides a cost-effective way to answer the query.

MRFs provide a slightly coarser grain of materialization if we compare them with a system that materializes views with arbitrary ranges for the attributes. However, if we allow fragments with arbitrary ranges to be stored in the pool, then the probability that a single stored fragment can solely be used to answer a new query is rather low, especially if most of the materialized results are small, i.e they correspond to small areas in the n-dimensional space. This means that we will need to use combinations of stored fragments and perform costly duplicate eliminations to compute an answer for a given query. In the general case that k fragments compute some portion of the query there might be up to 2^k combinations that need to be checked for finding the most efficient way to answer the query. Having too many small fragments with possible overlapping sections which require additional filtering in the pool, results in poor performance not only during query execution but also during updates. In most cases, updating fewer, larger fragments of views (as in a MRF-pool) is preferable. We denote the number of fragments in the pool as $|\mathcal{V}|$. In section 2.4.2 we show that the overhead of computing an update plan for the stored data grows linearly with $|\mathcal{V}|^2$, making the MRF approach more scalable.

2.3 Answering queries using the Directory Index

As we described, when a MR-query q is posted to the data warehouse, we scan $\mathcal{V}$ for candidate fragments that answer q. Given a MRF f and a query q, f answers q iff for every non-empty range R_i of the query, the fragment stores exactly the same range and for every empty range $R_i = ()$ the fragment's corresponding range is either empty or spans the whole domain of dimension i[2]. We say in this case that hyper-plane $\vec{f}$ *covers* $\vec{q}$.

Instead of testing all stored fragments against the query, DynaMat uses a directory, the *Directory Index* (see Figure 1), to further prune the search space. This is actually a set of indices connected through the lattice shown in Figure 4. Each node has a dedicated index that is used to keep track of all fragments of the corresponding view that are stored in the pool. For each fragment f there is exactly one entry that contains the following info:

- Hyper-plane $\vec{f}$ of the fragment
- Statistics (e.g number of accesses, time of creation, last access)
- The *father* of f (explained below).

For our implementation we used R-trees based on the $\vec{f}$ hyper-planes to implement these indices. When a query q arrives, we scan using $\vec{q}$ all views in the lattice, that might contain materialized results f whose hyper-planes $\vec{f}$ *cover* $\vec{q}$. For example if $\vec{q} = \{(1, 1000), (), Smith\}$ is the query hyperplane for dimensions $product$, $store$ and $customer$, then we first scan the R-tree index for view $(product, customer)$ using rectangle $\{(1, 1000), (Smith, Smith)\}$. Figure 6 depicts a snapshot of the corresponding R-tree for view $(product, customer)$ and the search rectangle. The shaded areas denote MRFs of that view that are materialized in the pool. Since no fragment is found, based on the dependencies defined in the lattice, we also check view $(product, store, customer)$ for candidate fragments. For this view, we "expand" the undefined in q $store$ dimension and search the corresponding R-tree using rectangle $\{(1, 1000), (min_{store}, max_{store}), (Smith, Smith)\}$. If a fragment is found, we "collapse" the $store$ column and aggregate the measure(s) to compute the answer for q.

Based on the content of the pool $\mathcal{V}$, there are three possibilities. The first is that a stored fragment f matches exactly the definition of the query. In this case, f is retrieved

[2] In the latter case we have to perform an additional aggregation to compute the result, as will be explained.

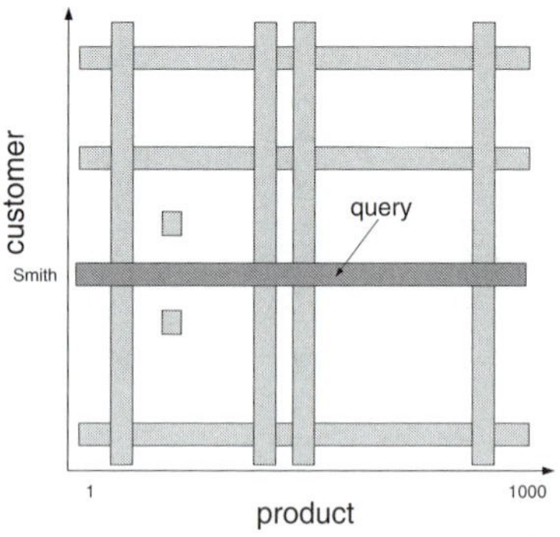

Figure 6: Directory for view $(product, customer)$

and returned to the user. If no exact match exists, assuming we are given a cost model for querying the fragments, we select the best candidate from the pool, to compute q. If view f is the materialized result of q, the fragment that was used to compute f is called the *father* of f and is denoted as $\acute{f}$. If however no fragment in $\mathcal{V}$ can answer q, the query is handled by the warehouse. In both cases the result is passed to the Admission Control Entity that checks if it can be stored in the pool.

As the number of MRFs stored in the pool is typically in the order of thousands, we can safely assume that in most cases the Directory Index will be memory resident. Our experiments validate this assumption and indicate that the look-up cost in this case is negligible. In cases where the index can not fit in memory, we can take advantage of the fact that the pool is reorganized with every update phase and use a packing algorithm [RL85] to keep the R-trees compact and optimized at all times.

2.4 Pool maintenance

For maintaining the MRF-pool, we need to derive a *goodness* measure for choosing which of the stored fragments we prefer. This measure is used in both the on-line and the update phases. Each time DynaMat reaches the space or time bounds we use the goodness for replacing MRFs. There can be many criteria to define such a goodness. Among those we tested, the following four showed the best results:

- The time that the fragment was last accessed by the system to handle a query:

  $$goodness(f) = t_{last\_access}(f)$$

  This information is kept in the Directory Index. Using this time-stamp as a goodness measure, results in an Least Recently Used (LRU) type of replacement in both cases.

- The frequency of access $freq(f)$ for the fragment:

  $$goodness(f) = freq(f)$$

  The frequency is computed using the statistics kept in the Directory Index and results in a Least Frequently used (LFU) replacement policy.

- The size $size(f)$ of the result, measured in disk pages:

$$goodness(f) = size(f)$$

The intuition behind this approach is that larger fragments are more likely to be hit by a query. An additional benefit of keeping larger results in the pool is that $|\mathcal{V}|$ gets smaller, resulting in faster look-ups using the Fragment Locator and less complexity while updating the pool. We refer to this case as the Smaller-Fragment-First (SFF) replacement policy.

- The expected penalty rate of recomputing the fragment, if it is evicted, normalized by its actual size:

$$goodness(f) = \frac{freq(f) * c(f)}{size(f)}$$

$c(f)$ is the cost of re-computing f for a future query. We used as an estimate of $c(f)$ the cost of re-computing the fragment from its father, which is computable in constant time. This metric is similar to the one used in [SSV96] for their cache replacement and admission policy. We refer to this case as the Smaller Penalty First (SPF).

In the remaining of this section we describe how the goodness measure is used to control the content of the pool.

2.4.1 Pool maintenance during queries

As long as there is enough space in the pool, results from incoming queries are always stored in $\mathcal{V}$. In cases where we hit the space constraint, we have to enforce a replacement policy. This decision is made by our `replace` algorithm using the $goodness$ measure of the fragments. The algorithm takes as input the current state of the pool $\mathcal{V}$, the new computed result f and the space restriction S. A stored fragment is considered for eviction only if its goodness is less than that of the new result. At a first step a set $F_{evicted}$ of such fragments with the smaller goodness values is constructed. If during this process we can not find candidate victims the search is aborted and the new result is denied storage in the pool. When a fragment f_{victim} is evicted the algorithm updates the $father$ pointer for all other fragments that point to f_{victim}. In section 2.4.2 we discuss the maintenance of the $father$ pointers.

2.4.2 Pool maintenance during updates

When the base relations (sources) are updated, the data stored in the MDW, and therefore the fragments in the pool, have to be updated too. Different update policies can be implemented, depending on the types of updates, the properties of the data sources and the aggregate functions that are being computed by the views. Several methods have been proposed [AAD+96, HRU96, ZDN97] for fast (re)-computation of Data Cube aggregates. On the other hand, incremental maintenance algorithms have been presented [GMS93, GL95, JMS95, MQM97, RKR97] that handle grouping and aggregation queries.

For our framework, we assume that the sources provide the differentials of the base data, or at least the log files are available. If this is the case, then an incremental update policy can be used to refresh the pool. In this scenario we also assume that all interesting aggregate functions that are computed are *self-maintainable* [MQM97] with respect to the updates that we have. This means that a new value for each function can be computed solely from the old value and from the changes to the base data.

Computing an initial update plan

Given a pool with $|\mathcal{V}|$ being in the order of thousands, our goal is to derive an *update plan* that allows us to refresh as many fragments as possible within a given update window W. Computing the deltas for each materialized result is unrealistic, especially if the deltas are not indexed somehow. In our initial experiments we found out that the time spent on querying the sources to get the correct deltas for each fragment is the dominant factor. For that reason our pool maintenance algorithm extracts, in a preprocessing step, all the necessary deltas and stores them in a separate view dV materialized as a Cubetree. This provides a efficient indexing structure for the deltas against multidimensional range queries. The overhead of loading a Cubetree with the deltas is practically negligible[3] compared to the benefit of having the deltas fully indexed. Assume that low_{d_i} and hi_{d_i} are the minimum and maximum values for dimension d_i that are stored in all fragments in the pool. These statistics are easy to maintain in the Directory Index. View dV includes all deltas within the hyper-plane:

$$\vec{dV} = \{(low_{d_1}, hi_{d_1}), \ldots, (low_{d_n}, hi_{d_n})\}$$

For each fragment f in $\mathcal{V}$ we consider two alternative ways of doing the updates:

- We can query dV to get the updates that are necessary for refreshing f and then update the fragment incrementally. We denote the cost of this operation as $UC_I(f)$. It consists of the cost of running the MR-query $\vec{f}$ against dV to get the deltas and the cost of updating f incrementally from the result.

- If the fragment was originally computed out of another result $\acute{f}$ we estimate the cost of recomputing f from its father $\acute{f}$, after $\acute{f}$ has been updated. The cost of computing f from its father is denoted as $UC_R(f)$ and includes the cost of running MR-query $\vec{f}$ against the fragment $\acute{f}$, plus the cost of materializing the result.

The system computes the costs for the two[4] alternatives and picks the minimum one, denoted as $UC(f)$ for each

[3] Cubetree's loading rate is about 12GB/hour in a Ultra 60 with a single SCSI drive.

[4] A third alternative, is to recompute each fragment from the sources. This case is not considered here, because the incremental approach is

fragment. Obviously, this plan is not always the best one. There is always the possibility that another result f_1 has been added in the pool after f was materialized. Since the selection of the father of f was done before f_1 was around, as explained in section 2.3, the above plan does not consider recomputing f from f_1. An eager maintenance policy of the father pointers would be to refine them whenever necessary, e.g set $father(f) = f_1$, if it is more cost effective to compute f from f_1 than from its current father $\acute{f}$. We have decided to be sloppy and not refine the father pointers based on experiments that showed negligible differences between the lazy and the eager policy. The noticeable benefit is that the lazy approach reduces the worst case complexity of the `replace` and the `makeFeasible` algorithm that is discussed in the next section from $O(|\mathcal{V}|^3)$ down-to $O(|\mathcal{V}|^2)$, thus making the system able to scale for large number of fragments. By the end of this phase, the system has computed the initial update plan, which directs the most cost-effective way to update each one of the fragments using one of the two alternatives, i.e incrementally from dV or by re-computation from another fragment.

Computing a feasible update plan for a given window

The total update cost of the pool is $UC(\mathcal{V}) = \sum_{f \in \mathcal{V}} UC(f)$. If this cost is greater than the given update window W we have to select a portion of $\mathcal{V}$ that will not be materialized in the new updated version of the pool. Suppose that we choose to evict some fragment f. If f is the father of another fragment f_{child} that is to be recomputed from f, then the real reduction in the update cost of the pool is less than $UC(f)$, since the update cost of f_{child} increases. For the lazy approach for maintaining the father pointer we *forward* the $father$ pointer for f_{child}: set $father(f_{child}) = father(f)$. We now have to check if recomputing f_{child} from $father(f)$ is still a better choice than incrementally updating f_{child} from dV. If $UC^{new}(f_{child})$ is the new update cost for f_{child} then the potential *update delta*, i.e the reduction in $UC(\mathcal{V})$, if we evict fragment f is:

$$U_{delta}(f) = UC(f) - \sum_{f_{child} \in \mathcal{V}: father(f_{child}) = f} (UC^{new}(f_{child}) - UC^{old}(f_{child}))$$

If the initial plan is not feasible, we discard at a first step all fragments whose update cost $UC(f)$ is greater than the window W. If we still hit the time constraint, we evict more fragments from the pool. In this process, there is no point in evicting fragments whose U_{delta} value is less or equal to zero. Having such fragments in the pool reduces the total update cost because all their children are efficiently updated from them. For the remaining fragments we use the goodness measure to select candidates for eviction until the remaining set is update-able within the given window W. If the `goodness` function is computable in constant time, the cost for k evictions is $O(k|\mathcal{V}|)$. In the extreme case where W is too small that only a few fragments can be updated this leads to an $O(|\mathcal{V}|^2)$ total cost for computing a feasible update plan. However, in many cases just a small fraction of the stored results will be discarded resulting in close to $O(|\mathcal{V}|)$ complexity.

expected to be faster. However, for sources that do not provide their differentials during updates, we can consider using this option.

3 Experiments

The comparison and analysis of the different aspects of the system made in this section is based on a prototype that we have developed for DynaMat. This prototype implements the algorithms and different policies that we present in this paper as well as the Fragment Locator and the Directory Index, but not the pool architecture. For the latter we used the estimator of the Cubetree Datablade [ACT97] developed for the Informix Universal Server for computing the cost of querying and updating the fragments.

We have created a random MR-query generator that is tuned to provide different statistical properties for the generated query sets. A important issue for establishing a reasonable set of experiments was to derive the measures to base the comparisons upon. The *Cost Saving Ratio* (CSR) was defined in [SSV96] as a measure of the percentage of the total cost of the queries saved due to hits in their cache system. This measure is defined as:

$$CSR = \frac{\sum_i c_i h_i}{\sum_i c_i r_i}$$

where c_i is the cost of execution of query q_i without using their cache, h_i is the number of times that the query was satisfied in the cache and r_i is the total number of references to that query. This metric is also used in [DRSN98] for their experiments. Because query costs vary widely, CSR is more appropriate metric than the common hit ratio: $\frac{\sum_i h_i}{\sum_i r_i}$. However, a drawback in the above definition for our case, is that it doesn't capture the different ways that a query q_i might "hit" the Pool. In the best scenario, q_i exactly matches a fragment in $\mathcal{V}$. In this case the savings is defined as c_i, where c_i is the cost of answering the query at the MDW. However, in cases where another result is used for answering q_i the actual savings depend on how "close" this materialized result is to the answer that we want to produce. If c_f is cost of querying the best such fragment f for answering q_i, the savings in this case is $c_i - c_f$.[5] To capture all cases we define the savings provided by the pool $\mathcal{V}$ for a query instance q_i as:

$$s_i = \begin{cases} 0 & \text{if } q_i \text{ can not be answered by } \mathcal{V} \\ c_i & \text{if there is an exact match for } q_i \text{ in } \mathcal{V} \\ c_i - c_f & \text{if } f \text{ from } \mathcal{V} \text{ was used to answer } q_i \end{cases}$$

using the above formula we define the Detailed Cost Saving

[5] c_i and c_f do not include the cost to fetch the result which is payable even if an exact match is found.

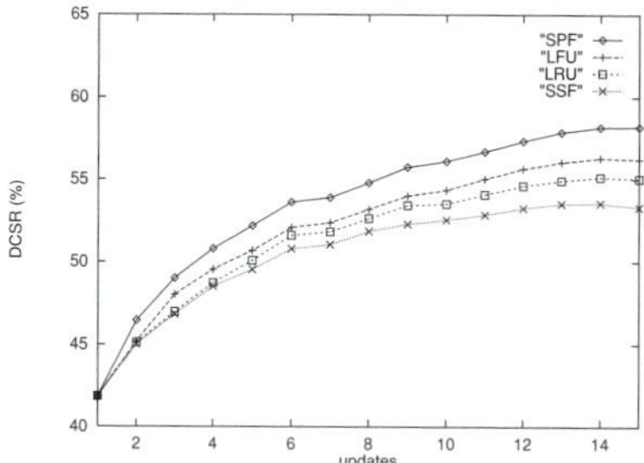

Figure 7: The **time bound** case, first 15x1500 queries

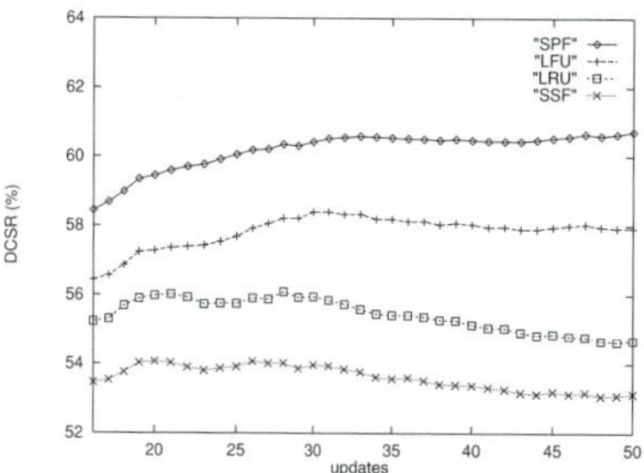

Figure 8: The **time bound** case, remaining 35x1500 queries

Ratio as:

$$DCSR = \frac{\sum_i s_i}{\sum_i c_i}$$

DCSR provides a more accurate measure than CSR for OLAP queries. CSR uses a "binary" definition of a hit: a query hits the pool or not. For instance if a query is computed at the MDW with cost $c_i = 10,000$ and from some fragment f with cost $c_f = 9,500$, CSR will return a savings of $10,000$ for the "hit", while DCSR will credit the system will only 500 units based on the previous formula. DCSR captures the different levels of effectiveness of the materialized data against the incoming queries and describes better the performance of the system.

The rest of this section is organized as follows: Subsection 3.1 makes a direct comparison of the different ways to define the goodness as described in 2.4. Subsection 3.2 compares the performance of DynaMat against a system that uses the optimal static view selection policy. All experiments were ran using an Ultra SPARC 60 with 128MB of main memory.

3.1 Comparison of different goodness policies

In this set of experiments we compare the DCSR under the four different goodness policies LRU, LFU, SFF and SPF. We used a synthetically generated dataset that models supermarket transactions, organized by the star schema. The MDW had 10 dimensions and a fact table containing 20 million tuples. We assumed 50 update phases during the measured life of the system. During each update phase we generated 250,000 new tuples for the fact table that had to be propagated to the stored fragments. The size of the full Data Cube for this base data after all updates where applied was estimated to be about 708GB. We generated 50 query sets with 1,500 MR-queries each, that were ran between the updates. These queries were selected uniformly from all $2^{10} = 1,024$ different views in the Data Cube lattice. In order to simulate hot spots in the query pattern the values asked by the queries for each dimension are following the 80-20 law: 80% of the times a query was accessing data from 20% of the dimension's domain. We also ran experiments for uniform and Gaussian distributions for the query values but are not presented here as they were similar to the 80-20% distribution.

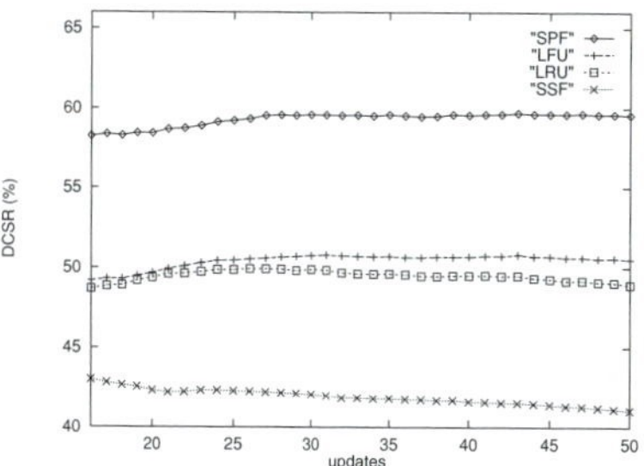

Figure 9: The **space bound** case

For the first experiment we tested the time-bound case. The size of the pool was chosen large enough to guarantee no replacement during queries and the time allowed for updating the fragments was set to 2% of W_{Data_Cube}, where W_{Data_Cube} is the estimated time to update the full Data Cube. For a more clear view we plot in Figure 7 the DCSR overtime for the first 15 sets of queries, starting with an empty pool. In the graph we plot the cumulative value of DCSR at the beginning of each update phase, for all queries that happened up to that phase. The DCSR value reaches 41.4% at the end of the first query period of 1,500 queries that were executed against the initially empty pool. This shows that simply by storing and reusing computed results from previous queries, we cut down the cost of accessing the MDW to 58.6%. Figure 8 shows how DCSR changes for the remaining queries. All four policies quickly increase their savings, by refining the content of the pool while doing updates, up to a point where all curves flatten out. At all times, SPF policy is the winner with 60.71% savings for the whole run. The average I/O per query, was 94.84, 100.08, 106.18 and 109.09 MB/query for the SPF, LFU, LRU and SFF policies respectively. The average write-back I/O cost due to the on-the-fly materialization was about the same in all cases ($\simeq$19.8MB/query). For the winner SPF policy the average time spend on searching the Directory Index was negligible (about 0.4msecs/query). Computing a feasible update plan took on the average 37msecs, and 51msecs in the worst case. The number of MRFs stored in the pool by the end of the last update phase was 206.

Figure 9 depicts DCSR overtime in the space-bound case for the last 35 sets of queries, calculated at the beginning

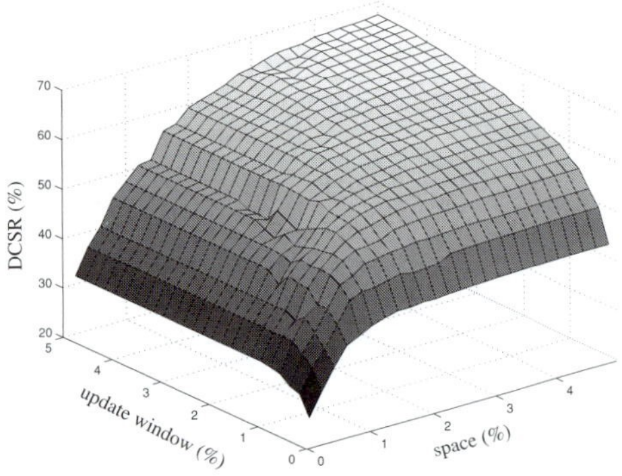

Figure 10: The **space & time bound** case

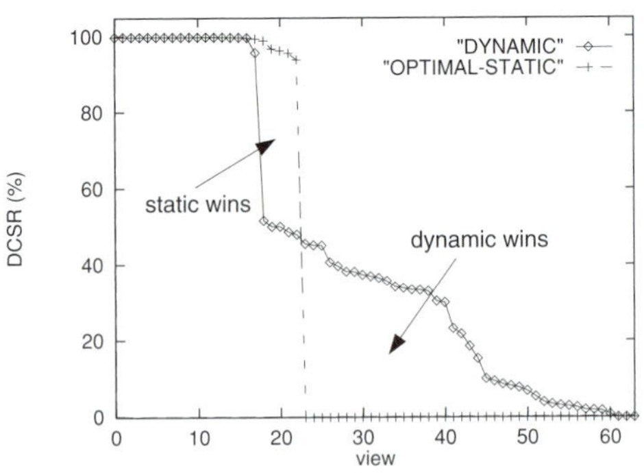

Figure 11: DCSR per view for uniform queries on the views

of each update phase. In this experiment there was no time restriction for doing the updates, and the space that was allocated for the pool was set to 14GB, i.e 2% of the full Data Cube size. In this case, the content of the pool is managed by the `replace` algorithm, as the limited size of the pool results in frequent evictions during the on-line mode. Again the SPF policy showed the best performance with a DCSR of 59.58%. For this policy, the average time spend on the `replace` algorithm, including any modifications on the Directory Index, was less that 3msecs per query. Computing the initial update plan for the updates, as explained in section 2.4.2, took 10msecs on the average. Since there was no time restriction and thus, the plan was always feasible, there was no additional overhead for refining this plan. The final number of fragments in the pool was 692.

In a final experiment we tested the four policies for the general case, where the system is both space and time bound. We varied the time window for the updates from 0.2% up to 5% of W_{Data_Cube} and the size of the pool from 0.2% up to 5% of the full Data Cube size, both in 0.2% intervals. Figure 10 shows the DCSR for each pair of time and space settings for the SPF policy, that outperformed the other three. We can see that even with limited resources DynaMat provides substantial savings. For example, with just 1.2% of disk space and 0.8% time window for the updates, we get over 50% savings compared to accessing the MDW.

3.2 Comparison with the optimal static view selection

In the experiments in the previous section we saw that the SPF policy provides the best goodness definition for a dynamic view (fragment) selection during both updates (time bound case) and queries (space bound case), or both. An important question however is how the system compares with a static view selection algorithm [HRU96, GHRU97, Gup97, BPT97] that considers only fully materialized views. Instead of comparing each one of these algorithms with our approach, we implemented SOLVE, a module that given a set of queries, the space and time restrictions, it searches exhaustively all feasible view selections and returns the optimal one for these queries. For a Data Cube lattice with n dimensions and no hierarchies there are 2^n different views. A static view selection, depending on the space and time bounds, contains some combination of these views. For for $n = 6$, the search space contains $2^{2^6} = 18,446,744,073,709,551,616$ possible combinations of the 64 views of the lattice. Obviously some pruning can be applied. For example, if a set of views is found feasible there is no need to check any of its subsets. Additional pruning of large views is possible depending on the space and time restrictions that are specified, however for non trivial cases this exhaustive search is not feasible even for small values of n.

We used SOLVE to compute the optimal static view selection for a six-dimensional subset of our supermarket dataset, with 20 million tuples in the fact table. There were 40 update phases, with 100 thousand new tuples being added in the fact table each time. The time window for the updates was set to the estimated 2% of that of the full Data Cube (W_{Data_Cube}). We created 40 sets of 500 MR-queries each, that were executed between the updates. These queries targeted uniformly the 64 different views in the 6-dimensional Data Cube lattice. This lack of locality of the queries represents the worst-case scenario for the dynamic case that needs to adapt on-the-fly to the incoming query pattern. For the static view selection this was not an issue, because SOLVE was given all queries in advance. The optimal set returned, after 3 days of computations in an Ultra SPARC 60, includes 23 out of the 64 full-views in the 6-dimensional Data Cube. The combined size of these views when stored as Cubetrees in the disk is 281MB (1.6% of the full Data Cube). For the most strict and unfavorable comparison for the dynamic case, we set the size of the pool to the same number. Since the dynamic system started with an empty pool, we used the first 10% of the queries as a training set and measured system's performance for the remaining 90%. We used the SPF policy to measure the goodness of the MRFs for the dynamic approach.

The measured cumulative DCSR for the two systems was about the same: 64.04% for the dynamic and 62.06% for the optimal static. The average I/O per query for the dynamic

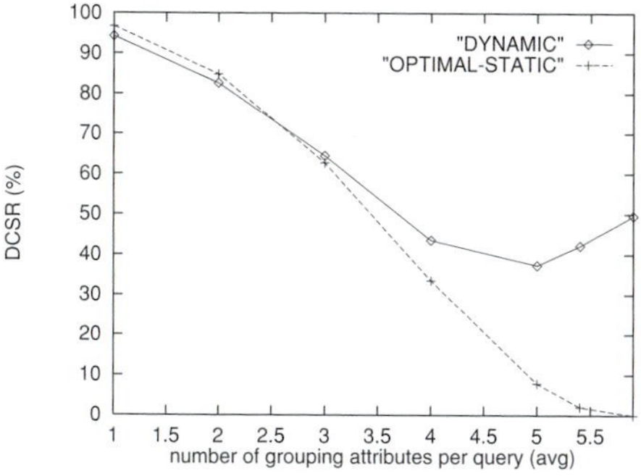

Figure 12: Dynamic vs Optimal-Static selection varying the average number of grouping attributes per query

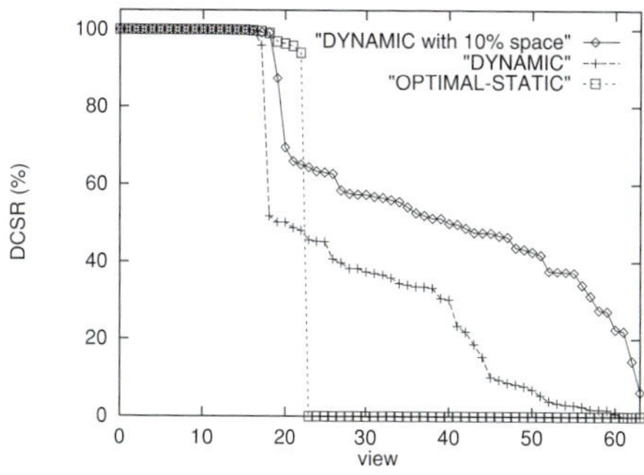

Figure 13: DCSR per view for space = 10%

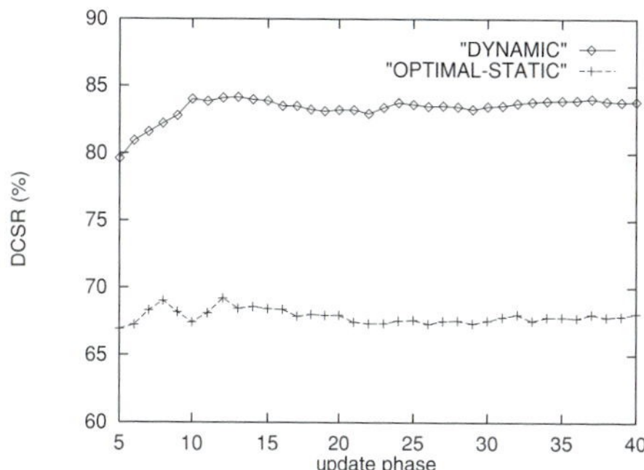

Figure 14: Dynamic vs Optimal-Static selection for drill-down/roll-up queries

system was 108.11MB and the average write-back I/O cost 2.18MB. For the optimal static selection the average I/O per query is 112.94MB and no write-back, without counting the overhead of materializing the statically selected views for the first time.

For a more clear view on the performance differences between the static and the dynamic approach, we computed the DCSR per view and plotted them in decreasing order of savings in Figure 11. Notice that the x-axis labeling does not correspond to the same views for the two lines. The plot shows that the static view selection performs well for the 23 materialized views, however for the rest 41 views its savings drops to zero. DynaMat on the other hand provides substantial savings for almost all the views. On the right hand side of the graph are the larger views of the Data Cube. Since most results from queries on these views are too big to fit in the pool, even DynaMat's performance decreases because they can not be materialized in the shared disk space.

Figure 12 depicts the performance of both systems for a non-uniform set of queries where the access to the views is skewed. The skewness is controlled by the number of grouping attributes in each query. As this number increases,[6] it favors accesses on views from the upper levels of the Data Cube lattice, which views are bigger in size and need larger update window. These views, because of the space and time constraints are not in the static optimal selection. On the other hand, the dynamic approach materializes results whenever possible and for this reason it is more robust than the static selection, as the workload shifts to the larger views of the lattice. As the average number of grouping attributes per query reaches 6, almost all queries in the workload access the single top-level six-dimensional view of the lattice. DynaMat adapts nicely to such workload and allocates most of the pool space to MRFs of that view. That explains the performance of DynaMat going up at the right hand side of the graph.

The pool size in the above experiments was set to 1.6% of the full Data Cube as this was the actual size of the views used by the optimal static selection. This number however is rather small for todays standards. We ran two more experiments with pool size 5% (878MB) and 10% (1.7GB) of the full Data Cube size. The optimal static selection does not refine the selected views because of the update window constraint (2%). DynaMat, on the other hand, capitalizes the extra disk space and increases the DCSR from 64.04% to 68.34 and 78.22% for the 5% and 10% storage. Figure 13 depicts the computed DCSR per view for this case. As more disk space is available, DynaMat achieves even more savings by materializing more fragments from the larger views of the Data Cube.

In the previous experiment the queries that we ran were selected uniformly from all 64 views in the Data Cube lattice. This is the worst case scenario for DynaMat which gains a lot more from locality of follow-up queries. Often in OLAP, users do drill-downs or roll-ups, where starting from a computed result, they refine their queries and ask for a more or less detailed view of the data respectively. DynaMat can enormously benefit from the roll-up queries because these queries are always computable from results that were previously added in the pool. To simulate such a workload we tuned our query-generator to provide 40 sets of 500 queries each with the following properties: 40% of the times a user asks a query for a randomly selected view from the Cube, 30% of the times the user performs a roll-up

[6]Having three grouping attributes per query, on the average, corresponds to the previous uniform view selection.

operation on the last reported result and 30% of the times the user performs a drill-down.

For this experiment, we used the previous set up for the 2% and 10% time and space bound and we re-computed the optimal static selection for the new queries. Figure 14 depicts DCSR for this workload. Compared to the previous example, DynaMat further increases its savings (83.84%) by taking advantage of the locality of the roll-up queries.

4 Conclusions

In this paper we presented DynaMat, a view management system that dynamically materializes results from incoming queries and exploits them for future reuse. DynaMat unifies view selection and view maintenance under a single framework that takes into account both the time and space constraints of the system. We have defined and used the Multidimensional Range Fragments (MRFs) as the basic logical unit of materialization. Our experiments show that compared to the conventional static paradigm that considers only full views for materialization, MRFs provide a finer and more appropriate granularity of materialization. The operational and maintenance cost of the MRFs, which includes any directory look-up operations during the online mode and the derivation of a feasible update plan during updates, remains practically negligible, in the order of milliseconds.

We compared DynaMat against a system that is given all queries in advance and the pre-computed optimal static view selection. These experiments indicate that DynaMat outperforms the optimal static selection and thus any sub-optimal view selection algorithm that has appeared in the literature. Another important result that validates the importance of DynaMat, is that just 1-2% of the Data Cube space and 1-2% of the update window for the full Data Cube are sufficient for substantial performance improvements.

However, the most important feature of DynaMat is that it represents a complete self-tunable system that dynamically adjusts to new patterns in the workload. DynaMat relieves the warehouse administrator from having to monitor and calibrate the system constantly regardless of the skewness of the data and/or of the queries. Even for cases that there is no specific pattern in the workload, like the uniform queries used for some of our experiments, DynaMat manages to pick a set of MRFs that outperforms the optimal static view selection. For more skewed query distributions, especially for workloads that include a lot of roll-up queries, the performance of DynaMat is even better.

5 Acknowledgments

We would like to thank Kostas Stathatos and Alexandros Labrinidis for their helpful comments and suggestions.

References

[AAD+96] S. Agrawal, R. Agrawal, P. Deshpande, A. Gupta, J. Naughton, R. Ramakrishnan, and S. Sarawagi. On the Computation of Multidimensional Aggregates. In *Proc. of VLDB*, pages 506–521, Bombay, India, August 1996.

[ACT97] ACT Inc. The Cubetree Datablade. http://www.act-us.com, August 1997.

[Aut] AutoAdmin Project, Database Group, Microsoft Research.

[BDD+98] R. G. Bello, K. Dias, A. Downing, J. Feenan, J. Finnerty, W. D. Norcott, H. Sun, A. Witkowski, and M. Ziauddin. Materialized Views In Oracle. In *Proc. of VLDB*, pages 659–664, New York City, New York, August 1998.

[BPT97] E. Baralis, S. Paraboschi, and E. Teniente. Materialized View Selection in a Multidimensional Database. In *Proc. of VLDB*, pages 156–165, Athens, Greece, August 1997.

[CR94] C.M. Chen and N. Roussopoulos. The implementation and Performance Evaluation of the ADMS Query Optimizer: Integrating Query Result Caching and Matching. In *Proc. of the 4th Intl. Conf. on Extending Database Technology*, pages 323–336, 1994.

[DDJ+98] L. Do, P. Drew, W. Jin, V. Junami, and D. V. Rossum. Issues in Developing Very Large Data Warehouses. In *Proceedings of the 24th VLDB Conference*, pages 633–636, New York City, New York, August 1998.

[DFJ+96] S. Dar, M.J. Franklin, B. Jonsson, D. Srivastava, and M. Tan. Semantic Data Caching and Replacement. In *Proc. of the 22th International Conference on VLDB*, pages 330–341, Bombay, India, September 1996.

[DR92] A. Delis and N. Roussopoulos. Performance and Scalability of Client-Server Database Architectures. In *Proc. of the 18th VLDB*, pages 610–623, Vancouver, Canada, 1992.

[DRSN98] P. M. Deshpande, K. Ramasamy, A. Shukla, and J.F. Naughton. Caching Multidimensional Queries Using Chunks. In *Proceedings of the ACM SIGMOD*, pages 259–270, Seattle, Washington, June 1998.

[GBLP96] J. Gray, A. Bosworth, A. Layman, and H. Piramish. Data Cube: A Relational Aggregation Operator Generalizing Group-By, Cross-Tab, and Sub-Totals. In *Proc. of the 12th ICDE*, pages 152–159, New Orleans, February 1996. IEEE.

[GHRU97] H. Gupta, V. Harinarayan, A. Rajaraman, and J. Ullman. Index Selection for OLAP. In *Proceedings of ICDE*, pages 208–219, Burmingham, UK, April 1997.

[GL95] T. Griffin and L. Libkin. Incremental Maintenance of Views with Duplicates. In *Proceedings of the ACM SIGMOD*, pages 328–339, San Jose, CA, May 1995.

[GMS93] A. Gupta, I.S. Mumick, and V.S. Subrahmanian. Maintaining Views Incrementally. In *Proceedings of the ACM SIGMOD Conference*, pages 157–166, Washington, D.C., May 1993.

[Gup97] H. Gupta. Selections of Views to Materialize in a Data Warehouse. In *Proceedings of ICDT*, pages 98–112, Delphi, January 1997.

[HRU96] V. Harinarayan, A. Rajaraman, and J. Ullman. Implementing Data Cubes Efficiently. In *Proc. of ACM SIGMOD*, pages 205–216, Montreal, Canada, June 1996.

[JMS95] H. Jagadish, I. Mumick, and A. Silberschatz. View Maintenance Issues in the Chronicle Data Model. In *Proceedings of PODS*, pages 113–124, San Jose, CA, 1995.

[KB96] A.M. Keller and J. Basu. A Predicate-based Caching Scheme for Client-Server Database Architectures. *VLDB Journal*, 5(1), 1996.

[Kim96] R. Kimball. *The Data Warehouse Toolkit*. John Wiley & Sons, 1996.

[KR98] Y. Kotidis and N. Roussopoulos. An Alternative Storage Organization for ROLAP Aggregate Views Based on Cubetrees. In *Proceedings of the ACM SIGMOD Conference*, pages 249–258, Seattle, Washington, June 1998.

[MQM97] I. S. Mumick, D. Quass, and B. S. Mumick. Maintenance of Data Cubes and Summary Tables in a Warehouse. In *Proceedings of the ACM SIGMOD Conference*, pages 100–111, Tucson, Arizona, May 1997.

[RK86] N. Roussopoulos and H. Kang. Preliminary Design of ADMS$\pm$: A Workstation-Mainframe Integrated Architecture for Database Management Systems. In *Proc. of VLDB*, pages 355–364, Kyoto, Japan, August 1986.

[RKR97] N. Roussopoulos, Y. Kotidis, and M. Roussopoulos. Cubetree: Organization of and Bulk Incremental Updates on the Data Cube. In *Proceedings of the ACM SIGMOD International Conference on Management of Data*, pages 89–99, Tucson, Arizona, May 1997.

[RL85] N. Roussopoulos and D. Leifker. Direct Spatial Search on Pictorial Databases Using Packed R-trees. In *Procs. of 1985 ACM SIGMOD*, pages 17–31, Austin, 1985.

[Rou91] N. Roussopoulos. The Incremental Access Method of View Cache: Concept, Algorithms, and Cost Analysis. *ACM–Transactions on Database Systems*, 16(3):535–563, September 1991.

[SDN98] A. Shukla, P.M. Deshpande, and J.F. Naughton. Materialized View Selection for Multidimensional Datasets. In *Proceedings of the 24th VLDB Conference*, pages 488–499, New York City, New York, August 1998.

[SS94] S. Sarawagi and M. Stonebraker. Efficient Organization of Large Multidimensional Arr ays. In *Proceedings of ICDE*, pages 328–336, Houston, Texas, 1994.

[SSV96] P. Scheuermann, J. Shim, and R. Vingralek. WATCHMAN: A Data Warehouse Intelligent Cache Manager. In *Proceedings of the 22th VLDB Conference*, pages 51–62, Bombay, India, September 1996.

[TS97] D. Theodoratos and T. Sellis. Data Warehouse Configuration. In *Proc. of the 23th International Conference on VLDB*, pages 126–135, Athens, Greece, August 1997.

[ZDN97] Y. Zhao, P.M. Deshpande, and J.F. Naughton. An Array-Based Algorithm for Simultaneous Multidimensional Aggregates. In *Proceedings of the ACM SIGMOD Conference*, pages 159–170, Tucson, Arizona, May 1997.

Chapter 8
Data Mining

At the beginning of the 1990's, there was increasing interest in pushing large-scale data analysis beyond the traditional "query-response" model used in database systems. This was particularly desired for *decision-support* applications, which try to help analysts use an organization's data to aid in strategic decision-making. One decision-support challenge we discussed earlier (Section 7) is to efficiently answer complex queries over enormous databases. But very often the most difficult problem is to figure out *what questions to ask* over a large, complex database. This is the grand challenge problem for data mining: the database system should be able to efficiently and effectively tell the analyst "what is interesting in my data"?

Data mining has roots in a number of fields, most significantly in database systems and a branch of AI known as *Machine Learning*. Perhaps because of the AI roots of Data Mining, there is a fog of quasi-anthropomorphic terminology surrounding the field. Data "mining" itself is a phrase meant to evoke the computer as a prospector searching for gold "nuggets" in "mountains" of data. The data mining process is often referred to as "Knowledge Discovery", with the emphasis on "Knowledge" rather than "data" implying an evolution from machines that just store bits into intelligent beings that "know" things.

The leading data mining conference is called "Knowledge Discovery and Data Mining" (SIGKDD). At the time of its founding, it was intended to bridge a gap between the database and AI communities. From the database side, there was a desire to break away from the querying metaphors that had driven the field, and look at algorithms for data analysis that didn't have simple declarative representations. From the AI side, there was a desire to deal more directly with real-world issues that hadn't received emphasis in that community: large-scale data collections, end-user interactivity and dirty data. SIGKDD caused concern in each community about unhealthy fracturing of the research landscape, and there was initial discussion about trying to avoid yet another research area. But it has proven to be a popular breakaway organization, and one that is reasonably healthy.

The name Data Mining seems quite general, but in fact is usually used in the research literature to describe a handful of simply-stated algorithm specifications for extracting patterns from large tables. By far the three most common of these are *Classification, Clustering,* and *Association Rules*. The first two problems originated in the statistics and machine learning communities, the third in the database community. We present one example of each in this chapter; for each example we present a paper that describes an intuitive, scalable, disk-oriented approach to the problem – one that is appropriate for large databases. We also present a fourth paper on emerging approaches toward integrating these techniques into the framework of a traditional database system.

Classification

The problem statement for classification is quite simple. You are given a table with n columns, and you are asked to predict the value of one additional "missing" column based on the data that you have. The missing column can take on one of k pre-specified values, or *class labels*. As one toy example, consider a table of credit card applicant data, including attributes like age, zip code, salary, home value, etc. The missing column could be called *risk*, taking on one of three possible classes: *low, medium,* or *high*.

Classification is typically an example of a *supervised learning* task, in which a human first "trains" the algorithm on some example data, by manually providing the value of the missing field for a number of example rows. Based on this training set, the classification algorithm should be able to predict the missing value for any future data that arrives. This *predictive* approach is often based on some statistical model, and in the context of the model provides a robust mathematical interpretation for the algorithm's choice of class labels. The "gotcha" with this worldview is that one has to trust that the statistical models being used are appropriate. We will return to this point at the end of this introduction.

The classification paper we present is an algorithm called SPRINT. It is not the most statistically sophisticated algorithm in the literature. However, it is approachable to a student of database systems, and it has the features that distinguish data mining from traditional machine learning: it scales up nicely to big, disk-based data sets, and it is naturally parallelizable. SPRINT builds a *decision tree*, which is a classic machine learning technique. Decision trees have various limitations. One typical pitfall is that they can *overfit* the training data, i.e., too carefully capture random distinctions among members of different classes in the training set. The result of overfitting is a classifier that cannot accommodate normal variations within members of a single class; various techniques can be parameterized to balance overfitting against over-generalizing. Another problem is that a decision tree breaks down the data hierarchically in a way that forbids "pivoting" along different attributes – e.g. if it first breaks down the credit card applicants by age, it may not do a good job describing how all the applicants should break down by salary. On the positive side, though, decision trees are very intuitive, and can be presented to end-users as output to explain the classification process. As a result, they are often used both in the research literature and in commercial data analysis tools such as CHAID, CART, and C4.5.

Clustering

Students often confuse clustering and classification on first exposure. In clustering, we again have an input table of *n* columns, and the challenge of generating a label for each row in a missing *n+1*'st column. However, there are two key differences from classification. First, clustering is typically an *unsupervised* task, with no training phase. Second, there are no pre-determined class labels involved in clustering. Instead, each row is to be assigned a *cluster ID;* intuitively, rows that are similar should have the same cluster ID, and rows that are different should have different cluster IDs. The cluster IDs themselves have no meaning; the description of a cluster is simply the members of the cluster itself (or some aggregate summary of the members). In SQL terms, clustering is a kind of generalized "GROUP BY" clause: rather than grouping together tuples with the same values on certain attributes, we group together tuples with *similar* values. Given these groups, we can compute aggregates (summaries) for each group to try and characterize its properties. As an example, it may be useful to cluster customers in a sales database into market segments, and try to summarize their buying patterns to decide how best to target ads.

Clustering hinges on a number of parameters. First, a fixed definition of "similarity" (or "distance") is typically defined to make the problem well-stated. Usually this is some combination of column-by-column distances. For a table with only numeric columns there are many natural distance metrics; three common ones include:

- The traditional Euclidean distance from geometry, i.e. the square root of the sum of squared columnwise distances (sometimes called the L2 norm).

- The so-called "Manhattan distance", which is analogous to moving on a fixed grid like the streets of Manhattan, measuring distance along the sides of rectangles rather than allowing diagonals. This is simply the sum of the columnwise distances (sometimes called the L1 norm).

- The maximum distance on any column (sometimes called the L-infinity norm).

In many cases one needs to scale each column in some way before computing distances, to account (for example) for the use of different units in each column. Also, some data types like "color" don't obviously map to a number line. Attributes from these unordered types (sometimes called *categorical* attributes) add complexity to the problem, since the distance between any two different values of a categorical attribute is not well defined.

Another parameter in clustering is to decide upon the "right" number of clusters to request. This is tightly tied to two other parameters, namely how wide each cluster is allowed to get (its "diameter"), and how close two separate clusters are allowed to get. Obviously if the algorithm is told to generate only a few clusters, they are likely to have big diameters. Similarly, with only a few clusters it may be impossible to cleanly separate all the nearby points.

We chose the BIRCH clustering algorithm for this collection of papers. Like SPRINT, it is not the most statistically sophisticated algorithm that has been proposed, but it has a number of attractive features. First, it should be approachable for a student of database systems, since it does not require a great deal of math or statistics to understand. Second, it has strong echoes of the Generalized Search Trees (GiSTs) of Chapter 5: it generates a hierarchy of partitions of the data, labeling each partition with a descriptor. Unlike the original GiST paper, these labels are not predicates but statistical *distribution* information – i.e., aggregate functions of the data below. These kind of extended GiST subtree descriptors were also proposed for near-neighbor searching and selectivity estimation by Aoki [Aoki98]. Hence BIRCH can be seen as a fairly natural extension to GiST that "shaves off" the bottom of the tree to ensure that it fits in memory. This tie-in between search structures (indexes) and data summarizations (mining models) is discussed further in [Bar97], and is a potential research direction we discuss below.

For the somewhat more statistically ambitious reader, a paper by Bradley *et al.* [BFR98] is a good alternative introduction to clustering for large tables. This work extends a traditional technique from statistics called *k-means* clustering, and shows how to make it efficient over large data sets. The k-means algorithm uses a Euclidean distance metric for distance. A follow-on paper by the same authors [BRF00] generalizes that work to richer probabilistic models using the *Expectation Maximization (E-M)* approach from statistics. E-M has two advantages over the prior approaches we have mentioned: it does not require a Euclidean distance metric, and – perhaps more significantly – it allows each row to be assigned to multiple clusters with varying probabilities ("20% likely to be in cluster 1, 30% likely to be in cluster 2", etc.) In essence, it changes the problem statement for clustering to one of assigning *k* new columns to the table – one for each cluster – and a probability value for each row in each of these columns. This shift in the problem statement again makes clustering a *predictive* approach; one that can be reasoned about probabilistically, under certain statistical models (a common one is a "mixture of Gaussians", i.e. a bunch of superimposed "bell curves"). By contrast, the other approaches we discussed are strictly about minimizing distances, and do not have a clear probabilistic interpretation.

Association Rules

The association rules problem comes out of the database community, and is the most recent of the popular data mining problems we present. The traditional example of association rules is to take as input a set of cash-register sales transactions – sometimes called "market baskets" – and from them try to compute associations of the form "*X _ Y (c%)*" where *X* and *Y* are sets of items, and the rule states that *c%* of transactions that contain *X* also contain *Y*. An example rule might be "when people buy chips and salsa, they also buy avocados 5% of the time". The value *c* is termed the *confidence* of the rule (we will have more to say about this terminology later.) If very few people bought the set of items *X U_Y*in the rule (the set {chips, salsa, avocados} in our case), then the above rule is probably not very significant. Hence these rules should only be generated when they are "supported" by a large number of sales transactions; the percentage of transactions that contain the set of items in the rule is called the *support* of the rule.

The paper we present here by Agrawal and Srikant is the best-known paper on association rule mining (though it is not the first and certainly not the last.) It breaks the problem down neatly into that of (a) first filtering down to only those sets with sufficient support, and (b) among those sets, finding the association rules. The solution to part (a) hinges on the insight that a set can only have sufficient support if all its subsets have sufficient support; hence sets of bigger and bigger numbers of items can be built up incrementally. The solution to part (b) uses a hashing scheme to find the associations.

There has been a huge number of follow-on papers to this one, including techniques to deal with scenarios where very many transactions have sufficient support (see [AY98] for a survey), techniques for doing the rule mining in an online and interactive fashion (e.g. [Hidber]), techniques for finding associations over quantities (e.g. age-brackets) not just item names (e.g. [MY97,SA96]), and myriad other variations and generalizations.

One reason for the popularity of association rule mining research is that it does not require a great deal of statistical sophistication; it is quite close to traditional relational query processing. As a result, the database community has invested more energy into this mining problem than into others; by contrast, the machine learning community has invested relatively little time on this technique, and members of that community have been known to question the utility of association rules.

A problem that the statistically-minded researchers have with association rules is that they are not predictive in any statistical sense. They simply count combinations of items in an existing database; they do not construct any statistical model with which to make predictions about future states of the database. In fact, the use of the term *confidence* for association rule mining is rather misleading, because it inaccurately echoes the notion of confidence intervals used in statistical estimation. In statistics, confidence intervals bound the value of a quantity (e.g. "the average value is 100, plus or minus 2"), and say how often the value should stay within those bounds for *all possible database states* containing the sample ("with 95% probability"). In this sense they are predictive measures over possible database states, while association rules are simply counts of the current database state.

Discussion

Briefly put, association rule mining is an example of a *combinatorial* (descriptive) approach to data mining, while classification and E-M clustering are examples of a *probabilistic* (predictive) approach.

At some level, it is a matter of religion whether descriptive or predictive approaches are better, or whether such a comparison is meaningful. Descriptive approaches don't provide any notion of whether the outcome is likely to recur in future data sets; they may only describe some happenstance in the current state of the database. On the other hand, predictive approaches typically make their predictions based on some *model*: i.e., some assumptions about underlying data distributions, which may or may not be a good match to the real-world phenomenon generating the data. In the end, either approach must be justified by its success in solving real problems.

This brings up another thorny issue in the current state of data mining. Despite the energy and hype behind the field, it has had limited broad-based practical application to date. The success stories mostly arise in narrow, custom-written applications; probably the best-known success is in credit-card fraud detection, which is a classification problem. General-purpose data mining tools like those sold by the SAS Institute have had modest success in the marketplace. Part of the problem is that many mining tools remain difficult to use: the choice of mining models and techniques to apply to a problem is often ambiguous, setting the various parameters of the various techniques remains a black art, and in the end there is always uncertainty about the significance of the results.

Another problem with current mining approaches is their limited scope: they typically operate on a single table, with fairly simple, full-scan access. Our last paper addresses this problem to some extent, by describing architectural and linguistic approaches to integrate mining algorithms into a richer database query environment. This is an area of research that took a surprisingly long time to emerge, perhaps because of the gap between the skill sets of database systems experts and statistical data analysis experts. This gap has narrowed significantly in the last decade, to the mutual benefit of both communities. We expect to see more integration of these approaches to querying and analyzing information in future; some interesting work has emerged melding data mining techniques with OLAP (e.g., [Sara01]). But much remains to be done, even in the first-order problem of efficiently integrating the favorite mining models into SQL systems.

Before parting, we note briefly that there are a number of other problems under investigation in the data mining community. These include the mining of *sequential patterns* (e.g. trends in stock prices over time), identifying *outliers* and "dirty" data, mining multiple tables for approximate relational dependencies (e.g. keys and foreign keys), etc. There are also twists on the traditional clustering and classification problems for specific settings, e.g. for text documents, for graphs (e.g. of hyperlinked documents), for XML, for unending data streams, etc. As with the earlier discussion, there are many algorithm variants for each of these tasks, and the success stories, when they exist, tend to be from carefully tuned solutions for specific domains.

In sum, data mining has come a long way in the past decade, and should now be part of any database expert's vocabulary and toolkit. On the other hand, there is still a huge distance between mining's current reality and the dream of an unsophisticated user asking the computer to "tell me what is important".

References

[Aok98] P.M. Aoki. "Generalizing 'Search' in Generalized Search Trees". In *Proc. 14th IEEE Int'l Conf. on Data Engineering* (ICDE '98), Orlando, FL, Feb. 1998, 380-389.

[AY98] Charu C. Aggarwal and Philip S. Yu. "Mining Large Itemsets for Association Rules". *IEEE Data Eng. Bull.* 21(1): 23-31, 1998.

[Bar97] D. Barbará, et al. "The New Jersey Data Reduction Report". *IEEE Bulletin of the Technical Committee on Data Engineering*, Dec. 1997.

[BFR98] Paul S. Bradley, Usama M. Fayyad and Cory Reina. "Scaling Clustering Algorithms to Large Databases". In *Proceedings of the Fourth International Conference on Knowledge Discovery and Data Mining* (KDD), August 27-31, 1998, New York City 9-15.

[BRF00] Paul S. Bradley, Cory Reina, Usama M. Fayyad. "Clustering Very Large Databases Using EM Mixture Models." In *International Conference on Pattern Recognition (ICPR)*, September 3-8, 2000, Barcelona, Spain, Volume II: 2076-2080.

[Hidber98] Christian Hidber. "Online Association Rule Mining." In *Proc. ACM SIGMOD International Conference on Management of Data*, June 1-3, 1999, Philadelphia, Pennsylvania, pp. 145-156.

[MY97] R. J. Miller and Y. Yang. "Association Rules over Interval Data", *Proc. of the ACM SIGMOD Int'l Conf. on the Management of Data*, Tuscon, AZ, May, 1997.

[SA96] Ramakrishnan Srikant and Rakesh Agrawal. "Mining quantitative association rules in large relational tables." In *ACM-SIGMOD International Conference on Management of Data*, pp. 1–12, 1996.

[Sara01] S. Sarawagi. "User-cognizant multidimensional analysis". *The VLDB Journal*, 10(2-3):224-239, 2001.

BIRCH: An Efficient Data Clustering Method for Very Large Databases

Tian Zhang
Computer Sciences Dept.
Univ. of Wisconsin-Madison
zhang@cs.wisc.edu

Raghu Ramakrishnan
Computer Sciences Dept.
Univ. of Wisconsin-Madison
raghu@cs.wisc.edu

Miron Livny*
Computer Sciences Dept.
Univ. of Wisconsin-Madison
miron@cs.wisc.edu

Abstract

Finding useful patterns in large datasets has attracted considerable interest recently, and one of the most widely studied problems in this area is the identification of *clusters*, or densely populated regions, in a multi-dimensional dataset. Prior work does not adequately address the problem of large datasets and minimization of I/O costs.

This paper presents a data clustering method named *BIRCH* (Balanced Iterative Reducing and Clustering using Hierarchies), and demonstrates that it is especially suitable for very large databases. *BIRCH* incrementally and dynamically clusters incoming multi-dimensional metric data points to try to produce the best quality clustering with the available resources (i.e., available memory and time constraints). *BIRCH* can typically find a good clustering with a single scan of the data, and improve the quality further with a few additional scans. *BIRCH* is also the first clustering algorithm proposed in the database area to handle "noise" (data points that are not part of the underlying pattern) effectively.

We evaluate *BIRCH*'s time/space efficiency, data input order sensitivity, and clustering quality through several experiments. We also present a performance comparisons of *BIRCH* versus *CLARANS*, a clustering method proposed recently for large datasets, and show that *BIRCH* is consistently superior.

1 Introduction

In this paper, we examine *data clustering*, which is a particular kind of data mining problem. Given a large set of multi-dimensional data points, the data space is usually not uniformly occupied. *Data clustering* identifies the sparse and the crowded places, and hence discovers the overall distribution patterns of the dataset. Besides, the derived clusters can be visualized more efficiently and effectively than the original dataset[Lee81, DJ80].

Generally, there are two types of attributes involved in the data to be clustered: *metric* and *nonmetric*[1]. In this paper, we consider metric attributes, as in most of the Statistics literature, where the clustering problem is formalized as follows: *Given the desired number of clusters K and a dataset of N points, and a distance-based measurement function (e.g., the weighted total/average distance between pairs of points in clusters), we are asked to find a partition of the dataset that minimizes the value of the measurement function.* This is a *nonconvex discrete* [KR90] optimization problem. Due to an abundance of local minima, there is typically no way to find a global minimal solution without trying all possible partitions.

We adopt the problem definition used in Statistics, but with an additional, database-oriented constraint: *The amount of memory available is limited (typically, much smaller than the data set size) and we want to minimize the time required for I/O.* A related point is that it is desirable to be able to take into account the amount of *time* that a user is willing to wait for the results of the clustering algorithm.

We present a clustering method named *BIRCH* and demonstrate that it is especially suitable for very large databases. Its I/O cost is linear in the size of the dataset: a *single scan* of the dataset yields a good clustering, and one or more additional passes can (optionally) be used to improve the quality further.

By evaluating *BIRCH*'s time/space efficiency, data input order sensitivity, and clustering quality, and comparing with other existing algorithms through experiments, we argue that *BIRCH* is the best available clustering method for very large databases. *BIRCH*'s architecture also offers opportunities for parallelism, and for interactive or dynamic performance tuning based on knowledge about the dataset, gained over the course of the execution. Finally, *BIRCH* is the first clustering al-

*This research has been supported by NSF Grant IRI-9057562 and NASA Grant 144-EC78.

SIGMOD '96 6/96 Montreal, Canada
© 1996 ACM 0-89791-794-4/96/0006...$3.50

[1] Informally, a *metric* attribute is an attribute whose values satisfy the requirements of *Euclidian* space, i.e., self identity (for any X, $X = X$) and triangular inequality (there exists a distance definition such that for any X_1,X_2,X_3, $d(X_1, X_2) + d(X_2, X_3) \geq d(X_1, X_3)$).

gorithm proposed in the database area that addresses *outliers* (intuitively, data points that should be regarded as "noise") and proposes a plausible solution.

1.1 Outline of Paper

The rest of the paper is organized as follows. Sec. 2 surveys related work and summarizes *BIRCH*'s contributions. Sec. 3 presents some background material. Sec. 4 introduces the concepts of clustering feature (CF) and CF tree, which are central to *BIRCH*. The details of *BIRCH* algorithm is described in Sec. 5, and a preliminary performance study of *BIRCH* is presented in Sec. 6. Finally our conclusions and directions for future research are presented in Sec. 7.

2 Summary of Relevant Research

Data clustering has been studied in the Statistics [DH73, DJ80, Lee81, Mur83], Machine Learning [CKS88, Fis87, Fis95, Leb87] and Database [NH94, EKX95a, EKX95b] communities with different methods and different emphases. Previous approaches, probability-based (like most approaches in Machine Learning) or distance-based (like most work in Statistics) , do not adequately consider the case that the dataset can be too large to fit in main memory. In particular, they do not recognize that the problem must be viewed in terms of how to work with a limited resources (e.g., memory that is typically, much smaller than the size of the dataset) to do the clustering as accurately as possible while keeping the I/O costs low.

Probability-based approaches: They typically [Fis87, CKS88] make the assumption that probability distributions on separate attributes are statistically independent of each other. In reality, this is far from true. Correlation between attributes exists, and sometimes this kind of correlation is exactly what we are looking for. The probability representations of clusters make updating and storing the clusters very expensive, especially if the attributes have a large number of values because their complexities are dependent not only on the number of attributes, but also on the number of values for each attribute. A related problem is that often (e.g., [Fis87]), the probability-based tree that is built to identify clusters is not height-balanced. For skewed input data, this may cause the performance to degrade dramatically.

Distance-based approaches: They assume that all data points are given in advance and can be scanned frequently. They totally or partially ignore the fact that not all data points in the dataset are equally important with respect to the clustering purpose, and that data points which are close and dense should be considered collectively instead of individually. They are *global* or *semi-global* methods at the granularity of data points. That is, for each clustering decision, they inspect all data points or all currently existing clusters equally no matter how close or far away they are, and they use global measurements, which require scanning all data points or all currently existing clusters. Hence none of them have linear time scalability with stable quality.

For example, using *exhaustive enumeration (EE)*, there are approximately $K^N/K!$ [DH73] ways of partitioning a set of N data points into K subsets. So in practice, though it can find the global minimum, it is infeasible except when N and K are extremely small. *Iterative optimization (IO)* [DH73, KR90] starts with an initial partition, then tries all possible moving or swapping of data points from one group to another to see if such a moving or swapping improves the value of the measurement function. It can find a local minimum, but the quality of the local minimum is very sensitive to the initially selected partition, and the worst case time complexity is still exponential. *Hierarchical clustering (HC)* [DH73, KR90, Mur83] does not try to find "best" clusters, but keeps merging the closest pair (or splitting the farthest pair) of objects to form clusters. With a reasonable distance measurement, the best time complexity of a practical *HC* algorithm is $O(N^2)$. So it is still unable to scale well with large N.

Clustering has been recognized as a useful spatial data mining method recently. [NH94] presents *CLARANS* that is based on randomized search, and proposes that *CLARANS* outperforms traditional clustering algorithms in Statistics. In *CLARANS*, a cluster is represented by its *medoid*, or the most centrally located data point in the cluster. The clustering process is formalized as searching a graph in which each node is a K-partition represented by a set of K medoids, and two nodes are neighbors if they only differ by one medoid. *CLARANS* starts with a randomly selected node. For the current node, it checks at most the *maxneighbor* number of neighbors randomly, and if a better neighbor is found, it moves to the neighbor and continues; otherwise it records the current node as a *local minimum*, and restarts with a new randomly selected node to search for another *local minimum*. *CLARANS* stops after the *numlocal* number of the so-called *local minima* have been found , and returns the best of these.

CLARANS suffers from the same drawbacks as the above *IO* method wrt. efficiency. In addition, it may not find a real local minimum due to the searching trimming controlled by *maxneighbor*. Later [EKX95a] and [EKX95b] propose focusing techniques (based on R^*-trees) to improve *CLARANS*'s ability to deal with data objects that may reside on disks by (1) clustering a sample of the dataset that is drawn from each R^*-tree data page; and (2) focusing on relevant data points for distance and quality updates. Their experiments show that the time is improved with a small loss of quality.

2.1 Contributions of *BIRCH*

An important contribution is our formulation of the clustering problem in a way that is appropriate for very large datasets, by making the time and memory constraints explicit. In addition, *BIRCH* has the following advantages over previous distance-based approaches.

- *BIRCH* is *local* (as opposed to global) in that each clustering decision is made without scanning all data points or all currently existing clusters. It uses measurements that reflect the natural *closeness* of points, and at the same time, can be incrementally maintained during the clustering process.
- *BIRCH* exploits the observation that the data space is usually not uniformly occupied, and hence not every data point is equally important for clustering purposes. A dense region of points is treated collectively as a single *cluster*. Points in sparse regions are treated as *outliers* and removed optionally.
- *BIRCH* makes full use of available memory to derive the finest possible subclusters (to ensure accuracy) while minimizing I/O costs (to ensure efficiency). The clustering and reducing process is organized and characterized by the use of an in-memory, height-balanced and highly-occupied tree structure. Due to these features, its running time is linearly scalable.
- If we omit the optional Phase 4 5, *BIRCH* is an incremental method that does not require the whole dataset in advance, and only scans the dataset once.

3 Background

Assume that readers are familiar with the terminology of vector spaces, we begin by defining centroid, radius and diameter for a cluster. Given N d-dimensional data points in a cluster: $\{\vec{X_i}\}$ where $i = 1, 2, ..., N$, the **centroid** $\vec{X0}$, **radius** R and **diameter** D of the cluster are defined as:

$$\vec{X0} = \frac{\sum_{i=1}^{N} \vec{X_i}}{N} \tag{1}$$

$$R = \left(\frac{\sum_{i=1}^{N} (\vec{X_i} - \vec{X0})^2}{N}\right)^{\frac{1}{2}} \tag{2}$$

$$D = \left(\frac{\sum_{i=1}^{N} \sum_{j=1}^{N} (\vec{X_i} - \vec{X_j})^2}{N(N-1)}\right)^{\frac{1}{2}} \tag{3}$$

R is the average distance from member points to the centroid. D is the average pairwise distance within a cluster. They are two alternative measures of the tightness of the cluster around the centroid. Next between two clusters, we define 5 alternative distances for measuring their closeness.

Given the centroids of two clusters: $\vec{X0_1}$ and $\vec{X0_2}$, the **centroid Euclidian distance** $D0$ and **centroid Manhattan distance** $D1$ of the two clusters are defined as:

$$D0 = ((\vec{X0_1} - \vec{X0_2})^2)^{\frac{1}{2}} \tag{4}$$

$$D1 = |\vec{X0_1} - \vec{X0_2}| = \sum_{i=1}^{d} |\vec{X0_1}^{(i)} - \vec{X0_2}^{(i)}| \tag{5}$$

Given N_1 d-dimensional data points in a cluster: $\{\vec{X_i}\}$ where $i = 1, 2, ..., N_1$, and N_2 data points in another cluster: $\{\vec{X_j}\}$ where $j = N_1 + 1, N_1 + 2, ..., N_1 + N_2$, the **average inter-cluster distance** $D2$, **average intra-cluster distance** $D3$ and **variance increase distance** $D4$ of the two clusters are defined as:

$$D2 = \left(\frac{\sum_{i=1}^{N_1} \sum_{j=N_1+1}^{N_1+N_2} (\vec{X_i} - \vec{X_j})^2}{N_1 N_2}\right)^{\frac{1}{2}} \tag{6}$$

$$D3 = \left(\frac{\sum_{i=1}^{N_1+N_2} \sum_{j=1}^{N_1+N_2} (\vec{X_i} - \vec{X_j})^2}{(N_1+N_2)(N_1+N_2-1)}\right)^{\frac{1}{2}} \tag{7}$$

$$D4 = \sum_{k=1}^{N_1+N_2} (\vec{X_k} - \frac{\sum_{l=1}^{N_1+N_2} \vec{X_l}}{N_1+N_2})^2$$

$$- \sum_{i=1}^{N_1} (\vec{X_i} - \frac{\sum_{l=1}^{N_1} \vec{X_l}}{N_1})^2 - \sum_{j=N_1+1}^{N_1+N_2} (\vec{X_j} - \frac{\sum_{l=N_1+1}^{N_1+N_2} \vec{X_l}}{N_2})^2 \tag{8}$$

$D3$ is actually D of the merged cluster. For the sake of clarity, we treat $\vec{X0}$, R and D as properties of a single cluster, and $D0$, $D1$, $D2$, $D3$ and $D4$ as properties between two clusters and state them separately. Users can optionally preprocess data by weighting or shifting along different dimensions without affecting the relative placement.

4 Clustering Feature and CF Tree

The concepts of **Clustering Feature** and **CF** tree are at the core of *BIRCH*'s incremental clustering. A **Clustering Feature** is a triple summarizing the information that we maintain about a cluster.

Definition 4.1 Given N d-dimensional data points in a cluster: $\{\vec{X_i}\}$ where $i = 1, 2, ..., N$, the **Clustering Feature (CF)** vector of the cluster is defined as a triple: **CF** $= (N, \vec{LS}, SS)$, where N is the number of data points in the cluster, $\vec{LS}$ is the linear sum of the N data points, i.e., $\sum_{i=1}^{N} \vec{X_i}$, and SS is the square sum of the N data points, i.e., $\sum_{i=1}^{N} \vec{X_i}^2$. □

Theorem 4.1 *(CF Additivity Theorem): Assume that* $\mathbf{CF_1} = (N_1, \vec{LS_1}, SS_1)$, *and* $\mathbf{CF_2} = (N_2, \vec{LS_2}, SS_2)$ *are the* **CF** *vectors of two disjoint clusters. Then the* **CF** *vector of the cluster that is formed by merging the two disjoint clusters, is:*

$$\mathbf{CF_1} + \mathbf{CF_2} = (N_1 + N_2, \vec{LS_1} + \vec{LS_2}, SS_1 + SS_2) \tag{9}$$

The proof consists of straightforward algebra. []

From the **CF** definition and additivity theorem, we know that the **CF** vectors of clusters can be stored and calculated incrementally and accurately as clusters are merged. It is also easy to prove that given the **CF** vectors of clusters, the corresponding $\vec{X0}$, R, D, $D0$, $D1$, $D2$, $D3$ and $D4$, as well as the usual quality metrics (such as weighted total/average diameter of clusters) can all be calculated easily.

One can think of a cluster as a set of data points, but only the **CF** vector stored as summary. This **CF** summary is not only efficient because it stores much less than all the data points in the cluster, but also accurate because it is sufficient for calculating all the measurements that we need for making clustering decisions in *BIRCH*.

4.1 CF Tree

A **CF** tree is a height-balanced tree with two parameters: branching factor B and threshold T. Each nonleaf node contains at most B entries of the form $[\mathbf{CF}_i, child_i]$, where $i = 1, 2, ..., B$, "$child_i$" is a pointer to its i-th child node, and $\mathbf{CF}_i$ is the **CF** of the subcluster represented by this child. So a nonleaf node represents a cluster made up of all the subclusters represented by its entries. A leaf node contains at most L entries, each of the form $[\mathbf{CF}_i]$, where $i = 1, 2, ..., L$. In addition, each leaf node has two pointers, "*prev*" and "*next*" which are used to chain all leaf nodes together for efficient scans. A leaf node also represents a cluster made up of all the subclusters represented by its entries. But all entries in a leaf node must satisfy a *threshold requirement*, with respect to a threshold value T: *the diameter (or radius) has to be less than T.*

The tree size is a function of T. The larger T is, the smaller the tree is. We require a node to fit in a page of size P. Once the dimension d of the data space is given, the sizes of leaf and nonleaf entries are known, then B and L are determined by P. So P can be varied for performance tuning.

Such a **CF** tree will be built dynamically as new data objects are inserted. It is used to guide a new insertion into the correct subcluster for clustering purposes just the same as a B+-tree is used to guide a new insertion into the correct position for sorting purposes. The **CF** tree is a very compact representation of the dataset because each entry in a leaf node is not a single data point but a subcluster (which absorbs many data points with diameter (or radius) under a specific threshold T).

4.2 Insertion into a CF Tree

We now present the algorithm for inserting an entry into a **CF** tree. Given entry "Ent", it proceeds as below:

1. *Identifying the appropriate leaf:* Starting from the root, it recursively descends the **CF** tree by choosing the **closest** child node according to a chosen distance metric: $D0$,$D1$,$D2$,$D3$ or $D4$ as defined in Sec. 3.
2. *Modifying the leaf:* When it reaches a leaf node, it finds the closest leaf entry, say L_i, and then tests whether L_i can "absorb" "Ent" without violating the threshold condition[2]. If so, the **CF** vector for L_i is updated to reflect this. If not, a new entry for "Ent" is added to the leaf. If there is space on the leaf for this new entry, we are done, otherwise we must *split* the leaf node. Node splitting is done by choosing the **farthest** pair of entries as seeds, and redistributing the remaining entries based on the **closest** criteria.
3. *Modifying the path to the leaf:* After inserting "Ent" into a leaf, we must update the **CF** information for each nonleaf entry on the path to the leaf. In the absence of a split, this simply involves adding **CF** vectors to reflect the addition of "Ent". A leaf split requires us to insert a new nonleaf entry into the parent node, to describe the newly created leaf. If the parent has space for this entry, at all higher levels, we only need to update the **CF** vectors to reflect the addition of "Ent". In general, however, we may have to split the parent as well, and so on up to the root. If the root is split, the tree height increases by one.
4. *A Merging Refinement:* Splits are caused by the page size, which is independent of the clustering properties of the data. In the presence of skewed data input order , this can affect the clustering quality, and also reduce space utilization. A simple additional merging step often helps ameliorate these problems: Suppose that there is a leaf split, and the propagation of this split stops at some nonleaf node N_j, i.e., N_j can accommodate the additional entry resulting from the split. We now scan node N_j to find the two **closest** entries. If they are not the pair corresponding to the split, we try to merge them and the corresponding two child nodes. If there are more entries in the two child nodes than one page can hold, we split the merging result again. During the resplitting, in case one of the seed attracts enough merged entries to fill a page, we just put the rest entries with the other seed. In summary, if the merged entries fit on a single page, we free a node space for later use, create one more entry space in node N_j, thereby increasing space utilization and postponing future splits; otherwise we improve the distribution of entries in the closest two children.

Since each node can only hold a limited number of entries due to its size, it does not always correspond to a natural cluster. Occasionally, two subclusters that should have been in one cluster are split across nodes. Depending upon the order of data input and the degree of skew, it is also possible that two subclusters that should not be in one cluster are kept in the same node. These infrequent but undesirable anomalies caused by page size are remedied with a global (or semi-global) algorithm that arranges leaf entries across nodes (Phase 3 discussed in Sec. 5). Another undesirable artifact is that if the same data point is inserted twice, but at different times, the two copies might be entered into distinct leaf entries. Or, in another word, occasionally with a skewed input order, a point might enter a leaf entry that it should not have entered. This problem can be addressed with further refinement passes over the data (Phase 4 discussed in Sec. 5).

5 The BIRCH Clustering Algorithm

Fig. 1 presents the overview of *BIRCH*. The main task of Phase 1 is to scan all data and build an initial in-memory **CF** tree using the given amount of memory

[2] That is, the cluster merged with "Ent" and L_i must satisfy the threshold condition. Note that the **CF** vector of the new cluster can be computed from the **CF** vectors for L_i and "Ent".

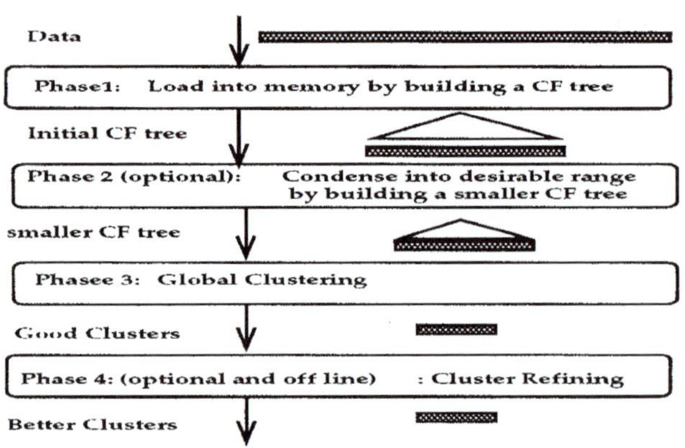

Figure 1: *BIRCH Overview*

and recycling space on disk. This **CF** tree tries to reflect the clustering information of the dataset as fine as possible under the memory limit. With crowded data points grouped as fine subclusters, and sparse data points removed as outliers, this phase creates a in-memory summary of the data. The details of Phase 1 will be discussed in Sec. 5.1. After Phase 1, subsequent computations in later phases will be:

1. fast because (a) no I/O operations are needed, and (b) the problem of clustering the original data is reduced to a smaller problem of clustering the subclusters in the leaf entries;
2. accurate because (a) a lot of outliers are eliminated, and (b) the remaining data is reflected with the finest granularity that can be achieved given the available memory;
3. less order sensitive because the leaf entries of the initial tree form an input order containing better data locality compared with the arbitrary original data input order.

Phase 2 is optional. We have observed that the existing global or semi-global clustering methods applied in Phase 3 have different input size ranges within which they perform well in terms of both speed and quality. So potentially there is a gap between the size of Phase 1 results and the input range of Phase 3. Phase 2 serves as a cushion and bridges this gap: Similar to Phase 1, it scans the leaf entries in the initial **CF** tree to rebuild a smaller **CF** tree, while removing more outliers and grouping crowded subclusters into larger ones.

The undesirable effect of the skewed input order, and splitting triggered by page size (Sec. 4.2) causes us to be unfaithful to the actual clustering patterns in the data. This is remedied in Phase 3 by using a global or semi-global algorithm to cluster all leaf entries. We observe that existing clustering algorithms for a set of data points can be readily adapted to work with a set of subclusters, each described by its **CF** vector. For example, with the **CF** vectors known, (1) naively, by calculating the centroid as the representative of a subcluster, we can treat each subcluster as a single point and use an existing algorithm without modification; (2) or to be a little more sophisticated, we can treat a subcluster of n data points as its centroid repeating n times and modify an existing algorithm slightly to take the counting information into account; (3) or to be general and accurate, we can apply an existing algorithm directly to the subclusters because the information in their **CF** vectors is usually sufficient for calculating most distance and quality metrics.

In this paper, we adapted an agglomerative hierarchical clustering algorithm by applying it directly to the subclusters represented by their **CF** vectors. It uses the accurate distance metric $D2$ or $D4$, which can be calculated from the **CF** vectors, during the whole clustering, and has a complexity of $O(N^2)$. It also provides the flexibility of allowing the user to specify either the desired number of clusters, or the desired diameter (or radius) threshold for clusters.

After Phase 3, we obtain a set of clusters that captures the major distribution pattern in the data. However minor and localized inaccuracies might exist because of the rare misplacement problem mentioned in Sec. 4.2, and the fact that Phase 3 is applied on a coarse summary of the data. Phase 4 is optional and entails the cost of additional passes over the data to correct those inaccuracies and refine the clusters further. Note that up to this point, the original data has only been scanned once, although the tree and outlier information may have been scanned multiple times.

Phase 4 uses the centroids of the clusters produced by Phase 3 as seeds, and redistributes the data points to its closest seed to obtain a set of new clusters. Not only does this allow points belonging to a cluster to migrate, but also it ensures that all copies of a given data point go to the same cluster. Phase 4 can be extended with additional passes if desired by the user, and it has been proved to converge to a minimum [GG92]. As a bonus, during this pass each data point can be labeled with the cluster that it belongs to, if we wish to identify the data points in each cluster. Phase 4 also provides us with the option of discarding outliers. That is, a point which is too far from its closest seed can be treated as an outlier and not included in the result.

5.1 Phase 1 Revisited

Fig. 2 shows the details of Phase 1. It starts with an initial threshold value, scans the data, and inserts points into the tree. If it runs out of memory before it finishes scanning the data, it increases the threshold value, rebuilds a new, *smaller* **CF** tree, by re-inserting the leaf entries of the old tree. After the old leaf entries have been re-inserted, the scanning of the data (and insertion into the new tree) is resumed from the point at which it was interrupted.

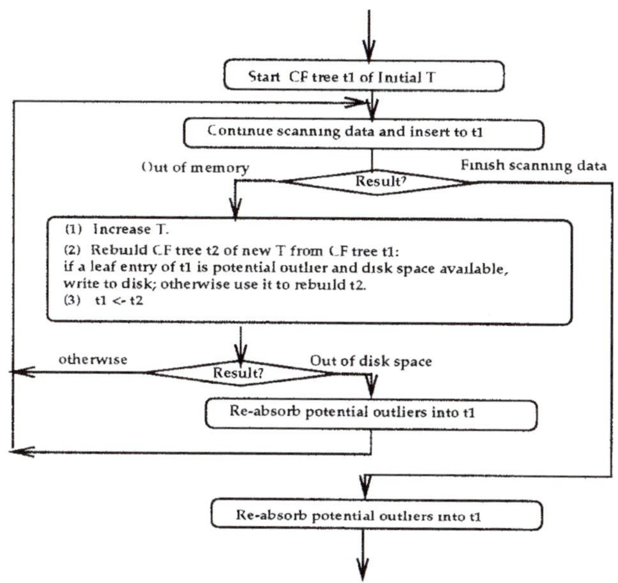

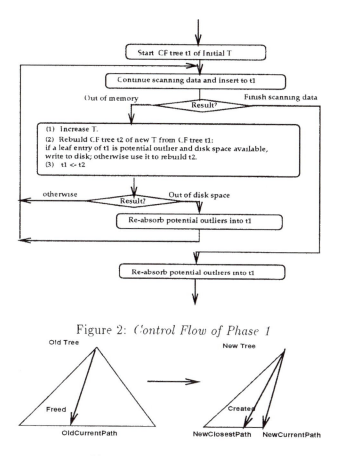

Figure 2: *Control Flow of Phase 1*

Figure 3: *Rebuilding CF Tree*

5.1.1 Reducibility

Assume t_i is a **CF** tree of threshold T_i. Its height is h, and its size (number of nodes) is S_i. Given $T_{i+1} \geq T_i$, we want to use all the leaf entries of t_i to rebuild a **CF** tree, t_{i+1}, of threshold T_{i+1} such that the size of t_{i+1} should not be larger than S_i. Following is the rebuilding algorithm as well as the consequent reducibility theorem.

Assume within each node of **CF** tree t_i, the entries are labeled contiguously from 0 to $n_k - 1$, where n_k is the number of entries in that node, then a **path** from an entry in the root (level 1) to a leaf node (level h) can be uniquely represented by $(i_1, i_2, ..., i_{h-1})$, where $i_j, j = 1, ..., h-1$ is the label of the j-th level entry on that path. So naturally, path $(i_1^{(1)}, i_2^{(1)}, ..., i_{h-1}^{(1)})$ is **before** (or $<$) path $(i_1^{(2)}, i_2^{(2)}, ..., i_{h-1}^{(2)})$ if $i_1^{(1)} = i_1^{(2)}$, ..., $i_{j-1}^{(1)} = i_{j-1}^{(2)}$, and $i_j^{(1)} < i_j^{(2)} (0 \leq j \leq h-1)$. It is obvious that a leaf node corresponds to a path uniquely, and we will use path and leaf node interchangeably from now on.

The algorithm is illustrated in Fig. 3. With the natural path order defined above, it scans and frees the old tree path by path, and at the same time, creates the new tree path by path. The new tree starts with NULL, and "OldCurrentPath" starts with the leftmost path in the old tree. For "OldCurrentPath", the algorithm proceeds as below:

1. *Create the corresponding "NewCurrentPath" in the new tree*: nodes are added to the new tree exactly the same as in the old tree, so that there is no chance that the new tree ever becomes larger than the old tree.
2. *Insert leaf entries in "OldCurrentPath" to the new tree*: with the new threshold, each leaf entry in "OldCurrentPath" is tested against the new tree to see if it can fit [3] in the "NewClosestPath" that is found top-down with the **closest** criteria in the new tree. If yes and "NewClosestPath" is **before** "NewCurrentPath", then it is inserted to "NewClosestPath", and the space in "NewCurrentPath" is left available for later use; otherwise it is inserted to "NewCurrentPath" without creating any new node.
3. *Free space in "OldCurrentPath" and "NewCurrent-Path"*: Once all leaf entries in "OldCurrentPath" are processed, the un-needed nodes along "OldCurrent-Path" can be freed. It is also likely that some nodes along "NewCurrentPath" are empty because leaf entries that originally correspond to this path are now "pushed forward". In this case the empty nodes can be freed too.
4. *"OldCurrentPath" is set to the next path in the old tree if there exists one, and repeat the above steps.*

From the rebuilding steps, old leaf entries are re-inserted, but the new tree can never become larger than the old tree. Since only nodes corresponding to "OldCurrentPath" and "NewCurrentPath" need to exist simultaneously, the maximal extra space needed for the tree transformation is h pages. So by increasing the threshold, we can rebuild a smaller **CF** tree with a limited extra memory.

Theorem 5.1 (**Reducibility Theorem:**): *Assume we rebuild CF tree t_{i+1} of threshold T_{i+1} from CF tree t_i of threshold T_i by the above algorithm, and let S_i and S_{i+1} be the sizes of t_i and t_{i+1} respectively. If $T_{i+1} \geq T_i$, then $S_{i+1} \leq S_i$, and the transformation from t_i to t_{i+1} needs at most h extra pages of memory, where h is the height of t_i.*

5.1.2 Threshold Values

A good choice of threshold value can greatly reduce the number of rebuilds. Since the initial threshold value T_0 is increased dynamically, we can adjust for its being too low. But if the initial T_0 is too high, we will obtain a less detailed **CF** tree than is feasible with the available memory. So T_0 should be set conservatively. *BIRCH* sets it to zero by default; a knowledgeable user could change this.

[3] Either absorbed by an existing leaf entry, or created as a new leaf entry without splitting.

Suppose that T_i turns out to be too small, and we subsequently run out of memory after N_i data points have been scanned, and C_i leaf entries have been formed (each satisfying the threshold condition wrt. T_i). Based on the portion of the data that we have scanned and the tree that we have built up so far, we need to estimate the next threshold value T_{i+1}. This estimation is a difficult problem, and a full solution is beyond the scope of this paper. Currently, we use the following heuristic approach:

1. We try to choose T_{i+1} so that $N_{i+1} = \mathrm{Min}(2N_i, N)$. That is, whether N is known, we choose to estimate T_{i+1} at most in proportion to the data we have seen thus far.
2. Intuitively, we want to increase threshold based on some measure of *volume*. There are two distinct notions of volume that we use in estimating threshold. The first is *average volume*, which is defined as $V_a = r^d$ where r is the average radius of the root cluster in the **CF** tree, and d is the dimensionality of the space. Intuitively, this is a measure of the space occupied by the portion of the data seen thus far (the "footprint" of seen data). A second notion of volume *packed volume*, which is defined as $V_p = C_i * T_i{}^d$, where C_i is the number of leaf entries and $T_i{}^d$ is the maximal volume of a leaf entry. Intuitively, this is a measure of the actual volume occupied by the leaf clusters. Since C_i is essentially the same whenever we run out of memory (since we work with a fixed amount of memory), we can approximate V_p by $T_i{}^d$.
   We make the assumption that r grows with the number of data points N_i. By maintaining a record of r and the number of points N_i, we can estimate r_{i+1} using least squares linear regression. We define the *expansion factor* $f = Max(1.0, \frac{r_{i+1}}{r_i})$, and use it as a heuristic measure of how the data footprint is growing. The use of *Max* is motivated by our observation that for most large datasets, the observed footprint becomes a constant quite quickly (unless the input order is skewed). Similarly, by making the assumption that V_p grows linearly with N_i, we estimate T_{i+1} using least squares linear regression.
3. We traverse a path from the root to a leaf in the **CF** tree, always going to the child with the most points in a "greedy" attempt to find the most crowded leaf node. We calculate the distance (D_{min}) between the closest two entries on this leaf. If we want to build a more condensed tree, it is reasonable to expect that we should at least increase the threshold value to D_{min}, so that these two entries can be merged.
4. We multiplied the T_{i+1} value obtained through linear regression with the expansion factor f, and adjusted it using D_{min} as follows: $T_{i+1} = Max(D_{min}, f * T_{i+1})$. To ensure that the threshold value grows monotonically, in the very unlikely case that T_{i+1} obtained thus is less than T_i then we choose $T_{i+1} = T_i * (\frac{N_{i+1}}{N_i})^{\frac{1}{d}}$. (This is equivalent to assuming that all data points are uniformly distributed in a d-dimensional sphere, and is really just a crude approximation, however, it is rarely called for.)

5.1.3 Outlier-Handling Option

Optionally, we can use R bytes of disk space for handling *outliers*, which are leaf entries of low density that are judged to be unimportant wrt. the overall clustering pattern. When we rebuild the **CF** tree by re-inserting the old leaf entries, the size of the new tree is reduced in two ways. First, we increase the threshold value, thereby allowing each leaf entry to "absorb" more points. Second, we treat some leaf entries as potential outliers and write them out to disk. An old leaf entry is considered to be a potential outlier if it has "far fewer" data points than the average. "Far fewer", is of course another heuristics.

Periodically, the disk space may run out, and the potential outliers are scanned to see if they can be re-absorbed into the current tree without causing the tree to grow in size. — An increase in the threshold value or a change in the distribution due to the new data read after a potential outlier is written out could well mean that the potential outlier no longer qualifies as an outlier. When all data has been scanned, the potential outliers left in the disk space must be scanned to verify if they are indeed outliers. If a potential outlier can not be absorbed at this last chance, it is very likely a real outlier and can be removed.

Note that the entire cycle — insufficient memory triggering a rebuilding of the tree, insufficient disk space triggering a re-absorbing of outliers, etc. — could be repeated several times before the dataset is fully scanned. This effort must be considered in addition to the cost of scanning the data in order to assess the cost of Phase 1 accurately.

5.1.4 Delay-Split Option

When we run out of main memory, it may well be the case that still more data points can fit in the current **CF** tree, without changing the threshold. However, some of the data points that we read may require us to split a node in the **CF** tree, A simple idea is to write such data points to disk (in a manner similar to how outliers are written), and to proceed reading the data until we run out of disk space as well. The advantage of this approach is that in general, more data points can fit in the tree before we have to rebuild.

6 Performance Studies

We present a complexity analysis, and then discuss the experiments that we have conducted on *BIRCH* (and *CLARANS*) using synthetic as well as real datasets.

6.1 Analysis

First we analyze the cpu cost of Phase 1. The maximal size of the tree is $\frac{M}{P}$. To insert a point, we need to follow a path from root to leaf, touching about $1 + \log_B \frac{M}{P}$ nodes. At each node we must examine B entries, looking for the "closest"; the cost per entry is proportional to the dimension d. So the cost for inserting all data points is $O(d * N * B(1 + \log_B \frac{M}{P}))$. In case we must rebuild the tree, let ES be the **CF** entry size. There are at most $\frac{M}{ES}$ leaf entries to re-insert, so the cost of re-inserting leaf entries is $O(d * \frac{M}{ES} * B(1 + \log_B \frac{M}{P}))$. The number of times we have to re-build the tree depends upon our threshold heuristics. Currently, it is about $\log_2 \frac{N}{N_0}$, where the value 2 arises from the fact that we never estimate farther than twice of the current size, and N_0 is the number of data points loaded into memory with threshold T_0. So the total cpu cost of Phase 1 is $O(d{*}N{*}B(1{+}\log_B \frac{M}{P}){+}\log_2 \frac{N}{N_0}{*}d{*}\frac{M}{ES}{*}B(1{+}\log_B \frac{M}{P}))$. The analysis of Phase 2 cpu cost is similar, and hence omitted.

As for I/O, we scan the data once in Phase 1 and not at all in Phase 2. With the outlier-handling and delay-split options on, there is some cost associated with writing out outlier entries to disk and reading them back during a rebuilt. Considering that the amount of disk available for outlier-handling (and delay-split) is not more than M, and that there are about $\log_2 \frac{N}{N_0}$ re-builds, the I/O cost of Phase 1 is not significantly different from the cost of reading in the dataset. Based on the above analysis — which is actually rather pessimistic, in the light of our experimental results — the cost of Phases 1 and 2 should scale linearly with N.

There is no I/O in Phase 3. Since the input to Phase 3 is bounded, the cpu cost of Phase 3 is therefore bounded by a constant that depends upon the maximum input size and the global algorithm chosen for this phase. Phase 4 scans the dataset again and puts each data point into the proper cluster; the time taken is proportional to $N * K$. (However with the newest "nearest neighbor" techniques, it can be improved [GG92] to be almost linear wrt. N.)

6.2 Synthetic Dataset Generator

To study the sensitivity of *BIRCH* to the characteristics of a wide range of input datasets, we have used a collection of synthetic datasets generated by a generator that we have developed. The data generation is controlled by a set of parameters that are summarized in Table 1.

Each dataset consists of K clusters of 2-d data points. A cluster is characterized by the number of data points in it(n), its radius(r), and its center(c). n is in the range of $[n_l,n_h]$, and r is in the range of $[r_l,r_h]$[4]. Once placed, the clusters cover a range of values in each dimension. We refer to these ranges as the "overview" of the dataset.

Parameter	Values or Ranges
Pattern	grid, sine, random
Number of clusters K	4 .. 256
n_l (Lower n)	0 .. 2500
n_h (Higher n)	50 .. 2500
r_l (Lower r)	0 .. $\sqrt{2}$
r_h (Higher r)	$\sqrt{2}$ .. $\sqrt{32}$
Distance multiplier k_g	4 (grid only)
Number of cycles n_c	4 (sine only)
Noise rate r_n (%)	0 .. 10
Input order o	randomized, ordered

Table 1: *Data Generation Parameters and Their Values or Ranges Experimented*

The location of the center of each cluster is determined by the *pattern* parameter. Three patterns — *grid*, *sine*, and *random* — are currently supported by the generator. When the *grid* pattern is used, the cluster centers are placed on a $\sqrt{K} \times \sqrt{K}$ grid. The distance between the centers of neighboring clusters on the same row/column is controlled by k_g, and is set to $k_g \frac{(r_l+r_h)}{2}$. This leads to an overview of $[0,\sqrt{K}k_g\frac{r_l+r_h}{2}]$ on both dimensions. The *sine* pattern places the cluster centers on a curve of sine function. The K clusters are divided into n_c groups, each of which is placed on a different cycle of the sine function. The x location of the center of cluster i is $2\pi i$ whereas the y location is $\frac{K}{n_c} * sine(2\pi i/(\frac{K}{n_c}))$. The overview of a sine dataset is therefore $[0,2\pi K]$ and $[-\frac{K}{n_c},+\frac{K}{n_c}]$ on the x and y directions respectively. The *random* pattern places the cluster centers randomly. The overview of the dataset is $[0,K]$ on both dimensions since the the x and y locations of the centers are both randomly distributed within the range $[0,K]$.

Once the characteristics of each cluster are determined, the data points for the cluster are generated according to a 2-d independent normal distribution whose mean is the center c, and whose variance in each dimension is $\frac{r^2}{2}$. Note that due to the properties of the normal distribution, the maximum distance between a point in the cluster and the center is unbounded. In other words, a point may be arbitrarily far from its belonging cluster. So a data point that belongs to cluster A may be closer to the center of cluster B than to the center of A, and we refer to such points as "outsiders".

In addition to the clustered data points, noise in the form of data points uniformly distributed throughout the overview of the dataset can be added to the dataset. The parameter r_n controls the percentage of data points in the dataset that are considered noise.

The placement of the data points in the dataset is controlled by the order parameter o. When the randomized option is used, the data points of all clusters and the noise are randomized throughout the entire

[4]Note that when $n_l = n_h$ the number of points is fixed and when $r_l = r_h$ the radius is fixed.

Scope	Parameter	Default Value
Global	Memory (M)	80x1024 bytes
	Disk (R)	20% M
	Distance def.	D2
	Quality def.	$(\bar{D})$
	Threshold def.	threshold for D
Phase1	Initial threshold	0.0
	Delay-split	on
	Page size (P)	1024 bytes
	Outlier-handling	on
	Outlier def.	Leaf entry which contains < 25% of the average number of points per leaf entry
Phase3	Input range	1000
	Algorithm	Adapted HC
Phase4	Refinement pass	1
	Discard-outlier	off
	Outlier def.	Data point whose Euclidian distance to the closest seed is larger than twice of the radius of that cluster

Table 2: *BIRCH Parameters and Their Default Values*

dataset. Whereas when the ordered option is selected, the data points of a cluster are placed together, the clusters are placed in the order they are generated, and the noise is placed at the end.

6.3 Parameters and Default Setting

BIRCH is capable of working under various settings. Table 2 lists the parameters of *BIRCH*, their effecting scopes and their default values. Unless specified explicitly otherwise, an experiments is conducted under this default setting.

M was selected to be 80 kbytes which is about 5% of the dataset size in the base workload used in our experiments. Since disk space (R) is just used for outliers, we assume that $R < M$ and set R = 20% of M. The experiments on the effects of the 5 distance metrics in the first 3 phases[ZRL95] indicate that (1) using $D3$ in Phases 1 and 2 results in a much higher ending threshold, and hence produces clusters of poorer quality; (2) however, there is no distinctive performance difference among the others. So we decided to choose $D2$ as default. Following Statistics tradition, we choose "weighted average diameter" (denoted as $\bar{D}$) as quality measurement. The smaller $\bar{D}$ is, the better the quality is. The threshold is defined as the threshold for cluster diameter as default.

In Phase 1, the initial threshold is default to 0. Based on a study of how page size affects performance[ZRL95], we selected P = 1024. The delay-split option is on so that given a threshold, the **CF** tree accepts more data points and reaches a higher capacity. The outlier-handling option is on so that *BIRCH* can remove outliers and concentrate on the dense places with the given amount of resources. For simplicity, we treat a leaf entry of which the number of data points is less than a quarter of the average as an outlier.

In Phase 3, most global algorithms can handle 1000 objects quite well. So we default the input range as 1000. We have chosen the adapted *HC* algorithm to use here. We decided to let Phase 4 refine the clusters only once with its discard-outlier option off, so that all data points will be counted in the quality measurement for fair comparisons.

6.4 Base Workload Performance

The first set of experiments was to evaluate the ability of BIRCH to cluster various large datasets. All the times are presented in *second* in this paper. Three synthetic datasets, one for each pattern, were used. Table 3 presents the generator settings for them. The weighted average diameters of the actual clusters[5], $\bar{D}_{act}$ are also included in the table.

Fig. 6 visualizes the actual clusters of DS1 by plotting a cluster as a circle whose center is the centroid, radius is the cluster radius, and label is the number of points in the cluster. The *BIRCH* clusters of DS1 are presented in Fig. 7. We observe that the *BIRCH* clusters are very similar to the actual clusters in terms of location, number of points, and radii. The maximal and average difference between the centroids of an actual cluster and its corresponding *BIRCH* cluster are 0.17 and 0.07 respectively. The number of points in a *BIRCH* cluster is no more than 4% different from the corresponding actual cluster. The radii of the *BIRCH* clusters (ranging from 1.25 to 1.40 with an average of 1.32) are close to, those of the actual clusters (1.41). Note that all the *BIRCH* radii are smaller than the actual radii. This is because *BIRCH* assigns the "outsiders" of an actual clusters to a proper *BIRCH* cluster. Similar conclusions can be reached by analyzing the visual presentations of DS2 and DS3 (but omitted here due to the lack of space).

As summarized in Table 4, it took *BIRCH* less than 50 seconds (on an HP 9000/720 workstation) to cluster 100,000 data points of each dataset. The pattern of the dataset had almost no impact on the clustering time. Table 4 also presents the performance results for three additional datasets – DS1o, DS2o and DS3o – which correspond to DS1, DS2 and DS3, respectively except that the parameter o of the generator is set to *ordered*. As demonstrated in Table 4, changing the order of the data points had almost no impact on the performance of *BIRCH*.

6.5 Sensitivity to Parameters

We studied the sensitivity of *BIRCH*'s performance to the change of the values of some parameters. Due to the lack of space, here we can only present some major conclusions (for details, see [ZRL95]).

[5] From now on, we refer to the clusters generated by the generator as the "actual clusters" whereas the clusters identified by *BIRCH* as "*BIRCH* clusters".

Dataset	Generator Setting	$\bar{D}_{act}$
DS1	grid, $K = 100, n_l = n_h = 1000, r_l = r_h = \sqrt{2}, k_g = 4, r_n = 0\%, o = randomized$	2.00
DS2	sine, $K = 100, n_l = n_h = 1000, r_l = r_h = \sqrt{2}, n_c = 4, r_n = 0\%, o = randomized$	2.00
DS3	random, $K = 100, n_l = 0, n_h = 2000, r_l = 0, r_h = 4, r_n = r_n = 0\%, o = randomized$	4.18

Table 3: *Datasets Used as Base Workload*

Initial threshold: (1) *BIRCH*'s performance is stable as long as the initial threshold is not excessively high wrt. the dataset. (2) $T_0 = 0.0$ works well with a little extra running time. (3) If a user does know a good T_0, then she/he can be rewarded by saving up to 10% of the time.

Page Size P: In Phase 1, smaller (larger) P tends to decrease (increase) the running time, requires higher (lower) ending threshold, produces less (more) but "coarser (finer)" leaf entries, and hence degrades (improves) the quality. However with the refinement in Phase 4, the experiments suggest that from $P = 256$ to 4096 , although the qualities at the end of Phase 3 are different, the final qualities after the refinement are almost the same.

Outlier Options: *BIRCH* was tested on "noisy" datasets with all the outlier options *on*, and *off*. The results show that with all the outlier options on, *BIRCH* is not slower but faster, and at the same time, its quality is much better.

Memory Size: In Phase 1, as memory size (or the maximal tree size) increases, the running time increases because of processing a larger tree per rebuilt, but only slightly because it is done in memory; (2) more but finer subclusters are generated to feed the next phase, and hence results in better quality; (3) the inaccuracy caused by insufficient memory can be compensated to some extent by Phase 4 refinements. In another word, *BIRCH* can tradeoff between memory and time to achieve similar final quality.

6.6 Time Scalability

Two distinct ways of increasing the dataset size are used to test the scalability of *BIRCH*.

Increasing the Number of Points per Cluster: For each of DS1, DS2 and DS3, we create a range of datasets by keeping the generator settings the same except for changing n_l and n_h to change n, and hence N. The running time for the first 3 phases, as well as for all 4 phases are plotted against the dataset size N in Fig. 4. Both of them are shown to grow linearly wrt. N consistently for all three patterns.

Increasing the Number of Clusters: For each of DS1, DS2 and DS3, we create a range of datasets by keeping the generator settings the same except for changing K to change N. The running time for the first 3 phases, as well as for all 4 phases are plotted against the dataset size N in Fig. 5. Since both N and K are growing, and Phase 4's complexity is now $O(K * N)$ (can be improved to be almost linear in the future), the total time is not exactly linear wrt. N. However the running time for the first 3 phases is again confirmed to grow linearly wrt. N consistently for all three patterns.

Dataset	Time	$\bar{D}$	Dataset	Time	$\bar{D}$
DS1	47.1	1.87	DS1o	47.4	1.87
DS2	47.5	1.99	DS2o	46.4	1.99
DS3	49.5	3.39	DS3o	48.4	3.26

Table 4: *BIRCH Performance on Base Workload wrt. Time, $\bar{D}$ and Input Order*

Dataset	Time	$\bar{D}$	Dataset	Time	$\bar{D}$
DS1	839.5	2.11	DS1o	1525.7	10.75
DS2	777.5	2.56	DS2o	1405.8	179.23
DS3	1520.2	3.36	DS3o	2390.5	6.93

Table 5: *CLARANS Performance on Base Workload wrt. Time, $\bar{D}$ and Input Order*

6.7 Comparisons of BIRCH and CLARANS

In this experiment we compare the performance of *CLARANS* and *BIRCH* on the base workload. First *CLARANS* assumes that the memory is enough for holding the whole dataset, so it needs much more memory than *BIRCH* does. In order for *CLARANS* to stop after an acceptable running time, we set its *maxneighbor* value to be the larger of 50 (instead of 250) and 1.25% of K(N-K), but no more than 100 (newly enforced upper limit recommended by Ng). Its *numlocal* value is still 2. Fig. 8 visualizes the *CLARANS* clusters for DS1. Comparing them with the actual clusters for DS1 we can observe that: (1) The pattern of the location of the cluster centers is distorted. (2) The number of data points in a *CLARANS* cluster can be as many as 57% different from the number in the actual cluster. (3) The radii of *CLARANS* clusters varies largely from 1.15 to 1.94 with an average of 1.44 (larger than those of the actual clusters, 1.41). Similar behaviors can be observed the visualization of *CLARANS* clusters for DS2 and DS3 (but omitted here due to the lack of space).

Table 5 summarizes the performance of *CLARANS*. For all three datasets of the base workload, (1) *CLARANS* is at least 15 times slower than *BIRCH*, and is sensitive to the pattern of the dataset. (2) The $\bar{D}$ value for the *CLARANS* clusters is much larger than that for the *BIRCH* clusters. (3) The results for DS1o, DS2o, and DS3o show that when the data points are ordered, the time and quality of *CLARANS* degrade dramatically. In conclusion, for the base workload, *BIRCH* uses much less memory, but is faster, more accurate, and less order-sensitive compared with *CLARANS*.

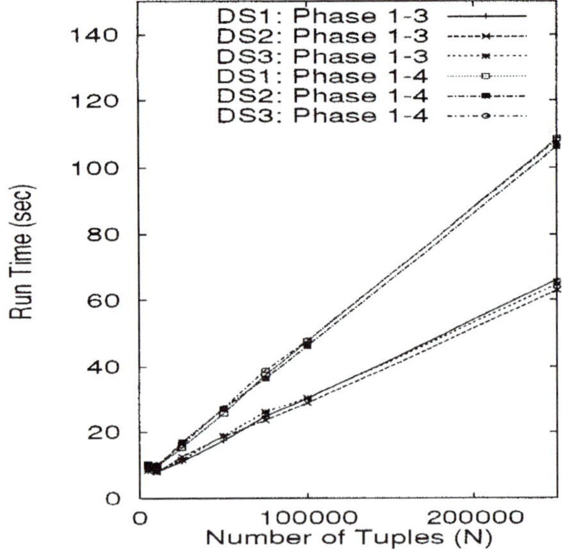

Figure 4: *Scalability wrt. Increasing* n_l, n_h

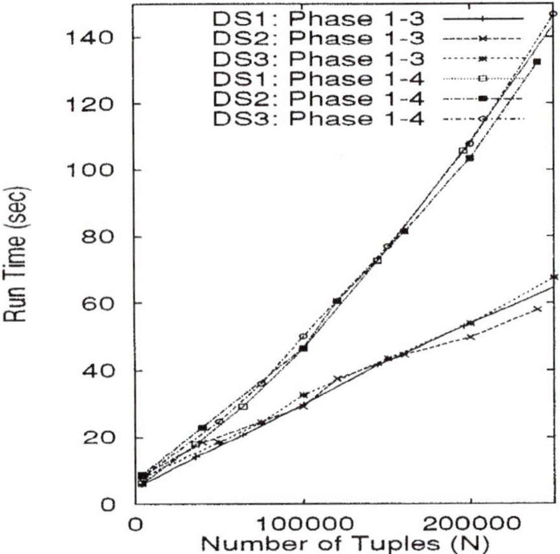

Figure 5: *Scalability wrt. Increasing K*

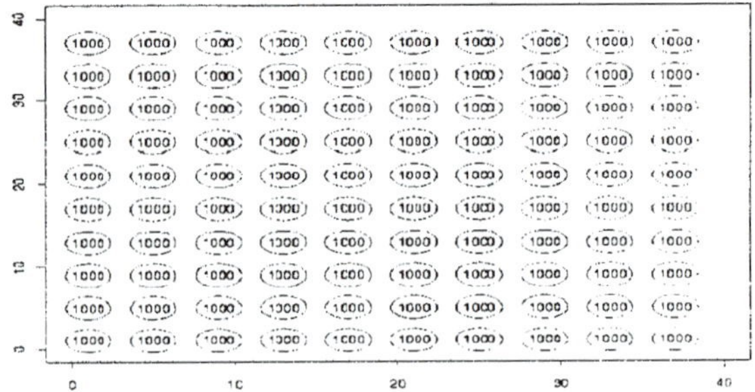

Figure 6: *Actual Clusters of DS1*

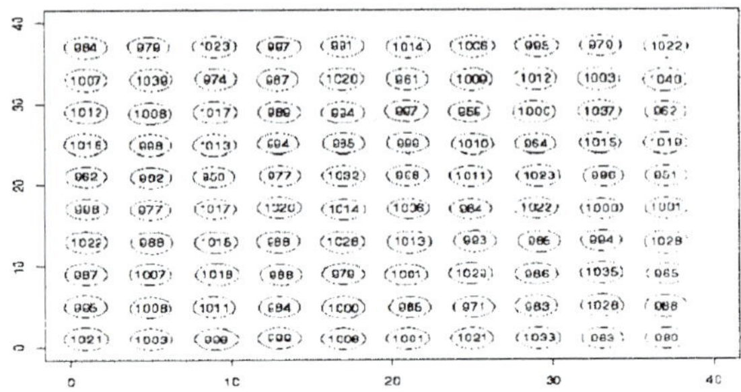

Figure 7: *BIRCH Clusters of DS1*

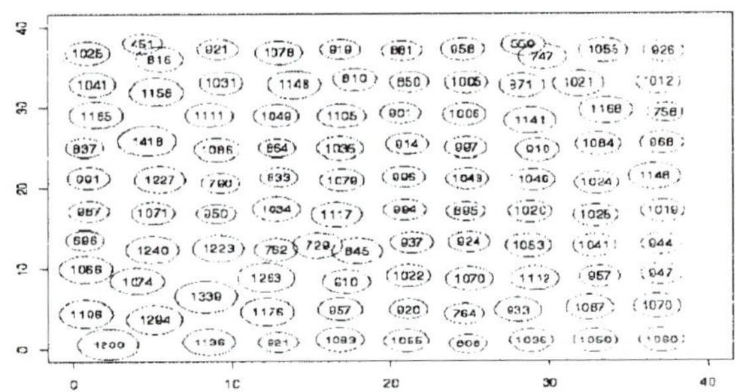

Figure 8: *CLARANS Clusters of DS1*

6.8 Application to Real Datasets

BIRCH has been used for filtering real images. Fig. 9 are two similar images of trees with a partly cloudy sky as the background, taken in two different wavelengths. The top one is in near-infrared band (NIR), and the bottom one is in visible wavelength band (VIS). Each image contains 512x1024 pixels, and each pixel actually has a pair of brightness values corresponding to NIR and VIS. Soil scientists receive hundreds of such image pairs and try to first filter the trees from the background, and then filter the trees into sunlit leaves, shadows and branches for statistical analysis.

We applied *BIRCH* to the (NIR,VIS) value pairs for all pixels in an image (512x1024 2-d tuples) by using 400 kbytes of memory (about 5% of the dataset size) and 80 kbytes of disk space (about 20% of the memory size), and weighting NIR and VIS values equally. We obtained 5 clusters that correspond to (1) very bright part of sky, (2) ordinary part of sky, (3) clouds, (4) sunlit leaves (5) tree branches and shadows on the trees. This step took 284 seconds.

However the branches and shadows were too similar to be distinguished from each other, although we could separate them from the other cluster categories. So we pulled out the part of the data corresponding to (5) (146707 2-d tuples) and used *BIRCH* again. But this time, (1) NIR was weighted 10 times heavier than VIS because we observed that branches and shadows were easier to tell apart from the NIR image than from the VIS image; (2) *BIRCH* ended with a finer threshold because it processed a smaller dataset with the same amount of memory. The two clusters corresponding to branches and shadows were obtained with 71 seconds. Fig. 10 shows the parts of image that correspond to

Figure 9: *The images taken in NIR and VIS*

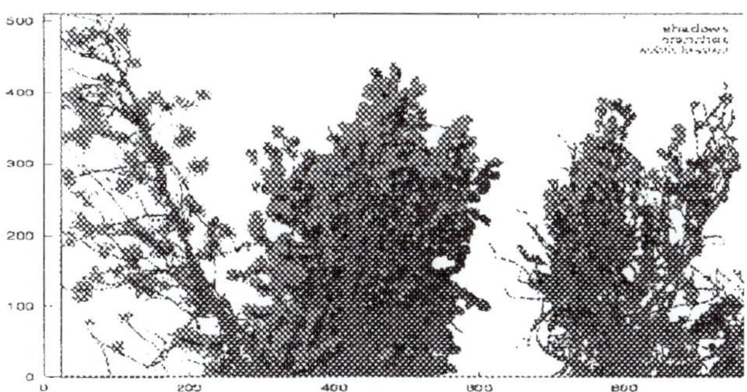

Figure 10: *The sunlit leaves, branches and shadows*

sunlit leaves, tree branches and shadows on the trees, obtained by clustering using *BIRCH*. Visually, we can see that it is a satisfactory filtering of the original image according to the user's intention.

7 Summary and Future Research

BIRCH is a clustering method for very large datasets. It makes a large clustering problem tractable by concentrating on densely occupied portions, and using a compact summary. It utilizes measurements that capture the natural closeness of data. These measurements can be stored and updated incrementally in a height-balanced tree. *BIRCH* can work with any given amount of memory, and the I/O complexity is a little more than one scan of data. Experimentally, *BIRCH* is shown to perform very well on several large datasets, and is significantly superior to *CLARANS* in terms of quality, speed and order-sensitivity.

Proper parameter setting is important to *BIRCH*'s efficiency. In the near future, we will concentrate on studying (1) more reasonable ways of increasing the threshold dynamically, (2) the dynamic adjustment of outlier criteria, (3) more accurate quality measurements, and (4) data parameters that are good indicators of how well *BIRCH* is likely to perform. We will explore *BIRCH*'s architecture for opportunities of parallel executions as well as interactive learnings. As an incremental algorithm, *BIRCH* will be able to read data directly from a tape drive, or from network by matching its clustering speed with the data reading speed. We will also study how to make use of the clustering information obtained to help solve problems such as storage or query optimization, and data compression.

References

[CKS88] Peter Cheeseman, James Kelly, Matthew Self, et al., *AutoClass : A Bayesian Classification System*, Proc. of the 5th Int'l Conf. on Machine Learning, Morgan Kaufman, Jun. 1988.

[DH73] Richard Duda, and Peter E. Hart, *Pattern Classification and Scene Analysis*, Wiley, 1973.

[DJ80] R. Dubes, and A.K. Jain, *Clustering Methodologies in Exploratory Data Analysis* Advances in Computers, Edited by M.C. Yovits, Vol. 19, Academic Press, New York, 1980.

[EKX95a] Martin Ester, Hans-Peter Kriegel, and Xiaowei Xu, *A Database Interface for Clustering in Large Spatial Databases*, Proc. of 1st Int'l Conf. on Knowledge Discovery and Data Mining, 1995.

[EKX95b] Martin Ester, Hans-Peter Kriegel, and Xiaowei Xu, *Knowledge Discovery in Large Spatial Databases: Focusing Techniques for Efficient Class Identification*, Proc. of 4th Int'l Symposium on Large Spatial Databases, Portland, Maine, U.S.A., 1995.

[Fis87] Douglas H. Fisher, *Knowledge Acquisition via Incremental Conceptual Clustering*, Machine Learning, 2(2), 1987

[Fis95] Douglas H. Fisher, *Iterative Optimization and Simplification of Hierarchical Clusterings*, Technical Report CS-95-01, Dept. of Computer Science, Vanderbilt University, Nashville, TN 37235.

[GG92] A. Gersho and R. Gray, *Vector quantization and signal compression*, Boston, Ma.: Kluwer Academic Publishers, 1992.

[KR90] Leonard Kaufman, and Peter J. Rousseeuw, *Finding Groups in Data - An Introduction to Cluster Analysis*, Wiley Series in Probability and Mathematical Statistics, 1990.

[Leb87] Michael Lebowitz, *Experiments with Incremental Concept Formation : UNIMEM*, Machine Learning, 1987.

[Lee81] R.C.T.Lee, *Clustering analysis and its applications*, Advances in Information Systems Science, Edited by J.T.Toum, Vol. 8, pp. 169-292, Plenum Press, New York, 1981.

[Mur83] F. Murtagh, *A Survey of Recent Advances in Hierarchical Clustering Algorithms*, The Computer Journal, 1983.

[NH94] Raymond T. Ng and Jiawei Han, *Efficient and Effective Clustering Methods for Spatial Data Mining*, Proc. of VLDB, 1994.

[Ols93] Clark F. Olson, *Parallel Algorithms for Hierarchical Clustering*, Technical Report, Computer Science Division, Univ. of California at Berkeley, Dec.,1993.

[ZRL95] Tian Zhang, Raghu Ramakrishnan, and Miron Livny, *BIRCH: An Efficient Data Clustering Method for Very Large Databases*, Technical Report, Computer Sciences Dept., Univ. of Wisconsin-Madison, 1995.

SPRINT: A Scalable Parallel Classifier for Data Mining

John Shafer* Rakesh Agrawal Manish Mehta

IBM Almaden Research Center
650 Harry Road, San Jose, CA 95120

Abstract

Classification is an important data mining problem. Although classification is a well-studied problem, most of the current classification algorithms require that all or a portion of the the entire dataset remain permanently in memory. This limits their suitability for mining over large databases. We present a new decision-tree-based classification algorithm, called SPRINT that removes all of the memory restrictions, and is fast and scalable. The algorithm has also been designed to be easily parallelized, allowing many processors to work together to build a single consistent model. This parallelization, also presented here, exhibits excellent scalability as well. The combination of these characteristics makes the proposed algorithm an ideal tool for data mining.

1 Introduction

Classification has been identified as an important problem in the emerging field of data mining[2]. While classification is a well-studied problem (see [24] [16] for excellent overviews), only recently has there been focus on algorithms that can handle large databases. The intuition is that by classifying larger datasets, we will be able to improve the accuracy of the classification model. This hypothesis has been studied and confirmed in [4], [5], and [6].

In classification, we are given a set of example records, called a *training set*, where each record consists of several fields or *attributes*. Attributes are either *continuous*, coming from an ordered domain, or *categorical*, coming from an unordered domain. One of the attributes, called the *classifying* attribute, indicates the *class* to which each example belongs. The objective of classification is to build a model of the classifying attribute based upon the other attributes. Figure 1(a) shows a sample training set where each record represents a car-insurance applicant. Here we are interested in building a model of what makes an applicant a high or low insurance risk. Once a model is built, it can be used to determine the class of future unclassified records. Applications of classification arise in diverse fields, such as retail target marketing, customer retention, fraud detection and medical diagnosis[16].

Several classification models have been proposed over the years, e.g. neural networks [14], statistical models like linear/quadratic discriminants [13], decision trees [3][20] and genetic models[11]. Among these models, decision trees are particularly suited for data mining [2][15]. Decision trees can be constructed relatively fast compared to other methods. Another advantage is that decision tree models are simple and easy to understand [20]. Moreover, trees can be easily converted into SQL statements that can be used to access databases efficiently [1]. Finally, decision tree classifiers obtain similar and sometimes better accuracy when compared with other classification methods [16]. We have therefore focused on building a scalable and parallelizable decision-tree classifier.

A decision tree is a class discriminator that recursively partitions the training set until each partition consists entirely or dominantly of examples from one class. Each non-leaf node of the tree contains a *split point* which is a test on one or more attributes and

---

*Also, Department of Computer Science, University of Wisconsin, Madison.

Proceedings of the 22nd VLDB Conference
Mumbai(Bombay), India, 1996

rid	Age	Car Type	Risk
0	23	family	High
1	17	sports	High
2	43	sports	High
3	68	family	Low
4	32	truck	Low
5	20	family	High

(a) Training Set

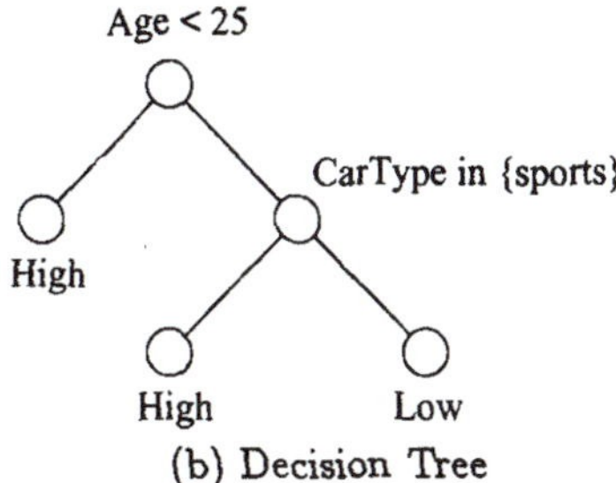

(b) Decision Tree

Figure 1: Car Insurance Example

determines how the data is partitioned. Figure 1(b) shows a sample decision-tree classifier based on the training set shown in Figure 1a. $(Age < 25)$ and $(CarType \in \{sports\})$ are two split points that partition the records into High and Low risk classes. The decision tree can be used to screen future insurance applicants by classifying them into the *High* or *Low* risk categories.

Random sampling is often used to handle large datasets when building a classifier. Previous work on building tree-classifiers from large datasets includes Catlett's study of two methods [4][25] for improving the time taken to develop a classifier. The first method used data sampling at each node of the decision tree, and the second discretized continuous attributes. However, Catlett only considered datasets that could fit in memory; the largest training data had only 32,000 examples. Chan and Stolfo [5] [6] considered partitioning the data into subsets that fit in memory and then developing a classifier on each subset in parallel. The output of multiple classifiers is combined using various algorithms to reach the final classification. Their studies showed that although this approach reduces running time significantly, the multiple classifiers did not achieve the accuracy of a single classifier built using all the data. Incremental learning methods, where the data is classified in batches, have also been studied [18][25]. However, the cumulative cost of classifying data incrementally can sometimes exceed the cost of classifying the entire training set once. In [1], a classifier built with database considerations, the size of the training set was overlooked. Instead, the focus was on building a classifier that could use database indices to improve the retrieval efficiency while classifying test data.

Work by Fifield in [9] examined parallelizing the decision-tree classifier ID3 [19] serial classifier. Like ID3, this work assumes that the entire dataset can fit in real memory and does not address issues such as disk I/O. The algorithms presented there also require processor communication to evaluate any given split point, limiting the number of possible partitioning schemes the algorithms can efficiently consider for each leaf. The Darwin toolkit from Thinking Machines also contained a parallel implementation of the decision-tree classifier CART [3]; however, details of this parallelization are not available in published literature.

The recently proposed SLIQ classification algorithm [15] addressed several issues in building a fast scalable classifier. SLIQ gracefully handles disk-resident data that is too large to fit in memory. It does not use small memory-sized datasets obtained via sampling or partitioning, but builds a single decision tree using the *entire* training set. However, SLIQ does require that some data per record stay memory-resident all the time. Since the size of this in-memory data structure grows in direct proportion to the number of input records, this limits the amount of data that can be classified by SLIQ.

We present in this paper a decision-tree-based classification algorithm, called SPRINT[1], that removes all of the memory restrictions, and is fast and scalable. The algorithm has also been designed to be easily parallelized. Measurements of this parallel implementation on a shared-nothing IBM POWERparallel System SP2 [12], also presented here, show that SPRINT has excellent scaleup, speedup and sizeup properties. The combination of these characteristics makes SPRINT an ideal tool for data mining.

The rest of the paper is organized as follows: In Section 2 we discuss issues in building decision trees and present the serial SPRINT algorithm. Section 3 describes the parallelization of SPRINT as well as two approaches to parallelizing SLIQ. In Section 4, we give a performance evaluation of the serial and parallel algorithms using measurements from their implementation on SP2. We conclude with a summary in Section 5. An expanded version of this paper is available in [22].

2 Serial Algorithm

A decision tree classifier is built in two phases [3] [20]: a growth phase and a prune phase. In the growth phase, the tree is built by recursively partitioning the

[1]SPRINT stands for Scalable PaRallelizable INndution of decision Trees.

data until each partition is either "pure" (all members belong to the same class) or sufficiently small (a parameter set by the user). This process is shown in Figure 2. The form of the split used to partition the data depends on the type of the attribute used in the split. Splits for a continuous attribute A are of the form $value(A) < x$ where x is a value in the domain of A. Splits for a categorical attribute A are of the form $value(A) \in X$ where $X \subset domain(A)$. We consider only binary splits because they usually lead to more accurate trees; however, our techniques can be extended to handle multi-way splits. Once the tree has been fully grown, it is pruned in the second phase to generalize the tree by removing dependence on statistical noise or variation that may be particular only to the training set.

The tree growth phase is computationally much more expensive than pruning, since the data is scanned multiple times in this part of the computation. Pruning requires access only to the fully grown decision-tree. Our experience based on our previous work on SLIQ has been that the pruning phase typically takes less than 1% of the total time needed to build a classifier. We therefore focus only on the tree-growth phase. For pruning, we use the algorithm used in SLIQ, which is based on the Minimum Description Length principle[21].

```
Partition(Data S)
    if (all points in S are of the same class) then
        return;
    for each attribute A do
        evaluate splits on attribute A;
    Use best split found to partition S into S1 and S2;
    Partition(S1);
    Partition(S2);

Initial call: Partition(TrainingData)
```

Figure 2: General Tree-growth Algorithm

There are two major issues that have critical performance implications in the tree-growth phase:

1. How to find split points that define node tests.
2. Having chosen a split point, how to partition the data.

The well-known CART [3] and C4.5 [20] classifiers, for example, grow trees depth-first and repeatedly sort the data at every node of the tree to arrive at the best splits for numeric attributes. SLIQ, on the other hand, replaces this repeated sorting with one-time sort by using separate lists for each attribute (see [15] for details). SLIQ uses a data structure called a *class list* which must remain memory resident at all times. The size of this structure is proportional to the number of input records, and this is what limits the number of input records that SLIQ can handle.

Age	Class	rid
17	High	1
20	High	5
23	High	0
32	Low	4
43	High	2
68	Low	3

Car Type	Class	rid
family	High	0
sports	High	1
sports	High	2
family	Low	3
truck	Low	4
family	High	5

Figure 3: Example of attribute lists

SPRINT addresses the above two issues differently from previous algorithms; it has no restriction on the size of input and yet is a fast algorithm. It shares with SLIQ the advantage of a one-time sort, but uses different data structures. In particular, there is no structure like the class list that grows with the size of input and needs to be memory-resident. We further discuss differences between SLIQ and SPRINT in Section 2.4, after we have described SPRINT.

2.1 Data Structures

Attribute lists

SPRINT initially creates an *attribute list* for each attribute in the data (see Figure 3). Entries in these lists, which we will call *attribute records*, consist of an attribute value, a class label, and the index of the record (*rid*) from which these value were obtained. Initial lists for continuous attributes are sorted by attribute value once when first created. If the entire data does not fit in memory, attribute lists are maintained on disk.

The initial lists created from the training set are associated with the root of the classification tree. As the tree is grown and nodes are split to create new children, the attribute lists belonging to each node are partitioned and associated with the children. When a list is partitioned, the order of the records in the list is preserved; thus, partitioned lists never require resorting. Figure 4 shows this process pictorially.

Histograms

For continuous attributes, two histograms are associated with each decision-tree node that is under consideration for splitting. These histograms, denoted as C_{above} and C_{below}, are used to capture the class distribution of the attribute records at a given node. As we will see, C_{below} maintains this distribution for attribute records that have already been processed, whereas C_{above} maintains it for those that have not.

Categorical attributes also have a histogram associated with a node. However, only one histogram is needed and it contains the class distribution for each value of the given attribute. We call this histogram a *count matrix*.

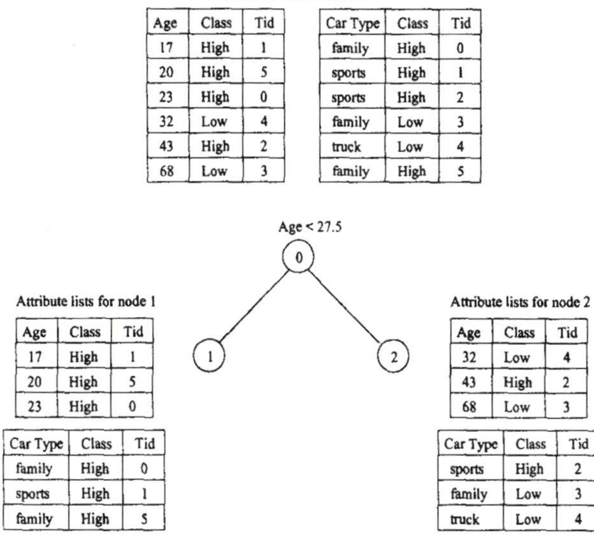

Figure 4: Splitting a node's attribute lists

Since attribute lists are processed one at a time, memory is required for only one set of such histograms. Figures 5 and 6 show example histograms.

2.2 Finding split points

While growing the tree, the goal at each node is to determine the split point that "best" divides the training records belonging to that leaf. The value of a split point depends upon how well it separates the classes. Several splitting indices have been proposed in the past to evaluate the goodness of the split. We use the *gini* index, originally proposed in [3], based on our experience with SLIQ. For a data set S containing examples from n classes, $gini(S)$ is defined as $gini(S) = 1 - \sum p_j^2$ where p_j is the relative frequency of class j in S. If a split divides S into two subsets S_1 and S_2, the index of the divided data $gini_{split}(S)$ is given by $gini_{split}(S) = \frac{n_1}{n} gini(S_1) + \frac{n_2}{n} gini(S_2)$. The advantage of this index is that its calculation requires only the distribution of the class values in each of the partitions.

To find the best split point for a node, we scan each of the node's attribute lists and evaluate splits based on that attribute. The attribute containing the split point with the lowest value for the gini index is then used to split the node. We discuss next how split points are evaluated within each attribute list.

Continuous attributes

For continuous attributes, the candidate split points are mid-points between every two consecutive attribute values in the training data. For determining the split for an attribute for a node, the histogram C_{below} is initialized to zeros whereas C_{above} is initialized with the class distribution for all the records for the node. For the root node, this distribution is obtained at the time of sorting. For other nodes this distribution is obtained when the node is created (discussed below in Section 2.3).

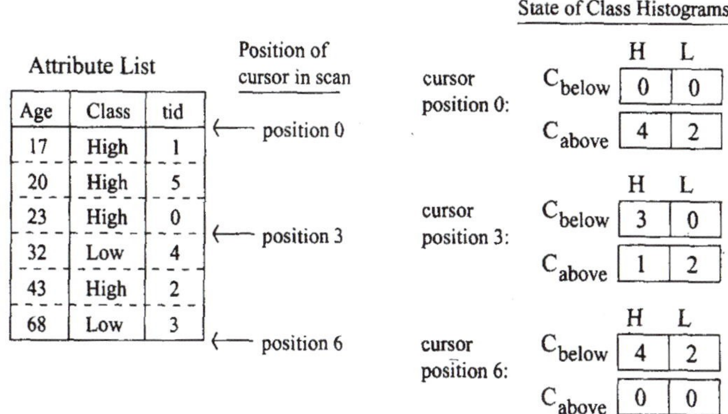

Figure 5: Evaluating continuous split points

Attribute records are read one at a time and C_{below} and C_{above} are updated for each record read. Figure 5 shows the schematic for this histogram update. After each record is read, a split between values (i.e. attribute records) we have and have not yet seen is evaluated. Note that C_{below} and C_{above} have all the necessary information to compute the gini index. Since the lists for continuous attributes are kept in sorted order, each of the candidate split-points for an attribute are evaluated in a single sequential scan of the corresponding attribute list. If a winning split point was found during the scan, it is saved and the C_{below} and C_{above} histograms are deallocated before processing the next attribute.

Categorical attributes

For categorical split-points, we make a single scan through the attribute list collecting counts in the count matrix for each combination of class label and attribute value found in the data. A sample of a count matrix after a data scan is shown in Figure 6. Once we are finished with the scan, we consider all subsets of the attribute values as possible split points and compute the corresponding gini index. If the cardinality of an attribute is above certain threshold, the greedy algorithm initially proposed for IND [17] is instead used for subsetting. The important point is that the information required for computing the gini index for any subset splitting is available in the count matrix.

The memory allocated for a count matrix is reclaimed after the splits for the corresponding attribute have been evaluated.

Attribute List

Car Type	Class	tid
family	High	0
sports	High	1
sports	High	2
family	Low	3
truck	Low	4
family	High	5

$\Longrightarrow$

Count Matrix

	H	L
family	2	1
sports	2	0
truck	0	1

Figure 6: Evaluating categorical split points

2.3 Performing the split

Once the best split point has been found for a node, we execute the split by creating child nodes and dividing the attribute records between them. This requires splitting the node's lists for every attribute into two (see Figure 4 for an illustration)[2]. Partitioning the attribute list of the winning attribute (i.e. the attribute used in the winning split point — *Age* in our example) is straightforward. We scan the list, apply the split test, and move the records to two new attribute lists — one for each new child.

Unfortunately, for the remaining attribute lists of the node (*CarType* in our example), we have no test that we can apply to the attribute values to decide how to divide the records. We therefore work with the *rids*. As we partition the list of the splitting attribute (i.e. *Age*), we insert the *rids* of each record into a probe structure (hash table), noting to which child the record was moved. Once we have collected all the *rids*, we scan the lists of the remaining attributes and probe the hash table with the *rid* of each record. The retrieved information tells us with which child to place the record.

If the hash-table is too large for memory, splitting is done in more than one step. The attribute list for the splitting attribute is partitioned upto the attribute record for which the hash table will fit in memory; portions of attribute lists of non-splitting attributes are partitioned; and the process is repeated for the remainder of the attribute list of the splitting attribute. If the hash-table can fit in memory (quite likely for nodes at lower levels of the tree), a simple optimization is possible. We can build the hash table out of the *rids* of only the smaller of the two children. Relative sizes of the two children are determined at the time the split point is evaluated.

During this splitting operation, we also build class

[2]Because file-creation is usually an expensive operation, we have a solution that does not require the creation of new files for each new attribute list. The details of this optimization can be found in [22].

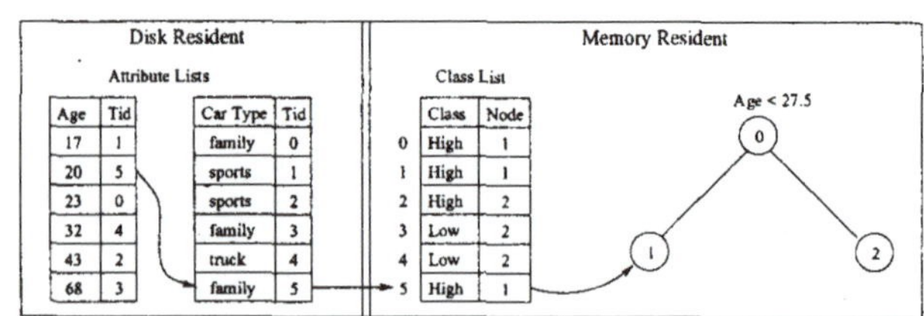

Figure 7: Attribute and Class lists in SLIQ

histograms for each new leaf. As stated earlier, these histograms are used to initialize the C_{above} histograms when evaluating continuous split-points in the next pass.

2.4 Comparison with SLIQ

The technique of creating separate attribute lists from the original data was first proposed by the SLIQ algorithm [15]. In SLIQ, an entry in an attribute list consists only of an attribute value and a *rid*; the class labels are kept in a separate data-structure called a *class list* which is indexed by *rid*. In addition to the class label, an entry in the class list also contains a pointer to a node of the classification tree which indicates to which node the corresponding data record currently belongs. Finally, there is only one list for each attribute. Figure 7 illustrates these data structures.

The advantage of not having separate sets of attribute lists for each node is that SLIQ does not have to rewrite these lists during a split. Reassignment of records to new nodes is done simply by changing the tree-pointer field of the corresponding class-list entry. Since the class list is randomly accessed and frequently updated, it *must* stay in memory all the time or suffer severe performance degradations. The size of this list also grows in direct proportion to the training-set size. This ultimately limits the size of the training set that SLIQ can handle.

Our goal in designing SPRINT was not to outperform SLIQ on datasets where a class list can fit in memory. Rather, the purpose of our algorithm is to develop an accurate classifier for datasets that are simply too large for any other algorithm, and to be able to develop such a classifier efficiently. Also, SPRINT is designed to be easily parallelizable as we will see in the next section.

3 Parallelizing Classification

We now turn to the problem of building classification trees in parallel. We again focus only on the growth phase due to its data-intensive nature. The pruning phase can easily be done off-line on a serial processor as it is computationally inexpensive, and requires access to only the decision-tree grown in the training phase.

In parallel tree-growth, the primary problems remain finding good split-points and partitioning the data using the discovered split points. As in any parallel algorithm, there are also issues of data placement and workload balancing that must be considered. Fortunately, these issues are easily resolved in the SPRINT algorithm. SPRINT was specifically designed to remove any dependence on data structures that are either centralized or memory-resident; because of these design goals, SPRINT parallelizes quite naturally and efficiently. In this section we will present how we parallelize SPRINT. For comparison, we also discuss two parallelizations of SLIQ.

These algorithms all assume a shared-nothing parallel environment where each of N processors has private memory and disks. The processors are connected by a communication network and can communicate only by passing messages. Examples of such parallel machines include GAMMA [7], Teradata [23], and IBM's SP2 [12].

3.1 Data Placement and Workload Balancing

Recall that the main data structures used in SPRINT are the attribute lists and the class histograms. SPRINT achieves uniform data placement and workload balancing by distributing the attribute lists evenly over N processors of a shared-nothing machine. This allows each processor to work on only $1/N$ of the total data.

The partitioning is achieved by first distributing the training-set examples equally among all the processors. Each processor then generates its own attribute-list partitions in parallel by projecting out each attribute from training-set examples it was assigned. Lists for categorical attributes are therefore evenly partitioned and require no further processing. However, continuous attribute lists must now be sorted and repartitioned into contiguous sorted sections. For this, we use the parallel sorting algorithm given in [8]. The result of this sorting operation is that each processor gets a fairly equal-sized sorted sections of each attribute list. Figure 3 shows an example of the initial distribution of the lists for a 2-processor configuration.

3.2 Finding split points

Finding split points in parallel SPRINT is very similar to the serial algorithm. In the serial version, processors scan the attribute lists either evaluating split-points for continuous attributes or collecting distribution counts for categorical attributes. This does not change in the parallel algorithm — no extra work or communication is required while each processor is scanning its attribute-list partitions. We get the full advantage of having N processors simultaneously and

Processor 0

Age	Class	rid
17	High	1
20	High	5
23	High	0

Car Type	Class	rid
family	High	0
sports	High	1
sports	High	2

Processor 1

Age	Class	rid
32	Low	4
43	High	2
68	Low	3

Car Type	Class	rid
family	Low	3
truck	Low	4
family	High	5

Figure 8: Parallel Data Placement

independently processing $1/N$ of the total data. The differences between the serial and parallel algorithms appear only before and after the attribute-list partitions are scanned.

Continuous attributes

For continuous attributes, the parallel version of SPRINT differs from the serial version in how it initializes the C_{below} and C_{above} class-histograms. In a parallel environment, each processor has a separate contiguous section of a "global" attribute list. Thus, a processor's C_{below} and C_{above} histograms must be initialized to reflect the fact that there are sections of the attribute list on other processors. Specifically, C_{below} must initially reflect the class distribution of all sections of an attribute-list assigned to processors of lower rank. The C_{above} histograms must likewise initially reflect the class distribution of the local section as well as all sections assigned to processors of higher rank. As in the serial version, these statistics are gathered when attribute lists for new leaves are created. After collecting statistics, the information is exchanged between all the processors and stored with each leaf, where it is later used to initialize that leaf's C_{above} and C_{below} class histograms.

Once all the attribute-list sections of a leaf have been processed, each processor will have what it considers to be the best split for that leaf. The processors then communicate to determine which of the N split points has the lowest cost.

Categorical attributes

For categorical attributes, the difference between the serial and parallel versions arises after an attribute-list section has been scanned to build the count matrix for a leaf. Since the count matrix built by each processor is based on "local" information only, we must exchange these matrices to get the "global" counts. This is done by choosing a coordinator to collect the count matrices from each processor. The coordinator process then sums the local matrices to get the global count-matrix.

As in the serial algorithm, the global matrix is used to find the best split for each categorical attribute.

3.3 Performing the Splits

Having determined the winning split points, splitting the attribute lists for each leaf is nearly identical to the serial algorithm with each processor responsible for splitting its own attribute-list partitions. The only additional step is that before building the probe structure, we will need to collect *rids* from all the processors. (Recall that a processor can have attribute records belonging to any leaf.) Thus, after partitioning the list of a leaf's splitting attribute, the *rids* collected during the scan are exchanged with all other processors. After the exchange, each processor continues independently, constructing a probe-structure with all the *rids* and using it to split the leaf's remaining attribute lists.

No further work is needed to parallelize the SPRINT algorithm. Because of its design, SPRINT does not require a complex parallelization and, as we will see in Section 4.3, scales quite nicely.

3.4 Parallelizing SLIQ

The attribute lists used in SLIQ can be partitioned evenly across multiple processors as is done in parallel SPRINT. However, the parallelization of SLIQ is complicated by its use of a centralized, memory-resident data-structure — the class list. Because the class list requires random access and frequent updating, parallel algorithms based on SLIQ require that the class list be kept memory-resident. This leads us to two primary approaches for parallelizing SLIQ : one where the class list is replicated in the memory of every processor, and the other where it is distributed such that each processor's memory holds only a portion of the entire list.

3.4.1 Replicated Class List

In the first approach, which we call SLIQ/R, the class list for the entire training set is replicated in the local memory of every processor. Split-points are evaluated in the same manner as in parallel SPRINT, by exchanging count matrices and properly initializing the class histograms. However, the partitioning of attribute lists according to a chosen split point is different.

Performing the splits requires updating the class list for each training example. Since every processor must maintain a consistent copy of the entire class list, every class-list update must be communicated to and applied by every processor. Thus, the time for this part of tree growth will increase with the size of the training set, even if the amount of data at each node remains fixed.

Although SLIQ/R parallelizes split-point evaluation and class-list updates, it suffers from the same drawback as SLIQ — the size of the training set is limited by the memory size of a single processor. Since each processor has a full copy of the class list, SLIQ/R can efficiently process a training set only if the class list for the entire database can fit in the memory of every processor. This is true regardless of the number of processors used.

3.4.2 Distributed Class List

Our second approach to parallelizing SLIQ, called SLIQ/D, helps to relieve SLIQ 's memory constraints by partitioning the class list over the multiprocessor. Each processor therefore contains only $1/Nth$ of the class list. Note that the partitioning of the class list has no correlation with the partitioning of the continuous attribute lists; the class label corresponding to an attribute value could reside on a different processor. This implies that communication is required to look up a "non-local" class label. Since the class list is created from the original partitioned training-set, it will be perfectly correlated with categorical attribute lists. Thus, communication is only required for continuous attributes.

Given this scenario, SLIQ/D has high communication costs while evaluating continuous split points. As each attribute list is scanned, we need to look-up the corresponding class label and tree-pointer for each attribute value. This implies that each processor will require communication for $N - 1/N$ of its data. Also, each processor will have to service lookup requests from other processors in the middle of scanning its attribute lists. Although our SLIQ/D implementation reduces the communication costs by batching the look-ups to the class lists, the extra computation that each processor performs in requesting and servicing remote look-ups to the class list is still high. SLIQ/D also incurs similar communication costs when the class list is updated while partitioning the data using the best splits found.

4 Performance Evaluation

The primary metric for evaluating classifier performance is *classification accuracy* — the percentage of *test* samples that are correctly classified. The other important metrics are *classification time* and the *size* of the decision tree. The ideal goal for a decision tree classifier is to produce compact, accurate trees in a short classification time.

Although the data structures and how a tree is grown are very different in SPRINT and SLIQ, they consider the same types of splits at every node and use identical splitting index (gini index). The two algorithms, therefore, produce identical trees for a given dataset (provided SLIQ can handle the dataset). Since SPRINT uses SLIQ 's pruning method, the final trees obtained using the two algorithms are also identical. Thus, the accuracy and tree size characteristics of SPRINT are identical to SLIQ. A detailed comparison of SLIQ's accuracy, execution time, and tree size with those of CART [3] and C4 (a predecessor of C4.5 [20]) is available in [15]. This performance evaluation shows that compared to other classifiers, SLIQ achieves comparable or better classification accuracy, but produces small decision trees *and* has small execution times. We, therefore, focus only on the classification time metric in our performance evaluation in this paper.

4.1 Datasets

An often used benchmark in classification is STATLOG[16]; however, its largest dataset contains only 57,000 training examples. Due to the lack of a classification benchmark containing large datasets, we use the synthetic database proposed in [2] for all of our experiments. Each record in this synthetic database consists of nine attributes four of which are shown in Table 1. Ten classification functions were also proposed in [2] to produce databases with distributions with varying complexities. In this paper, we present results for two of these function. Function 2 results in fairly small decision trees, while function 7 produces very large trees. Both these functions divide the database into two classes: Group A and Group B. Figure 9 shows the predicates for Group A are shown for each function.

Function 2 - Group A:
$((\textbf{age} < 40) \wedge (50K \leq \textbf{salary} \leq 100K)) \vee$
$((40 \leq \textbf{age} < 60) \wedge (75K \leq \textbf{salary} \geq 125K)) \vee$
$((\textbf{age} \geq 60) \wedge (25K \leq \textbf{salary} \leq 75K))$

Function 7 - Group A:
$\textbf{disposable} > 0$
where $\textbf{disposable} = (0.67 \times (\textbf{salary} + \textbf{commission})) - (0.2 \times \textbf{loan} - 20K)$

Figure 9: Classification Functions for Synthetic Data

Table 1: Description of Attributes for Synthetic Data

Attribute	Value
salary	uniformly distributed from 20k to 150k
commission	**salary** $\geq 75k \Rightarrow$ **commission** $= 0$ else uniformly distributed from 10k to 75k
age	uniformly distributed from 20 to 80
loan	uniformly distributed from 0 to 500k

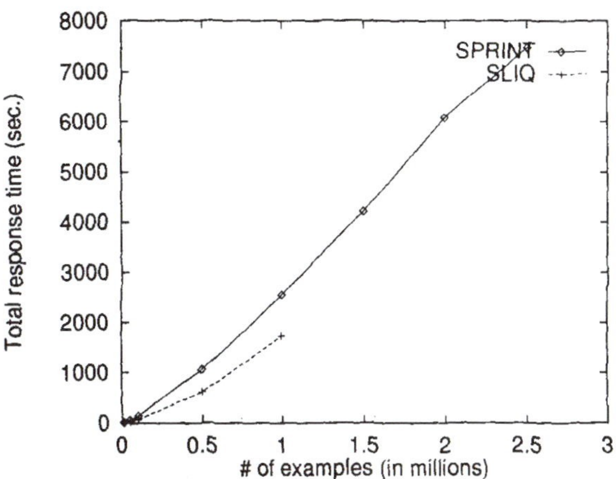

Figure 10: Response times for serial algorithms

4.2 Serial Performance

For our serial analysis, we compare the response times of serial SPRINT and SLIQ on training sets of various sizes. We only compare our algorithm with SLIQ because is has been shown in [15] that SLIQ in most cases outperforms other popular decision-tree classifiers. For the disk-resident datasets which we will be exploring here, SLIQ is the only other viable algorithm.

Experiments were conducted on an IBM RS/6000 250 workstation running AIX level 3.2.5. The CPU has a clock rate of 66MHz and 16MB of main memory. Apart from the standard UNIX daemons and system processes, experiments were run on an idle system.

We used training sets ranging in size from 10,000 records to 2.5 million records. This range was selected to examine how well SPRINT performs in operating regions where SLIQ can and cannot run. The results are shown in Figure 10 on databases generated using function 2.

The results are very encouraging. As expected, for data sizes for which the class list could fit in memory, SPRINT is somewhat slower than SLIQ. In this operating region, we are pitting SPRINT 's rewriting of the dataset to SLIQ 's in-memory updates to the class list. What is surprising is that even in this region SPRINT comes quite close to SLIQ. However, as soon as we cross an input size threshold (about 1.5 million records for our system configuration), SLIQ starts thrashing, whereas SPRINT continues to exhibit a nearly linear scaleup.

4.3 Parallel Performance

To examine how well the SPRINT algorithm performs in parallel environments, we implemented its parallelization on an IBM SP2 [12], using the standard MPI communication primitives [10]. The use of MPI allows our implementation to be completely portable to other

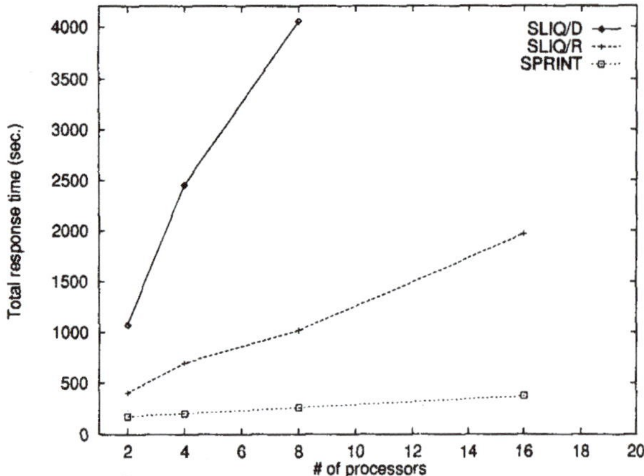

Figure 11: Response times for parallel algorithms

shared-nothing parallel architectures, including workstation clusters. Experiments were conducted on a 16-node IBM SP2 Model 9076. Each node in the multiprocessor is a 370 Node consisting of a POWER1 processor running at 62.5MHZ with 128MB of real memory. Attached to each node is a 100MB disk on which we stored our datasets. The processors all run AIX level 4.1 and communicate with each other through the High-Performance-Switch with HPS-tb2 adaptors. See [12] for SP2 hardware details.

Due to the available disk space being smaller than the available memory, we are prevented from running any experiments where attribute lists are forced to disk. This results in I/O costs, which scale linearly in SPRINT, becoming a smaller fraction of the overall execution time. Any other costs that may not scale well will thus be exaggerated.

4.3.1 Comparison of Parallel Algorithms

We first compare parallel SPRINT to the two parallelizations of SLIQ. In these experiments, each processor contained 50,000 training examples and the number of processors varied from 2 to 16. The total training-set size thus ranges from 100,000 records to 1.6 million records. The response times[3] for each algorithm are shown in Figure 11. To get a more detailed understanding of each algorithm's performance, we show in Figure 12 a breakdown of total response time into time spent discovering split points and time spent partitioning the data using the split points.

Immediately obvious is how poorly SLIQ/D performs relative to both SLIQ/R and SPRINT. The communication costs of using a distributed class-list and time spent servicing class-list requests from other processors are extremely high — so much so that SLIQ/D will probably never be an attractive algorithm despite its ability to handle training sets that are too large for either SLIQ and SLIQ/R. As shown in Figure 12, SLIQ/D pays this high penalty in both components of tree growth (i.e. split-point discovery and data partitioning) and scales quite poorly.

SPRINT performs much better than SLIQ/R, both in terms of response times and scalability. For both algorithms, finding the best split points takes roughly constant time, because the amount of data on each processor remains fixed as the problem size is increased. The increase in response times is from time spent partitioning the data. SPRINT shows a slight increase because of the cost of building the *rid* hash-tables used to split the attribute lists. Since these hash-tables may potentially contain the *rids* of all the tuples belonging to a particular leaf-node, this cost increases with the data size. SLIQ/R performs worse than SPRINT, because each processor in SLIQ/R must not only communicate but also apply class-list updates for every training example. As the problem size increase, so do the number of updates each processor must perform. While SPRINT may perform as much communication as SLIQ/R, it only requires processors to update their own local records.

The rest of this section examines the scalability, speedup, and sizeup characteristics of SPRINT in greater detail.

4.3.2 Scaleup

For our first set of sensitivity experiments, each processor has a fixed number of training examples and we examined SPRINT 's performance as the configuration changed from 2 to 16 processors. We studied three of these scaleup experiments, with 10, 50 and 100 thousand examples on each processor. The results of these runs are shown in Figure 13. Since the amount of data per processor does not change for a given experiment, the response times should ideally remain constant as the configuration size is increased.

The results show nice scaleup. The drop in scaleup is due to the time needed to build SPRINT 's *rid* hash-tables. While the amount of local data on each processor remains constant, the size of these hash-tables does not. The *rid* hash-tables grow in direct proportion to the total training-set size. Overall, we can conclude that parallel SPRINT can indeed be used to classify very large datasets.

4.3.3 Speedup

Next, we examined the speedup characteristics of SPRINT. We kept the total training set constant and changed the processor configuration. We did this for training-set sizes of 800 thousand and 1.6 million examples. Results for these speedup experiments are

[3] Response time is the total real time measured from the start of the program until its termination.

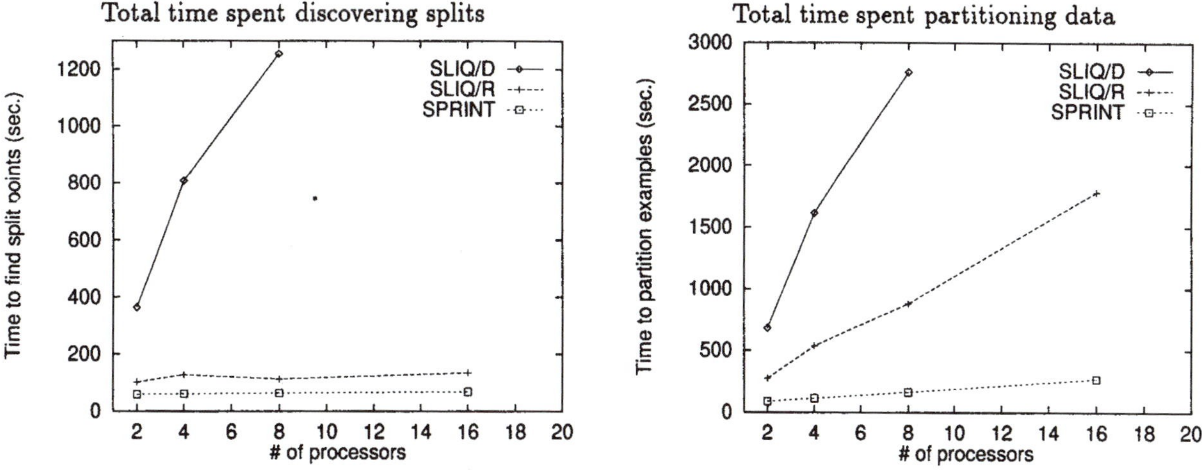

Figure 12: Breakdown of response times

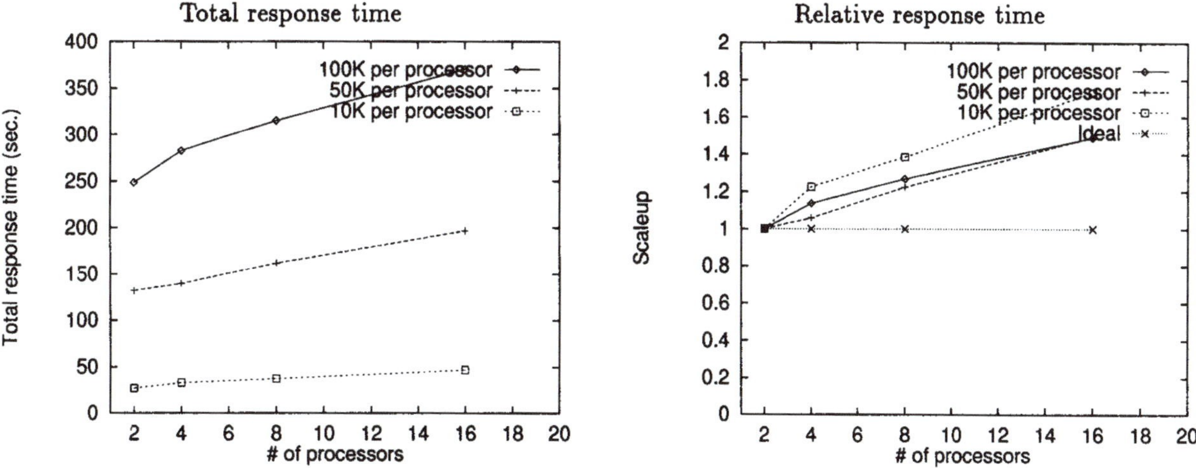

Figure 13: Scaleup of SPRINT

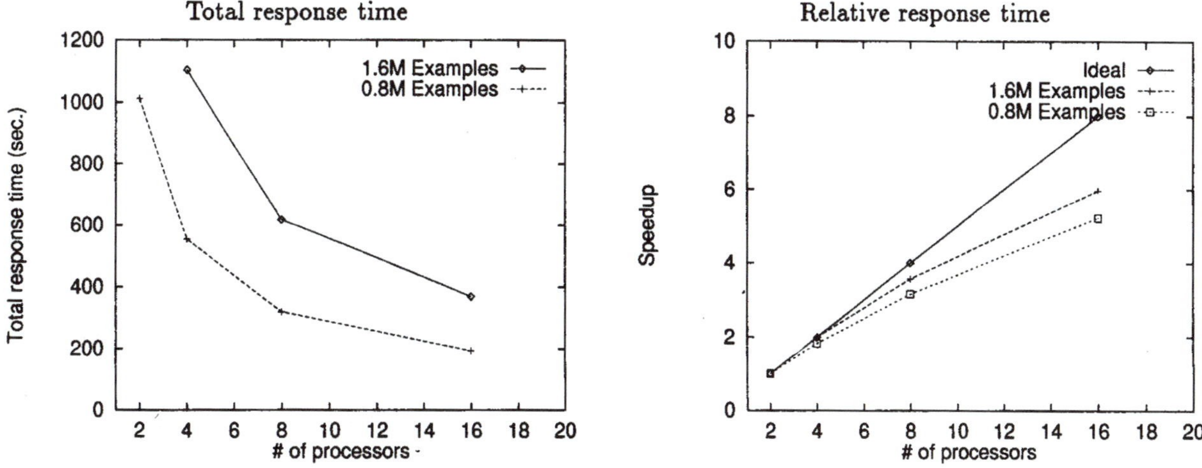

Figure 14: Speedup of SPRINT

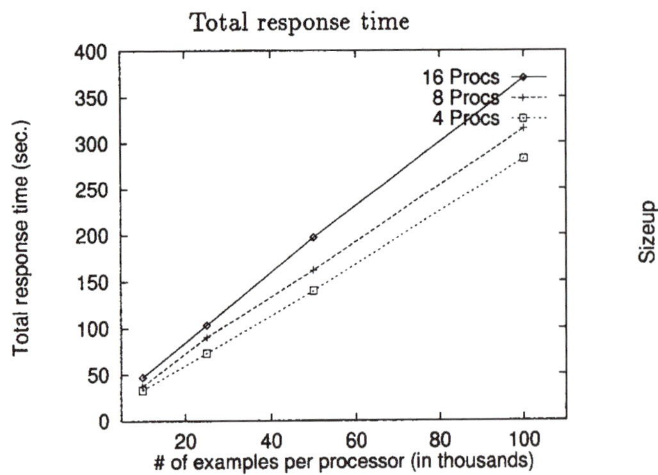

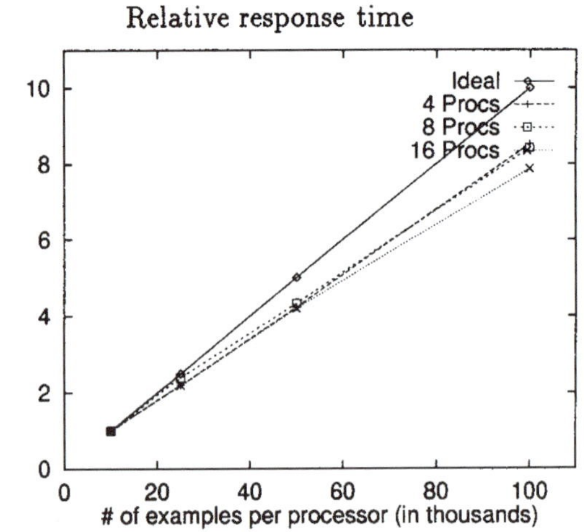

Figure 15: Sizeup of SPRINT

shown in Figure 14. Due to limited disk space, the 2-processor configuration could not create the dataset containing the 1.6 million examples. As can be expected, speedup performance improves with larger datasets. For small datasets, communication becomes a significant factor of the overall response time. This is especially true as the configuration sizes are increased to the point where there are only a few tens of thousand examples on each processor. Another factor limiting speedup performance is the *rid* hash-tables. These hash tables have the same size regardless of the processor configuration. Building these hash-tables thus requires a constant amount of time whether we are using 2 or 16 processors. These experiments show that we do get nice speed-up with SPRINT, with the results improving for larger datasets.

4.3.4 Sizeup

In sizeup experiments, we examine how SPRINT performs on a fixed processor configuration as we increase the size of the dataset. Figure 15 shows this for three different processor configurations where the per-processor training-set size is increased from 10 thousand to 100 thousand examples. SPRINT exhibits sizeup results better than ideal — processing twice as much data does not require twice as much processing time. The reason is that communication costs for exchanging split points and count matrices does not change as the training-set size is increased. Thus, while doubling the training-set size doubles most of the response costs, others remain unaffected. The result is superior sizeup performance.

5 Conclusion

With the recent emergence of the field of data mining, there is a great need for algorithms for building classifiers that can handle very large databases. The recently proposed SLIQ algorithm was the first to address these concerns. Unfortunately, due to the use of a memory-resident data structure that scales with the size of the training set, even SLIQ has an upper limit on the number of records it can process.

In this paper, we presented a new classification algorithm called SPRINT that removes all memory restrictions that limit existing decision-tree algorithms, and yet exhibits the same excellent scaling behavior as SLIQ. By eschewing the need for any centralized, memory-resident data structures, SPRINT efficiently allows classification of virtually any sized dataset. Our design goals also included the requirement that the algorithm be easily and efficiently parallelizable. SPRINT does have an efficient parallelization that requires very few additions to the serial algorithm.

Using measurements from actual implementations of these algorithms, we showed that SPRINT is an attractive algorithm in both serial and parallel environments. On a uniprocessor, SPRINT exhibits execution times that compete favorably with SLIQ. We also showed that SPRINT handles datasets that are too large for SLIQ to handle. Moreover, SPRINT scales nicely with the size of the dataset, even into the large problem regions where no other decision-tree classifier can compete.

Our implementation on SP2, a shared-nothing multiprocessor, showed that SPRINT does indeed parallelize efficiently. It outperforms our two parallel implementations of SLIQ in terms of execution time and scalability. Parallel SPRINT 's efficiency improves as the problem size increases. It has excellent scaleup, speedup, and sizeup characteristics.

Given SLIQ 's somewhat superior performance in problem regions where a class list can fit in memory, one can envision a hybrid algorithm combining SPRINT and SLIQ . The algorithm would initially run SPRINT until a point is reached where a class list could be constructed and kept in real memory. At this point, the algorithm would switch over from SPRINT to SLIQ exploiting the advantages of each algorithm in the operating regions for which they were intended. Since the amount of memory needed to build a class list is easily calculated, the switch over point would not be difficult to determine. We plan to build such a hybrid algorithm in future.

References

[1] Rakesh Agrawal, Sakti Ghosh, Tomasz Imielinski, Bala Iyer, and Arun Swami. An interval classifier for database mining applications. In *Proc. of the VLDB Conference*, pages 560–573, Vancouver, British Columbia, Canada, August 1992.

[2] Rakesh Agrawal, Tomasz Imielinski, and Arun Swami. Database mining: A performance perspective. *IEEE Transactions on Knowledge and Data Engineering*, 5(6):914–925, December 1993.

[3] L. Breiman, J. H. Friedman, R. A. Olshen, and C. J. Stone. *Classification and Regression Trees.* Wadsworth, Belmont, 1984.

[4] Jason Catlett. *Megainduction: Machine Learning on Very Large Databases.* PhD thesis, University of Sydney, 1991.

[5] Philip K. Chan and Salvatore J. Stolfo. Experiments on multistrategy learning by metalearning. In *Proc. Second Intl. Conference on Info. and Knowledge Mgmt.*, pages 314–323, 1993.

[6] Philip K. Chan and Salvatore J. Stolfo. Metalearning for multistrategy and parallel learning. In *Proc. Second Intl. Workshop on Multistrategy Learning*, pages 150–165, 1993.

[7] D. J. DeWitt, S. Ghandeharizadeh, D. A. Schneider, A. Bricker, H.-I. Hsiao, and R. Rasmussen. The Gamma database machine project. In *IEEE Transactions on Knowledge and Data Engineering*, pages 44–62, March 1990.

[8] D. J. DeWitt, J. F. Naughton, and D. A. Schneider. Parallel sorting on a shared-nothing architecture using probabilistic splitting. In *Proc. of the 1st Int'l Conf. on Parallel and Distributed Information Systems*, pages 280–291, December 1991.

[9] D. J. Fifield. Distributed tree construction from large data-sets. Bachelor's Honours Thesis, Australian National University, 1992.

[10] Message Passing Interface Forum. MPI: A Message-Passing Interface Standard, May 1994.

[11] D. E. Goldberg. *Genetic Algorithms in Search, Optimization and Machine Learning.* Morgan Kaufmann, 1989.

[12] Int'l Business Machines. *Scalable POWERparallel Systems*, GA23-2475-02 edition, February 1995.

[13] M. James. *Classificaton Algorithms.* Wiley, 1985.

[14] R. Lippmann. An introduction to computing with neural nets. *IEEE ASSP Magazine*, 4(22), April 1987.

[15] Manish Mehta, Rakesh Agrawal, and Jorma Rissanen. SLIQ: A fast scalable classifier for data mining. In *Proc. of the Fifth Int'l Conference on Extending Database Technology (EDBT)*, Avignon, France, March 1996.

[16] D. Michie, D. J. Spiegelhalter, and C. C. Taylor. *Machine Learning, Neural and Statistical Classification.* Ellis Horwood, 1994.

[17] NASA Ames Research Center. *Introduction to IND Version 2.1*, GA23-2475-02 edition, 1992.

[18] J. R. Quinlan. Induction over large databases. Technical Report STAN-CS-739, Stanfard University, 1979.

[19] J. Ross Quinlan. Induction of decision trees. *Machine Learning*, 1:81–106, 1986.

[20] J. Ross Quinlan. *C4.5: Programs for Machine Learning.* Morgan Kaufman, 1993.

[21] J. Rissanen. *Stochastic Complexity in Statistical Inquiry.* World Scientific Publ. Co., 1989.

[22] John C. Shafer, Rakesh Agrawal, and Manish Mehta. SPRINT: A scalable parallel classifier for data mining. Research report, IBM Almaden Research Center, San Jose, California, 1996. Available from `http://www.almaden.ibm.com/cs/quest`.

[23] Teradata Corp. *DBC/1012 Data Base Computer System Manual*, C10-0001-02 release 2.0 edition, November 1985.

[24] Sholom M. Weiss and Casimir A. Kulikowski. *Computer Systems that Learn: Classification and Prediction Methods from Statistics, Neural Nets, Machine Learning, and Expert Systems.* Morgan Kaufman, 1991.

[25] J. Wirth and J. Catlett. Experiments on the costs and benefits of windowing in ID3. In *5th Int'l Conference on Machine Learning*, 1988.

Fast Algorithms for Mining Association Rules

Rakesh Agrawal Ramakrishnan Srikant*

IBM Almaden Research Center
650 Harry Road, San Jose, CA 95120

Abstract

We consider the problem of discovering association rules between items in a large database of sales transactions. We present two new algorithms for solving this problem that are fundamentally different from the known algorithms. Empirical evaluation shows that these algorithms outperform the known algorithms by factors ranging from three for small problems to more than an order of magnitude for large problems. We also show how the best features of the two proposed algorithms can be combined into a hybrid algorithm, called AprioriHybrid. Scale-up experiments show that AprioriHybrid scales linearly with the number of transactions. AprioriHybrid also has excellent scale-up properties with respect to the transaction size and the number of items in the database.

1 Introduction

Progress in bar-code technology has made it possible for retail organizations to collect and store massive amounts of sales data, referred to as the *basket* data. A record in such data typically consists of the transaction date and the items bought in the transaction. Successful organizations view such databases as important pieces of the marketing infrastructure. They are interested in instituting information-driven marketing processes, managed by database technology, that enable marketers to develop and implement customized marketing programs and strategies [6].

The problem of mining association rules over basket data was introduced in [4]. An example of such a rule might be that 98% of customers that purchase tires and auto accessories also get automotive services done. Finding all such rules is valuable for cross-marketing and attached mailing applications. Other applications include catalog design, add-on sales, store layout, and customer segmentation based on buying patterns. The databases involved in these applications are very large. It is imperative, therefore, to have fast algorithms for this task.

The following is a formal statement of the problem [4]: Let $\mathcal{I} = \{i_1, i_2, \ldots, i_m\}$ be a set of literals, called items. Let $\mathcal{D}$ be a set of transactions, where each transaction T is a set of items such that $T \subseteq \mathcal{I}$. Associated with each transaction is a unique identifier, called its *TID*. We say that a transaction T *contains* X, a set of some items in $\mathcal{I}$, if $X \subseteq T$. An *association rule* is an implication of the form $X \Longrightarrow Y$, where $X \subset \mathcal{I}$, $Y \subset \mathcal{I}$, and $X \cap Y = \emptyset$. The rule $X \Longrightarrow Y$ holds in the transaction set $\mathcal{D}$ with *confidence* c if c% of transactions in $\mathcal{D}$ that contain X also contain Y. The rule $X \Longrightarrow Y$ has *support* s in the transaction set $\mathcal{D}$ if s% of transactions in $\mathcal{D}$ contain $X \cup Y$. Our rules are somewhat more general than in [4] in that we allow a consequent to have more than one item.

Given a set of transactions $\mathcal{D}$, the problem of mining association rules is to generate all association rules that have support and confidence greater than the user-specified minimum support (called *minsup*) and minimum confidence (called *minconf*) respectively. Our discussion is neutral with respect to the representation of $\mathcal{D}$. For example, $\mathcal{D}$ could be a data file, a relational table, or the result of a relational expression.

An algorithm for finding all association rules, henceforth referred to as the *AIS* algorithm, was presented in [4]. Another algorithm for this task, called the *SETM* algorithm, has been proposed in [13]. In this paper, we present two new algorithms, *Apriori* and *AprioriTid*, that differ fundamentally from these algorithms. We present experimental results showing

*Visiting from the Department of Computer Science, University of Wisconsin, Madison.

**Proceedings of the 20th VLDB Conference
Santiago, Chile, 1994**

that the proposed algorithms always outperform the earlier algorithms. The performance gap is shown to increase with problem size, and ranges from a factor of three for small problems to more than an order of magnitude for large problems. We then discuss how the best features of Apriori and AprioriTid can be combined into a hybrid algorithm, called *AprioriHybrid*. Experiments show that the AprioriHybrid has excellent scale-up properties, opening up the feasibility of mining association rules over very large databases.

The problem of finding association rules falls within the purview of database mining [3] [12], also called knowledge discovery in databases [21]. Related, but not directly applicable, work includes the induction of classification rules [8] [11] [22], discovery of causal rules [19], learning of logical definitions [18], fitting of functions to data [15], and clustering [9] [10]. The closest work in the machine learning literature is the KID3 algorithm presented in [20]. If used for finding all association rules, this algorithm will make as many passes over the data as the number of combinations of items in the antecedent, which is exponentially large. Related work in the database literature is the work on inferring functional dependencies from data [16]. Functional dependencies are rules requiring strict satisfaction. Consequently, having determined a dependency $X \rightarrow A$, the algorithms in [16] consider any other dependency of the form $X + Y \rightarrow A$ redundant and do not generate it. The association rules we consider are probabilistic in nature. The presence of a rule $X \rightarrow A$ does not necessarily mean that $X + Y \rightarrow A$ also holds because the latter may not have minimum support. Similarly, the presence of rules $X \rightarrow Y$ and $Y \rightarrow Z$ does not necessarily mean that $X \rightarrow Z$ holds because the latter may not have minimum confidence.

There has been work on quantifying the "usefulness" or "interestingness" of a rule [20]. What is useful or interesting is often application-dependent. The need for a human in the loop and providing tools to allow human guidance of the rule discovery process has been articulated, for example, in [7] [14]. We do not discuss these issues in this paper, except to point out that these are necessary features of a rule discovery system that may use our algorithms as the engine of the discovery process.

1.1 Problem Decomposition and Paper Organization

The problem of discovering all association rules can be decomposed into two subproblems [4]:

1. Find all sets of items (*itemsets*) that have transaction support above minimum support. The *support* for an itemset is the number of transactions that contain the itemset. Itemsets with minimum support are called *large* itemsets, and all others *small* itemsets. In Section 2, we give new algorithms, Apriori and AprioriTid, for solving this problem.

2. Use the large itemsets to generate the desired rules. Here is a straightforward algorithm for this task. For every large itemset l, find all non-empty subsets of l. For every such subset a, output a rule of the form $a \Longrightarrow (l - a)$ if the ratio of support(l) to support(a) is at least *minconf*. We need to consider all subsets of l to generate rules with multiple consequents. Due to lack of space, we do not discuss this subproblem further, but refer the reader to [5] for a fast algorithm.

In Section 3, we show the relative performance of the proposed Apriori and AprioriTid algorithms against the AIS [4] and SETM [13] algorithms. To make the paper self-contained, we include an overview of the AIS and SETM algorithms in this section. We also describe how the Apriori and AprioriTid algorithms can be combined into a hybrid algorithm, AprioriHybrid, and demonstrate the scale-up properties of this algorithm. We conclude by pointing out some related open problems in Section 4.

2 Discovering Large Itemsets

Algorithms for discovering large itemsets make multiple passes over the data. In the first pass, we count the support of individual items and determine which of them are *large*, i.e. have minimum support. In each subsequent pass, we start with a seed set of itemsets found to be large in the previous pass. We use this seed set for generating new potentially large itemsets, called *candidate* itemsets, and count the actual support for these candidate itemsets during the pass over the data. At the end of the pass, we determine which of the candidate itemsets are actually large, and they become the seed for the next pass. This process continues until no new large itemsets are found.

The Apriori and AprioriTid algorithms we propose differ fundamentally from the AIS [4] and SETM [13] algorithms in terms of which candidate itemsets are counted in a pass and in the way that those candidates are generated. In both the AIS and SETM algorithms, candidate itemsets are generated on-the-fly during the pass as data is being read. Specifically, after reading a transaction, it is determined which of the itemsets found large in the previous pass are present in the transaction. New candidate itemsets are generated by extending these large itemsets with other items in the transaction. However, as we will see, the disadvantage is that this results in unnecessarily generating and counting too many candidate itemsets that turn out to be small.

The Apriori and AprioriTid algorithms generate the candidate itemsets to be counted in a pass by using only the itemsets found large in the previous pass – without considering the transactions in the database. The basic intuition is that any subset of a large itemset must be large. Therefore, the candidate itemsets having k items can be generated by joining large itemsets having $k-1$ items, and deleting those that contain any subset that is not large. This procedure results in generation of a much smaller number of candidate itemsets.

The AprioriTid algorithm has the additional property that the database is not used at all for counting the support of candidate itemsets after the first pass. Rather, an encoding of the candidate itemsets used in the previous pass is employed for this purpose. In later passes, the size of this encoding can become much smaller than the database, thus saving much reading effort. We will explain these points in more detail when we describe the algorithms.

Notation We assume that items in each transaction are kept sorted in their lexicographic order. It is straightforward to adapt these algorithms to the case where the database $\mathcal{D}$ is kept normalized and each database record is a <TID, item> pair, where TID is the identifier of the corresponding transaction.

We call the number of items in an itemset its *size*, and call an itemset of size k a k-itemset. Items within an itemset are kept in lexicographic order. We use the notation $c[1] \cdot c[2] \cdot \ldots \cdot c[k]$ to represent a k-itemset c consisting of items $c[1], c[2], \ldots c[k]$, where $c[1] < c[2] < \ldots < c[k]$. If $c = X \cdot Y$ and Y is an m-itemset, we also call Y an *m-extension* of X. Associated with each itemset is a count field to store the support for this itemset. The count field is initialized to zero when the itemset is first created.

We summarize in Table 1 the notation used in the algorithms. The set $\overline{C}_k$ is used by AprioriTid and will be further discussed when we describe this algorithm.

Table 1: Notation

k-itemset	An itemset having k items.
L_k	Set of large k-itemsets (those with minimum support). Each member of this set has two fields: i) itemset and ii) support count.
C_k	Set of candidate k-itemsets (potentially large itemsets). Each member of this set has two fields: i) itemset and ii) support count.
$\overline{C}_k$	Set of candidate k-itemsets when the TIDs of the generating transactions are kept associated with the candidates.

2.1 Algorithm Apriori

Figure 1 gives the Apriori algorithm. The first pass of the algorithm simply counts item occurrences to determine the large 1-itemsets. A subsequent pass, say pass k, consists of two phases. First, the large itemsets L_{k-1} found in the $(k-1)$th pass are used to generate the candidate itemsets C_k, using the apriori-gen function described in Section 2.1.1. Next, the database is scanned and the support of candidates in C_k is counted. For fast counting, we need to efficiently determine the candidates in C_k that are contained in a given transaction t. Section 2.1.2 describes the subset function used for this purpose. See [5] for a discussion of buffer management.

```
L1 = {large 1-itemsets};
for ( k = 2; Lk-1 ≠ ∅; k++ ) do begin
    Ck = apriori-gen(Lk-1); // New candidates
    forall transactions t ∈ D do begin
        Ct = subset(Ck, t); // Candidates contained in t
        forall candidates c ∈ Ct do
            c.count++;
    end
    Lk = {c ∈ Ck | c.count ≥ minsup}
end
Answer = ∪k Lk;
```

Figure 1: Algorithm Apriori

2.1.1 Apriori Candidate Generation

The **apriori-gen** function takes as argument L_{k-1}, the set of all large $(k-1)$-itemsets. It returns a superset of the set of all large k-itemsets. The function works as follows. [1] First, in the *join* step, we join L_{k-1} with L_{k-1}:

```
insert into Ck
select p.item1, p.item2, ..., p.itemk-1, q.itemk-1
from Lk-1 p, Lk-1 q
where p.item1 = q.item1, ..., p.itemk-2 = q.itemk-2,
    p.itemk-1 < q.itemk-1;
```

Next, in the *prune* step, we delete all itemsets $c \in C_k$ such that some $(k-1)$-subset of c is not in L_{k-1}:

[1] Concurrent to our work, the following two-step candidate generation procedure has been proposed in [17]:

$$C'_k = \{X \cup X' | X, X' \in L_{k-1}, |X \cap X'| = k-2\}$$

$$C_k = \{X \in C'_k | X \text{ contains } k \text{ members of } L_{k-1}\}$$

These two steps are similar to our join and prune steps respectively. However, in general, step 1 would produce a superset of the candidates produced by our join step.

```
forall itemsets c ∈ C_k do
   forall (k−1)-subsets s of c do
      if (s ∉ L_{k−1}) then
         delete c from C_k;
```

Example Let L_3 be {{1 2 3}, {1 2 4}, {1 3 4}, {1 3 5}, {2 3 4}}. After the join step, C_4 will be {{1 2 3 4}, {1 3 4 5} }. The prune step will delete the itemset {1 3 4 5} because the itemset {1 4 5} is not in L_3. We will then be left with only {1 2 3 4} in C_4.

Contrast this candidate generation with the one used in the AIS and SETM algorithms. In pass k of these algorithms, a database transaction t is read and it is determined which of the large itemsets in L_{k-1} are present in t. Each of these large itemsets l is then extended with all those large items that are present in t and occur later in the lexicographic ordering than any of the items in l. Continuing with the previous example, consider a transaction {1 2 3 4 5}. In the fourth pass, AIS and SETM will generate two candidates, {1 2 3 4} and {1 2 3 5}, by extending the large itemset {1 2 3}. Similarly, an additional three candidate itemsets will be generated by extending the other large itemsets in L_3, leading to a total of 5 candidates for consideration in the fourth pass. Apriori, on the other hand, generates and counts only one itemset, {1 3 4 5}, because it concludes *a priori* that the other combinations cannot possibly have minimum support.

Correctness We need to show that $C_k \supseteq L_k$. Clearly, any subset of a large itemset must also have minimum support. Hence, if we extended each itemset in L_{k-1} with all possible items and then deleted all those whose $(k-1)$-subsets were not in L_{k-1}, we would be left with a superset of the itemsets in L_k.

The join is equivalent to extending L_{k-1} with each item in the database and then deleting those itemsets for which the $(k-1)$-itemset obtained by deleting the $(k-1)$th item is not in L_{k-1}. The condition $p.\text{item}_{k-1} < q.\text{item}_{k-1}$ simply ensures that no duplicates are generated. Thus, after the join step, $C_k \supseteq L_k$. By similar reasoning, the prune step, where we delete from C_k all itemsets whose $(k-1)$-subsets are not in L_{k-1}, also does not delete any itemset that could be in L_k.

Variation: Counting Candidates of Multiple Sizes in One Pass Rather than counting only candidates of size k in the kth pass, we can also count the candidates C'_{k+1}, where C'_{k+1} is generated from C_k, etc. Note that $C'_{k+1} \supseteq C_{k+1}$ since C_{k+1} is generated from L_k. This variation can pay off in the later passes when the cost of counting and keeping in memory additional $C'_{k+1} - C_{k+1}$ candidates becomes less than the cost of scanning the database.

2.1.2 Subset Function

Candidate itemsets C_k are stored in a *hash-tree*. A node of the hash-tree either contains a list of itemsets (a *leaf* node) or a hash table (an *interior* node). In an interior node, each bucket of the hash table points to another node. The root of the hash-tree is defined to be at depth 1. An interior node at depth d points to nodes at depth $d+1$. Itemsets are stored in the leaves. When we add an itemset c, we start from the root and go down the tree until we reach a leaf. At an interior node at depth d, we decide which branch to follow by applying a hash function to the dth item of the itemset. All nodes are initially created as leaf nodes. When the number of itemsets in a leaf node exceeds a specified threshold, the leaf node is converted to an interior node.

Starting from the root node, the subset function finds all the candidates contained in a transaction t as follows. If we are at a leaf, we find which of the itemsets in the leaf are contained in t and add references to them to the answer set. If we are at an interior node and we have reached it by hashing the item i, we hash on each item that comes after i in t and recursively apply this procedure to the node in the corresponding bucket. For the root node, we hash on every item in t.

To see why the subset function returns the desired set of references, consider what happens at the root node. For any itemset c contained in transaction t, the first item of c must be in t. At the root, by hashing on every item in t, we ensure that we only ignore itemsets that start with an item not in t. Similar arguments apply at lower depths. The only additional factor is that, since the items in any itemset are ordered, if we reach the current node by hashing the item i, we only need to consider the items in t that occur after i.

2.2 Algorithm AprioriTid

The AprioriTid algorithm, shown in Figure 2, also uses the apriori-gen function (given in Section 2.1.1) to determine the candidate itemsets before the pass begins. The interesting feature of this algorithm is that the database $\mathcal{D}$ is not used for counting support after the first pass. Rather, the set $\overline{C}_k$ is used for this purpose. Each member of the set $\overline{C}_k$ is of the form $< TID, \{X_k\} >$, where each X_k is a potentially large k-itemset present in the transaction with identifier TID. For $k = 1$, $\overline{C}_1$ corresponds to the database $\mathcal{D}$, although conceptually each item i is replaced by the itemset $\{i\}$. For $k > 1$, $\overline{C}_k$ is generated by the algorithm (step 10). The member of $\overline{C}_k$ corresponding to transaction t is $<t.TID, \{c \in C_k | c \text{ contained in } t\}>$. If a transaction does not contain any candidate k-itemset, then $\overline{C}_k$ will not have an entry for this transaction. Thus, the number of entries in $\overline{C}_k$ may be smaller than the number of transactions in the database, especially for large values of k. In addition, for large values of k, each entry may be smaller than the corresponding transaction because very few candidates may be contained in the transaction. However, for small values for k, each entry may be larger than the corresponding transaction because an entry in C_k includes all candidate k-itemsets contained in the transaction.

In Section 2.2.1, we give the data structures used to implement the algorithm. See [5] for a proof of correctness and a discussion of buffer management.

```
1)  L_1 = {large 1-itemsets};
2)  C̄_1 = database D;
3)  for ( k = 2; L_{k-1} ≠ ∅; k++ ) do begin
4)     C_k = apriori-gen(L_{k-1}); // New candidates
5)     C̄_k = ∅;
6)     forall entries t ∈ C̄_{k-1} do begin
7)        // determine candidate itemsets in C_k contained
          // in the transaction with identifier t.TID
          C_t = {c ∈ C_k | (c − c[k]) ∈ t.set-of-itemsets ∧
                (c − c[k−1]) ∈ t.set-of-itemsets};
8)        forall candidates c ∈ C_t do
9)           c.count++;
10)       if (C_t ≠ ∅) then C̄_k += < t.TID, C_t >;
11)    end
12)    L_k = {c ∈ C_k | c.count ≥ minsup}
13) end
14) Answer = ⋃_k L_k;
```

Figure 2: Algorithm AprioriTid

Example Consider the database in Figure 3 and assume that minimum support is 2 transactions. Calling apriori-gen with L_1 at step 4 gives the candidate itemsets C_2. In steps 6 through 10, we count the support of candidates in C_2 by iterating over the entries in $\overline{C}_1$ and generate $\overline{C}_2$. The first entry in $\overline{C}_1$ is { {1} {3} {4} }, corresponding to transaction 100. The C_t at step 7 corresponding to this entry t is { {1 3} }, because {1 3} is a member of C_2 and both ({1 3} - {1}) and ({1 3} - {3}) are members of t.set-of-itemsets.

Calling apriori-gen with L_2 gives C_3. Making a pass over the data with $\overline{C}_2$ and C_3 generates $\overline{C}_3$. Note that there is no entry in $\overline{C}_3$ for the transactions with TIDs 100 and 400, since they do not contain any of the itemsets in C_3. The candidate {2 3 5} in C_3 turns out to be large and is the only member of L_3. When we generate C_4 using L_3, it turns out to be empty, and we terminate.

Database

TID	Items
100	1 3 4
200	2 3 5
300	1 2 3 5
400	2 5

$\overline{C}_1$

TID	Set-of-Itemsets
100	{ {1}, {3}, {4} }
200	{ {2}, {3}, {5} }
300	{ {1}, {2}, {3}, {5}
400	{ {2}, {5} }

L_1

Itemset	Support
{1}	2
{2}	3
{3}	3
{5}	3

C_2

Itemset	Support
{1 2}	1
{1 3}	2
{1 5}	1
{2 3}	2
{2 5}	3
{3 5}	2

$\overline{C}_2$

TID	Set-of-Itemsets
100	{ {1 3} }
200	{ {2 3}, {2 5}, {3 5} }
300	{ {1 2}, {1 3}, {1 5}, {2 3}, {2 5}, {3 5} }
400	{ {2 5} }

L_2

Itemset	Support
{1 3}	2
{2 3}	2
{2 5}	3
{3 5}	2

C_3

Itemset	Support
{2 3 5}	2

$\overline{C}_3$

TID	Set-of-Itemsets
200	{ {2 3 5} }
300	{ {2 3 5} }

L_3

Itemset	Support
{2 3 5}	2

Figure 3: Example

2.2.1 Data Structures

We assign each candidate itemset a unique number, called its ID. Each set of candidate itemsets C_k is kept in an array indexed by the IDs of the itemsets in C_k. A member of $\overline{C}_k$ is now of the form $<$ TID, {ID} $>$. Each $\overline{C}_k$ is stored in a sequential structure.

The apriori-gen function generates a candidate k-itemset c_k by joining two large $(k-1)$-itemsets. We maintain two additional fields for each candidate itemset: i) *generators* and ii) *extensions*. The generators field of a candidate itemset c_k stores the IDs of the two large $(k-1)$-itemsets whose join generated c_k. The extensions field of an itemset c_k stores the IDs of all the $(k+1)$-candidates that are extensions of c_k. Thus, when a candidate c_k is generated by joining l^1_{k-1} and l^2_{k-1}, we save the IDs of l^1_{k-1} and l^2_{k-1} in the generators field for c_k. At the same time, the ID of c_k is added to the extensions field of l^1_{k-1}.

We now describe how Step 7 of Figure 2 is implemented using the above data structures. Recall that the t.set-of-itemsets field of an entry t in $\overline{C}_{k-1}$ gives the IDs of all $(k-1)$-candidates contained in transaction t.TID. For each such candidate c_{k-1} the extensions field gives T_k, the set of IDs of all the candidate k-itemsets that are extensions of c_{k-1}. For each c_k in T_k, the generators field gives the IDs of the two itemsets that generated c_k. If these itemsets are present in the entry for t.set-of-itemsets, we can conclude that c_k is present in transaction t.TID, and add c_k to C_t.

3 Performance

To assess the relative performance of the algorithms for discovering large sets, we performed several experiments on an IBM RS/6000 530H workstation with a CPU clock rate of 33 MHz, 64 MB of main memory, and running AIX 3.2. The data resided in the AIX file system and was stored on a 2GB SCSI 3.5" drive, with measured sequential throughput of about 2 MB/second.

We first give an overview of the AIS [4] and SETM [13] algorithms against which we compare the performance of the Apriori and AprioriTid algorithms. We then describe the synthetic datasets used in the performance evaluation and show the performance results. Finally, we describe how the best performance features of Apriori and AprioriTid can be combined into an AprioriHybrid algorithm and demonstrate its scale-up properties.

3.1 The AIS Algorithm

Candidate itemsets are generated and counted on-the-fly as the database is scanned. After reading a transaction, it is determined which of the itemsets that were found to be large in the previous pass are contained in this transaction. New candidate itemsets are generated by extending these large itemsets with other items in the transaction. A large itemset l is extended with only those items that are large and occur later in the lexicographic ordering of items than any of the items in l. The candidates generated from a transaction are added to the set of candidate itemsets maintained for the pass, or the counts of the corresponding entries are increased if they were created by an earlier transaction. See [4] for further details of the AIS algorithm.

3.2 The SETM Algorithm

The SETM algorithm [13] was motivated by the desire to use SQL to compute large itemsets. Like AIS, the SETM algorithm also generates candidates on-the-fly based on transactions read from the database. It thus generates and counts every candidate itemset that the AIS algorithm generates. However, to use the standard SQL join operation for candidate generation, SETM separates candidate generation from counting. It saves a copy of the candidate itemset together with the TID of the generating transaction in a sequential structure. At the end of the pass, the support count of candidate itemsets is determined by sorting and aggregating this sequential structure.

SETM remembers the TIDs of the generating transactions with the candidate itemsets. To avoid needing a subset operation, it uses this information to determine the large itemsets contained in the transaction read. $\overline{L}_k \subseteq \overline{C}_k$ and is obtained by deleting those candidates that do not have minimum support. Assuming that the database is sorted in TID order, SETM can easily find the large itemsets contained in a transaction in the next pass by sorting $\overline{L}_k$ on TID. In fact, it needs to visit every member of $\overline{L}_k$ only once in the TID order, and the candidate generation can be performed using the relational merge-join operation [13].

The disadvantage of this approach is mainly due to the size of candidate sets $\overline{C}_k$. For each candidate itemset, the candidate set now has as many entries as the number of transactions in which the candidate itemset is present. Moreover, when we are ready to count the support for candidate itemsets at the end of the pass, $\overline{C}_k$ is in the wrong order and needs to be sorted on itemsets. After counting and pruning out small candidate itemsets that do not have minimum support, the resulting set $\overline{L}_k$ needs another sort on TID before it can be used for generating candidates in the next pass.

3.3 Generation of Synthetic Data

We generated synthetic transactions to evaluate the performance of the algorithms over a large range of data characteristics. These transactions mimic the transactions in the retailing environment. Our model of the "real" world is that people tend to buy sets of items together. Each such set is potentially a maximal large itemset. An example of such a set might be sheets, pillow case, comforter, and ruffles. However, some people may buy only some of the items from such a set. For instance, some people might buy only sheets and pillow case, and some only sheets. A transaction may contain more than one large itemset. For example, a customer might place an order for a dress and jacket when ordering sheets and pillow cases, where the dress and jacket together form another large itemset. Transaction sizes are typically clustered around a mean and a few transactions have many items. Typical sizes of large itemsets are also clustered around a mean, with a few large itemsets having a large number of items.

To create a dataset, our synthetic data generation program takes the parameters shown in Table 2.

Table 2: Parameters

$\|D\|$	Number of transactions
$\|T\|$	Average size of the transactions
$\|I\|$	Average size of the maximal potentially large itemsets
$\|L\|$	Number of maximal potentially large itemsets
N	Number of items

We first determine the size of the next transaction. The size is picked from a Poisson distribution with mean μ equal to $|T|$. Note that if each item is chosen with the same probability p, and there are N items, the expected number of items in a transaction is given by a binomial distribution with parameters N and p, and is approximated by a Poisson distribution with mean Np.

We then assign items to the transaction. Each transaction is assigned a series of potentially large itemsets. If the large itemset on hand does not fit in the transaction, the itemset is put in the transaction anyway in half the cases, and the itemset is moved to the next transaction the rest of the cases.

Large itemsets are chosen from a set $\mathcal{T}$ of such itemsets. The number of itemsets in $\mathcal{T}$ is set to $|L|$. There is an inverse relationship between $|L|$ and the average support for potentially large itemsets. An itemset in $\mathcal{T}$ is generated by first picking the size of the itemset from a Poisson distribution with mean μ equal to $|I|$. Items in the first itemset are chosen randomly. To model the phenomenon that large itemsets often have common items, some fraction of items in subsequent itemsets are chosen from the previous itemset generated. We use an exponentially distributed random variable with mean equal to the *correlation level* to decide this fraction for each itemset. The remaining items are picked at random. In the datasets used in the experiments, the correlation level was set to 0.5. We ran some experiments with the correlation level set to 0.25 and 0.75 but did not find much difference in the nature of our performance results.

Each itemset in $\mathcal{T}$ has a weight associated with it, which corresponds to the probability that this itemset will be picked. This weight is picked from an exponential distribution with unit mean, and is then normalized so that the sum of the weights for all the itemsets in $\mathcal{T}$ is 1. The next itemset to be put in the transaction is chosen from $\mathcal{T}$ by tossing an $|L|$-sided weighted coin, where the weight for a side is the probability of picking the associated itemset.

To model the phenomenon that all the items in a large itemset are not always bought together, we assign each itemset in $\mathcal{T}$ a *corruption level* c. When adding an itemset to a transaction, we keep dropping an item from the itemset as long as a uniformly distributed random number between 0 and 1 is less than c. Thus for an itemset of size l, we will add l items to the transaction $1-c$ of the time, $l-1$ items $c(1-c)$ of the time, $l-2$ items $c^2(1-c)$ of the time, etc. The corruption level for an itemset is fixed and is obtained from a normal distribution with mean 0.5 and variance 0.1.

We generated datasets by setting $N = 1000$ and $|L| = 2000$. We chose 3 values for $|T|$: 5, 10, and 20. We also chose 3 values for $|I|$: 2, 4, and 6. The number of transactions was to set to 100,000 because, as we will see in Section 3.4, SETM could not be run for larger values. However, for our scale-up experiments, we generated datasets with up to 10 million transactions (838MB for T20). Table 3 summarizes the dataset parameter settings. For the same $|T|$ and $|D|$ values, the size of datasets in megabytes were roughly equal for the different values of $|I|$.

Table 3: Parameter settings

Name	$\|T\|$	$\|I\|$	$\|D\|$	Size in Megabytes
T5.I2.D100K	5	2	100K	2.4
T10.I2.D100K	10	2	100K	4.4
T10.I4.D100K	10	4	100K	
T20.I2.D100K	20	2	100K	8.4
T20.I4.D100K	20	4	100K	
T20.I6.D100K	20	6	100K	

3.4 Relative Performance

Figure 4 shows the execution times for the six synthetic datasets given in Table 3 for decreasing values of minimum support. As the minimum support decreases, the execution times of all the algorithms increase because of increases in the total number of candidate and large itemsets.

For SETM, we have only plotted the execution times for the dataset T5.I2.D100K in Figure 4. The execution times for SETM for the two datasets with an average transaction size of 10 are given in Table 4. We did not plot the execution times in Table 4 on the corresponding graphs because they are too large compared to the execution times of the other algorithms. For the three datasets with transaction sizes of 20, SETM took too long to execute and we aborted those runs as the trends were clear. Clearly, Apriori beats SETM by more than an order of magnitude for large datasets.

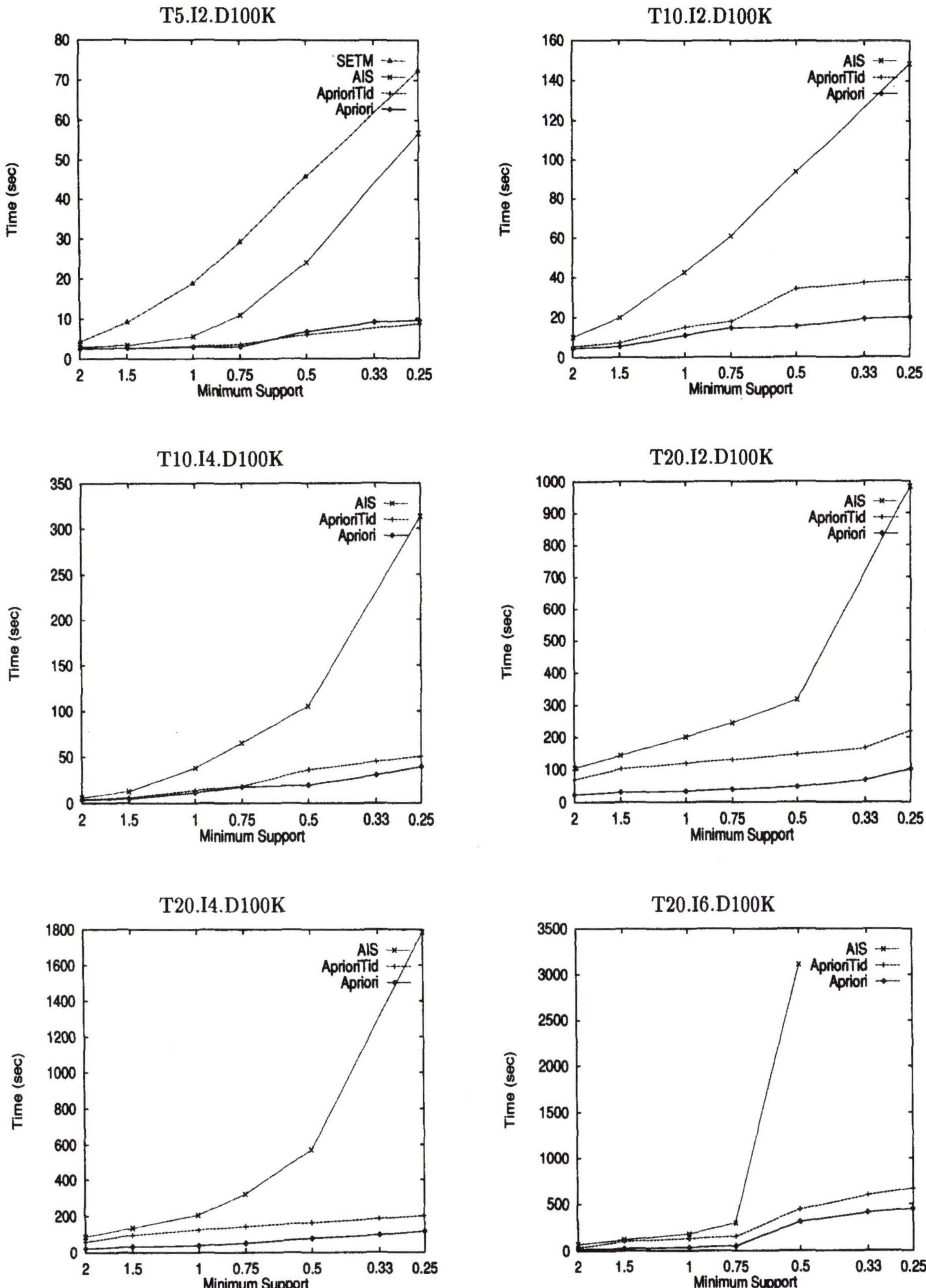

Figure 4: Execution times

Table 4: Execution times in seconds for SETM

Algorithm	Minimum Support				
	2.0%	1.5%	1.0%	0.75%	0.5%
Dataset T10.I2.D100K					
SETM	74	161	838	1262	1878
Apriori	4.4	5.3	11.0	14.5	15.3
Dataset T10.I4.D100K					
SETM	41	91	659	929	1639
Apriori	3.8	4.8	11.2	17.4	19.3

Apriori beats AIS for all problem sizes, by factors ranging from 2 for high minimum support to more than an order of magnitude for low levels of support. AIS always did considerably better than SETM. For small problems, AprioriTid did about as well as Apriori, but performance degraded to about twice as slow for large problems.

3.5 Explanation of the Relative Performance

To explain these performance trends, we show in Figure 5 the sizes of the large and candidate sets in different passes for the T10.I4.D100K dataset for the minimum support of 0.75%. Note that the Y-axis in this graph has a log scale.

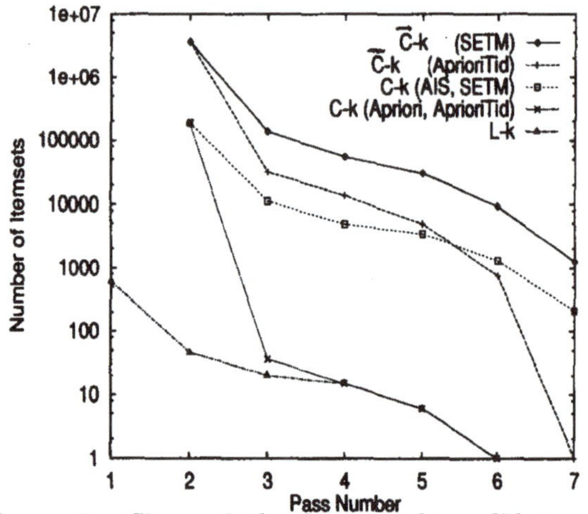

Figure 5: Sizes of the large and candidate sets (T10.I4.D100K, minsup = 0.75%)

The fundamental problem with the SETM algorithm is the size of its $\overline{C}_k$ sets. Recall that the size of the set $\overline{C}_k$ is given by

$$\sum_{\text{candidate itemsets } c} \text{support-count}(c).$$

Thus, the sets $\overline{C}_k$ are roughly S times bigger than the corresponding C_k sets, where S is the average support count of the candidate itemsets. Unless the problem size is very small, the $\overline{C}_k$ sets have to be written to disk, and externally sorted twice, causing the SETM algorithm to perform poorly.[2] This explains the jump in time for SETM in Table 4 when going from 1.5% support to 1.0% support for datasets with transaction size 10. The largest dataset in the scale-up experiments for SETM in [13] was still small enough that $\overline{C}_k$ could fit in memory; hence they did not encounter this jump in execution time. Note that for the same minimum support, the support count for candidate itemsets increases linearly with the number of transactions. Thus, as we increase the number of transactions for the same values of $|T|$ and $|I|$, though the size of C_k does not change, the size of $\overline{C}_k$ goes up linearly. Thus, for datasets with more transactions, the performance gap between SETM and the other algorithms will become even larger.

The problem with AIS is that it generates too many candidates that later turn out to be small, causing it to waste too much effort. Apriori also counts too many small sets in the second pass (recall that C_2 is really a cross-product of L_1 with L_1). However, this wastage decreases dramatically from the third pass onward. Note that for the example in Figure 5, after pass 3, almost every candidate itemset counted by Apriori turns out to be a large set.

AprioriTid also has the problem of SETM that $\overline{C}_k$ tends to be large. However, the apriori candidate generation used by AprioriTid generates significantly fewer candidates than the transaction-based candidate generation used by SETM. As a result, the $\overline{C}_k$ of AprioriTid has fewer entries than that of SETM. AprioriTid is also able to use a single word (ID) to store a candidate rather than requiring as many words as the number of items in the candidate.[3] In addition, unlike SETM, AprioriTid does not have to sort $\overline{C}_k$. Thus, AprioriTid does not suffer as much as SETM from maintaining $\overline{C}_k$.

AprioriTid has the nice feature that it replaces a pass over the original dataset by a pass over the set $\overline{C}_k$. Hence, AprioriTid is very effective in later passes when the size of $\overline{C}_k$ becomes small compared to the

[2] The cost of external sorting in SETM can be reduced somewhat as follows. Before writing out entries in $\overline{C}_k$ to disk, we can sort them on itemsets using an internal sorting procedure, and write them as sorted runs. These sorted runs can then be merged to obtain support counts. However, given the poor performance of SETM, we do not expect this optimization to affect the algorithm choice.

[3] For SETM to use IDs, it would have to maintain two additional in-memory data structures: a hash table to find out whether a candidate has been generated previously, and a mapping from the IDs to candidates. However, this would destroy the set-oriented nature of the algorithm. Also, once we have the hash table which gives us the IDs of candidates, we might as well count them at the same time and avoid the two external sorts. We experimented with this variant of SETM and found that, while it did better than SETM, it still performed much worse than Apriori or AprioriTid.

size of the database. Thus, we find that AprioriTid beats Apriori when its $\overline{C}_k$ sets can fit in memory and the distribution of the large itemsets has a long tail. When $\overline{C}_k$ doesn't fit in memory, there is a jump in the execution time for AprioriTid, such as when going from 0.75% to 0.5% for datasets with transaction size 10 in Figure 4. In this region, Apriori starts beating AprioriTid.

3.6 Algorithm AprioriHybrid

It is not necessary to use the same algorithm in all the passes over data. Figure 6 shows the execution times for Apriori and AprioriTid for different passes over the dataset T10.I4.D100K. In the earlier passes, Apriori does better than AprioriTid. However, AprioriTid beats Apriori in later passes. We observed similar relative behavior for the other datasets, the reason for which is as follows. Apriori and AprioriTid use the same candidate generation procedure and therefore count the same itemsets. In the later passes, the number of candidate itemsets reduces (see the size of C_k for Apriori and AprioriTid in Figure 5). However, Apriori still examines every transaction in the database. On the other hand, rather than scanning the database, AprioriTid scans $\overline{C}_k$ for obtaining support counts, and the size of $\overline{C}_k$ has become smaller than the size of the database. When the $\overline{C}_k$ sets can fit in memory, we do not even incur the cost of writing them to disk.

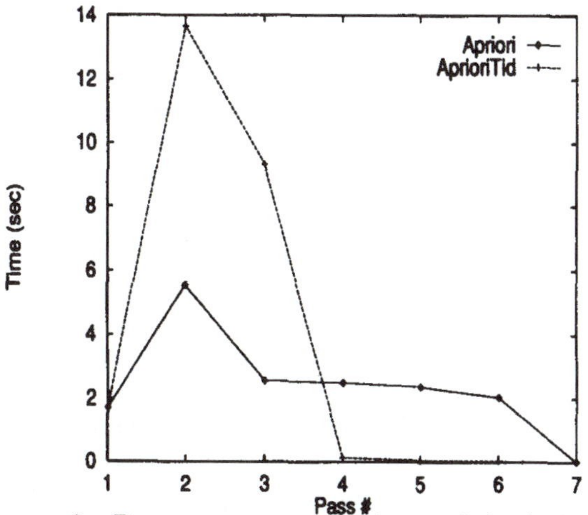

Figure 6: Per pass execution times of Apriori and AprioriTid (T10.I4.D100K, minsup = 0.75%)

Based on these observations, we can design a hybrid algorithm, which we call AprioriHybrid, that uses Apriori in the initial passes and switches to AprioriTid when it expects that the set $\overline{C}_k$ at the end of the pass will fit in memory. We use the following heuristic to estimate if $\overline{C}_k$ would fit in memory in the next pass. At the end of the current pass, we have the counts of the candidates in C_k. From this, we estimate what the size of $\overline{C}_k$ would have been if it had been generated. This size, in words, is ($\sum_{\text{candidates } c \in C_k} \text{support}(c)$ + number of transactions). If $\overline{C}_k$ in this pass was small enough to fit in memory, and there were fewer large candidates in the current pass than the previous pass, we switch to AprioriTid. The latter condition is added to avoid switching when $\overline{C}_k$ in the current pass fits in memory but $\overline{C}_k$ in the next pass may not.

Switching from Apriori to AprioriTid does involve a cost. Assume that we decide to switch from Apriori to AprioriTid at the end of the kth pass. In the $(k+1)$th pass, after finding the candidate itemsets contained in a transaction, we will also have to add their IDs to $\overline{C}_{k+1}$ (see the description of AprioriTid in Section 2.2). Thus there is an extra cost incurred in this pass relative to just running Apriori. It is only in the $(k+2)$th pass that we actually start running AprioriTid. Thus, if there are no large $(k+1)$-itemsets, or no $(k+2)$-candidates, we will incur the cost of switching without getting any of the savings of using AprioriTid.

Figure 7 shows the performance of AprioriHybrid relative to Apriori and AprioriTid for three datasets. AprioriHybrid performs better than Apriori in almost all cases. For T10.I2.D100K with 1.5% support, AprioriHybrid does a little worse than Apriori since the pass in which the switch occurred was the last pass; AprioriHybrid thus incurred the cost of switching without realizing the benefits. In general, the advantage of AprioriHybrid over Apriori depends on how the size of the $\overline{C}_k$ set decline in the later passes. If $\overline{C}_k$ remains large until nearly the end and then has an abrupt drop, we will not gain much by using AprioriHybrid since we can use AprioriTid only for a short period of time after the switch. This is what happened with the T20.I6.D100K dataset. On the other hand, if there is a gradual decline in the size of $\overline{C}_k$, AprioriTid can be used for a while after the switch, and a significant improvement can be obtained in the execution time.

3.7 Scale-up Experiment

Figure 8 shows how AprioriHybrid scales up as the number of transactions is increased from 100,000 to 10 million transactions. We used the combinations (T5.I2), (T10.I4), and (T20.I6) for the average sizes of transactions and itemsets respectively. All other parameters were the same as for the data in Table 3. The sizes of these datasets for 10 million transactions were 239MB, 439MB and 838MB respectively. The minimum support level was set to 0.75%. The execution times are normalized with respect to the times for the 100,000 transaction datasets in the first

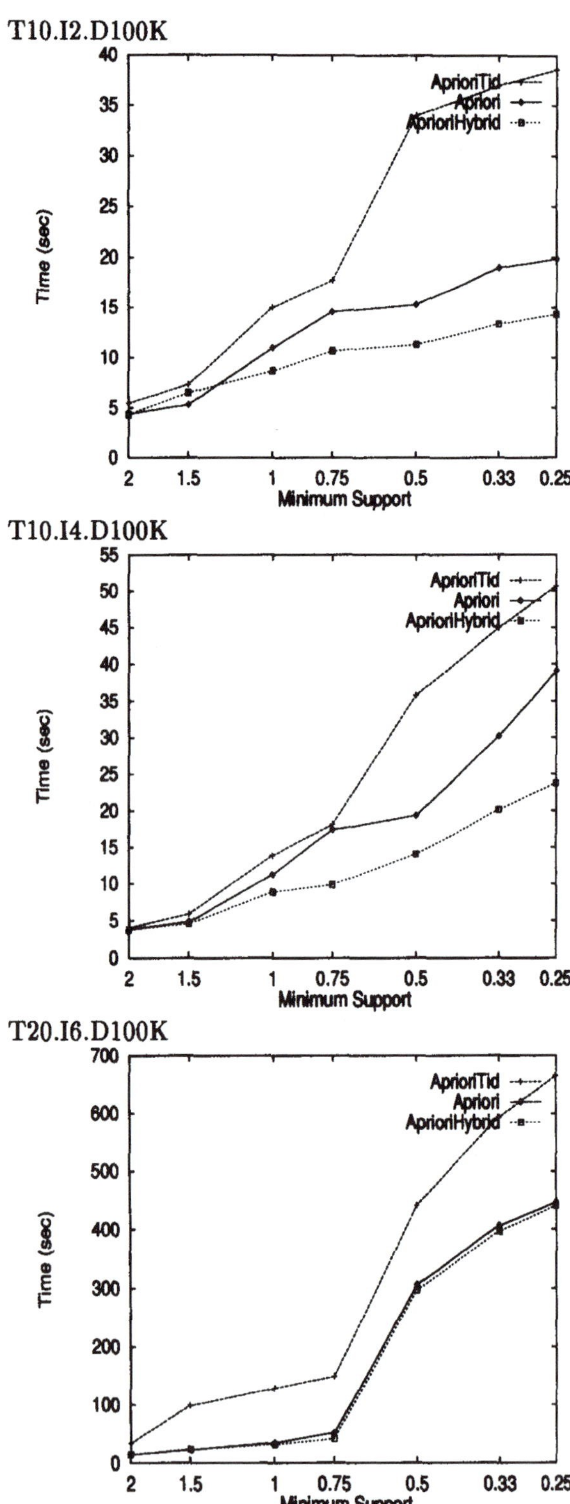

Figure 7: Execution times: AprioriHybrid

graph and with respect to the 1 million transaction dataset in the second. As shown, the executiȯn times scale quite linearly.

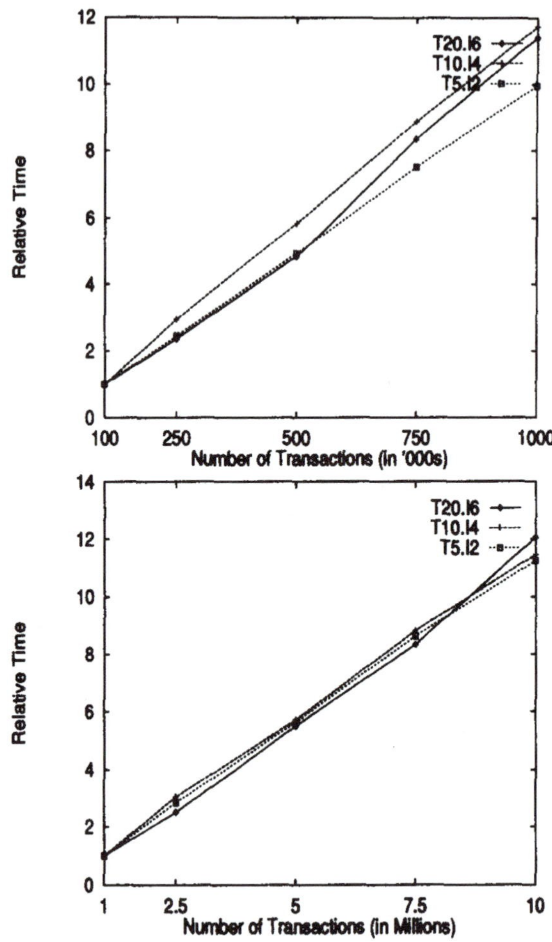

Figure 8: Number of transactions scale-up

Next, we examined how AprioriHybrid scaled up with the number of items. We increased the number of items from 1000 to 10,000 for the three parameter settings T5.I2.D100K, T10.I4.D100K and T20.I6.D100K. All other parameters were the same as for the data in Table 3. We ran experiments for a minimum support at 0.75%, and obtained the results shown in Figure 9. The execution times decreased a little since the average support for an item decreased as we increased the number of items. This resulted in fewer large itemsets and, hence, faster execution times.

Finally, we investigated the scale-up as we increased the average transaction size. The aim of this experiment was to see how our data structures scaled with the transaction size, independent of other factors like the physical database size and the number of large itemsets. We kept the physical size of the

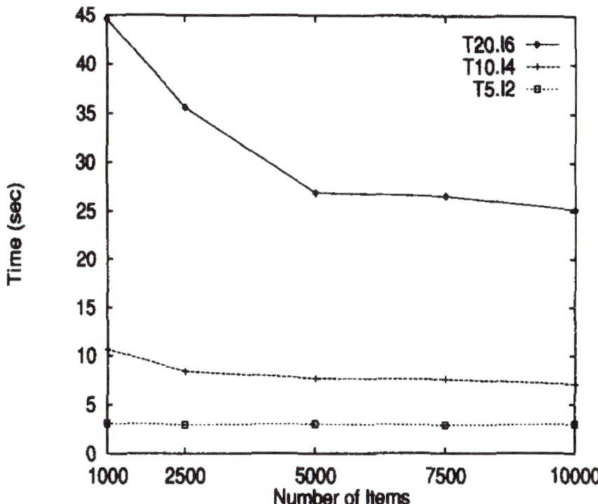

Figure 9: Number of items scale-up

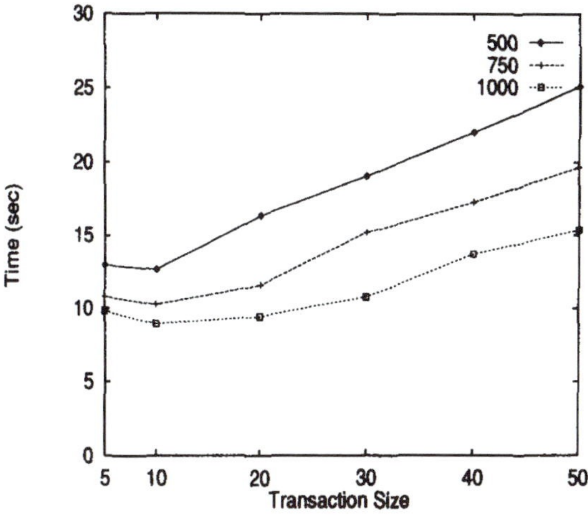

Figure 10: Transaction size scale-up

database roughly constant by keeping the product of the average transaction size and the number of transactions constant. The number of transactions ranged from 200,000 for the database with an average transaction size of 5 to 20,000 for the database with an average transaction size 50. Fixing the minimum support as a percentage would have led to large increases in the number of large itemsets as the transaction size increased, since the probability of a itemset being present in a transaction is roughly proportional to the transaction size. We therefore fixed the minimum support level in terms of the number of transactions. The results are shown in Figure 10. The numbers in the key (e.g. 500) refer to this minimum support. As shown, the execution times increase with the transaction size, but only gradually. The main reason for the increase was that in spite of setting the minimum support in terms of the number of transactions, the number of large itemsets increased with increasing transaction length. A secondary reason was that finding the candidates present in a transaction took a little longer time.

4 Conclusions and Future Work

We presented two new algorithms, Apriori and AprioriTid, for discovering all significant association rules between items in a large database of transactions. We compared these algorithms to the previously known algorithms, the AIS [4] and SETM [13] algorithms. We presented experimental results, showing that the proposed algorithms always outperform AIS and SETM. The performance gap increased with the problem size, and ranged from a factor of three for small problems to more than an order of magnitude for large problems.

We showed how the best features of the two proposed algorithms can be combined into a hybrid algorithm, called AprioriHybrid, which then becomes the algorithm of choice for this problem. Scale-up experiments showed that AprioriHybrid scales linearly with the number of transactions. In addition, the execution time decreases a little as the number of items in the database increases. As the average transaction size increases (while keeping the database size constant), the execution time increases only gradually. These experiments demonstrate the feasibility of using AprioriHybrid in real applications involving very large databases.

The algorithms presented in this paper have been implemented on several data repositories, including the AIX file system, DB2/MVS, and DB2/6000. We have also tested these algorithms against real customer data, the details of which can be found in [5]. In the future, we plan to extend this work along the following dimensions:

- Multiple taxonomies (*is-a* hierarchies) over items are often available. An example of such a hierarchy is that a dish washer *is a* kitchen appliance *is a* heavy electric appliance, etc. We would like to be able to find association rules that use such hierarchies.

- We did not consider the quantities of the items bought in a transaction, which are useful for some applications. Finding such rules needs further work.

The work reported in this paper has been done in the context of the Quest project at the IBM Almaden Research Center. In Quest, we are exploring the various aspects of the database mining problem. Besides the problem of discovering association rules, some other problems that we have looked into include the enhancement of the database capability with classification queries [2] and similarity queries over time sequences [1]. We believe that database mining is an important new application area for databases, combining commercial interest with intriguing research questions.

Acknowledgment We wish to thank Mike Carey for his insightful comments and suggestions.

References

[1] R. Agrawal, C. Faloutsos, and A. Swami. Efficient similarity search in sequence databases. In *Proc. of the Fourth International Conference on Foundations of Data Organization and Algorithms*, Chicago, October 1993.

[2] R. Agrawal, S. Ghosh, T. Imielinski, B. Iyer, and A. Swami. An interval classifier for database mining applications. In *Proc. of the VLDB Conference*, pages 560–573, Vancouver, British Columbia, Canada, 1992.

[3] R. Agrawal, T. Imielinski, and A. Swami. Database mining: A performance perspective. *IEEE Transactions on Knowledge and Data Engineering*, 5(6):914–925, December 1993. Special Issue on Learning and Discovery in Knowledge-Based Databases.

[4] R. Agrawal, T. Imielinski, and A. Swami. Mining association rules between sets of items in large databases. In *Proc. of the ACM SIGMOD Conference on Management of Data*, Washington, D.C., May 1993.

[5] R. Agrawal and R. Srikant. Fast algorithms for mining association rules in large databases. Research Report RJ 9839, IBM Almaden Research Center, San Jose, California, June 1994.

[6] D. S. Associates. The new direct marketing. Business One Irwin, Illinois, 1990.

[7] R. Brachman et al. Integrated support for data archeology. In *AAAI-93 Workshop on Knowledge Discovery in Databases*, July 1993.

[8] L. Breiman, J. H. Friedman, R. A. Olshen, and C. J. Stone. *Classification and Regression Trees*. Wadsworth, Belmont, 1984.

[9] P. Cheeseman et al. Autoclass: A bayesian classification system. In *5th Int'l Conf. on Machine Learning*. Morgan Kaufman, June 1988.

[10] D. H. Fisher. Knowledge acquisition via incremental conceptual clustering. *Machine Learning*, 2(2), 1987.

[11] J. Han, Y. Cai, and N. Cercone. Knowledge discovery in databases: An attribute oriented approach. In *Proc. of the VLDB Conference*, pages 547–559, Vancouver, British Columbia, Canada, 1992.

[12] M. Holsheimer and A. Siebes. Data mining: The search for knowledge in databases. Technical Report CS-R9406, CWI, Netherlands, 1994.

[13] M. Houtsma and A. Swami. Set-oriented mining of association rules. Research Report RJ 9567, IBM Almaden Research Center, San Jose, California, October 1993.

[14] R. Krishnamurthy and T. Imielinski. Practitioner problems in need of database research: Research directions in knowledge discovery. *SIGMOD RECORD*, 20(3):76–78, September 1991.

[15] P. Langley, H. Simon, G. Bradshaw, and J. Zytkow. *Scientific Discovery: Computational Explorations of the Creative Process*. MIT Press, 1987.

[16] H. Mannila and K.-J. Raiha. Dependency inference. In *Proc. of the VLDB Conference*, pages 155–158, Brighton, England, 1987.

[17] H. Mannila, H. Toivonen, and A. I. Verkamo. Efficient algorithms for discovering association rules. In *KDD-94: AAAI Workshop on Knowledge Discovery in Databases*, July 1994.

[18] S. Muggleton and C. Feng. Efficient induction of logic programs. In S. Muggleton, editor, *Inductive Logic Programming*. Academic Press, 1992.

[19] J. Pearl. Probabilistic reasoning in intelligent systems: Networks of plausible inference, 1992.

[20] G. Piatestsky-Shapiro. Discovery, analysis, and presentation of strong rules. In G. Piatestsky-Shapiro, editor, *Knowledge Discovery in Databases*. AAAI/MIT Press, 1991.

[21] G. Piatestsky-Shapiro, editor. *Knowledge Discovery in Databases*. AAAI/MIT Press, 1991.

[22] J. R. Quinlan. *C4.5: Programs for Machine Learning*. Morgan Kaufman, 1993.

Efficient Evaluation of Queries with Mining Predicates

Surajit Chaudhuri
Microsoft Corp.
surajitc@microsoft.com

Vivek Narasayya
Microsoft Corp.
viveknar@microsoft.com

Sunita Sarawagi
IIT Bombay
sunita@it.iitb.ac.in

Abstract

Modern relational database systems are beginning to support ad hoc queries on mining models. In this paper, we explore novel techniques for optimizing queries that apply mining models to relational data. For such queries, we use the internal structure of the mining model to automatically derive traditional database predicates. We present algorithms for deriving such predicates for some popular discrete mining models: decision trees, naive Bayes, and clustering. Our experiments on Microsoft SQL Server 2000 demonstrate that these derived predicates can significantly reduce the cost of evaluating such queries.

1. Introduction

Progress in database technology has made massive warehouses of business data ubiquitous [10]. There is increasing commercial interest in mining the information in such warehouses. Data mining is used to extract predictive models from data that can be used for a variety of business tasks. For example, based on a customer's profile information, a model can be used for predicting if a customer is likely to buy sports items. The result of such a prediction can be leveraged in the context of many applications, e.g., a mail campaign or an on-line targeted advertisement.

Recently, several database vendors have made it possible to apply predictive models on relational data using SQL extensions. The predictive models can either be built natively or imported, using PMML or other interchange format. This enables us to express queries containing *mining predicates* such as: "Find customers who visited the MSNBC site last week and who are *predicted* to belong to the category of baseball fans". The focus of this paper is to optimize queries containing such mining predicates. To the best of our knowledge, this is the first study of its kind. The techniques described in this paper are general and do not depend on the specific nature of the integration of databases and data mining.

We propose a technique that exploits knowledge of the mining model's content to optimize queries with mining predicates. Today's systems would evaluate the above query by first selecting the customers who visited the MSNBC site, then applying the mining model (treated as black-box) on the selected rows, and filtering the subset that are predicted to be "baseball fans". In contrast, we wish to exploit the mining predicate for better access path selection, particularly if "baseball fans" represent a very small fraction of MSNBC visitors. The main challenge in exploiting mining predicates is that each mining model has its own specific method of predicting classes as a function of the input attributes, and some of these methods are too complex to be directly usable by traditional database engines.

We present a general framework in which, given a mining predicate, a model-specific algorithm can be used to infer a simpler derived predicate expression. The derived predicate expression is constrained to be a propositional expression consisting of simple selection predicates on attribute values. Such a derived predicate, which we call an *upper envelope* of the mining predicate, can then be exploited for access path selection like any other traditional database predicate.

We concentrate on predictive mining models that when applied to a tuple $\vec{x}$ predict one of K discrete classes $c_1, \ldots c_K$. Most classification and clustering models fall in this category. For every possible class c that the model M predicts, its upper envelope is a predicate of the form $M_c(\vec{x})$ such that the tuple $\vec{x}$ has class c only if it satisfies the predicate $M_c(\vec{x})$, but not necessarily vice-versa. We require that $M_c(\vec{x})$ is a propositional predicate expression consisting of simple selection conditions on attributes of $\vec{x}$. Such upper envelopes can be added to the query to generate a semantically equivalent query that would result in the same set of answers over any database. Since $M_c(\vec{x})$ is a predicate on the attributes of $\vec{x}$, it has the potential of better exploiting index structures and improving the efficiency of the query.

The effectiveness of such semantic optimization depends on two criteria. First, we must demonstrate that the upper-envelope predicates can be derived for a wide set of commonly used mining models. Second, we need to show that the addition of these upper-envelope predicates can have a significant impact on the execution time for queries with mining predicates. In turn, this requires that our derivation of upper envelopes to be "tight" and the original mining predicate to be selective so that they are effective in influencing the access path selection. Our extensive experiments on Microsoft SQL Server provide strong evidence of the promise of such semantic optimization. Moreover, our experiments demonstrate that little overhead is incurred during optimization for using such upper envelopes.

Outline: The rest of the paper is organized as follows. In Section 2 we review existing support for mining predicates in SQL queries in two commercially available relational database engines: Microsoft SQL Server's Analysis Server and IBM DB2's Intelligent Miner Scoring facility. In Section 3 we present algorithms for deriving such predicates for three popular discrete mining models: decision trees, naive Bayes classifiers and clustering. In Section 4 we discuss the operational issues of using upper envelopes to optimize queries with mining predicates. In Section 5 we report the results of our experimental study to evaluate the effectiveness of our technique in improving the efficiency of queries with mining predicates. We discuss related work in Section 6.

2. Expressing Mining Queries in Existing Systems

In this section, we describe some of the possible approaches to expressing database queries with mining predicates. We emphasize that our techniques are general in the sense that they do not depend on the specific nature of such integration of databases and data mining.

2.1. Extract and Mine

The traditional way of integrating mining with querying is to pose a traditional database query to a relational backend. The mining model is subsequently applied in the client/middleware on the result of the database query. Thus, for the example in the introduction, the mining query will be evaluated in the following phases: (a) Execute a SQL query at the database server to obtain all the customers who visited MSNBC last week (b) For each customer fetched into the client/middleware, apply the mining model to determine if the customer is predicted to be a "baseball fan".

2.2. Microsoft Analysis Server

In the Microsoft Analysis Server product (part of SQL Server 2000) mining models are explicitly recognized as first-class table-like objects. Creation of a mining model corresponds to schematic definition of a mining model. The following example shows creation of a mining model that predicts risk level of customers based on source columns gender, purchases and age using Decision trees.

```
CREATE MINING MODEL Risk_Class          // Name of Model
(
Customer_ID LONG KEY,                   // source column
Gender TEXT DISCRETE,                   // source column
Risk TEXT DISCRETE PREDICT,             // prediction column
Purchases DOUBLE DISCRETIZED(),         // source column
Age DOUBLE DISCRETIZED,                 // source column
)
USING [Decision_Trees_101]              // Mining Algorithm
```

The model is trained using the INSERT INTO statement that inserts training data into the model (not discussed due to lack of space), Predictions are obtained from a model M on a dataset D using a prediction join [15] between D and M. A prediction join is different from a traditional equijoin on tables since the model does not actually contain data details. The following example illustrates prediction join.

```
SELECT D.Customer_ID, M.Risk
FROM [Risk_Class] M
PREDICTION JOIN
(SELECT Customer_ID, Gender, Age, sum(Purchases) as SP
  FROM Customers D Group BY Customer_ID, Gender, Age ) as D
  ON M.Gender = D.Gender
  and M.Age = D.Age
  and M.Purchases = t.SP
  Where M.Risk = "low"
```

In this example, the value of "Risk" for each customer is not known. Joining rows in the Customers table to the model M returns a predicted "Risk" for each customer. The WHERE clause specifies which predicted values should be extracted and returned in the result set of the query. Specifically, the above example has the mining predicate Risk = "low".

2.3. IBM DB2

IBM's Intelligent Miner (IM) Scoring product integrates the model application functionality of IBM Intelligent Miner for Data with the DB2 Universal Database [21] [1]. Trained mining models in flat file, XML or PMML format can be imported into the database. We show an example of importing a classification model for predicting the risk level of a customer into a database using a UDF called IDMMX.DM_impClasFile().

```
INSERT INTO IDMMX.ClassifModels values ('Risk_Class',
   IDMMX.DM_impClasFile('/tmp/myclassifier.x'))
```

Once the model is loaded, it can be applied to compatible records in the database by invoking another set of User Defined Functions (UDFs). An example of applying the above classification mining model ("Risk_Class") on a data table called Customers is shown below.

```
SELECT Customer_ID, Risk
FROM (
  SELECT Customer_ID, IDMMX.DM_getPredClass(
    IDMMX.DM_applyClasModel(c.model,
```

```
IDMMX.DM_applData(IDMMX.DM_applData('AGE',s.age),
    'PURCHASE',s.purchase))) as Risk
  FROM ClassifModels c, Customer_list s
  WHERE c.modelname='Risk_Class' and s.salary<40000
) WHERE Risk = 'low'
```

The UDF IDMMX.DM_applData is used to map the fields s.salary and s.age of the Customer_list table into the corresponding fields of the model for use during prediction. The UDF applyClasModel() applies the model on the mapped data and returns a composite result object that has along with the predicted class other associated statistics like confidence of prediction. A second UDF IDMMX.DM_getPredClass extracts the predicted class from this result object. The mining predicate in this query is: Risk = 'low'.

3. Deriving Upper Envelopes for Mining Predicates

We present algorithms for deriving upper envelopes for three popular mining models. We focus on mining models that produce a discrete class as output. The class of models whose prediction is real-valued is a topic of our future work. For some models like decision trees and rule-based classifiers, derivation of such predicates is straightforward as we show in Section 3.1. The process is more involved for naive Bayes classifiers and clustering as we show in Sections 3.2 and Sections 3.3 respectively.

In deriving these upper envelopes two conflicting issues that arise are the *tightness* and *complexity* of the upper envelope predicate. An upper envelope of a class c is said to be *exact* if it includes all points belonging to c and no point belonging to any other class. In most cases, where the model is complex we need to settle for looser bounds because both the complexity of the enveloping predicate and the running time for deriving the upper envelope might get intolerable. Complex predicates are also ineffective in improving the efficiency of the query because the DBMS might spend a lot of time in evaluating these otherwise redundant predicates. We revisit these issues in Sections 4.2.

3.1. Decision trees

In a decision tree [29] the internal nodes define a simple test on one of the attributes and the leaf-level nodes define a class label. An example of a decision tree is shown in Figure 1. The class label of a new instance is determined by evaluating the test conditions at the nodes and based on the outcome following one of the branches until a leaf node is reached. The label of the leaf is the predicted class of the instance. We extract the upper envelope for a class c, by ANDing the test conditions on the path from the root to each leaf of the class and ORing them together. Clearly, this envelope is *exact*. For the example in Figure 1 the upper envelope of class c_1 is "((lower BP $>$ 91) AND (age $>$ 63) AND (overweight)) OR ((lowerBP $\leq$ 91) AND (upper BP $>$ 130))". Similarly, of class c_2 is "((lower BP $>$ 91) AND (age $\leq$ 63)) OR ((lower BP $>$ 91) AND (age $>$ 63) AND (not overweight)) OR ((lowerBP $\leq$ 91) AND (upper BP $\leq$ 130))".

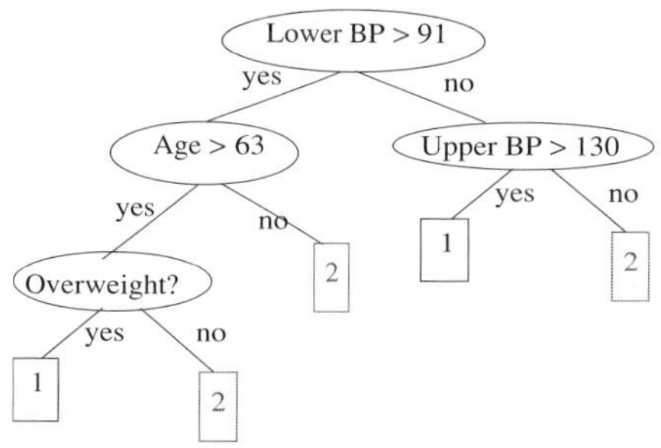

Figure 1. Example of a decision tree

Extraction of upper envelopes for rule-based classifiers [27, 14] is similarly straightforward. A rule-based learner consists of a set of if-then rules where the body of the rule consists of conditions on the data attributes and the head (the part after "then") is one of the k class-labels. The upper envelope of each class c is just the disjunction of the body of all rules where c is the head. Unlike for decision trees, the envelope may not be exact because some rule learners allow rules of different classes to overlap. Therefore, an input instance might fire off two rules, each of which predicts a different class. Typically, a resolution procedure based on the weights or sequential order of rules is used to resolve conflict in such cases. It may be possible to tighten the envelope in such cases by exploiting the knowledge of the resolution procedure.

3.2. naive Bayes Classifiers

Extracting the upper envelopes for naive Bayes classifiers is considerably more difficult than for decision trees. We first present a primer on naive Bayes classifiers in Section 3.2.1. Then we present two algorithms for finding upper envelopes in Sections 3.2.2. Finally, we present a proof of correctness in Section 3.2.3.

3.2.1. Primer on naive Bayes classifiers

Bayesian classifiers [27] perform a probabilistic modeling of each class. Let $\vec{x}$ be an instance for which the classifier needs to predict one of K classes $c_1, c_2, \ldots c_K$. The predicted class $C(\vec{x})$ of $\vec{x}$ is calculated as

$$C(\vec{x}) = \text{argmax}_k \Pr(c_k|\vec{x}) = \text{argmax}_k \frac{\Pr(\vec{x}|c_k)\Pr(c_k)}{\Pr(\vec{x})}$$

where $\Pr(c_k)$ is the probability of class c_k and $\Pr(\vec{x}|c_k)$ is the probability of $\vec{x}$ in class c_k. The denominator $\Pr(\vec{x})$ is the same for all classes and can be ignored in the selection of the winning class.

Let n be the number of attributes in the input data. Naive Bayes classifiers assume that the attributes $x_1, \ldots, x_n$ of $\vec{x}$ are independent of each other given the class. Thus, the above formula becomes:

$$C(\vec{x}) = \text{argmax}_k(\prod_{d=1}^{n} \Pr(x_d|c_k)\Pr(c_k)) \quad (1)$$

$$= \text{argmax}_k(\sum_{d=1}^{n} \log \Pr(x_d|c_k) + \log \Pr(c_k)) \quad (2)$$

Ties are resolved by choosing the class which has the higher prior probability $\Pr(c_k)$.

The probabilities $\Pr(x_d|c_k)$ and $\Pr(c_k)$ are estimated using training data. For a discrete attribute d, let $m_{1d} \dots m_{n_d d}$ denote the n_d members of the domain of d. For each member m_{ld}, during the training phase we learn a set of K values corresponding to the probability $\Pr(x_d = m_{ld}|c_k)$. Continuous attributes are either discretized using a preprocessing step (see [17] for a discussion of various discretization methods) or modeled using a single continuous probability density function, the most common being the Gaussian distribution. In this paper we will describe the algorithm assuming that all attributes are discretized.

Example An example of a naive Bayes classifier is shown in Table 1 for $K = 3$ classes, $n = 2$ dimensions, first dimension d_0 having $n_0 = 4$ members and the second dimension d_1 having $n_1 = 3$ members. The triplet along the column margin show the trained $\Pr(m_{j1}|c_k)$ values for each of the three classes for dimension d_1. The row margin shows the corresponding values for dimension d_0. For example, the first triplet in the column margin (.01, .7, .05) stands for $(\Pr(m_{01}|c_1), \Pr(m_{01}|c_2), \Pr(m_{01}|c_3))$ respectively. The top-margin shows the class priors. Given these parameters, the predicted class for each of the 12 possible distinct instances $\vec{x}$ (found using Equation 1) is shown in the internal cells. For example, the value 0.001 for the top-leftmost cell denotes $\Pr(\vec{x}|c_1)$ where $\vec{x} = (m_{00}, m_{01})$.

3.2.2. Finding the upper envelope of a class

We next present algorithms for finding the upper envelope to cover all regions in the n dimensional attribute space where the naive Bayes classifier will predict a given class c_k. For example, the upper envelope for class c_2 in the example of Figure 1 is $(d_0 \in \{m_{20}, m_{30}\}$ AND $d_1 \in \{m_{01}, m_{11}\})$ OR $(d_1 = m_{01})$. We will express this envelope as two regions described by their boundaries as $(d_0 : [2..3], d_1 : [0..1]) \vee (d_1 : [0..0])$.

A simple way to find such envelopes is to enumerate for each combination in this n dimensional space the predicted class as we have done for the example above. We can then cover all combinations where class c_k is the winner with a collection of contiguous regions using any of the known multidimensional covering algorithms [2, 30]. Each region will contribute one disjunct to the upper envelope. This is in fact a generic algorithm applicable to any classification algorithm, not simply naive Bayes. Unfortunately, it is impractically slow to enumerate all $\prod_{d=1}^{n} n_d$ (n_d is the size of the domain of dimension d) member combinations. A medium sized data set in our experiments took more than 24 hours for just enumerating the combinations. We next present a top-down algorithm that avoids this exponential enumeration.

A top-down algorithm The algorithm proceeds in a top-down manner recursively narrowing down the region belonging to the given class c_k for which we want to find the upper envelope. The main intuition behind this algorithm is to exploit efficiently computable upper bounds and lower bounds on the probabilities of classes to quickly establish the winning and losing classes in a region consisting of several combinations.

The algorithms starts by assuming that the entire region belongs to class c_k. It then estimates an upper bound $\text{maxProb}(c_j)$ and lower bound $\text{minProb}(c_j)$ on the probabilities of each class c_j as follows:

$$\text{maxProb}(c_j) = \Pr(c_j) \prod_{d=1}^{n} \max_{l \in 1 \dots n_d} \Pr(m_{ld}|c_j)$$

$$\text{minProb}(c_j) = \Pr(c_j) \prod_{d=1}^{n} \min_{l \in 1 \dots n_d} \Pr(m_{ld}|c_j)$$

Computation of these bounds requires time only linear in the number of members along each dimension. In Figure 2(a) we show the minProb (second row) and maxProb (third row) values for the region shown in Figure 1. For example, in the figure the minProb value of 0.0005 for class c_2 is obtained by multiplying the three values $\Pr(c_2) = 0.5$, $\min_{l \in 0..3} \Pr(m_{l0}|c_2) = \min(0.1, 0.1, 0.4, 0.4) = 0.1$, $\min_{l \in 0..2} \Pr(m_{l1}|c_2) = \min(0.7, 0.29, 0.01) = 0.01$.

Using these bounds we partially reason about the class of the region to distinguish amongst one of these three outcomes.

1. MUST-WIN: *All points in the region belong to class* c_k. This is true if the minimum probability of class c_k ($\text{minProb}(c_k)$) is greater than the maximum probability ($\text{maxProb}(c_j)$) values of all classes c_j.
2. MUST-LOSE: *No points in the region belong to class* c_k. This is true if there exists a class c_j for which $\text{maxProb}(c_k) < \text{minProb}(c_j)$. In this case class c_j will win over class c_k at all points in this region.
3. AMBIGUOUS: Neither of the previous two conditions apply, i.e., possibly a subset of points in the region belong to the class.

In Section 3.2.3 we sketch a proof of why these bounds are correct and also show how to improve them further.

When the status of a region is AMBIGUOUS, we need to first shrink the region and then split it into smaller regions, re-evaluate the upper and lower bounds in each region and recursively apply the above tests until all regions either satisfy one of the first two terminating conditions or the al-

	$d_1 \downarrow$	$p(c_1) = 0.33, p(c_2) = 0.5, p(c_3) = 0.17$			
m_{01}	.01, .7, .05	.001, .03, .0005 (c_2)	.001, .03, .0005 (c_2)	.0002, .1, .004 (c_2)	.0002, .1, .004 (c_2)
m_{11}	.5, .29, .05	.07, .01, .0005 (c_1)	.07, .01, .0005 (c_1)	.009, .06, .004 (c_2)	.009, .06, .004 (c_2)
m_{21}	.49, .1, .9	.07, .0005, .009 (c_1)	.07, .0005, .009 (c_1)	.009, .002, .07 (c_3)	.009, .002, .07 (c_3)
	$d_0 \rightarrow$	.4, .1, .05	.4, .1, .05	.05, .4, .4	.05, .4, .4
		m_{00}	m_{10}	m_{20}	m_{30}

Table 1. Example of a naive-Bayes classifier. Refer the Example paragraph of Section 3.2.1 for a description.

Region: d_0, d_1	[0..3], [0..2]	[0..3], [2..2]	[0..3], [0..1]	[0..1], [0..1]	[2..3], [0..1]
MinProb:	.0002, .0005, .0005	.0002, .03, .0005	.009, .0005, .0005	.07, .0005, .0005	.009, .002, .004
MaxProb:	.07, .1, .07	.0014, .1, .004	.07, .06, .07	.07, .01, .009	.009, .06, .07
Status:	AMBIGUOUS	MUST-LOSE	AMBIGUOUS	MUST-WIN	AMBIGUOUS
	(a) Starting region	*(b) Tighter bounds with member m_{21} of d_1*	*(c) Shrinking d_1 to [0..1]*	*(d) 1st child on splitting d_0 into [0..1] and [2..3]*	*(e) 2nd child*

Figure 2. First three steps of finding predicates for class c_1 of the classifier in Figure 1 showing a shrinkage step along dimension 1 followed by a split along dimension 0. In each box, the first line identifies the boundary of the region, the second and third lines show respectively the minProb and maxProb values of each of the three classes. The fourth line is the status of the region with respect to class c_1.

gorithm has made a maximum number of splits (an input parameter of the algorithm). A sketch of the algorithm appears below.

Algorithm 1 UpperEnvelope(c_k)

```
T: Tree initialized with the entire region as root;
while number of tree nodes expanded < Threshold do
  r= an unvisited leaf of T;
  r.status = Compute using c_k and maxProb, minProb
    values of r;
  if r.status = MUST-WIN then mark r as visited;
  if r.status = MUST-LOSE then remove r from T;
  if r.status = AMBIGUOUS then
    Shrink r along all possible dimensions;
    Split r into r_1 and r_2;
    Add r_1 and r_2 to T as children of r;
  end if
end while
Sweep T bottom-up merging all contiguous leaves;
Upper_Envelope(c_k) = disjunct over all leaves of T.
```

Shrink: We cycle through all dimensions and for each dimension d evaluate for each of its member m_{ld} the maxProb(c_j, d, m_{ld}) and minProb(c_j, d, m_{ld}) value as

$$\text{maxProb}(c_j, d, m_{ld}) = \Pr(c_j) \Pr(m_{ld}|c_j) \prod_{e \neq d} \max_r \Pr(m_{re}|c_j)$$

$$\text{minProb}(c_j, d, m_{ld}) = \Pr(c_j) \Pr(m_{ld}|c_j) \prod_{e \neq d} \min_r \Pr(m_{re}|c_j)$$

We use these revised tighter bounds to further shrink the region where possible. We test the MUST-LOSE condition above on the revised bounds and remove any members of an unordered dimension that satisfy this condition. For ordered dimensions, we only remove members from the two ends to maintain contiguity.

In Figure 2(a), from the minProb and maxProb values of the starting region [0..3], [0..2] we find that for class c_1 neither of the MUST-WIN or MUST-LOSE situation hold. Hence the situation is AMBIGUOUS for c_1 and we attempt to shrink this region. In Figure 2(b) we show the revised bounds for the last member m_{21} of dimension 1. This leads to a MUST-LOSE situation for class c_1 because in the region maxProb for class c_1 is smaller than minProb for class c_2. The new maxProb and minProb values in the shrunk region are shown in Figure 2(c). The shrunk region is again in an AMBIGUOUS state and we attempt to split it next.

Split: Regions are split by partitioning the values along a dimension. In evaluating the best split, we want to avoid methods that require explicit enumeration of the class of each combination. In performing the split our goal is to separate out (as best as possible) the regions which belong to class c_k from the ones which do not belong to c_k. For this, we rely on the well-known entropy function [27] for quantifying the skewness in the probability distribution of class c_k along each dimension. The details of the split are exactly as in the case of binary splits during decision tree construction. We evaluate the entropy function for split along each member of each dimension and choose the split which has the lowest average entropy in the two sub-regions. The only difference is that we do not have explicit counts of each class, instead we rely on the probability values of the members on each side of the splitting dimension.

Continuing with our example, in Figure 2(d) and (e) we show the two regions obtained by splitting dimension d_0 into [0..1] and [2..3]. The first sub-region shown in Figure 2(d) leads to a MUST-WIN situation and gives one disjunct for the upper envelope of class c_1. The second region is still in an AMBIGUOUS situation – however a second round of shrinkage along dimension d_1 on the region leads to an empty region and the top-down process terminates.

Merging regions: Once the above top-down split process terminates, we merge all regions that do not satisfy the MUST-LOSE condition. During the course of the above partitioning algorithm we maintain the tree structure of the split so that whenever all children of a node belong to the same class, they can be trivially merged together. This is followed by another iterative search for pairs of non-sibling regions that can be merged. The output is a set of non-overlapping regions that totally subsume all combinations belonging to a class.

Complexity The above top-down algorithm has a complexity of $O(tnmK)$ where t is the threshold that controls the depth of the tree to which we expand and $m = \max_{d=1}^{n}(n_d)$ is the maximum length of a dimension. Contrast this with the exponential complexity $K\prod_{d=1}^{n} n_d$ of just the enumeration step of the naive algorithm.

3.2.3. Formal Results

This section contains a sketch of the proof of correctness of the top-down algorithm and can be skipped on first reading.

The main concern about the correctness of the above algorithm arises from the use of the maxProb and minProb bounds in determining the two MUST-WIN and MUST-LOSE conditions. We sketch a proof of why these bounds are correct and also present a set of improved bounds for the special case of two classes. In this proof we do not explicitly discuss the case where there is a tie in the $\Pr(c_k|\vec{x})$ values of two classes.

Lemma 3.1 If a region satisfies the MUST-WIN condition minProb$(c_k) > \max_{j\neq k}$ maxProb(c_j) then for every possible cell v in the region the probability of class c_k is greater than the probability of every other class. Let $p_j(m_{ld})$ denote $\Pr(m_{ld}|c_j)$. We wish to prove that

$$\Pr(c_k)\prod_{d=1}^{n}\min_{l} p_k(m_{ld}) > \max_{j\neq k}\Pr(c_j)\prod_{d=1}^{n}\max_{l} p_j(m_{ld}) \quad (3)$$

implies

$$\forall v\left(\Pr(c_k)\prod_{d=1}^{n} p_k(v_d) > \max_{j\neq k}\Pr(c_j)\prod_{d=1}^{n} p_j(v_d)\right) \quad (4)$$

That is, (3) ⇒ (4). Similar results hold for the MUST-LOSE condition.

PROOF. Let $f(v,j)$ denote $\Pr(c_j)\prod_{d=1}^{n}\Pr(v_d|c_j)$. If $\min_v f(v,k) > \max_{j\neq k}\max_v(f(v,j))$ then $f(v,k) > f(v',j)$ for all values v' and all classes $j \neq k$. Also $\min_v(\Pr(c_k)\prod_{d=1}^{n}\Pr(v_d|c_k)) = \Pr(c_k)\prod_{d=1}^{n}\min_{v_d}\Pr(v_d|c_j)$ because all the terms within the product are non-negative. Similarly, moving the max() beyond the $\prod$ leaves the result unchanged. Thus, (3) ⇒ (4). ■

We next present a lemma that will help us get *exact* bounds for the case when the number of classes $K = 2$.

Lemma 3.2 When the number of classes $K = 2$, the MUST-WIN and the MUST-LOSE bounds are exact when the probability values $\Pr(v_d|c_j)$ in condition 3 of Lemma 3.1 are replaced with $\Pr'(v_d|c_j) = \frac{\Pr(v_d|c_j)}{\max_{i\neq k}\Pr(v_d|c_i)}$. Let $p'_j(m_{ld})$ denote $\Pr'(m_{ld}|c_j)$. We wish to prove that, when $K = 2$ condition 4 *is equivalent to*

$$\Pr(c_k)\prod_{d=1}^{n}\min_{l} p'_k(m_{ld}) > \max_{j\neq k}\Pr(c_j)\prod_{d=1}^{n}\max_{l} p'_j(m_{ld}) \quad (5)$$

Similar results hold for the MUST-LOSE condition.

PROOF. Omitted due to lack of space. ■

3.3. Clustering

Clustering models [22] are of three broad kinds: partitional, hierarchical and fuzzy. We concentrate on partitional clusters where the output is a set of k clusters and each point is assigned to exactly one of these k clusters. Hierarchical and fuzzy clusters are a subject of our ongoing work. Partitional clustering methods can be further subdivided based on the membership criteria used for assigning new instances to clusters. We consider three variants: centroid-based, model-based and boundary-based (commonly arising in density-based clusters).

In the popular centroid-based method each cluster is associated with a single point called the centroid that is most representative of the cluster. An appropriate distance measure on the input attributes is used to measure the distance between the cluster centroid and the instance. A common distance function is Euclidean or weighted Euclidean. The instance is assigned to the cluster with the closest centroid. This partitions the data space into K disjoint partitions where the i-th partition contains all points that are closer to the ith centroid than to any other centroid. A cluster's partition could take arbitrary shapes depending on the distance function, the number of clusters and the number of dimensions. Our goal is to provide an upper envelope on the boundary of each partition using a small number of hyper-rectangles.

A second class of clustering methods is model-based [25]. Model-based clustering assumes that data is generated from a mixture of underlying distributions in which each distribution represents a group or a cluster.

We show that both distance based and model-based clusters can be expressed exactly as naive Bayes classifiers for the purposes of finding the upper envelopes. Consider distance-based clustering first. Let $c_1, c_2 \ldots c_K$ be the K clusters, n be the number of attributes or dimensions of an instance $\vec{x}$ and $(c_{1k} \ldots c_{nk})$ be the centroid of the k-th cluster. Assume a weighted Euclidean distance measure. Let $(w_{1k} \ldots w_{nk})$ denote the weight values. Then, a point $\vec{x}$ is assigned to a cluster as follows:

$$\text{cluster of } \vec{x} = \text{argmax}_k \sum_{d=1}^{n} w_{dk}(x_d - c_{dk})^2$$

This is similar in structure to Equation 2 with the prior term missing. In both cases, for each component of $\vec{x}$, we have a set of K values corresponding to the K different clusters/classes. We sum over these n values along each dimension and choose of these K sums the class with the largest sum.

For several model-based clusters the situation is similar. Each group k is associated with a mixing parameter called τ_k ($\sum_{k=1}^{K} \tau_k = 1$) in addition to the parameters θ_k of the distribution function of that group. Thus, an instance will be assigned to the cluster with the largest value of

$$\text{cluster of } \vec{x} = \text{argmax}_k(\tau_k f_k(\vec{x}|\theta_k))$$

When the distribution function f_k treats each dimension independently, for example, mixtures of Gaussians with the covariance entries zero, we can again express the above expression in the same form as Equation 2.

Boundary-based clusters [18] explicitly define the boundary of a region within which a point needs to lie in order to belong to a cluster. Deriving upper envelopes is equivalent to covering a geometric region with a small number of rectangles. This is a classical problem in computation geometry for which several approximate algorithms exist [30, 2]. Further investigation of this problem is part of our future work.

4. Optimizing Mining Queries

So far we have considered examples of mining predicates of the form "Prediction_column = class_label". In Section 4.1, we show a wider class of mining predicates that may be optimized using upper envelopes for mining predicates of the above form. Then in Section 4.2 we discuss the key steps needed in enabling such optimization in a traditional relational database engine.

4.1. Types of mining predicates

We discuss three additional types of mining predicates that can be optimized using the derived per-class upper envelopes.

IN predicates: A simple generalization is mining predicates of the form: M.Prediction_column IN $(c_1, \ldots, c_l)$, where $c_1, \ldots, c_l$ are a subset of the possible class labels on M.Prediction_column. An example of such a query is to identify customers who a data mining model predicts to be either baseball fans or football fans. For such a mining predicate, the upper envelope is a disjunction of the upper envelopes corresponding to each of the atomic mining predicates. Thus, if M_{c_i} denotes the predicate (M.$Prediction\_column = c_i$), we can express the overall disjunct as: $\bigvee_{i=1}^{l} M_{c_i}$

Join predicates between two predicted columns: Another form of join predicates is M1.Prediction_column1 = M2.Prediction_column2. Such predicates select instances on which two models M1 and M2 concur in their predicted class labels. An example of such a query is "Find all microsoft.com visitors who are predicted to be web developers by two mining models $SAS\_customer\_model$ and $SPSS\_customer\_model$". In order to optimize this query using upper envelopes, we assume that the class labels for each of the mining models can be enumerated during optimization by examining the metadata associated with the mining models. In typical mining models we expect the number of classes to be quite small. Let the class labels that are common to these two mining models be $\{c_1, c_2, .., c_k\}$. Then, the above join predicate, is equivalent to this disjunction: $\bigvee_{i=1}^{k}$(M1.Prediction_column1 = M2.Prediction_column2 = c_i). Adopting the notation of the previous paragraph, this can be expressed as: $\bigvee_i (M1_{c_i} \wedge M2_{c_i})$. Note that if M1 and M2 are identical models, then the resulting upper envelope results in a tautology. Conversely, if M1 and M2 are contradictory, then the upper envelope evaluates to false and the query is guaranteed to return no answers. These observations can be leveraged during the optimization process to improve efficiency.

Join predicates between a predicted column and a data column: Consider predicates of the form M1.Prediction_column = T.Data_column that check if the prediction of a mining model matches that of a database column. An example of this type of predicate is: "Find all customers for whom predicted age is of the same category as the actual age"[1]. Such queries can occur, for example, in cross-validation tasks. Evaluation of the above query seems to require scanning the entire table. Fortunately, like in the previous paragraph, we can use the approach of enumerating the set of possible class labels. Once again, such an approach is feasible since in most mining models we expect the number of class to be small. If the set of classes are $\{c_1, c_2, .., c_k\}$, then, we can derive an implied predicate $\bigvee_i (M1_{c_i} \wedge T.Data\_column = c_i)$. This transforms the query to a disjunct or a union of queries. More importantly, we now have the option of leveraging the content of the mining model for access path selection. For exam-

[1] In this example, we consider age as a discretized attribute with the domain consisting of three categories: ''young", "middle-aged', "senior".

ple, for the i-th disjunct, the optimizer can potentially consider either the predicate $T.Data\_column = c_i$ or a predicate in $M1_{c_i}$ for access path selection. Of course, the final plan depends on other alternatives considered by the optimizer (including sequential scan) but our rewriting opens the door for additional alternatives. In addition to the above technique, the traditional approach of exploiting transitivity of predicates in the WHERE clause can also be effective. For example, if the query contains additional predicates on T.Data_columns that indirectly limits the possible domain values M1.Prediction_column can assume, then we can apply the optimization of the IN predicates discussed earlier in this section. For example, if the query were "Find all customers for which predicted age is the same as the actual age and the actual age is either old or middle-aged" then, via transitivity of the predicate, we get a predicate M.Prediction_column IN ('old', 'middle-aged') for which we can add the upper-enveloping predicates as discussed in the earlier paragraphs.

4.2. Key Steps in Optimization of Mining Predicates

The framework for optimizing queries with mining predicates has two key parts. First, during training of the mining models, upper envelopes for mining predicates of the form Model.Prediction_column = class_label have to be precomputed using the algorithms described in Section 3. Precomputation of such "atomic" upper envelopes reduces overhead during query optimization. Second, during query optimization we optimize queries with mining predicates using the following key steps:

1. Apply traditional normalization and transitivity rules to the given query to derive an equivalent query to be used for the following steps.
2. For each mining predicate f in the query, do the following. Assume that the mining predicate f references a mining model m_f:
   (a) Look up the information on class labels of m_f from the database, if needed.
   (b) Depending on the type of the mining predicate, derive an additional upper envelope u_f using the techniques described in Section 4.1. Computation of such an upper envelope requires looking up "atomic" upper envelopes computed during training (see earlier in this subsection).
   (c) Replace m_f with $m_f \wedge u_f$.
3. Apply normalization and transitivity rules to derive an equivalent query. If new mining predicates are inferred, return to step 2, else return.

Our experiments demonstrate that the additional work during training to derive "atomic" upper envelopes as well as step 2(b) during query optimization add little additional overhead in themselves. However, our strategy for optimization relies on the following assumptions about query optimization and evaluation.

Complexity of upper envelopes does not impact execution cost: We assume the following: (a) The evaluation of upper envelopes do not add to the cost of the query. This is consistent with traditional assumptions made in database optimization since every upper envelope consists of AND/OR expression of simple predicates. (b) The optimizer is well-behaved and is not misguided by the introduction of additional complex boolean predicates due to upper envelopes. We rely on optimizers whose selectivity computations and access path selections are robust for complex boolean expressions. Although we make the above two assumptions for simplicity, they rarely hold in all situations. Failure to satisfy condition (a) can be dealt by more careful rewriting. For example, if none of the predicates in the upper envelope is chosen for access path, the upper envelope can be removed at the end of the optimization. In general, we need to retain only a subset of relevant upper envelope for evaluation as filter conditions. We omit these details due to lack of space. Unfortunately, handling violation of condition (b) is more challenging, yet happens routinely. Today's query optimizers often degenerate to sequential scan when presented with a complex AND/OR expression. This would negate any benefits of upper envelopes as the latter typically consist of several disjuncts over conjuncts of atomic predicates on the data columns. Despite past work (e.g., [28]), handling complex filter conditions remains a core challenge for SQL query optimizers. This remains an area of our active research in the context of query optimization. However, for the time being, we rely on thresholding of the number of disjuncts (see Section 3.2) and simplification based on selectivity estimates to limit the complexity so that commercial optimizers are able to exploit upper envelopes. We omit detailed discussion due to lack of space.

Accessing content of mining models during query optimization should be enabled: Our strategies for deriving upper envelopes (as described in Section 4.1) requires access to content of the mining models (e.g., class labels) *during* optimization. Such information is different from the traditional statistical information about tables because the correctness of our optimization is impacted if the mining model is changed. In such cases, we need to invalidate an execution plan (if cached or persisted) in case it had exploited upper envelopes. Nonetheless, our approach of leveraging the content of mining models is justified because mining models evolve slowly and the size of a typical mining model is relatively small compared to data size. Therefore, optimization time is not severely impacted for accessing the content of a mining model.

Data Set	Test size in millions	Training size	# of classes	# of clusters
Anneal-U	1.83	598	6	6
Balance-Scale	1.28	416	3	5
Chess	1.63	2130	2	5
Diabetes	1.57	512	2	5
Hypothyroid	1.78	1339	2	5
Letter	1.28	15000	26	26
Pairty5+5	1.04	100	2	5
Shuttle	1.85	43500	7	7
Vehicle	1.73	564	4	5
Kdd-cup-99	4.72	100000	23	23

Table 2. Summary of Data Sets used in experiments

5. Experiments

In this section, we present results of experiments to evaluate the effectiveness of upper envelope predicates generated by algorithms presented in Section 3. Our experiments focussed on three important aspects: (i) Impact of upper envelope predicates on the running time and physical plan of queries. We study this in Section 5.2.1. (ii) Degree of tightness of the approximation, studied in Section 5.2.2. (iii) Time taken to generate upper envelope predicates. The significant outcome of the last experiment was that in almost all data sets the time to precompute the upper envelope predicate for each class (see Section 4.2) was a negligible fraction of the model training time. Likewise, the time to look up "atomic" upper envelope predicates was insignificant compared to the time for optimizing the query. We do not present further details of this experiment due to lack of space.

5.1. Experimental Setup

Mining Models: We have implemented the algorithms presented in Section 3 for the decision tree, naive Bayes and clustering mining models. We generated decision tree and clustering mining models using Microsoft Analysis Server that ships with Microsoft SQL Server 2000. For generating naive Bayes mining models we used the discrete naive Bayes inducer packaged with the MLC++ machine learning library [23].

Data Sets: We report numbers on 10 data sets consisting of 9 UCI [7] data sets and the 1999 KDDcup data set available at [5]. Table 2 summarizes various characteristics of each data set. We generated the test data set (for the UCI data sets) by repeatedly doubling all available data until the total number of rows in the data set exceeded 1 million rows. This way, the data distribution of each column (and hence selectivity of predicates on the column) in the test data set is the same as in the training data set. All data sets were stored in Microsoft SQL Server databases.

Implementation: When executing a mining query, we first identify the mining model object(s) referenced in the mining query and identify mining predicates for which generation of upper envelopes may be possible. In our current implementation, generation of upper envelope predicates is not integrated with the database engine; rather we rewrite the mining query externally to include the upper envelope predicates, and submit the rewritten query to the database engine. The upper envelopes are generated during training time by referring the MINING_MODEL_CONTENT schema rowset defined in the OLE DB for Data Mining [15] interface.

Evaluation Methodology: For each class (or cluster), we first generate the query with the upper envelope predicate for that class. Thus, if T is the table containing the test data, and $\langle p \rangle$ is the upper envelope predicate, we generate the query "SELECT * FROM T WHERE $\langle p \rangle$". We create a workload file containing all queries for the (data set, mining model) combination. Thus, the number of queries in the workload file is equal to the number of classes (or clusters) for that (data set, mining model) combination. To generate an appropriate physical design for this workload, we invoke the Index Tuning Wizard tool [12, 4] that ships with Microsoft SQL Server 2000 by passing it the above workload file as input, and implement the index recommendations proposed by the tool. We then execute the workload on the database and record the plan and running time of each query in the workload. We compare this with a query that performs a full scan of the table, i.e., "SELECT * FROM T".

Although in practice, mining queries may also contain other predicates, the above comparison with a "SELECT *" query is reasonable since our goal is to determine if addition of upper envelopes can reduce running time in a significant number of cases (due to indexed access path selection). Whether upper envelope predicates are indeed chosen over other predicates for indexing will of course depend on other predicates and their relative selectivity. Finally, a design that stores the class label with each tuple (e.g., as an additional column) in the base relation is not acceptable since (a) It does not scale well with the number of mining models and (b) In many cases, mining queries are issued not over the base relations but on queries (or views) over possibly multiple base relations Note that such precomputation of the class label may however be appropriate in limited cases (e.g., in materialized views).

5.2. Results

5.2.1. Impact of Upper Envelope Predicates on Running Time and Plan

We first evaluate the impact of upper envelope predicates on the running time of all queries for all mining models. The following table shows the average reduction in running time over all queries for each type of mining model, compared to a full scan of the data. We note that the reduction

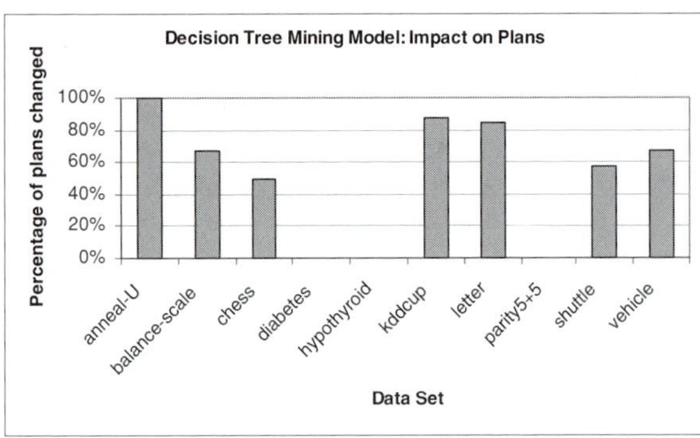

Figure 3. Impact of upper envelope predicates on physical plan for decision tree model

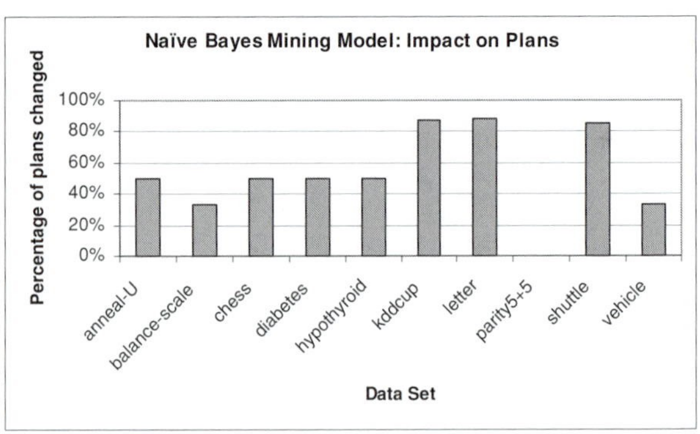

Figure 4. Impact of upper envelope predicates on physical plan for naive Bayes model

in running time we report here is in comparison to a "SELECT *", which does not include the time for actually invoking the mining model on the columns. If the application of mining models is time consuming, then we can expect to see an even greater percentage reduction.

Decision Tree	Naive Bayes	Clustering
73.7%	63.5%	79.0%

To further analyze the reason for the reduced running time, we measured the impact of the upper envelope predicates on the physical plan chosen by the query optimizer. For a given data set and mining model, we recorded for each query whether the plan chosen by the query optimizer changed compared to the query without upper envelope predicates. A plan is said to have *changed* if either: (a) The query optimizer chose one or more indexes to answer the query. (b) The query optimizer decided to use a "Constant Scan" operator since upper envelope predicate was NULL (i.e., it does not need to reference the data at all to answer the query). The table below shows the percentage of queries for which the plan changed over all data sets and mining models.

Decision Tree	Naive Bayes	Clustering
72.7%	75.3%	76.6%

As we can see from this table, for all types of mining models, a significant fraction of the queries had their physical plans altered as a result of introducing upper envelope predicates.

We now analyze these results further by drilling-down into the results for each data set. Figures 3, 4 and 5 show these numbers for the decision tree, naive Bayes and clustering mining models respectively. We observe that upper envelope predicates have greater impact on the plan for data sets where the number of classes is relatively large (e.g., kddcup, letter, shuttle etc.), and less impact for data sets where number of classes is small (e.g., Diabetes, Parity etc.). This is due to the fact that when the number of classes is large, there are typically more classes with small selectivity for which the query optimizer picks an index to answer the query. In fact, in some cases, the selectivity is 0, i.e., the

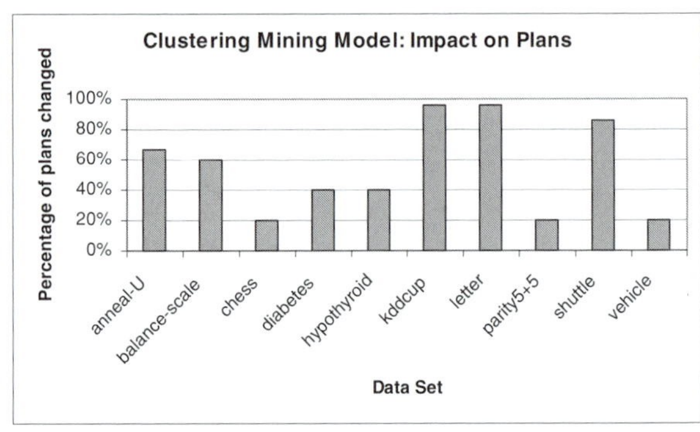

Figure 5. Impact of upper envelope predicates on physical plan for clustering model

upper envelope predicate is NULL. In such cases, the optimizer does not need to access any data to answer the query. A more detailed analysis of the average reduction in running time as a function of the selectivity (both original and upper envelope) of the class/cluster over all classes and clusters of all mining models and data sets is shown in Figure 6. We see that the reduction in running time is most significant when the selectivity is below 10%. Also, a comparison of the bars for original and upper envelope selectivities shows that the low reduction in running time for higher selectivities is not a reflection of the effectiveness of our algorithm. Rather, when a predicate's selectivity is high (e.g., above 10%) the optimizer rarely selects indexes, particularly non-clustered indexes. Thus, for high selectivity classes, adding upper envelope predicates is rarely useful, even if we could find *exact* predicates.

Finally, we noticed that in many cases, the upper envelope predicates generated by our algorithms for these data sets are relatively simple, i.e., consisting of few disjuncts. This increases the likelihood that the query optimizer can use an index lookup to answer the query. Overall, this experiment confirms our intuition that inclusion of upper envelope predicates significantly impacts the plan, and hence running times of queries with mining predicates.

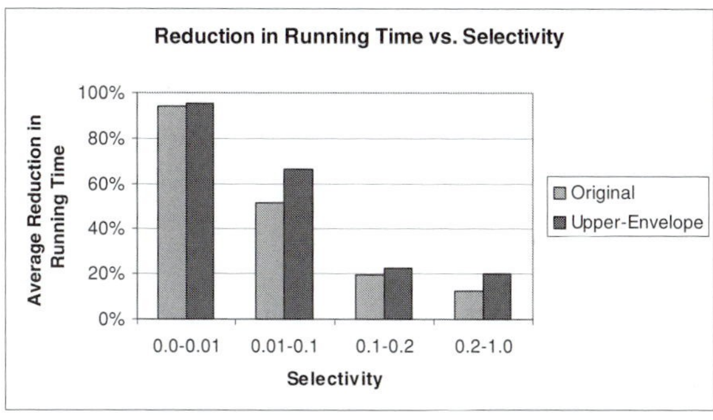

Figure 6. Running Time improvement vs. Original Selectivity: All mining models and data sets

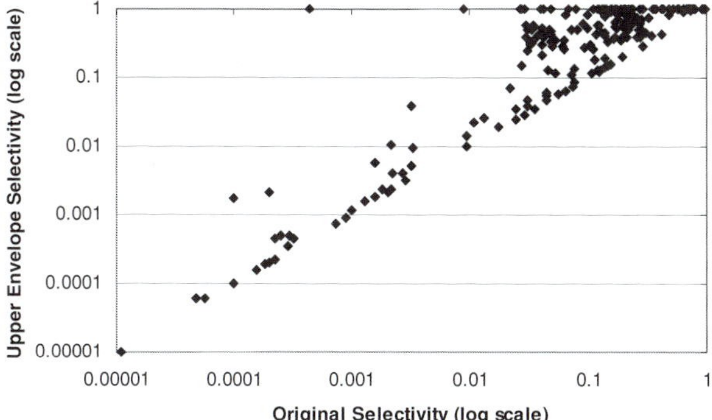

Figure 7. Tightness of approximation: naive Bayes and clustering

5.2.2. Tightness of Approximation

In this experiment, we compare the tightness of approximation of the upper envelopes for naive Bayes and clustering. For decision-trees, since the upper envelopes are exact, this comparison is not necessary. Figure 7 shows for all classes in all data sets for the naive Bayes and clustering mining models, a scatter plot of the original selectivity of each class vs. the selectivity of the corresponding upper envelope predicate (on a log scale). Each point in the scatter-plot corresponds to one class of a data set.

As we see from the figure, a significant fraction of the upper envelope predicates either have selectivities close to the original selectivity or have selectivity small enough that use of indexes for answering the predicate is attractive. Most cases where the algorithm failed to find a tight upper envelope correspond to cases where the original selectivity is large to start with. In such cases, the upper envelope predicates are unlikely to be useful for improving access paths even if they were exact.

6. Related Work

Our work falls in the broader area of integration of data mining and database systems and there are several pieces of related work in that area. The case for building the infrastructure for supporting mining on not only stored results but also on the result of an arbitrary database query was made in [9]. Agrawal et al [3] looked at the problem of generating decision tree classifiers such that the predicate could easily be pushed into the SQL query. However, they do not discuss how the method will work for other mining models. Other complementary areas of work include construction of mining models using SQL [31] and defining language extensions and application programming interfaces for integrating mining with relation DBMS [26], [1] and [15]. More recently, database systems, such as Microsoft Analysis Server or IBM DB2 have enabled specification of such queries. However, none of these systems exploit mining predicates for *optimization* in a general setting. Our paper represents the first work in that direction.

Our work can be viewed as part of the broader field of semantic query optimization. Early work in database systems recognized value of query modification (e.g., in INGRES) whereby a semantically implied predicate, perhaps derived from integrity constraints, is added to make evaluation of the query more efficient. Our technique follows the same approach but our novelty is in the specific information we exploit - the internal structure of the mining model to derive upper envelopes. To the best of our knowledge, this has not been attempted before. There has been past study of upper envelopes that represent approximation to given recursive queries [11, 8] but these do not apply to mining predicates.

Recently, there has been work on optimization of user-defined functions and predicates [19, 13, 32]. Mining predicates can certainly be viewed as user-defined predicates Thus, it is an interesting research question whether our idea of deriving implied database predicates based on content of mining models can be effectively applied to other examples of user-defined predicates as well.

The problem of rule extraction from hard to interpret models like Neural networks [24, 16] bears resemblance, but differs from our problem in that the extracted rules need to approximate the classification function but are *not* required to be implied predicates (upper envelopes). Moreover, the algorithm for rule learning as proposed in [24] requires an enumeration of the discretized input space, similar to our first-cut bottom up algorithm. Such an approach has been shown to be infeasible in our case.

The *coverage* problem has been addressed in several different contexts, including, covering a set of points with the smallest number of rectangles [30, 2], covering a collection of clauses with simpler terms in logic minimization problems [20] and constructing clusters with rectilinear boundaries [6]. Despite the apparent similarities, the coverage problems differ in a few important aspects. First, they assume that the points are already enumerated in the n-dimensional space. This is not a feasible option in our case. Next, the first two problems require an exact cover of smallest size whereas we only need an upper envelope. Finally, most of these approaches assume a small number of dimensions (two or three) and do not scale to higher dimensions.

References

[1] SQL multimedia and application packages part 6: Data mining, ISO draft recommendations, 1999.

[2] R. Agrawal, J. Gehrke, D. Gunopulos, and P. Raghavan. Automatic subspace clustering of high dimensional data for data mining applications. In *Proc. ACM SIGMOD International Conf. on Management of Data*, Seattle, USA, June 1998.

[3] R. Agrawal, S. Ghosh, T. Imielinski, B. Iyer, and A. Swami. An interval classifier for database mining applications. In *Proc. of the VLDB Conference*, pages 560–573, Vancouver, British Columbia, Canada, August 1992.

[4] S. Agrawal, S. Chaudhuri, L. Kollar, and V. Narasayya. Index tuning wizard for Microsoft SQL Server 2000. White paper. `http://msdn.microsoft.com/library/techart/itwforsql.htm`, 2000.

[5] S. D. Bay. The UCI KDD archive [http://kdd.ics.uci.edu]. Irvine, CA: University of California, Department of Information and Computer Science, 1999.

[6] M. Berger and I. Regoutsos. An algorithm for point clustering and grid generation. *IEEE Transactions on Systems, Man and Cybernetics*, 21(5):1278–86, 1991.

[7] C. Blake and C. Merz. UCI repository of machine learning databases, 1998.

[8] S. Chaudhuri. Finding nonrecursive envelopes for datalog predicates. In *Proceedings of the Twelfth ACM SIGACT-SIGMOD-SIGART Symposium on Principles of Database Systems, May 25-28, 1993, Washington, DC*, pages 135–146, 1993.

[9] S.Chaudhuri. Data mining and database systems: Where is the intersection? In *Bulletin of the Technical Committee on Data Engineering*, volume 21, Mar 1998.

[10] S. Chaudhuri and U. Dayal. An overview of data warehouse and OLAP technology. *ACM SIGMOD Record*, March 1997.

[11] S. Chaudhuri and P. G. Kolaitis. Can datalog be approximated? In *Proceedings of the Thirteenth ACM SIGACT-SIGMOD-SIGART Symposium on Principles of Database Systems, May 24-26, 1994, Minneapolis, Minnesota*, pages 86–96, 1994.

[12] S. Chaudhuri and V. R. Narasayya. An efficient cost-driven index selection tool for microsoft sql server. In *VLDB'97, Proceedings of 23rd International Conference on Very Large Data Bases, August 25-29, 1997, Athens, Greece*, pages 146–155, 1997.

[13] S. Chaudhuri and K. Shim. Optimization of queries with user-defined predicates. In *VLDB'96, Proceedings of 22th International Conference on Very Large Data Bases, September 3-6, 1996, Mumbai (Bombay), India*, pages 87–98, 1996.

[14] W. W. Cohen. Fast effective rule induction. In *Proc. 12th International Conference on Machine Learning*, pages 115–123. Morgan Kaufmann, 1995.

[15] M. Corporation. OLE DB for data mining. `http://www.microsoft.com/data/oledb`.

[16] M. W. Craven and J. W. Shavlik. Using neural networks for data mining. In *Future Generation Computer Systems*, 1997.

[17] J. Dougherty, R. Kohavi, and M. Sahami. Supervised and unsupervised discretization of continuous features. In *Proc. 12th International Conference on Machine Learning*, pages 194–202. Morgan Kaufmann, 1995.

[18] M. Ester, H.-P. Kriegel, J. Sander, and X. Xu. A density-based algorithm for discovering clusters in large spatial databases with noise. In *Proc. of the 2nd Int'l Conference on Knowledge Discovery in Databases and Data Mining*, Portland, Oregon, August 1996.

[19] J. M. Hellerstein and M. Stonebraker. Predicate migration: Optimizing queries with expensive predicates. In *SIGMOD Conference*, pages 267–276, 1993.

[20] S. J. Hong. MINI: A heuristic algorithm for two-level logic minimization. In R. Newton, editor, *Selected Papers on Logic Synthesis for Integrated Circuit Design*. IEEE Press, 1987.

[21] IBM. *IBM Intelligent Miner Scoring, Administration and Programming for DB2 Version 7.1*, March 2001.

[22] L. Kaufman and P. Rousseeuw. *Finding Groups in Data: An Introduction to Cluster Analysis*. John Wiley and Sons, 1990.

[23] R. Kohavi, D. Sommerfield, and J. Dougherty. Data mining using MLC++: A machine learning library in C++. In *Tools with Artificial Intelligence*, pages 234–245. IEEE Computer Society Press, available from `http://www.sgi.com/tech/mlc/`, 1996.

[24] H. Lu, R. Setiono, and H. Lui. Neurorule: A connectionist approach to data mining. In *Proc. of the Twenty first Int'l conf. on Very Large Databases (VLDB)*, Zurich, Switzerland, Sep 1995.

[25] G. McLachlan and K. Basford. Mixture models: Inference and applications to clustering, 1988.

[26] R. Meo, G. Psaila, and S. Ceri. An extension to sql for mining association rules. *Data Mining and Knowledge Discovery*, 2(2):195–224, 1998.

[27] T. Mitchell. *Machine Learning*. McGraw-Hill, 1997.

[28] C. Mohan, D. Haderle, Y. Wang, and J. Cheng. Single table access using multiple indexes: optimization, execution, and concurrency control techniques. In *Proc. International Conference on Extending Database Technology*, pages 29–43, 1990.

[29] J. R. Quinlan. *C4.5: Programs for Machine Learning*. Morgan Kaufman, 1993.

[30] R. A. Reckhow and J. Culberson. Covering simple orthogonal polygon with a minimum number of orthogonally convex polygons. In *Proc. of the ACM 3rd Annual Computational Geometry Conference*, pages 268–277, 1987.

[31] S. Sarawagi, S. Thomas, and R. Agrawal. Integrating association rule mining with databases: alternatives and implications. In *Proc. ACM SIGMOD International Conf. on Management of Data*, Seattle, USA, June 1998.

[32] G. M. Wolfgang Scheufele. Efficient dynamic programming algorithms for ordering expensive joins and selections. In *Proc. of the 6th Int'l Conference on Extending Database Technology (EDBT)*, Valencia, Spain, 1998.

Chapter 9
Web Services and Data Bases

In this section we include a collection of papers motivated by the emergence of the World Wide Web (WWW) as the major delivery mechanism for application services as well as information from both data bases and text files. There are three thrusts that we focus on. First, the web requires a different application architecture for DBMS services than commonly utilized in the past. Hence, we first discuss architectural issues. Next, the web has prominently showcased the retrieval and delivery of textual information. Hence, our second thrust is on querying textual data. We then close with a discussion of "nirvana", in the form of integrating textual data and conventional structured data.

When the web was envisioned by Tim Berners-Lee, he had in mind a hypertext-oriented system whereby users could link documents together with hyperlinks (URLs). In this way, a web of inter-related documents could be constructed. Hypertext is obviously not a new idea, and linking textual objects together has been a common theme for a long time. The web would have been yet another hypertext proposal without the contribution of Marc Andreesen, who added an easy-to-use GUI for the web called Mosaic. With Andreesen's browser, a user could easily navigate Berners-Lee's web of documents.

Web protocols (HTTP, HTML) were designed with documents in mind. However, the web quickly morphed into a delivery mechanism for conventional applications, especially ones that interact with data bases. Major web sites such as Amazon.com, Ebay.com, and United.com are front ends for large DBMS applications. As such, the web is now largely about delivery of application services and not textual documents. This use of the web for something that was never intended by the original developers has caused major headaches. Specifically, the web is "stateless", i.e. each HTTP request is independent of the previous one. In contrast, the interface between a GUI and a typical application as well as the interface between an application and the DBMS are very "stateful". For example, an application will often maintain state about a user session, such as the following:

- The user name and password for the session
- The application operations that the user is authorized to perform
- The maximum resource level that the user can consume

When an application is interacting with a DBMS, the state of this session includes:

- The user name and password on whose behalf the session is running
- The connection (socket) on which the user is communicating
- The current transaction
- The cursor position in a result set of records

As a result, web protocols present a big challenge to any system architect, namely how to simulate "state" on top of a protocol that is fundamentally stateless. The typical resolution of this dilemma is shown in Figure 9.1. On the user's computer, the only program that is run is a web browser. Hence, no part of the application exists on the client's machine, and this architecture is the ultimate in "thin client". Although Java applets can be added to most web browsers to run part of the clients application, they have never become popular. The reasons are varied, but revolve around universality (you have to run on everybody's browser), maintainability (what about site specific applet bugs), and load times (it takes forever to upload a large applet, especially over a modem to a home user).

The web browser specifies a URL to initiate communication via HTTP with a foreign web server. If the web server is part of a large application site such as Amazon, then it is really one of a hundred or more individual machines, often called "blade" servers because of their interchangeable nature – they are typically commodity "jelly bean" hardware running Linux and the Apache web server. Such computing "blades" can be cheaply expanded as traffic increases. In front of this "web server farm" is a "packet-spraying" router, which load-balances incoming messages among the farm. The only job of the web servers is to process HTTP requests and responses; no part of the application runs on this farm. Each web server has a simple "plugin" program (e.g. a script interpreter like PHP, PERL or Microsoft's ASP) to communicate with the next level, which is invariably an application server.

One might ask why the webserver tier is needed in this architecture. It is certainly possible to bypass the web server level and communicate directly from the client level to the app server level. To accomplish this, one must run a Java applet on the client that can open up a non-HTTP connection directly to the app server. Besides the applet disadvantage mentioned previously, there is one additional killer problem such an architecture faces: most firewalls are configured to admit HTTP traffic but no other protocols. Because there is invariably a firewall at the front of the site, guarding against unauthorized accesses, proprietary protocols are essentially never used at this level. Finally, there are usually certain very common simple tasks (e.g. delivering static content like the site's home page) that the web server can handle, thus offloading the application servers.

Each web server communicates with an application server, and there are typically a dozen or more "blades" performing this function. Again, one want to easily expand the number of machines as traffic grows. Moreover, most app servers are capable of performing load balancing across a collection of machines, so there is no need for a router in front of the "app server farm". The job of the app server is to run the application with which the user is communicating. WebLogic from BEA and WebSphere from IBM are the dominant app server products, with the remainder of the market spread over dozens of vendors.

The app server communicates with the underlying DBMS using native DBMS session-oriented protocols. There is often only a single large machine (say a Sun E10000 or E15000) running the DBMS. Architects often utilize a single large machine, rather than many small ones at the DBMS level, because of the difficulty of ensuring that each transaction touches only one machine. Otherwise, only two choices remain: the database and workload can be strictly partitioned (e.g. by having separate virtual "stores" for different product categories), or expensive two-phase commits are required to commit transactions across DBMS servers. Neither of these is attractive at the high end. If the capacity of a large shared memory multiprocessor (SMP) machine is exceeded, then the decision is often to move to a shared-disk parallel (cluster) architecture, again to minimize the difficulty of transaction commits.

The observant reader can note that the DBMS is essentially unaffected by the web. The major difference between Figure 1 and a traditional client-server architecture is that an app server is the object making DBMS requests, rather than a client machine. Moreover, on mainframe configurations where a large number of clients need application service, architects often use a transaction processing (TP) monitor such as CICS or IMS/DC. A TP monitor performs essentially the same function as the application servers do in Figure 1. In summary, the web is isolated above the DBMS by an app server, which functions very much like TP monitors have behaved on mainframes for a quarter of a century. This is a case where the statement that "the web changed everything" does not hold.

On the other hand, there are huge demands put on application servers by the web. Because DBMS experts must often get involved with application server issues, we have included a paper by Dean Jacobs of BEA as our first selection in this section. It highlights some of the distinctions between traditional TP monitors and modern app servers, and also focuses on the different kinds of state that have to be managed in web applications, and the way these kinds of state are managed, either in the app server or in the DBMS.

The second important aspect of web services is document retrieval. When the web is used for its original purpose as a document repository, a user has the problem of finding any particular document for which he is searching. Fairly early in the web's evolution, a collection of sites sprung up which "crawl" the web looking for publicly accessible documents. Then, they provide keyword indexing for these documents in a web-wide index. Subsequently, a user can request the documents that match a collection of keywords, and the site will return a collection of documents, sorted in perceived order of relevance. Example sites of this sort include AltaVista, Google, and Lycos, as well as subservices of portals like Yahoo!, Netscape and MSN. Obviously, these sites have a massive data management problem, yet none use packaged database systems as part of their solution. The next paper in this section by Eric Brewer, the architect of Inktomi (now owned by Yahoo!), explains how document indexing sites work in database system terms, why packaged DBMS solutions are not utilized in their design, and why the search engine design diverges from traditional DBMSs.

If you have ever typed an important but common query – e.g. the name of a frequently occurring medical condition that concerns you or a family member – you have experienced the frustration of receiving 10,000 or so "hits", and the resulting difficulty of finding the documents you are interested in and trust amid all the "clutter". The job of professional librarians is to organize large collections, so users can find documents of interest. However, it is clearly impossible to hire enough librarians to organize the web; hence the web will always be a place full of "clutter".

As such, it is important to develop better algorithms to determine relevance of a document to a particular user search. Traditional keyword indexing has its roots in the 1950's [Luhn59], and many of today's most common commercial techniques (e.g. inverted indexes and the well-known TFxIDF ranking metrics) have been around since the 1960's [SL68]. The interested reader is referred to an Information Retrieval textbook (e.g. [WMB99]) for more information on these. Unfortunately, these basic techniques alone do poorly in the presence of large amounts of clutter. To perform better a variety of add-on improvements have been suggested. One of the most interesting, proposed by the Google developers, was to leverage the web's additional hyperlink information to help determine relevance; a related scheme was proposed by researchers at Cornell and IBM [Klei99]. This tactic seems to work very well in practice, and for a while allowed Google to give better answers than its competitors. According to scuttlebutt, all of the major vendors now incorporate the Google technology, but that technology alone is still insufficient. The icing on the cake apparently comes from considering the visual aspects of web documents – essentially all search engines utilize the prominence of the word in the document (i.e. header, title, author, boldface, etc.) to improve relevance. Hopefully, the technology will gradually improve, leading to better facilities in the future. As an example of this class of system, we have included one of the original Google architecture papers as our next selection in this section. It reviews the Google ranking scheme, along with the architecture of Google's server farm, which is now fairly standard and was largely taken from Brewer and co.'s design at Inktomi.

The web has obviously catapulted information retrieval and document management into the forefront of Computer Science. However, word-oriented technology has fundamental limits of how well it can possibly perform. To do better, there are at least four directions being pursued.

First, one can develop sites that are specialized to a particular class of documents. In a specialized domain, one should be able to do much better than general purpose sites. For example, Charles Schwab is providing retrieval in the constrained universe of financial documents. Such a constrained universe has two desirable features. First, the set of reasonable queries is limited (you don't ask Charles Schwab about the meaning of God). Second, and perhaps more important, an expert can take the time to teach the system about the idioms and slang that are typically used in the limited world (Any Schwab system must know about insider trading, straddles, 401Ks, 403Bs, etc.). The next paper in this chapter is on BINGO!, a system for efficiently doing "focused" crawls for specialized search sites.[1]

Second, one can exploit natural language (NL) understanding techniques to parse documents and decipher their meaning. In addition, instead of accepting a collection of keywords from the user, one could accept a question, and then parse it using NL techniques. NL has been around since the 1950's, and slow steady improvements have been made. In our opinion, a general purpose NL system that works well is still considerably beyond the state of the art. In the meantime, techniques that use simpler notions of "understanding" taken from information retrieval – e.g. the frequencies and co-occurrences of words – tend to perform better than any sophisticated attempts at "understanding" language in a deep sense.

However, in constrained vertical markets NL systems are finding acceptance. Moreover, in constrained universes, an NL system can be front-ended by a speech understanding facility. This allows spoken input, rather than typed input, a definite advantage. Speaker-independent speech-understanding systems are currently in use for stock quotations, telephone number lookup, airport flight status, etc. We expect speech understanding and NL to make slow steady progress off into the future, thereby enlarging the collection of constrained universes for which they work well.

A third area of exploration is site description facilities. Often a user is looking for a site, rather than a specific document. For example, he might want a site that compares the safety records of various car models. This will not be answered by a specific document, but by a site like Consumers Report. To find such "services", one can use the keyword search available in a public indexing service and try to find the "home page" of a service using traditional technology. However, much better results would be obtained if all services entered a stylized description of what they do into a global repository. The user could then search though these descriptions for services of interest. This is the goal of UDDI, pioneered by Microsoft. Over time, we expect XML-based repositories of service capabilities to be widely available, and provide much better "site finding" capabilities than traditional techniques.

However, it is the fourth area in which we have the most interest. Obviously, there are a large number of unstructured documents available on the web. Such objects have no structure, other than what can be deciphered using NL techniques. As noted in the first paper of this book, there is a certain amount of "structured text" available on the web, such as want ads and resumes. However, we do not expect this kind of data to increase radically in the future, for the reasons that

[1] An added attraction of including the BINGO! paper in this collection is that it provides a whirlwind tour of techniques from Information Retrieval and Machine Learning: TFxIDF metrics, cross-entropy (a.k.a. Kullback-Leibler Divergence), Support Vector Machines, Kleinberg's HITS algorithm, etc.

were also noted in the first paper. Additionally, there is a considerable amount of "structured data with text fields". However, there is a truly massive amount of structured data available on the web. Not only is there a large amount of "facts and figures" such as telephone directories, demographic data, and weather data but also there is an even larger amount of transactional data. This data includes the status of your shipment, your credit card transactions, etc. The latter is usually available only through programmatic interfaces from the web. Hence, one must fill out a form and be authorized to receive the data in question.

Based on these observations, there is a huge amount of leverage that would result from being able to simultaneously query both structured data and text. For example a user might want to know any news reports that mentioned a stock that changed in value by more than 1%. This requires a "join" between financial ticker data and a news feed. This requires a federated data base system, which "wraps" disparate data sources with "gateways" to construct a common structured data model. The Mariposa system discussed in Chapter 4 of this book was an early example of this sort of architecture. This approach bases its underlying processing mechanism on SQL and an Object-relational data model.

Another approach would be to use XML and semi-structured data as the underlying model. In fact, BEA has recently introduced an XML-based federation system, called Liquid Data. Since XML is fundamentally semi-structured, this requires substantial changes to the federation optimizer in order to function on this kind of data. The last two papers in this section deal with XML processing. The first by Abiteboul presents a well written summary of the arguments for semi-structured data. For a counterpoint, the reader is advised to read the XML section of the first paper in this collection. The final two papers in this section discuss ways to perform query processing on semi-structured data.

We close this section with a final comment on XML. Many people now believe that future DBMSs will have to process both SQL-oriented data and XML data in the same system. Of course, it is a fairly traditional schema design problem to "shred" XML objects into a collection of tables, and then base all internal processing on SQL. A second approach is to build a native XML-based DBMS, which views SQL tables as a special case of XML objects. Of course, there is a lot of work to be done to figure out a sensible update model and view model for an XML-based world. This may be more difficult than it would appear, given the historical lesson from IMS logical data bases. A third option is to build a single DBMS that can switch modes, and process either kind of data. Essentially all vendors are taking the first approach in the short run. However, there is at least one large vendor that is actively pursuing each of the latter options. It will be interesting to see which approach is the long term winner.

References

[Luhn59] Hans Peter Luhn, "Auto-encoding of documents for information retrieval systems." In M. Boaz, *Modern Trends in Documentation* (pp. 45-58). London: Pergamon Press. 1959

[SL68] Gerard Salton and Michael Lesk. "Computer Evaluation of Indexing and Text Processing". *J. ACM* 15(1): 8-36 (1968).

[WMB99] Ian H. Witten, Alistair Moffat and Timothy C. Bell. *Managing Gigabytes (2nd ed.).* Morgan Kaufmann Publishers Inc. San Francisco, CA, USA. 1999.

[Klei99] Kleinberg, J.M. (1999) "Authoritative sources in a hyperlinked environment", *J. ACM*, Vol. 46, No. 5, pp.604--632.

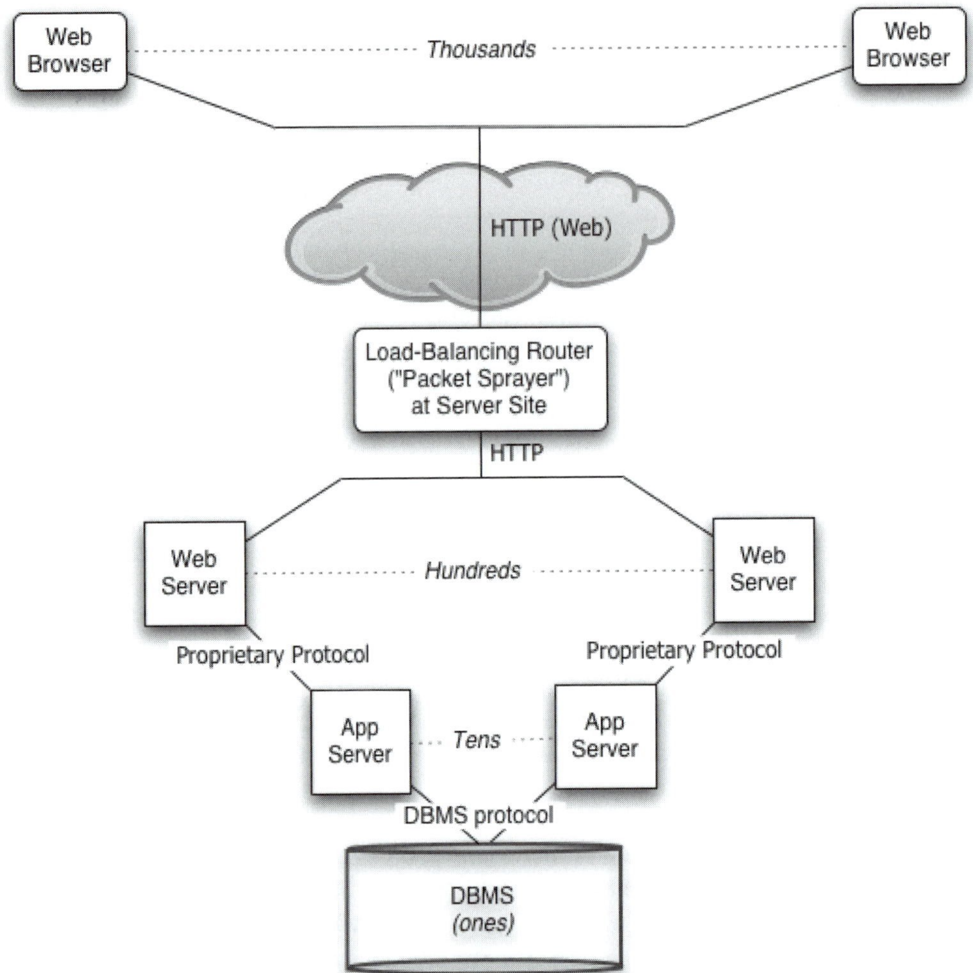

Figure 9.1: A Typical Web Application Architecture

Combining Systems and Databases: A Search Engine Retrospective

Eric A. Brewer
University of California at Berkeley

Although a search engine manages a great deal of data and responds to queries, it is not accurately described as a "database" or DMBS. We believe that it represents the first of many application-specific data systems built by the systems community that must exploit the principles of databases without necessarily using the (current) database implementations. In this paper, we present how a search engine should have been designed in hindsight. Although much of the material has not been presented before, the contribution is not in the specific design, but rather in the combination of principles from the largely independent disciplines of "systems" and "databases." Thus we present the design using the ideas and vocabulary of the database community as a model of how to design data-intensive systems. We then draw some conclusions about the application of database principles to other "out of the box" data-intensive systems.

1 Introduction

Search engines (SEs) are arguably the largest data management systems in the world; although there are larger databases in total storage there is nothing close in query volume. A modern search engine handles over 3 billion documents, involving on the order of 10TB of data, and handles upwards of 150 million queries per day, with peaks of several thousand queries per second.

This retrospective is based primarily on almost nine years of work on the Inktomi search engine, from the summer of 1994 through the spring of 2003. It also reflects some the general issues and approaches of other major search engines — in particular, those of Alta Vista, Infoseek and Google — although their actual specifics might differ greatly from the examples here.

Although queries tend to be short, there are more than ten million different words in nearly all languages. This is a challenge for two reasons. First, implies tracking and ranking ten million distinct words in three billion documents including the position and relative importance (e.g. title words) of every word. Second, with so few words per query, most queries returns thousands of hits and ranking these hits becomes the primary challenge.

Finally, search engines must be highly available and fresh, two complex and challenging data management issues. Downtime contributes directly to lost revenue and customer churn. Freshness is the challenge of keeping the index up to date with the data, nearly all of which is remote and relatively awkward to access. Most data is "crawled" using the HTTP protocol and some automation, although there is also some data exchange via XML.

Despite the size and complexity of these systems, they make almost no use of DBMS systems. There are many reasons for this, which we cover at the end, but the core hypothesis here is that, looking back, search engines should have used the *principles* of databases, but not the artifacts, and that other novel data-intensive systems should do the same (covered in Section 8).

These principles include:

Top-Down Design: The traditional systems methodology is "bottom up" in order to deliver capabilities to unknown applications. However, DBMSs are designed "top down", starting with the desired semantics (e.g. ACID) and developing the mechanisms to implement those semantics. SEs are also "whole" designs in this way; the semantics are different (covered below), but the mechanisms should follow from the semantics.

Data Independence: Data exists in sets without pointers. This allows evolution of representation and storage, and simplifies recovery and fault tolerance.

Declarative Query Language: the use of language to define queries that says "what" to return not "how" to compute it. The absence of "how" is the freedom that enables powerful query optimizations. We do not however use SQL (a DBMS artifact), but we do use the structure of a DBMS, with a query parser and rewriter, a query optimizer, and a query executor. We also define a logical query plan separate from the physical query plan.

The fundamental problem with using a DBMS for a search engine is that there is a semantic mismatch. The practical problem was that they were remarkably slow: experiments we performed in 1996 on Informix, which had cluster support, were an order of magnitude slower than the hand-built prototype, primarily due to the amount of specialization that we could apply (see Section 8). Most modern databases now directly support text search, which is sufficient for most search applications, although probably not for Yahoo! or Google.[1]

The semantics for a DBMS start with the goals of consistent, durable data, codified in the ideas of ACID transactions [GR97]. However, ACID transactions are not the right semantics for search engines.

First, as with other online services, there is a preference for high availability over consistency. The CAP Theorem [FB99,GL02] shows that a shared-data system must choose at most two of the following three properties: consistency, availability, and tolerance to partitions. This implies that for a wide-area system you have to choose between consistency and availability (in the presence of faults), and SEs choose availability, while DBMSs choose consistency.[2] In addition, the index is *always* stale to some degree, since updates to sites do not immediately affect the index. The explicit goal of freshness is to reduce the degree of inconsistency.

Second, SEs can avoid a general-purpose update mechanism, which makes isolation trivial. In particular, queries never cause updates, they are all read only. This implies query handling (almost) never deals with atomicity, isolation, or durability. Instead, updates are limited to atomic replacement of tables (covered in Section 5.2), and only that code deals with atomicity and isolation. Durability is even easier, since the SE is never the master copy: any lost data can generally be rebuilt from local copies or even recrawled (which is how it is refreshed anyway).

We start with an overview of the top-down design, followed by coverage of the query plan and implementation in Sections 3 and 4. Section 5 looks at updates, Section 6 at fault tolerance and availability, and Section 7 at a range of other issues. Finally, we take a broader look at data-intensive systems in Section 8.

2 Overview

In a traditional database, the focus is on a general-purpose framework for a wide variety of queries with much of the effort expended on data consistency in the presence of concurrent updates. Here we focus on supporting many concurrent read-only queries, with very little variation in the range of queries, and we focus on availability more than consistency.

These constraints lead to an architecture that uses an essentially static database to serve all of the read-only queries, and a large degree of offline work to build and rebuild the static databases. The primary advantage of moving nearly everything offline is that it greatly simplifies the online server and thus improves availability, scalability and cost.

We believe that most highly available servers should follow this "snapshot" architecture — the server uses a simple snapshot of the data, while most work, such as indexing, can be done offline without concern for availability. For example, any work done offline can be started and stopped at will, has a simple "start over" model for recovery, and in general is very low stress to modify and operate since these efforts are not visible to end users.

2.1 Crawl, Index, Serve

The first step is to "crawl" the documents, which amounts to visiting pages in essentially the same way as an end user. The *crawler* outputs collections of documents, typically a single file with a map at the beginning and thousands of concatenated documents. The use of large files improves system throughput, amortizes seek and directory operations, and simplifies management.[3] The crawler must keep track of which pages have been crawled or are in progress, how often to recrawl, and must have some understanding of mirrors, dynamic pages, and MIME types.

The *indexer* parses and interprets collections of documents. Its output is a portion of the static database, called a *chunk*, that reflects all of the scoring and normalization for those documents. In general, the goal is to move work from the (online) web servers to the indexer, so that the servers have the absolute minimum amount of work to do per query. For example, the indexer does all of the work of scoring, generating typically a single normalized score for every word in every document. The indexer does many other document analyses as well: determining the primary language and geographical region, checking for spam, and tracking incoming and outgoing links (used for scoring). One of the more interesting and challenging tasks is to track all of the *anchor text* for a document, which is the hyperlink text in *all other* (!) documents that point to this document.

Finally, the *server* simply executes queries against a collection of chunks. It performs query parsing and rewriting, query optimization, and query execution. Since the only update operation is the atomic replacement of a chunk (covered in Section 5), there are no locks, no isolation issues, and no need for concurrency control for queries.

2.2 Queries

Conceptually, a query defines some words and properties that a matching document should or should not contain. A *document* is normally a web page, but could also be a news article or an e-mail message. Each document is presumed unique, has a unique ID (DocID), a URL and some summary information.

Documents contain *words* and have *properties*. We distinguish words from properties in that words have a

---

1: As an aside, the databases were also very expensive. However, as we were among the first to build large web-database systems, we were charged per "seat", which in the fine print came down to distinct UNIX user IDs. But *all* of the end users were multiplexed onto one user ID, so this was quite reasonable! Later the database companies changes the definition of "user" and this trick was no longer valid.

2: Wide-area databases vary in their choice between availability and consistency. Those that choose availability operate some locations with stale data in the presence of partitions and generally have a small window that is stale (inconsistent) during normal operation (typically 30 seconds) [SAS+96]. Those that choose consistency must make one side of a partition unavailable until the partition is repaired.

3: In theory, a DBMS could be used for document storage, but it would be a poor fit. Documents have a single writer, are only dealt with in large groups, and have essentially no concurrent access. See the Google File System [GGL03] for more on these issues.

Property	Meaning
lang:english	doc is in english
cont:java	contains java applet
cont:image	contains an image
at:berkeley.edu	domain suffix is berkeley.edu
is:news	is a news article

Table 1: Example Properties

score (for this document) and properties are boolean (present or absent in the document). Table 1 lists some examples. A query *term* is a word or a property.

Simple queries are just a list of terms that matching documents must contain. Property matching is absolute: a matching document must meet all properties. Word matching is relative: documents receive relative scores based on how well they match the words.

Complex queries include boolean expressions of terms based on AND, OR and NOT. Boolean expressions for properties are straightforward, but those for words are not. In particular, the expression (NOT *word*) should not affect the scoring; it is really a property.

We cover scoring in more detail in the appendix, but for now we will use simple definitions. A query is just a set of terms:

$$\text{Query } Q \equiv \{w_1, w_2, .., w_k\} \tag{1}$$

The *score* of a document d for query Q is the sum of an overall score for the document and a score for each term in the query:

$$\begin{aligned}\text{Score}(Q, d) &\equiv \text{Quality}(d)\\ &+ \sum_i \text{Score}(w_i, d)\end{aligned} \tag{2}$$

The quality term is independent of the query words and reflects things like length (shorter is generally better), popularity, incoming links, quality of the containing site, and external reviews. The score for each word is a determined at index time and depends on frequency and location (such as in the title or headings, or bold).

There are some important non-obvious uses for words. In general, any property of a document that is not boolean is represented by a *metaword*. Metawords are artificial words that we add to a document to encode an affine property. For example, to encode how frequently a document contains images (rather than just yes or no), we add a metaword whose score reflects the frequency. You can use this trick to encode many other properties, such as overall document quality, number of incoming or outgoing links, freshness, complexity, reading level, etc. Implicitly, these metrics are all on the same scale, but we can change the weighting at query time to control how to mix them.

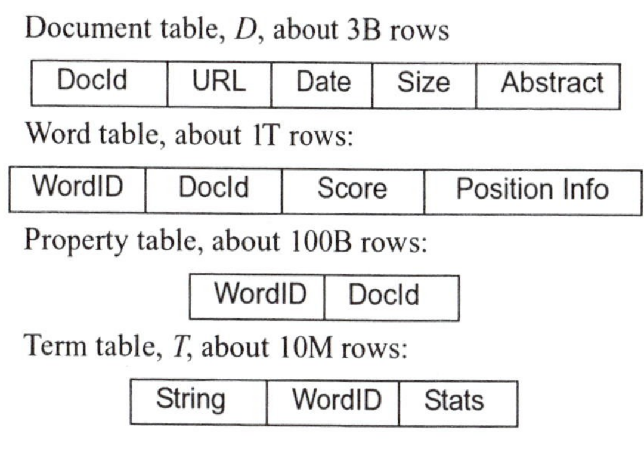

Figure 1: Basic Schema

3 Logical Query Plan

Given this simplified scoring, we turn to how to map a query into a query plan. This section looks at the logical query plan and the next section looks at the physical operators and plan implementation.

In the original development of this work, we were not cognizant that we were defining a declarative query language and that it should have a query plan, an optimizer, and a rewriter, and that we should cleanly separate the logical and physical query operators and plans. We did know we needed a parser. The absence of this view led to a very complicated parser that did ad-hoc versions of query rewriting and planning, and some optimization. The use of an abstract logical query plan is one of the important principles to take from database systems, and hence we retrospectively present the work based on a clean logical query plan.

For simplicity, we will limit the schema to three (large) tables: document info, word data and property data. Figure 1 shows the schema. Tables that we ignore include those for logging (one row per search), advertising, and users (for personalization); we talk about some of these in Section 7.

To simplify dealing with words and properties, we conceptually use an integer key for each word, the WordID. The term table, T, maps from the string of the term to the WordID for that word, and also keeps statistics about the word (or property). The stats are used for both scoring and to compute the *selectivity* for query optimization.[4] The simplest useful stat is the number of rows in the table, which tells you how common the term is in the corpus; high counts imply high selectivity and lower scores (since the word is common). Note that the

4: Selectivity is the fraction of the input that ends up in the output, and is thus a real number in the interval [0,1]. Ideally, a query plan should apply joins with low selectivity first, since they reduce the data for future joins. With multi-way equijoins (and semijoins), this is less important since we aim to do them all at once. Of great confusion to many is that *high* selectivity numbers imply the operation is *not* very "selective" in the normal English usage of the word.

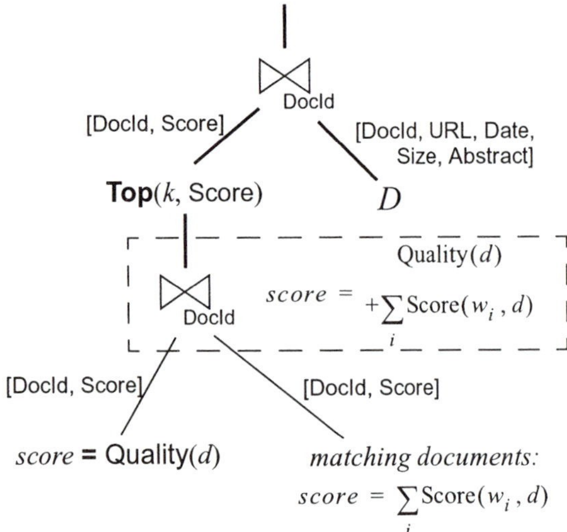

Figure 2: The General Query Plan
After finding the set of matching documents and their scores, the **Top** operator passes up the top k results (in order) to an equijoin that adds in the document information.

Operator	Meaning
e AND e	Equijoin with scoring
e OR e	Full outer join with scoring
e FILTER p	Semijoin: filter e by p
p AND p	Equijoin without scoring
p OR p	Full outer join without scoring
NOT p	s antijoin p (invert the set s)
NOT e	s antijoin e (invert, omit score)

Table 2: Logical Operators

```
prop:  prop AND prop
       | prop OR prop
       | NOT prop
       | NOT expr
       | property
```

term table is only used during query planning and is never referenced in the query itself.

Figure 2 shows the general plan for all queries. The fact that all queries have essentially the same plan is a significant simplification over general-purpose databases, and a key design advantage. The equijoins ($\bowtie_{\text{DocId}}$) join rows from each side that match on DocId, resulting in an output row that has the union of the columns. We refer to the top equijoin as the "document join," since it joins the top results with their document data.

The Top(k, *column*) operator returns the top k items from the input set ordered on *column*; it is not a common database operator, although it appears in some extensions to SQL and in the literature [CG99,CK98]. The input to Top is the set of fully scored documents, which combines the document quality score with the sum of the word scores from the matching documents. Top can be implemented in O(n) time using insertion sort into a k-element array.[5]

The next task is to produce the set of matching documents and their scores. Applying the top-down principle, we design a small query language for this application, rather than using SQL. Here is the BNF for one possible query language:

```
expr:  expr AND expr
       | expr OR expr
       | expr FILTER prop
       | word
```

There are seven corresponding logical operators as shown in Table 2. In this particular grammar, *expr* nodes have scores and *prop* nodes do not. The only way to join an *expr* and a *prop* is through the FILTER operator, which filters the word list on the left with the property list on the right. Note that the logical negation for an *expr*, NOT e, is a *prop* and not an *expr*. This is because there is no score for the documents not in the set. This implies that it is not possible to ask for "-foo" as a top-level query (i.e. the set of all documents that do not contain "foo"). In practice, we actually do allow properties and negated expressions as top-level queries, which are useful for debugging. Note that the Top operator (with query optimization) saves us from having to return (nearly) the whole database.

Normal queries are just a sequence of words with the implicit operator AND between them. For example, the query:

```
san francisco
```

maps to (san AND francisco). For properties:

```
bay area lang:english
```

maps to ((bay AND area) FILTER lang:english), which is the set of english-language documents that contain both words. A minus sign preceding a word normally means negation, so that:

```
bay area -hudson
```

maps to ((bay AND area) FILTER NOT hudson).

More complex queries usually come from an "Advanced Search" page with a form-based UI, or from a test interface that is amenable to scripting. We will use the parenthesized representation directly for these queries.

4 Query Implementation

Given the scoring functions and the logical operators, we next look at query optimization and the map-

5: Insertion sort is normally O(n lg n), but since we only keep a constant number of results, k, we have a constant amount of work for each of the n insertions.

ping of logical operators onto the physical operators. We start by defining the physical operators and then show how to map the logical operators and some possible optimizations. We finish with parallelization of the plan for execution on a cluster.

4.1 Access Methods and Physical Operators

There is really only one kind of access method: sequential scan of a sorted *inverted index*, which is just a sorted list of all of the documents that contain a given term. For properties, this is just the sorted list of documents; for expressions we add the score for each document. A useful invariant is to make expressions a subclass of properties, so that an expression list can be used for any argument expecting a property list. For example, this means we do not need a separate negation operator for expressions and properties. We cover the physical layout of the tables in Section 4.3, when we discuss implementation on a cluster.

An unusual aspect of the physical plan is that we cache all of the intermediate values (for use by other queries), and do not pipeline the plan. Caching works particularly well, since there are no updates in normal operation (updates are covered in Section 5). Given that we keep all intermediate results, there is no space savings for pipelining. Pipelining could still be used to reduce query latency, but we care more about throughput than latency, and throughput is higher without pipelining, due to lower per-tuple overhead and better (memory) cache behavior. Thus, we increase the latency of a single query that is not cached, but reduce the average latency (with caching) and increase throughput. [6]

Because the lists are sorted, binary operators become merging operations: every join is a simple (presorted) merge join. In fact, there is no reason to do binary operators: every join is a multiway merge join. The use of multiway joins is a win because it reduces the depth of the plan and thus the number of caching and scan steps (remember that intermediate results are not pipelined). In addition, it is useful to move negation into the multiway join as well, since the antijoin is a simple variation of a merge join. A consequence of this is that for every input to the multiway join, we add a boolean argument to indicate the positive or negative version of the input.

This leads us to have only four physical operators:

OR($e_1, e_2, \ldots e_k$)$\rightarrow$ *expr*

Compute the full outer multiway join, with scoring. We have left out the boolean flags; we will use "$\neg e$" as the input when we mean the negation.

ORp($p_1, p_2, \ldots p_k$)$\rightarrow$ *prop*

Multiway full outer join without scoring.

ANDp($p_1, p_2, \ldots p_k$)$\rightarrow$ *prop*

Multiway inner join without scoring

FILTER($e_1, e_2, \ldots e_k$)($p_1 \ldots p_n$) $\rightarrow$ *expr*

Multiway inner join with scoring for the expressions and no scoring for the properties.

Most queries map onto a one-deep plan using FILTER. It is essentially an AND of all of its inputs, with only the expressions used to compute the score. It implements (e AND e) if there are no properties. Although it could also subsume (p AND p), it is better to use ANDp, since the latter returns a property list rather than an expression list which avoids space for unused scores. Figure 3 shows some example queries with their logical and physical plans.

One nice property of using multiway joins is that it mitigates the need for estimating selectivity. Selectivity estimation is normally needed to compute the size of an input to another operator; increasing the fan in of an (inner) join limits the work to the actual size of the smallest input and thus decreases the need for estimates. For example, for FILTER and ANDp, the output is limited by the size of the smallest input (lowest selectivity). Thus selectivity only matters when we cannot flatten a subgraph to use a multiway join.

4.2 Query Optimizer

The optimizer has three primary tasks: map the logical query (including negations), exploit cached results, and minimize the number of joins by using large multiway joins. As expected these optimizations often conflict, leading us to either heuristics or simple models (as done in traditional optimizers). The basic heuristic is to focus first on caching, second on flattening (using larger multiway joins), and third on everything else.

The focus on caching all subexpressions leads to the atypical decision of using a top-down optimizer [Gra95], rather than the bottom-up style that is standard for traditional databases [Sel+79]. Although either could be made to work, the top-down approach makes it easy to find the highest cached subexpression: we simply check the cache as we expand downward. The bottom-up

```
"bay area lang:english"
⇩
(bay AND area) FILTER lang:english
⇩
FILTER(bay, area)(lang:english)
- - - - - - - - - - - - - - - - -
"san francisco contains:image
-contains:flash"
⇩
((san AND francisco) FILTER contains:image)
FILTER (NOT contains:flash)
⇩
FILTER(san, francisco)(contains:image,
¬contains:flash)
```

Figure 3: Two example queries and their logical and physical plans

6: In theory, we could choose to not cache some intermediate results that we believe unlikely to be used again, and pipeline the results, but this is not worth the extra complexity.

approach implies building many partial solutions as part of dynamic programming that are unnecessary if they are part of a cached subexpression: that is, you build up best subtrees before you realize that they are cached. Both approaches typically require building partial solutions and exploring parts of the space that are not used for the final plan.

The basic mapping of logical operators is straightforward, with the only subtlety being how to map negations:

```
a AND ¬b ⇨ FILTER(a)(¬b)

¬a AND ¬b ⇨ ANDp(¬a, ¬b)

a OR ¬b ⇨ OR(a, ¬b)

¬a OR ¬b ⇨ ORp(¬a, ¬b)
```

Note the use of ANDp and ORp when the output is a property and not an expression.

Given a correct tree of physical operators, the next step is to optimize it, which consists mostly of flattening the tree to use fewer but wider joins. The first step is to flatten all chains of pure AND or pure OR, making liberal use of the commutative and associative properties. For example:

```
(((a AND b) AND c) OR d)
   ⇨ OR(AND(a, b, c), d)
FILTER(a, FILTER(b)(c))(d)
   ⇨ FILTER(a, b)(c, d)
```

We can do more complicated forms of flattening by using DeMorgan's Law, which allows us to convert between and AND and OR operations. The basic conversion is:

```
a AND b ⇨ ¬(¬a OR ¬b)

a OR b ⇨ ¬(¬a AND ¬b)
```

An example use for flattening:

```
a AND b AND NOT (c OR d) ⇨
   AND(a, b, AND(¬c, ¬d)) ⇨
   FILTER(a, b)(¬c, ¬d)
```

However, we have to be careful to keep score information when applying DeMorgan's Law. For example, is (a OR ¬b) an expression or a property? If it is an expression, not all of the elements of the set have scores and we must make some up (typically zero). If it is a property, then we forfeit the scoring information (from a) for later expressions. Either policy can be made to work, although more flattening is possible when treating this case as a property, since otherwise (a OR ¬b) ≠ ¬ANDp(¬a,b).

The current heuristic is to flatten completely before looking for cached subexpressions, which is part of the general philosophy of using canonical representations for trees to ensure that only one form of a subexpression could appear in the cache. As a consequence, for a large multi-way join, we must look for subsets of the terms in the cache. We first look for the whole *k*-way join, then for each *k-1* subset, then each *k-2* subset, until we get to individual terms. Thus, if FILTER(a,b,e) and FILTER(d,f) were in cache (but larger subsets were not), we might map:

```
FILTER(a, b, c, d, e, f) ⇨
   FILTER(FILTER(a,b,e), c, FILTER(d,f))
```

One useful aspect of the cache is that we can keep the size of the cached set as part of its metadata, which allows us to exploit selectivity. In particular, given two overlapping sets in cache that each represent *k* terms, we choose the one with the smaller set size, since it is probably more selective. In the above example, if FILTER(a,c,d) was also in cache, we would select between it and FILTER(a,b,e) based either on selectivity, or the degree of caching of the remaining terms, or both. It is in the exploration of the remaining terms that the top-down approach may explore parts of the plan space that are not used.

As with traditional databases there are many other possible optimizations with increasing complexity, which we ignore here. To give the flavor of these, consider in the example above if c was not in cache, but FILTER(c)(e) was, then the latter could be used instead, since e is part of the larger conjunctive join, and ANDing it twice won't affect the final set. However, FILTER(c,e)() is not an acceptable replacement, since the score for e would be counted twice.[7]

4.3 Implementation on a Cluster

Once we have the optimized tree, we must map the query onto the cluster. The approach we take is to exploit symmetry, which simplifies design and administration of the cluster. In particular, the bulk of every query goes to every node and executes the same code on different data, as in the SPMD model from parallel computing [DGNP88].

From the database perspective, this means a mixture of replication for small tables and horizontal fragmentation (also known as "range partitioning") for large tables. In particular, the document, word and property tables are all horizontally fragmented by DocID, so that a self-contained set of documents (with a contiguous ranges of DocIDs) resides on each node. This structure simplifies updates to documents, and also makes it easy to mix nodes of different power, since we can give more powerful nodes more documents. The term table, which maps term strings to WordIDs, is replicated on each node, and we use global values for the WordIDs, so that WordIDs can be used in physical queries instead of the strings.

An important point is that the DocID is essentially random relative to the URL (such as a 128-bit MD5 or CRC), which means that documents are randomly spread across the cluster, which is important for load balancing and caching.

7: Under overload conditions, this might be an acceptable replacement, since it will be a small reranking of the same set of documents, and the scoring function is always magic to some degree anyway.

The word and property tables are (pre)sorted by WordID for that node's set of DocIDs, so that they are ready for sorted merge joins. We maintain a hash index on WordID for these tables to locate the beginning of the inverted index for each term. It is somewhat easier to think of the word and property tables as sets of "sub-tables", one for each WordID. This is because each sub-table is independently compressed and cached, as described below; the hash index on WordID is thus really in index of the sub-tables, and keeps track of whether or not they are in memory.

Initially, using a load balancer, a query is routed to exactly one node, called the *master* for that query. Most nodes will be the master for some queries and a *follower* for the others. The master node computes and optimizes the query plan, issues the query to all other nodes (the followers), and collates the results. Each follower computes *its* top k results, and the master then computes the top k overall. Finally, the last equijoin with the document table, D, is done via a distributed hash join with one lookup for each of the k results (which may also be cached locally). This is really a "fetch matches" join in the style of Mackert and Lohman [ML86], which means that you simply fetch the matching tuples on demand rather than doing any kind of movement or repartitioning of the table.

Using the master to compute the query plan has some subtle issues. The primary advantage is that the plan is computed only once, and all followers execute only physical queries. However, the cache contents are not guaranteed to be the same, since different nodes may have different amounts of cache space. In practice, the cache size is always proportional to the size of the fragment, so the contents usually agree, but not always. For example, a cache entry would be larger than usual if that node has more occurrences of a particular word, which may force something else out; however, since documents are spread randomly this effect tends to even out. Nonetheless, a follower may have to recompute something that the master expected to be in cache.

4.4 Other Optimizations

In addition to traditional database optimizations, search engines exploit some unusual tricks that merit discussion. We cover three of them here.

One of the most important optimizations is compression of inverted indices. Although compression has been covered in the literature [CGK01], it is not widely used in any major DBMS. It makes more sense for a search engine for a few reasons. First, there is no random access for these sub-tables, they are always scanned in their entirety as part of a sorted merge join. (The exception is the document table, which is random access and is not compressed.) Second, there are no updates to the tables, only whole replacement, so there is no issue of how to update a compressed table. The simplest good compression scheme is to use relative numbering for DocIDs, since they are in sorted order and the density may be high. This requires many fewer bits than the 32+ it would require to store the whole DocID. Similarly, it is important to make good use of all of the scoring bits, which can be done by a transformation of the scoring function.

It turns out that the compression not only increases the effective disk bandwidth, but also the cache size. By keeping the in-memory representation compressed, we increase the cache hit rate at the expense of having to decompress the table on every use. This turns out to be an excellent tradeoff, since modern processors can easily do the decompression on the fly without limiting the off-chip memory bandwidth, and the cost of a cache miss is millions of cycles (since it goes to disk).

A related optimization is preloading the cache on startup. This turns out to be pretty simple to do and greatly reduces the mean-time-to-repair for a node that goes down (for whatever reason). In the case of a graceful shutdown of the process, the node can write out its cache contents, and even reuse the memory via the file cache when the new process starts. For an unexpected shut down, the process can use an older snapshot of the cache, but will have to page it in, which is still faster that recomputing it (which requires reading all of the constituent tables). The primary limitation is that the snapshot must match the current version of the database; both are marked with version numbers for this reason.

Finally, the use of a master node enables a powerful kind of optimization based on the classic A* search algorithm (from AI) [RN02], which employs a conservative heuristic to prune the search space. In particular, instead of simply sending out the query, the master executes the query locally first (which adds some latency), and computes its top k local results, which it will have compute at some point anyway. The score of the kth local result is a conservative lower bound on the scores of the overall top k results. In particular, followers need not pursue any subquery that cannot beat this lower bound. For example, for a term in a multiway join, there is typically some score below which you need not perform the join, since even with the best values for the other terms the end score will not make the top k. Similarly, by keeping track of the best score for the whole table, we may be able to eliminate whole terms.

5 Updates

Although search engines are clearly read mostly, at some point we actually need to update the data. One huge benefit of the top-down strategy is that we can exploit our complete control over the timing and scope of updates.

We follow a few basic principles for updates. First, nodes are independent, so we can update one node without concern for the impact on other nodes. Replicas are clearly an exception to this, since they must be updated together, but their group is independent of other groups. Second, we only update whole tables and not individual rows. This means that we never insert, update or delete a row, and that we need at most one lock for the whole table. Third, updates should be atomic with respect to queries; that is, updates always occur between queries.

To simplify updates, we define a chunk to be the unit for atomic updates. Earlier we mentioned that the tables are partitioned by DocID among the nodes, but it is more accurate to say that the databases are partitioned into chunks, and that a node contains a contiguous range of chunks. Each chunk is a self-contained collection of documents with their word and property tables.

In practice, it is useful to split the cluster into multiple databases, called *partitions*. This allows each partition to have its own policies for replication and freshness. A query still goes to all nodes (of all partitions), and the DocIDs and WordIDs are still globally unique. For replicated partitions, which normally have two replicas, each node has the same chunks as it replica(s), and only one member of the replica group receives any given query in the normal case.

The next two sections looks at the creation and installation of chunks, and the following two look at more complex types of updates.

5.1 Crawling and Indexing

The first step for an update is to get the new content, which is usually done by crawling: visiting every document to verify that we have the current version, and retrieving a new version if we do not. Indexing is the process of converting a collection of documents into a chunk, and includes parsing and scoring, and the management of metadata, such as tracking incoming and outgoing links.

It is easiest to think of a chunk as a *range* of DocID values, which means that a chunk does not have a specific size per se, but rather an average size. This definition simplifies the addition and removal of documents from a chunk, since there is no effect on neighboring chunks. As a database grows, the average chunk size will grow until it reaches some threshold at which point it may be split into two or more chunks.

The simplest kind of crawl simply refreshes all of the documents in one chunk, and then reindexes them. Some documents may have to be recrawled multiple times if their site is down, or they can be left out for this version and recrawled next time, although eventually they are permanently removed.

The refresh rate is a property of the partition, and thus a property of all of its chunks. News partitions may be updated every fifteen minutes, while slow-changing content, such as home pages, may be refreshed every two weeks (or longer).

Document discovery, which is the process of finding new documents for the database, is primarily a separate process, although outgoing links are the main source of new documents. A separate database tracks metadata about all of the sites, including new links and global properties about spam sites, mirrors, paid content, etc. New documents can be added to existing chunks when they are next refreshed, or may be added to a new chunk in a separate partition, called the "new" partition.

Each chunk has a version number that is unique and monotonically increasing, typically a sequence number. The version number is used for cache invalidation, content debugging, and data rollback.

5.2 Atomic Updates

Once we have a new chunk, we need to install it atomically. Conceptually, this is done by updating a version vector [Cha+81], with one element for each chunk.

In the absence of caching this is trivial: it is sufficient to close and reopen the corresponding files. It is slightly better to open the new files first, which allows the existing queries to finish on the old version, while new queries go to the new version. When the last pre-update query completes, the old version files can be closed (and later deleted).

With caching, we must also invalidate the cache entries for the old version. The simplest implementation of caching uses a separate cache for each chunk, in which case we can just invalidate the whole cache for that chunk. This works pretty well; other chunks keep their caches intact and the overall performance impact is thus limited. Alternatively, caches can be unified for all of the chunks on a node, which improves performance, but chunk replacement invalidates the whole cache.

The replacement of a specific chunk does not require the node to be stopped. Rather by using UNIX signals, we can use a management process to install chunks remotely. We also use signals to initiate a rollback to the previous version of a chunk. With some automation, the management process can update all of the chunks in a smooth rolling upgrade, and likewise update all of the nodes. Updating chunks incrementally limits the impact of rebuilding the cache, since most of the cache remains intact; this makes it feasible to keep up with the ongoing load during an update.

5.3 Real-time Deletion and Updates

So far, we have said that we do not do updates to individual records. This is not strictly true, but is the right overall view, since the mechanism described here is relatively heavyweight. There are some occasions where it is useful to update a specific document immediately. For example, a document known to be illegal may need to be removed immediately upon discovery. For this purpose, we add a mechanism for real-time deletion, which also enables real-time updates.

The general approach to deletion is to *add* a row that means "item deleted" that we can then use as the right-hand side of an antijoin to cull the document from a set. For real-time deletion, we add a very small table (usually empty) to every chunk, which contains the list of deleted documents. It is a property table, where the property it represents is "has been deleted", and we apply it as a filter to every query. Since we add this filter before optimization, it will be optimized as well. In the normal case the top-most operator is already a FILTER, and the optimizer can just add the inverse of this table as an extra property. Thus to delete a document in real time, we simply add a row to this special table, and then atomically update the whole table (as with regular updates).

Given this mechanism, we can also do real-time updates. An update involves inserting the new version into a different chunk (usually in the "new" partition), and deleting the old version. Just doing the insert is not sufficient, since the master will see both versions, and may return both or the even just the old one (if it thinks they are duplicates).

5.4 System-Wide Updates

Occasionally, we perform updates that affect all of the nodes. The most common example is a change to the scoring algorithm, which makes the old scores incomparable with the new scores. Similarly, we may change the schema or the global ID mechanism. In such cases, we need to ensure that masters only use compatible followers.

The approaches to this are covered better elsewhere [Bre01], but the easiest solution is to update all of the nodes at once. By staging the updated versions ahead of time (i.e. loading them onto the disks in the background before the update), and using some automation, it is possible to update all of the nodes at once with less than a minute of downtime. The cold caches will perform poorly until they warm up, but since this kind of update is only done when the load is low, this is not a problem in practice.

6 Fault Tolerance

The primary goal of fault tolerance for search engines is high availability. We use a variety of techniques and optimizations to achieve this, few of which are novel, but together form a consistent strategy for availability.

The first task is to decide exactly what needs to be highly available, since there is always a significant cost to provide it. First, the snapshot approach means that all of the indexing and crawling process is independent to the server and thus need not be highly available. The only fault tolerance requirement for these elements is idempotency, to ensure that we can simply restart failed processes.

In addition, most documents are not worth replicating for high availability. In fact, most documents will never appear in a search result at all, but alas we cannot reliably predict which these are (or we would keep zero copies). Thus some partitions are replicated and some are not, and faults in non-replicated chunks or nodes simply reduce the database size temporarily. However, the use of pseudo-random DocIDs means that we lose a random subset of the documents in a partition, rather than, say, all the documents from one site. A typical policy might replicate popular sites and paid content.

6.1 Disk Faults

The most common fault is a disk failure, either of a block or a whole disk. A block fault only affects one chunk, but a disk failure might affect more than one. In both cases, new copies of the chunks can be loaded onto other blocks or disks in the background, and then atomically switched in. Note that chunks are never updated in place even in normal operation, so the replacement chunk is really just an atomic update to the same version. Nodes are limited by disk seeks, not space, so there is always plenty of free space for staging. In fact, given that space is cheap and staging areas are useful, it is worthwhile to cluster the active chunks onto contiguous tracks, which reduces the seek time during normal operation; other parts of the disk are used for staging.

Failed disks are left in active nodes until some convenient time, typically the scheduled maintenance window for that node. We replace whole nodes only, and then sort out the failed disks offline. This simplifies the repair process, as we always have spare nodes ready to swap in, which are then loaded with the proper chunks and put back online. Originally, we used RAID to hide disk faults, as most DBMSs do, but found this to be expensive and unnecessary, and those disks still needed some process for replacement.

For replicated chunks, if this node is the secondary, nothing special happens during recovery. If it is the primary, than the other replica becomes the primary and handles the queries until the local copy is restored. For caching purposes, it is best to have only one replica handle queries in the normal case (the primary), with the other replica idle. For load balancing, each member of a replica group will be the primary for some chunks and the secondary for others. The are lots of ways to determine which node should be the primary by default, but any simple (uniform) function of the chunk ID suffices.

6.2 Follower Faults

For node failures, we separate the case of followers from that of masters. A failed follower takes down all of its chunks. A master will detect this failure, if it doesn't already know, via a timeout. It will then either continue without the data in the unreplicated case, or contact the secondary in the replicated case. An important optimization is to spread the secondary copies across the partition, so that we spread out the redirected load that occurs during a fault [Bre01]. This can be done by "chained declustering" [HD90], but there are many suitable placements. For example, a typical partition might have ten nodes, 2-way replication, and nine primary chunks per node. Ideally, the nine secondaries that match the nine primaries for a given node, should be on nine different nodes, so that after a failure we have evenly spread out the load for the secondaries. Thus a replicated partition should have more nodes than the degree of replication, and a enough chunks per node to enable fine-grain load balancing after a failure.

Failed nodes are typically replaced later the same day, but they can be replaced at any time. The risk is that the secondary might fail before then.

6.3 Master Faults

Since masters are interchangeable, the basic strategy is to reissue the query on a different master. Originally, the master was also the web server, which meant that its failure was externally visible. A layer-7 switch [Fou01] can hide failed nodes for new queries, but it typically cannot reissue the outstanding queries at the time of the failure. For that, we depended on the end-user to hit reload, which they are remarkably happy to do.

The current approach separates the web server from the master, and the web server detects the failure and reissues failed queries to a new master (much like the relationship between masters and followers). This "smart client" approach [C+97] is strictly better for two reasons. First, the retry is transparent to the end user, much like a transactional queue [BHM90]. Second, it allows us to reissue the query to a different data center, which facilitates global load balancing and disaster recovery (covered below). The web servers are often owned by partners and are thus located in other data centers anyway. They use a client-side library within the web server to execute search queries, and the recovery and redirection code is part of this library.

6.4 Graceful Degradation

An important challenge for Internet servers that is not typically present for DBMSs is that of overload. There are many documented cases of huge load spikes due to human-scale events such as earthquakes or marketing successes [Mov99,WS00]. These spikes are too large for over-provisioning, which means we must assume that we will be overloaded and must degrade the quality of service gracefully. Overload detection is based on queue lengths: when queues become too long, the system enters overload mode until they drop below some low-water mark.

The details are beyond the scope of this paper, but there are two basic strategies that we use for graceful degradation (see [Bre01]). The first and simplest is to make the database smaller dynamically, which we can do by leaving out some chunks. This both reduces processing time per query and increases the effective cache size for the remaining data. Each chunk we take out increases our effective capacity by some amount, and we can continue this process until we are no longer saturated.

Second, we can decline to execute some queries based on their cost, which is a form of admission control. The naive policy simply denies expensive queries, such as those with many search terms. A more sophisticated version denies queries probabilistically, so that repeated queries will eventually get through, even if they are expensive.

6.5 Disaster Recovery

Disaster recovery is the process of recovering a whole data center, which might take considerable time, but should be very rare. So far we have not had any disasters, although we have moved data centers on multiple occasions, while keeping the system up, and thus know that our approach works.

The basic strategy is to combine master redirection and graceful degradation. When a data center fails or becomes unreachable, the client-side library in the web server will detect that the master has failed and will retry another master, probably in the same data center. At some point it will give up on that data center and try an alternate. The number of data centers varies, but the range is 2-10. Important partitions must be replicated at multiple data centers, in addition to local replication.

Although redirection is sufficient for a single query, it would not work in aggregate without automatic graceful degradation. If we simply redirect all queries from one data center to another, the new target will likely be overloaded. (At low load times, it would probably be fine.) Thus, we depend on graceful degradation to increase the capacity of the new data center to handle the load of both centers. Unlike a traditional load spike, which is relatively short lived, this state may persist for a while. Although it is possible to add some real capacity on short notice, full capacity may require major repairs or even the provisioning and setup of new space.

7 Other Topics

In this section we briefly visit a range a search engine challenges that differ from traditional database systems.

7.1 Personalization

Although personalization has become an important part of the web experience, e.g. "My Yahoo!", there is no equivalent in other media and thus search engines were the first systems to run into the problems of large-scale personalization. The first such site was the HotBot search engine, which (originally) allowed users to customize the search interface.

There are two general approaches: cookies and databases. In the cookie approach, user data is stored in a "cookie" and parsed as part of each visit, while the database approach stores only the user ID in the cookie, which it then uses to retrieve the appropriate row from a table. Although the cookie approach appears simpler, it suffers from two serious problems: the data is distributed and generally unreachable, which hinders analysis, and it is difficult to evolve the schema.

Essentially the cookie approach requires that all current and previous schema *overlap in time*, since there is no way to update the schema for a user until they next visit. For example, if the schema has gone through six versions, the current system must be able to handle cookies that use all six schemas, since which version a user follows depends only on the time of *their* last visit (from a given browser), which can be any time in the past. Given the large population of users, every schema will have some number of representatives. This can be addressed with version numbers (stored in the cookie), but remains awkward.

Although we used a DBMS to manage user data, it is actually a mediocre approach, primarily due to cost, complexity and availability. Indeed, there has been substantial work on how to solve this problem more directly, including some support in Enterprise Java Beans (backed by a database), the use a highly available cluster hash table [GBH+00,Gri00], and a new framework specifically for session-state management [LKF04]. Like the search engine itself, this component requires only a single query plan, in this case just a highly available hash table lookup (no joins, ranges, or projections).

7.2 Logging

Search engines, like other large-scale Internet sites, create enormous logs, often over 100GB per day. These logs are used primarily for billing advertisers, but also for improving the quality of the search engine, and debugging. (These are not the kind of logs used for durability in a DBMS.) Log management systems have become their own class of data-intensive systems, and they also do not fit well on top of existing databases. Although this material is covered much better by Adam Sah [Sah02], who worked on the original Inktomi log manager, it is worth some discussion here.

The two primary issues are 1) DBMSs traditionally do not handle large-scale real-time loading of data, and 2) the query language really needs to support regular expressions, relative timestamps, and partial string matches, none of which fit well within SQL. In addition, log records have a different and far simpler update model: logs are append only and log records are (generally) immutable. The concurrency control and fault tolerance decisions are thus quite different from a DBMS.

However, database principles and the top-down approach still apply, and in fact are the right approach. The log system has its own query language and its own optimizations, including compression, caching (of reverse DNS lookups), and parallelization.

7.3 Query Rewriting

As in DBMSs, query rewriting is a powerful and useful tool [PHH92,SJGP90]. In our case, there are two primary values. First and most important, it provides the easiest way to customize a query for a given user or population. For example, for users known to speak a certain language (based on their ISP for example), a rewritten query might increase the ranking of documents in that language or even filter the results for only that language. Similarly, personalization can be used to customize queries for a given user based on collections (e.g. more emphasis on news), topic, complexity, geographical location, etc.

Second, query rewriting is a clean way to encode the *context* of the query. An important direction for search engines is to provide different results based on the context of the query. For example, a query issued from a page about semiconductors that contains the word "chip" probably refers to semiconductors rather than corn chips or the TV show *Chips*. Rewriting the query to include a few terms about the context (with low weight) is one easy way to disambiguate an otherwise ambiguous query.

7.4 Phrase Queries

So far, we have only covered the simplest kinds of queries, those based on words and properties. However, the relative positions of words within a document are of great value for improved ranking. For example, searching for "New York" really should give much higher scores to documents in which the two words are adjacent and in the correct order. There are two general approaches to this problem: tracking proximity and tracking exact word positions.

Proximity techniques boost the scores of documents that have the words "near" each other, but not necessarily adjacent. This is a long-standing technique in information retrieval [Sal89], and there are many approaches. One typical one is to break a document into "pages" of some size and use one bit per page to track which pages contain a given word. "Nearness" is then defined by how many pages contain both words (which is just a bitwise AND). This requires building the bitmaps for every word/document pair, and then matching bitmaps once you know that document contains multiple words from the query.

The second approach is "phrase searching" in which the engine actually tracks every position of every word in every document. Remarkably, current search engines actually do this! Phrase queries are significantly more complex, as you need to do what amounts to a nested merge join for every word in the query. For example, given the sorted lists of positions for the words "New" and "York", you join them using an "off by one" equijoin: output a tuple exactly if the position of "New" is one less than the position of "York". The multiway join for phrases is analogous. Overall, the best ranking occurs by mixing the results of regular scoring, proximity boosts, and phrases.

8 Discussion and Conclusions

Up to now, the focus has been covering the design of a search engine from the perspective of a database system. In this section, we argue that is the right approach for other top-down data-intensive systems, and that such systems should employ the principles of databases if not the artifacts. We cover a few other example systems, each of which is a poor fit for existing databases, and yet a good fit for the principles.

First, it is worth summarizing why Informix did 10x worse than the hand-built search engine in 1996. Informix was among the best choices for a search engine at the time, and we in fact used it for other parts of the system, particularly personalization. It had cluster support and seemed to do a reasonable job with caching; it was also viewed as the best "toolbox" database, which is what we needed. The basic issue was *over generalization*, which presumably might limit modern DBMSs as well. Here is a partial list of the optimizations that account for the 10x difference: no locking, a single hand-optimized query plan, multiway joins, extensive compression, aggressive caching, careful data representation, hand-written access methods, single address space, and no security or access control (handled by the firewall). The representation of indexed text in mid-90's databases was typically 3x larger than the raw text; Inktomi and Alta Vista drove this number to well below one, which accounts a significant fraction of the overall performance gain, since this directly affects the number and size of I/O operations, and the hit rate of the cache. Finally, even if modern databases solved all of these problems, which they do not, the designers of the next big data-intensive system will surely find some mismatches, and will also have to apply the principles rather than the artifacts.

For the first example of such a system, we return to the logging system, discussed in Section 7.2. The best solution [Sah02] is a top-down design with data independence and a declarative language. Although based on Postgres, it is a large deviation from a traditional DBMS, as it includes Perl in the query language for string handling, strong support for loading data in real time, and changes for high availability. Predecessors, in fact, were not based on Postgres at all and used the file system for storage.

Another search-related example is the Google File System [GGL03], which is a distributed file system optimized for large files, constrained sharing, and atomic append operations. It is a top-down design driven by the need to handle more than one billion documents and millions of files; in particular, in handles all of the files used by the crawling and indexing systems. It has a relatively clean semantics for its important operations (concurrent append in particular), and support for high availability and replication. Although "navigational" rather than query based, it fits the top-down model proscribed here.

A more remote example is the Batch-Aware Distributed File System (BAD-FS) [BT+03]. This is a file system for large wide-area I/O intensive workloads such as cluster-based scientific applications. It is a top-down design with a simple declarative query language, which allows the scheduler to optimize communication, caching and replication by controlling both the placement and scheduling of jobs. Although not described this way, it has the usual phases: a parser, query planner and optimizer, and an execution engine. It also provides a variation of views. As with SQL, the declarative nature is critical for enabling optimizations. This project exhibits the proposed methodology in part because it has members from both the database and systems communities.

Although harder to show, many other systems fit this model of applying the principles without the artifacts. These include workflow systems, which have a query language and data independence, XML databases, and the emerging field of bioinformatics. All of these systems have top-down designs that do not map well on SQL and existing database semantics. The most common approach is to "make" them fit, however awkward that may be. A clean top-down design, as in the case of logging above, would lead to different implementation that is simpler, cleaner, and presumably more reliable and a better fit.

In the end, the hope is that projects on the "systems" side will benefit from top-down thinking, well-defined semantics, and declarative languages that leave room for optimization. Conversely, the hope on the "database" side would be for more modular and layered designs that are more flexible than current (monolithic) designs, and thus more useful for new kinds of systems. It is not clear that such layering is possible, but there is some evidence in the form of Berkeley DB and some of the novel uses of Postgres, such as the logging system.

Acknowledgments: We would like to thank Joe Hellerstein, Adam Sah, Mike Stonebraker, Remzi Arpaci-Dusseau, and many great Inktomi employees including Brian Totty, Paul Gauthier, Kevin Brown, Doug Cook, Eric Baldeschweiler, and Ken Lutz.

[Apa01] The Apache Web Server. http://www.apache.org.

[BEA01] *The BEA WebLogic Server Datasheet.* http://www.bea.com

[BHM90] P.A. Bernstein, M. Hsu and B. Mann. "Implementing Recoverable Requests Using Queues." *Proc.of ACM SIGMOD*. Atlantic City, NJ. 1990.

[Bre01] E. Brewer. "Lessons from Giant-Scale Services." *IEEE Internet Computing* 5(4): 46-55, April 2001. http://www.cs.berkeley.edu/~brewer/papers/GiantScale.pdf

[BT+03] J. Bent, D. Thain, A. Arpaci-Dusseau, R. Arpaci-Dusseau, and M. Livny. "Explicit Control in the Batch-Aware Distributed File System." *Proc. of SOSP 2003*. October 2003.

[C+97] C. Yoshikawa *et al.*, "Using Smart Clients to Build Scalable Services," *Proc of the.Usenix Annual Technical Conference*. Berkeley, CA, Jan. 1997.

[CG99] S. Chaudhuri and L. Gravano. "Evaluating Top-k Selection Queries." Proc. VLDB Conference, 1999. http://citeseer.nj.nec.com/chaudhuri99evaluating.html

[CGK01] Z. Chen, J. Gehrke, and F. Korn. "Query optimization in compressed database systems." *Proc. ACM SIGMOD 2001*. http://citeseer.nj.nec.com/chen01query.html

[Cha+81] D. Chamberlin *et al.* "A history and evaluation of System R." *Communications of the ACM*, 24(10), pp. 632–646, October 1981.

[CK98] M. J. Carey and D. Kossmann. "Reducing the braking distance of an SQL query engine." In *Proceedings of the 24th VLDB Conference*, pp. 158–169, New York, NY, August 1998. http://citeseer.nj.nec.com/carey98reducing.html

[DGNP88] F. Darema, D. A. George, V. A. Norton, and G. F. Pfister. "A single-program-multiple-data computational model for epex/fortran." *Parallel Computing*, 5(7), 1988.

[FB99] A. Fox and E. A. Brewer. "Harvest, Yield, and Scalable Tolerant Systems." *Proc. of HotOS-VII*. March 1999.

[FGCB97] A. Fox, S. D. Gribble, Y. Chawathe and E. Brewer. "Scalable Network Services" *Proc. of the 16th SOSP*, St. Malo, France, October 1997.

[Fou01] Foundry Networks ServerIron Switch. http://www.foundrynet.com/

[GBH+00] S. Gribble, E. Brewer, J. M. Hellerstein, and D. Culler. "Scalable, Distributed Data Structures for Internet Service Construction." *Proc. of OSDI 2000*, October 2000.

[GGL03] S. Ghemawat, H. Gobioff, and S.-T. Leung. "The Google File System." *Proc of the SOSP 2003*. October 2003.

[GL02] S. Gilbert and N. Lynch. "Brewer's conjecture and the feasibility of consistent, available, partition-tolerant web services." *Sigact News*, 33(2), June 2002.

[GR97] J. Gray and A. Reuter. *Transaction Processing*. Morgan-Kaufman, 1997

[Gra95] G. Graefe. "The Cascades framework for query optimization." *Data Engineering Bulletin*, 18(3):19–29, September 1995.

[Gri00] S. Gribble. *A Design Framework and a Scalable Storage Platform to Simplify Internet Service Construction*. Ph.D. Dissertation, UC Berkeley, September 2000.

[GWv+01] S. Gribble, M. Welsh, R. von Behren, E. Brewer, D. Culler, N. Borisov, S. Czerwinski, R. Gummadi, J. Hill, A. Joseph, R.H. Katz, Z.M. Mao, S. Ross, and B. Zhao. "The Ninja Architecture for Robust Internet-Scale Systems and Services." *Journal of Computer Networks*, March 2001.

[HD90] H. I. Hsiao and D. DeWitt. "Chained Declustering: A New Availability Strategy for Multiprocessor Database Machines." *Proc. of the 6th International Data Engineering Conference*. February 1990.

[Her91] Maurice Herlihy. *A Methodology for Implementing Highly Concurrent Data Objects*. Technical Report CRL 91/10. Digital Equipment Corporation, October 1991.

[LAC+96] B. Liskov, A. Adya, M. Castro, S. Ghemawat, R. Gruber, U. Maheshwari, A. C. Myers, M. Day and L. Shrira. "Safe and efficient sharing of persistent objects in Thor." *Proc. of ACM SIGMOD*, pp. 318–329, 1996.

[LKF04] B. C. Ling, E. Kiciman, A. Fox. Session State: Beyond Soft State *Proceedings of Networked Systems Design and Implementation (NSDI '04)*, San Francisco, CA, March 2004.

[LML+96] R. Larson, J. McDonough, P. O'Leary, L. Kuntz and R. Moon. Cheshire II: Designing a Next-Generation Online Catalog. *Journal for the American Society for Information Science*. 47(7), pp. 555–567. July 1996.

[ML86] L. F. Mackert and G. M. Lohman. "R* optimizer validation and performance evaluation for local queries." *Proceedings of SIGMOD 1986*, pp. 84–95, 1986.

[Mov99] MovieFone Corporation. "MovieFone Announces Preliminary Results From First Day of Star Wars Advance Ticket Sales." Company Press Release, *Business Wire*, May 13, 1999.

[PAB+98] V. S. Pai, M. Aron, G. Banga, M, Svendsen, P. Druschel, W. Zwaenepoel, and E. Nahum. "Locality-Aware Request Distribution in Cluster-based Network Servers." *Proc. of ASPLOS 1998*. San Jose, CA, October 1998.

[PDZ99] V. S. Pai, P. Druschel, and W. Zwaenepoel. "Flash: An efficient and portable Web server." *Proc. of the 1999 Annual USENIX Technical Conference*, June 1999.

[PHH92] H. Pirahesh, J. M. Hellerstein, and W. Hasan: "Extensible/Rule Based Query Rewrite Optimization in Starburst." *Proc. of SIGMOD 1992*. pp. 39-48. June 1992.

[RN02] S. Russell and P. Norvig. *Artificial Intelligence: A Modern Approach*. Prentice-Hall, 2002.

[Sah02] A. Sah. "A New Architecture for Managing Enterprise Log Data." *Proc. of LISA 2002*. November 2002.

[Sal89] G. Salton. *Automatic Text Processing: The transformation, analysis, and retrieval of information by computer*. Addison-Wesley, 1989.

[SAS+96] J. Sidell, P. M. Aoki, A. Sah, C. Staelin, M. Stonebraker, and A. Yu. "Data Replication in Mariposa." *Proc. of the 12th International Conference on Data Engineering*. February 1996.

[SBL99] Y. Saito, B. Bershad and H. Levy. "Manageability, Availability and Performance in Porcupine: A Highly Scalable, Cluster-based Mail Service." *Proc. of the 17th SOSP*. October 1999.

[Sel+79] P. G. Selinger, M. M. Astrahan, D. D. Chamberlin, R. A. Lorie and G. T. Price. "Access path selection in a relational database system." *Proc. of SIGMOD 1979*. Boston, MA. pp. 22–34. June 1979.

[SJGP90] M. Stonebraker, A. Jhingran, J. Goh, and S. Potamianos. "On rules, procedure, caching and views in data base systems." *Proc. of the 1990 ACM SIGMOD International Conference on Management of Data*. June 1990.

[WCB01] M. Welsh, D. Culler and E. Brewer. "SEDA: An Architecture for Well-Conditioned, Scalable Internet Services." *Proc. of the 18th SOSP*. October, 2001.

[WS00] L. A. Wald and S. Schwarz. "The 1999 Southern California Seismic Network Bulletin." *Seismological Research Letters*, 71(4), July/August 2000.

[ZBCS99] X. Zhang, M. Barrientos, J. B. Chen, and M. Seltzer. "HACC: An Architecture for Cluster-Based Web Servers." *Proc. of the 3rd USENIX Windows NT Symposium*, Seattle, WA, July 1999.

Appendix: Scoring

In this section we present a simple but representative scoring algorithm. Most of the research for current search engines is on improving the scoring algorithms or adding new components to the scoring systems, such as popularity metrics or incoming link counts.

We define a query as a set of words and their corresponding weights (W_i):

$$\text{Query } Q \equiv \{[w_1, w_2, \ldots, w_k], W_i\} \quad (3)$$

The score of a document for query Q is the weighted sum of an overall score for the document and a score for each word in the query:

$$\begin{aligned}\text{Score}(Q, d) &\equiv c_1 \text{Quality}(d) \\ &\quad + c_2 \sum_i W_i \text{Score}(w_i, d)\end{aligned} \quad (4)$$

The document quality term is independent of the query words and reflects things like length (shorter is better), popularity, incoming links, quality of the containing site, and external reviews.

The use of weighted sums for scoring is very common in information retrieval [Sal89] and this one is loosely based on Cheshire II [LML+96]. It has several advantages over more complex formulas: it is easy to compute, it can represent multiplication by using logarithms within components (commonly done), and the weights can be found using statistical regression (typically from human judgements on relevance). To simplify query execution, we define:[8]

$$\text{Score}(w_i, d) \equiv 0 \qquad \text{if } w_i \notin d \quad (5)$$

We don't actually require that $\sum W_i = 1$ and it useful to modify the weights individually at query time. Since we only care about the relative scoring within one query, there is no particular meaning to the sum of the weights. Nor do the words need to be unique; in fact, entering the same word twice usually gives it twice the weight.

The word score can be further broken down:

$$\text{Score}(w_i, d) \equiv c_3 \cdot f(w_i, d) + c_4 \cdot g(w_i) + c_5 \quad (6)$$

where f captures the relevance of the word in this document, and g captures the properties of the word in the overall corpus. For example, the specific version from Cheshire II is essentially [LML+96]:

$$\begin{aligned}\text{Score}(Q, d) \equiv\ & -0.0674\sqrt{length(d)} \\ & + \frac{1}{M}e \sum_{i=1}^{M} \begin{pmatrix} 0.679 \cdot \log Freq(w_i, d) \\ +0.223 \cdot \log IDF(w_i) \end{pmatrix}\end{aligned}$$

The top term is Quality(d) and the bottom term is the weighted sum, with even weights, of equation (6), where $f \equiv \log Freq(w_i, d)$ is the log of the count of w_i in d, and $g \equiv \log IDF(w_i)$ is the log of the *inverse document frequency* of w_i, which is one divided by the fraction of documents in which this word appears.

The scoring for AND and OR is trivial: just sum up the scores for the matching words. For example, (a AND b) has the same score as (a OR b), although the AND will usually return fewer documents.

8: Words that are in "anchor text" that point to the document are considered part of the document.

The Anatomy of a Large-Scale Hypertextual Web Search Engine

Sergey Brin and Lawrence Page

Computer Science Department,
Stanford University, Stanford, CA 94305, USA
sergey@cs.stanford.edu and page@cs.stanford.edu

Abstract

In this paper, we present Google, a prototype of a large-scale search engine which makes heavy use of the structure present in hypertext. Google is designed to crawl and index the Web efficiently and produce much more satisfying search results than existing systems. The prototype with a full text and hyperlink database of at least 24 million pages is available at http://google.stanford.edu/ To engineer a search engine is a challenging task. Search engines index tens to hundreds of millions of web pages involving a comparable number of distinct terms. They answer tens of millions of queries every day. Despite the importance of large-scale search engines on the web, very little academic research has been done on them. Furthermore, due to rapid advance in technology and web proliferation, creating a web search engine today is very different from three years ago. This paper provides an in-depth description of our large-scale web search engine -- the first such detailed public description we know of to date. Apart from the problems of scaling traditional search techniques to data of this magnitude, there are new technical challenges involved with using the additional information present in hypertext to produce better search results. This paper addresses this question of how to build a practical large-scale system which can exploit the additional information present in hypertext. Also we look at the problem of how to effectively deal with uncontrolled hypertext collections where anyone can publish anything they want.

Keywords

World Wide Web, Search Engines, Information Retrieval, PageRank, Google

1. Introduction

(Note: There are two versions of this paper -- a longer full version and a shorter printed version. The full version is available on the web and the conference CD-ROM.)

The web creates new challenges for information retrieval. The amount of information on the web is growing rapidly, as well as the number of new users inexperienced in the art of web research. People are likely to surf the web using its link graph, often starting with high quality human maintained indices such as Yahoo! or with search engines. Human maintained lists cover popular topics effectively but are subjective, expensive to build and maintain, slow to improve, and cannot cover all esoteric topics. Automated search engines that rely on keyword matching usually return too many low quality matches. To make matters worse, some advertisers attempt to gain people's attention by taking measures meant to mislead automated search engines. We have built a large-scale search engine which addresses many of the problems of existing systems. It makes especially heavy use of the additional structure present in hypertext to provide much higher quality search results. We chose our system name, Google, because it is a common spelling of googol, or 10^{100} and fits well with our goal of building very large-scale search engines.

1.1 Web Search Engines -- Scaling Up: 1994 - 2000

Search engine technology has had to scale dramatically to keep up with the growth of the web. In 1994, one of the first web search engines, the World Wide Web Worm (WWWW) [McBryan 94] had an index of 110,000 web pages and web accessible documents. As of November, 1997, the top search engines claim to index from 2 million (WebCrawler) to 100 million web documents (from Search Engine Watch). It is foreseeable that by the year 2000, a comprehensive index of the Web will contain over a billion documents. At the same time, the number of queries search engines handle has grown incredibly too. In March and April 1994, the World Wide Web Worm received an average of about 1500 queries per day. In November 1997, Altavista claimed it handled roughly 20 million queries per day. With the increasing number of users on the web, and automated systems which query search engines, it is likely that top search engines will handle hundreds of millions of queries per day by the year 2000. The goal of our system is to address many of the problems, both in quality and scalability, introduced by scaling search engine technology to such extraordinary numbers.

1.2. Google: Scaling with the Web

Creating a search engine which scales even to today's web presents many challenges. Fast crawling technology is needed to gather the web documents and keep them up to date. Storage space must be used efficiently to store indices and, optionally, the documents themselves. The indexing system must process hundreds of gigabytes of data efficiently. Queries must be handled quickly, at a rate of hundreds to thousands per second.

These tasks are becoming increasingly difficult as the Web grows. However, hardware performance and cost have improved dramatically to partially offset the difficulty. There are, however, several notable exceptions to this progress such as disk seek time and operating system robustness. In designing Google, we have considered both the rate of growth of the Web and technological changes. Google is designed to scale well to extremely large data sets. It makes efficient use of storage space to store the index. Its data structures are optimized for fast and efficient access (see section 4.2). Further, we expect that the cost to index and store text or HTML will eventually decline relative to the amount that will be available (see Appendix B). This will result in favorable scaling properties for centralized systems like Google.

1.3 Design Goals

1.3.1 Improved Search Quality

Our main goal is to improve the quality of web search engines. In 1994, some people believed that a complete search index would make it possible to find anything easily. According to Best of the Web 1994 -- Navigators, "The best navigation service should make it easy to find almost anything on the Web (once all the data is entered)." However, the Web of 1997 is quite different. Anyone who has used a search engine recently, can readily testify that the completeness of the index is not the only factor in the quality of search results. "Junk results" often wash out any results that a user is interested in. In fact, as of November 1997, only one of the top four commercial search engines finds itself (returns its own search page in response to its name in the top ten results). One of the main causes of this problem is that the number of documents in the indices has been increasing by many orders of magnitude, but the user's ability to look at documents has not. People are still only willing to look at the first few tens of results.

Because of this, as the collection size grows, we need tools that have very high precision (number of relevant documents returned, say in the top tens of results). Indeed, we want our notion of "relevant" to only include the very best documents since there may be tens of thousands of slightly relevant documents. This very high precision is important even at the expense of recall (the total number of relevant documents the system is able to return). There is quite a bit of recent optimism that the use of more hypertextual information can help improve search and other applications [Marchiori 97] [Spertus 97] [Weiss 96] [Kleinberg 98]. In particular, link structure [Page 98] and link text provide a lot of information for making relevance judgments and quality filtering. Google makes use of both link structure and anchor text (see Sections 2.1 and 2.2).

1.3.2 Academic Search Engine Research

Aside from tremendous growth, the Web has also become increasingly commercial over time. In 1993, 1.5% of web servers were on .com domains. This number grew to over 60% in 1997. At the same time, search engines have migrated from the academic domain to the commercial. Up until now most search engine development has gone on at companies with little publication of technical details. This causes search engine technology to remain largely a black art and to be advertising oriented (see Appendix A). With Google, we have a strong goal to push more development and understanding into the academic realm.

Another important design goal was to build systems that reasonable numbers of people can actually use. Usage was important to us because we think some of the most interesting research will involve leveraging the vast amount of usage data that is available from modern web systems. For example, there are many tens of millions of searches performed every day. However, it is very difficult to get this data, mainly because it is considered commercially valuable.

Our final design goal was to build an architecture that can support novel research activities on large-scale web data. To support novel research uses, Google stores all of the actual documents it crawls in compressed form. One of our main goals in designing Google was to set up an environment where other researchers can come in quickly, process large chunks of the web, and produce interesting results that would have been very difficult to produce otherwise. In the short time the system has been up, there have already been several papers using databases generated by Google, and many others are underway. Another goal we have is to set up a Spacelab-like environment where researchers or even students can propose and do interesting experiments on our large-scale web data.

2. System Features

The Google search engine has two important features that help it produce high precision results. First, it makes use of the link structure of the Web to calculate a quality ranking for each web page. This ranking is called PageRank and is described in detail in [Page 98]. Second, Google utilizes link to improve search results.

2.1 PageRank: Bringing Order to the Web

The citation (link) graph of the web is an important resource that has largely gone unused in existing web search engines. We have created maps containing as many as 518 million of these hyperlinks, a significant sample of the total. These maps allow rapid calculation of a web page's "PageRank", an objective measure of its citation importance that corresponds well with people's subjective idea of importance. Because of this correspondence, PageRank is an excellent way to prioritize the results of web keyword searches. For most popular subjects, a simple text matching search that is restricted to web page titles performs admirably when PageRank prioritizes the results (demo available at google.stanford.edu). For the type of full text searches in the main Google system, PageRank also helps a great deal.

2.1.1 Description of PageRank Calculation

Academic citation literature has been applied to the web, largely by counting citations or backlinks to a given page. This gives some approximation of a page's importance or quality. PageRank extends this idea by not counting links from all pages equally, and by normalizing by the number of links on a page. PageRank is defined as follows:

> *We assume page A has pages T1...Tn which point to it (i.e., are citations). The parameter d is a damping factor which can be set between 0 and 1. We usually set d to 0.85. There are more details about d in the next section. Also C(A) is defined as the number of links going out of page A. The PageRank of a page A is given as follows:*
>
> *PR(A) = (1-d) + d (PR(T1)/C(T1) + ... + PR(Tn)/C(Tn))*
>
> *Note that the PageRanks form a probability distribution over web pages, so the sum of all web pages' PageRanks will be one.*

PageRank or *PR(A)* can be calculated using a simple iterative algorithm, and corresponds to the principal eigenvector of the normalized link matrix of the web. Also, a PageRank for 26 million web pages can be computed in a few hours on a medium size workstation. There are many other details which are beyond the scope of this paper.

2.1.2 Intuitive Justification

PageRank can be thought of as a model of user behavior. We assume there is a "random surfer" who is given a web page at random and keeps clicking on links, never hitting "back" but eventually gets bored and starts on another random page. The probability that the random surfer visits a page is its PageRank. And, the *d* damping factor is the probability at each page the "random surfer" will get bored and request another random page. One important variation is to only add the damping factor *d* to a single page, or a group of pages. This allows for personalization and can make it nearly impossible to deliberately mislead the system in order to get a higher ranking. We have several other extensions to PageRank, again see [Page 98].

Another intuitive justification is that a page can have a high PageRank if there are many pages that point to it, or if there are some pages that point to it and have a high PageRank. Intuitively, pages that are well cited from many places around the web are worth looking at. Also, pages that have perhaps only one citation from something like the Yahoo! homepage are also generally worth looking at. If a page was not high quality, or was a broken link, it is quite likely that Yahoo's homepage would not link to it. PageRank handles both these cases and everything in between by recursively propagating weights through the link structure of the web.

2.2 Anchor Text

The text of links is treated in a special way in our search engine. Most search engines associate the text of a link with the page that the link is on. In addition, we associate it with the page the link points to. This has several advantages. First, anchors often provide more accurate descriptions of web pages than the pages themselves. Second, anchors may exist for documents which cannot be indexed by a text-based search engine, such as images, programs, and databases. This makes it possible to return web pages which have not actually been crawled. Note that pages that have not been crawled can cause problems, since they are never checked for validity before being returned to the user. In this case, the search engine can even return a page that never actually existed, but had hyperlinks pointing to it. However, it is possible to sort the results, so that this particular problem rarely happens.

This idea of propagating anchor text to the page it refers to was implemented in the World Wide Web Worm [McBryan 94] especially because it helps search non-text information, and expands the search coverage with fewer downloaded documents. We use anchor propagation mostly because anchor text can help provide better quality results. Using anchor text efficiently is technically difficult because of the large amounts of data which must be processed. In our current crawl of 24 million pages, we had over 259 million anchors which we indexed.

2.3 Other Features

Aside from PageRank and the use of anchor text, Google has several other features. First, it has location information for all hits and so it makes extensive use of proximity in search. Second, Google keeps track of some visual presentation details such as font size of words. Words in a larger or bolder font are weighted higher than other words. Third, full raw HTML of pages is available in a repository.

3 Related Work

Search research on the web has a short and concise history. The World Wide Web Worm (WWWW) [McBryan 94] was one of the first web search engines. It was subsequently followed by several other academic search engines, many of which are now public companies. Compared to the growth of the Web and the importance of search engines there are precious few documents about recent search engines [Pinkerton 94]. According to Michael Mauldin (chief scientist, Lycos Inc) [Mauldin], "the various services (including Lycos) closely guard the details of these databases". However, there has been a fair amount of work on specific features of search engines. Especially well represented is work which can get results by post-processing the results of existing commercial search engines, or produce small scale "individualized" search engines. Finally, there has been a lot of research on information retrieval systems, especially on well controlled collections. In the next two sections, we discuss some areas where this research needs to be extended to work better on the web.

3.1 Information Retrieval

Work in information retrieval systems goes back many years and is well developed [Witten 94]. However, most of the research on information retrieval systems is on small well controlled homogeneous collections such as collections of scientific papers or news stories on a related topic. Indeed, the primary benchmark for information retrieval, the Text Retrieval Conference [TREC 96], uses a fairly small, well controlled collection for their benchmarks. The "Very Large Corpus" benchmark is only 20GB compared to the 147GB from our crawl of 24 million web pages. Things that work well on TREC often do not produce good results on the web. For example, the standard vector space model tries to return the document that most closely approximates the query, given that both query and document are vectors defined by their word occurrence. On the web, this strategy often returns very short documents that are the query plus a few words. For example, we have seen a major search engine return a page containing only "Bill Clinton Sucks" and picture from a "Bill Clinton" query. Some argue that on the web, users should specify more accurately what they want and add more words to their query. We disagree vehemently with this position. If a user issues a query like "Bill Clinton" they should get reasonable results since there is a enormous amount of high quality information available on this topic. Given examples like these, we believe that the standard information retrieval work needs to be extended to deal effectively with the web.

3.2 Differences Between the Web and Well Controlled Collections

The web is a vast collection of completely uncontrolled heterogeneous documents. Documents on the web have extreme variation internal to the documents, and also in the external meta information that might be available. For example, documents differ internally in their language (both human and programming), vocabulary (email addresses, links, zip codes, phone numbers, product numbers), type or format (text, HTML, PDF, images, sounds), and may even be machine generated (log files or output from a database). On the other hand, we define external meta information as information that can be inferred about a document, but is not contained within it. Examples of external meta information include things like reputation of the source, update frequency, quality, popularity or usage, and citations. Not only are the possible sources of external meta information varied, but the things that are being measured vary many orders of magnitude as well. For example, compare the usage information from a major homepage, like Yahoo's which currently receives millions of page views every day with an obscure historical article which might receive one view every ten years. Clearly, these two items must be treated very differently by a search engine.

Another big difference between the web and traditional well controlled collections is that there is virtually no control over what people can put on the web. Couple this flexibility to publish anything with the enormous influence of search engines to route traffic and companies which deliberately manipulating search engines for profit become a serious problem. This problem that has not been addressed in traditional closed information retrieval systems. Also, it is interesting to note that metadata efforts have largely failed with web search engines, because any text on the page which is not directly represented to the user is abused to manipulate search engines. There are even numerous companies which specialize in manipulating search engines for profit.

4 System Anatomy

First, we will provide a high level discussion of the architecture. Then, there is some in-depth descriptions of important data structures. Finally, the major applications: crawling, indexing, and searching will be examined in depth.

4.1 Google Architecture Overview

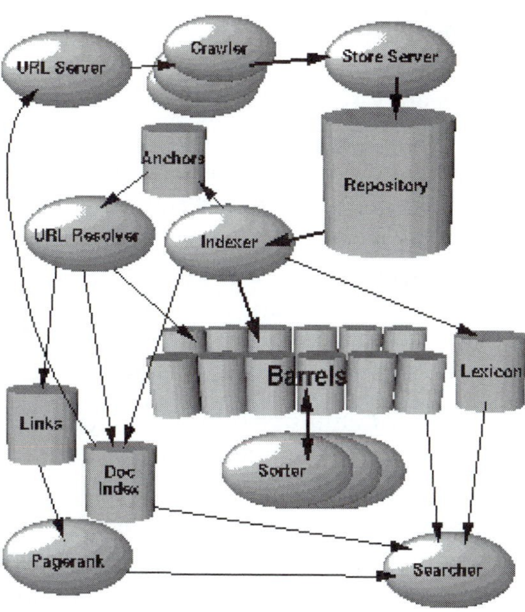

Figure 1. High Level Google Architecture

In this section, we will give a high level overview of how the whole system works as pictured in Figure 1. Further sections will discuss the applications and data structures not mentioned in this section. Most of Google is implemented in C or C++ for efficiency and can run in either Solaris or Linux.

In Google, the web crawling (downloading of web pages) is done by several distributed crawlers. There is a URLserver that sends lists of URLs to be fetched to the crawlers. The web pages that are fetched are then sent to the storeserver. The storeserver then compresses and stores the web pages into a repository. Every web page has an associated ID number called a docID which is assigned whenever a new URL is parsed out of a web page. The indexing function is performed by the indexer and the sorter. The indexer performs a number of functions. It reads the repository, uncompresses the documents, and parses them. Each document is converted into a set of word occurrences called hits. The hits record the word, position in document, an approximation of font size, and capitalization. The indexer distributes these hits into a set of "barrels", creating a partially sorted forward index. The indexer performs another important function. It parses out all the links in every web page and stores important information about them in an anchors file. This file contains enough information to determine where each link points from and to, and the text of the link.

The URLresolver reads the anchors file and converts relative URLs into absolute URLs and in turn into docIDs. It puts the anchor text into the forward index, associated with the docID that the anchor points to. It also generates a database of links which are pairs of docIDs. The links database is used to compute PageRanks for all the documents.

The sorter takes the barrels, which are sorted by docID (this is a simplification, see Section 4.2.5), and resorts them by wordID to generate the inverted index. This is done in place so that little temporary space is needed for this operation. The sorter also produces a list of wordIDs and offsets into the inverted index. A program called DumpLexicon takes this list together with the lexicon produced by the indexer and generates a new lexicon to be used by the searcher. The searcher is run by a web server and uses the lexicon built by DumpLexicon together with the inverted index and the PageRanks to answer queries.

4.2 Major Data Structures

Google's data structures are optimized so that a large document collection can be crawled, indexed, and searched with little cost. Although, CPUs and bulk input output rates have improved dramatically over the years, a disk seek still requires about 10 ms to complete. Google is designed to avoid disk seeks whenever possible, and this has had a considerable influence on the design of the data structures.

4.2.1 BigFiles

BigFiles are virtual files spanning multiple file systems and are addressable by 64 bit integers. The allocation among multiple file systems is handled automatically. The BigFiles package also handles allocation and deallocation of file descriptors, since the operating systems do not provide enough for our needs. BigFiles also support rudimentary compression options.

4.2.2 Repository

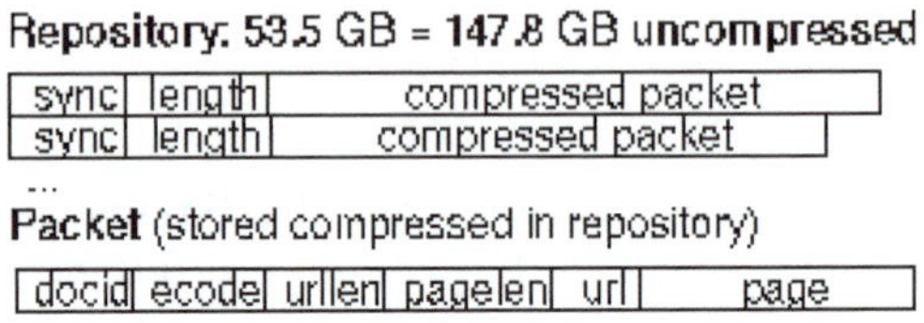

The repository contains the full HTML of every web page. Each page is compressed using zlib (see RFC1950). The choice of compression technique is a tradeoff between speed and compression ratio. We chose zlib's speed over a significant improvement in compression offered by bzip. The compression rate of bzip was approximately 4 to 1 on the repository as compared to zlib's 3 to 1 compression. In the repository, the documents are stored one after the other and are prefixed by docID, length, and URL as can be seen in Figure 2. The repository requires no other data structures to be used in order to access it. This helps with data consistency and makes development much easier; we can rebuild all the other data structures from only the repository and a file which lists crawler errors.

Repository: 53.5 GB = 147.8 GB uncompressed

sync	length	compressed packet
sync	length	compressed packet

...

Packet (stored compressed in repository)

docid	ecode	urllen	pagelen	url	page

Figure 2. Repository Data Structure

4.2.3 Document Index

The document index keeps information about each document. It is a fixed width ISAM (Index sequential access mode) index, ordered by docID. The information stored in each entry includes the current document status, a pointer into the repository, a document checksum, and various statistics. If the document has been crawled, it also contains a pointer into a variable width file called docinfo which contains its URL and title. Otherwise the pointer points into the URLlist which contains just the URL. This design decision was driven by the desire to have a reasonably compact data structure, and the ability to fetch a record in one disk seek during a search

Additionally, there is a file which is used to convert URLs into docIDs. It is a list of URL checksums with their corresponding docIDs and is sorted by checksum. In order to find the docID of a particular URL, the URL's checksum is computed and a binary search is performed on the checksums file to find its docID. URLs may be converted into docIDs in batch by doing a merge with this file. This is the technique the URLresolver uses to turn URLs into docIDs. This batch mode of update is crucial because otherwise we must perform one seek for every link which assuming one disk would take more than a month for our 322 million link dataset.

4.2.4 Lexicon

The lexicon has several different forms. One important change from earlier systems is that the lexicon can fit in memory for a reasonable price. In the current implementation we can keep the lexicon in memory on a machine with 256 MB of main memory. The current lexicon contains 14 million words (though some rare words were not added to the lexicon). It is implemented in two parts -- a list of the words (concatenated together but separated by nulls) and a hash table of pointers. For various functions, the list of words has some auxiliary information which is beyond the scope of this paper to explain fully.

4.2.5 Hit Lists

A hit list corresponds to a list of occurrences of a particular word in a particular document including position, font, and capitalization information. Hit lists account for most of the space used in both the forward and the inverted indices. Because of this, it is important to represent them as efficiently as possible. We considered several alternatives for encoding position, font, and capitalization -- simple encoding (a triple of integers), a compact encoding (a hand optimized allocation of bits), and Huffman coding. In the end we chose a hand optimized compact encoding since it required far less space than the simple encoding and far less bit manipulation than Huffman coding. The details of the hits are shown in Figure 3.

Our compact encoding uses two bytes for every hit. There are two types of hits: fancy hits and plain hits. Fancy hits include hits occurring in a URL, title, anchor text, or meta tag. Plain hits include everything else. A plain hit consists of a capitalization bit, font size, and 12 bits of word position in a document (all positions higher than 4095 are labeled 4096). Font size is represented relative to the rest of the document using three bits (only 7 values are actually used because 111 is the flag that signals a fancy hit). A fancy hit consists of a capitalization bit, the font size set to 7 to indicate it is a fancy hit, 4 bits to encode the type of fancy hit, and 8 bits of position. For anchor hits, the 8 bits of position are split into 4 bits for position in anchor and 4 bits for a hash of the docID the anchor occurs in. This gives us some limited phrase searching as long as there are not that many anchors for a particular word. We expect to update the way that anchor hits are stored to allow for greater resolution in the position and docIDhash fields. We use font size relative to the rest of the document because when searching, you do not want to rank otherwise identical documents differently just because one of the documents is in a larger font.

The length of a hit list is stored before the hits themselves. To save space, the length of the hit list is combined with the wordID in the forward index and the docID in the inverted index. This limits it to 8 and 5 bits respectively (there are some tricks which allow 8 bits to be borrowed from the wordID). If the length is longer than would fit in that many bits, an escape code is used in those bits, and the next two bytes contain the actual length.

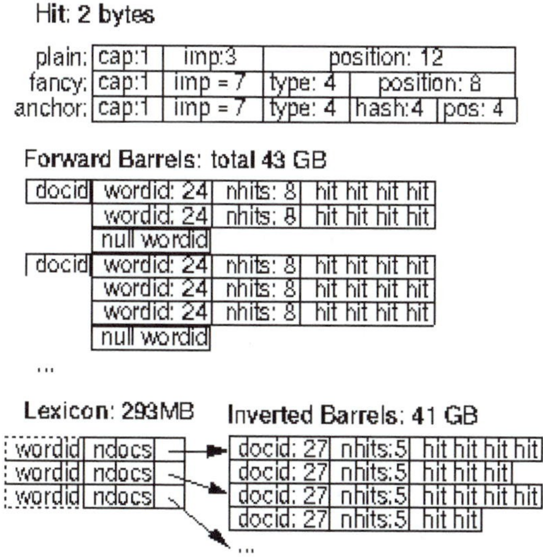

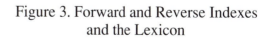

Figure 3. Forward and Reverse Indexes and the Lexicon

4.2.6 Forward Index

The forward index is actually already partially sorted. It is stored in a number of barrels (we used 64). Each barrel holds a range of wordID's. If a document contains words that fall into a particular barrel, the docID is recorded into the barrel, followed by a list of wordID's with hitlists which correspond to those words. This scheme requires slightly more storage because of duplicated docIDs but the difference is very small for a reasonable number of buckets and saves considerable time and coding complexity in the final indexing phase done by the sorter. Furthermore, instead of storing actual wordID's, we store each wordID as a relative difference from the minimum wordID that falls into the barrel the wordID is in. This way, we can use just 24 bits for the wordID's in the unsorted barrels, leaving 8 bits for the hit list length.

4.2.7 Inverted Index

The inverted index consists of the same barrels as the forward index, except that they have been processed by the sorter. For every valid wordID, the lexicon contains a pointer into the barrel that wordID falls into. It points to a doclist of docID's together with their corresponding hit lists. This doclist represents all the occurrences of that word in all documents.

An important issue is in what order the docID's should appear in the doclist. One simple solution is to store them sorted by docID. This allows for quick merging of different doclists for multiple word queries. Another option is to store them sorted by a ranking of the occurrence of the word in each document. This makes answering one word queries trivial and makes it likely that the answers to multiple word queries are near the start. However, merging is much more difficult. Also, this makes development much more difficult in that a change to the ranking function requires a rebuild of the index. We chose a compromise between these options, keeping two sets of inverted barrels -- one set for hit lists which include title or anchor hits and another set for all hit lists. This way, we check the first set of barrels first and if there are not enough matches within those barrels we check the larger ones.

4.3 Crawling the Web

Running a web crawler is a challenging task. There are tricky performance and reliability issues and even more importantly, there are social issues. Crawling is the most fragile application since it involves interacting with hundreds of thousands of web servers and various name servers which are all beyond the control of the system.

In order to scale to hundreds of millions of web pages, Google has a fast distributed crawling system. A single URLserver serves lists of URLs to a number of crawlers (we typically ran about 3). Both the URLserver and the crawlers are implemented in Python. Each crawler keeps roughly 300 connections open at once. This is necessary to retrieve web pages at a fast enough pace. At peak speeds, the system can crawl over 100 web pages per second using four crawlers. This amounts to roughly 600K per second of data. A major performance stress is DNS lookup. Each crawler maintains a its own DNS cache so it does not need to do a DNS lookup before crawling each document. Each of the hundreds of connections can be in a number of different states: looking up DNS, connecting to host, sending request, and receiving response. These factors make the crawler a complex component of the system. It uses asynchronous IO to manage events, and a number of queues to move page fetches from state to state.

It turns out that running a crawler which connects to more than half a million servers, and generates tens of millions of log entries generates a fair amount of email and phone calls. Because of the vast number of people coming on line, there are always those who do not know what a crawler is, because this is the first one they have seen. Almost daily, we receive an email something like, "Wow, you looked at a lot of pages from my web site. How did you like it?" There are also some people who do not know about the robots exclusion protocol, and think their page should be protected from indexing by a statement like, "This page is copyrighted and should not be indexed", which needless to say is difficult for web crawlers to understand. Also, because of the huge amount of data involved, unexpected things will happen. For example, our system tried to crawl an online game. This resulted in lots of garbage messages in the middle of their game! It turns out this was an easy problem to fix. But this problem had not come up until we had downloaded tens of millions of pages. Because of the immense variation in web pages and servers, it is virtually impossible to test a crawler without running it on large part of the Internet. Invariably, there are hundreds of obscure problems which may only occur on one page out of the whole web and cause the crawler to crash, or worse, cause unpredictable or incorrect behavior. Systems which access large parts of the Internet need to be designed to be very robust and carefully tested. Since large complex systems such as crawlers will invariably cause problems, there needs to be significant resources devoted to reading the email and solving these problems as they come up.

4.4 Indexing the Web

- **Parsing --** Any parser which is designed to run on the entire Web must handle a huge array of possible errors. These range from typos in HTML tags to kilobytes of zeros in the middle of a tag, non-ASCII characters, HTML tags nested hundreds deep, and a great variety of other errors that challenge anyone's imagination to come up with equally creative ones. For maximum speed, instead of using YACC to generate a CFG parser, we use flex to generate a lexical analyzer which we outfit with its own stack. Developing this parser which runs at a reasonable speed and is very robust involved a fair amount of work.
- **Indexing Documents into Barrels --** After each document is parsed, it is encoded into a number of barrels. Every word is converted into a wordID by using an in-memory hash table -- the lexicon. New additions to the lexicon hash table are logged to a file. Once the words are converted into wordID's, their occurrences in the current document are translated into hit lists and are written into the forward barrels. The main difficulty with parallelization of the indexing phase is that the lexicon needs to be shared. Instead of sharing the lexicon, we took the approach of writing a log of all the extra words that were not in a base lexicon, which we fixed at 14 million words. That way multiple indexers can run in parallel and then the small log file of extra words can be processed by one final indexer.
- **Sorting** -- In order to generate the inverted index, the sorter takes each of the forward barrels and sorts it by wordID to produce an inverted barrel for title and anchor hits and a full text inverted barrel. This process happens one barrel at a time, thus requiring little temporary storage. Also, we parallelize the sorting phase to use as many machines as we have simply by running multiple sorters, which can process different buckets at the same time. Since the barrels don't fit into main memory, the sorter further subdivides them into baskets which do fit into memory based on wordID and docID. Then the sorter, loads each basket into memory, sorts it and writes its contents into the short inverted barrel and the full inverted barrel.

4.5 Searching

The goal of searching is to provide quality search results efficiently. Many of the large commercial search engines seemed to have made great progress in terms of efficiency. Therefore, we have focused more on quality of search in our research, although we believe our solutions are scalable to commercial volumes with a bit more effort. The google query evaluation process is show in Figure 4.

To put a limit on response time, once a certain number (currently 40,000) of matching documents are found, the searcher automatically goes to step 8 in Figure 4. This means that it is possible that sub-optimal results would be returned. We are currently investigating other ways to solve this problem. In the past, we sorted the hits according to PageRank, which seemed to improve the situation.

1. Parse the query.
2. Convert words into wordIDs.
3. Seek to the start of the doclist in the short barrel for every word.
4. Scan through the doclists until there is a document that matches all the search terms.
5. Compute the rank of that document for the query.
6. If we are in the short barrels and at the end of any doclist, seek to the start of the doclist in the full barrel for every word and go to step 4.
7. If we are not at the end of any doclist go to step 4.
   Sort the documents that have matched by rank and return the top k.

Figure 4. Google Query Evaluation

4.5.1 The Ranking System

Google maintains much more information about web documents than typical search engines. Every hitlist includes position, font, and capitalization information. Additionally, we factor in hits from anchor text and the PageRank of the document. Combining all of this information into a rank is difficult. We designed our ranking function so that no particular factor can have too much influence. First, consider the simplest case -- a single word query. In order to rank a document with a single word query, Google looks at that document's hit list for that word. Google considers each hit to be one of several different types (title, anchor, URL, plain text large font, plain text small font, ...), each of which has its own type-weight. The type-weights make up a vector indexed by type. Google counts the number of hits of each type in the hit list. Then every count is converted into a count-weight. Count-weights increase linearly with counts at first but quickly taper off so that more than a certain count will not help. We take the dot product of the vector of count-weights with the vector of type-weights to compute an IR score for the document. Finally, the IR score is combined with PageRank to give a final rank to the document.

For a multi-word search, the situation is more complicated. Now multiple hit lists must be scanned through at once so that hits occurring close together in a document are weighted higher than hits occurring far apart. The hits from the multiple hit lists are matched up so that nearby hits are matched together. For every matched set of hits, a proximity is computed. The proximity is based on how far apart the hits are in the document (or anchor) but is classified into 10 different value "bins" ranging from a phrase match to "not even close". Counts are computed not only for every type of hit but for every type and proximity. Every type and proximity pair has a type-prox-weight. The counts are converted into count-weights and we take the dot product of the count-weights and the type-prox-weights to compute an IR score. All of these numbers and matrices can all be displayed with the search results using a special debug mode. These displays have been very helpful in developing the ranking system.

4.5.2 Feedback

The ranking function has many parameters like the type-weights and the type-prox-weights. Figuring out the right values for these parameters is something of a black art. In order to do this, we have a user feedback mechanism in the search engine. A trusted user may optionally evaluate all of the results that are returned. This feedback is saved. Then when we modify the ranking function, we can see the impact of this change on all previous searches which were ranked. Although far from perfect, this gives us some idea of how a change in the ranking function affects the search results.

5 Results and Performance

The most important measure of a search engine is the quality of its search results. While a complete user evaluation is beyond the scope of this paper, our own experience with Google has shown it to produce better results than the major commercial search engines for most searches. As an example which illustrates the use of PageRank, anchor text, and proximity, Figure 4 shows Google's results for a search on "bill clinton". These results demonstrates some of Google's features. The results are clustered by server. This helps considerably when sifting through result sets. A number of results are from the whitehouse.gov domain which is what one may reasonably expect from such a search. Currently, most major commercial search engines do not return any results from whitehouse.gov, much less the right ones. Notice that there is no title for the first result. This is because it was not crawled. Instead, Google relied on anchor text to determine this was a good answer to the query. Similarly, the fifth result is an email address which, of course, is not crawlable. It is also a result of anchor text.

Query: bill clinton
http://www.whitehouse.gov/
100.00% (no date) (0K)
http://www.whitehouse.gov/
    Office of the President
    99.67% (Dec 23 1996) (2K)
    http://www.whitehouse.gov/WH/EOP/OP/html/OP_Home.html
    Welcome To The White House
    99.98% (Nov 09 1997) (5K)
    http://www.whitehouse.gov/WH/Welcome.html
    Send Electronic Mail to the President
    99.86% (Jul 14 1997) (5K)
    http://www.whitehouse.gov/WH/Mail/html/Mail_President.html

mailto:president@whitehouse.gov
99.98%
    mailto:President@whitehouse.gov
    99.27%
The "Unofficial" Bill Clinton
94.06% (Nov 11 1997) (14K)
http://zpub.com/un/un-bc.html
    Bill Clinton Meets The Shrinks
    86.27% (Jun 29 1997) (63K)
    http://zpub.com/un/un-bc9.html
President Bill Clinton - The Dark Side
97.27% (Nov 10 1997) (15K)
http://www.realchange.org/clinton.htm
$3 Bill Clinton
94.73% (no date) (4K)
http://www.gatewy.net/~tjohnson/clinton1.html

Figure 4. Sample Results from Google

All of the results are reasonably high quality pages and, at last check, none were broken links. This is largely because they all have high PageRank. The PageRanks are the percentages in red along with bar graphs. Finally, there are no results about a Bill other than Clinton or about a Clinton other than Bill. This is because we place heavy importance on the proximity of word occurrences. Of course a true test of the quality of a search engine would involve an extensive user study or results analysis which we do not have room for here. Instead, we invite the reader to try Google for themselves at http://google.stanford.edu.

5.1 Storage Requirements

Aside from search quality, Google is designed to scale cost effectively to the size of the Web as it grows. One aspect of this is to use storage efficiently. Table 1 has a breakdown of some statistics and storage requirements of Google. Due to compression the total size of the repository is about 53 GB, just over one third of the total data it stores. At current disk prices this makes the repository a relatively cheap source of useful data. More importantly, the total of all the data used by the search engine requires a comparable amount of storage, about 55 GB. Furthermore, most queries can be answered using just the short inverted index. With better encoding and compression of the Document Index, a high quality web search engine may fit onto a 7GB drive of a new PC.

5.2 System Performance

It is important for a search engine to crawl and index efficiently. This way information can be kept up to date and major changes to the system can be tested relatively quickly. For Google, the major operations are Crawling, Indexing, and Sorting. It is difficult to measure how long crawling took overall because disks filled up, name servers crashed, or any number of other problems which stopped the system. In total it took roughly 9 days to download the 26 million pages (including errors). However, once the system was running smoothly, it ran much faster, downloading the last 11 million pages in just 63 hours, averaging just over 4 million pages per day or 48.5 pages per second. We ran the indexer and the crawler simultaneously. The indexer ran just faster than the crawlers. This is largely because we spent just enough time optimizing the indexer so that it would not be a bottleneck. These optimizations included bulk updates to the document index and placement of critical data structures on the local disk. The indexer runs at roughly 54 pages per second. The sorters can be run completely in parallel; using four machines, the whole process of sorting takes about 24 hours.

Storage Statistics	
Total Size of Fetched Pages	147.8 GB
Compressed Repository	53.5 GB
Short Inverted Index	4.1 GB
Full Inverted Index	37.2 GB
Lexicon	293 MB
Temporary Anchor Data (not in total)	6.6 GB
Document Index Incl. Variable Width Data	9.7 GB
Links Database	3.9 GB
Total Without Repository	**55.2 GB**
Total With Repository	**108.7 GB**

Web Page Statistics	
Number of Web Pages Fetched	24 million
Number of Urls Seen	76.5 million
Number of Email Addresses	1.7 million
Number of 404's	1.6 million

Table 1. Statistics

5.3 Search Performance

Improving the performance of search was not the major focus of our research up to this point. The current version of Google answers most queries in between 1 and 10 seconds. This time is mostly dominated by disk IO over NFS (since disks are spread over a number of machines). Furthermore, Google does not have any optimizations such as query caching, subindices on common terms, and other common optimizations. We intend to speed up Google considerably through distribution and hardware, software, and algorithmic improvements. Our target is to be able to handle several hundred queries per second. Table 2 has some sample query times from the current version of Google. They are repeated to show the speedups resulting from cached IO.

6 Conclusions

Google is designed to be a scalable search engine. The primary goal is to provide high quality search results over a rapidly growing World Wide Web. Google employs a number of techniques to improve search quality including page rank, anchor text, and proximity information. Furthermore, Google is a complete architecture for gathering web pages, indexing them, and performing search queries over them.

	Initial Query		**Same Query Repeated (IO mostly cached)**	
Query	**CPU Time(s)**	**Total Time(s)**	**CPU Time(s)**	**Total Time(s)**
al gore	0.09	2.13	0.06	0.06
vice president	1.77	3.84	1.66	1.80
hard disks	0.25	4.86	0.20	0.24
search engines	1.31	9.63	1.16	1.16

Table 2. Search Times

6.1 Future Work

A large-scale web search engine is a complex system and much remains to be done. Our immediate goals are to improve search efficiency and to scale to approximately 100 million web pages. Some simple improvements to efficiency include query caching, smart disk allocation, and subindices. Another area which requires much research is updates. We must have smart algorithms to decide what old web pages should be recrawled and what new ones should be crawled. Work toward this goal has been done in [Cho 98]. One promising area of research is using proxy caches to build search databases, since they are demand driven. We are planning to add simple features supported by commercial search engines like boolean operators, negation, and stemming. However, other features are just starting to be explored such as relevance feedback and clustering (Google currently supports a simple hostname based clustering). We also plan to support user context (like the user's location), and result summarization. We are also working to extend the use of link structure and link text. Simple experiments indicate PageRank can be personalized by increasing the weight of a user's home page or bookmarks. As for link text, we are experimenting with using text surrounding links in addition to the link text itself. A Web search engine is a very rich environment for research ideas. We have far too many to list here so we do not expect this Future Work section to become much shorter in the near future.

6.2 High Quality Search

The biggest problem facing users of web search engines today is the quality of the results they get back. While the results are often amusing and expand users' horizons, they are often frustrating and consume precious time. For example, the top result for a search for "Bill Clinton" on one of the most popular commercial search engines was the Bill Clinton Joke of the Day: April 14, 1997. Google is designed to provide higher quality search so as the Web continues to grow rapidly, information can be found easily. In order to accomplish this Google makes heavy use of hypertextual information consisting of link structure and link (anchor) text. Google also uses proximity and font information. While evaluation of a search engine is difficult, we have subjectively found that Google returns higher quality search results than current commercial search engines. The analysis of link structure via PageRank allows Google to evaluate the quality of web pages. The use of link text as a description of what the link points to helps the search engine return relevant (and to some degree high quality) results. Finally, the use of proximity information helps increase relevance a great deal for many queries.

6.3 Scalable Architecture

Aside from the quality of search, Google is designed to scale. It must be efficient in both space and time, and constant factors are very important when dealing with the entire Web. In implementing Google, we have seen bottlenecks in CPU, memory access, memory capacity, disk seeks, disk throughput, disk capacity, and network IO. Google has evolved to overcome a number of these bottlenecks during various operations. Google's major data structures make efficient use of available storage space. Furthermore, the crawling, indexing, and sorting operations are efficient enough to be able to build an index of a substantial portion of the web -- 24 million pages, in less than one week. We expect to be able to build an index of 100 million pages in less than a month.

6.4 A Research Tool

In addition to being a high quality search engine, Google is a research tool. The data Google has collected has already resulted in many other papers submitted to conferences and many more on the way. Recent research such as [Abiteboul 97] has shown a number of limitations to queries about the Web that may be answered without having the Web available locally. This means that Google (or a similar system) is not only a valuable research tool but a necessary one for a wide range of applications. We hope Google will be a resource for searchers and researchers all around the world and will spark the next generation of search engine technology.

7 Acknowledgments

Scott Hassan and Alan Steremberg have been critical to the development of Google. Their talented contributions are irreplaceable, and the authors owe them much gratitude. We would also like to thank Hector Garcia-Molina, Rajeev Motwani, Jeff Ullman, and Terry Winograd and the whole WebBase group for their support and insightful discussions. Finally we would like to recognize the generous support of our equipment donors IBM, Intel, and Sun and our funders. The research described here was conducted as part of the Stanford Integrated Digital Library Project, supported by the National Science Foundation under Cooperative Agreement IRI-9411306. Funding for this cooperative agreement is also provided by DARPA and NASA, and by Interval Research, and the industrial partners of the Stanford Digital Libraries Project.

References

- Best of the Web 1994 -- Navigators http://botw.org/1994/awards/navigators.html
- Bill Clinton Joke of the Day: April 14, 1997. http://www.io.com/~cjburke/clinton/970414.html.
- Bzip2 Homepage http://www.muraroa.demon.co.uk/
- Google Search Engine http://google.stanford.edu/
- Harvest http://harvest.transarc.com/
- Mauldin, Michael L. Lycos Design Choices in an Internet Search Service, IEEE Expert Interview http://www.computer.org/pubs/expert/1997/trends/x1008/mauldin.htm
- The Effect of Cellular Phone Use Upon Driver Attention http://www.webfirst.com/aaa/text/cell/cell0toc.htm
- Search Engine Watch http://www.searchenginewatch.com/
- RFC 1950 (zlib) ftp://ftp.uu.net/graphics/png/documents/zlib/zdoc-index.html
- Robots Exclusion Protocol: http://info.webcrawler.com/mak/projects/robots/exclusion.htm

- Web Growth Summary: http://www.mit.edu/people/mkgray/net/web-growth-summary.html
- Yahoo! http://www.yahoo.com/

- [Abiteboul 97] Serge Abiteboul and Victor Vianu, *Queries and Computation on the Web.* Proceedings of the International Conference on Database Theory. Delphi, Greece 1997.
- [Bagdikian 97] Ben H. Bagdikian. *The Media Monopoly*. 5th Edition. Publisher: Beacon, ISBN: 0807061557
- [Cho 98] Junghoo Cho, Hector Garcia-Molina, Lawrence Page. *Efficient Crawling Through URL Ordering*. Seventh International Web Conference (WWW 98). Brisbane, Australia, April 14-18, 1998.
- [Gravano 94] Luis Gravano, Hector Garcia-Molina, and A. Tomasic. *The Effectiveness of GlOSS for the Text-Database Discovery Problem.* Proc. of the 1994 ACM SIGMOD International Conference On Management Of Data, 1994.
- [Kleinberg 98] Jon Kleinberg, *Authoritative Sources in a Hyperlinked Environment*, Proc. ACM-SIAM Symposium on Discrete Algorithms, 1998.
- [Marchiori 97] Massimo Marchiori. *The Quest for Correct Information on the Web: Hyper Search Engines.* The Sixth International WWW Conference (WWW 97). Santa Clara, USA, April 7-11, 1997.
- [McBryan 94] Oliver A. McBryan. GENVL and *WWWW: Tools for Taming the Web. First International Conference on the World Wide Web.* CERN, Geneva (Switzerland), May 25-26-27 1994. http://www.cs.colorado.edu/home/mcbryan/mypapers/www94.ps
- [Page 98] Lawrence Page, Sergey Brin, Rajeev Motwani, Terry Winograd. *The PageRank Citation Ranking: Bringing Order to the Web.* Manuscript in progress. http://google.stanford.edu/~backrub/pageranksub.ps
- [Pinkerton 94] Brian Pinkerton, *Finding What People Want: Experiences with the WebCrawler.* The Second International WWW Conference Chicago, USA, October 17-20, 1994. http://info.webcrawler.com/bp/WWW94.html
- [Spertus 97] Ellen Spertus. *ParaSite: Mining Structural Information on the Web.* The Sixth International WWW Conference (WWW 97). Santa Clara, USA, April 7-11, 1997.
- [TREC 96] *Proceedings of the fifth Text REtrieval Conference (TREC-5).* Gaithersburg, Maryland, November 20-22, 1996. Publisher: Department of Commerce, National Institute of Standards and Technology. Editors: D. K. Harman and E. M. Voorhees. Full text at: http://trec.nist.gov/
- [Witten 94] Ian H Witten, Alistair Moffat, and Timothy C. Bell. *Managing Gigabytes: Compressing and Indexing Documents and Images.* New York: Van Nostrand Reinhold, 1994.
- [Weiss 96] Ron Weiss, Bienvenido Velez, Mark A. Sheldon, Chanathip Manprempre, Peter Szilagyi, Andrzej Duda, and David K. Gifford. *HyPursuit: A Hierarchical Network Search Engine that Exploits Content-Link Hypertext Clustering.* Proceedings of the 7th ACM Conference on Hypertext. New York, 1996.

Vitae

Sergey Brin received his B.S. degree in mathematics and computer science from the University of Maryland at College Park in 1993. Currently, he is a Ph.D. candidate in computer science at Stanford University where he received his M.S. in 1995. He is a recipient of a National Science Foundation Graduate Fellowship. His research interests include search engines, information extraction from unstructured sources, and data mining of large text collections and scientific data.

Lawrence Page was born in East Lansing, Michigan, and received a B.S.E. in Computer Engineering at the University of Michigan Ann Arbor in 1995. He is currently a Ph.D. candidate in Computer Science at Stanford University. Some of his research interests include the link structure of the web, human computer interaction, search engines, scalability of information access interfaces, and personal data mining.

8 Appendix A: Advertising and Mixed Motives

Currently, the predominant business model for commercial search engines is advertising. The goals of the advertising business model do not always correspond to providing quality search to users. For example, in our prototype search engine one of the top results for cellular phone is "The Effect of Cellular Phone Use Upon Driver Attention", a study which explains in great detail the distractions and risk associated with conversing on a cell phone while driving. This search result came up first because of its high importance as judged by the PageRank algorithm, an approximation of citation importance on the web [Page, 98]. It is clear that a search engine which was taking money for showing cellular phone ads would have difficulty justifying the page that our system returned to its paying advertisers. For this type of reason and historical experience with other media [Bagdikian 83], we expect that advertising funded search engines will be inherently biased towards the advertisers and away from the needs of the consumers.

Since it is very difficult even for experts to evaluate search engines, search engine bias is particularly insidious. A good example was OpenText, which was reported to be selling companies the right to be listed at the top of the search results for particular queries [Marchiori 97]. This type of bias is much more insidious than advertising, because it is not clear who "deserves" to be there, and who is willing to pay money to be listed. This business model resulted in an uproar, and OpenText has ceased to be a viable search engine. But less blatant bias are likely to be tolerated by the market. For example, a search engine could add a small factor to search results from "friendly" companies, and subtract a factor from results from competitors. This type of bias is very difficult to detect but could still have a significant effect on the market. Furthermore, advertising income often provides an incentive to provide poor quality search results. For example, we noticed a major search engine would not return a large airline's homepage when the airline's name was given as a query. It so happened that the airline had placed an expensive ad, linked to the query that was its name. A better search engine would not have required this ad, and possibly resulted in the loss of the revenue from the airline to the search engine. In general, it could be argued from the consumer point of view that the better the search engine is, the fewer advertisements will be needed for the consumer to find what they want. This of course erodes the advertising supported business model of the existing search engines. However, there will always be money from advertisers who want a customer to switch products, or have something that is genuinely new. But we believe the issue of advertising causes enough mixed incentives that it is crucial to have a competitive search engine that is transparent and in the academic realm.

9 Appendix B: Scalability

9. 1 Scalability of Google

We have designed Google to be scalable in the near term to a goal of 100 million web pages. We have just received disk and machines to handle roughly that amount. All of the time consuming parts of the system are parallelize and roughly linear time. These include things like the crawlers, indexers, and sorters. We also think that most of the data structures will deal gracefully with the expansion. However, at 100 million web pages we will be very close up against all sorts of operating system limits in the common operating systems (currently we run on both Solaris and Linux). These include things like addressable memory, number of open file descriptors, network sockets and bandwidth, and many others. We believe expanding to a lot more than 100 million pages would greatly increase the complexity of our system.

9.2 Scalability of Centralized Indexing Architectures

As the capabilities of computers increase, it becomes possible to index a very large amount of text for a reasonable cost. Of course, other more bandwidth intensive media such as video is likely to become more pervasive. But, because the cost of production of text is low compared to media like video, text is likely to remain very pervasive. Also, it is likely that soon we will have speech recognition that does a reasonable job converting speech into text, expanding the amount of text available. All of this provides amazing possibilities for centralized indexing. Here is an illustrative example. We assume we want to index everything everyone in the US has written for a year. We assume that there are 250 million people in the US and they write an average of 10k per day. That works out to be about 850 terabytes. Also assume that indexing a terabyte can be done now for a reasonable cost. We also assume that the indexing methods used over the text are linear, or nearly linear in their complexity. Given all these assumptions we can compute how long it would take before we could index our 850 terabytes for a reasonable cost assuming certain growth factors. Moore's Law was defined in 1965 as a doubling every 18 months in processor power. It has held remarkably true, not just for processors, but for other important system parameters such as disk as well. If we assume that Moore's law holds for the future, we need only 10 more doublings, or 15 years to reach our goal of indexing everything everyone in the US has written for a year for a price that a small company could afford. Of course, hardware experts are somewhat concerned Moore's Law may not continue to hold for the next 15 years, but there are certainly a lot of interesting centralized applications even if we only get part of the way to our hypothetical example.

Of course a distributed systems like G*l*oss [Gravano 94] or Harvest will often be the most efficient and elegant technical solution for indexing, but it seems difficult to convince the world to use these systems because of the high administration costs of setting up large numbers of installations. Of course, it is quite likely that reducing the administration cost drastically is possible. If that happens, and everyone starts running a distributed indexing system, searching would certainly improve drastically.

Because humans can only type or speak a finite amount, and as computers continue improving, text indexing will scale even better than it does now. Of course there could be an infinite amount of machine generated content, but just indexing huge amounts of human generated content seems tremendously useful. So we are optimistic that our centralized web search engine architecture will improve in its ability to cover the pertinent text information over time and that there is a bright future for search.

The BINGO! System for Information Portal Generation and Expert Web Search

Sergej Sizov, Michael Biwer, Jens Graupmann,
Stefan Siersdorfer, Martin Theobald, Gerhard Weikum, Patrick Zimmer

University of the Saarland
Department of Computer Science
Im Stadtwald, 66123 Saarbruecken
Germany

Abstract

This paper presents the BINGO! focused crawler, an advanced tool for information portal generation and expert Web search. In contrast to standard search engines such as Google which are solely based on precomputed index structures, a focused crawler interleaves crawling, automatic classification, link analysis and assessment, and text filtering. A crawl is started from a user-provided set of training data and aims to collect comprehensive results for the given topics.

The focused crawling paradigm has been around for a few years and many of our techniques are adopted from the information retrieval and machine learning literature. BINGO! is a system-oriented effort to integrate a suite of techniques into a comprehensive and versatile tool. The paper discusses its overall architecture and main components, important lessons from early experimentation and the resulting improvements on effectiveness and efficiency, and experimental results that demonstrate the usefulness of BINGO! as a next-generation tool for information organization and search.

1 Introduction

1.1 The Problem of Web and Intranet Information Search

Web search engines mostly build on the vector space model that views text documents (including HTML or XML documents) as vectors of term relevance scores [3, 19]. These terms, also known as features, represent word occurrence frequencies in documents after stemming and other normalizations. Queries are vectors too, so that similarity metrics between vectors, for example, the Euclidean distance or the cosine metric, can be used to produce a ranked list of search results, in descending order of (estimated) relevance. The quality of a search result is assessed a posteriori by the empirical metrics precision and recall: precision is the fraction of truly relevant documents among the top N matches in the result ranking (N typically being 10), and recall is the fraction of found documents out of the relevant documents that exist somewhere in the underlying corpus (e.g., the entire Web). More recently, the above basic model has been enhanced by analyzing the link structure between documents, viewing the Web as a graph, and defining the authority of Web sites or documents as an additional metric for search result ranking [5, 14]. These approaches have been very successful in improving the precision (i.e., "sorting out the junk" in more colloquial terms) for typical mass queries such as "Madonna tour" (i.e., everything or anything about the concert tour of pop star Madonna). However, link analysis techniques do not help much for expert queries where recall is the key problem (i.e., finding a few useful results at all).

Two important observations can be made about the above class of advanced information demands. First, the best results are often obtained from Yahoo-style portals that maintain a hierarchical directory of topics, also known as an ontology; the problem with this approach is, however, that it requires intellectual work for classifying new documents into the ontology and thus does not scale with the Web. Second, fully automated Web search engines such as Google, Altavista, etc. sometimes yield search results from which the user could possibly reach the actually desired information by following a small number of hyperlinks; here the problem is that exhaustively surfing the vicinity of a Web document may often take hours and is thus infeasible in practice. These two observations have motivated a novel approach known as focused crawling or thematic crawling [7], which can be viewed as an

Proceedings of the 2003 CIDR Conference

attempt to automate the above kinds of intellectual preprocessing and postprocessing.

1.2 The Potential of Focused Crawling

In contrast to a search engine's generic crawler (which serves to build and maintain the engine's index), a focused crawler is interested only in a specific, typically small, set of topics such as 19th century Russian literature, backcountry desert hiking and canyoneering, or programming with (the Web server scripting language) PHP. The topics of interest may be organized into a user- or community-specific hierarchy. The crawl is started from a given set of seed documents, typically taken from an intellectually built ontology, and aims to proceed along the most promising paths that stay "on topic" while also accepting some detours along digressing subjects with a certain "tunnelling" probability. Each of the visited documents is classified into the crawler's hierarchy of topics to test whether it is of interest at all and where it belongs in the ontology; this step must be automated using classification techniques from machine learning such as Naive Bayes, Maximum Entropy, Support Vector Machines (SVM), or other supervised learning methods [15, 17, 23]. The outcome of the focused crawl can be viewed as the index of a personalized information service or a thematically specialized search engine.

A focused crawler can be used for at least two major problems in information organization and search:

1. Starting with a reasonable set of seed documents that also serve as training data for the classifier, a focused crawl can populate a topic directory and thus serves as a largely automated *information portal generator*.
2. Starting with a set of keywords or an initial result set from a search engine (e.g., from a Google query), a focused crawl can improve the recall for an advanced *expert query*, a query that would take a human expert to identify matches and for which current Web search engines would typically return either no or only irrelevant documents (at least in the top ten ranks).

In either case the key challenge is to minimize the time that a human needs for setting up the crawl (e.g., provide training data, calibrate crawl parameters, etc.) and for interpreting or analyzing its results. For example, we would expect the human to spend a few minutes for carefully specifying her information demand and setting up an overnight crawl, and another few minutes for looking at the results the next morning. In addition, the focused crawler may get back to the user for feedback after some "learning" phase of say twenty minutes.

This mode of operation is in significant contrast to today's Web search engines which rely solely on precomputed results in their index structures and strictly limit the computer resource consumption per query in the interest of maximizing the throughput of "mass user" queries. With human cycles being much more expensive than computer and network cycles, the above kind of paradigm shift seems to be overdue for advanced information demands (e.g., of scientists).

1.3 Contribution and Outline of the Paper

This paper presents the BINGO! system that we have developed in the last two years at the University of the Saarland.[1]. Our approach has been inspired by and has adopted concepts from the seminal work of Chakrabarti et al. [7], but we believe it is fair to call our system a second-generation focused crawler. While most mathematical and algorithmic ingredients that we use in BINGO! (e.g., the classifier, cross-entropy-based feature selection, link analysis for prioritizing URLs in the crawl queue, etc.) are state-of-the-art, the overall system architecture is relatively unique (in the sense that most concepts have been around in the machine learning and information retrieval literature, but have not been considered in an integrated system context). The following are salient features of the BINGO! system:

- As human expert time is scarce and expensive, building the classifier on extensive, high-quality training data is a rare luxury. To overcome the potential deficiencies of the initial training documents, BINGO! uses a simple form of unsupervised, dynamic learning: during a crawl the system periodically identifies the most characteristic documents that have been automatically classified into a topic of interest and considers promoting these class "archetypes" to become new training data.
- The crawl is structured into two phases: a learning phase and a harvesting phase. The first phase performs a limited (mostly depth-first) crawl and uses a conservative tuning of the classifier in order to obtain a richer feature set (i.e., topic-specific terminology) and to find good candidates for archetypes. The second phase then switches to a much more aggressive breadth-first strategy with URL prioritization. Learning aims to calibrate the precision of the classifier, whereas harvesting aims at a high recall.
- BINGO! is designed as a comprehensive and flexible workbench for assisting a portal administrator or a human expert with certain information demands. To this end it includes a local search engine for querying the result documents of a crawl and various other data analysis techniques for postprocessing.

The paper describes the BINGO! architecture and its components, and it demonstrates the system's effectiveness by two kinds of experiments for information portal generation and expert search. The rest

[1]BINGO! stands for Bookmark-Induced Gathering of Information

of the paper is organized as follows. Section 2 gives an overview of the system's main concepts, the corresponding software components, and their interplay. When we had built the first prototype based on these concepts and started experimenting, we realized a number of shortcomings regarding the search effectiveness, i.e., the quality of the crawl results, and also efficiency, i.e., speed and resource consumption. These observations led to substantial improvements that are discussed in Sections 3 and 4 on effectiveness and efficiency. Section 5 presents our recent experimental results. We conclude with an outlook on ongoing and future work.

2 Overview of the BINGO! System

The BINGO! crawling toolkit consists of six main components that are depicted in Figure 1: the focused crawler itself, an HTML document analyzer that produces a feature vector for each document, the SVM classifier with its training data, the feature selection as a "noise-reduction" filter for the classifier, the link analysis module as a distiller for topic-specific authorities and hubs, and the training module for the classifier that is invoked for periodic re-training.

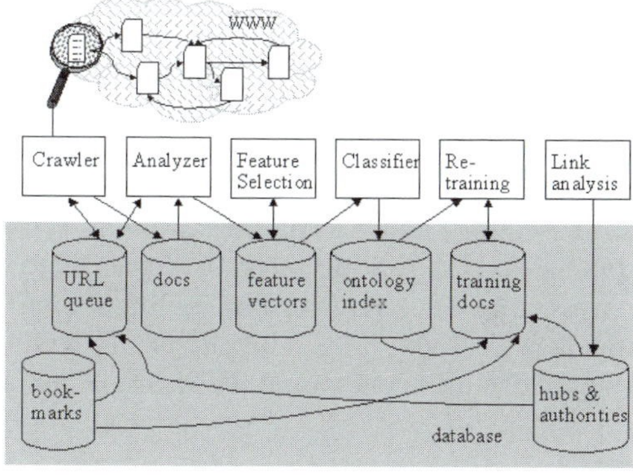

Figure 1: The BINGO! architecture and its main components

The crawler starts from a user's bookmark file or some other form of personalized or community-specific topic directory. These intellectually classified documents serve two purposes: 1) they provide the initial seeds for the crawl (i.e., documents whose outgoing hyperlinks are traversed by the crawler), and 2) they provide the initial contents for the user's topic tree and the initial training data for the classifier. Figure 2 shows an example of such a tree. Note that a single-node tree is a special case for generating an information portal with a single topic and no subclass structure or for answering a specific expert query. In the latter case the training data is a virtual document derived from the user query, and this training basis can be extended by prompting the user for relevance feedback after a short initial crawl and adding appropriate documents.

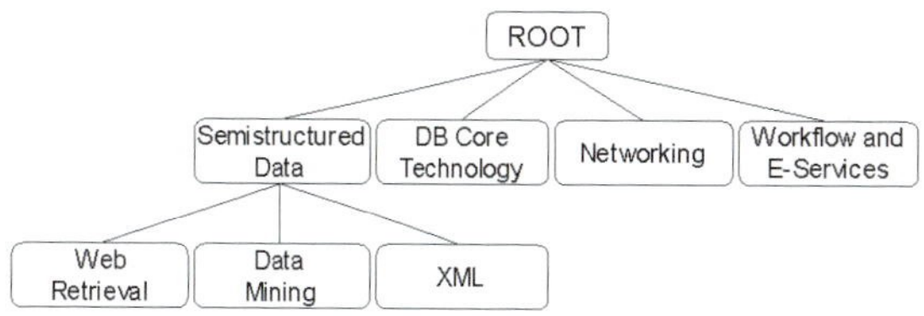

Figure 2: Example of a topic tree

All crawled documents, including the initial data, are stored in an Oracle9i database which serves as a cache. The role of the database system as a storage manager to BINGO! is further discussed in Section 4.

2.1 Crawler

The crawler processes the links in the URL queue using multiple threads. For each retrieved document the crawler initiates some analysis steps that depend on the document's MIME type (e.g., HTML, PDF, etc.) and then invokes the classifier on the resulting feature vector. Once a crawled document has been successfully classified, BINGO! extracts all hyperlinks from the document and adds them to the URL queue for further crawling; the links are ordered by their priority, i.e., SVM confidence in our case.

2.2 Document Analyzer

BINGO! computes document vectors according to the standard bag-of-words model, using stopword elimination, Porter stemming, and $tf * idf$ based term weighting [3, 16]. This is a standard IR approach where term weights capture the term frequency (tf) of the corresponding word stems in the document and the, logarithmically dampened, inverse document frequency (idf) which is the reciprocal of the number of documents in the entire corpus that contain the term. We consider our local document database as an approximation of the corpus for idf computation and recompute it lazily upon each retraining.

The document analyzer can handle a wide range of content handlers for different document formats (in particular, PDF, MS Word, MS PowerPoint etc.) as well as common archive files (zip, gz) and converts the recognized contents into HTML. So these formats can be processed by BINGO! like usual web pages. Many useful kinds of documents (like scientific publications, whitepapers, or commercial product specifications) are published as PDF; incorporating this material improves the crawling recall and the quality of the classifier's training set by a substantial margin.

2.3 Feature Selection

The feature selection algorithm provides the BINGO! engine with the most characteristic features for a given topic; these are the features that are used by the classifier for testing new documents. A good feature for this purpose discriminates competing topics from each other, i.e., those topics that are at the same level of the topic tree. Therefore, feature selection has to be topic-specific; it is invoked for every topic in the tree individually. As an example, consider a directory with topics mathematics, agriculture, and arts, where mathematics has subclasses algebra and stochastics. Obviously, the term *theorem* is very characteristic for math documents and thus an excellent discriminator between mathematics, agriculture, and arts. However, it is of no use at all to discriminate algebra versus stochastics. A term such as *field*, on the other hand, is a good indicator for the topic algebra when the only competing topic is stochastics; however, it is useless for a classifier that tests mathematics versus agriculture.

We use the Mutual Information (MI) measure for topic-specific feature. This technique, which is a specialized case of the notions of cross-entropy or Kullback-Leibler divergence [16], is known as one of the most effective methods [24]. The MI weight of the term X_i in the topic V_j is defined as:

$$MI(X_i, V_j) = P[X_i \wedge V_j] \, log \frac{P[X_i \wedge V_j]}{P[X_i]P[V_j]} \qquad (1)$$

Mutual information can be interpreted as measure of how much the joint distribution of features X_i and topics V_j deviate from a hypothetical distribution in which features and topics are independent of each other (hence the remark about MI being a special case of the Kullback-Leibler divergence which measures the differences between multivariate probability distributions in general).

The result of feature selection for a given topic is a ranking of the features, with the most discriminative features listed first. Our experiments achieved good results with the top 2000 features for each topic as the input to the classifier (compared to tens of thousands of different terms in the original documents). For efficiency BINGO! pre-selects candidates for the best features based on tf values and evaluates MI weights only for the 5000 most frequently occurring terms within each topic. As an example consider the class "Data Mining" in the topic tree of Figure 2 with home pages and DBLP pages of 5 to 10 leading researchers for each topic. Our feature selection finds the following word stems with the highest MI values: *mine, knowledg, olap, frame, pattern, genet, discov, cluster, dataset.*

2.4 Classifier

Document classification consists of a training phase for building a mathematical decision model based on intellectually pre-classified documents, and a decision phase for classifying new, previously unseen documents fetched by the crawler. For training BINGO! builds a topic-specific classifier for each node of the topic tree.

New documents are classified against all topics of the ontology tree in a top-down manner. Starting with the root, which corresponds to the union of the user's topics of interest, we feed the document's features into each of the node-specific decision models (including node-specific feature selection) and invoke the binary classifiers for all topics with the same parent. We refer to these as "competing" topics as the document will eventually be placed in at most one of them. Each of the topic-specific classifiers returns a yes-or-no decision and also a measure of confidence for this decision (see below). We assign the document to the tree node with the highest confidence in a positive decision. Then the classification proceeds with the children of this node, until eventually a leaf node is reached. If none of the topics with the same parent returns yes, the document is assigned to an artificial node labeled 'OTHERS' under the same parent.

Our engine uses support vector machines (SVM) [6, 23] as topic-specific classifiers. We use the linear form of SVM where training amounts to finding a hyperplane in the m-dimensional feature vector space that separates a set of positive training examples (document collection D_i^+ of the topic V_i) from a set of negative examples (document collection D_i^- of all competing topics V with the same parent as V_i) with maximum margin. The hyperplane can be described in the form $\vec{w} \cdot \vec{x} + b = 0$, as illustrated in Figure 3. Computing the hyperplane is equivalent to solving a quadratic optimization problem [23]. The current BINGO! version uses an existing open-source SVM implementation [1].

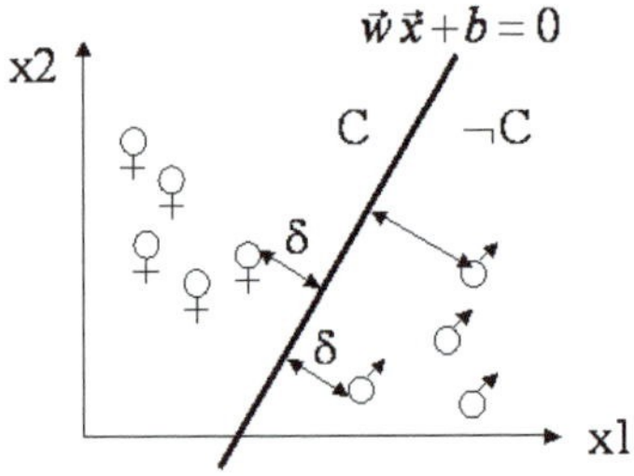

Figure 3: The separating hyperplane of the linear SVM classifier

Note that in the decision phase the SVM classifier is very efficient. For a new, previously unseen, document in the m-dimensional feature space $\vec{d} \in \mathbf{R}^m$ it merely needs to test whether the document lies on the "left" side or the "right" side of the separating hyperplane. The decision simply requires computing an

m-dimensional scalar product of two vectors.

We interpret the distance of a newly classified document from the separating hyperplane as a measure of the classifier's confidence. This computation is an inexpensive byproduct of the classifier. We use this kind of SVM confidence for identifying the most characteristic *"archetypes"* of a given topic. Note that training documents have a confidence score associated with them, too, by simply running them through the classifier's decision model after completed training. Further note that the initial training data does not necessarily yield the best archetypes, in particular, for expert Web search where the initial training data is merely a representation of the user's query terms. Therefore, BINGO! periodically considers promoting the best archetypes to become training documents for retraining the classifier. To estimate the precision of the new classifier, we use the computationally efficient $\xi\alpha$-method [13]. This estimator has approximately the same variance as leave-one-out estimation and slightly underestimates the true precision of the classifier (i.e., is a bit pessimistic). The prediction of the classifier's performance during a crawl is valuable for tuning the feature space construction; we will further discuss this issue in Section 3.

2.5 Link Analysis

The link structure between documents in each topic is an additional source of information about how well they capture the topic [4, 5, 7, 14]. Upon each retraining, we apply the method of [4], a variation of Kleinberg's HITS algorithm, to each topic of the directory. This method aims to identify a set S_A of authorities, which should be Web pages with most significant and/or comprehensive information on the topic, and a set S_H of hubs, which should be the best link collections with pointer to good authorities. The algorithm considers a small part of the hyperlink-induced Web graph $G = (S, E)$ with a node set S in the order of a few hundred or a few thousand documents and a set of edges E with an edge from node p to node q if the document that corresponds to p contains a hyperlink that points to document q. The node set S is constructed in two steps: 1) We include all documents that have been positively classified into the topic under consideration, which form the "base set" in Kleinberg's terminology. 2) We add all successors of these documents (i.e., documents that can be reached along one outgoing edge) and a reasonably sized subset of predecessors (i.e., documents that have a direct hyperlink to a document in the base set). The predecessors can be determined by querying a large unfocused Web database that internally maintains a large fraction of the full Web graph.

The actual computation of hub and authority scores is essentially an iterative approximation of the principal Eigenvectors for two matrices derived from the adjacency matrix of the graph G. Its outcome are two vectors with authority scores and hub scores. We are interested in the top ranked authorities and hubs. The former are perceived as topic-specific archetypes and considered for promotion to training data, and the latter are the best candidates for being crawled next and therefore added to the high-priority end of the crawler's URL queue. These steps are performed with each retraining.

2.6 Learning Phase vs. Harvesting Phase

Building a reasonably precise classifier from a very small set of training data is a very challenging task. Effective learning algorithms for highly heterogeneous environments like the Web would require a much larger training basis, yet human users would rarely be willing to invest hours of intellectual work for putting together a rich document collection that is truly representative of their interest profiles. To address this problem, we distinguish two basic crawl strategies:

- The *learning phase* serves to identify new archetypes and expand the classifier's knowledge base.
- The *harvesting phase* serves to effectively process the user's information demands with improved crawling precision and recall.

Depending on the phase, different focusing rules come into play to tell the crawler when to accept or reject Web pages for addition to the URL queue (see Section 4.2).

In the learning phase we are exclusively interested in gaining a broad knowledge base for the classifier by identifying archetypes for each topic. In many cases such documents can be obtained from the direct neighborhood of the initial training data, assuming that these have been chosen carefully. For example, suppose the user provides us with home pages of researchers from her bookmarks on a specific topic, say data mining; then chances are good that we find a rich source of topic-specific terminology in the vicinity of these home pages, say a conference paper on some data mining issue. i.e., a scientists homepage with links to her topic-specific publications. Following this rationale, BINGO! uses a depth-first crawl strategy during the learning phase, and initially restricts itself to Web pages from the domains that the initial training documents come from.

BINGO! repeatedly initiates re-training of the classifier, when a certain number of documents have been crawled and successfully classified with confidence above a certain threshold. At such points, a new set of training documents is determined for each node of the topic tree. For this purpose, the most characteristic documents of a topic, coined *archetypes*, are determined in two, complementary, ways. First, the link analysis is initiated with the current documents of a topic as its base set. The best authorities of a tree node are regarded as potential archetypes of the node. The second source of topic-specific archetypes builds on the confidence of the classifier's yes-or-no decision for a given node of the ontology tree. Among the automatically classified documents of a topic those documents whose yes decision had the highest confidence measure are selected as potential archetypes. The union of both top authorities and documents with high SVM confidence form a new set of candidates for promotion to training data.

After successfully extending the training basis with additional archetypes, BINGO! retrains all topic-specific classifiers and switches to the harvesting phase now putting emphasis on recall (i.e., collecting as many documents as possible). The crawler is resumed with the best hubs from the link analysis, using a breadth-first strategy that aims to visit as many different sites as possible that are related to the crawl's topics. When the learning phase cannot find sufficient archetypes or when the user wants to confirm archetypes before initiating a long and resource-intensive harvesting crawl, BINGO! includes a user feedback step between learning and harvesting. Here the user can intellectually identify archetypes among the documents found so far and may even trim individual HTML pages to remove irrelevant and potentially diluting parts (e.g., when a senior researcher's home page is heterogeneous in the sense that it reflects different research topics and only some of them are within the intended focus of the crawl).

3 Making BINGO! Effective

The BINGO! system described so far is a complete focused crawler with a suite of flexible options. When we started experimenting with the system, we observed fairly mixed success, however. In particular, some of the crawls lost their focus and were led astray by inappropriate training data or a bad choice of automatically added archetypes. Based on these lessons we improved the system in a number of ways that are described in this section.

3.1 Classifier Training on Negative Examples

An SVM classifier needs both positive and negative training examples for computing a separating hyperplane. As negative examples we used the positive training data from a topic's competing classes, which are the topic's siblings in the topic tree. For topics without proper siblings, e.g., for a single-topic crawl, we added a virtual child "OTHERS" to all tree nodes which was populated with some arbitrarily chosen documents that were "semantically far away" from all topics of the directory. This approach worked, but in some situations it was not sufficient to cope with the extreme diversity of Web data. In some sense, saying what the crawl should not return is as important as specifying what kind of information we are interested in.

As a consequence of this observation we now populate the virtual "OTHERS" class in a much more systematic manner. As the positive training examples for the various topics all contain ample common-sense vocabulary and not just the specific terms that we are interested in, we included training documents in the "OTHERS" classes that capture as much of the common-sense terminology as possible. In most of our experiments we use about 50 documents from the top-level categories of Yahoo (i.e., sports, entertainment, etc.) for this purpose. Since our focused crawls were mostly interested in scientific topics, this choice of negative examples turned out to be a proper complement to improve the classifier's learning.

3.2 Archetype Selection

The addition of inappropriate archetypes for retraining the classifier was a source of potential diffusion. To avoid the "topic drift" phenomenon, where a few out-of-focus training documents may lead the entire crawl into a wrong thematic direction, we now require that the classification confidence of an archetype must be higher than the mean confidence of the previous training documents. So each iteration effectively adds x new archetypes ($0 \leq x \leq min\{N_{auth}; N_{conf}\}$ where N_{auth} is the number of high-authority candidates from the link analysis and N_{conf} is the number of candidates with top ranks regarding SVM confidence), and it may also remove documents from the training data as the mean confidence of the training data changes. Once the up to $min\{N_{auth}; N_{conf}\}$ archetypes of a topic have been selected, the classifier is re-trained. This step in turn requires invoking the feature selection first. So the effect of re-training is twofold: 1) if the archetypes capture the terminology of the topic better than the original training data (which is our basic premise) then the feature selection procedure can extract better, more discriminative, features for driving the classifier, and 2) the accuracy of the classifiers test whether a new, previously unseen, document belongs to a topic or not is improved using richer (e.g, longer but concise) and more characteristic training documents for building its decision model. In the case of an SVM classifier, the first point means transforming all documents into a clearer feature space, and the second point can be interpreted as constructing a "sharper" (i.e., less blurred) separating hyperplane in the feature space (with more slack on either side of the hyperplane to the accepted or rejected documents).

3.3 Focus Adjustment and Tunnelling

Learning Phase with Sharp Focus

During the learning phase BINGO! runs with a very strict focusing rule. As the system starts only with a relatively small set of seeds, we can expect only low classification confidence with this initial classifier. Therefore, our top priority in this phase is to find new archetypes to augment the training basis. The crawler accepts only documents that are reachable via hyperlinks from the original seeds and are classified into the same topic as the corresponding seeds. We call this strategy *sharp focusing*: for all documents $p, q \in E$ and links $(p,q) \in V$ accept only those links where $class(p) = class(q)$.

The above strategy requires that at least some of the crawled documents are successfully classified into the topic hierarchy; otherwise, the crawler would quickly run out of links to be visited. This negative situation did indeed occur in some of our early experiments when the training data contained no useful links to related Web sources. Therefore, BINGO! also considers links from rejected documents (i.e., documents that do not pass the classification test for a given topic) for further crawling. However, we restrict the depth of traversing links from such documents to a threshold value, typically set to one or two. The rationale behind this threshold is that one often has to "tunnel" through topic-unspecific "welcome" or "table-of-contents" pages before again reaching a thematically relevant document.

Harvesting Phase with Soft Focus

Once the training set has reached $min\{N_{auth}; N_{conf}\}$ documents per topic, BINGO! performs retraining and the harvesting phase is started. The now improved crawling precision allows us to relax the hard focusing rule and to accept all documents that can successfully be classified into anyone of the topics of interest, regardless of whether this is the same class as that of its hyperlink predecessor. We call this strategy *soft focusing*: for all documents $p, q \in E$ and links $(p,q) \in V$ accept all links where $class(p) \neq ROOT/OTHERS$. The harvesting usually has tunneling activated.

3.4 Feature Space Construction

Single terms alone and the resulting $tf * idf$-based document vectors are a very crude characterization of document contents. In addition to this traditional IR approach we are also investigating various richer feature spaces:

- *Term pairs:* The co-occurrence of certain terms in the same document adds to the content characterization and may sometimes even contribute to disambiguating polysems (i.e., words with multiple meanings). The extraction of all possible term pairs in a document is computationally expensive. We use a sliding window technique and determine only pairs within a limited word distance.
- *Neighbor documents:* Sometimes a document's neighborhood, i.e., its predecessors and successors in the hyperlink graph, can help identifying the topic of the document. We consider constructing feature vectors that contain both the current document's terms and the most significant terms of its neighbor documents. This approach is somewhat risky as it may as well dillute the feature space (as reported in [8]); so it is crucial to combine it with conservative (MI based) feature selection.
- *Anchor texts:* The short texts in hyperlink tags of the HTML pages that point to the current document may provide concise descriptions of the target document. However, it is very crucial to use an extended form of stopword elimination on anchor texts (to remove standard phrases such as "click here").

The way we are using the above feature options in BINGO! is by constructing combined feature spaces or by creating multiple alternative classifiers (see next subsection). For example, BINGO! can construct feature vectors that have single-term frequencies, term-pair frequencies, and anchor terms of predecessors as components. For all components feature selection is applied beforehand to capture only the most significant of these features. The classifier can handle the various options that BINGO! supports in a uniform manner: it does not have to know how feature vectors are constructed and what they actually mean. Vectors with up to several thousand components can be handled with acceptable performance.

3.5 Meta Classification

BINGO! can construct a separate classifier (i.e., trained decision model) for each of the various feature space options outlined in the previous section (including combination spaces). Right after training it uses the $\xi\alpha$ estimator [13] for predicting the quality (i.e., classification precision) of each alternative and then selects the one that has the best estimated "generalization performance" for classifying new, previously unseen, documents. The same estimation technique can be used, with some extra computational effort, for choosing an appropriate value for the number of most significant terms or other features that are used to construct the classifier's input vectors after feature selection.

In addition, BINGO! can combine multiple classifiers at run-time using a meta classifier approach. Consider the set $V = \{v_1, \ldots, v_h\}$ of classifiers. Let $res(v_i, D, K) \in \{-1, 1\}$ be the decision of the i-th method for the classification of document D into class C, $w(v_i) \in \mathbf{R}$ be weights and $t_1, t_2 \in \mathbf{R}$ be thresholds. Then we can define a meta decision function as follows:

$$Meta(V, D, C) = \begin{cases} +1 \text{ when } \sum_{i=1}^{h} w_i \cdot res(v_i) > t_1 \\ -1 \text{ when } \sum_{i=1}^{h} w_i \cdot res(v_i) < t_2 \\ 0, \text{ otherwise} \end{cases} \quad (2)$$

The zero decision means that the meta classifier is unable to make a clear decision and thus abstains.

Three special instances of the above meta classifier are of particular importance (one of them using the $\xi\alpha$ estimators [13]):

1. *unanimous decision*: for definitively positive classification the results of all classifiers must be equal: as follows:
   $w(v_i) = 1$ for all $v_i \in V, \quad t_1 = h - 0.5 = -t_2$
2. *majority decision*: the meta result is the result of the majority of the classifiers:
   $w(v_i) = 1$ for all $v_i \in V, \quad t_1 = t_2 = 0.$
3. *weighted average* according to the $\xi\alpha$ estimators:
   $w(v_i) = precision_{\xi\alpha}(v_i)$ for all $v_i \in V, t_1 = t_2 = 0$

Such *model combination and averaging* techniques are well known in the machine learning literature [17]. They typically make learning-based decision functions more robust and can indeed improve the overall classification precision. This observation was also made in some of our experiments where unanimous and weighted average decisions improved precision from values around 80 percent to values above 90 percent. By default, BINGO! uses multiple alternative classifiers in parallel and applies the unanimous-decision meta function in the crawl's learning phase and the weighted average in the harvesting phase. Each of these parallel classifiers requires computing a scalar product between vectors with a few thousand components for each visited Web page that needs to be classified. When the crawler's run-time is critical, we therefore switch to a single feature space and a single classifier, namely, the one with the best $\xi\alpha$ estimator for its precision. This still requires training multiple classifiers, but in this run-time-critical case this is done only once before the harvesting phase is started. For the learning phase we always use the meta classifier.

3.6 Result Postprocessing

The result of a BINGO! crawl may be a database with several million documents. Obviously, the human user needs additional assistance for filtering and analyzing such result sets in order to find the best answers to her information demands. To this end BINGO! includes a local search engine that employs IR and data mining techniques for this kind of postprocessing.

The search engine supports both exact and vague filtering at user-selectable classes of the topic hierarchy, with relevance ranking based on the usual IR metrics such as cosine similarity [3] of term-based document vectors. In addition, it can rank filtered document sets based on the classifier's confidence in the assignment to the corresponding classes, and it can perform the HITS link analysis [14] to compute authority scores and produce a ranking according to these scores. Different ranking schemes can be combined into a linear sum with appropriate weights; this provides flexibility for trial-and-error experimentation by a human expert.

Filtering and ranking alone cannot guarantee that the user finds the requested information. Therefore, when BINGO! is used for expert Web search, our local search engine supports additional interactive feedback. In particular, the user may select additional training documents among the top ranked results that he sees and possibly drops previous training data; then the filtered documents are classified again under the retrained model to improve precision. For information portal generation, a typical problem is that the results in a given class are heterogeneous in the sense that they actually cover multiple topics that are not necessarily closely related. This may result from the diversity and insufficient quality of the original training data.

To help the portal administrator for better organizing the data, BINGO! can perform a cluster analysis on the results of one class and suggest creating new subclasses with tentative labels automatically drawn from the most characteristic terms of these subclasses. The user can experiment with different numbers of clusters, or BINGO! can choose the number of clusters such that an entropy-based cluster impurity measure is minimized [9]. Our current implementation uses the simple $K - means$ algorithm [16, 17] for clustering, but we plan to add more sophisticated algorithms.

4 Making BINGO! Efficient

Our main attention in building BINGO! was on search result quality and the effectiveness of the crawler. When we started with larger-scale experimentation, we realized that we had underestimated the importance of performance and that effectiveness and efficiency are intertwined: the recall of our crawls was severely limited by the poor speed of the crawler. In the last months we focused our efforts on performance improvement and reimplemented the most performance-critical function components.

BINGO! is implemented completely in Java and uses Oracle9i as a storage engine. The database-related components (document analysis, feature selection, etc.) are implemented as stored procedures, the crawler itself runs as a multi-threaded application under the Java VM. As crawl results are stored in the database, we implemented our local search engine as a set of servlets under Apache and the Jserv engine. Our rationale for Java was easy portability, in particular, our student's desire to be independent of the "religious wars" about Windows vs. Linux as the underlying platform.

This section discusses some of the Java- and database-related performance problems and also some of the key techniques for accelerating our crawler. We adopted some useful tips on crawl performance problems from the literature [10, 11, 20] and also developed various additional enhancements.

4.1 Lessons on Database Design and Usage

The initial version of BINGO! used object-relational features of Oracle9i (actually Oracle8i when we started), in particular, *nested tables* for hierarchically organized data. This seemed to be the perfect match for storing documents, as the top-level table, and the corresponding sets of terms and associated statistics as a subordinate table (document texts were stored in a LOB attribute of the top-level table). It turned out, however, that the query optimizer had to compute Cartesian products between the top-level and the subordinate table for certain kinds of queries with selections and projections on both tables. Although this may be a problem of only a specific version of the database system, we decide to drastically simplify the database design and now have a schema with 24 flat relations, and also simplified the SQL queries accordingly.

Crawler threads use separate database connections associated with dedicated database server processes. Each thread batches the storing of new documents and avoids SQL insert commands by first collecting a certain number of documents in workspaces and then invoking the database system's bulk loader for moving the documents into the database. This way the crawler can sustain a throughput of up to ten thousand documents per minute.

4.2 Lessons on Crawl Management

Networking aspects

A key point for an efficient crawler in Java is control over blocking I/O operations. Java provides the convenient `HTTPUrlConnection` class, but the underlying socket connection is hidden from the programmer. Unfortunately, it is impossible to change the default timeout setting; thus, a successfully established but very slow connection cannot be cancelled. The recommended way to overcome this limitation of the Java core libraries is to control the blocking connection using a parallel "watcher thread". To avoid this overhead, BINGO! implements its own socket-based HTTP connections following RFC 822 [18].

The Java core class `InetAddress`, used for the representation of network addresses and resolving of host names, is another potential bottleneck for the crawler [11]. It was observed that the caching algorithm of `InetAddress` is not sufficiently fast for thousands of DNS lookups per minute. To speed up name resolution, we implemented our own asynchronous DNS resolver. This resolver can operate with multiple DNS servers in parallel and resends requests to alternative servers upon timeouts. To reduce the number of DNS server requests, the resolver caches all obtained information (hostnames, IP addresses, and additional hostname aliases) using a limited amount of memory with LRU replacement and TTL-based invalidation.

Since a document may be accessed through different path aliases on the same host (this holds especially for well referenced authorities for compatibility with outdated user bookmarks), the crawler uses several fingerprints to recognize duplicates. The initial step consists of simple URL matching (however, URLs have an average length of more than 50 bytes [2]; our implementation merely compares the hashcode representation of the visited URL, with a small risk of falsely dismissing a new document). In the next step, the crawler checks the combination of returned IP address and path of the resource. Finally, the crawler starts the download and controls the size of the incoming data. We assume that the filesize is a unique value within the same host and consider candidates with previously seen IP/filesize combinations as duplicates. A similar procedure is applied to handle redirects. The redirection information is stored in the database for use in the link analysis (see Section 2.5). We allow multiple redirects up to a pre-defined depth (set to 25 by default).

Document type management

To avoid common crawler traps and incorrect server responses, the maximum length of hostnames is restricted to 255 (RFC 1738 [22] standard), the maximum URL length is restricted to 1000. This reflects the common distribution of URL lengths on the Web [2], disregarding URLs that have GET parameters encoded in them.

To recognize and reject data types that the crawler cannot handle (e.g., video and sound files), the BINGO! engine checks all incoming documents against a list of MIME types [12]. For each MIME type we specify a maximum size allowed by the crawler; these sizes are based on large-scale Google evaluations [2]. The crawler controls both the HTTP response and the real size of the retrieved data and aborts the connection when the size limit is exceeded.

Crawl queue management

The proper URL ordering on the crawl frontier is a key point for a focused crawler. Since the absolute priorities may vary for different topics of interest, the queue manager maintains several queues, one (large) incoming and one (small) outgoing queue for each topic, implemented as Red-Black trees.

The engine controls the sizes of queues and starts the asynchronous DNS resolution for a small number of the best incoming links when the outgoing queue is not sufficiently filled. So expensive DNS lookups are initiated only for promising crawl candidates. Incoming URL queues are limited to 25.000 links, outgoing URL queues to 1000 links, to avoid uncontrolled memory usage.

In all queues, URLs are prioritized based on their SVM confidence scores (see Section 2). The priority of tunnelled links (see 3.3) is reduced by a constant factor for each tunnelling step (i.e., with exponential decay), set to 0.5 in our experiments.

We also learned that a good focused crawler needs to handle crawl *failures*. If the DNS resolution or page download causes a timeout or error, we tag the corresponding host as "slow". For slow hosts the number of retrials is restricted to 3; if the third attempt fails the host is tagged as "bad" and excluded for the rest of the current crawl.

5 Experiments

5.1 Testbed

In the experiments presented here, BINGO! was running on a dual Intel 2GHz server with 4 GB main memory under Win2k, connected to an Oracle9i database server on the same computer. The number of crawler threads was initially restricted to 15; the number of parallel accesses per host was set to 2 and per recognized domain to 5. The engine used 5 DNS servers located on different nodes of our local domain. The maximum number of retrials after timeouts was set to 3. The maximum allowed tunneling distance was set to 2. The allowed size of the URL queues for the crawl frontier was set to 30,000 for each class. To eliminate "meta search capabilities", the domains of major Web search engines (e.g., Google) were explicitly locked for crawling. The feature selection, using the MI criterion, selected the best 2000 features for each topic.

In the following subsections we present two kinds of experiments: 1) the generation of an information portal from a small seed of training documents, and 2) an expert query that does not yield satisfactory results on any of the popular standard search engines such as Google.

5.2 Portal Generation for a Single Topic

To challenge the learning capabilities of our focused crawler, we aimed to gather a large collection of Web pages about *database research*. This single-topic directory was initially populated with only *two* authoritative sources, the home pages of David DeWitt and Jim Gray (actually 3 pages as Gray's page has two frames, which are handled by our crawler as separate documents).

The initial SVM classification model was built using these 2 positive and about 400 negative examples randomly chosen from Yahoo top-level categories such as sports and entertainment (see Section 3). In the learning phase, BINGO! explored the vicinity of the initial seeds and added newly found archetypes to the topic. To this end the maximum crawl depth was set to 4 and the maximum tunnelling distance to 2, and we restricted the crawl of this phase to the domains of the training data (i.e., the CS department of the University of Wisconsin and Microsoft Research, and also additional Yahoo categories for further negative examples). Since we started with extremely small training data, we did not enforce the thresholding scheme (3.2) (requirement that the SVM confidence for new archetypes would have to be higher than the average confidence of the initial seeds). Instead, we rather admitted all positively classified documents (including the ones that were positively classified into the complementary class "OTHERS", i.e., the Yahoo documents). Altogether we obtained 1002 archetypes, many of them being papers (in Word or PDF), talk slides (in Powerpoint or PDF), or project overview pages of the two researchers, and then retrained the classifier with this basis.

Property	90 minutes	12 hours
Visited URLs	100,209	3,001,982
Stored pages	38,176	992,663
Extracted links	1,029,553	38,393,351
Positively classified	21,432	518,191
Visited hosts	3,857	34,647
Max crawling depth	22	236

Table 1: Crawl summary data

The harvesting phase then performed prioritized breadth-first search with the above training basis and seed URLs, now without any domain limitations (other than excluding popular Web search engines). We paused the crawl after 90 minutes to assess the intermediate results at this point, and then resumed it for a total crawl time of 12 hours. Table 5.2 shows some summary data for this crawl.

To assess the quality of our results we used the DBLP portal (*http://dblp.uni-trier.de/*) as a comparison yardstick. The idea was that we could automatically construct a crude approximation of DBLP's collection of pointers to database researcher homepages. DBLP contains 31,582 authors with explicit homepage URLs (discounting those that have only a URL suggested by an automatic homepage finder). We sorted these authors in descending order of their number of publications (ranging from 258 to 2), and were particularly interested in finding a good fraction of the top ranked authors with BINGO!. To prevent giving BINGO! any conceivably unfair advantage, we locked the DBLP domain and the domains of its 7 official mirrors for our crawler. In evaluating the results, we considered a homepage as "found" if the crawl result contained a Web page "underneath" the home page, i.e., whose URL had the homepage path as a prefix; these were typically publication lists, papers, or CVs. The rationale for this success measure was that it would now be trivial and fast for a human user to navigate upwards to the actual homepage.

We evaluated the recall, i.e., the total number of found DBLP authors, and the precision of the crawl re-

Best crawl results	Top 1000 DBLP	All authors
1,000	27	91
5,000	79	498
all (21,432)	218	1,396

Table 2: BINGO! precision (90 minutes)

Best crawl results	Top 1000 DBLP	All authors
1,000	267	342
5,000	401	1,325
all (518,191)	712	7,101

Table 3: BINGO! precision (12 hours)

sult. For the latter we considered the number of pages found out of the 1000 DBLP-top-ranked researchers, i.e., the ones with the most publications, namely, between 258 and 45 papers. The crawl result was sorted by descending classification confidence for the class "database research", and we compared the top 1000 results to the top 1000 DBLP authors.

Tables 2 and 3 show the most important measures on crawl result quality. Most noteworthy is the good recall: we found 712 of the top 1000 DBLP authors (without ever going through any DBLP page). The precision is not yet as good as we wished it to be: 267 of these top-ranked authors can be found in the 1000 documents with highest classification confidence. So a human user would have to use the local search engine and other data analysis tools to further explore the crawl result, but given that the goal was to automatically build a rich information portal we consider the overall results as very encouraging. Note that our crawler is not intended to be a homepage finder and thus does not use specific heuristics for recognizing homepages (e.g., URL pattern matching, typical HTML annotations in homepages, etc.). This could be easily added for postprocessing the crawl result and would most probably improve precision.

5.3 Expert Web Search

To investigate the abilities of the focused crawler for expert Web search, we studied an example of a "needle-in-a-haystack" type search problem. We used BINGO! to search for *public domain open source implementations of the ARIES recovery algorithm.*

A direct search for "public domain open source ARIES recovery" on a large-scale Web search engine (e.g., Google) or a portal for open source software (e.g., sourceforge.net) does not return anything useful in the top 10 ranks; it would be a nightmare to manually navigate through the numerous links that are contained in these poor matches for further surfing. As an anecdotic remark, the open source software portal even returned lots of results about bin*aries* and libr*aries*.

Our procedure for finding better results was as follows. In a first step, we issued a Google query for "aries recovery method" and "aries recovery algorithm" to retrieve useful and starting points for a focused crawl. The top 10 matches from Google were intellectually inspected by us, and we selected 7 reasonable documents for training; these are listed in Figure 4.

1 http://www.bell-labs.com/topic/books/db-book/slide-dir/Aries.pdf
2 http://www-2.cs.cmu.edu/afs/cs/academic/class/15721-f01/www/lectures/recovery_with_aries.pdf
3 http://icg.harvard.edu/ cs265/lectures/readings/mohan-1992.pdf
4 http://www.cs.brandeis.edu/ liuba/abstracts/mohan.html
5 http://www.almaden.ibm.com/u/mohan/ARIES_Impact.html
6 http://www-db.stanford.edu/dbseminar/Archive/FallY99/mohan-1203.html
7 http://www.vldb.org/conf/1989/P337.PDF

Figure 4: Initial training documents

Note that Mohan's ARIES page (the 5th URL in Figure 4) does not provide an easy answer to the query; of course, it contains many references to ARIES-related papers, systems, and teaching material, but it would take hours to manually surf and inspect a large fraction of them in order to get to the source code of a public domain implementation.

These pages were used to build the initial SVM classification model. As negative examples we again used a set of randomly chosen pages from Yahoo top-level categories such as "sports". The focused crawler was then run for a short period of 10 minutes. It visited about 17,000 URLs with crawling depth between 1 and 7; 2,167 documents were positively classified into the topic "ARIES".

Finally, we used the result postprocessing component (see 3.6) and performed a keyword search filtering with relevance ranking based on cosine similarity. The top-10 result set for the query "source code release" contains links to open-source projects Shore and Minibase, which implement ARIES media recovery algorithm (Figure 5). Additionally, the third open source system, Exodus, is directly referenced by the Shore homepage. A MiniBase page (further up in the directory) was also among the top 10 crawl results according to SVM classification confidence; so even without further filtering the immediate result of the focused crawl would provide a human user with a very good reference.

We emphasize that the expert Web search supported by our focused crawler required merely a minimum amount of human supervision. The human expert had to evaluate only 30 to 40 links (20 for training set selection, and 10 to 20 for result postprocessing), collected into prepared lists with content previews. Including crawling time and evaluation, the overall search cost was about 14 minutes. This overhead is significantly lower than the typical time for manual surfing in the hyperlink vicinity of some initial authorities (such as IBM Almaden).

0.025 **http://www.cs.wisc.edu/shore/doc/** overview/node5.html
0.023 http://www.almaden.ibm.com/cs/ jcentral_press.html
0.022 http://www.almaden.ibm.com/cs/garlic.html
0.021 http://www.cs.brandeis.edu/~liuba/ abstracts/greenlaw.html
0.020 http://www.db.fmi.uni-passau.de/~kossmann/ papers/garlic.html
0.018 http://www.tivoli.com/products/index/ storage-mgr/platforms.html
0.015 **http://www.cs.wisc.edu/shore/doc/** overview/footnode.html
0.014 http://www.almaden.ibm.com/cs/clio/
0.011 **http://www.cs.wisc.edu/coral/minibase/** logmgr/report/node22.html
0.011 http://www.ceid.upatras.gr/courses/minibase/ minibase-1.0/documentation/html/minibase/ logmgr/report/node22.html

Figure 5: Top 10 results for query "*source code release*"

6 Conclusion

In this paper we have presented the BINGO! system for focused crawling and its applications to information portal generation and expert Web search. Many concepts in BINGO! have been adopted from prior work on Web IR and statistical learning, but we believe that the integration of these techniques into a comprehensive and versatile system like BINGO! is a major step towards a new generation of advanced Web search and information mining tools. The experiments that we presented in this paper have shown the great potential of the focused crawling paradigm but also some remaining difficulties of properly calibrating crawl setups for good recall and high precision.

Our future work aims to integrate BINGO! engine with a Web-service-based portal explorer and a semantically richer set of ontology services. On the other hand, we plan to pursue approaches to generating "semantically" tagged XML documents from the HTML pages that BINGO! crawls and investigate ways of incorporating ranked retrieval of XML data [21] in the result postprocessing or even as a structure- and context-aware filter during a focused crawl.

References

[1] The open-source biojava project. *http://www.biojava.org.*

[2] Google research project. *WebmasterWorld Pub Conference*, 2002.

[3] R. Baeza-Yates and B. Ribeiro-Neto. *Modern Information Retrieval.* Addison Wesley, 1999.

[4] K. Bharat and M. Henzinger. Improved algorithms for topic distillation in a hyperlinked environment. *ACM SIGIR Conference*, 1998.

[5] S. Brin and L. Page. The anatomy of a large scale hyper-textual Web search engine. *7th WWW Conference*, 1998.

[6] C.J.C. Burges. A tutorial on Support Vector Machines for pattern recognition. *Data Mining and Knowledge Discovery*, 2(2), 1998.

[7] S. Chakrabarti, M. van den Berg, and B. Dom. Focused crawling: A new approach to topic-specific Web resource discovery. *8th WWW Conference*, 1999.

[8] S. Chakrabarti, B. Dom, and P. Indyk. Enhanced hypertext categorization using hyperlinks. *SIGMOD Conference*, 1998.

[9] R. Duda, P. Hart, and D. Stork. *Pattern Classification.* Wiley, 2000.

[10] A. Heydon and M. Najork. Mercator: A scalable, extensible Web crawler. *WWW Conference*, 1999.

[11] A. Heydon and M. Najork. Performance limitations of the Java core libraries. *ACM Java Grande Conference*, 1999.

[12] The Internet Assigned Numbers Authority (IANA). http://www.iana.org.

[13] T. Joachims. Estimating the generalization performance of an SVM efficiently. *European Conference on Machine Learning (ECML)*, 2000.

[14] J.M. Kleinberg. Authoritative sources in a hyperlinked environment. *Journal of the ACM*, 46(5), 1999.

[15] D. Lewis. Naive (Bayes) at forty: The independence assumption in information retrieval. *European Conference on Machine Learning (ECML)*, 1998.

[16] C.D. Manning and H. Schuetze. *Foundations of Statistical Natural Language Processing.* MIT Press, 1999.

[17] T. Mitchell. *Machine Learning.* McGraw Hill, 1996.

[18] Hypertext Transfer Protocol. http://www.w3.org/protocols/http/.

[19] G. Salton and M.J. McGill. *Introduction to Modern Information Retrieval.* McGraw Hill, 1983.

[20] V. Shkapenyuk and T. Suel. Design and implementation of a high-performance distributed Web crawler. *International Conference on Data Engineering (ICDE)*, 2002.

[21] A. Theobald and G. Weikum. Adding relevance to XML. *3rd International Workshop on the Web and Databases (WebDB)*, 2000.

[22] RFC 1738: Uniform Resource Locators (URL). http://www.w3.org/addressing/rfc1738.txt.

[23] V. Vapnik. *Statistical Learning Theory.* Wiley, New York, 1998.

[24] Y. Yang and O. Pedersen. A comparative study on feature selection in text categorization. *International Conference on Machine Learning (ICML)*, 1997.

Data Management in Application Servers

Dean Jacobs

BEA Systems
235 Montgomery St
San Francisco, CA 94104, USA
dean@bea.com

Abstract

This paper surveys data management techniques used in Application Servers. It begins with an overview of Application Servers and the way they have evolved from earlier transaction processing systems. It then presents a taxonomy of clustered services that differ in the way they manage data in memory and on disk. The treatment of conversational state is discussed in depth. Finally, it describes a persistence layer that is specifically designed for and tightly integrated with the Application Server. Throughout this paper, examples are drawn from experiences implementing BEA WebLogic Server™.

1. Introduction

Transaction processing applications maintain data representing real-world concepts and field associated requests from client devices [1]. Transaction processing applications play an essential role in many industries, including:

- **Airlines** Managing flight schedules and passenger reservations.
- **Banking** Accessing customer accounts through tellers and ATMs.
- **Manufacturing** Tracking orders; Managing inventory; Planning and scheduling jobs
- **Telephony** Allocating resources during call setup and teardown; Billing across multiple companies.

The typical transaction processing workload consists of many short-running requests that include both queries and updates. In contrast, typical workloads for non-transactional applications, such as those for scientific computing or analytical processing, consist of smaller numbers of compute-intensive queries.

Transaction Processing Monitors provide a software infrastructure for building transaction processing applications. A key feature of TP Monitors is support for ACID properties of transactions to handle failures and other exceptional conditions. Other important features include support for security, administration, scalability, and high availability.

TP Monitors support both **synchronous** (two-way) and **asynchronous** (one-way) communication between distributed processes. In a synchronous remote procedure call (RPC), the sender of a request is blocked until a response is obtained from the receiver. In asynchronous messaging, no response is expected and the sender is free to continue as soon as the request has been queued by the infrastructure. In either case, reliable communication can be provided using distributed transactions. This technique is problematic in an administratively-heterogeneous environment however because a transaction started in one jurisdiction may end up holding resources, such as database locks, in another. An alternative is to use **store-and-forward messaging**, where messages are queued on the sender before being forwarded to queues on the receiver. Message forwarding can be reliably implemented using simple ACKing protocols. In addition, it provides a natural way of buffering work when a remote system is temporarily unavailable.

Early TP Monitors, in particular IBM CICS [2], were developed in the 1970s to run on monolithic mainframe systems. Distributed TP Monitors, such as BEA Tuxedo™ [3], were developed in the 1980s to run on collections of mid-sized computers. Distributed TP Monitors use software-level clustering to provide scalability and availability. **Application Servers**, such as BEA WebLogic Server™ [4], evolved from Distributed TP Monitors in the 1990s to meet new demands imposed by the Internet. Significant among these demands is support for loosely-coupled clients.

Tightly-coupled clients contain code from the Application Server and communicate with it using proprietary protocols. As a result, they can offer higher functionality and better performance. **Loosely-coupled** clients do not contain code from the Application Server and communicate with it using vendor-neutral, industry-standard protocols such as HTTP [5] and SOAP [6]. Loosely-coupled clients tolerate a wider variety of evolutionary changes to the server-side of an application and are easier to maintain. Prominent loosely-coupled clients include Web Browsers, for human-to-machine communication, and Web Services clients, for machine-to-machine communication. Web Services protocols for asynchronous communication usually employ store-and-forward messaging.

The choice of whether to use tightly- or loosely-coupled clients is affected not only by the degree of distribution of the system, but also by the extent to which it has a centralized administrative authority. For example, a chief architect might create a collection of tightly-coupled systems across widely-distributed outlets of a retail company or branches of a post office. On the other hand, highly-autonomous departments within the same enterprise might choose to use loosely-coupled clients so they can evolve their applications more independently.

As part of their evolution from TP Monitors, Application Servers have become increasingly dynamic in nature. Along with "systematic" applications, which are carefully planned and rolled out over a long period of time, Application Servers must handle "opportunistic" applications, which are rolled out quickly and modified often during their lifetimes. As a result, Application Servers greatly benefit by the ability to tune themselves, e.g., by automatically setting cache and thread pool sizes. In addition, Application Servers must handle traffic from unknown numbers of loosely-coupled clients across the Internet. As a result, Application Servers greatly benefit from the ability to dynamically enlist resources to handle peak loads [7]. Application Servers can be integrated into an enterprise-wide Grid Computing infrastructure that facilitates sharing of resources [8].

Application Servers provide most of the features of TP Monitors and thus embody the state of the art in transaction processing systems. In addition to traditional transaction processing applications, Application Servers are used for the following.

- **E-commerce** Catalog browsing and purchasing of consumer goods such as books
- **News Portals** Personalized consolidation of news from multiple sources
- **Financial Management** Control of financial holdings such as bank accounts or stocks
- **Packaged Applications** Single-purpose, vertical applications such as accounting, expense reporting, ERP, or CRM
- **Business Workflows** Automation of business processes such as bidding or ordering parts
- **Message Broker** Infrastructure for transforming and routing asynchronous messages

Application Servers offer a set of Application Programming Interfaces (APIs) to developers. Common APIs include the following.

- **Servlets** compute dynamic Web pages based on arguments to requests from Web Browsers. In contrast, static Web pages are always the same and can be hosted by a simple Web Server.
- **Web Services** are services that can be remotely invoked using industry-standard machine-to-machine protocols.
- **Components** are general-purpose objects with built-in support for features such as remote access, lifecycle management, and persistence. Components generally support object-relational mapping to allow persistence to RDBMSs.
- **Connectors** provide access to external back-end systems such as databases and mainframes.
- **Messaging** provides support for asynchronous communication.
- **Naming** services allow the externally visible parts of an application to be accessed by clients.

The Java™ 2 Enterprise Edition (J2EE™) [9] is a well-known set of industry-standard Application Server APIs that includes all of the above.

Application Servers are becoming increasingly distributed within the enterprise data center, both horizontally, from data-centric applications in the back-end to presentation-oriented applications in the front-end, and vertically, from stand-alone "stovepipe" applications to integrative applications that mediate access to many stovepipes. To provide desired qualities of service in the face of such distribution, Application Servers are increasingly maintaining data outside of centralized databases in the back-end. An Application Server may maintain the primary copy of data, for which it is then wholly responsible, or a secondary copy, which is drawn from a database. In either case, the net effect is often to relax ACID properties of transactions that manipulate the data [10].

This paper surveys data management techniques used in Application Servers. It identifies three basic types of clustered services - stateless, cached, and singleton - that differ in the way they manage data in memory and on disk. These service types provide different ways of relaxing ACID properties of transactions. The treatment of conversational state is discussed in depth. This paper also describes a persistence layer that is specifically designed for and tightly integrated with the Application Server. This persistence layer is lighter in weight than a conventional database and thus is better suited for distribution across a cluster. Throughout this paper, examples are drawn from experiences implementing WebLogic Server.

Two applications, which demonstrate the prominent loosely-coupled clients, will be used as running examples throughout this paper. The first is an **e-commerce application**, where consumers use Web Browsers to find and purchase goods. Items are selected one-by-one from a catalog and placed in a shopping cart, after which they may be purchased all together. The second is a **workflow application**, where a manufacturing business orders parts from a supplier using Web Services. Documents such as purchase orders and receipts flow back and forth as asynchronous messages according to an agreed-upon higher-level protocol.

This paper is organized as follows. Section 2 presents an overview of Application Server architectures. Section 3 presents the taxonomy of clustered services. Section 4 discusses the treatment of conversational state. Section 5 describes the Application Server persistence layer.

2. Application Server Architectures

Application Server systems are organized into logical tiers, each of which may contain multiple servers or other processes, as illustrated in Figure 1.

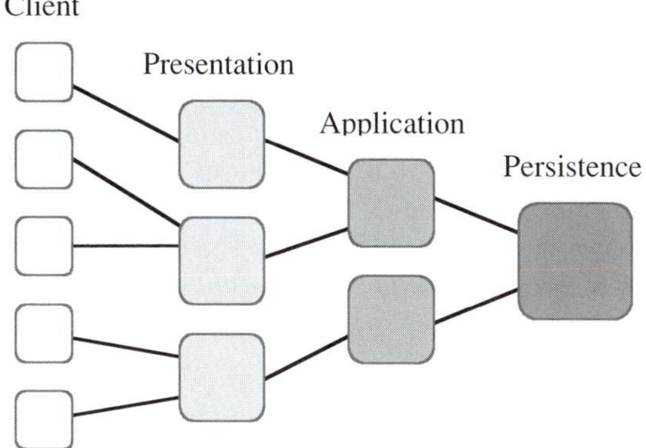

Figure 1 Multi-Tier Cluster Architecture

In this context, the example e-commerce application might be organized as follows. The client tier contains Web Browsers running on personal computers. The presentation tier contains Web Servers serving static Web pages. The application tier contains Application Servers running servlets, to generate personalized dynamic pages, and components, to access catalog and purchasing data. The persistence tier contains a database that maintains the catalog and purchasing data.

The example workflow application might be organized as follows. The client tier contains servers in the manufacturing business that place orders for parts. The presentation tier contains message routing processes. The application tier contains Application Servers running Web Services, to orchestrate the steps of the supplier's workflow, and components, to access inventory and purchasing data. The persistence tier contains a database that maintains the inventory and purchasing data.

More generally, the **client tier** may contain personal devices, such as workstations or handheld mobile units, embedded devices, such as network appliances or office machines, or servers in other enterprise systems. The **presentation tier** manages basic interactions with these clients over whatever protocols they require. Processes in the presentation tier do not run application code. The **application tier** contains Application Servers running all of the application code. The application tier may itself be divided, for example, into servlet and component tiers. The **persistence tier** provides durable storage in the form of databases and file systems. The persistence tier may also contain mainframes and other back-end systems.

The typical transaction processing workload consists of many short-running requests. In this setting, overall utilization of the system is improved by processing each request on as few servers as possible, since there is sufficient work to go around and the overhead for communication is relatively large. Consequently, all other factors being equal, it is preferable to minimize the number of physical tiers in the system.

The most common reason to segregate servers into actual physical tiers is for security, in particular, to support the placement of firewalls that filter traffic according to ports, protocols, and machines. Typically, firewalls are used to protect the application tier from the outside world, but they may also be used to restrict internal access to the persistence tier. Another common reason for segregating servers into physical tiers is to improve scalability by providing **session concentration**. The idea here is to place many smaller machines in the front end and multiplex socket connections to fewer, larger machines in the back end. In practice, a single machine can support thousands of connections and thus session concentration is required only to support tens of thousands of clients.

A **cluster** is a group of servers[1] that coordinate their actions to provide scalable, highly-available services. Scalability is provided by allowing servers to be dynamically added and removed and by balancing the load of requests across the system. Availability is provided by ensuring that there is no single point of failure and by migrating work off of failed servers. Ideally, a cluster should offer a **single system image** so that clients remain unaware of whether they are communicating with one or many servers [11]. The servers in a cluster may be contained within a single tier or they may span several tiers.

Simple round robin or data-dependent load balancing schemes generally suffice for the typical transaction processing workload. In particular, it is rarely worth the effort either to take actual server load into account or to redistribute on-going work when it occasionally becomes unbalanced. This is in contrast to practices commonly employed for compute-intensive applications [12].

Load balancing and failover for tightly-coupled clients is built into the Application Server infrastructure. For example, WebLogic Server integrates this functionality into its implementation of Remote Method Invocation (RMI), the basic Java API for invoking methods of a remote object. The caller-side RMI stub for a service obtains information about the instances of the service and makes load balancing and failover decisions.

Load balancing and failover for loosely-coupled clients must be implemented given the fixed vendor-neutral front-end of the cluster. One common approach relies on the fact that DNS allows multiple IP addresses to be listed under the same name and cycles through those addresses for each lookup. Using this feature, the front-end servers

[1] Throughout this paper, the term "server" refers to a software process rather than a piece of hardware. The latter is referred to as a "machine".

in a cluster can be co-listed under one name and clients can choose when to do lookups. This approach provides only coarse control over load balancing and failover. Moreover, it exposes details of the system so it is both less secure and harder to reconfigure. An alternative approach is to use a load balancing appliance (also known as a "packet sprayer") that exposes a single IP address and routes each request to one of the front-end servers behind it [13].

3. Clustered Services

This section describes three basic types of clustered services - stateless, cached, and singleton - that differ in the way they manage application data in memory and on disk.

Stateless services do not maintain application data between invocations, but rather load it into memory from shared back-end systems as needed for each request. A stateless service can be made scalable and highly available in a cluster by offering many instances of it, any one of which is as good as any other. Clients of the service are then free to switch between the instances as needed for load balancing and failover. While this approach is very simple, the large number of accesses to shared back-end systems can lead to long response times and can become a bottleneck to throughput.

To mitigate these problems, application data must be maintained privately by each server, either in memory, on disk, or both. **Cached services** maintain application data between invocations but keep it only loosely synchronized with the primary copy in a shared back-end system. This weak form of consistency allows there to be multiple instances of the service, for scalability and high availability, without incurring a high overhead for synchronizing copies of the data. **Singleton services** maintain application data between invocations and guarantee its strict transactional consistency. To achieve such guarantees without incurring excessive overhead, each individual data item is exclusively owned by a single instance of the service. If an instance of a singleton service fails, ownership of its data must be migrated to another server.

3.1 Stateless Services

Stateless services do not maintain application data between invocations. The simplest example of a stateless service is a component that computes a pure mathematical function of its arguments. A stateless service may maintain data internally as long as it does not directly effect results returned to clients. For example, database connection pools, which allow sharing and reuse of database connections by many clients, are stateless but keep track internally of which connections are in use. A stateless service may load application data into memory from a shared back-end system but only for the duration of an individual invocation. In the example e-commerce application, a stateless component might retrieve items from a large catalog that is stored in a database and pass them to a servlet for presentation in a browser. In the example workflow application, a stateless Web Service might retrieve the current workflow state from a database as each request arrives.

A stateless service can be made scalable and highly available by offering many instances of it in a cluster. WebLogic Server integrates this functionality into its implementation of RMI as follows. Each member of the cluster advertises the instances of stateless services it offers using a light-weight multicast protocol. This information is obtained by the caller-side stub for a service and used to make load balancing and failover decisions. The default load balancing algorithm uses a modified round-robin scheme that favors certain servers in order to minimize the spread of a transaction. The default failover algorithm retries a failed operation only if it can be guaranteed that there were no side-effects.

3.2 Cached Services

Cached services maintain application data between invocations but keep it only loosely synchronized with the primary copy in a shared back-end system. A cached service can be made scalable and highly available by offering many instances of it in a cluster. Cached data may be kept in memory and/or written out to a server's private disk. Data may be written out to avoid reacquiring it after a restart or to free up memory. Ideally, an Application Server should integrate caching into the implementation of its various APIs and, in addition, offer an explicit caching API.

Cached data may be the result of application-level processing of back-end data. In the example e-commerce application, HTML page fragments describing popular catalog items or special offers might be computed from relational data and cached by a servlet. In the example workflow application, aggregate historical data that is used for generating price quotes might be computed from relational data and cached by a Web Service. Cached data may also be a direct copy of back-end data. In the example applications, user or customer profiles that are retrieved from the database might be directly cached by a database connector or a component. Note that database connectors will cache the tabular results of relational queries while components will cache the fields of objects generated by object-relational mapping.

Cached data that is directly copied from the back-end may be updated by the service and written back. In the example applications, a component representing a user or customer profile might allow the data to be updated at the object level, producing a write to the backing relational data. Update anomalies can occur here because the read of the cached data occurs in a different transaction than the write. To prevent such anomalies from occurring, the data must be protected by optimistic concurrency control from within the cache.

WebLogic Server provides an option to use optimistic concurrency control to keep the cached fields of a component consistent with a database. At the beginning of a transaction, the server records the initial value of certain cached fields, either application-level version fields or actual data fields. At commit time, the generated UPDATE statement is predicated by a WHERE clause in which these values are compared with those in the database and a concurrency exception is thrown if they don't match. When such an exception occurs, it generally suffices for an application to retry the transaction. Overall, although this approach does not ensure serializability, its behavior may be desirable in that it increases concurrency in acceptable ways.

In **demand** caching, values are loaded as they are needed and **evicted** as they become out of date, as discussed in more detail below. Values may also be evicted to recover memory, a process that should be integrated with server-wide memory management. Demand caching is appropriate for large data collections with small working sets, such as user or customer profiles. In **materialized** caching, which is a form of replication, values are pre-loaded during initialization and **refreshed** when they become out of date. Values may not be evicted to recover memory. Materialized caching is appropriate for moderately-sized data collections that are frequently used, such as product catalogs. Since the set of data in memory is known at all times, this technique facilitates querying through the cache.

Cached values may be assigned a **time-to-live** until eviction or refresh. This approach does not require any communication between servers, so it scales well, but requires that the application tolerate a given window of staleness and inconsistency. This approach is attractive when the data is frequently updated, e.g., from a real-time data stream, in which case keeping up with the changes can be less efficient than not caching at all. Alternatively or in addition, values may be evicted or refreshed when updates occur. This approach is attractive when the data is infrequently updated, in which case the signalling overhead will be tolerable. Update signals may be sent with varying degrees of reliability, e.g., from best effort multicast to durable messaging.

Sending update signals requires identifying when relevant back-end data has changed. Doing so is straightforward if updates go through the Application Server itself, since it can then capture them in the course of its normal operations. For example, WebLogic Server can be configured to automatically evict all instances of a cached component in the event that any one of them is updated. After a transaction commits, the server multicasts a cluster-wide cache eviction signal containing the keys of any updated components. Identifying when relevant back-end data has changed is more difficult if updates go through other applications that share the data. In this case, the Application Server must rely on mechanisms such as database triggers or log-sniffing. Alternatively, the application can be made responsible for explicitly triggering cache evictions through a direct API.

For cached data that has been computed, sending update signals also requires identifying which pieces of back-end data are relevant in each case. There is a trade off here associated with the granularity of tracking of the data: finer granularity results in longer caching but is harder to implement efficiently. If the associated queries are known in advance, then it is possible to use database view maintenance techniques [14] for materialized caching and view invalidation techniques [15] for demand caching. This problem is compounded in the presence of ad-hoc queries, particularly if application-level processing of the back-end data makes it unclear which queries are relevant.

In a **partitioned** caching scheme [16], responsibility for subsets of the data is striped across subsets of the servers in the cluster. Partitioning makes it possible to scale up the effective memory size of the cluster so it can manage larger data collections. Partitioning requires data-dependent routing to forward requests to the appropriate servers. In contrast, without partitioning, data accesses always occur on the local server.

In a **two-tier** caching scheme, a first-tier cached service draws its data from a second-tier cached service, which draws its data from a shared back-end system as usual. Note that both tiers are contained within the application tier as illustrated in Figure 1. In the example e-commerce application, the first tier might contain servlets with small, demand caches of page fragments while the second tier contains components with large, materialized caches of catalog data. This architecture reduces the load on the back-end, since it allows a single lookup in the second tier to be shared by many members of the first tier. Moreover, it separates heavy-duty garbage collection, which is generated by application logic running in the first tier, from heavy-duty caching, which occurs in the second tier. Such a separation is advantageous because it allows the garbage collector to avoid needless scanning of cache elements.

3.3 Singleton Services

Singleton services maintain application data between invocations and guarantee its strict transactional consistency. To achieve such guarantees without limiting scalability of the cluster, each individual data item is exclusively owned by a single instance of the service. A data item may be accessed only by its owner; it may not be accessed by other members of the cluster nor shared with other applications.

The primary copy of a data item may be kept in a shared back-end system and cached in memory on the owner. In this case, performance is improved only for reads, since writes have to go through to the shared back-end. A second alternative is to keep the primary copy on a private disk of the owner as well as caching the data in memory. In addition to improving the performance of reads, this approach reduces the load on the shared back-end. A third alternative, which maximizes performance, is to keep the primary copy in memory on the owner rather than on a disk.

Examples of singleton services and their associated data items include the following.

- A **servlet container** (the Application Server module that executes servlets) and the data associated with browser sessions, such as the contents of shopping carts.
- A **messaging queue** and the messages on it that are awaiting delivery.
- A **transaction manager** and the data associated with its on-going transactions.
- A **distributed lock manager** and the status of locks in the system.
- An **in-memory database** and its current state.
- An **event correlation engine**, such as an alarm generator, and the current state of the system.

A large singleton service may be made scalable by partitioning it into multiple instances, each of which handles a different slice of the data. For example, WebLogic Server allows a logical messaging queue to be partitioned into many physical instances, each of which is responsible for certain messaging consumers. In the example workflow application, a logical queue holding requests to purchase parts might be partitioned into multiple physical queues, each associated with a group of customers. In the case of queues, partitioning also improves availability in that messages can continue to flow through the system even though an instance has failed, although certain messages or users may be stalled until the failed instance is recovered.

A request for a singleton service must be routed to the appropriate server. Routing must take into account partitioning if it occurs. Routing is straight-forward for tightly-coupled clients, since it is built into the Application Server infrastructure. For loosely-coupled clients, routing must be implemented given the fixed vendor-neutral front-end of the cluster, as discussed in the next section on conversational state. Routing introduces an extra network hop in processing a request. This overhead is acceptable if it is used to trade off server-to-database communication with server-to-server communication. Ideally, all of the singleton service instances needed to process a request should be co-located on the same server so that routing occurs only once per request.

If an instance of a singleton service fails, ownership of its data items must be **migrated** to a new server. If the primary copy of the data is kept in a shared back-end system, then it can be directly accessed by the new server. Alternatively, the primary copy can be kept on a private disk whose ownership can be transferred, such as a dual-ported disk. A third alternative is to replicate the data to a secondary server in the cluster. Note that in the latter case, the secondary is used only to recover the data, it does not process requests while the primary is active. There are three levels at which migration can occur: server, data, and service.

In **server migration**, a singleton service instance is pinned to a particular server and that server is migrated to a new machine as failures occur. The IP addresses of the server are usually migrated along with it, using routing protocols such as ARP, so external references do not need to be adjusted. One advantage of server migration is that it does not require any special effort on the part of the singleton service implementer; even pre-existing services can be made highly available without modification. In addition, it is compatible with the design of most High-Availability (HA) Frameworks [17], which offer whole-process migration.

A disadvantage of server migration is that it requires the administrator to manually distribute the set of singleton service instances across a fixed set of servers. Moreover, in order to provide headroom for the cluster to perform automatic load balancing in the event that machines are added, an unnecessarily large number of servers must be defined. As a result, some machines may be required to host several servers at the same time. Another disadvantage of server migration is that it may take a long time to start a server and initialize the application, increasing the downtime of the service. This problem can be mitigated using hot-standby techniques, which entail implementing some kind of server/service lifecycle API.

In **data migration**, ownership of data elements is distributed and migrated among existing singleton service instances, as illustrated by the following examples.

- Each server has one servlet container and failure of a server entails migrating its browser sessions to other servers.
- Each server has one physical instance of a logical messaging queue and failure of a server entails migrating its outstanding messages to other servers.
- Each server has one Transaction Manager and failure of a server entails migrating its outstanding transactions to other servers.
- Each server has one instance of an in-memory database that is in charge of some slices of the data and failure of a server entails migrating its slices to other servers.

Note that in the first three cases, any instance of the service is as good as any other until some kind of session or connection is created, after which a particular instance must be used. The advantage of data migration is that work distribution can be performed automatically without intervention on the part of the administrator. The disadvantage is that it complicates the task of writing a singleton service because ownership of data items may be assigned on-the-fly.

In **service migration**, complete singleton service instances are distributed and migrated among existing servers. As in server migration, this approach requires the administrator to manually distribute the work. A more serious problem is that this approach allows there to be multiple instances of the same service on the same server. This behavior is not acceptable for services, such as transaction managers, whose identity is uniquely associated with an individual server.

Regardless of the level at which it occurs – server, data, or service – migration usually requires sophisticated machinery to establish cluster membership. The problem is that, in an asynchronous network, there is no way to distinguish actual process failure from temporary process freezing or network partitioning [18]. Thus, a seemingly-failed process may reappear after migration has occurred, resulting in disagreement about the ownership of data. The standard solution is to have processes engage in a distributed agreement protocol [19] to establish cluster membership. Processes periodically prove their health to the rest of the system and, if that is not possible for any reason, shut themselves down. The decision to migrate is always postponed for at least one health-check period to give a seemingly-failed server the chance to shut itself down.

Among other options, WebLogic Server offers a novel technique for establishing cluster membership that uses a back-end database in place of server-to-server communication. Each server periodically writes to the database to prove its health and, within the same transaction, ensures that it has not been ejected from the cluster by another server. Other servers inspect the database to identify a timed-out server and, in the same transaction, eject it from the cluster. All timing data is taken from the database clock. This technique is particularly attractive for TP applications, which generally require a database and have one configured to the desired levels of scalability and availability. In contrast, distributed agreement protocols based on server-to-server communication introduce additional overhead that limits the size of a cluster. Moreover, such protocols often introduce a shared disk anyway in order to avoid "split-brain syndrome", where two sub-clusters function independently, which can result from network partitioning.

4. Managing Conversational State

A **conversation** between a client and the server-side of an application consists of a sequence of related requests intended to accomplish some goal. In the example e-commerce application, a conversation occurs when a browser client puts a series of items in a shopping cart and purchases them. In the example workflow application, a conversation occurs when a manufacturing client negotiates a bid for parts with a supplier. The participants of a conversation maintain **conversational state** to keep track of progress that has been made towards the desired goal.

Conversational state is ideal for management by a singleton service because a) requests that use it often benefit from short response times, b) it is not usually shared, and c) it can often tolerate reduced durability. This section discusses the use of singleton services to manage conversational state for the two prominent types of loosely-coupled clients, Web Browsers and Web Services clients.

To make use of singleton services, selection of the host for a conversation should occur when it is initially created and subsequent requests should be routed to the chosen server. Implementing such **session affinity** is straight-forward for tightly-coupled clients, since load balancing is built into the Application Server infrastructure. For loosely-coupled clients, which are discussed in this section, session affinity must be implemented given the fixed vendor-neutral front-end of the cluster.

4.1 Web Browser Clients

Web Browser conversations are called **servlet sessions** and the associated conversational state is called **servlet session state**. Web Browsers, Web Servers, and load balancing appliances provide mechanisms for implementing session affinity so servlet session state can be maintained in memory. When a servlet session is first created, the hosting server embeds its identity in a cookie that is returned to the client. The client then includes this cookie in each subsequent request, where it can be used to implement session affinity. One approach is for the Application Server vendor to provide a Web Server plug-in that inspects the cookie and routes requests from the presentation tier to the application tier. This approach introduces an extra network hop in processing each request. Alternatively, load balancing appliances can be configured to key session affinity to data such as cookies or client IP addresses.

If servlet session state is maintained only in memory on a single server, then it will be lost when that server fails. Availability can be improved by placing servlet session state under the control of a singleton service and migrating it in the event of failure. The sophisticated machinery to establish cluster membership is unnecessary in this case because a given servlet session is accessed by only a single client, which can unambiguously drive ownership and migration.

WebLogic Server supports replication of servlet session state to a secondary server in the cluster and migration of the data between servlet containers in the event of failure. All requests are handled by the primary server, which synchronously transmits a delta for any updates to the secondary before returning the response to the client. To support migration, the identity of both the primary and the secondary are embedded in the cookie. In the event that either server fails, a new primary/secondary pair is established lazily when the next request arrives, since that is the first opportunity to rewrite the cookie.

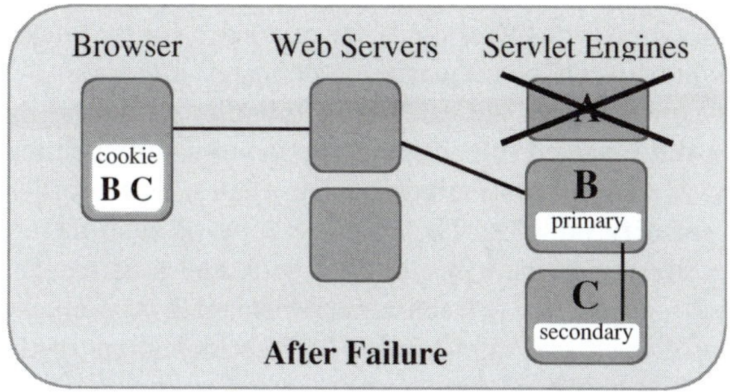

Figure 2 Replication with Routing in the Web Server

Figure 3 illustrates the case where a load balancing appliance performs routing. The primary is created on the server that was initially selected by the appliance and for which it set up session affinity. If the primary becomes unreachable, the appliance switches to some arbitrary member of the cluster. When the next request arrives there, the servlet engine inspects the cookie, contacts the secondary to get a copy of the state, becomes the primary, and rewrites the cookie leaving the secondary unchanged.

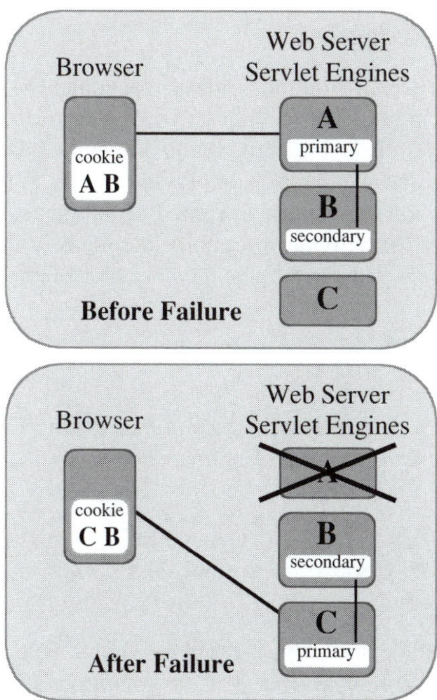

Figure 3 Replication with External Routing

4.2 Web Services Clients

Web Service conversations may in general involve multiple participants, each of which maintains conversational state. In the example workflow application, suppose manufacturer A negotiates a bid for parts with broker B which then negotiates the bid with supplier C, as illustrated in Figure 4. Broker B should maintain a single piece of state for both conversations and thus it effectively has a single multi-party conversation. Note that in this example, A, B, and C each have their own cluster.

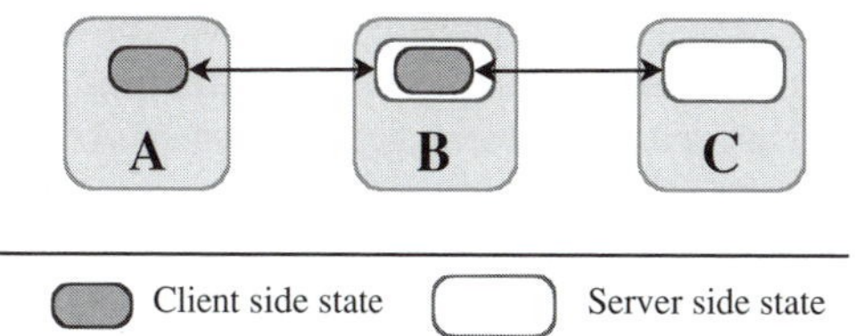

Figure 4 Subordinate Web Service Conversations

Web Service conversational state should nominally be kept in a shared database and accessed through a stateless service each time a request arrives. However, conversations that are short-lived or that have bursty access patterns are attractive to maintain in memory under the management of a singleton service. Depending on the durability requirements, the data can be written through to a shared database, replicated to a passive secondary, or lost on failure. The latter two alternatives might be acceptable for read-only applications, shopping-cart-style applications where only the last fulfilment step is crucial, and forwarding applications where reliability is provided by the external end-points. It is not possible to ensure that session affinity is set up in all cases for all transport protocols, thus routing is in general required.

If a Web Service conversation is maintained in memory, then any associated in-bound or out-bound asynchronous messages should be co-located with it. Assuming it is prohibitive to maintain a queue per conversation, this behavior can be accomplished by partitioning a single logical queue into one physical instance per server and assigning a set of conversations to each instance. Again, depending on durability requirements, messages can be written through to a shared database, replicated to a passive secondary, or lost on failure. Treating a conversation and its messages in the same way provides a consistent unit of failure.

The difficulty of migrating multi-party conversations is illustrated in Figure 4. If A or C were to drive migration decisions about B in isolation, in the same way that a browser drives decisions about servlet sessions, then there could be disagreement as to which server owns the data. Instead, there must be cluster-wide agreement about migration and servers that are deemed to have failed must be shut down. Thus multi-party conversations require the sophisticated machinery to establish cluster membership

WebLogic Server allows Web Service conversations to be managed by singleton services. The implementation makes use of a Conversation Manager that is also a singleton service. The Conversation Manager mediates between clients to choose the initial host of a conversation at the point it is created. A client uses this mechanism to attempt to accommodate session affinity that has been set up for it by the vendor-neutral front-end of the cluster.

After this point, a client has no say as to which server hosts a conversation; migration decisions are entirely under the control of the clustering infrastructure. The Conversation Manager also provides a service for finding the locations of conversations to facilitate routing. The locations of conversations are cached on each server to reduce the load on the Conversation Manager.

5. An Application Server Persistence Layer

As Application Servers become increasingly distributed within the enterprise, they increasingly maintain **middle-tier data** outside of centralized databases in the back-end. This paper has characterized this practice in terms of cached services, which maintain loosely-synchronized secondary copies of the data, and singleton services, which maintain strict transactional consistency by granting exclusive ownership of each data item to a single service instance.

An Application Server instance may write middle-tier data to a private disk, either to avoid reacquiring it from the back-end (for cached services) or because it is the primary copy and must be made durable (for singleton services). Conventional databases are less than ideal for this purpose for several reasons. First, since the data is accessed by only one server at a time, conventional distributed concurrency control is unnecessary. Second, since the data is often accessed only in limited ways, e.g., by key or through a sequential scan, conventional database access mechanisms are overbuilt. Third, conventional databases are relatively expensive and hard to maintain, making them inappropriate to install on every member of a cluster.

Middle-tier data is better handled by a persistence layer that is specifically designed for the Application Server. This persistence layer should be tightly integrated with Application Server instances to decrease communication costs and simplify administration. It should also be lighter weight than a conventional database so it is more appropriate to install on every member of a cluster.

Messages, both in-bound and out-bound, are the most significant category of middle-tier data. Gray argues that databases should be enhanced with TP-monitor-like features to handle messaging; for example, triggers and stored procedures should evolve into worker thread/process pools for servicing queue entries [20]. The counter-argument is that Application Servers should be enhanced with persistence, since they also provide much of the required infrastructure, including security, configuration, monitoring, recovery, and logging. Specialized file-based message stores are in fact common, for all of the reasons described above, and can be used as a starting point for building an Application Server persistence layer.

WebLogic Server has a file-based message store and it is being generalized to handle other kinds of data. Of particular importance is the state associated with Web Service conversations. In addition to the benefits described above, having the same resource manager handle this data along with its messages eliminates the need for two-phase commit between the messaging system and a database.

Another significant category of middle-tier data is the **meta-data** needed to configure the server and its applications. Meta-data can include business rules, user profiles, and security policies. The primary copy of such data is generally maintained in a shared back-end system. The data is pushed out to each server instance in the cluster where it is cached on a local disk. The local copy of the data can significantly reduce server and application start up times as well as making restarts more autonomous.

It may also be useful to cache a copy of back-end application data on disk in the middle tier. This technique can isolate operational systems in the back-end from the distribution, load-handling, and error-handling requirements of presentation-oriented applications in the front-end. And the extraction, transformation, and loading process can optimize the data for the needs of these applications. For example, relational data might be pre-digested into object or XML form to avoid runtime mapping.

Acknowledgements

This paper reports on the work of many talented people at BEA, including Juan Andrade, Adam Bosworth, Ed Felt, Steve Felts, Eric Halpern, Anno Langen, Adam Messinger, Prasad Peddada, Sam Pullara, Seth White, Rob Woollen, and Stephan Zachwieja. Special thanks to Adam Messinger for helping to organize the ideas in this paper. This paper is dedicated to the memory of Ed Felt.

References

[1] J. Gray, A. Reuter. *Transaction Processing: Concepts and Techniques.* Morgan Kaufman, 1993.

[2] CICS/VS Version 1.6, General Information Manual, GC33-1055, IBM Corp., Armonk, N.Y., 1983.

[3] J. Andrade, M. Carges, T. Dwyer, and S. Felts. *The Tuxedo System - Software for Constructing and Managing Distributed Business Applications.* Addison-Wesley Publishing, 1996.

[4] BEA Systems. The WebLogic Application Server. http://www.bea.com/products/ weblogic/ server/index.shtml.

[5] Hypertext Transfer Protocol -- HTTP/1.1. http://www.ietf.org/rfc/rfc2616.txt

[6] Simple Object Access Protocol (SOAP) 1.1. http://www.w3.org/TR/SOAP.

[7] A. Fox, S. Gribble, Y. Chawathe, E. Brewer, and P. Gauthier. Cluster-Based Scalable Network Services. *Proceedings of ACM Symposium on Operating Systems Principles*. Vol. 31, October 1997.

[8] I. Foster, C. Kesselman, and S. Tuecke. The Anatomy of the Grid: Enabling Scalable Virtual Organizations. *International Journal of Supercomputer Applications*. 2001.

[9] Sun Microsystems. Java™ 2 Platform, Enterprise Edition (J2EE™). http:// java.sun.com/ j2ee.

[10] J. Gray. The Transaction Concept: Virtues and Limitations. *Proceedings of VLDB*. Cannes, France, September 1981.

[11] G. F. Pfister. *In Search of Clusters, 2nd Edition*. Prentice Hall, 1998.

[12] D. L. Eager, E. D. Lazowska, and J. Zahorjan. Adaptive load sharing in homogeneous distributed systems. *IEEE Transactions on Software Engineering*. Vol. 12, 1986.

[13] T. Bourke. *Server Load Balancing*. O'Reilly & Associates, August 2001.

[14] A. Gupta, I. S. Mumick (Editors). *Materialized Views: Techniques, Implementations, and Applications*. The MIT Press, 1999.

[15] K. S. Candan, D. Agrawal, W. S. Li, O. Po, W. P. Hsiung. View Invalidation for Dynamic Content Caching in Multitiered Architectures. *Proceedings of the 28th Very Large Data Bases Conference*, August 2002.

[16] B. Devlin, J. Gray, B. Laing, G. Spix. Scalability Terminology: Farms, Clones, Partitions, and Packs: RACS and RAPS. Microsoft Technical Report MS-TR-99-85, December 1999.

[17] E. Marcus, H. Stern. *Blueprints for High Availability: Designing Resilient Distributed Systems*. Wiley, January 2000.

[18] N. A. Lynch. *Distributed Algorithms*. Morgan Kaufmann, San Francisco 1996.

[19] B. Lampson. How to Build a Highly Available System Using Consensus. In *Distributed Algorithms, Lecture Notes in Computer Science 1151*, (ed. Babaoglu and Marzullo), Springer, 1996.

[20] J. Gray. Queues are Databases. *Proceedings 7th High Performance Transaction Processing Workshop*. Asilomar CA, Sept 1995.

Querying Semi-Structured Data

Serge Abiteboul*

INRIA-Rocquencourt
Serge.Abiteboul@inria.fr

1 Introduction

The amount of data of all kinds available electronically has increased dramatically in recent years. The data resides in different forms, ranging from unstructured data in file systems to highly structured in relational database systems. Data is accessible through a variety of interfaces including Web browsers, database query languages, application-specific interfaces, or data exchange formats. Some of this data is *raw* data, e.g., images or sound. Some of it has structure even if the structure is often implicit, and not as rigid or regular as that found in standard database systems. Sometimes the structure exists but has to be extracted from the data. Sometimes also it exists but we prefer to ignore it for certain purposes such as browsing. We call here *semi-structured data* this data that is (from a particular viewpoint) neither raw data nor strictly typed, i.e., not table-oriented as in a relational model or sorted-graph as in object databases.

As will seen later when the notion of semi-structured data is more precisely defined, the need for semi-structured data arises naturally in the context of data integration, even when the data sources are themselves well-structured. Although data integration is an old topic, the need to integrate a wider variety of data-formats (e.g., SGML or ASN.1 data) and data found on the Web has brought the topic of semi-structured data to the forefront of research.

The main purpose of the paper is to isolate the essential aspects of semi-structured data. We also survey some proposals of models and query languages for semi-structured data. In particular, we consider recent works at Stanford U. and U. Penn on semi-structured data. In both cases, the motivation is found in the integration of heterogeneous data. The "lightweight" data models they use (based on labelled graphs) are very similar.

As we shall see, the topic of semi-structured data has no precise boundary. Furthermore, a theory of semi-structured data is still missing. We will try to highlight some important issues in this context.

The paper is organized as follows. In Section 2, we discuss the particularities of semi-structured data. In Section 3, we consider the issue of the data structure and in Section 4, the issue of the query language.

---

* Currently visiting the Computer Science Dept., Stanford U. Work supported in part by CESDIS, NASA Goddard Space Flight Center; by the Air Force Wright Laboratory Aeronautical Systems Center under ARPA Contract F33615-93-1-1339, and by the Air Force Rome Laboratories under ARPA Contract F30602-95-C-0119.

2

2 Semi-Structured Data

In this section, we make more precise what we mean by semi-structured data, how such data arises, and emphasize its main aspects.

Roughly speaking, semi-structured data is data that is neither raw data, nor very strictly typed as in conventional database systems. Clearly, this definition is imprecise. For instance, would a BibTex file be considered structured or semi-structured? Indeed, the same piece of information may be viewed as unstructured at some early processing stage, but later become very structured after some analysis has been performed. In this section, we give examples of semi-structured data, make more precise this notion and describe important issues in this context.

2.1 Examples

We will often discuss in this paper BibTex files [Lam94] that present the advantage of being more familiar to researchers than other well-accepted formats such as SGML [ISO86] or ASN.1 [ISO87]. Data in BibTex files closely resembles relational data. Such a file is composed of records. But, the structure is not as regular. Some fields may be missing. (Indeed, it is customary to even find compulsory fields missing.) Other fields have some meaningful structure, e.g., author. There are complex features such as abbreviations or cross references that are not easy to describe in some database systems.

The Web also provides numerous popular examples of semi-structured data. In the Web, data consists of files in a particular format, HTML, with some structuring primitives such as tags and anchors. A typical example is a data source about restaurants in the Bay Area (from the Palo Alto Weekly newspaper), that we will call Guide. It consists of an HTML file with one entry per restaurant and provides some information on prices, addresses, styles of restaurants and reviews. Data in Guide resides in files of text with some implicit structure. One can write a parser to extract the underlying structure. However, there is a large degree of irregularity in the structure since (i) restaurants are not all treated in a uniform manner (e.g., much less information is given for fast-food joints) and (ii) information is entered as plain text by human beings that do not present the standard rigidity of your favorite data loader. Therefore, the parser will have to be tolerant and accept to fail parsing portions of text that will remain as plain text.

Also, semi-structured data arises often when integrating several (possibly structured) sources. Data integration of independent sources has been a popular topic of research since the very early days of databases. (Surveys can be found in [SL90, LMR90, Bre90], and more recent work on the integration of heterogeneous sources in e.g., [LRO96, QRS$^+$95, C$^+$95].) It has gained a new vigor with the recent popularity of the Web. Consider the integration of car retailer databases. Some retailers will represent addresses as strings and others as tuples. Retailers will probably use different conventions for representing dates, prices, invoices, etc. We should expect some information to be missing from some sources. (E.g., some retailers may not record whether non-automatic transmission is available).

More generally, a wide heterogeneity in the organization of data should be expected from the car retailer data sources and not all can be resolved by the integration software.

Semi-structured data arises under a variety of forms for a wide range of applications such as genome databases, scientific databases, libraries of programs and more generally, digital libraries, on-line documentations, electronic commerce. It is thus essential to better understand the issue of querying semi-structured data.

2.2 Main aspects

The structure is irregular:
This must be clear from the previous discussion. In many of these applications, the large collections that are maintained often consist of heterogeneous elements. Some elements may be incomplete. On the other hand, other elements may record extra information, e.g., annotations. Different types may be used for the same kind of information, e.g., prices may be in dollars in portions of the database and in francs in others. The same piece of information. e.g., an address, may be structured in some places as a string and in others as a tuple.

Modelling and querying such irregular structures are essential issues.

The structure is implicit:
In many applications, although a precise structuring exists, it is given implicitly. For instance, electronic documents consist often of a text and a grammar (e.g., a DTD in SGML). The parsing of the document then allows one to isolate pieces of information and detect relationships between them. However, the interpretation of these relationships (e.g., SGML exceptions) may be beyond the capabilities of standard database models and are left to the particular applications and specific tools. We view this structure as implicit (although specified explicitly by tags) since (i) some computation is required to obtain it (e.g., parsing) and (ii) the correspondence between the parse-tree and the logical representation of the data is not always immediate.

It is also sometimes the case, in particular for the Web, that the documents come as plain text. Some ad-hoc analysis is then needed to extract the structure. For instance, in the Guide data source, the description of restaurant is in plain text. Now, clearly, it is possible to develop some analysis tools to recognize prices, addresses, etc. and then extract the structure of the file. The issue of extracting the structure of some text (e.g., HTML) is a challenging issue.

The structure is partial:
To completely structure the data often remains an elusive goal. Parts of the data may lack structure (e.g., bitmaps); other parts may only unveil some very sketchy structure (e.g., unstructured text). Information retrieval tools may provide a limited form of structure, e.g., by computing occurrences of particular words or group of words and by classifying documents based on their content.

An application may also decide to leave large quantities of data outside the database. This data then remains unstructured from a database viewpoint. The loading of this external data, its analysis, and its integration to the database have to be performed efficiently. We may want to also use optimization techniques to

4

only load selective portions of this data, in the style of [ACM93]. In general, the management and access of this *external data* and its interoperability with the data from the database is an important issue.

Indicative structure vs. constraining structure:
In standard database applications, a strict typing policy is enforced to protect data. We are concerned here with applications where such strict policy is often viewed as too constraining. Consider for instance the Web. A person developing a personal Web site would be reluctant to accept strict typing restrictions.

In the context of the Lore Project at Stanford, the term *data guide* was adopted to emphasize non-conventional approaches to typing found in most semi-structured data applications. A *schema* (as in conventional databases) describes a strict type that is adhered to by all data managed by the system. An update not conforming is simply rejected. On the other hand, a *data guide* provides some information about the current type of the data. It does not have to be the most accurate. (Accuracy may be traded in for simplicity.) All new data is accepted, eventually at the cost of modifying the data guide.

A-priori schema vs. a-posteriori data guide:
Traditional database systems are based on the hypothesis of a fixed schema that has to be defined prior to introducing any data. This is not the case for semi-structured data where the notion of schema is often posterior to the existence of data.

Continuing with the Web example, when all the members of an organization have a Web page, there is usually some pressure to unify the style of these home-pages, or at least agree on some minimal structure to facilitate the design of global entry-points. Indeed, it is a general pattern for large Web sources to start with a very loose structure and then acquire some structure when the need for it is felt.

Further on, we will briefly mention issues concerning data guides.

The schema is very large:
Often as a consequence of heterogeneity, the schema would typically be quite large. This is in contrast with relational databases where the schema was expected to be orders of magnitude smaller than the data. For instance, suppose that we are interested in Californian Impressionist Painters. We may find some data about these painters in many heterogeneous information sources on the Web, so the schema is probably quite large. But the data itself is not so large.

Note that as a consequence, the user is not expected to know all the details of the schema. Thus, queries over the schema are as important as standard queries over the data. Indeed, one cannot separate anymore these two aspects of queries.

The schema is ignored:
Typically, it is useful to ignore the schema for some queries that have more of a discovery nature. Such queries may consist in simply browsing through the data or searching for some string or pattern without any precise indication on where it may occur. Such searching or browsing are typically not possible with SQL-like languages. They pose new challenges: (i) the extension of the query languages; and (ii) the integration of new optimization techniques such as full-text indexing [ACC+96] or evaluation of generalized path expressions [CCM96].

The schema is rapidly evolving:
In standard database systems, the schema is viewed as almost immutable, schema updates as rare, and it is well-accepted that schema updates are very expensive.

Now, in contrast, consider the case of genome data [DOB95]. The schema is expected to change quite rapidly, at the same speed as experimental techniques are improved or novel techniques introduced. As a consequence, expressive formats such as ASN.1 or ACeDB [TMD92] were preferred to a relational or object database system approach. Indeed, the fact that schema evolves very rapidly is often given as the reason for not using database systems in applications that are managing large quantities of data. (Other reasons include the cost of database systems and the interoperability with other systems, e.g., Fortran libraries.)

In the context of semi-structured data, we have to assume that the schema is very flexible and can be updated as easily as data which poses serious challenges to database technology.

The type of data elements is eclectic:
Another aspect of semi-structured data is that the structure of a data element may depend on a point of view or on a particular phase in the data acquisition process. So, the type of a piece of information has to be more eclectic as, say in standard database systems where the structure of a record or that of an object is very precise. For instance, an object can be first a file. It may become a BibTex file after classification using a tool in the style of [TPL95]. It may then obtain *owner*, *creation-date*, and other fields after some information extraction phase. Finally, it could become a collection of reference objects (with complex structures) once it has been parsed. In that respect also, the notion of type is much more flexible.

This is an issue of objects with multiple roles, e.g., [ABGO93] and objects in views, e.g., [dSAD94].

The distinction between schema and data is blurred:
In standard database applications, a basic principle is the distinction between the schema (that describes the structure of the database) and data (the database instance). We already saw that many differences between schema and data disappear in the context of semi-structured data: schema updates are frequent, schema laws can be violated, the schema may be very large, the same queries/updates may address both the data and schema. Furthermore, in the context of semi-structured data, this distinction may even logically make little sense. For instance, the same classification information, e.g., the sex of a person, may be kept as data in one source (a boolean with *true* for male and *false* for female) and as type in the other (the object is of class *Male* or *Female*). We are touching here issues that dramatically complicate database design and data restructuring.

2.3 Some issues

To conclude this section, we consider a little more precisely important issues in the context of semi-structured data.

6

Model and languages for semi-structured data:
Which model should be used to describe semi-structured data and to manipulate this data? By languages, we mean here languages to query semi-structured data but also languages to restructure such data since restructuring is essential for instance to integrate data coming from several sources. There are two main difficulties (i) we have only a partial knowledge of the structure; and (ii) the structure is potentially "deeply nested" or even cyclic. This second point in particular defeats calculi and algebras developed in the standard database context (e.g., relational, complex value algebra) by requiring recursion. It seems that languages such as Datalog (see [Ull89, AHV94]) although they provide some form of recursion, are not completely satisfactory.

These issues will be dealt with in more details in the next two sections.

Extracting and using structure:
The general idea is, starting with data with little explicit structure, to extract structuring information and organize the data to improve performance. To continue with the bibliography example, suppose we have a number of files containing bibliography references in BibTex and other formats. We may want to extract (in a data warehousing style) the titles of the papers, lists of authors and keywords, i.e., the most frequently accessed data that can be found in every format for references, and store them in a relational database. Note that this extraction phase may be difficult if some files are structured according to formats ignored by our system. Also, issues such as duplicate elimination have to be faced. In general, the issue of recognizing an object in a particular state or within a sequence of states (for temporal data) is a challenging issue.

The relational database then contains links to pieces of information in the files, so that all data remains accessible. Such a structured layer on top of a irregular and less controlled layer of files, can provide important gains in answering the most common queries.

In general, we need tools to extract information from files including classifiers, parsers, but also software to extract cross references (e.g., within a set of HTML documents), information retrieval packages to obtain statistics on words (or groups of words) occurrences and statistics for relevance ranking and relevance feedback. More generally, one could envision the use of general purpose data mining tools to extract structuring information.

One can then use the information extracted from the files to build a structured layer above the layer of more unformed data. This structured layer references the lower data layer and yields a flexible and efficient access to the information in the lower layer to provide the benefits of standard database access methods. A similar concept is called *structured map* in [DMRA96].

More ways to use structure: the data guide
We saw that many differences with standard databases come from a very different approach to typing. We used the term *data guide* to stress the differences. A similar notion is considered in [BDFS97]. Now, since there is no schema to view as a constraint on the data, one may question the need for any kind of typing information, and for a data guide in particular. A data guide provides a computed loose description of the structure of data. For instance, in a particular

application, the data guide may say that *persons* possibly have ougoing edges labelled *name, address, hobby* and *friend,* that an *address* is either a `string`, but that it may have outgoing edges labelled *street,* and *zipcode.* This should be viewed as more or less accurate indications on the kind of data that is in the database at the moment.

It turns out that there are many reasons for using a data guide:

1. *graphical query language*: Graphical interfaces use the schema in very essential ways. For instance, QBE [Zlo77] would present a query frame that consists of the names of relations and their attributes. In the context of semi-structured data, one can view the data guide as an "encompassing type" that would serve the role of a type in helping the user graphically express queries or browse through the data.
2. *cooperative answer*: Consider for instance the mistyping of a label. This will probably result in a type error in a traditional database system, but not here since strict type enforcement is abandoned. Using a data guide, the system may still explain why the answer is empty (because such label is absent from the database.
3. *query optimization*: Typing information is very useful for query optimization. Even when the structure is not rigid, some knowledge about the type (e.g., presence/absence of some attributes) can prove to be essential. For instance, if the query asks for the Latex sources of some documents and the data guides indicate that some sources do not provide Latex sources, then a call to these sources can be avoided. This is also a place where the system has to show some flexibility. One of the sources may be a very structured database (e.g., relational), and the system should take advantage of that structure.

The notion of the *data guide associated to* some particular data with various degrees of accuracy, its use for expressing and evaluating queries, and its maintenance, are important directions of research.

System issues:
Although this is not the main focus of the paper, we would like to briefly list some system issues. We already mentioned the need for new query optimization techniques, and for the integration of optimization techniques from various fields (e.g., database indexes and full text indexes). Some standard database system issues such as transaction management, concurrency control or error recovery have to be reconsidered, in particular, because the notion of "data item" becomes less clear: the same piece of data may have several representations in various parts of the system, some atomic, some complex. Physical design (in particular clustering) is seriously altered in this context. Finally, it should be observed that, by nature, a lot of the data will reside outside the database. The optimization of external data access (in particular, the efficient and selective loading of file data) and the interoperability with other systems are therefore key issues.

3 Modeling Semi-Structured Data

A first fundamental issue is the choice of a model: should it be very rich and complex, or on the contrary, simple and lightweight? We will argue here that it should be *both*.

Why a lightweight model? Consider accessing data over the Internet. If we obtain new data using the Web protocol, the data will be rather unstructured at first. (Some protocols such as CORBA [OMG92] may provide a-priori more structured data.) Furthermore, if the data originates from a new source that we just discovered, it is very likely that it is structured in ways that are still unknown to our particular systems. This is because (i) the number of semantic constructs developers and researchers may possibly invent is extremely large and (ii) the standardization of a complex data model that will encompass the needs of all applications seems beyond reach.

For such novel structures discovered over the network, a *lightweight* data model is preferable. Any data can be mapped to this *exchange* model, and becomes therefore accessible without the use of specific pieces of software.

Why also a heavyweight data model? Using a lightweight model does not preclude the use of a compatible, richer model that allows the system to take advantage of particular structuring information. For instance, traditional relations with indexes will be often imported. When using such an indexed relation, ignoring the fact that this particular data is a relation and that it is indexed would be suicidal for performance.

As we mentioned in the previous section, the types of objects evolve based on our current knowledge possibly from totally unstructured to very structured, and a piece of information will often move from a very rich structure (in the system where it is maintained); to a lightweight structure when exchanged over the network; to a (possibly different) very rich structure when it has been analyzed and integrated to other pieces of information. It is thus important to dispose of a flexible model allowing both a very light and a very rich structuring of data.

In this section, we first briefly consider some components of a rich model for semi-structured data. This should be viewed as an indicative, non-exhaustive list of candidate features. In our opinion, specific models for specific application domains (e.g., Web databases or genome databases) are probably more feasible than an all-purpose model for semi-structured data. Then, we present in more details the Object Exchange Model that is pursuing a minimalist approach.

3.1 A maximalist approach

We next describe primitives that seem to be required from a semantic model to allow the description of semi-structured data. Our presentation is rather sketchy and assumes knowledge of the ODMG model. The following primitives should be considered:

9

1. The ODMG model: the notions of objects, classes and class hierarchy; and structuring constructs such as set, list, bag, array seem all needed in our context.
2. Null values: these are given lip service in the relational and the ODMG models and more is needed here.
3. Heterogeneous collections: collections need often to be heterogeneous in the semi-structured setting. So, there is the need for some union types as found for instance in [AH87] or [AK89].
4. Text with references: text is an important component for semi-structured information. Two important issues are (i) references to portions of a text (references and citations in LaTex), and (ii) references from the text (HTML anchors).
5. Eclectic types: the same piece of information may be viewed with various alternative structures.
6. Version and time: it is clear that we are often more concerned by querying the recent changes in some data source that in examining the entire source.

No matter how rich a model we choose, it is likely that some weird features of a given application or a particular data exchange format will not be covered (e.g., SGML exceptions). This motivates the use of an underlying minimalist data format.

3.2 A minimalist approach

In this section, we present the Object Exchange Model (OEM) [AQM+96], a data model particularly useful for representing semi-structured data.

The model consists of graph with labels on the edges. (In an early version of the model [PGMW95], labels were attached to vertices which leads to minor differences in the description of information and in the corresponding query languages.) A very similar model was independently proposed in [BDHS96]. This seems to indicate that this model indeed achieves the goals to be simple enough, and yet flexible and powerful enough to allow describing semi-structured data found in common data sources over the net. A subtle difference is that OEM is based on the notion of objects with object identity whereas [BDHS96] uses tree markers and *bisimulation*. We will ignore this distinction here.

Data represented in OEM can be thought of as a graph, with objects as the vertices and labels on the edges. Entities are represented by *objects*. Each object has a unique *object identifier* (oid) from the type `oid`. Some objects are atomic and contain a value from one of the disjoint basic atomic types, e.g., `integer`, `real`, `string`, `gif`, `html`, `audio`, `java`, etc. All other objects are complex; their value is a set of *object references*, denoted as a set of (*label*, *oid*) pairs. The labels are taken from the atomic type `string`. Figure 1 provides an example of an OEM graph.

OEM can easily model relational data, and, as in the ODMG model, hierarchical and graph data. (Although the structure in Figure 1 is *almost* a tree, there is a cycle via objects &19 and &35.) To model semi-structured information sources, we do not insist that data is as strongly structured as in standard database models. Observe that, for example, (i) restaurants have zero, one or more addresses; (ii) an address is sometimes a string and sometimes a complex structure; (iii) a zipcode may be a string or an integer; (iv) the zipcode occurs in the address for some and directly under restaurant for others; and (v) price information is sometimes given and sometimes missing.

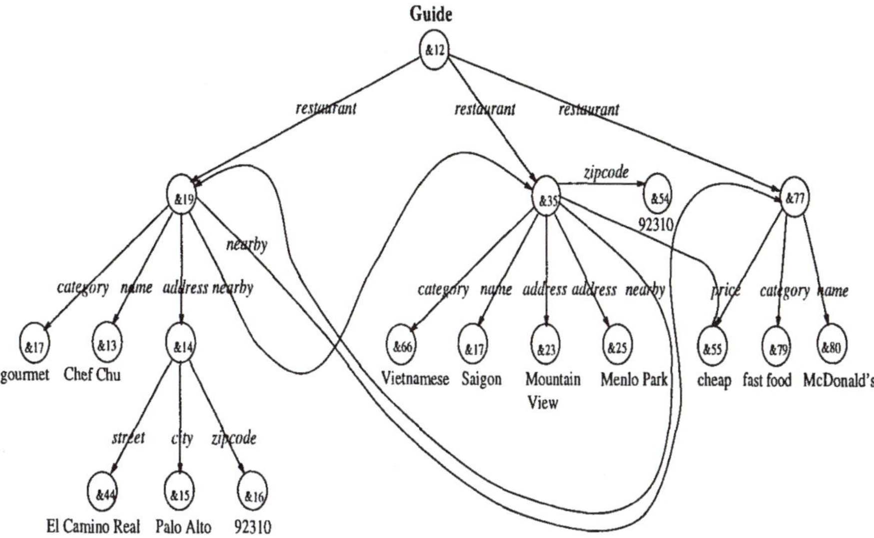

Fig. 1. An OEM graph

We conclude this section with two observations relating OEM to the relational and ODMG models:

OEM vs. relational: One can view an OEM database as a relational structure with a binary relation *VAL(oid, atomic_value)* for specifying the values of atomic objects and a ternary relation *MEMBER(oid, label, oid)* to specify the values of complex objects. This simple viewpoint seems to defeat a large part of the research on semi-structured data. However, (i) such a representation is possible *only* because of the presence of object identifiers, so we are already out of the relational model; (ii) we have to add integrity constraints to the relational structure (e.g., to prohibit dangling references); and (iii) it is often the case that we want to recover an object together with its subcomponents and this recursively, which is certainly a feature that is out of relational calculus.

OEM vs. ODMG: In the object exchange model, all objects have the same type, namely OEM. Intuitively, this type is a tuple with one field per possible label containing a set of OEM's. Based on this, it is rather straightforward to have a type system that would incorporate the ODMG types and the

OEM type (see [AQM+96]). This is a first step towards a model that would integrate the minimalist and maximalist approaches.

4 Querying and Restructuring

In the context of semi-structured data, the query language has to be more flexible than in conventional database systems. Typing should be more liberal since by nature data is less regular. What should we expect from a query language?

1. standard database-style query primitives;
2. navigation in the style of hypertext or Web-style browsing;
3. searching for pattern in an information-retrieval-style [Rie79];
4. temporal queries, including querying versions or querying changes (an issue that we will ignore further on);
5. querying both the data and the type/schema in the same query as in [KL89].

Also, the language should have sound theoretical foundations, possibly a logic in the style of relational calculus. So, there is a need for more works on calculi for semi-structured data and algebraizations of these calculi.

All this requires not only revisiting the languages but also database optimization techniques, and in particular, integrating these techniques with optimization techniques from information retrieval (e.g., full text indexing) and new techniques for dealing with path expressions and more general hypertext features.

There has been a very important body of literature on query languages from various perspectives, calculus, algebra, functional, and deductive (see [Ull89, AHV94]), concerning very structured data. A number of more recent proposals concern directly semi-structured data. These are most notably Lorel [AQM+96] for the OEM model and UnQL [BDHS96] for a very similar model. Although developed with different motivations, languages to query documents satisfy some of the needs of querying semi-structured data. For instance, query languages for structured documents such as OQL-doc [CACS94] and integration with information retrieval tools [ACC+96, CM95] share many goals with the issues that we are considering. The work on query languages for hypertext structures, e.g., [MW95, BK90, CM89b, MW93] and query languages for the Web are relevant. In particular, query languages for the Web have attracted a lot of attention recently, e.g., W3QL [KS95] that focuses on extensibility, WebSQL [MMM96] that provides a formal semantics and introduce a notion of locality, or WebLog [LSS96] that is based on a Datalog-like syntax. A theory of queries of the Web is proposed in [AV97].

W3QL is typical from this line of works. It notably allows the use of Perl regular expressions and calls to Unix programs from the `where` clause of an SQL-like query, and even calls to Web browsers. This is the basis of a system that provides bridges between the database and the Web technology.

We do not provide here an extensive survey of that literature. We more modestly focus on some concepts that we believe are essential to query semi-structured data. This is considered next. Finally, we mention the issue of data restructuring.

12

4.1 Primitives for querying semi-structured data

In this section, we mention some recent proposals for querying semi-structured data.

Using an object approach: The notion of objects and the flexibility brought by an object approach turn out to be essential. Objects allow to focus on the portion of the structure that is relevant to the query and ignore portions of it that we (want to) ignore.

To see that, consider first the relational representation of OEM that was described in Section 3.2 and relational query languages. We can express simple queries such as *what is the address of Toto?* even when we ignore the exact structure of *person* objects, or even if all persons do not have the same structure:

```
select unique V'.2
from   persons P, MEMBER N, MEMBER A, VAL V, VAL V'
where  P = N.1 and P = A.1 and
       N.2 = "name" and N.3 = V.1 and V.2 = "Toto" and
       A.2 = "address" and A.3 = V'.1
```

assuming a unary relation *persons* contains the oid's of all persons. Observe that this is only assuming that persons have names and addresses.

In this manner, we can query semi-structured data with almost no knowledge on the underlying structure using the standard relational model. However, the expression of the query is rather awkward. Furthermore, this representation of the data results in losing the "logical clustering" of data. The description of an object (a tuple or a collection) is split into pieces, one triplet for each component. A more natural way to express the same query is:

```
Q1   select A  from persons P, P.address A
     where  "Toto" = P.name
```

This is actually the correct OQL syntax; but OQL would require *persons* to be an homogeneous set of objects, fitting the ODMG model. On the other hand, Lorel (based on OEM) would impose no restriction on the types of objects in the *persons* set and Q1 is also a correct Lorel query. In OEM, *persons* object will be allowed to have zero, one or more names and addresses. Of course, the Lorel query Q1 will retrieve only persons with a name and an address. Lorel achieves this by an extensive use of coercion.

Using coercion: A simple example of coercion is found with atomic values. Some source may record a distance in kilometers and some in miles. The system can still perform comparison using coercion from one measure to the other. For instance, a comparison $X < Y$ where X is in kilometer and Y in miles is coerced into $X < mile\_to\_km(Y)$.

The same idea of coercion can be used for structure as well. Since we can neither assume regularity nor precise knowledge of the structure, the name or address of a person may be atomic in some source, a set in other sources, and not be recorded by a third. Lorel allows one to use Q1 even in such cases. This is done by first assuming that all properties are set-valued. The empty set (denoting the absence of this property) and the singleton set (denoting a functional property) are simply special cases. The query Q1 is then transformed by coercing the equality in *P.Name = "Toto"* into a set membership *"Toto" in P.Name.*

So, the principle is to use a data model where all objects have the same interface and allow a lot of flexibility in queries. Indeed, in Lorel, all objects have the same type, OEM.

Path expressions and Patterns: The simplest use of path expressions is to concatenate attribute names as in "Guide.restaurant.address.zipcode". If Guide is a tuple, with a restaurant field that has an address field, that has a zipcode field, this is pure field extraction. But if some properties are set-valued (or all are set-valued as for OEM), we are in fact doing much more. We are traversing collections and flattening them. This is providing a powerful form of navigation in the database graph. Note that now such a path expression can be interpreted in two ways: (i) as the set of objects at the end of the paths; and (ii) as the paths themselves. Languages such as OQL-doc [CACS94] consider paths as first class citizen and even allow the use of path variables that range over concrete paths in the data graph.

Such simple path expressions can be viewed as a form of browsing. Alternatively, they can be viewed as specifying certain line patterns that have to be found in the data graph. One could also consider non-line patterns such as `person { name , ss# }`, possibly with variables in the style of the psi-terms [AKP93].

Extended path expressions: The notion of path expression takes its full power when we start using it in conjunction with wild cards or path variables. Intuitively, a sequence of labels describes a directed path in the data graph, or a collection of paths (because of set-valued properties). If we consider a regular expression of the alphabet of labels, it describes a (possibly infinite) set of words, so again a set of paths, i.e., the union of the paths described by each word. Indeed, this provides an alternative (much more powerful way) of describing paths.

Furthermore, recall that labels are string, so they are themselves sequences of characters. So we can use also regular expressions to describe labels. This is posing some minor syntactic problems since we need to distinguish between the regular expressions for the sequence of labels and for the sequence of characters for each label. The approach taken in Lorel is based on "wild cards". We briefly discuss it next.

To take again an example from Lorel, suppose we want to find the names and zipcodes of all "cheap" restaurants. Suppose we don't know whether the zipcode occurs as part of an address or directly as subobject of restaurants. Also, we do not know if the string "cheap" will be part of a category, price, description, or other subobject. We are still able to ask the query as follows:

```
select R.name,  R(.address)?.zipcode
from   Guide.restaurant R
where  R.% grep "cheap"
```

The "?" after *.address* means that the address is optional in the path expression. The wild-card "%" will match any label leading a subobject of restaurant. The comparison operator grep will return true if the string "cheap" appears anywhere in that subobject value. There is no equivalent query in SQL or OQL, since neither allow regular expressions or wild-cards.

This last example seems again amenable to a relational calculus translation although the use of a number of % wildcards may lead to some very intricate relational calculus equivalent, and so would the introduction of disjunction. Note that the Kleene closure in label sequences built in path expressions in [AQM+96] and OQL-doc [CACS94] takes immediately out of first order. For instance, consider the following Lorel query:

```
select t  from MyReport.#.title t
```

where "#" is a shorthand for for a sequence of arbitrary many labels. This returns the title of my report, but also the titles of the section, subsections, etc., no matter how deeply nested.

The notion of path expression is found first in [MBW80] and more recently, for instance, in [KKS92, CACS94, AQM+96]. Extended path expressions is a very powerful primitive construct that changes the languages in essential ways. The study of path expressions and their expressive power (e.g., compared to Datalog-like languages) is one of the main theoretical issues in the context of semi-structured data. The optimization of the evaluation of extended path expressions initiated in [CCM96] is also a challenging problem.

Gluing information and rest variables: As mentioned above, a difficulty for languages for semi-structured data is that collections are heterogeneous and that often the structure of their components is unknown. Returning to the *persons* example, we might want to say that we are concerned only with *persons* having a name, an address, and possibly other fields. MSL [PGMW95] uses the notion of *rest* variables to mention "possibly other fields" as for instance in:

```
res(name:X, address:Y; REST1) :- r(name:X, address:Y; REST1),
                                 Y = (city:"Palo Alto"; REST2)
```

Here r is an collection of heterogeneous tuples. The first literal in the body of the rule will unify with any tuple with a *name* and *address*. The $REST1$ variable will unify with the remaining part of the tuple. Observe that this allows filtering the tuples in r without having to specify precisely their internal structure.

This approach is in the spirit of some works in the functional programming community to allow dealing with heterogeneous records, e.g, [Wan89, CM89a, Rem91]. One of the main features is the use of extensible records that are the basis of inheritance for objects as records. However, the situation turns out to be much simpler in MSL since: (i) there is much less emphasis on typing; and

(ii) in particular, it is not assumed that a tuple has at most one l-component for a given label l.

Object identity is also used in MSL [PAGM96] to glue information coming from possibly heterogeneous various objects. For instance, the following two rules allow to merge the data from two sources using *name* as a surrogate:

```
&person(X) ( name:X, ATT:Y ) :- r1 ( name:X, ATT:Y )
&person(X) ( name:X, ATT:Y ) :- r2 ( name:X, ATT:Y )
```

Here *&person(X)* is an object identifier and *ATT* is a variable. Intuitively, for each tuple in *r1* (or *r2*) with a name field X, and some *ATT* field Y, the object *&person*(X) will have an *ATT* field with value Y. Observe the use of object identity as a substitute for specifying too precisely the structure. Because of object identity, we do not need to use a notion such as *REST* variable to capture in one rule instantiation all the necessary information.

We should observe again that these can be viewed as Datalog extensions that were introduced for practical motivations. Theoretical result in this area are still missing.

4.2 Views and restructuring

Database languages are traditionally used for *extracting* data from a database. They also serve to specify *views*. The notion of view is particularly important here since we often want to consider the same object from various perspectives or with various precisions in its structure (e.g., for the integration of heterogeneous data). We need to specify complex restructuring operations. The view technology developed for object databases can be considered here, e.g., [dSAD94]. But we dispose of much less structure to start with when defining the view and again, arbitrarily deep nesting and cycles pose new challenges.

Declarative specification of a view: Following [dSAD94], a view can be defined by specifying the following: (i) how the object population is modified by hiding some objects and creating virtual objects; and how the relationship between objects is modified by hiding and adding edges between objects, or modifying edge labels.

A simple approach consists of adding hide/create vertices/edges primitives to the language and using the core query language to specify the vertices/edges to hide and create. This would yield a syntax in the style of:

```
define view Salary with
       hide select P.salary from persons P
            where P.salary > 100K
       virtual add P.salary := "high" from persons P
            where P.salary > 100K
```

For vertex creation one could use a Skolem-based object naming [KKS92].

The declarative specification of data restructuring for semi-structured data is also studied in [ACM97].

A more procedural approach A different approach is followed in [BDHS96] in the languages UnQL and UnCAL. A first layer of UnQL allows one to ask queries and is in the style of other proposals such as OQL-doc or Lorel, e.g., it uses wild cards. The language is based on a comprehension syntax. Parts of UnQL are of a declarative flavor. On the other hand, we view the restructuring part as more procedural in essence. This opinion is clearly debatable.

A particular aspect of the language is that it allows some form of restructuring even for cyclic structures. A *traverse* construct allows one to transform a database graph while traversing it, e.g., by replacing all labels A by the label A'. This powerful operation combines tree rewriting techniques with some control obtained by a guided traversal of the graph. For instance, one could specify that the replacement occurs only if particular edge, say B, is encountered on the way from the root.

A lambda calculus for semi-structured data, called UnCAL, is also presented in [BDHS96] and the equivalence with UnQL is proven. This yields a framework for an (optimized) evaluation of UnQL queries. In particular, it is important to be able to restructure a graph by local transformations (e.g., if the graph is distributed as it is the case in the Web). The locality of some restructuring operations is exploited in [Suc96].

Acknowledgements This paper has been quite influenced by discussions on semi-structured data with many people and more particularly with Peter Buneman, Sophie Cluet, Susan Davidson, Tova Milo, Dallan Quass, Yannis Papakonstantinou, Victor Vianu and Jennifer Widom.

References

[ABGO93] A. Albano, R. Bergamini, G. Ghelli, and R. Orsini. An object data model with roles. In *VLDB*, 1993.

[ACC+96] S. Abiteboul, S. Cluet, V. Christophides, T. Milo, G. Moerkotte, and Jerome Simeon. Querying documents in object databases. Technical report, INRIA, 1996.

[ACM93] S. Abiteboul, S. Cluet, and T. Milo. Querying and updating the file. In *Proc. VLDB*, 1993.

[ACM97] S. Abiteboul, S. Cluet, and T. Milo. Correspondence and translation for heterogeneous data. In *Proc. ICDT*, 1997.

[AH87] S. Abiteboul and R. Hull. IFO: A formal semantic database model. *ACM Trans. on Database Systems*, 12:4:525–565, 1987.

[AHV94] S. Abiteboul, R. Hull, and V. Vianu. *Foundations of Databases.* Addison-Wesley, Reading-Massachusetts, 1994.

[AK89] S. Abiteboul and P. C. Kanellakis. Object identity as a query language primitive. In *Proc. ACM SIGMOD Symp. on the Management of Data*, pages 159–173, 1989. to appear in *J. ACM.*

17

[AKP93] Hassan Ait-Kaci and Andreas Podelski. Towards a meaning of Life. *Journal of Logic Programming*, 16(3-4), 1993.

[AQM+96] S. Abiteboul, D. Quass, J. McHugh, J. Widom, and J. Wiener. The lorel query language for semistructured data, 1996. ftp://db.stanford.edu//pub/papers/lorel96.ps.

[AV97] S. Abiteboul and V. Vianu. Querying the web. In *Proc. ICDT*, 1997.

[BDFS97] P. Buneman, S. Davidson, M. Fernandez, and D. Suciu. Adding structure to unstructured data. In *Proc. ICDT*, 1997.

[BDHS96] P. Buneman, S. Davidson, G. Hillebrand, and D. Suciu. A query language and optimization techniques for unstructured data. In *SIGMOD*, San Diego, 1996.

[BK90] C. Beeri and Y. Kornatski. A logical query language for hypertext systems. In *VLDB*, 1990.

[Bre90] Y. Breitbart. Multidatabase interoperability. *Sigmod Record*, 19(3), 1990.

[C+95] M.J. Carey et al. Towards heterogeneous multimedia information systems: The Garlic approach. In *Proc. RIDE-DOM Workshop*, 1995.

[CACS94] V. Christophides, S. Abiteboul, S. Cluet, and M. Scholl. From structured documents to novel query facilities. In *SIGMOD'94*. ACM, 1994.

[CCM96] V. Christophides, S. Cluet, and G. Moerkotte. Evaluating queries with generalized path expressions. In *SIGMOD*, Canada, June 1996.

[CM89a] Luca Cardelli and John C. Mitchell. Operations on records. In *Proceedings of the Fifth Conference on the Mathematical Foundations of Programming Semantics*. Springer Verlag, 1989.

[CM89b] Mariano P. Consens and Alberto O. Mendelzon. Expressing structural hypertext queries in graphlog. In *Proc. 2nd. ACM Conference on Hypertext*, Pittsburgh, 1989.

[CM95] M. Consens and T. Milo. Algebras for querying text regions. In *Proc. on Principles of Database Systems*, 1995.

[DMRA96] L.M.L. Delcambre, D. Maier, R. Reddy, and L. Anderson. Structured maps: Modelling explicit semantics over a universe of information, 1996. unpublished.

[DOB95] S.B. Davidson, C. Overton, and P. Buneman. Challenges in integrating biological data sources. *J. Computational Biology 2*, 1995.

[dSAD94] C. Souza dos Santos, S. Abiteboul, and C. Delobel. Virtual schemas and bases. In *Intern. Conference on Extending Database Technology*, Cambridge, 1994.

[ISO86] ISO 8879. Information processing—text and office systems—Standard Generalized Markup Language (SGML), 1986.

[ISO87] ISO. Specification of astraction syntax notation one (asn.1), 1987. Standard 8824, Information Processing System.

[KKS92] M. Kifer, W. Kim, and Y. Sagiv. Querying object-oriented databases. In *SIGMOD*, 1992.

[KL89] M. Kifer and G. Lausen. F-logic: A higher-order language for reasoning about objects. In *sigmod*, 1989.

[KS95] D. Konopnicki and O. Shmueli. W3QS: A query system for the World Wide Web. In *VLDB*, 1995.

[Lam94] L. Lamport. *Latex*. Addison-Wesley, 1994.

[LMR90] W. Litwin, L. Mark, and N. Roussopoulos. Interoperability of multiple autonomous databases. *Computing Surveys*, 22(3), 1990.

18

[LRO96] A. Levy, A. Rajaraman, and J.J. Ordille. Querying heterogeneous information sources using source descriptions. In *Proc. VLDB*, 1996.

[LSS96] Laks V. S. Lakshmanan, Fereidoon Sadri, and Iyer N. Subramanian. A declarative language for querying and restructuring the Web. In *RIDE*, New Orleans, February 1996. In press.

[MBW80] J. Mylopoulos, P. Bernstein, and H. Wong. A language facility for designing database-intensive applications. *ACM Trans. on Database Sys.*, 5(2), June 1980.

[MMM96] A. Mendelzohn, G. A. Mihaila, and T. Milo. Querying the world wide web, 1996. draft, available by ftp: milo@math.tau.ac.il.

[MW93] T. Minohara and R. Watanabe. Queries on structure in hypertext. In *Foundations of Data Organization and Algorithms, FODO '93*. Springer, 1993.

[MW95] A. O. Mendelzon and P. T. Wood. Finding regular simple paths in graph databases. *SIAM J. Comp.*, 24(6), 1995.

[OMG92] OMG ORBTF. *Common Object Request Broker Architecture*. Object Management Group, Framingham, MA, 1992.

[PAGM96] Y. Papakonstantinou, S. Abiteboul, and H. Garcia-Molina. Object fusion in mediator systems. In *VLDB*, Bombay, 1996.

[PGMW95] Y. Papakonstantinou, H. Garcia-Molina, and J. Widom. Object exchange across heterogeneous information sources. In *Data Engineering*, Taipei, Taiwan, 1995.

[QRS+95] D. Quass, A. Rajaraman, Y. Sagiv, J. Ullman, and J. Widom. Querying semistructured heterogeneous information. Technical report, Stanford University, December 1995. Available by anonymous ftp from db.stanford.edu.

[Rem91] D. Remy. Type inference for records in a natural extension of ml. Technical report, INRIA, 1991.

[Rie79] C.J. Van Riejsbergen. *Information retrieval*. Butterworths, London, 1979.

[SL90] A. Sheth and J. Larson. Federated database systems for managing distributed, heterogeneous, and autonomous databases. *Computing Surveys*, 22(3), 1990.

[Suc96] D. Suciu. Query decomposition and view maintenance for query languages for unstructured data. In *Proc. VLDB*, 1996.

[TMD92] J. Thierry-Mieg and R. Durbin. Syntactic definitions for the acedb data base manager. Technical report, MRC Laboratory for Molecular Biology, Cambridge, CB2 2QH, UK, 1992.

[TPL95] M. Tresch, N. Palmer, and A. Luniewski. Type classification of semistructured data. In *Proc. of Intl. Conf. on Very Large Data Bases*, 1995.

[Ull89] J.D. Ullman. *Principles of Database and Knowledge Base Systems, Volume I,II*. Computer Science Press, 1989.

[Wan89] M. Wand. Complete type inference for simple objects. In *Proceedings of Symp. on Logic in Computer Science*, 1989.

[Zlo77] M. Zloof. Query-by-example: A data base language. *IBM Systems Journal*, 16:324–343, 1977.

DataGuides: Enabling Query Formulation and Optimization in Semistructured Databases*

Roy Goldman
Stanford University
royg@cs.stanford.edu

Jennifer Widom
Stanford University
widom@cs.stanford.edu

Abstract

In *semistructured* databases there is no schema fixed in advance. To provide the benefits of a schema in such environments, we introduce *DataGuides*: concise and accurate structural summaries of semistructured databases. DataGuides serve as dynamic schemas, generated from the database; they are useful for browsing database structure, formulating queries, storing information such as statistics and sample values, and enabling query optimization. This paper presents the theoretical foundations of DataGuides along with an algorithm for their creation and an overview of incremental maintenance. We provide performance results based on our implementation of DataGuides in the *Lore* DBMS for semistructured data. We also describe the use of DataGuides in Lore, both in the user interface to enable structure browsing and query formulation, and as a means of guiding the query processor and optimizing query execution.

1. Introduction

Traditional relational and object-oriented database systems force all data to adhere to an explicitly specified schema. Yet a typical site on the World-Wide Web demonstrates that much of the information available on-line is *semistructured*. Although the data may exhibit some structure, it is too varied, irregular, or mutable to easily map to a fixed schema. Recent research has focused on data models, query languages, and systems that do not require a schema to accompany each database [AQM+96, BDHS96, BDS95, KS95, MAG+97].

Beyond its use to define the structure of the data, a schema serves two important purposes:

- A schema, in the form of either tables and their attributes or class hierarchies, enables users to understand the structure of the database and form meaningful queries over it.
- A query processor relies on the schema to devise efficient plans for computing query results.

Without a schema, both of these tasks become significantly harder. Although it may be possible to manually browse a small database, in general forming a meaningful query is difficult without a schema or some kind of structural summary of the underlying database. Further, a lack of information about the structure of a database can cause a query processor to resort to exhaustive searches. To address these challenges in "schema-free" environments, we introduce *DataGuides*, dynamically generated and maintained structural summaries of semistructured databases. This paper makes several contributions:

- We give a formal definition of DataGuides as concise, accurate, and convenient summaries of semistructured databases. Further, we motivate and define *strong* DataGuides, well-suited for implementation within a DBMS.
- We provide a simple algorithm to build strong DataGuides and describe how to keep them consistent when the underlying database changes.
- We show how to store sample values and other statistical information in a DataGuide.
- We demonstrate how DataGuides have been successfully integrated into *Lore* [MAG+97] (for *Lightweight Object Repository*), a DBMS for semistructured data under development at Stanford University. DataGuides are vital to Lore's user interface: users depend on the DataGuide to learn about the structure of a database so they can formulate meaningful queries. In addition, users may specify and submit queries directly from the DataGuide.
- Finally, we explain how a query processor can use a strong DataGuide to significantly optimize query execution.

Our work is cast in the context of the Lore system. All data in Lore follows a simple, graph-based data model called *OEM*, for *Object Exchange Model* [PGW95]. Thus, our work can be applied easily to any graph-based data model. A Lore database is queried using *Lorel* [AQM+96], an OQL-based language designed for easy and effective queries over semistructured data.

Within Lore, DataGuides serve much the same role as traditional metadata. For example, DataGuides are stored directly in Lore as OEM objects. As with metadata in relational or object-oriented systems, user interfaces or client applications may access and query the DataGuide through Lore's standard interfaces [MAG+97]. And in the same way that a traditional query processor consults metadata, the DataGuide is available to guide Lore's query processor. Of course, DataGuides also differ significantly from metadata, since they are dynamically generated: DataGuides conform to the data, rather than forcing data to conform to the DataGuides.

1.1 Related Work

DataGuides extend initial work presented in [NUWC97], which gives a theoretical foundation to the concept of dynamically generated structural summaries of graph-structured databases, called *Representative Objects* (ROs). Their foundational work defines these summaries in a functional style, with less emphasis on implementation.

* This work was supported by the Air Force Rome Laboratories and DARPA under Contracts F30602-95-C-0119 and F30602-96-1-031.

Proceedings of the 23rd VLDB Conference
Athens, Greece, 1997

Other related theoretical research is presented in [BDFS97], which discusses schemas for graph-structured databases. A formal definition of a *graph schema* is given, along with an algorithm to determine whether a database conforms to a specific schema. The work in [BDFS97] is presented with a more traditional view of a schema than we take. Optimization and browsing functionality depend on having a database (or at least large fragments of the database) conform to an explicitly specified schema. In contrast, our work focuses directly on the case where it is inconvenient or implausible to specify and maintain a schema: DataGuide summaries are dynamically generated and maintained to always represent the current state of the database. A DataGuide never includes information that does not exist in the database, and by definition any database always "conforms" to its DataGuide. A graph schema, on the other hand, could be a superset of any database that conforms to it.

As with many research and commercial user interfaces that use a schema (or structural summary) to guide browsing and query formulation, our work has been influenced by the seminal work on *Query By Example* [Zlo77]. In addition to early research efforts such as Timber [SK82], many commercial relational front-ends such as Access and Paradox have sophisticated interfaces for visually specifying queries. Several visual database browsers have also been developed for richer, object-oriented data models, including KIVIEW [MDT88] and OdeView [AGS90]. PESTO [CHMW96] is a visual tool for exploring object databases that integrates browsing and querying into a single interface. The DataGuide is unique as a graphical browsing and query tool, since it presents a template dynamically generated directly from a database without regard to any fixed schema or class hierarchy.

For query optimization, we show how the DataGuide can be used as a *path index*. Substantial research on object-oriented query optimization has focused on the design and use of path indexes, e.g., [BK89, CCY94, KM92]. In general, previous work has required explicit specification of the paths to index. The issues of how to create, maintain, and use a path index in a semistructured data model like OEM, where the set of paths in a database may often change over time, have not to the best of our knowledge been addressed.

1.2 Paper Outline

Section 2 first reviews the data model and query language with which we are working. It then provides the motivation and definition for DataGuides, along with a simple algorithm for creating them. In Section 3 we present experimental results showing the time and space required to build and store typical DataGuides. Section 4 explains how to incrementally maintain a DataGuide in response to database modifications. Section 5 describes how DataGuides are used in practice to browse structure and guide query formulation through a graphical interface to the Lore system. In Section 6 we see how a strong DataGuide can improve query processing in Lore. We discuss future research in Section 7.

2. Foundations

In this section we describe our basic data model and query language. We then motivate and define DataGuides and their properties, and we provide an algorithm for building them.

2.1 Object Exchange Model

Our research is based on the *Object Exchange Model* (*OEM*), a simple and flexible data model that originates from the *Tsimmis* project at Stanford University [PGW95]. OEM itself is not particularly original, and the work presented here adapts easily

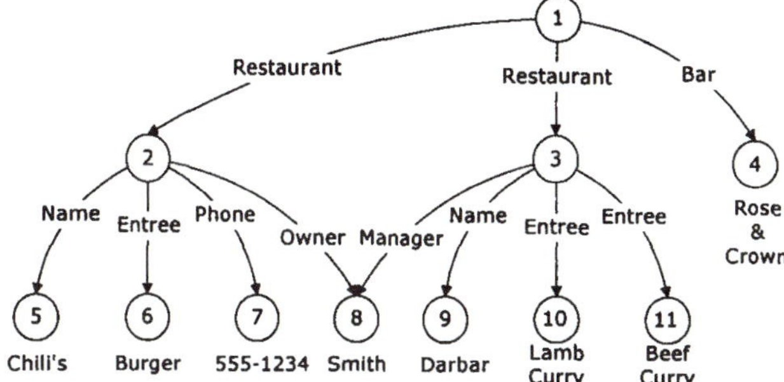

Figure 1. A sample OEM database

to any graph-structured data model. In OEM, each object contains an object identifier (oid) and a value. A value may be atomic or complex. Atomic values may be integers, reals, strings, images, programs, or any other data considered indivisible. A complex OEM value is a collection of 0 or more OEM subobjects, each linked to the parent via a descriptive textual label. Note that a single OEM object may have multiple parent objects and that cycles are allowed. For more details on OEM and its motivation see [AQM+96, PGW95].

Figure 1 presents a very small sample OEM database, representing a portion of an imaginary eating guide database. Each object has an integer oid. Our database contains one complex root object with three subobjects, two Restaurants and one Bar. Each Restaurant is a complex object and the Bar is atomic, containing the string value "Rose & Crown." Each Restaurant has an atomic Name. The Chili's restaurant has atomic data describing its Phone number and one available Entree. We can see that the database structure is irregular, since restaurant Darbar, with two Entrees, doesn't include any phone number information. Finally, we see that OEM databases need not be tree-structured—Smith is the Owner of one restaurant and Manager of the other.

Next, we give several simple definitions useful for describing an OEM database and subsequently for defining DataGuides.

Definition 1. A *label path* of an OEM object o is a sequence of one or more dot-separated labels, $l_1.l_2...l_n$, such that we can traverse a path of n edges $(e_1...e_n)$ from o where edge e_i has label l_i. ❑

In Figure 1, Restaurant.Name and Bar are both valid label paths of object 1. In an OEM database, queries are based on label paths. For example, in Figure 1, a valid query might request the values of all Restaurant.Entree objects that satisfy a given condition. Queries are further discussed in Section 2.2.

Definition 2. A *data path* of an OEM object o is a dot-separated alternating sequence of labels and oids of the form $l_1.o_1.l_2.o_2...l_n.o_n$ such that we can traverse from o a path of n edges $(e_1...e_n)$ through n objects $(x_1...x_n)$ where edge e_i has label l_i and object x_i has oid o_i. ❑

In Figure 1, Restaurant.2.Name.5 is a data path of object 1.

Definition 3. A data path d is an *instance* of a label path l if the sequence of labels in d is equal to l. ❑

Again in Figure 1, Restaurant.2.Name.5 is an instance of Restaurant.Name and Bar.4 is an instance of Bar.

Definition 4. In an OEM object s, a *target set* is a set t of oids such that there exists some label path l of s where $t = \{o \mid l_1.o_1.l_2.o_2...l_n.o$ is a data path instance of $l\}$. That is, a target set t is the set of all objects that can be reached by traversing a given label path l of s. We say that t is "the target set of l in s," and we write $t = T_s(l)$. Each element of t is *reachable* via l, and likewise l *reaches* any element of t. ❑

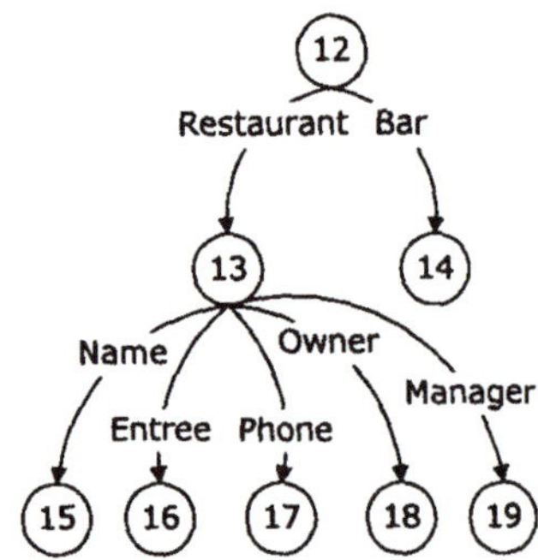

Figure 2. A DataGuide for Figure 1

For example, the target set of Restaurant.Entree in Figure 1 is {6, 10, 11}. Note that two different label paths may share the same target set. {8}, for instance, is the target set of both Restaurant.Owner and Restaurant.Manager.

2.2 Lorel Query Language

Lorel (for *Lore language*) was developed at Stanford to enable queries over semistructured OEM databases. Lorel is based on OQL [Cat93], with modifications and enhancements to support semistructured data; for details see [AQM+96]. As an extremely simple example, in Figure 1 the Lorel query

```
Select Restaurant.Entree
```

returns all entrees served by any restaurant, the set of objects {6, 10, 11}. As another simple example, we may request the names of all restaurants that serve burgers:

```
Select Restaurant.Name
Where  Restaurant.Entree = "Burger"
```

In Figure 1, the answer to the query is the single object 5.

As these brief examples indicate, some knowledge of the structure of the database is important for forming meaningful queries. The Lorel language does provide several facilities, such as "wildcards" in label paths, to enable queries when the database structure isn't entirely known. Still, a summary of the structure of the underlying database is invaluable for guiding the formulation of meaningful queries in Lorel.

2.3 DataGuides

We are now ready to define a DataGuide, intended to be a *concise, accurate*, and *convenient* summary of the structure of a database. Hereafter, we refer to a database that we summarize as the *source database*, or simply the *source*. We assume a given source database is identified by its root object. To achieve *conciseness*, we specify that a DataGuide describes every unique label path of a source exactly once, regardless of the number of times it appears in that source. To ensure *accuracy*, we specify that the DataGuide encodes no label path that does not appear in the source. Finally, for *convenience*, we require that a DataGuide itself be an OEM object so we can store and access it using the same techniques available for processing OEM databases. The formal definition follows.

Definition 5. A *DataGuide* for an OEM source s is an OEM object d such that every label path of s has exactly one data path instance in d, and every label path of d is a label path of s. ❑

Figure 2 shows a DataGuide for the source OEM database shown in Figure 1. Using a DataGuide, we can check whether a given label path of length n exists in the original database by

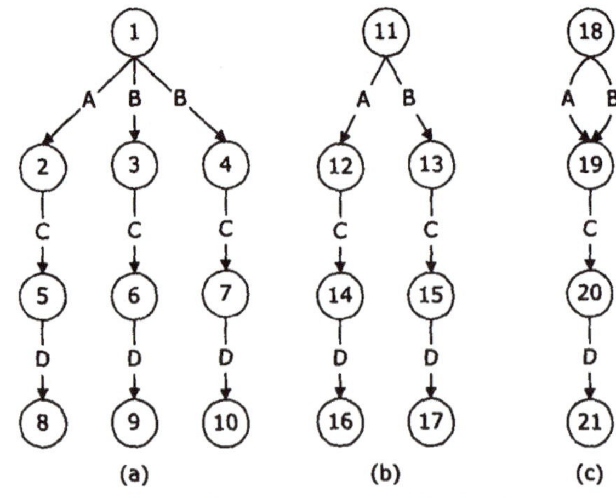

Figure 3. A source and two DataGuides

considering at most n objects in the DataGuide. For example, in Figure 2 we need only examine the outgoing edges of objects 12 and 13 to verify that the path Restaurant.Owner exists in the database. Similarly, if we traverse the single instance of a label path l in the DataGuide and reach some object o, then the labels on the outgoing edges of o represent all possible labels that could ever follow l in the source database. In Figure 2, the five different labeled outgoing edges of object 13 represent all possible labels that ever follow Restaurant in the source. Notice that the DataGuide contains no atomic values. Since a DataGuide is intended to reflect the structure of a database, atomic values are unnecessary. Later we will see how special atomic values, when added to DataGuides, can play an important role in query formulation and optimization. Note that every target set in a DataGuide is a singleton set. Recalling Definition 4, a target set denotes all objects reachable by a given label path. Since any DataGuide label path has just one data path instance, the target set contains only one object—the last object in that data path.

A considerable theoretical foundation behind DataGuides can be found in [NUWC97]. That paper proved that creating a DataGuide over a source database is equivalent to conversion of a non-deterministic finite automaton (NFA) to a deterministic finite automaton (DFA), a well-studied problem [HU79]. When the source database is a tree, this conversion takes linear time. However, in the worst case, conversion of a graph-structured database may require time (and space) exponential in the number of objects and edges in the source. Despite these worst-case possibilities, experimental results in Section 3 are encouraging, indicating that for typical OEM databases, the running time is very reasonable and the resulting DataGuides are significantly smaller than their sources. Unfortunately, no research known to the authors formally identifies those NFAs that do or do not require exponential time or space to be converted to equivalent DFAs.

2.4 Existence of Multiple DataGuides

From automata theory, we know that a single NFA may have many equivalent DFAs [HU79]. Similarly, as shown in Figure 3, one OEM source database may have multiple DataGuides. Figures 3(b) and (c) are both DataGuides of the source in Figure 3(a). Each label path in the source appears exactly once in each DataGuide, and neither DataGuide introduces any label paths that do not exist in the source. Figure 3(c) is in fact *minimal*: the smallest possible DataGuide. (Well-known state minimization algorithms can be used to convert any DataGuide into a minimal one [Hop71].) Given the existence of multiple DataGuides for a source, it is important to decide what kind of DataGuide should be built and maintained in a semistructured database system. Intuitively, a minimal DataGuide might seem desirable, furthering our goal of having as concise a summary as possible; [NUWC97] also suggests building a minimal DataGuide. Yet, as we now explain, a minimal DataGuide is not always best.

First, incremental maintenance of a minimal DataGuide can be very difficult. In Figure 3(a), suppose we add a new child object to 10, via the label E. To correctly reflect this source insertion in Figure 3(b), we simply add a new object via label E to object 17. But to reflect the same insertion in the minimal DataGuide in Figure 3(c), we must do more work in order to somehow generate the same DataGuide as our updated version of Figure 3(b), since it now is the minimal DataGuide for the source. In general, maintaining a minimal DataGuide in response to a source update may require much of the original database to be reexamined. The next subsection describes a second significant problem with minimal DataGuides.

2.5 Annotations

Beyond using a DataGuide to summarize the structure of a source, we may wish to keep additional information in a DataGuide. For example, consider a source with a label path l. To aid query formulation, we might want to present to a user sample database values that are reachable via l. (Such a feature is very useful in OEM, since there are no constraints on the type or format of atomic data.) As another example, we may wish to provide the user or the query processor with the statistical odds that an object reachable via l has any outgoing edges with a specific label. Finally, for query processing, direct access through the DataGuide to all objects reachable via l can be very useful, as will be seen in Section 6. The following definition classifies all of these examples.

Definition 6. In a source database s, given a label path l, a property of the set of objects that comprise the target set of l in s is said to be an *annotation* of l. That is, an annotation of a label path is a statement about the set of objects in the database reachable by that path. ❑

A DataGuide guarantees that each source label path l reaches exactly one object o in the DataGuide. Object o seems like an ideal place to store annotations for l, since we can access all annotations of l simply by traversing the DataGuide's single data path instance of l. Unfortunately, nothing in our definition of a DataGuide prevents multiple label paths from reaching the same object in a DataGuide, even if the label paths have different target sets in the source. Referring to Figure 3(c), we see that label paths A.C and B.C both reach the same object. Thus, if we store an annotation on object 20, we cannot know if the annotation applies to label path A.C, label path B.C, or both. In the DataGuide in Figure 3(b), however, we have two distinct objects for the two label paths, so we can correctly separate the annotations. Next, we formalize DataGuide characteristics that enable unambiguous annotation storage.

2.6 Strong DataGuides

We define a class of DataGuides that supports annotations as described in the previous subsection. Intuitively, we are interested in DataGuides where each set of label paths that share the same (singleton) target set in the DataGuide is the set of label paths that share the same target set in the source. Formally:

Definition 7. Consider OEM objects s and d, where d is a DataGuide for a source s. Given a label path l of s, let $T_s(l)$ be the target set of l in s, and let $T_d(l)$ be the (singleton) target set of l in d. Let $L_s(l) = \{m \mid T_s(m) = T_s(l)\}$. That is, $L_s(l)$ is the set of all label paths in s that share the same target set as l. Similarly, let $L_d(l) = \{m \mid T_d(m) = T_d(l)\}$. That is, $L_d(l)$ is the set of label paths in d having the same target set as l. If, for all label paths l of s, $L_s(l) = L_d(l)$, then d is a *strong* DataGuide for s. ❑

```
// MakeDG: algorithm to build a strong DataGuide
// Input:  o, the root oid of a source database
// Effect: dg is a strong DataGuide for o

targetHash: global empty hash table, to map source
            target sets to DataGuide objects
dg: global oid, initially empty

MakeDG (o) {
  dg = NewObject()
  targetHash.Insert({o}, dg)
  RecursiveMake({o}, dg)
}

RecursiveMake(t1, d1) {
  p = all children <label, oid> of all objects in t1
  foreach (unique label l in p)  {
    t2 = set of oids paired with l in p
    d2 = targetHash.Lookup(t2)
    if (d2 != nil) {
      add an edge from d1 to d2 with label l
    } else {
      d2 = NewObject()
      targetHash.Insert(t2, d2)
      add an edge from d1 to d2 with label l
      RecursiveMake(t2, d2)
    }
  }
}
```

Figure 4. Algorithm to create a strong DataGuide

For example, Figure 3(c) is not a strong DataGuide for Figure 3(a). The source target set T_s(B.C) is {6, 7}, and the DataGuide target set T_d(B.C) is {20}. In the source, L_s(B.C) is {B.C}, since no other source label paths have the same target set. In the DataGuide, however, L_d(B.C) is {B.C, A.C}. Since L_s(B.C) $\neq$ L_d(B.C), the DataGuide is not strong. The reader may verify that Figure 3(b) is in fact a strong DataGuide.

Next, we show that a strong DataGuide is sufficient for storage of annotations. A proof appears in [GW97].

Theorem 1. Suppose d is a strong DataGuide for a source s. If an annotation p of some label path l is stored on the object o reachable via l in d, then p describes the target set in s of each label path that reaches o. ❑

We also show that a strong DataGuide induces a straightforward one-to-one correspondence between source target sets and DataGuide objects (again the proof appears in [GW97]). This property is useful for incremental maintenance (Section 4) and query processing (Section 6).

Theorem 2. Suppose d is a strong DataGuide for a source s. Given any target set t of s, t is by definition the target set of some label path l. Compute $T_d(l)$, the target set of l in d, which has a single element o. Let F describe this procedure, which takes a source target set as input and yields a DataGuide object as output. In a strong DataGuide, F induces a one-to-one correspondence between source target sets and DataGuide objects. ❑

If a DataGuide is not strong, it may be impossible to find a one-to-one correspondence between source target sets and DataGuide objects. For example, Figure 3(a) has seven different target sets, each corresponding to one of the label paths A, A.C, A.C.D, B, B.C, B.C.D, and the empty path. Since Figure 3(c) has only 4 objects, we cannot have a one-to-one correspondence.

Source					DataGuide		
Description	Objects	Links	Labels	Height	Objects	Links	Time (secs)
Sports (Tree)	3,095	3,094	41	5	75	74	1.37
DBG (Graph)	947	1,102	32	--	138	168	1.52

Table 1. DataGuide performance for operational Lore databases

Source										DataGuide		
DB No	Tree ?	Objects	Links	Height	Labs. per Level	Fan-out	Full ?	Objs. per Level	Backlink Freq/ Level	Objects	Links	Time (secs)
1	Y	37,449	37,448	5	1	8	Y	--	--	6	5	11.3
2	Y	329,176	329,175	12	2	8	N	--	--	1,802	1,801	127.3
3	N	37,111	311,111	12	2	10	Y	500	--	156	288	123.1
4	N	26,700	93,151	12	2	10	N	500	--	3,074	3,073	712.6
5	N	11,134	44,346	5	4	80	N	2000	10/2	198	720	22.6
6	N	4,524	13,151	8	4	10	N	200	10/0	14,326	29,101	78.5
7	N	3,108	6,787	8	4	10	N	200	15/3	8,736	16,805	36.2

Table 2. DataGuide performance for synthetic databases

2.7 Building a Strong DataGuide

Strong DataGuides are easy to create. In a depth-first fashion, we examine the source target sets reachable by all possible label paths. Each time we encounter a new target set *t* for some path *l*, we create a new object *o* for *t* in the DataGuide—object *o* is the single element of the DataGuide target set of *l*. Theorem 2 guarantees that if we ever see *t* again via a different label path *m*, rather than creating a new DataGuide object we instead add an edge to the DataGuide such that *m* will also refer to *o*. A hash table mapping source target sets to DataGuide objects serves this purpose. The algorithm is specified in Figure 4. Note that we must create and insert DataGuide objects into `targetHash` before recursing, in order to prevent a cyclic OEM source from causing an infinite loop. Also, since we compute target sets to construct the DataGuide, we can easily augment the algorithm to store annotations in the DataGuide.

3. Experimental Performance

As described in Section 2.3, computing a DataGuide for a source is equivalent to converting a non-deterministic finite automaton into an equivalent deterministic finite automaton. For a tree-structured source, this conversion always runs in linear time, and the size of the DataGuide is bounded by the size of the source. Yet for an arbitrary graph-structured source, creating a DataGuide may require exponential running time and could feasibly generate a DataGuide exponentially larger than the source. Needless to say, we are very concerned about the potential for exponential behavior, and as far as we know no research has tried to formalize automaton characteristics that lead to better or worse behavior.

In this section, we show that for many classes of OEM databases, experimental performance results are very encouraging. We begin by discussing performance on two operational OEM databases that, although admittedly are relatively small, require very little time for DataGuide creation and yield DataGuides significantly smaller than the source. In the future we plan to build and analyze larger, realistic OEM databases. For now, we describe further experiments conducted on synthetic OEM databases. For a wide range of parameters, we find that many large graph-structured databases still yield good performance. All measurements are taken running the Lore system on a Sun Ultra 2 with 256MB RAM.

3.1 Operational Databases

We first consider two medium-sized databases used in Lore. One is a tree, and the other is a graph with significant data sharing. We believe tree-structured sources will be common in Lore; any relational database, for example, can be modeled as an OEM tree. Our tree-structured database contains a snapshot of data imported from a large and popular Web site covering many different sports, with the OEM database following the structure of the menus and links at the site. While the overall structure is quite regular, data for each sport differs significantly. We captured only a small portion of the Web site, building a database with about 3,000 objects and links, 40 unique labels, and a maximum height of 5. Building a strong DataGuide requires 1.37 seconds, and the DataGuide contains 75 objects and 74 links.

Our second operational database contains information about the Stanford Database Group, describing the group's members, projects, and publications. (We will see this database again in Section 5 when we discuss Lore's user interface.) The database uses extensive data-sharing (graph structure). As an example, a single group member might be reachable as a member of one or more projects and as an author of any number of publications. The graph also contains numerous cycles; for example, each group member reachable by a link from a project also has links to all projects he or she works on. Our database currently contains about 950 objects and 1,100 links, with 32 unique labels. Building a strong DataGuide takes 1.52 seconds; the resulting DataGuide has 138 objects and 168 links. Performance for both databases is summarized in Table 1.

3.2 Synthetic Databases

To further study performance, we generated numerous large synthetic databases, both trees and graphs, with and without cycles. Tree-structured databases have the following parameters.

- *Height*, or number of levels, in the tree.
- For each level in the tree, the number of unique labels on outgoing edges (*labels per level*). The sets of labels corresponding to different levels are disjoint.

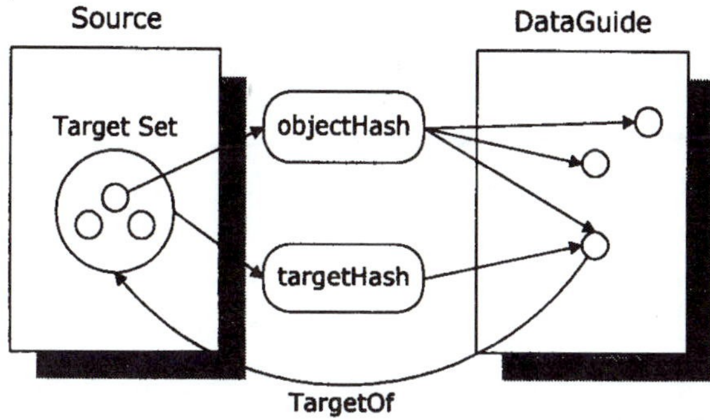

Figure 5. Data structures for DataGuide maintenance

- Maximum outgoing edges from any non-leaf (*fan-out*).
- Whether to use maximum fan-out for each object (*full*) or to simulate irregular structure by varying the number of outgoing edges of any object from zero to the maximum fan-out (*irregular*).

For graph-structured databases we modify and supplement the above tree parameters as follows.

- *Height* is defined as the longest path in a breadth-first traversal from the root of the graph. Level *n* includes all objects whose shortest path from the root has *n* edges.
- *Fan-out* no longer is sufficient to specify the number of objects at a level, since many edges of one level may point to the same object. Hence, a new parameter is the maximum number of *objects per level*, as an integer to be multiplied by the level number. Until this number is exceeded, every edge from the previous level points to a different object. When the limit is reached, all remaining edges are evenly distributed among existing objects in the level.
- Rather than sending all outgoing edges to objects in the next level, any proportion of outgoing edges (*backlink frequency*) may be redirected to objects in previous levels; here we always redirect edges to objects a fixed number of levels (*backlink level*) above the current level.

Results describing numerous synthetic databases are captured in Table 2. We summarize the results briefly here; for further discussion see [GW97]. While it is impossible to explore all possible graphs, we see that as expected, space and time performance for any tree is good (*DB1*, *DB2*). Acyclic graphs with repetitive structure do not cause problems in common situations (*DB3*, *DB4*). For relatively shallow graphs with a large number of outgoing edges per object, cycles do not pose much of a problem either (*DB5*). For much deeper graphs, however, cycles can cause DataGuides to be larger than the source (*DB6*, *DB7*). While the examples presented here yield reasonable performance, the potential does certainly exist for very poor performance. Many unconstrained backlinks in deep graphs, for instance, can cause significant problems.

While we are confident that in practice OEM databases will rarely exhibit structure that results in poor performance, we plan to build and analyze additional operational Lore databases for empirical testing. Also, we hope to formalize properties that can guarantee (or prohibit) good performance, or to find heuristics to help an algorithm detect when a database may result in poor performance. In such cases, we may be able to achieve better performance by building a strong DataGuide over only the first few levels. This way, DataGuides can still be useful for guiding queries that do not examine long paths. Finally, we plan to measure the performance impact of annotations (Section 2.5) and incremental DataGuide maintenance (Section 4).

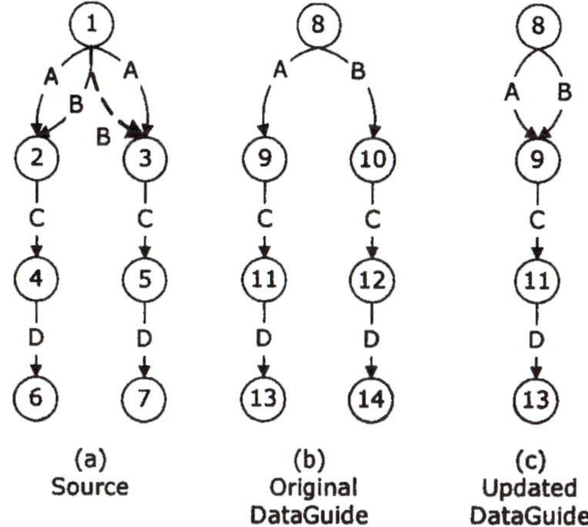

Figure 6. Insertion of an edge

4. Incremental Maintenance

If a DataGuide is to be useful for query formulation and especially optimization, we must keep it consistent when the source database changes. In this section we address how to update a strong DataGuide to reflect insertions or deletions of edges in the source. Note that updates to atomic values do not affect the DataGuide. We modify the DataGuide creation algorithm for incremental maintenance, using the following structures depicted in Figure 5.

- As we construct target sets in the DataGuide algorithm, we store them within the database as auxiliary OEM objects.
- We make persistent the `targetHash` table, which maps source target sets to DataGuide objects.
- For each DataGuide object, we add an edge labeled `TargetOf` connecting it to its corresponding target set (guaranteed to exist by Theorem 2).

In parallel, we build an additional persistent hash table, `objectHash`, to map a source object *o* to all DataGuide objects that correspond to target sets containing *o*. Our algorithm updates the DataGuide in response to any number of edge insertions or deletions on the source. Each edge can be written as *u.l.v*, indicating an edge from object *u* to object *v* via the label *l*. We refer to *u* as the *update point*. The algorithm can directly handle the insertion of a complete subgraph, given an update point connecting the new graph to the existing database. First, the algorithm identifies all DataGuide regions that might be affected by the changes: for each update point *u*, we use `objectHash` to find every DataGuide object whose corresponding source target set contains *u*. Each such DataGuide object is a "sub-DataGuide" that describes the potential structure of any object in the corresponding source target set (including one or more of the update points). The updates may affect each such sub-DataGuide, so we must recompute all of them, relying on `targetHash` to avoid excessive recomputation; if we encounter a target set that already has a corresponding DataGuide object, we can halt our recursion. The algorithm is a slightly modified version of the DataGuide creation algorithm from Figure 4, and is specified in full in [GW97]. Next, we trace one insertion example to demonstrate the algorithm. An example for deletion can be found in [GW97].

Example 4.1. Figure 6 shows one of the trickier cases for insertion. Figure 6(a), without the dashed B edge between objects 1 and 3, is our original source, and Figure 6(b) is a

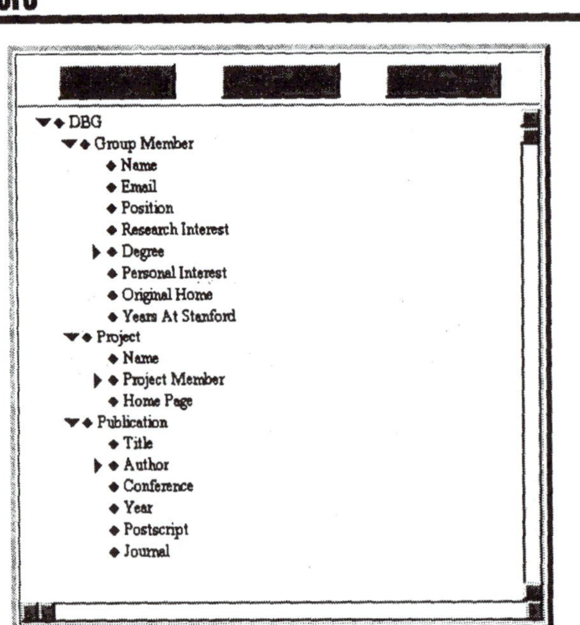

Figure 7. A Java DataGuide

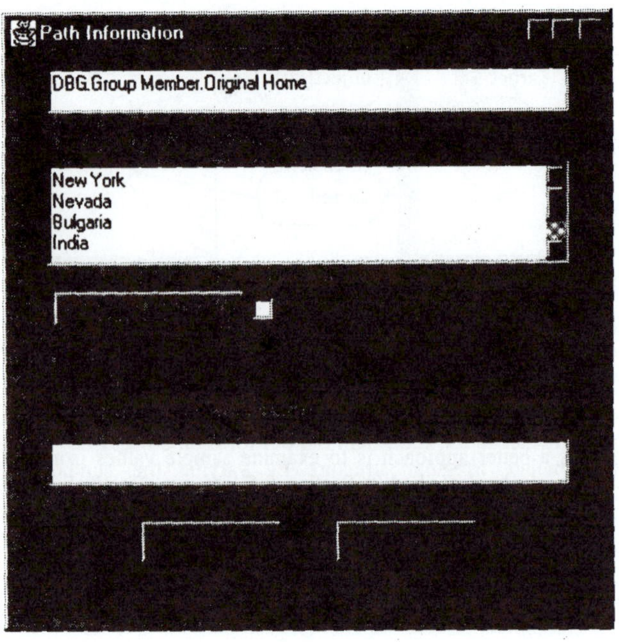

Figure 8. DataGuide path information

strong DataGuide for this source (with `TargetOf` links omitted). Suppose we insert the B edge. Object 1 is the sole update point, and DataGuide object 8 corresponds to the only target set that object 1 is a part of. Hence, we recompute the sub-DataGuide beginning at 8. As in the original algorithm, we examine the children of all objects in the initial source target set, label by label. Suppose we consider children via label A first. The target set is {2, 3}. From our persistent `targetHash`, we see that object 9 corresponds to this set. We catch the fact that an edge from 8 to 9 with the label A already exists, so no additional work is required for that label. Proceeding to examine children via label B, we see that the target set is now also {2, 3}. Hence we add a new edge from 8 to 9 with the label B. Before doing so, we remove the existing B edge. The detached subgraph is garbage collected, and the final result is the strong DataGuide shown in Figure 6(c).

Notice that deleting the edge we just inserted would regenerate a DataGuide equivalent to Figure 6(b). After the deletion, the target set of A remains {2, 3}, but the target set of B is now {2}. Hence, the B edge from 8 to 9 is removed, and recursive calls generate a new DataGuide path from the root for B.C.D. ❑

The work required to maintain the DataGuide depends entirely on the structural impact of the updates. For example, inserting a new leaf into a tree-structured database requires only one target set to be recomputed (and one new object added to the DataGuide). At the other extreme, in a graph-structured database extensive sharing may cause many sub-DataGuides to be recomputed after an update. Regardless, keeping accurate target set data prevents any excessive recomputation: recursion is halted whenever a target set lookup in `targetHash` is successful, indicating that the sub-DataGuide corresponding to that target set is already correct.

5. Query Formulation

Without some notion of the structure of a database, formulating queries can be extremely difficult. The user is limited to an ad-hoc combination of browsing the entire database, issuing exploratory queries, and guesswork. Since DataGuides provide concise, accurate, and up-to-date summarizing information about the structure of a database, they are very useful for query formulation. In this section we demonstrate the value of DataGuides in the context of a Java-based Web user interface we have created for Lore. From the interface, a user can interactively explore the DataGuide to aid formulation of Lorel queries. Further, the DataGuide enables end-users to specify a large class of queries in a "by example" style, without any knowledge of the Lorel query language.

In all of our examples we refer to a medium-sized database we have built describing members, projects, and publications of the Stanford Database Group, first introduced in Section 3. The database mirrors much of the information available on the Database Group Web site, and in fact contains links to many of our site's home pages, images, and publications. Once a connection to the database is made, the user is presented with an HTML page framing a Java DataGuide, as shown in Figure 7.

The user can explore the DataGuide by clicking on the arrows (triangles), which expand or collapse complex objects within the DataGuide. Immediately, we see how the DataGuide guides the specification of path expressions used in queries (recall Section 2.2): every valid path expression must begin with the `DBG` label, followed by `Group_Member`, `Project`, or `Publication`. Expanding a DataGuide complex object lists all potential subobject labels that are found in the database, and we never see two subobjects with the same label. Therefore, we can determine whether any label path of length n exists in the database by clicking on at most n-1 DataGuide arrows. In contrast, when browsing a semistructured database directly, we may have to examine many like-labeled objects before finding one with a specific outgoing label.

While the DataGuide is useful for deducing valid path expressions, values in the database at this point remain a mystery. A user interested in locating all group members from Nevada doesn't know if `Original_Home` for someone from Las Vegas would be stored as `"Las Vegas, NV"`, `"Nevada"`, or `"Nevada, USA"`. One option is to use

```
▼◆ DBG
  ▼◆ Group Member
      ◆ Name
      ◆ Email
      ◆ Position like "%Student"
      ◆ Research Interest
    ▶ ◆ Degree
      ◆ Personal Interest
      ◆ Original Home = "Nevada" or = "New York"
      ◆ Years At Stanford > 2
  ▶ ◆ Project
  ▶ ◆ Publication
```

Figure 9. A DataGuide query specification

Lorel's pattern matching features [AQM+96] to write a query that attempts to encompass all possible formats, but in many cases a better approach is to examine sample values from the database. As described in Section 2.5, we can effectively store such sample values as annotations in the DataGuide. In Figure 7, notice that a diamond accompanies every label, corresponding to a distinct label path from the root. Clicking on the diamond brings up a dialog box such as the one shown in Figure 8, which was obtained by clicking on the diamond next to the `Original_Home` label.

The top portion of the dialog box identifies the path expression and shows two DataGuide annotations: the total number of database objects reachable by that path expression, and a list of sample values. Currently, a fixed number of values are chosen arbitrarily from the database, although clearly we could be more sophisticated here. Annotations are stored as specially marked children of DataGuide objects that are interpreted by the user interface. They are easily computed during DataGuide creation and maintenance.

The other elements in the dialog box allow users to specify queries directly from the DataGuide without writing Lorel, in a style reminiscent of *Query By Example* [Zlo77]. As shown, a user can click a button to select a path for the query result. Further, value-filtering conditions may be specified using common arithmetic and logical operators, as well as custom operators such as the UNIX utility `grep` and the SQL function `like`. (These comparisons correspond to Lorel "where" conditions, but users need not be aware of that fact.) The on-screen DataGuide is updated to reflect any query specifications, highlighting diamonds for selected path expressions and displaying filtering conditions next to the corresponding labels. Figure 9 shows the DataGuide after a user has specified to select all graduate students in the group that are originally from Nevada or New York and have been at Stanford for more than two years. (The `like` predicate will satisfy any `PhD Student` or `Masters Student`.) When the user clicks the Go button from Figure 7, the Java program generates a Lorel query equivalent to the DataGuide query specification, and sends it to Lore to be processed. Lore returns query results in HTML, using a hierarchical format that is easy to browse and navigate: like-labeled objects are grouped together, and complex objects are represented as hyperlinks. At any point the user may return to the DataGuide to modify the original query or submit a new one.

Currently, DataGuide queries can specify any Lorel query with simple path expressions (no path wildcards) and "where" clauses that are conjunctive with respect to unique path expressions. Also, all value comparisons must be made against constants. We hope to add techniques that expand the expressive power of DataGuide queries; e.g., disjunctions across path expressions, path wildcard specifications, and variables to enable joins.

On a larger scale, we believe that there is much opportunity for blurring the distinction between formulating a query and browsing a query result, in the spirit of PESTO [CHMW96]. For example, suppose that instead of supplying just a few sample values, the dialog box for each path expression always displayed all values. Then clicking on a diamond answers the simple query to find all values reachable by a given path. Furthermore, by integrating the query processor with our DataGuide maintenance algorithms, we could quickly respond to a filtering condition specified in the DataGuide by updating the DataGuide and its value lists to reflect that condition. For example, suppose the user specified the condition in Figure 9 on `Position` first, restricting the query to only consider students. It may be that the database has no `Research_Interest` data for any such group members, so that path could be removed temporarily from the DataGuide. More importantly, clicking on the diamond next to `Original_Home` would now display the homes of students only. In the same manner, restricting `Years_At_Stanford` and `Original_Home` would evaluate the entire desired query, since clicking on the diamonds for labels under `Group_Member` would only display data that matched our query conditions. At that point, it may be desirable to revert to the current model of result browsing, allowing a user to examine one by one the group members that satisfied the query.

The DataGuide-driven user interface described here is accessible to the public via the Lore Home page on the Web, at `www-db.stanford.edu/lore`.

6. Query Optimization

In this section we discuss one technique that uses information maintained by a strong DataGuide to significantly speed up query processing for a broad class of Lorel queries. Essentially, a strong DataGuide can also serve as a *path index*. While path indexes have been studied for traditional object-oriented database systems, e.g., [BK89, CCY94, KM92], they are typically created for user-specified path expressions; in a semistructured environment, the set of path expressions may be in flux, and isolating useful paths to index may be difficult. Conveniently, we can build and incrementally maintain a comprehensive path index for all possible path expressions using a strong DataGuide. As shown in Section 4 for incremental maintenance, each object in the strong DataGuide can have a link to its corresponding target set in the source. Hence, in time proportional to the length of a label path, we can use the DataGuide to find all source objects reachable via that path, independent of the size of the source. In this section we analyze a sequence of queries to show the benefits of having fast access to target sets during query processing.

All of our query processing comparisons are based on the number of objects examined. We use a very simple cost model that assigns a uniform cost to every object examination since, in general, it is difficult to make guarantees about clustering in a graph-based model like OEM; each object examination may therefore require a random disk access. Note that the value of a complex object is a sequence of <label, oid> pairs representing its subobjects [MAG+97], so time spent to examine only the labels and oids of those subobjects is included in the cost of examining the complex object itself. For some queries, we need to find parents of an OEM object. Parent pointers need not be stored explicitly within the database; Lore, for example, instead uses a hash-based index to map an object o and a label l to all parents that reach o via l [MAG+97]. For simplicity, we assume that examining an object yields that object's parents at no additional cost.

Example 6.1. We begin with a very simple Lorel query over a sample database, showing how the DataGuide can dramatically reduce query execution cost. Suppose we wish to execute the following Lorel query (recall Section 2.2) over a database with structure similar to the Stanford Database Group database described in Section 5. It finds all publications in Troff format.

```
Select DBG.Group_Member.Publication.Troff
```

The result is a set of oids. For this example, let us consider an extreme database that has one DBG object containing 10,000 group members (among other objects). Each GroupMember has an average of 100 Publications, but only one Troff subobject exists in the entire database. Without any a priori knowledge of the structure of the database, a query processor would be forced to examine each GroupMember, in turn each Publication of each GroupMember, and finally return every Troff object of each such Publication. We see that, in addition to the root and the DBG object, the query processor must examine 1,000,000 objects. Note that Lore's current indexing schemes are not applicable to this query [MAG+97].

In this example, the query result is exactly the objects in the target set of DBG.GroupMember.Publication.Troff. To find the target set, we simply traverse the path from the root of the DataGuide, and we know there is only one such path. Hence, we need examine only six objects to find the result: the DataGuide root, the DBG object, the GroupMember, the Publication, the Troff object, and the object containing the path's target set. (As in Section 4, the object in the DataGuide reachable by DBG.GroupMember.Publication.Troff includes as part of its value a TargetOf link to a special complex object whose children are all objects in the path's target set.)

Note that when traversing the DataGuide, we may find that a path does not exist. For this query and many others, such a finding guarantees that the query result is empty. This type of optimization does not require a strong DataGuide and was in fact suggested by [NUWC97]. ❑

Example 6.2. We now show a somewhat more interesting query. Suppose we wish to find the publication years of some of the group's older publications:

```
Select DBG.Group_Member.Publication.Year
Where DBG.Group_Member.Publication.Year < 1975
```

This query introduces a filtering condition. For such conditions Lore includes a B-tree based *value index* (*Vindex*) that takes a label, operator, and value and returns the set of oids of objects that satisfy the given value constraint and have the specified incoming label [MAG+97]. Note that this index is based only on the last label in a label path to an object. Using the DataGuide, we can compute the intersection between the set of objects returned by the Vindex on (Year, <, 1975) and the target set of the full label path, DBG.GroupMember.Publication.Year. Because the DataGuide algorithm in Figure 4 constructs each target set in one step (and never modifies a target set), we can typically expect target sets to be stored contiguously on disk. Further, since oids returned by the Vindex are stored efficiently in a B-tree, we expect computation of this intersection to be fast, with few additional random disk accesses.

We now specify a sample database for analyzing the performance of both this query and Example 6.3 below. While the numbers are contrived in this particular database, they are representative of the size and structure of databases we are likely to encounter in practice. Suppose the path DBG.GroupMember. Publication.Year has a target set Y of 20,000 objects. Assume 1,000 of these objects satisfy the value constraint, each reachable via a single Publication along that path. Also, suppose that these 1,000 Year objects are referenced by 1,000 other Publications along the path DBG.Project.Publication.Year, and that 9,000 other Year objects with value less than 1975 are reachable from 9,000 more Publications on that same path. Hence, a Vindex lookup on (Year, <, 1975) returns 10,000 objects, pointed to by 11,000 different Publications.

To process the query using the DataGuide, we first examine 5 DataGuide objects to find the oid identifying Y. Next, we retrieve the 10,000 valid oids from the Vindex and intersect them with the 20,000 oids of Y to compute the result. Now consider processing the query without the DataGuide. A "top-down" exploration that does not use the Vindex would need to examine the values of all 20,000 objects in Y, and as in the previous example we might examine many GroupMember or Publication objects that do not even have the appropriate subobjects. Alternatively, Lore can build a query plan to take advantage of the Vindex by traversing "bottom-up" to identify objects reachable by valid paths [MAG+97]. In this example, for each object o returned by the Vindex, the system would find all objects that have a Year link to o, check to see which of those objects have incoming links with the label Publication, and so on up to the root until it can determine whether or not the object is indeed reachable via the label path DBG.GroupMember. Publication.Year. To begin processing our example, we first examine all 10,000 objects returned by the Vindex to find the 11,000 Publications with links to those objects. Next, we must find the parents of all 11,000 Publication objects as well. Hence, processing the query "bottom-up" requires at least 21,000 objects to be examined. ❑

Example 6.3. Suppose we now wish to find the actual older publications:

```
Select DBG.Group_Member.Publication
Where DBG.Group_Member.Publication.Year < 1975
```

Let P denote the target set of the "select" path and Y the target set of the "where" path, both found by traversing a single data path in the DataGuide. As mentioned in Example 6.1, if either path does not exist then the query result is empty. Otherwise, we proceed as in Example 6.2 to intersect oids in Y with the set of oids returned by the Vindex to identify candidate Year objects, Y^*. Next, we examine all objects in Y^* to find the set P^* of (parent) objects that have Year links to objects in Y^*. Since P^* may include objects not in the query result, we intersect the oids of P^* and P to compute the final result R.

As before, Y has 20,000 objects. We assume each Publication has a single Year, so P has 20,000 objects as well. Y^*, essentially the query result from the previous example, has 1,000 objects. Because of data-sharing, P^* contains 2,000 objects. In addition to the work required from the previous example to compute Y^*, we need to examine the 1,000 objects in Y^* to find the parent objects in P^*, and we must intersect P and P^* to find R. Hence, the total cost using the DataGuide is 1,000 expensive object examinations, plus the relatively small costs involved in retrieving 10,000 oids from the Vindex and performing two oid set intersections: one between the 10,000 oids returned by the Vindex and the 20,000 oids in Y, and the other between the 20,000 oids in P and the 2,000 oids in P^*. In comparison, a top-down approach without the Vindex or DataGuide would again have to examine at least 20,000 objects. Similarly, as in the previous example, combining the Vindex with parent traversal would retrieve 10,000 oids from the Vindex and then examine at least 21,000 objects. ❑

The techniques used in these examples can be generalized to many other queries as well. For instance, we can optimize queries that use Lorel's support for "wildcards" and regular expressions in path specifications [AQM+96]. As an example,

```
Select DBG(.Group_Member|.Project).Publication
```

selects Publications of either GroupMembers or Projects. Because the DataGuide is an OEM object, we can reuse the same code that handles such constructs over data to find target sets of such paths in the DataGuide.

In practice, the impact of the DataGuide on query processing certainly depends on the structure of the database. Even so, direct access to target sets always enables the query processor to prevent the search space from growing needlessly large. As follow-on work, we plan to run benchmarks to carefully compare the performance of the different query processing approaches described in this section. Ultimately, we hope to build an optimizer that uses statistics and detailed performance characteristics to combine DataGuides, Vindexes, and child/parent link traversal into efficient query plans.

7. Future Work

From a theoretical standpoint, we would like to investigate the possibility of performance guarantees for DataGuide creation over certain classes of databases. Ideally, we could formalize database characteristics that guarantee good performance. Heuristics that quickly identify databases that may result in poor DataGuide performance would also be helpful. Strategies for dealing with such cases are also important. We also plan to measure the performance of DataGuide creation and maintenance over large, realistic OEM databases.

As mentioned in Section 5, we plan to continue to exploit DataGuides to enhance our user interface to Lore. In addition to allowing more expressive queries to be specified directly from the DataGuide, we plan to work towards blurring the distinctions between metadata and data (or alternatively, query formulation and result browsing). This process will demand considerable cooperation between the query processor and DataGuide management, in addition to quickly and repeatedly updating a (potentially remote) user's view of the database.

With regard to query optimization, we plan to run extensive benchmarks comparing query processing in Lore with and without DataGuides. In the process, we seek to classify the queries and database characteristics for which DataGuides improve performance.

Acknowledgments

The authors wish to thank Svetlozar Nestorov, Jeff Ullman, Janet Wiener, and Sudarshan Chawathe for their initial work on Representative Objects. We are also grateful to Serge Abiteboul, Jason McHugh, Svetlozar Nestorov, and Jeff Ullman for helpful suggestions on our work, and to the rest of the Lore group at Stanford for enabling this research.

References

[AGS90] R. Agrawal, N. Gehani, and J. Srinivasan. OdeView: The Graphical Interface to Ode. In *Proceedings of the ACM SIGMOD International Conference on Management of Data*, pp. 34-43, Atlantic City, NJ, May, 1990.

[AQM+96] S. Abiteboul, D. Quass, J. McHugh, J. Widom, and J. Wiener. The Lorel Query Language for Semistructured Data. *Journal of Digital Libraries*, 1(1), November, 1996.

[BDFS97] P. Buneman, S. Davidson, M. Fernandez, and D. Suciu. Adding Structure to Unstructured Data. In *Database Theory: Sixth International Conference Proceedings*, pp. 336-350, Delphi, Greece, 1997.

[BDHS96] P. Buneman, S. Davidson, G. Hillebrand, and D. Suciu. A Query Language and Optimization Techniques for Unstructured Data. In *Proceedings of the ACM SIGMOD International Conference on Management of Data*, pp. 505-516, Montreal, Canada, 1996.

[BDS95] P. Buneman, S. Davidson, and D. Suciu. Programming Constructs for Unstructured Data. In *Proceedings of the 1995 International Workshop on Database Programming Languages*, 1995.

[BK89] E. Bertino and W. Kim. Indexing Techniques for Queries on Nested Objects. *IEEE Transactions on Knowledge and Data Engineering*, pp. 196-214, 1(2), June, 1989.

[Cat93] R.G.G. Cattell, ed. *The Object Database Standard: ODMG-93*. Morgan Kaufmann, San Francisco, CA, 1994.

[CCY94] S. Chawathe, M. Chen, and P. Yu. On Index Selection Schemes for Nested Object Hierarchies. In *Proceedings of the Twenty-First International Conference on Very Large Data Bases*, pp. 331-341, Santiago, Chile, 1994.

[CHMW96] M. Carey, L. Haas, V. Maganty, and J. Williams. PESTO: An Integrated Query/Browser for Object Databases. In *Proceedings of the Twenty-Second International Conference on Very Large Data Bases*, pp. 203-214, Bombay, India, August, 1996.

[GW97] R. Goldman and J. Widom. DataGuides: Enabling Query Formulation and Optimization in Semistructured Databases. Technical Report, Stanford University, 1997. Available at `http://www-db.stanford.edu`.

[Hop71] J. Hopcroft. An $n \log n$ Algorithm for Minimizing the States in a Finite Automaton. In *The Theory of Machines and Computations*, pp. 189-196, New York, 1971.

[HU79] J. Hopcroft and J. Ullman. *Introduction to Automata Theory, Languages, and Computation*. Addison-Wesley, Reading, MA, 1979.

[KM92] A. Kemper and G. Moerkotte. Access Support Relations: An Indexing Method for Object Bases. *Information Systems*, pp. 117-145, 17(2), 1992.

[KS95] D. Konopnicki and O. Shmueli. W3QS: A Query System for the World Wide Web. In *Proceedings of the Twenty-First International Conference on Very Large Data Bases*, pp. 54-65, Zurich, Switzerland, 1995.

[MAG+97] J. McHugh, S. Abiteboul, R. Goldman, D. Quass, and J. Widom. Lore: A Database Management System for Semistructured Data. *SIGMOD Record*, 26(3), September, 1997.

[MDT88] A. Motro, A. D'Atri, and L. Tarantino. The Design of KIVIEW: An Object-Oriented Browser. In *Proceedings of the Second International Conference on Expert Database Systems*, April, 1988.

[NUWC97] S. Nestorov, J. Ullman, J. Wiener, and S. Chawathe. Representative Objects: Concise Representations of Semistructured Hierarchical Data. In *Proceedings of the Thirteenth International Conference on Data Engineering*, Birmingham, U.K., April, 1997.

[PGW95] Y. Papakonstantinou, H. Garcia-Molina, and J. Widom. Object Exchange Across Heterogeneous Information Sources. In *Proceedings of the Eleventh International Conference on Data Engineering*, pp. 251-260, Taipei, Taiwan, 1995.

[SK82] M. Stonebraker and J. Kalash. TIMBER - A Sophisticated Relational Browser. In *Proceedings of the Eighth International Conference on Very Large Data Bases*, Sept., 1982.

[Zlo77] M. Zloof. Query By Example. *IBM Systems Journal*, pp. 324-343, 16(4), 1977.

NiagaraCQ: A Scalable Continuous Query System for Internet Databases

Jianjun Chen David J. DeWitt Feng Tian Yuan Wang
Computer Sciences Department
University of Wisconsin-Madison

{jchen, dewitt, ftian, yuanwang}@cs.wisc.edu

ABSTRACT

Continuous queries are persistent queries that allow users to receive new results when they become available. While continuous query systems can transform a passive web into an active environment, they need to be able to support millions of queries due to the scale of the Internet. No existing systems have achieved this level of scalability. NiagaraCQ addresses this problem by grouping continuous queries based on the observation that many web queries share similar structures. Grouped queries can share the common computation, tend to fit in memory and can reduce the I/O cost significantly. Furthermore, grouping on selection predicates can eliminate a large number of unnecessary query invocations. Our grouping technique is distinguished from previous group optimization approaches in the following ways. First, we use an incremental group optimization strategy with dynamic re-grouping. New queries are added to existing query groups, without having to regroup already installed queries. Second, we use a query-split scheme that requires minimal changes to a general-purpose query engine. Third, NiagaraCQ groups both change-based and timer-based queries in a uniform way. To insure that NiagaraCQ is scalable, we have also employed other techniques including incremental evaluation of continuous queries, use of both pull and push models for detecting heterogeneous data source changes, and memory caching. This paper presents the design of NiagaraCQ system and gives some experimental results on the system's performance and scalability.

1. INTRODUCTION

Continuous queries [TGNO92][LPT99][LPBZ96] allow users to obtain new results from a database without having to issue the same query repeatedly. Continuous queries are especially useful in an environment like the Internet comprised of large amounts of frequently changing information. For example, users might want to issue continuous queries of the form:

> *Notify me whenever the price of Dell or Micron stock drops by more than 5% and the price of Intel stock remains unchanged over next three month.*

In order to handle a large number of users with diverse interests, a continuous query system must be capable of supporting a large number of triggers expressed as complex queries against web-resident data sets.

The goal of the Niagara project is to develop a distributed database system for querying distributed XML data sets using a query language like XML-QL [DFF+98]. As part of this effort, our goal is to allow a very large number of users to be able to register continuous queries in a high-level query language such as XML-QL. We hypothesize that many queries will tend to be similar to one another and hope to be able to handle millions of continuous queries by grouping similar queries together. Group optimization has the following benefits. First, grouped queries can share computation. Second, the common execution plans of grouped queries can reside in memory, significantly saving on I/O costs compared to executing each query separately. Third, grouping makes it possible to test the "firing" conditions of many continuous queries together, avoiding unnecessary invocations.

Previous group optimization efforts [CM86] [RC88] [Sel86] have focused on finding an optimal plan for a small number of similar queries. This approach is not applicable to a continuous query system for the following reasons. First, it is computationally too expensive to handle a large number of queries. Second, it was not designed for an environment like the web, in which continuous queries are dynamically added and removed. Our approach uses a novel incremental group optimization approach in which queries are grouped according to their signatures. When a new query arrives, the existing groups are considered as possible optimization choices instead of re-grouping all the queries in the system. The new query is merged into existing groups whose signatures match that of the query.

Our incremental group optimization scheme employs a query-split scheme. After the signature of a new query is matched, the sub-plan corresponding to the signature is replaced with a scan of the output file produced by the matching group. This optimization process then continues with the remainder of the query tree in a bottom-up fashion until the entire query has been analyzed. In the case that no group "matches" a signature of the new query, a new query group for this signature is created in the system. Thus, each continuous query is split into several smaller queries such that inputs of each of these queries are monitored using the same techniques that are used for the inputs of user-defined continuous queries. The main advantage of this approach is that it can be implemented using a general query engine with only minor modifications. Another advantage is that the approach is easy to implement and, as we will demonstrate in Section 4, very scalable.

Since queries are continuously being added and removed from groups, over time the quality of the group can deteriorate, leading to a reduction in the overall performance of the system. In this case, one or more groups may require "dynamic re-grouping" to re-establish their effectiveness.

Continuous queries can be classified into two categories depending on the criteria used to trigger their execution. *Change-based* continuous queries are fired as soon as new relevant data becomes available. *Timer-based* continuous queries are executed only at time intervals specified by the submitting user. In our previous example, day traders would probably want to know the desired price information immediately, while longer-term investors may be satisfied being notified every hour. Although change-based continuous queries obviously provide better response time, they waste system resources when instantaneous answers are not really required. Since timer-based continuous queries can be supported more efficiently, query systems that support timer-based continuous queries should be much more scalable. However, since users can specify various overlapping time intervals for their continuous queries, grouping timer-based queries is much more difficult than grouping purely change-based queries. Our approach handles both types of queries uniformly.

NiagaraCQ is the continuous query sub-system of the Niagara project, which is a net data management system being developed at University of Wisconsin and Oregon Graduate Institute. NiagaraCQ supports scalable continuous query processing over multiple, distributed XML files by deploying the incremental group optimization ideas introduced above. A number of other techniques are used to make NiagaraCQ scalable and efficient. 1) NiagaraCQ supports the incremental evaluation of continuous queries by considering only the changed portion of each updated XML file and not the entire file. Since frequently only a small portion of each file gets updated, this strategy can save significant amounts of computation. Another advantage of incremental evaluation is that repetitive evaluation is avoided and only new results are returned to users. 2) NiagaraCQ can monitor and detect data source changes using both push and poll models on heterogeneous sources. 3) Due to the scale of the system, all the information of the continuous queries and temporary results cannot be held in memory. A caching mechanism is used to obtain good performance with limited amounts of memory.

The rest of the paper is organized as follows. In Section 2 the NiagaraCQ command language is briefly described. Our new group optimization approach is presented in Section 3 and its implementation is described in Section 4. Section 5 examines the performance of the incremental continuous query optimization scheme. Related work is described in Section 6. We conclude our paper in Section 7.

2. NIAGARACQ COMMAND LANGUAGE

NiagaraCQ defines a simple command language for creating and dropping continuous queries. The command to create a continuous query has the following form:

CREATE *CQ_name*
XML-QL query
DO *action*
{**START** *start_time*} {**EVERY** *time_interval*} {**EXPIRE** *expiration_time*}

To delete a continuous query, the following command is used:

Delete *CQ_name*

Users can write continuous queries in NiagaraCQ by combining an ordinary XML-QL query with additional time information. The query will become effective at the *start_time*. The *Time_interval* indicates how often the query is to be executed. A query is timer-based if its *time_interval* is not zero; otherwise, it is change-based. Continuous queries will be deleted from the system automatically after their *expiration_time*. If not provided, default values for the time are used. (These values can be set by the database administrator.) *Action* is performed upon the XML-QL query results. For example, it could be ``MailTo dewitt@cs.wisc.edu" or a complex stored procedure to further processing the results of the query. Users can delete installed queries explicitly using the delete command.

3. OUR INCREMENTAL GROUP OPTIMIZATION APPROACH

In Section 3.1, we present a novel incremental group optimization strategy that scales to a large number of queries. This strategy can be applied to a wide range of group optimization methods. A specific group optimization method based on this approach is described in Section 3.2. Section 3.3 introduces our query-split scheme that requires minimal changes to a general-purpose query engine. Section 3.4 and 3.5 apply our group optimization method to selection and join operators. We discuss how our system supports timer-based queries in Section 3.6. Section 3.7 contains a brief discussion of the caching mechanisms in NiagaraCQ to make the system more scalable.

3.1 General Strategy of Incremental Group Optimization

Previous group optimization strategies [CM86] [RC88] [Sel86] focused on finding an optimal global plan for a small number of queries. These techniques are useful in a query environment where a small number of similar queries either enter the system within a short time interval or are given in advance. A naive approach for grouping continuous queries would be to apply these methods directly by reoptimizing all queries whenever a new query is added. We contend that such an approach is not acceptable for large dynamic environments because of the associated performance overhead.

We propose an incremental group optimization strategy for continuous queries in this paper. Groups are created for existing queries according to their signatures, which represent similar structures among the queries. Groups allow the common parts of two or more queries to be shared. Each individual query in a query group shares the results from the execution of the group plan. When a new query is submitted, the group optimizer considers existing groups as potential optimization choices. The new query is merged into those existing groups that match its signatures. Existing queries are not, however, re-grouped in our approach. While this strategy is likely to result in sub-optimal groups, it reduces the cost of group optimization significantly. More importantly it is very scalable in a dynamic environment. Since continuous queries are frequently added and removed, it is possible that current groups may become inefficient. "Dynamic re-grouping" would be helpful to re-group part or all of the queries either periodically or when the system performance degrades below some threshold. This is left as future work.

3.2 Incremental Group Optimization using Expression Signature

Based on our incremental grouping strategy, we designed a scalable group optimization method using expression signatures. Expression signatures [HCH+99] represent the same syntax structure, but possibly different constant values, in different queries. It is a specific implementation of the signature concept.

3.2.1 Expression Signature

For purposes of illustration, we use XML-QL queries on a database of stock quotes.

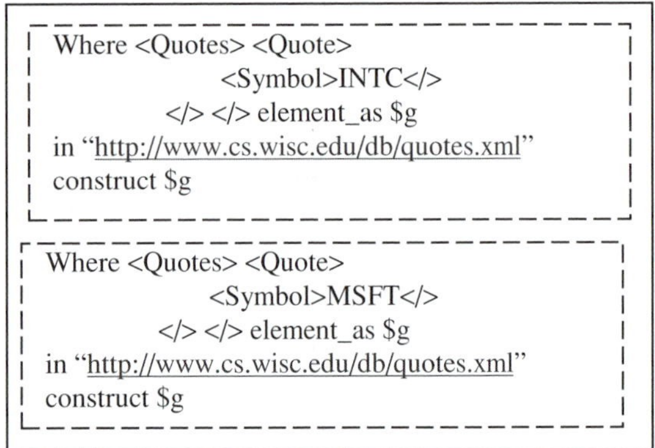

```
Where <Quotes> <Quote>
          <Symbol>INTC</>
      </> </> element_as $g
in "http://www.cs.wisc.edu/db/quotes.xml"
construct $g
```

```
Where <Quotes> <Quote>
          <Symbol>MSFT</>
      </> </> element_as $g
in "http://www.cs.wisc.edu/db/quotes.xml"
construct $g
```

Figure 3.1 XML-QL query examples

The two XML-QL queries in Figure 3.1 retrieve stock information on either Intel (symbol INTC) or Microsoft (symbol MSFT). Many users are likely to submit similar queries for different stock symbols. An expression signature is created for the selection predicates by replacing the constants appearing in the predicates with a placeholder. The expression signature for the two queries in Figure 3.1 is shown in Figure 3.2.

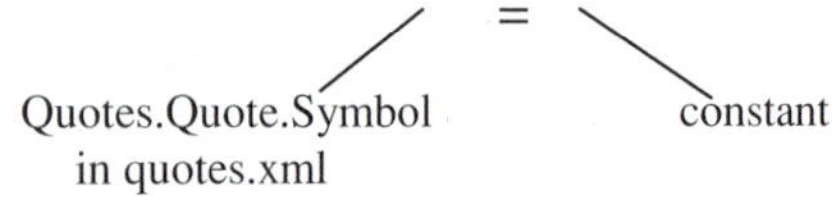

Figure 3.2 Expression signature of queries in Figure 3.1

A query plan is generated by Niagara query parser. Figure 3.3 shows the query plans of the queries in Figure 3.1. The lower part in each query plan corresponds to the expression signature of the queries. A new operator TriggerAction is added on the top of the XML-QL query plan after the query is parsed. Expression signatures allow queries with the same syntactic structure to be grouped together to share computation [HCH+99]. Expression signatures for different queries will be discussed later. Note, in NiagaraCQ, users can specify an XML-QL query without specifying the destination data sources by using a "*" in the file name position and giving a DTD name. This allows users to specify continuous queries without naming the data sources. Our group query optimizer is easily extended to support this capability by using a mapping mechanism offered by the Niagara Search Engine. Without losing generality for our incremental grouping algorithm, we assume continuous queries are defined on a specific data source in this paper.

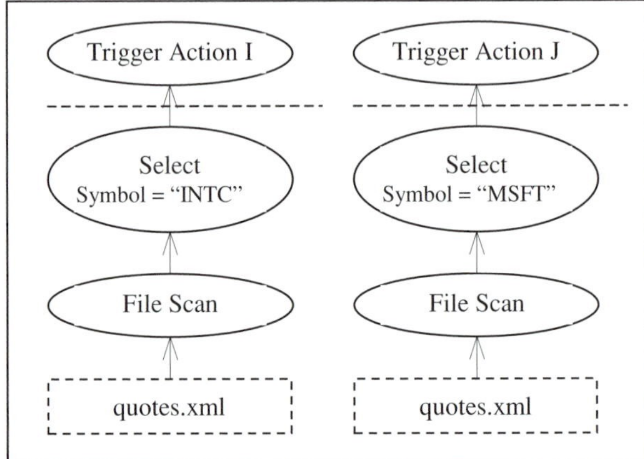

Figure 3.3 Query plans of queries in Figure 3.1

3.2.2 Group

Groups are created for queries based on their expression signatures. For example, a group is generated for the queries in Figure 3.1 because they have same expression signature. We use this group in following discussion. A group consists of three parts.

1. Group signature

The *group signature* is the common expression signature of all queries in the group. For the example above, the expression signature is given in Figure 3.2.

Constant_value	Destination_buffer
....	....
INTC	Dest. i
MSFT	Dest. j
....	....

Figure 3.4 an example of group constant table

2. Group constant table

The *group constant table* contains the signature constants of all queries in the group. The constant table is stored as an XML file. For the example above, "INTC" and "MFST" are stored in this table (Figure 3.4). Since the tuples produced by the shared computation need to be directed to the correct individual query for further processing, the destination information is also stored with the constant.

3. Group plan

The *group plan* is the query plan shared by all queries in the group. It is derived from the common part of all single query plans in the group. Figure 3.5 shows the group plan for the queries in Figure 3.1.

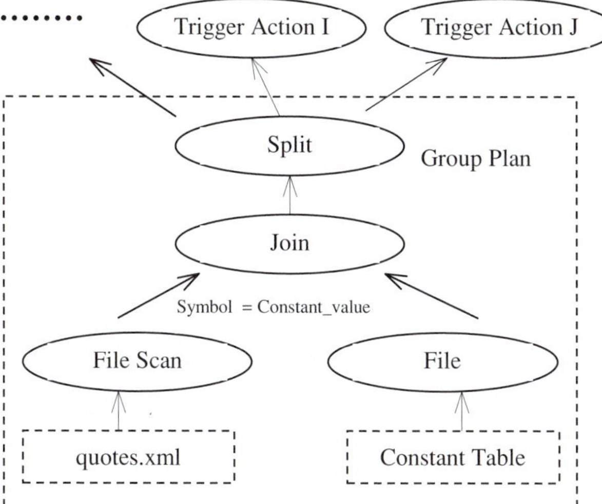

Figure 3.5 Group plan for queries in Figure 3.1

An expression signature allows queries in a group to have different constants. Since the result of the shared computation contains results for all the queries in the group, the results must be filtered and sent to the correct destination operator for further processing. NiagaraCQ performs filtering by combining a special ***Split*** operator with a Join operator based on the constant values stored in the constant table. Tuples from the data source (e.g. Quotes.xml) are joined with the constant table. The *Split* operator distributes each result tuple of the Join operator to its correct destination based on the destination buffer name in the tuple (obtained from the Constant Table). The *Split* operator removes the name of the destination buffer from the tuple before it is put into the output stream, so that subsequent operators in the query do not need to be modified. In addition, queries with the same constant value also share the same output stream. This feature can significantly reduce the number of output buffers.

Since generally the number of active groups is likely to be on the order of thousands or ten of thousands, group plans can be stored in a memory-resident hash table (termed a *group table*) with the group signature as the hash key. Group constant tables are likely to be large and are stored on disk.

3.2.3 Incremental Grouping Algorithm

In this section we briefly describe how the NiagaraCQ group optimizer performs incremental group optimization.

When a new query (Figure 3.6) is submitted, the group optimizer traverses its query plan bottom up and tries to match its expression signature with the signatures of existing groups. The expression signature of the new query, which is the same as the signature in Figure 3.2, matches the signature of the group in Figure 3.5. The group optimizer breaks the query plan (Figure 3.7) into two parts. The lower part of the query is removed. The upper part of the query is added onto the group plan. If the constant table does not have an entry "AOL", it will be added and a new destination buffer allocated.

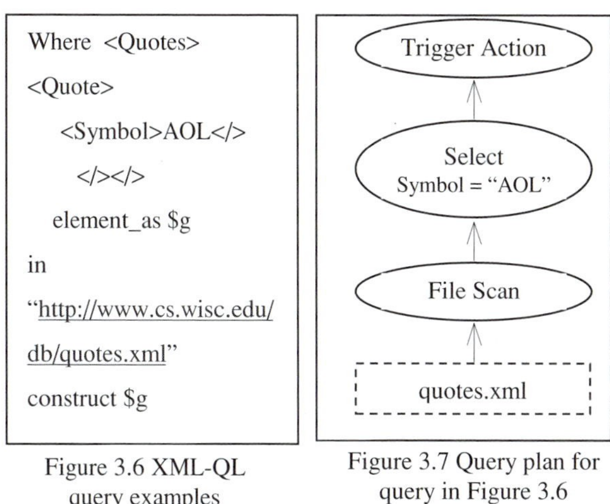

Figure 3.6 XML-QL query examples

Figure 3.7 Query plan for query in Figure 3.6

In the case that the signature of the query does not match any group signature, a new group will be generated for this signature and added to the group table.

In general, a query may have several signatures and may be merged into several groups in the system. This matching process will continue on the remainder of the query plan until the top of the plan is reached. Our incremental grouping is very efficient because it only requires one traversal of the query plan.

In the following sections, we first discuss our *query-split* scheme and then describe how incremental group optimization is performed on selection and join operators.

3.3 Query Split with Materialized Intermediate Files

The destination buffer for the split operator can be implemented either in a pipelined scheme or as an intermediate file. Our initial design of the split operator used a pipeline scheme in which tuples are pipelined from the output of one operator into the input of the next operator. However, such a pipeline scheme does not work for grouping timer-based continuous queries. Since timer-based queries will only be fired at specified time, output tuples must be retained until the next firing time. It is difficult for a split operator to determine which tuples should be stored and how long they should be stored for.

In addition, in the pipelined approach, the ungrouped parts of all query plans in a group are combined with the group plan, resulting in a single execution plan for all queries in the group. This single plan has several disadvantages. First, its structure is a directed graph, and not a tree. Thus, the plan may be too complicated for a general-purpose XML-QL query engine to execute. Second, the combined plan may be very large and require resources beyond the limits of some systems. Finally, a large portion of the query plan may not need to be executed at each query invocation. For example, in Figure 3.5, suppose only the price of Intel stock changes. Although the destination buffer for Microsoft is empty, the upper part of the Microsoft query (Trigger Action J) is also executed. This problem can be avoided only if the execution engine has the ability to selectively load part of a query plan in a bottom-up manner. Such a capability would require a special implementation of the XML-QL query engine.

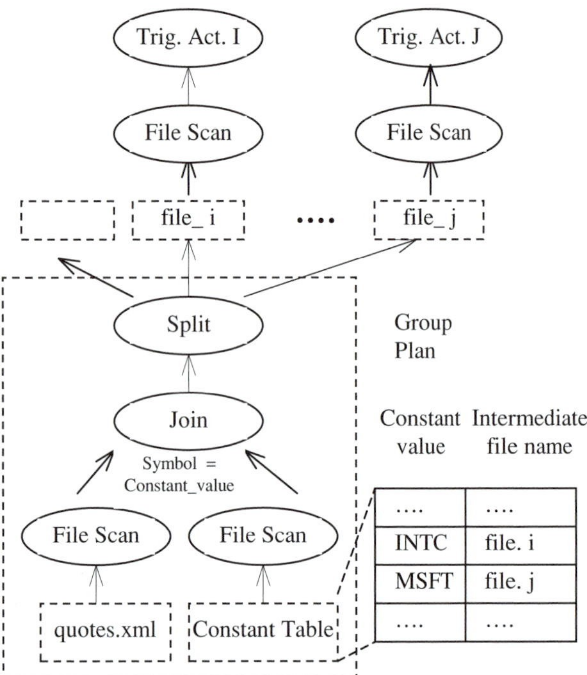

Figure 3.8 query-split scheme using intermediate files

Since a split operator has one input stream and multiple (possibly tens of thousands) output streams, split operators may become a bottleneck when the ungrouped parts of queries consume output tuples from the split stream at widely varying rates. For example, suppose 100 queries are grouped together, 99 of which are very simple selection queries, and one is a very expensive query involving multiple joins. Since this expensive query may process the input from the split operator very slowly, it may block all the other simple queries.

The pipeline scheme can be used in systems that support only a small number of change-based continuous queries. Since our goal is to support millions of both change-based and timer-based continuous queries, we adopt an approach that is more scalable and easier to implement. We also try to use a general query engine to the maximal extent possible.

In our new design (Figure 3.8), the split operator writes each output stream into an intermediate file. A query plan is cut into two parts at the split operator and a file scan operator is added to the upper part of plan to read the intermediate file. NiagaraCQ treats the two new queries like normal user queries. In particular, changes to the intermediate files are monitored in the same way as those to ordinary data sources! Since a new continuous query may overlap with multiple query groups, one query may be split into several queries. However, the total number of queries in the system will not exceed the number of groups plus the number of original user queries. Since we assume that no more than thousands of groups will be generated for millions of user queries, the overall number of queries in the system will increase only slightly. Intermediate file names are stored in the constant table and grouped continuous queries with the same constant share the same intermediate file.

The advantages of this new design include:

1. Each query is scheduled independently, thus only the necessary queries are executed. For example, in Figure 3.8, if only the price of Intel stock changes, queries on intermediate files other than "file_i" will not be scheduled. Since usually only a small amount of data is changed, only a few of the installed continuous queries will be fired. Thus, computation time and system resource usage is significantly reduced.

2. Queries after a split operator will be in a standard, tree-structured query format and thus can be scheduled and executed by a general query engine.

3. Each query in the system is about the size of a common user query, so that it can be executed without consuming an unusual amount of system resources.

4. This approach handles intermediate files and original data source files uniformly. Changes to materialized intermediate files will be processed and monitored just like changes to the original data files.

5. The potential bottleneck problem of the pipelined approach is avoided.

There are some potential disadvantages. First, the split operator becomes a blocking operator since the execution of the upper part of the query must wait for the intermediate files to be completely materialized. Since continuous queries run over data changes that are usually not very large, we do not believe that the impact of this blocking will be significant. Second, reading and writing the intermediate files incurs extra disk I/Os. Since most data changes will be relatively small, we anticipate that they will be buffered in memory before the upper part queries consume them. There will be disk I/Os in the case of timer-based queries that have long time intervals because data changes may be accumulated. In this situation, data changes need to be written to disk no matter what strategy is used. As discussed in Section 3.7, NiagaraCQ uses special caching mechanisms to reduce this cost.

3.4 Incremental Grouping of General Selection Predicates

Our primary focus is on predicates that are in the format of "*Attribute op Constant.*" *Attribute* is a path expression without wildcards in it. Op includes "=", "<", ">". Such formats dominate in selection queries. Other predicate formats could also be handled in our approach, but we do not discuss them further in this paper.

Figure 3.9 shows an example of a range selection query that returns every stock whose price has risen more than 5%. Figure 3.9 also gives its expression signature. The group plan for queries with this signature is the same in Figure 3.5, except the join condition is *Change_Ratio > constant.*

A general range-query has both lower_bound and upper_bound values. Two columns are needed to represent both bounds in the constant table. Thus each entry of the constant table will be [lower_bound, upper_bound, intermediate_file_name]. The join condition is *Change_Ratio < upper_bound and Change_Ratio > lower_bound.* A special index would be helpful to evaluate this predicate. For example, an interval skip list [HJ94] could be used for this purpose when all the intervals fit in memory. We are considering developing a new index method that handles this case more efficiently.

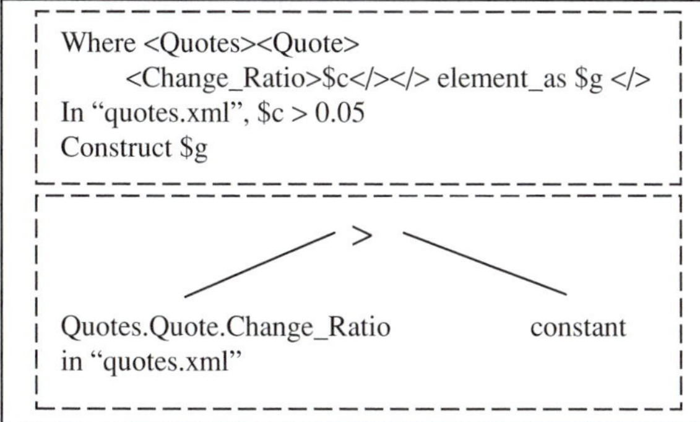

Where <Quotes><Quote>
<Change_Ratio>$c</></> element_as $g </>
In "quotes.xml", $c > 0.05
Construct $g
>
Quotes.Quote.Change_Ratio
in "quotes.xml"
constant

Figure 3.9 Range selection query example and its expression signature

One potential problem for range-query groups is that the intermediate files may contain a large number of duplicate tuples because range predicates of the different queries might overlap. "Virtual intermediate files" are used to handle this case. Each virtual intermediate file stores a value range instead of actual result tuples. All outputs from the split operator are stored in one real intermediate file, which has a clustered index on the range attribute. Modification on virtual intermediate files can trigger upper-level queries in the same way as ordinary intermediate files. The value range of a virtual intermediate file is used to retrieve data from the real intermediate file. Our query-split scheme need not be changed to handle virtual intermediate files.

In general, a query may have multiple selection predicates, i.e. multiple expression signatures. Predicates on the same data source can be represented in conjunctive normal form. The group optimizer chooses the most selective conjunct, which does not contain "or", to do incremental grouping. Other predicates are evaluated in the upper levels of the continuous query after the split operator.

```
Where <Quotes><Quote><Symbol>"INTC"</>
        <Current_Price>$p</></> element_as $g </>
in "quotes.xml", $p < 100
Construct $g
```

Figure 3.10 an example query with two selection predicates

Figure 3.10 shows a query with two selection predicates, which retrieves Intel stock whenever its price falls below \$100. This query has two expression signatures, one is an equal selection predicate on *Symbol* and the other is a range selection predicate on *Current_price*. The expression signature on the equal selection predicate (i.e. on *Symbol*) is used for grouping because it is more selective. In addition, a new select operator with the second selection predicate (i.e. the range select on *Current_price*) will be added above the file scan operator.

3.5 Incremental Grouping of Join Operators

Since join operators are usually expensive, sharing common join operations can significantly reduce the amount of computation. Figure 3.11 shows a query with a join operator that, for each company, retrieves the price of its stock and the company's profile. The signature for the join operation is shown on the right side of the figure. A join signature in our approach contains the names of the two data sources and the predicate for the join. The group optimizer groups join queries with the same join signatures. A constant table is not needed in this case because there is only one output intermediate file, whose name is stored in the split operator. This file is used to hold the results of the shared join operation.

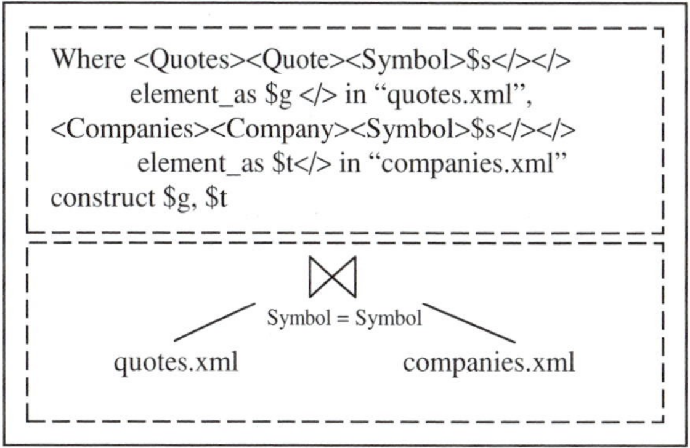

Figure 3.11 an example query with join operator and its signature

There are two ways to group queries that contain both join operators and selection operators. Figure 3.12 shows such an example, which retrieves all stocks in the computer service industry and the related company profiles. The group optimizer can place the selection either below or above the join, so that two different grouping sequences can be used during incremental group optimization process. The group optimizer chooses the better one based on a cost model. We discuss these alternatives below using the query example in Figure 3.12.

```
Where <Quotes><Quote><Symbol>$s</>
   <Industry>"Computer Service"</></>
        element_as $g </> in "quotes.xml",
<Companies><Company><Symbol>$s</></>
        element_as $t</> in "companies.xml"
construct $g, $t
```

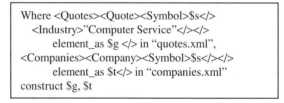

Figure 3.12 an example query with both join and selection operators

If the selection operator (e.g., on *Industry*) is pulled above the join operator, the group optimizer first groups the query by the join signature. The selection signature, which contains the intermediate file, is grouped next. The advantage of this method is that it allows the same join operator to be shared by queries with different selection operators. The disadvantage is that the join, which will be performed before the selection, may be very expensive and may generate a large intermediate file. If there are only a small number of queries in the join group and each of them has a highly selective selection predicate, then this grouping method may be even more expensive than evaluating the queries individually.

Alternatively, the group optimizer can push down the selection operator (e.g., on *Industry)* to avoid computing an expensive join. First, the signature for the selection operator is matched with an existing group. Then a file scan operator on the intermediate file produced by the selection group is added and the join operator is rewritten to use the intermediate file as one of its inputs. Finally, the group optimizer incrementally groups the join operation using its signature. Compared to the first approach, this approach may create many join groups with significant overlap between them. Note, however, that this same overlap exists in the non-grouping approach. Thus, in general, this method always outperforms than non-grouping approach.

The group optimizer will select one of these two strategies based on a cost model. To date we have implemented the second approach in NiagaraCQ. In the future we plan on implementing the first strategy and compare the performance of the two approaches.

3.6 Grouping Timer-based Continuous Queries

Since timer-based queries are only periodically executed their use can significantly reduce computation time and make the system more scalable. Timer-based queries are grouped in the same way as change-based queries except that the time information needs to be recorded at installation time. Grouping large number of timer-based queries poses two significant challenges. First, it is hard to monitor the timer events of those queries. Second, sharing the common computation becomes difficult due to the various time intervals. For example, two users may both request the query in Figure 3.1 with different time intervals, e.g. weekly and monthly. The query with the monthly interval should not repeat the weekly query's work. In general, queries with various time intervals should be able to share the results that have already been produced.

3.6.1 Event Detection

Two types of events in NiagaraCQ can trigger continuous queries. They are data-source change events and timer events. Data sources can be classified into push-based and pull-based. Push-based data sources will inform NiagaraCQ whenever interesting data is changed. On the other hand, changes on pull-based data sources must be checked periodically by NiagaraCQ.

Timer-based continuous queries are fired only at specified times. However, queries will not be executed if the corresponding input files have not been modified. Timer events are stored in an event list, which is sorted in time order. Each entry in the list corresponds to a time instant where there exists a continuous query to be scheduled. Each query in NiagaraCQ has a unique id. Those query ids are also stored in the entry. Whenever a timer event occurs, all related files will be checked. Each query in the entry will be fired if its data source has been modified since its last firing time. The next firing times for all queries in the entry are calculated and the queries are added into the corresponding entries on the list.

3.6.2 Incremental Evaluation

Incremental evaluation allows queries to be invoked only on the changed data. It reduces the amount of computation significantly because typically the amount of changed data is smaller than the original data file. For each file, on which continuous queries are defined, NiagaraCQ keeps a "delta file" that contains recent changes. Queries are run over the delta files whenever possible instead of their original files. However, in some cases the complete data files must be used, e.g., incremental evaluation of join operators. NiagaraCQ uses different techniques for handling delta files of ordinary data sources and those of intermediate files used to store the output of the split operator. NiagaraCQ calculates the changes to a source XML file and merges the changes into its delta file. For intermediate files, outputs from the split operators are directly appended to the delta file.

In order to support timer-based queries, a time stamp is added to each tuple in the delta file. Since timer-based queries with different firing times can be defined on one file, the delta file must keep data for the longest time interval among those queries that use the file as an input. At query execution time, NiagaraCQ fetches only tuples that were added to the delta file since the query's last firing time.

Whenever a grouped plan is invoked, the results of its execution are stored in an intermediate file regardless of whether or not queries defined on these intermediate files should be fired immediately. Subsequent invocations of this group query do not need to repeat previous computation. Upper level queries defined on intermediate files will still be fired at their scheduled execution time. Thus, the shared computation is totally transparent to these subsequent operators.

3.7 Memory Caching

Due to the desired scale of the system, we do not assume that all the information required by the continuous queries and intermediate results will fit in memory. Caching is used to obtain good performance with a limited amount of memory. NiagaraCQ caches query plans, system data structures, and data files for better performance.

1. Grouped query plans tend to be memory resident since we assume that the number of query groups is relatively small. Non-grouped change-based queries may be cached using an LRU policy that favors frequently fired queries. Timer-based queries with shorter firing intervals will have priority over those with longer intervals.
2. NiagaraCQ caches recently accessed files. Small delta files generated by split operators tend to be consumed and discarded. A caching policy that favors these small files saves lots of disk I/Os.
3. The event list for monitoring the timer-based events can be large if there are millions of timer-based continuous queries. To avoid maintaining the whole list in memory, we keep only a "time window" of this list. The window contains the front part of the list that should be kept in memory, e.g. within 24 hours.

4. IMPLEMENTATION

NiagaraCQ is being developed as a sub-system of Niagara project. The initial version of the system was implemented in Java (JDK1.2). A validating XML parser (IBM XML4J) from IBM is used to parse XML documents. We describe the system architecture of NiagaraCQ in Section 4.1 and how continuous queries are processed in Section 4.2.

4.1 System Architecture

Figure 4.1 shows the architecture of Niagara system. NiagaraCQ is a sub-system of Niagara that handles continuous queries. NiagaraCQ consists of

1. A continuous query manager, which is the core module of NiagaraCQ system. It provides a continuous query interface to

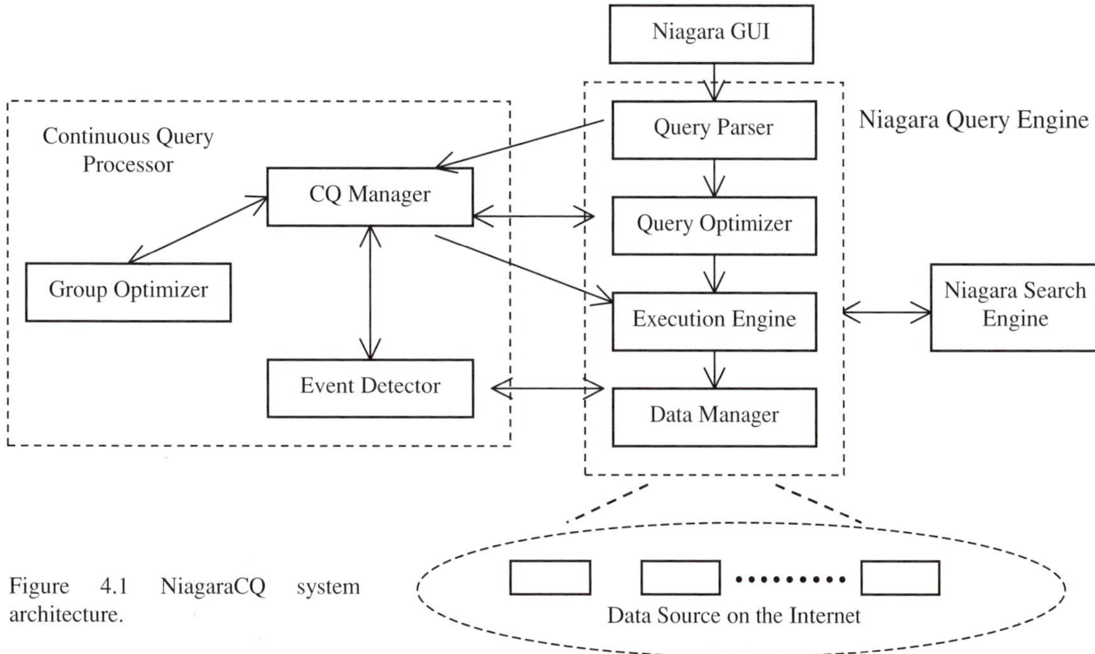

Figure 4.1 NiagaraCQ system architecture.

users and invokes the Niagara query engine to execute fired queries.

2. A group optimizer that performs incremental group optimization.
3. An event detector that detects timer events and changes of data sources.

In addition, the Niagara data manager was enhanced to support the incremental evaluation of continuous queries.

4.2 Processing Continuous Queries

Figure 4.2 shows the interactions among the Continuous Query Manager, the Event Detector and the Data Manager as continuous queries are installed, detected, and executed. Continuous query processing is discussed in following sections.

4.2.1 Continuous Query Installation

When a new continuous query enters the system, the query is parsed and the query plan is fed into the group optimizer for incremental grouping. The group optimizer may split this query into several queries using the query-split scheme described in Section 3. The continuous query manager then invokes the Niagara query optimizer to perform common query optimization for these queries and the optimized plans are stored for future execution. Timer information and data source names of these queries are given to the Event Detector (Step 1 in Figure 4.2). The Event Detector then asks the Data Manager to monitor the related source files and intermediate files (Step 2 in Figure 4.2), which in turn caches a local copy of each source file. This step is necessary in order to detect subsequent changes to the file.

The Event Detector monitors two types of events: *timer events* and *file-modification* events. Whenever such events occur, the Event Detector notifies the Continuous Query Manager about which queries need to be fired and on which data sources.

The Data Manager in Niagara monitors web XML sources and intermediate files on its local disk. It handles the disk I/O for both ordinary queries and continuous queries and supports both push-based and pull-based data sources. For push-based data sources, the Data Manager is informed of a file change and notifies Event Detector actively. Otherwise, the Event Detector periodically asks the Data Manager to check the last modified time.

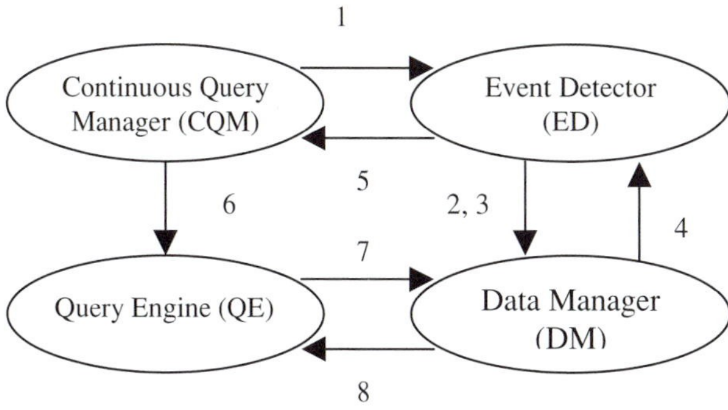

1. CQM adds continuous queries with file and timer information to enable ED to monitor the events.
2. ED asks DM to monitor changes to files.
3. When a timer event happens, ED asks DM the last modified time of files.
4. DM informs ED of changes to push-based data sources.
5. If file changes and timer events are satisfied, ED provides CQM with a list of firing CQs.
6. CQM invokes QE to execute firing CQs.
7. File scan operator calls DM to retrieve selected documents.
8. DM only returns data changes between last fire time and current fire time.

Figure 4.2 Continuous Query processing in NiagaraCQ

4.2.2 Continuous Query Deletion

A system unique name is generated for every user-defined continuous query. A user can use this name to retrieve the query status or to delete the query. Queries are automatically removed from the system when they expire.

4.2.3 Execution of Continuous Queries

The invocation of a continuous query requires a series of interactions among the Continuous Query Manager, Event Detector and Data Manager.

When a timer event happens, the Event Detector first asks the Data Manager if any of the relevant data sources have been modified (Step 3 in Figure 4.2). The Data Manager returns a list of names of modified source files. The Data Manager also notifies the Event Detector when push-based data sources have been changed (Step 4 in Figure 4.2). If a continuous query needs to be executed, its query id and the names of the modified files are sent to the Continuous Query Manager (Step 5 in Figure 4.2). The Continuous Query Manager invokes the Niagara query engine to execute the triggered queries (Step 6 in Figure 4.2). At execution time, the Query Engine requests data from the Data Manager (Step 7. in Figure 4.2). The Data Manager recognizes that it is a request for a continuous query and returns only the delta file (Step 8 in Figure 4.2). Delta files for source files are computed by performing an XML-specific "diff" operation using the original file and the new version of the file.

5. EXPERIMENTAL RESULTS

We expect that for a continuous query system over the Internet, incremental group optimization will provide substantial improvement to system performance and scalability. In the following experiments, we compare our incremental grouping approach with a non-grouping approach to show benefits from sharing computation and avoiding unnecessary query invocations.

5.1 Experiment Setting

The following experiments were conducted on a Sun Ultra 6000 with 1GB of RAM, running JDK1.2 on Solaris 2.6.

```
<!ELEMENT Quotes ( Quote )*>
<!ELEMENT Quote ( Symbol, Sector, Industry,
Current_Price, Open, PrevCls, Volume, Day's_range,
52_week_range?, Change_Ratio>
<!ELEMENT Day's_range (low, high)>
<!ELEMENT 52_week_change (low, high)>
```

Figure 5.1 DTD of quotes.xml

```
<!ELEMENT Companies ( Company )*>
<!ELEMENT Company ( Symbol, Name, Sector, Industry,
Company_profiles?>
<!ELEMENT Company_profiles (Capital, Employees,
Address, Description)>
<!ELEMENT Address (City, State)>
```

Figure 5.2 DTD of companies.xml

Data Sets

Our experiments were run against a database of stock information consisting of two XML files, "quotes.xml" and "companies.xml". "Quotes.xml" contains stock information on about 5000 NASDAQ companies. The size of "quotes.xml" is about 2 MB. Related company information is stored in "companies.xml", whose size is about 1MB. The DTDs of these two XML files are given in Figure 5.1 and 5.2, respectively. Data changes on "quotes.xml" are generated artificially to simulate the real stock market and continuous queries are triggered by these changes. The "companies.xml" file was not changed during our experiments.

We give a brief description of the assumptions that we made to generate "quotes.xml". Each stock has a unique *Symbol* value. The *Industry* attribute takes a value randomly from a set with about 100 values. The *Change_Ratio* represents the change percentage of the current price to the closing price for the previous session. It follows a normal distribution with a mean value of 0 and standard deviation of 1.0.

Since time spent calculating changes in source files is the same for both the grouped and non-grouped approaches, we run our experiments directly against the data changes. Unless specified, the number of "tuples" modified is 1000, which is about 400K bytes.

Queries

Although users may submit many different queries, we hypothesize that many queries will contain similar expression signatures. In our experiments, we use four types of queries to represent the effect of grouping queries in a stock environment by their expression signatures.

```
Where <Quotes><Quote><Symbol>"INTC"</></>
element_as $g </> in "quotes.xml", construct $g
```

Query Type-1 Example: Notify me when Intel stocks change.

```
Where <Quotes><Quote><Change_Ratio>$c</></>
element_as $g </> in "quotes.xml", $c > 0.05
construct $g
```

Query Type-2 Example: Notify me of all stocks whose prices rise more than 5 percent.

```
Where <Quotes><Quote><Symbol>"INTC"</>
<Current_Price>$p</></> element_as $g </>
in "quotes.xml", $p < 100,  construct $g
```

Query Type-3 Example: Notify me when Intel stock trades below 100 dollars.

```
Where <Quotes><Quote><Symbol>$s</><Industry>
"Computer Service"</></> element_as $g </>
in "quotes.xml",
<Companies><Company><Symbol>$s</></>
element_as $t</> in "companies.xml"
construct $g, $t
```

Query Type-4 Example: Notify me all of changes to stocks in the computer service industry and related company information.

- Type-1 queries have the same expression signature on the equal selection predicate on *Symbol*.
- Type-2 queries have the same expression signature on the range selection predicate on *Change_ratio*.

- Type-3 queries have two common expression signatures, one is on the equal selection predicate on *Symbol*, and the other is on the range selection predicate on *Current_price*. The expression signature of the equal selection predicate is used for grouping Type-3 queries because it is more selective than that of the range predicate.
- Type-4 queries contain expression signatures for both selection and join operators. Selection operators are pushed down under join operators. The incremental group optimizer first groups selection signatures and then join signatures.

Queries of Type-3 are generated following a normal distribution with a mean value of 3 and a standard deviation of 1.0. Queries of the other types are generated using different constants following a uniform distribution on the range of values in the data unless specified.

5.2 Interpretation of Experimental Result

The parameters in our experiments are:

1. **N**, the number of installed queries, is an important measure of system scalability.

2. **F**, the number of fired queries in the grouping case. The number of fired queries may vary depending on triggering conditions in the grouping case. For example, in a Tye-1 query, if Intel stock does not change, queries defined on "INTC" are not scheduled for execution after the common computation of the group. This parameter does not affect non-grouping queries.

3. C, the number of tuples modified.

In our grouping approach, a user-defined query consists of grouped part and non-grouped part. $\mathbf{T_g}$ and $\mathbf{T_{ng}}$ represent the execution time of each part. The execution time **T** for evaluating **N** queries is the sum of $\mathbf{T_g}$ and $\mathbf{T_{ng}}$ of each of **F** fired queries, $T = T_g + \sum_F T_{ng}$, because the grouped portion is executed only once.

Since the non-grouping strategy needs to scan each XML data source file multiple times, we cache parsed XML files in memory so that both approaches scan and parse XML files only once. This ensures that the comparison between the two approaches is fair. However, in a production system, parsed XML files probably could not be retained in memory for long periods of time. Thus, many non-grouped queries may each have to scan and parse the same XML files multiple times.

5.2.1 Experimental results on single type queries

We studied how effectively incremental group optimization works for each type of query. We measured and compared execution time for queries of each type for both the grouping and non-grouping approaches.

Experiment results on type-1 queries

Experiment 1. (Figure 5.3) C =1000 tuples.

- **Case 1**: **F** = **N**, i.e. all queries are fired in both approaches.

The execution time of the non-grouping approach grows dramatically as N increases. It cannot be applied to a highly loaded system. On the other hand, the grouping approach consumes significantly less execution time by sharing the computation of the selection operator. It also grows more slowly because in a single Type-1 query $\mathbf{T_{ng}}$ is much smaller than $\mathbf{T_g}$.

- **Case 2: F = 100**, i.e., 100 queries are invoked in the grouping approach.

In the grouping approach, the execution time of Case 2 is almost constant when **F** is fixed. The execution time of the grouping approach depends on number of fired queries **F**, not on the total number of installed queries **N**. The reason is that, although $\mathbf{T_g}$ increases as **N** grows, this shared computation is executed only once and is a very small portion of total execution time. The execution time for the upper queries, which is proportional to the number of fired queries F, dominates the total execution time. On the other hand, the execution time for the non-grouping approach is proportional to **N** because all queries are scheduled for execution.

Experiment 2. (Figure 5.4) F = N = 2000 queries

In this experiment we explore the impact of **C**, the number of modified tuples, on the performance of the two approaches. **C** is varied from 100 tuples (about 40K bytes) to 2000 tuples (about 800K bytes). Increasing **C** will increase the query execution time. For the non-grouping approach, the total execution time is proportional to **C** because the selection operator of every installed query needs to be executed. For the grouping approach, the execution time is not sensitive to the change of **C** because the increase of $\mathbf{T_g}$ only counts for a small percentage of the total execution time and the sum of $\mathbf{T_{ng}}$ of all fired queries does not change because of the predicate's selectivity.

Experiment results for Type-2, 3, 4 queries (Figure 5.5, 5.6, 5.7) C =1000 tuples, F = N

We discuss the influence of different expression signatures in this set of experiments.

Figure 5.5 and Figure 5.6 show that our group optimization works well for various selection predicates. Type-2 queries are grouped according to their range selection signature. Type-3 queries have two signatures. The group optimizer chooses an equal predicate to group queries since it is more selective.

Figure 5.7 shows the results for Type-4 queries. Type-4 queries have one selection signature and one join signature. The selection operator is pushed below the join operator. Queries are first grouped by their selection signature. There are 100 different industries in our test data set. The output of the selection group is written to 100 intermediate files and one hundred join groups are created. Each join group consumes one of the intermediate files as its input. The difference between the execution time with and without grouping is much larger than in the previous experiments because a join operator is more expensive than a selection operator.

5.2.2 Experiment results on mixed queries of Type-1 and type-3 (Figure 5.8) C =1000 tuples, F = N (N/2 Type-1 queries and N/2 Type-3 queries)

Previous experiments studied each type of query separately for the purpose of showing the effectiveness of different kinds of expression signatures. Our incremental group optimizer is not limited to group only one type of queries. Different types of queries can also be grouped together if they have common

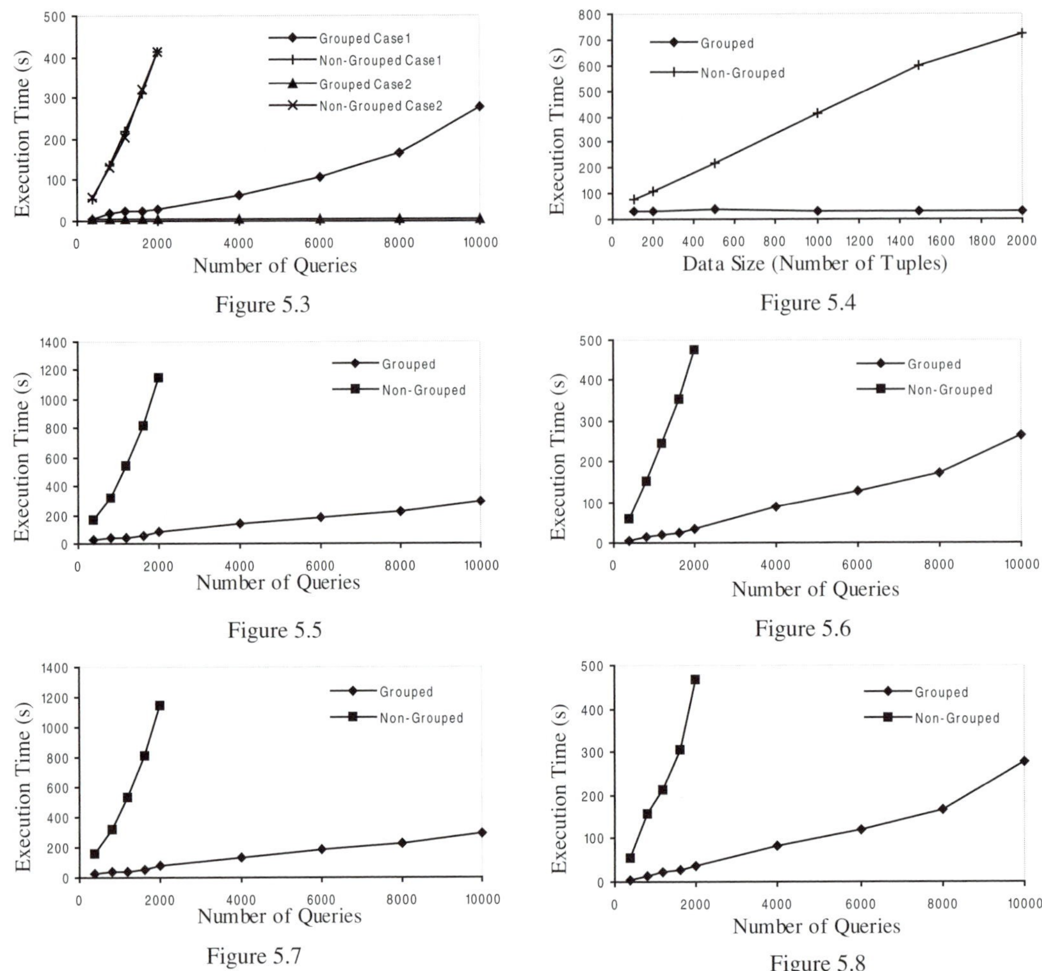

Figure 5.3

Figure 5.4

Figure 5.5

Figure 5.6

Figure 5.7

Figure 5.8

signatures. In this experiment, Type-1 queries and Type-3 queries are grouped together because they have the same selection signature. Figure 5.8 shows the performance difference between the grouped and non-grouped cases.

5.3 System Status and Future Work

A prototype version of NaigraCQ has been developed, which includes a Group Optimizer, Continuous Query Manager, Event Detector, and Data Manager. As the core of our incremental group optimization, the Group Optimizer currently can incrementally group selection and join operators. Our incremental group optimizer is still at a preliminary stage. However, incremental group optimization has been shown to be a promising way to achieve good performance and scalability. We intend to extend incremental group optimization to queries containing operators other than selection and join. For example, sharing computation for expensive operators, such as aggregation, may be very effective. "Dynamic regrouping" is another interesting future direction that we intend to explore.

6. RELATED WORK AND DISCUSSION

Terry et al. first proposed the notion of "continuous queries" [TGNO92] as queries that are issued once and run continuously. He used an incremental evaluation approach to avoid repetitive computation and return only new results to users. Their approach was restricted to append-only systems, which is not suitable for our target environment. NiagaraCQ uses an incremental query evaluation method but is not limited to append-only data sources. We also include action and timer events in Niagara continuous queries.

Continuous queries are similar to triggers in traditional database systems. Triggers have been widely studied and implemented [WF89][MD89][SJGP90][SPAM91][SK95]. Most trigger systems use an Event-Condition-Action (ECA) model [MD89]. General issues of implementing triggers can be found in [WF89].

NiagaraCQ is different from traditional trigger systems in the following ways.

1. The main purpose of the NiagaraCQ is to support continuous query processing rather than to maintain data integrity.
2. NiagaraCQ is intended to support millions of continuous queries defined on large number of data sources. In a traditional DBMS, a very limited number of triggers can be installed on each table and a trigger can usually only be defined on a single table.
3. NiagaraCQ needs to monitor autonomous and heterogeneous data sources over the Internet. Traditional trigger systems only handle local tables.
4. Timer-based events are supported in NiagaraCQ.

Open-CQ [LPT99] [LPBZ96] also supports continuous queries on web data sources and has functionality similar to NiagaraCQ. NiagaraCQ differs from Open-CQ in that we explore the similarity among large number of queries and use group optimization to achieve system scalability.

The TriggerMan [HCH+99] project proposes a method for implementing a scalable trigger system based on the assumption that many triggers may have common structure. It uses a special selection predicate index and an in-memory trigger cache to achieve scalability. We share the same assumption in our work and borrow the concept of an expression signature from their work. We mainly focus on the incremental grouping of a subset of the most frequently used expression signatures, which are in the format "Attribute op Constant", where op is one of "<", "=" and ">". The major differences between NiagaraCQ and TriggerMan are:

1. NiagaraCQ uses an incremental group optimization strategy.
2. NiagaraCQ uses a query-split scheme to allow the shared computation to become an individual query that can be monitored and executed using a slightly modified query engine. TriggerMan uses a special in-memory predicate index to evaluate the expression signature.
3. NiagaraCQ supports grouping of timer-based queries, a capability not considered in [HCH+99].

Sellis's work [Sel86] focused on finding an optimal plan for a small group of queries (usually lower than ten) by recognizing a containment relationship among the selection predicates of queries with both selection and join operators. This approach for group optimization was very expensive and not extendable to a large number of queries.

Recent work [ZDNS98] on group optimization mainly focuses on applying group optimization to solve a specific problem. Our approach also falls into this category. Alert [SPAM91] was among the earliest active database systems. It tried to reuse most parts of a passive DBMS to implement an active database.

7. CONCLUSION

Our goal is to develop an Internet-scale continuous query system using group optimization based on the assumption that many continuous queries on the Internet will have some similarities. Previous group optimization approaches consider grouping only a small number of queries at the same time and are not scalable to millions of queries. We propose a new "incremental grouping" methodology that makes group optimization more scalable than the previous approaches. This idea can be applied to very general group optimization methods. We also propose a grouping method using a query-split scheme that requires minimal changes to a general purposed query engine. In our system, both timer-based and change-based continuous queries can be grouped together for event detection and group execution, a capability not found in other systems. Other techniques to make our system scalable include incremental evaluation of continuous queries, use of both pull and push models for detecting heterogeneous data source changes and a caching mechanism. Preliminary experiments demonstrate that our incremental group optimization significantly improves the execution time comparing to non-grouping approach. The results of experiments also show that the system can be scaled to support very large number of queries.

8. ACKNOWLEDGEMENT

We thank Zhichen Xu for his discussion with the first author during initial writing of the paper. We are particularly grateful to Ashraf Aboulnaga, Navin Kabra and David Maier for their careful review and helpful comments on the paper. We also thank the anonymous referees for their comments. Funding for this work was provided by DARPA through NAVY/SPAWAR Contract No. N66001-99-1-8908 and NSF award CDA-9623632.

9. REFERENCES

[CM86] U..S. Chakravarthy and J. Minker. Multiple Query Processing in Deductive Databases using Query Graphs. VLDB Conference 1986: 384-391.

[DFF+98] A. Deutsch, M. Fernandez, D. Florescu, A. Levy, D. Suciu. XML-QL: A Query Langaage for XML. http://www.w3.org/TR/NOTE-xml-ql.

[HCH+99] E. N. Hanson, C. Carnes, L. Huang, M. Konyala, L. Noronha, S. Parthasarathy, J.B.Park and A. Vernon. Scalable Trigger Processing. In proceeding of 15th ICDE, page 266-275, Sydney, Australia, 1999.

[HJ94] E. N. Hanson and T. Johnson. Selection Predicate Indexing for Active Databases Using Interval Skip List. TR94-017. CIS department, University of Florida, 1994.

[LPBZ96] L. Liu, C. Pu, R. Barga, T. Zhou. Differential Evaluation of Continual Queries. ICDCS 1996: 458-465.

[LPT99] L. Liu, C. Pu, W. Tang. Continual Queries for Internet Scale Event-Driven Information Delivery. TKDE 11(4): 610-628 (1999).

[MD89] D. McCarthy and U. Dayal. The architecture of an active database management system. SIGMOD 1989: 215-224.

[RC88] A. Rosenthal and U. S. Chakravarthy. Anatomy of a Modular Multiple Query Optimizer. VLDB 1988: 230-239.

[Sel86] T. Sellis. Multiple query optimization. ACM Transactions on Database Systems, 10(3), 1986.

[SJGP90] M. Stonebraker, A. Jhingran, J. Goh and S. Potamianos. On Rules, Procedures, Caching and Views in Data Base Systems. SIGMOD Conference 1990: 281-290.

[SK95] E. Simon, A. Kotz-Dittrich. Promises and Realities of Active Database Systems. VLDB 1995: 642-653.

[SPAM91] U. Schreier, H. Pirahesh, R. Agrawal, and C. Mohan. Alert: An architecture for transforming a passive dbms into an active dbms. VLDB 1991: 469-478.

[TGNO92] D. Terry, D. Goldberg, D. Nichols, and B. Oki. Continuous Queries over Append-Only Databases. SIGMOD 1992: 321-330.

[WF89] J. Widom and S.J. Finklestein. Set-Oriented Production Rules in Relational Database Systems. SIGMOD Conference 1990: 259-270.

[ZDNS98] Y. Zhao, P. Deshpande, J. F. Naughton, A. Shukla. Simultaneous Optimization and Evaluation of Multiple Dimensional Queries. SIGMOD 1998: 271-282.

Chapter 10
Stream-Based Data Management

Introduction

There are two driving forces behind the research presented in this section. The first concerns a collection of applications that are poorly served by conventional DBMS technology, while the second deals with the emergence of microsensors as an economically viable technology.

In financial services, there are many applications that deal with "data feeds". These are typically streams of stock market "tick" data, foreign exchange transactions, etc. Commercial feeds are available from a variety of vendors, and all the major brokerage houses perform processing on these feeds. Example applications include deciding where to send a trade request, determining whether a given feed is damaged or late, deciding whether a given fund is in compliance with SEC or brokerage house rules, and performing automated trading strategies. Essentially all of these applications are currently written with "roll your own" technology. The brokerage houses have looked for commercial solutions and come up empty-handed. There are two market requirements that are not currently being met; namely scalable time series operations and real time response. Real time means that the stream must be processed before it is stored in a DBMS. Direct stream processing should be contrasted with store-and-query processing, where the data is stored, indexed and then queried. Store-and-query processing has little chance of meeting the real time requirements of Wall Street. Also, most of the Wall Street applications entail time-series operations, which have historically been difficult for traditional DBMSs to deal with.

A similar state of affairs exists in industrial process control (IPC) applications. Continuous feed factories, such as oil refineries, glass factories, chemical plants and food processing operations generate substantial streams of real time data from individual processing steps. When the bottles start breaking in the glass factory, automated software is desired that will quickly identify the problem and adjust the machines in the factory to correct it. Again, we see time series operations correlating multiple streams of data that must be performed in real time.

A third area with similar issues is network and system monitoring. Virtually all enterprises want to perform real time network monitoring. Intrusion detection is the foremost application, including denial of service attacks. Additionally, worm and virus detection costs enterprises millions of dollars annually. The current solution is to run detection programs that look for offensive code in incoming packets. However, this is only successful after the new threat has been identified, a signature bit string in the threat discovered, and then loaded into anti-virus software. By then, it is way too late. System administrators want to find threats in real time, before they have an opportunity to wreak havoc. One possible scenario is to quarantine incoming messages for a short while and look for patterns (for example, identical payloads from the same set of sources addressed to many different people in the enterprise). Clearly, this is high volume stream processing. Lastly, real time spam detection may be amenable to the same sort of architecture.

In addition to network monitoring, similar applications can be built to monitor the health of large computer systems. The individual hardware components (CPU, SAN, disk system, etc.) all generate messages concerning their health and status; similar messages are generated by server software (webservers, appservers, mailservers, DBMSs, etc.) Putting these disparate events together into a coherent whole for delivery to a system administrator is a stream-based application with high data rates.

It is worth mentioning a cautionary tale from "click stream" analysis. In the late 1990's there were startups that focused on specialized systems to watch the clicks from a typical shopping site, such as Amazon, with the idea of detecting interesting patterns in the sequence of clicks. However, the commercial enterprises that tried this application reported that it was not worthwhile, and click stream analysis as a standalone application fell out of favor. This is an example where a single-app engine was not worth building. However, there may well be more traction for more general-purpose stream analysis systems that monitor all kinds of system logs, spanning a variety of hardware and software.

One of the main challenges in any of the above application settings is keeping up with the rate of data production. Financial services feeds are typically running several thousand messages a second, while network monitoring applications are a couple of orders of magnitude higher. Database researchers in search of a high-volume, homogeneous-schema, structured data source need look no further than the output of a packet sniffer on their local network. Running "tail -f" on system logs adds a number of additional sources, leading to a fairly rich, high-volume streaming database. An example of an interesting database-style query processor custom-designed for high-volume network monitoring is Gigascope [CJSS03].

The second driving force behind streaming research is the emergence of low-cost microsensor technology. This comes in a variety of forms.

At the low end are RFID tags. These are small, coin-sized devices that cost pennies per unit, and are capable of transmitting a value (e.g. an ID) and perhaps computing a handful of instructions (e.g. decrement a counter) when brought in proximity to an RFID reader. RFID readers are much more expensive (currently from hundreds to thousands of dollars, though prices are falling) and they require non-trivial power to run – hence they typically are connected to a fixed power source and immobile. Over time, RFID will replace bar codes on most individual items in retail applications. Currently, most retail stores use bar codes to track items as they are "swiped" at the cash register; RFID can in principle allow retailers to know when an item leaves the shelf, allowing perfect supply chain optimization. Similar benefits are available in warehouses, where tracking pallets or cases by RFID can minimize misplaced merchandise. We expect that in the next decade, RFID and similar tagging technologies will be cheap enough that every object of material could be tagged and tracked.

Wireless sensor networks (sensornets) are a more intriguing technology, some years further away from widespread deployment than RFID. Sensornets are made up of devices that combine inexpensive sensors (e.g. temperature, pressure, acceleration, humidity, magnetic field, etc.) with a low-function microprocessor (think of a 1980's PC, or a PDP-11), a radio for communication, and a battery for power. A set of such devices can autoconfigure themselves into a communication network, and do modest computation while routing sensor readings toward some base station. Sensornets can actively monitor their environment, and band together to do distributed sensing and computation tasks.

Current generations of these devices are the size of a coin, but there are working, programmable prototypes the size of a grain of salt. The vision is for these to become small and cheap enough in the next decade to realize the science fiction idea of "Smart Dust" – disposable clouds of sensing and computing infrastructure that could be easily deployed without careful installation or configuration. A major challenge in these environments is to minimize battery drain by keeping data acquisition and communication to a minimum. The design of "in-network" distributed data acquisition and query systems for sensornets is in its infancy; the earliest proposal appeared in

2000 in Cornell's Cougar project [BS00]. However, database-style querying has become a hot topic in the sensornet research community, and the TinyDB system [MFHH03] is in steady use and being supported by a leading commercial sensornet vendor.

There are (at least!) two major social issues that stand in the way of widespread deployment of sensing technologies. The first is privacy. People are understandably wary of the possibility of being monitored by third parties who do not have their interests at heart. A recent high-profile story concerned Benetton, which backed down on plans to deploy RFID in each garment, when public outcry developed about privacy considerations after the sale. At the very least, RFID technology must be able to be permanently disabled in order to overcome end-customer concerns about personal tracking. A second issue concerns the environmental impact of billions of "disposable" computing devices. Some researchers are investigating biodegradable materials for microsensing, which would certainly be a big change for the computer hardware industry.

Impact on DBMS Technology

The various instantiations of sensor devices will cause a whole new collection of applications to emerge, such as the ones mentioned above. We will call these **monitoring applications**, and the big question is "What impact will these applications have on data management systems?" Some say current DBMSs can adequately deal with monitoring apps, while others claim new technology is required.

There are several reasons why new DBMS technology might be required. First, monitoring applications often require time-series operations. In a military monitoring application, one wants to know the route of a particular vehicle over the last hour. In stock monitoring apps, one wants to compute moving averages of particular securities. Although time series data was included in the Informix Universal Server as a "blade", efficient utilization of the blade required considerable server changes. Also, the Informix blade was only able to handle "regular" time series data, where events happened at specified intervals. Irregular time series, such as those resulting from very thinly traded securities, required additional technology. It is fair to say that current servers are not very good even at traditional time series applications like those from Wall Street.

Second, if a monitoring application becomes overloaded, it is sometimes acceptable to drop observations on the floor or coalesce multiple observations into one synopsis, on the presumption that more pressing fresh information will arrive shortly. Hence, in a condition of overload it can be useful to trade off precision for unimportant objects to get good response time on important matters. Priority scheduling and non-ACID behavior have long been tactics in networks and real-time systems, but this sort of technology has not found its way into commercial DBMSs.

Third, monitoring applications have a big component that is "event-driven". By this we mean that a large volume of incoming messages must be processed to see which of a (perhaps large) set of monitoring conditions becomes true. In effect the monitoring conditions are predicates and act like queries. Hence, the "queries" are stored and the data is "pushed" through them. This is the reverse of commercial DBMSs where the data is stored and the queries act against the stored data.

Put differently, monitoring applications are mostly events with a little querying on the side. In contrast, OLTP applications are mostly querying. Current DBMSs have been optimized for querying, and triggers (which act like monitoring conditions) have been added as an afterthought. It is possible that there is a better architecture than that of commercial DBMSs for a mix of events and queries.

Lastly, incoming events typically have a fair amount of processing done on them. For example, they are often noisy and must be cleaned. They often must be correlated with other events (so-called sensor fusion). In addition, they must be converted to a common clock and/or a common co-ordinate system. One possible architecture to perform this processing is to run such programs in an application server in middleware, and then perform the DBMS functions in a back-end DBMS. Such a multi-tier architecture will lead to many boundary crossings between middleware and the DBMS, perhaps one per event processed. This could lead to serious performance degradation. An alternative is to collapse the DBMS and middleware functions into a single system specialized for stream processing.

Research Issues

It remains to be seen whether stream processing will have a long term impact on commercial systems. However, the topic is being widely researched at the present time, not only in the database systems community, but also in the theory community. There is a large body of literature, for example [GGR02] that focuses on limited-memory, single-pass algorithms for computing aggregates and mining results on stream-based information. This research has similarities to the papers presented in the data mining section of this book. However, this class of work assumes that only single-pass algorithms are acceptable on streams, and that limitations on the size of the "state" that can be kept during the mining process may be present. We will not discuss this stream mining in this section, but focus instead on the execution of explicit monitoring queries.

The first issue in any stream processing system is the application program interface, i.e. how to extend or change SQL to express the tasks of stream-oriented applications. Our first paper in this chapter is the pioneering work of Seshadri et. al. on a stream-oriented query algebra from 1994; a followon SQL-like language appeared a couple years thereafter [SLR96]. In our opinion, much of the recent query language work in this area borrows heavily from these papers.

Then, we turn our attention to the challenges of handling a large number of standing queries over streaming events. The query conditions may entail checking a predicate against each message, or they may be more complex and involve joins with other message streams. For efficiency, it is important to handle the batch of standing queries together, sharing work when possible. Early research in this area focused on Rete networks [Forg82], and some of the later work has been variants on this kind of discrimination network technology. The current best practice in this area appears to be the work of Eric Hanson on Ariel, and we include his most recent paper as our second selection in this chapter. It is instructive to view recent stream query work through the lens of more traditional discrimination network ideas.

Current commercial systems support database triggers; however we know of no major vendor that can support more than a few triggers per table. The basic problem is that these vendors merely check each triggering condition individually on each update. Hence, supporting a large number of triggering conditions will lead to very bad performance. To provide scalable performance on large numbers of triggering conditions, an Ariel-style data structure must be used.

An alternate approach to discrimination networks borrows from conventional cost-based query optimization. The result of query optimization is a query plan, which is a graph of operators, through which tuples are either pulled or pushed. If tuples arrive at random times, they look like messages, and the nodes look like monitoring operations. In conventional query optimization, the sizes and data distributions of all the tables are known in advance, and the best query plan can be obtained. However, in a message processing framework, messages may arrive according to unknown distributions in arrival times and in data values, and an optimal plan cannot be generated in advance. In this scenario, it is important that a query plan be able to adapt to changes in the arrival rate and contents of messages. A survey of adaptive query optimization schemes appears in [HFC+00]. Our third paper in this section presents the Berkeley work on eddies, which is the first paper from the Telegraph project. Eddies are the most aggressive proposal for allowing query plans to monitor and adapt to changes in the input distributions. This first eddy paper does not particularly discuss streaming data sources, but it does discuss the way in which various join operators allow for adapting a query plan mid-stream. The eddy mechanism has been extended in a number of directions: [MSH02] and [CF03] extend eddies to share work among multiple continuous queries over streams, and [RDH03] extends eddies to consider multiple access and join methods.

One natural question concerning eddies is whether a system would need to adapt on every tuple. In effect, the cost of adaptation must be balanced against the benefit of fine granularity alteration. It turns out that the overhead of eddies can be largely masked by adapting at a slightly coarser grain; say every 100 tuples or so [DESH04].

The last paper in this chapter, a description of the Aurora prototype, contains four features of note. First, it represents an example of a complete specialized stream-processing system. Other prototypes include Telegraph [CCD+03], and STREAM [MOTW03], and the interested reader is encouraged to compare the architectures. As a second contribution, Aurora focuses on the issue that stream processing engines are fundamentally real-time systems. As such, they must be aware of latency and other quality-of-service issues, and Aurora has explored the benefits of building quality-of-service deeply into the engine. Third, like the Berkeley work, Aurora recognizes the need for adaptability in the query processing strategy. However, it stakes out a different point in the adaptivity spectrum, trading fine-grained adaptivity for reduced overhead. A final feature of Aurora is its focus on an algebra-style "boxes-and-arrows" approach to query composition, rather than an extension to SQL. It is an open question whether dataflow diagrams or SQL queries will be more natural for users of streaming systems.

The curious reader is also encouraged to consider the multi-query sharing focus of TelegraphCQ [CCD+03], and the memory-minimization approach of STREAM [MOTW03,BBDM03,etc]. In sum, these three systems focus on a mixture of adaptivity, controlled quality of service in the face of overload, and multi-query sharing. In the absence of realistic applications, it is very hard to tell what balance of these features is most important. Hopefully in the next few years these projects will tackle some real problems and these lessons will come clear. We expect to see continued research activity in this area, and attempts to move it into commercial systems. It will be interesting to see the long term impact of this activity.

References

[BBDM03] Brian Babcock, Shivnath Babu, Mayur Datar and Rajeev Motwani. "Chain: Operator Scheduling for Memory Minimization in Data Stream Systems". In *Proc. of the ACM-SIGMOD International Conference on Management of Data*, June 2003.

[BS00] Philippe Bonnet and Praveen Seshadri. "Device Database Systems." In *Proc. 16th International Conference on Data Engineering (ICDE)*. San Diego, CA, February-March, 2000.

[CCD+03] Sirish Chandrasekaran, Owen Cooper, Amol Deshpande, Michael J. Franklin, Joseph M. Hellerstein, Wei Hong, Sailesh Krishnamurthy, Samuel Madden, Vijayshankar Raman, Fred

Reiss and Mehul A. Shah. "TelegraphCQ: Continuous Dataflow Processing for an Uncertain World". In *Proc. First Biennial Conference on Innovative Data Systems Research (CIDR)*, Asilomar, Ca., January 2003.

[CJSS03] Charles D. Cranor, Theodore Johnson, Oliver Spataschek and Vladislav Shkapenyuk. "The Gigascope Stream Database". *ACM SIGMOD International Conference on Management of Data*, June, 2003.

[Forg82] Charles Forgy: Rete: A Fast Algorithm for the Many Patterns/Many Objects Match Problem. *Artificial Intelligence* 19(1): 17-37 (1982).

[GGR02] Minos Garofalakis, Johannes Gehrke and Rajeev Rastogi. "Querying and Mining Data Streams: You Only Get One Look" .Tutorial, *ACM SIGMOD International Conference on Management of Data*, Madison, Wisconsin, June 2002. http://www.bell-labs.com/user/minos/Talks/streams-tutorial02.ppt.

[HFC+00] Joseph M. Hellerstein, Michael Franklin, Sirish Chandrasekaran, Amol Deshpande, Kris Hildrum, Sam Madden, Vijayshankar Raman and Mehul A. Shah. "Adaptive Query Processing: Technology in Evolution". *IEEE Data Engineering Bulletin*, June, 2000.

[MFHH03] Samuel R. Madden, et al. "The Design of an Acquisitional Query Processor for Sensor Networks". In *Proceedings ACM-SIGMOD International Conference on Management of Data*, June 2003.

[MOTW03] Rajeev Motwani, Jennifer Widom, Arvind Arasu, Brian Babcock, ShivnathBabu, Mayur Datar, Gurmeet Manku, Chris Olston, Justin Rosenstein, and Rohit Varma. "Query Processing, Approximation, and Resource Management in a Data Stream Management System." In *Proc. First Biennial Conference on Innovative Data Systems Research (CIDR)*, Asilomar, Ca., January 2003.

[MSH02] Samuel R. Madden, Mehul A. Shah and Joseph M. Hellerstein. "Continuously Adaptive Continuous Queries over Streams". In *Proceedings ACM-SIGMOD International Conference on Management of Data*, Madison, WI, June 2002.

[RDH03] Vijayshankar Raman, Amol Deshpande and Joseph M. Hellerstein. Using State Modules for Adaptive Query Processing. In *Proc. International Conference on Data Engineering (ICDE)*, 2003.

[SLR96] Praveen Seshadri, Miron Livny, Raghu Ramakrishnan: The Design and Implementation of a Sequence Database System. In *Proc. International Conference on Very Large Data Bases (VLDB)*, 1996, pp. 99-110

Scalable Trigger Processing

Eric N. Hanson, Chris Carnes, Lan Huang, Mohan Konyala, Lloyd Noronha,
Sashi Parthasarathy, J. B. Park and Albert Vernon
301 CSE, CISE Department, University of Florida
Gainesville, FL 32611-6120
hanson@cise.ufl.edu, http://www.cise.ufl.edu/~hanson

Abstract[†]

Current database trigger systems have extremely limited scalability. This paper proposes a way to develop a truly scalable trigger system. Scalability to large numbers of triggers is achieved with a trigger cache to use main memory effectively, and a memory-conserving selection predicate index based on the use of unique expression formats called expression signatures. A key observation is that if a very large number of triggers are created, many will have the same structure, except for the appearance of different constant values. When a trigger is created, tuples are added to special relations created for expression signatures to hold the trigger's constants. These tables can be augmented with a database index or main-memory index structure to serve as a predicate index. The design presented also uses a number of types of concurrency to achieve scalability, including token (tuple)-level, condition-level, rule action-level, and data-level concurrency.

1. Introduction

Trigger features in commercial database products are quite popular with application developers since they allow integrity constraint checking, alerting, and other operations to be performed uniformly across all applications. Unfortunately, effective use of triggers is hampered by the fact that current trigger systems in commercial database products do not scale. Numerous database products only allow one trigger for each type of update event (insert, delete and update) on each table. More advanced commercial trigger systems have effective limits of a few hundred triggers per table.

Application designers could effectively use large numbers of triggers (thousands or even millions) in a single database if it were feasible. The advent of the Internet and the World Wide Web makes it even more important that it be possible to support large numbers of triggers. A web interface could allow users to interactively create triggers over the Internet. This type of architecture could lead to large numbers of triggers created in a single database.

This paper presents strategies for developing a highly scalable trigger system. The concepts introduced here are being implemented in a system we are developing called TriggerMan, which consists of an extension module for an object-relational DBMS (a DataBlade for Informix with Universal Data Option, hereafter simply called Informix [Info99]), plus some additional programs to be described later. The approach we propose for implementing a scalable trigger system uses asynchronous trigger processing and a sophisticated predicate index. This can give good response time for updates, while still allowing processing of large numbers of potentially expensive triggers. The scalability concepts outlined in this paper could also be used in a trigger system inside a DBMS server.

A key concept that can be exploited to develop a scalable trigger system is that if a large number of triggers are created, it is almost certainly the case that many of them have almost the same format. Many triggers may have identical structure except that one constant has been substituted for another, for example. Based on this observation, a trigger system can identify unique *expression signatures*, and group predicates taken from trigger conditions into equivalence classes based on these signatures.

The number of distinct expression signatures is fairly small, small enough that main memory data structures can be created for all of them. In what follows, we discuss the TriggerMan command language and architecture, and then turn to a discussion of how large numbers of triggers can be handled effectively using expression signature equivalence classes and a novel selection predicate indexing technique.

[†] This research was supported by the Defense Advanced Research Projects Agency, NCR Teradata Corporation, and Informix Corporation.

2. The TriggerMan Command Language

Commands in TriggerMan have a keyword-delimited, SQL-like syntax. TriggerMan supports the notion of a *connection* to a local Informix database, a remote database, or a generic data source program. A connection description for a database contains information about the host name where the database resides, the type of database system running (e.g. Informix, Oracle, Sybase, DB2 etc.), the name of the database server, a user ID, and a password. A single connection is designated as the default connection. There can be multiple *data sources* defined for a single connection. Data sources normally correspond to tables, but this is not essential.

Triggers can be defined using this command:

```
create trigger <triggerName> [in setName]
[optionalFlags]
from fromList
[on eventSpec]
[when condition]
[group by attributeList]
[having groupCondition]
do action
```

Triggers can be added to a specific trigger set. Otherwise they belong to a default trigger set. The **from**, **on**, and **when** clauses are normally present to specify the trigger condition. Optionally, **group by** and **having** clauses, similar to those available in SQL [Date93], can be used to specify trigger conditions involving aggregates or temporal functions. Multiple data sources can be referenced in the **from** clause. This allows multiple-table triggers to be defined.

An example of a rule, based on an **emp** table from a database for which a connection has been defined, is given below. This rule sets the salary of Fred to the salary of Bob:

```
create trigger updateFred
from emp
on update(emp.salary)
when emp.name = 'Bob'
do execSQL 'update emp set
salary=:NEW.emp.salary where emp.name=
''Fred'' '
```

This rule illustrates the use of an execSQL TriggerMan command that allows SQL statements to be run against a database. The :NEW notation in the rule action (the **do** clause) allows reference to new updated data values, the new emp.salary value in this case. Similarly, :OLD allows access to data values that were current just before an update. Values matching the trigger condition are substituted into the trigger action using macro substitution. After substitution, the trigger action is evaluated. This procedure binds the rule condition to the rule action.

An example of a more sophisticated rule (one whose condition involves joins) is as follows. Consider the following schema for part of a real-estate database, which would be imported by TriggerMan using **define data source** commands:

```
house(hno,address,price,nno,spno)
salesperson(spno,name,phone)
represents(spno,nno)
neighborhood(nno,name,location)
```

A rule on this schema might be "if a new house is added which is in a neighborhood that salesperson Iris represents then notify her," i.e.:

```
create trigger IrisHouseAlert
on insert to house
from salesperson s, house h, represents r
when s.name = 'Iris' and s.spno=r.spno and
r.nno=h.nno
do raise event
NewHouseInIrisNeighborhood(h.hno, h.address)
```

This command refers to three tables. The **raise event** command used in the rule action is a special command that allows rule actions to communicate with the outside world [Hans98].

3. System Architecture

The TriggerMan architecture is made up of the following components:

1. the TriggerMan DataBlade which lives inside of Informix,
2. **data sources**, which normally correspond to local or remote tables. Most commonly, a data source will be a local table. In that case, standard Informix triggers are created automatically by TriggerMan to capture updates to the table. We use the one trigger per table per update event available in Informix to capture updates and transmit them to TriggerMan by inserting

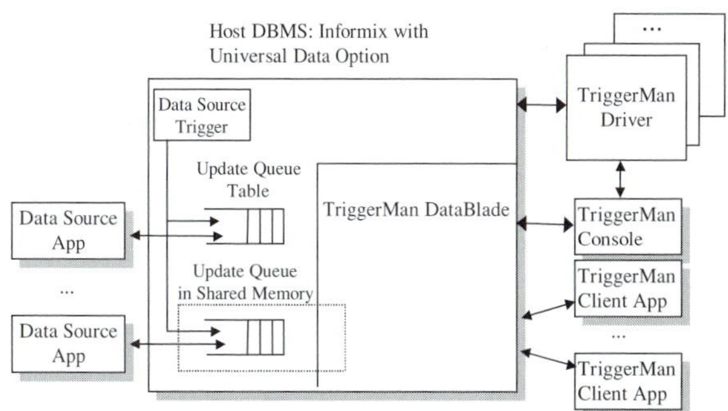

Figure 1. The architecture of the TriggerMan trigger processor.

them in an update descriptor table. For remote data sources, data source applications transmit update descriptors to TriggerMan through the data source API (defined below).

3. **TriggerMan client applications**, which create triggers, drop triggers, register for events, receive event notifications when triggers fire, etc.,
4. one or more instances of the **TriggerMan driver** program, each of which periodically invokes a special TmanTest() function in the TriggerMan DataBlade, allowing trigger condition testing and action execution to be performed,
5. the **TriggerMan console**, a special application program that lets a user directly interact with the system to create triggers, drop triggers, start the system, shut it down, etc.

The general architecture of the TriggerMan system is illustrated in Figure 1. Two libraries that come with TriggerMan allow writing of client applications and data source programs. These libraries define the TriggerMan *client application programming interface* (API) and the TriggerMan *data source API*. The console program and other application programs use client API functions to connect to TriggerMan, issue commands, register for events, and so forth. Data source programs can be written using the data source API. Updates received from update capture triggers or data source programs are consumed on the next call to TmanTest().

As Figure 1 shows, data source programs or triggers can place update descriptors in a table acting as a queue. This works in the current implementation. We plan to allow updates to be delivered into a main-memory queue as well in the future. This will deliver updates faster, but the safety of persistent update queuing will be lost. Trigger processing in the current system is asynchronous. If simple Informix triggers are used to capture updates, TriggerMan could process triggers synchronously as well. We plan to add this feature in a later implementation.

TriggerMan is based on an object-relational data model. The current implementation supports char, varchar, integer, and float data types. Support for user-defined types is being added.

Trigger Condition Testing Algorithm

TriggerMan uses a discrimination network called an *A-TREAT network* [Hans96] a variation of the TREAT network [Mira97] for trigger condition testing. In the future, we plan to implement an optimized type of discrimination network called a Gator network in TriggerMan [Hans97b].

This paper focuses primarily on efficient and scalable selection condition testing and rule action execution. The results are applicable to TREAT, Rete [Forg82] and Gator networks when used for trigger condition testing. The results could also be adapted to other trigger systems.

4. General Trigger Condition Structure

Trigger conditions have the following general structure. The **from** clause refers to one or more data sources. The **on** clause may contain an event condition

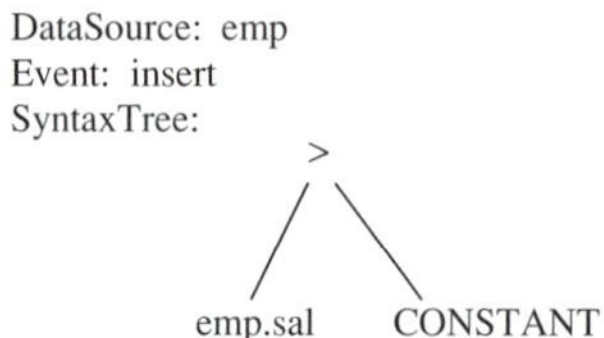

Figure 2. Example expression signature syntax tree.

for at most one of the data sources referred to in the **from** list. The **when** clause of a trigger is a Boolean-valued expression. For a combination of one or more tuples from data sources in the **from** list, the **when** clause evaluates to true or false.

A canonical representation of the **when** clause can be formed in the following way:

1. Translate it to conjunctive normal form (CNF, i.e. and-of-ors notation).
2. Each conjunct refers to zero, one, two, or possibly more data sources. Group the conjuncts by the set of data sources they refer to.

If a group of conjuncts refers to one data source, the logical AND of these conjuncts is a selection predicate. If it refers to two data sources, the AND of its conjuncts is a join predicate. If it refers to zero conjuncts, it is a trivial predicate. If it refers to three or more data sources, we call it a hyper-join predicate.

These predicates may or may not contain constants. The general premise of this paper is that very large numbers of triggers will only be created if predicates in different triggers contain distinct constant values. Below, we will examine how to handle selection and join predicates that contain constants, so that scalability to large numbers of triggers can be achieved.

5. Scalable Predicate Indexing Using Expression Signatures

In what follows, we treat the event (**on**) condition separately from the **when** condition as a convenience. However, event conditions and **when** clause conditions are both logically selection conditions [Hans96] that can be applied to update descriptors submitted to the system.

A *tuple variable* is a symbol, defined in the **from** clause of a trigger, which corresponds to a usage of a particular data source in that trigger. The general form of a selection predicate is:

$(C_{11} \text{ OR } C_{22} \text{ OR} \ldots \text{OR } C_{1N_1}) \text{ AND} \ldots \text{ AND} (C_{K1} \text{ OR } C_{K2} \text{ OR} \ldots \text{OR } C_{KN_K})$

where all clauses C_{ij} appearing in the predicate refer to the *same* tuple variable. Furthermore, each such clause is an atomic expression that does not contain Boolean operators, other than possibly the NOT operator. A single clause may contain constants.

For convenience, we assume that every data source has a data source ID. A data source corresponds to a single table in a remote or local database, or even a single stream of tuples sent in messages from an application program. An expression signature for a general selection or join predicate expression is a triple consisting of a data source ID, an operation code (insert, delete, update, or insertOrUpdate), and a generalized expression. If a tuple variable appearing in the **from** clause of a trigger does not have any event specified in the **on** clause, then the event is implicitly insert *or* update for that tuple variable. The format of the generalized expression is:

$(C'_{11} \text{ OR } C'_{22} \text{ OR} \ldots \text{OR } C'_{1N_1}) \text{ AND} \ldots \text{AND} (C'_{K1} \text{ OR } C'_{K2} \text{ OR} \ldots \text{OR } C'_{KN_K})$

where clause C'_{ij} is the same as C_{ij} except that all constants in C_{ij} are substituted with placeholder symbols. If the entire expression has m constants, they are numbered 1 to m from left to right. If the constant number $x, 1 \le x \le m$, appears in the clause C_{ij} in the original expression, then it is substituted with placeholder CONSTANT_X in C_{ij} in the expression signature.

As a practical matter, most selection predicates will not contain OR's, and most will have only a single clause. Consider this example trigger condition:

on insert to emp
when emp.salary > 80000

In an implementation, the generalized expression in an expression signature can be a *syntax tree* with placeholders at some leaf nodes representing the location where a constant must appear. For example, the signature of the trigger condition just given can be represented as shown in

Figure **2**. The condition:

on insert to emp
when emp.salary > 50000

has a different constant than the earlier condition, but it has the same signature. In general, an expression signature defines an *equivalence class* of all instantiations of that expression with different constant values.

If an expression is in the equivalence class defined by an expression signature, we say the expression *matches* the expression signature.

Expression signatures represent the logical structure or schema of a part of a trigger condition. We assert that in a real application of a trigger system like TriggerMan, even if very large numbers of triggers are defined, only a relatively small number of unique expression signatures will ever be observed - perhaps a few hundred or a few

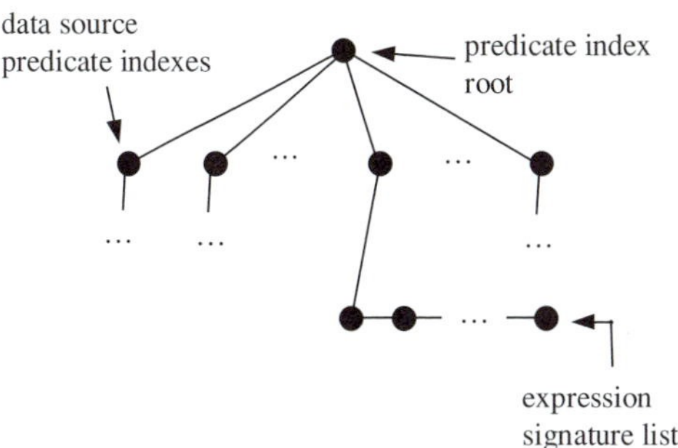

Figure 3. Predicate Index Structure.

thousand at most. Based on this observation, it is feasible to keep a set of data structures in main memory to represent all the distinct expression signatures appearing in all triggers. Since many triggers may have the same signature but contain different constants, tables will be created to store these constants, along with information linking them to their expression signature. When these tables are small, low-overhead main-memory lists or indexes can be used to cache information from them. When they are large, they can be stored as standard tables (with an index when appropriate) and queried as needed, using the SQL query processor, to perform trigger condition testing. We will elaborate further on implementation issues below.

5.1. Processing a Trigger Definition

When a **create trigger** statement is processed, a number of steps must be performed to update the trigger system catalogs and main memory data structures, and to "prime" the trigger to make it ready to run. The primary tables that form the trigger catalogs are these:

trigger_set(tsID, name, comments, creation_date, isEnabled)

trigger(triggerID, tsID, name, comments, trigger_text, creation_date, isEnabled, ...)

The purpose of the isEnabled field is to indicate whether a trigger or trigger set is currently enabled and eligible to fire if matched by some update. The other fields are self-explanatory. A data structure called the *trigger cache* is maintained in main memory. This contains complete descriptions of a set of recently accessed triggers, including the trigger ID and name, references to data sources relevant to the trigger, and the syntax tree and Gator network skeleton for the trigger. Given current main memory sizes, thousands of trigger descriptions can be loaded in the trigger cache simultaneously. E.g. if a trigger description takes 4K bytes (a realistic number), and 64Mbytes are allocated to the trigger cache, 16,384 trigger descriptions can be loaded simultaneously.

Another main memory data structure called a *predicate index* is maintained. A diagram of the predicate index is shown in Figure 3. The predicate index can take an update descriptor and identify all predicates that match it.

Expression signatures may contain more than one conjunct. If a predicate has more than one conjunct, a single conjunct is identified as the most selective one. Only this one is indexed directly. If a token matches a conjunct, any remaining conjuncts of the predicate are located and tested against the token. If the remaining clauses match, then the token has completely matched the predicate clause. See [Hans90] for more details on this technique.

The root of the predicate index is linked to a set of *data source predicate indexes* using a hash table on data source ID. Each data source predicate index contains an *expression signature list* with one entry for each unique expression signature that has been used by one or more triggers as a predicate on that data source. For each expression signature that contains one or more constant placeholders, there will be a *constant table*. This is an ordinary database table containing one row for each expression occurring in some trigger that matches the expression signature.

When triggers are created, any new expression signatures detected are added to the following table in the trigger system catalogs:

expression_signature(sigID, dataSrcID, signatureDesc,
constTableName, constantSetSize,
constantSetOrganization)

The sigID field is a unique ID for a signature. The dataSrcID field identifies the data source on which the signature is defined. The signatureDesc field is a text field with a description of the signature. We will define the other fields later.

When an expression signature E is encountered at trigger creation time, it is broken into two parts: the indexable part, E_I, and the non-indexable part, E_NI, as follows:

E = E_I AND E_NI

The non-indexable portion may be NULL. The format of the constant table for an expression signature containing K distinct constants in its indexable portion is:

const_tableN(exprID, triggerID, nextNetworkNode,
const1, … constK, restOfPredicate)

Here, N is the identification number of the expression signature. The fields of const_tableN have the following meaning:

1. exprID is the unique ID of a selection predicate E,
2. triggerID is the unique ID number of the trigger containing E,
3. nextNetworkNode identifies the next A-TREAT network node of trigger triggerID to pass a token to after it matches E (an alpha node or a P-node),
4. const1 … constK are constants found in the indexable portion of E, and
5. restOfPredicate is a description of the non-indexable part of E. The value of restOfPredicate is NULL if the entire predicate is indexable.

If the table is large, and the signature of the indexable part of the predicate is of the form attribute1=CONSTANT1 AND … attributeK=CONSTANTK, the table will have a clustered index on [const1, … constK] as a composite key. If the predicate has a different type of signature based on an operator other than "=", it may still be possible to use an index on the constant fields. As future work, we propose to develop ways to index for non-equality operators and constants whose types are user-defined [Kony98].

Putting a clustered index on the constant attributes will allow the triggerIDs of triggers relevant to a new update descriptor matching a particular set of constant values to be retrieved together quickly without doing random I/O. Notice that const_tableN is not in third normal form. This was done purposely to eliminate the need to perform joins when querying the information represented in the table.

Referring back to the definition of the expression_signature table, we can now define the remaining attributes:

1. constTableName is a string giving the name of the constant table for an expression signature,
2. constantSetSize is the number of distinct constants appearing in expressions with a given signature, and
3. constantSetOrganization describes how the set of constants will be organized in either a main-memory or disk-based structure to allow efficient trigger condition testing. The issue of constant set organization will be covered more fully later in the paper.

Given the disk- and memory-based data structures just described, the steps to process a **create trigger** statement are:

1. Parse the trigger and validate it (check that it is a legal statement).
2. Convert the **when** clause to conjunctive normal form and group the conjuncts by the distinct sets of tuple variables they refer to, as described in section 4.
3. Based on the analysis in the previous step, form a trigger condition graph. This is an undirected graph

with a node for each tuple variable, and an edge for each join predicate identified. The nodes contain a reference to the selection predicate for that node, represented as a CNF expression. The edges each contain a reference to a CNF expression for the join condition associated with that edge. Groups of conjuncts that refer to zero tuple variables or three or more tuple variables are attached to a special "catch all" list associated with the query graph. These will be handled as special cases. Fortunately, they will rarely occur. We will ignore them here to simplify the discussion.

4. Build the A-TREAT network for the rule.
5. For each selection predicate above an alpha node in the network, do the following:
   Check to see if its signature has been seen before by comparing its signature to the signatures in the expression signature list for the data source on which the predicate is defined (see Figure 3). If no predicate with the same signature has been seen before,
   - add the signature of the predicate to the list and update the expresssion_signature catalog table.
   - If the signature has at least one constant placeholder in it, create a constant table for the expression signature.

   If the predicate has one or more constants in it, add one row to the constant table for the expression signature of the predicate.

5.2. Alternative Organization Strategies for Expression Equivalence Classes

For a particular expression signature that contains at least one constant placeholder, there may be one or more expressions in its equivalence class that belong to different triggers. This number could be small or large. To get optimal performance over a wide range of sizes of the equivalence classes of expressions for a particular expression signature, alternative indexing strategies are needed. Main-memory data structures with low overhead are needed when the size of an equivalence class is small. Disk-based structures, including indexed or non-indexed tables, are needed when the size of an equivalence class is large.

The following four ways can be considered to organize the predicates in an expression signature's equivalence class:

1. main memory list
2. main memory index
3. non-indexed database table
4. indexed database table

Strategies 3 and 4 *must* be implemented to make it feasible to process very large numbers of triggers containing predicate expressions with the same signature but different constants -- they are mandatory in a scalable trigger system. Strategies 1 and 2 are also required in order to make the common case (a few thousand triggers or less) fast. A cost model that illustrates the tradeoffs is presented in [Hans98b]. Strategies 1 and 2 have been implemented in TriggerMan and strategies 3 and 4 are under construction.

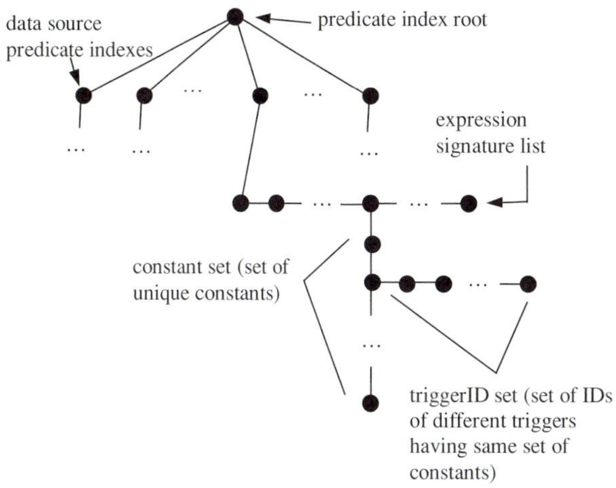

Figure 4. Expanded View of Normalized Predicate Index Structure.

5.3. Common Sub-expression Elimination for Selection Predicates

An important performance enhancement to reduce the total time needed to determine which selection predicates match a token is common sub-expression elimination. This can be achieved by normalizing the predicate index structure. Figure 4 shows an expanded view of the predicate index given in Figure 3. The *constant set* of an expression signature contains one element for each constant (or tuple of constants [const1, ... ,constK]) occurring in some selection predicate that matches the signature. Each constant is linked to a triggerID set, which is a set of the ID numbers of triggers containing a particular selection predicate. For example, if there are rules of the form:

create trigger T_I from R when R.a = 100 do ...

for I=1 to N, then there will be an expression signature R.a=CONSTANT, the constant set for this signature will contain an entry 100, and the triggerID set for 100 will contain the ID numbers of T_1 ... T_N.

We will implement constant sets and triggerID sets in a fully normalized form, as shown in Figure 4, when these sets are stored as either main memory lists or indexes (organizations 1 and 2). This normalized main-memory data structure will be built using the data retrieved from the constant table for the expression signature.

5.4. Processing Update Descriptors Using the Predicate Index

Recall that an update descriptor (token) consists of a data source ID, an operation code, and an old tuple, new tuple, or old/new tuple pair. When a new token arrives, the system passes it to the root of the predicate index, which locates its data source predicate index. For each expression signature in the data source predicate index, a specific type of predicate testing data structure (in-memory list, in-memory lightweight index, non-indexed database table, or indexed database table) is in use for that expression signature. The predicate testing data structure of each of these expression signatures is searched to find matches against the current token.

When a matching constant is found, the triggerID set for the constant contains one or more elements. Each of these elements contains zero or more additional selection predicate clauses. For each element of the triggerID set currently being visited, the additional predicate clause(s) are tested against the token, if there are any.

When a token is found to have matched a complete selection predicate expression that belongs to a trigger, that trigger is *pinned* in the trigger cache. This pin operation is analogous to the pin operation in a traditional buffer pool; it checks to see if the trigger is in memory, and if it is not, it brings it in from the disk-based trigger catalog. The pin operation ensures that the A-TREAT network and the syntax tree of the trigger are in main-memory. After the trigger is pinned, ensuring that it's A-TREAT network is in main memory, the token is passed to the node of the network identified by the nextNetworkNode field of the expression that just matched the token.

Processing of join and temporal conditions is then performed if any are present. Finally, if the trigger condition is satisfied, the trigger action is executed.

6. Concurrent Token Processing and Action Execution

An important way to get better scalability is to use concurrent processing. On an SMP platform, concurrent tasks can execute in parallel. Even on a single processor, use of concurrency can give better throughput and response time by making scarce CPU and I/O resources available to multiple tasks so any eligible task can use them. There are a number of different kinds of concurrency that a trigger system can exploit for improved scalability:

1. **Token-level concurrency:** multiple tokens can be processed in parallel through the selection predicate index and the join condition-testing network.

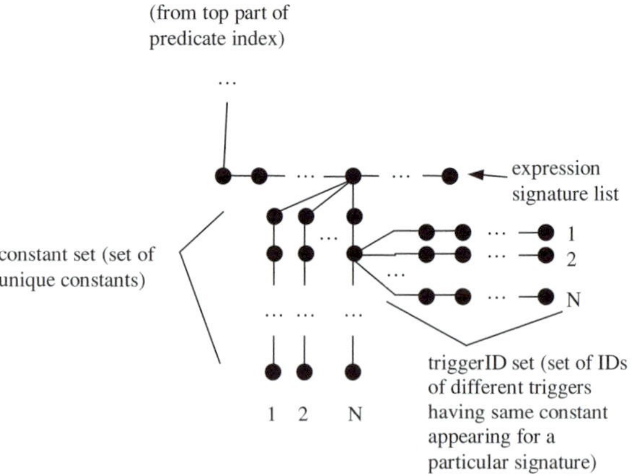

Figure 5. Illustration of partitioned constant sets and triggerID sets to facilitate concurrent processing.

2. **Condition-level concurrency:** multiple selection conditions can be tested against a single token concurrently.
3. **Rule action concurrency:** multiple rule actions that have been fired can be processed at the same time.
4. **Data-level concurrency:** a set of data values in an alpha or beta memory node of an A-TREAT or Gator network [Hans97] can be processed by a query that can run in parallel.

For ideal scalability, a trigger system must be able to capitalize on all four of these types of concurrency. The current implementation supports token level concurrency only. We plan to support the other types of concurrency in future versions of the system. Such a future version will make use of a task queue kept in shared memory to store incoming or internally generated work. An explicit task queue must be maintained because it is not possible to spawn native operating system threads or processes to carry out tasks due to the process architecture of Informix [Info99].

The concurrent processing architecture, as illustrated in **Figure** 1, will make use of N driver processes. We define NUM_CPUS to be the number of real CPUs in the system, and TMAN_CONCURRECY_LEVEL to be the fraction of CPUs to devote to concurrent processing in TriggerMan, which can be in the range (0%,100%]. The TriggerMan administrator can set the TMAN_CONCURRENCY_LEVEL parameter. Its default value is 100%. N is defined as follows:

$$N = \lceil NUM\_CPUS * TMAN\_CONCURRENCY\_LEVEL \rceil$$

Each driver process will call TriggerMan's TmanTest() function every T time units. Each driver will also call back immediately after one execution of TmanTest() if work is still left to do. We propose a default value of T equal to 250 milliseconds; determining the best value of T is left for future work. TmanTest will do the following:

```
while(total execution time of this invocation of
   TmanTest < THRESHOLD and work is left in the
   task queue)
{
   Get a task from the task queue and execute it.
   Yield the processor so other Informix tasks can use it
   (call the Informix mi_yield routine [Info99]).
}
if task queue is empty
      return TASK_QUEUE_EMPTY
return TASKS_REMAINING
```

The driver program will wait for T time units if the last call to TmanTest() returns TASK_QUEUE_EMPTY. Otherwise, the driver program will immediately call TmanTest() again. The default value of THRESHOLD will be 250 milliseconds also, to keep the task switch overhead between the driver programs and the Informix processes reasonably low, yet avoid a long user-defined routine (UDR) execution. A long execution inside TriggerMan should be avoided since it could result in higher probability of faults such as deadlock or running out of memory. Keeping the execution time inside TriggerMan reasonably short also avoids the problem of excessive lost work if a rollback occurs during trigger processing.

Tasks can be one of the following:

1. process one token to see which rules it matches
2. run one rule action
3. process a token against a set of conditions
4. process a token to run a set of rule actions triggered by that token

Task types 1 and 2 are self-explanatory. Tasks of type 3 and 4 can be generated if conditions and potential actions (triggerID structures containing the "rest of the condition") in the predicate index are partitioned in advance so that multiple predicates can be processed in parallel. An example of when it may be beneficial to partition predicates in advance is when there are many rules with the same condition but different actions. For example, suppose there are M rules of the form:

```
create trigger T_K
from R
when R.company = "IBM"
  do raise event notify_user("user K", R.company,
                             R.sharePrice)
```

for K=1..M. If M is a large number, a speedup can be obtained by partitioning this set of triggers into N sets of equal size. This would result in a predicate index substructure like that illustrated in Figure 5.

Here, the triggerID set would contain references to triggers T_1 ... T_M. These references would be partitioned round robin into N subsets of approximately equal size. Multiple subsets would be processed in parallel to achieve a speedup.

7. Trigger Application Design

The trigger system proposed in this paper is designed to be highly scalable. However, just because programmers *can* create a large number of triggers does not mean that is always the best approach. If triggers have extremely regular structure, it may be best to create a single trigger and a table of data referenced in the trigger's **from** clause to customize the trigger's behavior. This is discussed in more detail in a longer version of this paper [Hans98b].

8. Related Work

There has been a large body of work on active database systems, but little of it has focussed on predicate indexing or scalability. Representative works include HiPAC, Ariel, the POSTGRES rule system, the Starburst Rule System, A-RDL, Chimera, RPL, DIPS and Ode [Hans96,McCa89,Ston90,Wido96]. Most active database systems follow the event-condition-action (ECA) model proposed for HiPAC in a straightforward way, testing the condition of every applicable trigger whenever an update event occurs. The cost of this is always at least linear in the number of triggers associated with the relevant event since no predicate indexing is normally used. Moreover, the cost per trigger can be high since checking the condition can involve running an expensive query.

Work by Hanson and Johnson focuses on indexing of range predicates using the interval skip-list data structure [Hans96b], but this approach does not scale to very large numbers of rules since it may use a large amount of main memory. Work on the Rete [Forg82] and TREAT [Mira87] algorithms for efficient implementation of AI production systems is related to the work presented here, but the implicit assumption in AI rule system architectures is that the number of rules is small enough to fit in main memory. Additional work has been done in the AI community on parallel processing of production rule systems [Acha92], but this does not fully address the issue of scaling to large numbers of rules. Issues related to high-performance parallel rule processing in production systems are surveyed by Gupta et al. [Gupt89]. They cite several types of parallelism that can be exploited, including node, intranode, action, and data parallelism. These overlap with the types of concurrency we outlined in section 6. Work by Hellerstein on performing selections after joins in query processing [Hell98] is related to the issue of performing expensive selections after joins in Gator networks and A-TREAT networks [Kand98]. Proper placement of selection predicates in Gator networks can improve trigger system performance, and thus scalability.

The developers of POSTGRES proposed a marking-based predicate indexing scheme, where data and index records are tagged with physical markers to indicate that a rule might apply to them [Ston87,Ston90]. Predicates that can't be solved using an index result in placement of a table-level marker. This scheme has the advantage that the system can determine which rules apply primarily by detecting markers on tables, data records, and index records. Query and update processing algorithms must be extended in minor ways to accomplish this.

A disadvantage of this scheme is that it complicates implementation of storage and index structures. Moreover, when new records are inserted or existing records are updated, a large number of table-level markers may be disturbed. The predicate corresponding to every one of these disturbed markers must be tested against the records, which may be quite time-consuming [Ston87,Ston90]. This phenomenon will occur even for simple predicates of the form attribute=constant if there is no index on the attribute.

Research on the RPL system [Delc88a,Delc88b] addressed the issue of execution of production-rule-style triggers in a relational DBMS, but its developers did not use a discrimination network structure. They instead used an approach that runs database queries to test rule conditions as updates occur. This type of approach has limited scalability due to the potentially large number of queries that could be generated if there are many rules. Work on consistent processing of constraints and triggers in SQL relational databases [Coch96] has helped lead to recent enhancements to the SQL3 standard. However, the focus of this work is on trigger and constraint semantics. An implicit assumption in it is that constraints and triggers will be processed using a query-based approach, which will not scale up to a large number of triggers and constraints. We speculate that it may be possible to work around this assumption. A predicate index like the one proposed in this paper potentially could be used.

The DIPS system [Sell88] uses a set of special relations called COND relations for each condition element (tuple variable) in a rule. These COND relations are queried and updated to perform testing of both selection and join conditions of rules. Embedding *all* selection predicate testing into a process that must query database tables is not particularly efficient – it will not compare favorably to using some sort of main-memory predicate index. A main-memory predicate index should be used to get the best performance for a small-to-medium number of predicates, which is the common case. However, DIPS was capable of utilizing parallelism via the database query processor to test rule conditions, a feature in common with the system described in this paper. The DATEX system addresses the issue of executing large expert systems when working memory is kept in a database [Bran93], and is thus related to rule system scalability. A contribution of the DATEX system was an improved way to represent information normally kept in alpha-memory nodes in TREAT networks. However, DATEX was focussed on large-scale production systems, whereas the work presented in this paper is oriented to handling large numbers of triggers that operate in conjunction with databases and database applications, so our work is not directly comparable to DATEX. In summary, what sets our work apart from prior research efforts on database trigger systems and database-oriented expert systems tools is our focus on scalability from multiple dimensions. These include the capacity to accommodate large numbers of triggers, handle high rates of data update, and efficiently fire large numbers of triggers simultaneously. We achieve scalability through careful selection predicate index design, and support for four types of concurrency (token-level, condition-level, rule-action-level, and data-level).

9. Conclusion

This paper describes an architecture that can be used to build a truly scalable trigger system. As of the date of this writing, this architecture is being implemented as an Informix DataBlade along with a console program, a driver program, and data source programs. The architecture presented is a significant advance over what is currently available in database products. It also generalizes earlier research results on predicate indexing and improves upon their limited scalability [Forg82,Mira87,Ston87,Hans90,Hans96]. This architecture could be implemented in any object-relational DBMS that supports the ability to execute SQL statements inside user-defined routines (SQL callbacks). A variation of this architecture could also be made to work as an external application, communicating with the database via a standard interface (ODBC [Geig95]).

One topic for future research includes developing ways to handle temporal trigger processing [Hans97,AlFa98] in a scalable way, so that large numbers of triggers with temporal conditions can be processed efficiently. Another potential future research topic involves ways to support scalable trigger processing for trigger conditions involving aggregates. Finally, a third potential research topic is to develop a technique to make the implementation of the main-memory and disk-based structures used to organize the constant sets illustrated in Figure 4 extensible, so they will work effectively with new operators and data types. In the end, the results of this paper and the additional research outlined here can make highly efficient, scalable, and extensible trigger processing a reality.

References

[Acha92] Acharya, A., M. Tambe, and A. Gupta, "Implementation of Production Systems on Message-Passing Computers," *IEEE Transactions on Knowledge and Data Engineering*, 3(4), July 1992.

[AlFa98] Al-Fayoumi, Nabeel, *Temporal Trigger Processing in the TriggerMan Active DBMS*, Ph.D. dissertation, Univ. of Florida, August, 1998.

[Bran93] Brant, David A. and Daniel P. Miranker, "Index Support for Rule Activation," *Proceedings of the ACM SIGMOD Conference*, May, 1993, pp. 42-48.

[Coch96] Cochrane, Roberta, Hamid Pirahesh and Nelson Mattos, "Integrating Triggers and Declarative Constraints in SQL Database Systems," *Proceedings of the 22nd VLDB Conference*, pp. 567-578, Bombay, India, 1996.

[Date93] Date, C. J. And Hugh Darwen, *A Guide to the SQL Standard*, 3rd Edition, Addison Wesley, 1993.

[Delc88a] Delcambre, Lois and James Etheredge, "The Relational Production Language: A Production Language for Relational Databases," *Proceedings of the Second International Conference on Expert Database Systems*, pp. 153-162, April 1988.

[Delc88b] Delcambre, Lois and James Etheredge, "A Self-Controlling Interpreter for the Relational Production Language," *Proceedings of the ACM-SIGMOD Conference on Management of Data*, pp. 396-403, June 1988.

[Forg82] Forgy, C. L., Rete: "A Fast Algorithm for the Many Pattern/Many Object Pattern Match Problem," *Artificial Intelligence*, vol. 19, pp. 17-37, 1982.

[Geig95] Geiger, Kyle, *Inside ODBC*, Microsoft Press, 1995.

[Gupt89] Gupta, Anoop, Charles Forgy and Allen Newell, "High Speed Implementations of Rule-Based Systems," *ACM Transactions on Computer Systems*, vol. 7, no. 2, pp. 119-146, May, 1989.

[Hans90] Hanson, Eric N., M. Chaabouni, C. Kim and Y. Wang, "A Predicate Matching Algorithm for Database Rule Systems," *Proceedings of the ACM-SIGMOD Conference on Management of Data, pp. 27*1-280, Atlantic City, NJ, June 1990.

[Hans96] Hanson, Eric N., "The Design and Implementation of the Ariel Active Database Rule System," *IEEE Transactions on. Knowledge and Data Engineering*, vol. 8, no. 1, pp. 157-172, February 1996.

[Hans96b] Hanson, Eric N. and Theodore Johnson, "Selection Predicate Indexing for Active Databases Using Interval Skip Lists," *Information Systems*, vol. 21, no. 3, pp. 269-298, 1996.

[Hans97] Hanson, Eric N., N. Al-Fayoumi, C. Carnes, M. Kandil, H. Liu, M. Lu, J.B. Park, A. Vernon, "TriggerMan: An Asynchronous Trigger Processor as an Extension to an Object-Relational DBMS," University of Florida CISE Dept. Tech. Report 97-024, December 1997. http://www.cise.ufl.edu.

[Hans97b] Hanson, Eric N., Sreenath Bodagala, and Ullas Chadaga, "Optimized Trigger Condition Testing in Ariel Using Gator Networks," University of Florida CISE Dept. Tech. Report 97-021, November 1997. http://www.cise.ufl.edu.

[Hans98] Hanson, Eric N., I.C. Chen, R. Dastur, K. Engel, V. Ramaswamy, W. Tan, C. Xu, "A Flexible and Recoverable Client/Server Database Event Notification System," *VLDB Journal*, vol. 7, 1998, pp. 12-24.

[Hans98b] Hanson, Eric N. et al., "Scalable Trigger Processing in TriggerMan," TR-98-008, U. Florida CISE Dept., July 1998. http://www.cise.ufl.edu

[Hell98] Hellerstein, J., "Optimization Techniques for Queries with Expensive Methods," to appear, *ACM Transactions on Database Systems (TODS)*. Available at www.cs.berkeley.edu/~jmh.

[Info99] "Informix Dynamic Server, Universal Data Option," http://www.informix.com.

[Kand98] Kandil, Mohktar, *Predicate Placement in Active Database Discrimination Networks*, Ph.D. Dissertation, CISE Department, Univ. of Florida, Gainesville, August 1998.

[Kony98] Konyala, Mohan K., *Predicate Indexing in TriggerMan*, MS thesis, CISE Department, Univ. of Florida, Gainesville, Dec. 1998.

[McCa89] "McCarthy, Dennis R. and Umeshwar Dayal, "The Architecture of an Active Data Base Management System," *Proceedings of the. ACM SIGMOD Conference on Management of Data*, Portland, OR, June, 1989, pp. 215-224.

[Mira87] Miranker, Daniel P., "TREAT A Better Match Algorithm for AI Production Systems," *Proceedings of the AAAI Conference*, August 1987, pp. 42-47.

[Sell88] Sellis, T., C.C. Lin and L. Raschid, "Implementing Large Production Systems in a DBMS Environment: Concepts and Algorithms," Proceedings *of the 1988 ACM SIGMOD Conference*.

[Ston87] Stonebraker, M., T. Sellis and E. Hanson, "An Analysis of Rule Indexing Implementations in Database Systems," *Expert Database Systems: Proceedings from the First International Workshop*, Benjamin Cummings, 1987, pp. 465-476.

[Ston90] Stonebraker, Michael, Larry Rowe and Michael Hirohama, "The Implementation of POSTGRES," *IEEE Transactions on Knowledge and Data Engineering*, vol. 2, no. 7, March, 1990, pp. 125-142.

[Wido96] Widom, J. And S. Ceri, *Active Database Systems*, Morgan Kaufmann, 1996.

The Design and Implementation of a Sequence Database System *

Praveen Seshadri **Miron Livny** **Raghu Ramakrishnan**
Computer Sciences Department
U.Wisconsin, Madison WI 53706
praveen,miron,raghu@cs.wisc.edu

Abstract

This paper discusses the design and implementation of SEQ, a database system with support for sequence data. SEQ models a sequence as an ordered collection of records, and supports a declarative sequence query language based on an algebra of query operators, thereby permitting algebraic query optimization and evaluation. SEQ has been built as a component of the PREDATOR database system that provides support for relational and other kinds of complex data as well.

There are three distinct contributions made in this paper. (1) We describe the specification of sequence queries using the $\mathcal{SEQUIN}$ query language. (2) We quantitatively demonstrate the importance of various storage and optimization techniques by studying their effect on performance. (3) We present a novel nested design paradigm used in PREDATOR to combine sequence and relational data.

1 Introduction

Much real-life information contains logical ordering relationships between data items. "Sequence data" refers to data that is ordered due to such a relationship. Traditional relational databases provide no abstraction of ordering in the data model, and do not support queries based on the logical sequentiality in the data. In earlier work, we had described a data model that could describe a wide variety of sequence data, and a query algebra that could be used to represent queries over sequences [SLR95]. We had also observed that sequence query evaluation could benefit greatly from algebraic optimizations that exploited the order information [SLR94]. This paper describes the issues that were addressed when building the SEQ sequence database system based on these ideas.

SEQ is a component of the PREDATOR[1] multi-threaded, client-server database system which supports sequences, as well as relations and other kinds of complex data. The system uses the SHORE storage manager library [CDF+94] for low-level database functionality like buffer management, concurrency control and recovery. A novel design paradigm provides query processing support for multiple data types, including both sequences and relations. The system implementation has been in progress for more than a year and is currently at approximately 35,000 lines of C++ code (excluding the SHORE libraries). In this paper, the focus is on the SEQ component which provides the $\mathcal{SEQUIN}$ language to specify declarative sequence queries, and an optimization and execution engine to process them. The PREDATOR system is described in detail in [Ses96], and only a high-level overview is presented here.

1.1 The State Of The Art

Financial management products like MIM [MIM94] provide special purpose systems for analyzing stock market data. Current general-purpose database systems provide limited support for sequence data. The Order-By clause in SQL only specifies the order in which answers are presented to the user. Most existing support deals with *temporal* data. While SQL-92 provides a timestamp data type, there are few constructs that can exploit sequentiality. Many temporal queries can be expressed in SQL-92 using features like correlated subqueries and aggregation, these are typically very inefficient to execute. Research in the temporal database community has focused on enhancing relational data models with temporal semantics [TCG+93], but there have been few implementations. Most commercial database systems will allow a sequence to be represented as a 'blob' which is managed by the system, but interpreted solely by the application program. Some object-oriented systems

* Praveen Seshadri was supported by IBM Research Grant 93-F153900-000 and an IBM Cooperative Fellowship. Miron Livny and Raghu Ramakrishnan were supported by NASA Research Grant NAGW-3921. Raghu Ramakrishnan was also supported by a Packard Foundation Fellowship in Science and Engineering, a Presidential Young Investigator Award with matching grants from DEC, Tandem and Xerox, and NSF grant IRI-9011563.

Proceedings of the 22nd VLDB Conference
Mumbai(Bombay), India, 1996

[1] "PREDATOR" is (recursively) the PRedator Enhanced DAta Type Object-Relational DBMS.

like O2 [BDK92] provide array and list constructs that allow collections of data to be ordered. The object-relational database system Illustra [Ill94] provides database support for time-series data along with relational data. A time-series is an ADT(Abstract Data Type) value implemented as a large array on disk. A number of ADT methods are implemented to provide primitive query functionality on a time-series. The methods may be composed to form meaningful queries.

1.2 Desired Sequence Functionality

The abstract model of a data sequence is shown in Figure 1. An *ordering domain* is a data type which has a total order and a predecessor/successor relation defined over its elements (also referred to as 'positions'). Examples of ordering domains are the integers, days, seconds, etc. A *sequence* is a mapping between a collection of similarly structured records and the positions of an ordering domain. While every record must be mapped to at least one position, there is no requirement that there be a record mapped to *every* position. The 'empty' positions correspond intuitively to 'holes' in the sequence. The DBMS should efficiently process queries over large disk-based sequences. Further, in most applications, there is sequence data as well as relational and other kinds of data. Complex values like images, or even entire relations can be associated with a single position in a sequence [SLR96], and conversely, there can be a sequence associated with a single relational tuple.

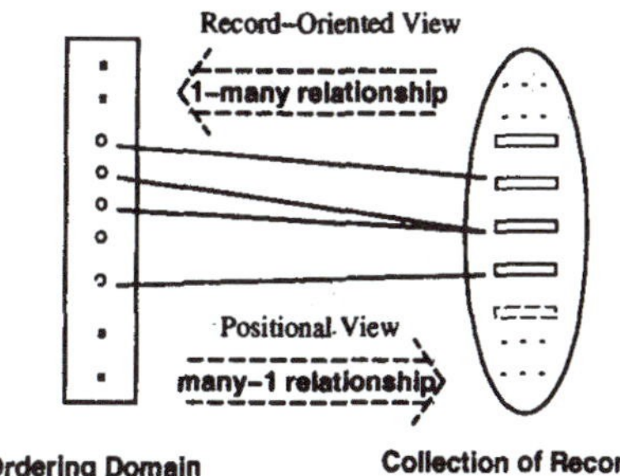

Figure 1: Data Sequence

In [SLR95], we proposed an algebra of Positional sequence query operators. In terms of Figure 1, these operators "view" the sequence mapping from the left (positions) to the right (records). While we do not describe the operators in detail in this paper, the $\mathcal{SEQUIN}$ query language is based on this algebra. The dual mapping from right (records) to the left (positions) leads to operators that are extensions of the relational algebra. Such operators have been extensively investigated in the temporal database community [TCG+93], and they are not considered here.

2 PREDATOR System Design

Object-relational systems like Illustra [Ill94], and Paradise [DKLPY94] allow an attribute of a relational record to belong to an Abstract Data Type (ADT). Each ADT defines methods that may be invoked on values of that type. An ADT can itself be a structured complex type like a sequence, with other ADTs nested inside it. Relations are the *top-level* type, and all queries are posed in the relational query language SQL. There has been much research related to ADT technology, beginning with [Sto86].

The PREDATOR design enhances the ADT notion by supporting "Enhanced Abstract Data Types"(E-ADTs). Both sequences and relations are modeled as E-ADTs . Each E-ADT supports one or more of the following:

Storage Management: Each E-ADT can provide multiple physical implementations of values of that type. The particular implementation used for a specific value may be specified by the user when the value is created, or determined automatically by the system.

Catalog Management: Each E-ADT can provide catalogs that maintain statistics and store schema information. Further, certain values may be named.

Query Language: An E-ADT can provide a query language with which expressions over values of that E-ADT can be specified (for example, the relation E-ADT may provide SQL as the query language, and the sequence E-ADT may provide $\mathcal{SEQUIN}$).

Query Operators and Optimization: If a declarative query language is specified, the E-ADT must provide optimization abilities that will translate a language expression into a query evaluation plan in some evaluation algebra.

Query Evaluation: If a query language is specified, the E-ADT must provide the ability to execute the optimized plan.

The E-ADT paradigm is a novel contribution that differentiates PREDATOR from the traditional ADT-method based approach to providing support for collection types in databases. The difference is crucial to the usability, functionality and performance of queries over complex data types like sequences. The ability to name objects belonging to different E-ADTs allows *any* E-ADT to be the top-level type. This allows users who are primarily interested in sequence data, for example, to directly query named sequences without having to embed the sequences inside relational tuples. While we believe that the E-ADT paradigm can and should be applied to provide database support for *any* complex data type, a detailed discussion of E-ADTs is beyond the scope of this paper. In this current paper, we only wish to place the support for sequence data in the context of the larger database system. The reader is referred to [Ses96] for further details on E-ADTs and the PREDATOR system.

The design philosophy of E-ADTs is carried directly over into the system architecture. PREDATOR is a client-server database in which the server is a loosely-coupled system of E-ADTs . The high-level picture of the system is shown in Figure 2. An underlying theme in the implementation of most components of the system is to allow for extensibility by specifying uniform interfaces. The server is built on top of a layer of common database utilities that all E-ADTs can use. Code to handle arithmetic and boolean expressions, constant values and functions is part of this layer. An important component

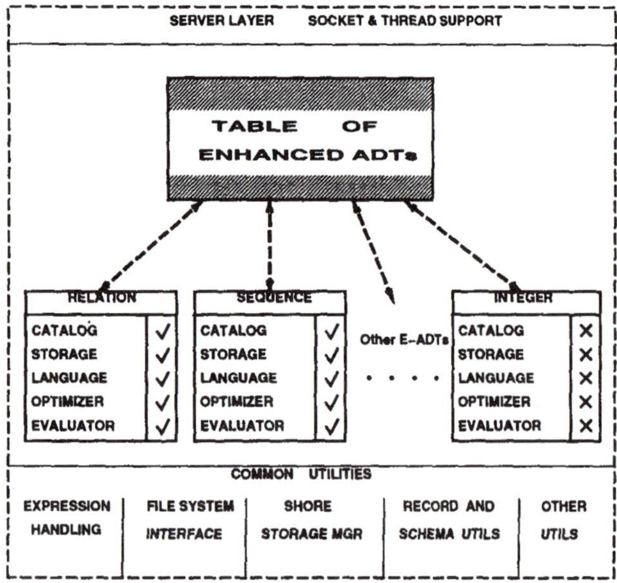

Figure 2: System Architecture

of the utility layer is the SHORE Storage Manager [CDF+94]. SHORE provides facilities for concurrency control, recovery and buffer management for large volumes of data. It also provides a threads package that interacts with the rest of the storage management layers; PREDATOR uses this package to build a multi-threaded server.

The core of the system is an extensible table in which E-ADTs are registered. Each E-ADT may (but does not have to) support and provide code for the enhancements described. As shown in the figure, some of the basic types like integers do not support any enhancements. Two E-ADTs that do support enhancements are sequences and relations. The important question to ask is: how does the interaction between sequences and relations occur? The answer is difficult to explain with meaningful examples at this stage because the sequence E-ADT has not yet been described. Instead, we first provide an isolated discussion of the sequence E-ADT . We then return to the issue of how sequences and relations interact in Section 4.

3 The Sequence E-ADT

An important component of the model of a sequence is the ordering domain. Each ordering domain is modeled as a data type with some additional methods that make it an *ordered* type. *LessThan(Pos1, Pos2)*, *Equal(Pos1, Pos2)* and *GreaterThan(Pos1, Pos2)* allow comparisons to be made among positions. *NumPositions(Pos1, Pos2)* counts the number of positions between the two specified end points. *Next(StartPos, N)* and *Prev(StartPos, N)* compute the Nth successor and predecessor of the starting position. All ordering domains are registered in an extensible table maintained by the sequence E-ADT . Additionally, we need to capture the hierarchical relationship between various ordering domains. For instance, Figure 3 shows one set of hierarchical relationships between common temporal ordering domains. A table of *Collapses* is maintained by the sequence E-ADT . Each *Collapse* represents an edge in the hierarchy and provides methods that map a position in one ordering domain to a position or set of positions in the other domain. For example, a Collapse involving 'days' and 'weeks' maps each day to the week it belongs in, and each week to the set of days of that week.

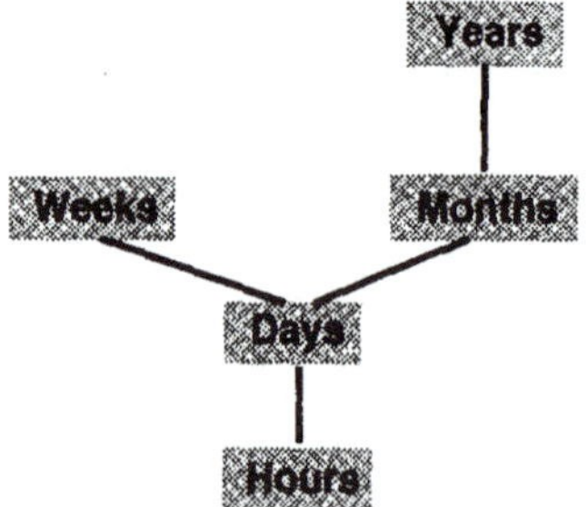

Figure 3: Sample Ordering Hierarchy

As shown in Figure 1, a sequence models a many-to-one mapping between positions in the ordering domain and a set of records. As a simplification, we restrict each record to be mapped to a single position (the one-to-many abstraction is modeled by making copies of the record). In SEQ, the position mapping is maintained as an explicit attribute of each record. Although there are different storage implementations of sequences in the system, they all provide certain common interface methods:

OpenScan(Cursor), GetNext(Cursor), CloseScan(Cursor). These methods provide a scan of the sequence in the forward order of the ordering domain. Any positions in the domain which are not mapped to a record are ignored in the scan.

GetElem(Pos). This finds the record at the specified position in the sequence (or fails if none exists at that position).

3.1 Experimental Database

We wish to quantitatively demonstrate (a) some possible choices of storage techniques for sequences, and (b) the importance of various optimization techniques. The sequences used in the experimental database were generated synthetically. While we could have used a real-life data set instead, it would have been more difficult to control various properties of each sequence. The properties of interest in each sequence are: (1) the *cardinality*, i.e., the number of records in the sequence, (2) the *record width*, i.e., the number of bytes in each record, (3) the *density*, i.e. the percentage of the positions in the underlying ordering domain that are non-empty. All the sequences have an *hourly* ordering domain and start at midnight on 0100/01/01 (i.e. January 1st in the year 100 AD). We considered sequences with two different densities: 100% and 20%. The cardinality of each sequence was either 1000 (1K), 10000(10K) or 100000(100K) records. For sequences of each density, the final time-points are shown in Table 1[2].

Notice that because of empty positions, the 20% density sequences span about 5 times as many positions as the 100%

[2] The entries in the table are approximate since they only show the last day, not the last hour.

	Cardinality		
Density	1K	10K	100K
100%	0100/02/15	0101/04/02	0112/07/16
20%	0100/08/16	0106/05/09	0162/11/15

Table 1: Synthetic Data Upper Bounds

density sequences. The empty positions were chosen randomly so that the overall density was 20%. The first field of every sequence record is an SQL time-stamp value. Different sequences were generated with 1, 5, 10 and 20 fields in addition to the timestamp. The values in the fields were 4-byte integers generated randomly between 0 and 1000. All experiments were performed on a SUN-Sparc 10 workstation equipped with 24MB of physical memory. The data was loaded into a SHORE storage volume implemented on top of the Unix file system. The SHORE storage manager buffer pool was set at 200 8K pages, which is smaller than the available physical memory, but is realistic for this small sample database. Logging and recovery was turned off to mimic a query-only environment. In all the experiments, the queries used contain a final aggregate over the entire sequence, thereby minimizing any time spent in printing answers. Each query was executed four times in succession, the maximum and minimum execution times were excluded, and the average of the other two times was used as the performance metric.

3.2 Storage Implementation

SEQ supports two repositories for sequence data, the Unix file system and the SHORE storage manager. The default repository is built using the SHORE storage manager library. Data volumes maintained by SHORE can reside either directly on raw disk, or on the file system; our experiments used the latter approach. A sequence can also be stored as an ascii file on the Unix file system. Much real-world sequence data currently exists in this format. It may be more expedient to directly run queries off this data, instead of first loading it into the database. Of course, this repository does not provide any of the database properties of concurrency control, recovery, etc. We studied three alternative implementations of a sequence using SHORE:

File: SHORE provides the abstraction of a 'file' into which records can be inserted. A scan of the file returns the records in the order of insertion; this enabled us to implement a sequence as a SHORE file. One advantage of this implementation was that we could code it with minimal effort. The major drawback is that the storage manager imposes several bytes (at least 24) of space overhead for every record, in addition to a large space overhead for creating a file. While concurrency control is available at the record level, inserts in the middle of a sequence are difficult to implement without an index.

IdList: In order to eliminate the space overhead per file, a sequence is stored as an array of record-ids. Each such array is a SHORE large object, which can grow arbitrarily large. Each record-id occupies 4 bytes, and identifies the appropriate record. All records are created in a single "super" file. While the space overhead for each file is eliminated, the other drawbacks still remain (primarily, the storage overhead per record). Further, since the record-id is a logical identifier in SHORE, this needs to be mapped to an internal physical identifier when the record needs to be retrieved. This problem could be avoided by using the less portable solution of actually storing the list of physical identifiers instead. Concurrency control is now at the level of the entire sequence, but inserts are easier to code because SHORE allows new data to be inserted into the middle of a large object.

Array: In this implementation, a sequence is an array of records. The array is implemented using a single SHORE large object which contains all the records. Since we expect many sequences to be irregular (i.e., have empty positions), we chose a compressed array representation in which no space is wasted for an empty position. This can dramatically reduce space utilization for data sets of very low density. However, this makes some operations within a sequence (like positional lookup, insert and delete) more expensive to implement. Variable length records require additional complex code. However, there are two important benefits to this implementation: the per-record space overhead is minimal and there is physical sequentiality for the records of a sequence. With fixed-size records in a mostly-query environment, this should be the implementation of choice.

Experiment 1: We measured the time taken to scan each of the example sequences stored using each of the implementation techniques just described. A scan is the most basic sequence operation that is used in almost every query. Consequently, the time taken to scan a sequence is a suitable indicator of the efficiency of the storage implementation. The results for the sequences with density 100% are shown (there was no significant difference with the 20% density sequences, hence they have been omitted). The actual $\mathcal{SEQUIN}$ query run was:

```
PROJECT count(*)
FROM    <data_sequence>
ZOOM  ALL;
```

Figures 4, 5, and 6 show the results for the sequences of cardinality 100K, 10K and 1K respectively. In all the graphs, the number of fields in each record varies along the X-axis, while the runtime is plotted on the Y-axis. For all the implementations, the scan cost grows with the width of the records. Note that the SHORE Array implementation is the most efficient whatever the cardinality or width of the sequence. Therefore, in all the remaining experiments, this was the storage implementation used. The SHORE File implementation is worse than SHORE Array because of the file handling overhead per record. IdList is the worst SHORE implementation primarily because of the added cost of converting from logical to physical identifiers. The Unix ascii file implementation is the most sensitive to the width of the data records because each attribute needs to be parsed at run-time to convert it from ascii to binary format.

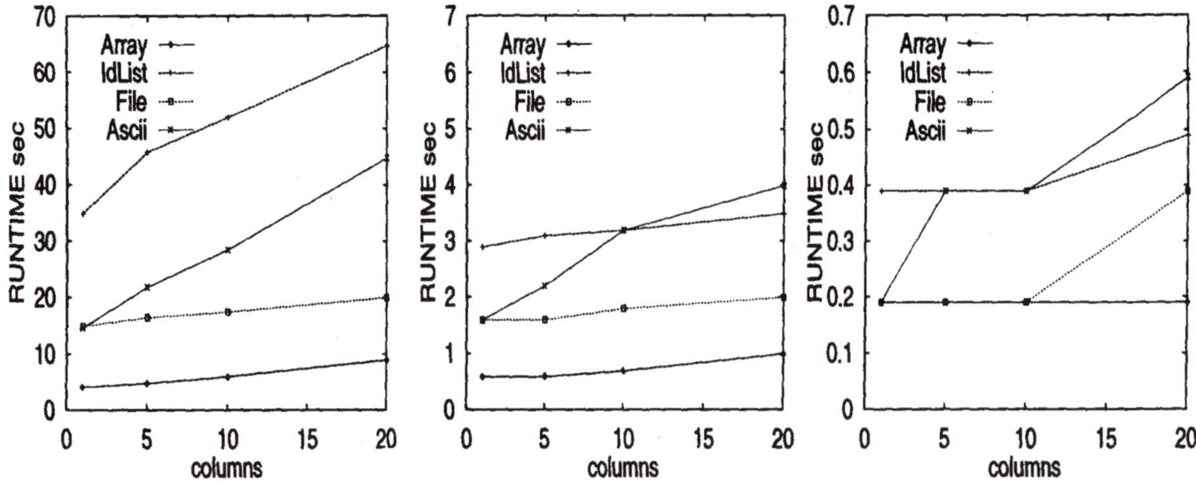

Figure 4: Expmt.1 : Card 100K Figure 5: Expmt.1 : Card 10K Figure 6: Expmt.1 : Card 1K

3.3 SEQUIN query language

SEQUIN [3] is a declarative language for sequence queries, similar in flavor to SQL. The result of a SEQUIN query is always a sequence. The overall structure of a SEQUIN query is:

```
PROJECT   <project-list>
FROM      <sequences-to-be-merged-on-position>
[WHERE    <selection-conditions>]
[OVER     <start-window> TO <end-window>]
[ZOOM     <zoom-info>];
```

We now explain the various constructs using simple examples based on the following sample database. Consider the sequences Stock1 and Stock2 representing the hourly price information on two stocks. Both sequences have the same schema: {time:Hour, high:Double, low:Double, volume:Integer}, where the 'time' field is underlined to show that it defines the order.

The first query estimates the monetary value of Stock1 traded in each hour when the low price fell below 50. The answer is a sequence with the monetary value computed for each such hour.

```
PROJECT ((A.high+A.low)/2)*A.volume
FROM    Stock1 A
WHERE   A.low < 50;
```

The query demonstrates the use of the PROJECT and WHERE clauses. The PROJECT clause with a target list of expressions is similar to the SELECT clause of SQL.There is no output record for positions at which the WHERE clause condition fails; these are empty positions in the output sequence. Since the result is a sequence of the desired values, it should have an ordering attribute; however none exists in the PROJECT list. In such cases, the ordering attribute from the input sequence is automatically added to the output schema.

We now consider finding the 24-hour moving average of the difference between the high prices of the two stocks.

```
PROJECT avg(A.high - B.high)
FROM    Stock1 A, Stock2 B
OVER    $P-23 TO $P
```

This query demonstrates the use of the FROM clause, and the OVER clause for moving window aggregates. When there is more than one sequence specified in the FROM clause, there is an implicit join between them on the position attribute (in this case, on 'time'). Since this is a declarative query, the textual order of the sequences in the FROM clause does not matter. Note that the PROJECT clause uses the *avg* aggregate function. The set of records over which the aggregate is computed is defined by the moving window of the OVER clause. In this case, the window spans the last 24 hours, but in general, the bounds of the window can use any arithmetic expression involving addition, subtraction, constant integers and the special $P symbol representing the 'current' position for which the record is being generated. Empty positions in the input sequence are ignored as long as there is at least one valid input record in the aggregation window.

Next, we show a rather complex query that demonstrates the possible variations in the FROM clause. The desired answer is a sequence containing for every hour, the difference between the 24-hour moving average of the high price of Stock1, and the high price of Stock2 at the most recent hour when the volume of Stock2 traded was greater than 25,000. The answer sequence is only of interest to the user after hour 2000.

```
// first define the moving average as a view
CREATE VIEW MovAvgStock1 AS (
       PROJECT avg(C.high) as avghigh
       FROM    Stock1 C
       OVER    $P-23 TO $P);
// then use the view in the query
PROJECT A.avghigh - B.high
FROM MovAvgStock1 A,
     Previous(PROJECT D.high
              FROM    Stock2 D
              WHERE   D.volume > 25,000) B
WHERE $P > 2000;
```

Note that the sequences in the FROM clause may themselves be defined using another SEQUIN query block. This may be effected

[3] SEquence QUery INterface.

using a view (as is the MovAvgStock1 sequence A), or a nested query block defining a sequence expression (as is the sequence B). Three special modifiers with functional syntax are allowed in the FROM clause: *Next, Previous and Offset. Previous* (as in this example) defines a sequence which associates with every position the record at the most recent non-empty position in the input sequence. Remember that sequences need not be regular, and consequently there can be positions which are not associated with any records. The Previous modifier fills these 'holes' with the most recent record. Similarly, *Next* defines a sequence in which the holes are filled with the most imminent record. Both these modifiers can take a second optional argument which specifies how many such steps to take (which is 1 by default); for example, Previous(S, 2) defines a sequence of the second-most recent input record at each position. The *Offset* modifier defines a sequence in which the position-to-record mapping of the input sequence is shifted by a specified number of positions. Finally, note that the WHERE clause can also use the $P notation to access the 'current' position attribute.

The next query demonstrates the use of the ZOOM clause to exploit the hierarchical relationship between ordering domains[4]. Here is the $\mathcal{SEQUIN}$ query to compute the daily minimum of the volume of Stock1 traded every hour.

```
PROJECT min(A.volume)
FROM    Stock1 A
ZOOM    days
```

We assume that 'days' is the name of an ordering domain known to the system, and that there is a Collapse registered with the system from 'hours' (the ordering domain of the input) to 'days'. The answer sequence has an implicit attribute of type 'days' that provides the ordering. If the resulting ordering domain is at a coarser granularity in the hierarchy than the source ordering domain, as in this example, then the PROJECT clause must be composed of aggregate expressions.

Our final example shows how the ZOOM clause can perform conditional collapses. Suppose that just as in the previous query, we want to compute the minimum volume of Stock1 traded over consecutive periods of time. However, these periods are not well-defined like 'days' or 'weeks'. Instead, they depend on the data. Specifically, the periods may be bounded by those times when the high and low values were very close (implying an hour of stability for the stock). This can be expressed as follows:

```
PROJECT min(A.volume)
FROM    Stock1 A
ZOOM    BEFORE (A.high - A.low < 0.1);
```

The query states that the aggregation window includes records upto but not including the record which satisfies the stability condition. If the last record is also to be included in the aggregation window, the word BEFORE is replaced by AFTER. As a final variant, the ZOOM clause could simply be 'ZOOM ALL', specifying that the aggregation is to be performed on the entire sequence. These versions of the ZOOM operator generate sequences that are ordered by an implicit integer field that starts at value 1 and increases in increments of 1 (since this is the only meaningful sequence ordering for the result).

In this paper, we have omitted discussion of some other features of $\mathcal{SEQUIN}$ including a construct to re-define the ordering field of a sequence, update constructs and DDL features. A $\mathcal{SEQUIN}$ query is parsed into a directed acyclic graph of algebraic operators, which is then optimized by the query optimizer. We have described the algebra operators and some optimization techniques in [SLR95, SLR94].

[4]The word "zoom" is used because the action of moving down or up through the ordering hierarchy is similar to zooming in and out with a lens.

3.4 Query Optimizations

This section describes the effects of four categories of implemented optimizations. Each optimization is first explained in principle, and then demonstrated by means of a performance experiment. We have tried to keep the queries in the experiments as simple as possible, in order to isolate the effects of each optimization.

3.4.1 Propagating Ranges of Interest

This class of optimizations deals with the use of information that limits the range of positions of interest in the query answer. There are two sources of such information: one is from selection predicates in the query that use the position attribute. Experiment 2 demonstrates the benefits of propagating such selections into the sequence scans. The other source is from statistics on the valid ranges of positions in each sequence. These valid ranges can be propagated through the entire query as described in [SLR94]. Experiment 3 demonstrates how the valid-range can be used for optimization.

Experiment 2:

```
PROJECT count(*)
FROM 100K_10flds_100dens S
WHERE S.time > "<timestamp1>"
ZOOM ALL;
```

This query is a variant of the query used earlier to measure the performance of a sequence scan. In this case, the scan is over only a portion of the sequence. SEQ can optimize the query by pushing the selection predicate into the scan of the sequence. Since the default implementation of sequences in SEQ expects irregular sequences and uses a compressed Array implementation, there is no simple way to directly access a specific position. If the selection range is from Pos1 to Pos2, the first record within the range (at Pos1) is difficult to locate exactly. Based on the density of the sequence, the valid range of the sequence, and the desired selection range, SEQ performs a weighted binary search to get close to the correct starting position. However, if the query is modified so that the > is replaced by a < (i.e. the desired range is at the beginning of the sequence), then the binary positioning is not needed.

We studied the effect of varying the predicate selectivity from 1% to 100%. We ran the experiment twice, once with the selection windows at the start of the valid-range (**at_start**), and once with the selection windows at the end(**at_end**). Three algorithms were considered: no selection push-down (NO_PD), simple push-down with no binary-positioning (ORD_PD), and selection push-down with binary positioning (BP_PD).

The results for **at_start** are shown in Figure 7. The predicate selectivity is shown on the X-axis, and the query execution time is on the Y-axis. While there is no difference between BP_PD and ORD_PD (since the predicate is at the start of the window), NO_PD performs much worse because the entire sequence is scanned. As the selectivity increases, all the algorithms become more expensive because there is additional work being done in the final count aggregate.

The results for **at_end** are shown in Figure 8. The performance of NO_PD is the same as in the **at_start** experiment. The performance of BP_PD is almost the same as in the **at_start** experiment, because it is able to use the selection information to position the scan at the appropriate start position. On the other hand, ORD_PD cannot do

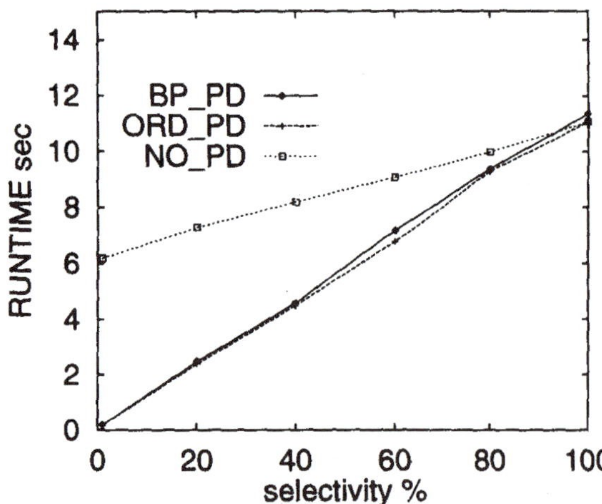

Figure 7: Range Selections At Start: Expmt. 2

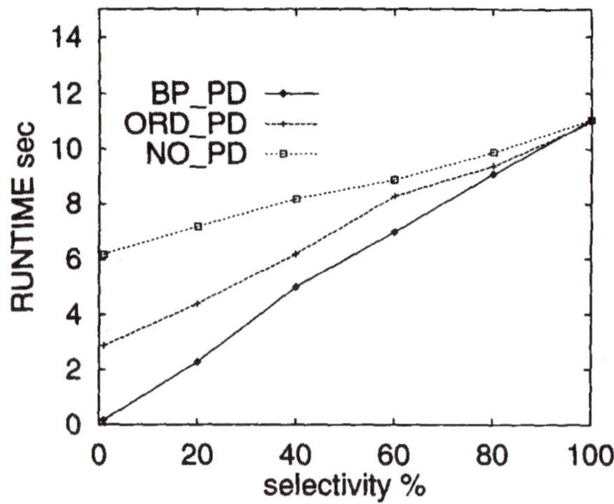

Figure 8: Range Selections At End: Expmt. 2

this, and therefore scans the entire sequence. However, ORD_PD can apply the selection predicate at a lower level in the system and therefore performs better than NO_PD. Note that the BP_PD algorithm, which performs best, can only be applied if the valid range and density statistics are maintained for the sequences.

Experiment 3:

```
// View applies selection to the base sequence
CREATE VIEW ViewSeq AS (
        PROJECT A.fld2
        FROM a100K_10_100 A
        WHERE A.fld1 > 900);
// Merge B with offset ViewSeq
PROJECT count(*)
FROM 100K_5flds_100dens B,
     Offset(ViewSeq, <offset_distance>) C;
```

This query joins two sequences on position; however, one of the sequences is first shifted by some specified number of positions. Each of the base sequences in this query has 100K records spanning an identical range (see Table 1). However, since one of them is shifted, neither of the sequences needs to be scanned in its entirety; only the mutually overlapping region needs to be scanned. This is shown intuitively in Figure 9. The valid-range propagation optimization is able to recognize such optimization opportunities in all SEQ queries.

We varied the overlap from 90% of the valid-range to 10%, and executed the query with (RNG_PROP) and without (NO_PROP) the valid-range optimization. The results are shown in Figure 10. The smaller the overlap between the two sequences, the better is the relative performance of RNG_PROP. The difference between the two lines is due to the work saved in scanning the sequence.

3.4.2 Moving Window Aggregates

All aggregate functions in SEQ (used in both relational and sequence query processing) are implemented in an extensible manner. Each aggregate function provides three methods: *Initialize(), Accumulate(record), Terminate()*. This abstract interface allows the aggregation operator to compute its result incrementally, independent of the specific aggregate function computed. The presence of moving window aggregates in SEQ creates new opportunities for optimization. Note that in relational aggregates, the input data is partitioned into *disjoint* portions over which the aggregation is performed. Contrast this with the moving window sequence aggregates in which there is an *overlap* between successive aggregation windows. For example, consider the 3-position moving average of a sequence 1,2,3,4,5. Once the sum $1 + 2 + 3$ has been computed as 6, this computation can be used to reduce the work done for the next aggregate. Instead of adding $2 + 3 + 4$, one could instead compute $6 - 1 + 4$. Due to the small aggregation window in this example, there is little benefit. However, when the windows become larger and the operations are more expensive, there can be significant improvements due to this approach. Importantly, the time required for aggregation is independent of the size of the window.

While some aggregates like Count, Sum, Avg and Product are directly amenable to this optimization, others like Min, Max, Median and Mode are not. We call this the *symmetry* property of an aggregate function. In order to exploit the symmetry property in an extensible manner, we require each aggregate function to provide two more methods: *IsSymmetric()* and *Drop(record)*. Experiment 4 demonstrates the importance of exploiting symmetric aggregates.

Experiment 4: We considered queries of the form

```
// Define the moving aggregate
CREATE VIEW MovAggr AS
   (PROJECT <aggr_function>(S.fld1)
    FROM    <data_sequence> S
    OVER    $P-<window_size> TO $P);

// Count records to minimize printing
PROJECT count(*)
FROM    MovAggr
ZOOM ALL;
```

Moving window aggregates are among the most important sequence queries posed in stock market analysis applications. Our example query is the simplest form of a moving aggregate (with a final count operator thrown in as usual to eliminate the time for printing answers). This experiment was restricted to only the 100K_10cols_100dens and 100K_10cols_20dens sequences. The window size was varied from 5 to 100, while the aggregate functions tried were MIN (non-symmetric) and AVG(symmetric).

The results for the 100% density sequence are shown in Figure 11. Notice that the performance of MIN100 grows linearly with the size of the aggregation window. This is because the entire aggregation window has to be processed for each MIN aggregate computed. In comparison, the performance of AVG100 is almost independent of the

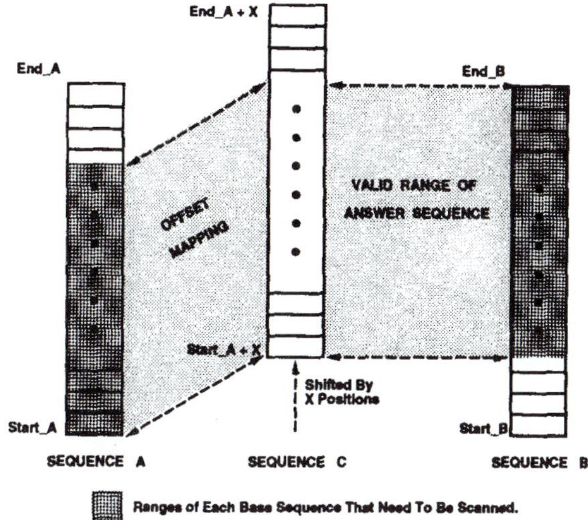

Figure 9: Range Propagation: Intuition

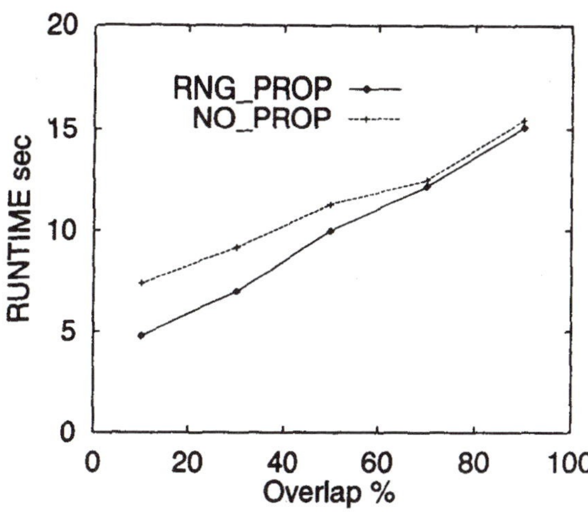

Figure 10: Range Propagation: Expmt. 3

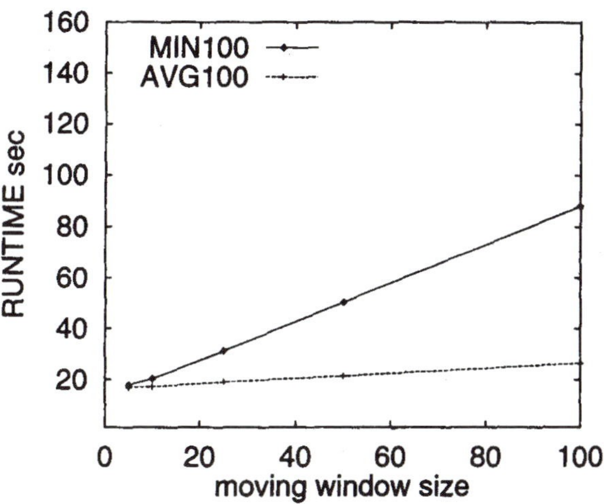

Figure 11: Expmt.4: 100% Density

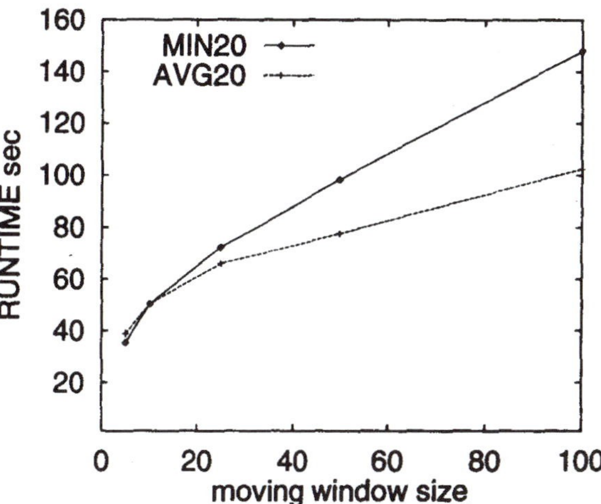

Figure 12: Expmt.4: 20% Density

size of the aggregation window. The slight dependence of AVG100 on the window size has an interesting reason. Given a particular timestamp, it is more expensive to compute the 100th previous timestamp, than the 10th previous timestamp. Simple arithmetic cannot be applied to temporal ordering domains because the variable number of days in a month has to be accounted for.

The results for the 20% density sequence are shown in Figure 12. Note that a moving aggregate over a sequence with holes generates many more records than exist in the input sequence. Assume that there is an input record at hour 100 and the next record is at hour 102. A 3-hour moving aggregate sequence has a value at hour 101 as well, because there is at least one record in its aggregation window from hour 99 to hour 101. This explains why the cost of both aggregates increases with window size. Since the density is low (20%), there are also fewer records in each aggregation window, and the relative difference between the AVG20 and MIN20 grows more slowly with the size of the aggregation window. The relative difference between AVG20 and MIN20 at window size 100 is about the same as the relative difference between AVG100 and MIN100 at window size 20. This is to be expected, because the ratio of the densities of the two sequences is also 100:20.

3.4.3 Common Sub-Expressions

The same sequence may be accessed repeatedly in different parts of a query. For example, the following query compares the values of a moving average at successive positions looking for stability in the stock prices.

```
// View: moving average over last 24 hours
CREATE VIEW MovAvgStock1 AS
      (PROJECT avg(S.high) as avghigh
       FROM    Stock1 S
       OVER    $P-23 to $P);

// Check change in moving average
PROJECT *
FROM MovAvgStock1 T1, Offset(MovAvgStock1, 1) T2
WHERE T1.avghigh - T2.avghigh < 10.
```

Figures 13 and 14 show two possible algebraic query graphs that can be constructed from this query. The meaning of each query graph is obvious. The difference between the two query graphs is that one uses a common sub-expression, while the other does not. Common sub-expressions occur frequently in sequence queries, so this is an important issue. When a query graph with a common sub-expression

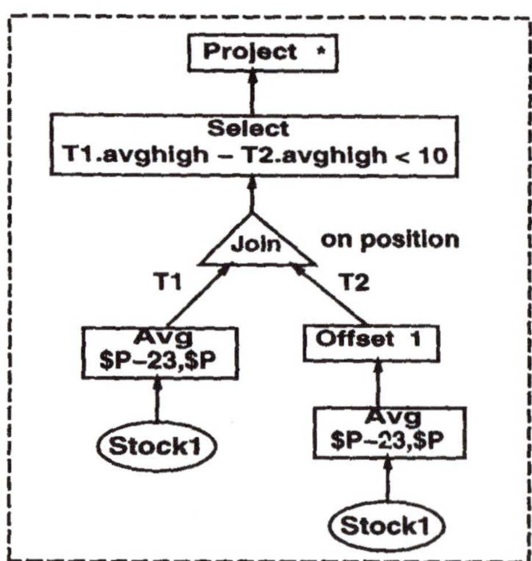

Figure 13: Graph 1: Repeated Computation

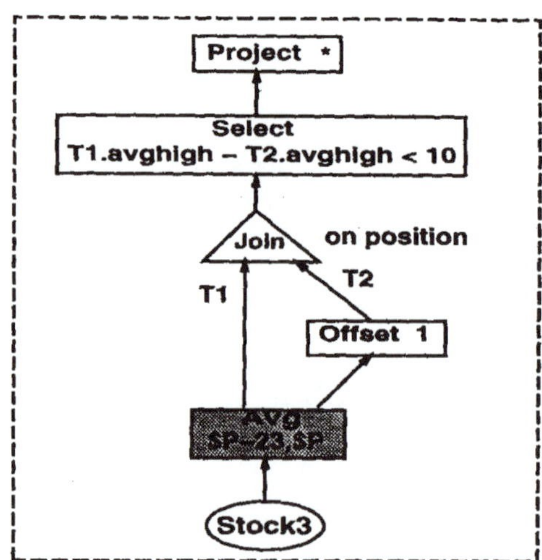

Figure 14: Graph 2: Common Sub-Expression

is constructed for a *relational* query, the query optimizer chooses one of two options. One option is to repeatedly evaluate the common sub-expression; this is equivalent to using the version of the query graph without a common sub-expression(Figure 13). The other option is to compute the sub-expression once, store the result, and repeatedly access the stored result. For sequence queries, we will show that materializing intermediate results is not a desirable option.

By an analysis of the query graph and the scopes of the various operators involved, SEQ can determine exactly how much of the common sub-expression result should be cached, so that the entire query can be evaluated with a single stream access of the common sub-expression. In other words, neither is the common-subexpression evaluated multiple times, nor is it materialized [Ses96].

Experiment 5: We ran the very same query shown above (except

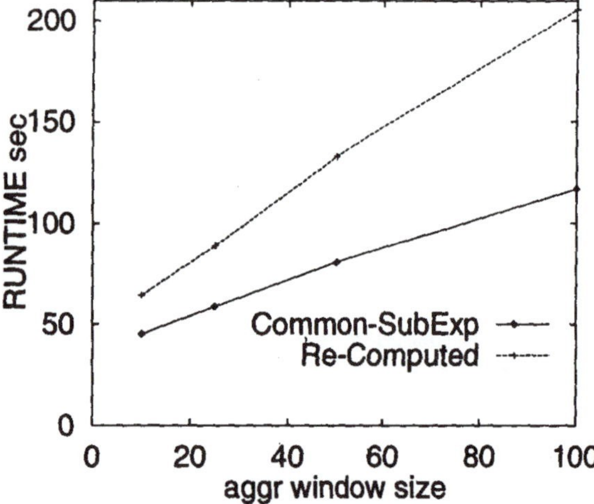

Figure 15: Common Subexpressions: Expmt. 5

that the Stock1 sequence was replaced by 100K_10flds_100dens). We varied the size of the aggregation window from 10 to 100; as the window size increases, so does the cost of the common sub-expression. The query execution time was measured with the SEQ optimization (Common-Subexp) and with repeated evaluation (Re-Computed). The results are shown in Figure 15. The common sub-expression optimization used by SEQ obviously performs much better than repeated evaluation. As the cost of the common sub-expression increases (i.e., as the window size grows), this optimization becomes extremely important. While we have ignored the possibility of materializing the intermediate result, the next experiment will show that materialization is very inefficient in general.

3.4.4 Operator Pipelining

An important optimization principle in SEQ is to try and ensure *stream access* [SLR94] to the stored sequence data as well as to intermediate data; i.e., each sequence is read in a single continuous pipelined stream without materializing it. This is accomplished by associating buffers with each operator, to-cache some relevant portion of the most recent data from its inputs. In our example of the hourly sequences, a 24-hour moving aggregate would need a buffer of no more than the 24 most recent input records. This 'window' of recent data is called the *scope* of the operator. All the operators in the algebra have fixed size scopes in a particular query. Consider the simple query below that scans a sequence and computes an aggregate over the entire data:

```
PROJECT count(*)
FROM    <data_sequence>
ZOOM  ALL;
```

Experiment 6 will show that there is a tremendous penalty to pay for failing to pipeline even such a simple query between the Scan operator and the Count operator. Experiment 7 shows that when the query becomes complex, with several nested operators, the relative importance of pipelining becomes even more clearly defined.

Experiment 6: We ran the query shown above over all the sequences in the sample database. The results with the pipelining optimization (Pipelined) and without it (Materialized) are shown in the 3-D graph of Figure 16. The number of columns in each record varies along the X-axis, while the sequence cardinality varies on a logarithmic scale on the Y-axis. The Z-axis shows the query execution time on a logarithmic scale. Once again, we only show the results for the 100% density sequences (the 20% density results are similar). Notice that materialization increases the cost by almost an order of magnitude!

Experiment 7: In this experiment, we want to show the effects of increased query complexity on materialized execution. Section 3.3 had several examples of non-trivial queries. By using the view mechanism, many complex queries can be generated. It is difficult to choose a single representative for all complex queries. Instead, since the purpose of this experiment is to isolate and study the performance of pipelining and materialization, we use a query that, though not intuitively meaningful, can be varied in a controlled manner. We

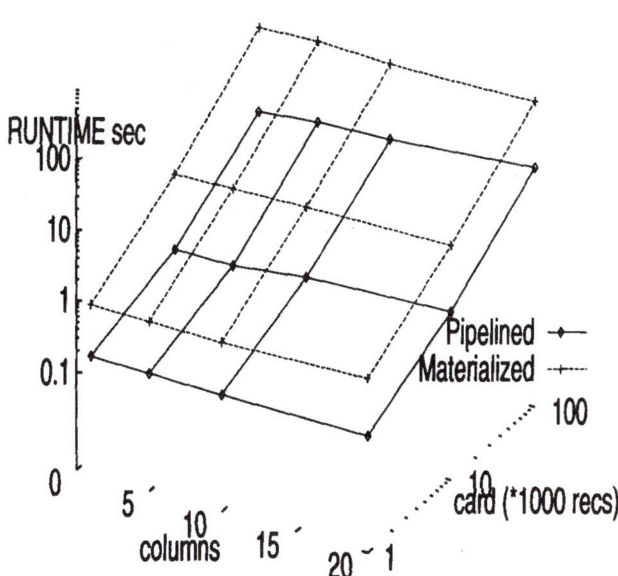

Figure 16: Pipelining: Expmt. 6

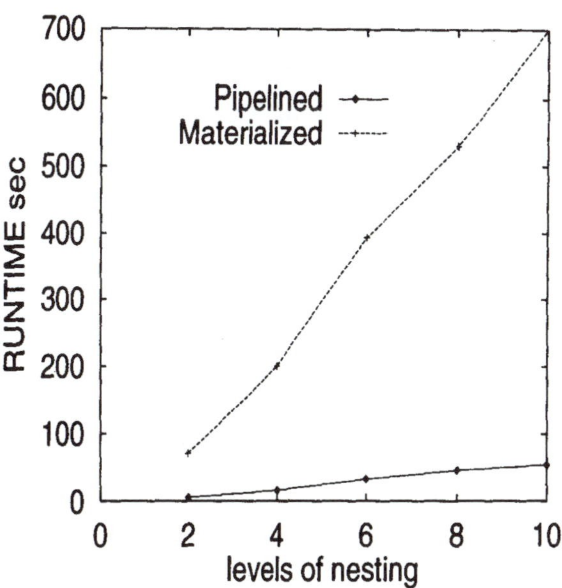

Figure 17: Pipelining: Expmt. 7

consider one particular data sequence (100K_10flds_100dens) and vary the number of levels of operators in the query from 2 to 10. For instance, with 4 levels, the corresponding *SEQUIN* query is

```
PROJECT count(*)
FROM    (PROJECT *
         FROM (PROJECT *
                FROM 100K_10flds_100dens)) S;
ZOOM  ALL;
```

We disabled the SEQ optimization that merges consecutive scans which would otherwise reduce all these queries to a common form. The results with and without the pipelining optimization are shown in Figure 17. The X-axis shows the number of levels of nesting in each query, while the Y-axis shows the query execution time. Notice that while the cost of the default SEQ execution with pipelining grows moderately (due to the presence of more operators on the query execution path), the cost of the materialized execution grows dramatically with the complexity of the query expression.

4 Combining Sequences and Relations

We now return to the issue of how sequences and relations interact in PREDATOR. The important questions are: how does a query access both relational and sequence data, how does optimization of this query occur, and how is the query evaluated? In order to discuss these questions, we slightly extend the example that we used to explain the *SEQUIN* language in Section 3.3. Consider a relation *Stocks* of securities that are traded on a stock exchange, with the schema *(name:String, stock_history:Sequence)*. The *stock_history* is a sequence of hourly information on the high and low prices, and the volume of the stock traded in each hour.

4.1 Nested Language Expressions

In this example, since the sequence data is nested within the relational data, it is appropriate for the user to think of the relational E-ADT as the top-level type. A query will therefore be posed in the relational query language (SQL) with nested query expressions in the sequence query language (*SEQUIN*).

Let us consider the SQL query to find for each stock, the number of hours after hour 3500 when the 24-hour moving average of the high price was greater than 100.

```
SELECT S.name, SEQUIN(
  "PROJECT count(*)
   FROM (PROJECT avg(H.high) as avghigh
         FROM   $1  H
         OVER   $P-23 TO $P ) A
         WHERE  A.avghigh > 100 AND $P > 3500
         ZOOM ALL",
   S.stock_history)
FROM   Stocks S;
```

The SQL query has the usual SELECT clause target list of expressions. One of these expressions is a *SEQUIN* query, whose syntax is functional. There is one such implicit function for every E-ADT language registered in the system. The first argument to the *SEQUIN* function is a query string in that language. Any parameters to be passed from SQL (the calling language) to the embedded query in *SEQUIN* are provided as additional arguments. These parameters are referenced inside the embedded query using the positional notation \$1, \$2, etc. In this particular query, the passed parameter (S.stock_history) is a sequence. Note that the SQL language parser does not know about the grammar of the embedded language, and merely treats the *SEQUIN* subquery as a function call whose first argument is some string. For the SQL parser, this query is treated in the same manner as the following query would be:

```
SELECT S.name, Foo("hello", S.stock_history)
FROM   Stocks S;
```

As part of the type-check of the SQL query, the type of the *SEQUIN* function is also checked. This causes the embedded *SEQUIN* query to be parsed by the parser of the sequence E-ADT. It is no longer sufficient to identify the type of every parameter passed. In this example, the parameter is of a sequence type, but this is not sufficient to type-check the embedded query. The schema information for the sequence must also be specified along with the type. This implies that throughout the system code that handles values and expressions, meta-information like the schema must be maintained as part of the type information. The return type of the $\mathcal{SEQUIN}$ query expression is a sequence as usual. Expressions of a particular type may be cast to another type using cast functions that are registered with the system. The cast mechanism is also used to convert sequences into relations. The cast from relations to sequences additionally requires the specification of the order attribute.

When optimizing a nested query, each E-ADT is responsible for optimizing its own query blocks. Since the nested languages are introduced in the guise of functions, each optimizer must be sure to 'plan' any function invoked. Planning a function like $\mathcal{SEQUIN}$ causes the optimization of the embedded query to be performed. In this example, the SQL optimizer is called on the outer query block, and the $\mathcal{SEQUIN}$ optimizer operates on the nested query block. There is currently no optimization performed across query blocks belonging to different E-ADTs . During execution of the SQL query, the nested $\mathcal{SEQUIN}$ expression is evaluated just as any other function would be. There are several other implementation details that are described in [Ses96].

4.2 Comparison with Existing Systems

Some current systems like Illustra [Il194] support sequences (more specifically, time-series) as ADTs with a collection of methods providing query primitives. A query is a composition of the primitive functions or methods. Here is approximately how the example of the last section would be written using ADT methods:

```
SELECT S.name,
 count(filter("time > 3500",
  filter("high > 100",
   mov_avg(-23, 0,
    project("time,high",S.stock_history)))))
FROM   Stocks S;
```

The user writes the query using SQL, but the part of the query that manipulates the time-series uses a composition of special time-series primitive functions. Note that a query language based on function composition can be more awkward to use than a high-level language like $\mathcal{SEQUIN}$. In just the same way, it is often easier to express a complex query in SQL than in the relational algebra.

The more important observation is that there are several equivalent *different* functional expressions that could be used in this query. These different alternatives are not considered by the system. While queries in $\mathcal{SEQUIN}$ are declarative, queries based on the functional composition of methods have a procedural semantics. When a query expression involves the composition of more than one of these methods, little or no inter-function optimization is performed, and each individual method is evaluated separately. While we did perform a performance comparison with Illustra [Il194], we are not permitted to discuss those results. Instead, we provide a qualitative comparison.

Experiments 6 and 7 showed that materialization can perform an order of magnitude worse than pipelining with stream-access. In the ADT-method approach, pipelining is not possible without inter-function optimization. The simple query of Experiment 6 is expressed in a form similar to *Count(Scan(S))*. Since methods are independently evaluated, the result of the scan is materialized, and then the count of this materialized result is computed. The optimizations that propagate valid ranges and selection predicates (Experiments 2 and 3) once again require the ability to push range selections from one function to another. Consequently, ADT-method based systems do not exploit these optimizations. Experiment 5 showed that the common subexpression optimization could reduce query execution time by almost a factor of two. An ADT-method approach cannot identify common sub-expressions without inter-function optimization, let alone take advantage of them to optimize query execution. Putting these together, the ADT-method approach is unable to apply optimization techniques that could result in overall performance improvements of approximately two orders of magnitude! We should stress that these differences are symptoms of a basic design difference between SEQ and ADT-method systems. In order for these systems to derive some of the efficiencies of the SEQ approach, they will have to adopt some or all of the system design used by SEQ. We have elaborated on this at length in [SLR96, Ses96].

5 Related Research

Research work directed at modeling time-series data [SS87, CS92, Sto90] provided initial direction to our efforts. The model of a time-series in [SS87] is similar to ours, and an SQL-like language was also proposed; implementation issues were discussed in the context of how the model could be mapped to a relational data model.The Tangram Stream Processor [Sto90] uses transducers and stream processing to query sequences in a logic programming context; there are many similarities between the stream processing ideas in this work and in SEQ. The dual nature of sequences (Positional versus Record-Oriented) is recognized by the temporal query language of [WJS93]. The extensive work on temporal database modeling, query languages, and query processing [TCG+93] is mostly complementary to our work, because it involves changes to relations and to SQL [TSQL94]. However, it would be interesting to study how time-ordered sequences can be efficiently converted into relations with time-stamps, and vice-versa.

While most object-oriented database proposals include constructors for complex types like lists and arrays [VD91, BDK92], they can either be treated as collections, or manipulated using a primitive set of methods; no facilities for sequence queries are provided. The work described in [Ric92] is an exception, and proposes an algebra based on temporal logic to ask complex queries over lists. There have also been languages proposed to match regular patterns over sequence data [GW92, GJS92], and the proposal of [GJS92] has been implemented as an event recognition system. This work is complementary to ours, since SEQ is oriented to more traditional database queries, and currently does not have powerful pattern-matching capabilities.

6 Conclusions

We have described the design and implementation of the support for sequences in SEQ. The primary contribution of this research is to underscore the importance of algebraic optimization for sequence queries along with a declarative language in which to express them. We have demonstrated the effects of query optimization by means of performance experiments. The PREDATOR system (of which SEQ is a component) supports relational data as well as sequence data, using a novel design paradigm of enhanced abstract data types (E-ADTs). The system implementation based on this paradigm allows sequence and relational queries to interact in a clean and extensible fashion.

We have compared the merits of our approach with the alternative ADT-method approach used by some current systems. If issues like usability and performance are important, our conclusion is that it is inadequate to rely upon procedural methods of a sequence ADT to express queries.

There are many sources of sequence data that will pose future challenges to the system implementation. The most exciting of these are real-time sequences (where the implementation of query evaluation may have to be modified to use one thread to read each real-time sequence), sequences stored on tape (where stream access becomes absolutely critical for performance) and multi-dimensional sequences (where the zooming features may have to be enhanced to allow queries that drill down and up the dimensions). There are also several open research issues in the design of systems based on the E-ADT paradigm, and in extensions of the paradigm to handle optimizations that span data types.

Acknowledgements

The persistent data support for SEQ was built on top of the SHORE storage manager developed at the University of Wisconsin. Mike Zwilling was very patient in tracking down SHORE 'problems' that almost always turned out to be bugs in SEQ. Illustra Information Technologies, Inc. give us a free version of their database and time-series datablade, and free access to their user-support personnel. David DeWitt and Mike Carey gave helpful advice and support during the performance evaluation of SEQ. Kurt Brown, Mike Carey, Joey Hellerstein, Navin Kabra, Jignesh Patel, Kristin Tufte, and Scott Vandenberg provided useful discussions on the subject of E-ADTs .

References

[BDK92] F. Bancilhon, C. Delobel, and P. Kanellakis (eds). Building an Object-Oriented Database System: The Story of O2.. Morgan Kaufmann Publishers, 1992.

[CDF+94] M.J. Carey, D.J. DeWitt, M.J. Franklin, N.E. Hall, M. McAuliffe, J.F. Naughton, D.T. Schuh, M.H. Solomon, C.K. Tan, O. Tsatalos, S. White and M.J. Zwilling. Shoring Up Persistent Objects. In *Proceeding of the ACM SIGMOD Conference on Management of Data*, May 1994.

[CS92] Rakesh Chandra and Arie Segev. Managing Temporal Financial Data in an Extensible Database. In *Proceedings of the International Conference on Very Large Databases(VLDB)*, pages 238–249, 1992.

[DKLPY94] D.J. DeWitt, N. Kabra, J. Luo, J.M. Patel and J. Yu. Client-Server Paradise. In *Proceedings of the International Conference on Very Large Databases (VLDB)*, Santiago, Chile, September 1994.

[MIM94] Logical Information Machines. MIM User Manual. 6869 Marshall Road, Dexter, MI 48130.

[GJS92] N.H. Gehani, H.V. Jagadish, and O. Shmueli. Composite Event Specification in Active Databases: Model and Implementation. In *Proceedings of the International Conference on Very Large Databases(VLDB)*, pages 327-338, 1992.

[GW92] S. Ginsburg and X. Wang. Pattern Matching by Rs-operations: Towards a Unified Approach to Querying Sequenced Data. In *Proceeding of the ACM SIGMOD Conference on Management of Data*, 1992.

[Ill94] Illustra Information Technologies, Inc. Illustra User's Guide, June 1994. 1111 Broadway, Suite 2000, Oakland, CA 94607.

[Ric92] Joel Richardson. Supporting Lists in a Data Model. In *Proceedings of the International Conference on Very Large Databases(VLDB)*, pages 127–138, 1992.

[SLR96] Praveen Seshadri, Miron Livny and Raghu Ramakrishnan. Design and Implementation of a Sequence Database. Technical Report. *University of Wisconsin, CS-Dept*, 1996.

[Ses96] Praveen Seshadri. Management of Sequence Data. Ph.D. Thesis. *University of Wisconsin, CS-Dept*, 1996.

[SLR95] Praveen Seshadri, Miron Livny and Raghu Ramakrishnan. SEQ: A Model for Sequence Databases. In *Proceedings of the IEEE Conference on Data Engineering*, March 1995.

[SLR94] Praveen Seshadri, Miron Livny and Raghu Ramakrishnan. Sequence Query Processing. In *Proceeding of the ACM SIGMOD Conference on Management of Data*, pages 430-441, May 1994.

[SS87] Arie Segev and Arie Shoshani. Logical Modeling of Temporal Data. In *Proceedings of ACM SIGMOD '87 International Conference on Management of Data, San Francisco, CA*, pages 454–466, 1987.

[Sto86] Michael Stonebraker. Inclusion of New Types in Relational Data Base Systems. In *Proceedings of the IEEE Conference on Data Engineering*, pages 262-269, 1986.

[Sto90] D. Stott Parker. Stream Data Analysis in Prolog. In *The Practice of Prolog*, Chapter 8, MIT Press, 1990.

[TCG+93] A. Tansel, J. Clifford, S. Gadia, S. Jajodia, A. Segev, R. Snodgrass (eds). Temporal Databases, Theory, Design and Implementation. Benjamin/Cummings Publishing Company, 1993.

[TSQL94] TSQL2 Language Design Committee. TSQL2 Language Specification. In *ACM SIGMOD Record*, 23, No.1, pages 65–86, March 1994.

[VD91] S.L. Vandenberg and D.J. DeWitt. Algebraic Spport for Complex Objects with Arrays, Identity, and Inheritance. In *Proceedings of ACM SIGMOD '91 International Conference on Management of Data*, pages 158–167, 1991.

[WJS93] Sean X. Wang, Sushil Jajodia, and V.S. Subrahmanian. Temporal Modules: An Approach Toward Federated Temporal Databases. In *Proceedings of ACM SIGMOD '93 International Conference on Management of Data, Washington, DC*, pages 227–237, 1993.

Eddies: Continuously Adaptive Query Processing

Ron Avnur Joseph M. Hellerstein
University of California, Berkeley
avnur@cohera.com, jmh@cs.berkeley.edu

Abstract

In large federated and shared-nothing databases, resources can exhibit widely fluctuating characteristics. Assumptions made at the time a query is submitted will rarely hold throughout the duration of query processing. As a result, traditional static query optimization and execution techniques are ineffective in these environments.

In this paper we introduce a query processing mechanism called an *eddy*, which continuously reorders operators in a query plan as it runs. We characterize the *moments of symmetry* during which pipelined joins can be easily reordered, and the *synchronization barriers* that require inputs from different sources to be coordinated. By combining eddies with appropriate join algorithms, we merge the optimization and execution phases of query processing, allowing each tuple to have a flexible ordering of the query operators. This flexibility is controlled by a combination of fluid dynamics and a simple learning algorithm. Our initial implementation demonstrates promising results, with eddies performing nearly as well as a static optimizer/executor in static scenarios, and providing dramatic improvements in dynamic execution environments.

1 Introduction

There is increasing interest in query engines that run at unprecedented scale, both for widely-distributed information resources, and for massively parallel database systems. We are building a system called Telegraph, which is intended to run queries over all the data available on line. A key requirement of a large-scale system like Telegraph is that it function robustly in an unpredictable and constantly fluctuating environment. This unpredictability is endemic in large-scale systems, because of increased complexity in a number of dimensions:

Hardware and Workload Complexity: In wide-area environments, variabilities are commonly observable in the bursty performance of servers and networks [UFA98]. These systems often serve large communities of users whose aggregate behavior can be hard to predict, and the hardware mix in the wide area is quite heterogeneous. Large clusters of computers can exhibit similar performance variations, due to a mix of user requests and heterogeneous hardware evolution. Even in totally homogeneous environments, hardware performance can be unpredictable: for example, the outer tracks of a disk can exhibit almost twice the bandwidth of inner tracks [Met97].

Data Complexity: Selectivity estimation for static alphanumeric data sets is fairly well understood, and there has been initial work on estimating statistical properties of static sets of data with complex types [Aok99] and methods [BO99]. But federated data often comes without any statistical summaries, and complex non-alphanumeric data types are now widely in use both in object-relational databases and on the web. In these scenarios – and even in traditional static relational databases – selectivity estimates are often quite inaccurate.

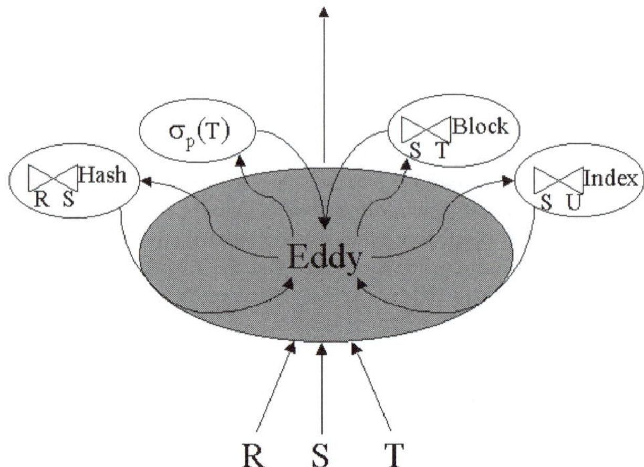

Figure 1: An eddy in a pipeline. Data flows into the eddy from input relations R, S and T. The eddy routes tuples to operators; the operators run as independent threads, returning tuples to the eddy. The eddy sends a tuple to the output only when it has been handled by all the operators. The eddy adaptively chooses an order to route each tuple through the operators.

User Interface Complexity: In large-scale systems, many queries can run for a very long time. As a result, there is interest in Online Aggregation and other techniques that allow users to "Control" properties of queries while they execute, based on refining approximate results [HAC$^+$99].

For all of these reasons, we expect query processing parameters to change significantly over time in Telegraph, typically many times during a single query. As a result, it is not appropriate to use the traditional architecture of optimizing a query and then executing a static query plan: this approach does not adapt to intra-query fluctuations. Instead, for these environments we want query execution plans to be reoptimized regularly during the course of query processing, allowing the system to adapt dynamically to fluctuations in computing resources, data characteristics, and user preferences.

In this paper we present a query processing operator called an *eddy*, which continuously reorders the application of pipelined operators in a query plan, on a tuple-by-tuple basis. An eddy is an n-ary tuple router interposed between n data sources and a set of query processing operators; the eddy encapsulates the ordering of the operators by routing tuples through them dynamically (Figure 1). Because the eddy observes tuples entering and exiting the pipelined operators, it can adaptively change its routing to effect different operator orderings. In this paper we present initial experimental results demonstrating the viability of eddies: they can indeed reorder effectively in the face of changing selectivities and costs, and provide benefits in the case of delayed data sources as well.

Reoptimizing a query execution pipeline on the fly requires significant care in maintaining query execution state. We highlight query processing stages called *moments of symmetry*, during which operators can be easily reordered. We also describe *synchronization barriers* in certain join algorithms that can restrict performance to the rate of the slower input. Join algorithms with frequent moments of symmetry and adaptive or non-existent barriers are thus especially attractive in the Telegraph environment. We observe that the Ripple Join family [HH99] provides efficiency, frequent moments of symmetry, and adaptive or nonexistent barriers for equijoins and nonequijoins alike.

The eddy architecture is quite simple, obviating the need for traditional cost and selectivity estimation, and simplifying the logic of plan enumeration. Eddies represent our first step in a larger attempt to do away with traditional optimizers entirely, in the hope of providing both run-time adaptivity and a reduction in code complexity. In this paper we focus on continuous operator reordering in a single-site query processor; we leave other optimization issues to our discussion of future work.

1.1 Run-Time Fluctuations

Three properties can vary during query processing: the costs of operators, their selectivities, and the rates at which tuples arrive from the inputs. The first and third issues commonly occur in wide area environments, as discussed in the literature [AFTU96, UFA98, IFF+99]. These issues may become more common in cluster (shared-nothing) systems as they "scale out" to thousands of nodes or more [Bar99].

Run-time variations in selectivity have not been widely discussed before, but occur quite naturally. They commonly arise due to correlations between predicates and the order of tuple delivery. For example, consider an employee table clustered by ascending age, and a selection `salary > 100000`; age and salary are often strongly correlated. Initially the selection will filter out most tuples delivered, but that selectivity rate will change as ever-older employees are scanned. Selectivity over time can also depend on performance fluctuations: e.g., in a parallel DBMS clustered relations are often horizontally partitioned across disks, and the rate of production from various partitions may change over time depending on performance characteristics and utilization of the different disks. Finally, Online Aggregation systems explicitly allow users to control the order in which tuples are delivered based on data preferences [RRH99], resulting in similar effects.

1.2 Architectural Assumptions

Telegraph is intended to efficiently and flexibly provide both distributed query processing across sites in the wide area, and parallel query processing in a large shared-nothing cluster. In this paper we narrow our focus somewhat to concentrate on the initial, already difficult problem of run-time operator reordering in a single-site query executor; that is, changing the effective order or "shape" of a pipelined query plan tree in the face of changes in performance.

In our discussion we will assume that some initial query plan tree will be constructed during parsing by a naive *pre-optimizer*. This optimizer need not exercise much judgement since we will be reordering the plan tree on the fly. However by constructing a query plan it must choose a spanning tree of the query graph (i.e. a set of table-pairs to join) [KBZ86], and algorithms for each of the joins. We will return to the choice of join algorithms in Section 2, and defer to Section 6 the discussion of changing the spanning tree and join algorithms during processing.

We study a standard single-node object-relational query processing system, with the added capability of opening scans and indexes from external data sets. This is becoming a very common base architecture, available in many of the commercial object-relational systems (e.g., IBM DB2 UDB [RPK+99], Informix Dynamic Server UDO [SBH98]) and in federated database systems (e.g., Cohera [HSC99]). We will refer to these non-resident tables as *external tables*. We make no assumptions limiting the scale of external sources, which may be arbitrarily large. External tables present many of the dynamic challenges described above: they can reside over a wide-area network, face bursty utilization, and offer very minimal information on costs and statistical properties.

1.3 Overview

Before introducing eddies, in Section 2 we discuss the properties of query processing algorithms that allow (or disallow) them to be frequently reordered. We then present the eddy architecture, and describe how it allows for extreme flexibility in operator ordering (Section 3). Section 4 discusses policies for controlling tuple flow in an eddy. A variety of experiments in Section 4 illustrate the robustness of eddies in both static and dynamic environments, and raise some questions for future work. We survey related work in Section 5, and in Section 6 lay out a research program to carry this work forward.

2 Reorderability of Plans

A basic challenge of run-time reoptimization is to reorder pipelined query processing operators while they are in flight. To change a query plan on the fly, a great deal of state in the various operators has to be considered, and arbitrary changes can require significant processing and code complexity to guarantee correct results. For example, the state maintained by an operator like hybrid hash join [DKO+84] can grow as large as the size of an input relation, and require modification or recomputation if the plan is reordered while the state is being constructed.

By constraining the scenarios in which we reorder operators, we can keep this work to a minimum. Before describing eddies, we study the state management of various join algorithms; this discussion motivates the eddy design, and forms the basis of our approach for reoptimizing cheaply and continuously. As a philosophy, *we favor adaptivity over best-case performance*. In a highly variable environment, the best-case scenario rarely exists for a significant length of time. So we will sacrifice marginal improvements in idealized query processing algorithms when they prevent frequent, efficient reoptimization.

2.1 Synchronization Barriers

Binary operators like joins often capture significant state. A particular form of state used in such operators relates to the interleaving of requests for tuples from different inputs.

As an example, consider the case of a merge join on two sorted, duplicate-free inputs. During processing, the next tuple is always consumed from the relation whose last tuple had the lower value. This significantly constrains the order in which tuples can be consumed: as an extreme example, consider the case of a slowly-delivered external relation slowlow with many low values in its join column, and a high-bandwidth but large local relation fasthi with only high values in its join column – the processing of fasthi is postponed for a long time while consuming many tuples from slowlow. Using terminology from parallel programming, we describe this phenomenon as a *synchronization barrier*: one table-scan waits until the other table-scan produces a value larger than any seen before.

In general, barriers limit concurrency – and hence performance – when two tasks take different amounts of time to complete (i.e., to "arrive" at the barrier). Recall that concurrency arises even in single-site query engines, which can simultaneously carry out network I/O, disk I/O, and computation. Thus it is desirable to minimize the overhead of synchronization barriers in a dynamic (or even static but heterogeneous) performance environment. Two issues affect the overhead of barriers in a plan: the frequency of barriers, and the gap between arrival times of the two inputs at the barrier. We will see in upcoming discussion that barriers can often be avoided or tuned by using appropriate join algorithms.

2.2 Moments of Symmetry

Note that the synchronization barrier in merge join is stated in an order-independent manner: it does not distinguish between the inputs based on any property other than the data they deliver. Thus merge join is often described as a symmetric operator, since its two inputs are treated uniformly[1]. This is not the case for many other join algorithms. Consider the traditional nested-loops join, for example. The "outer" relation in a nested-loops join is synchronized with the "inner" relation, but not vice versa: after each tuple (or block of tuples) is consumed from the outer relation, a barrier is set until a full scan of the inner is completed. For asymmetric operators like nested-loops join, performance benefits can often be obtained by reordering the inputs.

When a join algorithm reaches a barrier, it has declared the end of a scheduling dependency between its two input relations. In such cases, the order of the inputs to the join can often be changed without modifying any state in the join; when this is true, we refer to the barrier as a *moment of symmetry*. Let us return to the example of a nested-loops join, with outer relation R and inner relation S. At a barrier, the join has completed a full inner loop, having joined each tuple in a subset of R with every tuple in S. Reordering the inputs at this point can be done without affecting the join algorithm, as long as

[1] If there are duplicates in a merge join, the duplicates are handled by an asymmetric but usually small nested loop. For purposes of exposition, we can ignore this detail here.

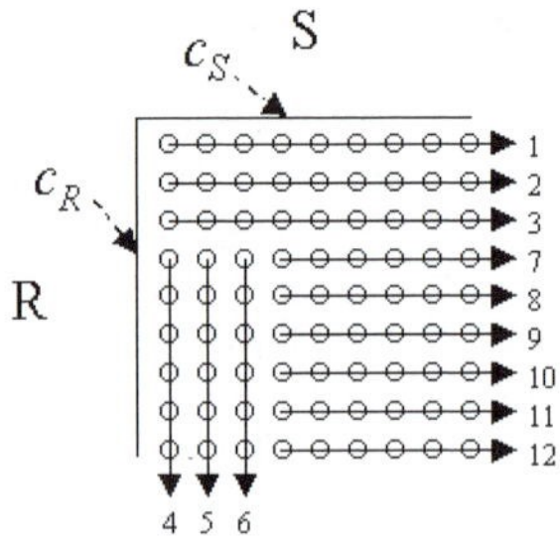

Figure 2: Tuples generated by a nested-loops join, reordered at two moments of symmetry. Each axis represents the tuples of the corresponding relation, in the order they are delivered by an access method. The dots represent tuples generated by the join, some of which may be eliminated by the join predicate. The numbers correspond to the barriers reached, in order. c_R and c_S are the cursor positions maintained by the corresponding inputs at the time of the reorderings.

the iterator producing R notes its current cursor position c_R. In that case, the new "outer" loop on S begins rescanning by fetching the first tuple of S, and R is scanned from c_R to the end. This can be repeated indefinitely, joining S tuples with all tuples in R from position c_R to the end. Alternatively, at the end of some loop over R (i.e. at a moment of symmetry), the order of inputs can be swapped again by remembering the current position of S, and repeatedly joining the next tuple in R (starting at c_R) with tuples from S between c_S and the end. Figure 2 depicts this scenario, with two changes of ordering. Some operators like the pipelined hash join of [WA91] have no barriers whatsoever. These operators are in constant symmetry, since the processing of the two inputs is totally decoupled.

Moments of symmetry allow reordering of the inputs to a single binary operator. But we can generalize this, by noting that since joins commute, a tree of $n-1$ binary joins can be viewed as a single n-ary join. One could easily implement a doubly-nested-loops join operator over relations R, S and T, and it would have moments of complete symmetry at the end of each loop of S. At that point, all three inputs could be reordered (say to T then R then S) with a straightforward extension to the discussion above: a cursor would be recorded for each input, and each loop would go from the recorded cursor position to the end of the input.

The same effect can be obtained in a binary implementation with two operators, by swapping the positions of binary operators: effectively the plan tree transformation would go in steps, from $(R \bowtie_1 S) \bowtie_2 T$ to $(R \bowtie_2 T) \bowtie_1 S$ and then to $(T \bowtie_2 R) \bowtie_1 S$. This approach treats an operator and its right-hand input as a unit (e.g., the unit $[\bowtie_2 T]$), and swaps units; the idea has been used previously in static query optimization schemes [IK84, KBZ86, Hel98]. Viewing the situation in this manner, we can naturally consider reordering multiple joins and their inputs, even if the join algorithms are different. In our query $(R \bowtie_1 S) \bowtie_2 T$, we need $[\bowtie_1 S]$ and $[\bowtie_2 T]$ to be mutually commutative, but do not require them to be the same join algorithm. We discuss the commutativity of join algorithms further in Section 2.2.2.

Note that the combination of commutativity and moments of symmetry allows for very aggressive reordering of a plan tree. A single n-ary operator representing a reorderable plan tree is therefore an attractive abstraction, since it encapsulates any ordering that may be subject to change. We will exploit this abstraction directly, by interposing an n-ary tuple router (an "eddy") between the input tables and the join operators.

2.2.1 Joins and Indexes

Nested-loops joins can take advantage of indexes on the inner relation, resulting in a fairly efficient pipelining join algorithm. An index nested-loops join (henceforth an "index join") is inherently asymmetric, since one input relation has been pre-indexed. Even when indexes exist on both inputs, changing the choice of inner and outer relation "on the fly" is problematic[2]. Hence for the purposes of reordering, it is simpler to think of an index join as a kind of unary selection operator on the unindexed input (as in the join of S and U in Figure 1). The only distinction between an index join and a selection is that – with respect to the unindexed relation – the selectivity of the join node may be greater than 1. Although one cannot swap the inputs to a single index join, one can reorder an index join and its indexed relation as a unit among other operators in a plan tree. Note that the logic for indexes can be applied to external tables that require bindings to be passed; such tables may be gateways to, e.g., web pages with forms, GIS index systems, LDAP servers and so on [HKWY97, FMLS99].

2.2.2 Physical Properties, Predicates, Commutativity

Clearly, a pre-optimizer's choice of an index join algorithm constrains the possible join orderings. In the n-ary join view, an ordering constraint must be imposed so that the unindexed join input is ordered before (but not necessarily directly before) the indexed input. This constraint arises because of a *physical property* of an input relation: indexes can be probed but not scanned, and hence cannot appear before their corresponding probing tables. Similar but more complex constraints can arise in preserving the ordered inputs to a merge join (i.e., preserving "interesting orders").

The applicability of certain join algorithms raises additional constraints. Many join algorithms work only for equijoins, and will not work on other joins like Cartesian products. Such algorithms constrain reorderings on the plan tree as well, since they always require all relations mentioned in their equijoin predicates to be handled before them. In this paper, we consider ordering constraints to be an inviolable aspect of a plan tree, and we ensure that they always hold. In Section 6 we sketch initial ideas on relaxing this requirement, by considering multiple join algorithms and query graph spanning trees.

2.2.3 Join Algorithms and Reordering

In order for an eddy to be most effective, we favor join algorithms with frequent moments of symmetry, adaptive or nonexistent barriers, and minimal ordering constraints: these algorithms offer the most opportunities for reoptimization. In [AH99] we summarize the salient properties of a variety of join algorithms. Our desire to avoid blocking rules out the use of hybrid hash join, and our desire to minimize ordering constraints and barriers excludes merge joins. Nested loops joins have infrequent moments of symmetry and imbalanced barriers, making them undesirable as well.

The other algorithms we consider are based on frequently-symmetric versions of traditional iteration, hashing and indexing schemes, i.e., the Ripple Joins [HH99]. Note that the original pipelined hash join of [WA91] is a constrained version of the hash ripple join. The external hashing extensions of [UF99, IFF$^+$99] are directly applicable to the hash ripple join, and [HH99] treats index joins as a special case as well. For non-equijoins, the block ripple join algorithm is effective, having frequent moments of symmetry, particularly at the beginning of processing [HH99]. Figure 3 illustrates block, index and hash ripple joins; the reader is referred to [HH99, IFF$^+$99, UF99] for detailed discussions of these algorithms and their variants. These algorithms are adaptive without sacrificing much performance: [UF99] and [IFF$^+$99] demonstrate scalable versions of hash ripple join that perform competitively with hybrid hash join in the static case; [HH99] shows that while block ripple join can be less efficient than nested-loops join, it arrives at moments of symmetry much more frequently than nested-loops joins, especially in early stages of processing. In [AH99] we discuss the memory overheads of these adaptive algorithms, which can be larger than standard join algorithms.

Ripple joins have moments of symmetry at each "corner" of a rectangular ripple in Figure 3, i.e., whenever a prefix of the input stream R has been joined with all tuples in a prefix of input stream S and vice versa. For hash ripple joins and index joins, this scenario occurs between each consecutive tuple consumed from a scanned input. Thus ripple joins offer very frequent moments of symmetry.

Ripple joins are attractive with respect to barriers as well. Ripple joins were designed to allow changing rates for each input; this was originally used to *proactively* expend more processing on the input relation with more statistical influence on intermediate results. However, the same mechanism allows *reactive* adaptivity in the wide-area scenario: a barrier is reached at each corner, and the next corner can adaptively reflect the relative rates of the two inputs. For the block ripple join, the next corner is chosen upon reaching the previous corner; this can be done adaptively to reflect the relative rates of the two inputs over time.

The ripple join family offers attractive adaptivity features at a modest overhead in performance and memory footprint. Hence they fit well with our philosophy of sacrificing marginal speed for adaptability, and we focus on these algorithms in Telegraph.

3 Rivers and Eddies

The above discussion allows us to consider easily reordering query plans at moments of symmetry. In this section we proceed to describe the eddy mechanism for implementing reordering in a natural manner during query processing. The techniques we describe can be used with any operators, but algorithms with frequent moments of symmetry allow for more frequent reoptimization. Before discussing eddies, we first introduce our basic query processing environment.

3.1 River

We implemented eddies in the context of River [AAT$^+$99], a shared-nothing parallel query processing framework that dy-

[2] In unclustered indexes, the index ordering is not the same as the scan ordering. Thus after a reordering of the inputs it is difficult to ensure that – using the terminology of Section 2.2 – lookups on the index of the new "inner" relation R produce only tuples between c_R and the end of R.

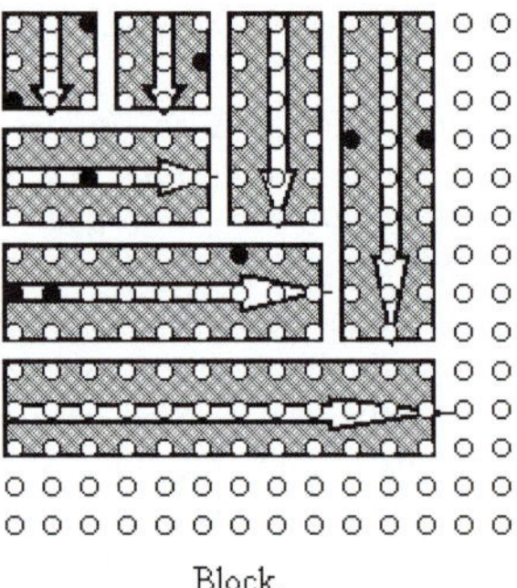

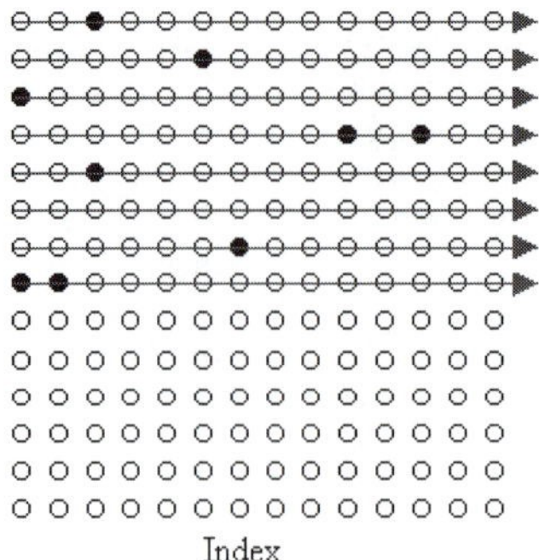

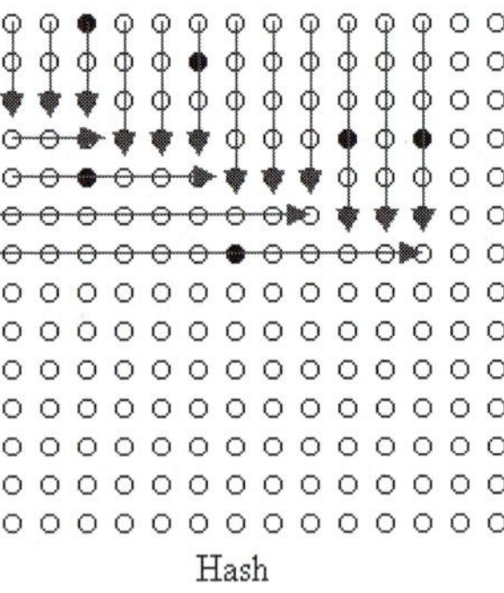

Figure 3: Tuples generated by block, index, and hash ripple join. In block ripple, all tuples are generated by the join, but some may be eliminated by the join predicate. The arrows for index and hash ripple join represent the *logical* portion of the cross-product space checked so far; these joins only expend work on tuples satisfying the join predicate (black dots). In the hash ripple diagram, one relation arrives 3× faster than the other.

namically adapts to fluctuations in performance and workload. River has been used to robustly produce near-record performance on I/O-intensive benchmarks like parallel sorting and hash joins, despite heterogeneities and dynamic variability in hardware and workloads across machines in a cluster. For more details on River's adaptivity and parallelism features, the interested reader is referred to the original paper on the topic [AAT+99]. In Telegraph, we intend to leverage the adaptability of River to allow for dynamic shifting of load (both query processing and data delivery) in a shared-nothing parallel environment. But in this paper we restrict ourselves to basic (single-site) features of eddies; discussions of eddies in parallel rivers are deferred to Section 6.

Since we do not discuss parallelism here, a very simple overview of the River framework suffices. River is a dataflow query engine, analogous in many ways to Gamma [DGS+90], Volcano [Gra90] and commercial parallel database engines, in which "iterator"-style *modules* (query operators) communicate via a fixed dataflow graph (a query plan). Each module runs as an independent thread, and the edges in the graph correspond to finite message queues. When a producer and consumer run at differing rates, the faster thread may block on the queue waiting for the slower thread to catch up. As in [UFA98], River is multi-threaded and can exploit barrier-free algorithms by reading from various inputs at independent rates. The River implementation we used derives from the work on Now-Sort [AAC+97], and features efficient I/O mechanisms including pre-fetching scans, avoidance of operating system buffering, and high-performance user-level networking.

3.1.1 Pre-Optimization

Although we will use eddies to reorder tables among joins, a heuristic pre-optimizer must choose how to initially pair off relations into joins, with the constraint that each relation participates in only one join. This corresponds to choosing a spanning tree of a query graph, in which nodes represent relations and edges represent binary joins [KBZ86]. One reasonable heuristic for picking a spanning tree forms a chain of cartesian products across any tables known to be very small (to handle "star schemas" when base-table cardinality statistics are available); it then picks arbitrary equijoin edges (on the assumption that they are relatively low selectivity), followed by as many arbitrary non-equijoin edges as required to complete a spanning tree.

Given a spanning tree of the query graph, the pre-optimizer needs to choose join algorithms for each edge. Along each equijoin edge it can use either an index join if an index is available, or a hash ripple join. Along each non-equijoin edge it can use a block ripple join.

These are simple heuristics that we use to allow us to focus on our initial eddy design; in Section 6 we present initial ideas on making spanning tree and algorithm decisions adaptively.

3.2 An Eddy in the River

An eddy is implemented via a module in a river containing an arbitrary number of input relations, a number of participating unary and binary modules, and a single output relation (Figure 1)[3]. An eddy encapsulates the scheduling of its participating operators; tuples entering the eddy can flow through its operators in a variety of orders.

In essence, an eddy explicitly merges multiple unary and binary operators into a single n-ary operator within a query plan, based on the intuition from Section 2.2 that symmetries can be easily captured in an n-ary operator. An eddy module maintains a fixed-sized buffer of tuples that are to be processed by one or more operators. Each operator participating in the eddy has one or two inputs that are fed tuples by the eddy, and an output stream that returns tuples to the eddy. Eddies are so named because of this circular data flow within a river.

A tuple entering an eddy is associated with a tuple descriptor containing a vector of *Ready* bits and *Done* bits, which indicate respectively those operators that are elgibile to process the tuple, and those that have already processed the tuple. The eddy module ships a tuple only to operators for which the corresponding Ready bit turned on. After processing the tuple, the operator returns it to the eddy, and the corresponding Done bit is turned on. If all the Done bits are on, the tuple is sent to the eddy's output; otherwise it is sent to another eligible operator for continued processing.

[3]Nothing prevents the use of n-ary operators with $n > 2$ in an eddy, but since implementations of these are atypical in database query processing we do not discuss them here.

When an eddy receives a tuple from one of its inputs, it zeroes the Done bits, and sets the Ready bits appropriately. In the simple case, the eddy sets all Ready bits on, signifying that any ordering of the operators is acceptable. When there are ordering constraints on the operators, the eddy turns on only the Ready bits corresponding to operators that can be executed initially. When an operator returns a tuple to the eddy, the eddy turns on the Ready bit of any operator eligible to process the tuple. Binary operators generate output tuples that correspond to combinations of input tuples; in these cases, the Done bits and Ready bits of the two input tuples are ORed. In this manner an eddy preserves the ordering constraints while maximizing opportunities for tuples to follow different possible orderings of the operators.

Two properties of eddies merit comment. First, note that eddies represent the full class of bushy trees corresponding to the set of join nodes – it is possible, for instance, that two pairs of tuples are combined independently by two different join modules, and then routed to a third join to perform the 4-way concatenation of the two binary records. Second, note that eddies do not constrain reordering to moments of symmetry across the eddy as a whole. A given operator must carefully refrain from fetching tuples from certain inputs until its next moment of symmetry – e.g., a nested-loops join would not fetch a new tuple from the current outer relation until it finished rescanning the inner. But there is no requirement that *all* operators in the eddy be at a moment of symmetry when this occurs; just the operator that is fetching a new tuple. Thus eddies are quite flexible both in the shapes of trees they can generate, and in the scenarios in which they can logically reorder operators.

4 Routing Tuples in Eddies

An eddy module directs the flow of tuples from the inputs through the various operators to the output, providing the flexibility to allow each tuple to be routed individually through the operators. The routing policy used in the eddy determines the efficiency of the system. In this section we study some promising initial policies; we believe that this is a rich area for future work. We outline some of the remaining questions in Section 6.

An eddy's tuple buffer is implemented as a priority queue with a flexible prioritization scheme. An operator is always given the highest-priority tuple in the buffer that has the corresponding Ready bit set. For simplicity, we start by considering a very simple priority scheme: tuples enter the eddy with low priority, and when they are returned to the eddy from an operator they are given high priority. This simple priority scheme ensures that tuples flow completely through the eddy before new tuples are consumed from the inputs, ensuring that the eddy does not become "clogged" with new tuples.

4.1 Experimental Setup

In order to illustrate how eddies work, we present some initial experiments in this section; we pause briefly here to describe our experimental setup. All our experiments were run on a single-processor Sun Ultra-1 workstation running Solaris 2.6, with 160 MB of RAM. We used the Euphrates implementation of River [AAT+99]. We synthetically generated relations as in Table 1, with 100 byte tuples in each relation.

To allow us to experiment with costs and selectivities of selections, our selection modules are (artificially) implemented

Table	Cardinality	values in column a
R	10,000	500 - 5500
S	80,000	0 - 5000
T	10,000	N/A
U	50,000	N/A

Table 1: Cardinalities of tables; values are uniformly distributed.

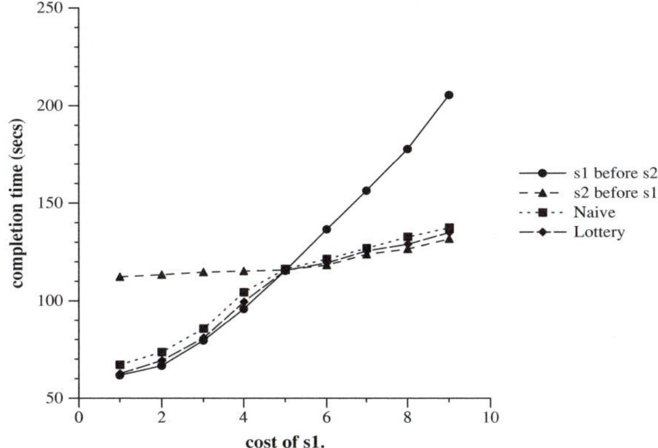

Figure 4: Performance of two 50% selections, $s2$ has cost 5, $s1$ varies across runs.

as spin loops corresponding to their relative costs, followed by a randomized selection decision with the appropriate selectivity. We describe the relative costs of selections in terms of abstract "delay units"; for studying optimization, the absolute number of cycles through a spin loop are irrelevant. We implemented the simplest version of hash ripple join, identical to the original pipelining hash join [WA91]; our implementation here does not exert any statistically-motivated control over disk resource consumption (as in [HH99]). We simulated index joins by doing random I/Os within a file, returning on average the number of matches corresponding to a pre-programmed selectivity. The filesystem cache was allowed to absorb some of the index I/Os after warming up. In order to fairly compare eddies to static plans, we simulate static plans via eddies that enforce a static ordering on tuples (setting Ready bits in the correct order).

4.2 Naive Eddy: Fluid Dynamics and Operator Costs

To illustrate how an eddy works, we consider a very simple single-table query with two expensive selection predicates, under the traditional assumption that no performance or selectivity properties change during execution. Our SQL query is simply the following:

```
SELECT *
  FROM U
 WHERE s1() AND s2();
```

In our first experiment, we wish to see how well a "naive" eddy can account for differences in costs among operators. We run the query multiple times, always setting the cost of $s2$ to 5 delay units, and the selectivities of both selections to 50%. In each run we use a different cost for $s1$, varying it between 1 and 9 delay units across runs. We compare a naive eddy of the two selections against both possible static orderings of

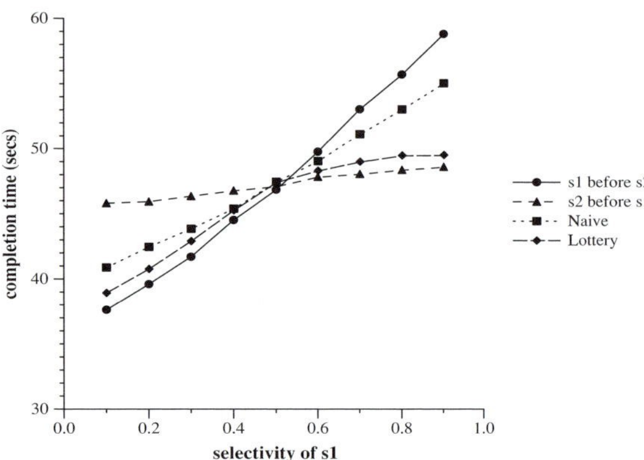

Figure 5: Performance of two selections of cost 5, $s2$ has 50% selectivity, $s1$ varies across runs.

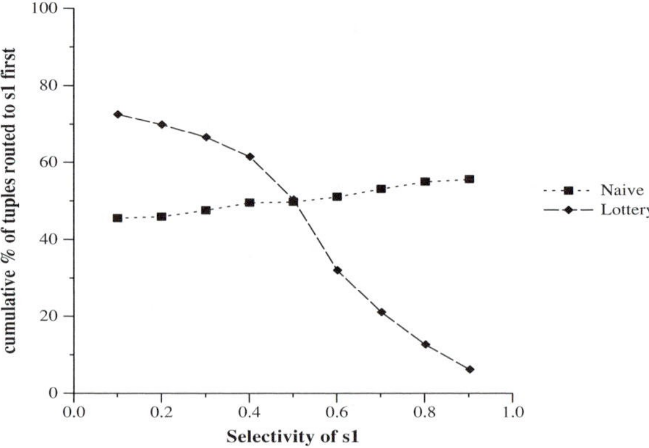

Figure 6: Tuple flow with lottery scheme for the variable-selectivity experiment(Figure 5).

the two selections (and against a "lottery"-based eddy, about which we will say more in Section 4.3.) One might imagine that the flexible routing in the naive eddy would deliver tuples to the two selections equally: half the tuples would flow to $s1$ before $s2$, and half to $s2$ before $s1$, resulting in middling performance over all. Figure 4 shows that this is not the case: the naive eddy nearly matches the better of the two orderings in all cases, without any explicit information about the operators' relative costs.

The naive eddy's effectiveness in this scenario is due to simple fluid dynamics, arising from the different rates of consumption by $s1$ and $s2$. Recall that edges in a River dataflow graph correspond to fixed-size queues. This limitation has the same effect as *back-pressure* in a fluid flow: production along the input to any edge is limited by the rate of consumption at the output. The lower-cost selection (e.g., $s1$ at the left of Figure 4) can consume tuples more quickly, since it spends less time per tuple; as a result the lower-cost operator exerts less back-pressure on the input table. At the same time, the high-cost operator *produces* tuples relatively slowly, so the low-cost operator will rarely be required to consume a high-priority, previously-seen tuple. Thus most tuples are routed to the low-cost operator first, even though the costs are not explicitly exposed or tracked in any way.

4.3 Fast Eddy: Learning Selectivities

The naive eddy works well for handling operators with different costs but equal selectivity. But we have not yet considered differences in selectivity. In our second experiment we keep the costs of the operators constant and equal (5 units), keep the selectivity of $s2$ fixed at 50%, and vary the selectivity of $s1$ across runs. The results in Figure 5 are less encouraging, showing the naive eddy performing as we originally expected, about half-way between the best and worst plans. Clearly our naive priority scheme and the resulting back-pressure are insufficient to capture differences in selectivity.

To resolve this dilemma, we would like our priority scheme to favor operators based on both their consumption and production rate. Note that the consumption (input) rate of an operator is determined by cost alone, while the production (output) rate is determined by a product of cost and selectivity. Since an operator's back-pressure on its input depends largely on its consumption rate, it is not surprising that our naive scheme does not capture differing selectivities.

To track both consumption and production over time, we enhance our priority scheme with a simple learning algorithm implemented via *Lottery Scheduling* [WW94]. Each time the eddy gives a tuple to an operator, it credits the operator one "ticket". Each time the operator returns a tuple to the eddy, one ticket is debited from the eddy's running count for that operator. When an eddy is ready to send a tuple to be processed, it "holds a lottery" among the operators eligible for receiving the tuple. (The interested reader is referred to [WW94] for a simple and efficient implementation of lottery scheduling.) An operator's chance of "winning the lottery" and receiving the tuple corresponds to the count of tickets for that operator, which in turn tracks the relative efficiency of the operator at draining tuples from the system. By routing tuples using this lottery scheme, the eddy tracks ("learns") an ordering of the operators that gives good overall efficiency.

The "lottery" curve in Figures 4 and 5 show the more intelligent lottery-based routing scheme compared to the naive back-pressure scheme and the two static orderings. The lottery scheme handles both scenarios effectively, slightly improving the eddy in the changing-cost experiment, and performing much better than naive in the changing-selectivity experiment.

To explain this a bit further, in Figure 6 we display the percent of tuples that followed the order $s1, s2$ (as opposed to $s2, s1$) in the two eddy schemes; this roughly represents the average ratio of lottery tickets possessed by $s1$ and $s2$ over time. Note that the naive back-pressure policy is barely sensitive to changes in selectivity, and in fact drifts slightly in the wrong direction as the selectivity of $s1$ is increased. By contrast, the lottery-based scheme adapts quite nicely as the selectivity is varied.

In both graphs one can see that when the costs and selectivities are close to equal ($s1 = s2 = 50\%$), the percentage of tuples following the cheaper order is close to 50%. This observation is intuitive, but quite significant. The lottery-based eddy approaches the *cost* of an optimal ordering, but does not concern itself about strictly observing the optimal ordering. Contrast this to earlier work on runtime reoptimization [KD98, UFA98, IFF+99], where a traditional query optimizer runs during processing to determine the optimal plan remnant. By focusing on overall cost rather than on finding the optimal plan, the lottery scheme probabilistically provides nearly optimal performance with much less effort, allowing re-optimization to be done with an extremely lightweight technique that can be executed multiple times for every tuple.

A related observation is that the lottery algorithm gets closer to perfect routing ($y = 0\%$) on the right of Figure 6 than it does ($y = 100\%$) on the left. Yet in the corresponding performance graph (Figure 5), the differences between the lottery-based eddy and the optimal static ordering do not change much in the two settings. This phenomenon is explained by examining the "jeopardy" of making ordering errors in either case. Consider the left side of the graph, where the selectivity of $s1$ is 10%, $s2$ is 50%, and the costs of each are $c = 5$ delay units. Let e be the rate at which tuples are routed erroneously (to $s2$ before $s1$ in this case). Then the expected cost of the query is $(1 - e) \cdot 1.1c + e \cdot 1.5c = .4ec + 1.1c$. By contrast, in the second case where the selectivity of $s1$ is changed to 90%, the expected cost is $(1 - e) \cdot 1.5c + e \cdot 1.9c = .4ec + 1.5c$. Since the jeopardy is higher at 90% selectivity than at 10%, the lottery more aggressively favors the optimal ordering at 90% selectivity than at 10%.

4.4 Joins

We have discussed selections up to this point for ease of exposition, but of course joins are the more common expensive operator in query processing. In this section we study how eddies interact with the pipelining ripple join algorithms. For the moment, we continue to study a static performance environment, validating the ability of eddies to do well even in scenarios where static techniques are most effective.

We begin with a simple 3-table query:

```
SELECT *
  FROM R, S, T
 WHERE R.a = S.a
   AND S.b = T.b
```

In our experiment, we constructed a preoptimized plan with a hash ripple join between R and S, and an index join between S and T. Since our data is uniformly distributed, Table 1 indicates that the selectivity of the RS join is 1.8×10^{-4}; its selectivity *with respect to* S is 180% – i.e., each S tuple entering the join finds 1.8 matching R tuples on average [Hel98]. We artificially set the selectivity of the index join w.r.t. S to be 10% (overall selectivity 1×10^{-5}). Figure 7 shows the relative performance of our two eddy schemes and the two static join orderings. The results echo our results for selections, showing the lottery-based eddy performing nearly optimally, and the naive eddy performing in between the best and worst static plans.

As noted in Section 2.2.1, index joins are very analogous to selections. Hash joins have more complicated and symmetric behavior, and hence merit additional study. Figure 8 presents performance of two hash-ripple-only versions of this query. Our in-memory pipelined hash joins all have the same cost. We change the data in R, S and T so that the selectivity of the ST join w.r.t. S is 20% in one version, and 180% in the other. In all runs, the selectivity of the RS join predicate w.r.t. S is fixed at 100%. As the figure shows, the lottery-based eddy continues to perform nearly optimally.

Figure 9 shows the percent of tuples in the eddy that follow one order or the other in all four join experiments. While the eddy is not strict about following the optimal ordering, it is quite close in the case of the experiment where the hash join should precede the index join. In this case, the relative cost of index join is so high that the jeopardy of choosing it first drives the hash join to nearly always win the lottery.

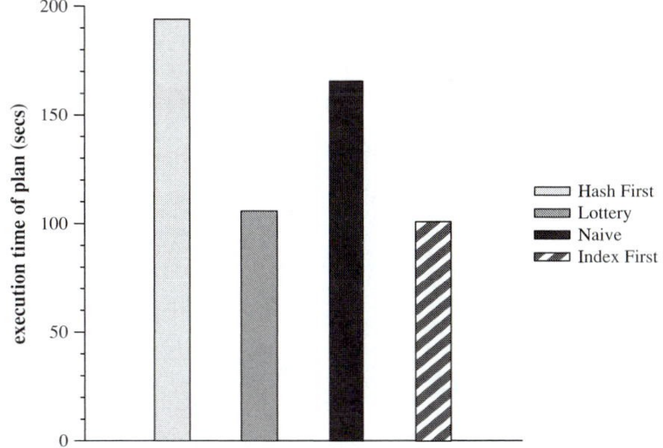

Figure 7: Performance of two joins: a selective Index Join and a Hash Join

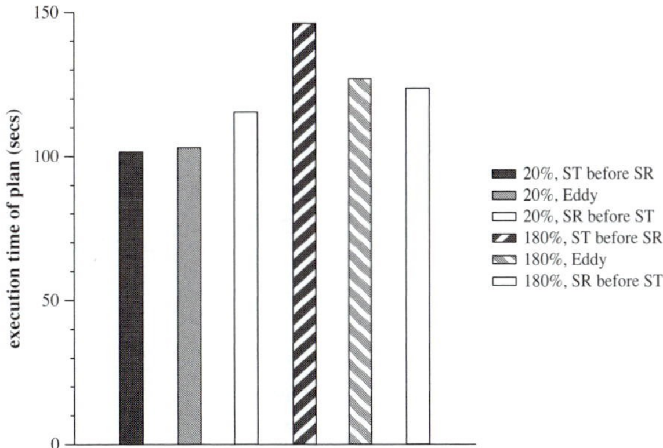

Figure 8: Performance of hash joins $R \bowtie S$ and $S \bowtie T$. $R \bowtie S$ has selectivity 100% w.r.t. S, the selectivity of $S \bowtie T$ w.r.t. S varies between 20% and 180% in the two runs.

4.5 Responding to Dynamic Fluctuations

Eddies should adaptively react over time to the changes in performance and data characteristics described in Section 1.1. The routing schemes described up to this point have not considered how to achieve this. In particular, our lottery scheme weighs all experiences equally: observations from the distant past affect the lottery as much as recent observations. As a result, an operator that earns many tickets early in a query may become so wealthy that it will take a great deal of time for it to lose ground to the top achievers in recent history.

To avoid this, we need to modify our point scheme to forget history to some extent. One simple way to do this is to use a *window* scheme, in which time is partitioned into windows, and the eddy keeps track of two counts for each operator: a number of *banked* tickets, and a number of *escrow* tickets. Banked tickets are used when running a lottery. Escrow tickets are used to measure efficiency during the window. At the beginning of the window, the value of the es-

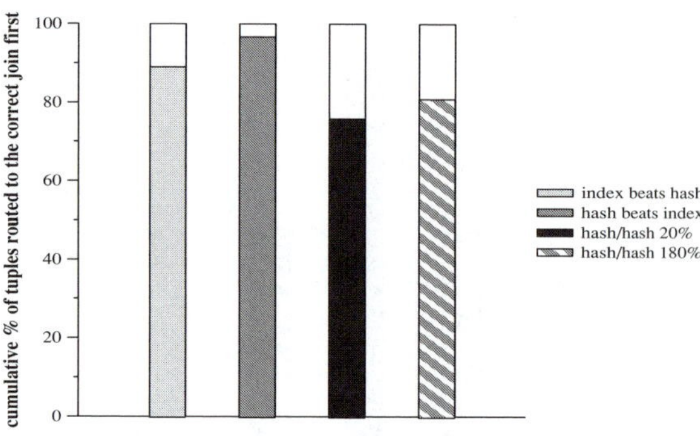

Figure 9: Percent of tuples routed in the optimal order in all of the join experiments.

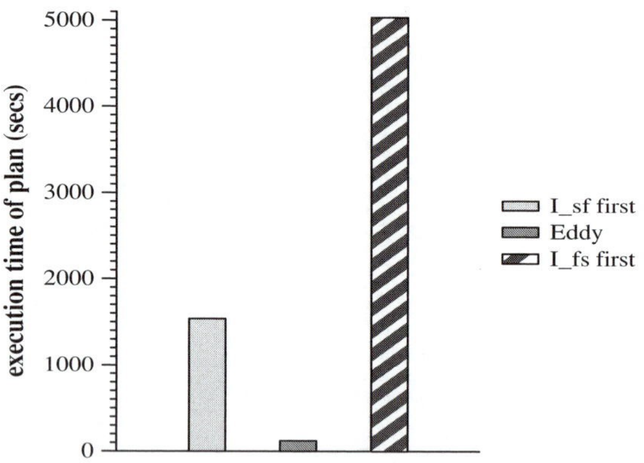

Figure 10: Adapting to changing join costs: performance.

crow account replaces the value of the banked account (i.e., `banked = escrow`), and the escrow account is reset (`es-crow = 0`). This scheme ensures that operators "re-prove themselves" each window.

We consider a scenario of a 3-table equijoin query, where two of the tables are external and used as "inner" relations by index joins. Our third relation has 30,000 tuples. Since we assume that the index servers are remote, we implement the "cost" in our index module as a time delay (i.e., `while (gettimeofday() < x) ;`) rather than a spin loop; this better models the behavior of waiting on an external event like a network response. We have two phases in the experiment: initially, one index (call it I_{fs}) is fast (no time delay) and the other (I_{sf}) is slow (5 seconds per lookup). After 30 seconds we begin the second phase, in which the two indexes swap speeds: the I_{fs} index becomes slow, and I_{sf} becomes fast. Both indexes return a single matching tuple 1% of the time.

Figure 10 shows the performance of both possible static plans, compared with an eddy using a lottery with a window scheme. As we would hope, the eddy is much faster than either static plan. In the first static plan (I_{sf} before I_{fs}), the initial index join in the plan is slow in the first phase, processing only 6 tuples and discarding all of them. In the remainder of the run, the plan quickly discards 99% of the tuples, passing 300 to the (now) expensive second join. In the second static plan (I_{fs} before I_{sf}), the initial join begins fast, processing about 29,000 tuples, and passing about 290 of those to the second (slower) join. After 30 seconds, the second join becomes fast and handles the remainder of the 290 tuples quickly, while the first join slowly processes the remaining 1,000 tuples at 5 seconds per tuple. The eddy outdoes both static plans: in the first phase it behaves identically to the second static plan, consuming 29,000 tuples and queueing 290 for the eddy to pass to I_{sf}. Just after phase 2 begins, the eddy adapts its ordering and passes tuples to I_{sf} – the new fast join – first. As a result, the eddy spends 30 seconds in phase one, and in phase two it has less then 290 tuples queued at I_{sf} (now fast), and only 1,000 tuples to process, only about 10 of which are passed to I_{fs} (now slow).

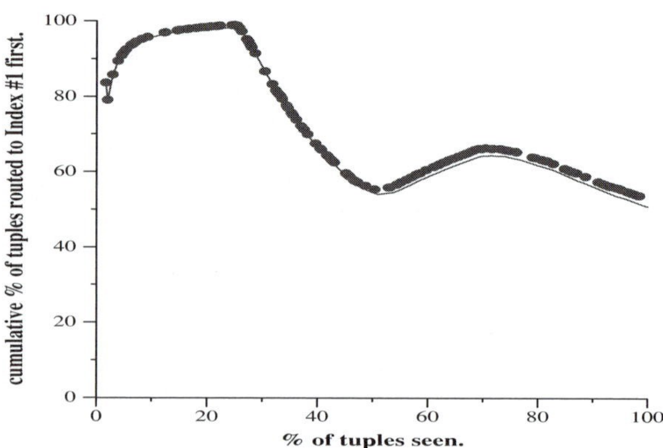

Figure 11: Adapting to changing join costs: tuple movement.

A similar, more controlled experiment illustrates the eddy's adaptability more clearly. Again, we run a three-table join, with two external indexes that return a match 10% of the time. We read 4,000 tuples from the scanned table, and toggle costs between 1 and 100 cost units every 1000 tuples – i.e., three times during the experiment. Figure 11 shows that the eddy adapts correctly, switching orders when the operator costs switch. Since the cost differential is less dramatic here, the jeopardy is lower and the eddy takes a bit longer to adapt. Despite the learning time, the trends are clear – the eddy sends most of the first 1000 tuples to index #1 first, which starts off cheap. It sends most of the second 1000 tuples to index #2 first, causing the overall percentage of tuples to reach about 50%, as reflected by the near-linear drift toward 50% in the second quarter of the graph. This pattern repeats in the third and fourth quarters, with the eddy eventually displaying an even use of the two orderings over time – always favoring the best ordering.

For brevity, we omit here a similar experiment in which we fixed costs and modified selectivity over time. The results were similar, except that changing only the selectivity of two operators results in less dramatic benefits for an adaptive scheme. This can be seen analytically, for two operators of cost c whose selectivites are swapped from low to hi in a manner analogous to our previous experiment. To lower-bound the performance of either static ordering, selectivities should be toggled to their extremes (100% and 0%) for equal amounts of time – so that half the n tuples go through both operators. Either static plan thus takes $nc+1/2nc$ time, whereas an optimal

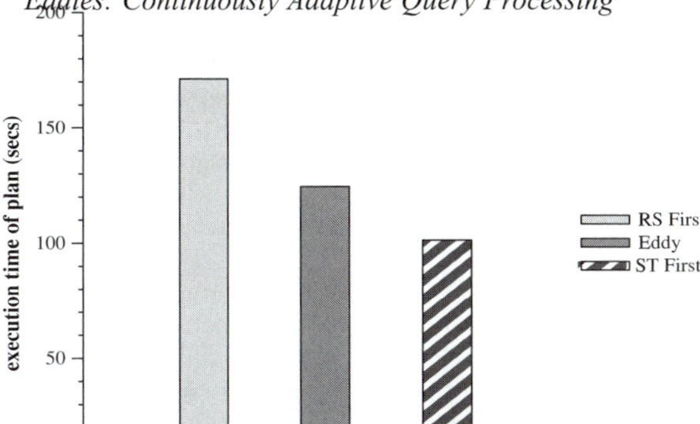

Figure 12: Adapting to an initial delay on R: performance

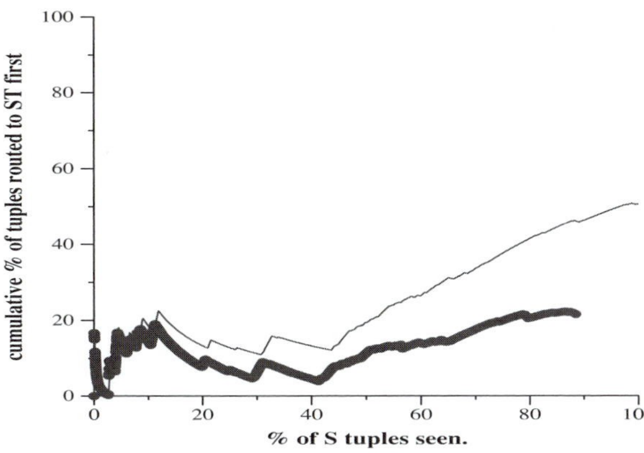

Figure 13: Adapting to an initial delay on R: tuple movement.

dynamic plan takes nc time, a ratio of only 3/2. With more operators, adaptivity to changes in selectivity can become more significant, however.

4.5.1 Delayed Delivery

As a final experiment, we study the case where an input relation suffers from an initial delay, as in [AFTU96, UFA98]. We return to the 3-table query shown in the left of Figure 8, with the RS selectivity at 100%, and the ST selectivity at 20%. We delay the delivery of R by 10 seconds; the results are shown in Figure 12. Unfortunately, we see here that our eddy – even with a lottery and a window-based forgetting scheme – does not adapt to initial delays of R as well as it could. Figure 13 tells some of the story: in the early part of processing, the eddy incorrectly favors the RS join, even though no R tuples are streaming in, and even though the RS join should appear second in a normal execution (Figure 8). The eddy does this because it observes that the RS join does not produce any output tuples when given S tuples. So the eddy awards most S tuples to the RS join initially, which places them in an internal hash table to be subsequently joined with R tuples when they arrive. The ST join is left to fetch and hash T tuples. This wastes resources that could have been spent joining S tuples with T tuples during the delay, and "primes" the RS join to produce a large number of tuples once the Rs begin appearing.

Note that the eddy does far better than pessimally: when R begins producing tuples (at 43.5 on the x axis of Figure 13), the S values bottled up in the RS join burst forth, and the eddy quickly throttles the RS join, allowing the ST join to process most tuples first. This scenario indicates two problems with our implementation. First, our ticket scheme does not capture the growing selectivity inherent in a join with a delayed input. Second, storing tuples inside the hash tables of a single join unnecessarily prevents other joins from processing them; it might be conceivable to hash input tuples within multiple joins, if care were taken to prevent duplicate results from being generated. A solution to the second problem might obviate the need to solve the first; we intend to explore these issues further in future work.

For brevity, we omit here a variation of this experiment, in which we delayed the delivery of S by 10 seconds instead of R. In this case, the delay of S affects both joins identically, and simply slows down the completion time of all plans by about 10 seconds.

5 Related Work

To our knowledge, this paper represents the first general query processing scheme for reordering in-flight operators within a pipeline, though [NWMN99] considers the special case of unary operators. Our characterization of barriers and moments of symmetry also appears to be new, arising as it does from our interest in reoptimizing general pipelines.

Recent papers consider reoptimizing queries at the ends of pipelines [UFA98, KD98, IFF+99], reordering operators only after temporary results are materialized. [IFF+99] observantly notes that this approach dates back to the original INGRES query decomposition scheme [SWK76]. These inter-pipeline techniques are not adaptive in the sense used in traditional control theory (e.g., [Son98]) or machine learning (e.g., [Mit97]); they make decisions without any ongoing feedback from the operations they are to optimize, instead performing static optimizations at coarse-grained intervals in the query plan. One can view these efforts as complementary to our work: eddies can be used to do tuple scheduling within pipelines, and techniques like those of [UFA98, KD98, IFF+99] can be used to reoptimize across pipelines. Of course such a marriage sacrifices the simplicity of eddies, requiring both the traditional complexity of cost estimation and plan enumeration along with the ideas of this paper. There are also significant questions on how best to combine these techniques – e.g., how many materialization operators to put in a plan, which operators to put in which eddy pipelines, etc.

DEC Rdb (subsequently Oracle Rdb) used competition to choose among different access methods [AZ96]. Rdb briefly observed the performance of alternative access methods at runtime, and then fixed a "winner" for the remainder of query execution. This bears a resemblance to sampling for cost estimation (see [BDF+97] for a survey). More distantly related is the work on "parameterized" or "dynamic" query plans, which postpone some optimization decisions until the beginning of query execution [INSS97, GC94].

The initial work on Query Scrambling [AFTU96] studied network unpredictabilities in processing queries over wide-area sources. This work materialized remote data while processing was blocked waiting for other sources, an idea that can be used in concert with eddies. Note that local materialization ameliorates but does not remove barriers: work to be done locally after a barrier can still be quite significant. Later work focused on rescheduling runnable sub-plans during initial delays in delivery [UFA98], but did not attempt to reorder in-flight operators as we do here.

Two out-of-core versions of the pipelined hash join have been proposed recently [IFF+99, UF99]. The X-Join [UF99] enhances the pipelined hash join not only by handling the out-of-core case, but also by exploiting delay time to aggressively match previously-received (and spilled) tuples. We intend to experiment with X-Joins and eddies in future work.

The Control project [HAC+99] studies interactive analysis of massive data sets, using techniques like online aggregation, online reordering and ripple joins. There is a natural synergy between interactive and adaptive query processing; online techniques to pipeline best-effort answers are naturally adaptive to changing performance scenarios. The need for optimizing pipelines in the Control project initially motivated our work on eddies. The Control project [HAC+99] is not explicitly related to the field of control theory [Son98], though eddies appears to link the two in some regards.

The River project [AAT+99] was another main inspiration of this work. River allows modules to work as fast as they can, naturally balancing flow to whichever modules are faster. We carried the River philosophy into the intial back-pressure design of eddies, and intend to return to the parallel load-balancing aspects of the optimization problem in future work.

In addition to commercial projects like those in Section 1.2, there have been numerous research systems for heterogeneous data integration, e.g. [GMPQ+97, HKWY97, IFF+99], etc.

6 Conclusions and Future Work

Query optimization has traditionally been viewed as a coarse-grained, static problem. Eddies are a query processing mechanism that allow fine-grained, adaptive, online optimization. Eddies are particularly beneficial in the unpredictable query processing environments prevalent in massive-scale systems, and in interactive online query processing. They fit naturally with algorithms from the Ripple Join family, which have frequent moments of symmetry and adaptive or non-existent synchronization barriers. Eddies can be used as the sole optimization mechanism in a query processing system, obviating the need for much of the complex code required in a traditional query optimizer. Alternatively, eddies can be used in concert with traditional optimizers to improve adaptability within pipelines. Our initial results indicate that eddies perform well under a variety of circumstances, though some questions remain in improving reaction time and in adaptively choosing join orders with delayed sources. We are sufficiently encouraged by these early results that we are using eddies and rivers as the basis for query processing in the Telegraph system.

In order to focus our energies in this initial work, we have explicitly postponed a number of questions in understanding, tuning, and extending these results. One main challenge is to develop eddy "ticket" policies that can be formally proved to converge quickly to a near-optimal execution in static scenarios, and that adaptively converge when conditions change. This challenge is complicated by considering both selections and joins, including hash joins that "absorb" tuples into their hash tables as in Section 4.5.1. We intend to focus on multiple performance metrics, including time to completion, the rate of output from a plan, and the rate of refinement for online aggregation estimators. We have also begun studying schemes to allow eddies to effectively order dependent predicates, based on reinforcement learning [SB98]. In a related vein, we would like to automatically tune the aggressiveness with which we forget past observations, so that we avoid introducing a tuning knob to adjust window-length or some analogous constant (e.g., a hysteresis factor).

Another main goal is to attack the remaining static aspects of our scheme: the "pre-optimization" choices of spanning tree, join algorithms, and access methods. Following [AZ96], we believe that competition is key here: one can run multiple redundant joins, join algorithms, and access methods, and track their behavior in an eddy, adaptively choosing among them over time. The implementation challenge in that scenario relates to preventing duplicates from being generated, while the efficiency challenge comes in not wasting too many computing resources on unpromising alternatives.

A third major challenge is to harness the parallelism and adaptivity available to us in rivers. Massively parallel systems are reaching their limit of manageability, even as data sizes continue to grow very quickly. Adaptive techniques like eddies and rivers can significantly aid in the manageability of a new generation of massively parallel query processors. Rivers have been shown to adapt gracefully to performance changes in large clusters, spreading query processing load across nodes and spreading data delivery across data sources. Eddies face additional challenges to meet the promise of rivers: in particular, reoptimizing queries with intra-operator parallelism entails repartitioning data, which adds an expense to reordering that was not present in our single-site eddies. An additional complication arises when trying to adaptively adjust the degree of partitioning for each operator in a plan. On a similar note, we would like to explore enhancing eddies and rivers to tolerate failures of sources or of participants in parallel execution.

Finally, we are exploring the application of eddies and rivers to the generic space of dataflow programming, including applications such as multimedia analysis and transcoding, and the composition of scalable, reliable internet services [GWBC99]. Our intent is for rivers to serve as a generic parallel dataflow engine, and for eddies to be the main scheduling mechanism in that environment.

Acknowledgments

Vijayshankar Raman provided much assistance in the course of this work. Remzi Arpaci-Dusseau, Eric Anderson and Noah Treuhaft implemented Euphrates, and helped implement eddies. Mike Franklin asked hard questions and suggested directions for future work. Stuart Russell, Christos Papadimitriou, Alistair Sinclair, Kris Hildrum and Lakshminarayanan Subramanian all helped us focus on formal issues. Thanks to Navin Kabra and Mitch Cherniack for initial discussions on run-time reoptimization, and to the database group at Berkeley for feedback. Stuart Russell suggested the term "eddy".

This work was done while both authors were at UC Berkeley, supported by a grant from IBM Corporation, NSF grant IIS-9802051, and a Sloan Foundation Fellowship. Computing and network resources for this research were provided through NSF RI grant CDA-9401156.

References

[AAC+97] A. C. Arpaci-Dusseau, R. H. Arpaci-Dusseau, D. E. Culler, J. M. Hellerstein, and D. A. Patterson. High-Performance Sorting on Networks of Workstations. In *Proc. ACM-SIGMOD International Conference on Management of Data*, Tucson, May 1997.

[AAT+99] R. H. Arpaci-Dusseau, E. Anderson, N. Treuhaft, D. E. Culler, J. M. Hellerstein, D. A. Patterson, and K. Yelick. Cluster I/O with River: Making the Fast Case Common. In *Sixth Workshop on I/O in Parallel and Distributed Systems (IOPADS '99)*, pages 10–22, Atlanta, May 1999.

[AFTU96] L. Amsaleg, M. J. Franklin, A. Tomasic, and T. Urhan. Scrambling Query Plans to Cope With Unexpected Delays. In *4th International Conference on Parallel and Distributed Information Systems (PDIS)*, Miami Beach, December 1996.

[AH99] R. Avnur and J. M. Hellerstein. Continuous query optimization. Technical Report CSD-99-1078, University of California, Berkeley, November 1999.

[Aok99] P. M. Aoki. How to Avoid Building DataBlades That Know the Value of Everything and the Cost of Nothing. In *11th International Conference on Scientific and Statistical Database Management*, Cleveland, July 1999.

[AZ96] G. Antoshenkov and M. Ziauddin. Query Processing and Optimization in Oracle Rdb. *VLDB Journal*, 5(4):229–237, 1996.

[Bar99] R. Barnes. Scale Out. In *High Performance Transaction Processing Workshop (HPTS '99)*, Asilomar, September 1999.

[BDF+97] D. Barbara, W. DuMouchel, C. Faloutsos, P. J. Haas, J. M. Hellerstein, Y. E. Ioannidis, H. V. Jagadish, T. Johnson, R. T. Ng, V. Poosala, K. A. Ross, and K. C. Sevcik. The New Jersey Data Reduction Report. *IEEE Data Engineering Bulletin*, 20(4), December 1997.

[BO99] J. Boulos and K. Ono. Cost Estimation of User-Defined Methods in Object-Relational Database Systems. *SIGMOD Record*, 28(3):22–28, September 1999.

[DGS+90] D. J. DeWitt, S. Ghandeharizadeh, D. Schneider, A. Bricker, H.-I Hsiao, and R. Rasmussen. The Gamma database machine project. *IEEE Transactions on Knowledge and Data Engineering*, 2(1):44–62, Mar 1990.

[DKO+84] D. J. DeWitt, R. H. Katz, F. Olken, L. D. Shapiro, M. R. Stonebraker, and D. Wood. Implementation Techniques for Main Memory Database Systems. In *Proc. ACM-SIGMOD International Conference on Management of Data*, pages 1–8, Boston, June 1984.

[FMLS99] D. Florescu, I. Manolescu, A. Levy, and D. Suciu. Query Optimization in the Presence of Limited Access Patterns. In *Proc. ACM-SIGMOD International Conference on Management of Data*, Phildelphia, June 1999.

[GC94] G. Graefe and R. Cole. Optimization of Dynamic Query Evaluation Plans. In *Proc. ACM-SIGMOD International Conference on Management of Data*, Minneapolis, 1994.

[GMPQ+97] H. Garcia-Molina, Y. Papakonstantinou, D. Quass, A Rajaraman, Y. Sagiv, J. Ullman, and J. Widom. The TSIMMIS Project: Integration of Heterogeneous Information Sources. *Journal of Intelligent Information Systems*, 8(2):117–132, March 1997.

[Gra90] G. Graefe. Encapsulation of Parallelism in the Volcano Query Processing System. In *Proc. ACM-SIGMOD International Conference on Management of Data*, pages 102–111, Atlantic City, May 1990.

[GWBC99] S. D. Gribble, M. Welsh, E. A. Brewer, and D. Culler. The MultiSpace: an Evolutionary Platform for Infrastructural Services. In *Proceedings of the 1999 Usenix Annual Technical Conference*, Monterey, June 1999.

[HAC+99] J. M. Hellerstein, R. Avnur, A. Chou, C. Hidber, C. Olston, V. Raman, T. Roth, and P. J. Haas. Interactive Data Analysis: The Control Project. *IEEE Computer*, 32(8):51–59, August 1999.

[Hel98] J. M. Hellerstein. Optimization Techniques for Queries with Expensive Methods. *ACM Transactions on Database Systems*, 23(2):113–157, 1998.

[HH99] P. J. Haas and J. M. Hellerstein. Ripple Joins for Online Aggregation. In *Proc. ACM-SIGMOD International Conference on Management of Data*, pages 287–298, Philadelphia, 1999.

[HKWY97] L. Haas, D. Kossmann, E. Wimmers, and J. Yang. Optimizing Queries Across Diverse Data Sources. In *Proc. 23rd International Conference on Very Large Data Bases (VLDB)*, Athens, 1997.

[HSC99] J. M. Hellerstein, M. Stonebraker, and R. Caccia. Open, Independent Enterprise Data Integration. *IEEE Data Engineering Bulletin*, 22(1), March 1999. http://www.cohera.com.

[IFF+99] Z. G. Ives, D. Florescu, M. Friedman, A. Levy, and D. S. Weld. An Adaptive Query Execution System for Data Integration. In *Proc. ACM-SIGMOD International Conference on Management of Data*, Philadelphia, 1999.

[IK84] T. Ibaraki and T. Kameda. Optimal Nesting for Computing N-relational Joins. *ACM Transactions on Database Systems*, 9(3):482–502, October 1984.

[INSS97] Y. E. Ioannidis, R. T. Ng, K. Shim, and T. K. Sellis. Parametric Query Optimization. *VLDB Journal*, 6(2):132–151, 1997.

[KBZ86] R. Krishnamurthy, H. Boral, and C. Zaniolo. Optimization of Nonrecursive Queries. In *Proc. 12th International Conference on Very Large Databases (VLDB)*, pages 128–137, August 1986.

[KD98] N. Kabra and D. J. DeWitt. Efficient Mid-Query Reoptimization of Sub-Optimal Query Execution Plans. In *Proc. ACM-SIGMOD International Conference on Management of Data*, pages 106–117, Seattle, 1998.

[Met97] R. Van Meter. Observing the Effects of Multi-Zone Disks. In *Proceedings of the Usenix 1997 Technical Conference*, Anaheim, January 1997.

[Mit97] T. Mitchell. *Machine Learning*. McGraw Hill, 1997.

[NWMN99] K. W. Ng, Z. Wang, R. R. Muntz, and S. Nittel. Dynamic Query Re-Optimization. In *11th International Conference on Scientific and Statistical Database Management*, Cleveland, July 1999.

[RPK+99] B. Reinwald, H. Pirahesh, G. Krishnamoorthy, G. Lapis, B. Tran, and S. Vora. Heterogeneous Query Processing Through SQL Table Functions. In *15th International Conference on Data Engineering*, pages 366–373, Sydney, March 1999.

[RRH99] V. Raman, B. Raman, and J. M. Hellerstein. Online Dynamic Reordering for Interactive Data Processing. In *Proc. 25th International Conference on Very Large Data Bases (VLDB)*, pages 709–720, Edinburgh, 1999.

[SB98] R. S. Sutton and A. G. Bartow. *Reinforcement Learning*. MIT Press, Cambridge, MA, 1998.

[SBH98] M. Stonebraker, P. Brown, and M. Herbach. Interoperability, Distributed Applications, and Distributed Databases: The Virtual Table Interface. *IEEE Data Engineering Bulletin*, 21(3):25–34, September 1998.

[Son98] E. D. Sontag. *Mathematical Control Theory: Deterministic Finite-Dimensional Systems, Second Edition*. Number 6 in Texts in Applied Mathematics. Springer-Verlag, New York, 1998.

[SWK76] M. R. Stonebraker, E. Wong, and P. Kreps. The Design and Implementation of INGRES. *ACM Transactions on Database Systems*, 1(3):189–222, September 1976.

[UF99] T. Urhan and M. Franklin. XJoin: Getting Fast Answers From Slow and Bursty Networks. Technical Report CS-TR-3994, University of Maryland, February 1999.

[UFA98] T. Urhan, M. Franklin, and L. Amsaleg. Cost-Based Query Scrambling for Initial Delays. In *Proc. ACM-SIGMOD International Conference on Management of Data*, Seattle, June 1998.

[WA91] A. N. Wilschut and P. M. G. Apers. Dataflow Query Execution in a Parallel Main-Memory Environment. In *Proc. First International Conference on Parallel and Distributed Info. Sys. (PDIS)*, pages 68–77, 1991.

[WW94] C. A. Waldspurger and W. E. Weihl. Lottery scheduling: Flexible proportional-share resource management. In *Proc. of the First Symposium on Operating Systems Design and Implementation (OSDI '94)*, pages 1–11, Monterey, CA, November 1994. USENIX Assoc.

Retrospective on Aurora

Hari Balakrishnan[3], Magdalena Balazinska[3], Don Carney[2], Uğur Çetintemel[2], Mitch Cherniack[1], Christian Convey[2], Eddie Galvez[1], Jon Salz[3], Michael Stonebraker[3], Nesime Tatbul[2], Richard Tibbetts[3], Stan Zdonik[2]

[1] Department of Computer Science, Brandeis University, Waltham, MA 02454, USA (e-mail: {mfc, eddie}@cs.brandeis.edu)
[2] Department of Computer Science, Brown University, Providence, RI 02912, USA (e-mail: {dpc, ugur, cjc, tatbul, sbz}@cs.brown.edu)
[3] Department of EECS and Laboratory of Computer Science, Massachussetts Institute of Technology, Cambridge, MA 02139, USA (e-mail: {hari, mbalazin, jsalz, stonebraker, tibbetts}@lcs.mit.edu)

Edited by ♣. Received: ♣/ Accepted: ♣
Published online: ♣♣ 2004 –

Abstract. This experience paper summarizes the key lessons we learned throughout the design and implementation of the Aurora stream-processing engine. For the past 2 years, we have built five stream-based applications using Aurora. We first describe in detail these applications and their implementation in Aurora. We then reflect on the design of Aurora based on this experience. Finally, we discuss our initial ideas on a follow-on project, called Borealis, whose goal is to eliminate the limitations of Aurora as well as to address new key challenges and applications in the stream-processing domain.

Keywords: Data stream management – Stream-processing engines – Monitoring applications – Distributed stream processing – Quality-of-service

1 Introduction and history

Over the last several years, a great deal of progress has been made in the area of stream-processing engines (SPEs) [7,9, 15]. Three basic tenets distinguish SPEs from current data-processing engines. First, they must support primitives for streaming applications. Unlike OLTP, which processes messages in isolation, streaming applications entail time series operations on streams of messages. Although a time series "blade" was added to the Illustra Object-Relational DBMS, generally speaking, time series operations are not well supported by current DBMSs. Second, streaming applications entail a real-time component. If one is content to see an answer later, then one can store incoming messages in a data warehouse and run a historical query on the warehouse to find information of interest. This tactic does not work if the answer must be constructed in real time. Real time also dictates a fundamentally different storage architecture. DBMSs universally store and index data records before making them available for query activity. Such *outbound processing*, where data are stored before being processed, cannot deliver real-time latency, as required by SPEs. To meet more stringent latency requirements, SPEs must adopt an alternate model, *inbound processing*, where query processing is performed directly on incoming messages before (or instead of) storing them. Lastly, an SPE must have capabilities to gracefully deal with spikes in message load. Fundamentally, incoming traffic is bursty, and it is desirable to selectively degrade the performance of the applications running on an SPE.

The Aurora stream-processing engine, motivated by these three tenets, is currently operational. It consists of some 100K lines of C++ and Java and runs on both Unix- and Linux-based platforms. It was constructed with the cooperation of students and faculty at Brown, Brandeis, and MIT. The fundamental design of the engine has been well documented elsewhere: the architecture of the engine is described in [7], while the scheduling algorithms are presented in [8]. Load-shedding algorithms are presented in [18], and our approach to high availability in a multisite Aurora installation is covered in [10,13]. Lastly, we have been involved in a collective effort to define a benchmark that described the sort of monitoring applications that we have in mind. The result of this effort is called Linear Road and is described in [4].

Recently, we have used Aurora to build five different application systems. Throughout the process, we have learned a great deal about the key requirements of streaming applications. In this paper, we reflect on the design of Aurora based on this experience.

The first application is an Aurora implementation of Linear Road, mentioned above. In addition to Linear Road, we have implemented a pilot application that detects late arrival of messages in a financial-services feed-processing environment. Furthermore, one of our collaborators, a military medical research laboratory [20], asked us to build a system to monitor the levels of hazardous materials in fish. We have also worked with a major defense contractor on a pilot application that deals with battlefield monitoring in a hostile environment. Lastly, we have used Aurora to build Medusa, a distributed version of Aurora that is intended to be used by multiple enterprises that operate in different administrative domains. Medusa uses an innovative agoric model to deal with cross-system resource allocation and is described in more detail in [5].

We start with a short review of the Aurora design in Sect. 2. Following this, we discuss the five case studies mentioned above in detail in Sect. 3 so the reader can understand the con-

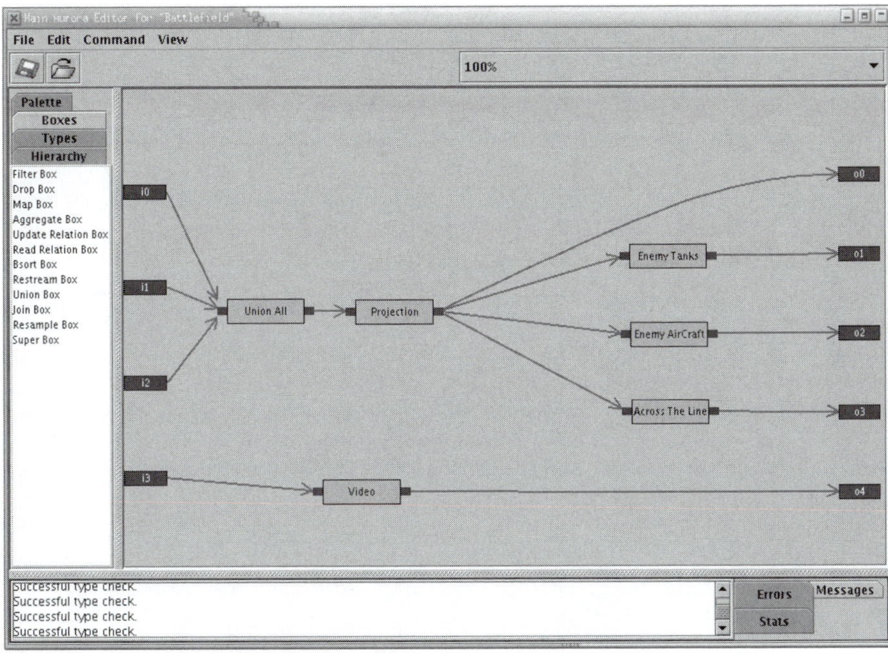

Fig. 1. Aurora graphical user interface

text for the retrospection that follows. In Sect. 4, we present the lessons we have learned on the design of SPEs. These include the necessity of supporting stored tables, the requirement of synchronization primitives to main consistency of stored data in a streaming environment, the need for supporting primitives for late-arriving or missing messages, the requirement for a myriad of adaptors for other feed formats, and the need for globally accessible catalogs and a programming notation to specify Aurora networks (in addition to the "boxes and arrows" GUI). Since stream-processing applications are usually time critical, we also discuss the importance of lightweight scheduling and quantify the performance of the current Aurora prototype using a microbenchmark on basic stream operators. Aurora performance on the Linear Road benchmark is documented elsewhere [4].

The current Aurora prototype is being transferred to the commercial domain, with venture capital backing. As such, the academic project is hard at work on a complete redesign of Aurora, which we call Borealis. The intent of Borealis is to overcome some of the shortcomings of Aurora as well as make a major leap forward in several areas. Hence, in Sect. 5, we discuss the ideas we have for Borealis in several new areas including mechanisms for dynamic modification of query specification and query results and a distributed optimization framework that operates across server and sensor networks.

2 Aurora architecture

Aurora is based on a dataflow-style "boxes and arrows" paradigm. Unlike other stream-processing systems that use SQL-style declarative query interfaces (e.g., STREAM [15]), this approach was chosen because it allows query activity to be interspersed with message processing (e.g., cleaning, correlation, etc.). Systems that only perform the query piece must ping-pong back and forth to an application for the rest of the work, thereby adding to system overhead and latency. An Aurora network can be spread across any number of machines to achieve high scalability and availability characteristics.

In Aurora, a developer uses the GUI to wire together a network of boxes and arcs that will process streams in a manner that produces the outputs necessary for his or her application. A screen shot of the GUI used to create Aurora networks is shown in Fig. 1. The black boxes indicate input and output streams that connect Aurora with the stream sources and applications, respectively. The other boxes are Aurora operators, and the arcs represent dataflow among the operators. Users can drag and drop operators from the palette on the left and connect them by simply drawing arrows between them. It should be noted that a developer can name a collection of boxes and replace it with a "superbox". This "macrodefinition" mechanism drastically eases the development of big networks.

The Aurora operators are presented in detail in [3] and summarized in Fig. 2. Aurora's operator choices were influenced by numerous systems. The basic operators Filter, Map, and Union are modeled after the Select, Project, and Union operations of the relational algebra. Join's use of a distance metric to relate joinable elements on opposing streams is reminiscent of the relational band join [12]. Aggregate's sliding-window semantics is a generalized version of the sliding-window constructs of SEQ [17] and SQL-99 (with generalizations including allowance for disorder (`SLACK`), timeouts, value-based windows, etc.). The `ASSUME ORDER` clause (used in Aggregate and Join), which defines a result in terms of an order that may or may not be manifested, is borrowed from AQuery [14].

Each input must obey a particular schema (a fixed number of fixed- or variable-length fields of the standard data types). Every output is similarly constrained. An Aurora network accepts inputs, performs message filtering, computation, aggregation, and correlation, and then delivers output messages to applications. Moreover, every output is optionally tagged with a Quality-of-Service (QoS) specification. This specification indicates how much latency the connected application can tolerate as well as what to do if adequate responsiveness cannot

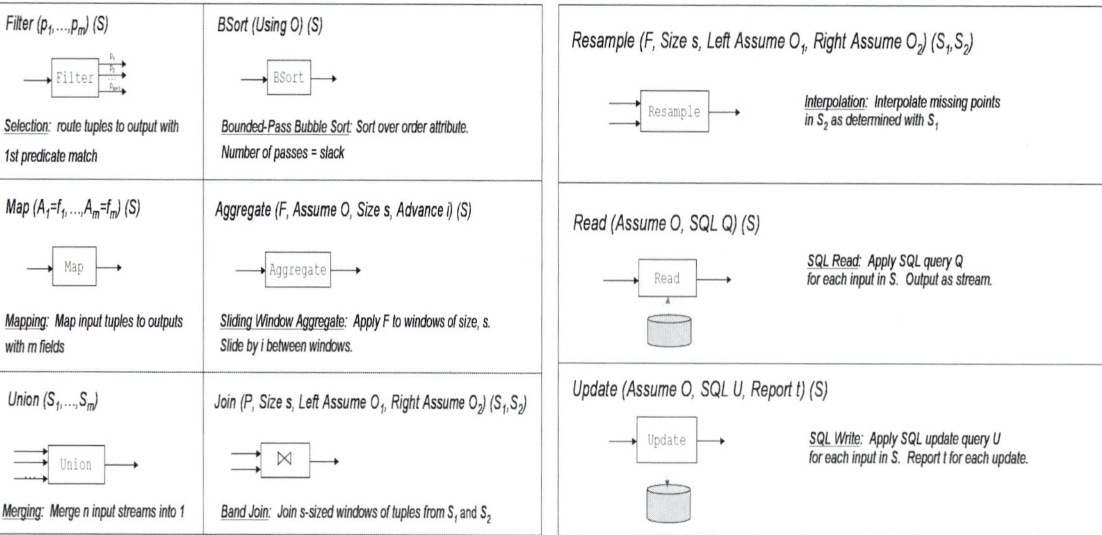

Fig. 2. Aurora operators

be assured under overload situations. Note that the Aurora notion of QoS is different from the traditional QoS notion that typically implies hard performance guarantees, resource reservations, and strict admission control.

On various arcs in an Aurora network, the developer can note that Aurora should remember historical messages. The amount of history to be kept by such "connection points" can be specified by a time range or a message count. The historical storage is achieved by extending the basic message-queue management mechanism. New boxes can be added to an Aurora network at connection points at any time. History is replayed through the added boxes, and then conventional Aurora processing continues. This processing continues until the extra boxes are deleted.

The Aurora optimizer can rearrange a network by performing box swapping when it thinks the result will be favorable. Such box swapping cannot occur across a connection point; hence connection points are arcs that restrict the behavior of the optimizer as well as remember history.

When a developer is satisfied with an Aurora network, he or she can compile it into an intermediate form, which is stored in an embedded database. At run time this data structure is read into virtual memory and drives a real-time scheduler. The scheduler makes decisions based on the form of the network, the QoS specifications present, and the length of the various queues. When queues overflow the buffer pool in virtual memory, they are spooled to the embedded database. More detailed information on these various topics can be obtained from the referenced papers [3,7,8,18].

3 Aurora case studies

In this section, we present five case studies of applications built using the Aurora engine and tools.

3.1 Financial services application

Financial service organizations purchase stock ticker feeds from multiple providers and need to switch in real time between these feeds if they experience too many problems. We worked with a major financial services company on developing an Aurora application that detects feed problems and triggers the switch in real time. In this section, we summarize the application (as specified by the financial services company) and its implementation in Aurora.

An unexpected delay in the reporting of new prices is an example of a feed problem. Each security has an expected reporting interval, and the application needs to raise an alarm if a reporting interval exceeds its expected value. Furthermore, if more than some number of alarms are recorded, a more serious alarm is raised that could indicate that it is time to switch feeds. The delay can be caused by the underlying exchange (e.g., NYSE, NASDAQ) or by the feed provider (e.g., Comstock, Reuters). If it is the former, switching to another provider will not help, so the application must be able to rapidly distinguish between these two cases.

Ticker information is provided as a real-time data feed from one or more providers, and a feed typically reports more than one exchange. As an example, let us assume that there are 500 securities within a feed that update at least once every 5 s and they are called "fast updates". Let us also assume that there are 4000 securities that update at least once every 60 s and they are called "slow updates".

If a ticker update is not seen within its update interval, the monitoring system should raise a *low alarm*. For example, if MSFT is expected to update within 5 s, and 5 s or more elapse since the last update, a low alarm is raised.

Since the source of the problem could be in the feed or the exchange, the monitoring application must count the number of low alarms found in each exchange and the number of low alarms found in each feed. If the number for each of these categories exceeds a threshold (100 in the following example), a *high alarm* is raised. The particular high alarm will indicate what action should be taken. When a high alarm is raised, the low alarm count is reset and the counting of low alarms begins

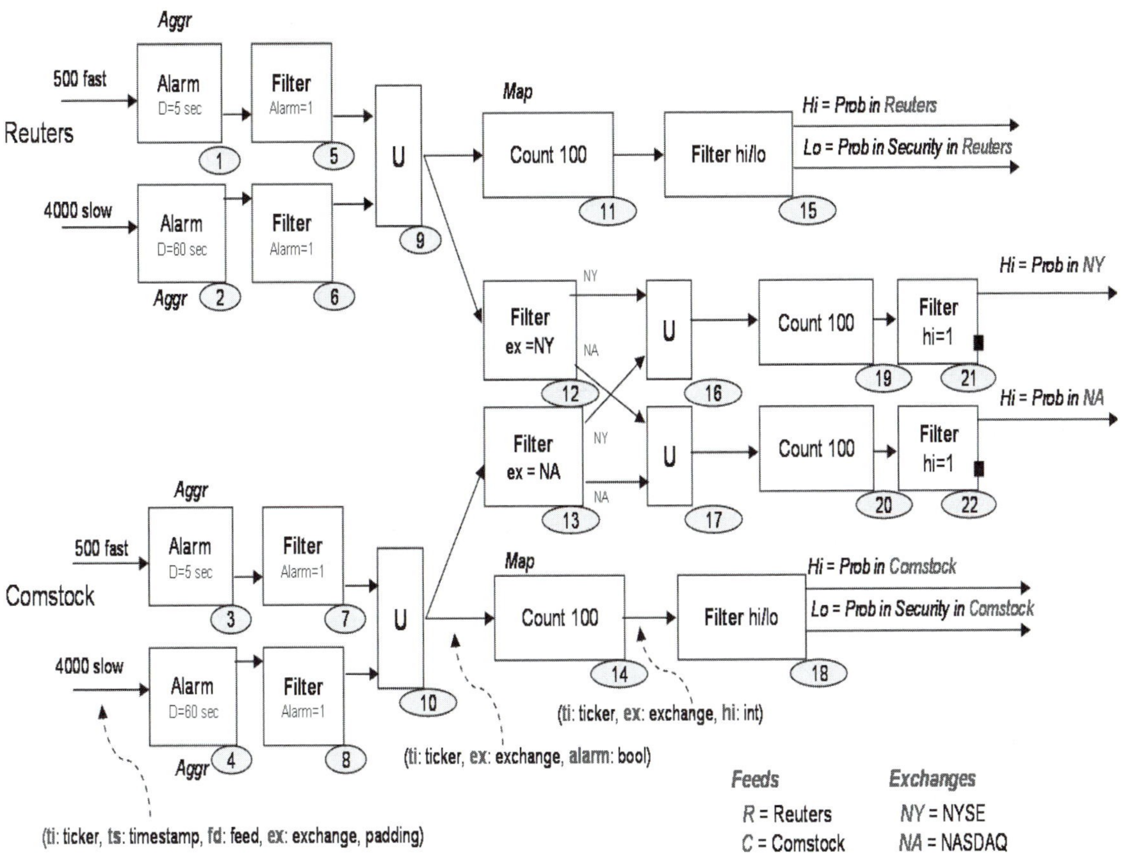

Fig. 3. Aurora query network for the alarm correlation application

again. In this way, the system produces a high alarm for every 100 low alarms of a particular type.

Furthermore, the posting of a high alarm is a serious condition, and low alarms are suppressed when the threshold is reached to avoid distracting the operator with a large number of low alarms.

Figure 3 presents our solution realized with an Aurora query network. We assume for simplicity that the securities within each feed are already separated into the 500 fast updating tickers and the 4000 slowly updating tickers. If this is not the case, then the separation can be easily achieved with a lookup. The query network in Fig. 3 actually represents six different queries (one for each output). Notice that much of the processing is shared.

The core of this application is in the detection of late tickers. Boxes 1, 2, 3, and 4 are all Aggregate boxes that perform the bulk of this computation. An Aggregate box groups input tuples by common value of one or more of their attributes, thus effectively creating a substream for each possible combination of these attribute values. In this case, the aggregates are grouping the input on common value of ticker symbol. For each grouping or substream, a window is defined that demarcates interesting runs of consecutive tuples called *windows*. For each of the tuples in one of these windows, some memory is allocated and an aggregating function (e.g., Average) is applied. In this example, the window is defined to be every consecutive pair (e.g., tuples 1 and 2, tuples 2 and 3, etc.) and the aggregating function generates one output tuple per window with a boolean flag called *Alarm*, which is a 1 when the second tuple in the pair is delayed (call this an *Alarm tuple*) and a 0 when it is on time.

Aurora's operators have been designed to react to imperfections such as delayed tuples. Thus, the triggering of an Alarm tuple is accomplished directly using this built-in mechanism. The window defined on each pair of tuples will *timeout* if the second tuple does not arrive within the given threshold (5 s in this case). In other words, the operator will produce one alarm each time a new tuple fails to arrive within 5 s, as the corresponding window will automatically timeout and close. The high-level specification of Aggregate boxes 1 through 4 is:

```
Aggregate(Group by ticker,
          Order on arrival,
          Window (Size = 2 tuples,
                  Step = 1 tuple,
                  Timeout = 5 sec))
```

Boxes 5 through 8 are Filters that eliminate the normal outputs, thereby letting only the Alarm tuples through. Box 9 is a Union operator that merges all Reuters alarms onto a single stream. Box 10 performs the same operation for Comstock.

The rest of the network determines when a large number of Alarms is occurring and what the cause of the problem might be.

Boxes 11 and 15 count Reuters alarms and raise a high alarm when a threshold (100) is reached. Until that time, they simply pass through the normal (low) alarms. Boxes 14 and 18 do the same for Comstock. Note that the boxes labeled *Count*

100 are actually Map boxes. Map takes a user-defined function as a parameter and applies it to each input tuple. That is, for each tuple t in the input stream, a Map box parameterized by a function f produces the tuple $f(x)$. In this example, *Count 100* simply applies the following user-supplied function (written in pseudocode) to each tuple that passes through:

```
F (x:tuple) = cnt++
if (cnt % 100 != 0)
    if !suppress
        emit lo-alarm
    else
        emit drop-alarm
else
    emit hi-alarm
    set suppress = true
```

Boxes 12, 13, 16, and 17 separate the alarms from both Reuters and Comstock into alarms from NYSE and alarms from NASDAQ. This is achieved by using Filters to take NYSE alarms from both feed sources (Boxes 12 and 13) and merging them using a Union (Box 16). A similar path exists for NASDAQ alarms. The results of each of these streams are counted and filtered as explained above.

In summary, this example illustrates the ability to share computation among queries, the ability to extend functionality through user-defined Aggregate and Map functions, and the need to detect and exploit stream imperfections.

3.2 The Linear Road benchmark

Linear Road is a benchmark for stream-processing engines [2, 4]. This benchmark simulates an urban highway system that uses "variable tolling" (also known as "congestion pricing") [11,1,16], where tolls are determined according to such dynamic factors as congestion, accident proximity, and travel frequency. As a benchmark, Linear Road specifies input data schemas and workloads, a suite of continuous and historical queries that must be supported, and performance (query and transaction response time) requirements.

Variable tolling is becoming increasingly prevalent in urban settings because it is effective at reducing traffic congestion and because recent advances in microsensor technology make it feasible. Traffic congestion in major metropolitan areas is an increasing problem as expressways cannot be built fast enough to keep traffic flowing freely at peak periods. The idea behind variable tolling is to issue tolls that vary according to time-dependent factors such as congestion levels and accident proximity with the motivation of charging higher tolls during peak traffic periods to discourage vehicles from using the roads and contributing to the congestion. Illinois, California, and Finland are among the highway systems that have pilot programs utilizing this concept.

The benchmark itself assumes a fictional metropolitan area (called "Linear City") that consists of 10 expressways of 100-mile-long segments each and 1,000,000 vehicles that report their positions via GPS-based sensors every 30 s. Tolls must be issued on a per-segment basis automatically, based on statistics gathered over the previous 5 min concerning average speed and number of reporting cars. A segment's tolls are overridden when accidents are detected in the vicinity (an accident is detected when multiple cars report close positions at the same time), and vehicles that use a particular expressway often are issued "frequent traveler" discounts.

The Linear Road benchmark demands support for five queries: two continuous and three historical. The first continuous query calculates and reports a segment toll every time a vehicle enters a segment. This toll must then be charged to the vehicle's account when the vehicle exits that segment without exiting the expressway. Again, tolls are based on current congestion conditions on the segment, recent accidents in the vicinity, and frequency of use of the expressway for the given vehicle. The second continuous query involves detecting and reporting accidents and adjusting tolls accordingly. The historical queries involve requesting an account balance or a day's total expenditure for a given vehicle on a given expressway and a prediction of travel time between two segments on the basis of average speeds on the segments recorded previously. Each of the queries must be answered with a specified accuracy and within a specified response time. The degree of success for this benchmark is measured in terms of the number of expressways the system can support, assuming 1000 position reports issued per second per expressway, while answering each of the five queries within the specified latency bounds.

An early Aurora implementation of this benchmark supporting one expressway was demonstrated at SIGMOD 2003 [2].

3.3 Battalion monitoring

We have worked closely with a major defense contractor on a battlefield monitoring application. In this application, an advanced aircraft gathers reconnaissance data and sends them to monitoring stations on the ground. These data include positions and images of friendly and enemy units. At some point, the enemy units cross a given demarcation line and move toward the friendly units, thereby signaling an attack.

Commanders in the ground stations monitor these data for analysis and tactical decision making. Each ground station is interested in particular subsets of the data, each with differing priorities. In the real application, the limiting resource is the bandwidth between the aircraft and the ground. When an attack is initiated, the priorities for the data classes change. More data become critical, and the bandwidth likely saturates. In this case, selective dropping of data is allowed in order to service the more important classes.

For our purposes, we built a simplified version of this application to test our load-shedding techniques. Instead of modeling bandwidth, we assume that the limited resource is the CPU. We introduce load shedding as a way to save cycles.

Aurora supports two kinds of load shedding. The first technique inserts random drop boxes into the network. These boxes discard a fraction of their input tuples chosen randomly. The second technique inserts semantic, predicate-based drop filters into the network. Based on QoS functions, system statistics (like operator cost and selectivity), and input rates, our algorithms choose the best drop locations and the drop amount as indicated by a drop rate (random drop) or a predicate (semantic drop). Drop insertion plans are constructed and stored in a table in advance. As load levels change, drops are automati-

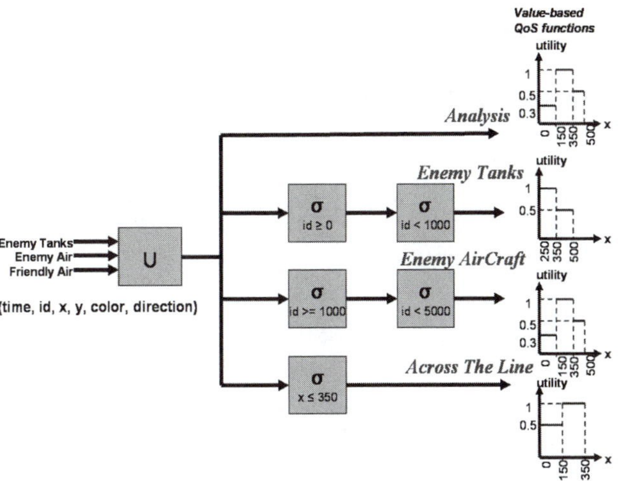

Fig. 4. Aurora query network for battlefield monitoring application

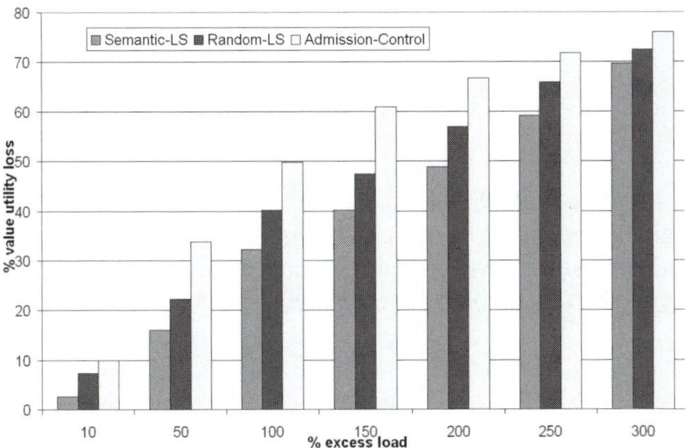

Fig. 5. Comparison of various load-shedding approaches (%excess load vs. % value utility loss)

cally inserted and removed from the query networks based on these plans [18].

One of the query networks that we used in this study is shown in Fig. 4. There are four queries in this network. The *Analysis* query merges all tuples about positions of all units for analysis and archiving. The next two queries, labeled *Enemy Tanks* and *Enemy Aircraft*, select enemy tank and enemy aircraft tuples using predicates on their IDs. The last query, *Across The Line*, selects all the objects that have crossed the demarcation line toward the friendly side.

Each query has a value-based QoS function attached to its output. A value-based QoS function maps the tuple values observed at an output to utility values that express the importance of a given result tuple. In this example, the functions are defined on the *x-coordinate* attribute of the output tuple, which indicates where an object is positioned horizontally. The functions take values in the range [0, 500], of which 350 corresponds to the position of the vertical demarcation line. Initially all friendly units are on the [0, 350] side of this line whereas enemy units are on the [350, 500] side. The QoS functions are specified by an application administrator and reflect the basic fact that tuples for enemy objects that have crossed the demarcation line are more important than others.

We ran this query network with tuples generated by the Aurora workload generator based on a battle scenario that we got from the defense contractor. We fed the input tuples at different rates to create specific levels of overload in the network; then we let the load-shedding algorithm remove the excess load by inserting drops to the network. Figure 5 shows the result. We compare the performance of three different load-shedding algorithms in terms of their value utility loss (i.e., average degradation in the QoS provided by the system) across all outputs at increasing levels of load.

We make the following important observations. First, our semantic load-shedding algorithm, which drops tuples based on attribute values, achieves the least value utility loss at all load levels. Second, our random load-shedding algorithm inserts drops of the same amounts at the same network locations as the semantic load shedder. Since tuples are dropped randomly, however, loss in value utility is higher compared to the semantic load shedder. As excess load increases, the performance of the two algorithms becomes similar. The reason is that at high load levels, our semantic load shedder also drops tuples from the high utility value ranges. Lastly, we compare both of our algorithms against a simple admission control algorithm, which sheds random tuples at the network inputs. Both our algorithms achieve lower utility loss compared to this algorithm. Our load-shedding algorithms may sometimes decide to insert drops on inner arcs of the query network. On networks with box sharing among queries (e.g., the union box is shared among all four queries, Fig. 4), inner arcs may be preferable to avoid utility loss at multiple query outputs. On the other hand, at very high load levels, since drops at inner arcs become insufficient to save the needed CPU cycles, our algorithms also insert drops close to the network inputs. Hence, all algorithms tend to converge to the same utility loss levels at very high loads.

3.4 Environmental monitoring

We have also worked with a military medical research laboratory on an application that involves monitoring toxins in the water. This application is fed streams of data indicating fish behavior (e.g., breathing rate) and water quality (e.g., temperature, pH, oxygenation, and conductivity). When the fish behave abnormally, an alarm is sounded.

Input data streams were supplied by the army laboratory as a text file. The single data file interleaved fish observations with water quality observations. The alarm message emitted by Aurora contains fields describing the fish behavior and two different water quality reports: the water quality at the time the alarm occurred and the water quality from the last time the fish behaved normally. The water quality reports contain not only the simple measurements but also the 1-/2-/4-hour sliding-window deltas for those values.

The application's Aurora processing network is shown in Fig. 6 (snapshot taken from the Aurora GUI): The input port (1) shows where tuples enter Aurora from the outside data source. In this case, it is the application's C++ program that reads in the sensor log file. A Union box (2) serves merely to split the stream into two identical streams. A Map box (3) eliminates all tuple fields except those related to water quality. Each superbox (4) calculates the sliding-window statistics for

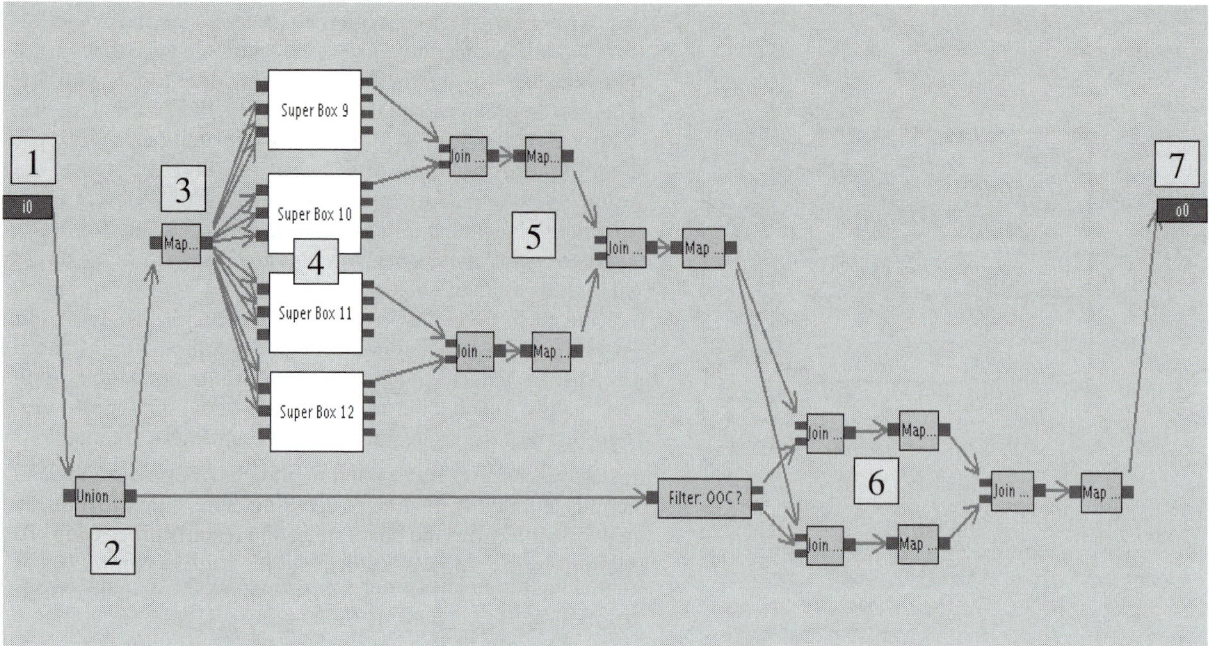

Fig. 6. Aurora query network for the environmental contamination detection applications (GUI snapshot)

one of the water quality attributes. The parallel paths (5) form a binary join network that brings the results of (4)'s subnetworks back into a single stream. The top branch in (6) has all the tuples where the fish act oddly, and the bottom branch has the tuples where the fish act normally. For each of the tuples sent into (1) describing abnormal fish behavior, (6) emits an alarm message tuple. This output tuple has the sliding-window water quality statistics for both the moment the fish acted oddly and for the most recent previous moment that the fish acted normally. Finally, the output port (7) shows where result tuples are made available to the C++-based monitoring application. Overall, the entire application ended up consisting of 3400 lines of C++ code (primarily for file parsing and a simple monitoring GUI) and a 53-operator Aurora query network.

During the development of the application, we observed that Aurora's stream model proved very convenient for describing the required sliding-window calculations. For example, a single instance of the aggregate operator computed the 4-h sliding-window deltas of water temperature.

Aurora's GUI for designing query networks also proved invaluable. As the query network grew large in the number of operators used, there was great potential for overwhelming complexity. The ability to manually place the operators and arcs on a workspace, however, permitted a visual representation of "subroutine" boundaries that let us comprehend the entire query network as we refined it.

We found that small changes in the operator language design would have greatly reduced our processing network complexity. For example, Aggregate boxes apply some window function [such as `DELTA(water-pH)`] to the tuples in a sliding window. Had an Aggregate box been capable of evaluating multiple functions at the same time on a single window [such as `DELTA(water-pH)` and `DELTA(watertemp)`], we could have used significantly fewer boxes. Many of these changes have since been made to Aurora's operator language.

The ease with which the processing flow could be experimentally reconfigured during development, while remaining comprehensible, was surprising. It appears that this was only possible by having both a well-suited operator set and a GUI tool that let us visualize the processing. It seems likely that this application was developed at least as quickly in Aurora as it would have been with standard procedural programming.

We note that, for this particular application, real-time response was not required. The main value Aurora added in this case was the ease of developing stream-oriented applications.

3.5 Medusa: distributed stream processing

Medusa is a distributed stream-processing system built using Aurora as the single-site query-processing engine. Medusa takes Aurora queries and distributes them across multiple nodes. These nodes can all be under the control of one entity or be organized as a loosely coupled federation under the control of different autonomous participants.

A distributed stream-processing system such as Medusa offers several benefits:

1. It allows stream processing to be incrementally scaled over multiple nodes.
2. It enables high availability because the processing nodes can monitor and take over for each other when failures occur.
3. It allows the composition of stream feeds from different participants to produce end-to-end services and to take advantage of the distribution inherent in many stream-processing applications (e.g., climate monitoring, financial analysis, etc.).
4. It allows participants to cope with load spikes without individually having to maintain and administer the computing, network, and storage resources required for peak operation. When organized as a loosely coupled federated sys-

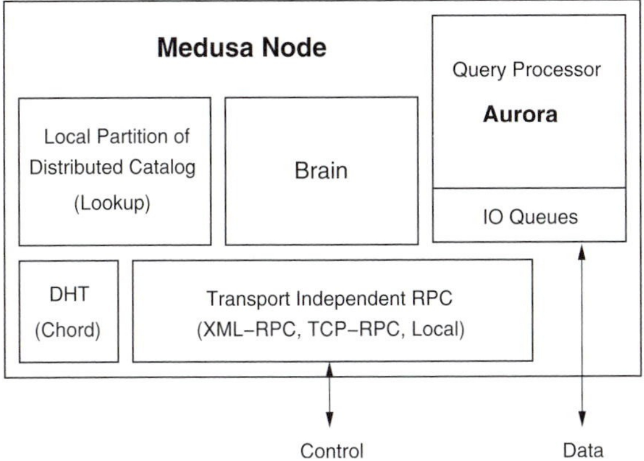

Fig. 7. Medusa software architecture

tem, load movements between participants based on predefined contracts can significantly improve performance.

Figure 7 shows the software structure of a Medusa node. There are two components in addition to the Aurora query processor. The *Lookup* component is a client of an internode distributed catalog that holds information on streams, schemas, and queries running in the system. The *Brain* handles query setup operations and monitors local load using information about the queues (*IOQueues*) feeding Aurora and statistics on box load. The *Brain* uses this information as input to a *bounded-price* distributed load management mechanism that converges efficiently to good load allocations [5].

The development of Medusa prompted two important changes to the Aurora processing engine. First, it became apparent that it would be useful to offer Aurora not only as a stand-alone system but also as a library that could easily be integrated within a larger system. Second, we felt the need for an Aurora API, summarized in Table 1. This API is composed of three types of methods: (1) methods to set up queries and push or pull tuples from Aurora, (2) methods to modify query networks at runtime (operator additions and removals), and (3) methods giving access to performance information.

Table 1. Overview of a subset of the Aurora API

`start` and `shutdown`: Respectively starts processing and shuts down a complete query network.
`modifyNetwork`: At runtime, adds or removes schemas, streams, and operator boxes from a query network processed by a single Aurora engine.
`typecheck`: Validates (part of) a query network. Computes properties of intermediate and output streams.
`enqueue` and `dequeue`: Push and pull tuples on named streams.
`listEntities` and `describe(Entity)`: Provide information on entities in the current query network.
`getPerfStats`: Provides performance and load information.

Load movement. To move operators with a relatively low effort and overhead compared to full-blown process migration, Medusa participants use *remote definitions*. A remote definition maps an operator defined at one node onto an operator defined at another node. At runtime, when a path of operators in the boxes-and-arrows diagram needs to be moved to another node, all that is required is for the corresponding operators to be instantiated remotely and for the incoming streams to be diverted to the appropriately named inputs on the new node.

For some operators, the internal operator state may need to be moved when a task moves between machines, unless some "amnesia" is acceptable to the application. Our current prototype restarts operator processing after a move from a fresh state and the most recent position of the input streams. To support the movement of operator state, we are adding two new functions to the Aurora API and modifying the Aurora engine. The first method freezes a query network and removes an operator with its state by performing the following sequence of actions atomically: stop all processing, remove a box from a query network, extract the operator's internal state, subscribe an outside client to what used to be the operator's input streams, and restart processing. The second method performs the converse actions atomically. It stops processing, adds a box to a query network, initializes the box's state, and restarts processing. To minimize the amount of state moved, we are exploring freezing operators around the windows of tuples on which they operate rather than at random instants. When Medusa moves an operator or a group of operators, it handles the forwarding of tuples to their new locations.

Medusa employs an agoric system model to create incentives for autonomous participants to handle each other's load. Clients outside the system pay Medusa participants for processing their queries and Medusa participants pay each other to handle load. Payments and load movements are based on *pairwise contracts* negotiated offline between participants. These contracts set tightly bounded prices for migrating each unit of load and specify the set of tasks that each participant is willing to execute on behalf of its partner. Contracts can also be customized with availability, performance, and other clauses. Our mechanism, called the *bounded-price mechanism*, thus allows participants to manage their excess load through private and customized service agreements. The mechanism also achieves a low runtime overhead by bounding prices through offline negotiations.

Figure 8 shows the simulation results of a 995-node Medusa system running the bounded-price load management mechanism. Figure 8a shows that convergence from an unbalanced load assignment to an almost optimal distribution is fast with our approach. Figure 8b shows the excess load remaining at various nodes for increasing numbers of contracts. A minimum of just seven contracts per node in a network of 995 nodes ensures that all nodes operate within capacity when capacity exists in the system. The key advantages of our approach over previous distributed load management schemes are (1) lower runtime overhead, (2) possibility of service customization and price discrimination, and (3) relatively invariant prices that one participant pays another for processing a unit of load.

High availability. We are also currently exploring the runtime overhead and recovery time tradeoffs among different approaches to achieve high availability (HA) in distributed stream processing, in the context of Medusa and Aurora* [4]. These approaches range from classical Tandem-style process-pairs [6] to using upstream nodes in the processing flow as backup for their downstream neighbors. Different approaches also provide different recovery semantics where: (1) some tuples are lost, (2) some tuples are reprocessed, or (3) operations

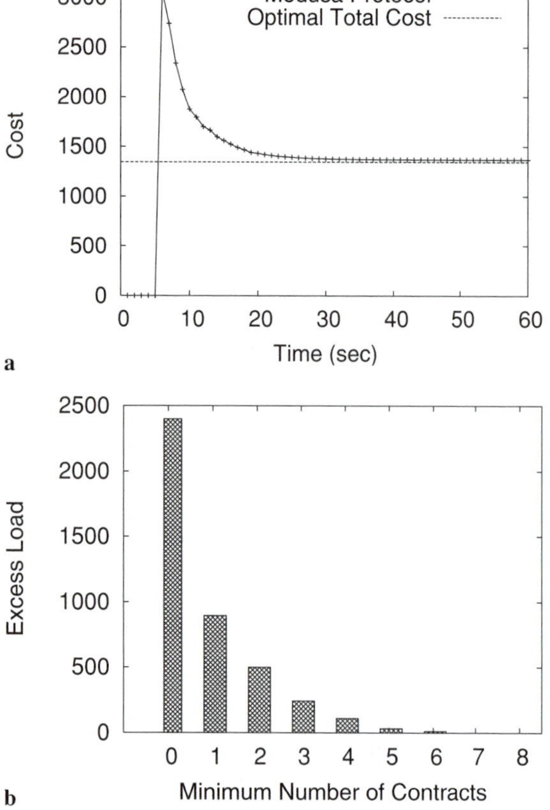

Fig. 8a,b. Performance of Medusa load management protocol. **a** Convergence speed with a minimum of 7 contracts/node. **b** Final allocation for increasing number of contracts

take over precisely where the failure happened. We discuss these algorithms in more detail in [13]. An important HA goal for the future is handling network partitions in addition to individual node failures.

4 Lessons learned

4.1 Support for historical data

From our work on a variety of streaming applications, it became apparent that each application required maintaining and accessing a collection of historical data. For example, the Linear Road benchmark, which represents a realistic application, required maintaining 10 weeks of toll history for each driver, as well as the current positions of every vehicle and the locations of accidents tying up traffic. Historical data might be used to support *historical queries* (e.g., tell me how much driver X has spent on tolls on expressway Y over the past 10 weeks) or serve as inputs to *hybrid* queries involving both streaming and historical data [e.g., report the current toll for vehicle X based on its current position (streamed data) and the presence of any accidents in its vicinity (historical data)].

In the applications we have looked at, historical data take three different forms. These forms differ by their *update patterns* – the means by which incoming stream data are used to update the contents of a historical collection. These forms are summarized below.

1. **Open windows (connection points)**: Linear Road requires maintaining the *last 10 weeks' worth of toll data for each driver* to support both historical queries and integrated queries. This form of historical data resembles a window in its FIFO-based update pattern but must be shared by multiple queries and therefore be openly accessible.
2. **Aggregate summaries (latches)**: Linear Road requires maintaining such aggregated historical data as: the current toll balance for every vehicle (`SUM(Toll)`), the last reported position of every vehicle (`MAX(Time)`), and the average speed on a given segment over the past 5 min (`AVG(Speed)`). In all cases, the update patterns involve maintaining data by key value (e.g., vehicle or segment ID) and using incoming tuples to update the aggregate value that has the appropriate key. As with open windows, aggregate summaries must be shared by multiple queries and therefore must be openly accessible.
3. **Tables**: Linear Road requires maintaining tables of historical data whose update patterns are arbitrary and determined by the values of streaming data. For example, a table must be maintained that holds every accident that has yet to be cleared (such that an accident is detected when multiple vehicles report the same position at the same time). This table is used to determine tolls for segments in the vicinity of the accident and to alert drivers approaching the scene of the accident. The update pattern for this table resembles neither an open window nor an aggregate summary. Rather, accidents must be deleted from the table when an incoming tuple reports that the accident has been cleared. This requires the declaration of an arbitrary update pattern.

Whereas open windows and aggregate summaries have fixed update patterns, tables require update patterns to be explicitly specified. Therefore, the Aurora query algebra (SQuAl) includes an Update box that permits an update pattern to be specified in SQL. This box has the form

```
UPDATE (Assume O, SQL U, Report t)
```

such that U is an SQL update issued with every incoming tuple and includes variables that get instantiated with the values contained in that tuple. O specifies the assumed ordering of input tuples, and t specifies a tuple to output whenever an update takes place. Further, because all three forms of historical collections require random access, SQuAl also includes a Read box that initiates a query over stored data (also specified in SQL) and returns the result as a stream. This box has the form

```
READ (Assume O, SQL Q)
```

such that Q is an SQL query issued with every incoming tuple and includes variables that get instantiated with the values contained in that tuple.

In short, the streaming applications we have looked at share the need for maintaining and randomly accessing collections of historical data. These collections, used for both historical and hybrid queries, are of three forms differing by their update patterns. To support historical data in Aurora, we include an update operation (to update tables with user-specified update patterns) and a read operation (to read any of the forms of historical data).

4.2 Synchronization

As continuous queries, stream applications inherently rely on shared data and computation. Shared data might be contained in a table that one query updates and another query reads. For example, the Linear Road application requires that vehicle position data be used to update statistics on highway usage, which in turn are read to determine tolls for each segment on the highway. Alternatively, box output can be shared by multiple queries to exploit common subexpressions or even by a single query as a way of merging intermediate computations after parallelization.

Transactions are required in traditional databases because data sharing can lead to data inconsistencies. An equivalent synchronization mechanism is required in streaming settings, as data sharing in this setting can also lead to inconsistencies. For example, if a toll charge can expire, then a toll assessment to a given vehicle should be delayed until a new toll charge is determined. The need for synchronization with data sharing is achieved in SQuAl via the WaitFor box whose syntax is shown below:

```
WaitFor (P: Predicate, T: Timeout).
```

This binary operator buffers each tuple t on one input stream until a tuple arrives on the second input stream that with t satisfies P (or until the timeout expires, in which case t is discarded). If a Read operation must follow a given Update operation, then a WaitFor can buffer the Read request (tuple) until a tuple output by the Update box (and input to the second input of WaitFor) indicates that the Read operation can proceed.

In short, the inherent sharing possible in streaming environments makes it sometimes necessary to synchronize operations to ensure data consistency. We currently implement synchronization in SQuAl with a dedicated operator.

4.3 Resilience to unpredictable stream behavior

Streams are by their nature unpredictable. Monitoring applications require the system to continue operation even when the unpredictable happens. Sometimes, the only way to do this is to produce approximate answers. Obviously, in these cases, the system should try to minimize errors.

We have seen examples of streams that do not behave as expected. The financial services application that we described earlier requires the ability to detect a problem in the arrival rate of a stream. The military application must fundamentally adjust its processing to fit the available resources during times of stress. In both of these cases, Aurora primitives for unpredictable stream behavior were brought to bear on the problem.

Aurora makes no assumptions that a data stream arrives in any particular order or with any temporal regularity. Tuples can be late or out of order due to the nature of the data sources, the network that carries the streams, or the behavior of the operators themselves. Accordingly, our operator set includes user-specified parameters that allow handling such "damaged" streams gracefully.

For many of the operators, an input stream can be specified to obey an expected order. If out-of-order data are known to the network designer not to be of relevance, the operator will simply drop such data tuples immediately. Nonetheless, Aurora understands that this may at times be too drastic a constraint and provides an optional slack parameter to allow for some tolerance in the number of data tuples that may arrive out of order. A tuple that arrives out of order within the slack bounds will be processed as if it had arrived in order.

With respect to possible irregularity in the arrival rate of data streams, the Aurora operator set offers all windowed operators an optional timeout parameter. The timeout parameter tells the operator how long to wait for the next data tuple to arrive. This has two benefits: it prevents blocking (i.e., no output) when one stream is stalled, and it offers another way for the network designer to characterize the value of data that arrive later than they should, as in the financial services application in which the timeout parameter was used to determine when a particular data packet arrived late.

4.4 XML and other feed formats adaptor required

Aurora provides a network protocol that may be used to enqueue and dequeue tuples via Unix or TCP sockets. The protocol is intentionally very low-level: to eliminate copies and improve throughput, the tuple format is closely tied to the format of Aurora's internal queue format. For instance, the protocol requires that each packet contain a fixed amount of padding reserved for bookkeeping and that integer and floating-point fields in the packet match the architecture's native format.

While we anticipate that performance-critical applications will use our low-level protocol, we also recognize that the formats of Aurora's input streams may be outside the immediate control of the Aurora user or administrator, for example, stock quote data arriving in XML format from a third-party information source. Also, even if the streams are being generated or consumed by an application within an organization's control, in some cases protocol stability and portability (e.g., not requiring the client to be aware of the endian-ness of the server architecture) are important enough to justify a minor performance loss.

One approach to addressing these concerns is to simply require the user to build a proxy application that accepts tuples in the appropriate format, converts them to Aurora's internal format, and pipes them into the Aurora process. This approach, while simple, conflicts with one of Aurora's key design goals – to minimize the number of boundary crossings in the system – since the proxy application would be external to Aurora and hence live in its own address space.

We resolve this problem by allowing the user to provide plug-ins called *converter boxes*. Converter boxes are shared libraries that are dynamically linked into the Aurora process space; hence their use incurs no boundary crossings. A user-defined *input converter box* provides a hook that is invoked when data arrive over the network. The implementation may examine the data and inject tuples into the appropriate streams in the Aurora network. This may be as simple as consuming fixed-length packets and enforcing the correct byte order on fields or as complex as transforming fully formed XML documents into tuples. An *output converter box* performs the inverse function: it accepts tuples from streams in Aurora's internal format and converts them into a byte stream to be consumed by an external application.

Input and output converter boxes are powerful connectivity mechanisms: they provide a high level of flexibility in dealing with external feeds and sinks without incurring a performance hit. This combination of flexibility and high performance is essential in a streaming database that must assimilate data from a wide variety of sources.

4.5 Programmatic interfaces and globally accessible catalogs are a good idea

Initially, Aurora networks were created using the GUI and all Aurora metadata (i.e., catalogs) were stored in an internal representation. Our experience with the Medusa system quickly made us realize that, in order for Aurora to be easily integrated within a larger system, a higher-level, *programmatic interface* was needed to script Aurora networks and metadata needed to be globally accessible and updatable.

Although we initially assumed that only Aurora itself (i.e., the runtime and the GUI) would need direct access to the catalog representation, we encountered several situations where this assumption did not hold. For instance, in order to manage distribution operation across multiple Aurora nodes, Medusa required knowledge of the contents of node catalogs and the ability to selectively move parts of catalogs from node to node. Medusa needed to be able to create catalog objects (schema, streams, and boxes) without direct access to the Aurora catalog database, which would have violated abstraction. In other words, relying on the Aurora runtime and GUI as the sole software components able to examine and modify catalog structures turned out to be an unworkable solution when we tried to build sophisticated applications on the Aurora platform. We concluded that we needed a simple and transparent catalog representation that is easily readable and writable by external applications. This would make it much easier to write higher-level systems that use Aurora (such as Medusa) and alternative authoring tools for catalogs.

To this end, Aurora currently incorporates appropriate interfaces and mechanisms (Sect. 3.5) to make it easy to develop external applications to inspect and modify Aurora query networks. A universally readable and writable catalog representation is crucial in an environment where multiple applications may operate on Aurora catalogs.

4.6 Performance critical

During the development of Aurora, our primary tool for keeping performance in mind was a series of "microbenchmarks". Each of these benchmarks measured the performance of a small part of our system, such as a single operator, or the raw performance of the message bus. These benchmarks allowed us to measure the merits of changes to our implementation quickly and easily.

Fundamental to an SPE is a high-performance "message bus". This is the system that moves tuples from one operator to the next, storing them temporarily, as well as into and out of the query network. Since every tuple is passed on the bus a number of times, this is definitely a performance bottleneck. Even such trivial optimizations as choosing the right `memcpy()` implementation gave substantial improvements to the whole system.

Second to the message bus, the scheduler is the core element of an SPE. The scheduler is responsible for allocating processor time to operators. It is tempting to decorate the scheduler with all sorts of high-level optimization such as intelligent allocation of processor time or real-time profiling of query plans. But it is important to remember that scheduler overhead can be substantial in networks where there are many operators and that the scheduler makes no contribution to the actual processing. All addition of scheduler functionality must be greeted with skepticism and should be aggressively profiled.

Once the core of the engine has been aggressively optimized, the remaining hot spots for performance are to be found in the implementation of the operators. In our implementation, each operator has a "tight loop" that processes batches of input tuples. This loop is a prime target for optimization. We make sure nothing other than necessary processing occurs in the loop. In particular, housekeeping of data structures such as memory allocations and deallocation needs to be done outside of this loop so that its cost can be amortized across many tuples.

Data structures are another opportunity for operator optimization. Many of our operators are stateful; they retain information or even copies of previous input. Because these operators are asked to process and store large numbers of tuples, efficiency of these data structures is important. Ideally, processing of each input tuple is accomplished in constant time. In our experience, processing that is linear in the amount of states stored is unacceptable.

In addition to the operators themselves, any parts of the system that are used by those operators in the tight loops must be carefully examined. For example, we have a small language used to specify expressions for Map operators. Because these expressions are evaluated in such tight loops, optimizing them was important. The addition of an expensive compilation step may even be appropriate.

To assess the relative performance of various parts of the Aurora system, we developed a simple series of microbenchmarks. Each microbenchmark follows the following pattern:

1. Initialize Aurora using a query network q.
2. Create d dequeuers receiving data from the output of the query network. (If d is 0, then there are no dequeuers, i.e., tuples are discarded as soon as they are output.)
3. Begin a timer.
4. Enqueue n tuples into the network in batches of b tuples at a time. Each tuple is 64 bytes long.
5. Wait until the network is drained, i.e., every box is done processing every input tuple and every dequeuer has received every output tuple. Stop the timer. Let t be the amount of time required to process each input tuple, i.e., the total amount of time passed divided by n.

For the purposes of this benchmark, we fixed n at 2,000,000 tuples. We used several different catalogs. Note that these networks are functionally identical: every input tuple is output to the dequeuers, and the only difference is the type and amount of processing done to each tuple. This is necessary to isolate the impact of each stage of tuple processing; if some networks returned a different number of tuples, any performance differential might be attributed simply to there

Table 2. Microbenchmark results

	Query(q)	# Dequers(d)	Batch size(b)	Average latency
A	NULL	0	1	1211 ns
B	NULL	0	10	176 ns
C	NULL	0	100	70 ns
D	NULL	0	1000	60 ns
E	NULL	1	10	321 ns
F	NULL	1	100	204 ns
G	NULL	1	1000	191 ns
H	NULL	5	1000	764 ns
I	NULL	10	1000	1748 ns
J	FILTER	1	1000	484 ns
K	UNION	1	1000	322 ns
L	UNION-CHAIN	1	1000	858 ns

being less or more work to do because of the different number of tuples to enqueue or dequeue.

- NULL: A catalog with no boxes, i.e., input values are passed directly to dequeuers.
- FILTER: A catalog with a filter box whose condition is true for each tuple.
- UNION: A union box that combines the input stream with an empty stream.
- UNION-CHAIN: A chain of five union boxes, each of which combines the input stream with an empty stream.

Table 2 shows the performance of the benchmark with various settings of q, d, and b.

We observe that the overhead to enqueue a tuple in Aurora is highly dependent on the batch size but for large batch sizes settles to 60 ns. Dequeuers add a somewhat higher overhead (between 130 ns (G–D) and 200 ns (I–H)/5] each) because currently one copy of each tuple is made per dequeuer. Comparing cases G and K, or cases G and L, we see that adding a box on a tuple path incurs a delay of approximately 130 ns per tuple; evaluating a simple comparison predicate on a tuple adds about 160 ns (J–K).

These microbenchmarks measure the overhead involved in passing tuples into and out of Aurora boxes and networks; they do not measure the time spent in boxes performing nontrivial operations such as joining and aggregation. Message-passing overhead, however, can be a significant time sink in streaming databases (as it was in earlier versions of Aurora). Microbenchmarking was very useful in eliminating performance bottlenecks in Aurora's message-passing infrastructure. This infrastructure is now fast enough in Aurora that nontrivial box operations are the only noticeable bottleneck, i.e., CPU time is overwhelmingly devoted to useful work and not simply to shuffling around tuples.

5 Future plans: Borealis

The Aurora team has secured venture capital backing to commercialize the current code line. Some of the group is morphing into pursuing this venture. Because of this event, there is no reason for the Aurora team to improve the current system. This section presents the initial ideas that we plan to explore in a follow-on system, called Borealis, which is a distributed stream-processing system. Borealis inherits core stream-processing functionality from Aurora and distribution functionality from Medusa. Borealis modifies and extends both systems in nontrivial and critical ways to provide advanced capabilities that are commonly required by newly emerging stream-processing applications.

The Borealis design is driven by our experience in using Aurora and Medusa, in developing several streaming applications including the Linear Road benchmark, and several commercial opportunities. Borealis will address the following requirements of newly emerging streaming applications.

5.1 Dynamic revision of query results

In many real-world streams, corrections or updates to previously processed data are available only after the fact. For instance, many popular data streams, such as the Reuters stock market feed, often include messages that allow the feed originator to correct errors in previously reported data. Furthermore, stream sources (such as sensors), as well as their connectivity, can be highly volatile and unpredictable. As a result, data may arrive late and miss their processing window or be ignored temporarily due to an overload situation. In all these cases, applications are forced to live with imperfect results, unless the system has means to correct its processing and results to take into account newly available data or updates.

The Borealis data model will extend that of Aurora by supporting such corrections by way of revision records. The goal is to process revisions intelligently, correcting query results that have already been emitted in a manner that is consistent with the corrected data. Processing of a revision message must replay a portion of the past with a new or modified value. Thus, to process revision messages correctly, we must make a query diagram "replayable". In theory, we could process each revision message by replaying processing from the point of the revision to the present. In most cases, however, revisions on the input affect only a limited subset of output tuples, and to regenerate unaffected output is wasteful and unnecessary. To minimize runtime overhead and message proliferation, we assume a closed model for replay that generates revision messages when processing revision messages. In other words, our model processes and generates "deltas" showing only the effects of revisions rather than regenerating the entire result. The primary challenge here is to develop efficient revision-processing techniques that can work with bounded history.

5.2 Dynamic query modification

In many stream-processing applications, it is desirable to change certain attributes of the query at runtime. For example, in the financial services domain, traders typically wish to be alerted of *interesting* events, where the definition of "interesting" (i.e., the corresponding filter predicate) varies based on current context and results. In network monitoring, the system may want to obtain more precise results on a specific subnetwork if there are signs of a potential denial-of-service attack. Finally, in a military stream application that MITRE [19] explained to us, they wish to switch to a "cheaper" query when the system is overloaded. For the first two applications, it is sufficient to simply alter the operator parameters (e.g., window size, filter predicate), whereas the last one calls for altering the operators that compose the running query. Another motivating application comes again from the financial services community. Universally, people working on trading engines wish to test out new trading strategies as well as debug their applications on historical data before they go live. As such, they wish to perform "time travel" on input streams. Although this last example can be supported in most current SPE prototypes (i.e., by attaching the engine to previously stored data), a more user-friendly and efficient solution would obviously be desirable.

Two important features that will facilitate online modification of continuous queries in Borealis are *control lines* and *time travel*. Control lines extend Aurora's basic query model with the ability to change operator parameters as well as operators themselves on the fly. Control lines carry messages with revised box parameters and new box functions. For example, a control message to a Filter box can contain a reference to a boolean-valued function to replace its predicate. Similarly, a control message to an Aggregate box may contain a revised window size parameter. Additionally, each control message must indicate when the change in box semantics should take effect. Change is triggered when a monotonically increasing attribute received on the data line attains a certain value. Hence, control messages specify an <attribute, value> pair for this purpose. For windowed operators like Aggregate, control messages must also contain a flag to indicate if open windows at the time of change must be prematurely closed for a clean start.

Time travel allows multiple queries (different queries or versions of the same query) to be easily defined and executed concurrently, starting from different points in the past or "future" (typically by running a simulation of some sort). To support these capabilities, we leverage three advanced mechanisms in Borealis: enhanced connection points, connection point versions, and revision messages. To facilitate time travel, we define two new operations on connection points. The *replay operation* replays messages stored at a connection point from an arbitrary message in the past. The *offset operation* is used to set the connection point offset in time. When offset into the past, a connection point delays current messages before pushing them downstream. When offset into the future, the connection point predicts future data. When producing future data, various prediction algorithms can be used based on the application. A connection point version is a distinctly named logical copy of a connection point. Each named version can be manipulated independently. It is possible to shift a connection point version backward and forward in time without affecting other versions.

To replay history from a previous point in time t, we use revision messages. When a connection point receives a replay command, it first generates a set of revision messages that delete all the messages and revisions that have occurred since t. To avoid the overhead of transmitting one revision per deleted message, we use a macro message that summarizes all deletions. Once all messages are deleted, the connection point produces a series of revisions that insert the messages and possibly their following revisions back into the stream. During replay, all messages and revisions received by the connection point are buffered and processed only after the replay terminates, thus ensuring that simultaneous replays on any path in the query diagram are processed in sequence and do not conflict. When offset into the future, time-offset operators predict future values. As new data become available, these predictors can (but do not have to) produce more accurate revisions to their past predictions. Additionally, when a predictor receives revision messages, possibly due to time travel into the past, it can also revise its previous predictions.

5.3 Distributed optimization

Currently, commercial stream-processing applications are popular in industrial process control (e.g., monitoring oil refineries and cereal plants), financial services (e.g., feed processing, trading engine support and compliance), and network monitoring (e.g., intrusion detection, fraud detection). Here we see a *server-heavy* optimization problem – the key challenge is to process high-volume data streams on a collection of resource-rich "beefy" servers. Over the horizon, we see a very large number of applications of wireless sensor technology (e.g., RFID in retail applications, cell phone services). Here we see a *sensor-heavy* optimization problem – the key challenges revolve around extracting and processing sensor data from a network of resource-constrained "tiny" devices. Further over the horizon, we expect sensor networks to become faster and increase in processing power. In this case the optimization problem becomes more balanced, becoming *sensor-heavy/server-heavy*. To date, systems have exclusively focused on either a server-heavy environment or a sensor-heavy environment. Off into the future, there will be a need for a more flexible optimization structure that can deal with a very large number of devices and perform cross-network sensor-heavy/server-heavy resource management and optimization.

The purpose of the Borealis optimizer is threefold. First, it is intended to optimize processing across a combined sensor and server network. To the best of our knowledge, no previous work has studied such a cross-network optimization problem. Second, QoS is a metric that is important in stream-based applications, and optimization must deal with this issue. Third, scalability, sizewise and geographical, is becoming a significant design consideration with the proliferation of stream-based applications that deal with large volumes of data generated by multiple distributed sensor networks. As a result, Borealis faces a unique, multiresource, multimetric optimization challenge that is significantly different than the optimization problems explored in the past. Our current thinking is that Borealis will rely on a hierarchical, distributed optimizer that runs at different time granularities.

Another part of the Borealis vision involves addressing recovery and high-availability issues. High availability demands that node failure be masked by seamless handoff of processing to an alternate node. This is complicated by the fact that the optimizer will dynamically redistribute processing, making it more difficult to keep backup nodes synchronized. Furthermore, wide-area Borealis applications are not only vulnerable to node failures but also to network failures and more importantly to network partitions. We have preliminary research in this area that leverages Borealis mechanisms including connection point versions, revision tuples, and time travel.

5.4 Implementation plans

We have started building Borealis. As Borealis inherits much of its core stream-processing functionality from Aurora, we can effectively borrow many of the Aurora modules including the GUI, the XML representation for query diagrams, portions of the runtime system, and much of the logic for boxes. Similarly, we are borrowing some networking and distribution logic from Medusa. With this starting point, we hope to have a working prototype within a year.

Acknowledgements. This work was supported in part by the National Science Foundation under Grants IIS-0086057, IIS-0325525, IIS-0325703, IIS-0325838, and IIS-0205445 and by Army contract DAMD17-02-2-0048. We would like to thank all members of the Aurora and the Medusa projects at Brandeis University, Brown University, and MIT. We are also grateful to the anonymous reviewers for their invaluable comments.

References

1. A guide for hot lane development: A U.S. Department of Transportation Federal Highway Administration. http://www.itsdocs.fhwa.dot.gov/JPODOCS/REPTS_TE/13668.html
2. Abadi D, Carney D, Çetintemel U, Cherniack M, Convey C, Erwin C, Galvez E, Hatoun M, Hwang J, Maskey A, Rasin A, Singer A, Stonebraker M, Tatbul N, Xing Y, Yan R, Zdonik S (2003) Aurora: A data stream management system (demo description). In: ACM SIGMOD
3. Abadi D, Carney D, Çetintemel U, Cherniack M, Convey C, Lee S, Stonebraker M, Tatbul N, Zdonik S (2003) Aurora: A new model and architecture for data stream management. VLDB J 12(2):120–139
4. Arasu A, Cherniack M, Galvez E, Maier D, Maskey A, Ryvkina E, Stonebraker M, Tibbetts R (2004) Linear Road: A benchmark for stream data management systems. In: VLDB conference, Toronto (in press)
5. Balazinska M, Balakrishnan H, Stonebraker M (2004) Contract-based load management in federated distributed systems. In: NSDI symposium
6. Barlett J, Gray J, Horst B (1986) Fault tolerance in tandem computer systems. Technical Report TR-86.2, Tandem Computers
7. Carney D, Çetintemel U, Cherniack M, Convey C, Lee S, Seidman G, Stonebraker M, Tatbul N, Zdonik S (2002) Monitoring streams – a new class of data management applications. In: VLDB conference, Hong Kong
8. Carney D, Çetintemel U, Rasin A, Zdonik S, Cherniack M, Stonebraker M (2003) Operator scheduling in a data stream manager. In: VLDB conference, Berlin, Germany
9. Chandrasekaran S, Deshpande A, Franklin M, Hellerstein J, Hong W, Krishnamurthy S, Madden S, Raman V, Reiss F, Shah M (2003) TelegraphCQ: Continuous dataflow processing for an uncertain world. In: CIDR conference
10. Cherniack M, Balakrishnan H, Balazinska M, Carney D, Çetintemel U, Xing Y, Zdonik S (2003) Scalable distributed stream processing. In: CIDR conference, Asilomar, CA
11. Congestion pricing: a report from intelligent transportation systems (ITS). http://www.path.berkeley.edu
12. DeWitt D, Naughton J, Schneider D (1991) An evaluation of non-equijoin algorithms. In: VLDB conference, Barcelona, Catalonia, Spain
13. Hwang J, Balazinska M, Rasin A, Çetintemel U, Stonebraker M, Zdonik S (2003) A comparison of stream-oriented high-availability algorithms. Technical Report CS-03-17, Department of Computer Science, Brown University, Providence, RI
14. Lerner A, Shasha D (2003) AQuery: Query language for ordered data, optimization techniques, and experiments. In: VLDB conference, Berlin, Germany
15. Motwani R, Widom J, Arasu A, Babcock B, Babu S, Datar M, Manku G, Olston C, Rosenstein J, Varma R (2003) Query processing, approximation, and resource management in a data stream management system. In: CIDR conference
16. Poole RW (2002) Hot lanes prompted by federal program. http://www.rppi.org/federalhotlanes.html
17. Seshadri P, Livny M, Ramakrishnan R (1995) SEQ: A model for sequence databases. In: IEEE ICDE conference, Taipei, Taiwan
18. Tatbul N, Çetintemel U, Zdonik S, Cherniack M, Stonebraker M (2003) Load shedding in a data stream manager. In: VLDB conference, Berlin, Germany
19. The MITRE Corporation. http://www.mitre.org/
20. US Army Medical Research and Materiel Command. https://mrmc-www.army.mil/

Sources

Chapter 1

Stonebraker, Michael and Joseph M. Hellerstein, "*What Goes Around Comes Around*." Not previously published.

Hellerstein, Joseph M. and Michael Stonebraker, "*Anatomy of a Database System*." Not previously published.

Chapter 2: Query Processing

Selinger, P. G., M. M. Astrahan, D. D. Chamberlin, R. A. Lorie, and T. G. Price, "Access Path Selection in a Relational Database Management System." In *Proceedings of the 1979 ACM SIGMOD International Conference on Management of Data*. New York: ACM Press, 1979.

Shapiro, Leonard. "Join Processing in Database Systems with Large Main Memories." *ACM Transactions on Database Systems* 11:3 (1986).

DeWitt, David J., and Jim Gray. "Parallel Database Systems: The Future of High Performance Database Processing." *Communications of the ACM* 35:6 (1992): 85–98.

Graefe, Goetz. "Encapsulation of Parallelism in the Volcano Query Processing System." In *Proceedings of the 1990 ACM SIGMOD International Conference on Management of Data*. New York: ACM Press, 1990.

Nyberg, C., T. Barclay, Z. Cvetanovic, J. Gray, and D. Lomet. "AlphaSort: A RISC Machine Sort." In *Proceedings of the 1994 ACM SIGMOD International Conference on Management of Data*. New York: ACM Press, 1994.

Mackert, Lothar F., and Guy M. Lohman. "R* Optimizer Validation and Performance Evaluation for Distributed Queries." In *Proceedings of the Twelfth International Conference on Very Large Data Bases*, edited by Wesley W. Chu et al. San Francisco: Morgan Kaufmann, 1986.

Stonebraker, Michael, Paul M. Aoki, Witold Litwin, Avi Pfeffer, Adam Sah, Jeff Sidell, Carl Staelin, and Andrew Yu. "Mariposa: A Wide-Area Distributed Database System." *The Very Large Data Base Journal* 5 (1996): 48-63.

Chapter 3: Data Storage and Access Methods

Beckmann, Norbert, Hans-Peter Kriegel, Ralf Schneider, and Bernhard Seeger. "The R*- tree : An efficient and robust access method for points and rectangles," In *Proceedings of the 1990 ACM SIGMOD International Conference on Management of Data*. New York: ACM Press, 1990.

Stonebraker, Michael. "Operating System Support for Database Management." *Communications of the ACM*. 7:24 (1981): 412–418.

Gray, Jim, and Goetz Graefe. "The Five-Minute Rule Ten Years Later, and Other Computer Storage Rules of Thumb." *ACM SIGMOD Record* 26:4 (1997): 63–68.

Patterson, David A., Garth A. Gibson, and Randy H. Katz. "A Case for Redundant Arrays of Inexpensive

Disks (RAID)." In *Proceedings of the 1988 ACM SIGMOD International Conference on Management of Data*. New York: ACM Press, 1988.

Chapter 4: Transaction Management

Gray, Jim, Raymond A. Lorie, Gianfranco R. Putzolu, and Irving L. Traiger. "Granularity of Locks and Degrees of Consistency in a Shared Data Base." In *Modelling in Data Base Management Systems: Proceedings of the IFIP Working Conference on Modelling in Data Base Management Systems*, edited by G.M. Nijssen. North-Holland, 1976.

Kung, H. T., and John T. Robinson. "On Optimistic Methods for Concurrency Control," *ACM Transactions on Database Systems* 6:81 (1986): 213–226.

Agrawal, Rakesh, Michael J. Carey, and Miron Livny. "Concurrency control performance modeling: alternatives and implications." *ACM Transactions on Database Systems* 12:4 (1987): 609–654.

Lehman, Philip L., and S. Bing Yao. "Efficient Locking for Concurrent Operations on B-trees." *ACM Transactions on Database Systems* 6:4 (1981): 650–670.

Mohan, C., Don Haderle, Bruce Lindsay, Hamid Pirahesh, and Peter Schwartz. "ARIES: A Transaction Recovery Method Supporting Fine-Granularity Locking and Partial Rollbacks Using Write-ahead Logging," *ACM Transactions on Database Systems* 17:1 (1993): 94–162.

Mohan, C., Bruce Lindsay, and R. Obermarck. "Transaction Management in the R* Distributed Database Management Systems." *ACM Transactions on Database Systems* 11:4 (1986): 378–396.

Gray, Jim, Pat Helland, Patrick O'Neil, and Dennis Shasha. "The Dangers of Replication and a Solution." In *Proceedings of the 1996 ACM SIGMOD International Conference on Management of Data*. New York: ACM Press, 1996.

Chapter 5: Extensibility

Stonebraker, Michael. "Inclusion Of New Types In Relational Data Base Systems." In *Proceedings of the Second International Conference on Data Engineering*. Washington, D.C.: IEEE Computer Society, 1986.

Hellerstein, Joseph M., Jeffrey F. Naughton, and Avi Pfeffer. "Generalized Search Trees for Database Systems." In *Proceedings of the Twenty-First International Conference on Very Large Data Bases*, edited by Umeshwar Dayal. San Francisco: Morgan Kaufmann, 1995.

Lohman, Guy M. "Grammar-like Functional Rules for Representing Query Optimization Alternatives." In *Proceedings of the 1988 ACM SIGMOD International Conference on Management of Data*. New York: ACM Press, 1988.

Chapter 6: Database Evolution

Chaudhuri, Surajit, and Vivek Narasayya. "AutoAdmin 'What-if' Index Analysis Utility." In *Proceedings of the 1988 ACM SIGMOD International Conference on Management of Data*. New York: ACM Press, 1988.

Bernstein, Philip A. "Applying Model Management to Classical Meta Data Problems," In *Proceedings of the First Biennial Conference on Innovative Data Systems Research*. New York: ACM Press, 2003.

Mohan, C., and Inderpal Narang. "Algorithms for Creating Indexes for Very Large Tables Without Quiescing Updates." In *Proceedings of the 1992 ACM SIGMOD International Conference on Management of Data*. New York: ACM Press, 1992.

Chapter 7: Data Warehousing

Chaudhuri, Surajit, and Umeshwar Dayal. "An Overview of Data Warehousing and OLAP Technology." *SIGMOD Record* 26:1 (1997) 65–74.

O'Neil, Patrick, and Dallan Quass. "Improved Query Performance with Variant Indexes." In *Proceedings of the 1997 ACM SIGMOD International Conference on Management of Data*. New York: ACM Press, 1997.

Gray, Jim, Surajit Chaudhuri, Adam Bosworth, Andrew Layman, Don Reichart, and Murali Venkatrao. "DataCube: A Relational Aggregation Operator Generalizing Group-By, Cross-Tab, and Sub-Totals." *Data Mining and Knowledge Discovery* 1 (1997): 29–53.

Zhao, Yihong, Prasad Deshpande, and Jeffrey F. Naughton. "An Array-Based Algorithm for Simultaneous Multidimensional Aggregates." In *Proceedings of the 1997 ACM SIGMOD International Conference on Management of Data*. New York: ACM Press, 1997.

Ceri, Stefano, and Jennifer Widom. "Deriving Production Rules for Incremental View Maintenance." *Proceedings of the Seventeenth International Conference on Very Large Data Bases*, edited by Guy M. Lohman et al. San Francisco: Morgan Kaufmann, 1991.

Hellerstein, Joseph M., Ron Avnur, and Vijayshankar Raman. "Informix under CONTROL: Online Query Processing." *Data Mining and Knowledge Discovery* 12 (2000): 281–314.

Kotidis, Yannis, and Nick Roussopoulos. "DynaMat: A Dynamic View Management System for Data Warehouses." In *Proceedings of the 1999 ACM SIGMOD International Conference on Management of Data*. New York: ACM Press, 1999.

Chapter 8: Data Mining

Zhang, Tian, Raghu Ramakrishnan, and Miron Livny. "BIRCH: An Efficient Data Clustering Method for Very Large Databases." In *Proceedings of the 1996 ACM SIGMOD International Conference on Management of Data*. New York: ACM Press, 1996.

Shafer, John, Rakesh Agrawal, and Manish Mehta. "SPRINT: A Scalable Parallel Classifier for Data Mining." In *Proceedings of the Twenty-Second International Conference on Very Large Data Bases*, edited by T. M. Vijayaraman, et al. San Francisco: Morgan Kaufmann, 1996.

Agrawal, Rakesh and Ramakrishnan Srikant. "Fast Algorithms for Mining Association Rules." In *Proceedings of the Twentieth International Conference on Very Large Data Bases*, edited by Jorge B. Bocca, et al. San Francisco: Morgan Kaufmann, 1994.

Chaudhuri, Surajit, Vivek Narasayya, and Sunita Sarawagi. "Efficient Evaluation of Queries with Mining Predicates." *Proceedings of the Eighteenth International Conference on Data Engineering*. Washington, D.C.: IEEE Computer Society, 2002.

Chapter 9: Web Services and Data Bases

Brewer, Eric A. "Combining Systems and Databases: A Search Engine Retrospective." Not previously published.

Brin, Sergey, and Lawrence Page. "The Anatomy of a Large-Scale Hypertextual Web Search Engine." *Proceedings of the Seventh International World Wide Web Conference (WWW7) on Computer Networks* 30:1-7 (1998):107–117.

Sizov, Sergej, Michael Biwer, Jens Graupmann, Stefan Siersdorfer, Martin Theobald, Gerhard Weikum, and Patrick Zimmer. "The BINGO! System for Information Portal Generation and Expert Web Search." In *Proceedings of the First Biennial Conference on Innovative Data Systems Research*. New York: ACM Press, 2003.

Jacobs, Dean. "Data Management in Application Servers." *Datenbank-Spektrum* 8 (2004): 5–11.

Abiteboul, Serge. "Querying Semi-Structured Data." In *Proceedings of the Sixth International Conference on Database Theory*, edited by Foto N. Afrati, et al. Springer-Verlag, 1997.

Goldman, Roy, and Jennifer Widom. "DataGuides: Enabling Query Formulation and Optimization in Semistructured Databases." In *Proceedings of the Twenty-Third International Conference on Very Large Data Bases*, edited by Matthias Jarke, et al. San Francisco: Morgan Kaufmann, 1997.

Chen, Jianjun, David DeWitt, Fend Tian, and Yuan Wang. "NiagaraCQ: A Scalable Continuous Query System for the Internet Databases." In *Proceedings of the 2000 ACM SIGMOD International Conference on Management of Data*. New York: ACM Press, 2000.

Chapter 10: Stream-Based Data Management

Hanson, Eric N., Chris Carnes, Lan Huang, Mohan Konyala, Lloyd Noronha, Sashi Parthasarathy, J. B. Park, and Albert Vernon. "Scalable Trigger Processing." In *Proceedings of the Fifteenth International Conference on Data Engineering*. Washington, D.C.: IEEE Computer Society, 1999.

Seshadri, Praveen, Miron Livny, and Raghu Ramakrishnan. "The Design and Implementation of a Sequence Database System." In *Proceedings of the Twenty-Second International Conference on Very Large Data Bases*, edited by T. M. Vijayaraman, et al. San Francisco: Morgan Kaufmann, 1996.

Avnur, Ron, and Joseph M. Hellerstein. "Eddies: Continuously Adaptive Query Processing." In *Proceedings of the 2000 ACM SIGMOD International Conference on Management of Data*. New York: ACM Press, 2000.

Balakrishnan, Hari, Magdalena Balazinska, Don Carney, Uğur Çetintemel, Mitch Cherniack, Christian Convey, Eddie Galvez, Jon Salz, Michael Stonebraker, Nesime Tatbul, Richard Tibbetts, and Stanley Zdonik. Retrospective on Aurora. *VLDB Journal* (2004).